The Family Letters

The Family Letters

A Portrait of an American Family Through Letters

From the 18th to the 20th Century

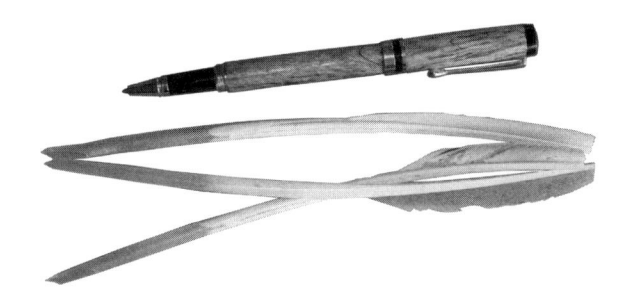

Edited by John T. B. Mudge

The Durand Press
Lyme, New Hampshire

Published by The Durand Press
25 Lamphire Hill, Lyme, New Hampshire 03678-3108
www.durandpress.com

Copyright © 2008 by John T. B. Mudge.
All rights reserved.

No part of this publication may be reproduced, translated, stored in or introduced into a retrieval system, or transmitted, in any form or by any means (electronic, mechanical, photocopying, recording, or otherwise), without the prior written permission of the publisher, except by a reviewer, who may quote brief passages in a review.

If this book is stamped "SAMPLE" or "REVIEW COPY," it has been supplied free of charge to a person, institution, or publication for specific purposes and neither the publisher nor the author has received any compensation for it. If it is so stamped, please do not purchase it.

Sale of this book without a cover is unauthorized. If this book has no cover, it may have been reported to the publisher as "unsold or destroyed" by a bookstore or distributor and neither the author nor publisher may have received payment for it.

Book and cover design by May 10 Design, West Lebanon, New Hampshire.
Typeset in Adobe Minion.

Title page illustration: Quill pens belonging to Francis Thayer, 1822–1880, and a modern pen, made from the Wye Oak in Wye Mills, Maryland, belonging to the author.

ISBN 978-0-9708324-5-0

Library of Congress control number: 2008910294

Printed in the United States of America

10   9   8   7   6   5   4   3   2   1

First Edition

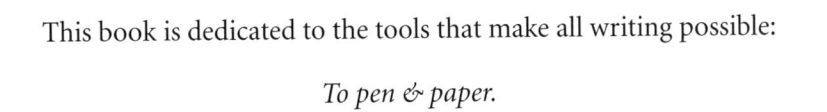

This book is dedicated to the tools that make all writing possible:

To pen & paper.

Letters

I particularly request you to write me by next opportunity with your own hand— and recommend you to practice reading & writing 'till I return home.
—*John Cropper to his wife Margaret "Peggy" Cropper, May 29, 1778, written from Valley Forge.*

Two letters from you, have been duly received (and I think I may add duly appreciated) by me since I last wrote you; and they certainly deserve, a long letter in return… —*Anne E. Wise to Henry A. Wise, January 8, 1835.*

It is of the greatest importance to write letters well; as this is a talent which unavoidably occurs every day of one's life, as well in business as in pleasure; and inaccuracies in orthography or in style are never pardoned *but in ladies.*
—*from a clipping found in the papers of Annie Jennings Wise Hobson, source unknown.*

I hurried on up to the P.O. with a light heart & buoyant step almost sure of the rich treasure. But on looking into Box No. 40– "lo and behold" it was empty. I was not a little disappointed.
—*Francis Thayer to Catherine McKie, October 30, 1847.*

Letter writing is the bane of my happiness as regards my duty to friends, and a neglect of duty is ever staring me in the face, to mar my happiness. But when I commence writing to one I love, as now, in a few moments I seem to see them, to take them by the hand, and after a few moments I am only surprised that I receive no answer, and then comes the thought that the Lord and remembered, are far away.
—*Catherine McKie to Francis Thayer, December 2, 1847.*

Your Mother and I came to the conclusion that for once at least you have been up to your promise, that is, you would not write home any more unless you received a few lines from your Father or Mother. Now in order to stir you up to do your duty and to get you in the way of communicating once more with your old and truest friends (except Frank) I have thought it proper to write you a few lines that you may know how we all are at home.
—*George McKie to Catherine McKie Thayer, January 12, 1853.*

Three packets have come and gone and not a note from you. Sabbath last and Thursday last I was sure of a letter— of some sign or token at least from you and none came. Did you forget to mail your letters Tuesday or Saturday to be certain of reaching our ferry at Norfolk by Friday and by Tuesday?
—*Henry A. Wise to Mary Lyons, October 1, 1853.*

Have you no paper? If so write.
   —*Catherine McKie Thayer to Sophia Whiteside McKie, 1859.*

I rather expected a letter from you this morning but was disappointed. Of course I would not have you neglect your studies to write letters, but I assure you my good boy, we are all hungry for your letters and hope you will continue to write often… Write as often as you have the time…
   —*Francis S. Thayer to Francis McKie Thayer at Amherst College, October 5, 1875.*

The length of my last letter was conclusive evidence that I had quite forgotten Sam Weller's idea of the great art of letter writing, 'make them short, so that the reader will wish they had been longer.'
   —*Francis S. Thayer in a newspaper column, May 31, 1879.*

We had no Eastern mail yesterday, and there is no prospect of one today. Morning paper says three of the roads (R.R.) are again blocked by snowdrifts. However we had a *Times* of Monday the 18th yesterday. There seems to be no accounting for the way some mail comes and other mail is delayed…
   —*Catherine McKie Thayer to Katherine Jermain, January 23, 1886.*

Dearest, sweetest I thank you so for all your letters and if mine seem cold remember that I am not much learned in the art of saying nice things and that my epistolary practice has been for years in the field of business correspondence…
   —*Henry Wise Hobson to Katherine Thayer Jermain, November 12, 1887.*

I spent yesterday straightening up my receipts etc. and last evening I looked over a box of letters… Indeed they came to me not only as voices of love and friendship from the past, but as spirit voices from the dear ones in Paradise…
   —*Annie Jennings Wise Hobson to her son, Henry Wise Hobson, December 12, 1888.*

If anyone should ever take the trouble to investigate our married life they will find a large part of our relations existing in letters written by me from RR trains. I wonder how many letters I have sent you from way stations?
   —*Henry Wise Hobson to Katherine Thayer Hobson, January 25, 1896.*

By the way, in going through Mother's letters & papers, be careful what you throw away… I wish you would keep my letters to her. I should like to have these again, as they form a kind of diary of the past and what has been.
   —*Katherine Hobson Kraus to Eleanor Whiteside Hobson, June 11, 1916.*

…Wasn't it strange that last night we both should have written to each other about the pleasure derived from writing?
   —*Eleanor Hobson Mackenzie to George M. Mackenzie, July 12, 1916.*

Table of Contents

Introduction		xi
I	An Annotated Genealogy	1
II	1777–1838 • Virginia, Pennsylvania, and Tennessee	19
III	1806–1860 • Virginia, Henry A. Wise and His family	39
IV	1835–1844 • Early Papers from Cambridge, New York	79
V	1844–1850 • Letters from Cambridge and Troy, Part One	95
VI	1851–1854 • Letters from Cambridge and Troy, Part Two	153
VII	1855–1859 • Letters from Cambridge and Troy, Part Three	185
VIII	1860–1861 • Letters from Cambridge and Troy, Part Four	231
IX	1860–1865 • Life in Virginia	259
X	1862–1869 • Letters from Cambridge and Troy, Part Five	319
XI	1866–1876 • Virginia	345
XII	1870–1877 • Letters from Cambridge and Troy, Part Six	379
XIII	1878–1880 • The Thayer Family in Colorado	429
XIV	The Summer of 1882 • Disease, Marriage, and Death	445
XV	The 1880s • A Young Lawyer Goes West	465
XVI	1887, Part One • A Very Busy Year	503
XVII	1887, Part Two • Henry Wise Hobson and the Mormon Church	561
XVIII	1888–1889 • Colorado	583
XIX	1890 • The Robert E. Lee Memorial	625
XX	1890–1897 • A Growing Family in Denver	637
XXI	1898, Part One • Henry W. Hobson and the Practice of Law	749
XXII	1898, Part Two • August	809
XXIII	1898–1916 • A Widow and Her Children	835
Appendix A	Timeline • Selected Dates in Family History	935
Appendix B	Handwriting Samples	943
Appendix C	Selected Portraits and Photographs	956
Appendix D	Bibliography	960
Acknowledgments		963
Index		965

Introduction

THIS is a book of letters, and it may be difficult for some to read. The authors and recipients of these letters are the characters in this story, and they were real people. No effort has been made to change or disguise their identity and the lives they led. Some had very distinguished lives— four biographies have been previously published about two of them. In a work of fiction the reader meets characters in the early chapters and then follows them through the rest of the story until they succeed, fail, ride off into the sunset, or die at the end. Here the reader will meet "characters" in the early chapters and then follow them through the rest of the book, but this is not a work of fiction, and the successes, failures, sunset rides, and deaths are all real. Some may say that this is a genealogical study. It is that, but it is not about census records, birth certificates, or charts and descriptions of how everyone in a group of people is related to each other. This is the story of an American family as found in the written record that it created and left behind. I have included some material that describes their professional work, but for the most part that has been omitted in favor of focusing on their personal lives. We all have an equal number of ancestors that we can put onto charts to show their relationships, but we do not all have a well documented record of who our ancestors were and how and where they lived. This is that record for a part of my family. It is also a record of how America grew and changed from its birth in the 18th century, through the growth and turmoil of the 19th century, and finally to the challenges of the early 20th century. Hopefully readers will be able to relate to that time and place and imagine the roles that their own ancestors played in the greater story that is here—the story of America.

~

Old steamer trunks and cardboard boxes, all filled with assorted papers, have been stored in different barns for many years. Though always referred to as the "the family letters," there are also diaries, newspaper clippings, photographs, and other miscellaneous things that have been saved for these hundred-plus years. I first knew about these letters in the early 1960s during visits to my grandmother's when my mother would go out to the barn and bring folders of letters back into the house to read, but I was younger, doing other things, and had little interest in old letters at that time. Then, maybe thirty-five years ago, the boxes and trunks were moved to my parents' barn in New Hampshire. From time to time my mother would retrieve some folders from the barn and transcribe a few letters on an old typewriter. Then, about seven years ago, I took a look inside the trunks and boxes and realized that there was a story there—a story that will now be told.

These letters, from six generations over three centuries, tell an American story. Specifically it is the story of my ancestors—their lives, education, interests, politics, travels, marriages, families, illnesses, births, deaths, friends, successes, failures, and more. As single letters they are very simple writings that describe their sad and happy times, their ordinary lives, and their hopes for the future. As a collection of letters they tell a much larger story that you will find. Some of the letters are from the New York side of the family—the McKies, Whitesides, and Thayers. Other letters are from the Virginia side of the family—the Croppers, Wises, and Hobsons. Finally, there are the letters and papers of Henry Wise Hobson and Katherine Thayer Hobson, one from Virginia and the other from New York, who met and married while living in Colorado and had four children, Katherine, Henry, Eleanor, and Thayer.

I searched for but found no conventions for transcribing and publishing letters. No one will ever again have the same experience that I had of removing these envelopes from a trunk and then opening, unfolding, and reading the letters for the first time in over a century. Then there were the tasks of organizing the letters so that they told their story and of preparing this book in such a way that readers would be able to have a sense of adventure and discovery as they read through this material—either the entire book or only selected chapters. One unavoidable problem was that the very act of transcribing the letters dramatically changes them, for they are no longer pieces of paper, held first by the author, then by the recipient, and then perhaps shared with other family members. Transcribing the letters moved them into a word processing system that would have been unimaginable when they were written.

Some may consider this to be a book of original source material with little interpretation. Others might call this the data of history, first person testimony as found in letters and diaries, that are the very personal records of a given time and place. It is through reading and studying this material about the past that we are better able to understand those times. The reader will not find a sentence that includes a brief quotation as the evidence for some thesis or interpretation that I am anxious to prove. There is a story in these letters, but it is one that readers must put together and interpret for themselves. Just imagine an old trunk filled with unsorted letters—well, some of the sorting has now been done.

A collection of letters is often very one-sided, for it most likely consists only of the letters that someone has received and saved. In this collection there are instances where *both sides* of the correspondence have been preserved. It is then that the letters come alive and the reader is in the middle of a conversation from another century. In one instance I had the letters *from* a distant uncle and then I found that the letters written *to him* were at the Virginia Historical Society. Today the entire conversation can be put together.

Readers will find that this book is in the voices of the letter writers and that there has been no attempt to edit and put the many voices into a single voice. Much historical writing presents and analyzes facts but provides few opportunities to explore and understand personal feelings with first-hand and anecdotal information. The many voices found here provide that opportunity, and as we read about their personal lives, we begin to understand and relate to more than just the facts of the times when they lived. My voice as the editor, and I use that word with caution to describe my role, will be found only when I believe that some "explanation" is necessary. I will not try to tell this story in my words, for the letters and diaries tell it so well.

As with many "collections," material about some time periods and events is missing. For example, many of the letters were written by someone who was traveling but when that person was "at home," there would have been no need to write a letter and therefore none exist about those domestic times. There are some diaries of those times, but, as the reader will discover, diaries are in a different "voice" and are written for a different purpose than letters. Another example is the correspondence of Annie Jennings Wise Hobson of Virginia. Many of her letters to her son still exist, but of his letters to her, only the one written on his fortieth birthday has survived. In my research and travels I found some "family letters" in a number of libraries. Where I have included that material, I have always indicated the institution where the original letters may be found. I have made no effort to "fill in the gap" with conjecture and story telling when my search for "missing materials" was unsuccessful. Novelists can write so that there are no gaps in the fictional worlds that they create, but the historical record of the real world is incomplete and there are some things that will never be known. If and when other letters from this extended family are found and archived, they will only add to the story that is here.

This book contains more than just letters and diaries. Some members of the family wrote books and articles that are reprinted here in appropriate places. This includes material by John Sergeant Wise, Ellen Wise Mayo, and Barton Haxall Wise. This and other previously published material compliments the material in the letters that is now published for the first time.

All of that said, there were some general rules that I followed as I worked my way through this project:

Organization: The different chapters of the book are by time period and by related groups of letters. In many chapters the correspondence is between two people. Where appropriate, other letters have been included in order to add another dimension and voice to that time and place.

Editing: Nothing has been edited from these letters because it was embarrassing or might seem scandalous. The material has been edited only because of its volume, for without that editing, this would be volume one of many.

Spelling: Our language and spelling has changed over time, and my preference has been to use the original spelling rather than modern spelling. Some of the writers spelled better than others, and where I did "correct" the spelling it was only out of a desire not to put "[sic]" after every spelling "mistake." Some words had a different meaning or usage in the past that might be considered obsolete or perhaps unknown today, and those are explained in the sidebars. In order to be consistent, all of the letters have been "signed" in italics.

Verb tenses: I have left them as I found them, and for the most part they are correct. However, the reader may be disturbed by something such as an occasional "was" where it should be "were." That was what was written and spoken at the time, and that is what is published here. When either spelling or verb tenses are "corrected," it is all too easy to next edit the sentences and then rearrange and reorganize whole paragraphs. The result would be that the letter is no longer in the voice of its author. I did not want to do that, and I did not do that.

Abbreviations: Many abbreviations have been left as they were originally written. Therefore, an original letter may read "phila" but I have not spelled out "Philadelphia." They often said "Cam" when they wrote from Cambridge, and I have left it that way. The abbreviations used in these letters might be compared to those used today in e-mail and text messaging.

Punctuation: The letters have, for the most part, been transcribed with the original punctuation. Some of the letters were filled with ampersands (&s), and I have changed some of those to read "and."

Sidebars: In reading the letters and putting the book together I thought that some explanatory information would be useful in different places. Throughout the book that material is in the sidebars on each page rather than lost in footnotes at the bottom of the page or at the end of a chapter. In a few instances, where the explanatory material was longer than would be permitted along the side of the page, it was incorporated into the general text. In a few places, a letter has been put in the sidebar. This will all be obvious to the reader.

Photographs: The old trunks and boxes contained many of the photographs and illustrations that have been used throughout the book. Additional photographs have been generously provided by different libraries and museums. Unless otherwise credited, all of the photographs were either in the boxes and trunks with the letters or taken in the course of my travels to North Carolina, Virginia, Maryland, West Virginia, Pennsylvania, New York, Massachusetts, Colorado, and Utah.

News events: Sometimes a letter refers to news events of the day. I have gone back to *The New York Times* and other newspapers to read the related news stories, and I have quoted some of that material. In 1876 *The New York Times* described itself as follows: "*The New York Times* is the best family paper published. It contains the latest news and correspondence. It is free from all objectionable advertisements and reports, and may be safely admitted to every domestic circle. The disgraceful announcements of quacks and medical pretenders, which pollute so many newspapers of the day, are not admitted into the columns of *The Times* on any terms." In other words, "All the news that's fit to print." In order to provide some historical context for the writings, the introduction to each chapter includes brief summaries of historical events for the time period covered in that chapter.

∽

It was a fascinating experience to read and study these letters— sometimes with a sense of apprehension of what I might find and at other times with an eagerness to learn as much as possible about the lives of these ancestors. These letters provided a rare opportunity to "touch history," but there were times when I felt as though I was stuck in a maze of bewildering and confusing letters from a distant past and I regretted my venture into those boxes and trunks. Exciting were the moments when I "put something together" and part of the adventure was more complete. Slowly the project "came together" and I could see the story that the letters told. More work, transcribing, researching, editing, and traveling, and the project has been completed, and it is now time for others to read the story. I truly hope that I have done justice to *The Family Letters*.

I

An Annotated Genealogy

HAVING stated in the introduction that this book is more than a genealogical study, this chapter is exactly that, genealogical information. First, it must be made clear that this information is incomplete. Persons wishing to continue the charts with more generations may do so. Secondly, purists may be upset that the information here does not include all branches of the different families. Again, that is not the purpose of this section. The purpose here is solely to show some of the ancestry of the primary characters in the rest of this book, whose roots in America went back to the early 1600s, and also give some anecdotal information about those early settlers. Readers interested in more genealogical information and all of the relationships may find that information in other sources. Some may want to just skim through this chapter at first and then, from time to time, return to it in order to clarify the relationship between different people. One technique used here will clearly indicate that people are missing from this chapter. If the end of a line reads "(four children)" and the next line begins, "(third child, 3rd)" then that means– that the first generation mentioned had four children, that the person on the following line is the third child, and that other children have been omitted from this material. To repeat, this summary does not attempt to follow all branches of the extended family. In addition, there may be a small amount of redundancy as one goes from one part of this chapter to another. This is meant to clarify the relationships rather than to complicate the readings.

Every effort has been made to use multiple sources to verify the information that is published here. However, errors often creep into genealogical information. In doing this research there was one reference to an uncle stating that he had died in 1890. It can be so easily be documented that this individual died in a Civil War battle in 1862 that one can only wonder how "1890" was ever published. Elsewhere there exists a chart stating that one ancestor died in 1858, but it is very easily documented that she had five children after that date and died in 1914. There is a book that incorrectly describes Annie Jennings Wise Hobson as Henry A. Wise's sister. She was his daughter. Another book claims that George Wise, killed at Petersburg in 1864, was Wise's son. George Wise was Henry Wise's nephew. Please be careful when using genealogical information.

In the below material, generations are indicated by Roman numerals and "b," "d," "m," and "div" are standard abbreviations for "born," "died," "married," and "divorced."

Obscurity, birthplace of John Cannon Hobson, July 20, 1791. Photograph courtesy of Hobson Goddin.

The Virginia Ancestry

The Virginia ancestry begins with the arrival of immigrants from England in the early 17th century. In the ensuing years these settlers traded with and fought wars with the Indians, cleared and farmed their land, and then fought in the American Revolution. They held county offices and were members of the House of Burgesses. They were early settlers in this part of the new world.

The Hobson family genealogy:

I. Thomas Hobson, 1665–1717: m. Clark Winder, d. 1743.

II. John Hobson, 1701–1777: m. 1733: Sarah (otherwise unknown).

III. William Hobson, d. 1764: m. January 28, 1750: Elizabeth Merryman (otherwise unknown).

IV. John Miller Hobson, d. September 19, 1824: m. October 30, 1777: Susanna "Susan" Hatcher, d. August 6, 1825.

V. John Cannon Hobson (fifth son), b. July 20, 1791 at Obscurity in Cumberland County, Virginia: d. April 11, 1873: m. October 2, 1823: Mary Shaw Maben (also Maban), b. April 10, 1795: d. April 3, 1871, (five children below).

VI. 1. John David Hobson, b. January 24, 1824: d. August 22, 1901: m. Martha Bland Selden, b. March 10, 1830: d. June 10, 1911. Lived at Howard's Neck Farm in Goochland County, Virginia.
2. William C. Hobson, b. April 3, 1826: d. July 5, 1853 (or 1855): m. Virginia K. Pemberton, 1834–1860, of Clover Forest in Goochland County, Virginia.
3. Alexander Maben Hobson, 1829–1863: m. Polly Pemberton of Clover Forest in Goochland County, Virginia. Lived at Snowden in Goochland County, Virginia.
4. Frederick Plumer Hobson, b. February 24, 1833: d. April 4, 1868: m. July 9, 1856: Annie Jennings Wise, b. April 28, 1837: d. June 3, 1914. Lived at Eastwood in Goochland County, Virginia.
5. Mary Morrison Hobson, m. December 4, 1855: William H. Lyons, d. June 18, 1867, of Richmond.

Howard's Neck, Goochland County, home of John David Hobson. Photo from Historic Virginia Homes and Churches *by Robert A. Lancaster, Jr.*

Mary Shaw Maben

Mary Shaw Maben was born in Dumfries, Scotland, the daughter of David Maben Jr. and Mary Morrison. Family letters say that this Mary Morrison was the subject of Robert Burns' poem "Mary Morison." In 1897, Mary Maben Lyons, researched the Family Bibles and on January 20, 1897, wrote to Henry Wise Hobson, her cousin, the following: "I can tell you nothing about the Morisons except that Grandma Hobson told Mother that Burns' 'Mary Morison' was your Great–Grandmother. Great–Great Uncle David Maben had several of Burns' poems in manuscript. He has a worthless grandson living in Amelia. I suppose he has them." There is another sheet in an unidentified handwriting that reads: "There has been a good deal of confusion relative to Mary Morrison, there being two of the name resident in Dumfries County, Scotland at about the same period. The letters, documents, data, etc. in possession of the family prove however without doubt that Burns' "Bonnie Mary Morrison" and of his poems, is identical with Mary Morrison the wife of David Maben 2nd, who came to America with her husband, and is buried in Petersburg, Virginia, and who was the daughter of Robert Morrison and that Mary Morrison the daughter of Adjutant John Morrison, has no claim whatsoever to the honor of having inspired Burns to write his poem."

VI. Frederick Plumer Hobson (fourth child), b. February 24,1833 in Petersburg Virginia. [Named after the Rev. Dr. Plumer, a distinguished Presbyterian.]: d. April 4, 1868: m. July 9, 1856: Ann "Annie" Jennings Wise, b. April 28, 1837: d. June 3, 1914: (six children; two, John Cannon Hobson, 1857–1890, and Henry Wise Hobson, 1858–1898, survived to adulthood).

VII. 1st. John Cannon Hobson, (oldest child) b. April 22, 1857 in the Executive Mansion, Richmond, Virginia: d. February 15, 1890: m. May 20, 1878: Alice Virginia Pettit, b. May 18, 1860, (daughter of John M. Pettitt of Accomac County): d. February 17, 1933, (seven children below).

VIII. 1. John Cannon Hobson, b. July 31, 1880: d. January 17, 1960: m–1st. Maude Douthit, b. December 17, 1888: d. February 14, 1941: m-2nd. Nellie Elizabeth King, b. May 30, 1913. d. Nov. 30, 1995.
2. Henry Wise Hobson, b. October 9, 1880: d. July 1898.
3. George Richardson Hobson, b. April 13, 1883: m. September 28, 1918: Atilda Marie Wunderlicht, b. 1884.
4. Mary Morrison Hobson, b. December 2, 1884: d. February 14, 1947: m. August 15, 1907: John W. Bryan, b. August 16, 1911: d. February 13, 1947.
5. Otelia Armistead Hobson, b. May 5, 1886: d. September 9, 1886.
6. Jennings Wise Hobson, b. August 15, 1887: d. December 6, 1955: m. November 5, 1913: Mary Louise Berkley, b. August 12, 1887: d. January 9, 1947.
7. Alice Virginia Hobson, b. October 16, 1888: d. May 6, 1972: m. June 14, 1909: Harwood Syme Haynes, b. August 27, 1883.

VII. 2nd. Henry Wise Hobson (second child), b. July 9, 1858 at Eastwood, Goochland County, Virginia: d. August 13,1898 in New York City: m. December 17, 1887: Katherine Thayer Jermain, b. December 3, 1859 in Troy, New York: d. December 3, 1915 in Central Valley, New York, (four children below, all born in Denver, Colorado).

VIII. 1. Katherine Thayer Hobson, b. April 11, 1889: d. September 9, 1982. Two marriages, no issue. m-1: Herbert Kraus, div.: m-2: Diether Thimme, div.
2. Henry Wise Hobson, b. May 16, 1891: d. February 1983: m. Edmonia Taylor Bryan, (four children).
3. Eleanor Whiteside Hobson, b. January 7, 1893: d. April 28, 1985: m. June 22, 1916: George M. Mackenzie, b. Aug. 13, 1885: d. March 25, 1952. (four children). [The editor of this book is the third son of their eldest child.]
4. Francis Thayer Hobson, b. September 4, 1897: d. October 17, 1967: m-1st. Janet Camp, div.: m-2nd. Priscilla Fansler, div. (one son): m-3rd. Laura Zametkin, div.: m-4th. Isabelle Garrabrants, b. September 3, 1903: d. January 7, 1960. (two children): m-5th. Elizabeth Davis.

Hobson family plot, Hollywood Cemetery. Graves of John Cannon Hobson, right monument, and his wife, left. The stones read: "Mary S. wife of John C. Hobson Born at Dumfries Scotland April 10, 1795 Died April 3, 1871" and "John C. Hobson Born in Cumberland Col. July 20,1791 Died April 11, 1873".

Grave of Col. John Wise. Wise family cemetery near Chesconessex Creek, Onancock, Virginia.

Grave of Scarburgh Robinson, "Wife of John Wise and Daughter of Co. Tully Robinson and his wife Sara West," Wise family cemetery near Chesconessex Creek, Onancock, Virginia.

> The Wise family genealogy:

I. John Wise 1st, b. 1617: d. 1695: m. June 4, 1636: Hannah Scarburgh. Wise sailed from Gravesend, England on July 4, 1635 and settled on Chesconessex Creek near Accomack. In Virginia he married Hannah Scarburgh who had come from Norfolk, England with her father Capt. Edmund Scarburgh. John Wise reportedly purchased just over 1,000 acres, on the Chesconnessex and Onancock creeks, from the Indians in exchange for seven Dutch blankets.

II. John Wise 2nd, d. 1717: m. Matilda West, d. 1722, (otherwise unknown).

III. John Wise 3rd, d. 1767: m. Scarburgh Robinson.

IV. John Wise 4th, b. July 27, 1723: d. March 1769: m. Margaret Douglas, b. 1736: d. 1808.

V. John Wise 5th, b. @ 1765: d. March 30, 1812: m–1st. Mary "Polly" Henry, d. (no issue) [Mary Henry was the niece of Patrick Henry.]: m–2nd. April 18, 1799: Sarah "Sally or Sallie" Corbin Cropper, b. 1777: d. 1813: (three of six children lived to adulthood). This John Wise is often referred to as Major John Wise and was Speaker of the House of Delegates, 1794–1799.

VI. Henry Alexander Wise, (fifth child of above second marriage), b. December 3, 1806: d. September 12, 1876: m–1st. October 8, 1828: Ann Elizabeth Jennings, b. December 31, 1808: d. May 4, 1837: m–2nd. November 1840: Sarah Sergeant, b. 1817: d. 1850: m–3rd. November 1853, Mary Lyons, b. 1814: d. July 17, 1901.

Henry A. Wise had fourteen children, but only seven, four by his first wife and three by his second, lived to adulthood. There is strong circumstantial evidence that Wise fathered a son, William Henry Grey (also Gray), by Elizabeth Gray, one of his slaves. The children of Henry A. Wise that lived to adulthood:

m–1st to Ann Elizabeth Jennings, 1808–1837:
   1. Mary Elizabeth Wise, 1829–1898, m. Alexander Y. P. Garnett.
   2. Obadiah Jennings Wise, 1831–1862.
   3. Henry A. Wise Jr., 1834–1869, m. Harriet Haxall.
   4. Annie Jennings Wise, 1837–1914, m. Frederick Plumer Hobson.
m–2nd to Sarah Sergeant, 1817–1850:
   1. Richard Alsop Wise, 1843–1900, m. Maria Peachy.
   2. Margaretta Ellen "Néné" Wise, 1844–1909, m. William Carrington Mayo.
   3. John Sergeant Wise, 1846–1913, m. Evelyn "Eva" Byrd Beverley Douglas, 1851–1925. [John S. Wise and his wife had nine children. Letters from two of them, John S. "Jack" Wise Jr. and Hugh D. Wise are included in this book.]

VII. Annie Jennings Wise (fourth child of first marriage above), b. April 28, 1837: d. June 3, 1914: m. July 9, 1856: Frederick Plumer Hobson, b. February 24, 1833: d. April 4, 1868. (Six children, two survived to adulthood. See Hobson family genealogy above.)

I   An Annotated Genealogy

Located beside Chesconessex Creek near Onancock, Virginia, is the Wise family burial ground, where John Wise I through John Wise VI are buried with their wives and other family members. The brick wall surrounding the cemetery includes memorial plaques for some members of the family who are buried elsewhere. The plaques shown in the background in this photo, from left to right, are in memory of: Obadiah Jennings Wise, (1831–1862, son of Henry A. Wise and buried in Hollywood Cemetery), Eva Douglas Wise, (1851–1925, wife of John S. Wise and buried in Hollywood Cemetery), John S. Wise, (1846–1913, son of Henry A. Wise and buried in Hollywood Cemetery), Mary E. Lyons, (1814–1901, third wife of Henry A. Wise and buried in Hollywood Cemetery), Ann Jennings Wise, (1808–1837, first wife of Henry A. Wise, formerly buried in this cemetery but now buried in Hollywood Cemetery), Henry A. Wise, (1806–1876, buried in Hollywood Cemetery), Sarah Sergeant Wise, (1817–1850, second wife of Henry A. Wise and buried in Philadelphia), Richard Alsop Wise, (1843–1900, son of Henry A. Wise and buried in Hollywood Cemetery), Hugh Douglas Wise, (1871–1942, son of John S. Wise), Ida Hungerford Wise, (wife of Hugh D. Wise), and Henry A. Wise, (son of Jennings Wise & Elizabeth Anderson).

Henry Alexander Wise on his ancestry:

Accomack June 29th, 1848
To Mr. Hunt, author
Albany, N. York

Sir.
   The death of all the aged paternal relations, the last in 1842, of my family, makes it difficult for me to furnish you the requisite materials for the compilation of a genealogical record. I will give my recollections of facts, independent of records.
   The name Wise, Wies originally, perhaps, is I believe of German origin, the root of which you will find in Burke's heraldry, the motto: *Ande sapere*. I can't fix the exact period to which to trace my European ancestry. You will find in Burke something curious respecting one of the ancestor's coat of arms, three eremites & the "fleur de lis," his wit making him, by a certain response to Henry VIII, I think a favorite or favored at least by the King. The wit was in a poem upon "lis" & "louse." His armorial bearings you'll see in Burke.

Near Wise Point on Chesconessex Creek, Onancock, Virginia, where John Wise settled in 1635.

My American ancestor was an emigrant from the North, I think, of England. I don't know the date & place of his birth. He was a Col. in the Kings commission and was a member of the Executive Council in Accomack Va. I don't know when he emigrated, but it was not long after the first settlement of Virginia. My father's patrimony, a tract of about 1,000 acres of land, still held by the male descendants of his oldest son, situated on Chesconessex Creek, Accomack Va., under this grant of the Crown of England was purchased from the Indians, of the hills called A— [illegible] by our first emigrant ancestor, Col. John Wise for 7 Dutch blankets. The date of this grant I am not able to ascertain, for the reason that the records of Accomack County were, many years ago, destroyed by fire.

Our Ancestor, the said Col. John Wise, settled on Chesconessex Creek, Accomack County Eastern shore of Virginia. He was married but I don't know whom he married. He and his wife died at Chesconessex, a place called Fort George, when I don't know, and there they were buried. They had two children whom only I know of, John (my grandfather) and Tully Robinson Wise (Robinson I suspect was their mother's patronymial. The dates of their birth I don't know. When they married I am not informed; but they married two sisters, daughters of an emigrant Scotch barrister, George Douglas (whose very old law books and whose coat of arms I now have.)…

John Wise, the elder brother, married Margaret (called Peggy) Douglas, and Tully R. Wise married Tabitha (called Tabby) Douglas. John inherited the estate, the manor place on Chesconessex, and Tully a large body of land on the west creek north called Deep Creek. I don't know when Tully died, but he was buried at Deep Creek… John was born the ~ day of ~ A. D. 17~, I don't know when he was married. He settled at Chesconessex, Fort George. There died, the ~ day of ~ A. D. 17~, and was there buried. He left two sons, the oldest named John (my father) and the younger named Tully Robinson Wise, and three daughters, Cassy, Elizabeth, & Mary. The 3 daughters all died childless. Tully Robinson Wise was a physician, married first a Miss Bowdoin of Northampton County Va, and after her decease, a widow (Mrs. Fisher) whose maiden name was White…

John Wise, my father… was a lawyer by profession and was as such highly esteemed for his integrity & success; he was Speaker for several years of the H of delegates of Virginia, from the year 1794 to the year 1799; and at the time of his death was clerk of the County and Superior Courts of Accomack. He married first, Mary the daughter of James Henry, one of the judges of the Genl. Court of Virginia, of [illegible] Bay in Northumberland Co. Va. Several years after her death he married Sarah (called Sally) Cropper, the oldest daughter of [John Cropper] — [End of four page letter.]

Other Family Connections

❦ The Jennings family genealogy:

I. Jacob Jennings, b. @ 1711: d. 1787: m. unknown.

II. Jacob (eldest child), b. 1744: d. February 17, 1813: m. Mary Kennedy, d. 1791, (eight children).

III. Obadiah Jennings, (fifth child), b. December 13, 1778: d. January 12, 1832: m-1st. Mary Becket, (one child): m-2nd. Ann "Anna" Wilson, b. 1787, (daughter of Dr. James Wilson of Wye Mills, Maryland): d. 1841 (or 1842), (seven children).

IV. Ann Elizabeth Jennings (second child of second marriage), b. December 31, 1808: d. May 4, 1837: m. October 8, 1828 in Nashville, Tennessee: Henry Alexander Wise, b. December 3, 1806: d. September 12, 1876. See Wise family genealogy above.

V. Annie Jennings Wise, (fourth child), b. April 28, 1837: d. June 3, 1914: m. July 9, 1856: Frederick Plumer Hobson, b. February 24, 1833: d. April 4, 1868. Six children, two survived to adulthood. See Hobson family genealogy above.

The Jennings family
Jacob Jennings, 1711–1787, served in the American Revolution and is buried in Bound Brook, New Jersey. His son, also Jacob, studied medicine and was wounded at the Battle of Trenton during the American Revolution. After the war he was ordained in the Dutch Reformed Church and moved to Virginia where he continued to practice medicine and minister to two congregations. His son, Obadiah, was a lawyer and Presbyterian minister, living at different times in Washington, Pennsylvania, Steubenville, Ohio, and Nashville, Tennessee. In 1892 Annie Jennings Wise Hobson responded to an inquiry about her Jennings ancestors: "I have written requesting my sister Mrs. Garnett to send you the dates you ask for of the birth, marriage & death of my mother Ann Jennings—as she could give you more accurate data than I can. My Mother died when I was three days old…" Ann Elizabeth Jennings Wise, 1808–1837, was originally buried in Accomack but her remains were moved to the Hollywood Cemetery in Richmond after the death of Henry A. Wise.

❦ The Littleton and Scarburgh family genealogy:

I. Nathaniel Littleton, emigrated to Accomack County, Virginia @ 1638: d. 1654: m. Anne Southey, d. 1656. He became Chief Justice of Accomack County, a Member of the House of Burgesses in 1652, and a member of Governor Richard Burnett's Executive Council.

Grave of Ann Elizabeth Jennings Wise, 1808–1837, Hollywood Cemetery, Richmond, Virginia. "Ann Elizabeth Wise — Daughter of O. Jennings D. C. and the wife of Henry A. Wise. Born the 31st day of December 1808 and Died the 4th day of May 1837 Be of good cheer it is I. Be not afraid." At the time of her death she was buried in Accomac, Virginia. Her body and this stone were moved to the Hollywood Cemetery and the back of the stone reads: "Moved from Deep Creek Accomac Virginia May 1928 by her descendants". See photo page 46.

II. Mary Littleton m. Edmund Scarburgh (also Scarborough, Scarbrugh and Skarborowgh)

III. Matilda Scarburgh m. Lt. Col. John West.

IV. Matilda West, d. 1722: m. John Wise 2nd, d. 1717. (See Wise family genealogy above.)

The Scarburgh family

Col. Edmund Scarburgh, born in England about 1617, came to Virginia with his father, Capt. Edmund Scarburgh. Col. Scarburgh has been described as being "very independent" and was a personal friend of Peter Stuyvesant of New Netherlands (New York). He owned a large number of trading vessels that sailed between New England, New Amsterdam, the West Indies, and Accomack, and he owned several thousand acres of land in Accomack and Maryland. Between 1629 and 1630 Capt. Scarburgh, the father, had been the first burgess from the Eastern Shore. In 1659 Col. Scarburgh commanded a force of 600 men in a campaign against the Assateague Indians and in that same year he imported thirty negroes from the Dutch in Manhattan—then the largest number of slaves ever brought into Virginia by an individual. In 1661 he was appointed a commissioner by Philip Calvert of Maryland to assist in surveying the boundary line between Maryland and Virginia. Taking advantage of this position, Scarburgh greatly extended the territory of Accomack to the north to include his Maryland land holdings and also took the opportunity to drive the Quakers out of Accomack county.

≫ The Bowman & Cropper family genealogy:

I. Edmund Bowman, emigrated to Accomack @ 1643: d. @ 1691: m. Catherine, three daughters. When Bowman came to Virginia he was given a grant of seven square miles of land upon Folly Creek where he built the house that would be known as Bowman's Folly.

II. Gertrude Bowman m. John Cropper who had come to Virginia from Scotland.

III. Sebastian Cropper, d. spring 1727: m. Rachel Parker, d. 1727

IV. Bowman Cropper, d. 1757: m. unknown.

V. Sebastian Cropper Jr., d. spring 1776: m. Sarah Corbin, d. 1776.

VI. John Cropper, b. December 23, 1755 in Accomack County, Virginia: d. January 15, 1821: m-1st. August 1776: Margaret Pettitt, daughter of William Pettit, (two children lived to adulthood, Sarah "Sally" Corbin Cropper and Margaret Pettit Cropper. Margaret m. Thomas M. Bayly). m-2nd. Catherine Bayly, (six children). Catherine Bayly, Cropper's second wife, was the sister of Thomas M. Bayly, Cropper's son–in–law.

VII. Sarah "Sally" Corbin Cropper, oldest child, first marriage, b. 1777: d. 1813: m. April 18, 1799: John Wise 5th, b. @1765: d. March 11, 1812. (See Wise family genealogy above.)

Left, the Cropper family cemetery and above, the view from the cemetery, Bowman's Folly, Accomac, Virginia.

John Cropper

A Memoir of General John Cropper by Barton Haxall Wise was published by the Virginia Historical Society in 1892 and reprinted by the Eastern Shore of Virginia Historical Society in 1974. As a boy of nineteen, Cropper was selected to be the captain of the local company of volunteers from Accomack, and in December 1776 he left his home and joined General Washington. He saw service at many of the early battles of the Revolutionary War including Trenton, Brandywine, and Germantown, was with the Virginia troops during the winter of 1777–1778 at Valley Forge, and throughout his life had a very close relationship with George Washington. His wife, Margaret Pettit Cropper died in 1781 when she swallowed some pins as she was helping her husband bandage his wounds. John Cropper later married Catherine Bayly and had six more children. The inscriptions on the tombstones of Margaret Cropper and John Cropper in the cemetery at Bowman's Folly read:

Margaret Cropper

Wife of John Cropper Jun. Daughter of William Pettit and Mary his wife of Northampton. Died 3rd June 1781, Aged 29 years, 1 month 21 days. At her feet lies Sabra Corbin Cropper, daughter of John Cropper Jun. and Catherine his wife, died 2nd November 1791, Aged 12 days.

In memory of General John Cropper oldest son of Sebastian and Sabra was born at Bowmans Folley in the County of Accomac E. S. Virginia December 23rd 1753. He was an officer in the revolutionary war and continued untill the end. He died January 15th 1821 being 65 years and 22 days old leaving a wife, seven children and 10 grandchildren.

༄ The Thoroughgood family genealogy:

I. William Thoroughgood b. c. 1560 Norfolk County, England m. Anne Edwards.
There is no evidence that either William Thoroughgood or his wife ever came to America.

II. Capt. Adam Thoroughgood b. 1603/ (or 1604) of Lynnhaven, England. Came to Virginia in 1621: d. 1640: m. 1624: Sara Offley, b. 1609, who came to America in 1626. (four children).

III. Elizabeth Thoroughgood m. Capt. John Michael who had come to Virginia about 1656.

IV. Margaret Michael m. Col. John Custis b. 1653: d. January 26, 1713.

V. Col. Henry Custis m. Anne Kendall (otherwise unknown).

VI. Robinson Custis m. Mary (otherwise unknown).

VII. Mary Custis m. William Pettit.

VIII. Margaret Pettit m. August 1776: John Cropper, b. December 23, 1755 at Bowman's Folly: d. January 15, 1821. (See Bowman and Cropper genealogy above.)

IX. Sara "Sally" Corbin Cropper (oldest child, 1777–1813), m. April 18, 1799: John Wise 5th, b. @1765: d. March 11, 1812. (See Wise family genealogy above.)

Adam Thoroughgood

Adam Thoroughgood, 1603/1604–1640, came to America as an indentured servant in 1621 aboard the *Charles* and was a prosperous tobacco farmer when his indenture ended in 1624. He then returned to England to recruit more settlers for the Virginia colony. In England he married Sarah Offley who was only fifteen years old (some sources say she was 18 years old). She was the daughter of a wealthy investor in The Virginia Company and granddaughter of the Lord Mayor of London. For each indentured servant that Thoroughgood brought to Virginia he was granted 50 acres. Ultimately he owned over 5,000 acres along the Lynnhaven River and at one time was a member of House of Burgesses at Jamestown. The Lynnhaven River and Norfolk County were named by him after his birthplace. The Adam Thoroughgood House still stands in a residential area of Virginia Beach and is said to be the oldest brick home in America. Different sources give the date of its construction as either 1635 or 1680. If the latter date, then the house that bears Adam Thoroughgood's name was built by one his descendants and not by him.

Right: The Adam Thoroughgood House, Virginia Beach, Virginia, before restoration and removal of dormers. Photo from Tidewater Virginia *by Paul Wilstach.*

Far right: The Adam Thoroughgood House. Photo from Historic Virginia Homes and Churches *by Robert A. Lancaster, Jr.*

The New York and Massachusetts Ancestry

The Massachusetts ancestry begins with the arrival of immigrants from England in the early 17th century but it was not until the middle of the next century that ancestors arrived in New York. As in Virginia, in the ensuing years these settlers traded with and fought wars with the Indians, cleared and farmed their land, and then fought in the American Revolution.

❧ The Thayer family genealogy:

I. Thomas Thayer, from Braintree, Essex County, England, emigrated to Braintree Massachusetts. around 1630: d. June 2, 1665: m. April 16, 1616 (or 1618): Margery Wheeler, d. February 11, 1672 (or 1673).

II. Fernando Thayer, b. in England (baptized April 18, 1625) and came to America with his parents: d. March 28, 1713: m. Jan. 14, 1651 (or 1652) Huldah Hayward, d. September 1 , 1690.

III. Isaac Thayer, m. February 1, 1691 (or 1692): Mercy Ward. b. January 27, 1669: d. December 18, 1700.

IV. Ebenezer Thayer, b. September 6, 1697: m. May 9, 1719 (or August 9, 1721) at Mendon, Massachusetts: Mary Wheelock, b. January 21, 1701 (or 1702) at Mendon, Massachusetts, (eight children).

V. Ebenezer Thayer (oldest child), b. June 6, 1720: m. April 24, 1734: Hannah Greene of Mendon, Massachusetts. d. 1783.

VI. Ebenezer Thayer, b. May 21, 1737: m. Martha White b. October 8, 1737.

VII. Thaddeus Thayer, b. August 10, 1760: m. October 1, 1783: Rhoda Smith, b. 1759: d. December 24, 1817.

VIII. Adin (also Aden) Thayer, b. January, 28, 1785 in Bellingham Cross, Massachusetts: d. Feb. 7, 1858 in Hoosick Falls, New York: m. December 1815 in Wilmington, Vermont: Mary Ball, b. March 19, 1795: d. March 15, 1864, (eleven children).

IX. Francis S. Thayer, (fourth child), b. September 11, 1822 in Dummerston, Vermont: d. November 26, 1880 in Colorado Springs, Colorado: m. April 30, 1850: Catherine Whiteside McKie, b. June 16, 1827 in Cambridge, New York: d. January 4, 1901 in Colorado Springs Colorado, (two children below).

X. 1. Francis McKie Thayer, b. June 13, 1857: d. May 24, 1902: m. May 1898, Harriet Jones: (no children).
2. Katherine Thayer, b. December 3, 1859 in Troy, New York: d. December 3, 1915 in Central Valley, New York: m–1st. June 7, 1882: Barclay Jermain, d. July 7, 1882, (no children). m–2nd. December 17, 1887: Henry Wise Hobson, b. July 9, 1858 at Eastwood, Goochland County, Virginia: d. August 13,1898 in New York City, (four children below, all born in Denver, Colorado).

XI. 1. Katherine Thayer Hobson, b. April 11, 1889: d. September 9, 1982. Two marriages, no issue. m-1: Herbert Kraus, div.: m-2: Diether Thimme, div.
2. Henry Wise Hobson, b. May 16, 1891: d. February 9, 1983: m. Edmonia Taylor Bryan, (four children).
3. Eleanor Whiteside Hobson, b. January 7, 1893: d. April 28, 1985: m. June 22, 1916: George M. Mackenzie, b. August 13, 1885: d. March 25, 1952, (four children).
4. Francis Thayer Hobson, b. September 4, 1897: d. October 17, 1967: m-1st. Janet Camp, div.: m-2nd. Priscilla Fansler, div. (one son.): m-3rd. Laura Zametkin, div.: m-4th. Isabelle Garrabrants, b. September 3, 1903: d. January 7, 1960, (two children): m-5th. Elizabeth Davis.

൙ The McKie family genealogy:

I. John McKie, b. 1705: d. October 27, 1782: m. Mary Ann Wilson, b. 1718: d. March 31, 1806, (six children below).

II. 1. Alexander McKie, died in Scotland.
2. Peter McKie, died in Scotland.
3. Mary McKie, came to America with her parents.
4. John McKie, came to America with his parents but later moved to Canada.
5. James McKie, 1760–1843, came to America with his parents. At age 22, James took over the management of the farm. (See below.)
6. Elizabeth McKie, came to America with her parents.

II. James McKie (fifth child above), b. 1760: d. June 14, 1843: m. Elizabeth Wilson, b. 1765: d. December 27, 1849, (eleven children, below).

III. 1. Sarah McKie, 1786–1860: m-1st. William Armitage: m-2nd. John Reid, 1766–1842.
2. Mary McKie, 1787–1845, no other information known.
3. John McKie, June 1, 1789–September 9, 1864: m. Catharine Whiteside, 1793–1824.
4. George McKie, August 14, 1791–January 15, 1861, (see below).
5. Elizabeth McKie, 1793–1855: m. Henry Mathews, 1784–1843.
6. William McKie, 1795– April 15, 1863: m-1st. Nancy Law, d. 1838: m-2nd. Julia Smith, 1805–1879.
7. Ann McKie, 1798–1856, never married.
8. Margaret McKie, 1800–1874: m. William Wilcox, 1803–1870.
9. Almy McKie, 1802–June 24, 1868, never married.
10. James McKie, 1805–May 5, 1869: m. Lucy Campbell, 1811–1875. James is the author of a diary excerpted in the following chapters.
11. Peter McKie, 1808–1856: m. Letitia McFarland.

III. George McKie, (fourth child above), b. August 14, 1791: d. January 15, 1861: The seven children of George McKie by the two Whiteside sisters are:
m-1st Catherine Whiteside, b. February 12, 1793: d. February 20, 1824.
1. Neil W. McKie, June 17, 1815–April 27, 1862.
2. Edwin J. McKie, October 29, 1818–March 7, 1895: m-1st Antoinette Mosher: m-2nd Jane Short. There are no living descendants of Edwin McKie.

McKie Hollow Road, 2000.

m-2nd Sophia Whiteside, b. April 6, 1796: d. January 21, 1878.
1. George Wilson McKie, August 23, 1825–May 27, 1860.
2. Catherine McKie, b. June 16, 1827: d. January 4, 1901: m. April 30, 1850: Francis S. Thayer, b. September 11, 1822 in Dummerston, Vermont: d. November 26, 1880 in Colorado Springs, Colorado. See Thayer family genealogy.
3. Henry M. McKie, September 6, 1829–April 22, 1851.
4. James McKie, September 13, 1831–November 1, 1855.
5. Peter McKie, December 25, 1833–November 1853.

The McKie family

Born in Bargaly Glen, Minnigaff Parish, Newton–Stewart, Galloway, Scotland, in 1705, John McKie married Mary Ann Wilson and lived in Minnigaff, Scotland, until 1767 when, at the age of sixty-two, they emigrated to America. He purchased a large tract of land, perhaps 400 acres, in the Wilson Patent in what is now the town of White Creek, New York, about four miles east of Cambridge and moved there in 1774. This land, remote, hard to work, and covered with virgin forest, was reportedly purchased because he wanted to live in the hills to remind him of Scotland. *The History of Washington County*, published in 1878, described Whitecreek as follows: "The hilly districts afford extensive and excellent pasturage. The town on the whole is adapted to husbandry of a varied character… The broken and mountainous districts in the north part of the town are less adapted for tillage than the lands in most of the other towns of the county. Extensive tracts were possessed by single individuals and stocked mostly with sheep." Though an elderly man when he arrived there, John McKie and his teenage sons carved a farm out of this wilderness where four generations of the family would live over the next 100 years.

James McKie, 1760–June 14, 1843, was born in Minnigaff Parish, District of Galloway, Scotland, and came to America with his parents when he was seven years old. He was fourteen when the family cleared the farm in what is now McKie Hollow. In 1780, James McKie, then twenty, was one of sixty mili-

McKie Valley showing Snake Hill and Sugar Loaf Mountain in the distance. Stereoscopic Views published by L. F. Hurd, Greenwich, New York.

Looking up McKie Valley, showing Two-top and Pittstown Mountains. Stereoscopic Views published by L. F. Hurd, Greenwich, New York.

Farms in McKie Hollow, 2000.

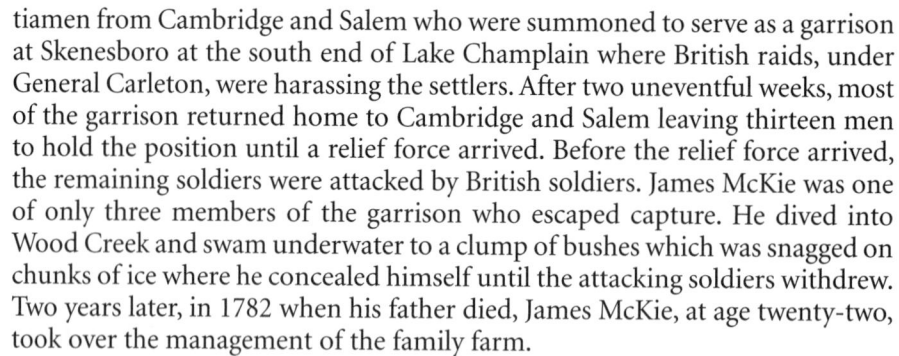

tiamen from Cambridge and Salem who were summoned to serve as a garrison at Skenesboro at the south end of Lake Champlain where British raids, under General Carleton, were harassing the settlers. After two uneventful weeks, most of the garrison returned home to Cambridge and Salem leaving thirteen men to hold the position until a relief force arrived. Before the relief force arrived, the remaining soldiers were attacked by British soldiers. James McKie was one of only three members of the garrison who escaped capture. He dived into Wood Creek and swam underwater to a clump of bushes which was snagged on chunks of ice where he concealed himself until the attacking soldiers withdrew. Two years later, in 1782 when his father died, James McKie, at age twenty-two, took over the management of the family farm.

In 1785 James McKie married his first cousin Elizabeth Wilson, 1765–December 27, 1849, of New York City. Elizabeth Wilson was the daughter of George Wilson, 1737–February 7, 1808, and Sarah Dawson, 1737–November 1797. George Wilson was the brother James McKie's mother, Mary Ann Wilson McKie.

George McKie, 1791–1861, James' second son, was a farmer, first in White Creek and later on the Peter Whiteside farm in Cambridge, New York, where the family prospered for many years. Though he was twice married and had seven children, George McKie's only living descendants are through his daughter Catherine McKie, 1827–1901, who married Francis Thayer, 1822–1880. As the Episcopal Church forbids the marriage of in-laws, George McKie became a Presbyterian when he married Sophia Whiteside, the sister of his first wife.

William McKie's Residence, McKie Hollow, Hurd's Stereoscopic Views, Greenwich, New York.

Grave of James McKie, 1760–1843, Woodland Cemetery, Cambridge, New York. "Born in Galloway Shire, Scotland, A Revolutionary War Soldier."

The Whiteside family genealogy:

I. Phineas Whiteside, b. January 31, 1716, County Tryone, Ireland: d. April 1, 1793: m. Ann Cooper, 1731–March 13, 1800 (seven children below).

II. 1. John Whiteside, 1752–1841: m. Margaret Robertson, 1754–1849.
2. William Whiteside, 1754–1803: m. Lois Freeman, 1761–1840.
3. Peter Whiteside, 1755–1835: m. Ann Robertson, 1756–1815.
4. Thomas Whiteside, 1758–1830: m. Elizabeth Cramer, 1762–1838.
5. Ann Whiteside, 1761–1806: m. John Cochran, 1763–1838.
6. Edward Whiteside, 1763–1844: m-1st. Ann French, 1768–1806: m-2nd. Asenath Murray, 1782–1836.
7. Oliver Whiteside, 1766–1804: m. Susanna Prendergast, 1766–1804.

II. Peter Whiteside (third child), b. 1755: d. May 26, 1835: m. March 12, 1789: Ann Robertson, 1756–1815. (Three children, Niel, 1791–1814, Catherine, 1793–1824, and Sophia, 1796–1878.)

III. 2nd. Catherine Whiteside (second child), b. February 12, 1793: d. February 20, 1824: m. December 17, 1812: George McKie, b. August 14, 1791: d. January 15, 1861. (Two children, see McKie family genealogy above.)

III. 3rd. Sophia Whiteside (third child), b. April 6, 1796: d. January 21, 1878: m. George McKie (his 2nd marriage), b. August 14, 1791: d. January 15, 1861. (Five children, see McKie family genealogy above.) Sophia's headstone is clearly engraved "1796" and that date is used in this book. Two other publications, Ida

Whiteside's *A History of Phineas Whiteside and His Family* and Islay V. H. Gill's *The McKie Family of the Cambridge Valley*, incorrectly state that she was born in 1795.

IV. Catherine McKie, second child of second marriage, b. June 16, 1827: d. January 4, 1901: m. April 30, 1850: Francis S. Thayer, b. September 11, 1822, in Dummerston, Vermont: d. November 26, 1880, in Colorado Springs, Colorado. (Two children, see Thayer family genealogy above.)

V. Katherine Thayer, second child, b. December 3, 1859: d. December 3, 1915: m-1st June 7, 1882: Barclay Jermain, d. July 7, 1882 (no children); m-2nd December 17, 1887: Henry Wise Hobson, b. July 9,1858, at Eastwood, Goochland County, Virginia: d. August 13,1898, in New York City. (Four children, see Thayer or Hobson genealogies above.)

It was a small world in the 1800s. Barclay Jermain's mother, Catherine Ann Rice, had been born in White Creek, New York, on February 27, 1823, the daughter of Clark Rice and Ann Hutton Rice. Catherine Ann Rice married James Barclay Jermain and had three daughters and one son. Catherine Ann Rice Jermain and Catherine McKie Thayer, 1827–1901, were very close friends in Cambridge, White Creek, Albany, and Troy.

The Whiteside family

Born in 1716, Phineas Whiteside came to America about 1735–1736 from County Tyrone in North Ireland, but little is known of his forebears. He had some education to prepare him for the ministry, and when he came to America he settled in the Pequea Valley in Lancaster County, Pennsylvania, where, in 1752, he married Ann Cooper of Leacock township. In 1754 he was ordained an elder in the Covenanter Church at Octararo, Pennsylvania. In 1764 he traveled north from Pennsylvania with a missionary from Scotland. Two years later

Graves of Peter Whiteside, 1755–1835, and Ann Robertson Whiteside, 1756–1815, Whiteside Cemetery, Cambridge, New York. Ann's stone reads: "A loving wife, a tender parent. A friend of the poor & a sincere Christian. She died esteemed of her friends and acquaintance."

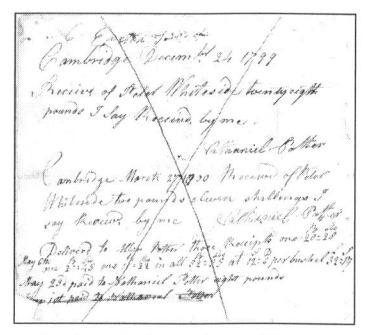

1799 & 1800 Promissory Notes of Peter Whiteside's: "Cambridge, December 24, 1799, Received of Peter Whiteside twenty-eight pounds I say received by me. Nathaniel Potter"

Whiteside family graves. Graves of Phineas and Anne Whiteside, right, and row of gravestones for their descendants. Whiteside Cemetery, Cambridge, New York.

Grave of Phineas Whiteside, 1716–1793, "He saw Columbia struggling for liberty," Whiteside Cemetery, Cambridge, New York.

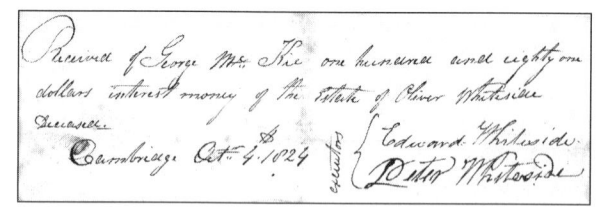

Receipt for funds from the estate of Oliver Whiteside, 1766–1804. Includes signatures of brothers Edward Whiteside and Peter Whiteside: "Received of George McKie one hundred and eighty one dollars interest money of the estate of Oliver Whiteside, deceased. Cambridge, October 4, 1824. Edward Whiteside & Peter Whiteside, Executors."

he repeated the journey and decided to settle in the Cambridge, New York, area where he purchased 800 acres of land and obtained a perpetual lease on an additional 600 acres. One story claims that he climbed the tallest tree he could find in West Cambridge and vowed to purchase all of the land that he could see. The *History of Washington County* notes that during the American Revolution Phineas Whiteside "was one of the few who pledged himself for the credit of his country to the amount of £10,000."

Phineas Whiteside was the second person buried in the Whiteside cemetery, a small cemetery adjoining the Whiteside Church in Cambridge, New York. His wife, Ann Cooper Whiteside, died in 1800 and is buried beside him. His epitaph reads:

In Memory Of — Phineas Whiteside Esq., by birth an Hibernian was born Jan. 31, 1716. He saw this and many parts of America a wilderness. He saw Columbia struggling for liberty, in which he took an active part; He saw her successful. He died April 1st, 1793 in the 77th year of his age.

"Full ripe in virtue as in age, For endless bliss he quit the stage."

Catherine McKie Thayer, 1827–1901, once copied the following letter from Mary Whiteside, (born August 26, 1718), in Ireland to her brother Phineas who had come to America. Phineas never saw this letter since it was written after his death but before that news had reached his sister.

Killycolpy June 2, 1793.
Mr. Phineas Whiteside Cambridge, County Albany York State America
Much Regarded Brother—

We and friends here are well thanks to God for it. We continue writing every year to you but very seldom get a letter from you. Therefore I entreat you or family to continue writing to us and to let us know in what occupation your family is in or if they are married all yet or not.

Dear Brother, my eldest son is in England this three years again the 12th of August next, learning to be a doctor and I expect him home again November and my two daughters and other son are living at home with me yet.

I hope if this reaches you that you will not omit to let me hear how you all are and give us an account of the Circumstances, form, and state of that part of America– or if you expect peace will continue in it. The English is very much engaged in war against the French at present and has or is about raising a militia in almost every County in this Kingdome. My kind love to you and family. –*Mary Whiteside.*

❧ The Wheelock family genealogy:

I. Ralph Wheelock, b. at Shropshire, England in 1600: Left England in 1637: d. Medfield, Massachusetts. January 11, 1682: m. Rebecca, (nine children).

Ralph Wheelock matriculated at Cambridge University in England in 1623 and there received his education. An ordained minister, Wheelock was much more interested in education than the ministry. He left England and sailed to the Massachusetts Bay Colony in 1637. He was to teach in the free school in Dedham, Massachusetts, from 1644–1651, the first free school in Massachusetts and one of the first schools in New England supported by a town tax. In 1651 he was one of the founders of Medfield, Massachusetts, and later a teacher in the first school established there. In the 1650s he took up collections for Harvard College, the first college in America, founded in 1636.

II. Benjamin Wheelock (fourth child), b. January 8, 1639 (or 1640) in Dedham, Massachusetts: d. about 1720 in Mendon, Massachusetts, m. May 21, 1668, in Medfield, Massachusetts: Elizabeth Bullen d. 1689 (three children).

III. Benjamin Wheelock (second child), b. December 12, 1678, in Medfield, Massachusetts: d. September 13, 1746, in Mendon, Massachusetts, m. December 9, 1700 in Mendon, Massachusetts: Huldah Thayer b. March 11, 1682.

Huldah Thayer was possibly the daughter of Fernando Thayer, 1625–1673, and Huldah Hayward (d. 1690), see Thayer family genealogy. If that was the case, then Mary Wheelock and Ebenezer Thayer, "IV" below, were first cousins. Benjamin Wheelock had a cousin, Eleazar Wheelock, who founded Dartmouth College.

IV. Mary Wheelock, b. January 21, 1701, (or 1702) at Mendon, Massachusetts, m. August 9, 1721, at Mendon, Massachusetts: Ebenezer Thayer of Bellingham, Massachusetts, b. September 6, 1697 (eight children, see Thayer family genealogy above).

In 1895, when Katherine Thayer Hobson, 1859–1915, sought to join the Colonial Dames, she listed Ralph Wheelock on her application, she being a ninth generation descendant of his. Her application was approved.

❧ Some family confusion:

There has been confusion ever since two Whiteside brothers, Peter and John, married two sisters, Ann and Margaret Robertson. Each family had a daughter named Catherine. The two Catherines married two brothers, George and John McKie. Peter's daughter married George McKie and John's daughter married John McKie. Islay V. H. Gill's pamphlet *The McKie Family of the Cambridge Valley* (1960) and Ida Whiteside's *A History of Phineas Whiteside and His Family* (1961) both incorrectly give the years of John's daughter as being the years of Peter's daughter. John's daughter lived August 6, 1793 –November 21, 1880, and had three children and Peter's daughter lived February 12, 1793–February 20, 1824, and had two children.

∼

The story of these different families, the Hobsons, Wises, Whitesides, Thayers, and McKies, is now best told in the letters, diaries, and other writings that survive them, and that is the rest of this book.

II

1777–1838

Virginia, Pennsylvania, and Tennessee

AMERICA was born and began to grow up during these tumultuous years as the descendants of the early settlers created a new nation. From Accomac, Virginia, a young John Cropper went to Valley Forge and wrote letters home to his wife and newborn child. From Readington, New Jersey, a young surgeon, Jacob Jennings, went to war and was wounded at the Battle of Trenton. A son of his was born in 1778. It would not be until 1828 when, in Nashville, Tennessee, Cropper's grandson would marry Jennings' granddaughter and the grandson would embark on a career that would make him a political power and household name in Virginia.

America experienced great growing pains during these years. Uncertain of the form of government that the new nation would have, its founders first wrote the Articles of Confederation whose lack of success caused them to convene again and write the Constitution which was ratified in 1788. During these formative years, the nation's capital would move from New York to Philadelphia and then finally to the District of Columbia. The census of 1790 showed that this was a nation of four million people and that Philadelphia was the largest city in the country. Ten years later the census would report a population of 5.3 million people, including half a million slaves. In 1808 Congress prohibited the importation of slaves from Africa, and in 1810 the census reported a population of 7.2 million, including 1.2 million slaves.

There were other things happening in America and around the world during these years. In 1793 Eli Whitney patented the cotton gin and in that same year yellow fever killed an estimated five thousand people in Philadelphia. Elsewhere, Merino sheep were first imported to the United States from Spain in 1802, establishing the sheep raising industry in America, and the 1802 purchase of the Louisiana Territory doubled the size of the new nation.

Letters and writings by:
George Corbin
John Cropper
Sarah Corbin Cropper, daughter of John Cropper
S. Ellis
Obadiah Jennings
Samuel Jennings
John Wise 5th, father of Henry A. Wise

Letters written from: Morristown, New Jersey; Valley Forge, Steubenville, and Philadelphia, Pennsylvania; and Accomac and Richmond, Virginia.

The Birth of a Nation — Valley Forge

John Cropper's letters to his wife are addressed in three ways: Margaret, Marget, and Peggy.

a great Battle in the Jersys Washington defeated British troops at Princeton on January 3, 1777.

Mr. Abbot George Abbot and his wife had raised Margaret Pettit after the deaths of her parents. When Margaret married John Cropper, the reception was at the Abbot home.

January 12, 1777, Philadelphia
Dear Peggy—   This Day I am leaving Philadelphia with the Regiment to go to Camp. Last night we heard the king's seventh regiment was intirely taken. To Day we hear by a Major who comes from Camp that there has been a great Battle in the Jersys, and that Howe's army is half taken Prisoners and Kill'd. Soldiers are flocking from every part, which I hope will put an End to the War this Winter, if our People behave as well as they have. Within three Weeks two thousand Hessians and Englishmen have been brought to this City. Inclosed I send you a Saturday's Paper. Give my love to all Relations and Compliments to Friends, and write by the first opportunity direct your Letters to be left at the [illegible], in Philadelphia, and I shall get them. I expect to be home in about 3 months. beg Mr. Abbot to write to me. Our Soldiers are all dressed in Regimentals at the Expense of the Continent, and have received all their Wages. God bless You and my Brothers. I am your most Affectionate Husband where ever I goe,   —*John Cropper*.
(From a photo facsimile of the letter. The letter was also published in Barton Haxall Wise's *Memoir of General John Cropper* first published in 1892 and reprinted in 1974 by the Eastern Shore of Virginia Historical Society.)
Addressed to: Mrs. Marget Cropper, Accomack County, Virginia
Fav'd by Doct. Fousher

Philada. Jan. 16th 1777
Dear Peggy—   Twas my intention to write to you by every opportunity; therefore I now write by Doctr. Fousher. Thank God, I am yet tollerable hearty & hope you are the same, however do let me hear from you by first opportunity.
     Our Regimt. has never marchd before today. [torn page] are this minute setting of for camp. Last Monday I sent of my horse & chair; please take the best care of Bearer. I now send you three yards of narrow lace which cost me 3 dollars, such is the dearness.
     It would give me great pleasure to hear from my Brothers, Mr. & Mrs. Abbot, but much more to hear particularly from my dear Peggy. I shall leave all my things at the Tavern call'd the Conesstougou Waggon where I have left every thing prepared in the best manner I cou'd, if Fate shou'd snatch me out of the World. If you write or shou'd want any thing of mine, the Conesstougou Waggon is the place.
     I am you'rs 'till Death, *John Cropper*. (*John Cropper Correspondence*, Mortimer Rare Book Room, Smith College Library.)

Addressed to— Mr. Geo. Abbot, Accomack County, Virginia
From— Jno Cropper's Camp, Morris T. April 1, 1777.
Headquarters, Morristown. Apl 1st, 1777.
Dear Sir: Just now, Wm. Widgon, from Accomack arrived at my lodgings, and informed me of something that gives me the greatest anxiety & pain, unless I am better informed: He tells me that on Monday 23rd of March he came by Assawaiman & that Mrs. Cutler told him that my dear Peggy was deliv'd of a Girl, that the child was expect'd to die & that my Peggy was not very bad; I am afraid he does not tell me the worst. I beg'd Mr. Joyne to call

Assawaiman probably Assawoman on a modern map

at your house & deliver this letter. Be so good as to send John Cropper up immediately. tell him I will pay his asking, I will allow him one week to get ready. Send up my summer clothes by him.

I shall be impatient to hear from your house. Dear Friend— &c, *John Cropper*. (Smith College Library)

Addressed to— Major John Cropper, Head Quarters, Morris Town, New Jersey.
From— George Corbin.
Dr. Jack: Yours of [torn page] was duely handed me, and afforded me great satisfaction as it gave me information of your health and convinced me that some reports propagated by your Enimies were false and malitious. It was reported but the author I could not found out, that you was returned to the *General* as a deserter, and that you was sure to be broke when ever you reached Head Quarters. I suspect your friend Capt I. Snead to have been the Reporter, from what other people told me, but when I asked him myself about the matter he told me that some report of the kind had prevailed, but he believed it to be groundless. —You have heard before that I expect that Captn. Joine has lost his cause with Ingram.

Our Election was yesterday,—Simpson Senator— Fr. Henry & I. Arbuckle Delegates— & In. Teackle offered as Delegates no other candidates. Many people have been much alarmed with us expecting the seat of War would be here, but their fears begin to vanish. Sunday last came into Chingoteague a schooner in ballast commanded by a Frenchman, the hands on board appeared to be all men belonging to the King's ships of War from which with other circumstances a guard is ordered to bring them tomorrow to the Ct. House for further examination.

Your wife is well after being delivered of a daughter said to be a fine child. Tom. continues at school— Coventon is at my house at present but is going to live with his G. Father & to go to school— Purnel is at the Plantation, cannot as yet get a master for him. Mr. Scott's family and my own are all well. Should be glad to hear from you by every opportunity.

I am with affection, Yours' *Geo. Corbin*, April 30, 1777. (Smith College Library)

Addressed to— Mr. George Abbot, Acco. County, Virginia
From— Jno Cropper, Camp at Short Hills, May 24, 1777.
Dear Friend—   I have recd. your kind letters from time to time, for which I sincerely thank you, & am exceeding glad to have hear'd by I. Cropper of the welfare of all your family, in particular I thank almighty God for his kind benevlence to my dear *Wife* & *child*; may the same almighty God never fail dispensing his blessings to them, to you & your family.

I observe in many of your letters you address me as if you desir'd I shou'd come home, & am informed by I. Cropper that many of my friends blame me for not coming & that my dear Peggy thinks *my love for her* in some measure degenerat'd because I do not come; which rather makes me uneasy under my *absence* from home.— In answer to which, let me tell you my reasons for not returning & then do you judge of them: My first motive in interceeding for a commission was a love for *liberty* and the *rights of mankind*; agreeable to, indeed above my expectations I was honour'd by my countrymen with a Captaincy, then by the affection & thro' the means

Peggy was deliv'd of a Girl   This is the first reference to John Cropper's oldest child, Sarah Corbin Cropper, 1777–1813. In later years she would marry John Wise 5th, 1765–1812, and be the mother of Henry Alexander Wise, 1806–1876.

Geo. Corbin   John Cropper's mother's maiden name was Sarah Corbin. Therefore, George Corbin was her brother and John Cropper's uncle.

Snead and *Joine*   John Cropper, Thomas Snead, and Levin Joynes were the three captains in the regiment from Accomack County that marched north to join with the Revolutionary army. The spelling of the names sometimes varies.

Tom and *Coventon*   John Cropper's brothers.

of a people I shar'd a greater honour, that of getting the first company in my regimt. march'd to actual [hole in paper] had I given up my commission, then, what wou'd have been the suggestions & language of the people; upon my going to [hole in paper] I immediately found myself promoted; if I had resign'd then & left my men (who would certainly have desert'd if I'd left them) before there was an opportunity of action, wou'd not my men exclaim'd ag. me for bringing them into a business that I myself was afraid of; yes! & justly might have call'd me a coward; again consider the advantage of experience that a young man in my station may reap at camp, consider also that 'tis the duty a man owes to almighty God & his dear posterity, to contribute every means in his power to the defence & protection of his Country. Believe me sir, to be sensible of the pleasure I should enjoy with my dear Peggy & the rest of my friends, also that I well consider the disadvantage my estate must be under in my absence, & that my mind & heart are frequently with her though the Jersy contains my person; but I can get over it for one year for the sake of my posterity forever. I suppose my Peggy will think me exceeding unlucky not to come down recruiting the other time nor now— either, this is the reason, before, I was sick in Philada. at the time of sending the recruiting officers & now I cannot as no field officer goes a recruiting.

I am shure to get leave to come home in the fall; I expect to go to my own Regimt. in a few days, which will be the 1st or 4th Virg. Regimt. I have the pleasure to inform that I'm at present very healthy and don't fear but I shall continue so. & am as happy as I can be 300 mile from......

Lieut. Waples this minute arriv'd, & Geo Barnes from Virga. We are just informed by a packet from England taken by one of our privateers that the king depends upon the force now in America to subdue it, & tells Genl. Carlton to reinforce Genl. How with part of his army from Canada, as he supposes that half Carlton's force is sufficient to maintain his ground there, but the devil is, that Carlton has sent all his troops here before, to reinforce after their loss of the Hessians at Trentown & P. Town; some deserters from the Enemy today inform that they are moving out of the Jersies now, into N. York for [hole in paper] of our troops that come in so fast; whether that is true or false, we dont much depend, but we are sure they'll be forc'd to leave the Jersies in a month or two, as our force is by far greater than ever it was, & the troops flock in daily.

The Jersy people begin to be all Whigs now, before they were mostly Tories; our troops are in the highest spirits, live very well, & every thing seems to go easy;— [hole in paper] from one Regimt. frequently skirmish with the enemy; but they have not yet learnt bush dodging. Shou'd be glad if you'd inform by your next letter how my plantation goes on & how my little brothers & cousin are & give whatever news you have in your quarter.

To Mrs. Cropper:
Old woman, what makes you uneasy about your husband, I'm shure he's not worth having as he keeps two women here, and wou'd get married if he cou'd get any body to have him; he's as corkey as can be; A'nt you asham'd to be afraid of your husband doing amiss when you know how modest I am & ever was, why I'm not afraid of you.

Genl. Carlton Sir Guy Carleton, commander of British soldiers near Lake Champlain and Canada.

Genl. How Sir William Howe, a Major General in the British army, who defeated Washington at Brandywine in September 1777 and at Germantown in October 1777.

The Jersy people Some residents of New Jersey were slow to support the American Revolution and waited to see who might win the war before committing themselves.

But to be serious, I'm surpris'd the lies of any person about me shou'd make you uneasy, especially such as you must have been sure were the most atrocious ones; you certainly know me.

Come cheer up, I'd not give you for two Jersey girls— Tell my little daughter I give my love to her & shou'd be glad to see her. Farwell my dear……

Mr. Abbot will please to give my love to Mrs. Abbot & children. Mrs. Wilkins— oh! I'm glad to hear Mr. Wilkins has turn'd a Whig, I hope he'll not turn Tory again before I come home, give my love to Wm. Pettit & every friend, particularly Sakor Parker, Jas. Berry & wife, In. Abbot, widow, nay every body.

Tell little Polly to nurse her little cousin & I'll fetch her some pretty thing. —I told Mrs. Cropper by I. Cropper that if she continu'd to be so unhappy in my absence I wou'd resign & come home immediately & so I will if you'll only inform it by next letter.

Cap. Parraman, Cap. Poulson & many other officers give their love to you & your family.

J. Cropper Jun.
My horse ever must be kept fat. (Smith College Library)

Addressed to— Major John Cropper at New.Ark, New Jersey per. Captn. J. Snead.
From— George Corbin
Accomack, June 8th, 1777.
Dear Jack—   Being closely confined to Mr. Scott's family which is now in the small pox with my children, but not so far advanced in the disorder as to enable me to give you an account what will be the event.— Have just time to inform you, that since my last to you have been agreeably entertained by the receipt of two of your favours, the last of which was dated the 31st of April [*sic*], in which you request me to give you a detail of your affairs. As to your private affairs they are nothing changed, save what you must expect from the change of the season, your crop of wheat, oats, corn &c— are promising for the time of year, you stock of Negroes &c well and thriving— The children continue as when I wrote you, Thos. at Eden School & Coventon at his G. Father's goes to English school. Purnell your wife has removed from the Plantation a few days ago to Geo. Abbotts to send to school as I am informed.

As to your publick affairs little has or can be done I am afraid, Rinold has not returned from the Northward, therefore could not call on him, for your acct. agt. the State, thought proper to send it pr. Collin. Simpson who is now on the Assembly, who promised to procure payment if in his power. Cannot inform you what our Assembly are doing as nothing has transpired since their siting, therefore must be excused for private news; and as to public news you are at the fountain head; we have little but flying reports not worth relating; pardon me, there is one piece of great news here, but with you I expect is is a trifling— last week a cannonaiding began at Tynepuren by a number of small vessels of the Enimy's at five armed vessels of ours in that harbour, the fire was returned by our Vessels but little, if any damage was done on either side. — Our Capes are well watched by Frigates & tenders, which occasions Chingoteague to have a considerable share of trade. — Should be oblige to you in your next to give me a small plan of the situation of our Army and the Enimy's— their numbers , &c. The price of Commodities & Salt very scarce with us, has been sold with us for 20 3/4 pr. Bushl.

Am glad to hear of your preferment, hope you will endeavour to merit *Honour* more than wear it. —And I must repeat my satisfaction at your advancement as it affords you the pleasure of [torn page]ing your private enimies, beneath you who have taken not a little pains to blast your character, both as a soldier and Christian. *God save you*. Hope to hear from you by first opportunity.

I am with affection, Your uncle, Geo. Corbin. (Smith College Library)

Addressed to— Major John Cropper of the 7th Regt. Virga. Regulars, Pennsylvania
From— George Corbin, Onancock, October 20, 1777.
Favd. By Mr. Geo Parker.
Dear Nephew—   Yours of the 17th Inst. came duely to hand, and as it gave me the most positive proof of your being in the land of the living, afforded me great satisfaction. I lament the fate of the unhappy tho' brave 9th Regt. which I am informed suffered by being too eager.—

Should have been glad to have recd. from you a list of the prisoners of the 9th Regt. as I could much better have complied with your request in their favour; which I should still be oblige to you for together with an account of the wounded and dead of the same.

Your request to me for 100 Dollars in specie to relieve the necessities of your friends, this convinces me that you profess a heart capable of true friendship, which alone exists with the virtuous. Your feeling & affection for your friends has made you forget that tomorrow the fortune of war may place you in their situation; should this happen you will stand in need of more hard money than I at present have. By the next safe oppertunity however you may expect to receive 40 or 50 or more hard dollars if I can purchase them, should have sent them now, but knew not of this oppertunity when I left home. Your friends are all well nothing has happened remarkable in your private affairs— the account you sent me agt. the state of Virga I delivered to Col. Simpson, but he could do nothing for you he told me. Mr. Scott is poorly. Mrs. Scott and the children have had bad colds but are recruiting. Dr. Jack I should be exceeding glad to see you as soon as your honour and the duty you owe to your country will permit you, and in the mean time may God of his infinite mercy & goodness keep you in the ways of virtue, and may he cover your head in the day of battle— this my dear Nephew is the constant prayer of, Your Affectionate Uncle, *Geo. Corbin*. October 28, 1777.

N.B. Should time & oppertunity permit, inform me fully of the Germantown affair and how matters stand in yr. opinion by Mr. Parker. (Smith College Library)

October 29th, 1777
Dear Jack: Since writing the within we have recd. per Mr. Tyson and Tompkins of Northampton the agreeable news of How's evacuating Philada.

and retreating to his shiping and it is also reported that by that Retreat a number of our Soldiers their prisoners obtained their liberty, and that Genl. Lee was taken by a party of our light Horse.— I am afraid this information, like a castle in the air, has no foundation to support it, and you will be surprised that I at a distance should hear ten times as much news as you who are on the spot, and indeed it would be strange if the facts were true; and I can account for it no other way (should the news be false) than by supposing the Tories who are deeply indebted to the United States for lies told to their disadvantage, now intend to prove themselves friends and repay their debt by lying in their favour, however I hope the States will not receive such trash in discharge of a debt *bona fide* due, but will insist on the penalty.

Methink, I heard you say, I am tyred of hearing the name *Tory*. I would rather hear something of the Whigs. Well I can inform you with trust that all the Tories, Tories did I say, I mean *Whigs*, in Accomack have taken the Oath of fidelity to the state, and that no one person in the County from sixteen to fifty have refused I mean whites.

On friday last arrived at Hampton 2 Transports under convoy of a Ship of War, have not heared their design, the Western shore militia are called upon to watch them. If you were to see our militia parade you would at least suppose, Genl. Washing had passed through the County and left some of his military knowledge behind him.

You begin to look as if you was frightened at so long a letter from me, but I have many good reasons for it, two of which shall give you. Since writing the within your favor of the 1st Octr. came to hand, in which it was your last request and you will remember it has been a long time since you recd. one from me. Therefore make no doubt but will readily excuse my taking up your time with trifles.

I am, affectionately Yours, *Geo. Corbin*. (Smith College Library. Included in the files is a typed transcript of this letter with a note, "Original not included in the collection.")
Addressed to— Mr. George Abbott, Accomack County.
From— Jn. Cropper

Bethlehem, 10th November 1777.
D. Sir, I rec'd your two several letters by Major Johnstone & Teakle— You desire an acct. of the different actions; all I know or can tell is that we had pretty hard work both at Brandewine and Germantown, at the latter the 9th V. Regiment made a considerable mistake, and indeed a great many Continentals slipped their winds; you know nought is never in danger, therefore I escap'd.

To give you no more news than a quire of paper wou'd hold, only'd serve to raise your curiosity. The Enemy have drubb'd us, & we have paid them with interest; 600 were killed on 5th inst. & 200 taken at the Fort; the brave fellows had fix'd their ladders to scale the fort & were cut down to a man almost; which you know we cant help, if they attempt to climb over, we shoud crack their knuckles— Since Mr. Teakle left me I've had a very dangerous illness at this place, which has been the consequence of cathing much cold; I now am perfectly recover'd, and had my horse come up shou'd have set of for home by this time; please send him up as soon as possible, I shall wait for him 'till 13th Decem. Give all the love, Esteem & every thing else for me. I'll come & cure all. I am &c, &c *J. Cropper.*

Brandewine and Germantown… a considerable mistake Over 1,000 Americans were killed at Brandywine, Pennsylvania on September 9, 1777. On October 5, 1777, American troops attacked the British encampment at Germantown, Pennsylvania where over 1,000 Americans were killed in part because American soldiers accidentally fired on each other.

N.B. I'd almost forgot to inform that they call me L. Colo., 'tis a great thing but must not carry it home, I suppose.— Tell any of your family that shou'd enquire for me, I begin to be full of home. J.C. (Smith College Library)

Addressed to— Mrs. Margaret Cropper, Accomack County, Virginia. Favored by Mr. Snead.
From— John Cropper, Camp Valley Forge, 13th March 1778.
Dear Peggy— At the receipt of this letter I feel your trouble and disappointment, but am in some degree comforted, from a consciousness of its being occasion'd by an over fondness in Me to ofset & in saving my distress'd Country, tottering at this time on the brink of ruin: My dear! Excuse your husband for doing what he thinks is right! Excuse in him an overfondness for his Country's cause! Don't think him insensible of a *husband's* affection or the distress of an absent wife. I know the whole, but the interest of my Country, my wife, my angel inphant (than the two latter nothing except the former can be more dear), united & jointly call upon Me, to struggle in this cause of Virtue, Justice, millions & Posterity.— After the actions of Brandewine and Germantown, I thought nothing upon earth shou'd keep Me 2 weeks from the arms of my *dear wife*, and from taking in my arms the dear delightful *sweet daughter* (I think I see it in the mama's arms!) but unfortunately was taken sick and retir'd to Bethlehem abt. 50 miles North of Philada. where I continu'd ill 'till the latter end of Novem. at which time his Excellency was pleas'd to order Me upon Duty to relieve Col. Wood who had the comm'd of the troops, and care of the hospitals at & abt. Bethlehem, from which duty could never get reliev'd untill February, when I immediately set off & came to Camp; upon my arrival, apply'd to Genl. Woodford for a recommendation to his Excellency for permission to visit my friends, upon which he gave me the most repeated assurances of his willingness to serve Me, but at the same time, delar'd that 'twas impossible for Me to be spar'd, as so many officers in the Virga. line had either resign'd, or teaz'd his Excellency so as to gain leave of absence, at the expence of their reputation; upon seeing the brigade found out the truth of G. Woodford's assertions, for there were not but two field officers, and myself commdr. of the brigade, therefore concluded to stay a few weeks; When Mr. Lyon came, I was determin'd to go home wt. him & Major Snead, & accordingly went again to the Genl. & inform'd that fond as I was of the service of my Country must resign or get leave of absence; at hearing that he expressed his sorrow, and said he'd go next morning, (which was this morning) and himself apply to his Excellency to get me a permission, which he did and rec'd for answer that his Excellency was sensible of my necessitous situation, but begged that I wou'd endeavour to content myself 2 or 3 Weeks, and farther directed Genl. Woodford to send immediately to Virginia for the absent field-officer. Inconsistent with the interests of this Country and my honor, I know my dear Peggy has too much virtue & esteem for her husband to desire him from the Army, and so soon as he can, will come to his dear wife. The letter I rec'd from your own hand gave me a great pleasure, yet I hope to see you before another reaches Me. I have a piece of fine holld. that I intend to send by Major Snead, but can't get it time enough from a country house where it is. I have several other things but can't send them but hope to bring them myself within a month from now.

his Excellency George Washington.

holld holland, heavy cotton or linen fabric.

My Dear give love to all our friends. I am your most loving Husband, *John Cropper.*
N.B. I have try'd to purchase a chaise, but am afraid I can't get one.— please have my watch taken care of, also my horse. *J. C.*
Major Snead will hand you this, who notwithstanding report is mine & your good friend.   *Mr. Cropper.* (Smith College Library)

Addressed to— Mrs. Margaret Cropper, Accomack County, Virginia.
From— John Cropper, Camp Valley Forge, 10th May 1778.
My Dear Peggy—   My not coming home agreeable to the times promised in my two last letters had been occasion'd by my promising at the time of getting leave, to stay untill an officer of my rank shou'd come, to take care of Genl. Woodford's Brigade, which I have commanded since his absence 'till within these few days, when the officer before mention'd came, but yet 'tis necessary for me to stay a few days tho shall be home by the first of June, or at any rate (by God's permission) before the beggining of the campain.

My Dear Peggy, I beg You'll have patience to go thro my absence with the same virtue and heroism, you have done. I think it too ridiculous to endeavour to convince you of my persevering in the same love I left you with, for I am sure my *Angel* cou'd never doubt my sincerity,— I now anticipate the pleasure I shall shortly have in the company of my little daughter & its mama, how I will caress & fondle upon the sweet infant; But no more of that, the thoughts only make me unhappy, at the distance of 250 miles.

My most fervent prayer is that this may meet you & the dear daughter in the enjoyment of health, peace & prosperity— My esteem to our good sister, our mother & all other friends.

I am, dear Peggy, Yours untill time shall be no more, *John Cropper.*
N.B. The 6th Instant was a day of rejoicing with our army, in which all the artillery & muskettry of our army was discharged, and the three following toasts drank—
    Long live the King of France—
    Success to the friendly European powers—
    Success to the United States of America.
and many patriotick songs; the whole was upon the court of France's declaring us independant.   —*J. C.*

N.B. Enclos'd I send you a pair of clasps for my little girl, and a newspaper. I send you a plain gold ring, an exact fellow to which I have on my finger. I send it you mark'd wt. the first letters of my name; please receive it as a sincere pledge of my faith & constancy. —*J. C.* (Smith College Library)

Addressed to—Mrs. Margaret Cropper, Accomack County, Virginia.
From— John Cropper, Camp Valley Forge, 29th May 1778.
My Dear Peggy—   Having a favorable opportunity I do myself the pleasure of writing you as fully as possible, and must beg your patience and attention.— You are much surprised, and I'm afraid unhappy, that I've disappointed in my several promises to come home from time to time; nor do I wonder at your surprise, neither shou'd I think strange if you believ'd it my intention never to come home; for I have deceiv'd myself, and wou'd not have believ'd an angel, if he'd told me that I shou'd have stay'd so long

France's declaring us independant   Treaties with France were signed on February 2, 1778, and news of this alliance reached New York and America on May 2, 1778, only eight days before the date of this letter.

from the arms of my *dear wife*, my *darling infant*, and the management of my unsettled estate at home— but, so it is, —and as sure as there is a god in heaven, or that you and I exist, my motives are laudible, and my intentions innocent.— Let it be sufficient for the present to say, that the exigency of my country's cause, my over fondness for a military profession, and the advice of those I esteem my friends, have so long kept me from the enjoyment of domestick happiness, with an *amiable wife, delightful little daughter,* and *social friends.* It is with the greatest reluctance I stay in camp, when I consider what you suffer in my absence— but, my country's call, the greatest of all calls, demands my presence with the army for a time, to pay for the blessings I have enjoy'd, and expect to enjoy under the auspices of *liberty.*— My dear, when you consider my conduct since our first acquaintance— when you consider I was faithful & constant at a time when I might have ruin'd your reputation forever— when you consider I marry'd you ags. the will & consent of not only my father & mother, but ags. the advice and persuasion of all those who call'd themselves my friends— when you reflect upon those considerations for which I don't pretend to claim the smallest merit, I hope; I beg you by the remembrance of the pleasures we have enjoy'd together, to content yourself untill next fall; as the spouse of him who is serving in the cause of his country, himself, and every thing that can be near & dear: But, if you think you cannot wait 'till that time, that it will destroy your happiness, inform me by Lieut. Curtis, and I will (however disagreeable it may be) resign immediately upon his return—

The campain is now begun, and I am desirous to see the end of it— By those who came last from Virginia, indeed I was inform'd before, that there was a misunderstanding between you & Uncle Corbin, for which I am excessive sorry.— I am afraid you've been mis inform'd, or misled by some of your friends— I'm afraid Mr. Abbot is to blame for this— be it as it will, I beseech you to loose no time in making it up, for I cannot be happy while there is any difference between you & him— I have wrote to him very fully on the subject, & positively insisted to have it made up, and said I was shure you'd not be against it.— I beg you to be satisfy'd my dear, that I never promised you to come home, or indeed made you any other promise, but what at the time I intended to perform, and be satisfy'd that however strange my conduct may have appear'd, that it has ever been for the honor & happiness of my family. Lieutn. Curtis who has stay'd with me several days, since his escape from the Enemy, waits upon you with this, who is & has been my good friend. From him you may learn my situation & my intentions.— I send you one piece of linen abt. 20 yds. coarse, also one half piece and 2 1/2 yds of superfine, abt. 13 yds wraped up in two new shirts, which I drew from the Continental store; but they are so badly made, as you will see, that they are not fit to wear till made over again— Also 3 pr. stockings, two of which I had made at Bethlehem, & send them home to be whitened; the other pair are yours, which I dont want as I have stockings enough to last me 'till next winter— Also 1 pr. of leather shoes made at Bethlehem, I am afraid they are too small, and am certain they are very homely ones— One pr. of black shammy flower'd, done at Bethlehem— I send you a plain gold ring which if you please present to our good sister, & request her to wear it until I return— it is like yours sent by Lieut. Kindale. The fine linen sent down is for yourself— I want the two shirts made over again & ruffled, also 6 shirts made of the coarse linen & ruffled wt. fine cambrick if possible to be got.— When Lieut. Curtis returns to camp, you will please send me two or three shirts & stocks, and if you've any stuff for summer waistcoats & breeches— Lieut. Curtis will also bring up my horse & watch.

 I shou'd be extreemly glad to see our brother Wm. Pettit at camp; if he will come up he will be at no expense while he stays in camp— at any rate I shou'd be glad to see any one that cou'd give an acct. of my affairs.— I particularly request you to write me by next opportunity with your own hand— and recommend you to practice reading & writing 'till I return home.

 My Dear Peggy, I am, your sincere & ever faithfull husband, *John Cropper*. (Smith College Library)

Addressed to— John Cropper, Valley Forge
From— George Corbin, Onancock, July 18, 1778.
My dear Nephew— Your very kind and affectionate favor of the 28th of May last, came duely to hand, than which, nothing could have afforded me more real satisfaction, except a personal interview with yourself.— It gave me the greatest pleasure to find that you still (after representation to my disadvantage as I conjecture) view me in the character of an *affectionate sincere Friend*. God grant me grace to deserve the sacred Epithet. I am sorry to inform you that your suspicions of a misunderstanding between Mrs. Cropper and myself are not without some foundation, this information I have carefully avoided giving you, as I thought it very imprudent to mention it untill all parties were face to face, and as I was very certain it would render you very unhappy; nor can I now enter into the particulars with the approbation of my Judgment, but hope you will at present be contented with my conduct, when I inform you— that at the sale of your father's Estate I had purchased every necessary towards housekeeping that you stood in need of to support your wife genteelly, and at the same time I informed her that whatever she stood in need of at any time for the use of her family I would willingly provide, and desired she might apply to me for that purpose. This I did under an expectation that your wife would settle on your plantation, and as far as the province of a wife extended take care of your Interest: and I was confirmed in this Expectation from her own declaration and other circumstances: but you have long since known my disappointment, the reasons for which I have never yet learned; but supposed they were made known to you, and were satisfactory: under this supposition I have taken the same care of your Estate, as I did of my own in like circumstances, both of which you may reasonably conclude suffered from my multiplicity of business, to which you are not a stranger. I shall conclude this disagreeable subject after informing that Peggy has never been at my house since I saw you, nor ever spoke to me but once, which was to clear herself to me of a report which prevailed of her having spoke disrespectful of some one of our family; it being at a public place, I observed to her that it was very improper to say any thing about the matter then, but told her I should be exceeding glad to talk the matter over privately when none were present but friends; thus the conversation ended, this happened a 12 Month or upwards ago; but I hope when it pleases God to restore you to us (as you are our mutual friend,) it will be in your power

to reconcile all misunderstandings between us, and excite a *firm disinterested Esteem* which only can be a proper and lasting foundation for Friendship. I leave it to the searcher of Hearts to determine who is right and who is wrong, and hope I shall never be so lost to myself, as not to acknowledge and ask pardon for my offences when sensible of them, and wish on all occasion to hold myself open to conviction. My dear Johnny, Do not infer from any thing I have said that I have the most distant wish to lessen your exalted affection for *her* who *is*, and I hope always will be to you: as *your dearer Self*— Believe me your fervent love to your Wife, Infant, and Orphan Brothers, which so agreeably filled the whole of your last favour to me, if possible, brightened my affection for you.

As to information concerning your Brothers, I can with pleasure and truth inform you, they are false. Thomas Cropper I have kept constant at Eden School where he now is, even at the extravagant price of £60 per annun for board, determined if it stripped him of every shilling of his property, to keep him at School; the profits of his Estate you know does not equal his expense, yet I have not, nor do not intend to brake upon his Principle. And I do with greater pleasure inform you that his progress in learning is very rapid, and he is become as I am informed by Mr. Adams with whom he boards, a very good boy.— Coventon is still with his Grandfather, sometimes at school and sometimes not, as schools with us you know are very precarious.

Your poor old G. Father is very poorly— I much doubt if you ever see him again in this World. Mr. Scott is also in a very poor state of health. Mrs. Scott and the children are well and join in Compliments to you.—

Such cloth as you deserved me to procure for you is not to be had with us. I made inquiry and found one piece of the colour you mentioned but was not fine, it was such as we used to buy for 28 or 30 per Yard for which they now ask £15 pr Yard—the price and coarse quality of the cloth prevented me from buying. All kind of merchandise is very dear with us. Sugar 8/ per lb. Rum 45/ pr Galn. Mollasses 30/. Country produce also high except Wheat— Indian Corn 6/ Oats 3/ Wheat from 6/ to 10/ agreeable to quality by retail— at Wholesale no price— Your crop of Wheat on the Plantation last year's unsold, the I. Corn chiefly sold, Lambs 8 dollars— We are just informed that the English Fleet with all their Troops sailed from N. York the day before the French Fleet arrived there, and that all our prisoners were set at liberty— should this important piece of Intelligence be true, I shall expect to see you in Acomack shortly.

The Sloop *Supply* commanded by William Selby and owned by myself and others is in the French Fleet laden with Tobo. They took our Captn. for a Pilot— A 26 Gun ship fell into the hands of the Fleet opposite Chingstraper Inlett— The frigate of 28 Guns run ashore, and the crew delivered themselves up prisoners at Snow Hill.— We are all Whigs now, those who not long since were suspected of Torism are now violent Whigs, Good God what a change! but not to be wondered at, for those who could for the prospect of Interest spill their Country's blood will now, as their Interest is more obvious on the side of their Country take part with it, or wish to take part with it.

Give my kind compliment to my worthy friends and old living acquaintance Mrs. B. Bush and Brother if in the land of the living, also Mr. John Haley & Family, the two Mr. Finleys and any other Gentn. of my former acquaintance. If they should desire to know what part I am acting on the stage of Life, you may inform them I have been advocate for the good and I am afraid sometimes for the bad: but am not about to curtail my public business, and live more retired.— Danl. Rodgers, whom you mentioned in your last, was taken upon suspicion of Treason; but for want of Testimony has been acquited of that charge; and is now under a prosecution of which I expect will deprive him of his liberty for 5 years or during the War, and all his property; Esau Kellom, his associate, made his escape to the West Indies as soon as he found he was to answer for his Conduct.— God grant that America may earnestly endeavor to merit the Blessings now confered on her, and may we as virtuous as we are like to be free. Farewell, —*G. C.* (Smith College Library)

1779

◐ John Cropper's Diary:

January 1st, 1779— Pretty day. Wm. Pettit and myself divided our negroes.
January 2nd— Peggy and I went from Mr. Wilkin's to Accomac Courthouse. I bought old Jacob, and hired three of my brother Tom's negro's.
January 17th—Deep snow on the earth. I went down the Creek to see in what situation Major Simpson's boat lay in the marsh.

Sunday, 4th July— Anniversary of Independency. An eligant ball at the courthouse tomorrow evening.
Monday, 5th— An eligant ball and entertainment at courthouse.
Friday, 16th— Peggy and I set off for camp. Went to Mr. Abbot's.
Monday, August 2nd— Arrived at the Virginia camp, a place called Suffering's. The troops are healthy and in high spirits, and are commanded by Lord Stirling. Drank tea wt. Gen. Woodford.

Saturday, September 21st— I set off for Virginia; lodged at Chester…
Friday, September 27th— Peggy and I went to Bowman's Folly— lodged at Latin House.
*Saturday, 28th Augus*t— Nothing, only that I moved my furniture from Latin House to Bowman's Folly.
Thursday, 16th— I amused myself during the excessive high tides, occasioned by the N. Easter) shooting curlews, willets, and other birds.

Friday, December 25th— Christmas. Mr. Abbott and myself went to Assawaman Church. Snowy day.

William Pettit was his wife's brother.

When Barton Haxall Wise wrote the *Memoir of General John Cropper* he noted that he had in his possession Cropper's diary from 1779 and described it as follows: "The entries contained in it exhibit the exposed condition of the Accomack people and the numerous conflicts they had with the enemy. However, despite the trying ordeals to which they were subjected, John Cropper and his wife appear to have dined out frequently, and enjoyed social intercourse with their neighbors." Wise quotes extensively from the diary in his piece and some of that material is quoted here. Wise's papers were given to the Virginia Historical Society but the original copy of Cropper's diary is not in that collection.

1797

Published in Barton Haxall Wise's *The Life of Henry A Wise* is the following exchange of letters between Major John Wise and General John Cropper from early in 1797:

John Wise 5th to John Cropper: Feeling myself irresistibly impelled by inclination, and prompted by a sense of propriety, I have presumed now to address you upon a subject of importance and delicacy. Having conceived an affection for your daughter (Miss Sally) I beg leave to solicit your permission to make my addresses to her, and at the same time, let me express a hope that should I be so fortunate as to succeed in obtaining her affections, my first wishes may not be frustrated by your disapprobation, I have thought proper to make the application to you on the subject in this manner, rather than in person, because my character, (if I have acquired any,) my condition and my situation in life are not altogether unknown to you, and if objections are to be made they can be more freely communicated in this than in any other way. I have hitherto proceeded no further with the lady than merely to obtain her permission to make this application, and Sir, I now pledge you the honor of a Gentleman, that in case you have objections, of an insuperable nature, to the proposed union, whatever may be the chagrin, regret and mortification which I may feel upon the occasion, I will not disturb the quiet of a parent anxiously solicitous, no doubt, for the happiness of a beloved daughter, by persisting any further with her. Permit me to assure you that I am with much consideration and respect, your obedient servant, *John Wise.*

Bowman's Folly, 11 of May 1797.
Sir: Although the application made by letter of this day was unexpected, yet my reflections heretofore on that subject have prepared me to answer: That however solicitous I may be for the temporal felicity of my daughter and future respectability of my daughter and future respectability of my child, she is the only proper Judge of the person best calculated to make her happy. Respect and impartiality ought to be shown by me to you or any gentleman that might make his address to my daughter, and I confide in your candor and justice. I am, sir, with due respect, Your obedient servant, *John Cropper.*

Sarah Cropper and John Wise were married in 1799.

1798

 Sarah Cropper writes to her father:

Philadelphia, February 27, 1798
To: Col John Cropper Accomac county Eastern Shore, Virginia
Nothing here has a greater affect upon the mind than good spirits; with them we are more agreeable to our friends and still more so to ourselves, nothing has a greater tendency to raise mine… I need not say to you how much pleasure your affectionate letter gave me; your advice was perfectly just, and truly good, human nature is fallable [*sic*], could I always do right I should be happy, but as I often err, I hate my own depravity, and am induced to think myself the most abject wretch on earth. Again reason comes to aide me and tell me to value myself more highly. Experience is good: such things try the mind: and *virtue* alone can understand temptations. Do I possess that? No: Can I not endeavor to gain it: shurely I can, then my first concern shall be to possess that invaluable gem. I have said so much to you about myself you will think I have forgotten my sister. I can tell you she is well, and continues to learn. She says, sister tell papa I will

write to him very soon, so that you may expect a letter. We are sorry to hear of our little sister's indisposition, though children of her age are subject to complaints more or less, she has been a very remarkable healthy child. Our friend Mr. Evans is very kind, he calls often to see me and I believe enjoys a good state of health. We have now fine sleighing. I was out yesterday with a party on Schuykill where we had an elegant supper. I had the pleasure of seeing a Mr. Fist, who was just going to Mr. Jefferson's and was so polite as to take my commands. I have lately been at a party at Doctor P—'s, was much pleased particularly with his *Daughter,* who is an accomplished woman. I have not been to the assembly yet though design going the next. Your friends are all well here. I know of nothing particularly interesting to communicate except my sister's and my love to Mama, Anna, Aunt Betsy, Uncle and all our Friends. Give my love to Johnny and Louisa. Remember us to John Cropper and Mr. A— . believe me my dear Papa with every sentiment of love, Your Daughter, *Sally Cropper.* (Virginia Historical Society)

1799

A letter from John Cropper's son-in-law:

Addressed to—Colo. John Cropper, Accomack
Richmond. Dec. 11th, 1799
Dr. Sir—   I last evening, by mere accident, recd. information that your Kentucky lands had been advertised in the papers of that state to be sold for the taxes due on them. Supposing it to be a matter of moment to you, I this morning waited upon Mr. Jas. Heron, to whom I was referred for particulars, & from whom I recd. an account, that while he was in Kentucky during the last summer he saw in the papers of that state an advertisement containing a list of lands to be sold for payt. of taxes (one of which papers he showed me) and among others contained in that list was 6666 2/3 acres in your name to be

Bowman's Folly, Eastern Shore, Virginia. Original house built on this site in 1653 by Edward Bowman. John Cropper, a descendant of Bowman, tore down the original house and had slaves haul earth to build a mound on which he had the present house built. Photo from Tidewater Virginia *by Paul Wilstach.*

John Cropper, 1755–1821, by Charles Wilson Peale. Peale was a friend of Cropper's, and they had served together during the Revolution. The portrait was painted in 1792–1793, when Cropper was in his mid-thirties. Cropper is shown in his uniform of the Continental army, with scarlet facings representing the Corps of Engineers. Photograph courtesy of the National Museum of American History, Smithsonian Institution.

Catherine Cropper, John Cropper's second wife, by Charles Wilson Peale. Photograph courtesy of the National Museum of American History, Smithsonian Institution.

sold for the tax of 1798 amounting to 50/. —He also informed me that he had offered to pay for you as well as for several of his friends in this state, but the Auditor do's not receive the taxes after sending out the advertisements & lists. —He informs me that you have every thing to apprehend from the villainy of those concerned in those sales, it frequently happening that large & valuable tracts are sold for the payment of small and inconsiderable sum due for taxes; & that it is made so much a jobbing business that persons were going down with money to Christian Court House (the place where these lands were to be sold) to buy them in at a small price.

Mr. Heron says that the place ofrd. was 250 miles from that where he was & that he could not provide a mean of making a remittance so as to save the rights of his friends.

The foregoing is all I am able to collect abt. it, save only that the sale was to have been, by the advertisements in Octo. last.— The paper in which it is, is dated in Augt.— If I can glean any further information relative to it, I will communicate it instantly, & should you wish any thing done here which I can do, you will take the liberty to command me.

I have just snatched time enough to give you this information, which I fear I have scarcely made intelligible, & can only now say that I am with sincerity, Your Fr. *Jn. Wise.* (Smith College Library)

In later years, John Cropper tore down Bowman's Folly, the ancestral home that Edmund Bowman had built and he had a new home, described by one historian as "the most pretentious house in Virginia on this side (the Eastern shore side) of the bay," constructed on an artificial mound that had been built up by the slaves. The "new home" still stands today. An unidentified newspaper clipping in the family papers reads as follows:

After the Revolution Colonel Cropper passed the remaining years of his life on his estate. The stately old mansion was pleasantly situated about one hundred yards from the bank of a creek running up from the ocean, and was surrounded by venerable trees, smooth green lawns, gardens and the deer park. Near it was the family cemetery, where the dead of two centuries rested. Across the creek were the remains of an old fortification, and beside it was planted a piece of old artillery to mark the height of an unusual tide. From the beach to the blue horizon stretched the broad Atlantic, and in the nearer distance were the islands of Chincoteague and Assateague, lively with their herds of wild ponies, and silver—framed in the waves that dashed on their shores. In this quiet retreat the veteran delighted to imitate the virtues and to cherish the memory of his former illustrious commander. Mr. Custis, in his "Recollections," says that Colonel Cropper had but one toast, which he gave every day to all companies; it was "God bless General Washington!" John Cropper died in 1821.

∾ A military pension:

Addressed to: Mrs. Catherine Cropper, Accomack C.H. VA.
Washington City, Nov. 15, 1838
Madam,   I have the pleasure of saying to you, that yr. pension claim is allowed, & I have recd. the certificate. Upon averaging the terms of Col. Croppers services in his different grades, whilst in *actual* service, it was found that you were entitled to $570.83 cts. per year, commencing on the 4th of March

1831, & payable half yearly. The 1st payment will be made in January & will amount to the sum of $1427.07 cts. for 2 1/2 years in arrears, & there will be 2 1/2 years more to be recd. if you live so long, payable $285.41 cts. every half year. I shall return to Accomack before going to Richmond, in time to prepare the necessary powers of attorney to receive the money.

I remain, Madam, most respectfully your ob. Servant, *Vr. S. Ellis.*
(Smith College Library)

❧ Another side of the family: Obadiah Jennings, A lawyer and minister from Pennsylvania and Tennessee.

The following Memoir has been prepared at the request of the friends of the deceased [Obadiah Jennings], especially his bereaved partner… it is hoped, the narrative will be read with interest, especially by friends and acquaintances. It presents a bright example of Christian character, which may be profitable for instruction and reproof, as well as for encouragement and animation to the people of God, amidst the conflicts of life, and the agonies of death…

Rev. Obadiah Jennings, D. D., was born 13th December, 1778, near Baskingridge, in the state of New Jersey. He was the fourth son of the Rev. Jacob Jennings, a minister of the Presbyterian Church, who united the character of Clergyman and Physician. Not long after his birth, his father removed to Virginia… Of the youthful years of Mr. Jennings little is known… Having enjoyed a strictly religious education, under the care and direction of eminently pious parents, impressions were made on his mind which were never entirely obliterated, and had an influence in forming correct moral habits, and restraining him from vicious excesses… Having given early indication of genius, his father determined to afford him a liberal education. He was according sent to Canonsburg, at that time the seat of a flourishing Academy, which was afterwards, in 1802, organized into a College, called "Jefferson College." Here he pursued with diligence and success the study of the classics, mathematic, and sciences. Having acquired the best education which the Western Country could then afford, he commenced the study of the law, with John Simonson, Esq., of Washington, where he was first admitted to the bar in the fall of 1800. He immediately removed to Steubenville… soon after his removal to Steubenville, he was united in marriage with Miss Becket, the daughter of Col. Becket of Westmoreland county, Pa. This amiable lady was early removed by death, leaving an only daughter… He was again married, to Miss Ann Wilson, daughter of a respectable clergyman of the state of Delaware… At the bar, he ever maintained a high standing, and fully realized the expectations excited by his first efforts… In the language of one who knew him well, "his *forté* lay in addressing a jury: in this he had no superior. In an argument to the court on a point of law, when the occasion called for preparation, and required him to put forth all his strength, he was surpassed by few." He was much esteemed by his brethren of the bar, and greatly confided in by the community at large…

…In the year 1810, Mr. Jennings connected himself with the Presbyterian church, by a profession of his faith, and not long after, as already stated, removed to the town of Washington, Pa. Here he was elected to the office of Ruling Elder… Upon his first attaching himself to the church, and for some time afterwards, it does not appear that he had any intention of relinquishing the profession of the law. His first serious thoughts on this subject, were occasioned by a visit from an obscure Christian, who happened to tarry at his house all night… To himself, the practice of the bar had

The Reverend Obadiah Jennings, 1778–1832, (father of Ann Elizabeth Jennings Wise). Photograph courtesy of the Virginia Historical Society, Richmond, Virginia.

become, in many respects, irksome, and contrary to his renovated taste and habits. Of the two professions, he had no difficulty in determining which would best accord his own taste and feelings. The courts of God's house, he greatly preferred to the courts of earthly litigation… While his mind was vibrating on the great question of his duty, he was laid on a bed of sickness, and brought to a decision in the light of eternity. The disease with which he was attacked was violent, and he was brought down to the very verge of the grave… Agonizing prayers were offered up in his behalf, which were graciously answered. A physician of eminence, from Steubenville, who attended him constantly, scarcely entertained a hope of his recovery, and when he opened a vein to bleed him, he remarked that it might possibly be favorable, but that it was done more with a view of lessening the pains of dying, that with a hope of restoring him. Soon afterwards a change was visible, and he was restored in a manner almost miraculous. He was also cheered with the returning light of God's countenance. The cloud was dispelled, and he was enabled to rejoice in God his Saviour. "The question," said he, "is decided. If God spare my life, it shall be devoted to his service in preaching the gospel of Christ." …in the fall of 1816, he was licensed by the Presbytery of Ohio to preach the gospel… Having accepted of the call, he removed to Steubenville in the spring of 1817, and was ordained and installed pastor… Having received a call from Nashville, Tennessee, his mind was again in great perplexity as to the path of duty… In April, 1828, he removed to Nashville, where he remained until his decease.

The closing scene was such as might have been anticipated from a life so devoted to the service of the Redeemer. "Precious in the sight of God is the death of his saints." Precious too, in the recollection of pious friends, is the "death-bed of the just." With a mind calm and composed, in full view of death and judgment, he called his family around him, to bid them a final farewell. With his dying benediction and prayer, he gave to each of his children that were present, his last counsel, in a manner most tender, solemn, and beautifully appropriate. He left his blessing, also, to those who were absent. Silver and gold he had none to leave them. The riches of the world he had renounced for the gospel's sake: but he had that to leave them which was of more value than all the riches of the world. In faith on the divine promises, he cheerfully committed his family to God, expressing a strong confidence the *He* would provide. When reminded of the promise made to the fatherless and the widow; "that," said he, with emphasis and animation, "is the legacy, that is the legacy."

When his son Thomas, who had been his constant nurse and physician, said to him, "Father you are dying" —he immediately replied, "Bless the Lord, O my soul."

In a moment of great suffering, he remarked with characteristic energy of thought, "If this be the way to heaven, what must be the way to hell?" His mind however was calm and resigned, and even triumphant, in the near prospect of death. As a draught of water was presented to his dying lips, he said, "I shall soon drink from the river of life, which issues from the throne of God and the Lamb."

He asked his wife to repeat to him the answer to the question in the Shorter Catechism, "What benefits do believers receive from Christ at their death? and several times afterwards repeated with great delight, "the souls of believers are at their death made perfect in holiness, and do immediately pass into glory." Thus while his mind was absorbed in the contemplation of those glorious prospects which were opening upon him, he sunk, with peaceful serenity, into the slumber of death—resting, with unshaken confidence, in the merits of the Redeemer, *for an abundant entrance into the everlasting kingdom of God*—"animated with a hope full of IMMORTALITY."

After his death, every suitable mark of respect was shown by the people of Nashville. His funeral was one of the largest ever seen in that place…

As to his *private* life, it may be truly said, he was exemplary in all its relations. Few men have passed through life more generally beloved and esteemed, and more completely without reproach.

He was peculiarly interesting and engaging as a companion, and in his social intercourse… There was a captivating urbanity of manners, which spread an irresistible charm over all his intercourse with society. These amiable qualities, which belonged to him as a man, became doubly interesting, when consecrated by religion. In him were combined the gentleman and the Christian… …As a testimony of the estimation in which he was held, it may be mentioned, that a short time before his decease, the college of New Jersey conferred on him the degree of Doctor of Divinity. During his practice at the bar, accustomed to write only in haste and on business, he had given little attention to *style*, and when he commenced the composition of sermons, he labored under no small difficulty, which however, he was enabled to surmount, so as to write with great facility, though his style is characterized more by perspicuity and force, than by ornament and elegance…

…His *style of preaching*, as has been justly described, "was characterized by strength, rather than polish; by solid sense, rather than elegance of language; by clearness of exposition, rather than ornament; by force of argument, rather than beauty of illustration." His eloquence was the eloquence of thought, rather than delivery. Few persons could sit under his ministry with indifference. The serious and pious heard him with interest and delight, while the more careless could not fail to be impressed with the solemnity and force of his addresses, and whatever opinion they formed of the sermon or the speaker, retired with a less favorable opinion of themselves.

We have been favored with a copy of several letters, addressed to Doctor Samuel K. Jennings of Baltimore, the eldest brother, a highly respectable physician, and a minister of the gospel of the Methodist church…

Steubenville, Jan 23, 1810.
Dear Brother—
…The day you wrote your letter, I spent with our father at his house. He, with all his parental anxiety and pious solicitude for my eternal welfare, urged me, as he had frequently done before, to begin the worship of God in my family. I did not, at that time, comply. I thought I saw so many difficulties in the way, it would be impossible for me to attempt it. Since my return home, however, and since the commencement of this year, I have been enabled, after the most violent struggle, which you can better conceive than I can describe, to attempt to acknowledge God in my family. My Ann is rejoiced, and renders praise to God for bringing me to see, in some measure, the necessity and importance of religion. But alas! I fear her joy will be very short lived! My performances of all religious duties which I attempt, especially family worship, is so wretched, I have been frequently ready to conclude I must give it up… Thus, my dear brother, I have endeavored to let you know something of the state of my mind. What will be the event, God only knows. Whether these dry bones can live, "O Lord thou knowest," Pray for me, my brother, pray without ceasing. Yours, O. J.
—Excerpted from *Debate on Campbellism; Held at Nashville, Tennessee*, by Obadiah Jennings, D. D. published in 1832.

III

1806–1860

Virginia, Henry A. Wise and His Family

IN the young and growing new nation, these were years of increasing regional animosity engendered by one issue—slavery. Each admission of a new state, slave or free, was cause for hostile feelings that were only resolved through a compromise that would have to be re-visited when another territory wished to become a state. In 1849 it took sixty-three ballots to elect a Speaker of the House of Representatives, and at different times there were a variety of gag rules against abolitionist petitions to Congress. Abolitionists were very active: The American Anti-Slavery Society was formed in 1833; by 1836 there were over 500 abolitionist societies active in the north; the "Underground Railway" was established in 1838 to assist slaves fleeing to Canada, and northern states enacted Personal Liberty Laws to obstruct the Federal Fugitive Slave Act. Feelings in the south were equally strong: In 1835 a mob in Charleston, South Carolina, burned abolitionist literature impounded by the local postmaster; some of the southern states enacted laws prohibiting the distribution of abolitionist literature, and in 1859 a convention in Vicksburg urged the repeal of all laws prohibiting the importation of slaves. In 1851 Charles Sumner, an outspoken abolitionist, was elected Senator from Massachusetts. Five years later he was beaten unconscious by Representative Preston Brooks of South Carolina in response to Sumner's criticism of Brooks' uncle. It took Sumner, now a martyr in the North, three years to recover from the attack while at the same time Brooks was being praised in the South.

However, there were also other things happening in America and around the world during these years. The Troy Female Seminary was opened in 1821 by Emma Willard in Troy, New York. In 1825 the Erie Canal was opened which greatly reduced the cost of transporting goods and materials between New York and the Ohio and Mississippi River valleys. Joseph Smith founded the Church of Jesus Christ of Latter-day Saints in 1830. The following year Nat Turner led an unsuccessful slave revolt in Virginia and William Lloyd Garrison founded *The Liberator*, an abolitionist periodical urging the release of all slaves. In 1834 slavery was abolished in the British Empire and Cyrus McCormick patented his reaper, forever changing wheat farming in America and around the world. Charles Dickens' *Oliver Twist* was published in 1837. In 1839 Charles Darwin published the first summary of his 1832–1836 voyage on the *HMS Beagle*, and in 1857 he published the outline of his theory of evolution and natural selection. In 1839 Abner Doubleday laid out the first baseball diamond in Cooperstown, New York. It would be another twenty years before the first collegiate baseball game was played in Williamstown, Massachusetts, between Amherst College and Williams College. James Fenimore-Cooper published *The Deerslayer* in 1841. In 1844 Joseph Smith was killed by a mob in Nauvoo, Illinois, and Brigham Young became head of the Mormon Church. In 1857 a mass murder at Mountain Meadows, Utah, resulted in the deaths of 140 non-Mormons. In that same year some Mormons rebelled against the appointment of a non-Mormon as the territorial governor and in 1858 U. S. Troops were used to restore order. However, as a rule, little attention was being paid to Mormonism by anyone in Virginia during these years. America again greatly expanded its territory after the Mexican-American war of 1846–1847. The fight against slavery became a part of American literature when in 1851 *Uncle Tom's Cabin* was serialized in *National Era*, an anti-slavery periodical based in Washington, D. C.

Letters and writings by:
William H. Brown, *Portrait Gallery—Distinguished American Citizens with Biographical Sketches and Fac-Similes of Original Letters*
William E. Cameron, a former Governor of Virginia
John Cropper
James P. Hambleton, *A Biographical Sketch of Henry A. Wise*
William Prime, excerpts from his book, *Boat Life on the Nile*
Barton Haxall Wise, a grandson of Henry A. Wise, excerpts from his biography of his grandfather
Henry A. Wise
The children of Henry A. Wise:
   Mary Elizabeth Wise, the oldest daughter by his first wife, married to Dr. Alexander Y. P Garnett.
   Obadiah Jennings Wise, the oldest son by his first wife.
   Annie Jennings Wise, a daughter by his first wife, married to Frederick Plumer Hobson.
   John Sergeant Wise, a son by his second wife, excerpts from *The End of An Era*.
Ann Elizabeth Wise, Henry A. Wise's first wife and a daughter of Obadiah Jennings
Mary Lyons Wise, Henry A. Wise's third wife.

Letters written from: Twifordville, Accomack, Onancock, Williamsburg, Richmond, Lynchburg, and Eastwood, Goochland County, Virginia; Bloomington, Indiana; Washington, D. C.; and Berlin, Germany.

∽

While no letters or other documents survive about Henry A. Wise's early years, there are some important facts that should be summarized:
- 1806, Henry A. Wise born December 3rd in Accomac, Virginia.
- 1812, Wise's father, John Wise 5th, died. The below letter from John Cropper to his daughters tells of this death:

Drummond town, Virginia, 2d April 1812
My dear children, Ann and Eliza— I have to communicate the melancholy news of the death of Major John Wise. He departed this life the 28th ultimo at eleven o'clock in the forenoon. Major Wise had been declining ever since last summer, but his situation was flattering, and his friends hoped he would recover until about the middle of last month, when he declined more rapid, and death put a period to his affliction at the time I have mentioned, leav-

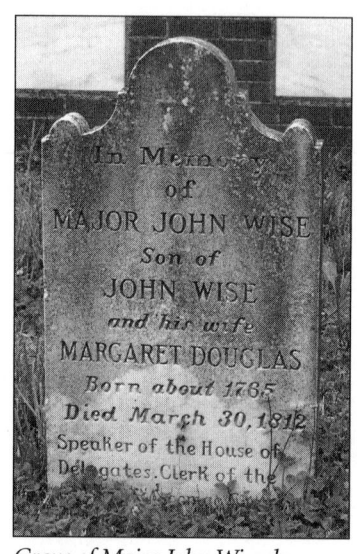

Grave of Major John Wise, born about 1765, died March 30, 1812, Wise family burial ground near Chesconessex Creek, Onancock, Virginia.

ing behind him a widow and six children, all of them to bear the severe loss of an affectionate husband, tender parent, and valuable protector. Let us not moan, but remember to imitate his talents and copy his virtues. I intend to go to Philadelphia the last of this month prepared to bring you both home, Ann to remain at home, but Eliza to return to school in the fall. I received a letter from each of you, by the last mail, written on the same sheet of paper, which was very satisfactory. Eliza improves now, and Ann loses in handwriting, owing to hurry and heedlessness. Your affectionate Father *Jno. Cropper, Jr.* (Virginia Historical Society, typed copy of letter.)

~ Henry Alexander Wise—A self description of his boyhood:

"He was a pale and puny boy in body, of large eyes and mouth and ugly, and so odd and oldish he wouldn't make with the children, but sought the old folks and learned their saying, and was fond of sweethearts older than himself, and spent his pocket money for red ribbons and climbed after nuts and fruit for their favors. He delighted in old stories, loved curious things; caught up quaint sayings, made something or much of what others threw away as nothing; was called by hard nicknames, but especially by the name of Prince Hal, because of a high-strung nervous temperament; and, fondled by black nurses, he was willful in his humors and sharp and quick and imperious in his temper; he loved fun and was fond of sport, precocious in mischief, tough and wiry in his tissues, an active, daring bad boy who could learn whatever he tried, but wouldn't learn what he didn't love, and could fight hard or run fast. There was a strange admixture of hardy recklessness and extreme caution in his nature; he was a great mimic and game maker, often offended by his broad humor, but was frank and genial, and so warm in his affections, and generous in his disposition, that he was generally popular, though he could when he tried make some hate him with a bitter hate."
—Barton Haxall Wise, *The Life of Henry A. Wise of Virginia.*

Henry Alexander Wise, photo by Rockwood, Holland Building, 1440 Broadway (40th Street), New York.

- 1813, Wise's mother, Sarah Corbin Cropper Wise, died. Wise then went to live at Bowman's Folly near the Atlantic Ocean, the home of his maternal grandfather, General John Cropper.
- 1814–1815, Wise went to live with two aunts near Chesconnessex Creek on the Chesapeake Bay side of Accomac.
- At age eight, Wise attends Margaret Academy near Accomac.
- 1822, before he was sixteen, Wise goes to Washington College, (now Washington and Jefferson College in Washington, Pennsylvania), where Dr. Andrew Wylie was the President.
- 1823, Wise meets Anne Elizabeth Jennings, the daughter of the Reverend Obadiah Jennings, pastor of the Presbyterian Church in Washington, Pennsylvania.
- 1825, Wise graduates and commences the study of law with Judge Henry St. George Tucker.
- 1827, Wise emancipates Elizabeth Grey and her two children, Mary Jane and William Henry. In later years William Henry Grey, a young mulatto boy, accompanied Wise into the House of Representatives.
- August 1828, Wise leaves Virginia for Nashville, Tennessee where Anne Elizabeth Jennings was then living with her parents. Anne's father, Obadiah Jennings, was a close friend of Andrew Jackson and the wedding party visited Jackson's home, The Hermitage, after the wedding.

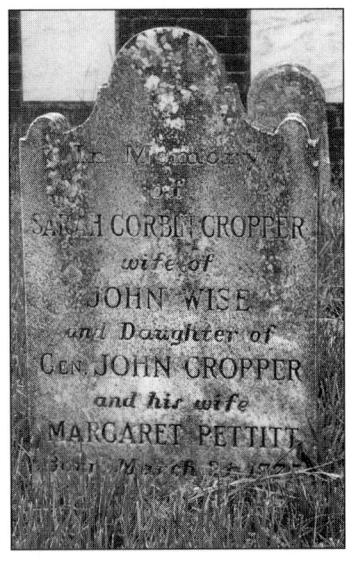

Grave of Sara Corbin Cropper Wise, 1777–1813, wife of John Wise 5th, 1765–1812, Wise family burial ground near Chesconessex Creek, Onancock, Virginia.

On May 3, 1811, John Cropper wrote the following letter in search of a new teacher:
Dear Sir— ...I indulge myself in the pleasure of writing to you, and enquiring after the health and welfare of yourself, Mrs. Jones, and your children—and also to ask of you your opinion, whether a teacher could be employed in New York for the Margaret academy in Accomack. A single man well recommended for capacity and moral character is required, and if such a one could be employed he might expect a liberal salary. The trustees have about the last of March Mr. David Comfort the principal left the academy on account of a spell of sickness which he had and an apprehension that he might have his health in the future… Please answer this letter by Mr. Snead, or by mail to Drummond Town, Virginia.   Your respectful servant, Jno. Cropper Jr."
(Letter, John Cropper to Reverend Cave Jones, Virginia Historical Society.)

Margaret Academy, Cheriton vicinity, Accomack County, Virginia. The Virginia General Assembly granted a charter to establish this school in 1786, but it was not built until 1806, opening in 1807. John Cropper was one of the founders and benefactors of the school, and it was named after his first wife, Margaret Pettit Cropper. The school was described as "a high-grade classical school, at which many of the leading men of the Eastern Shore have been educated." The school building was destroyed in the late 19th century. Photograph from Virginia Homes and Churches *by Robert Lancaster, Jr.*

The first marriage—Wise's love for Anne Jennings, their marriage, and the return to Virginia have been described as follows:

He became enamored of this lady whilst at college, and never rested until the marriage rites were celebrated, on the 8th day of October 1828, in the city of Nashville, Tennessee, where her father had been called as pastor of the Presbyterian congregation of that place. Mr. Wise had made his arrangements previously to leaving Virginia to settle in Nashville, which he did… But still he sighed for the 'milk of the ocean,' his 'own' native Virginia. To gratify his wife, he made every effort to be satisfied in Nashville. But despite all that he could do, he was unhappy outside his native State… Finally to gratify this wish of his heart, he determined, with the consent of his wife, to return to Accomack: which he did in the fall of 1830. When he returned home, the scenes of his boyhood exhilarated and enlivened a feeble frame which had almost fallen a prey to melancholy."   —James P. Hambleton, *A Biographical Sketch of Henry A. Wise.*

Henry A. Wise was elected to Congress in April 1833.

"A reporter, in an article entitled *Glances at Congress*, thus describes his [Henry A. Wise's] personal appearance and manner of speaking: "He is pale and thin, about thirty years of age, perhaps not so much. He dresses like an old man, though his general appearance is very youthful. He is very slovenly in his apparel, his coat hanging like a miller's bag on his shoulders… His forehead is projecting and massive, and his mouth large, but firmly set. Without being handsome, his face has a general pleasing character… To see him sauntering about the hall, with his long Indian strides, you would at

once be tempted to ask who he was; to hear him speak your attention would be riveted upon him. You no longer see the loose garment on the ungainly figure, the *outré* neckerchief vanishes, and your eyes are fixed on the excited and earnest orator. All his prominent characteristics are brought out with great rapidity—firmness, impetuosity, a disdain for honeyed words, fierce sarcasm and invective, all gather into a hurricane and startle the drowsy members from the lounges and wake up those victims of dull hours, the reporters... Mr. Wise may not always say anything remarkable or striking, but there is an intensity about his manner that fastens on the attention and clutches it until he has finished. He is remarkably quick in arriving at conclusions, and generally, too, in a way that would not have been struck upon by any one else. He is very independent in his disposition, fearless, and, to use a common expression, above board... He has undoubtedly very high talents, and I have heard him, upon more than one occasion, soar into the regions of commanding eloquence. His forte lies in invective; then he becomes, to those whose party sympathies follow his own excited train of feeling, thrilling; his pale and excited face, his firm and compact head thrown back, his small bony hand clenched in the air, or with the forefinger quivering there, his eyes brilliant and fixed, his voice high yet sonorous, impress a picture too vivid to be easily erased from the mind. A stranger, a few days ago, of his own party, on coming into the hall for the first time, at such a moment, compared his appearance to that of a corpse galvanized! Mr. Wise, as is well known, is a prominent member of the opposition. He cannot be ranked as a leader; certain it is, however, he is not led. He is much beloved by those who know him in private life, being jovial, free-hearted, and full of hilarity.'"
 —Barton Haxall Wise, *The Life of Henry A. Wise of Virginia.*

Governor Henry Alexander Wise, about 1828–1830, artist uncertain. One source attributes this portrait to John Gadsby Chapman, one of Wise's close personal friends and a frequent visitor to the Wise home in Accomac, Virginia. Collection of the Executive Mansion, courtesy of The Library of Virginia.

1834–1837

Letters to Henry A. Wise in Congress:

December 14, [1834], Twifordville.
My dear Husband—   I received your welcome letter informing me of your safe arrival... Friday morning before day, George with the assistance of Mr. Gillet's men killed the hogs; and after dinner I attended to the weighing of them. The largest weighed 289 pounds, the other 255. Old Lydia seemed much pleased, with the result of their weight, said she had earned her dress, as you had promised it to her, if she made them weigh 5 hundred... In the evening as I promised to go, though it was really inconvenient for me to do so, I took all the children and went to Margaret's to meet Mrs. Custis. We got there a little before dark. Mrs. Custis did not arrive, until an hour afterwards. We sat up until twelve talking. I learnt all the news of Washington from Mr. McMaster's. You will hear it all from Mr. McHennan I expect, therefore I will not repeat it, lest it will be Thomson's news... Saturday morning I left, though it was raining, as the hogs demanded my attention at home. I left Mary and Oby however; they were both very glad that the rain came, and prolonged their visit to Deep Creek... I had my fat fried up and my sausages made Saturday. I got a half a bushel of leaf lard from the hogs. In the afternoon, I sent George to Onancock, as I heard Captain Hopkins had come. He brought me a barrel of fine pippin apples, and a box of Candles... Saturday night Mr. Gillett's men came and salted my meat away for me. I told Tully to purchase a thousand weight more for us. He sent to Baltimore for his own and our winter stores... Yesterday as the morning was

Ann Elizabeth Jennings Wise, 1808–1837, wife of Henry A. Wise. Photograph courtesy of the Virginia Historical Society, Richmond, Virginia.

"Henry A. Wise, Representative from Virginia," early political poster. Courtesy of the Virginia Historical Society, Richmond, Virginia.

unfavourable I did not go to meeting. Charlotte took the gig and went to Deep Creek for the children. I spent the morning reading… I need not tell you that I very much desire to see you and that it will be a fortnight tomorrow since you left us. Farewel [sic] my dear husband may every blessing attend. Your wife, *Ann E. Wise*. (Virginia Historical Society)

January 8, 1835.
My dear Husband—   Two letters from you, have been duly received (and I think I may add duly appreciated) by me since I last wrote you; and they certainly deserve, a long letter in return. But our life here is so secluded, so barren of incident, that I fear I will not be able to fill a sheet to you today. We have not seen any one, since I last wrote, except Tully, who yesterday peeped at us, for a few minutes. He came to bring some beef, and was obliged to ride on horseback, as the roads are impassable in a gig… The children are all well, and often talk of you & ask me to read them, what you write. Mary says I must tell you, "she can count a hundred, and can *most* read, in the Bible, and those books you sent, with the pretty pictures in them. That she has commenced learning the multiplication table, and wants to know it all, to say to you when you come home." I must add, that she finds multiplication a vexation, as the old rhyme says, and wished the other day "that the people would not make books with it in them." …Oby says "tell papa; I am a good boy, and that I put on my trousers myself this morning." …Do not my dear husband, think of me, as being constantly unhappy, & discontented, in your absence. I have a *great deal* this winter, to beguile time of its weariness, and alleviate the pain of separation from you, in the presence & society of my *dear Mother* & sisters. We are all well, and I think as happy, as we can or should be, separated from some of those, we love as well, if not "best of any." …I will not apologize *to you* for manner or matter, as you well know, I am not gifted, in epistolary writing, and I well know that for me write what I will, it will be acceptable to you because I wrote it… Believe me to be your affectionate devoted wife.   —*Ann E. Wise*. (Virginia Historical Society)

January 16, 1835.
My dear Henry—   You have spoilt me writing two letters a week; how much was I disappointed, on Sunday last, when the servant returned with only a bundle of papers… I do not like to hear of that heart burn you mention. I have heard my *dear father* say, that that it was the lowest grade of the dyspepsia. So do have a care of it, if it continues to trouble you, be careful of your diet until rid of it… We all continue as well as usual. My own health still gradually improving. I will attend to your directions about taking exercise &c. Margaret & Tully spent yesterday with us. They had considerable difficulty in getting here, the roads are so dreadful… I need scarcely tell you, that I did not get my pen mended to write you, as I intended. It is almost worn out in the service. I will try and have a new one when I write next… Good night my dear husband and believe me as ever your affectionate wife.   —*A. E. Wise*. (Virginia Historical Society)

January 24, 1835.
My dear Husband—   It is a bright beautiful morning here, almost as mild as spring. Much would I like, to transport myself to Washington, and climb

Capitol hill with you today. But if I had Aladdin's lamp with the permission of only rubbing it once and wishing, I would prefer bringing you here to see the children and all, unless perchance I knew you were to occupy the floor of the house to-day... Today I have done various little things about the house, have been often enough to the kitchen to afford me some exercise; and have written you this dull account of how I have spent my time since I wrote you. It was not quite twelve when I commenced writing but is now almost seven o'clock, as I have met with many little interruptions, and you know I do not hold the pen, of a very ready writer... I want you my dear Husband to think of me, not "as striving to be contented and happy" but as being most generally quite as much so as you would wish, during your absence. I keep myself fully occupied, and do not sit down to brood over trouble, as you fear. Do not again refer to any trouble you give me when you are here, for it is but trifling, and would not be half what it is, if it were not for my morbid feelings and want of attention to trifles. I do know that you love me as your life, that you love me with an affection equal to mine for you, and more I could not wish for. I have perfect confidence in your unalienable affection. I have put by most carefully your two pumpin [sic] seeds, and will have them narrowly watched and particularly taken care of, when the time comes for planting them. Before I opened your letter I felt them and thought it was money, and when I opened it they were done up so much like medicine that I might have supposed it to be a love powder, if I have had the least idea, that you thought I needed one from you. The children are all well...   Your affectionate wife, —*Ann E. Wise.* (Virginia Historical Society)

February 2, 1835.
My dear Husband—   ...Mother has been quite sick with the influenza since I wrote you but is now getting better. The children are all well and all fast asleep. You need not fear that Oby wants for exercise. He has grown wonderfully since you left home & has become a most incessant talker and master of mischief. I do not think I ever knew as mischievous a child; it really distresses me to see him delight in it so much...   —*Ann E. Wise.* (Virginia Historical Society)

February 13, 1835.
My dear Husband—   I wrote you a hasty line last mail and did not intend to write again until next Monday, but you express so much anxiety at not having received a letter from me, that I write this mail lest my two last may not reach you... I am writing in the midst of the noise of the children. Mother is engaged writing; they are all dismissed into my room and I have had several times to lay down my pen to try to command quiet and tap Oby for his mischief, pulling the girls hair &c. We are all as well as usual... You must have been indeed surprised by Uncle James Wilson's visit. I do not think that I ever gave you an account of him. If I have not I will do so on your return. Mother and all his relatives thought him dead for a number of years until about a year since. I would write more though I do not know that I have any thing to write that would interest you but it is just dark and I want to send my letter before your good Uncle retires for the night... The children say "tell papa he must come home we want to see him *so bad.*"   ...Ever yours, *Ann E. Wise.* (Virginia Historical Society)

December 26, 1835.
A pleasant, (if not a merry) Christmas to you, my dear husband. I suppose that you and the other public servants have now a few days respite from attending the house. Would you could employ them in paying us a visit. But this I know cannot be; as the broad Chesapeake rolls between us, and no steamboat waits to convey you here despite wind or weather… You want to know how Henry comes on; he is very fat and becomes more lively and interesting every day. The other children are well, except slight colds… My own health is very delicate. I try to take all the care I can of it. I think I am much thinner than when [you] left home. I feel better this evening however than I have done for several days past… Your books & papers are all safely moved here. I believe I have nothing more to write at present; unless it be to tell you what you very well know, that I am very anxious to see you, and often feel impatient at your long absence, and often or still anticipate your glad return. Let me know when you write next how many sermons you have heard. Who is Mr. Smith that I see is elected Chaplain to the lower house? Is he not a Presbyterian minister and does he preach well? Good night my dear husband, and believe me to be ever your affectionate wife. —*Ann E. Wise.* (Virginia Historical Society)

December 28, 1835.
My dear Husband—   Yesterday I received your *very short* letter of the 22d inst. Though I am much obliged to you for it, short as it is, for it assures me of your good health and constant remembrance of me; yet I could not but feel disappointed at its brevity… We have all been blessed with health since I wrote you this day week ago… John called this morning and gave me your letter to read, and the thirty dollars you sent. You say in it you have had constant colds. Whereas you have reported yourself constantly well, except for one day and night to me. Do not my dear Henry ever attempt to deceive me respecting your health, or I shall feel constantly uneasy… The children send love to you: Do take care of your health and do not go to bed with cold feet I beg of you… Farewel my dear Husband and believe me to be as ever your affectionate wife. —*Ann E. Wise.* (Virginia Historical Society)

January 4, 1836.
My dear Henry—   Yesterday I received your well filled sheet of the 26th, and your letter of the 29th. I have read them already, a half dozen times… Thursday was my birthday. I completed that day my 27th year. To how little purpose have I spent my life. I hope the years which are yet to come to me, be their number many or few, will be spent more profitably to myself and others… I shall count the hours almost the moments, until the arrival of the Wednesday mail; as I expect not only a letter from you, but your speech which you said in your last you should be engaged writing off for the press… Good night my dear dear husband and believe me to be as ever your devoted wife.   —*Ann E. Wise.* (Virginia Historical Society)

༄ Misfortune and tragedy, 1837:

During the spring of 1837, before Mr. Wise reached home from Washington, his dwelling-house with nearly all of his valuable books and papers were consumed by fire. His family were removed to a friend's house in the village of Drummondtown, and that house, in a

Grave of Ann Jennings Wise, 1808–1837, near Chesconessex Creek, Accomack, Virginia, before being moved in 1928 to Hollywood Cemetery in Richmond, Virginia. Photograph part of the Doran S. Callahan Photograph Collection, 1890–1900 housed in the Eastern Shore of Virginia Room at the Eastern Shore Public Library. Photo courtesy of the Library of Virginia and reprinted with permission of the Eastern Shore Public Library.

very mysterious manner, was set on fire also. This so affected the nervous system of his wife, that she never recovered from it, and died in the month of June [May 4] following. She was the mother of seven children, but left only four living. Mary Elizabeth… Obadiah Jennings (the eldest son)… Henry Alexander Wise, Jr… and Ann Jennings Wise, the second daughter… who was an infant at the death of her mother…
—James P. Hambleton, *A Biographical Sketch of Henry A. Wise.*

Accomack C. H. E. S. Va. Oct. 27th, 1837.
My dear Madam—   Often have I undertaken to thank you, affectionately and gratefully, for the kind letter of condolence which your good heart prompted you to write to me last summer. Oh! My dear Madam, you know not how misfortune stunned every faculty and all the energy of my weak spirit. I have not been and never shall be the same man you once knew. Again and again did I try hard to rouse myself, but will you believe me that I wrote not even to Balie Peyton a line until late last month? Judge White's letter was a recipe, yours a balm… I have uplifted a pile, a monstrous weight of business since he directed me to busy myself in the active duties of life, to restore my wounded balance of mind and spirit. God knows care has been heaped upon me— relation after relation, near & dear, has died, one in quick succession after another and their estates have fallen on me to settle. My own affairs have long been neglected… When I got to Balt. [Baltimore] some client stopped me "in transition" as the lawyers say, & carried me on business to Hampton so that I was delayed in reaching *my children* until Monday last. I write by the first mail— ours are bi-weekly only. I found my babes all well but one. My youngest boy [Henry Alexander Wise] is yet pale with a short but severe attack of bilious fever. When the news reached me he was sick I was sure he would die— the fortune of the year has so run with me. Thank God that every one of *her* children are yet spared to me! …I cannot write a letter now to a friend without sickening with grief… My sister was in Washington a moment, and, though a plain Virginia house-wife, I wanted you to see that she was so. Her domestic habits are all in all to me now. She is very much attached to my children and my youngest— the babe, little Ann E., is now a healthy, fat, fine child. She is nursed by Ann's favorite servant and thrives like a pig on fat meat and milk. I am, at this moment, engaged in writing out an interminable speech which I made at 12 o'clock at night on the 14th inst. You must therefore excuse the incoherence of this epistle & take it, as it was intended, a mere apology for my long apparent neglect. I hope to meet you *at Philippi* next month. In the meantime believe me to desire you all the health & happiness you can enjoy with the Judge, who I hope arrived at home safe & in good health.   Yours Truly, *Henry A. Wise.* (Virginia Historical Society)

↝ In the years that followed, some of the most interesting correspondence is from Obadiah Jennings Wise, Henry A. Wise's oldest son:

Henry A. Wise M.C. Washington City, D.C.
Philadelphia, February 27.
My dear Father—   I wish to see you very much, pray come and see us as we cannot go to see you but we expect you soon. We are busy attending to our studies. I am learning geography, arithmetic, reading writing and definitions. Sister and I have just traveled through the map of Asia. Give my love to

My dear Madam   Henry A. Wise is writing to Mrs. Ann White of Knoxville in response to her letter of condolence after the death of his wife.

Balie Peyton   1803–1878, a Congressman from Tennessee from 1833–1837 and Minister to Chile, 1849–1853.

bilious fever   Sometimes misspelled *billious* by one uncle, a term used to generally describe digestive disorders with any, or perhaps all, of the following symptoms– jaundice, constipation, headache, vertigo, anorexia, and diarrhea.

Ann E.   Known throughout her life as "Annie," the daughter had been christened "Ann Jennings Wise." Her father's reference to *"Ann E."* suggests the possible derivation of "Annie." Her mother, Ann Elizabeth Wise after whom she had been named, had died three days after her birth. The use of the name "Ann E.", subsequently spelled "Annie" and with an emphasis on the pronunciation of the "E," would become a lifelong memorial to a Mother whom she never knew. Had it been spelled "Anne," the "e" would have been silent. Her gravestone reads *Annie.*

all enquiring friends, particularly George and Mrs. White. Dear Father please excuse this bad writing for it is my first attempt at letter writing my dear Father, your affectionate son, *O. J. Wise.* (Virginia Historical Society)

Henry A. Wise, Drummond town, Accomack County, Virginia
Philadelphia (not dated)
Dear Father—   I have delayed too long replying to your kind and excellent and dear letter— but my dear father that it was want of love from his own loving boy, who loves him better him that all the world beside— But the weather has been so fine and when school was out I was so full of play that I knew that you will excuse me. I am glad dear father that the very book that I study at school is the one that you recommended. Tell cousin George that he must not be long in answering my letter. I am very much pleased with my school. I am learning Orthography, reading, writing, Arithmetic, grammer [*sic*], geography history and philosophy. The Miss Sergeants invited us to spend the evening and Mrs. Sergeant sent her love to you. We are all well and join me in love to you dear father. Uncle Tully, Aunt Margaretta Uncle John and Aunt Ann, Aunt Betsey, Aunt Harriet and all my cousins. Write soon dear father to your affectionate son. *O. J. Wise.* (Virginia Historical Society)

Henry A. Wise M.C. Washington City, D.C.
Philadelphia. December 9, 1839.
Dear Father—   And are you really at Washington. I hope you will be able to come and see us for we want to see you very much indeed. Grandma says it is her humble opinion indeed that you ought to come and see your children. We are all well except Henry who has got the jaundice and my teacher says that we will go in Natural History. I have been committing the song of English History which tells me all about all the kings that ever reigned in England which I hope I shall soon have the pleasure of repeating to you. One day when Grandma was singing to little Anne she said Grandma sing about my papa and every time she gets up from saying her prayers she says Grandma I love papa. We all send love. *O. Jennings Wise.* (Virginia Historical Society)

֍ 1840–1853: The second marriage and Minister to Brazil.

In November 1840 Henry Wise married Sarah Sergeant of Philadelphia. He continued to serve in Congress until after the election of 1843.

his friends Wise was appointed to the post in Brazil by President John Tyler, one of his close personal friends. Wise and his family sailed to Brazil aboard the frigate *Constitution.*

"On Mr. Wise's return to Congress it was discovered that his physical health was giving away rapidly from the constant excitement of about ten years. Consequently his friends sent his name again to the Senate for the Court of Rio Janeiro… On the 8th day of February 1844, he resigned his seat in Congress, and sailed from New York for Rio in the month of May following his resignation."
—James P. Hambleton, *A Biographical Sketch of Henry A. Wise.*

Others were taking note of Henry Wise and the following appeared in 1845:

"In person, he is nearly six feet tall, extremely thin, and has not enjoyed a very great share of good health. His features are strongly marked and expressive; his mouth large but firmly set; his hair is light and carelessly worn; his forehead high and prominent, denoting strong intellectual powers; his eyes are dark and piercing, and his complexion pale and colorless, and rendered still more pallid by his cravat, which is always white.

In debate, Mr. Wise is particularly happy; his manner is animated, and he easily becomes excited by his subject… As a speaker, he is pleasing, and always commands the fullest attention from his auditors. His peculiar forte is in sarcasm and invective, and on occasions when he is compelled to resort to the exercise of these weapons, he is exceedingly severe and sometimes withering.

Mr. Wise may now be said to occupy a situation seldom attained by public men of our day. He may now be stated to belong to no party, and to be independent of any. His constituents are of all parties, and among them he is uncommonly popular…

His social and familiar habits, his easy and affable manners, render him at all times an agreeable companion, and the sincerity which characterizes him on all occasions adapts him particularly as a companion and friend. It must be evident to every observing mind, that Mr. Wise possesses talents of the first order, and when the experience of a few years in public life is added to the information he now possesses, he promises to rank high amongst the most talented and distinguished men of our country."
—William H. Brown, *Portrait Gallery—Distinguished American Citizens with Biographical Sketches and Fac-Similes of Original Letters.*

Henry A. Wise Portrait Gallery—Distinguished American Citizens with Biographical Sketches *and* Fac-Similes of Original Letters *by William H. Brown, Hartford, Connecticut, 1845 (Reissued 1931).*

In 1847 Wise returned to Virginia from Brazil and in 1850 he was elected to the State Convention that revised the Virginia Constitution. During that convention he received the news of the death of his second wife, the mother of seven children, only four of whom survived their mother and one of them died later in infancy.

༄ The Virginia Constitutional Convention, Richmond, August 1850:

"A writer of the time, in the *Southern Literary Messenger*, in describing the members of the convention, thus speaks of him [Henry A. Wise]:— 'In appearance he was one of the most remarkable looking men in the Assembly, and would attract attention wherever seen. His face seemed full of cavities, —hollow cheeks, large, hollow eye-sockets, and the most cavernous mouth; when he spoke, the eyebrow seemed thrown up toward the top of his head, and his mouth immensely opened, like a gate on its hinges, so that he appeared to be all eyes and all mouth—two very good features in an orator. His face is full of flexibility and, by the easy play of its muscles, expresses every emotion and passion of the mind. In fact, the whole face speaks in every muscle and fibre of it. When at rest, his relaxed features, tall, loose-jointed figure, and slight, spare form give no promise of physical power; yet the length and frequency of his speech and his earnest, violent gesticulation show that he possesses great power of endurance. From out this cavernous mouth flow streams of eloquence; these hollow eye-sockets are filled up with the blaze of the eye; and the very flexibility of his features adds force and emphasis to his words. His hazel eye, even when quiet, has a daring outlook that well expresses the character of the man; and in his excited moments it blazed and burned in the fire of his own vehemence, as if it would consume all opposition and intimidate all resistance. His action is always abundant and is of the most vehement and excited character. Totally devoid of grace, which his loose, angular figure forbids, it yet possesses much power and eccentric force; his use of the long forefinger reminds us of Randolph, and, like him, he excels in denunciation. His voice is the most perfect and beautiful feature that, as an orator, he possesses; it is at once powerful and sweet,

John Tyler Portrait Gallery—Distinguished American Citizens with Biographical Sketches *and* Fac-Similes of Original Letters *by William H. Brown, Hartford, Connecticut, 1845 (Reissued 1931).*

Henry A. Wise. Engraved by H. B. Hall & Sons, New York. Used as the frontispiece in The Life of Henry A. Wise of Virginia *by Barton H. Wise.*

as flexible as the muscles and features of his face, and as perfectly under control; it has compass, variety, depth, and clearness, and, besides this, it has that peculiarity of sound or accent which constitutes the winning spell of the orator and which so effectually charms an audience… Mr. Wise spoke on every question that came up, and, in fact, scarcely a day passed that he did not have something to say. His greatest speech was made upon the Basis Question, toward the close of the debate upon that subject, he was five days in delivering it… The effect of his speech was so strikingly evident; and if the true test of an orator is in his power to convince a mixed audience of the truth of his own opinions and to carry with him their attention and their sympathies, then Henry A. Wise is one of the most eloquent men in Virginia.'"
—Barton Haxall Wise, *The Life of Henry A. Wise of Virginia.*

Letters from two of Henry Wise's children, Mary Elizabeth and Obadiah, describe the family between 1848 and 1853:

August 5, 1848   …If Father [Henry A. Wise] leaves Accomac, I hope he will not leave Henry [Henry A. Wise Jr.] there by himself so long; it would do him a great deal of harm. He is a very good boy if he has Father to keep him in order, but he ought not to be there without anyone to command him. As to his going to college next fall, it would be the ruin of him; he must be kept at home a while longer till he learns to be more of a man so far as studying and behaving without being forced to it. Annie has improved with regard to her temper and behavior; altogether Richard is the same sober old-mannish child, but he is more healthy and plays more. Néné is as wild as ever and just as much of a pet with Father. Johnnie is too sweet to describe…
—*Mary Elizabeth Wise,* as quoted by William M. Adkins in *Obadiah Jennings Wise '50: A Sketch of His Life,* Indiana University Alumni Quarterly.

Bloomington, April 2nd, 1849.
My dear Father—   As the bustle of examinations, exhibitions & moving from one boarding house to another is now completely over; as it is time to send on my quarterly accounts, and moreover as I feel like corresponding with "mine honorsive" here I am snugly seated in the room appropriated to me by mine host (Cousin John Parker's friend, the worshipful brother John Onchard) surrounded by pen ink &c with little to say, but wishing to say much.

The Philomatheau exhibition came off on last Monday evening. Your two nephews did about as well as any there. Their declamation was about the best on the exhibition. With regard to the composition of their essays, you can have a shame of judging for yourself, as I presume Aunt Margaret will send them on to you… I have come to the sage determination that I will spend this vacation without loafing. I have several tremendous projects on hand, such as making gardens, reading Greek (some question about that though) and— but stop! I'll let you into a secret which *no one else knows:* your son, has of late taken several small dives into authorship. Besides furnishing several fictions for the *Indiana Tribune,* he has had the pleasure of seeing half a dozen pieces of his own verse in print. I have come to the conclusion that there is nothing so much needed by our country as poetry, and have determined to try my hand at the business. I have commenced a translation of Voltaire's *Henriade* into verse, which I hope to complete before leaving college. What think you of it? Please write to me and tell me all about things at home… As the mail closes in about half an hour, and as I have nothing more to say my epistle must be cut short…   love to all, Your affectionate son, *O. Jennings Wise.* (Virginia Historical Society)

January 21, 1850—   They always mention, when writing from home the receipt of a letter from you, but that is a very unsatisfactory way of hearing from a brother, particularly one who has always been in every way so closely connected in all my doings and pleasures until you went to college. Indeed, Obe, I have been thinking much of late about the times we have had together, studying, walking, riding, and it seems to me everything we did together, the recollection of it all is so very delightful, I wish we had it to do over. Do you? I cannot believe you will be home next June.
—*Mary Elizabeth Wise Garnett,* as quoted by William M. Adkins in *Obadiah Jennings Wise '50: A Sketch of His Life.*

Bloomington, April 18th, 1850.
My dear Father—   I received you last letter, dated April 4th, on Tuesday last. With regard to my extravagance I thank you for your kind reproof; but must say that my extravagance has been owing no more to my *being a child* than to my *being treated as a child*. I have been utterly ignorant as to the state of your affairs. When I left home I knew you to be free from debt… I have heard repeatedly since that you had your hands full of practice, which together with your reputation was increasing daily. All this led me to believe that you were making more than enough for all the necessaries and comforts of the family. And I can not believe that I would knowingly have prevented Henry and Annie from receiving their share of your liberality. As I have done so, I can only promise to try every means in my power when I return home to make amends at least to Annie for the deprivation… I have paid off my debts and have $20 and some cents remaining. I will try to do on $150.00 more; but I doubt whether I shall be able to do so. I do not think that my clothes will cost less than 40 or 45 dollars; my winter clothes being nearly all worn out, and my summer ones outgrown. Besides this at the end of the next session I shall owe my washerwoman $18.00. This bill I have allowed to run on for some time, forgetting sometimes and several times offering to pay her, but she refused, stating that she would prefer to receive it "all in a lump;" afraid most probably that I wished to take it from her. Under the hand of "other expenses" I have included fuel, (which I shall have to use until the middle of May) candles, stationary [sic], postage, library subscriptions. The boys are all well. College commences again on Wednesday week. Please write to me and forgive, Your son, *O. Jennings Wise.* (Virginia Historical Society)

Only, Monday, March 22, 1852.
My dear Father—   Having nothing else to interest you, I must give you another detail of farming operations, which will not, I fear be as pleasing as it is interesting, since it is an epitomoe [sic] of agricultural disasters. On Monday and Tuesday we managed to finish the guano land, Spenser being too much indisposed to work. On Wednesday we had a perfect storm of wind and rain, which continuing all day, prevented all labor that day. The hands were employed during the better part of Thursday in organizing the fences and

fodder stacks, which suffered severely on the preceding day. A freeze having succeeded (or succeeded rather) the storm. All hands were employed for the rest of the week in cutting and mauling logs for the oat-field fence, which is now partly constructed— that is, it is made about six logs high… On Saturday the snow fell about two inches deep. This morning I had Fred, Spenser and little John Poulson helping to ship the cattle on board William Finney's vessel for *Natts Island,* while the other hands carted out manure. We got them all safely in the hold and then the vessel started round to Toppings Creek to take in the house logs, but ran hard aground where she is now waiting for high water to lift her off… I forgot to tell you that we finished rolling the oats on Tuesday. The box from Philadelphia arrived here today, bringing all the things you sent for by John Sergeant. All are well. Your affectionate son, *O. Jennings Wise.* (Virginia Historical Society)

Friday, Nov. 6th, 1852.
My dear Father—   I take the opportunity, which Jim's departure this evening affords me, to drop you a line. Henry is getting along finely. He is on good terms with all the professors, and has already graduated in French. He has been mainly instrumental in getting up a new literary society, which now rivals in numbers the one previously initiated. He has been elected by its members to deliver an address, in contest against an orator chosen by the other society, on the 22nd February next. I was of opinion that he would make a much better speech by waiting till next year; but, as he will then have to prepare his graduating address, he preferred to take a chance this time.

The Judge keeps me busy. Our class, near twenty in number, attends lectures every day in the week, besides the extra duty of the moot court on Saturday… I do not think that I shall need $300 for this session. Henry will need more. Give love to all. Your affectionate son, *O. Jennings Wise.* (Virginia Historical Society)

By this time Obadiah Wise was studying law.

Williamsburg, Jan. 9th, 1853.
My dear Father— …I spent Christmas week with Uncle John in Princess Anne. All the family were in excellent health except himself— he was confined to his room all the time by a severe attack of inflammatory rheumatism, but was getting getter when I left. I am entirely out of money, and I find that Henry is in the same situation. I shall soon owe $50 for board, Henry has paid his up to the 22nd of February. I also owe $60 for books… for this debt I gave my note payable at the end of six months— so you see that if it is not convenient for you to let me have it now, the money need not be forthcoming till then. Henry owes I believe, about $30, in small debts… Our initiation fees &c cost us together about $30 and my trip to Princess Anne $15— washing bills $10. This statement will show how the greater part of our money has gone. We need at present at least $100–$200 would perhaps [be] better, as it would enable us to go upon the cash system for the future. The reason why I have not written to you sooner is that I did not know exactly where to find you. All the boys are well. Your affectionate son, *O. Jennings Wise.* (Virginia Historical Society)

Williamsburg, March 13, 1853.
My dear Father—   I received your letter yesterday. I shall certainly graduate in July, when I wish immediately to take out a law license. I should be very

much pleased if you can find nothing better for me to do, to return here next fall, and take the law… Henry returned from Richmond yesterday, where he has been on account of his teeth, for the last few days: they were decaying rapidly and began to be painful to him. I am sorry that I was not aware of the state of his mouth while Dr. S— was here. His teeth cost him $45, his other expenses $20, in all $65. This necessitates a draft for this amount, as soon as you can conveniently send it. I have received but two letters from Washington since I have been here, one from sister and the other from Annie. It is, I expect, my own fault; I have lost the habit of writing affectionate letters, But I trust that you, at least, will believe that, with all my selfishness, I love you dearly, yes more dearly than ever, Your affectionate son, *O. Jennings Wise.* (Virginia Historical Society)

Williamsburg, April 10, 1853.
My dear Father— Today being my birthday, I have determined to send you a few lines, notwithstanding the fact that I have little or nothing to say… Last week Jimmie and the other two candidates for the degree of A. M., together with myself, were elected by the faculty members of the Phi Beta Kappa Society. How the honor came to be conferred on me, and on no other member of the law class I cannot tell; but I am more the less thankful for it. As you are aware no doubt, it is the most honorable, as well as the oldest and most widely extended literary society in this country. The faculty are determined to make a big show on "the 4th." They are stimulating the candidates for graduation with present exhortations as well as with prospective gold medals. One or two of them have indicated that a poem on my part would be acceptable. I really don't believe that I *could* prepare one, even if I had the time and inclination— the poetic fire is so feint within me. My daydreams are becoming daily more prosaic— principally concerning a series of very learned legal arguments to be delivered in future, and I must confess it— of future fees also… I have not set my heart on going abroad… I have but little preference as to which court of Europe I should reside at… though I would somewhat prefer an English or a German residence, the first in order to become acquainted with the English courts, the latter to learn the German language… Give love to all and kiss the children for me. Your affectionate son, *O. Jennings Wise.* (Virginia Historical Society)

1853–1860

❧ The third marriage:

Only, near Onancock, Va. August 13, 1853.
My dearest Mary Lyons— My heart bounds to you— it wells up to gush forth to you in its fullness & freshness. And is it so— that I am yet blest "in woman & love"? Again, again, again! I thank thee, I bless thee, I praise thee, I love thee. And this is not impious adoration, but is truly a part of the Divinity, which stirs within us— an earnest devotion, satisfying as nature's law which Heaven approves and sends to earth to light it up and lift us to the grace & gladness & glory above… Yes, Mary Lyons, you have thrice blessed me & "I am yours and you are mine" forever! And this intensity of realization

shall grow with time and deepen… I will teach thee all I know of love like a little child… I was called to dinner. Since I have called Annie to my side and told her all and requested her to write to you. Oh! She is too sweet. The child wept but not bitterly— she kissed me and was happy & recovered herself and immediately wrote the inclosed. It is her own spontaneous self and just what you will always find her— generous, sensible, sensitive, conscientious and Christian-like. [Annie was then 16 years old.] In the midst of this "joy of grief" with her a letter is just handed to me from my son in London— a beautiful & manly letter from one whom you will respect when you know him as you will love Annie on sight. He [Obadiah Jennings Wise] left for Hamburgh en route to Berlin July 22nd at 1 o'clock at night…

—Saturday, Aug 14th. I have again slept upon it and talked with Annie, and my dear dear Mary Lyons! I fear not for you nor for my children. You will unite at once by instantaneous fusion with us all. *I feel it so*. I am not a fool in my love. No! Mary Lyons you have only just made me happy, thrice happy in the hope of all in you to make a wife & mother. Say when I may fly to you and say it soon & may God keep you in His keeping forever for your own *Henry A. Wise*.

Washington, August 28th. [1853]
My dear Miss Lyons—   Father has just informed me of his engagement to yourself. I hope you will understand me when I confess it is with mixed feeling I think of his marriage. They must arise from selfishness, however for I know it will be better for him and his children to have a good wife and Mother, and from what everyone has told me I feel sure he could not have made a happier choice. May God bless you both and make you as good a Mother to my little brothers and sisters as theirs was to me and He could not give them a greater blessing… Yours, *Mary W. Garnett*.

Mary Elizabeth Wise Garnett, 1829–1898, a daughter of Henry A. Wise by his first marriage and married to Dr. Alexander Y. P. Garnett.

Washington City— Sept 13th, 1853.
My dear Mary Lyons—   The Omnibus from Alexandria brought me here early last evening, half sick and more than half sad at waving adieu to that pale face which beamed on me at parting from the Hotel door and which has been before my mind's eye ever since, waking and last night dreaming. Yes! Last night I did dream of you for the first time and it was a dream which I would *not* have had "all a dream"— it was so bright and beautiful and full of delight. That dream I will tell to you some of these days when it may make you as happy as it did me this glorious morning, so glittering with light and the hopes which light always inspires… I met my nephew at the cars and bade him ride out to see you. I trust he did so and that you found him a promising fellow. He said Dr. Garnett told him to inform *you*, not me, of the newborn grand daughter & the thought of that babe made me anxious to hasten on to Mary [Mary Wise Garnett]. I found her very well, but the child, though very large and apparently healthy, will not live, I think. Why, the Doctors cannot tell. She has sent for a clergyman to christen it & lest it may die, I forego naming it *Mary Lyons*. The mother is perfectly resigned to let it sleep and— wake in Heaven… The *Balt Sun* says I am writing a scathing article against the Pacific R. Road and am soon to lead a Richmond beauty to the altar. How they get hold of those things I can't tell, but sometimes "what everybody says

must be true." Speed the day! Say I when I am to be one with my own pure loved Mary Lyons. Your own *Henry A. Wise.*

September 20, 1853.
I do not write to offer you comfort my dear Mrs. Lyons in your sore affliction, for earthly friends can give little or no consolation under such circumstances. I only wish to tell you that you have my sincerest sympathy and love. Much I have thought of you in your trouble & prayed that my heavenly Father would console not only yourself but all the sorrowing ones of your family, and I am sure my prayers will be answered. Father read me your kind message. I love you for it… I had determined before to love you for my father's sake. I feel sure now that my heart's warmest affection must be yours for your own sake… Father received a letter from Sister [Mary Wise Garnett] today in which she sent her love and warmest sympathy to you. She too sorrows, her little babe died last Wednesday, and though all must rejoice that it was taken in its purity to God, without ever having known earthly sin and care, still it had its place in a mother's heart and that heart could not help grieving when it was taken from her. I desire so much to see you, and hope it will not be very long before I shall meet you. My best wishes for your welfare and happiness are always yours and again I assure you that I will do everything in my power to promote the latter. That you may find consolation in your afflictions is the sincere prayer of   —Yours Truly & Affectionately, *Annie J. Wise.*

∾ Tragedy in the family, two letters:

Only, near Onancock Va. Sept 24th, 1853.
My dear Mary Lyons— … Mary Garnett has lost her dear little babe & I have just finished a note of condolence to her. Write to her. Write to me. I pray God to guard you…   Your Own *Henry A. Wise.*

Only, Oct. 1st, 1853.
My dear Mary Lyons—   Annie brings me this letter to inclose to you. It excites me more than I could describe to do so. For two weeks I have not recd. a line from you and my anxiety is almost intolerable. Yet, I am *chained* here! I am *compelled* to remain at home for the present and would fly to you. How are you?— Sick? —Overwhelmed with grief? —Forgotten me? Three packets have come and gone and not a note from you. Sabbath last and Thursday last I was sure of a letter— of some sign or token at least from you and none came. Did you forget to mail your letters Tuesday or Saturday to be certain of reaching our ferry at Norfolk by Friday and by Tuesday? Tuesday week coming, Oct. 11th, I shall leave here for Richmond. May I not? Ah! If tomorrow's mail should forbid it, I shall be most unhappy. I am very disturbed now.   Your own *Henry A. Wise.*

Only, near Onancock, Va. October 6th, 1853.
My dear Mary Lyons—   I fear you will tire of my frequent letters, but I am a little sad about you & my solicitudes must plead my apology. You have been much distracted and I was not near you and I have been anxious without being able to relieve my doubts or my fears. By the side of me a maid,

in the bloom of health and childish in age, and cut down; and by your side a youth full— full of hope & promise— to admonish us how short life is & uncertain everything around & about us. This has actually made me nervously anxious about our wedding day. Are you *ever— never* to be mine? I have asked that question a thousand times, knowing too how you are & have been lately sorrowing. This has made me jump to work— the work of rapid preparation for your coming & coming soon. The house has been torn up from top to bottom and the work is still going on but will be finished by next week. And I have been pitching my wheat crop and have not much hindrance from interruptions of labor and from the drought this fall. But it will all come right… We must— indeed we *must* be married soon. I shall go on next Tuesday week unless I hear something from you to forbid. I have gone forth to the woods and knelt alone & prayed God *for you*. I weep when the love of you comes right full over me. Your own *Henry A. Wise.*

Only, Oct. 12th, 1853.
My dear Mary Lyons—   …Yesterday I rec'd a letter from Mary Garnett and it inclosed your sweet— exquisitely sweet letter to her on the death of her babe. I gratefully thank you for it. You need not fear, my love— these dear children already all love you and they will all bless you. I *know* they will and am therefore so anxious for you to *come* to them and to come quickly. Mary promises to meet you here. I don't intend that anyone else for some time, except the children, shall be here to divert us in the least from each other. I am your own, *Henry A. Wise.*

Henry A. Wise and Mary Elizabeth Lyons of Richmond were married in November 1853.

Perhaps the most complete description of the Wise family for the 1840s and 1850s is a letter written by Obadiah Jennings Wise to Mrs. John Gadsby Chapman who was living in Rome. An artist, John Gadsby Chapman, 1808–1889, was a close friend of Henry A. Wise and had often visited with the Wise family. Obadiah's letter:

Berlin, Germany, January 5, 1854.
Dear Mrs. Chapman—   Six months and more have elapsed since Mrs. Brown, on her return from Italy, delivered me some kind messages from yourself which stirred up a host of old remembrances, and led to repeated determinations to open a correspondence with you. Business, indolence and every other sort of hindering circumstance have continually interposed to prevent the accomplishment of these good intentions, and I am at last moved to the undertaking by the greatest motive power of this life— selfishness. I have a favor to ask of you, of which I will speak directly.

You wish to know what we have all been doing since we parted from you at New York nearly eleven years ago. My energies are entirely insufficient to furnish anything like a satisfactory *exposé* of even the domestic occurrences of our own little family circle during so long a period of time. I can only give you a sketch of the appearance and character of each member of the circle, together with a recital of some of the most important events.

We lived a pleasant life in Brazil. The only great grief that befell us was the news of the death of my uncle Mr. Tully R. Wise, which reached us shortly

Obadiah Jennings Wise, 1831–1862. Photograph courtesy of the Virginia Historical Society, Richmond, Virginia.

after our arrival. We luxuriated in a climate and scenery which I cannot believe to be surpassed by those of Italy itself— made but little advance in social intercourse with the Portuguese inhabitants, who were inapproachable and although we mingled considerably with a mixed society of English, American, French and Spaniards, permanent and transitory, were obliged to find in each other our chief resources of entertainment.

Father employed his energies in exercising a strict patriarchal government over a large household composed of various nations and complexions and speaking three languages which he did not understand, —in cultivating two or three acres of garden land, —in suppressing the slave trade, —and in asserting and maintaining the rights and privileges of our republican citizens. Our sojourn in the country was marked by two additions to the family —a flaxen haired, blue-eyed girl, whose real name is Margaret, but who is known to this day only by the name of Néné (the Portuguese synonym for "baby") —and a hearty *buster* of a boy, who received the bluff and appropriate cognomen of "John."

Early in the spring of 1847, I left the rest of the family at Rio, and betook myself to the University at Bloomington, Indiana, at the head of which was Father's old master, the late Dr. Andrew Wylie. Entering a class of which I was much in advance, and relishing the independence of college life and western manners, I was soon at my ease there.

The rest of the family returned home in the fall and in spite of positive orders to the contrary, found me on the ground to welcome their arrival; —a matter which, you may be sure, was the immediate cause of very severe parental admonitions. A few days at home brought to my eyes the fact that, during the passage home and for some time previous to it, Dr. Garnett (a young naval surgeon from Essex County Virginia) and my sister Mary had done some damage to each other's hearts, —and in time, that a matrimonial engagement was pending. Having sufficiently bedeviled the young lady about this delicate situation of affairs, I returned to college, leaving my brother Henry in an indignant state of mind because he was not allowed to accompany me. The fact was that, although we loved each other dearly, our fraternal affection was enlivened by almost daily pugilistic encounters; —so it was thought best to keep us apart.

I did not return home again until my college term was over, varying it only by a long visit to my uncle Dr. Jennings, at Nashville, Tennessee. He impressed me as a most incorrigible old bachelor, which impression he has since (some two years ago) disproved by taking to wife a comely young damsel of seventeen summers, who, in addition to her other charms, threw into his possession a comfortable estate of some $50,000. The Dr. is now the only surviving member of my mother's family. Just before leaving Rio de Janeiro, I received the news of my aunt Sarah's death. Shortly after arriving at college, I wrote to my aunt Mary, and was answered by a black-sealed letter from my aunt Rebecca, announcing that aunt Mary died shortly before my letter was received. My answer to my aunt Rebecca's letter did not reach her before her own death.

My college career was not very creditable as far as acquirement and distinction were concerned. Ardently attached to my dear old master, Dr. Wylie, for whose memory I still retain the liveliest affection and admiration, —I devoted myself particularly to his instructions— political, metaphysical and religious and caught from his clear head and manly heart those moral and religious convictions which are to me now as a "pillar of strength." Snubbed by all the other professors for neglect of their departments, I became an active member of one of the debating societies of the college, —wrote quite a quantity of very mediocre political essays, and having thus wasted most of my time in declamation and dreaming, at last took my diploma almost *de gratia.*

I returned home in 1850, and found Henry more than six feet high (overtopping me by more than three inches) —Annie almost a woman, and sister Mary a wife and mother. Within a few months after my return my stepmother died suddenly. Blessings on her memory! —for nine years she loved us all with a mother's love and cared for us with a mother's care; and her children are as dear to me as if one mother had given us birth. During the following year we also lost little Spencer, the baby who was born while I was at college. He was a black-eyed little boy with curly hair, and resembled very much the picture Mr. Chapman painted of me at three years old.

I remained at home for two years, acting as family tutor, farmer, law student and lieutenant of militia, —all of which occupations I partially attended to by fits and starts.

In the fall of 1852, I went to the law school at Williamsburg Va:, which is under the direction of Judge Scarburgh, a gentlemen with whom you were doubtless acquainted in Accomac some twenty years ago, and who was then Mr. George P. Scarburgh. Determined to compensate in some degree the mortification which my previous neglect to study had caused to Father, I worked diligently, and in nine months time took my law diploma and law license. Just after I obtained these, President Pierce was kind enough to tender me an appointment to the office which I now hold and father consented that I should take it for four years, under the condition that any leisure hours should be applied to a study of the civil law.

A short time after my arrival here, I received a letter from Father, announcing his approaching marriage with Miss Mary Lyons of Richmond, Virginia. Except a correspondence which I have had with that lady since the marriage, I am entirely unacquainted with her; —but the letters which I have received from all quarters are such as to assure me that Father has made a most excellent selection. His wife is without fortune, but bears the character of a pious and amiable woman, —and as she is already 38 years of age no inconvenience can result from too great a disparity in this respect. Thus having brought matters up to the present time, I will try to give you an idea of the changes which time has wrought upon each one of us.

Father's hair is now plentifully mixed with grey, his form is not quite so straight as it used to be, and he is obliged to use glasses when he reads. His mind is in the ripeness of its vigor, and his energy is as unshaken as ever. He is even a better orator than he used to be, and much more of a philosopher. Since he returned from Brazil he has devoted himself to the cultivation of a farm on Onancock creek, and to his law practice. During the time, he has held office only for one year. Aiming all his energies at striking from our state constitution the aristocratic features which it so long displayed, he was elected a member of the constitutional convention 1850–51. Acknowledged as a leader of the reform party in that convention, he achieved the proudest triumph of his life, carrying through the principal reform measures, in spite of an original majority of seventeen against them. His great speech was on the question of the basis of representation, and for five successive days an overcrowded audience favored him with its attendance and applause. Nor has he at any time neglected either state or general politics. He was a democratic elector in the two presidential campaigns of '48 and '52, and has at all time placed his shoulder to the wheel whenever political issues of any description have been in agitation. I have just read two long long letters which he has lately published— one is on the slavery question, and the other is a blow which he has dealt with all his strength at the new political association of Know Nothings. I have also just received the news of his nomination as the Democratic candidate for Governor of Virginia, and do not doubt that he will be elected next spring by a large majority.

Don't blame me for boasting in this way, for I am very proud of him, —and he is, as he always was, the dearest and best of fathers.

You would know my sister Mary at a glance. Mr. Chapman's portrait of her is still an excellent likeness. She has also preserved the cheerfulness and truthfulness of her childhood, —and she possesses more of Father's decision and energy than any of the rest of us. She has two children, a boy and girl. Her husband is an estimable gentleman, and is rapidly making a fortune in the practice of his profession at Washington.

Henry is very tall and very slender, and as much like Father as he used to be. The most *striking* feature of his character is an unconquerable pugnacious tendency. On returning from college I was obliged in self defence to give him two sound drubbings. At seventeen years of age, he administered a caning to his schoolmaster, and commenced making stump speeches. These evidences of precocity induced a family consultation, in which it was determined to send him to the Virginia Military Academy at Lexington. After a few months residence at this place he was courtmartialed [sic] and dismissed for a slight mistake— that of fixing his bayonet in one of the cadets instead of on his musket. He then went to William and Mary College, where a year's intimacy with the able and pious President of that university, Bishop Johns, awoke him to religious convictions. He joined the Episcopal church, determined to enter the ministry and applied himself so intently to his studies that his health has lately begun to fail, and he has been obliged to leave college and take my old part of farmer and schoolmaster at home, where he will remain a year to recruit his strength.

Annie is the beauty of the family. Her face is a perfect oval— her hair a light chestnut, and although her forehead is too large for the artist's standard of female beauty, yet the expression of her large dark eyes, her long jetty eyelashes and black and well penciled eyebrows, together with the perfect regularity and fine chiseling of the rest of the features, set off by a complexion very much like my mother's was— all this makes up a very lovely face. She is also taller than Sister Mary, who is rather inclined to the *petite*. Annie is also inclined to be a blue, scribbles verses and puzzles me with the toughest sort of metaphysical problems. In spite of these foibles, however, she is a dear affectionate sister and, I believe, a sincere and earnest Christian. She is still at school, and will not be set free from it till next spring.

Dick is the blue-eyed baby you saw at New York. He is a queer boy, very quiet and old, manish [sic] in his ways, but a good child and evinces much decision of character. His brother John worships him.

John is a thickset ruffian with a head much too large for his body (when he was six years old, I could wear his hat). He overflows with animal spirits and doesn't fear the devil— and has a sharp grey eye with a light in it that looks like Father's: this is perhaps the reason why the latter considers him the smartest of all his children.

Néné is perfectly blonde. She has a *retrousé* nose and is not pretty; but she is as agile as a deer and as full of deviltry as a young fox.

I received several days ago a letter from Father, in which he says—

"Henry is at home teaching and taking care of Richard and Johnny. Henry's health is improving and I hope his energy is coming back to him. Richard is an *intense* child and John a *locomotive*! Néné is the dearest little witch in the world and is constantly and inseparably with her mother. Annie is now well, doing her duty faithfully and dutifully at school in Richmond. Her health was bad last winter. Mary is the same sterling woman, —much loved and respected by your mother, to whom she has been devotedly kind, and she is as hard in health as she is firm in principle…

There! I have given you a sketch of all of them— such a sketch as I would give to no one but a valued friend, —for they are the dearest treasures I have and I hold them sacred in my heart of hearts.

But perhaps you'd like to have an additional portrait— that of the humble indicter of these lines. Very well: You must know, in the first place, that I have lost all my beauty (I am vain enough to believe that I formerly possessed an uncommon share of the commodity). Picture to yourself a man 5 feet 9 inches tall, with an attenuated frame, rather short in the legs and very long in the arms, —a small head, —a hatchet face embellished with a large nose, hair inclined to curl and very coarse and bushy— *voila tout!* If asked for a picture of my moral disposition I would only say with Wilde—

"I never knelt at glory's shrine,
To wealth I never bowed the knee,
Beauty has heard no vows of mine.
I love thee, ease and only thee!"

Indeed, if circumstances permitted it, I should be apt to sink into a Sybarite; but something in the shape of moral sentiment and filial duty is slowly converting me into a s-t-e-a-d-y, r-o-u-t-i-n-e businessman. You may be surprised at my temerity in presenting this commonplace picture to the eye of a lady whose sentiment and taste are those of a cultivated artist, and who is the wife of a great artist; —but honest truth dictates the measure and I have long since ceased to be a coxcomb.

Now to the immediate cause of this letter. —It is barely possible that I may soon start for Italy. If I do, I shall accompany some friends, who will leave here next week —whether I go or not. Now it is most probable that I shall not be able to go, —and if I do go, I am an independent bachelor— sufficiently able to take care of myself under any circumstances: but it is not so with my friends— …The party will be at Rome on the 11th of February next. They are anxious to have apartments secured, if any are to be rented *at that time*; but are willing to take the risk of procuring apartments after their arrival, rather than go to the expense of renting them at once to be kept vacant until then…

…I will be very grateful for any attention which Mr. Chapman and yourself will show the party in question during their stay in Rome. I think it hardly possible that I shall accompany them.

I shall be much disappointed if this letter does not insure me a correspondence with you. Rest assured that you have all never ceased to be remembered and loved in Accomac. Mr. Chapman's pictures have looked down upon us continually, and your names are household words around our fireside. Some time ago, we had several family readings of Mr. Chapman's letters, which were forwarded to Father by their mutual friend, Mr. Holmes Conrad, to whom they were addressed. I remember in one of them Mrs. Chapman expressed his intention of making an artist of Jack…

Remember me affectionately to Mr. Chapman and the boys— also to the little girl with whose name and face I am as yet unacquainted, —and believe me, Yours very truly, *O. Jennings Wise*
To: Mrs. John G. Chapman, at Rome. (Virginia Historical Society)

◠ Letters from Annie Wise:

Richmond, February 6, 1854.
My dear Father— I received your letter yesterday afternoon and must acknowledge that it worried me a great deal, as I do not think that Mrs. B— was the right person to inform you of my being "too delicate" to remain at school. But I must tell you at once what Dr. Conway's opinion is, for as soon as I read your letter I wrote a note to him requesting that he would come around here this morning. He left about a half an hour ago and I will tell you now his message, word for word as nearly as possible. He said to tell you and Dr. Garnett that in the beginning of the winter (or rather at Christmas) I had quite a severe attack of cold accompanied with fever and a very bad sore throat, but that the fever soon left me as also did all other symptoms of cold except an irritation of the throat and a cough…I became so much better that he thought further treatment useless. (He did not see me again for some time, and in the mean while the weather being very changeable I caught slight colds which always settled in my throat but as the annoyance from it was very slight, I did not call in Dr. Conway.) But (to continue the Dr.'s message) that the last attack I had, had again thrown me back, and as my cold and cough still cling to me and [illegible] me for my regular school duties for a time at least, that it would be better for me to go home, as change of air and riding on horse-back would benefit me, though he does not think my health in any very immediate danger at all, and that by proper exercise and following his prescription (which is pretty much the same as Dr. Garnett's) I can recover here. He also said to tell you that this winter in Richmond had been a very trying one for any body's constitution and to tell Dr. Garnett that his prescription is exactly what I now require and what he would have prescribed for me before I had not become so much better.

And now dear Father, hear what I have to say— I cannot tell you how it would distress me to give up my present course of studies and though perhaps for a week or so, I cannot attend the school room as regularly as usual, still I can attend to my music and French, and recover just as well as at home, and though Dr. Conway thinks it would be better for me to be in the country, still he says there is no doubt but what by care and prudence, and not applying myself to my studies too much for a week or so, will get well, and then too Father, the spring weather will soon be here. At any rate please let me stay until you and Mother come up the last of this month, and then if I am not well you can take me home. Last week I did suffer a great deal from my cough, but that is now better, though still troublesome, and I have no doubt but what it will leave me soon. I really think that the disappointment from leaving school will be just as bad for me, as allowing me to stay here… Mrs. B— says to tell you that if she had thought it really necessary for me to go home she would have written you word. But if you think I must return I will try to do so cheerfully and I can easily go on to Washington before the last of this week and meet you there…Your affectionate child, *Annie J. Wise.*   —Let me hear from you Father at once.

February 6, 1854.
Dear Father—   Your letter has just been handed me dated from Accomac. And as I see you say Dr. Garnett thinks I ought to leave Richmond I suppose I must go. My cough is caused by a tickling in my throat which Dr. Conway says is bronchitis. If you wish me to join you in Washington you had better telegraph to me tomorrow and I can return with Maria H—'s brother who is now here.   —Your daughter *Annie.*

Richmond, February 21, 1854.
My dear Father—   I am writing to you sitting up in bed for I am sorry to say that I have again been sick, though by no means seriously so. The weather for the last two weeks has been so very changeable, that it has caused me to take cold, and this is the second day that I have been in bed. I was quite sick yesterday and last night with fever and *aching in my bones*, but though somewhat weak, I am better today, Dr. Conway having prescribed a hot foot-bath…

Dear Father, when are you coming to Richmond? I want to see you so much, and have thought about you and all of home, all the time since I have been sick. When you do come here, be sure to bring Mother with you, —it will make your coming *doubly welcome*… The intermediate examination is now very near… I know that I have *really studied* far more than I ever did before and have learnt some things. I think I shall stand it about as well as any of the girls. Indeed Father, though I do not always succeed, I do try to do my duty.

…I am tired and weak, and must therefore stop. Kiss all at home for me, and give my love to the servants and Eliza. Also give my love to Aunt Harriet… God bless you my darling Father. Write when you care to. —Your own affectionate child, *Annie J. Wise.*

❧ Letters from Mary Lyons Wise:

Only, March 3rd, 1854.
Shall I address you as My dear Husband— the first time I have used that *comprehensible* word which conveys to *me* so much of love and trust. You did not expect to hear from us so soon but a letter came from Annie this evening, which I am anxious for you to see. I hope you will go on to Richmond. You can then better judge her condition. I received a letter from Wm. Henry Lyons dated Feb 26th— he says Annie has been staying with Mary several days, and has been quite sick with a cold, but when he wrote, was "nearly well." I also received an affectionate letter from Henry and one came to you from Mrs. Sergeant, the chief object of which was to ask you to send the children to Phila, the first of April. The children are all hanging about me, (just after supper)— Eliza begging them to go upstairs but they are not inclined to obey the summons. Johnny is pretending to have the nightmare, and can't be awakened, both Jim and Eliza

---

Eliza   in some letters *Ida,* was a white nurse from Philadelphia, who began working for Henry A. Wise when he married Sarah Sergeant who had also come from Philadelphia. After Sarah Sergeant died Eliza stayed with the family during Wise's third marriage, throughout the Civil War, and then, in her old age, she was cared for by Annie Jennings Wise Hobson.

Mrs. Sergeant   the grandmother of Henry Wise's children by his second marriage to Sarah Sergeant.

are shaking him. Ah! He is up with a scream of laughter, and I hear his sweet voice singing along the stairs. Richard is very busy writing by my side… Néné is incessantly calling out "Mother, Mother" so you can form a pretty good idea of our position tonight… Today I have been in the garden with George, but he don't like "Book gardening." Write me, if only a line. Give my brother my affectionate love. The children send much love. Mine to all at the Dr's. Good night. May angels guard you, prays, your devoted wife, *M. L. Wise.*

Washington Sept. 30th 1854   … Dr. Garnett is very kind indeed— he is looking at my case, not doing much yet. He begs you will send him your "Know-Nothing" letter to read before you publish it. He wrote an article for the *Enquirer* against your opponent & it was too caustic that Mr. Payor would not publish it. Please don't become too much excited in speaking. I am afraid you will injure yourself… When do you think you may be here! …I told dear Johnny & Richard that they should not go into the bush alone, or go shooting without Henry till I got back, tho' they protested that "Papa" said they might go. Néné is well & happy. The waning light reminds me 'tis time to say Adieu. May a kind Providence watch over & guide you tonight—   Your devoted wife, *M. L. Wise.*

Only. Jan 8th, 1855.
My beloved husband—   The Boat did not cross on Friday, consequently I received no letter from you yesterday. I did not bear my disappointment as I should… You have hardly time to think of a little scene, "way across the Bay," where a poor sick good for nothing mother reclines on a couch, the elder son reading aloud, one son sitting at her feet & one dear little fellow, the father's *softened* image, lying by her side… Johnny enclosed his first attempt at letter writing— I hope you won't think it is Dutch! I have written to ask Willie to hire me a cook. Mrs. Poulson has just left me— she is a kind neighbor… I wrote to you on Saturday. If you return through Richmond please bring me something interesting and instructive to read. Today is gloomy without…
—Your devoted wife, *M. L Wise.*

Johnny John Sergeant Wise, born 1846, son of Henry A. Wise and Sarah Sergeant Wise.

Only, Jan. 13th, 1855.
My dear Husband—   Richard insists on sending his letter, and as it is *unique* in its style, I enclose it for your amusement. I hope he will soon be able to write you a better one. He would tell you I was sick, but today I am much better, tho' compelled to lie in bed—
    …I am not depressed. My firm trust is in the strong arm of the Lord Jehovah. I am resigned to whatever he deems best for me… May the Lord speed you in your work & undertake for you is the constant prayer of your devoted wife. The children are with me frequently and read to me. I wish you could have seen them last night— all on my bed, while Richard read aloud. Henry will write you of domestic matters. I can't write more now… Take care of yourself & please don't speak too vehemently. God bless you my husband, now & forever… —Your own wife. *M. L. Wise.*

Richard Richard Wise, born 1843, son of Henry W. Wise and Sarah Sergeant Wise.

Only, Jan. 17th, 1855.
I have only heard from you once my dearly loved husband, since we parted, but I must again send my little messenger to seek you out, and ask for tidings of your precious self. I am constantly thinking and dreaming of you. Last

night I dreamt we were traveling together in the water, had some alarm, but were safely put on shore. May it be prophetic that we may be safely landed at last, on the "fair shores of Canaan." The children have just left me, after saying their lessons, & Néné written a *nice* letter to Annie. Richard begs so hard to say his English lessons to me that I have consented to it. He does not like Henry & treats him so badly. Today I am much better, but am keeping very quiet and don't intend to work about till you get home. Dr. Lyons has only paid me one visit. I was suffering so much that Mrs. Poulson urged me to send for him. Mrs. P— has been very kind to me… Eliza is very attentive to me indeed. I take Dr. Garnett's pills every day… Be careful of yourself my dear husband. I shall try to get well ere you return & trust you may find everybody and everything doing well. I can't get a cook… George has nearly finished the fruit trees. I am putting him about the garden. …I can't write more now. Do write to me my dear Husband. I feel that you will succeed. At early dawn I have thoughts of you ever since you left me & often at the midnight have too. I am always your devoted wife. *M. L. Wise.*

Jan 19th, 1855.
Tonight, I hope you reach Lynchburg, my wandering husband so that you may take time to rest and refresh yourself for tomorrow's appointment. I don't know why your letters have not reached me, as the papers & letters, both North & South, have arrived regularly for the last two weeks. I feel *somewhat anxious* about you, as I did not hear from you & the papers told me you did not meet the people in Petersburg by appointment… By tomorrow you will have received two letters from me and one from Néné & Johnny. I have sent two to Charlottesville. What would I not give to be with you tonight. Probably you are cold & wearied & have not a comfortable room, whilst I am sitting by *your fire*, everything around me, a little black sketch before me, reminding me of "one I love so dear." The children have gone down to supper & much to their delight have Peggy Bagswell as their guest— a few moments since, I had them all sitting by my side, save Johnny, who was in my lap talking of you. They are now entertaining Miss Peggy with their books… Henry Baine has been in my room tonight, giving me an account of matters on the farm… You have 6 white lambs and 1 black one— one was born dead. The carpenters & bricklayers have neither appeared yet. I have tried to make George fasten up the broken gates, but the sheep will steal in, and despair me of all my lily flowers… they have dainty appetites. I wish they would comfort themselves on myrtle. I have forgotten to tell you that I am walking about my room a *little* today. I feel almost well again… The children I have had with me constantly— teaching them & reading to them. Néné has read to me frequently and is behaving much better than she did shortly after you left us. I have never seen a child who so *detests* books as she does… —*M.W.*

∾ Letters from Annie Wise:

Richmond, January 30, 1855.
My dear Father—   It is not without consideration that I have concluded to write you this letter. Every week has of late has brought me a letter from home stating that Mother was confined to her bed, & I cannot tell you how unhappy it makes me feel to think of her as sick & alone while I am here enjoying every

pleasure & blessing, gratifying my tastes and ambitions, when I feel assured that my presence at home is so much needed and could contribute a great deal to the happiness of those I love. On the first of March the half session here will be completed & I now leave it for you to say dear Father whether I had not better leave school at that time & return to Only. You know that I am as ambitious to cultivate my mind as you are desirous that I should do so, —that the pursuit of knowledge is to me a great pleasure, and you cannot therefore infer that I am wearied of school-life, when I tell you that on the whole I would prefer returning home. Let me give you my reasons, & I then leave it for you to decide for me. If Mother still continues sick, she will (I presume) be obliged to again consult the Physician in Philadelphia, & the household at home would be left to manage itself, & the children to run wild; if I am there I can prevent both. Even if Mother does not go to Philadelphia she is too delicate, too little capable of bearing fatigue & of exertion to have the care of the *ménage* & to be constantly watching & training the children; if I was with her I could assist her in both, & in so doing could be training my own mind, heart and body. Néné particularly is now at an age when she requires constant watching & instruction, —and remember my dear Father that I am no longer a child… That I would like to finish the course here I do not deny, but by proper diligence at home I do not think that I should lose a great deal by returning there soon. From my experience last year I am convinced that I could not remain here during the month of June, so that I should lose but three months of the session. Music is the only study which I should materially lose in at present, & that at some future time I could make up for. I could take a selection of French books home with me & would regularly correspond in French with Mrs. V— (my present teacher) …And lastly I feel more and more each day how greatly I need physical strength, & am convinced that the confined life of the school-room does me no good bodily. I need active & constant exercise which it is here impossible to take. The weather during the Spring in Richmond is also very trying to my throat on account of the constant dampness which pervades the atmosphere. I have now given you my views dear Father, & leave it for you to decide "the question." …Please reply to this at once, as Mrs. P— could probably supply my place if she knew in time whether I will certainly leave. I should have written to you before but never knew where you were. I often think of your labors & the fatigue which you are undergoing & wish that I could prevent both. I have written somewhat hurriedly having a recitation to prepare for. God bless you dear Father.   —Your devoted child *Annie J. Wise.*

Richmond, February 6, 1855.
My dear Father—   …Every week brings me the tidings from Only that Mother is constantly sick and confined to her couch— and so miserable does it make me to think of her as sick, suffering, and alone, so fully am I convinced that home is now my proper sphere of duty that I am willing, even prefer, to return there at the end of this half session… I wish you to reply at once dear Father, as Mrs. P— may have to refuse new boarders if I do not leave, & if I do she can by knowing in time supply the vacancy which my departure would occasion… I now leave it for you to decide what I am to do, & shall anxiously await your reply. I often think of you dear Father amidst your labors & wish that I could share your fatigue. That God will bless and protect you is ever the prayer of Your devoted Child, *Annie J. Wise.*

◧ Mary Lyons Wise:

Writing to Joseph Fuqua on November 14, 1855, Henry A. Wise described his wife's condition:

My dear Sir—   I got home from Washington, last Saturday, and found yours dated the 1st and 27th October. I did not go to Bedlam for politics but to see my sweet, suffering wife who has been a patient there for months in the hand of the Doctor. Thank God! She is now better and may be able to go with me to Richmond at the end of the year…" (Library of Virginia)

Mary Lyons may have been an invalid much of the time, and was often sick with diarrhea, which at the time was treated with opium. As described in George B. Wood's *Treatise on the Practice of Medicine*, 1858, diarrhea was treated as follows: "In bilious diarrhea, with bright-yellow or green passages, a gentle cathartic may first be administered with or without laudanum, and then small doses of calomel and opium, about the sixth of a grain of the former to the twelfth of a grain of the latter, for example, every hour or two… [after discussing other remedies]. With all these remedies it is usually proper to combine opium." There is a clear reference to opium in Annie Jennings Wise Hobson's *Diary*, Chapter 9, written at Eastwood where Mary Lyons visited during the Civil War. Several pages have been removed from the diary suggesting that someone may have wanted to delete the mention of opium.   —*Editor's note*.

◧ Two letters about a letter:

February 3rd, 1855. [Mary Lyons Wise to Henry A. Wise]
The papers tell me you are doing too much & will break down. Please don't speak all the way home, let the Democrats do something for themselves. Richard and Néné have gone to spend the day with "Peggy." Johnny didn't care to go, and is busy waiting on me— he is the most energetic & attractive child I ever saw, is bad sometimes like other children, but his very badness has a charm about it! Now you'll say I am partial. I am, but he studies well & if I reprove him he thinks it all right and behaves so properly that I can hardly refrain from putting him in my heart and kissing him while in the same act of looking *grave displeasure*. He wrote you his first letter on the 8th Jan., enclosed in mine. You have not received them I suppose, but he watches the mail with the utmost intent for a reply… The garden is being prepared for peas, cabbages and I wish your oats were in. Unless Monday should be cold I suppose Henry will have them hard at work finishing them. I have written twice to Obe since you left me, enclosed one of your letters to him and gave him everything I could gather of your movements & probable success. I wrote to Mr. Parker to send *my* sheep by Cpt. Hopkins. He wrote back a very polite note, offering to do anything for me, and informing me that he sent the animals in November… Your sheep look very well— they pay me frequent visits, attracted by the pretty prospect & prettier shrubs. If you have any *change to spare* won't you get me a few flower seed in Richmond… Adieu. May heaven bless you & speed you safely to your wife. *M. L. Wise.*

Lynchburg, Va. January 19th, 1855.
My dear "Manchild" John—   Your note was the sweetest note in the world,

except Mother's and Néné. Do, my boy, take care of my lambs— your lambs. I will pay you and black John a nine pence for every one you save… You must not join your words so close together that two words seem one word. But you did first rate for the first trial, and I have no doubt that you will be a full man by Mother's training, if you will but mind her & attend your book. Now, how do you get around my wife so that she can't whip you when you are bad? Don't you see how she loves you? Then you must love her… Kiss Mother & Richard & Néné all for me. Why don't Richard write? Be good children, Take care of Mother for your father, *Henry A. Wise*.

Feb. 12th 1855.
I fear you will be quite exhausted reading my numerous letters… I only know I feel like reading one from you ever day, but alas I am a "forlorn woman" (and not such a *belle* as you are.) … On Saturday I wrote you that my *sickness*, after lasting 7 days, has passed away. Today I am compelled to lie down because it has returned. Why, I know not, for I have not left my room since the 3rd February & then only went to the parlor. I have no pain, no uncomfortable feeling, but a little debility from this continued drain on me. Henry encloses a letter from Phil— which came last night… The ice-house is full, aren't you glad? I can't write anymore… Why don't your other letters come. Your devoted *M. L.*

◦∽ A letter from one brother to another:

Berlin, September 18th, 1855.
Dear brother John—   I was very glad to receive your letter of last June, —glad to see that you can write me a letter all by yourself without spelling a single word wrong, and in a handwriting just about as good as your elder brother himself can scratch off; and above all I was glad to learn by it that my dear old *Buster* is just what he used to be, and still loves me well enough to quarrel because I don't write to him. But, John you're a savvy dog— just as savvy as you ever were. What business have you got telling me that "I think myself so grand that I can't write to a little boy in old Virginia"? Eh! Sir, what do you mean? Don't you see that that isn't the style of respect and reverence, and all that sort of thing, in which you ought to address your elder? And besides, it is all your own fault that I didn't write to you. Don't you remember that you wrote to me last winter a year ago, and asked me to get you a little book like the German boys read out of? Well, I kept putting off writing to you to see if I couldn't find one to suit, and I can't now. So, I have just picked over a pile of newspapers to get two or three funny ones for you. I think you will like the pictures. The reading is very funny too, and you must get some Dutchman to translate it for you, —and if you'll write to me again, I'll send you some more. And when I come home I'll bring you a parcel of books, —and you'll have to learn German, so as to read them. And I've got a whole pile of pictures. When I went traveling last year, I bought pictures of all the places I came to. I've got about two hundred of them, and I'm going to have them all bound in a book; so that we can look over them and talk about them, and search out all the places on the map. Won't that be nice? I send you with this a letter for Mother; and you must tell Néné and Dick to write to me, and give my love to Ida; —and when you write to me again, you must tell me what you are going to do with all the horses when you go to Richmond. Your affectionate brother, *O. Jennings Wise*. (Virginia Historical Society)

The Campaign for Governor

James Hambleton's description of the campaign in 1856:

Mr. Wise is five feet eleven inches high; his average weight is 130 pounds; he is remarkably lean; was originally fair skinned, but is now swarthy, his hair is a light auburn, and was, when young, almost flaxen, which he generally wears long, and behind his ears; his head is large, with great depth between the temples; his forehead is low, but broad; his eyes large, gray and deep set, arched by a heavy and remarkably expressive brow, which by turns shows all the workings of the inner man; his nose is large and prominent, and is what might be termed a *Virginia nose*; his mouth is capacious; his lips rather thick; his jaws lank and florid; chin broad and prominent, with furrough from the centre downwards; he was originally very strait and active, but begins to stoop a little. Upon the whole he is not a handsome man, but one that will in any assemblage impress the beholder with his manly and defiant features. He is an excessive chewer of tobacco, but never smokes, and rarely drinks anything of an alcoholic character. Mr. Wise is remarkably abstemious and regular in all his habits except chewing tobacco.

Thus we have sketched, in as succinct a manner as possible, the life of one of the most illustrious men ever reared in this commonwealth. Mr. Wise combines qualities that eminently befit him to steer the helm of State through troubled times, especially through this threatening crisis. Thoroughly acquainted and largely experienced in the machinery of government, possessing wide and comprehensive views of the requirements of the nation, firm, decided and inflexible, the fearless tribune of the people, he is competent to the highest duties of State. His course, triumphant defence of the Democratic faith in the late gubernatorial campaign in this State, entitle him to the highest consideration and lasting endearment of all who live and wish to perpetuate the Union of the States.

Jefferson has made his memory immortal as the author of the Declaration of Independence and Religious Toleration; Mason as the author of the Bill of Rights; Jackson by severing Bank and Government; and Henry A. Wise by "crushing out," from all law-abiding States, that most detestable, insidious, loathsome, Protean-like, baneful, and contemptible of all isms—Know Nothingism. He is the great benefactor of the people of the nineteenth century. Long may he live to enjoy with his fellow citizens the fruits of his labours. May he wear, with republican simplicity and fidelity, the honors of his country, and preserve unsullied and untarnished those that still await him.
—James P. Hambleton, *A Biographical Sketch of Henry A. Wise*.

Shortly after he became Governor, Wise County, Virginia, was named after Henry A. Wise.

Ex-Governor William E. Cameron describing Wise's campaign for Governor:

He was then in the prime of life, and in person, manner, voice, and mental equipment the ideal leader of a forlorn hope. Elected to Congress in 1833, he had, by lengthy service in that body and by intimate association with the ruling intellects of the age, acquired knowledge of public affairs and a readiness in debate which gave the fullest play to his natural powers of oratory. Tall, lithe, yet muscular, a frame of steel, knit with nerves; his face, clean-shaven, had the rigid lines of a classic cameo, but his expression varied to suit his rapid moods so that the auditor could almost anticipate his words. His gesture was eloquence itself, powerful, yet restrained. His command of language was unequalled… His voice, too, had the compass of an organ pipe, and ranged from the persuasive softness of a lute to the metallic ring of the bugle note. Add to all this the magnetism which defies analysis, which forces other men to listen

and then compels them to believe; a courage as uncalculating as that of a sea-hawk, a strength of conviction as absolute as ever sustained a martyr at the stake; and there you have an imperfect portrait of the man who flung himself single-handed against an epidemic of fanaticism (the Know-nothings), and won the fight... The model of a campaign speaker and a master of invective, Wise was in every way fitted to strike terror to the hearts of the members of the new secret order, and from the Chesapeake to the banks of the Ohio and to the Tennessee line, he canvassed the State, delivering speeches of impassioned eloquence and convincing logic. Everywhere enormous crowds greeted him with unbounded enthusiasm and people rode on horseback fifty miles across the mountains to hear him.
—Barton Haxall Wise, *The Life of Henry A. Wise of Virginia.*

Know-Nothings— The Know-Nothing party originated in New York City as a secret anti-immigrant and anti-Catholic society. Members of the party proclaimed that "Americans must rule America" and by 1854 it was a national organization. Article VI of The Constitution of the United States reads: "No religious test shall ever be required as a qualification for any office of public trust under this government." The Constitution of Virginia reads: "No man shall be compelled to frequent or support any religious worship, place or ministry whatever; nor shall any man be enforced or restrained, molested or burthened in his body or goods, or otherwise suffer, on account of his religious opinion or belief; but all men shall be free to profess, and by argument to maintain, their opinions in matters of religion, and the same shall in no wise affect, diminish or enlarge their civil capacities." The Constitution of the Know-Nothing Party read: "The object of this organization shall be to resist the insidious policy of the Church of Rome, and other foreign influences against the institutions of the country, by placing in all offices in the gift of the people, or by appointment, none but native born Protestant citizens." The Know-Nothing oath: "You furthermore promise and declare that you will not vote nor give your influence for any man for any office in the gift of the people, unless he be an American born citizen, in favor of Americans ruling America, nor if he be a Roman Catholic." The party disbanded after 1856. Writing in his book, *Seven Decades of the Union*, Henry A. Wise described the Know-Nothing movement: "It was the most impious and unprincipled affiliation by bad means, for bad ends, which ever seized upon large masses of men of every opinion and party, and swayed them for a brief period blindly, as if by a Vehmgerichte!"
—*Editor's note.*

The Campaign as described by Barton Haxall Wise:

In his addresses Wise did not confine himself to the issue of Know-nothingism alone, but dwelt at length upon his favorite topics of public improvements and the industrial development of the State. Oftentimes his hearers, who came expecting to hear a political discussion solely, were entertained for hours by a dissertation upon the minerals, woods, and water-power of the State, the encouragement of manufacturers, and the need of improved transportation facilities, etc... He urged the need of a complete system of public education, such as was contemplated by Jefferson, and a State school of scientific agriculture. Virginia, he described as being 'in the anomalous condition of an old State that has all the capacities of a new one— of a new State that has all the capacities of an old one.' On the subject of slavery, he pointed out the steady growth of abolitionism throughout the North, and declared that the Know-nothings were abolitionists in disguise, which assertion seemed in a measure confirmed, by the large

Henry A. Wise, Governor of Virginia. Engraved by A. B. Walter, Philadelphia. Used as the frontispiece in James P. Hambleton's Biographical Sketch of Henry A. Wise.

Virginia State Capitol, Richmond. Photo from Historic Virginia Homes and Churches *by Robert A. Lancaster, Jr.*

number of extremists throughout the North and New England who were prominent in the secret order. He was unsparing in his denunciation of this class, and of what he considered the encroachments upon the rights of the South…

On the 24th day of May, 1855, what had been one of the most exciting campaigns that has ever occurred in this country came to an end, and the *viva voce* of the people of Virginia was given for the Democratic standard-bearer. The total vote of the State was 156,668, of which Wise received 83,424 votes, Flournoy 73,244, being a majority of 10,180 for the former. Throughout the Northern States the result in Virginia had been watched with intense interest… The triumphant march of the secret order in America was thenceforward broken, and the 'dark lantern' had lost it attractiveness, for in addition to Virginia, Georgia, Alabama, Louisiana, and Mississippi gave their verdict against the new movement, and Know-nothingism, instead of successfully invading the South, received an overwhelming defeat…

…On the 1st of January, 1856, he took the oath of office as governor, without any inaugural ceremony, and entered upon the discharge of his duties.

—Barton Haxall Wise, *The Life of Henry A. Wise of Virginia.*

1856

On July 9, 1856 Annie Jennings Wise was married to Frederick Plumer Hobson in the Governor's Mansion in Richmond. Annie had earlier written to her brother, Obadiah, then in Paris, about the wedding. Obadiah responded:

Your letter of June 5th reached me just in time to let me know beforehand that today is your wedding day. A very bright, pleasant day it is here, and strange to say, not at all different from several other days previous; …The whole thing mixes up all sorts of ideas and remembrances, —pleas-

Frederick Plumer Hobson, 1833–1868.

ant and unpleasant, —serious and comical, —and carried me backward and forward through all the scenes of our nineteen years' acquaintance—and it seems to me that some man whose face I am unacquainted with is about to take unto himself for a wife, —a little red-faced infant, —a little girl in short frocks, —a slender damsel of thirteen summers, —a maiden of sixteen who has begun to wear her hair and bodice like a woman, —and a full grown woman whom I think about, but have never seen, —all in a heap, —and that somehow I ought to feel a little more pathetic about the transaction than I really do.
   —William M. Adkins, *Obadiah Jennings Wise '50: A Sketch of His Life,* Indiana University Alumni Quarterly, 1937–1938.

On April 22, 1857 Annie Wise Hobson gave birth to John Cannon Hobson in the Executive Mansion in Richmond, perhaps the only time that a Governor's grandson has been born in that house. Soon, Annie would move to Eastwood in Goochland County, west of Richmond. John Cannon Hobson had given Eastwood to his son Plumer Hobson, and he had given other large farms, Howard's Neck and Snowden to two other sons.

Governor's Mansion, Photo from Historic Virginia Homes and Churches *by Robert A. Lancaster, Jr.*

1858

Eastwood, September 23, 1858.
My dear Father—   I must no longer delay thanking you for the beautiful cup you sent to *my little Henry Wise*. It is as handsome a one as I ever saw, & much handsomer than babies usually receive. May he prove himself worthy of the gift, & of the name he bears!
   To me it is valuable as an evidence of my dear Father's affection, & of the honor conferred upon me *in being permitted to name a son* after *the Governor* of my state, & one who shall stand amongst my country's great men in the annals of her history— *who is now in my estimation her greatest man.*
   You will see by my letter to Mother that Mr. Hobson is absent… He seems very cheerful. He occupies himself attending to his correspondence & reading. In the evening we take a quick game of chess together. I hope that you will bring Mother up & pay me a visit soon.   —Your devotedly attached daughter, *Annie J. W. Hobson.*

my little Henry Wise   Henry Wise Hobson, named after his grandfather Henry Alexander Wise, was born on July 9, 1858.

Eastwood, Dec. 11th, 1858.
My dear Mother—   I write an exciting day has just passed for our little household. Henry was baptized between father & me by his Uncle Henry. As I desired somewhat to honor the event I invited the neighbors to witness it. Mrs. & Mrs. Seddon & their children, Mr. & Mrs. G—, Mrs. Billing and all the young folks from Mrs. Morison's were here. I gave them all a kind of cold collation. As Tom was sick I had to exert myself considerably to have things *comme il faut* & I feel quite tired tonight. I wish that you could have witnessed with Father how Henry behaved. He was laughing & cooing all the time. When the water was put on him he laughed in his Uncle's face. Dedicating a child to God is truly a solemn duty in life. I endeavored today to take hold of all God's gracious promises with earnest faith and to send my whole heart to God in prayer from my little one.

Uncle Henry   Henry A. Wise, Jr., 1834–1869

I am greatly gratified that you all liked the sausage meat so well. I have some sauce for Father which I hope you will find equally as good as I have taken a great deal of pain with them. I'll endeavor to send you some eggs for Xmas. Not only Mr. Hobson & I regret that the children cannot come up at Xmas but all the young people in the neighborhood are disappointed that they will not be here. My Xmas will be truly dull without them. We shall have a quiet time at Eastwood. I am sure my dear Mother that you will not regret half as much as I do that I cannot take the New Year's dinner with you & Father. But that is a time that it is almost impossible on these large plantations to leave home. And then too it is such a bad season of the year to travel about with young children. Any change is so apt to give them cold. Henry and Cannon seem so well now that I want to keep them so, the whole winter. I'd not expect that we will go down again sooner than the Spring. I wish that I could have enjoyed Father's birthday with you all. God grant it that he may be spared to see many more. Ah! it is such a sad thing to me to think that you will so soon leave Richmond. I shall feel so far away from you all… I think of you very very often and never forget you in my prayers. I love you very dearly Mother. I have wanted more of late to be with you than I ever did before. Often I have thought— "if I could only enjoy one hour's talk with Mother!" A press of household cares & duties has been my cross and temptation since my return home… I have enjoyed some pleasant evenings lately reading *Boat Life on the Nile* by Prime. He writes in an easy, agreeable style & gives me a delightful idea of Boat life in Egypt… Tell Johnny and Néné that I am so poor this Xmas they must not expect a present. I have told Dick the same… I received such a kind letter from Mrs. Hobson by Richard. She is so truly good and kind to me. Having heard I still had a cold she sent me the recipe of a remedy for it, and offered to do a great deal of work for me, as she knows that Tom is sick & Maria, the cook, also. The latter has a daughter. If Dr. Deane thinks it advisable, we are at once going to send the mother Maria to the Infirmary in Richmond. Our love to all. I do hope that you are better.   —Truly your attached daughter, A. J. W. Hobson.

Tom, a butler and slave at Eastwood

"I have enjoyed some pleasant evenings lately reading *Boat Life on the Nile* by Prime"

"The bazaars of Cairo have been frequently described. The streets are a little wider where the shops abound, and are usually roofed over, admitting sunshine by windows in the matting or close roof, only at mid-day. Business hours are from about eleven to three. No shop is open longer in the principal bazaars. I have more than once found a merchant closing his shop and have been refused an article I wished to purchase… At mid-day the bazaars are crowded, jammed, with passers-by or purchasers, women with vailed [sic] faces, and donkeys loaded with water-skins, Turks, Bedouins, camels, dromedaries, and horses, all mingled together, for side-walk or pavement there is none, and it is therefore at the risk of constant pressure against the filthiest specimens of humanity, and constant collisions with nets of fleas and lice, that one passes through the narrow streets…

"…Here it was the Nile. No dream, no half river, no small stream of dashing water, but that great river of which we had read, thought, and dreamed; the river on which princes in long-forgotten years had floated palaces and temples from far up, down to their present abode; the river which Abraham saw, and over which Moses stretched out his arm in vengeance; where the golden barge of Cleopatra swept with perfumed breezes, and when, but a few years later, she was dead and her magnificence gone, the feeble footsteps of the Son of God, in infancy on earth, hallowed the banks that the idolatry of thousands of years had cursed; the river of which Homer sang, and Isaiah prophesied, and in whose dark waters fell the tears of the weeping Jeremiah; the river of which all poets wrote, and philosophers taught, all learning, all science, all art spoke for centuries. The waters at our feet, murmuring dashing, brawling against the foundation of the palace, come by the stately front of Abou Simbal, had loitered before the ruins of Philæ, had dashed over the cataracts and danced in the starlight by Luxor and Karnak. From what remote glens of Africa, from what Ethiopian plains they rose, we did not now pause to think, but having looked long and earnestly up the broad reach of the river, we turned into the palace, and after pipes and coffee, the universal gift of hospitality here, we returned to our boat.

"The Nile itself, at first, sadly disappointed me. I confess to ideas of a clear and glorious river, like the swift Ohio, flowing over golden sand and shining stones. I had never paused to ask myself whence came its fertilizing powers, or whence the vast deposits of soft mud that enrich the lower part of Egypt; and when I saw the strong stream in the hot sunshine, looking more like flowing mud than water, I was unwilling to call this the Nile. Utility was not what I wanted to see in the river. Beauty, majesty, power, all these I had looked for, and there was nothing of them until the sun went down, and the moon gilded—not silvered—the stream. Then it was the river of my imagination— a strong, a mighty flood, glorious in its deep, strong flow, and the unsightly banks, which, in the day, are abrupt walls of black mud, in layers looking like huge unbaked brick, become picturesque and fairly beautiful with waving groves of sont and palms, and glistening fields of doura."   —William C. Prime, *Boat Life in Egypt and Nubia*.

October–December 1859

From *The End of an Era* by John S. Wise:

The attack of John Brown upon Harper's Ferry came upon Virginia like a clap of thunder out of a clear sky.

In the afternoon of October 17, 1859, I [John S. Wise] was passing along Main Street in Richmond, when I observed a crowd of people gathering about the bulletin board of a newspaper. In those days, news did not travel so rapidly as now; besides which, the telegraph lines at the place from which the news came were cut.

The first report read— "*There is trouble of some sort at Harper's Ferry. A party of workmen have seized the Government Armory.*"

Soon another message flashed: "*The men at Harper's Ferry are not workmen. They are Kansas border ruffians, who have attacked and captured the place, fired upon and killed several unarmed citizens, and captured Colonel Washington and other prominent citizens of the neighborhood. We cannot understand their plans or ascertain their numbers.*"

By this time an immense throng had assembled, agape with wonder. Naturally reflecting that the particulars of an outbreak like this would first reach the governor, I darted homeward. I found my father in the library, roused from his afternoon siesta, in the act of reading the telegrams which he had just received. They were simply to the effect that the arsenal and government property at Harper's Ferry were in possession of a band of rioters, without describing their character. I promptly and breathlessly told what I had

John Brown's Fort, the armory engine house where John Brown was captured after his unsuccessful raid on the United States Armory in Harper's Ferry, October 16, 1859. This incident, and all of the events surrounding it, contributed significantly to the disintegration of the Union and the outbreak of the Civil War in 1861. Harper's Ferry was then in Virginia but is now in West Virginia.

seen on the bulletin boards, and, while I was hurriedly delivering my news, other messengers arrived with telegrams to the same effect as those posted in the streets. The governor was by this time fully aroused. He was prompt in action. His first move was to seize the Virginia code, take a reference, and indite a telegram addressed to Colonel John Thomas Gibson, of Charlestown, commandant of the militia regiment within whose territory the invasion had occurred, directing him to order out, for the defense of the State, the militia under his command, and immediately report what he had done…

…I was promptly dispatched to summon the Secretary of the Commonwealth, the Adjutant-General, and the colonel and adjutant of the First Regiment…

In those days, the track ran down the centre of the street, and the depot was in the most popular portion of the city. News of the disturbance having gone abroad, it was an easy task to assemble the regiment; and, by the time appointed, all Richmond was on hand to learn the true meaning of the outbreak, and witness the departure of the troops…

The masses of the populace swarming about the soldiers presented every variety of excitement, interest, and curiosity.

As for me, my "mannishness" (there is no other word expressive of it) was such that, forgetting what an insignificant chit I was, I actually attempted to accompany the troops.

Transported by enthusiasm, I rushed home, donned a little blue jacket with brass buttons and a navy cap, selected a Virginia rifle nearly half as tall again as myself, rigged myself with a powder-horn and bullets, and, availing myself of the darkness, crept into the line of K Company. The file-closers and officers knew me, and indulged me to the extent of not interfering with me, never doubting the matter would adjust itself. Other small boys, who got a sight of me standing there, were variously affected. Some were green with envy, while others ridiculed me with pleasant suggestions concerning what would happen when father caught me.

In time the order to embark was received. I came to "attention" with the others, went through the orders, marched into the car, and took my seat. It really looked as if the plan was to succeed. Alas and alas for these hopes! One incautious utterance had thwarted all my plans. When I went home to comparison myself for war, the household had been too much occupied to observe my preparations. I succeeded in donning my improvised uniform, secured my arms, and had almost reached the outer door of the basement, when I encountered Lucy, one of the slave chambermaids.

"Hi! Mars' John. Whar is you gwine?' exclaimed Lucy surprised.

"To Harper's Ferry," was the proud reply, and off I sped.

"I declar', I b'leeve that boy thinks hisself a man, sho' 'nuff," said Lucy, as she glided into the house. It was not long before she told Eliza, the housekeeper, who in turn hurried to my invalid mother with the news. She summoned Jim, the butler, and sent him to father with the information.

Now Jim, the butler, was one of my natural enemies. However, the Southern man may have been master of the negro, there were compensatory processes whereby certain negroes were masters of their masters' children. Never was autocracy more absolute than that of a Virginia butler. Jim may have been father's slave, but I was Jim's minion, and felt it. There was no potentate I held in greater reverence, no tyrant whose mandates I heard in greater fear, no ogre whose grasp I should have felt with greater terror. This statement may not be fully appreciated by others, but will touch a responsive chord in the heart of every Southern-bred man who passed his youth in a household where "Uncle Charles," or "Uncle Henry," or "Uncle Washington," or uncle somebody, wielded the sceptre of authority as family butler. Bless their old souls, dead and gone, what did they want with freedom? They owned and commanded everything and everybody that came into their little world. Even their own masters and mistresses were dependent upon them to an extent that only increased their sense of their own importance. What Southern boy will ever forget the terrors of that frown which met him at the front door and scanned his muddy foot-marks on the marble steps? What roar was every more terrible—what grasp more icy or relentless—than those of his father's butler surprising him in the cake-box or the preserve-jar? What criminal, dragged to justice, ever appeared before the court more thoroughly cowed into subjection than the Southern boy led before the head of the house in the strong grip of that domestic despot?

"What!" exclaimed the governor, on hearing Jim's report of my escapade, "is that young rascal really trying to go? Hunt him up, Jim! Capture him! Take away his arms, and march him home in front of you!" Laughing heartily, he resumed his work, well knowing that Jim understood his orders and would execute them.

Think of such authority given to a negro, just when John Brown was turning the heads of the slaves with ideas of their own importance! Is it not monstrous? I was sitting in a car, enjoying the sense of being my country's defender starting for the wars, when I recognized a well-known voice in the adjoining car, inquiring, "Gentlemen, is any ov you seed anythin' ov de Gov'ner's little boy about here? I'm a-lookin' fur him under orders to take him home."

I shoved my long squirrel-rifle under the seats and followed it, amid the laughter of those about me. I heard the dread footsteps approach, and the inquiry repeated. No voice responded; but, by the silence and the tittering, I knew I was betrayed. A great, shiny black face, with immense whites to the eyes, peeped almost into my own, and, with a broad grin, said, "Well, I declar'! Here you is as las'! Cum out, Mars' John." But John did not come. Jim, after coaxing a little, seized a leg, and, as he drew me forth, clinging to my long rifle, he exclaimed, "Well, 'fore de Lord! How much gun has dat boy got, anyhow?" and the soldiers went wild with laughter.

In full possession of the gun, and pushing me before him, Jim marched his prisoner home. Once or twice I made a show of resistance, but it was in vain. "Here, you boy! You better mind how you cut yo' shines. You must er lost you' senses. Yo' father told me to take you home. I gwine to do it, too, you understand? Ef you don't mind, I'll take you straight to him, and you know and I know dat if I do, he'll tare you up alive fur botherin' him with you' foolishiss, busy ez he is." I realized that it was even so, and, sadly crestfallen, was delivered into my mother's chamber, where, after a lecture upon the folly of my course, I was kept until the Harper's Ferry expedition was fairly on its way…

John Brown was tried for treason, murder, and inciting slaves to insurrection. His trial occupied six days. He was defended by able counsel, of his own selection, from Massachusetts and Ohio. Every witness he desired summoned appeared. The evidence of his guilt was overwhelming, and he was sentenced to death. Any other penalty would have been a travesty of justice, and a confession that the organized governments which he assailed were mockeries, affording no protection to their citizens against midnight murder and assassination. Did the Virginians exult over the wretched victim of his own lawlessness? NO!

The *New York Herald* published the account of how that verdict was received: "Not the slightest sound was heard in the vast crowd, as this verdict was returned and read; not the slightest expression of elation or triumph was uttered from the hundreds present… Nor was this strange silence interrupted during the whole of the time occupied by the forms of the court."

Henry A. Wise. Courtesy of the Valentine Richmond History Center, Richmond, Virginia.

...The Virginians took the life of John Brown to preserve their own lives, and the lives of their wives and children, from destruction. He had, indeed, "whetted knives of butchery" for them, and had come a thousand miles to kill people who had never heard his name...

...To one who knows the truth, the most tantalizing reflections upon the John Brown raid are these: The man who, as colonel in the army of the United States, captured Brown; the governor of Virginia, under whose administration he was justly hung; ay, a majority of the people of Virginia— were at heart opposed to slavery. Uninterrupted by madmen like Brown, they would have accomplished, in good time, the emancipation of the slave without the awful fratricidal scenes which he precipitated. Of course there are those who will still deny this, and conclusive proof is impossible. History took its course... Neither Colonel Lee nor the governor of Virginia were champions of slavery. Both rejoiced at its final overthrow...

When Virginia had performed her duty in executing Brown, her next step was to inquire what sympathy she received in the hour of her trial. She expected, as she had a right to expect, that the North, boasting of its superior civilization and its greater regard for the maintenance of the laws protecting person and property, would be practically unanimous in condemnation...

When it was learned that, in many parts of the North, churches held services of humiliation and prayer; that bells were tolled; that minute-guns were fired; that Brown was glorified as a saint; that even in the legislature of Massachusetts, eight out of nineteen senators had voted to adjourn at the time of his execution; that Christian ministers had been parties to his schemes of assassination and robbery; that women had canonized the bloodthirsty old lunatic as "St. John the Just;" that philanthropists had pronounced him "most truly Christian;" that Northern poets like Whittier and Emerson and Longfellow were writing panegyrics upon him; that Wendell Phillips and William Lloyd Garrison approved his life, and counted him a martyr, —then Virginians began to feel that an "irrepressible conflict" was indeed upon them...

...When the troops came back from Harper's Ferry, they were amply supplied with songs. The first and most popular was one upon John Brown, sung to the tune of *The Happy Land of Canaan*. It had a number of verses, only one of which I remember, running something after this fashion:—

> "In Harper's Ferry section, there was an insurrection,
> John Brown thought the niggers would sustain him,
> But old master Governor Wise
> Put his specs upon his eyes,
> And he landed in the happy land of Canaan.
>
> REFRAIN
> "Oh me! Oh my! The Southern boys are a-trainin',
> We'll take a piece of rope
> And march 'em up a slope,
> And land 'em in the happy land of Canaan."

It is surprising how popular this rigmarole became through the South, and many a time during the war I heard the regiments, as they marched, sing verses from it. It is in contrast with the solemn swell of *John Brown's Body*, as rendered by the Union troops. The latter is only an adaptation of a favorite camp-meeting hymn which I often heard the negroes sing, as they worked in the fields, long before the days of John Brown. The old words were:

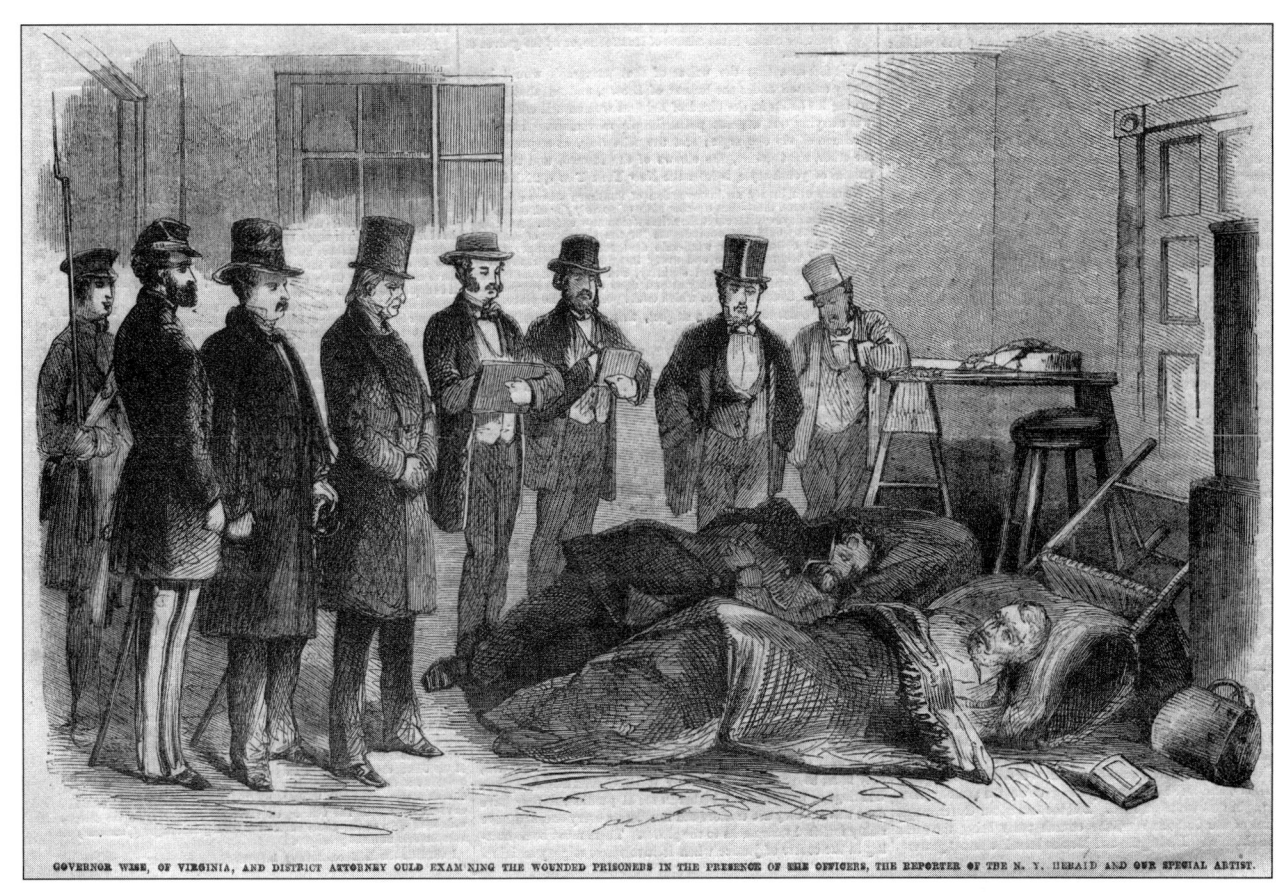

"The Insurrection at Harper's Ferry, Va. — *Governor Wise, of Virginia, and District Attorney Ould Examining the Wounded Prisoners in the Presence of the Officers, the Reporter of the N. Y. Herald and our own Special Artist.*" John Brown is on the floor at right, being interrogated a few hours after his capture. Known to have been present when Brown was questioned were: Virginia Governor Henry A. Wise, Colonel Robert E. Lee, Virginia Senator James M. Mason, Ohio Congressman Clement Vallandigham, District of Columbia District Attorney Robert Ould, and a reporter from the *New York Herald*. In this illustration from Frank Leslie's Illustrated News, *October 29, 1859, Wise is probably fourth from left. Robert E. Lee, known to have been there in civilian clothes is probably third from left, with his sword. One of Brown's supporters wrote of the meeting:* "In contrast with so many Northern journalists, and to some extent with Vallandigham, the two Virginians (Wise and Mason) proved themselves perfect gentlemen on this occasion." *Photo courtesy of the Virginia Historical Society, Richmond, Virginia.*

"My poor body lies a-mouldering in the clay,
My poor body lies a-mouldering in the clay,
My poor body lies a-mouldering in the clay,
While my soul goes marching on.

REFRAIN
"Glory, glory, hallelujah,
Glory, glory, hallelujah,
Glory, glory, hallelujah,
As my soul goes marching on."

1860

Henry A Wise's term as Governor of Virginia ended on January 1, 1860.

my little daughter Annie Wise Hobson, born March 4, 1860, at Eastwood.

asafaetida gum resin, of various oriental plants of the carrot family, formerly used in medicine.

Eastwood, March 29, 1860.

Many thanks my own beloved Father for your sweet blessing upon myself and my little daughter. This morning's mail brought it to me. Ever since the birth of the little one I have desired to write and tell you about it, but of course could not use my eyes.

One of the first desires I expressed after its birth was, "Oh! If I could only show it to Father," and every day since I have wished the same thing. You have doubtless heard that her Father named it after me. I am very proud of *my little Annie Wise* for she really is an *uncommon baby*. She weighed at least twelve pounds at her birth and grows finely. She is by far the largest & healthiest baby I have had. She has my brown eyes & nose exactly with very dark hair. Her mouth is like Cannon's & everyone noticed the strong likeness between them. Her head is very large, & her shoulders very broad. She does nothing but eat & sleep. Thank God, after some days of trying sickness I have been doing wonderfully well & I gain strength as rapidly as I could expect. My nervous system was sadly out of sorts and had it not been for *asafaetida*, I should have been very ill, if not have died. May it please God to answer your prayer my dear Father, that I may have a grace given me to bring up my children for an eternity in Heaven. May I be as conscientious in the discharge of my duty towards them as my Father has been towards me. And I must add, may my daughter prove "more faithful and true" to us than I have been towards my beloved parent, for well do I know that I have often failed & been wanting in dutifulness.

The little one is waking & is as usual ravenously hungry. Cannon & Henry are well & hearty. Cannon prays to God every day "please bring my Grandpa back." I wish that I could run down & help you in your *lonely home*. Mr. H— & I join in love.   —Your devoted daughter, *A.J.W.H.*

P.S. Excuse such a poor letter, for my hands are unsteady & eyes weak.

IV

1835–1844

Early Papers from Cambridge, New York

THESE were simple times on a farm in Cambridge, New York, where they raised Merino sheep. The seven McKie children were growing up, being educated, and beginning to leave the family farm. The records of this period are sparse, but the papers that do exist, give some insight into their lives.

These were busy times for a growing America. A fire destroyed over 500 buildings in New York City in 1835 causing an estimated $20 million in damages. Arkansas became the twenty-fifth state in 1836 and Michigan the twenty-sixth state in the following year. In 1836 Texas won its independence from Mexico, and in 1840, the sixth census showed that the United States had a population of 17 million of which an estimated 600,000 were immigrants who had come to America since the 1830 census. In 1843, 1,000 pioneering settlers left Independence, Missouri, and began what would become the great westward migration along the Oregon Trail. The institution of slavery was becoming increasingly controversial during these years and northern states passed laws that sought to obstruct the Fugitive Slave Act that required run-away slaves be returned to their owners in the South. At the same time, the "underground railroad" emerged for slaves fleeing from the South to Canada. In 1837 Victoria became Queen of Great Britain and Ireland. News still traveled slowly during these times but that too was beginning to change. Samuel Morse introduced Morse code in 1838 and in 1843 Congress made a grant of $30,000 to establish a forty-mile telegraph line between Baltimore and Washington. The means of remembering things was about to change with Louis Daguerre's invention of the daguerreotype process, the first form of photography, in 1839.

Letters, a schoolbook, and essays by:
Catherine McKie
George McKie
Sophia Whiteside McKie
Noah Webster Jun.

Letters written from: Albany and Schaghticoke, New York; Poultney, Vermont; and school essays.

∽

Sophia Whiteside
   Born in 1796, Sophia was the second daughter of Peter Whiteside and Ann Robertson Whiteside. The only record of her education, undoubtedly in the one

room schoolhouse near the farm in Cambridge, New York, is her schoolbook from 1808 and a comment that she was a student of French which she read daily. Her small schoolbook, inscribed by her and dated "1808" is excerpted below. The original spelling has been retained, including the use of "ƒ" where modern spelling would use an "s."

～ Sophia's schoolbook:

An AMERICAN SELECTION of Leƒƒons in Reading and Speaking. Calculated to Improve the MINDS and Refine the TASTE of YOUTH and also to Instruct them in the GEOGRAPHY, HISTORY, and POLITICS OF THE UNITED STATES. To Which Are Prefixed, RULES in ELOCUTION and DIRECTIONS for Expressing the Principal Passions of the Mind. Being the THIRD PART of a GRAMMATICAL INSTITUTE of the ENGLISH LANGUAGE, To Which is Added, An APPENDIX, Containing Several New Dialogues. By Noah Webster, Jun. Esquire. (Printed at Boston, 1800.)

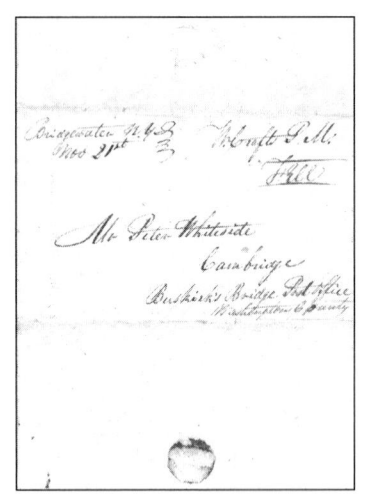

Undated envelope addressed: Mr. Peter Whiteside, Cambridge, Buskirk's Bridge Post Office, Washington County.

PREFACE
The deƒign of this Third Part of the Grammatical Inƒtitute of the Engliƒh Language is to furniƒh schools with a variety of Exerciƒes for Reading and Speaking… In America, it will be uƒeful to furniƒh schools with additional eƒƒays, containing the history, geography and tranƒactions of the United States. Information on theƒe ƒubjects, is neceƒƒary for youth, both in forming their habits and improving their minds. A love of our country and an acquaintance with its true ƒtate, are indiƒpenƒable: They ƒhould be acquired in early life.

RULES for READING and SPEAKING
Rule I. *Let your articulation be clear and diƒtinct.* A good articulation conƒiƒts in giving every letter and ƒyllable its proper pronunciation of ƒound.
Rule II. *Observe the Stops, and mark the proper Pauƒes, but make no pauƒe where the ƒenƒe requires none.* The characters we uƒe as ƒtops are extremely arbitrary, and do not always mark a ƒuƒpenƒion of the voice. On the contrary, they are often employed to ƒeparate the ƒeveral members of a period, and ƒhow the grammatical conƒtruction…
Rule III. *Pay the ƒtricteƒt attention to Accent, Emphaƒis, and Cadence.* Let the accented ƒyllables be pronounced with a proper ƒtreƒs of voice, the unaccented with little ƒtreƒs of voice, but distinctly…
Rule IV. *Let the ƒentiments you expreƒs be accompanied with proper Tones, Looks and Geƒtures.* By *tones* are meant the various modulations of voice by which we naturally expreƒs the emotions and paƒƒions. By *looks* we mean the expreƒƒion of the emotions and paƒƒions in the countenance. *Geƒtures* are the various motions of the hands or body which correƒpond to the ƒeveral ƒentiments and paƒƒions, which the ƒpeaker deƒigns to expreƒs. All theƒe ƒhould be perfectly natural. They ƒhould be the ƒame which we uƒe in common converƒation. A speaker ƒhould endeavor to feel what he ƒpeaks; for the perfection of reading and ƒpeaking is, to pronounce the words as if the ƒentiments were our own……

GENERAL DIRECTIONS for expreƒƒing certain Passions or Sentiments.
[*From the* Art of Speaking]
   MIRTH or *Laughter* opens the mouth, criƒps the noƒe, leƒƒens the aperture of the eyes, and ƒhakes the whole frame.

Perplexity draws down the eyebrows, hangs the head, crafts down the eyes, clofes the eyelids, fhuts the mouth, and pinches the lips; then fuddenly the whole body is agitated, the perfon walks about bufily, ftops abruptly, talks to himfelf, &c.

Vexation adds to the foregoing, complaint, fretting, and lamenting.

Pity draws down the eyebrows, opens the mouth, and draws together the features.

Grief is expreffed by weeping, ftamping with the feet, lifting up the eyes to heaven.

Melancholy is gloomy and motionlefs, the lower jaw falls, the eyes are caft down and half fhut, words few, and interrupted with fighs…

Commanding acquires a peremptory tone of voice, and a fevere look…

Wonder opens the eyes, and makes them appear prominent. The body is fixed in a contracted ftooping pofture, the mouth is open, the hands often raifed. Wonder at firft ftrikes a perfon dumb; then breaks forth into exclamations.

Curiofity opens the eyes and mouth, lengthens the neck, bends the body forward, and fixes it in one pofture, &c.

Anger is expreffed by rapidity, interruption, noife and trepidation, the neck is ftretched out, the head nodding in a threatening manner. The eyes red, ftaring, rolling, fparkling; the eyebrows drawn down over them, the forehead wrinkled, the nostrils ftretched, every vein fwelled, every mufcle ftrained. When anger is violent, the mouth is opened, and drawn towards the ears, fhewing the teeth in a gnafhing pofture, the feet ftamping, the right hand thrown out, threatening with a clenched fift, and the whole frame agitated.

Peevifhnefs is expreffed in nearly the fame manner, but with more moderation; the eyes a-fquint upon the object of difpleafure, the upper lip drawn up difdainfully……

GEOGRAPHY
Chap. XXIII.
Explanation of the Terms in Geography.
1. The *terraqueous globe* is the world or earth, confifting of land and water
2. About three fifths of the furface of the earth is covered with water.
3. The land is divided into two great continents, the eaftern and weftern.
4. The eaftern continent is divided into Europe, Afia, and Africa and the weftern into North and South America.
5. A Continent is a vaft tract of land, not feparated into parts by feas.
6. An Ifland is a body of land, lefs than a continent, and furrounded with water…

Chap. XXIV.
GEOGRAPHY OF THE UNITED STATES
The United States of America are fixteen; New Hampfhire, Maffachufetts, Rhode Ifland, Connecticut, (which four are ufually called New England) New York, New Jerfey, Pennfylvania, Delaware, Maryland, Virginia, North Carolina, South Caroline, Georgia, Vermont, Kentucky, and Tenneffee.

The territory granted to thefe States, extends from Canada and the lakes to Florida; and from the Atlantic Ocean, to the river Miffifippi: It is about fourteen hundred miles in length, from northeaft to fouthweft; and from eaft to weft, its breadth, at the northern extremity, is about twelve hundred miles; but at the fouthern, not more than feven hundred.

The northern part of this land upon the fea, is called the *District of Maine*; but it belongs to the State of Maffachufetts…

NEW YORK STATE

Extends from the ocean to Lake Champlain and Canada, and comprehends about twenty miles on the eaſt, and forty on the weſt of the river Hudſon. It has Connecticut, Maſſachuſetts and Vermont on the eaſt, and New Jerſey and Pennſylvania on the weſt.

The city of New York is ſituated upon a peninſula, or rather upon an iſland; for the water flows around it, and it is connected the continent by a small bridge only, called King's Bridge, fifteen miles from the city. The city contains nearly three thouſand five hundred houſes. It is an excellent ſituation for trade, having a ſafe ſpacious harbor, which is ſeldom or never obſtructed with ice...

...The college in New York, called Columbia College, is well endowed and furniſhed with profeſſors; but its ſtudents are not numerous.

VIRGINIA

This state is bounded by the Atlantic on the eaſt; by Maryland, Pennſylvania, and the Ohio on the north; by the Miſſiſippi and Ohio on the weſt, and by North Carolina on the ſouth...

...James River admits veſſels of two hundred and fifty tons burthen to Warwick, and of one hundred twenty-five tons to Richmond, about ninety miles from its mouth...

...The towns in Virginia are not large; the people mostly reſiding on their plantations...

...Richmond, at the head of navigation on James' river, and the ſeat of government, contains about three hundred houſes...

...Williamſburg was formerly a flouriſhing and beautiful town. It contained about two hundred and fifty houſes, and was the ſeat of government.

The principal ſtreet is one mile in length on a plain, with the college at one end, and the capital or ſtate-houſe, at the other, exhibiting a pleaſant proſpect. But ſince the ſeat of government has been fixed at Richmond, the city has decayed. Williamſburg is the ſeat of a univerſity, but the inſtitution is not in a flouriſhing ſtate.

The large and numerous rivers which water Virginia are very favorable for commerce. The principal article of exportation is tabacco, of which about 60,000 hogſheads are exported annually. Wheat is alſo raiſed in abundance, eſpecially in the mountainous parts of the State. Corn is the principal article of food for the negroes, yet a ſurplus is raiſed for exportation.

֍ Slavery in Cambridge, New York:

Slavery in America is most often associated with the southern states, but it is a mistake to think that slavery did not exist in the northern states. New York had a slave population of 19,000 adults in 1756, and slavery was not abolished there until 1827. It was not until 1860 that New Jersey became the last northern state to abolish slavery. There is very strong evidence that there were slaves on the Whiteside farm in Cambridge, New York. In the archives at Cornell University is a copy of a bill-of-sale signed by Phineas Whiteside dated August 18, 1800 that refers to: "one female negro slave named Deon of the age of twenty—one or thereabouts, to have and to hold bargained slave so mentioned and sold to the said John Whiteside, his Heirs and assigns forever..." A second document has more recently been found that describes another "negro boy" on the Whiteside farms. This handwritten copy of another document reads:

"'Sale of negro boy by my ancestors' — Know all men by these present that we Susannah Whiteside widow [widow of Oliver Whiteside, 1766–1804, the youngest son of Phineas Whiteside], Peter Whiteside, Edward Whiteside of the Town of Cambridge, County of Washington and State of New York and James Prendergast [possibly the brother of the widow whose maiden name was Susannah Prendergast] of the Town of Pittstown, County of Rensselaer and State aforesaid, Executors of Oliver Whiteside, late of the Town of Cambridge, deceased, for and in consideration of the sum of one dollar paid at or before the sealing and delivery of these presents by Abraham Van Trugh of the Town of Cambridge, County of Washington and State of New York, the receipt whereof is hereby acknowledged, have granted bargained and sold by these presents do grant bargain and sell unto the above named Abraham Van Trugh his heirs executors, administrators and assigns the term of service of a negro boy named Ben, born the tenth day of February one thousand eight hundred and two as will appear on record in the clerks office of the Town of Cambridge and until the said boy shall come to the age of twenty-eight years the term of service proscribed by law, to have and to hold the above named Ben so sold to the said Abraham Van Trugh his heirs executors administrators and assign and [illegible] against every person or persons lawfully claiming the above named Ben unto the said Abraham Van Trugh… In witness we have herewith set out hands and seals this ninth day of May in the year of our Lord one thousand eight hundred and five. [Signed & sealed] Susanna Whiteside, Peter Whiteside, Edward Whiteside. [Witnessed by] Peter Whiteside & James Whiteside."

This three-year old boy would appear to be the second slave that was sold from the Whiteside farm. It is not known if the two slaves were related.
—*Editor's note*

❧ Miscellaneous receipts:

Rec. Cambridge Jan 28th, 1832 of George McKie fifty two dollars in full for one hundred bushels of corn. —*H. Darrow & Co* by *John H. Willard.*

Cambridge, April 3, 1832. $7.04. Received of George McKie one of the Commissioners of common schools for the town of Cambridge seven dollars and four cents being the amount of public money owe [sic] unto school district No. 17 in Cambridge.
—*E. Hatch.*

Cambridge, April 3, 1832. $16.28. Received of George McKie one of the Commissioners of common schools for the town Cambridge sixteen dollars and twenty-eight cents being the amount of public money owe until school district No. 15 in Cambridge.
—*Edward Johnson.*

Received of G. McKie on this sixth day of September 1841 the sum of thirty-five dollars, pay in full, for hay bought of me to this date. —*E. F. Whiteside.*

❧ George McKie to his wife Sophia:

Albany, Feb 9th, 1835.
My Dear Wife—   Having a little leisure and a good many thoughts of home and you particularly, I have been compelled to scratch a few lines and forward them on to you. I am in good health and feel grateful for the bless-

George McKie, 1791–1861. F. Forshew, Photographer, Hudson, New York.

Sophia Whiteside McKie, 1796–1878. Sophia must have been a very unusual woman for she reportedly had twenty-two proposals of marriage before her twenty-first birthday. When she did marry, she married her brother-in-law. C. R. Clark, Photographer, 338 River Street, Troy, New York.

Wilson Wilson was most likely the schoolmaster. The letter is very difficult to read and much has been omitted.

ing. I am anxious to know how your Father and Niel is doing and conclude the best will be to return home on Friday so you may send Edwin to Troy Friday morning. Judge Skinner concludes to go home with me. William Wilcox and Margaret have been to Albany and I expect them at our House friday [*sic*] evening. Margaret has purchased a new Hat— quite nice too. I cannot describe it. You will probably see it soon. Tell Edwin if he comes with the wagon to put both seats in it and the buffaloes. I have not anything more, quite barren you will perceive, but never forgetting the one who above all others have the strongest claims on my affections and esteem.   —Yours with additional fondness if possible.   —*G. McKie.*

Catherine McKie is away at school:

Schaghticoke, May 27th, 1836.
My Dear Mother—   Mrs. Wilson told me that Mr. Lee was in town. She said also that I might return with him if I chose. I should like to go but I think that I had better not for I am afraid that you can not bring me back before school on Monday. I think of you every day more and more and love you more and more although I am quite happy here. I like Mr. F— very much & the little girls are all very pleasant. I do not think that I could find any fault with them if I should try. Mr. Slocum came home last night… you sent me more than enough cloth for two towels. I will send the towels but keep the piece. Perhaps you may want something else made out of it. My teacher says that I recite my lesson very well… I went down street and got four oranges that night you left me.   —Your Affectionate Daughter, *Catherine McKie.*

My Dear friend—   I am extremely happy to have it in my favor to inform you that your little daughter appears to be happy and contented with us beyond my expectations…   —your friend *Wilson.*

Catherine McKie was nine years old when she was sent to school in Schaghticoke, New York, about ten miles from the family farm in Cambridge. In addition to this letter from that time period, a penmanship lesson from 1831 and her "algebra" lessons from 1838 have been preserved. All of the below are solved in longhand in the workbook (her answers are in brackets). From the book of algebra lessons:

- Reduce 31472 farthings to pounds. [32]
- Bought a hogshead of rum containing 114 gallons at 96.00 cents per gallon and sold it again at 100.32 [cents] per gallon; what was the whole gain and what was the gain percent? [4.5 percent]
- Extraction of the Square root — What is the square root of 18,420? [135.72]
- Suppose a man had put out one cent at compound interest in 1620, what would have been the amount in 1824, allowing it to double once in 12 years? [131,072]
- What is the present worth of $100 annuity to be continued 4 years, but not to commence till 2 years hence, allowing 6 percent compound interest? [308.39]
- Suppose I lend a friend $500 for 4 months, he promising to do me a like favor some time afterward. I have need of $300. How long may I keep it to balance the favor? [$6 \, 2/3$]

Sixteen years later, on October 30, 1854, Catherine recalled this period in Schaghticoke when she wrote to her mother: "George said you had been taking one of those powders which 'make you well when you are sick and when you are well will make you sick.' This reminder of Mr. Wilson, and my home in Schaghticoke, brings also to mind the homesickness I had so much when I was there, and it was on one of these memorable occasions of illness that Mr. Wilson told me 'Tobacco lie' by way of diversion."

Between 1843 and 1844 Catherine McKie studied at the Troy Conference Academy, now Green Mountain College, in Poultney, Vermont, about forty miles north of Cambridge. Her brother George was also a student there as was a young man from Hoosick Falls, New York, named Francis Thayer. Preserved are some of Catherine's letters home to her parents, some of her essays, and one of her Mother's letters to her children away at school.

~ Poultney letters:

Saturday aft. Oct. 29 — 1843.
Dear Mother—   I suppose you are wondering by this time, what I am doing— how I am situated, whether I am contented or not; I will give you a description, and then you can judge. George and myself left the Bridge, as I suppose father told you, about 1 o'clock, and came on, full of going to school at Poultney. The stage dined at Cam—, and I sat in the parlor half an hour and never thought of any India-rubbers, until we were halfway to Salem. I regret it very much as I shall need them, but I will do the best I can. We stayed but a few moments in Salem and neither George or myself saw any of Uncle Matthew's family. The next place at which we stopped was Bishops Corners, where we stayed about 15 minutes, and the next and last place was the Troy Conference Academy— which we reached at 9 o'clock in the evening. Judge of our surprise on being told that the quarter does not end until next Wednesday. But I will endeavor to improve my time as much as possible.

George and myself had tea and then I was put in a room with a Miss Cochran, from Rupert with whom I am to remain [share] until next Wednesday, when I shall change. I intend to room alone as there are none here that

the Bridge   Probably Buskirk, site of Burkirk's Bridge.

Buskirks Bridge, rebuilt 2004. First bridge here built in 1804, serving the Great Northern Turnpike, by Martin Buskirk, a tavern-keeper on the Cambridge, New York, side of the Hoosick River, re-built about 1850.

I fancy for a chum. My room will be on the third floor, a back room on the southwest corner of the building, in it is one window looking south and another west. Miss Cochran is a real Yankee in every sense of the word but a very good and pious girl. I did not eat anything after I left home until I got here, and I had a bad sick headache and was anxious to get to bed as soon as possible. I went into the room with Miss Cochran and as there was but one lamp in the room I did not see— but all looked as well as could be expected. I prepared to retire, and turned down the bedclothes; and what do you think the bed was; well just take one of the comforters; and spread one thickness over the straw bed, and you have it. It seemed rather hard I can assure you, after a ride of 45 miles and a sick headache for my comfort, to seek repose on such a bed; but I have become accustomed to it now, and sleep as well as if it were made of down. The next morning, at 5 o'clock, was wakened by the bell and at six went to the chapel for prayers. At 7, breakfast. The young ladies called, and all said, "Now I hope you will not be homesick," and it reminded me of home, so much, and the difference between home and this place that if ever there was a homesick girl, I was one. I cried myself almost sick, went to bed, took a nap, and woke up in much better spirits. In the evening went to church with all the other girls to attend a musical concert given by several of the quires [choirs] of the County.

Thursday morning came and with it hot biscuit (or dingbats as they are called here) for breakfast. At noon, mush and milk for dinner, Sumptuous, is it not: No danger of having the gout here. There was a music convention here which commenced with the concert I have spoken of. Thursday afternoon we went to the church where we were highly entertained with music and an address from Prof. Wentworth which was excellent. We went in the evening also, at which time the convention closed. The music through the whole was grand. Yesterday we had a good breakfast— broiled beef for dinner and good slap-jacks (pancakes) for tea, and today all is good.

I like the Teachers very much, and as far as I am capable of judging, they fill their places well. I went to see Miss Wright (Preceptress) in reference to my studies today, and think I shall study Latin, Rhetoric, Geometry, and Writing. It is just as George said in regard to the ladies. With the exception of twelve or fourteen, they look as if they never were out of the woods until they came here, the same with the gents. The bell rings for prayers so goodbye. —Prayers over. I hope my selection of studies will meet with your approbation. I may take something in the place of Latin. I am now reviewing Arithmetic in my room before next quarter. There are 80 boarders here. Tell Wina Sally to have a bed like mine and see how nice it is. The tea bell rings.

—Friday evening 10 o'clock. It is two weeks tomorrow since I commenced scribbling on this sheet, and then I supposed that it would have reached you long ere this. But if I have not written, it is not because I have not thought of home. No, not an hour has passed in which home has been forgotten: and at the lone hour of midnight when every room in the building is dark save mine, then, and not heartlessly, do I wish myself in that loved home once more. Tis then when fatigued by constant application from 6 o'clock in the morning until 12 o'clock at night, (meals included), I wish for a friendly chitchat by my own Father's fireside and truly appreciate the truth of the phrase, "There is no place like home." But I will turn to my studies… [page torn].

Wednesday evening 12 o'clock. I expected to have sent this scrawl last Monday, but will give my reasons for not doing so. I have said before that we have class meetings on Sat. evenings and Prayer meetings Sabbath evening. The first Sat. eve I requested Prayer for George. I did the same the next Sat. eve and the next also— which was last Sat. eve. He was present every time. Last Sabbath morning immediately after breakfast the Preceptress came to... [page torn]   —Kate.

West Poultney. Feb. 17, 1844.
Dear Mother—   It seems like an age since I left home and all Friends connected with it. I do not wish you to infer that I have been homesick again, yet I must confess that I have been a little bit lonely, but as studying has commenced, I'll bid farewell to everything belonging to the order of the "blues". We had a long tiresome ride coming up in the stage. The stage came to the Bridge at 12 o'clock. Mr. Pick and six students in one stage and Miss Marvin in another. We went up with her. At Cambridge we found Lib Beadle and some other old school girls, waiting for the stage. We arrived in Salem about 4 o'clock. Mary Mathews was at Mr. Gile's. There was but one stage going North so we were obliged to ride from Salem to Granville very much crowded, as there were 18 in the stage. At Granville there was an extra provided and we rode more comfortably. There was a gentleman of the name of Worthington who rode up in the stage, and was formerly connected with Lansing Taylor when in Albany. He brought a son to school who is about the size of J— and a very interesting little fellow. He (Mr. Worthington) gave me a history of Mr. T—'s family, and to sum it all up in one word, he had an exalted view of the whole family. The school is much larger than it was last quarter and everything goes on smoothly. We have 76 boarding at present and more are expected. Our Steward and Lady give unusual satisfaction, & our board is one of the first class. My studies are French, Logic, Mental Ph-y, and Writing. I have been in the spelling class but have been sent out. You may think this is rather strange but I will give you an explanation. When Mr. Peck was organizing the classes, he said he would call the class in spelling and he should like all who thought it necessary to take their seats for that class, to do so. But he said if any of the teachers found a word spelled incorrectly in any of the compositions, the author would be sent into the orthography class even if it were the best scholar in the school. He said too that if any went into class who were found by the Teacher to be good spellers, that they would be sent out of the class. So you see that it is rather a compliment not to be allowed to stay in the spelling class.

Esther Marvin, of who I have spoken, has a bad cough and I fear that unless she has it cured soon, she will be obliged to leave school. I have made her come and room with me & I shall keep her in the room until it is safe for her to go into the cold air. Olive Allen, who you heard me speak of, has been quite sick and under the doctor's care more than a week but is a little better today... In regard to a carpet, if you choose to sew two breadths of your rag carpet together, 13 feet in length and put in a box and leave it at V. & D. Marvin, Troy (Father knows where they are) and Mr. Marvin can send it to me. That is, put the direction on the box & Mr. M— will send it by some acquaintance. You can do just as you think best about it. The carpet that I have is almost worn out. Is Mr. Campbell with you now? If he is, you cannot be

Mr. T— probably refers to Francis Thayer whom Catherine McKie met while studying at the Troy Conference Academy in Poultney, Vermont.

lonely. In regard to light clothes I will write in the future. I would like to write more but have no time as I want to take this to the Office so that it can go in mail tonight for you recollect that you told me to write if it were but six lines. Mary M— told me that Mr. R— was not expected to live. I am anxious to hear from her. Give my love to all at home, Father and all enquiring friends. If you should send me a carpet, a fruitcake or anything with it would be acceptable. Write soon as convenient. George is well and wishes to be remembered to all.   —Your Daughter *Kate*.

Tuesday, West Poultney, March 25, 1844.
Dear Mother—   Perhaps you may have wondered why I have been silent so long. But could you see how I have been situated perhaps you would not find so great cause for surprise.

In the first place then, you recollect that when I was at home, you told me that I should write oftener, and I supposed that I would; but after I had written and waited for an answer, I hoped that by keeping silent you would remember that a letter from home would be as dear to me as one from me could be to anyone. But since I received Henry's letter, I have felt that if you was not worn out with sick ones I ought to be thankful to say nothing of writing letters. Well then to justify myself, sickness is my plea. Not that I have been sick, but Olive Allen of whom I have spoken to you. She rooms next to me and for a week we did not know but she might be taken away any moment. Esther Marvin has been sick too. I made her come and room with me until she recovers so as to be able to go in the halls. She was with me two weeks, when her Physician said she might go to her own room, and not expose herself to the cold air any more than was absolutely necessary. Her lungs are very much affected, and I never saw a person have a worse cough. Last Friday afternoon she was taking some tea in her room, when she was seized with a violent pain in her head— her face turned almost as red as was possible except a small spot on her cheek which was very white. Her face and neck very much swollen. A physician was sent for immediately. He came in a few moments and attempted to bleed her but her blood seemed so thick that it would not run but very little. Several things were done for her and she was relieved. Her Physician said that it was congestion of the lungs and brain and that if she had not been relieved in a very short time, the eruption of a blood vessel would have been the consequence. He said that there was much danger of another attack during the night, and if she had another, she could not live through it. I can assure you that it was solemn enough. Two young ladies and myself took the directions and sat up with her that night, and we may truly say that we watched— for I presume that she drew not a breath without being heard as we stood over her constantly. The night passed and her life was spared. She told me that if she had another spell, she could not live; and that if her face began to turn red when she was asleep to wake her, for she did not wish to go to sleep and wake at the judgment bar of God. You may imagine that it was a solemn time. Her Mother was written for that night, and she came today. Esther will go home next week probably if she is no worse. Mr. Newman, of whom you have heard me speak, has lost his child. I sat up with that one night. Mr. Pick is sick now.

He has taken a severe cold, and has a bad cough, and some fever, but we hope that he may soon be restored to health. By what I have written, you will readily conclude that there has been much illness among us as well as others. Henry wrote that Clara was sick at our house, poor thing. Would that she were happy in another world, I hope she is better now. And as for "Shany," as Clara calls her, I know not what to say. To wish her happiness were vain, yet I have a wish for her— it is that she may always sit behind the stove, and laugh, as much as she pleases.

As to the school this quarter, everything moves onwards in fine [letter torn]. George is doing well in his studies and appears anxious to go on. As for myself I have nothing to say except that I like my studies very much. As to staying until the close of the term, we wish to know as soon as possible— you and Father know what we wish to do, and of course it is for you to decide as you think best. If I am not to stay longer than this quarter, do not send my carpet, if you say that I can, then let me know as soon as convenient, and I will send for some other things that I shall need. Give my best love to Father and all br-s [brothers]… Remember me to E.P. Beadle if home, and tell her how I have been situated that I could not write her— also to her Mother, & Lee, Sarah & S. and Mr. and Mrs. Akin. Finally to all enquiring friends. Write me as soon as possible, all the particulars will highly interest me, although they may seem unimportant to others. George wishes to be affectionately to all. Tell the little ones I should like to kiss them all a dozen times. From *Kate*, as ever.

Mother it is at this hour, when the sun is disappearing behind the western hills, that I wish myself with thee, that I wish myself at home by my own Mother's side but I must cease for the scalding teardrop tells me, that now I can not sit by the fireside of my own loved home.

Wednesday, West Poultney, 8th May.
Dear Mother.   I received by George all that was sent, and I can assure you, that I was much pleased. I received more than I expected, and tender my sincere thanks to the different Donors. I was surprised to hear that I had a silk dress, but cannot say that I am sorry that it has come… I have received a hat and parasol from Esther Marvin. I sent her the money for the parasol, four dollars, and my hat was seven. Do not exclaim I beg of you. I wanted a handsome straw hat and it is so, truly. Perhaps the price will appear too great to '*some of the family*'. But let Ed call to Mr. W— and leave seven dollars for Esther from me— and say nothing more to her. She will know what it is for. And let it pass paying for parasol and hat that she purchased for me. What deception: but is it not for the best? I am doing well in my studies, and my health is good. I have the pieces to my worsted dress. It was the pink one that I cared most for. The school is increasing in number every day. There are ninety-six boarders here at present. If there is good letter paper in the store I wish you would get me a quire. The girls have come in and put a nightcap and a pair of spectacles on me and now I am showing them how Grandmother can write. And it seems as though you might hear them laugh, if it is 45 miles. I cannot write any more and send this out tonight so I must bid you good night. My love to all.   —*Kate McKie.*
P.S. Put up a cake of Father's shaving soap with my dresses.

Enclosed handwritten receipt:

Miss Catherine McKie
To: Mrs. Hannah Cobb Dr.
To 8 weeks Board 12 / $12.00
Received Payment in full for the above bill— Hannah Cobb.

90 THE FAMILY LETTERS

༄ A letter from Sophia Whiteside McKie:

George Wilson McKie, West Poultney, Vermont.
Cambridge, May 20th, 1844.
Dear Children—   I have delayed writing a few days expecting a letter from you before Edwin would go to N.Y., and I did not know but there was something here that you would like to have sent you. As I suppose you have learned by Edwin's letter that we intended you should stay until the end of the term and did not know that you understood it so before your Father left you. You have had reason to expect your piece of carpeting before this but it is only a few days since this much was woven and cut off and sent home. When you see it, you will say what a splendid roll but it will do so for a short time. I hope you will soon write and let me know what things you both will require for summer. George will you want a vest and pants? Can they be made there if you need them? You recollect you have the pattern for summer pants here.

    I feel very much interested for those persons that you have spoken and written to me about that were sick, particularly Miss Marvin. I think her case must be a very critical one but I sincerely hope she is much better. If you know how she is when you write, say how she is… Sickness continues in our place. Jane is in a very reduced state, sits up but a few minutes in her bed at a time except when she is compelled to on account of severe fits of coughing. She appears to realize her situation and has a great desire to get better but seems composed, resigned— death has no terrors to her. I watched last night with her and came home this morning with as bad a cold as you almost ever saw me have and you can judge how I look and how well I can see which will be some apology for this scrawl… Your Father has a very bad cold with considerable toothache and has been very busy with almost all the men clearing the stumps and stones of the cranbury hill for Hiram Starbuck. He has taken it for three years. The meadows in the hollow are let out to mow which you know will be a great relief to us all. Your Father has received a letter from Gardner, the Schuyler debt Lawyer. He says the Slade case is decided and the probability is we may get 2000$ and it will enable us to assist Niel and that would be very gratifying… It is now getting dark again as has been the case every time I have set down to write. You perceive I have been disappointed again about sending the box, but I hope you will get it safe and will be well to enjoy your fruit if you cannot get maple sugar. Your lemons will be almost past— there is none to be had here. Now I have told you all the little news I think of at present that is worth writing and some that is not. Time passes on about as usual. No preaching except one Sabbath from Mr. Bullians since Mr. C— left us, and we felt quite at a loss what to do with ourselves for a few sabbaths. The traveling has been unusually bad this spring— almost impassable on accounts of the drifts they were bad until nearly the last of March, and then came the mud which has prevented us from going to the Bridge until last Sabbath. Sally went with Mr. Beach. The family have all retired. The 3 boys have kissed me good night. Almost nine. May God be with [you / us] this night and through life is the sincere wish of your Mother [*and written around the edge of paper*—] I have been brought up very short I did not know but I had another page until I was on the last line. The boys left kisses for you both. You will have business enough for the ensuing week to read this. I feel a little

---

Letter is unsigned, but is in the handwriting of Sophia Whiteside McKie.

assist Niel Niel McKie was attempting to establish himself as a grocer in New York City at this time.

unpleasant that I am not sending much of anything to George but whatever you need you will have sent when we hear from you and E— gets back.

West Poultney, June 27, 1844.
Dear Mother—   After so long a silence I do not know as you will care to hear from me, thinking perhaps that I have almost forgotten home. But appearances are deceitful— and I can only say that I have thought of home as much as ever, but have not had time to express my thoughts through the medium of pen and ink. The only reason is that, my studies and preparation for the Exhibition have taken my attention from 4 o'clock in the morning until 11, or 12 o'clock at night. Last evening the Ladies Ex, took place. The compositions were all most excellent (excepting my own)... Perhaps you may not know that Troy Annual Conference is in session here at present, consisting of 175 Ministers. The Church is very large and was, to use a low expression, crammed full. As usual George has crept out of Exhibition, he does it to the injury of himself, but neither the persuasion or threats of the teachers produced any effect on him. The dresses you sent me were beautiful and I hope the time will come when I can repay those who are so kind to me at present. I endeavor to improve my time as much as possible. The bell has rung for 6 o'clock and I must send to the Post Office— I cannot write to Niel immediately and I wish you would write to him and say that I have received his gifts and am much gratified with them. My best love to all—   —Kate.
Keep this letter on account of the scheme.

Letter written on the back of a school program, *Gentlemen's Exhibition*, Troy Conference Academy, June 26, 1844.

❧ Catherine McKie's Essays:

Some of the essays are dated while others are not:

What is your life? It is ever a vapour that appeareth for a very little time and then vanisheth away.
  How true and yet how little realized.
  Life has frequently been compared to a day. Youth has been considered analogous to the morning, ripening manhood to noonday, and old age to the shades of evening. How striking the analogy.
  In the morning of life we are gay and thoughtless. We think only of the present and cast not a thought on the morrow.
  In the meridian of life the joys of the past seem to be in some measure forgotten and our minds are occupied with anticipation of the future.
  In the evening of life we realize our situations, the shortness of life and the necessity of preparing ourselves while young for another world. Conscious as we are of the shortness of life we should engage (employ) ourselves in such a manner so that if spared 'til old age we can look back upon the days of our youth without the sad reflection that we have misspent the time which has been so graciously allotted to us by our maker.

After being absent for some months from my native village, I with pleasure retraced my steps and finally reached it late Sat. eve. The next day being Sabbath, I resolved to go to church, and hear our own minister preach once more. I went to church, and after taking my seat I cast my eye around expecting to meet a glance of recognition from those

On January 13, 1840, the steamship *Lexington* left its pier on Manhattan's East River at 4:00 p.m. bound for Stonington, Connecticut, carrying 143 passengers and crew and a cargo of cotton. In the early hours of the evening a crew member noticed that some of the woodwork around the smokestack was on fire. Unable to extinguish the fire, the crew unsuccessfully attempted to launch the lifeboats. The cotton quickly ignited and the fire soon spread to the entire ship and passengers and crew were forced to jump from the ship, a few lucky ones using bales of cotton as rafts. The frigid waters in Long Island Sound caused many to die of hypothermia and many who clung to the bales of cotton fell off and drowned. A nearby sloop failed to respond with aid, and there were only four survivors of this, the worst steamboat disaster on Long Island Sound.

I loved, but here in many cases I was disappointed. During intermission I walked out of the church, and the first thing that attracted my attention was the old church-yard. I at once felt a desire to look upon the graves of those friends whom I had laid beneath the cold sod and I hastened to gratify my desire. While passing along to the grave of a relative, my attention was attracted to one newly made— at the head of which was placed a plain but neat stone. There was something about it that seemed to forbid me to go on, something that seemed to say to me "see whose name is inscribed here." I unconsciously stepped back that I might read the name, and if I at that moment had heard a peal of thunder, I could not have been more startled. It was the name of one who I had supposed till this moment to be among the living. This was indeed a time for reflection. When I had left my home, this friend, now beneath the tomb, was enjoying everything that health and prosperity could bestow. I had heard nothing of her death and I knew not whether she was in a state of happiness or misery, and I feared for her, unless she had experienced a change. I hesitated not a moment, but hastened from the church-yard, determined to ascertain the state of her feelings before death. I soon met with a person who I knew would be able to give what information I wanted. I enquired about her sickness, death etc. I was told that she had been taken away very suddenly, and that her last words were, "I cannot die." There could be no hope then that she was among the blest. It did seem to me awful, that she, whom I had known from childhood, whom I had ever loved, should suffer eternal death. Oh! thought I, had she prepared herself to meet her God, she might now be happy, she might be in the presence of her God, and his [His] smile would now rest upon her. She had Christian friends, but perhaps they had never warned her of the necessity of preparing for death: but was that an excuse! No a just God had required this duty of her, and she had neglected it, and it was but just, that she should suffer the consequences. —*Kate McKie.* (Catherine McKie. Oct. 25)

Death has ever been considered the great enemy of mankind, and in whatever form he presents himself, [he] seldom fails to produce an emotion of dread of which it seems almost impossible to divest ourselves. But there is much difference in the degree to which this sensation is awakened under different circumstances. Take for instance the burning of the *Lexington*, several of her passengers at that time were on their return to friends whom they had not seen for years; and as they drew near their native homes how many sad hearts became glad in view of meeting those who were near and near. The alarm of fire was given and in a few moments the boat was wrapped in flames. What must have been the feelings of the passengers as they were driven by the flames from the boat and obliged to commit themselves to the mercy of the waves; what the feelings of a mother too who, with her infant in her arms, spent her last moments in endeavoring to catch at some object by which she might save herself and child; but all in vain for they too had been chosen by the [illegible] destroyer. No one could have beheld this awful scene without the most painful feelings. But let us enter the chamber of death and view a scene entirely different. There lies a young female apparently in the arms of death, one who a few weeks since was enjoying good health and little thought she would so soon lie on a death-bed. But it came to see her now, the same smile plays upon her features that was wont to be there in the bloom of health, and it seems as if the very angels themselves are waiting with impatience for her to bid a last farewell to earth and its trivial enjoyments that they may fulfill their duty by conducting her redeemed spirit to a happier sphere. But see?— She bids farewell to earth, and now, her spirit is winging its way to mansions of eternal rest. When we behold such a scene as this there certainly can be no anxiety in regard to the departed; for who can but say that an individual in such circumstances would be far happier than if permitted to live; but at the same time there is, in seeing an individual calmly resign himself to the sleep of death, something that is calculated to startle. But why is it so? Is it because we feel that the same hand that takes one individual from this world has the power to call us, and we know not how soon that hand may think proper to do so. Why should we tremble then and fear to die: since Death but unbinds the soul and frees it for the sky. And in connection with this we feel as we stand around the bed of death, that great preparation is necessary in order that we can pass the boundary to that bourn "whence no traveler returns." And if we are prepared, should it not rather be considered a kind messenger that has come to sever the link that binds our spirits to this earth and give them opportunity to commence an eternity of happiness.

> Then " "Aft' as the bell with solemn tole [*or:* toll]
> Speaks the departing of a soul
> Let each one ask himself, am I
> Prepared should I be called to die"
>
> —*Catherine McKie,* Sept 7.

The proper study of mankind is Man.

Some time since while traveling in a stage-coach, I had an opportunity of verifying the truth of this maxim. At the time to which I allude I stepped myself into a coach and after securing myself a comfortable seat, the first thing I did was to ascertain who were my companions. The first one, who attracted my attention, was a young lady, who I soon learned without much exertion on my part, and apparently none on hers, was a graduate from the Albany Female Academy. According to her account, she had left school about a year previous loaded with the highest honors. Her dress showed plainly that she was a *faithful votary of fashion*. The small delicate hand, on which many brilliant diamonds found a resting place, evidently had not been familiar with domestic utensils. A showy gold chain glistened upon her neck, attached to which a splendid watch plainly showed the wealth of the owner, and were I to judge from her constant reference to it for the time, I should suppose the hours passed slowly. As the result of my observations, I concluded she would be called a *fashionable lady*. The second of my companions, whom I proceeded to notice, was a man whose very existence almost seemed to depend upon the passing of some tariff law, or the erection of a United States bank. He firmly believed that unless such and such bills were passed in Congress, that the people of the United States would be in a worse condition than those under a despotic government; that there was so much extravagance existing, as to affect the morals of the country and that it was time for something to take place, to put a stop to such proceedings. Seated beside him was an individual who in one respect seemed to have avoided the curse pronounced upon man, for judging from appearances he had not eaten his bread by the sweat of his face. He seemed to find his principal amusement in twirling the key of his watch, or in minutely examining his gold-headed cane. Perhaps a more full description would be conveyed, by saying he was a flop. The next one of our number whom I observed was a lady and from her irritable disposition and from the state of her nerves, I concluded that she had taken a strong cup of coffee before starting. She was not at a loss for occasions to express dissatisfaction and was constantly making some exclamation about bad roads and careless drivers. The remaining passenger was a lady. She, I judged, was one whom sorrow had taught to look to the right source for happiness. Her countenance bore an expression so high and noble, and at the same time so calm. A humility that it seemed as if none but pure thoughts would dare to approach and seek to find a home within a breast so holy. She sat alone, apparently insensible of surrounding occurrences. I had now formed some idea of the characters of my companions and wished for an opportunity for each to display some of the traits that dame nature had bestowed on them.

As I was musing upon these differences, we were suddenly started from our seats by the stage turning to one side and on asking the driver what had happened, he told us that the vehicle had received a slight injury and that he would be obliged to go back about a mile to a place where he could get it repaired in a short time; our company seemed disposed to wait there, until he returned, and accordingly all left the coach. We had not proceeded far, when suddenly the sun was darkened, and on looking up we saw that we might expect a thunder-storm; and as there were no building that we could reach before rain might fall, there was no alternative but to remain where we were. Our anticipations were soon realized. A flash of lightning and the sound of thunder, told us that the storm was near. In a few moments large drops of rain began to fall, flashes of lightning came in quick succession and peal after peal of thunder rolled over our heads. The rain now fell in torrents, and it seemed as if the next flash would wither some tall oak or pine, in the adjoining forest. Now was time for reflection, but most all of our company but me were not of that kind to enjoy such a time as this. All save one was struck with fear, she, who put her trust in him who rules the storm, was calm. You might see her viewing the lightning and listening to catch the sound of the thunder as it died away at a distance. To her it appeared sublime, for it was the voice of God. The storm passed, and again the sun made his appearance. How changed the scene: All nature seemed to rejoice, and as we were passing by an old hedge, our plain lady, as she was called by some, perceived an insect and in the next moment had it in her hand, viewing it with a magnifying glass. This was more than the young lady could bear, with such delicate feelings as she had been cultivated, and while the others crowded around to see the beautiful insect, she stood at a distance and said that she was *extremely surprised* to see anyone *so vulgar* as to be gratified by the sight of a *worm*; and seemed upon the point of fainting when we requested her to look at it. At this time our coachman returned and again we took our seats, the fashionable lady suffering *intensely* from the disarrangement of her nervous system occasioned by the sight of a *worm*. The businessman seemed wrapt in thought, apparently devising some way to make money and the irritable lady contented herself by saying, "that it was just as she expected with such a driver." Whilst the plain lady was still busily engaged examining the worm, I read in the expression of her countenance.   —*Kate McKie.*

In an unidentified handwriting worm not an insect.

V

1844–1850

Letters from Cambridge and Troy, Part One

IN the spring of 1842 twenty-year-old Francis S. Thayer left his home in Hoosick Falls, New York, and took a $100 a year job at a flour mill in Troy, New York, the city that would be his home for the next thirty-five years. He had saved his money to attend college, but his father urged him to give the money to an older brother so that the brother could go to college. Francis Thayer would go into the world of business with no formal education other than the time he had studied at the Troy Conference Academy in Poultney, Vermont. After studying in Poultney, Thayer spent a year teaching in North Bennington, Vermont, but he decided that he did not want to be a teacher. Prior to moving to Troy he had met Catherine McKie of Cambridge, New York, who had also studied in Poultney and whose brothers were his friends. There are many letters and diaries from this time period that tell about their lives.

The years 1844 to 1850 were years of growth and political controversy in America. The great national controversy of this time was slavery—both the practice of slavery in the south and its spread in the west. The term "sold down the river" would become a part of our language in reference to the practice of selling slaves to distant plantations. Slavery was always an issue as the United States either acquired new territory or territories became states. In 1844 the United States negotiated a Treaty of Annexation with Texas that was ratified the following year. Henry A. Wise, a Congressman from Virginia, had urged President Tyler, Wise's close friend, to follow that course, and in recognition of his work, a county in Texas would be named after the Virginia Congressman. Between 1845 and 1848 Florida, Texas, Iowa, and Wisconsin would become states. This expansion of America coincided with new means of communications. In 1844 Samuel Morse sent the first telegraph message between Washington and Baltimore: "What hath God wrought!" Three years later the Post Office introduced adhesive stamps, and in 1850 the first overland mail delivery west of the Mississippi was organized with monthly mail between St. Louis and Salt Lake City. In 1845 the potato crop failed in Ireland causing a famine. In 1847 an influenza epidemic in London killed an estimated 15,000 people, and in that same year Brigham Young and his followers arrived in the valley of the Great Salt Lake and founded the "State of Deseret" which would later become Utah. By 1849 trans-Atlantic crossings between Liverpool and New York took thirty-three days and passage in steerage cost $10. A fire in 1849 burned over 400 buildings in St. Louis. The 1850 publication of Nathaniel Hawthorne's *The Scarlet Letter* caused controversy with both its discussion of adultery and its attack on Puritan hypocrisy. Nobody in 1850 was using the term "non-native species" as part of an environmental protection project, but some might later think that the term would apply to an experiment in Brooklyn where English

Receipt for hay: "Received of G. McKie on the sixth day of September 1841, the sum of thirty five dollars, pay in full for hay bought of me to this date. E. F. Whiteside."

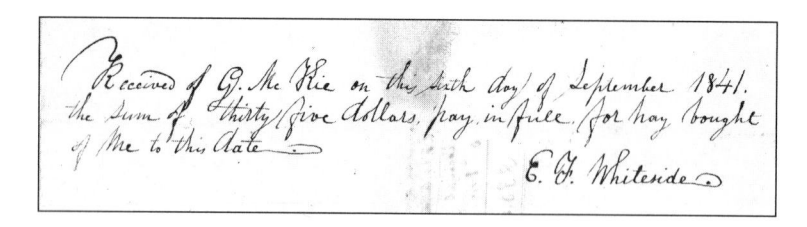

sparrows were imported to eat the caterpillars in the shade trees. The sparrows thrived, and the city of New York had to import starlings to prey on the sparrows in Central Park.

This was America in the 1840s as Catherine McKie of Cambridge wrote her diary and exchanged letters, for a several years a "secret" correspondence, with Francis Thayer of Troy. When Catherine wrote letters to Francis, her brothers would discreetly deliver them to him in Troy. Francis placed his letters in magazines that Catherine's brothers would bring home to her. Francis saved Catherine's letters in envelopes that were numbered and dated and Catherine saved the letters from Francis. It may seem extraordinary, but Francis also saved the *handwritten drafts* of his letters to Catherine. This was certainly not the fastest means of communications.

Letters and diaries by:
Catherine (Cate and Kate) Sophia McKie married, Catherine McKie Thayer
George McKie
George Wilson McKie (son of George & Sophia McKie)
Niel W. McKie
Francis (Frank) S. Thayer

Letters written from: Troy and Cambridge, New York; New York City; at sea, Chile, and Panama.

∽

☙ Catherine McKie's diaries:

Between 1845 and 1850, when Catherine McKie was between eighteen and twenty-three, she kept a daily journal, three little volumes of unlined pages on which she made very short entries. One of the volumes is written in pencil and is perhaps a "draft" for one of the others which is written in ink. At the end of one volume is the "draft" and at the end of another is a more complete chronology. Both are printed below:

The draft:
C. McKie born June 16, 1827
1836 At school at Schaghticoke
1839 At school at Buskirks Bridge
1840 At home.
1841 Went to Cam— [Cambridge] School in May
1842 At school in Cam—
1843 At home. At Reed's Hollow, Salem. from November went to Poultney to school.

Schaghticoke is a community about ten miles southwest of Cambridge.

1844 At school in Poultney— Left P. in July.
1845 At home. In Salem, winter.
1846 At home. Uncle James'

A more complete chronology:
1836 At school at Schaghticoke.
1839 At school at Buskirks Bridge
1840 In Fairfield
1841 Went to Cambridge to school in May.
1842 At school in Cambridge
1843 In the winter at Reed's Hollow. In Salem.
	In Nov. went to Poultney to school.
1844 At school in Poultney — left July 17
1845 At home. Salem during the winter.
1846 At Uncle James'. Salem during the winter.
	Br. George went to China in May.
1847 Br. George returned in March
1848 Went to New York with Louisa Whiteside
1849 Edwin McKie married to Maria A. Mosher, October 31st.
1850 April 30th. F. S. Thayer & C. McKie married.
	May. George went to California
	Nov. George returned from California
1851 April 22 Brother Henry died
1852 Sept. Brother Edwin was robbed of $48,000 at Cleveland, Ohio.
1853 February 7th. Brother Peter left home for Australia.
	Sept. 28. Brother Edwin left New York for Australia.
1854 July. Edwin J. McKie returned from Australia.

1844–1845

Troy, August 12th, 1844, Monday morning, 5 o'clock.
Miss Catherine McKie—   Permit me to address you respecting a subject which has much interested me since my return from a very pleasant visit with you of late. I have often resolved to express to you my regards for you and as often doubted what course to pursue for fear of being defeated in my expectations. Kate, I know you have an honest heart and will not expose me should you not reciprocate the regard I cherish for you. I therefore *frankly* express to you that it is my earnest desire to become more acquainted with you and continue my visits to you if it should be your pleasure. You will please inform me by mail your feelings in relation to this subject which I assure you will, if it meets your approbation, be a source of much happiness to me and I trust will not be a step to be regretted by you. My health, since my return from your house, I am happy to say is very much improved. I hope you will favor me with reply to this letter as soon as convenient.   —Yours very sincerely, *Francis S. Thayer.*

In the following section, Catherine McKie's diaries, where quoted, are at the end of every year as a summary of the year that is ending.

Cambridge, August 15th, 1844, Thursday eve, 11 o'clock.
Mr. Thayer—   Your letter, dated Monday morning, was received in the evening and in compliance with your request I answer it by return mail—

(ours twice a week). With regards to your letter, I wish to be perfectly frank. In reference to a non intimate acquaintance with you, I have not even the shadow of an objection for I have ever considered you one of my most worthy acquaintances, but I cannot approve of the cultivation of that acquaintance with regards to any particular subject— to do so would be injustice to you and of course meanness in me— not that I am engaged— no— I am as free as the mountain air.

A statement of facts may not be improper. When you was [sic] here you saw my Mother, perhaps you heard her say that her health was very poor— if you did not, such it is, and has been for twenty years. Her family is large— she has but one daughter, and her couch, when a child was ever the sick child's couch. The Mother watched over her with all a Mother's tenderness, and when the Mother's eyes grow dim, and when her cheek grows pale, is it the duty of that child to cultivate an acquaintance in such a manner, as may tend to alienate her affections from that Mother? Is it not rather her province to smooth her pathway to the grave? And with this view of this subject, would I not practice injustice to you to comply with your request to visit me as you describe? And besides Frank *I dare not trust myself* to form such an acquaintance. I have thus blindly given you my opinion and hope that I have not offended you— if so it has been done unintentionally. I intend to spend a few days in Troy next month. If I should see you I would be more explicit. I am happy to hear that your health is improved— neglect nothing that will preserve it. Until we meet Frank, may your own prayers and the prayers of friends shield you from temptation and guide you in the way of purity and happiness.   —Your friend as ever, *Kate*.

Troy, August 19th, 1844, Monday morning, 5 o'clock.
My Friend Kate—   Your letter of Thursday eve came to hand Saturday afternoon. Although it was not such as I wished it might be— yet I am not offended but disappointed. If I have offended you I hope you will forgive me for I was honest. I thank you for your prompt and frank reply. Your reasons are good for not complying with my request even if there was no other obstacle in the way but the poor health of your kind and affectionate Mother who has watched over you in sickness and in health with such tenderness and affection as a fond Mother only knows. I would be committing a sin which would haunt me by day, and by night as long as I live, to ask you to comply with my request while it would alienate your affections from that Mother who above all others under heaven merits your unceasing love and affection now in her declining years.

Kate, I have a dear Mother whose health is much like your Mother's. I know what it is to love such a Mother but I cannot find words to express it when I gaze upon my Mother's pale cheek or think of her. I ask myself this question: how I shall ever pay her the great debt I owe her for all her kindness from the moment of my existence to the present time. I answer: Leave nothing undone which will make her happy and do nothing which will make her unhappy, which I shall do as long as reason holds her power over my mind. Kate I do hope that what has passed between us since I saw you will not in the least *mar* our former friendship. The periodicals which I promised to send you I will leave at the Washington Hall done up in a bundle addressed to your brother Edwin with directions to have them

forwarded the first opportunity. I intended to have sent them by George Saturday but I was so much engaged in business that I did not have time even to treat him (Geo) with common civility. I hope he will excuse me this time and I will promise to give him my undivided attention next time he takes the trouble to call on me which I trust will be the first time he comes to the City… I would be glad to receive another letter from you as a friend if you think it best. Please overlook all errors in this hastily written letter and believe me to be your sincere friend as ever.   —*Frank*.
PS *May the last clause of your letter have effect.*

Cambridge, August 29th, 1844, Thursday eve, 11 o'clock.
Friend Frank—   Your letter of Monday morning was received in the evening. In reference to what has passed between us through the medium of pen and paper, I trust you will not dream of having offended me, for you have given me no occasion for offence…

I received the periodicals last Sat eve and have read three numbers of the *Knickerbockers*— am much pleased with the work, and think it the best of the kind I ever met with… And Frank, will you not come up to attend the Barbecue— be assured we shall be happy to see you. It is late and the hour bids me close…'tis an hour for reflection and is it not a season for reflection? The sun and yellow leaf are but types of the fading scenes of earth— and each leaf that falleth hath in itself a lesson… Nature is a silent teacher too— she tells a 'mystic lesson,' but they who watch her well may prophet by her teachings. Now Frank, do not think that you are under obligations to answer this scrawl— *merely* because you may not think it polite to leave it unanswered— for I shall think you deserve a compensation if you read it. As a friend, I shall always be happy to hear from you— and hope you will soon let me know whether you will attend the meeting in Saratoga or not. "Good night" Frank, and may your pillow be guarded by him who dispenses health and happiness in this life and that which is to come.   —*Kate*.

Troy, Sept 2nd, 1844.
My Friend Kate—   …With regard to attending the Whig Barbecue to be held at Saratoga on the 19th inst. I would say that when I first heard that there was to be such a meeting I promised myself that if possible I would attend it, and now since receiving your letter that resolution has been strengthened and I now promise you that I will attend the said meeting… I would like very much to be at Cambridge on the 14th or 15th but I cannot ask my worthy employers to let me be absent so long at this very busy season of the year when my humble services are needed most… As the mail which takes this closes at 7 o'clock I am obliged to stop, fondly anticipating that I shall soon see you— when we can talk over matters and things in general. Hoping that this may find you and all your friends in good health, I subscribe myself your sincere friend as ever.   —*Frank*.

Troy, October 1st, 1845, Wednesday evening.
Dear Friend—   In a most welcome letter which I received from you a little more than a year since, I find these pleasing words— "As a friend I shall always be happy to hear from you." With this view Kate, I am disposed to break in occasionally upon your quiet and leisure and claim a little of your

your letter   The letter of August 15, 1844.

Knickerbockers   First published in January 1833, *Knickerbockers* quickly became the most popular and influential literary magazine of the period. It ceased publication in 1859.

friends   Francis Thayer and Catherine McKie used this term when they wrote about their families.

precious time for my own pleasure and satisfaction. If I intrude you can tell me so and that will be the end of it. It would please me greatly to hear from you now and then. We have known something of each other. We once traveled a short way together in common pursuits and enjoyments. Those school days and the images they wrought on my mind have not passed away. Memory goes back often and seems to delight to linger long on the scenes of those few months that made so bright a spot in my life. I could wish for my own improvement and the friends I made there that they have been many years instead of months. And yet I believe I have not lost all the friends I made there. At any rate I have endeavored to retain some of them and whether I have succeeded or not in one instance, for the present and future, I submit to you. Kate I do love a sincere and open friend. One whose sympathies are kindred with my own. And when in youth such a friend, one or more of them, is found, and you feel and know that such a one has a spirit akin to your own, one whose moral sentiments and social qualities are responsive to your own, it is ennobling and elevating to strengthen and cultivate that friendship, to brighten its links and add to them one by one, as the years roll on and cares and sorrows chill the glow and warmth of our first associations… George called on me on his return to College…

George McKie, Catherine's brother, was a student at Union College.

I have not been out of the City since the day I left your house, since which time I have been much engaged in business, so much so that I long to get away from the counting room and spend a few of these *charming* days in the country with my friends, which I regret to say I am unable to do at present. My duties are arduous now, and will be so until the close of navigation when I shall (Providence permitting) have the inexpressible pleasure of again visiting my friends… In conclusion I would say, that if I have in writing you this epistle intruded, I hope you will pardon me. On the other hand should you consider it worthy an answer, be assured it will meet with a most hearty reception. Until we meet Kate, "may good angels and happy thoughts be your companions."   —Your sincere friend, *Frank*.

A Summary of 1845:
1845 *Cambridge, Washington Co.*
Jan 23. Left home for Salem.
Jan 25. Went to Poultney
Feb. 9. George came home.
Feb. 11. Finished quilt.
June 13. Father & Mother went to Whitecreek
June 16. My birthday.
June 18. F. S. Thayer called.
June 17. F. S. Thayer left.
July 26. E. P. Beadle & Miss Jones called.
Aug 9. …Mother & myself called at Mr. Beadle's.
Aug 11. Niel returned to New York.
Aug 22. Went to J. J. Lee. F. S. Thayer here.
Aug 25. F. S. left…
Nov. 13. Father & Mother went to White creek. Eliza W— here.
Nov. 14. Father & Mother returned. Aunt Mary very low.
Nov. 27. Aunt Mary died.
Nov. 28. Attended funeral.

Mary McKie (also Aunt Polly), 1787–1845, second of eleven children of James McKie, 1760–1843, and Elizabeth Wilson McKie, 1765–1849. There is no record of her ever marrying.

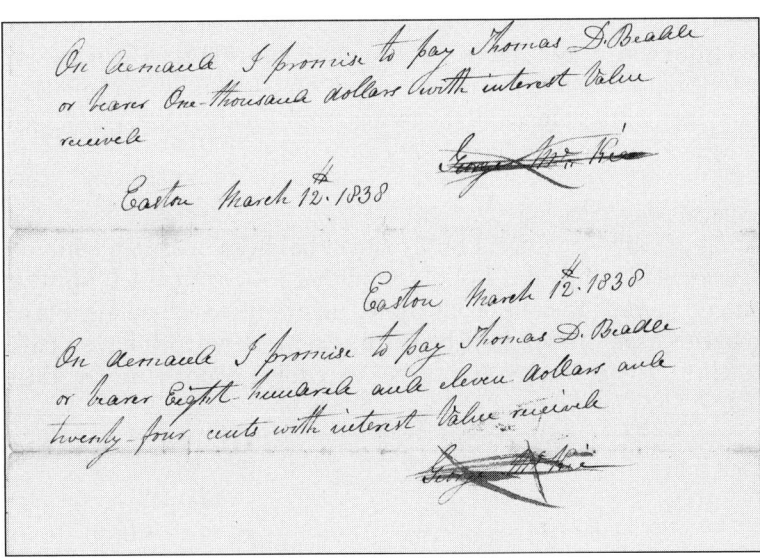

Promissory note from George McKie: "On demand I promise to pay Thomas D. Beadle or bearer one-thousand dollars with interest value received. George McKie, Easton March 12, 1838"

Nov. 30. Snow fell— the first this fall.
Dec. 1. Snow all day.
Dec. 31. The year has passed and what changes has it wrought— sure, time must leave its impress and years are pilferers. The poet has said. There is "not a year but pilfers as he goes some youthful grace that age would gladly keep."
 —*Excerpts from the 1845 diary of Catherine Sophia McKie.*

1846

New York, May 16, 1846.
Dear Father—   Yours of the 13th just came duly to hand & seen George & done the best in my power to have him return home but all to no purpose. He has left this day for Canton in the ship *Rainbow*. I have given him a good outfit & everything to make him comfortable. It is a splendid ship & first-rate men are the owners & Captain I have seen them both and told them under what circumstances he goes out. They calculate to be gone 10 months. She is the fastest ship in the world & George goes out under favorable circumstances. If he is disposed to do well he can do so. I have given George all the good advice I was capable of doing & think he is determined to try to do well. There is quite a number of young men gone out in the *Rainbow* out of first rate families in this city. George received 2 coats & a letter from Benj Fish enclosing 10 dollars. I think I shall be up home in 2 weeks or so. Tell Ed I want to know when he is coming down or whether he intends to come or not. Remember me to all the family—   Your affectionate son, *N. W. McKie*. [Niel Whiteside McKie]

New York, May 19, 1846.
Dear Brother—   When I wrote Father on Saturday last I had not time to say what I wanted to. It rained all day here on Saturday last & George did not

leave the harbor until Monday morning (yesterday). George says he was not expelled from college nor did he cut up any scrape there... He owes 8 or 9 dollars for board & a little at the college & 3 or 4 dollars at Dorlons Troy is all he owes... Remember me to all the family, Your Brother, *Niel W. McKie.*

George's trunk is all packed up & I have the key.

Schenectady, May 19th, '46.
Mr. George McKie—   Dear Sir, Your son has been boarding with me & has left a small bill unpaid & I understand that your son has left home and don't intend coming to college any more. He promised to pay me this term. I should like to have you send the ballance [sic] on to me for I have a payment to make. Let me hear from you soon & by so doing you will much oblige me. Yours etc. *P. V. R. Livingston.*

[Itemized bill]

July 7th to eight weeks board, $2.00 per week.	*$16.00*
July 31 to 3 weeks & 3 days Board & Room $3.50	*12.00*
1846 March 11th to 17 weeks & 2 days Board $2.00	*34.58*
July 22nd to use of horse & wagon & Sundries	*11.69*
	74.27
March 10th Cr. By Cash at 3 different times	*50.00*
	24.27

˷ George McKie's trip to China:

A far bit at sea, May 31, 1846.
Dear Brother—   Little did you think or did I, of the toils and hardships which a person in my situation has to undergo. Had I imagined that the life of a sailor was so burdensome— never, never would I have stepped my foot on board a ship. The first day or two out it was pretty pleasant— smooth sea and gentle breezes. But the fourth day we had a strong gale— the ship pitched bows under every wave. I was drenched to the skin all day long and at night got into a cold— wet— damp— dreary berth— and had hardly got to sleep when "all hands on deck" aroused me and from that time until morning, there I stood, wet— wet— wet clear through to the skin.

And to give you any further history of our further voyage would only be a repetition of the above. Every other day we begin work at 4 o'clock and work like the D— until 8 o'clock, then we have until 12 o'clock to ourselves. From 16 o'clock work again until 6 o'clock— when "clane up the decks" keeps us about an hour. Then we stand watch 4 hours on and 4 off all night.

The food is the next consideration. Salt beef and pork with dry hard navy crackers, tea for supper, coffee, breakfast— sweetened with molasses. This with what they call "Duff" at sea made out of flour— put in a bag and boiled and eaten with molasses. This is fare for an epicure you may well say. You cannot appreciate my feelings when I think of home and all its pleasant endearing associations, brother, Cate and all dwell continually in my mind. But still I think that it will be of great benefit to me.

I was seasick about ten minutes— but for two or three days I felt a qualmish sensation at my stomach— but now my appetite is perfectly wolfish. It is the opinion of some of the crew that we will be gone from New York 2 years on a trading expedition in the Indian Ocian. The Captain has his wife with him. The ship is prepared with sails and rigging enough for a three year cruise— so the conjecture may be a true one…

June 9th— Some days have elapsed since I wrote the above. Since then things have passed off much as usual on shipboard. Yesterday about 2 o'clock PM, while I was painting some iron, the cheering cry of "Land ho" was shouted from the crop-trees. The land appeared to be about 30 or 40 miles off and as the weather was somewhat misty we did not get a good sight. It was one of the Cape de Verde Islands, St. Antonia by name, so that you can see about where we are. If I live, won't my heart pound when the cry of "Land ho" is heard in latitude 41 of thereabouts and New York bay is made.

I would give all that is in the power of mortal to give, to take one look upon our family on one of these beautiful summer evenings. Niel— you know nothing about beautiful climates away up there. The nights are beautiful— clear— stars very bright— the ship sailing along at about 10 knots an hour. The wind such as we would call a fine summer's evening breeze. Last night we caught for the first time a flying fish and a queer fish he was— about 10 inches and shaped like our brook suckers or rather more slim. The wings were simply an elongation of the fins, just behind the gills. The wings were about 4 inches in length.

We have seen several sail but have spoken none yet. While I am writing there is a sail off to Leeward about 8 miles, standing on the same course that we are. I shall be satisfied to stay at home when the voyage is out, and be perfectly contented with country life. If ever a person was disappointed in these expectations, that person can appreciate my feelings. Any respectably connected person casting his life in such a mould, as the life of a sailor, is only to be wept as lost, if he allows himself to be led by many of his companions. If anything ever had a moral effect upon a sensitive mind, it is the shock caused by the utterance of the vilest oaths of the most uncouth language— the most degraded conversation— must have a very bad or a good effect. With me I hope the latter has been the case. Time to think and deep thought have caused me to deeply to regret my first course of life as to shed tears of repentance over the ruins, and when you see me again, if God in his providence ever permits you to do so, you will not see your wild unprincipled rogue of a brother, but a man. I hope Father will forgive my youthful indiscretions. I do not hope that he will, only wish it, as I know that he cannot do it, but when I say the pecuniary difficulties that he would soon find out if not settled were what drove me away from home (for think not Niel that I wanted to go to sea) it will be something of a plea in my defense. But could father know my feelings when I left home or when we left the port of New York, he would consider it sufficient punishment for all my faults. The 2nd day out my hands were covered with work blisters within and blistered without by the sun. If I recollect there were 17 blisters on the insides of my hands and fingers. How is Mother and all the rest of the family? I don't ask to be answered, but only because it is natural. Many have been the times my night watches on deck, that I have sat on the rail and thought of you and all the family and almost wept as I thought of the kindly brotherly feeling which you showed when you parted with me when the ship was about sailing— yes hot blistering tears of repentance have I shed over my past misspent life— but none over this last rash act the greatest of all— which has separated me from family— home— friends— and in fact almost all that makes life endurable. But if after one year and I return, the meeting will be all the sweeter and that little knowledge picked up will interest friends. I will write every opportunity so goodby and God bless you and all the family. Bid all the family a kind farewell for me— tell Cate that I will bring her something as a remembrance— and that she must not get married until I get back again. To Mother a kiss of affection and a son's blessing, to Father the same— to Ed, a warm brotherly hug— and goodbye to Henry, James, and Peter and the warmest well wishes and prayers of your affectionate brother to yourself. —G. W. McKie.

Valparaiso [Chile], August 8, 1846.
Dear Brother— …We entered this port this morning about daylight and cast anchor in 28 fathoms water. A beautiful place is Valparaiso— built on the side of a range of hills that rise from "old ocean's" bed to the height of three or four hundred feet almost perpendicularly, covered with green verdure down to the very waters edge— not a tree to been seen— just over this range— inland the Andes raise their snow clad tops. The air on the water is almost insupportable— (although we have a sea breeze)— on account of the heat, and just overhead the snow is piled up to the very heavens. We have not been ashore yet but the crew hopes to get on shore over Sunday— and if ever the Sabbath was broken by rambling about, it will be broken that day. We had a cold passage around Cape Horn. The rigging covered with ice for a week without a thawing day, the deck with snow and ice. But thank God we weathered the cape without losing a man or spar or sail. The rest of the voyage will be in warm weather. We shall stay in this port about a week, then for Callao, the port of Lima, then for Canton…

I hope that all difficulties will be settled up before I get home and allusion made afterwards. I know that it was wrong and have applied the corrective— all that can be said will only aggravate not cure the matter. My mind is made up… if I am received as formerly, with kindness and kisses, I'll go to work and be a farmer or go through college, but if on the other hand, if kicks & cuffs await me, the sea is my home ever after— and so mote it be. That is enough and finishes the subject forever on my part. You might have written me to Canton, and I hope you have as a letter from home would be to me a world of interest at present. When we were in the bay at New York I wrote a short letter to Father detailing the state of my financial concerns, and I sincerely hope that they are all settled. When I went up to Troy from N. Y. and borrowed the 40 dollars of John White, I paid 33 dollars to different individuals that had lent me in their innocence.

You are all enjoying good health I hope at home. The warm weather and exercise is conducive to health as I have found by experience as the erysipelas has troubled me but once or twice, and then only in the eyes, although I have not had a dry foot or shirt from one week to another for three weeks in succession. My time is about up and I must draw this letter to a close— commending the blessing of God on you all. Kindest love to all— Father, Mother, Sister, Brothers— and all enquiring friends. We will not take a two or three year cruise as I have predicted in the others, but will be home in less than a year from the time of starting— if God spares our ship and crew. Ask Louisa or Cate Whiteside (Fuller) if they know a young fellow by the name of Pound,

From this series of letters it appears that George McKie may have left Union College with some financial problems and debts, but there is no other information about that. The only records of the 1846 trip to China are the following: 1) his sister's entries in her diary, 2) a lacquered box that he brought back with him, and 3) this letter. Unfortunately the original copy of the letter has been misplaced or lost.

a minister's son. He knows them and is a doctor on board this craft with me— Once more love to all—
As ever you affectionate brother, *George.*

Troy, August 27th, 1846.
Dear Friend Kate—   When I visited you a few weeks ago I intended to have disclosed to you what was uppermost in my mind. But no favorable moment offered itself… Yes Kate, I love you and have long loved you. "I know you but to love you." Years ago, when I first knew you, this attachment was formed. I hardly knew myself then. It might be a boyish fancy and sober thoughts and mature years might efface the first bright and beautiful image that love impressed on my heart, but I have lived long enough, haven't I Kate, to trust myself to know my own constancy. And I now avow to you that with every year and month of my life, you who first touched my heart with love, have become more and more the object of my affection until you are now interwoven and bound up in all the hopes, desires and ambition of my life. And now Kate do you respond to this fond and devoted affection of one who has loved you for years— and loves you alone. If you do, I am happy and O how bright the promise of the future… I have thus *honestly* and *frankly* made known to you my feelings towards you, and I hope I have not offended you. If I have I trust you will be kind enough to forgive me. Do let me hear from you soon that I may know my destiny and meet it brave hearted and firm like a man— this I shall do Kate come what may, both for your sake and my own. With these deep and heartfelt feelings I subscribe myself. Your sincere Friend, *yes more than friend, Frank Thayer.*

This letter was written on my 24th birthday. May it never be so celebrated again. K.
Troy, Sept. 11th, 1846.
Friend Kate—   Your letter of 3rd inst. came to hand the 5th and however surprising it may seem to you, my own feelings will not permit me to let it pass unanswered. This is probably the last letter I shall ever write to you and I wish to be *frank* in every sense of the word, as I was in my letter to you of Aug. 27th in which I made a *sincere* and *devoted* avowal of love. And with equal frankness you have answered that you did not respond to it. The simple truth is that I loved you and you did not love me and there is now left no room for doubt. I have but one course to pursue and that is to veil the memories of the past and fill up the future with other hopes and this precludes the propriety or wish on my part to continue an intimate association as *friend*… You will not understand me Kate when I tell you that our association except as we may by accident be thrown together will now cease and that in this is my safety. If you loved me you would understand. My task is now *to forget you and my association with you*… Do not imagine that in all this there is anything of wounded pride that gives me this tone. My own happiness requires that I should not seek your society. It tells me that separation and time are the messengers of my peace. You need not as you suggest "be pained" on my account. I am too keenly alive to your happiness to wish that even in memory for me one drop of bitterness should ever come to that overflowing cup of pleasure which I pray God may be yours through life. My task to forget you may not be easy but in time it will be accomplished… I am grieved to learn that you

have been called upon to watch over the sick bed of a dear brother. I know by painful experience that the care and anxiety under such circumstances is very great and am not surprised that you are almost worn out with watching. I hope and pray too that your dear brother may soon regain his usual health and that each and every one of you may enjoy health, happiness and prosperity. I shall return you your letters, the first *safe and convenient opportunity* and I wish you to return mine *including this*. Good bye Kate. Your Friend and well wisher, *Frank*.

Troy, October 10th, 1846, Saturday evening.
Dear Kate—   Your letter of 1st inst. (mailed at the Junction P.O. 5th) came to hand Monday afternoon. *Welcome, thrice welcome.* I never before knew how much there was in those words "better late than never." The connection in which they now come to me will make them forever cherished. In my letter to you of Aug. 27th I opined to you my full heart. I loved you and I loved you so well and truly that I did not approach the matter perhaps as I should. I did not adopt any prudential steps to ascertain how much and well you thought of me. If I had been experienced at all in such affairs I never should have walked boldly up to you with my heart in my hand as I did but cautiously and by slow degrees. I should have revealed my attachment in some doubtful expressions and in this way sought in some manner to ascertain your feeling towards me. But Kate this is not my way or character. I know my own feelings…

When I received your reply to my letter, your first reply I mean, I felt that the brightest promise of the future was darkened to me. I felt that my earliest and first love was disappointed. O Kate you do not know how sad and heavy some of those gloomy hours were when I had fully made up my mind that you did not reciprocate my attachment and that I must turn away and leave to some other person more fortunate the precious treasure of your affection. But I made up my mind to do it. And now if I mistake not (Do I?) a new light breaks in and I may believe that there are *two* who in inclination and feeling are *one*. Your philosophy and observation so far as much of the world goes is good no doubt, but it is not all so. Heaven has planted some flowers of "frail and delicate growth" that when nursed and watched with affection, care, and tenderness will grow up and strengthen with the years of life and diffuse around our path sweeter blessings and richer joys, as we go on our journey through life… The clouds have now rolled away and I feel myself in a sunlight of pleasure that I never before experienced and while I ask may I not now hope for your love. I wish you would write me by week from Monday's mail, (sooner if you have time), and tell me all you think of me. I don't care much for anybody else opinion just now. Kate I want to see you much— very much and I now hope that I shall be able to avail myself of that pleasure in two weeks from this afternoon, perhaps three— at any rate as soon as I can. I can hardly deny myself the pleasure of attending your county fair but business is so pressing at this season of the year. I am obliged to adopt for my motto, "business before pleasure" and stay at home. I should really like to hear the Ladie's report read… There was no need of your making an apology for the appearance of your last letter for it was the best letter I ever received, and may I not look for another soon. Please accept this scrawl from your sincere and devoted lover. *Frank*, always.

◦ The Ladies report:

The Committee of Ladies experience great pleasure in being able to state, that the large variety and superior quality of articles presented, furnish good evidence that the Ladies of the County feel an increasing interest in these annual assemblies.

This fact leads us to anticipate a brighter, better day— a day when the industry of woman, usefully applied, shall have triumphed over indolence and *profitless* employment. For upon woman, as a being of *useful* industry, depend her happiness, her elevation, and the morals of those associated with her. Every lady has duties to perform in her own private sphere; and nothing can give her more real enjoyment than a consciousness of having discharged those duties faithfully.

Useful employment is no less necessary for the mind, than active exercise for the body. Both are required to sustain under present exertion, as well as to strengthen and mature for greater trials and more strenuous effort. When indolence governs the body, inactivity creeps over the mind. It becomes dull and spiritless, appears to have lost the elements of happiness, and evinces none of its former energy, except in seeking for one of two things, as circumstances may require: either external opiates, to drown imaginary evils, or external stimulants, calculated to create a fitful, feverish glare of happiness—happiness which soon expires, and the mind is left in the same dull state as before…

We are told with truth that "there is beauty all around our paths," and all may cull the flowers; yet experience, that potent tutor, tells us that in this life the sunshine, the cloud, and the storm, rapidly succeed each other, and in order to be prepared to meet the changes of life, we should early acquire a thorough practical knowledge of all its duties.

Without industry, no woman can attain the position for which she is designed. There are those who plead as an excuse for their want of intelligence, that their domestic, or other active duties, require all their time. This should not, need not be. We are not required to cultivate and strengthen the mortal, to the total neglect of the immortal. Every individual should devote a portion of each day, to reading such books as would be calculated to call forth and awaken into energy, latent principles of thought, which may be improved and matured by future examination…

In conclusion, your committee would remark that if the views which they have advanced be just— and they hope they are—the Ladies of this County must feel deep gratification for the institution of this Society, which generously smiles upon, and greatly encourages female industry. Untrammeled by those invidious distinctions caused by imposing titles and high sounding pedigree, as well as by any false standard of superiority, we are free to reward and appreciate true merit, without regard to name or station.

The scene which is about to close has been a happy one; yet we look forward to a brighter, happier scene than this—a day when woman shall banish indolence from the fireside; when a correct taste, and a mature judgment, shall give elegance to plainness, combine beauty with utility and economy, and when the influence of woman shall be, like that of the moon upon the ocean, —unseen, but felt, —in the *noiseless* but *dignified* duties of her home.   —C. McKie.
—From the report of the Washington County Agricultural Society, *Washington County Post*, October 27, 1846.

Catherine's father, George McKie, strongly disapproved of her giving this report and having her name and the report published in the newspaper.

Troy, Nov. 4th, 1846, Wednesday night, 11 o'clock.
My Dear Kate—   In compliance with your request and my promise I herewith return to you *the letter* which has given us both some unhappy hours.

You have explained to my *full satisfaction* why you penned such a letter and I now hope and trust that you will not for *one moment* harbor a single painful thought in regard to it. Although my neck was bowed down for a while I now walk erect and elastic in the hope and promise of future joys. Yes Kate, that same love which I have so long cherished for you still burns with a pure and quenchless flame and believe me when I tell you that my letter of Aug. 27th was a "candid one" *without* the slightest "coloring of imagination."

That I had a delightful ride after leaving you on the bright and charming morning I need not tell you— for how could it have been otherwise? When the sun shone out with unusual splendor upon all nature clothed in the garb of autumn presenting to the eye a scene truly grand and sublime. As I glided swiftly along over hills and dales towards my much loved home I could think of little else but the happy happy hour I had just passed with you that made an impression upon my memory which never can be effaced. In a few minutes (as it seemed to me) after I left you I was with my friends at Hoosick. As I expected I was asked some questions in regard to the route which I took to get there so early in the day. I *frankly* told them that I came via Cambridge (a fact which they would have soon learned from some other source) which I thought the better course. My visit at home was necessarily *short & sweet*, only 4 or 5 hours— a longer one next time I hope… Good night Kate and may our affection for each other be deep-rooted, sincere, and growing which I trust it is. Affectionately your, ever faithful and true, *Frank*.

Thursday, Nov. 19th, 1846.
My Dear Kate—   …I must confess Kate that I can hardly reconcile myself to *this sly way* of corresponding and when I think of the time that must elapse before I can see you. I am half (if not more) inclined to believe that it would be better for us both to let your folks know the feelings that we cherish towards each other and ask their approbation which I hope and pray too, they may be pleased to grant. I will not argue this but merely suggest the idea, leaving it entirely with you to act as you think best. I now think I shall go up home and spend Thanksgiving and I assure you it would give me much pleasure to return via Cambridge and make you a short visit, which pleasure I must forego until the *proper time* arrives. I am as usual hard at work over Journal & Ledger, day after day, week after week & so on. When it will end I know not. Business has been such this fall as to require my whole time and attention. I hope for cold weather soon to close navigation, when I shall have a little more leisure. I know you will write me the first convenient opportunity which I hope may present itself soon… Your sincere and devoted *Frank*.

Wednesday evening, 6 o'clock.
Dear Frank—   I have just been told by Ed that he could take a package to you if I wished him to do so. Last evening he did not know that he would have time. A month since I received "said letter" from you, read it, and then gave it to the flames. I trust it will be forgotten by both. Two weeks since in a note you expressed a dislike to this "*sly correspondence*," I can but agree with you. Truth and good intentions require no covering and yet Frank I cannot think of giving publicity to what *we only* are acquainted with, not even my Mother. It is far

this sly way of corresponding Francis Thayer and Catherine McKie exchanged these letters without the knowledge of her parents.

more for her sake than my own, that I would keep it from her. How can I give her any uneasiness now on my account. Wait 'till I see you again, and then you can tell me your best method of arranging matters. You need not fulfill your promise of sending a note in each one of the periodicals unless you choose. I would love to hear from you, yes and *see you very often* but I do not wish you to do anything merely to gratify me, which you very much dislike particularly when there results no *real* lasting benefit to either. However I must hear from you once more before you come home in winter… I should have written before, but I have had no opportunity. Henry has been in Troy but had not time to "take a package." …Ed says he is waiting for my "bundle of books," so good bye this time. Your own *Kate*. —I am perfectly well.

Thursday afternoon, December 17th, 1846.
My Dear Kate—   …In regard to giving publicity to our affairs, I have only to say that your own wishes should be strictly adhered to. Yes Kate, I love you and your dear Mother too much to ask you to take one step that would give her any uneasiness on your account at this time. When I see you we will talk over this matter if we have an opportunity. We will for the present move along in *quiet loveliness* at the same time having an eye on the many bright and happy days which I trust we may be permitted to spend together. Glad was I to hear that the "said letter" had been given to the flames— a wise disposition of it. I think it is my wish, as well as yours, that it should be forgotten for I am quite certain that there was nothing in that I have the least desire to remember… —Ever thine faithful & true *Frank*.

A Summary of 1846:
Feb. 16. Mother quilted
Feb. 18. Finished the quilts. At work on four quilts about 18 days.
March 10. F. S. Thayer
March 11. F.S.T. left in the aft.
April 20. Libby Beadle came here, went to [illegible] and procured plants, returned & took tea. Lib went home.
May 18. Br. G— left New York for China.
Oct 24. F. S. Thayer came
Oct 25. F. S. Thayer and Ed went to Church
Oct 26. F. S. left.
Nov 23. Ed went to Glens Falls.
Nov. 24. Henry went to Troy on horseback
Nov. 25. The first snowfall. Dreadful wind storm.
Nov. 26. Ed returned. Sleighing
   —*Excerpts from the 1846 diary of Catherine Sophia McKie.*

1847

February 22, 1847. Pleasant. Started from Troy in the stage for Hoosick, arrived home about 1 o'clock, found our folks all well, also my friends in the village. Was glad to get home— all it lacked to fill up the cup of pleasure was good sleighing…
   —*Diary of Francis S. Thayer.*

April 19, 1847. Monday morning.

My dear Kate—   I have passed a long night in painful thought— such thoughts as I once cast from me. I felt myself the happiest man on earth. I have thought of everything that has been said or written on this subject which weighs heavily on my mind at present. Kate, when I am gone, I wish you to review the past, lay the whole matter before your dear Mother— make up your mind and write me the result; which I pray God may be such as will make me the happiest man on earth. Is it right that we should go along in doubt much longer. I can write no more. Anxiously awaiting your reply I subscribe myself your sworn and devoted *Frank*.

Troy, May 5th, 1847.

My own dear Kate—   I waited long and anxiously for your letter of 22nd which was not received till the evening of the 28th. I almost dreaded to receive it for it was to convey to me so much of joy or disappointment. I had staked my happiness on my love for you and you had answered in words of sweet response that you loved me… I have had some dark and gloomy hours in this my *first* and *only* love. At one time I almost despaired of winning your affections and at the moment when I had given up all, a few words from you broke the gloom— the clouds rolled away and with a joyous heart I saw and hailed the light of a new day— it was fair and beautiful for with it then came your smile, your welcome, your promise of love. This was almost a new being to me and I have lived in it ever since. And now Kate shall I not always live in it? …In your letter you desired me to write you a good long letter which I am happy to do. I could find no time to write before this evening on account of having more business than usual. I am very busy in closing up the business of my old employers and commencing the business of *Howland, Bills & Thayer*. You will of course excuse the delay. This is a long letter and I will leave you to decide whether it is a good one or not. I have only to say that it has one merit and that it is a *true one*. Kate I want you to write me a good long letter. You can't tell how happy I shall be to receive it— just say how soon I may visit you— name the day. I want to see you more than ever.   —Your own devoted *Frank* always.

July 2, 1847. This is a yellow day. I would like to get away into the country but cannot at present. Hope to about the 17th this month & then won't I have a good time…

July 17. This is a scorching day indeed. Started from Troy with Mr. H's man & our wagon about 11 o'clock… Arrived home about 1/2 past 4 P.M. found friends all well and glad to see me…

July 28. Weather continues fine. Just the kind of weather for harvesting the abundant crops which this County is again blessed with…   —*Diary of Francis S. Thayer*.

Troy, July 31st, 1847.

My dear Kate—   …O Kate— you can't tell how happy I should be if I could hear from you once a week and see you once a month. How long before this state of things may be brought about? I leave it with you to decide. With no small amount of pleasure shall I improve every opportunity of writing to you and I shall expect you to write to me in return… Kate don't say that you can't write to me for such is not the case. If I could write half as well as you can I would promise you a good long letter every week. You write *just exactly* to suit me and that is enough when you are writing to me. Next time you are writing to me, if Miss Thomas asks you to put out the lights, just tell her to go to sleep and dream about her *sweetheart* if she has got one— if she has not, it is *high time* she had… When I commenced scribbling on this sheet of paper I did not think of getting as far as the fourth page, but here I am and here I will stop. If I was not quite so sleepy I would fill up this page and then copy it and make some attentions for the better as there is much need of. But here you have it, just as I have scribbled it off, without much thought. So good night. Sweet dreams & happy thoughts to thee   —Your own devoted *Frank*.

August 21, 1847. One of the loveliest days that ever smiled upon the earth— not a cloud to be seen, the air is cool & refreshing. Busy at work…   —*Diary of Francis S. Thayer.*

Sep 3.
Dear Frank—   I have just been told by Ed that he is going to Troy… Had I known that I would have an opportunity to write you today I might have written more than I am now. Your notes (how welcome) have been received and I only wished that I could answer them verbally. In response to your visiting here before the end of Oct, I can say this, I shall attend the State and perhaps the Rensselaer Co. Fair if nothing prevents… but if I should not see you at either of these gatherings, I would like to see you here about the last of Sep… The truth is Frank, many gents come here much oftener than you do, and about some of them & myself there are sundry memoirs; now I can not deny myself the pleasures of seeing you occasionally… How often I have thought of you these quiet, moonlit evenings. I never so much enjoyed a summer as I have this last, most beautiful one. Ed is ready and has sadly *crumpled* this scrawl trying, or pretending, to *see* its contents. He returns tomorrow. Write by him will you not? Tell me what you think of my plan.   —Yours always *Kate*.

Troy, Sept. 3rd, 1847, Friday evening, 10 o'clock.
My own dear Kate—   I have just rec'd your note from Ed. Glad indeed was I to learn that there is a *fair* prospect of meeting before the last of Oct… I don't know as there is anything going on here worthy of note save the heat of the Eternal Sun beating down upon the brick walls and stone pavements. I would like to be in the country about three days— O the green carpet that God has spread out for those who live far from Cities. I would like to cast myself upon it and look up to Heaven and thank Him for the summer's verdure and the summer's shade… I want to see you very much. My thoughts are always with you.   —Your own true *Frank*.

Troy, Oct 30th, 1847, Saturday evening.
My own dear Kate—   I left the store a little earlier than usual tonight rejoicing in the hope that tonight's mail would bring me a letter from my own dear Kate. I hurried on up to the P.O. with a light heart & buoyant step almost sure of the rich treasure. But on looking into Box No. 40— "lo and behold" it was empty. I was not a little disappointed. I assure you for I had said to myself all the week— Well this is the last week in Oct & I shall see or hear from Kate

this week sure... I have no notion of letting an opportunity pass without reminding you that there is a certain young man in the City of Troy by the name of Frank Thayer who thinks more of you than he does of all the rest of creation and that he is very anxious to hear from a certain young lady up in Cambridge. Who do you guess it is? Well to tell you the plain truth— it's Kate McKie & "it's nobody else." It is now some seven weeks since I have seen or heard a word from you. This is my third letter (you can hardly call them letters) and I do hope you will not let it remain long unanswered... I am waiting to hear from you before naming the time when I shall be up to see you. You know my feelings on this subject & I will be governed as your own good judgment shall dictate. Now Kate be sure and write me soon & remember that I am more than ever your own *Frank*.

Troy, Nov. 25th, 1847.
My own dear Kate—   ...This morning Mr. Bills and myself drew lots to see which should go to hear Dr. Berman's Thanksgiving Sermon. As fate would have it, it fell to my lot to stay in the Office and attend to business. I quietly seated myself at the desk and waited till about sermon time & then got a man to stay in the office and I walked over to the church, slipped in slyly, took a back seat, and then remained *chained to my seat* for nearly two hours. I will not now attempt to give you even a faint outline of the Doctor's discourse. It was grand indeed and worthy of the Doctor... Kate how much do you suppose I would give to see you tonight?— To take you by the hand, to meet those lips and to call you my own. Why I would give anything in the world... In a little more than two weeks I shall hope to see you & then what a grand time we will have— the thought of it makes me happy. I hope we shall be alone awhile Monday night. Now Kate don't forget to write to me soon. I have a hundred things to tell you— amongst others is this, that I love you better than ever—   Your own *Frank*.

December 2, 1847, Thursday eve, 10 o'clock.
My dear Frank—   I am all alone now, and of course my thoughts are with you... Now *do not* think that I do not enjoy writing to you. I know but one greater pleasure, and you can guess what it is. Is there nothing that you are in duty bound to do, that you try to forget, until the very moment arrives, in which your task must be performed; and when that moment comes you go about it— soon your task is completed and you find yourself in a very happy mood and realise in fact, that the very thing to which you looked forward with dislike, has really afforded you much enjoyment. Well, if you are so situated, you know precisely how I feel. Letter writing is the *bane* of my happiness as regards my duty to friends, and a neglect of duty is ever staring me in the face to mar my happiness. But when I commence writing to one I love, as now, in a few moments I seem to see them, to take them by the hand, and after a few moments I am only surprised that I receive no answer, and then comes the thought that the Lord and remembered, are far away. Well, Frank I give you permission to write an essay on *Snakes* or *serpents* as you please, a [illegible] earthy subject I grant, but a sufficient return for this dissertation on writing.

I believe that you have given me your views in reference to writing to friends on the Sabbath, and asked me what I thought on the subject— Well as I look at it now, it seems to me that all thoughts which may be verbally expressed on the Sabbath with perfect propriety are equally innocent if expressed on paper, but neither of us I believe would think it right to use the Sabbath as a day "very convenient," as I have heard some remark, for keeping up a general correspondence with friends. I hope and trust dear Frank that we value the privileges of the sacred day too much to spend it so. This afternoon I heard Mr. Jones preach, and so headless and pointless was his discourse, that I could get but this one idea from it, that the Kingdom of God, and the Gospel of God are synonymous— so you see that I have but little to reflect upon as regards the sermon… Thanksgiving passed off like *any other day*, more of that when I see you. Write here by Ed if you wish to, and tell him when you will be here… Good night ever more. Oh if I could see you. Yours, *Kate*.

Troy, December 12th, 1847.
My own dear Kate—   The elements have conspired against me and I cannot see you tomorrow as I had so fondly anticipated. So I must do the next best way— and I will write you a letter. I shall defer writing an essay on "*Snakes & Serpents*" until I can find nothing else to write to you about; and think you my dearest that time will ever come? I know your answer will be, "no." I shall always have a story of love to tell you and though I may tell it a thousand times over, I will try and tell it in a different way so as to make it more interesting to you than an *essay* on "*Snakes & Serpents*." …My sheet is nearly written over and I have yet a thousand things to tell you. Oh that I could see you one hour tonight— the time is coming when I can see you every day and night and then we will be happy… I am glad that our views in regard to writing to each other on the Sabbath coincide. I don't believe I could have spent this evening any better than I have. Now Kate I have written you a long and loving letter— perhaps it is too loving— if it doesn't' suit you tell me so for I can write in another style… Good night my own dear Kate.   —More than ever, your own *Frank*.

December 21, 1847. At Mr. McKie's, Cambridge. Staid in the house all day or till 5 o'clock when I started for Hoosick after enjoying one of the happiest times anyone ever enjoyed. Never have I enjoyed myself so well before. Every renewal of my association with that family makes them to me dearer. Was invited by all to come again as soon as I could. Had rather a cold ride home, got home about 7 o'clock. Spent the evening in calling on friends. Was asked any number of questions about my visit at Cambridge— all of which I answered as I pleased.   —*Diary of Francis S. Thayer.*

A Summary of 1847:
Feb. 15. F. S. Thayer
Feb. 16. F. S. left
March 10. George Wilson came home.
March 26. Rain & snow, dreadful wind
March 27. A perfect hurricane
March 28. Bright & clear
March 29. Breaking roads
April 17. F. S. Thayer & Uncle William
April 18. All at home
April 19. F. S. Thayer left in the aft.

A souvenir from China. A small lacquered box brought back from China by George Wilson McKie in 1847.

October 24. All at home— dark & gloomy without. Pleasant & cheerful within.
Nov. 16. Went to Troy.
Dec. 2. Rainy & very warm.
Dec. 3. Father went to Salem. Uncle William here.
Dec. 20. F. S. Thayer. Attended Dr. Mosher's funeral.
Dec. 31. …The year is about to close. This with other years has gone from the earth forever…   —*Excerpts from the 1847 diary of Catherine Sophia McKie.*

1848

≈   About a letter:

Troy, January 2d, 1848.
My own dear Kate—   With all my heart I wish you a happy thrice-happy New Year— rather late, but "better late than never." In my last "short note" I asked you if my style of writing suited you. I again asked you the same question when I last saw you. Your reply was "I will let you know when I write to you." I have since heard nothing from you so *I am still in the dark*. However, I shall keep on in the old style. Our loving communications, my dear Kate, are not to be restrained and I hope there is *but one* opinion in regard to the freedom to be used in the interchange of feeling. The pleasure I take in receiving & writing to you my dear girl is the pleasure of heart responding to heart, akin to that we enjoy when together, and does not that surpass all that we are blessed with anywhere else? …Kate I have thought much about "*the letter*" since my return, and the more I think of it the more I wish for the time to come when you may *think it best to present the said letter*. Or if you do not wish to present it just say to me that I may send something of *that sort* by mail. I am aware that it is a delicate subject to broach but just think my dear Kate how much happier we should be if the matter was settled as I pray God it may be soon. I cannot think of opposition on the part of your Father. No Kate, I shall not have it, shall I? …Now my dear Kate, just remember how punctual I am and write me soon.   —More than ever your own *Frank*.

Troy, January 16th, 1848.
My own dear Kate—   Many thanks for your *kind* note per Ed. Every day for a week past I have *looked anxiously* for that letter which you said you should write "the first suitable and convenient opportunity." Which I hope may present itself soon, *yes, very soon*… What do you suppose your father would say if he knew all about our affairs? Suppose you *hand over that letter* and see what he will say. I hope and trust nothing— only what we would have him say. Many no doubt, unacquainted with the joys of *true love,* would say that it is foolish business to *get in love*. But we Kate can give them the *lie*— till then they know nothing about it… I have noted with some care the different ways in which men seek for enjoyment. And amongst the young, the pleasures of society and friendship is one of the greatest sources of happiness. But if the bosom thrills at the name of friend, what emotions will fill it when the heart has learned to love? …Now Kate *observe how faithful* I have been in writing to you and answer this as soon as *possible*. May I not expect an answer this week? Good night my own dear Kate. Your own forever *Frank*.

Troy, January 23rd, 1848, Sunday evening.
My own dear Kate—   Has the appointed time arrived yet Kate? Or according to established rules ought I to wait a week longer? …With regard to "that letter," I must say that it is my *honest* opinion that the sooner you hand it over the better. Will it be any *easier* to deliver it two months hence than it will in one hour after you receive this? I cannot see that it will. I am aware that it is a very delicate matter and am not surprised that you *dread woefully* to say a word about it to your parents. I can wait till I see you "*once more*" if you say so. *I hope you will not say so…* Just think favorably about "that letter" —won't you my dear Kate? Give it to your Mother first for she is not wholly unacquainted with our affairs. Now Kate do answer this just as soon as possible— this week won't you. I don't know as there is anything going on here that would interest you, so I will bid you Good night and go to bed. I subscribe myself *Your own Frank*, ever faithful & ever true.

Cambridge, January 28th, 1848, Friday, 11 o'clock.
My dear Frank—   …Now Frank do not think hard of me if I say that I felt that I cannot present it now, do not think either that I would not rather consult your wishes than my own however trying it might be to me at the time, if I thought it would make any *material* difference. In this case I can hardly think that a few weeks or three or four months would do so. The same uncertainty hangs over us that ever has. I am only certain of one thing, of the sincerity and fervor of my regard for you. Every day and week that passes but bind me more closely to you— and now I will answer your question in a letter written about three weeks since— That wherever others may be, whatever others may say, you will always find your own Kate with you in thought and feeling… I can write no more. Good bye your own *Kate*.

Troy, Feb. 6th, 1848.
My own dear Kate—   Your last was received a week ago this morning and it came as ever Kate, thrice welcome. It was a *first rate* letter Kate, long & loving— that is the kind. Isn't it rather singular that I haven't another correspondent who *can write* such letters as you do? …Now, if it should happen that the sleighing should not last till Saturday you will not see me. Now Kate you must not think that I feel hard towards you for not presenting that letter. *No. No. No. No.* I do not. More about this when I see you. If I did not expect to see you soon I would write more. Good night my own dear Kate. *You are Frank's more than ever, a good deal.*

February 12, 1848. Very cold at Hoosick. Spent the day in visiting friends. All of whom I found in good health…
February 13. Very cold but pleasant. Went to Bennington with Liz to Church— heard two very good sermons…
February 14. Beautiful day, sleighing first rate. 11 o'clock started for Cambridge, found my friends at home and such a good time as I had I have not room enough in this book to describe.   —Diary of Francis S. Thayer.

Wednesday evening, 6 o'clock, Feb. 16, 1848.
Do not write *that* letter until you hear from me again. I would write more but I have not been up a moment today, and am now writing sitting up in bed. Nothing but a *very bad headache* and cold.   —Your own *Kate* as ever.

Troy, Feb 18th, 1848, Friday evening, 11 o'clock.
My own dear Kate—   I cannot let Ed go home tomorrow without taking a few words to you from your own Frank... I hope & pray too that you will be quite well when you get this. It seems to me Kate that you have a good deal more of the headache than you used to have... Kate I wish I could be with you when you have such turns of the headache. O if I could only be with you at such times and sit down by your side... I would give anything if I could see you tonight. I must close. Good night dearest. More than ever your own *Frank.*

Cambridge, Feb. 20, 1848.
My dear Frank—   In your unexpected but *very welcome* letter received yesterday by Ed, you say that you shall expect to hear from me by Monday's mail. I will not disappoint you... Besides I had not read the copy I have in some time, thinking that I would read it over with you, when you came, but I did not. You know I spoke to you of one slight change, I have now looked over that letter, and see nothing else to alter unless it be this one trifle. I merely suggest the alteration, leaving it to your better judgment to decide. You say in the first place. 'Custom of duty' and so on. You then say, 'A reciprocal attachment exists between— and myself, which has induced us to exchange the vows of marital love.' You tell the truth, and the whole truth, and surely your own Kate should not be the one to teach you to keep back the truth— but would not parental advice seem to be more *strictly consulted* if nothing were said of vows on our part. Would it not be better for Father to suppose that no vows had been exchanged... I would not even have him think for a moment, that I would make any binding promises that would permanently affect my happiness, without consulting him. I would not, I could not, do anything that might have the least tendency to make him think that his wishes have been un-cared for... These are my reasons, and I merely suggest the suppression of the last clause of the sentence— 'A reciprocal attachment exists between— and myself'— does not that *completely tell the whole story on both sides.* Do as you please. I can trust you at all times. Just let me have undisputed possession of "Old Sarsaparilla" (Have I spelled that word right?— if not, tell me in your next) and I shall be happy. Now that I have said all I have to say about the letter, I suppose you wish to know when to send it. All I have to say is this— that I wish you to send it just as soon as is convenient after you receive and read this. If it must come, and Mother and you say it must, why the sooner the better... Your own *Kate.*

❧ The Letter:

Troy, February 24th, 1848.
Mr. and Mrs. George McKie—
Respected Friends—   Custom and duty demand that I should make to you a disclosure which concerns alike the happiness of your daughter and myself. A reciprocal attachment exists between Catherine and myself. I therefore as in duty bound solicit your favor to my suit and assent to a union when situation and circumstances shall render it proper. I make the request at this time in order that a correspondence and intercourse desirable to both may receive the sanction of parental authority and advice. You know my char-

acter and disposition and should you deem me worthy of the hand of your daughter it will ever be my highest aim to merit the alliance. With the highest respect and esteem I am, as ever, your obedient servant, *Francis S. Thayer.*

Troy, February 27th, 1848.
My own dear Kate—   …Well my dear Kate have you seen or heard anything from "*the letter*" yet, or have you observed anything unusual in your Father's looks or actions. I reckon you have by this time for the said letter was altered as suggested by you and mailed last Friday morning. I hope and pray too that on the *third reading* it will pass by a unanimous vote. I shall look for an answer next Tuesday evening. I dare not think of opposition for I know not how I could *stand it*. If I get a favorable answer to *that letter,* and the traveling is pretty good, I shall be up to see you two weeks from yesterday P.M., that is if you have *no objection*… But the icy chill has gathered upon a nation's heart and there is weeping all over the Country. I refer to the death of Mr. Adams [John Quincy Adams, 1767–1848]… I think that letter was much better after altering it as you suggested… I did not say that *that letter must* be submitted to a third reading soon. I only said I thought it would be better to have the matter settled before long and I still think so. Kate, I did have the blues between the reception of your two last letters. How often did I wish that I could be with you but as you say, it could not be… Now my dear Kate just take care of yourself and think of me as always your own *Frank.*

I have only one excuse for writing such a *prosy* letter as this— that is I have got a horrid toothache which would stop me from writing to anybody except my own dear Kate.

Cambridge, March 7, 1848.
My dear Frank—   It is now after 12 o'clock and I can write you but a few lines for I must be up in the morning early… Niel leaves early in the morning for New York… Your very kind and good (not prosy) letter was received in due season. It did not read like a letter coming from one who had the toothache. Indeed I think you must have forgotten it just at the time. I never had the *vile ache*, and cannot *really* sympathize with you, but for your sake I heartily concur with all that Burns has said. You ask me if the letter was received by Fri. mail? It was— at least I saw it and gave it to Mother Friday eve, and I presume it was soon read. Now Father has said nothing *directly* to me in reference to it. I suppose that it would have been answered last week had not Father been very much engaged. And now as to what it contains, I am perfectly dependent on you for information. The truth of the matter is just this, I think— Since the day that you left here, I have not been very well any of time. I think I took cold that morning, but what if I did. I shall soon get over it… Mother and Father, they seem to think that because I am somewhat subject to the headaches, and have not been very well for the last three weeks, that I am in a deplorable state of health. Now from what I have heard said, I believe that in the letter, no objection is made whatever, but I think that some bit of sermon is made to my health. Let me know will you not? …This morning I received word from Uncle James McKie saying that he would come for me on Thursday, to go home with him, to stay a few days— he will return on Friday and I suppose I must go with him. You know now Frank that I would dearly love to see you and yet I honestly believe that you had better wait at least

two months… I must say no more except to ask you to write by Ed. I have scrawled much but written nothing. You deserve something better in return for your last. But good night, pleasant dreams, and happy waking thoughts to you.   —Your own *Kate*.

—I persuaded Mother to let me have the letter to deposit, and although it may seem a little strange, I send it with mine instead of by the mail.

 The Response:

Cambridge, March 6, 1848.
Mr. Francis Thayer—   Sir, your letter was duly received and I do not know but that I have violated the rules of modern etiquette not returning an answer at an earlier day— but in answer to your request I cannot say that we have any reasonable objections in relation to your entering into a correspondence with Catherine provided it has its origin in mutual affection. Anything further than a correspondence at present would, when taking into consideration the delicate state of Catherine's health, be considered by us imprudent and rather premature.   —Respectfully yours etc. *George McKie*.

Troy, March 23, 1848.
My own dear Kate—   "Better late than never." You would have heard from me a week or more ago had you not said in your last that you were soon intending to spend a few days from home— so I thought it would be just as well if I took a few days *grace*… Kate, you were right in your suspicion that allusion was made to the state of your health in your Father's letter which was received with yours. It grieves me to the heart to know that you are suffering at all. But I am consoled on this point by your own assurance that you are not seriously ill. The letter of your Father's allows a correspondence but says that nothing more can be thought of in your present state of health. I could have wished for an *unqualified* assent but I suppose we must "take the good the Gods send and watch the clouds"— this is the old maxim… How much I always gain by being with you. I never go away from you without feeling that my heart is *fuller* and *stronger* and my hopes *firmer* and *fonder*. The seed that is planted needs the sun every day. Cover it up, the earth grows dry around it, it may sicken or die. Let it have the dew and sunshine of each morning and it will spring up in life and beauty. Don't think that I am sentimental or that I fear that our affection will die. I only mean to say that the oftener we meet the better we shall love each other. But you are the best judge of this and I shall yield to all you say. Your wish in this matter shall be my law, and I shall school myself as well as I can, and this is best after all, for from your Father's letter is it not certain that he will ever consent that you may leave him for me… It is now March— let the spring pass away— April and May— *long long* months they will be to me. And then I think in all propriety I can come and see you early in June. And the fond greeting may have the double joy of long absence. It is hard for me my dear Kate to bring myself to this, but I see by your suggestions that you would rather it should be so. In the meantime we can keep up a correspondence as often as we have during the past six months. My sheet is almost full and I must close…   —Good night my own dear Kate. More than ever your *Frank*.

When Francis Thayer had first met Catherine McKie, years before in Poultney, Vermont, she was wearing a white muslin dress with a pattern of little pink sprigs. When they became engaged, he asked whether there were any pieces of that dress in existence. A remnant was found amongst the odd pieces of material always kept for rag carpets, and Francis carried a small piece of it in his wallet until he died.

Cambridge, March 28, 1848, Friday evening, 9 o'clock.
My dear Frank—   Friday you know is deemed an unlucky day, but Friday last proved a perfect gala day to me— and why? —Just because I received such a good letter from you. It was almost four weeks since I had heard from you, and that is a long time for me. I have read your letter a dozen times or more, and not once without feeling sober enough. I think that you must have been sad from some good cause, for you saw only the *darkest* side of the present and future— and this is unusual for you always have said *hope on* to me. Now do not think Frank that I wish your letter had been different, no, I love you the better for it, sad though it made me. I only regret that you do not look upon things concerning us as I do just now. I think my exposition will be better than yours. We will see. You say that Father's letter allows only a correspondence now— you wish that it had been different, and finally almost concludes that Father will never consent for me to leave him for you. I understand it very differently. Perhaps because with my parents all the time and know them better. Had Father entertained any objections in my respect whatever he would have talked with me on the subject. As it was, he said nothing to me directly. Nothing more than a sly insinuation occasionally. Again, he allows only a correspondence now, and not even that unless it has its "origin in mutual affection." You cannot believe Frank that a *kind* Father would sanction a correspondence prompted by reciprocal attachment only, and at the same time intend to give a death-blow to all the hopes of happiness which might arise from that intercourse…

   When Father wrote, he and Mother both thought that my health was such, that he could not think it best for us to meet frequently unless I got better— (When he sees me eat now I wonder what he thinks.)— I honestly believe that a headache, once in two weeks, will be a sufficient excuse in Father's estimation to ward off the consummation of affairs until the proper time arrives. Not that he will make any objection in the end, if I am well, but he thinks that I cannot be spared, and that the only way to keep me will be to allow of little intercourse between us. I have not heard him say this, but I know that he thinks so. However, I think we can convince him that we may meet occasionally, and be happy in the performance of duty. You say that Father's letter and suggestions in mine have made you conclude not to come until June. Now my dear fellow, I do not know what I wrote you except that I thought you had better not come in two weeks as you spoke of, but I had not the least idea of waiting until June. My heart aches when I think of it, and even now it seems as if I can hardly consent to it… When you come here the weather can be talked over, and I think that Father can be made to believe that we are in no haste to change the even time of our lives, except it may be in seeing each other more than once in three and a half months… It is not pleasant for me to be separated for so long a time, but if it is best, it must be so. 'Tis true the oftener I see you the more I wish to be with you— but my affection Frank, while I have the right and privilege to cherish it, will neither "sicken nor die" —as you say.   —Your *Kate* always.

April 16, 1848, Sabbath evening, 10 o'clock.
My dear Frank—   …I believe too as you say that there need not be, perhaps should not be any restraint in our intercourse but Frank I have more

than once told you that it was a long time before I would believe that there was one living, who was dearer to me than my own Mother, and now since *I can doubt it no longer,* I can hardly grant it to myself, except when necessity requires me to speak in regard to our matters, and then courage comes easily… I cannot tell you the half of what I feel towards you. I cannot even tell myself— but I can "sit and shut my eyes" and think of you until my heart bounds with gladness— until it seems that to be with you would be happiness without alloy… Expression teaches us that joy and sorrow are ever mingled, but I believe that he has least of sorrow who acts "heart within and God o'er head"… Well my dear fellow just excuse this essay, and I will trouble you with no more this time. Ed leaves home tomorrow for Ohio. I shall send this by him to you. He is to be absent three or four months. I feel lonely already, for, of all my brothers, he seems most to me like a sister, I can go to him with less restraint than to my other brothers, and he has ever been so very, very good and kind to me, that it is very hard to bid him good bye. I fear that I cannot write to you as often now as I have done, unless I mail my letters at our Office, which, you know that I hardly like to do. But be assured that your Kate will send you a scrawl as often as she can. She only wishes that they could contain better matters. In regard to July instead of June as the time for you to come up, I shall hear nothing of it now. June, *to* me, is a *long way off*. We shall see when summer comes, something new may appear…   —I only wish you were here, *Kate*, more than ever.

Most of the entries in the diary are seven lines long, but this entry is sixteen lines long and very difficult to read. There are first eight lines written regularly, and then the diary was turned upside down and the next eight lines are written in-between the first lines.

May 1, 1848. Pleasant, wrote up books in AM… About 1/2 past 9 heard a cry of fire… burning every building on River St… whole amount of loss will be 150,000 dollars. We shall lose about 1,500 over insurance. About 3 o'clock another fire broke out in the upper part of the city, at both fires 34 houses burned…
May 4. Fine weather. We are now all settled in our new office & ready to do business…
May 5. Beautiful weather, the pleasantest day of the season so far. All nature is putting on her green robe & the trees are in bloom. Amount of loss over insurance is $3,691.25 according to statement made out this day…   —*Diary of Francis S. Thayer.*

Troy, May 7th, 1848, Sunday evening.
My own dear Kate—   …I suppose you have seen an account of the terrible fire we had here last Monday night. I will not dwell on this subject for it is by no means pleasing to me. Our store was completely destroyed, saved only our most valuable books and papers and a few articles which we threw out of the back doors and windows, a part of which were stolen before we could carry them to a safe place. Luck another time I hope never to see. Our loss over insurance will be $1,500 or $2,000. We have taken another store (No. 159 River Street) and shall go on with business just as though nothing of the kind had happened. I felt "sorter" bad for a while but I am all over it now. Lost my dog & cat, both were burnt. I worked so hard that night that it made me almost sick. Am now much better in health and *spirits.* When are you coming down here? I heard that you was here a few days ago. I don't believe you would come to Troy without letting *your own Frank* know it, would you? *I reckon not.*

Cambridge, May 8th, 1848.
My own dear Frank—   I have just received and read your letter of last evening, and it seems to bring you nearer to me. When I think that you were

writing to me so few hours since, and that now, I can talk to you again… You say that you heard a few days since that I was in Troy. I have not been in Troy since last November. I shall probably be down in the course of three or four weeks and shall try to see you if I can… By the way, did you ever hear the story that I was married to a somebody who had lived here about the time that Islando Lee was married? It seems that my name was confused with hers, and I had the credit of the affair to a considerable extent… —Your *Kate*.

May 27, 1848. Beautiful weather, could not be more so. Busy at my desk all the A.M. When Bills came from dinner told me that Kate McKie had been at his home… I immediately went to Mr. Bills' & waited till Kate came back 1/2 past 2. Spent 3/4 of an hour with her… —*Diary of Francis S. Thayer.*

May 28, 1848, Sabbath morning.
I am sober tonight and indeed have been all day, and just for this reason I wished to see you and could not, for you are not here… The earth is turning with life and beauty, the skies are bright above all day long, the air is filled with fragrances and melody, and the cheering voices of kind friends are ever in my ear and yet amid all these my very heart is far away… One word in reference to your last best letter— It came in the evening: after reading it again and again, I watched the stars awhile, (*we will study the Geography of the heavens together*), left the blinds open and laid down to sleep. I had pleasant dreams that night, and was wakened in the morning by two doves tapping on my window with their beaks. I called it a good omen, and believe me I was gloriously happy that day. So good night to you dearest Frank, thoughts of you tonight will bring a bright and sunny morrow.
    —Monday morning. I told you that I should feel better this morning, and so I do. All things look fairer, and two weeks does not seem an age to me. After leaving Troy Sat. eve, my thoughts were all with you, but you know that it would not do for me to have your company home, oh no, that would *make a talk*… Now Frank, this letter is done. I just heard a knock at the door, and have received an old acquaintance of Mother's, a Miss Richards, who has been South teaching some ten years or more, has not been here in some fifteen yeas, and of course must and should receive every attention we can give her. Mother is not well… Goodbye— Do write me once more before you come.   —Your own *Kate* as always.

June 16, 1848. Very warm & sultry. This is my dear Kate's birthday. She is 21. I wish I could celebrate this anniversary by being with her…   —*Diary of Francis S. Thayer.*

Monday morning, July 17th, 1848.
My own dearest Kate—   Your good letter of Saturday morning came to hand in the evening and would have been answered last night but for the reason I had a *horrid* headache, and no lover ever sought the idol of his heart more eagerly than I did my pillow last night. I wished a thousand times that I could give you a better letter to read tonight but I could not. So of course you will excuse me 'till next Sunday evening as I shall be alone in business this week and may not feel in the right mood to write you a long letter after working hard all day in the office… My friends in Hoosick are all getting better. Adin is able to ride out. Lib & Port just able to sit up in bed a few minutes.

I now think I shall go home to make my summer's visit in about two weeks. Will write you more about that in my next... —Your own affectionate *Frank.*

Troy, July 23, 1848, Sunday evening.
My own dear Kate— You remember dearest what I said to you in my last, and now I shall fulfill and you know with how much pleasure I always write to you... I well remember the severe thunder-storm we had a week ago last Thursday eve. My thoughts were with you constantly and if I could have been with you in person I would have taken you by the hand and drawn you close to my side and said to you— Remember Dearest Kate that there is One who watches over us in storm and in sunshine and let us put our trust in Him and all will be well with us... High-ho, a week from next Wednesday I intend to leave these brick walls and stone pavements for a ten-day visit in the Country. And where do you think I shall go— Well I will tell you for I reckon that you are somewhat interested. Wednesday go to Hoosick. Thursday P.M. come up to see you. Yes, you my dearest Kate. Friday proceed north to Glens Falls, Lake George etc. and return to Hoosick the first of the next week... Do write soon, very soon and be very careful of your health. More than ever your own *Frank.*

August 14, 1848. Very hot...
August 15. Weather continues very hot, about 90°...
August 16. Hot as blazes...
August 17. No let-up on the weather. Hot as ever... Terrible fire in Albany, 5 or 600 buildings destroyed, loss estimated at 2 or 3, 000,000. The whole city was threatened with destruction. 6 o'clock it commenced raining and checked the fire...
August 18. Rainy AM...
August 19. Cool & pleasant... went to Albany to look at the ruins and such a vast field of ruin and devastation I never want to see again. —*Diary of Francis S. Thayer.*

DREADFUL FLAGRATION — *Most of the business portion of the City in Ruins. Hundreds of building and millions of property Destroyed. Our city is literally desolate.* A fire broke out at about noon yesterday, in a stable in the rear of the Albion Hotel, corner of Broadway and Herkimer St., between Broadway and the river. The wind was a gale from the south, the heat of the weather and the fire intense, and everything dry and combustible. In an inconceivably short time, the fire spread over a wide surface, prostrating everything before it. The efforts of the firemen, aided by the Troy, West Troy, Greenbush, Arsenal, and Schenectady companies, were directed as well as they could be under such appalling circumstances, but they were powerless against such an amazing force of flame, of raging wind, and the fierce hat of the wide-spreading and all-consuming element... Full four hundred buildings are consumed, and property probably not less than two or three millions, although no estimate of value is yet attainable... The area of the fire embraces many acres, perhaps fifty or sixty, of the most compact and valuable part of the city... —*Albany Argus,* August 18, 1848.

The Burnt District was visited yesterday by throngs of citizens, and many from abroad. It is a scene of desolation never before witnessed here, and we trust we many never look upon the like again. A view of it from the roof the Exchange presents a vast field of ruin and devastation. —*Albany Argus,* August 19, 1848.

Cambridge, August 27, 1848, Sabbath evening, 10 o'clock.
My own dear Frank—   Your very excellent letter written a week ago this evening lies before me— as yet unanswered, and now it is 10 o'clock— and Mother's "Don't' sit up late Kitty" is even more in my ear… I should have written you last week if I could have found an opportunity but company at home and the sickness of friends used up the week so closely that you were neglected, but not forgotten night or day… You say that you have never been "so happy and so sad, as since you last visited here—" and ask me if it is not so? Now my dear fellow, you have by your own acknowledgement been convinced of the truth of what I have been telling you for some time about frequent visits. I have always told you that it was better for me not to see you often, with all the uncertainty of the future before us. As you say the pang comes not with the last word or look, but 'tis when sights and hearing fail to bring the idol near— when I am left to myself, that such a *dreary loneliness* rising from the very depths of the heart serves to cast a shade of melancholy over my mind. Of course I *shake it off* as soon as possible and guard against it again as well as I can, but *these are hours* when it seems to me that I can hardly wait your coming… Yesterday I received a letter from Uncle James. He says he is coming for me a week from Tuesday— that we are to visit Salem, and attend the wedding of a cousin in Argyle, and what more I cannot tell… I do not write a very long letter tonight for I must be up early in the morning. So good night to you dearest and nearest…   —Your own *Kate*.

Troy, Sept 3, 1848, Sabbath evening.
My own Dear Kate—   Your *most admirable* letter of last Sabbath evening came to hand Tuesday eve and now it shall be answered. It was a good letter Kate, and not only *good* but *kind* and *loving*— such a letter as I think you like to write to me and such as I am sure I like to receive… When I look around among those of my acquaintances who have been coupled together I cannot but think that some of them are "unequally yoked together." There does not seem to be that strength of affection, that overflowing of happiness, which I am sure will be exhibited when you and *your own* are brought together. From all that I have observed in my intercourse with those who are pledged to each other, I am led to believe that we love each other better than most others do. *Has this idea ever struck you*? You ask me if I recollect what I was writing two years ago— Yes, my dear Kate, I well remember that letter which revealed to you my *love*. I shall never forget the 27th day of Aug and the 19th of Sept 1846. The time between the above dates I will not speak of now. Only to say that whatever passed between us is all *settled and promised to be forgotten*. Yes dearest, you have since made it all up. Notwithstanding all our *reasoning* and *good judgment* I cannot deny myself the happiness of seeing you oftener in the future than I have in the past… My own dearest Kate I would not be *guilty* of visiting you *too often* and on the other hand I wish from the bottom of my heart that I could visit you as often as once a month. I know that you would be glad to see me every day and it is only for our *mutual benefit* that you would have me use a little more *discretion for awhile*. What say you to my coming up Saturday 16th Sept! Nothing I am sure would suit me better… I have been to Church twice today. Heard one of Mr. Halley's best in the A.M. and it's *equal* from Mr. James of Albany this P.M. Dr. Berman is out

of town so I have a *perfect* right to run away to other churches… I must now close… —Your own *Frank*.

September 11, 1848. Delightful weather. This is my birthday, 26 years old— good health, bright prospects and everything around me to make me happy and indeed I think I am as happy as any one that I am acquainted with… —*Diary of Francis S. Thayer.*

Cambridge, Oct. 1, 1848, Sabbath evening, 9 o'clock.
My own dear Frank— I have just learned from Bro. Henry that he is going to Troy tomorrow. He made me acquainted with his intentions before the whole McKie clan, adding that if I wished to send a letter, I had better write it, for he intended to leave early. I said yes… It is often said that girls seldom fully appreciate the kindness and comforts of home until forever separated from that home— that few justly estimate the value of a Mother's advice and encouragement even in the most trivial affairs— and I fully believe it. I know that it is so in regard to myself. When here I do not know my own dependence, but if I am from home a week, I have scores of questions for Mother when I am home again… I have just been looking over your letters and find one dated Oct. 1, 1845— a very good letter written just three years ago tonight. You say in one place, "It would please me greatly to hear from you now and then." Well I hardly thought it all time then, and will not say that I think it time now. As I did not answer the letter at the time, I will just notice it now… I have not been to Church today, have spent most of the time reading… —Your *Kate*.

Cambridge, Nov. 12, 1848, Sabbath evening, 9 o'clock.
My own dear Frank— I have taken a letter sheet and yet I am inclined to think that I should have commenced on note paper; and why?— for this reason— It is now 9 o'clock and I must be up early in the morning. You and the promise I made you a week ago have been in my heart and before my mind in every waking hour… Mother has not been able to sit up today, is somewhat feverish and chilly by turns. I have been trying to do something for her during the day, but she is much the same this evening. I hope she may be better tomorrow. Since I have returned I notice that Mother coughs a good deal in the morning— she tells me that her lungs seem somewhat oppressed. I shall not be easy a moment until her cough is removed. Oh, my Mother I could not live without her… We have had two or three very cold days and now the ground is white with snow, as *one I love too much to tell wished*. I am very careful, and am perfectly well, never as well in my life as for two months. A week ago this very hour we were alone and tell me, was I not happy? With you I am always so— What would I give to bring you here tonight? I believe our spirits commune with each other, and that is joy… I would rather see your own dear self, than all others, I love you better after every greeting and good-bye. Now Frank, do not scold me if I stop writing just in a minute. I do it out of kindness for you, and besides Mother's, "Do not sit up Kitty, for you will have to be up very early in the morning," has some influence on me, just excuse this perfectly awful scrawl and when I write again I'll try and do better… —Your own *Kate* always.

Troy, Nov. 19th, 1848, Sunday evening, 10 o'clock.
My own dearest Kate— Two hours & a half ago I came to my room for

the purpose of writing to you. I had hardly got my fire fixed & seated myself before Gil Robertson came in, and I have had to make myself as agreeable as possible under the circumstances. Every minute I wished he would start, but no go. I suppose if I had told him that I wished to write to my own dear Girl he would have left me alone much sooner. Well Kate, as late as it is, you see I have commenced at the top of the page and, if I have *good luck,* shall fill up this letter sheet with something and if it is an awful scrawl I hope you will excuse it. You will won't you? ...I am grieved to learn that your dear Mother is not as well as usual. I hope that I shall soon hear that she is much better and I pray God that she may live many long years in the enjoyment of health & happiness. I found my friends at Hoosick all well and happy. Three hours I passed with them the day I left you... What a political hurricane we have seen since I last saw you... The tall oaks that had stuck their roots deep in the soil of corruption have bent before the storm of popular vengeance. I trust the good Whigs will use their victory like men— they have labored like good soldiers to obtain it...   —Once more good night, Your own *Frank.*

political hurricane Zachary Taylor was elected President on November 7, 1848.

December 6, 1848, Wed. afternoon.
My own dear Frank—   I have just leaned from brother Peter that he is going to Easton for Ed's lecture... Well, as to how we are, Mother has suffered very much with the pain in her shoulders all this week, had a very bad night last night... As for myself, I suffered a good deal Monday night with the pain in my side, yesterday could not sit up at all, but have been up nearly all day today. Otherwise I am perfectly well... I am happy to say that the rest of the family are perfectly well. It has rained here for the last forty-eight hours. I am glad that I do not depend on the bright blue sky for my enjoyment. I never wanted to see you as much as I do now. I think of you all the time. I think we are doing very well now as regards the sick. Edwin makes Mother's bed, and Henry makes mine. The Irish girl does up the cooking in *French style,* so you see that we are doing very well. When we all get well and can make you comfortable I shall say "*come,*" with many thanks for your kind offer. Peter has come and I can write no more. Your *Kitty.*

Troy, Dec. 7th, 1848, Thursday P.M.
My own dear Kate—   Yesterday morn your *precious* letter of Sabbath eve came to hand and I cannot *begin* to tell you how much *joy* it gave to me. I hope and trust you will soon write me that you are all well again and then I shall come and see you. My own dearest Kate— What a happy meeting that will be for I can *hardly* wait for the time to come, but as you say, "I must make the most of my present comforts."...I haven't time this P.M. to answer your dear good letter and if I had plenty of time I haven't the power to write what you deserve for that most *excellent* letter. Write soon and remember that I am your own *Frank*... I have *strong* hopes of seeing you in a little more than one week and may not write you a long letter before that time... Goodbye for this time. Your *Frank.*

Troy, Dec. 10th, 1848.
My own dear Kitty—   This has been a very dark, rainy, gloomy day corresponding with my feelings for I expected a note from you this morning and was disappointed. I fear that you are worse or you would have sent me

a word… You wrote me a note Wednesday P.M. containing the good news that you were better than you were the day before. My own dear Girl, you do not know with how much anxiety I look for a word from you concerning the state of your health. I think of but little else these days and can say with you "I never wanted to see you as much as I do now." You need not write long letters, no Kate I would not have you sit up to write me as late as you did a week ago tonight. I was fearful that the pain in your side would come on again after writing such a long letter… There is a good deal of talk here about the Cholera in New York. Up to yesterday morning about 30 cases had been reported and nearly half proved fatal. The dreadful scourge seems as yet to be confined (with the exception of one or two cases) to the ship *New York* which brought it to our shores. I pray that this awful calamity may not come upon us. I heard yesterday & today that there was three cases of small pox at Miss Willard's Seminary. About half of the scholars have left and such a state of excitement never was known in the institution before. I hope the young ladies are more frightened than hurt. Did you ever see such weather as we have had for the past week? Nothing but rain, rain, rain and mud, mud, mud. I am sick of such disagreeable weather and hope for a change soon… My dearest Kate I would give anything if I could see you tonight. Do let me hear from you *soon very soon*. Good night Kitty. I am *more than ever* your *Frank*.

Cambridge, Dec. 12th, Mon eve.
My own dear Frank—   Your good letter of last evening has just been rec'd. I need not tell you that I am much cheered by these letters and kind notes from you, coming when words of love and comfort from you are more than ever welcome. You say that you expected a line from me by Fri's mail. Thurs I exercised too much, and had a night of suffering to pay for it. Had I been well I should have sent you a remembrance. Mother has suffered more pain every day since I wrote you last until today. She has rested better the last three nights. Today she has been easier, has not set up any since she was first taken. She can walk, but a sitting posture brings on the most excruciating pains in her shoulders. Dr. Hale from the Bridge, in whom we have much confidence, says that it is neuralgia and perhaps something of rheumatism, that it will be some time before she can be well because so worn out body and mind during the last four or five weeks. In regard to myself, you need not be alarmed…   —Your *Kate* always.

Troy, Dec. 14th, 1848.
My own dear Kate—   Your very kind note of Mon. eve. came duly to hand Tues. eve for which please accept a *thousand thanks*. I am *right glad* to hear you say that you are going to be *lazy* and get well as soon as possible. Now my dear Girl do not, as soon as you get a little better, throw off that *lazy* fit (which I know is so unnatural for you) and go to work and get down sick again. You won't will you? I think I hear you say *No*… The cholera excitement seems to be *totally eclipsed* by the "Yellow fever" or rather Gold Hunting in California which is all the rage nowadays. I haven't taken the fever yet— shall give you due notice before I leave this part of the country… Four to six new cases of Cholera occur at Staten Island daily. Only one case in New York City yet and this one was immediately sent to the Hospital… I hope this dreadful pestilence may be arrested before it hurries thousands of human beings to the grave. No more cases of Small Pox at the Seminary since I last wrote you and

Gold Hunting   The discovery of gold in California was first reported in the *New York Herald* in August 1848. By 1849 over 100,000 gold seekers from all parts of the United States and many foreign countries had gone to California.

of course the great excitement somewhat abates… I cannot close this letter without telling you that you must be *very very* careful. I hope and pray that you and your dear Mother will soon be well. Your own *Frank* always.

Cambridge, Dec. 17th 1848, Sabbath eve.
My own dear Frank—   It is now after 11 o'clock and yet I must say a word to you as Ed goes to Troy tomorrow morning… Your dear good letter, just like yourself, was received this eve or aft, rather as we had the mail earlier than usual from the Office. Your letter does me a *world* of good. I cannot tell you how charming they are to me… Yesterday morn, Mother said for the first time that she felt better, and today she says that she really thinks that she is a little better… Until yesterday she has had no appetite. Now, she eats a little and I hope and pray she may soon be well… I have been looking at your *likeness* and how have I wished that I had the *original* by my side. *My very heart aches to see that original* but it cannot be yet… Oh, how wisely is the future hidden from us— how well that we may not raise the veil, and see the joy and sorrow with which coming years are laden… I do not know when I may say "come" to you. I only know that it will be as soon as I can do so. All fear of the Small Pox with us is over, yet few can come home— in reality there is *not the least* danger— the house is thoroughly purified. Would that New York were as free from cholera. I pray God that the awful disease may be arrested now in the bud… —*Kate*.

Cambridge, Dec. 31, 1848, Sabbath evening.
My own dear Sam—   …My heart tells me tonight that I have not much improved the past year, of a hundred things done and undone— all wrong. I wish I was a better girl— that my heart, my very thoughts were all right in the eye of that heavenly Father who has so graciously watched over me thus far through life. I have had countless blessings— the comforts of home, of parents, of kind friends, have been around me, and last but not least I have, I *trust*, been blessed with your love, thoughts of which shed joy around my heart, not only when all is sunny overhead but most, when this my light of life is dearest— in the lonely hour of sickness, when the heart must receive rather than give consolation. I wish you my dear Frank the happiest New Year you have ever seen. If you could be with me tomorrow I *think* I should be thrice happy… and believe me when I tell you— you are dearer to me than *ever before*. Yes I never loved you as I do now. —Your *Kitty*.

Sam Francis Thayer's middle name was "Samuel," but it was seldom used.

Troy, Dec. 31st, 1848, Sabbath eve, 9 o'clock.
My own dearest Kate—   We gave the parting hand and *kiss* without making any definite arrangement who should write first. Now Kate if you should wait for me and I should wait for you to write it would be more than "six weeks" before we should hear from each other by letter and such a state of things would be *intolerable* for us. Mr. & Mrs. B— might get along with it, but we can't. I have written you so much nonsense of late perhaps it would be nice in me to keep silent for a fortnight at least, But my dear Girl you are so near & dear to me I cannot let this last morning of 1848 pass without saying a few words to you. In the first place let me tell you "*Frankly*" that I love you more than I ever can begin to tell and the knowledge that you love me as well as I do you makes me happy, thrice happy… Here I am comfortably seated in my pleasant room (no smoke tonight) and I thought it would be as sweet a fare-

Mr. & Mrs. B Mr. Bills was Francis Thayer's business partner.

well to the Old Year as I could have to commune with you for a few moments. How I wish that I could spend the first day of 1849 with you… Yesterday I went down to Albany to witness the presentation of a magnificent gold sword (cost $1,700) to General Wood by Gov. Young. All the military companies turned out here and in Albany and such a turn out of citizens must have been very gratifying to the Old Hero. I volunteered to go down with the City Corps as Paymaster. I put on the uniform of an officer and it was remarked by not a few that I never looked so well before in my life. I guess they didn't see me when 18 years old & Captain of that Company of Green Mountain Boys. We now have firm sleighing and should it last two weeks you may expect to see me… Now a Happy New Year to you my own dear Kate. May you always love me as well as you do now and may many many years, long and happy, pass before we live in another world. I have no doubt that we shall love better there than we do here but this love on earth is dear, is sweet— is it not Kate? Now dearest let me hear from you soon very soon and often and let me have good tidings too and once more a happy, thrice happy new year to you with all the love of your own *Frank*.

—I broke my gold pen the other day so I had to take an old quill pen which will account for the perfectly horrid appearance of this scrawl… If you can't read this letter send it back, and the next time I write you I will take a little more pains. I must now say good night and wish you again a happy New Year. Your own *Frank*.

A Summary of 1848:
Jan 9. Snow for sleighing, cold.
Feb. 14. F. S. Thayer
Feb 15. Bro. Niel went to Troy… F. S. T. left
Feb. 16. A very bad headache, could not sit up at all.
March 17. A very pleasant quiet day.
March 19. Alone all day.
April 17. Ed went West.
May 26. Headache all day.
June 10. F. S. Thayer
June 11. Went to Cam— to Church
June 12. F. S. Thayer left in the morn. A bright & beautiful morning.
June 15. …Br. Niel came home.
June 16. My birthday…
June 19. Br. Niel left in the morning.
August 10. F. S. Thayer
August 11. F. S. Thayer left in aft.
—*Excerpts from the 1848 diary of Catherine Sophia McKie.*

1849

Cambridge, January 7th, 1849, Sabbath evening, 10 o'clock.
My own dear Frank—   It is late to begin a letter to you, for I have a world of thoughts for you always and now I have a heart full of the warmest thanks to offer you for your last best letter written a week ago tonight… I have been to Church today. Mr. Scales' text from Ecclesiastes (11:9): "Rejoice, O young

man in thy youth and let thy heart cheer thee." His sermon was good and so plain that I easily think I could give every idea advanced by him. Henry says that Allison B— took notes— I cannot think it, and I pity the head not capable of taking in that sermon. I call it good because it would be *generally* understood, and better appreciated than a discourse pondered by real thought and study. Perhaps I do not see this in a proper light. The truth is that he, being a young man, a Minister of "great promise," fills the eyes of all the scheming Mothers in the congregation, and no one can receive too frequent visits from him. I am much amused by the remarks I hear… In regard to your coming up here before you go home, which will be in the course of three weeks, you say, I would like to ask you one question: Did you not *know* what I would say about your coming up here this week? Now Frank I think I need not tell you that I should be glad to see you every hour. You knew that long long ago and yet I think that I must wait until the month has passed away and then you will make my heart glad on your way to or from Hoosick… Br. Ed has gone to bed sick with a cold. I have done everything for him that he would let me do, and I hope that he may be better in the morning. He tells me that the reason I wait on him so willingly is because I want him to carry a letter to you tomorrow… I'll write no more, or rather one thing more—that Mother continues to gain strength… Your own *Kate* who loves you so much.

Troy, January 21st, 1849.
My Own Dearest Kate—   …I hope Kate that you have concluded to go with your own Frank to his sister Liz's wedding. Don't, my dear girl, mind what the gossiping community may say. But let your own good judgment be your guide. I would like *very very* much to have you go, still I shall not urge the matter. Do as you think best and I shall be satisfied. I hope I shall not feel as bad at Liz's wedding as I did at Mary's. I well remember my feelings more than six years ago when my sister Mary was married. All at once it rushed upon me that I must bid her *good bye* for a long time and that she was going far away to a new home and could not be what she had been to me— a sister at home. And I tell you when I took her by the hand and said good-bye to the Dear Girl, my heart and eyes were fuller than parting with friends ever made them before. It came upon me all of a sudden. I let the feeling have its way and in a short time I was quite in a different vein thinking what a fine fellow she had got for a husband and how instead of dropping tears in the opening path of her love and happiness, I should ring a merry round in her bridal ear and wish her all the happiness this world can afford. I hope to see this dear sister next summer. Our folks at home will feel bad to have Liz leave home, and no doubt there will be some *wet eyes*. As far as I am concerned I am glad that she is to be married and coming here to live. I shall then have a place something like home to go to, such a place as I have not been accustomed to visit often for many years. It is now ten years since I lived at home, and I must say that I am getting *dissatisfied* with this way of living. And often *long* for that happy home of *ours* where we shall be so happy. Won't you take pity on a poor fellow without a home? Did you ever think of the happiness that will be ours when we shall live together? I have thought of this much and only wish that the time was nearer at hand. I am ready any day. I think that I have heard you say that you don't believe in long engagements. I don't either *so we agree*… Now don't fail to take care of yourself and always remember that

I love you better and better every day of my life. *Adieu* my own Kitty for this time, —Your own *Frank*.

Troy, February 1st, 1849.
My Own Dearest Kate—   Your charming little note of last Sabbath eve came duly to hand Monday eve for which please accept many thanks from the heart that loves you above everything else. *I love you more and more…* My Sister Liz and her husband (how strange that sounds) arrived here last Monday and have taken rooms, at Mrs. Roberts', No. 30 2nd Street. I have called on them every evening thus far and it really does my heart good to see them so pleasantly situated and so happy. I only regret that I am not a *married man* myself… About 5 o'clock this morning I was awake by the bells ringing for fire. I looked out and saw a very bright light in the immediate vicinity of our store and I assure you I was a little *frightened* and not many minutes elapsed before I was here on the spot and found all safe. The fire was on the block below us— destroying a "ruin hole" and three or four old wooden houses. A number of poor families were turned into the street, houseless and penniless. One poor man I heard begging this morning for fifty cents to buy his children some shoes, saying that he had lost everything— scarcely had time to escape with their lives. I have just this moment heard that a negro boy had been found in the ruins, burnt to a crisp— this is horrid… The appearance of this scrawl is good evidence that I am in a great hurry. Would write more if I had time.   —*Frank*.

February 19, 1849. At Mr. McKie's. Very cold, up 8 o'clock. Niel & Ed went to the Point to take the stage for Troy. Spent the day till 6 o'clock with Kate & nothing wanting to make me happy but Kate's good health. Hope & pray that she will be better soon. Spent the eve at home with my good Mother. Had the *blues*.   —*Diary of Francis S. Thayer*.

Troy, March 9th 1849, Friday evening, 1/2 past 11 o'clock.
My own dear Kitty—   …Kate you must let me know when you go away from home and remember and write me as soon as you get back and what do you suppose I would like to have you say to me? Something like this— "My own Frank never mind about staying away *the eight long weeks* but just come up and see your own Kate who wants to see you 'not a bit' but 'a good deal.'" There is my sentiment… I think of you the whole time and long for the time to come when we shall live & love together. Next Sabbath eve I will try and write you a letter as I promised, *not merely to fulfill a promise but because I love you dearly, tenderly & truly*. Good night Dearest Kate.   —Your *Frank*.

Troy, March 11th, 1849, Sabbath evening.
My own dear Kate—   Now for another letter and really, to tell you the plain simple truth my dear girl, I am somewhat puzzled to know what to say first. If I could have a seat by your side this still quiet Sabbath eve I could tell you much more than I could put on paper from this time till tomorrow morning— and in a better style too. I would in the first place take you by the hand and give & receive the same sweet kiss of love and then we would talk of love and what we are to each other, which is nothing more nor less than all in all… Kate— I imagine that you are now (1/2 past 8 o'clock) engaged in writ-

ing to me one of your sweet letters. Now Dearest, just think how much paper, ink etc. we might save if I could just step in and spend the eve with you. But this cannot be so we will go on with our letters… I have ten thousand things to say to you but it is getting late and I must close this scrawl and take it to the P.O. My dear Kate just give me one kiss— there I have it in imagination. When shall I have it in reality? You will of course be very careful & take good care of yourself. Your own *faithful* Frank says truly that he loves you more and more every day. Good night Dearest Kate. More than ever your own *Frank*.

Cambridge, March 11th, 1849, Sabbath evening, 9 o'clock.
My own dear Frank—   Are you really writing to me now? If so, is it not to be regretted that we are separated by twenty long miles— for were you here, I should be relieved from the burden of writing. (*You know that I hate to write letters.*)… I regret to hear that Charlie V. Scharnick is married, and particularly to the woman he is united to for life. I attended school with her in Poultney, and understand her character exactly. I only hope that she is changed, for unless she is, she has little claim upon the affections of *his* friends, and none upon their respect. I will say no more just now, perhaps I have said too much already. But of the woman I attended school with, I *all but* hate her for this reason— Her father a minister, she a daily listener to his teachings. Her Father sent her to school, and while there she was only a disgrace to her friends, and her sex. I was in class with her and was obliged for my own sake to teach her civility, while at the same time I felt degraded by the association. This may account for my dislike. I know that it is not a proper feeling… Should I not rather pray for any one than give way to weakened feelings in regard to them… I am perfectly well now. Mother has been sick today, but is better this evening— only a headache… Your *Kitty*.

April 13, 1849. Cloudy & very little rain. Went to Waterford to see about some flour barrels… George McKie took the *Empire* for NY to seek his fortune…
—*Diary of Francis S. Thayer.*

Troy, April 16th, 1849.
My Own Dearest Kate—   I have just seen Ed who tells me that he is going home tomorrow morning and I have no doubt he will think it a little strange if I don't hand him a note for you… Do you have any idea of what I am going to say? Well my *own* Kate— 'tis nothing more nor less than this. I love you with my *whole heart* and am *well satisfied* that that love is returned. And my dear Girl as long as you give me such *proof* as you have for more than two years I shall never doubt you.— Doubt you my *own* dearest Kate, *no never* and I trust that you will never think of such a thing again… Did you ever see such weather as we are having now a days? I never did. You must be *very careful* and not get cold. You will, won't you? When we parted your Mother promised me that you should be careful. A week ago today we were together and *O how happy*. It seems to me more than a month since we gave the parting hand and *kiss before the eyes of your Mother*. I hope to hear from George in a day or two and then I will write you again. You must let me know from you *often, very often* and I will do the same by you a *thousand* times more than ever.   —Your own *Frank*.

Troy, May 20th, 1849, Sunday evening.

My own dearest Kate—   Here I am in my own room for the purpose of fulfilling the promise I made you last Thursday when I saw you but a moment. It was too bad that we could not have a longer time together— wasn't it? …A week ago this very hour we were together, *all alone* and O how happy. My heart if full when I think of those happy thrice happy hours. We are together in thought tonight and I imagine you up in your quiet room writing me one of your good long letters. I only wish that what I may write tonight will give you one tenth part of the real solid comfort your dear good letters always give your own Frank. Enough of this. 'Tis Sabbath evening and is it possible that we are twenty long miles apart— methinks that I am with you even now and perhaps you are thinking of me. You are surrounded by dear and kind friends but I must think that you sometimes feel lonely because I am away… Last Friday morning our normally quiet City was thrown into a state of the most intense excitement by the news of the awful accident to the Steam Boat *Empire*… You cannot imagine the gloom that was in every heart. The downcast look of the citizens as they passed along the streets and the low tone of conversation as they met in groups, here and there, all gave painful evidence that there was grief in every heart. My feelings were not such as I experienced when the ill-fated *Swallow* was wrecked for then I had a near & dear sister onboard and knew not for a while whether she was among the saved or lost. I was sitting at my desk Friday noon when a man came into the office and told me that the *Empire* was run into by a sloop and such and from 50 to 100 lives lost. I thought of Niel the first thing and the first question I asked "was she going down or coming up" and when told that she was coming up I was somewhat relieved. Up to yesterday P.M. nine bodies had been removed from the wreck and it is feared that many more will be found when the boat is raised. Just one week before this terrible accident the awful riot in New York took place. Truly, "In the midst of life we are in death."…I will now seal up this scrawl, read my Bible and go to bed. Good night Kate. I here seal it with a kiss. I shall have a letter from you Tuesday evening.   —More than ever your own *Frank*.

THE EMPIRE *Steamboat Empire Sunk. Great Loss of Life.* The first serious steamboat casualty upon the North River which it has been our duty to record this season, occurred last night by the steamer *Empire*, on her way from this city to Albany. About ten o'clock last evening, when opposite Newburgh, she discovered a schooner on her starboard bow, loaded with lumber, beating down. The wind was blowing fresh and the schooner under rapid way, when danger of collision was first apparent. The pilot of the *Empire*, Mr. Levi Smith, called out to the schooner to halt, but no attention was paid to him.   —*New York Evening Post*, May 18, 1849

The Wreck of the Empire — The following graphic and impressive account of the earlier particulars of the loss of the Empire, were addressed by a prominent physician in Newburgh to a friend in this city, and not intended for publication. The intense anxiety felt to learn anything that can be known of this disaster, has seemed a sufficient excuse for laying this communication, from an eye witness, before the public without waiting to obtain the permission of its writer. Newburgh, May 18, 1849 — 6 o'clock A. M. Gloom rests upon our village… I had just returned to my home from a professional visit about ten last evening, when a scream— nay, a mass, a column of shrieks reached me from

off the water... We made our way to the steamboat landing... We soon made our way down to the railroad crossing, and from thence to Wells's dock. We were just in time to behold the splendid *Empire* yield herself a prize to the remorseless water. What a night! ...Imagination can not convey to you our feelings; standing in safety on the shore, without any means in our power to render assistance, we were the lookers on, in this sad tragedy... At the United States Hotel we had a large number of rescued passengers. One lady with two children was lamenting the absence of two more, whether drowned or not we did not know. Another was clasping a fond little girl to her bosom, having lost one on board the boat of the age of ten months— she sat in mute but agonizing silence. We made her as comfortable as possible. One family of Ladds, from Stonington, Ct., had lost four sons, young lads— no tidings of them last night...
—*New York Evening Post,* May 19, 1849.

Troy, May 27th, 1849, Sabbath eve, 7 o'clock.
My own dearest Kate—   I have just returned to my own quiet room from a long pleasant walk on the hill east of the City and now for a letter to my own dear Girl... How delightful it is in Spring to go out into the woods when the eye is refreshed by the sight of flowers and green foliage that adorns everything around you. The ear greeted by the melody of nature's choirs warbling forth their sweet songs and the other scenes delighted by the sweet fragrance and the rich luxuriance of the season. I know that you enjoy all this, and I hope and pray that the time may soon come when we can together go out into the woods... and then if our hearts are right we shall be happy. I have thought much about what you said in regard to those two birds you saw a week ago today. Truly it was an important lesson & may we profit by it... I hope Uncle Sam will do his duty and take this to you in due course... Write often, very often. More than ever, your own *Frank*.

Cambridge, May 31, 1849, Thursday evening, 11 o'clock.
My own dear Frank—   It is not early you see, but I will not rest my head on my pillow until I have written you a word... Mother has gone to Cousin Robert McMurray to sit up with his Grandmother, my Mother's Aunt you know. She has been sick some ten days— we suppose her last sickness, she is ninety-five years of age and Mother's nearest relative. Brothers George & Peter are away fishing and I feel quite alone. I only wish that you were with me and I should be more than happy...   —Good night, your *Kitty*.

Troy, May 31st, 1849, Thursday evening, 10 o'clock.
My Own Dearest Kate—   I am always thinking of you and ever keep in mind that you have a mail every Monday and Friday. I have nothing new or interesting to communicate tonight, but write I will a few words, knowing as I do that you are always happy to hear from this fellow who loves you so *well & truly*... One thing more I must tell you that is my good Mother went to Church last Sabbath for the second time since she lived in Hoosick which is almost ten years— *this is one of the wonders of the age.* There is a great deal of talk here about the Cholera. I try to think as little about it as possible, live temperately and hope for the best. No cases here yet... This is the last day of May 1849, a month which will long be remembered, a month in which many disasters have taken place. Riots in Canada. Riot in N. Y., wreck of the *Empire*, Great fire in St. Louis, flood in New Orleans and last but not least the appear-

My Mother's Aunt Margaret Robertson, 1754–1849, who had married John Whiteside, 1752–1841. Margaret was the sister of Ann Robertson who had married Peter Whiteside. Ann Robertson Whiteside was Catherine "Kitty" McKie Thayer's grandmother. Here there is a genealogical nightmare: It is the story of two sisters, Ann & Margaret Robertson, marrying two brothers, Peter and John Whiteside. Each couple had a daughter named Catherine. The two Catherines, double-first cousins, married two brothers, John and George McKie. After the death of "his" Catherine, George McKie, a widower, married Catherine's sister, Sophia Whiteside.

ance of Cholera in New York. Who knows not what is before us— ...*Write soon*. Good night Dear Kate, sweet dreams to thee.   —*Frank*.

༄ Newspaper stories:

Reports of the Cholera at Richmond — The members of the legislature, having become considerable alarmed about the reports of cholera in this city, have made a proposition to adjourn to White Sulphur Springs. It however was not adopted. A Committee of Health has been appointed, with orders to report to the House from day to day. Several respectable physicians have assured the members of the House that there was no Asiatic cholera in the city.   —*New York Evening Post*, May 31, 1849.

The Cholera in Philadelphia — The Board of Health reports three cases of Cholera, all of which have proved fatal. Two of them occurred in the Richmond district and one by Southwark. The latter was an Irish emigrant, said to be from New York.
    —*New York Evening Post*, May 31, 1849.

Reported Cholera — Baltimore, A case of Cholera was reported in this city, but it was not authenticated.   —*New York Evening Post*, May 31, 1849.

STEAMBOAT EXPLOSION — LOSS OF LIFE — CHOLERA   St. Louis, May 30. The Steamer *San Francisco* collapsed a flue last evening while she was leaving this port for Missouri. Mr. Parker, the mate, was badly scalded, and many persons were blown overboard, several of whom are supposed to have been drowned. The steamboat *Cora*, lying alongside, was much damaged, and the captain and the crew were more or less injured by the explosion. The cholera is disappearing from the towns of the Upper Missouri, although it is said to be making sad havoc among the California emigrants on the plains. The health report of this city for the week ending the 28th has created some excitement—286 deaths having occurred, 118 of which were cholera.
    —*New York Evening Post*, May 31, 1849.

No new cases of cholera have been reported this morning. Cholera in Troy. A young man named Norton, a printer, who had worked in the office of the *Troy Daily Whig*, died of the cholera today at 1 o'clock, P.M. He was first attacked with dysentery on Saturday, which assumed the form of cholera, with violent spasms, &c. He suffered great agony. This is the second case of cholera in this city.   —*Troy Budget*, June 4, 1849.

CHOLERA New York. The Sanitary Commission reports 39 cases and 11 deaths as having occurred during the last 24 hours. Of these, 10 cases and 3 deaths occurred in the Hospital, and 29 cases and 8 deaths in private practice.
    —*New York Evening Post*, June 5, 1849.

Troy, June 3rd, 1849, Sabbath eve, 10 o'clock.
My own dearest Kate—   Your last *most excellent* letter of Thursday eve was rec'd last eve about 8 o'clock and here let me say to you my own dear Kitty that you have all the thanks & *love too* of the heart that loves you above everything else... You say that you may be in Troy an hour or two during the present week. Now Kate I don't think you can do a *wiser* thing than to come down as early in the week as you can & stay till Saturday and then I will be most happy to carry you home and such a ride as we would

have no two lovers ever had yet. No matter if we are *six* hours on the road think of this my dear Girl & do if possible come down & stay here two or three days at least… We have had no cases of cholera here yet. A public meeting is to be held tomorrow eve for the purpose of adopting some plan by which the City may be thoroughly cleaned and a fine use can be made of disinfecting agents. 13 cases were reported in New York yesterday… I hope and pray that you are well and happy this morning.   —Good-bye for this time, your *Frank*.

June 9, 1849—
I do hereby faithfully promise my own Dear Kate that ever after this date under no circumstances whatever will I use intoxicating liquor except in case of sickness. Signed with my hand, sealed with my seal, and dated June 9th 1849.   —*Francis S. Thayer*.

Written on a card in an envelope.

June 8, 1849. …took Kate… called on Mrs. Jermain. Had a fine time…
June 9. Pleasant AM and cloudy PM. Attended to business till 5 o'clock, then took Kate & carried her home— *had one of the rides* such as does my very heart good. Started 6 o'clock arrived home 1/2 past 10. Passed a *thrice* happy evening.
—Diary of Francis S. Thayer.

Jermain The reader should remember this name.

Troy, June 11th, 1849, Thursday P.M.
My own Dearest Kate—   I hope and pray that you are well & happy this lovely afternoon… There is nothing new going on here in this quiet little City. No new cases of Cholera this week that I have heard of— In New York from 25 to 40 cases per day. I have yet much to say to you but no more time to write now. You shall have another scrawl next Monday. Write often and I will do the same. —More than ever your own *Frank*.
    P.S. Do excuse this miserable scrawl. I am in a hurry, as you will plainly see by the writing. Will do better next time.

Troy, July 1st, 1849, Sabbath evening, 10 o'clock.
My own dearest Kate—   …Our City never was in a more healthy state than at present. Only three or four cases of Cholera during the past two weeks. In New York the Cholera seems to be on the increase a little. I pray God that this dreadful scourge may be averted… More than ever your own *Frank*.

Troy, July 22nd, 1849, Sabbath evening, 10 o'clock.
My own dearest Kate—   Only two days ago we were together and passed a *thrice happy* two hours for which I am indebted to our mutual friend Liz. …How sorry I was that you left quite so soon. You must have got completely drenched and I fear took a severe cold. What a sudden shower that was and how it did pour down for a few minutes— the windows of heaven seemed to have been opened all at once… Yesterday I heard good news from home. Father is much better & will soon go to Saratoga Springs where he always enjoys himself so well. Hought has concluded to remain at home until Sept & then go back to New York to a good and profitable situation… Two good sermons I have heard from Dr. Berman today, A.M. and evening…   —Your own *Frank*.

Troy, July 26th, 1849, Thursday evening, 9 o'clock.
My own dear Kate—   …Just five years ago today I was at your home for the first time. Do you my own dear Kate recollect the time? I do. What would you have said then if I had told you that I loved you? I did love you long before that time & have loved you more & more ever since. We have passed through some dark days within the past five years, but all is *bright & lovely* with us now & I pray God that our way through life may be such as will give us much happiness… I wish from the bottom of my heart that you could think that we *should* meet as often as once in two weeks. I have said & written too much perhaps about the propriety of our meeting often. I will say no more about it and try and think as you do. I am *sure* that you love me and would be happy to see me every hour…   —More than ever your own *Frank*.

July 28, 1849. Very pleasant. Jim (older brother) arrived here this morning & says I must carry him home. Very busy till 1/2 past 3 when Jim & I started for Hoosick. Drove out in 3 1/4 hours, stayed at home about an hour & then left for Cambridge, where I arrived a little past 9 o'clock. A thrice happy time with my own Kate.
July 29. (Sunday) Delightful weather. Stayed in house till about noon. Charlie B— drove up and Kate & I took ourselves to the woods where we spent a happy two hours, 5 o'clock Niel & Geo came home from Clarendon. Geo & I went to the Old Whiteside Church, Mr. M— preached.
July 30. Very warm. 10 o'clock left Mr. McKie's for Hoosick, Geo in Company with me. Took dinner at home then took Jim in & came back to Troy, came near killing my horse, it was awful hot. Jim & H— took the *Columbia* to NY. Wrote a letter to Geo & a note to Kate.   —Diary of Francis S. Thayer.

Troy, Aug 5th, 1849, Sabbath eve, 9 o'clock.
My own dearest Kitty—   …How much do you suppose I would give to be with you tonight. Why Kate I would give anything but your love for me & mine for you. Just let the mind run back one week & ask your own heart if we were not happy then. Yes Kate it was such happiness as but few, very few, experience… How often during the past week have I thought of those *bright* two hours we spent in our sylvan retreat last Sabbath— that tree which had fallen across the brook, my hat falling off in to the water— killing that snake and many other little incidents…   —I am more than ever your own *Frank*.
     —Do let me hear from you soon, very soon and often. If I write too often just say so. I will either send a paper or write again in a week.

Troy, Aug 7th, 1849, Tuesday eve, 10 o'clock.
My own dear Kitty—   I am just this moment through with the labors of the day and now let me write a line or two to you which I will drop in the office on my way up to my room… You intimate that you may go to Montreal. Now Kate you know that I would have you in the perfect enjoyment of every pleasure which this world & the hope of a brighter & happier one can bestow. But I must say to you Dearest Kate that I do not feel very well about your going to Montreal at this time when there is so much of Cholera there. However if you think there is no danger & you wish to go, why then go & I will hope & pray for your health and happiness… You must keep me well advised of your movements so that I can direct my letters accordingly…   —Good night— More than ever your own *Frank*.

Troy, Aug. 19th, 1849.
My own dear Kitty—   …I see by the papers that they are having great times in Montreal— fires, riots etc. Have you been there to witness any of these awful scenes? The spirit of Revolution seems to pervade the whole world and I think the trouble in Canada has just begun. Henry Clay passed through here last Thursday on his way to Newport. A great crowd of good and true Whigs assembled in front of the Troy House to see and cheer the old man who ought to have been made President years ago. He staid here only about half an hour. I never saw him before and it really done me good to look upon him— A Great Man that Henry Clay— A man every true Whig loves. I wish he was in Old Zach's place… I have heard three sermons today— the best one was from a young Unitarian minister who is preaching here on trial… Now Good night Dearest Kitty. Sweet dreams & happy thoughts be with you. I am more than ever your own *Frank*.

August 27, 1849. Very warm. Stayed at Mr. McKie's till 5 P.M. when I started for Troy after having the best visit in my life…   —Diary of Francis S. Thayer.

Troy, Sept. 2nd, 1849, Sabbath eve. 8 o'clock.
My own dearest Kate—   Just about this time last Sabbath eve we returned to the house from the Old Mill where we passed a thrice happy hour. How I wish that we could be together tonight… "I recon" that you are now up in your room writing to this Boy and such a dear good letter as I shall expect to receive Tuesday eve makes my very heart glad and I only wish that you could take even half as much real solid comfort in reading my letter as I do in yours. I hope to hear good news in regard to the matter referred to your Mother. You know my wishes and what I think is for the best. Now Kitty I would have you weigh the reasons pro & con *candidly* and let me know the decision at your earliest convenience. Again I ask, would it be any easier for you to leave home six months or a year hence than in six weeks? I do not wish to hurry the matter but I do really think that we ought to be married in the year 1849. Every one of my near & dear friends advise me to get married this fall, and as this advice is in accordance with my own feelings & judgment, I think that we should take up with it… We are old enough. In a very few days and I shall be 27 years old and I trust in such circumstances as to be able to support a wife… I have heard two good sermons today… My health is first rate, never better. Haven't had the headache again. How is Ed? You must make him take better care of himself. Good night Kitty. Your own *Frank*.

Sept. 11, 1849.
My own Frank—   I am about to say a word to you as I can by Br. Henry tomorrow… I have talked long and candidly with my Mother. She says but this— that she would not be wholly selfish yet she cannot let me go from her before "the time of the singing of birds has come." She says that she has never really thought of my going from home, until within a very few weeks, that she knows that it must come sometime, but she has never allowed herself to think of it… I of course was silent on that one point, and this fact, with her own hopes, made me suppose that at some *indefinite* time away in the future I would, as it were, be taken from her, and she felt, as she has often said to me, that she should not let it trouble her until she was obliged to. And now

she says that she must have time to think of it, to become familiar with the subject. Mother says too, that for years she had no female friend in whom she could perfectly confide, with whom she might share her joys and sorrows, my schooldays passed away, and I was with her, a few short years have hurried by, and now I am almost gone. "Catherine," she says, "my heart will not give you up now. I cannot: I need think of it, in a few months I shall feel differently. Tell Frank that he must bear with me in this one thing if he wishes you with him, then may he know something of the trial before me… Tell him too that I do not, cannot claim you because circumstances require you here. I do really think of that. I can only say that I cannot give you up. Tell him not to think me wholly selfish but to think it all for the best. And in justice to him say that I would not have it otherwise than it is."

   Thus have I tried to tell you Frank in few words what you wished to know, my Mother's opinion. It is as I anticipated, but not as you appeared to hope when here. When you too see and know my Mother's grief when she speaks of the matter in question, you could *not ask* her to do as you yourself wish… I feel that it is all truth when she says, "give me time" and shall feel very differently. I shall not look for a note from you by Henry. He will stay no longer than necessary in the City… Now Frank, my dearest and kindest friend, care nothing about what I have written, except to feel that it is all for the best. I believe it is this and I know, that my conscience would not let me leave my Mother while she feels as at present…   —Yours *Kitty*.

September 11, 1849. Weather continues fine. My birthday, 27 years old, hope to be married before another year rolls around…   —Diary of Francis S. Thayer.

Troy, Sept. 30th, 1849, Sabbath evening, 10 o'clock.
My own Dearest Kitty—   I must give you another short letter tonight for the reason it is late. My room is damp & chilly and I have something of a cold— perhaps should take more cold if I should sit up long enough to fill this sheet as I would like to do. I have taken the precaution to put on my thick overcoat & hat so you can see that I am careful… I was agreeably surprised to hear that Father & Mother made you a visit with Mr. & Mrs. Bills Friday. What will folks say now? Well let them talk, who cares? I don't. Mr. & Mrs. B— say that they had a delightful visit at Hoosick and at your home— never passed two days more pleasantly… O it is a joy to think that I shall see you in a very few days, and receive to my bosom the dear good Girl I love so well & truly. Heaven bless you dearest and speed the hour that shall bring us together. Good night dearest Kitty. More than ever your own *Frank*.

Cambridge, Sept. 30, 1849, Sabbath eve.
My own dearest Frank—   …You wished me to write you this evening, coaxed me saying, "That's a good girl"— Willing to *attempt* to gratify you, I came to my room, full two hours since, intending to commence scribbling at once. I thought that I would look in my box of *written treasures*, and during the last one hundred and twenty minutes, I have been looking over some of your good old letters. I find among the letters of this summer an envelope post-marked June 1st or 7th, and no letter with said envelope. It troubles me a little, I cannot find the letter, neither can I imagine in what way it has strayed

away from its enclosure. Tomorrow if all is well I'll find it, if it is to be found. I cannot bear to lose one single line that you have written me. You said in your letter of Thurs. eve that "you would send the scrawl, I might read it and then burn it." Pretty truly— you know Frank that I could not be induced to destroy a word you send me by way of note or letter. Why then will you say anything about such an impossibility?... Brother Henry is able to help himself better than when I wrote you last. He can walk about very well, for two days has laid down without assistance, but cannot rise alone. I fear that it will be a long time before he fully recovers— and yet we hope for the best. I hope my own Frank that you will find it convenient to come up next Sat eve. I have at times this week thought that I could not wait until that time without seeing you. —Mon. morning. *Patter patter* goes the rain this dark morning. I hope your mind's sky is free from clouds and darkness and I cannot but wish that next Sat aft. may be clear and pleasant! Do you know why? —Surely you do, just so that I may see my own Frank. Good bye until I see you. I hope Uncle James has a long letter for me from you know who. —Your *Kate*.

Troy, October 18th, 1849, Thursday evening, 10 o'clock.
My own Dearest Kate— I am tired and 'tis late *for a man of a family to be out* so I will only say a word or two to you my own dear good girl. What kind of time did you have going home last eve? I hope that you was well protected from the rain and did not take cold. I watched the clouds and wished a thousand times that it would stop raining, but it would come down "just as long as the boy knows his father." After you left I regretted very much that I did not say more to you about staying here until Saturday and I was almost if not quite sorry that I did not just put my foot down to say that you should not go. Wouldn't you like to see me show my authority?... Why is it that you are always in such a hurry when you come to Troy? I hope to make you contented and happy here before next February. I'll try, and think you that I shall fail to do it? Ask your own heart and then tell me. Our love for each other will always make us happy together. Have you talked with your Mother about January? If you have not I trust you will before our next meeting so that you can let me know the result. You don't know how much I think of it... My heart loves you more than ever before 'tho my letters are so *very poor*. I have been very busy today and now have lots of work which ought to be done but I can do no more tonight. If "Mr. Howland" would only do the work I used to do when I first came here my task would not be so hard. I will not complain, no I should not, for I am much better off than those who have nothing to do. I was a little mad yesterday when I found out that Mr. Bills sent Charlotte to the Store and left word with "Mr. Howland" to have me come to the house and don't you think the "little old gentleman" never said a word about it. Didn't I have some cause to be a *little mad*? I had no idea of writing half as much as this when I commenced. The fact is I couldn't stop, so please excuse me. I would give anything for one sweet hour with you tonight. One sweet kiss & then Good Night to you my own dearest Kitty. —Your own *Frank*.

November 3, 1849. Charming weather. Indian summer... Wrote to Brother Henry to start for Poultney to school next Wednesday. I have agreed to pay his expenses as long as he will go...   —*Diary of Francis S. Thayer.*

Troy, Nov. 15th, 1849, Thursday evening.

My own Dearest Kate—   Your last dear good kind letter is before me and should be answered by a better letter than you ever received from this Boy… I was thinking today what I should do if I couldn't see you only once in four weeks. You don't now think it best not to meet oftener than once a month do you? I know you don't. Nothing new here save that Mr. Howland has got a new suit of plaid. Liz says he looks like a monkey dressed up to ride on the pony as they do at the circus. You would laugh to see him… I'll just say that I love you more than ever before and stop scribbling.   —Your own devoted *Frank*.

P.S. I hope and pray too that you are well and happy tonight. You will be careful. Always remember that we must have health to make us happy. I have written in a great hurry as you plainly see…

November 19, 1849. Very rainy day. Could not leave Mr. McKie's and I was not sorry. Spent the day as pleasantly as I could wish— all sunshine & happiness indoors but dark clouds & rain without. I always have been & ever shall be happy when with my own Kate. To bed between 12 & 1 o'clock.

November 20. Dark cloudy day. Left Mr. McKie's about 11 o'clock & came to Troy in the rain… Rec'd a letter from Henry in West Poultney.   —*Diary of Francis S. Thayer.*

Troy, Dec. 6th, 1849, Thursday evening.

My own dearest Kate—   Do you know who wants to see you, talk with you, take you by the hand & give you the sweetest kiss you ever dreamed of? I will leave you to answer this question. I reckon you can guess… Well my dear Girl, how are you and what is the news? I haven't heard from you in a whole week and it seems a long month to me… Tuesday Mr. Bills had a very severe attack of the colic & has not been out of the house since. I was up with him till 4 o'clock Tuesday night. Dr. Robbins was with him all night. He is better today 'tho not able to sit up much. I must now close this & go over to Mr. Bills' to stay all night. If I could go to my own room you should have a long letter in place of this scrawl. Will write more Sabbath eve. Hope you will write soon. —More than ever your own *Frank*.

—My love to your dear good Mother. I do want to see you more than ever before. Would that I could be with you tonight— What joy would be ours. One sweet kiss, sweet dreams to thee.

Troy, Dec. 13th, 1849, Thursday eve. 9 o'clock.

My own darling Kate—   *Highho*! In a little less than forty-eight hours I hope to be with you. Yes Dearest Kitty, I see nothing now to prevent my leaving this little City Saturday P.M. and you know how glad I shall be to set my face towards your home where my thoughts always are… I have not been home in some time & I now think that I shall go from your house to Hoosick. I would like to have you go with me. Will you? More than ever your own *Frank*.

Troy, Dec. 20th, 1849, Thursday evening.

My own dearest Kate—   You will recollect that I left you Monday about 1/2 past 12 o'clock P.M. after having much the happiest time we ever had together. I only wish that I could come up this week and have another just such time. I cannot, or rather you do not think it best so I shall stay home… I cannot tell you how sorry I was that you had the headache so bad last Saturday & Sabbath evenings and you do not know how gladly I would have taken it from you— this I could not do, but you had all the sympathy a loving heart only knows. I arrived at home about two o'clock & staid till after tea. Had a short but pleasant visit, found our folks all well. My ride to Troy that night was a cold & lonely one. Our folks said that I must stay till morning as it was dark & stormy… I was very sorry to hear at Hoosick that Mrs. Ball was sick with fever… She went up there on a visit and was taken sick. She was better & Mr. Ball went up to bring her home the day I was at Hoosick. Do they not have a great deal of sickness & trouble? …I am a thousand times more than ever your own *Frank*.

P.S. How have you been this week? I hope & pray well & happy. You must be very careful. I wish that I could be with your own home tonight. How much happiness we could crowd into one short hour. You know I don't like to send you such a scrawl as this but 'tis the best I can do now. —Your own devoted *Frank*.

Mr. & Mrs. Ball Most likely Francis Thayer's grandparents as his mother's maiden name was Mary Ball.

Troy, Dec. 23rd, 1849, Sabbath evening.
My own dearest Kate—   Again I am seated in my own room for the agreeable purpose of writing to my own dear good Girl in whose presence I was so happy just one week ago this very hour… It is true that my letters outnumber yours but when I come to compare their intrinsic value I have not the heart to complain of you for not writing oftener. I could only wish that my scrawls were good letters such as would be satisfactory to myself. In my last I promised to write a better letter tonight. Well Kate I am fearful that I shall not be able to fulfill my promise for I am not exactly in the writing mood… —Your own *Frank*. P.S. Kate do you recollect the last half-hour we spent together up in "my room" last Sabbath night? I have thought of that same time a thousand times. I wish that we could have another just such time now. One thing I am going to do next time I come up to see you— go to bed before 1 o'clock. It is too bad to sit up 'til— (I don't think it would look well to write it down.) I have blamed myself a good deal for keeping you up so late. Now hear me— I am not going to do so any more. Give me just one sweet kiss, there I have it in imagination, once more Goodnight…

A Summary of 1849:
January 16, 1849. Frank left in the morning.
February 21. …Brothers George, Jimmie & Peter have gone to White Creek…
May 17. …*Empire* lost.
May 18. A bright beautiful moon. Last night the *Empire* sank— a sad accident…
August 14. …at 3 o'clock Mr. & Mrs. T. H—, Mrs. G. H— & self left in rain for Montreal. Reached there 1/2 past 7-eve.
August 15. Rose at 4 o'clock. Rode around the mountain before breakfast & visited the Cathedral. Such a prospect over a city I never saw…
October 6. Raining a little all day. Frank came at eve. Rained very hard in the night…
October 7. Frank left for Glens Falls in the morning. A beautiful day.
November 22. Peter and myself went to Grandmother's in aft.…
December 8. Busy doing nothing all the morning. Mother had some headache…
December 28. Finished pants for Father. Uncle John came with word of Grandmother's

Grandmother McKie Elizabeth Wilson McKie, 1765–1849, is now buried in the Woodland Cemetery in Cambridge. See diary of James McKie, October 26, 1865, page 332.

death. I went home with him.
December 29. Grandmother's funeral at 1 o'clock p.m. Returned from White Creek with Br. H— and Antoinette…
Grandmother McKie died Dec. 27, 1849— Would have been 85 years of age June 19.
—*Excerpts from the 1849 diary of Catherine Sophia McKie*

1850

Troy, January 13th, 1850.
My own darling Kitty— What shall I say to you? Let me in the first place tell you that I love you with my whole heart and would give much if I could only have a seat by your side for a few hours tonight… Now we are twenty long miles apart, but do not our spirits commune with each other and is not this joy indeed? I am with you in thought every hour and I pray that the time may soon come when we can live and love together. I look forward with the eye of faith to the coming spring as the *happy* time when we shall consummate our fondest wishes and plans— when we shall be linked together in those bonds which are never ended except by death. We have loved each other for years and every day we live we love better and better… I am sure that we shall be happy, thrice happy together.

The bells are ringing for fire and I have just looked out to see where it is. I should think it was down in the lower end Fourth Street. Well Kitty, as I have nothing to burn up in that vicinity and not being a fireman, I'll keep on writing to my own dear good Girl… Today I have heard two most excellent sermons from Dr. Hopkins of Williams College. Could I take a seat by your side, I would tell you something of these splendid sermons… I do wish that you could have heard these sermons, and I do hope & pray that my hearing them will not be in vain… We have not yet completed the arrangements for keeping house in the spring. We talk about it every day and I am in hopes we shall soon be able to make the arrangements I spoke to you about… I have got an *ugly* boil on the side of my neck and that or something else gives me the headache— so you must excuse this perfectly awful scrawl. Kitty, I'll promise you a better letter sometime when I feel perfectly well. My love to your dear good Mother. Good night. God bless you. —Your own *Frank*.

Troy, January 14th, 1850.
My own Darling Kitty— Your kind brother Ed has gone over to Mr. Hughes' and will be back here in a few minutes. Now as I *haven't* anything in particular to do I'll just say a word or two to you my darling girl… Liz received a letter from home today in regard to our plans for housekeeping. Our folks at home think well of it, and I have no doubt we shall have it all arranged this week. I don't mean that we shall move into the house this week but shall take a share of it. Liz says you will have to learn her many things in regard to housekeeping— you will won't you? …The weather is cold this week. I wish we had a little more snow to make good sleighing— then I would come up to your house with Liz this week. *You must be very careful in this cold weather. Now remember this* my darling Kitty. Good-bye for this time. Write soon. Your own *Frank*.

❧ A case of the flu:

January 15, 1850. Busy at the store all the A.M. & down to Albany as a witness in P.M.… Had a cold ride & took a severe cold somehow or other. On going to bed at 11 o'clock took some hot rum. Sick all night, vomited, high fever etc. etc.
January 16. Up about 10 o'clock after a sick night. Took a very little breakfast & then dressed myself… called Dr. Thomas in the eve, very high fever, headache & many other things too numerous to mention…
January 17. Another sick night, very little sleep; no appetite & I've got the blues. Dr. says I am not going to be sick but what more can he ask to come upon me to make me a sick man. Wrote to Kate.
January 18. I am getting no better very fast. Dr. doesn't attend to me as he should, comes only once a day & keeps telling me there is no danger…
January 19. Suffered a good deal of pain. Dr. did not come to see me & I don't like it… Ed McKie called to see me & I sent a letter to Kate.
January 20. Had a hard night of it last night. Sent Graves for the Dr. this morn. He came about 11 o'clock & gave me some relief… I have to keep my bed most of the time.
January 21. Was in great pain all night… Got no sleep till morn. Dr. came in A.M. & made me better. He says I must be careful for a week & then I can leave my room. Wrote a note to Kate.
January 22. I feel better this morning, not so much pain & I now think that I am on the road to renewed health… Dr. comes twice a day now & he is determined to get me up soon.
January 23. A good deal better this morning. Up & dressed. I shaved myself for the first time in a week…
January 24. Still continue to grow better… Dr. says I may go out in two or three days.
January 25. Better indeed. I am almost well…
January 26. Pleasant. Dr. called to see me in A.M. & said I might go out. Walked down to the store for the first time since a week ago… —*Diary of Francis S. Thayer.*

Troy, January 20th, 1850, Sabbath morning, 11 o'clock.
My own dearest Kitty—   I did not rest very well last night and I don't know as I am any better today than I was yesterday. I am no worse. The Dr. has just been here and says I must take some medicine this P.M. which will make me sick for a few hours and then I shall be better. I'll take anything if it will only make me well…   —*Frank*
    —7 o'clock P.M. I have kept this open 'till this time just so I could tell you that I feel better this eve. Hope you will write tonight. Good night dearest— …*Frank.*
    —Oh for one sweet kiss from my darling Kitty. You are with me in thought every minute.

Cambridge, Jan 20th, 1850, Sabbath aft, 4 o'clock.
My own dear Frank—   And you are sick my own good Frank, and I cannot do or say anything to relieve you. I am comforted in knowing you are better. I would have you always well and happy. But I am thankful that you are better… In regards to the housekeeping arrangement, I have only to say on my own part that your kind Sister Liz need have no fears on my account, that is in regard to making me happy… I should like to see Liz at any time

with you. If I do not see you before next Saturday, shall hope to see you then. I trust we will have some snow by that time… I can write no more. Brother Ed is going to Easton and I wish him to take this with him. I hope I shall have good news tomorrow from you. God grant that you may soon be restored to perfect health.   —Your *Kitty*.

Troy, January 21st, 1850, Monday eve. 6 o'clock.
My own darling Kitty—   I have just eaten my supper and would you like to know of what it consisted? Well Kate, Liz got me a bowl of cocoa and two Boston crackers which tasted very good. I say that I am better today and Dr. Thomas says ditto and what is better still, he says I may ride out tomorrow or next day if it is pleasant. We have had a heavy fall of snow which will I hope make good sleighing by the time I get ready for it. I don't know what I shall do. I shan't be able to drive my Harry until I get a good deal more strength than I have got now. Suppose you come down and drive for me. If I get along as well as I expect, I shall come up to see you Friday or Saturday this week and then won't we have a time?   —*Frank*.

Cambridge, January 25th, 1850, Sabbath aft. 4 o'clock.
My own dear Frank—   And you are sick, my own good Frank, and I cannot do or say anything to relieve you. I am comforted in knowing you are better. I would have you always well and happy. But I am thankful that you are better, and doubly so that you were so situated, that your good sister could watch over you. She has all my hearts gratitude for every kind word and deed, yet I know her kindness would be prompted by a Sister's love, not by a sense of duty… A mist or something comes before my eyes when I think of you sick, and sad fearful thoughts are ever coming up to make me but a child… In regards to the housekeeping arrangement, I have only to say on my own part that it "bears acquaintance"— Your kind Sister Liz need have no fears on my account, that is in regard to making me happy… Let her be assured then that it will be the first wish of my heart to do as she would have me in all things. The arrangement would be of advantage to me, yet I would not be the only one to enjoy or be benefited by it. I would not have her feel that my presence would impose a single restraint, or add one to the cares of life… I would like to see Liz very much at any time with you… Now my own dearest Frank, but a word and then good-bye for this time. *You will not forget to be careful.* And we will not forget to thank our God for his goodness, to ask his mercy. I wish I could be with you one hour, all alone with you just one hour. Yet we can say "God bless us when we're parted. God bless us when we're near"… God grant that you may soon be restored to perfect health.   —Your *Kitty*.

Troy, January 27th, 1850, Sabbath P.M. 3 o'clock.
My own darling Kitty—   …The Dr. called to see me yesterday morning and told me that I might walk down to the store. I immediately *bundled* up and started on rather a *slow gait*. I had to stop once or twice but finally I arrived at the store— staid there about two hours and then walked back. I stepped on the scales and was astounded to find that I had lost 20 pounds in 10 days. Almost everyone I met said to me, "You have been sick, haven't you?" "Yes a little."   …Kate I want to see you more than I can tell and if we had sleighing I think I should be with you in a day or two but as it is I may put

off coming up 'till the last of the week as I have some writing which ought to be done this week. I feel pretty well now 'tho I haven't strength to do much yet. I am careful and shall get well just as soon as I can. Suppose you come down here this week and I'll carry you home Friday or Saturday. Liz would give anything to see you. She speaks of you a dozen times every day and very often asks me if I think she can visit you in regard to housekeeping. I tell her she must do the best she can and we will find no fault. Liz says she is willing to learn and with your advice and assistance hopes to make it pleasant for all… Now Kate, write soon and often and your own Frank will do the same. My love to your dear good Mother. Liz sends her love… God bless you dearest and may He bless us both in the prayer of *your own Frank* who loves you better than ever before.   —Do come down here this week. I want to see you.

Troy, February 14th, 1850, Thursday P.M.
My own Darling Kitty—   …This is Valentine's Day and I cannot let it pass without just telling you in a very plain & simple manner that I love you with my *whole heart.* Now Kitty is not this as good a Valentine as you could wish for? I am sure you will say "Yes Francis my own 'naughty' boy."…Graves took a leave of the House today. We are to have it put in first rate repair inside & out, and I have no doubt we shall find in it a very comfortable & happy home, much more pleasant it will be for us than to board at any boarding house in the City. I think on the whole we had better take the back chamber— more about this when you come down to look for yourself…   —Your own devoted *Frank*.

Troy, Febry. 21st, 1850, Thursday evening.
My own darling Kitty—   …Dearest Kitty, are you well & happy tonight? Would that I could hear that you are so from your own soft lips. I shall expect to hear from you Saturday eve and I pray God that you may be able to say that you are all well & happy…Yesterday morning I went to Hoosick to attend the funeral of my Aunt Wilder who died Monday very suddenly of inflammation of the stomach and bowels. She had been in feeble health for some time, but we little thought she was so soon to be taken away. Last Saturday she was about the house and Monday noon was no more. This is indeed a very sudden and melancholy bereavement. Uncle Wilder and the children are overwhelmed with grief and we all feel her loss more than words can tell. She has left four children… What a loss to those children— a mother who was perfectly devoted to them. Oh that she could have been spared to them a few years longer. "God gave & he taketh away." And we should learn to submit to his will… The mail will close in a few minutes and I must close now. So Good night my dearest darling girl. God bless you and be with us both. More than ever   —Your own *Frank*.
   —Love to your dear Ma. *Be very careful.*

Troy, March 3rd, 1850, Sabbath evening, 1/2 past 6 o'clock.
My own dearest Kitty—   You must excuse me from writing a long letter this eve for I am in duty bound to go down to the Troy House to see Mr. & Mrs. Ball who have been here since Friday and I never knew it until this P.M. when coming home from church… Let me remind you that it is now March— the first month of spring. And what does this bring to mind— why

the most delightful thought and prospect of the season, this, that the *last* of April is near at hand when I hope to claim you as the wife of my bosom. Now Kate, do not start back and feel horrified when I talk about our getting married… I ask you my dearest girl if there ever will be a more favorable time than this spring. I know and feel that your home and home friends are very near and dear to you and it will be hard indeed for you to leave them. But do you not know that there is one who loves you with his whole heart and soul, and here I tell you that it will ever be his highest aim to make you happy. You have known him and loved him for years and have all the confidence in the world in him. You should bear in mind that you are not to be removed far from home and your dear good kind Mother… Yesterday I met Mrs. Stowe in the street and she asked me when I was going to be married. She said she had a particular reason for making the inquiry, said she must know just two weeks before the time. I told her I couldn't give her any information on so delicate a subject. Perhaps you can give her the desired information. I have no objections 'tho I wish you would tell me *first*… I have heard two good sermons today. I suppose you have heard one from the Boy at the Bridge. It is high time for me to close, so Good-night my darling Kitty. Love to your Mother. God bless you and your own *Frank*.

Troy, March 7th, 1850, Thursday P.M.
My own dearest Kitty—   Your kind note of Sabbath eve was handed to me by your obliging brother Ed, Monday P.M., and it has been read & re-read time and again. I have it before me now and as my eyes rest upon it my heart longs to be with you my own darling Kitty. I wish you to understand that the note paper is paid for, and all I ask of you in regard to it is to use it up just as fast as you can— always keeping in mind that I shall claim no small portion of it. It was decidedly too bad for Ed & Niel to laugh & talk to you in a *mean* way. Next time they do not conduct themselves as good kind brothers should do, why just send for me and I'll take your part and see if both can't make them behave… It grieves me to the very heart to hear that you dear good Mother gains strength so slowly. I know that she has all the care & attention, duty & affection can give and I hope, trust, & pray that she may be better, yes well soon. A heart full of love to her from your own Frank. When I see you I shall have a few words to say in regard to the *publicity* of our affairs and I hope & trust that I shall be able to *exculpate* myself from all blame. I have always endeavored to be very cautious about what concerned us more than anybody else and I do hope you will not accuse me of being too communicative in regard to our plans for the future… —Your own *Frank*.

April 7, 1850. Charming day. Kate quite sick & had to take to bed: not able to sit up a moment. Sat by the bedside an hour or two during the day and all the eve till 10 o'clock when I went out in the kitchen… and to bed near 11 o'clock.
April 8. Up about 8 o'clock. Kate better this morn & able to walk about…
—Diary of Francis S. Thayer.

Troy, April 17th, 1850, Wednesday evening.
My own darling Girl—   I have been very busy indeed all day long and I have only time to write a few words… Enclosed I hand you the key to your

trunk which I will see *shipped* onboard the stage tomorrow morning and I hope & trust that it will reach you in due time and in good order. I had a cold & lonely ride from your house Monday but took no more cold… Now Kitty dear, don't you be *frightened* when you think of the great change that is about to come over us for I'm going to make you happy if it is in my power to do so. You have all my heart's best affections and I'll try to make you the happiest of the happy. I intend to go home Saturday eve and up to see you Sabbath P.M. You'll be glad to see me, won't you? Although it will be only a week from the time I last saw you. Did you ever see such cold disagreeable weather in April as we have had for a week? I long to see a pleasant spring-like day… If you want anything here just write me & I'll bring it… Good night. God bless you & your own *Frank*.

Cambridge, April 18, 1850, 11 o'clock.
My own dearest Frank—   Did I promise to write a word to you this week. I believe so, but if you knew how well I have been this past week you would not think a message in reference to health necessary. Did you take some cold last Monday— I fear so, for it was a raw chilly day. You will take good care of yourself, will you not Francis? …My heart flutters and I want to hide my head in a good resting place when I think of the last day of this month. You know I do not say this for want of love to you, but thoughts of such a change, and more than all my lonely Mother, will come over me, and give me dreams most grave and sober. I can write but a word more now… Mother is pretty well now… God bless us with His love and our own as his children now and always.   —Your *Kitty McKie*.

Troy, April 18th, 1850, Thursday evening.
My own dearest darling Kitty—   If I am not mistaken I promised that you should hear from me on Friday and now I am seated at my own desk for the purpose of fulfilling that promise… Aaron went to New York tonight to be gone till next Tuesday or Wednesday. Liz will go home with me Saturday and I shall return via Hoosick Monday and bring her back. Should the weather be unpleasant Saturday I shall not leave the City and in that case you will not see me at your house until next week Saturday as we talked of. Today I wrote to Jim, Hought & Port to be on hand the 30th. I hope & trust they will come. This P.M. I rec'd a letter from Henry saying that he should come to the *wedding*. Now Kate, if you think of anything you want here just say so to me and I'll show you that I shall be most happy to serve you. I saw your trunk onboard the stage this morning and ere this I suppose you have rec'd it… Kiss your dear good Mother for me and tell her that I know but little difference between her and my own dear Mother. Good night. God bless you and your own devoted *Frank*.

Troy, April 25th. 1850, Thursday, evening 8 o'clock.
My own dearest darling Kitty—   Are you well and happy this charming evening? I only wish that I could take a seat by your side and hear you say "Yes Francis." As for myself I can truly say that I am now better than I have been for two weeks past. My cold is taking leave of me and am I not glad of it! Yes indeed. …I intend to have our room all in order Saturday and I hope and trust that when you take a look at it you will be fully satisfied with everything

it contains *not excepting the carpet* about which so much has been said. It is a pretty carpet and I'll stick to it notwithstanding what others may say… Jim & Hought write me that it will be next to impossible for them to come up to the wedding. Jim says that his engagements are positive and cannot leave even for a day. He also says that he is well aware that the occasion is one which calls for sacrifices but I am too good a businessman to require important matters to be neglected for any other occurrence except one's own wedding. Hought says he will certainly make us a visit when we get settled in our new home. Port will be on hand. I cannot realize that in five days I shall be a married man. I have for years looked forward to this event with joy and as the time is near at hand I have no misgivings. My prayer is that I shall be able to make you happy and here I tell you again that it shall ever be highest aim to make you happy through life. I hope, trust, and pray too that on the sea of life all prosperous gales may waft us and that we may reach in the end the sure heaven of rest. Now Kitty just keep up good courage and not feel badly about what may happen next Tuesday. Are you careful my darling Girl? Now don't work too hard and get yourself sick— You *must* not. I must close, one sweet kiss. Good night. God bless you & your own *Frank*.

New York, April 26th, 1850.
My Dear Sister—   Your favour of the 18th just came duly to hand… I have been rather under the weather with a cold this week but am now better, only quite hoarse. I find it impossible to leave here on Saturday to be with you on Tuesday next as I had intended & much regret it. I am so drove with business it's impossible to leave & be gone so long having to work night & day. The spring has been so cold that business is backward. Kate, God bless you. Tell Father I have not seen Trowbridge yet but do so on Sunday next. He lives so far up Town & never to home, it's hard to find him. My love to all.   —Your affectionate Brother, *Niel W. McKie*.

New York, April 30, 1850.
Dear Father—   [letter is mostly about a lawsuit but ends—] …I must close. My love to all. I regret I could not go up home to Kate's wedding.
—Your affectionate son. *N. W. McKie*. [Niel Whiteside McKie]

April 30, 1850. A more delightful day could not be wished for. This day is one full of interest to me & the dear good girl I am this day joined to for life. Married at 3 o'clock by Rev. T. C. McLorry, started for Troy about 5. Aaron & Liz met us. Mr. & Mrs. Bills & Hatty came in & took tea with us.
May 1, 1850. Cold & windy. Up a little before 6 o'clock & over to the store before breakfast. How strange it seems that I am indeed a married man. How dreamlike. Spent the day about my business as usual. Flour market firm & improving.
—*Diary of Francis S. Thayer.*

Francis S. Thayer and Catherine McKie Thayer daguerreotypes, dates unknown.

➣ Excerpts from the letters of George W. McKie describing his trip to California:

Friend Frank etc etc—   After two weeks of steaming we have at last arrived at the Isthmus and right glad are all of us once more to get a firm hold of Terra Firma— although the temperature of this place is a great drawback on the enjoyment anticipated— boiling heat it is. My health and spirits were never better and if Providence will continue the blessing, will remain so. We stopped in Havana two days but in consequence of the turbulent state of the times, were not allowed to land and consequently cannot write *descriptively* of the place and people. Didn't know at our time, but that we might have something to do with the raid, reports flying of all kinds, none to be relied on and you are probably better informed of the state of affairs than I am. We have about 900 passengers on board and all are acquaintances now… —*May 25, 1850*

Dear Father— After a long and somewhat fatiguing journey I have arrived here (Panama, New Grenada) safe and healthy…

Chagres is a low filthy place, defiled by all sorts and conditions of vice. Gamblers seem to be doing the most lucrative business— the natives having the most uncontrollable passion for games of chance— women and all. All I say and all surely it is as the Priests frequent the gambling table and the altar alternatively. The town is composed of low huts, covered with large leaves common to the tropics— bamboo sides, open as a crib— no floors— and pigs, mules, men, women and children lodge and victual indiscriminately. The children as bare as when born and the adults not much better clad… You cannot imagine the appearance of the forests here— one continuous impenetrable brake, vines clustering about trees in such a manner as to make it perfectly impossible to force a passage through…

…The Gold— silver, diamonds about the alter are valued at millions while the majority of the worshippers are remarkable for nothing but their squalid wretchedness. The priests who officiate number about a dozen and look well fed and sensual. There is a dozen or more services a day for ought I know— or at least a continual squalling— which they call chanting. The population of this place is about 5,000 to 8,000, mostly natives or Indian and negro mixed with Spanish blood— very few pure blooded Spanish. The Governor of the Province held a Subscription ball on Saturday night which I attended— or rather I went about 11 o'clock— walked upstairs saw a little insignificant person bowing at the door, paid him no notice, not even bowed, but walked in. When the interpreter informed me that the bowing individual at the door was the governor, whew— my exclamation was not calculated to win favor of his excellency if he could have understood it— but thank Babel he did not and I was presented to the man that a moment before I had called a *fussy little squirt*. The ball was about over and after stopping a few moments, I again shook hands with the Governor— and thot [sic] in my heart that a weak nation had well chosen its ruler and left. —*June 2, 1850.*

Dear Father— The vessel to which I was appointed has arrived and will leave this port (Panama, New Grenada) on Tuesday night and from that out my letters to you and the rest of the family will be infrequent— as it takes about two months to make the voyage, and there is no opportunity of sending by a quicker conveyance than from this place when we return.

My health has been very good so far… The agent has made me second mate of the *Isthmus* and if my qualifications had been good enough— that is if my knowledge of navigation had not become faint from long inattention to it, he would have made me capt of her, he having no confidence whatever in the present Capt.…

The officers with whom I am to be associated are ignorant men and of no force or business capacity— which will make it somewhat unpleasant, but I hope to make it a season of improvement.

This place is as remarkable for the inflation that has taken place in the price of goods etc. as California. I paid $7.50 for the washing of 20 pieces last— almost the original cost of the articles. I am paying $12.00 per week for board and not very good at that, no butter, no potatoes, no milk, and no cleanliness. On Tuesday last I went on board the *Isthmus* and took [illegible] of coal— was three days receiving— took about 200 tons at $45.00 a ton— so that you can see what it costs to run steamers on this side as it takes about 500 and over tons to make the voyage. This climate is very much like our August— that is an August day during which you have alternate rain and sunshine. Hot very hot— the rain not cooling the air but making it more close and warm— but nevertheless were the streets kept clean and proper attention paid to diet, there is not a doubt but that it would be healthy. Situated immediately on the lea and sufficiently elevated to admit of drainage, all that is necessary is a will to make it a perfect garden. All grains will grow here— corn is produced in abundance and that too by as indolent a people as the world knows. The cattle are very fine in the bone, clean build, beautifully coated and are allowed to roam at large— each owner having his mark burned on the hip. They do not get fat but still are good eating. Horses are small and good for nothing and are only used to ride— and for that, mules are considered the better and safer riding beast. Animals of all kinds are seen led about the streets here daily. Today I saw a Peccary— or Mexican hog shaped very much like a pig but limbs very slight, and covered with fur or coarse hair like a raccoon. Monkeys in abundance of all varieties and colours. Parrots salute you at every door with an oath in Spanish which may not startle you when I say that all, men, women, and children make use— and that freely too, of an oath equivalent to damn— and consider it rather beautifying to the construction of the language. This place, of all others that I ever saw, is most infested with gamblers, hundreds and hundreds of tables piled high with gold and silver, anxious faces, fixed eyeballs intent upon the game circle the tables about. Many who leave home, with scarcely sufficient to get to California, hear of the success of some fortunate fool and stake a few dimes at first and perchance win— and be betting on their luck changes— but the unfortunate fool plays on to win back what he has lost— and stops when he finds himself pennyless. Many here are in that situation…

I shall look anxiously for letters from home when I return here… —*June 16, 1850.*

Cambridge, July 11, 1850, Thursday morning, 7 o'clock.
My dearest Frank—   I have just learned from Niel that he passes through Easton this morning on his way north, and I at once concluded to avail myself of this opportunity to send to Easton as a letter by our mail would not reach you before Sat… Father received a letter from Br. George Tuesday. I was dated June 16th Panama. He wrote that he was well and should leave the next Tuesday for San Francisco. The papers tell us however that the *Isthmus* left Panama the 22nd. He says, "I am looking anxiously for letters from home by the *Falcon* which arrives in a day or two, and shall expect to hear at this place when I return which will be in about three months." How disappointed must he have

been, not one word from the home and friends of his childhood. I have nothing to say in regard to others but this willful neglect of mine in regard to writing is a sin… I must try and do right in this respect. I shall remember that a right course always brings its own reward… I can write no more now as Niel is packing and would like some assistance. So good-bye my darling Frank. Let us not forget that this life is but the beginning of an eternity of years for which our hearts tell us that we should be prepared… My kindest love to Liz & Aaron. Mother send love to you. —Your own *Kitty*.

◆ More from George McKie:

Brother Niel—   We have arrived nearly back to Panama… Our voyage had been a successful one as far as the profits of the vessel are concerned— but a mighty uncomfortable one for those on board of her. From the time we left Panama till we arrived at San F— it rained almost continually— night and day and the consequence of that is that I have had the Erysipelas all the way back. Don't say anything to Mother about it— but it took the Land from under me for a few days, extended up my arms, down my neck, back, legs, face swelled etc and in fact was much worse than ever before— so much so that I made up my mind to go home at the end of the voyage— but since I left Acapulco have been better and will try one more trip and if the E does not trouble me, shall stay on…

Erysipelas inflammation of the skin, sometimes treated at this time by bleeding.

Say to all fever stricken people who wish to see California to stay at home— nine tenths who come here do not make expenses and half, if not all, the yarns you hear in the States are gammon to gull the simple. I saw thousands in S. F. who had not money enough to buy a dinner, men who had been at the mines, hardworking men, not addicted to gambling or kindred vices and not the ghost of a cent to jingle with a button.

I am looking with a deal of anxiety for news from home which I shall receive at Panama I hope. Next to seeing our friends is hearing from them… Give my love to all and ask them to write me at Panama Steamer *Isthmus* care of the American Consul and there will be no miscarriage. This letter I send by Capt Rodgers, a passenger on the *Isthmus* and a fine man. I have not time to give you any descriptive account of the voyage but will do so at my leisure which I have not had as yet. Write of Father's suit etc. Love again to all the family.   —*August 5, 1850.*

Troy, May 30th, 1850, Thurs eve, 7 o'clock.
My dearest Mother—   You may be surprised to hear from me so soon from Troy, but you know what Burns says that "the best laid schemes of mice and men aft gang agly"—so with ours in regard to our Western trip. When we arrived here we found Mr. Howland with inflammation in the eyes which prevented his doing anything in the office. Mr. Bills could not confine himself, so Frank and myself concluded to stay at home from necessity and finally thought it all for the best… Monday, coming down I lost my parasol, and we went back two miles and found it in the mud and water. Fortunately no one was cross about it and we had some fun holding up the dissolved thing to dry in the sun. I must not write much more, my eyes ache, but they will be better soon I think. I hope you have been well this week, better than last week or the week before…   —With the warmest love of your daughter *Kitty*.

June 3, 1850. At Cambridge. Weather pleasant. Took Ed's horse to the Blacksmith, worked in the garden. Horseback ride with Kate up to the P.O. Kate rode my horse & I rode Ed's. Have nothing to do but just eat, sleep & enjoy myself to the best advantage. *June 5.* At Cambridge. Weather hot. 10 o'clock left Father McKie's for White Creek. Got over to Uncle James' little after noon, all gone to Church except Aunt Almy. They returned from Church about 1/2 past 3…   —*Diary of Francis S. Thayer.*

Troy, July 11th, 1850, Thursday evening
My own dearest Kitty— How is my Kitty this charming eve? I would give anything to know and more than a good deal if I could just be with her for a while. I hope & trust that you have been well and happy this week… I had a pleasant ride with Niel— took the stage at Lansingburgh and arrived here before noon since which time I have been pretty busily engaged— more so this week than usual. The weather has been delightful and I have only wanted my own darling with me & freedom from the toothache, to make all things "perfectly agreeable." My old stump of a tooth has troubled me nearly all the time… The melancholy intelligence of the death of President Taylor has come upon us so unexpectedly that all hearts are oppressed with grief. God in his Providence has seen fit for the second time to remove by death the Chief Magistrate of the Nation and sadness is upon every brow— A Nation in tears. A great and good man has fallen… What a lesson this sudden bereavement should teach us and may God grant that we who live may profit by it. I send the *Express* in which there is an affecting notice of the death of President Taylor. There was a meeting of the Common Council of our City today and it was recommended by them that all business should be suspended on Saturday for three hours— from 11 till 2 o'clock… Kitty I can hardly bear the thought of not being with you Sat. eve and yet I dare not calculate upon it with too much certainty… Much love to your dear Mother and all my heart's best love to you my own dearest Kitty. More than ever your own devoted *Frank*.

September 11, 1850. My birthday. I am 28 years old in the enjoyment of perfect health & everything around me calculated to make me happy for which I thank Him the giver of every good & perfect gift. Ed McKie brot [sic] a note to me from my dearest Kitty. *December 2.* Very cold stormy day. In the Home all day long reading & attending to the wants of my sick wife. Have now about 20 inches snow which makes firm sleighing. Kate better today so that she sat up two hours. —*Diary of Francis S. Thayer.*

President Zachary Taylor, November 24, 1784–July 9, 1850, died of cholera and was succeeded by Vice-President Millard Fillmore.

VI

1851–1854

Letters from Cambridge and Troy, Part Two

AS 1851 began, Francis and Catherine Thayer were living in Troy, New York, and making occasional visits to their parents in the nearby towns of Cambridge and Hoosick Falls.

In American politics, slavery continued to be the controversial and divisive issue. Praised in the North but condemned in the South, Harriet Beecher Stowe's *Uncle Tom's Cabin*, published in 1852, had a profound affect both on the slavery debate and on the conscience of America. A year earlier Herman Melville had published *Moby Dick* and Nathaniel Hawthorne had published *The House of Seven Gables*. In 1851 Congress had reduced postage rates and a letter could be mailed 3,000 miles for 3¢. America was growing. In 1853 the Washington Territory was created out of part of the Oregon Territory, and for $10 million, the United States completed the Gadsden Purchase of 30,000 square miles from Mexico. A year later 13,000 Chinese immigrants would arrive in America to be employed in building the trans-continental railroad. American ingenuity continued to respond to the nation's demands for new and better things. In 1851 Isaac Singer patented a continuous-stitch sewing machine, and in 1854 Horace Smith and Daniel Wesson invented the Smith & Wesson revolver. Fire was often the scourge of cities and over 2,500 buildings were destroyed in the San Francisco fire of 1851. In that same year, Frederick Scott Archer, an Englishman, introduced the collodion or "wet plate" technique to photography and people's perception of themselves and everything around them would be forever changed. It was on September 18, 1851 that the first edition of the *New York Daily Times* appeared.

In Cambridge and Troy these were very normal times on the farm, but they were also times of both happiness and tragedy for the large family.

Letters and diaries by:
Edwin McKie
George McKie
George Wilson McKie
Niel McKie
Peter McKie
Catherine McKie Thayer
Francis S. Thayer

Letters written from: Troy, Cambridge, and New York, New York, Massachusetts, New Jersey, Brazil, Scotland, England, and Australia.

∼

Population of the United States:

1790	3,929,827
1800	5,305,941
1810	7,239,814
1820	9,638,191
1830	12,866,020
1840	17,068,666

(Including 6,100 seamen in the United States Navy)

Population of the Principal Cities and Towns in the United States
New York, 425,000
Philadelphia, 258,832
Richmond, 20,150
Nashville, 11,000

—*Statistical information published in the front of Francis S. Thayer's 1851 diary.*

1851

Receipt for school expenses, firewood: "Cambridge March 21, 1851, Received of George McKie fifteen dollars in full for four cords of wood fitted for the School House Stove in District No. 19 in the town of Easton Washington County N. York State. Daniel Hunt. Witness A. Perry."

Receipt for school expenses, boarding the teacher: "Recd of George McKie one of the trustees of school district No. 19 in Easton and Cambridge, twenty five dollars and fifty cents for boarding teacher 17 weeks a 12/ per week and eighteen cents for pay postage on school district journal from October 1850 to April 1st 1851. —Easton, March 21st, 1851. —A. Perry."

South Easton, April 10, 1851.
Dear Sister— At the request of Father & Mother I wrote you this morning to come up home on Saturday next if you could, but since then, the Doctor has been here and says that George has canker & rash and think as you have not had it, you had better not come. Your Mother thinks

it would be imprudent for you to come home at this time and consequently will not expect you. George continues about the same (that is) his throat is very sore and cannot swallow anything with the exception of something in a liquid state. The rest of the family are all well.   —Your Brother, *N. W. McKie.*

Troy, April 12, 1851.
Dear Mother—   I learn by Niel's letter of Thurs. afternoon that George has the Scarlet fever. I hope and pray that he may not have a hard time with that awful disease. You must do one thing— that is take Peter from his outdoors work and have him assist you in the house— If you want me at home or George is very sick let me know, and I will come up in the Stage. My fear of Scarlet fever seems to have gone a little since one of my own friends has it— I shall expect to hear Mon. or Tues. certainly. I do very much hope that George may have a light attack and no one else takes it— I hope and pray that you may get along comfortably   —*Kitty.*

April 19, 1851.
Dear Br. Ed—   Your letter in reference to George was received last evening, and we are very sorry indeed to hear that he was getting along nicely and then took cold. I wish he could have been careful.

From your letter I hardly know what to conclude. You say G— is very sick… It seems that this sickness cannot be at all alarming under the circumstances. I hope not certainly— Now matters here stand just in this way— Mr. Graves is in N. Y., returns tomorrow morning. Frank has been unusually busy this week. The affairs of the Howland estate as well as the Firm have occupied the time. Frank has not been in until 10 & 11 o'clock all the week. Mr. I. Howland leaves Monday at which time matters will be arranged and this great hurry over with. We expect to hear by mail today, and if G— is no better or (as I hope not) any worse, then Frank and myself will come up this evening. But if we do not hear at all today, we will come up Monday aft. without fail, if we are all well. You will probably get this letter at 1 or 2 o'clock. Now if G's situation is at all *alarming* or my services are very much needed, can you not send someone to the Point and telegraph us, and we will come up this evening. I wish I was home now— I would like to be with George and I know Mother is weary enough. I hope and pray the boy may be better soon and that we shall today hear. If he is dangerously ill or I am needed, Frank is ready to take me any moment without regard to business. I can write no more as this must go to the Office very very soon. I am very anxious to know today how G— is. Give my love to Niel and all at home. Poor sick G— in particular. Good bye.

Mon afternoon we expect to see all, sick and well. Tell Mother to give herself no trouble on our account.   —Your aff sister *Kate.*

❧ Death in the family:

April 22, 1851. About 1/2 past 4 am— Giltrop came to our Home with the sad news that Br. Henry McKie was very sick and the friends at home wished us to come up as soon as possible. We started about 6 and arrived there at 9 o'clock, one hour and a

Henry McKie, 1829–1851, died when he was twenty-two years old and is buried in the Whiteside Church Cemetery in Cambridge, New York.

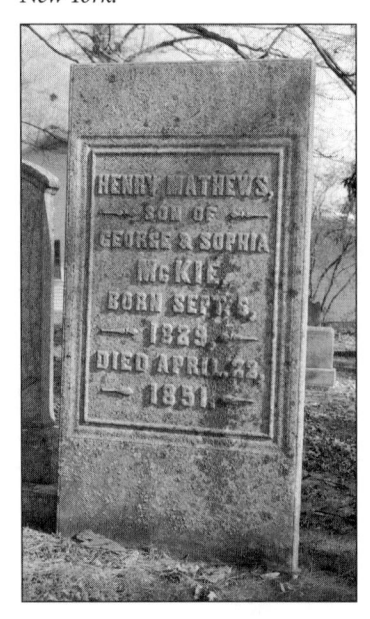

half after the dear fellow died. I can say nothing but that we are all buried in grief and mourning. Came back to Troy PM.

April 23. Beautiful day. Everything in the world without looks pleasant and cheerful but our hearts are afflicted by the death of a dear good kind brother. May God bless us and prepare us for the change that awaits us. About 4 PM left Troy to go & attend Henry's funeral tomorrow. Arrived at Cambridge about 7 and found a house of mourning.

April 24. Beautiful day. At 10 o'clock met with many others to pay the last tribute to the dead body of Henry McKie. Prayer at the house by Mr. McLoury. After burying the body, a good sermon was preached in the Whiteside Church by Mr. McLoury.

April 25. At Cambridge. Charming day. Busy most all day putting up a frame for woodbine at the back stoop. Over to the mill after the saw & a piece of plank. Was somewhat tired when night came. I am truly in the house of mourning.

April 26. At Cambridge. Busy at making frame etc. P.M. took a girl up near Union Village. She had been working at Mr. McKie's two weeks. Came back via Ann Whiteside's and left her hat. Ed went over to Easton. Niel sold his carriage for $175.

April 27. Charming day. Down to the Bridge to church. Peter with me. Heard a very good sermon from Mr. Strong. Kate not very well. Spent the PM & eve reading the *Bible*— read several chapters to my good Mother McKie.

May 4. Cloudy & looks like rain. I did not go off to Church. Went with Niel down into John Lee's pasture after two stray sheep, picked some wild flowers. P.M. Ed & wife came over & stayed two hours or more. Peter & Jimmie affected with sore eyes. 9 o'clock to bed.
—*Diary of Francis S. Thayer.*

Troy, May 16, 1851, Fri morn. 6 o'clock.
Dearest Mother— This is a bright beautiful morning, Mother, and I hope you are well and not worn out. I am to write you a *little* note which Frank is to take with the rest to the Stage Officer hoping that this package may go directly and reach you this eve. I am sorry indeed to have to send you such things to anchor so much sadness in your poor heart, and not be able to comfort you in the least, but know my good Mother that whether with or away from you, I would only say to you and myself that God has afflicted us all in mercy. We had wandered far from duty and we must be recalled to a sender of it, made to feel that our strength is not enough for life or death, but at how sad is this change. May God bless this affliction to our comfort and eternal good. My heart is with you and poor Father all the time. But one above must be your only firm support… Frank sends love to you and all. My love to Father and Brothers. I hope you are well and have plenty of good help. This is an awful scrawl but God be with you Mother, Love *Kitty*.

Troy, November 16th, 1851, Sabbath eve, 7 o'clock, Our own room.
My own dearest Kitty— You know with how much anxiety I watched the clouds yesterday and how I longed to have the *happiness* of meeting you last eve. You did not expect me did you? …I am more than ever yours. Have you heard how I reached Troy last Monday morn in the snow-storm? Well I will tell you. I came on very comfortably until I got to that small bridge near Col. Talmadge. (You probably don't recollect said bridge.) Then and there in consequence of said bridge being in a broken down state, my wagon broke down and rendered it impossible for me to proceed further. The forward axlebar broken and you can imagine my disappointment. I was anxious to get

to Troy early and to have such an accident happen was provoking. As good luck would have it Mr. Beadle soon came along and I put my things into his wagon and led Charlie, stopped at the Valley, and sent a man back after my wagon. Myself and Charlie came to Troy with Mr. Beadle, arrived here about 1/2 past 8 o'clock. When I come up after you I shall ride Charlie up to the Valley and then try my wagon again. I am getting used to riding on horseback and I like it very well— the greatest objection is that it is too much work to keep my pants and boots clean in this muddy weather. I have had quite enough to attend to the past week. Mr. Bills went to New York Tuesday night and returned Wednesday night. Mrs. Howland remains about the same as she was weeks ago. Libby has had the measles. She is now most well. Eda is well again— the sweet little creature said when you was going away, "Now Aunty Thayer wouldn't go away if she only knew how sick I am." ... Tell your good kind Father that I have *feasted* on the apples he put up for me. I am growing an addition to my whiskers and if I don't see you before next Saturday eve you will hardly know me. I am a little afraid you will suggest some *cutting down*... —Frank.

Beadle Hill from the Poplars. Hurd's Stereoscopic Views, Greenwich, New York.

1852

Troy, Jan. 4, 1852, Sabbath aft 5 o'clock.
My dear good Mother—   We have just returned from Church and already it begins to grow dark. Nearly all day has it been snowing a little but there is not yet snow enough for sleighing. Now I have my lamp lighted and can see better now. I cannot say that we had a very pleasant ride down on Mon. Frank got out about a mile this side the Valley and walked most of the way to Lansingburgh from whence we came in the Stage. Edwin took Cambridge stage at Grants, leaving horse and cart there— he went up next day for them. I drove Charlie, he was tame enough in the mud. Frank got his feet wet and finished out his tooth-ache by an ulcer on the gum which broke and then he was much relieved, but he had the worst swollen face for two or three days that I ever saw— which prevented his going to Albany. Frank and Edwin mean to go this week. The New Year has come. The last year gone. One year ago how little we knew of the future— how little know we now... I have succeeded in getting one kind of the calico but have not found the other. I can say nothing of coming home... I should be happy indeed if I could sit down with you until 11 o'clock. It would do much good to hear from you all... So good by for this time, my love to Father and Brothers all. God bless us all. Frank sends his love to you.   —Your *Kitty*.

Troy, March 11, 1852, Thursday P.M.
My own dearest Kitty—   I'm all alone in the office & nothing to do but write to you. And what shall I say to you dearest? To tell you that I love you more & more with every passing moment would be an old story. But old as it is, I reckon you like to have me repeat it now & then... This eve Oliver Wendell Holmes is to lecture. I wish you could be here to go with me. I expect a rich treat... If the traveling is not too bad you may look for me Sat eve. I may conclude to wait until the first of next week and then come up after you... Love to all. I am more than ever your own *Frank*.

March 14, 1852. At Cambridge, rainy day. Did not go out to Church. Kate took a Lobelia emetic & was sick four or five hours, after which she got up & ate heartily & was well again. Such is the power of Lobelia.
—*Diary of Francis S. Thayer.*

Troy, April 1, 1852.
My dear Mother—   We have just taken dinner, Frank has gone to the Store, and I am seated to write you a few lines on this "All Fools Day."…I have never been here so long without writing you and I have often thought that perhaps you had been disappointed… Oh Mother how do I wish from my heart that you and Father could walk in and sit down with me and be with us a few days or many days as you would be happy… George said to me that you talk some of Peter going to sea for his health. I should regret very much to see him leave us all… I was in hopes that the constant use of Sarsaparilla would cure him. At any rate, good Physicians should be consulted in regard to this voyage, and if we are assured that it may be of great benefit we must sacrifice our feelings for his good. I hope to see you all in a week or few days, and hope too that Peter may get so well and strong that he will forget that he has ever seen Lobelia or any other medicines. I shall think of you and him all the time. Give my best love to Father, Peter & others. Frank sends love…   —Good-bye Mother, *Kitty.*

Peter going to sea for his health The reader should remember this comment.

April 25, 1852. Pleasant day. Did not go to church. Spent the day walking about the farm & in the home reading. The new dog, "Don," takes up a good deal of time & attention. This is the first really warm & pleasant day of the season.
—*Diary of Francis S. Thayer.*

Troy, May 16, 1852, Sabbath aft.
My dear Mother—   I wish you was with me and then I would not have to write a note, what you do not do *very often.* But you are at my old home, and I am in my new one with the best Frank in the world and I hope you are as happy as we are and more so if you can be… I do hope that you and Father have had your likenesses taken, if you have not and still have an opportunity, do have it done for me… I hear nothing of Peter, he may or may not be going East. It seems that I must come home to know anything of home. I have heard two good sermons today, one from Dr. Berman. We hope to be with you in a few days. My love with Frank's to you and all. God bless you and keep you always.   —Your own *Kitty.*

September 7, 1852. …up at 5 o'clock. Kate, her mother, Ed & wife & wife's mother all to the 6:35 N.Y. car to go to Long Beach…   —*Diary of Francis S. Thayer.*

༄ A vacation by the sea:

Pavilion Hotel, Long Branch, New Jersey Sep. 10th, 1852, Friday morn 10 o'clock.
Dear Father [Catherine McKie Thayer writing to George McKie, her father]—
I suppose before this will reach you, Edwin has seen you and told you of our safe arrival here. Mother was somewhat sick on the way but could not throw anything up or off her stomach. Since Edwin left we have been very well indeed. Yesterday, Thursday was a very fine day, a bright sun overhead,

Catherine McKie Thayer, a hand-painted miniature based on the daguerreotype page 148.

but such a cool breeze from the ocean that we did not feel the heat. This morning the sun is shut in by clouds and there is some prospect of rain. We do not wish for rain here but hope you have had rain for it has been needed so much. Yesterday Mother and I walked about three miles… You would not know Mother I think, in her bathing dress, which is a real Bloomer— Full drawers, fastened around the ankle, a full frock coming about to the knees, head mounted by a big straw hat with its broad brim turned straight up behind— such is Mother in bathing trim. She calls herself Black Hawk and enjoys the bathing very much. I wish you could be with us. Suppose you come down with Edwin and have just one look at the ocean. I know you must enjoy it. I could sit on the beach and look at the breakers and listen to the roaring of the waters all day long. The sound is like the deep rumbling of thunder but there is no lightning to alarm me. Young and old gaze many times a day and sit on the beach to look and listen. All seem awed in mind, yet over all there seems to come a lively exhilaration of feeling, perhaps owing to the bracing air coming from the water. We breakfast at 1/2 past 7 o'clock, bathe from 10 to 11 o'clock or thereabout, dine at 2 o'clock and take tea at 7 o'clock. We have excellent board. Everything well cooked and comes on the table in a hot eatable state. We have about 20 or 25 boarders now and if the weather remains pleasant we shall have company while we wish to stay. Not that we are so dependent on others, but four boarders in a house that will accommodate 250 are rather too much alone. I hardly know what to say about coming home. It will seem to depend on the weather and Mother's and Netty's feelings… Mother sends all her love to you and what you will spare to the rest. She hopes you are doing very well without her, that you feel well and not very lonely. I wish you could be here with us, But I must stop and write a word to Frank. So good-bye. Love to all. God bless you my good Father. Your affectionate daughter,   —*Kate.*

∽ Theft:

Tuesday, September 21, 1852. Went to Cleveland by cars. R— left us as we got in. Had my money stolen— lost $48,700
Wednesday, September 22, 1852. At Cleveland, went Pittsburgh. Saw Police officer & was up till 2 A.M. Porter Thayer at Cleveland.   —*Diary of Edwin McKie.*

Friday, September 24, 1852. Pleasant. Down to Greenbush & Albany. On my return at 1/2 past 11 AM heard that Ed McKie was robd [*sic*] in Cleveland, Ohio of $48,700 on the 21st. 1/2 past 3 PM left for Cambridge to tell Ed's folks at home the awful news…
Sunday, September 26, 1852. Fine rain last night. Port arrived in Troy last night directly from Cleveland and today about 11 AM he came to Father McKie to give him some consolation about Ed. After dinner Port went to Hoosick…
  —*Diary of Francis S. Thayer.*

In 1852 Edwin McKie, brother of Catherine McKie Thayer, was engaged in the wool and pork business and traveled extensively to Ohio, Virginia, Michigan, and western New York. There is no other mention of this theft of money, a large amount even by modern standards. This theft undoubtedly contributed to business losses that he had, for after this he was much less active. A year later he went to England and Australia.

∽ A group letter to Catherine Thayer:

Cambridge, Nov 1852.
Dear Sister—   I will write you a few lines to let you know how we are getting along. Mother and Father are well, Peter is trying the Cold Water Practice for his complaint, George has gone North a hunting, he is going to

be gone about two weeks. Father would like to have you get him two large cotton neck hankerchiefs. [*sic*] I want you to get me 2 1/2 yds of cloth to line a coat and 1 doz of Smoked Pearl Buttons. The cloth wants to be single fold. I am going to have a coat out of the gray cloth. We expect you will come up home Saturday. The boys are all well, tell Francis, Niel has got a horse to match his. Good-bye, your Br. *James McKie.*

Kate—   Your letter to me at Easton is at home. The package is here all safe. Tell Miss Graves that my wife will have a better Baby than hers when she does have one. It may not be larger or better looking, but it will have a slight *variation*, as you say hers is a gal.   —*Your Uncle Edwin.* All well. Come up Saturday, Bring Frank. Let him come up with you. —*Ed.*

Monday morning.

Kitty—   Yesterday Jimie left his letter open that I might scratch a few lines to you. I intended last week to have surprised you with a long scrawl but your father would say tomorrow we *will* write but he was kept very busy. George gone, Peter and I engaged in the cold water and Lobelia. We expect George the last of this week... Your father has come in and says give next to my best love to them, take a kiss yourself and same for Francis from your Mother. —*S. [Sophia] McKie.* Kitty may God bless you both, hope to see you soon. My new girl does well. Edwin got the start of me.

December 31, 1852. Weather mild & looks like rain. Gave note to Farmer's Bank at 45 days for $3,700. The last day of the year & I thank God for all his mercy & goodness during the year now about to close & pray for His blessing in future.

—*Diary of Francis S. Thayer.*

1853

༄ George McKie to his daughter:

Cambridge, Jan. 12th, 1853.

Well Catherine my Child—   Your Mother and I came to the conclusion that for once at least you have been up to your promise, that is, you would not write home any more unless you received a few lines from your Father or Mother. Now in order to stir you up to do your duty and to get you in the way of communicating once more with your old and truest friends (except Frank) I have thought it proper to write you a few lines that you may know how we all are at home. Your Mother's health is to all appearance improving. She has had a slight cold since you left home but soon recovered from it. I feel somewhat flattered that she will continue to improve until her ordinary health is restored. I am quite well, likewise the remainder of the family. I suppose you have heard there Peter left N. York... and I trust hope and pray that the vessel and passengers may be safely landed at the place of which she was destined. Anne Whiteside spent a few days with us this week which made it quite pleasant for us. We are expecting that Frank will have some leisure toward the last of next week when we may reasonably expect a visit from you. Hope you will not fail. Your mother's love to you and Frank... From your Father. Children, my love to you both.   —*G. McKie.*

◦ Brother to sister:

So Easton, 1853.
Dear Kate—   Mother wishes me to write a few words descriptively. The pork season was gotten along with— without much trouble. James' lambs (the twins) are growing rapidly and promise to be the progenitors of a long line of celebrated sheep. Mother and Father have both had outrageous colds— in their backs and limbs but the unusual flow of sap indicates a change for the better. Peter also has a bad cold and has been homeopathically— Totonically— and Hydropathically treated and from the abundant flow of watery fluid from his proboscis— I conclude the Hydropath is the effective agent in the removal of the disease. Mother and Father are just home suggesting various ideas to transmit to you. Mother says that Father is getting so large in and below the waist that his drawers pinch him— and Father says that it is the fault of the drawers and not from any enlargement of the breadbasket— "tam sit."

    Ed and Nette are expected this afternoon to stay the week— Say? Why can't you and Frank come up on Friday and help eat one of the eight turkeys that I killed the day I took you to the Bridge? Love from all the family to you and Frank etc.   —Yours affectionately, *G. W. McKie.*

Morse's American Telegraph
Troy Jan 13, 1853
By Telegraph from: NY
To: Peter Gordon
The *Eagle* will not sail before Thursday or Saturday of next week. —*James Boone*, Purser.

January 13, 1853. Up at 1/2 past 6… Heard Peter McKie was soon to start for Australia
January 17. The coldest day of this season… Peter McKie getting ready to start for Australia Thursday next.
January 20. Mild & pleasant. Peter McKie went to N.Y. to sail Saturday for Australia…
                                                —*Diary of Francis S. Thayer.*

Jan. 27th, 1853, Cambridge, Thurs aft. 1 o'clock.
Dearest Frank—   …We had a telegram from Peter yesterday. He is still in N. Y. Expects to sail Saturday…   —Your own *Kitty.*

Catherine McKie Thayer's journal records that Peter McKie left home for Australia on February 7, 1853.

◦ Letters from Peter McKie:

Brother George—   I am now sitting in the cabin and writing to you… Tell Jim and Ed (brothers James and Edwin McKie) to be good boys and write to me very soon after the departure of the *Eagle*. Direct to Port Phillip. We will leave our address at that port at Post Office and if absent Post Office, at Sydney. If George does not come, if E— do not come, I will write as soon as I arrive and continue to every three weeks.

Father and Mother—   I was very glad to hear that you were a getting better, yes, very glad. I will let you know what I have been a doing since I arrived here. At first I spent two nights at Mr. Fuller's after hearing that the ship was not to go until Monday. The Purser told me that confidentially soon after my arrival. Well, after spending a night or so with Mr. Fuller, I came to New York and purchased all I wanted and counseled a worthy physician. He told me it was the best thing as I could do as there was no danger of me.   —*January 29 or 30, 1853.*

Brother George—   We are within a few rods of another vessel bound for London, England, and I take this opportunity to write home. (Longitude 21 1/2 Latitude 4 1/2) We have had a very good passage so far but it is nearly a calm now. I have been but middling well. I feel rather better at present but I am not feeling as well as anticipated. I think I will get along very well though if not I will return first opportunity. It is pretty warm here at present. I think I had better return as soon as I can conveniently on account of leaving Mother in ill health. This ship is a very good sailer. We have passed everything whether on our course or not. She proves herself good so far. If you should come, don't leave before I might have time to return as I may return immediately. If I don't feel better than I do now we may run into Cape Town. I will write again. I am in hopes I will find all well on my return. Good by all.   —*March 5.*

Dear Father—   We have just arrived at this place. (Rio de Janeiro). As I supposed to spend a few days but finding the yellow fever prevailing we leave very soon. Therefore, I cannot write many particulars. I will now let you know how I have been during the warm passage. I have not felt very well. The warm weather is very weakening but I am in hopes that when I get into cooler climes I will get better. All the passengers have suffered. Our vessel proves to be as good as any we have seen on the ocean. Sails fast under a good breeze, but we have not been in a calm since we left the Gulf Stream. Had no trade winds, only a gentle breeze during the night to drive us to Rio. We came here on account of being out of water. I can write no more to you father but to wish that you are enjoying the blessings of a savior.

   Dear Mother—   I will write a little for you to read. I have thought of you by day and night, hoping that you were enjoying good health. God grant that you are and that I may find you very well when I get home. But should we never see each other again in this world, I hope we may meet in a better. I shall be prepared to meet whatever may befall me so don't give yourself any trouble on my account. We have to part sometime. God bless you dear Mother. I trust in God and will willingly give myself up to his charge so goodby.

   Dear Sister—   I will write a few lines to you. I hope you are enjoying good health and F— too. I can but refer you to what I have written if I or you should be taken away we will meet in a better world— that is a comfort to think of.

   God bless you dear sisters and brothers. I will write also in reference to George leaving for Australia. He has later news than I have. He better not leave until he hears from us, but he will judge for himself. Tell James never to think of putting himself under the control of a captain and mates. I bid you all farewell. A kiss and goodby. Hope you may enjoy good health. Give my love to Wina and Sally. Tell them I wish them enjoying good health. Love to all friends.   —*April 9, 1853.*

We arrived in Callao (Brazil) on Friday week. On Sunday went over the bows with Dahl— Desbrow Pound— and run about the town for one hours or two— and then Dahl and myself went out to the view of Old Gallao destroyed by an earthquake in 1800. The houses were buried or thrown down to the ground so that but few traces of them remain… On Friday morning last the President of Peru, Don Castillio and his suite paid the vessel a visit. The Pres— is a fine looking man, tall, strait, dark complexion— *dark as tartarus* mustaches— The ladies of this country are small in stature and features, hair as black as the raven's wing— Eyes and teeth white as ivory, wear their dresses loose fitting, a coiffure about their heads covering their faces entirely with the exception of one sparkling black eye… —*Sept. 13th.* [fragment of a letter]

Troy, March 27, 1853.
My dear Mother—   I have half an hour to write before the aft. service and I will improve it. If you received a note from me last week, you probably know that we designed going to N. York on Tues. or Wed. We went Tues. morn and returned last eve at 11 o'clock. We had a very pleasant time. A good visit at Jim's— and found nice things for housekeeping— too good I fear. I said something I thought I ought to say in favor of less impressive furniture for parlor and some other things. But my money buys nothing, and Frank said he would have good articles and few in number, rather than many poor ones. So what we have should be of good quality. Do not think from what I have said that we have been terribly extravagant— for we have not. I only wished to be very plain and prudent and Frank would have a good quality of everything. His way is the better I presume…   —Your *Kitty.*

April 11, 1853. Weather continues cold & unpleasant. Getting ready for closing up the business of the old firm & commencing the new.
April 15. The last day of the business of the firm of Howland, Bills & Thayer. Busy all day & until 1/2 past 12 o'clock at night posting up Books. Then home & could not get to sleep till about 2 o'clock.
April 16. The firm of Bills & Thayer commences today… —*Diary of Francis S. Thayer.*

Springfield (Massachusetts), April 28th, 1853.
Dearest Kitty—   I arrived here last eve and shall leave for Northampton and Greenfield in a few minutes. The weather is charming and I have had a pleasant time of it thus far. I have seen many of our old customers and they all say they will continue business with us. You may look for me in Troy Saturday night about 11 o'clock. I shall go to Brattleboro and Keene and return to Troy via Rutland. The cars are about to start and I must close. Yours in haste, Your own *Frank.*

Troy, May 17, 1853, Tues aft 4 o'clock.
Dear Father & Mother—   Your letter of May 11 was duly received, and last evening Frank brought in one dated the 15th, Sab, and enclosing one from Peter, which I need not say I was glad to receive. We are disappointed with you all that Peter has not already received some benefit from the voyage. I had great confidence in it and still hope that after a time his health will improve. I cannot but feel that it will. You know Father I *will look on*

the brighter side. It does this much if nothing more, it makes a happier present, and the unknown future will bring its trials sooner than we are fit to meet them… In regard to Peter, we are assured by Physicians and may believe that his lungs are sound and after the ills of his voyage, I trust he may have a more than corresponding improvement in health… I am glad to hear that there is now a slight improvement in Mother's health, I wish I could hear of a more speedy change for the better… I took cold just after or the day I came down, and went out yesterday, the first time in twelve days. For about nine days I took everything that a good nurse of the olden time would have given, but *would not* have a doctor. I am afraid of them. I think it is easier falling into the hands of a Doctor than climbing out… and Frank would consult someone so I told him he might go to Dr. Cook and last Friday I began the little pills, and my cough has been loose ever since and is very much better, almost well. Indeed I should be quite well again, if I were only strong as usual. The medicines I took for my cough at first had only this effect— kept me sick and have left my back and bowels in a very weak state. But time and care will do for me all I need now I think… I presume it will be better for me not to ride 20 miles Sat. unless necessary. Just remember Mother I am doing well now and could wish you were as well. Good bye. Frank sends love to you. My love to all. Your affec. Daughter, *C. McKie Thayer*.   —I enclose Peter's letter as I presume you would like to have it.

May 29, 1853. Beautiful day. Dr. Berman's in A.M. & heard a most excellent sermon from him. As usual Kate not able to go out so I stayed at home in P.M.
June 4. Pleasant. Busy at Home most of the day. Moved from 104 to 147 First Street. We are to sleep under our own room tonight for the first time. Tired & to bed at 11 o'clock.
July 27. Pleasant A.M. & Rainy P.M. All alone at the store. Bills gone & Wm. sick. Lost dog & found him at the R. R. depot…   —*Diary of Francis S. Thayer.*

Mrs. Thayer 147 1st —Kitty— If not much trouble have Mary make some biscuit for tea out of this flour. —*Frank*
The handwritten reply— Not trouble for you my darling. —your *Kitty*.

[In an envelope addressed: *To my dear Frank only.*]
Oct. 19, 1853.
Dear Frank—   I am now about to take this lace upstairs and lay it away for another summer. God only knows if I shall live to see it needed. I have many inward fears and some dark hours, but these I would not share with you my darling Frank. *Let ours be pleasant hours together.* I pray God to give me heart to meet and strength to bear the coming future, but if it shall be his will to take me from you, from *this sweet home of ours*, I will trust his love and mercy for another better home in Heaven for *us both* my precious Frank. God bless us *my Frank*. Good bye.

This note was written and dated by Catherine McKie Thayer. A note in the handwriting of her granddaughter, Katherine Thayer Hobson, reads: "Probably written by C. McKie Thayer before birth of first baby in 1854."

December 31, 1853. …This has been a prosperous year for business & I am thankful for it. I have enjoyed good health & I thank God for all his mercy & goodness towards me & mine and pray for his blessing to rest upon us.   —*Diary of Francis S. Thayer.*

❧ Letters from Edwin McKie in Scotland & Liverpool:

Bro George— Here I am [Edinburgh] in the land of the plaids and the ponies. I have been at London for a few days, and have also been at some small towns. I went about the county of York, and stopped one day on the estate of the Duke of Devonshire, who has the largest estate of any one man in England, his income is over 400,000 dollars yearly... Well England is a great country. The land is fine and well tilled. All the fields are small, say from 4 to 10 acres, and the soil is, or looks very rich. The fences are all hawthorn or stone. I have not seen a rail fence either in Scotland or England. Neither have I seen a yoke of oxen, the work is all done with horses, or with a horse and cart. Labor is very scarce. I have seen large quantities of wheat uncut or standing, and any quantity standing in the shock in the field. They have no barns here, the grain and hay being all stacked and threshed on the ground. The cattle are fine and large and very generally fat. I never saw such sheep as they have here. I have not seen a poor sheep, and such large fat sheep you nor I never saw, all coarse wooled. I have seen many places here which are of very ancient origin, and of which many persons would be highly delighted, but my temperament and disposition does not find anything very marvelous in them, but still very interesting. There are buildings or castles here so old, no one knows anything of their date, not even the Duke himself, and from their appearance, I would think he did not, or could not have much recollection, as I saw Adam and Eve in one of them. Consequently it must have been the house that Adam built according to the best of my recollection... I shall go see the cottage of Robert Burns, which is at Ayr, which will interest me more than all else...

...The *Golden Age* has put off going till the 10th of November, and if she does not get a good number of passengers, I do not think she will go. When I left Liverpool no one had spoken for passage, and the excitement is all over, and it yet remains to be seen whether the *Golden Age* will go or not... I will write after I get back to Liverpool so it will go by the *Baltic* on Wednesday next. This goes on Saturday this week in a *Cunard*. Give my love to Father, Mother, Niel, James and all and now as I always was— Your Brother, —*Ed.* October 27, 1853.

Uncle— [to an unidentified uncle] The *Golden Age* does not leave for Australia till Nov. 10th. I have been to London, Edinburgh, and Glasgow & have been in the best part of England and have seen a good share of all the old ancient places on my route. This place interests me most. I have found one family of McKies but they are a queer set. The old man is William McKie, him I did not see, he was sick. His sons and daughters, of which he has five, some married and live near him and some with him...

I find many here by the name of Wilson but none who ken aught about the one I have inquired for.

I go back to Liverpool tomorrow & will see if any news there, and if so will add a postscript...

I have been to see Burns' cottage, and there is still in it the bed he was born in, the cradle he was rocked in, and many other things he once had. I also called on a sister of Burns, who lives near his birthplace. She is an old

the name of Wilson Edwin McKie's grandmother was Elizabeth Wilson, 1765–1849, daughter of George Wilson, 1737–1808, from Ireland.

Cottage in which Burns was born, visited by Edwin McKie in October 1853. From The Complete Poetical Works of Robert Burns, *Houghton Mifflin Company, 1897.*

An enclosed envelope reads "Sprigs of heather from the foot of Burns' monument sent me by my good Br. E. J. McKie —C. McKie Thayer" *—November 15, 1853.*

Lady, and lives with her two daughters who are maiden ladies. I had a very interesting time with them. They told me many things Rob had done & of many things he had said of which I never before heard… The people here have erected a fine monument to his memory & they all love the name of Burns. There are many interesting places about Edinburgh, of which I have many a memoranda, as well as of other places I have seen…

The farmers of Scotland are a fine set of men, and men who know how to farm it. There is some of the best-looking farms here I ever saw. A large quantity of wheat is yet uncut in England, and thousands of acres yet standing in the shock in the fields. It has been raining for weeks every day. I hardly think I have seen one whole fine day since I have been here…

I hope our ship will go on the 10th Nov. but the bad news from there may put her back a while… —*October 30, 1853.*

Enclosed is a sprig of heather from Burns' monument.

Dear Father— The *Golden Age* has been at her old tricks. We were to sail on the first of November, then the 10th, then 19th, now 26th and when we start 'tis hard to say. After I wrote George from Edinboro I went to Ayr in Ayrshire, I found a family of McKies there who were formerly from Galwayshire, but I could not learn much from them as they would not say much about their ancestors. They said they had no relatives in America, & I was glad they said so for I did not like their actions at all, and I left them…

I have been back here for some time waiting for the *Golden Age* to sail for Australia…

There is nothing new here. The people here are a very ignorant set. They have no more idea of America, than I have of Jerusalem. A lady said to one of our passengers that he spoke with very good English she thought & asked if the Americans all used the English language as well as he. His reply was, no, the most of them used the Choctaw. I have been asked many times if we had railroads, and if we lived on game and such things. No one takes a paper here unless he is rich, or well to do in this world. There is but one daily paper in this whole kingdom and that the *London Times*, and costs 6d each (or 12 1/2 cts). All other papers are weekly or semi and tri weekly, and are also very dear. Merchants will club together and take a semi weekly paper and each have his regular time to read it and so it goes around. There is much poor people in Liverpool alone than in all America. The Dutchess [*sic*] of Sutherland had better look to her own degraded white slaves here than sending or meddling with the slaves in America, for slavery is in its worst form here. Men, women, and children go bare footed and bare assed here— now begging for half penny to get some bread, and one cannot go a single block without having half a dozen or more after him. About half-past-one every day the swill is taken on the dock from the ship & then there is fun. Men, women, and boys are all on hand, ready as soon as it is set on the dock. They pitch in & such a melee is great sport, fight & scratch, pull hair and dive in and eat the whole up & then they are off 'til the next day again. The people are taxed to death, everybody pays a tax who does anything. There are women who pick up horse dung in the street who have to pay for a license, this is all true, every word of it.

Kiss Mother for me and remember me to all of them— Niel and the boys… The weather is warm here. One does not want an overcoat— I will write again before I go.   —*November 15, 1853.*

Dear Father—   The *Golden Age* leaves tomorrow at 8 A. M. & no mistake. Yesterday they put on cattle, sheep, hogs, geese, turkeys, ducks, chickens, and a large quantity of fresh dressed meat for the voyage…

I have nothing new or worth writing. I am in first rate health myself. I now pull up 178 pounds. Everything looks green here. Cattle and sheep in good pasture, and not much frost, but considerable rain. The fields look as fresh as ours do in June. Stock here good. Grass all the year round. I expect to find Peter in Australia, will look him up as soon as I get there. I was in hope to hear from you before I left, and I may tomorrow morning before we sail, as a steamer is due tonight from New York…   —*November 27, 1853.*

Dear Brother—   We left the dock [Liverpool] on Monday last for Australia and our pilot run the ship across the river into the dock on the opposite side and tore away our cutwater and about fifteen feet of the keel and made a hole in the bottom that compelled the ship to put into dock again, for repairs. The men have been at work all week, and they will get her done tonight, and we shall start again at 12 tomorrow with about 160 passengers, about 30 in the cabin, the balance in steerage…

I will write from the Cape of Good Hope, so goodbye & I remain truly your affectionate Brother

I send this in an envelope with a letter to Nette & save postage.
                                              —*December 4, 1853.*

1854

January 30, 1854. Weather moderate… Geo McKie came. He is on his way to New York to engage in the grocery business which I hope & trust may prove successful…
                                              —*Diary of Francis S. Thayer.*

◦ George Wilson McKie to his father:

New York, February 13, 1854.
Dear Father—   Yours of Saturday last was received on Monday and was very glad to get a letter from home and pleased to hear that you were all well.

Last week I caught a very bad cold and Sunday I was obliged to go to bed, took some pills and some other stuff and continued about the same until last night and this morning I feel much better. Bones all ached and head also. Bowels bound up and in fact I was threatened with a fever.

I came near coming home so late as yesterday— but concluded to wait until today and then if no better to come home. This morning I am much better, but not as well as I should have been if I had taken a good sweat and an emetic.

We are doing a very good business for the season and the prospect looks very fair now but who can tell how soon it may be clouded? …Write me as often as you can, and give my love to all the family and a cookie to Charm & Drive.   —Affectionately your son *George.*

New York, February 22, 1854.
Burdick McKie and Cundall, Wholesale Grocers
No. 236 Front Street, New York

Dear Father—   This morning, having nothing in particular to do and feeling anxious to hear from home, I thought I would advise you and Mother of the mutuality there was in the matter of correspondence. I have written you three times and have not heard from home but once since I have been here. Last week I had a very bad cold but have got the better of it now. We have had a very severe snowstorm here as you will see by the papers. The snow is piled up six feet high in some streets and the first thaw will make the water almost as high.

The business season has not as yet opened although we are doing a little business daily, say from $2 to $500 per day, enough to pay expenses. Our people don't come down much until after the river opens. From the present aspect of affairs we shall do very well, but anyone who thinks it is play is very much mistaken. The work here is harder than any farming work I know of. In some seasons of the year it is not as bad but 2/3ds of time the time is all occupied. Saw Mr. Harrison Hunley yesterday— He said Uncle James and friends were all well, and Aunt Julia some better. The smallpox is very prevalent here and seems to be on the increase. I do not know when I can get home, may be about the middle of March but can't say positively. Write me as often as you can and believe me yours, Affectionately,   —*G. W. McKie.*

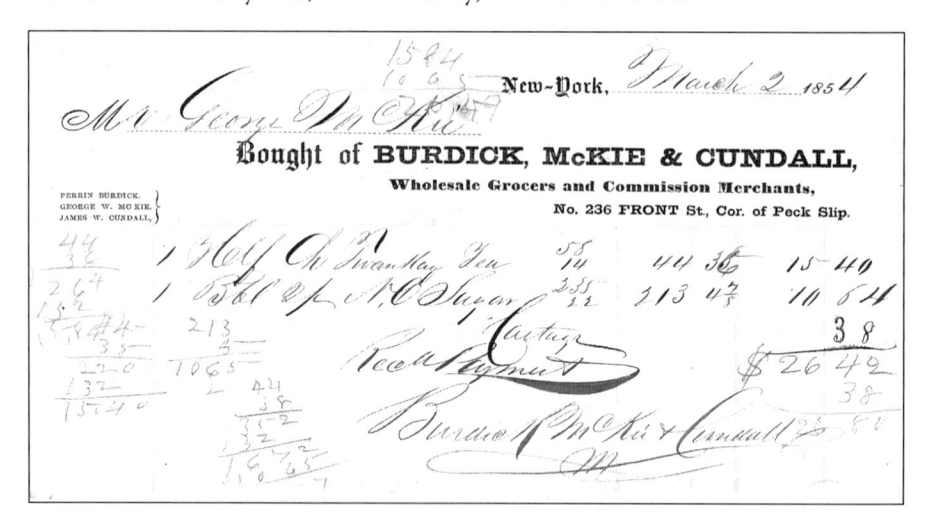

Invoice from Burdick, McKie & Cundall for tea & sugar, $26.80.

Troy, March 5, 1854, Sabbath aft. 4 o'clock.
My dear Mother—   Frank is in Church and I am alone, so will write you a few lines for Frank to take to the office when he comes home. I have given up Church going for the present— Frank is kind enough to take notes and with some filling up from memory, I feel as if I have almost been to Church and listened to a Sermon… I wish you and Father could step in, take tea with us and then be home again at bed time, then Father would hardly have time to get lonely… So now write me often, once in two weeks at least, and tell me what you do each day, how you feel and so I can know a little of your everyday life. If we do not visit for some weeks, we can keep pretty well acquainted… I trust we shall hear from Peter from some source very soon… I have been

improving every day since I came home in some respects, and feel better than I have in a month, have slept well the last three nights… Frank sends love. My love to all. God bless you and us.   —*Kitty.*

❧ A letter from Edwin McKie in Australia:

Dear Father—   We arrived at Melbourne on the 13th February, after a passage of 51 days running time and 71 days in all from Liverpool. I came up here (Sydney) to find Peter, and Mr. Gordon and I find that Peter did not stay here long but went to San Francisco in the brig *Julia Ann*. The brig has been back here since, and gone to California again… I am staying on the *Golden Age* here, and shall go back to Melbourne in her on Wednesday of this week…

…Tell George and James to stay where they are & they will do well enough. I am going up to the mines, when I get to Melbourne, but where I shall bring up eventually, I can't say, but I shall keep going till I find some place where I can make something. I may go back to Liverpool. That is one good place. The Captain of the clipper ship *Queen of the East* offers me a free passage if I will go with him to Canton & then to London. He will be gone about six months. If I can't do anything at the mines I may go with him, but I can't say… I can't write half I would like to, but I hope to see you all in a year or two. No rain here for five months & the hot winds and dust is awful. Fleas, flies, & muskitoes in millions, no sleep to be had unless covered with something. Where I shall go or what I shall do I can't say, don't write me till you hear from me again, can't say where I shall be. My health is first rate. Never better, costs me nothing to live on the ship. Captain Porter says he will take me to Panama free, and wants me to go, but I shan't leave yet. No use to go home again till I have seen the Elephant all over.

The wool trade is about over for this year… Peter was well and hearty when he was here. I saw a passenger who came with him in the *Eagle*, went with Peter to San Francisco. Hoping you are all well and in good health. I will close by sending my best love to Mother and to you and all the boys, Niel, George, James, and many kisses to my dear Mother, and much love to yourself.   —*March 5, 1854.*

Troy, March 12, 1854, Sabbath aft. 5 o'clock.
My dear good Mother—   …My new woman Ellen has come, and does very well— is not as fast on foot as I could wish, but seems to be a well disposed person. If she is contented and willing to stay in this quiet place, I hope to make her what will be necessary for our comfort. Of one thing I am satisfied— that she can cook well— I mean make everything taste good. If she does not stay, someone else will come, it will all come out right I presume… Well I will pause soon. The bell has rung for tea, and we will go down. I only wish you and Father were with us.— We have had a good plain tea and Henry must go and take my letter. So good-bye. My love to Father, Jimmy etc. Frank sends love to all. God bless you my dear good Mother.   —Your daughter *Kitty.*

March 18, 1854. A terrible tornado visited this City & vicinity. Roofs blown off, buildings demolished etc. etc. It is estimated that $50,000 will not cover the damage done in the City, $20,000 damage to windows…   —*Diary of Francis S. Thayer.*

Troy, March 19, 1854, Sabbath eve.

My dear Mother—   Instead of writing to you as I intended two hours ago I laid down and thought I would take a little nap in your *warm bedroom*, but Francis soon came up and since he came we have been talking about this and that thing… We hear nothing directly from the absent brothers [Peter McKie & Edwin McKie] except that the *Golden Age* left Cape of Good Hope Jan 16th for Melbourne. I suppose we must hear from Edwin soon. I trust we will soon get some news from Peter. Nothing from George the last week. So much for the absent ones. I have not heard from you in more than two weeks and I hope you have been well, but it would be a comfort to me to get a few lines from you once in a while… Yesterday we had the greatest blow we have had in years: buildings were blown down and unroofed by the dozens and a great amount of damage done. It is said from 150 to 200 thousand dollars worth of property destroyed and some lives lost. Albany has suffered still more… My woman Ellen goes on well in the kitchen and very well through the house, if she remains as she has been thus far I should be very sorry to part with her… But I must close. Frank and Nettie send love to all. My own to Father and brothers. Now remember you *shan't have your silk apron* if you do not write to me soon. Good-bye my good Mother. I hope you are well.   —Your *Kitty*.

Troy, April 9, 1853 [1854], Sabbath eve, 8 o'clock. [Marked "*Private*" both on the envelope and inside.]

My dear Mother—   I intended to have written a line to you before this time but with some toothache this afternoon (which is all gone) and Mr. Graves this eve, I have now but a little while to write… yet if you was here by my side I should have much to say… so Frank and I are alone for the first time in four weeks… Cousins Eliza, Libbie, and Nettie said they should see you very soon… They can tell you that I am very well indeed— better that I ever thought anyone could be, and be as I am, and what does me more good than all is to hear that you keep pretty well for you… I hope to get some cleaning done this week and to be fully prepared for coming events by another Sat. if all is well. I have been to see Mrs. Lee (nurse) and she says if I keep on regularly and carefully, that from the first to the middle of May will be my time… I feel that if I should remain as I am that I should like to have you come in two weeks or about that time.— If I could know just when I should be sick I should have you stay at home until two or three days before that time on Father's account— and my own too, for I would rather you would be here after, than some time before the event. Rhoda went Thursday and comes back here tomorrow to stay until you come— so shall not be alone yet you know. I love to be alone *sometimes*. Frank sends love to all. My own to Father & Brothers. God bless you all, let me hear from you this week. —Your *Kitty*.

This letter is clearly dated 1853 but it refers to "my time." Catherine McKie Thayer had no children in 1853 but was expecting a child in the spring of 1854.

Troy, Apr. 16, 1854, Sabbath aft. 5 o'clock.

My dear good Mother—   We received a line from Father some three days since, stating that Jimie was quite sick… I do hope Jimie is well before this time… Rhoda came on Monday and will stay until you can come, or if anything should prevent your coming (I hope it may not be so), would stay with me I presume. She is very kind & does everything for my comfort. I have had a good deal of tooth and headache the past week, and have had all the two upper stories of the house cleaned… My *clothes of all kinds* are put up in order and ready for use *I believe*. I have a little embroidery on flannel to do, and that I believe is all. It has been concluded by my *friends generally* I believe that I must not be left alone long at a time, so Frank stayed home with me this morn and Rhoda this night. So you see I am well cared for… If there is any change this week I will let you know in some way. I can say nothing of your coming as I do not know how Jimie is or how you are yourself. I would not have you anxious about me or think too much of me… Mrs. Lee has not been to see me yet, and I fancy thinks I *cannot* need her before the first of May. I am in no hurry I assure you. I only hope the time will be the right time. My best love to Jimie. I trust he is better…   —God bless you my good Mother, bless us always, *Kate*.

◦∽ George Wilson McKie writes to his father:

New York, April 18, 1854.
Dear Father—   Yours is received and am sorry to hear that Jimmie is unwell, as it will throw all onto you— but I am in hopes that he has recovered before this or I should have heard from you. I am expecting news from Troy every day— and hope to hear that all things will go off well there. I see by the papers that the *Golden Age* has arrived at Melbourne and presume that Ed has written and that you have received letters from him— if so please to inform me. You have sheared the sheep before this I suppose— If not, they should be shorn the first thing— as the weather will be moderate after this probably, and if they are to do anything this fall they must have their wool well out. If you cannot get them washed I would not wait to do it, or would do it at once, and shear them as soon as they are dry. Now don't keep putting it off until a more convenient time Father, or it will be too late to do any good in a few days. The weather has been very disagreeable here for the last two or three days and business consequently dull— but today the sun is out and the snow is leaving very fast. It has been the worst storm we have had this year here. Write me often. My love to all and a kiss to Mother.   —Yours Affectionately, *G. W. McKie*.

New York, April 25, 1854.
Dear Father—   A letter from Jimmie says that you are going to Troy with Mother to visit Frank and Kate— also that he is getting better. Well I hope that your visit at Kate's will be one that none will regret. I am anxiously looking for news from Troy. Have looked for a line from Frank daily for some time. James Kenyon is here and gives me a budget of information. The weather here has been very pleasant for some days back. Last night we had a regular Spring rain and last night we also had a melancholy loss of life at a fire. James Kenyon and myself got to the ruins after the fall. There were several killed and many wounded. We heard some poor fellow crying out for help lustily under the ruins, but when we left they had not reached him. Another man caught under the safe, weighing some 1500 pounds, he was out this morning I believe. Take it all in all, it was a mournful scene. My love to all the family and friends. Yours affectionately,   —*George*.

◖   Birth and tragedy:

May 1, 1854. About 3 o'clock this morn. my own Kitty was taken sick. I immediately called her mother & went after the Nurse & Doctor. Hour after hour I watched over the darling of my soul and saw her suffer as one in perfect agony. God grant that I may never know another day as this. The hour of 12 came & with it another day and no relief.   —*Diary of Francis S. Thayer.*

Troy, May 2, 1854.
Dear Father—   [Francis Thayer to George McKie] I am grieved to write you that Catherine was this morning about 4 o'clock delivered, by the aid of instruments, of a still-born daughter after being sick twenty-five hours. We all feel very bad that we could not save the child but when we know that Catherine is doing very well we really have reason to thank God that it is no worse. God grant that Catherine may be restored to health & strength. Mother is pretty well and getting rest today. I will write you again Thursday. No more time to write now. Yours Truly,   —*F. S. Thayer.*

May 2, 1854. A little past 12 this morn. Dr. B— became alarmed and I went for Dr. Seymour and the instruments to deliver my worn out wife of her child which was done a little before 4 o'clock this morn. The little daughter never breathed & oh how my heart was grieved & oh how thankful that Kitty was relieved from such agony as she had borne for 25 hours.
May 3. Beautiful day. Kitty as comfortable as we could expect after so much suffering. My heart is sad when I think of the little one God gave & took away so soon. Would that it had lived, for I know not how to give it up. My own & Kitty's child— the first born and not to see it alive. It is God's hand and we should not murmur.
May 4. Pleasant most of the day. My heart is full of thanks to God for his goodness & mercy. Oh how thankful I am that my dear good Kitty is doing well. I stay with her about half the time and the other half at the store, but my thoughts are with my Kate the whole time. Fannie and M— went home in the noon train.
   —*Diary of Francis S. Thayer.*

Troy, May 4th, 1854, Thursday evening.
Dear Father—   I am very happy to inform you that Catherine is doing as well as could be expected after so much suffering. She is of course yet very weak and requires the very best of care and watching which she receives from her dear good Mother and most excellent nurse. Mother begins to think about going home, and after discussing the matter, we have concluded to say to you that in case you should come down on Saturday she will return home with you on Monday provided Catherine should continue to improve as we hope and pray she may. If you do not find it convenient to come down then Mother will take the Monday morning train for Johnsonville, that is, if Catherine gets along well. We all feel the loss of the little child which we had hoped would live to be a comfort to us— But God saw fit to take it from us and we should be reconciled. I suppose you cannot very well leave home long just now, but if you can come Saturday P.M. and return Monday morning— it will not take much time. Mother & Kitty send much love.   —Truly Yours, *F. S. Thayer.*

New York, May 9th, 1854.
My dear Father—   Your letter of the 3rd of this month is received and I am glad to hear that you are all well. Am sorry to learn that the Spring business is so backward— but it is a relief to believe that we shall have a fine season, after all— a "seed time and harvest." The probability is that there will be a warm Spring and a growing one when it does come.

    I learn this morning that the booms have all given out up the River and that the lumbermen have lost all their logs— so that we see that others have their troubles as well as us farmers. I had a letter from Frank some days since bearing the sad intelligence of the loss of their child— But it is well probably and should be a consolation to us to know that Kate has been spared through such danger. I shall go up to Troy in a few weeks— and see them. There is reason to hope that you have sheared the sheep as the weather has been fine now for some days. Old Bill will get along I hope until grass and then probably he will make out to live. Will write you again in a day or two— meanwhile believe me affectionately you son,   —*G. W. McKie.*

Troy, May 10th, 1854.
Dear Father—   Agreeable to your request I write to inform you that Catherine is slowly improving and doing as well as we could expect. Mother will take the cars Saturday morning, as agreed upon when you was here. Your brother Wm. was here yesterday and he informed me that Aunt Julia was better and recovering very slowly. Your salt was sent to the Depot yesterday and I suppose it went up today.   —Yours in haste, *F. S. Thayer.*

Your brother Wm.   William McKie, 1795–1863, married Julia Smith, 1805–1879, and lived in Salem, New York.

Troy, May 16th, 1854.
Dear Mother—   At tea time Kitty told me to write to "Mammy" and let her know that she was doing well and gaining strength every day. I hope and trust she will soon be able to sit up and keep on gaining until she is perfectly well… The little puppys [*sic*] do their duty finely— the black one is better of his cough and the other one barks like a little hero when he is left alone. We have had very pleasant weather this week. Good times for farmers.   —Your *Francis*   —Love to all.

Troy, May 21st, 1854.
Dear Mother—   Yours and Father's letter was duly received and we were glad to hear that you were all getting along so well at home. Kitty continues to improve. I can see that she is gaining strength every day. She has just been sitting up in the armchair a few minutes. I hope before another Sabbath she will be able to leave her room— and Oh how glad we shall be when we can live as we have done. The little pups are doing very well— sometimes when they get very hungry they nurse rather too hard. George came up last eve per Rail Road and returns tonight per boat. He was glad to see us and we were glad to see him. He is very well and seems to be in good spirits.   —Love to all. Your son *Francis.*

Troy, May 25th, 1854.
Dear Mother—   Kitty continued to improve gradually until Tuesday afternoon when she was taken with severe pain in her back hips and limbs which

Milk leg disease The swelling of legs after a pregnancy, so called because of the notion that the swelling was due to a metastasis of the mother's milk.

continued for some hours and then the pain was confined to her left limbs where it still continues, although not quite as bad as it has been. Her left foot is swollen some today. The Doctor says it may be a mild form of a milk leg but he says it will not be long before she will be better of it as the remedies which we have applied has checked its course. I am grieved that Kitty has to suffer so much and I pray God that she may soon be relieved and restored to health & strength. If you can leave home and I do hope you can, I think you had better come down Saturday in the morning train and stay a few days. Kitty says it would be a comfort to her to have you here but she knows it will be very lonely for Father for you to be away from home. Tell Father to be reconciled to your absence for a few days, and when Kitty gets able to ride, she will make you a long visit. I do hope you can come Saturday. At any rate I will be at the Depot on the arrival of the morning train Saturday morning. I will write tomorrow evening & direct my letter to Johnsonville so that whoever brings you to the cars will get a letter at the Post Office at Johnsonville. —Your affectionate son, *Francis*.

May 28th, 1854, Sabbath evening, 7 o'clock.
Dear Mother—   I went to the Depot yesterday twice expecting to meet you but was disappointed. I came to the conclusion that you did not get my letter as you should have done. Kitty, we are in hopes, is really better today. She does not suffer so much pain and the Doctor says he thinks she has passed the worst of it. There is no denying the fact that it is a mild form of Milk Leg which is bad enough to give a great deal of pain and trouble. Mrs. Lee is liable to be called away any time after the 1st of June but she may stay a week or two longer. Kitty has just said that perhaps you better not come until Mrs. Lee is obliged to leave. If you can leave home it would be a good thing for you to be here with Kitty who thinks so much of you and it would be so much comfort for her to have Mammy with her. You must do as you think best. I should be very glad to see you here at any time not so much on my own account, but I know it would be such a comfort to Kitty. I will write a line every opportunity.   —Your son, *Francis*.

As Peter McKie had not been heard from directly since April 1853, the family became increasingly concerned and began to search for him.

~ Searching for Peter McKie:

Cambridge, May 29, 1854.
George: I have received a letter today from S. E. Shirtleff. He writes me that Peter came to his house on the 14th of October last and that he left on Sunday the 15th. He took passage on the *Golden Gate* on his way home via Panama. Peter had some letters with him for a Mr. Seamans from Lansingburgh to his family. Mr. Shirtleff says he saw Mr. Seamans on the 30th of April… that he saw Peter when he purchased his ticket and that his ticket was purchased for an assumed name of John Hill. Mr. Seamans asked him why he did that. Peter said that he did not want his people to know that he was coming home, so I suppose he would go by the name of John Hill. Mr. Seamans said further that he saw him leave on the steamer, also that he was in company with some three or four of his acquaintances, one man from Cincinnati, Ohio by the name of Michael Longfellow. He was on his way home likewise. Mr. Shirtleff says he will see the Purser of the *Golden Gate* and by his memorandum he can learn

whether Peter died before he reached Panama. I want you to go to the Office in New York and see what steamer connected with the *Golden Gate* of the 25th of October, and by the purser's book you can learn if any such person as John or William Hill, or Peter McKie ever came on board at Aspinwall and if he did, you can learn whether or not he died at sea. These are heartrending news George, and I pray that God in his infinite mercy will support us in this sore trial. One misfortune has been following close after another since poor Henry left us—

George— I want you to make all necessary inquiry and write me immediately as our anxiety is intense. Your poor Mother's feelings as well as my own is more that I can describe. Why cannot you come home if it is only for a day or two. It will be very consoling to see you particularly at this distressing period. We are all in our usual health, except your Mother. She has taken some cold and quite feeble today, but I hope it will not last long.
A Father's and Mother's love to you George,   —*George McKie.*

New York, N.Y. May 31, 1854.
Dear Father—   I have had a friend of mine who is well acquainted with the management of steam boat matters… I wrote you yesterday that Peter had not shipped in his own name, but after getting your letter, I sent my friend again— and he showed your letter to me and the people in the office gave him all the information he desired. W. Hill did sail from San Francisco on the 16th of October last, on the *Golden Gate*, and from Aspinwall he went to New Orleans, and there gave up his ticket…

There is no doubt but that Peter went to New Orleans… From the 1st of October for three months after and so you may feel confident that Peter got to New Orleans safely and is now somewhere in the South or West and we will hear from him before long. At any rate we can rest assured that he is alive or we should have heard from him in a great hurry. Affectionately,   —*G. W. McKie.*

Troy, June 1st, 1854.
Dear Mother—   Kitty remains about the same as when I wrote last eve, perhaps she is a little better 'tho the change is so slight we can hardly perceive it. Today Mrs. Lee was obliged to leave us which we all regretted very much indeed. We have got a Mrs. Demming who is said to be a good nurse but I hardly think she will be able to do everything a sick person needs as well as Mrs. Lee. We are now more than ever anxious to have you come Saturday and I hope & trust you will come if you are able. What are a few lonely days to Father compared to the comfort [of] our dear one. I will be at the Depot on arrival of the cars Saturday morning at 1/2 past 9.   —Yours affectionately *Francis.*

Troy, June 18th, 1854.
Dear Mother—   Kitty continues to improve and we hope to have her out riding in the course of another week. Her leg does not pain her much now and the swelling has nearly all subsided— there is some stiffness in the knee yet and of course the whole limb is very weak. Marcia is with us and Mrs. Demming will stay as long as she is needed. Kitty's teeth trouble her but we hope she will be able to have them out soon and end that troublesome matter.

I have been permitted to sleep downstairs the past two nights for which favor I feel very grateful. Tell Father that we shall send up that horse I spoke to him about tomorrow or next day. My hens are doing finely— 5 eggs yesterday and 4 today— Are you not glad we have eggs of our own? —As ever your affectionate *Francis.*

Sabbath eve, June 25, 1854.
Dear Mother—   The first thing you will want to know is, "how is Kitty." Well Mama, Kitty is really better & seems quite like herself. She walks out into the Parlor & all about on her crutches, with a little assistance. I have taken her out to ride twice & we hope to come up to see you in about two weeks… Kate has no pain in her leg now & the cords are gradually relaxing & soon I hope she will be able to walk without the aid of crutches. She eats all that is set before her. Our hens are doing bravely, 6 or 7 eggs a day. *Don Jr.* nurses occasionally & Mary does the rest very well. Kitty has found your thimble & we will send it to you at the first opportunity.   —Your boy *Francis.*

My dearest Mother—   My good Frank has brought me the pen and paper that I may write you a line. I have the most pleasant thing for you to hear is that I am improving a little every day. "Many nickels make a muckle" and so I shall soon be strong and well I trust. "Good bye." Hope you are well. Love to all. God bless you dear Mother.   —Your loving *Kitty.*

July 12, 1854.
Dear Father—   I have not written you for some time because I believed that every week would bring me home…

   I received a letter from Edwin yesterday, dated at Panama, New Grenada on the 20th June. He was to start immediately for Liverpool in the English Steamer & if matters did not look favorable he would come home about 1st of August— was in good spirits etc but wished his movements kept secret for some reason or other. I bought the John Lee oxen yesterday or the *Hastings* oxen or the big oxen and am now the owner of the biggest cattle in the world. Shall send them to Conn to exhibit tomorrow or next day— and am confident that they will pay— was offered $400.00 more than I paid for them in a hour after I bot them. Shall come home some time next week… I hope to stay on a day or two… Hope you will not work me too hard.

   Money is getting closer and closer here & failures are an everyday occurrence and no letting up for some time to come— is to be expected… Cholera is raging here and people are much frightened & I never saw New York as dull as it is at present…

   …Don't let Mother do much this weather if you have to keep another girl to superintend. Kiss her for me and believe me, affectionately as ever, —Your son, *George.*

 ᑡ Catherine Thayer's recovery:

Troy, July 13, 1854, Thurs. afternoon, 5 o'clock.
My dearest Mother—   I thought I would commence a letter to you earlier in the week by writing some every day, would make out a long and very interesting letter. But the *rush of business* has prevented me from time to time. I think of you oftener than of any absent one, and I know you often

think of me and wish you could step in and sit with me a little while, know just what we are doing and see *for yourself* how well I am. I will tell you how I spend my time— It may interest a Mother, it may not anyone else. At about 6 or 1/2 past I begin operations for the day. I sit up in bed, have a washbowl, towels, hairbrush, toothbrush given me. I use them and by this time breakfast is ready. I have my breakfast on the stand beside the bed. Soon Mary comes up, draws my breasts and rubs my limb and puts on the cotton bandage. Then she helps me to put on my skirts and double gown, fixes my chair for me, puts me into it, gives me a handkerchief, footstool and flybrush, and with my crutches nearby, she leaves me to take care of the room. During the forenoon I use Mrs. Bills' chair with or without assistance, and lay down once or twice before dinner. About three o'clock Mary comes up and draws my breasts and rubs my limb again. After this I generally fall asleep for an hour or so. At teatime, as at dinner, Frank carries me down to the dining room, and after meals brings me up. I have a good appetite and enjoy eating of course. I walk about as much during the day, as to go six times to the front door and back— that is since this cool weather came on. When it was so warm, I could not walk much, my ancle [*sic*] and foot would puff up in an hour after I was up in the morn, so that I did not try to walk.— But for three days I have travel'd considerable. Today my limbs pain me some but not severely. I rode out once last week and this morn. I like to go out and get the *open air* and think it strengthens me. About 1/2 past 8 in the eve. Mary goes through her 3rd performance and finishes by bathing me with alcohol. I will tell you just how my breasts are. It is more than two weeks since "Don Junior" (a puppy) has drawn them (except for a moment last night to see if he had forgotten— not he and very gentle too.) I supposed I would have no milk by this time, but I think now that it may last a week longer, perhaps ten days. By using the puppy once a week I could keep milk in my breasts a month or two longer I think, if not more. Still I am inclined to let it go now as it will be with Mary's drawing. I heard from you yesterday by Uncle James… I was sorry you hurried home to see George and you would be disappointed. He came here from the West Sab morn. and left Mon aft., is going home soon. Love to all— I must stop. Good bye. —Your *Kitty*.

Mrs. Bills Mrs. Bills was the wife of Francis Thayer's business partner at Bills & Thayer.

July 26, 1854. Very warm again. Ten or twelve cases of Cholera…
—Diary of Francis S. Thayer.

❧ From George Wilson McKie in New York City:

New York City, July 31, 1854.
My dear Father—   I supposed that I should be able to get home this week but in consequence of being obliged to go out to Hartford Conn, with the cattle tomorrow… I am in hopes that Edwin will be here before I go out to Saratoga as he thought he would come home about the first of August. I sent his trunk to Johnsonville last week marked in your name by Express. The key I have & will bring it home when I come and you will find also a quintal of nice codfish at the Lick the last of this week probably. Will bring Mother a basket of pure apples for preserves when I come up if I can get them reasonably cheap. Love to all & a kiss to Mother.   —Affectionately your son, *George*.

New York, August 7, 1854.
Dear Father—   It was my intention to have been at home before this—but as Cundall has not returned in consequence of the sickness of his wife I am obliged to stay here until he returns & am in hopes that he will be here on the cars this afternoon or by the boat tomorrow morning. I then shall be able to start for home on Wednesday. Now I have to go to the Springs direct from here in relation to a mortgage that we hold on some property there as security for bill of goods & shall probably get home by Saturday or Monday. I have been expecting Edwin daily & hope he may get here before I come home if he is coming soon. The cholera is increasing a little as you will see by the papers but am in hopes that the change in the weather will prove favorable. It is cool and pleasant this morning and if should continue a few days the disease would diminish and people feel less alarmed. I sent Ed's trunk home some days since— but kept the key thinking that I would be home myself as soon as the trunk & will now keep it until I do come. The fish I believe have not been sent yet but will see about it today. Give my love to Mother and Kate & the rest.   —Yours affectionately, *George.*

Troy, Aug 13, 1854, Sabbath evening.
Dear Mother—   Kitty has had a little headache this P.M. and now her eyes don't feel like writing & she just said "Francis you must write a few lines to Mammy." Your letter with Father's came to hand last Monday & we hope to get another one from you tomorrow. The prospect for our being with you for a few days begins to brighten… My brother Porter was married last Wednesday & we expect him here with our new sister-in-law to spend a day or two with us this week. Kitty is gradually improving in strength, she walks all over the house, upstairs, downstairs and in the ladies chamber and says nothing to nobody. Don is as cunning as he can be. He took Kate's shoe this morning before she got up and carried it off. He is very watchful and takes care that no one enters the yard without giving the alarm… We have very little cholera here now. Only two or three cases per day. Kitty sends much love.   —Your boy *Francis.*

August 13, 1854. Weather warm in A.M. & more comfortable in P.M. Church in A.M. & heard a good sermon from Dr. Smith of New York— took notes for Kitty. After dinner put away our little Baby's clothes in which we had hoped to see a living baby to give our hearts' joy & gladness. God saw fit to take it from us.
August 25. Warm & pleasant. Awful dry & dusty. At 1/2 past 12 o'clock P.M. a fire broke out in the Planning Mill which swept everything in the lower part of the City…Our sweet home a mass of smoking ruins, a good share of our furniture saved…
—*Diary of Francis S. Thayer.*

Troy, August 27, 1854, Sabbath eve. 8 o'clock.
My dearest Mother—   I suppose you will expect a line from us tomorrow. Kitty has just turned to me & says I must write to Mammy, and so I will. As far as our pleasant home is concerned, we are situated differently from what we were last Sabbath eve. Yes Mother, our first sweet home all alone by ourselves is in ashes and now we must look up another or rather we have found a house where we shall be happy if we don't have everything around us quite so pleasant and convenient. I presume you have seen an

account of the fire so I will not attempt a description. Our furniture was nearly all saved in a damaged condition— the insurance on it will cover the loss. The house, shed, & barn were insured for $2,000, not enough into $1,000 to $1,500. We have taken a comfortable house up on the second block above this *near the candy store*, No. 41 First Street… All our best things and those we prized most highly were saved. Your feather bed is all safe, *also your cup*. Our furniture is at the store piled up, one thing on top of another just as it came from the fire. We shall probably get settled in our new home in a week or ten days and then we shall make you a visit. It is a sorry sight to go over the burnt district, the extent of which is about 30 acres. Nearly 200 buildings destroyed… Don jr. was snatched from the flames by Mr. Graves' faithful Dennis and is now the happiest of puppies. Kitty was more stronger or seemed able to do more than she was from the time we commenced moving until I took her in my arms and carried her out of the burning house up this way until I found a wagon in which I placed her and sent her up here. Geo Lee was here and rendered us much assistance in moving etc. *We lost our house and we shall not be quite so independent about eggs and chickens in future*. The house we have taken is about as far from the store as it is to the North Barn. I don't mean from the Store to the north barn but from your house to the north barn. We were very sorry to give up our sweet home, but when we think of our situation compared to others who have lost their all, we thank God that we are not left without the means of obtaining another home and possessing all that is necessary to make us comfortable and happy… Kitty says don't you give yourself any uneasiness about us.   —Your boy *Francis*.
   —Kitty sends much love to all.

CONFLAGRATIONS — *Several Blocks of Buildings and a Railroad Depot Burned $1,250,000 Worth or Property Destroyed* — Between 12 and 1 o'clock yesterday, a most destructive fire commenced burning in Troy, and at 5 o'clock it had destroyed nearly $300,000 worth of property. The fire originated in the steam planning mill on the corner of Division and Front streets, and extending three blocks east to Second Street, then down four blocks to the Hudson River Railroad depot, destroying all the buildings on the way.
   The depot of the Hudson River Railroad Company was also entirely destroyed, together with their engine house and about 1,000 cords of wood… The cars and engines of the Hudson River Company were all saved.
                              —*New York Daily Times*, August 26, 1854.

Large Fire in Troy — Loss not less than a Million Dollars
A fire broke out at 1 o'clock today and spread with irresistible fury over a space equal to about eight blocks, consuming probably not less than two or three hundred buildings, and destroying property amounting to not less than one million dollars… Our city has never before been visited with such a conflagration. Fortunately, no fatal accidents occurred.   —*New York Daily Times*, August 26, 1854.

September 8, 1854. Weather cool & pleasant. Geo. McKie came from New York & went up home. Wish we could go with him but we must stay & get settled again— Then I hope for a few days of leisure. Kate not very well…
September 11. Weather cool. My birthday. 32 years old this day. I thank God for his

goodness & mercy towards me & I pray for His blessing to attend me & mine. Kitty sick with diarrhea & severe pain. Went to Stoddards for some cholera medicine for Kate. Business rather dull. We buy only just enough wheat to supply our orders for Town.
—*Diary of Francis S. Thayer.*

Troy, Oct. 15, 1854, Sabbath eve. 6 o'clock.
My dear Mother—   Frank has just said "I wish I was up to old George McKie's" and I can truly say that I wish we could be with you until 10 o'clock and then step into our own comfortable room, but we cannot and wishing is vain… I have just been reading some of the evidence with regard to the *Arctic's* loss. Of course you have it before this. How dreadful does it seem to those who are not personally distressed. How much more painful to those whose friends have gone down beneath the dark water. And here on Friday was a very sad accident. Eleven persons were drowned by the upsetting of a skiff crossing to West Troy— many of those leave families. Truly it seems that this is a year of calamities. But I would not dwell on the darker side of life's journey. There is a brighter side than this view would give. Only yesterday I saw a lady, Mrs. Wales of whom you have heard me speak, and as soon as she met me she burst out crying and said I did not know how much she had felt for me during the summer and more recently since we had lost our pleasant home and asked me how I had borne it? I could only say that I *would* not murmur, and hardly dared to wish it otherwise than as it is and so I try to feel, and almost all the time do feel that "God doeth all things well." Yet even now while I write there is a springing up of tender thoughts within me… Father's gift of potatoes, apples etc. was received in good order, and today we had some of both kinds of eatables and can testify to their good qualities. You will receive our best thanks for all these with the many other favors you are always showing… But good Mamma I begin to see the end of this sheet. I have written very hastily. Perhaps you will wish I had written less and that more plainly. It is too late now to amend. Frank sends love. Our love to you, Father and all. Good-bye. God bless you. Do let me hear from you soon and that you are well.   —Your daughter *Kitty McKie Thayer.*

LOSS OF THE ARCTIC — Collision Between the Steamer and a Propeller off Cape Race. — PROBABLE LOSS OF TWO TO THREE HUNDRED LIVES — INSTANT DESTRUCTION OF THE ARCTIC —   Five Boat Loads of Passengers Missing. — Rescue of Thirty-Two persons — The melancholy particulars of the loss of the Collins steamship *Arctic* were spread before our readers yesterday in an Extra Edition of the Daily Times, and in a large part of our regular edition. The City was filled with mourning for the loss of so many valuable lives, and all classes of the community felt for the calamities of others as though they had been their own. We do not remember an occasion when sympathy so universal and unaffected has been bestowed upon the sufferers by a terrible catastrophe. Authentic details of the loss of the *Arctic* were gathered yesterday by our Reporters and are this morning published in our columns at full length. The facts ascertained are briefly these. The *Arctic* when off Cape Race, at noon on the 27th September, came into collision with a first-class steam propeller and by the violence of the shock both vessels sprang a leak at the same moment. The propeller being built with water-tight compartments, is supposed to have escaped destruction. But not so the *Artic* which sank in a very short time, taking down with her the Captain of the vessel… and other prominent citizens of New York… The

Telegraphic dispatches received from Halifax report the arrival of a considerable number of the survivors at that port and hopes are held out that more lives have been saved than was at first reported…
—*The New York Daily Times*, October 12, 1854.

THE ARCTIC — Additional Particulars — The Propeller ascertained to be the *Vesta*, of France — Thirteen persons lost from the *Vesta* — …The vessel which came in collision with the *Arctic* is ascertained to have been the French steam propeller *Vesta*. She arrived at St. John's (Newfoundland) on the 30th September, three days after the collision, in a shattered condition. Her bows and foremast were damaged to a very great extent… All the passengers and crew who arrived at Halifax, as reported yesterday, have left that port for Boston, by the Cunard steamship *Europe*.
—*The New York Daily Times*, October 13, 1854.

Dreadful Accident at Troy — Eleven Persons Drowned by the Upsetting of a Ferry Skiff— A ferry skiff was upset in the river when near Steamboat Dock, about 7 o'clock this morning. It contained 17 persons, including the skiffman, only 6 of whom were saved. The skiffman, named George Yetto, was drowned. The unfortunate victims were, principally, young men employed in Wheeler & Taylor's Chair Factory, West Troy, and were at the time going over to their work.

— SECOND DISPATCH —   The skiff was upset by the swell from a steam tow-boat. Eight of the bodies have been recovered. The following is a list of the drowned: Jerry Cavanagh, aged 25, leaves a wife; Patrick Cokely, aged 23; Thomas Morton, aged 45, leaves a family; John Mahan, aged 15; George Yetto, the ferryman, aged 20, leaves a wife; Charles Daly, 24 years, leaves a wife, Anthony Meach, 13 years; Robert Douglas (colored) 23 years; Barney Riley, Michael Egan and Thomas Nolan.
—*The New York Daily Times*, October 14, 1854.

Troy, Oct. 30, 1854, Mon evening, 6 o'clock.
My dear Mother—   I intended to commence writing to you some two hours ago, but Mrs. Mann (who is now a near neighbor) came in and has since 3 o'clock been sitting with me. We have had a very pleasant chat in which you was not forgotten. My Frank has just come in to tea and he says "tell Mama she is a good woman." …With regard to the potatoes you "sent" us I am requested by George and Frank to say a word. We are using the good white ones and in the middle of many of them there is a black spot. George called it dry rot, and thought you had better use what you have of the kind or you would lose them entirely. So much for the potatoes which we are eating as fast as we find convenient… My love to Father and Brothers all— and much to yourself. I am getting stronger every day and feel very well indeed. Write me very soon, and come as soon as you can to see me. I fear you make yourself sick housecleaning. Do be very careful Mother.   —Your *Kitty* as ever.

Troy, Nov. 16, 1854.
My dear Mother—   I received your good long letter (long for you) yesterday morn and since I read it I have felt as if I must see you very soon. I can hardly wait until you can come. I am glad to hear that you are quite well for you. I only hope you will remain so and gain as much stronger as anyone can. But I fear you will work too much and get sick— that is what I fear… Yester-

day Frank and I rode to the Mill and up to Mrs. Stow's to hear how their little girl Ella was. She has been sick with a disease of the brain about two weeks. We found little Ella alive, but oh how changed in one week by suffering. I expect every hour to hear she is gone to the home of children. Little Ella is five years old, the first three years of her life was one continued watch, day and night, so delicate, sickly, and feeble was she— within two years she had grown plump and healthy and now, as her Mother thought she had gained a hold on life, she must give her up. The first words Esther said to me were, "Thank God Kate that your baby was not spared and taken away from you in this way." Such trials have parents: yet Mother, I think it is because the gift is sweet and precious that the parting is so sad… —God bless you and us all, Your *Kitty McKie Thayer.*

December 2, 1854. Cold windy day. Father McKie came in A.M. to spend the Sabbath with us. He couldn't stand it without Sophia any longer. Fathers & Mothers Thayer & McKie, Liz & Aaron, Kate & self took tea at Mr. Bills'…

December 31. Beautiful Sabbath moon, the last of the year 1854 which has been a year of some sad changes to us. Our little baby was born & God took it to heaven to dwell with angels. We would have kept it with us in this wicked world but God said nay. Our first & beautiful home was consumed to ashes but we have yet a happy home & a multitude of blessings for which we should ever feel thankful to Him, the giver of every good & perfect gift. Heard three good sermons. —*Diary of Francis S. Thayer.*

A summary of 1854:

January 7, 1854. A.M. cold… Mother (Sophia McKie visiting in Troy) had her likeness taken which I keep as a treasure…

January 11. Uncle James called in the morn and I went out with him to do a little "Shop." He bought a beautiful $40 shawl for Aunt Lucy…

March 2. A beautiful pleasant morn. Frank gave me a sleigh ride. How I love to breathe this clear cool air— House heat seems like the air in a sick room…

May 2. I saw my little one taken from me by my own Frank. He went out and made a tiny grave and in it laid our little one… My Frank came back from his lonely task and sat by me to give my lonely heart comfort…

May 13. My dear Mother went home this morning. It was a trial to bid her good bye. But I was thankful that I had so good a Mother and that she could be with me in this first trial of suffering.

June 1. My good kind nurse Mrs. Lee was called away this aft. and I felt very sorry indeed to see her go. I do love her very much. Mrs. Deming came and I saw that she was a poor afflicted woman.

June 16. This is my birthday… Frank slept with me tonight— the first time. How good to rest on his arm once more.

June 22. Mrs. Deming went home this eve. She has been very very kind to me. I feel that I have been blessed in having the attention of the best nurses.

August 13. This was a warm morn. My Frank went to Church, took notes & read them to me. After dinner rolled up our little Baby's clothes and my Frank took them away… And now the outward work is done. It was a hard struggle indeed to put away the clothes in which I had so often pictured a baby… God's will be done…

August 25. This morn was pleasant but pretty warm… our home never looked more pleasant. At 1/2 past 12 o'clock the Planning Mill took fire. At 1/2 past 2 we began to clear our house and at 5 o'clock our sweet home was but a smoking ruin. We left our home and came to Mrs. Graves'… We have saved most of the furniture but Oh, *our home* is gone.

August 26. A little rain fell this morn… After dinner Frank brought me to 104 1st via the ruins. We stopped and looked on what was our home of yesterday. No leafy trees, no hanging vine— But one thing makes me love this spot. There lies our Baby. A precious mound is that to me. Our hopes and our Home have perished. Our Home is a thing of memory, there we first lived together alone, there we were happy. There we welcomed a child though suffering… (See diaries of October 20 & 22, 1856.)

September 24. Frank not quite like himself. Bowels out of order. How pleasant it is to be with my Parents in our old home again. When I left here last February I had strange fearful thoughts and I feared I should not come here again, still I thought, hoped that I would.

December 25. This is Merry Christmas day. Twenty-one years ago this morn my poor lost Brother was born. Is he lost to Earth and Heaven or is he a "choiring angel now" or is he given over to the man of sin. Would to God this question might be settled. I dare not hope and yet cannot give him up.

December 31. This beautiful Sab morning Frank and self went to church and heard Dr. Berman preach a most excellent sermon… This year was born with many hopes… but those hopes were never realized. We looked to see a little one, a child of *ours* make our sweet home more than full of quiet happiness but to that little frame God granted no life, nor sound nor breath and— and— the child of many prayers and of such agony as but one can never realize was laid away when buds and blossoms sprang. Strength came back by slow degrees and when we together could go about our home, our hearts were glad and thankful. Then came the sweeping desolation of a fire and our happy home… was a smoking ruin… Ere the smoke ceased to ascend, my Frank had found this home and here we have been just as happy as in our first home… We have lost no comforts… We may gather comfort by contrast and those who have *enough* should be thankful. But who will take care of the poor. Our near friends who were with us a year ago are with us now. But where oh where is that lost Brother— Is he a wanderer or has he joined the spirits of a better world. Would that God would lift the veil that shuts his destiny out. I hope if he has been taken away (and I cannot but feel that he has) that he was prepared to go and if he was it matters but little— life will soon be over and he is not lost but gone before. May we be kept by his Spirit and ere long be joined to his family on Earth & finally to His heavenly kingdom.

—Excerpts from the 1854 diary of Catherine McKie Thayer.

lost Brother Peter W. McKie.

VII

1855–1859

Letters from Cambridge and Troy, Part Three

BETWEEN 1855 and 1859 America continued to become increasingly divided over the issue of slavery. The U. S. Supreme Court decision in March 1857, *Dred Scott v. Sandford,* was cause for protest and anger throughout the country. The Court's ruling—that a slave's residence in a free state did not make him a free person and that Congress had no right to prohibit slavery in the Territories, would be overturned by a Civil War. The Lincoln-Douglas Debates of 1858 introduced America to a new figure in the anti-slavery debate, and in 1859 the slavery debate turned violent in Harpers Ferry, Virginia. America would soon be at war with itself. Before that war began, Minnesota and Oregon became the 32nd and 33rd states. America was growing in other ways. In 1855 over 400,000 immigrants arrived in New York City, and stagecoach service was introduced between San Francisco and St. Louis in 1858—a distance of 2,812 miles that could be covered in twenty-three days. There were changes in communications: in 1856 the post office *required* the use of adhesive postage stamps; in 1857 *The New York Daily Times* became *The New York Times,* and in 1858 the Atlantic cable was completed. During this time period, Francis Thayer was very successful at his business in Troy and by 1857, after recovering from the tragedies of 1854, he and his wife were starting a family.

In February 1855 James McKie began what would become a three-volume diary written in large ledger books which are excerpted below. The style of these journals, written entirely in Cambridge, is a very simple statement of facts with little or no personal comment. There is mention of the weather, visitors to his house, the persons whom he visited, church services, business activities, farm activities, and family affairs. Two conclusions may be quickly drawn from these journals: first, with the number of visitors to his house, James McKie and his wife seldom dined alone; second, the Troy home of Francis and Catherine Thayer was a busy place with many family members, McKies and Thayers, siblings and parents, and friends and other relatives, all stopping there for a meal or the night. James McKie was the brother of George McKie and was therefore Catherine McKie Thayer's uncle.

Letters and diaries by:
P. Mallon, a family friend
Edwin McKie
James McKie
Sophia Whiteside McKie
Catherine McKie Thayer
Francis S. Thayer

Letters and diaries written from: Troy, Cambridge, Buffalo, and New Utrecht, New York; Cincinnati, Ohio; Chicago, Illinois; Dubuque, Iowa; and England.

	U. S. Population figures for 1850	
	Free	Slaves
Free states	13,574,797	
Slave states	6,294,938	3,067,234
District and Territories	197,985	3,500
	20,067,720	3,070,734

—Statistical information published in the front of Francis S. Thayer's 1855 diary.

1855

January 1, 1855. The New Year came in bright and beautiful. Mild & pleasant as a May morning. Attended to business until 2 o'clock. After dinner made about twenty calls on my most particular friends. Kate recd a few calls. Eve spent at home.
—*Diary of Francis S. Thayer.*

February 24, 1855. Saturday. I, James McKie, commence this journal on this the fiftieth anniversary of my birthday. —*Diary of James McKie.*

Troy, Jan. 5, 1855, Fri. eve. 7 o'clock.
My dear Mother—   Merry Christmas and Happy New Year to you good Mamma. Better late than never in my congratulations. How strangely does *55* look on paper, but we shall soon get accustomed to it— and so the years go by… But *we* must write letters and if our epistles do not prove edifying to our neighbors, they will be very pleasing and satisfactory to ourselves, and is not this a great source of happiness. [words crossed out] You see I make many mistakes, I always have some excuse of course and now my excuse is this— Don seems to be disputing for his territory, the yard, with our neighbor's white cat, and I am every moment expecting to hear unmistakable evidence that Master Don has got the worst of the fight. As yet however it is rather a skirmish than a battle. I have just let Don in. He has licked my face for the kindness and laid down on his mat for a snooze. We have been sewing some and are still doing slowly. Have made drawers for Frank, chemise and am just finishing the last of four short night gowns which you know I promised myself when I was sick… Yesterday I cut out three linen shirts and today I have bought a dress for myself of which I send you a sample… I am very well indeed… I only wish Mother that you was so situated that you could enjoy life as you go as much as I do— surely you are a thousand times more worthy… I do very much fear that I shall soon hear that you are sick, overworked— and who will take your place, and how long does it take to bring you up again, when you have taken your bed. Do remember how you was two years ago and do not bring on such pain and weakness again…   —Your *Kitty* as ever.

February 27, 1855, Tuesday. Went to Cambridge in the morning— heard much said of *General Samuel Houston of Texas* who had spent a portion of the day previous in that place, while passing through, leaving a favorable impression behind him. *Afternoon.* Lucy & I visited our school kept by Miss Eastman. The day mostly pleasant.

March 6. Mild day. Went to depot in the morning with Almy on her way to Salem. Met… Joseph McAdue who informed me that Sister Betsey had died the evening previous at 6 o'clock… severe thunder and lightning last night.

March 7. Went to Salem with Lucy to attend the funeral of Sister Betsey at 1 o'clock P.M… Of the friends present, there were Brothers John & George and myself and wives. Peter & son George. Sisters Ann & Almy, Mrs. Isabella Safford, John Miller & wife, Wm. Armitage & Sister Margaret Barclay, John Armitage, John McKie jr. and Francis S. Thayer & wife. Mr. Farrington addressed the audience. Funeral conducted by John C. Beaty. Called at William's with Mr. & Mrs. Thayer, found him quite unwell of a cold. Julia as usual, improving slowly… The day pleasant.

March 27. Winter day. Snow four inches deep— cold and blustering. Went to Town Meeting… two tickets were run— a Know-Nothing and a fusion ticket from both parties (Whigs & Democrats). Know-Nothing ticket elected…

April 16. Clear beautiful day— much like spring… Called at Mrs. Bills to see Mrs. Jas. Jermain…

June 6. Cool pleasant day— went to Troy with Maria, took dinner at Mr. Thayer's…

—Diary of James McKie.

Sister Betsey Elizabeth "Betsey" McKie, 1793–1855, had married Henry Matthews, 1784–1845, of Salem, New York. They had one daughter, Mary, who married Charles Crary a lawyer from Salem and later New York City. Over the years, Mary remained in close contact with the family.

April 27, 1855. Weather cooler & wind blows hard. Libby Beadle came to make us a visit. She is a good girl & finer friend…

April 28. Pleasant day. Brother Adin here… Libby Beadle with us and she & Kate have "good time" together. Eve at home early, took a bath & to bed.

June 3. Weather showery. Listened to a most excellent sermon from Dr. Berman. Studied lesson & went to Bible class at 2 o'clock. At 3 o'clock attended most solemn services. My dear good wife, Sister Liz, & self were baptized by Dr. Berman & we for the first time sat down at our Lord's table. A blessed Sabbath may it prove to be.

July 9. Pleasant summer weather. At 1/4 to 11 A.M. I saw my good Kitty off for Bath with her Uncle James, Aunt Lucy & Miss Fassett. God bless them & grant that they may return in much better health. I am lonely & wish to be with the one I love best in the world.

July 15. Pleasant summer weather. P.O. before breakfast & expected to get a letter from my Kitty but none came. Dr. Berman preached a most excellent sermon in morning. After Bible class wrote a long letter to my good wife. Eve to church & heard Mr. Booth.

July 20. Weather cooler after the rain of last night. Getting ready to go & see my Kitty tomorrow. Flour market dull… Eve went to prayer meeting. Very few attended. Why should it be so…

July 21. Cool & Rainy… Jas McKie came down in morn train & we left for New York & Bath 1/4 to 11. Rainy passage, arrived at Bath about 1/2 past 7— found our good wives better & happy to see us.

July 22. At Bath. Very pleasant day. A.M. took my first bath in salt water. P.M. went to church & heard a man from New York…

July 23. At Bath. A pleasant day. Went to New York by 7 o'clock stage…

July 27. At Bath. This morn Uncle James, Aunt Lucy & Miss Fassett left for home. Sorry to have them go. Dull times here without acquaintances. Nothing to do but loaf about but sleep & bathe.

August 1. Beautiful day, after breakfast went all around to get a carriage to take us to Coney Island. Couldn't find anything in the shape of a vehicle until after dinner when

Landscape looking North from Mrs. Beadle's. Hurd's Stereoscopic Views, Greenwich, New York.

we all stepped into a carriage & were born to Coney Island...
August 3. Beautiful day. At 6 o'clock A.M. took carriage at Bath for New York...
August 4. At Niagara. Weather warm, started for church but was too late...
August 7. River St. Lawrence. Cloudy morning & we woke among the Thousand Islands. A lovely spot in the St. Lawrence. Changed boats at Ogdensburg & went down the River over the rapids to Montreal where we arrived safely 1/2 past 6 P.M.
August 8, 9, 10 & 11. (visiting Montreal, Quebec, Lake George & then home to Troy) "...home at 8 o'clock & we were thankful & happy." —*Diary of Francis S. Thayer.*

July 9, 1855. Pleasant day. Went to *Bath, Long Island* with Lucy, Maria & Katy Thayer. Got there same evening... Ephraim ploughing potatoes and cutting briers in cornfield.
July 10. I staid at *Bath.* Came to *New York* in afternoon and went back again. Ephraim hoeing potatoes.
July 11. I left Bath at 7: A.M. Arrived in Troy at 3 P.M. Got dividend at Union Bank of 4 per ct. (On Monday previous I got cash on five coupons of N. Road Bonds at Union Bank.) Arrived home at 7 o'clock P.M...
July 21. Rainy morning. I went to Bath (L. Island). Mr. Thayer went from Troy with me. When we arrived at 7 o'clock P.M. and found our folks comfortable...
July 22. At Bath. Pleasant morning. Mr. & Mrs. Thayer, Lucy & I bathed at 11 o'clock. At 3 o'clock P.M. Mr. & Mrs. Thayer & I went to Church...
July 23. Cool morning at Bath. Mr. Thayer went to N. York to buy wheat. Catherine, Maria, Lucy & I bathed. Mr. Thayer returned at 7 o'clock...
July 24. Cool. Mr. Thayer went to N. York after breakfast. Catherine, Maria & I bathed... After dinner Maria & I went to Brooklyn. I had two daguerreotypes taken of myself, gave one to Catherine, we returned to Bath at 7 o'clock. At 3 o'clock Mr. Thayer returned with his Mother & sister (Mrs. Lovell of Michigan). James Thayer of N. York accompanied them and returned to New York. A smart shower in afternoon.
July 25. Cloudy wet morning, hot through the day. Mr. Thayer, Mrs. Lovell, Maria, Catherine & I bathed. A Mr. Elliot & daughter of Williamsburgh were drowned at Coney Island, went in too far and were carried out by the current. Two young men and one young lady of the same party escaped narrowly.
July 27. Pleasant morning. Mr. Thayer, Mrs. Lovell & Lucy bathed before breakfast at half past 9 o'clock... I will mention in this place that on Thursday of last week, Lucy & Catherine Thayer, while bathing at Bath, were *Providentially saved from drowning*—being alone, and getting in too far, were nearly carried out, but Lucy having a little more strength was enabled to pull Catherine out. They were much frightened, and felt that they had been saved by a kind *Providence* alone. —*Diary of James McKie.*

༄ A vacation by the sea:

Troy, July 6, 1855, Fri. morn. 7 o'clock.
My dear good Mother—   I intended to write you yesterday but was out in the morn... I send you the lost pin and samples of two new dresses for my excursion. I had supposed that Aunt Almy was going but from what I hear it is, Aunt Lucy and... Maria. I do not care if Uncle James takes her to the moon if Aunt Almy will only go... I have hopes Mother that you and your family would think best for you to go but you do not speak of it. I suppose it is of no use to say anything. What I think is this— that if you had a chance to get away from home and have a little change as the Aunts do and have done,

your health would be better. But I cannot give you all the rest and comforts I would be so glad to see you have. Not that you have not comfort, but there are changes that would do you good… —Your *Kitty* as ever.
P.S. Frank will get the post office direction of the place. Bath L. Island and will let you know so that you can write me.

July 16, 1855, New Utrecht, Mon aft. 2 o'clock.
My Dear Frank— Your kind letter of July 12th was handed me Saturday eve… You would like to know how we spend our time. We rise at or about 6 o'clock, breakfast at 7. Our breakfast is composed of fish, beefsteak, corn pancakes, boiled eggs, bakers and home made bread, butter, tea, coffee etc., for the most part very well cooked. After breakfast we walk about a little, mend our gloves, hose etc. read and talk until about 10 o'clock when we prepare to go out and bathe, which preparation is divesting ourselves of rings, and all things not necessary to a decent appearance in going to and from the beach. We there put on our bathing dresses in our six foot square bath house, run into the water & stay from about five to eight minutes and then back to the house where we don our dry clothing again and go home. If we choose we have a lunch of a tumbler of milk, some gingerbread and then retire until it is time to get ready for dinner, which is on the table at 1 o'clock. Dinner today was made up of roast beef, boiled ham, clam pie, peas, beans, beets, potatoes, bread, tea, pie etc.— a sufficient variety. The beef not quite as tender a selection as a certain *dear friend* of mine would have made but on the whole very good. In the aft we read, sew, and chat and at 7 o'clock we have tea. Cold meat, bread, butter, cheese, cake, and preserves make up this meal. We do not have fresh fruit as I supposed we would. I have seen none since I passed Poughkeepsie. After tea someone goes to the Post office— some are gladdened by a letter from a dear friend and another feels a little or very much disappointed because she receives nothing. About 10 o'clock we read and retire— and now you have the changes of one day before you. But my last look before our little lamp is put out is upon your face my darling Frank. It is so quiet, so gentle, and yet decided that I want to put my arms about the neck of the good original, my own Frank. But I cannot for five days more and then I feel as if I could not be disappointed next Sat… Bring a pair of wool pants to bathe in and an extra nightshirt for the same use… —Your loving *Kitty*.

July 17th, 1855, Tues aft. 6 o'clock. A very hot morn in New Utrecht
My very dear Frank— …Until today the weather has been pretty warm, but with a fine breeze from the water we have kept comfortable. Last eve Aunty proposed going to Brooklyn today to do a little shopping. We went and so uncomfortable a day I have not spent this summer. So hot, yes hot and with the headache of course. I have had little or no enjoyment since morn. We returned at 4 o'clock, took a wash bath in cool water, laid down and rested and now I am dressed and writing to my best friend. I shall keep away from shops after this… You spoke to me writing to Mother. I wrote her before I came and have written once since and much as I would like to have her here, I think I can offer no more inducement. But I must pause. I shall write you again. The boy Isaac (Jew) is waiting to take this to the Office and bring paper or *letter* from you I hope. Good bye. Dearest. —God bless you and your *Kitty*.

July 18th, 1855, New Utrecht.
Mercury 90°. Wed aft 1/2 past 5 o'clock.
My dearest Frank—   I received your kind and welcome letter of Monday last eve. You say that nearly all the people are coming. I am very glad indeed, but I do not know that this house will be perfectly agreeable to all parties— *Not that Aunty or myself are any less neat than anyone who is coming but we can tolerate better perhaps…* If anyone is coming expecting to find anything except the ocean they are ignorant and better stay at home. Now, come one come all, and someone may go to Weights. I am almost melted. There is *great sport* in bathing and strength in sea air and we shall all be comfortable somewhere. Do not repeat, say one half I have said for I have underrated. I believe only— do not let the friends think this a Saratoga…   —God bless you Darling, Your *Kitty*.

July 19th, 1855, New Utrecht, Thurs morn. 8 o'clock.
My dear Mother—   I have a moment to write you and will embrace it. I have just written to Frank, who comes down here Sat, leaves Troy 1/4 to 11 in company with Mother Thayer, Mrs. Lowell, Mrs. Adams, Fanny, & Alice. I fear some of them think they are coming to a shady delightful Saratoga, but they are not and I fear will be disappointed. I think I am stronger than when I came but it is not easy to tell with the mercury at 88° in the house.   —Your daughter *Kitty* as ever.

August 1, 1855, New Utrecht, alias Bath. Wednesday P.M.
Dear Edwin— [to Edwin McKie in Cambridge]   I take my pen in hand to inform you that we are in good health. I came down here with your Uncle James a week ago last Saturday, found our friends doing finely on sea bathing and breezes. Uncle J., Aunt Lucy, and Miss Fassett left for home last Friday. My Mother, sister Mary, and her husband have been here with us about a week. Kate is stronger and much better than when she left home and I hope by the time we return home she will be strong enough to take a bull by the horns. Day after tomorrow morning (Friday) we expect to leave here for Buffalo & Niagara via Erie R. R., stop a day or two at the Falls & then through Lake Ontario down the St. Lawrence to Montreal where we shall stop a short time & then set our faces towards home via Lake Champlain & Lake George. We have marked out the above route & shall take it if Kate stands traveling well… Today we went down to Coney Island to bathe, about 3 miles from here. A great place for bathing— much better than here altho' not so safe for feeble women and men who can't swim. I have learned to swim a little and after this when I go over to the Mill Pond with "the Boys" I'll show you how to swim like a fish out of water. We have had very hot weather for two weeks, & I hear bad stories about the wheat crop in western New York & Michigan. Yesterday & today have been good hay days… Kate has written to Mamma twice since she left home & not a word has she heard from the home of her childhood this three weeks… We expect to reach home the last of next week. Kate sends much love and so do I.   —Yours very respectfully, *F. S. Thayer*.

Troy, Aug 22nd, 1855. Wednesday evening.
Dearest Kitty—   I have just come over from the tea and now for a few minutes I will talk to you with pen & paper, would that I could do so by word

o' mouth. Well Kitty, how do you do? With your good Mother I know you pass happy hours but when night comes you feel somewhat lonely and wish to be with your Francis… Often I have thought of the sad news we have heard of poor Peter. Many months have passed and we have hoped on & could not give him up. How many prayers have been offered up for him that he might be spared and brought home to us. And now when hope almost fades away there is consolation in looking up to Him who has promised to be with His children in every hour of trial and affliction. If we should never hear from the dear Boy again we can, I think, hope that he has passed from a world of conflict & sin to a brighter & better world where I trust we shall meet him. There is yet some hope that Peter may be among the living & my prayer is that we may not remain in such awful suspense much longer. Our Hoosick friends returned from Saratoga yesterday after having a very pleasant time… Don is delighted to see me every time I meet him at the door & the little fellow almost asked me where his mistress has gone. Yesterday Mrs. Wales called while I was at dinner. I went into the Parlor & sat with her a few minutes and what do you think Don did while I was gone. Why the knowing pup hopped up into my chair & took the chicken bone I had picked & never touched another thing on the table when he might have helped himself to a good dish of chicken & toast— "remarkable."…I hope & trust that the country air will give you strength & that you will go right straight along & be as well and strong as ever… Good night, God bless you, My own dearest Kitty.   —Your own *Francis*.

September 4, 1855. Fine hay day. *J. B. Jermain*, wife & children, *servants*, man & woman, here to dinner. Children's names, *Catherine, Anna, Marie, Julia* & *Barclay*. Mans name Charles Brown, Scotchman, girl's, Susan (Protestant Irish)…
September 5. Clear fine day…I mailed a letter today for Geo. Rice, also a catalog of Holyoke Seminary to Mrs. J. B. Jermain. David worked for long afternoon.
—*Diary of James McKie.*

September 11, 1855. Beautiful day. I am 33 years old this day. How swiftly time is passing away & should not this teach us to live nearer & nearer to God who prolongs our lives. During the past year I trust that I have expressed a hope in Christ & by the grace of God I hope to live a Christian life and receive a Christian's reward.
—*Diary of Francis S. Thayer.*

Troy. Sept. 17, 1855, Monday evening.
My dearest Mother—   I can write you a few lines before Frank goes to the Office and will do so. As you have heard before this, Father Thayer had a turn of paralysis a week ago last Wed night. Frank went out in the night and found his Father very comfortable. On the Sat. following Dr. B— went out and when he returned he said Father was much more comfortable and had a far better use of his limbs than many after so severe an attack. Since this time he has been gaining strength, walks to the Store and on to Adin's. All now seems to depend on prudence in eating and exercise. With it he may live years. So say the physicians. We hope and pray he may be spared many years yet… I wish you would come down before peaches are gone. We have a large dish full every night for tea. Now will you not come a little sooner. I have preserved some black berries for you and will send them, not, not before *cool*

J. B. Jermain   Here begins a genealogical jigsaw puzzle. James McKie's journal includes numerous references to James B. (Barclay) Jermain and his family of Albany, New York. These names will come up again and again throughout this book. For the moment the reader should only try to understand this: James McKie was married to Lucy Campbell. James and Lucy had no children, but they took Lucy's nephew, Clark Rice, into their home and raised him as a son. Clark Rice was the son of George Rice and Catherine Campbell. George Rice had a sister, Catherine Rice Jermain, February 27, 1823–April 21, 1873, who was married to James Jermain. Therefore, James Jermain was Clark's uncle, and the Jermain children and Clark Rice were first cousins. Catherine Rice Jermain of Albany had been a childhood friend of Catherine McKie Thayer of Troy. As children, Catherine Rice had grown up in White Creek, New York, not far from where Catherine McKie Thayer had lived in nearby Cambridge. Persons yet unborn as of this 1855 journal will play a role in this story, and the "connection" between the families continues into the 21st century.

weather. The mercury stands at 78° here in the dining room. We are all glad to have such good weather to harden corn and ripen tomatoes… I must stop. Do write me how you are. I am glad you are through haying. Good bye. God bless you. Give my love with Frank's to Father and Brothers all—   —Your *Kitty.*

Troy, Oct. 15, 1855, Monday evening.
My dear Mother—   Just now while Mary is setting the table, and I am expecting Frank to tea every moment. I will write a few lines to my good Mamma. I have just been out to make a few calls… Frank has come and we must have tea. I wish you could sit down with us. Well tea is over and I am left alone to finish up my scribble to you. Nettie wrote that you was not very well after you got home. I was very sorry to hear it. You ought to try and be bright and well and they will let you come again the sooner… Frank's Father remains about the same— very comfortable. With care I think he may live years… Nettie wrote me that Father would spare us some winter apples. Frank says he will send four barrels to Johnsonville tomorrow… Frank sends love   —Your *Kitty.*

༄ Death in the family:

Saturday, October 20.
This morning Edward Hunt came in and told us that Jimie is sick of Bilious Fever and they would like us to come home. We left at 11 o'clock reached home at 2—. Jimie bled at the nose some 4 1/2 hours last night which has reduced him much.   —*Diary of Catherine McKie Thayer.*

Charming day. Warm and pleasant as summer. 10 o'clock A.M. Ed Hunt came for us to go home on account of Jimie being sick with fever. Car to Schaghticoke and "Jack" & wagon from there. Found Jimie quite sick but hope he will soon be better. Dr. Cook attending him and I think well of his treatment.   —*Diary of Francis S. Thayer.*

Sunday, October 21
This morning Jimie was moved upstairs into my room. Father did not like to have him moved there on Henry's account because he died there but it can make no difference to the living. It is certainly a better room for Jimie than Mother's small room.
   —*Diary of Catherine McKie Thayer.*

Pleasant at Cambridge. Jimie no better if quite as well. Moved him up into the north room. Dr. Cook tells us that the Boy is doing well, but we don't know what a day may bring forth. We all hope & pray to be spared from affliction.
   —*Diary of Francis S. Thayer.*

Monday, October 22.
Frank went home this morning— Who knows how he may find us on Saturday— or before.   —*Diary of Catherine McKie Thayer.*

Weather cool & pleasant. Niel took me to the Lick for the morn car for Troy. Sent oranges & lemons to Jimie…   —*Diary of Francis S. Thayer.*

VII 1855–1859 • Letters from Cambridge and Troy, Part Three

Monday eve, 7 o'clock.
Dearest Kitty—   We came very slowly to the Lick this morning and until we got in sight of the depot, I was very much afraid that I should be too late. As it was, the cars were nearly an hour behind time and I arrived here safely about 1/2 past 10 o'clock… Now Kitty I must close and go to our church to hear J. B. Gough who lectures tonight. I do wish you could be here just for two hours. I hope and pray too that Jimie may very soon be better and that you will take good care of your dear good self and always believe me more and dearer to you than ever before.   —Your *Frank*.

Wed, October 23 morn. 12 o'clock.
Dear Frank—   I have an opportunity to send a line by Dr. C— and gladly embrace it. Jimie is no worse, I hope, than when you left us. Until last evening he seemed just about the same. But last night he had more fever and when the Dr. came he said Jimie appeared to have taken cold. The Dr. gave him medicine and in the course of three hours he was in a perspiration and has been so ever since. I hope it will prove no serious drawback. I hoped to be able to say to you that Jimie was better and that I could come Saturday but as it is now I must wait before I say anything of coming home. I have just been talking with the Dr. and he says there will be a change in the disease by Sat. *if and probably not before,* that Jimie is very sick but has no *alarming symptoms*. And so Dr. tells me,—How it is I do not know… I was glad to get your letter. It did me good… I hear the car whistle now, I wish I could see it. Will you come Sat— and how?…   —Your *Kitty* as ever.

Troy, Wednesday, October 23 evening, 7 o'clock.
My Dearest Kitty—   Your kind note came to hand just now. Would that you could have written that Jimie was better as I had hoped and prayed. This has been a very rainy day— much like a week ago last Friday. Shall have high water again and perhaps Mr. Mosher will make me another early call in the morning… I will come up Saturday eve by cars to Johnsonville and I do hope and pray too that I may find Jimie much better. You must favor yourself as much as you can and not get sick yourself. Do take good care of yourself my darling. I must close and go to our good Wed. eve meeting.   —Your own *Frank*.

Thursday, October 25. We have had strong winds and the trees are naked. They have lost all their rich foliage that draped them six days ago. The wind has blown them away in crowds and it has brought very sad thoughts as I have seen them leave their summer home.   —*Diary of Catherine McKie Thayer.*

Catherine McKie Thayer made no diary entries for October 23rd and 24th. Francis Thayer was in Troy during the week, and his diary has no references to Jimie.

Friday, October 26. Jimie has seemed much the same through the week. Very restless at times but his only complaint has been: "that it is rather uncomfortable." So patient so peaceful does he seem I dared not say it to my own heart but Jimie did not look like recovery.   —*Diary of Catherine McKie Thayer.*

Saturday, October 27.
Today Jimie seemed a little different from what he has done— a moisture covers his entire body— Frank came up this eve and brought Don with him. I was glad to see him but Jimie is so sick. I fear he may be disturbed.   —*Diary of Catherine McKie Thayer.*

…Took eve cars to Johnsonville. Niel met me there. Jimie not as well as when I left him last Monday. —*Diary of Francis S. Thayer.*

Sunday, October 28.
Jimie remains about the same. The perspiration rather increasing. The Dr. here for the night— Sally came over this aft to have the care of Jimie tonight. No one but very near ones have been with him before. —*Diary of Catherine McKie Thayer.*

Cloudy unpleasant day. A little rain. Did not go to Church as no one seemed inclined to go with me. Mrs. Mosher & Henry came in the P.M. Jimie not as well today and I have some fears. Dr. Cook says he is doing well & there are no alarming symptoms. God grant that he may live. —*Diary of Francis S. Thayer.*

Monday, October 29.
This morning about 5 o'clock Mother called us. Jimie had a bad sinking turn. The Dr. was in the room in a moment, and Jimie was revived, but oh how deathly he looked. Today the perspiration has been very profuse. Cos. Margaret and Libby here today. Cos. Jimie McKie brought his mother. —*Diary of Catherine McKie Thayer.*

At 4 o'clock this morning Jimie had a sinking turn and we were all very much alarmed. I thought of going to Troy this morn but I cannot leave Jimie who I fear will never be well again. All hearts in this house are sad indeed. Oh God spare us from affliction.
—*Diary of Francis S. Thayer.*

Tuesday, October 30.
Poor Jimie seems weaker every day but has his reason perfectly— "says he can trust in God" We are doing all that love can do but the result is with God. Oh if he would spare him to us. Libby, Cos. Eliza, Aunt Catherine, Sally, and us all who love him best.
—*Diary of Catherine McKie Thayer.*

Jimie no better and very little hope of his recovery. He seems to be aware of his situation and expresses a hope and trust in our blessed Savior. God grant that the dear boy may be reconciled to the will of Him who doeth all things well, and we pray that his life may be spared. —*Diary of Francis S. Thayer.*

Wednesday, October 31.
This morn Jimie seems much the same, weaker if anything. Frank went to Troy this after. returned at eve.— Tonight Frank and the Dr. take care of Jimie. Cos. Margaret and Libby are ready to wait on them. I went in and bid Jimie "Goodnight." I felt I might never see him alive again. Oh may God spare him.
—*Diary of Catherine McKie Thayer.*

Jimie continues about the same as for two days past. Dr. Cook said this morn that he could not live longer than a day or two. P.M. Went to Troy per R.R. from Eagle Bridge for some things for Jimie. Dr. Cook and I watched with Jimie & I thought him more comfortable. —*Diary of Francis S. Thayer.*

Fine clear day. I went to Br. George's to see James who was lying very sick of a fever. Found Mr. & Mrs. Thayer, Mr. H. Whiteside, Mr. Mallary, & Sally Miller there. Wm. Stevenson died yesterday of consumption… —*Diary of James McKie.*

Thursday, November 1.
This morn Frank came in at 6 o'clock and said Jimie had been quite comfortable through the night. I went in and he said to me with difficulty, "morning Caty," and my heart sank within me. I saw he was almost gone. At 12 o'clock he called for all the family and gradually sinking, died at 5 o'clock. Oh can it be that our Jimie has gone from the earth forever. I went in to see him when he was dressed for the grave, and little did he think when he last wore those clothes how soon they would be put on his body cold in death— and I hardly knew the dear Brother, so thin so emaciated— But as calm as he had been in his sickness— the same peaceful expression. Frank went to T. [Troy]. Oh this lonely home Henry, Peter, Jimie— gone "the little boys" in their graves. George and I are all poor Mother has left of her five children. Oh that these afflictions might— our hearts from this world and by the spirit— fit us for Heaven. God is able and is he not willing to do us good in this hour. —*Diary of Catherine McKie Thayer.*

Our dear Boy Jimie had another sinking turn this morn which left us no hope of his recovery. Oh how we have watched over him and every human effort is exhausted. At 5 minutes past 5 o'clock P.M. the dear Boy, without a struggle, passed to a brighter and better world I hope and trust. Oh what an hour of mourning. —*Diary of Francis S. Thayer.*

Friday, November 2.
I cannot realize that death has taken from us our dear brother Jimie, but there he is cold and lifeless and tomorrow we are to consign him to the grave. Went to Troy in morn and returned in eve… —*Diary of Francis S. Thayer.*

Saturday, November 3.
This has been a rainy day. At 11 o'clock was the funeral of our lost brother Jimie. Mr. Short and Mr. Shaw attended. Oh how dark is this home and how lonely. Poor Father and Mother. May they find in this affliction that "earth has no sorrow that Heaven cannot heal." Libby here and is better than anyone else. —*Diary of Catherine McKie Thayer.*

Very rainy day. This day at 11 o'clock the funeral of our dear kind brother Jimie took place… —*Diary of Francis S. Thayer.*

A very rainy day. Almy, Clark & I attended the funeral of James McKie (son of George). Mr. Shortt went with us, he preached in the church from Revelations, 1st Chapt — 17 & 18 verses… at the funeral were Brother John, wife, three sons, & son William's wife. Brother William, Brother Peter, & son George. Chas. Crary & wife, George Wilcox & wife, and Willie Wilcox, and Thos. Shepherd, also Frances Thayer. Rev. Mr. Shaw made concluding prayer. —*Diary of James McKie.*

Sunday, November 4. Father and Frank went to church. Libby went home with her Mother after church. Oh 'tis a lonely house. How the winds will howl and the snow blow cold over the graves of the Brothers. God knows, we do not, if Peter had a natural grave. We must trust.
Monday, November 5. This morn George took Frank to Johnsonville. I am to stay until Wed. Nettie and I went to work on Mother's doublegown, and how out of place does sewing seem in this house. "The gay will laugh when thou art gone, the busy brood of care plod on" and so it is, must be & should be.
Tuesday, November 6. Nettie and I at work on doublegown. Everyone is quiet, everyone speaks low— steps quietly and even a stranger would know that death has summoned

James McKie, 1831–1855. According to family history, Jimie was once injured in the head by a pitchfork. Though he was recovering and returned to school, his parents had an understanding with the teacher that he would be given very little work. One day, Jimie repeatedly dropped his pencil and this annoyed the teacher who grabbed the poker and hit the boy on the head. Dazed, Jimie was led home by the other children. His father, George McKie, was enraged at this and immediately went to the school where he dragged the teacher out into the snow and gave him a horse whipping. Jimie was twenty-four years old when he died, and is buried in the Whiteside Church Cemetery in Cambridge, New York. Photographer, H.M. Wells, Cambridge, New York.

a loved one from our circle. Poor Father and Mother how hard it is for them. This is Election Day. All went a little while.

Wednesday, November 7. This morn cut a pair of pants for Father. In the aft. Parish took me to Eagle Bridge where I waited 3/4 of an hour. Came home and met my Frank at the Depot. I was glad to get home.

Thursday, November 8. This morn I went out to buy mourning— oh black clothes for little br. Jimie— A week ago dear Br Jimie breathed his last. When I would see Jimie I must turn to that dying bed. I cannot follow him beyond, but we must trust him with his Maker. —*Diary of Catherine McKie Thayer.*

༄ The search for Peter McKie:

Cincinnati, Ohio, Sunday, November 25, 1855.
Friend Thayer: [P. Mallon or Mallen to Francis Thayer.] Since writing you I saw the German attorney who stated that he had seen a man who knew Klinefelter as Mr. Cone, a client of mine. I called on Cone who said that he knew Klinefelter, that he was now on a steamboat running in the White River down south, that Klinefelter had told him of his Australia trip, and spoke of a young man who accompanied him back. Cone remembered that Klinefelter had mentioned the fact that the young man had got out of money and sold his pistols, the last thing to get money, but Cone did not remember where K— had parted with him and referred me to Klinefelter's sister at the Allegheny House, corner of Walnut Street and the River, a third class tavern. I found her the maid of the dining room. She had heard her brother speak of his California trip and of young men but knew nothing further. She is not a bright girl, expected her brother up about Christmas but it was uncertain when he would come, she did not know what boat he was on, nor how to direct a letter. The proprietor of the house and barkeeper knew Klinefelter well, had heard him tell of California etc., but remembered nothing of Peter. Said the owners of the boat, Dean & Hale, could tell me about him and how to direct a letter and that the widow of Klinefelter's brother could tell me more than anyone else about what I desired to know, that she lived at the Railroad House near the Hamilton Depot. I called at Dean & Hale's. The young man did not know which of the two boats Klinefelter was on, but he owned and kept the *Bar*, the *Sangarmon* or the *Jacob Lazcar* and that he would get a letter directed to Michael Klinefelter, Napoleon, Arkansas care Captain John D. Adams.

I then went to see the sister-in-law, whom I found more intelligent. She remembered Klinefelter speaking of a young man who came from Australia with him to Cincinnati and she thought that the name I gave was the same, was not sure. She said Klinefelter was quite sick and that this young man came up the river to take care of him as they had traveled so far together and that after he got Klinefelter home he left for New Orleans. I asked her if Klinefelter ever spoke of sickness on the Isthmus. She said that he had mentioned that but two died there and that they were ladies. I left with her name, particulars, etc., and she will write at once for full particulars.

You will observe by the above that Peter is not identified, but there are strong probabilities that he arrived here in good health and is now alive. I have stated the facts as I got them without color one way or the other— there is ground for hope. I will have a full statement from Klinefelter either personally when he comes here or by letter through his sister-in-law. You can write to him too if you choose. I do hope your anxiety on this subject will soon be relieved. I write today as I spent all my spare time yesterday in looking up the various parties. Truly Yours, Friend, *P.M.*

Troy, Dec. 21, 1855. Fri. eve. 10 o'clock.
My dear Mother—   I have just received your letter written this morning, and it has done me good. Now Mother you have been almost out of the habit of writing for years, but the sheet before proves that you have not forgotten how and if you had, do you remember what you have so often said— "Never too old to learn." It does indeed seem a long time since I have seen you, and I did expect to be at home long before this, if but for a day or two. If we had had snow I should have come up for a few days before Frank could come… And again I have thought we should hear from Klinefelter. Every time Frank comes in I ask for a letter or look to see if he is about to hand me one. I have just asked Frank and he says perhaps we will go to Hoosick from here next week and drive over from there for a day or so. I hope we can do so… I will not write more, as I hope to see you soon. I hope you are better than you have been but you do not say. Love to all. Frank sends love. God bless you.   —Your *Kitty*.

December 24, 1855. Pleasant day. Mr. Bills sold 1/4 of the mill to M— for $5,500 & from 1st March next we take M— into business with us. Myself one half, Bills 1/4, M— 1/4. I am to furnish $32,000 capital, Bills, $16,000, M— $2,000…
December 25, 1855. At store till 1 o'clock then shut up & told the boys to be off & enjoy Christmas. Two or three inches snow & hail, sleighs out in abundance… Recd a letter from George giving some information of Peter we hope…
—Diary of Francis S. Thayer.

Troy, December 25, 1855, Christmas morn. 11 o'clock.
My dear good Mother—   …This is Peter's birthday, and if he is living he must think of it. If he is well and *willfully* silent I pray God may this day give him such a sign of his ungrateful conduct to his parents as will bring him back to duty, a penitent indeed. Do not think I am harsh or unkind Mother. I have not a thought for myself or the Brothers but no child of yours has or can have the shadow of justification in causing you such anguish for years— wearing away your very life as it were. We who are with you have a right to feel indignant if Peter is indeed alive and well in our own Country and the willing cause of such anxiety. I hope and pray the boy is alive, honest and industrious and that you may soon see or hear from him… I have just written to Dr. C— for medicine if he has any for me. And again we expect every day to hear from Kleinfeldter. Frank says about week after next we may come. Good-bye. Love to all Franks sends love. God bless you.   —Your *Kitty*.

December 25, 1855. Troy, N.Y.
George [George W. McKie]: …It certainly does look as though Peter is yet among the living and yet I can hardly believe the boy could give his friends so much grief and mourning. A few days will probably clear or deepen the mystery. I hope for good news of the dear boy and God speed the time… Yours truly, *Frank*.

Father Adin Thayer, father of Francis Thayer.

December 31, 1855. A very pleasant cold winter's day, most excellent sleighing… The year which is now about to close has been one of great changes among our intimate friends. Death has been busy & has entered our own circle— a dear brother had been taken from us & we hope that he was not unprepared to meet his maker— God help us to do our whole duty. —*Diary of Francis S. Thayer.*

A summary of 1855:
January 1, 1855. This first day of the year has been a delightful one. Frank has made and I have received calls, the first time since *we* have been in Troy. My mind is cleared and my heart feels better for the truthful confiding conversation we had last night. I hope this year will find us members of a better family in its close…
February 4. Cambridge. This morn was cold and windy and no one went to Church. How pleasant it seems to be with my good Mother and all the home friends. It would seem that there should be no real trouble here, but where is the family to which no trials come.
February 5. Cambridge. Mother and I busy almost all day. I made pies in the morn. This has been a cold day and this eve is colder still. But Father's large wood-house furnishes material for driving out Jack Frost.
April 22. This has been a beautiful day… Five years ago my poor Bro. Henry died on just such a bright Spring day as this has been. Oh with what suffering to my heart has that day of death been reminded. But I know that God doeth all things well and I am glad that we have just such a Being to order our ways, mark our paths…
August 24. …At eve I went to see "Libby Butler" and called to see our Mr. Gordon hoping to hear something definite of our poor lost Brother, but he could tell me nothing.
September 6. This morning at 1 o'clock we were waked by Rus Parsons who came to tell us that Father had a bad attack last night and it was feared that he would not recover. My poor Frank left here with his *Charlie* at 2 or 3 o'clock and my heart was with [him] through all his lonely ride. I met him at the cars at 1/2 past 9 and he said Father is better…
December 6. This morn was pleasant. My Frank and I went up to the Cemetery where we drive sometimes, without selecting our last resting place. It matters little if the Spirit is with God who gave it, where the body lies…
December 31. … I have never known so many deaths among my Friends and acquaintances as during the past year… Oh little did I think when I left here that I was going home to watch by the bedside of a dear dying Brother. For days and nights we watched, and all that human could do to sooth and relieve was done. Every brother ready to catch every look or half expressed wish, dear Parents almost wishing to lay down in the child's place. But neither Father nor tender Mother, Brothers nor Sister can take thy place before God. The cup is given by His hand and must be drained. And after days of fever and thirsts, a change came— and the shadow of death came over him. We called it weakness and strove by stimulants and nourishing food to keep the body up, but its vital strength was spent drop by drop and he could not rally.

Monday— Tues— Weds— and Thursday came and at 12 o'clock the dear Bro— in perfect consciousness of his condition, felt that the end was come. With wishful eyes he called for each one of the home circle and gently passed away. He closed his eyes in death at 5 o'clock and we were alone— no little younger brother.

The old home is very lonely now, more so than ever. I, who am away, do not feel it as those who have never left it… Most of our departed friends died in Christ and is not this assurance better than a life in sin. Jimie apparently conscious and sensible of his condition said, "he could trust himself." "'Twas all he could do." Oh, we thank thee our Father for this… —*Excerpts from the diary of Catherine McKie Thayer.*

1856

January 14, 1856. At Hoosick. Weather cold & pleasant… Spent the day around among my friends. My good father quite feeble & confined to the house. My prayer is that he may soon be better & he may yet enjoy a good old age.   —*Diary of Francis S. Thayer.*

January 11, 1856. Cold morning. At 11 o'clock B. Pitney came for me to go to Peter's— he was not expected to live long. John Armitage & I went immediately over. Peter died calmly and peacefully about 3 o'clock P.M. after being confined but three days. He had been unwell since August, his disease was a collection of water about the heart. Mr. Crary, wife & Almy came in from Salem just in time to see him die. We thought he did not know them. Brother John was there also. We sent for Mr. Shortt, he came up and made a prayer. Soon after Peter expired without a struggle or groan. Mr. Shortt again prayed in a most impressive manner. It was a solemn scene. We were much comforted from the fact that the summons did not come unexpectedly and that he met it with humble resignation to the Divine Will… John Armitage & Mary Crary went to Miss Lands to get shroud made. I went to graveyard with old Mr. Mitchell, engaged him to dig grave…

Peter Peter McKie, 1808–1856, brother of James McKie, author of this journal, and uncle of the missing Peter Whiteside McKie.

January 13. Snowy morning accompanied by a most terrific hurricane. We were unable to go to the funeral of Brother Peter… I regret extremely that we were unable to attend the funeral and lost the hearing of the sermon. Peter would have been 48 years old the 16th of this month (next Wednesday).

January 14. Pleasant day, some little snow fell. I went in morning to Peter's, after Almy. Ann was taken sick Saturday night (having taken cold, giving her a severe pain in the side and head and was so bad this morning that she wanted Almy… Bro. John was with Ann all forenoon.

January 15. Clear cold day. We called Doctor Gray to see Ann. He bled and prescribed for her but gave it as his opinion that she could not live long. I wrote a Will for Ann, got Sarah Gillette & David Leggett to witness it. David went to Salem after Mary Crary. They arrived at 9 o'clock— Ann in great distress. Brother John here twice today…

Ann Ann McKie, 1798–1856, sister of both James McKie, writer of this journal and Peter McKie, above.

January 16. Clear cold morning. Br. William came at 9 o'clock, George at 10. John in the morning. Doctor Gray came in the morning and said there was no change in Ann… David went for Mr. Shortt in morning. He came, had some conversation with Ann and made a most impressive prayer. David took him home before noon. He came again at evening…

January 17. Pleasant day. Doctor Gray called to see Ann— said she was failing. John came down and took Catherine home. She had set up with Ann night before…

January 18. Pleasant day. Sister Ann died this morning at 1/2 past 4 o'clock in a firm hope of a blissful immortality. Mary Crary, Katy Thayer, Almy & I sat up with her. She fell asleep at 6 o'clock last evening and did not awake again in this world. She slept soundly and almost without moving a muscle till she breathed her last. We feel that the hand of God has been laid heavily upon us, but we hope to recognize in all our affliction the hand of a Merciful and Gracious God who doth not afflict his children willingly but in great kindness. Catherine & Minerva McKie came (David went for them) and laid out the body. Brother George came at noon and staid a short time…

January 19. Cold day, some storm in morning… Our Sister Ann's funeral took place at noon. Mr. Shortt made some appropriate remarks from Philippians, 1st Chapt. 20th verse… Among the friends present were Brother John & wife & son John, Bro. George, Mr. Thayer & wife, Edwin & wife, and Neil. Bro. William & John Armitage, Mr. Crary &

Peter Whiteside McKie, 1833–1853. No one ever determined what happened to Peter Whiteside McKie. At an unknown date a memorial stone for him was placed in the Whiteside Church Cemetery in Cambridge, New York. Photographer, H. M. Wells, Cambridge, New York.

wife, Wm. McKie 2nd & wife and Mr. Wilcox and his Bro. George's wife… Mary Crary came home with us to stay over Sabbath with her Aunt Almy…

February 4. Extremely cold. David found a sheep dead this morning which had got hung in the fence a few days previous. —*Diary of James McKie.*

The search for Peter McKie continues:

Cincinnati, Ohio, Sunday, February 20, 1856.
Friend Thayer: [P. Mallon or Mallen to Francis Thayer.] I have had an interview this morning with Michael Klinefelter. He says that Peter and himself came on together as far as the Isthmus. He, Klinefelter, wished to come from there by New York as the fever was at New Orleans and the Rivers might be low. So he could not get up to Cinti. Peter complained of ill health and desired to visit the "Hot Springs of Arkansas," then to come by Cincinnati home to New York, that Peter left Aspinwall in the Steamer *Young America* for New Orleans, since which time he has not been heard from, and thinks if not at home, he is dead. Klinefelter inclines to the opinion that Peter is dead. He thinks you had better write to the Hot Springs, Arkansas and inquire about him. You had better, or rather, you might write to the Post Master there giving a description of Peter and ask him to inquire of the boarding house keepers about him.

It is most probable that Peter died in New Orleans as Klinefelter thinks that fever was then bad in New Orleans.

I will make further inquires and find out how the Mississippi River was at the time. The Hot Springs from New Orleans would be up the Mississippi to the mouth of the Arkansas… Klinefelter is a pleasant appearing young man about Peter's age or a little older, is of German descent but reared here, and made rather a favorable impression upon me. He stated that Peter said he had money enough to take him home if he was not confined by his sickness. It might be well for you to come on and go to New Orleans and no doubt by a search through the hospitals and the office and books of the Steamers, you could find what had become of Peter and relieve [*sic*] from the uncertainty that hangs over the matter.

I had hoped that Klinefelter would at least have reduced it to a certainty one way or the other. I had but a few moments with Klinefelter and will endeavor to have a further conversation with him. With regards to Mrs. Thayer, I remain, Yours truly, P. Mallon.

February 28, 1856. Very pleasant day… Wrote advertisements for Peter to be published in the *New York Herald* & New Orleans papers. God grant that we may learn the fate of the boy. —*Diary of Francis S. Thayer.*

INFORMATION WANTED — OF PETER W. MCKIE of South Easton, Washington County, N. Y. About 22 years of age, five feet eight inches in height— rather dark red hair and whiskers, dark blue eyes, somewhat high cheekbones and face, tapered considerably to the chin: sailed from San Francisco, en-route from Australia in the steamer *Golden Gate*, Oct. 16, 1853, with passage ticket in the name of William Hill; supposed to have arrived in New Orleans, Nov. 7, 1853, per steamer *El Dorado*, from Aspinwall; had a black trunk marked G. W. McKie, Panama. Anyone knowing anything about said McKie, who will communicate with F. S. Thayer, Troy, N.Y. will be suitably rewarded.
—*Unidentified newspaper clipping in the files.*

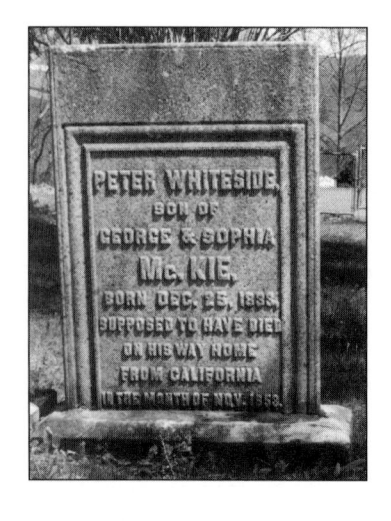

February 25, 1856. Pleasant day… John Fisher called in the evening to get a petition signed to the legislature for the passage of a law for paying the soldiers of 1812– expenses while out at that time…

February 29. Pleasant day. Another winter has passed away, one of the coldest and most severe on record. How impressively should the passing away of Winter, Spring, Summer, and Autumn remind us of our rapid approach to the eternal world and the importance of preparing for Death, Judgment, and Eternity…   —*Diary of James McKie.*

March 23, 1856. At Cambridge, a pleasant spring-like day. Traveling very bad & we did not go to Church. Out with the boys in the morning among the cattle, sheep etc. The three dogs caught & killed a skunk & such a perfumery as we had was a commotion…

April 25. Delightful day. Kate & I went to Albany & bought a carpet for our Parlor… Didn't like the idea of going to Albany to buy goods but we couldn't suit ourselves here.

June 29. At Cambridge. Very hot & no one went to Church. Down to the brook with Ed & washed off, saw the colts, sheep, etc… We had a thunder shower.
     —*Diary of Francis S. Thayer*

April 20, 1856. Snow began to fall early and continued to fall all day, was quite deep at sun down, when it mostly stopped snowing. The storm was so severe that no one went to church. These silent Sabbaths afford a valuable opportunity for reading and meditation. Happy will it be for us if we improve these with strict reference to our final account at the judgment day of God.

April 21. Mild morning. Snow a good deal melted. David & Clark went to Bennington after breakfast— after noon the wind began to blow, and increased in violence through the afternoon, until it became one of the most terrific hurricanes we have had for a long time. We were a good deal damaged. It blew the roof clear from the corn house, stripped the back part of the wagon shed a good deal and injured hog pen roof. It blew down 20 apple trees, mostly an old grafted orchard, two sumacs in front yard and much to our sorrow, it blew down most of the old walnut tree at the dooryard. It has stood there for a long time, an ornament to our place, and had almost become venerable. The willow also back of old house, on which our Father used to hang his salt basket is nearly destroyed. William King's barn door blew down so that he was afraid to leave his horses, and he brought them down to our stalls for the night. Ellen Lynch came along from Cambridge, going to William McKie's. She stopped and stayed all night.

April 22. Mild day— some rain falling through the day…

April 24. Warm day. Lewis, Henry & James Austin here at corn house…I paid Lewis 20/ for two days, and the other 16/ each for the same, in cash… I went to town in morning and mailed a Certificate of Deposit for 360 dols to George Rice, belonging to his wife. I paid 5 cents extra and had the letter registered and took a receipt from L. M. Green.

July 7. Fine day. On the morning we Doctored our sheep for hoof rot. Afternoon David & I went to the village and worked at house…I went to Albert H— to see a pair of oxen.
     —*Diary of James McKie.*

❧ A vacation at the beach:

Troy, July 31st, 1856.
My own dearest Kitty— We have another hot day. Would that you could send us a refreshing sea breeze. It may be as it was last Sabbath, ie, none to spare. Today I have had my hair cut, got a new straw hat, bread and milk for dinner

and now at 1/4 past 3 back to the office writing to you my darling… That little steamer boat on Lake George was burned Tuesday P.M. and five lives lost by jumping overboard— All who stuck by the burning boat were taken off by small boats. There is not another steamer boat on Lake George nor can one be taken there— so the travel through that beautiful place will be very little until another boat can be built on the spot…   —Your own *Frank*.

Rockaway, Aug 1, 1856, 10 minutes to 3 o'clock.
My dearest Frank—   I sit down to write you a few lines to send by the stage leaving a little after 3. It may not reach you any sooner than if I send tomorrow morning and it *may*. I was on the bed reading at 2 o'clock when your most welcome letters of Wed & Thurs were handed me… It is as I feared, very dry and hot with you… I rise about 6, go down to the beach soon after breakfast and stay until it gets pretty warm there, go down again about 1/2 past 5 and stay until tea time and really try to do the best I can here… May God bless and keep us where ere we may be—   Your *Kitty* in haste.
   —1/2 past 4 o'clock—   Well my darling, I went down to the Office and learned that there is no mail before morning, so I put this sheet in my pocket and went in to dinner… Mr. Sanderson, who you remember was sick, was taken home this morning. A gent who went with him and his parents has just returned. He says Mr. S— bore the journey well, that he had one short spasm only. Poor fellow, he has paid dearly for the champaign [sic] he drank last Sat. May it teach him a salutary lesson… 1/2 past 8 o'clock… I left this sheet to go to the beach. I stayed and watched the rising tide until after 7, then came up and took tea… I write these things my darling as if I do not expect you tomorrow eve— but I do most confidently, and if you are now in Troy instead of sailing on the Hudson, you *will pity* me tomorrow eve at 6 o'clock when the stages come in and you are not there. I *know* you will come if you can come, and if you cannot, I must come home soon. I have written this much knowing that if you cannot be here you will be happier in receiving more than a few lines…   —Your own *Kitty*.

August 4, 1856. Rockaway. Cloudy & looks like rain. Bathed with Kitty this morn. Don't feel very well & wrote home that I should stay here till Wednesday. Would that I could stay here with Kitty till Sept.
August 5, 1856. Heavy rain all the A.M. at Rockaway. I feel better today. Took a lesson in playing Billiards. Just at eve took a long walk up to the store & got a straw hat for Kitty.
   —*Diary of Francis S. Thayer*.

Far Rockaway, Aug 7, 1856, Thurs eve.
My dear good Mother—   Well Mother, I received your good and most welcome letter about 6 o'clock. I read it over three times and then went down and had a long walk on the beach and thought of you and all you have to do— and of poor Niel. Oh if he would but ask God for strength and *trust* Him, all would be well with him. I am glad to hear as much of your affairs, and yet there are many questions I want to ask… Frank came down last Sat. eve and went home Wed morn. I am to stay here until a week from Sat. next, the 15th, when I go home without Frank coming for me, which I can do as well as not… You ask me what of my health? I felt better for two weeks before I left Troy than I had done in some time. Last night I had headache, the first

I have had in some weeks, and I really feel very well. I only wonder that I do not grow strong *faster*. One trouble I always have here at the sea shore, my bowels will not move without a good dose of rhubarb every night, yet I drink a bottle of water every morning. I think I might as well let it alone for all the perceivable effects… I am doing better than I *thought* I could when I wrote you last. I was so lonely without Frank. It seemed as if I *could not* stay here without him or some friend to be with me. But I have made some pleasant acquaintances… Now Mother do write me a good long letter as soon as you have time— poor woman you ought to have all your time… Give my best to Father, Edwin, George, and Nettie. My kindest love to Niel… Oh if he would but *continue* in prayer all would be as it once was. May God bless and love us all.   —Your *Kitty* as ever.

Troy, Aug 7th. 1856.
Dearest Kitty—   It was a charming day in New York. About 4 o'clock, after I had finished up my business, I went over to the Steam Ship Co.'s office in West Street. Could learn nothing then but was told that I might possibly gain some information of Peter at the Office No. 88 Wall Street. I had not time to go there and another reason the office would have been closed if I had gone. Next time I am in New York I will certainly go and see what can be learned…   —Frank.

Troy, August 8th, 1856.
Dearest Kitty—   …Your good long letter met me in New York. I put it in my pocket and said to myself, 'Now I'll read this when I get home and feel lonely.' And last night when the boys had left the office I took out the *little treasure* and my heart was made glad by its perusal. Let me have another one soon if you please. I send you enclosed a draft on New York for $75, on which you can write your name on the back "C. McKie Thayer" whenever you wish to pay your bill. You may think I am very particular in instructing you how to endorse a draft. It is necessary to have these matters exact. For instance, a draft made payable to *Francis S. Thayer* would not go if I should endorse it *F. S. Thayer*… If you can feel contented and are doing well I hope you will not come back until the last of Aug. or 1st Sept. for I think it is a matter of *Great* importance to you and me too that you should gain all the strength you possibly can and if the sea air and bathing will give you health and strength do avail yourself of it. You must weigh the matter well and let your own good judgment be your guide… I hope and trust that you are well taken care of. If you are not, go right straight to the office and make complaints. No more time to write now. Will say something more tomorrow.   —Your ever devoted *Frank*.

The Rockaway, August 10, 1856, Sabbath eve. 9 o'clock.
My dearest Frank—   Your letter of Thursday and one by Mr. Heath were handed me yesterday and I have read them over and over again… In regard to coming home I hardly know what to say. If I really should feel that I am gaining strength I would try and stay another week. I feel very well indeed, have had one headache, but not from impurient air. You know it is difficult to tell what your strength is here because you do not test your powers of endurance. A walk to and from and on the beach is not a fair trial of strength. I'll write you again in

time for you to come down in case it should seem best for me to stay over. Write me what you think. I have had *the feeling that I might as well, if not better, leave here a little sooner and go to Saratoga and take the tonic waters there for strength and the sulphur to act on the stomach and bowels. But this may be a foolish notion "not grounded in reason."* What say you? …In my last letter to Mother I said that it was possible that I might go to Saratoga and if I should she must go with me— and George must send her… If I should go I do want her to go if she can. It will be a rest for a few days at least. If you see G— ask if Mother can get away. If I do not go there she can come to Troy and rest with us. I wish I could step into your presence my own kind Frank, but long miles separate us, yet I trust our thoughts are one… May God keep and bless us and soon unite us in body as we are now in spirit united. You will write me soon. I will write Wed. Good night my dear Frank. —Your own *Kitty*.

Troy, Our Room, Sabbath P.M. Aug. 10th. 1856.
Dearest Kitty—   …Last eve after 8 o'clock I walked down to the Mill and what a beautiful eve it was. My thoughts were with you the whole time. How many wives who had not seen their husbands for a week were made happy when the stage arrived at the Pavilion last eve about 6 o'clock. There was one there who was not disappointed but lonely. Well, Kitty if you should not come home Saturday I shall be with you. I hope and trust I am glad that you have a front room and I now think that I shall prevail upon you to stay another week so that I can enjoy a night of old ocean from your window. Mr. Bills will return from Saratoga this week and if you are doing well ie, gaining flesh and strength would it not be wise for you to stay another week. I will not ask you to stay if I cannot make you a visit. The hot weather will soon be over and if you wait until it is comfortable here before you come back I trust there will be nothing to hinder your coming right straight along gaining health and strength… Donny is in a chair at my side & no doubt wishes to be remembered. He is a good "popies (puppy)," follows me every time he gets a chance…   —Your own *Frank*.

The Rockaway, August 12th, 1856, Tuesday evening 10 o'clock.
My own dear Frank—   It is three weeks tonight since we came to this place and it seems *an age*. I intended to write you directly after tea but have spent the eve with a Mrs. Afterbury and sister from New York who leave tomorrow because they do not like it here. I am very sorry they go for they are very agreeable. I can assure you Frank that this has been a *rich* day for me, *three letters* from you… Ever since I have been here my bowels have been in such a *confined* state that my head could not be right clear, but today there has been a favorable change… I stated matters to you in my last letter and asked your opinion and advice. You see that I may lose my best acquaintances this week and it will be rather lonely for me again. If I could look in your heart and know what you think best, I could decide positively, and I must, for you must not be left in doubt whether to come Sat or not. I will only say that if you express yourself positively in favor of my coming home Sat after what I wrote you in my last, I shall come with pleasure… I shall want to see you Sat very much my darling. How much I cannot tell, but you may not think it worth-while to come if I go home so soon after. Should you in answer to my

letter of Sabbath eve advise my remaining, I will do so and hope I may hear in answer to this whether you come Sat. or not... But I must say good night. How happy shall I be if here on Sat. and your dear self appears at 6 o'clock. I hope to hear tomorrow. I cannot express all my thanks for your frequent letters. Take good care of yourself and may God bless and keep us for his sake.   —Your *Kitty* always.

September 4, 1856. Clear fine day. David went to town in morning, I afternoon. Wm's folks here to dinner, John also. Wm. Staying all night. Clark went to town with me to see his Uncle Jermain's family...
September 6. Warm day. David & I worked at house. Clark went home with his Uncle Jermain to make a visit...
September 9. Clear warm day... Clark came home from his Uncle Jermain's in morning train...
September 30. Cloudy morning. Lucy & I went to Albany...We came to Jas B. Jermain's and staid all night...
October 20. Beautiful day. David & I went to town, he took down two load of wood...I painted church steps. Saw Brother William in Cambridge. I wrote Mr. Thayer to buy me some cedar posts. I recd a letter from Charles Crary containing notices for creditors in the matter of the estates of Ann & Peter McKie...
October 23. Clear cool day. David & I at the village at work. Julia & Clark came there at noon. Julia cleaned upper rooms. I sent Mr. Thayer a New York draft for 40 dols to pay for 100 cedar posts which he purchased for me...
October 25. Clear cold day...I recd a letter from Frank Thayer acknowledging the receipt of a draft for 40 dols which I sent him to pay for cedar posts.
October 29. Cloudy cold day...I recd from Troy by railroad 100 cedar posts bot [*sic*] by Frank Thayer.
December 1. Cold wintry morning. Chas. Robertson came and put up our clothes reel...   —*Diary of James McKie.*

September 11, 1856. Very warm & pleasant until near noon when we had a shower... God in his goodness & mercy has spared me to see another birthday & my prayer & hearts desire is that every year may find me a better & better man.
October 20. Another charming day. A.M. up to cemetery with Kate & selected a lot where we hope to lay our little Baby soon. A solemn duty but we shall feel better when it is done...
October 22. Dark & foggy morning... Took up our little Baby & laid it in our lot at the Cemetery, forever from our sight. God Grant that we may meet that little Spirit, our first born, in a better & brighter world...
December 5, 1856. At Hoosick. Came up last eve to see my kind Father who is failing in health from month to month...   —*Diary of Francis S. Thayer.*

December 31, 1856. Mild day. David & Clark went to the farm and got a load of wood. Mrs. Shortt spent the afternoon here. Mr. Shortt came to tea. John Armitage called at evening. Mrs. & Mrs. Beals called in the evening. I gave John Armitage one hundred dollars to give his Mother, as legacy left her by Ann. Ann Ruggles with us yet. This is the end of another year (1856), two of our members (Ann & Peter) died since it came in and Maria Fassett also. God only knows who will be called next.
                            —*Diary of James McKie.*

Grave marker for infant child of Francis and Catherine Thayer, May 2, 1854.

A summary of 1856:

January 12. This morn made preparations for going home… Took the cars for Hoosick at 1/2 past 5 and at 7— we were with our good friends there. Found Father better but confined to the house.

January 14. Hoosick. This morn Adin went to Troy. Frank called on some of his kin. I had headache and stayed at home. Aunt Lydia here, whom I have never seen before. Time has touched her lightly, only with the tip of his wing. Father is restless under his confinement to the house. May God give him a patient spirit for *his sake.*

January 17. … Poor Aunt Ann laid down at 6 and awoke not again in this world.

January 18. She died at 1/2 past 4 o'clock. Her work is done and she has gone to a better world— so we all feel. Uncle Peter buried last Sabbath, Aunt Ann tomorrow— Truly their separation is short. This seems a very solemn day. Father came up in the morn…

January 19. …Poor Aunt Ann's body was left in the old Churchyard but her spirit is where neither cold nor wind nor storm can reach her. I am glad to get home.

January 21. This Monday has been a pleasant day. Mother and I in the kitchen a while as we used to be…

February 28. This morn I took a short ride with Frank. He gave me the letter from Klinefelter this morn and one from George saying that the young man in [illegible] is not Peter. Oh how heavy is the load on my poor Mother's heart today. Frank wrote advertisements for *Herald* & New Orleans papers.

April 1. This is All Fool's day from an old custom of doubtful origin. Five months today since Jimie died…

April 8. …Frank has had a tooth ache all day and goes to bed in misery. I hope he may obtain relief…

April 9. …Frank had toothache all last night and has had it all day. My skill is exhausted, yet how glad would I be to relieve him.

April 10. …Frank had the toothache last night, no sleep nor rest and yet he is very patient…

April 11. …Frank is suffering terrible with his teeth, slept some last night…

April 12. …My Frank went this morning and had a sound tooth out— it had a tumor at the root. Frank has borne this almost intolerable toothache four days and nights, has had no rest— and has been as patient as a lamb…

May 1. This has been a bright but windy day… Two years ago today was my day of suffering. Oh if our baby were playing beside me I could almost forget it, but it is not so. Oh let me feel and say, "not my will but *Thine* be done."

May 2. Rained. Two years ago today our Baby was born and at eve was laid away neath the springing grass and bursting leaves. Oh I'll never forget how I felt when Frank and Mr. Becker went out and took our baby. The door closed— and in that little grave how many bright hopes and sweet expectations are buried. "Suffer little children to come unto—"

May 19. Showery in the morn but the sunset was clear and beautiful. Frank made his will and I hope and pray long years may pass before it need be read by any eyes save his. It was wise to make it… Little know we what is just behind the curtain.

July 23. Rockaway. There are about 400 people in the house and it is a dreary place for a person to be without friends…

July 29. Rockaway. This morn my Frank left me for Troy. —I do not know how I can get along here without him— alone too, in such a crowd of strangers. I know what I will do tomorrow. Eat. Bathe, walk, sleep, and read as seems to be for my best good.

August 1. Rockaway. Well I have passed four days without my dearest friend, one more

During these four days, the diary also describes the carpenters, painters, and wall paperers who were working at the house.

night's rest and another day spent like very other day here and Frank will come and I shall be happy as a child. Tonight he is on the River and I hope will reach here in safety tomorrow.
August 2. Rockaway. At 6 o'clock this eve Frank came and I want nothing now…
October 20, 1856. This morn Frank and I rode up to the Cemetery and chose a lot for our last resting place. Wednesday, if pleasant, we take our Baby up and lay it in its little grave…
October 22. This morning was very cloudy and foggy but Frank took up our little baby and we took it up to the Cemetery and the little coffin was covered forever from our sight. God grant that we may meet that little spirit in the angel's world…
November 2. A year ago this pleasant Sabbath was a sad one to us at the Old Home. How soon the year has passed. Another may glide as rapidly away and where will be those of us who live now…
—*Excerpts from the 1856 diary of Catherine McKie Thayer.*

1857

January 19, 1857. A cold morning. Mercury 8° below zero. A most boisterous snow storm— wind blowing from the Northeast, and blocking up the roads at a great rate. We fear great damage has been done. Alexander H— here to dinner. I wrote to Susan Watson in answer to one from her.
January 20. Pleasant day. We were shoveling snow from sidewalk all forenoon. Afternoon I went to Bank… Lucy & Miss Ruggles spent the afternoon at Mr. Shortt's. I went in time to take tea… —*Diary of James McKie.*

January 19, 1857. Hoosick. A day long to be remembered as the coldest & most severe day the "oldest inhabitant" has ever seen. Mercury down to 25° to 28° below zero. Railroads blocked up or nearly so…
January 29. Hoosick. Weather pleasant & milder. Everybody out breaking roads in A.M. After dinner started for our Cambridge home…
January 23. The coldest day of the season. Out just long enough to do the chores. Mercury down near 30° below zero. With good fires we made out to keep comfortable. Only one train passed by during the day.
March 2. Cambridge. As Father says, "this is remarkable weather." Wind blowed a perfect hurricane all day & the way some three or four inches light snow flew about was a caution to that old gentleman, "the oldest inhabitant." Could not go to Troy so stayed at home. —*Diary of Francis S. Thayer.*

March 24, 1857. Beautiful morning. I heard a Robin for the first time. John Campbell went home this morning… —*Diary of James McKie.*

Troy, April 30, 1857, Thurs eve, 9 o'clock.
My dear Mother—   Seven years ago today I left your good home and came to Troy with my Frank. We came up from our house this eve just about the time that we arrived in Troy seven years ago, and if I were set back Mother, I would do the same thing over again. I cannot say, as I have heard others, do not get married. I know that we have been blessed beyond many, yes far more than I deserve. May God make our future as happy as our past has been… Write me very soon…   —Your *Kitty*.

Troy, May 18th, 1857.
Dear Brother [to George W. McKie]—   …We have got moved & all settled in our new home. Kate is pretty well, better and stronger than she has been for months and I do hope and pray she may be the happy mother of a living child before another two weeks. We expect the young visitor the very last of this month and you will be duly advised of our domestic affairs. We expect Mother a week from today… —Good-bye, *Frank.*

Greenbush, May 18, 1857, Tues aft. 1 o'clock.
Dear Mamma—   Well Mother I am sorry enough to hear that your second girl was not worth keeping, and particularly just at this time. We hope Edwin is better and Nettie too, so that you will not be obliged to have a plurality of invalids at home. At first I felt greatly troubled at the state of affairs, but I concluded that I could not make any changes in my arrangements, that on the whole it has been thought best for you to be with me, and if you came, those at home would be provided for in some way. So I try to think that it will be "all right." I only fear that you are working yourself sick to get ready to leave home. We are well and delightfully situated, if we only have pleasant weather. I *long* for a little sunshine. You say you will come the 25th. I cannot ask you to defer it longer… My love to Father, Niel, and Brothers. May God bless & keep you and us   —Your *Kitty.*

a fine boy The letter announces the birth of Francis McKie Thayer, known as Uncle Frank in later years.

Troy, June 13, 1857.
Dear Father—   I am indeed rejoiced to say that your dear daughter gave birth to a fine boy this A.M. She was sick about six hours and had a severe time but nothing like what she passed through three years ago. The Doctor says everything is favorable and we hope and pray too that all may go on well. The Boy is a "*bouncer*" weighing 11 pounds and ready to see his Grandfather. We shall of course be glad to see you here at any time. Mother is comfortable and happy that Kitty has got along thus far so well. I will write again soon, Yours most affectionately, *Frank.*

June 13, 1857. Delightful day. Cool & pleasant. At 1/2 past 4 my good Kate called me & said she was going to be sick. Called Mother & Mrs. Lee & then started for Dr. B— who arrived about 8 & at just 10 o'clock & 10 minutes my darling Kitty presented me with a fine boy & O how thankful.
June 14, 1857. Pleasant. Kitty & the Baby doing finely. God has been kind to us & our hearts are full of joy & gladness. Up to church in A.M. Dr., Berman preached a most excellent sermon…   —*Diary of Francis S. Thayer.*

Troy, June 15, 1857.
Dear Father—   I wrote you Saturday that you had a grandson down here and all doing well. We expected you down this morning to take a look at the young gentleman. He is indeed a *lusty* fellow and those who have seen him say he is a fine boy. Mother says if she does not see you or hear from you she will take the morning cars Wednesday for Johnsonville where you will meet her. Kate is very comfortable and we see nothing to hinder her from getting along in good time…   —Yours in haste, *Frank.*

June 17, 1857. Mother McKie took morn cars for Lick where she will meet Granddaddy George who will be happy to see Sophia & to hear from his grandson.
—*Diary of Francis S. Thayer*

June 29, 1857. Pleasant morning. I went to Troy. I dined with Mr. Thayer— saw their son for the first time…
—*Diary of James McKie.*

Troy, July 15, 1857.
Dear George—   …Father and Mother came down on Monday to see us & the Baby. Father will go home tonight and he says Sophia must go too, but Kate says she shant— which will carry the day I don't know, Kate I reckon… Yours as ever, *Frank.*

Greenbush, Fri 11 o'clock. [sometime in the summer of 1857]
My dear Mamma—   I trust you will be glad to get a line from me as you want to know just how we are doing. I am nicely washed and dressed and Mrs. Lee is washing the baby in the parlor by the stove— fire every day, what weather! Baby kept us awake all night after you left and let us sleep all last night… My breasts are now very comfortable and I think can be kept so easily, nipples a little tougher I think. Have not taken a drop of anything of medicine— have eaten figs and prunes and last night I had the *largest* passage from the bowel I ever saw from a *human*… But I must stop— As you will perceive I have not looked on the paper much for fear of straining my eyes. God bless you and us.   —*Kitty*.

July 19, 1857. Weather continues very hot. Up to Church in A.M. Dr. Berman preached as normal a most excellent sermon: *Duty of Parents Towards Their Children*. Now that I am a Father I should heed & profit by this appeal.   —*Diary of Francis S. Thayer.*

Greenbush, Aug 25, 1857.
My dearest Mother—   Do you think that I have forgotten you or how to write. I hope not for I do well remember and I can scribble… Father Thayer has lost the use of his limbs within a week and Henry who has just come from Ionia, with his strong arms and willing heart, can be of great service at home. I should not be surprised to know of a change there very soon. Frank is here talking to his boy. I have asked him two or three questions but he pays no attention to *me*. Baby has a fine vaccine scab on his arm. Frank has just said "I guess your Grandma would like to see you."   —Your *Kitty*.

August 29, 1857. Port & family left in A.M. for Utica. Went to Hoosick to see my poor feeble Father who is wasting away both in body & mind…
—*Diary of Francis S. Thayer.*

Port Porter Thayer, Francis Thayer's brother.

Mon eve 1/2 past 9. [summer 1857]
My dear good Mother—   I received your note by George and am glad to feel that you are not working harder and have not more cares than ever. You must take care of yourself anyway. Well you wrote me that you wished 1/2 yd lace. Do you mean trimming lace or do you mean plain lace for the body

of the cap? Write and let me know at once. I send you black ribbon as you desired. Our baby grows fast enough as George can tell… Is my carpet bag at your house? If so, will you send it the first good opportunity. I cannot find it here and it rather seems to me that you have it up there… Father Thayer fails very gradually… How much I do want to see you, come just as soon as you can. God bless you—   Your *Kitty*.

September 28, 1857. Pleasant morning. I went to Troy and back at noon. William went down also. Philadelphia Banks suspended specie payment on Saturday. New England banks out of Boston suspended today. I deposited my check today for 530 dols in full for my new stock. I deposited the money the 1st day of August. I took a draught to draw interest from 1st September.   —*Diary of James McKie.*

Buffalo, Oct. 10th, 1857, Saturday P.M.
Dearest Kitty—   I arrived here safely about 2 o'clock this morning, was detained four or five hours by a collision 18 miles this side of Rochester. The train running east was behind time, our train waited the required time and moved on very slowly and in a few moments both trains came together, smashing the front part of both engines and breaking three or four cars. The fireman on the train going east jumped off and was very badly hurt about the head and face. One passenger in the forward car saw something wrong and started to go out, got out on the platform when the crunch came and had his leg broken. If he had kept his seat no doubt he would have escaped. Several passengers got scratched and bruised I was in the rear car and was by a kind providence preserved without the least injury. This is a beautiful day and now I wish I could step in and stay with you and "Babies"…Kiss "Babies" and tell the dear little fellow to kiss you for me.   —Your own *Frank*.

Accident on the Erie Railroad — Buffalo, Thursday, Oct. 8.
At noon today an engine on the New York and Erie Railroad ran into the way express train, east of the Buffalo and Erie Road, at the crossing of the two roads in this City. Several persons were seriously but not fatally injured. Nobody was killed. The train was heavily loaded with passengers on their way to the State Fair. There were no through passengers on the train.   —*The New York Times,* October 9, 1857.

Oct. 14, 1857, Wed 3 o'clock P.M.
My dearest Frank—   I have just put Baby on his pillow and wish you could see how sweet and peaceful he lies in his infant slumber… —Your *Kitty*

October 14, 1857. Pleasant day in Buffalo. Banks throughout the State suspending specie payments. Business at a perfect standstill. Could not buy wheat for State Bank Drafts on Metropolitan Bank, New York. A pretty state of affairs truly. Eve raining.
                                                —*Diary of Francis S. Thayer.*

The Money panic reached its climax yesterday, and the banks in the City of New York, fifty-odd in number, all suspended Specie payments! The run which terminated in this resolution, involuntary or compulsory with eighteen or twenty of the banks before 3 o'clock, and voluntary by the subsequent action last night of the remainder commenced about noon in Wall Street, after it became generally known that all the banks on the North River or West side of the town had stopped payment. The old Bank of

New York was the first among the large banks to exhaust its specie... The Bank panic yesterday seriously disturbed general business—and there was a partial pause in operations. Flour declined... wheat fell... and corn was a trifle cheaper...
—*The New York Times*, October 14, 1857.

October 30, 1857. Weather cloudy with an occasional streak of sun... Noon train Kate, Baby & self went to Hoosick. Little Frank's first visit to Hoosick. Mother was delighted to see grandson. My poor father lies on his bed almost gone in body & mind...
—*Diary of Francis S. Thayer.*

November 14, 1857. Cool morning. I went to Troy. Took dinner at Mr. Thayer's...
—*Diary of James McKie.*

Troy, December 4, 1857, Fri eve 8 o'clock.
My dearest Frank—   If you were as near me in person as you are in thought I should not need a pen to tell you that we are well and doing well—what you wish most to hear... Baby is about over his cold, and I am better of mine. It is now confined to me "ed." I wish you could take him (Baby) in your arms as I know you would like to. My dear Frank— I make so many mistakes writing that I almost wish it were not necessary for me to write, indeed I could quite wish it. I wish you were through your business with satisfaction to yourself... Good night my Darling. May God bless and keep you and us.
—*Kitty*

Chicago, Dec. 8th, 1857.
Dearest Kitty—   I am getting along bravely in the way of buying wheat and at the rate I have bot [*sic*— bought] today it will take only two or three days more to find the bottom of my purse. Have bot a little more than half my money's worth. A week tomorrow since I left home and I assure you it seems a month to me. How often I think of you and our darling boy up in our room, and Oh how happy two hearts will be when we can again meet under our own "vine & fig tree." I wonder if Baby will know me? I cannot now tell when I shall be able to leave here and I will not name the time for fear of disappointment. Now dearest you must write a line, if no more, very often. I expected a letter from you this morn but none came... Weather today mild and a little rain. Any quantity of mud.   —More than ever your own *Frank.*

Chicago, Dec. 9th, 1857.
My own dearest Kitty—   ...Yesterday I did a "Land office business" in the way of buying wheat & today nothing. Hope to do something tomorrow & close up my purchases in this market this week & be ready to start for Iowa next Monday morning...   —More than ever your own *Frank.*

December 31, 1857. Last night about three inches of snow & a few sleighs slipping about. Hardly enough for good sleighing. Brother Adin here & took dinner with us. Geo. W. McKie also took dinner with us. Business very dull, average sales this week about 10 bls per day. This day closes up another year & I am truly thankful to a kind & merciful God for all His mercies towards me & mine. We have indeed been blessed with health, happiness & prosperity which I pray God may be continued to us.
—*Diary of Francis S. Thayer.*

A summary of 1857:

June 13, 1857. This morn at 10 o'clock a perfectly formed and healthy boy was given us and we were so thankful.

September 1. The Summer is past and Autumn is here— When Summer came I thought—who will live to see the Autumn come, perhaps all here but me. But I tried to Trust and now we have our boy, strong & well. We are thankful…

—*Excerpts from the 1857 diary of Catherine McKie Thayer.*

1858

January 1, 1858. A beautiful New Years day. I continued in a good deal of distress in my head. Doctor Kennedy was very attentive and nursed me very well…

January 2. A pleasant morning. Almy came down in morning train to stay a few days. Wm. Came down again this afternoon and staid until evening. Bro. George came in before dinner and staid until 3 o'clock. About 10 o'clock P.M. Doctor Kennedy came in and bathed my head thoroughly with Arnica which relieved my head almost entirely from pain.

January 3. Clark went to Meeting. I was quite comfortable through the day.

January 4. Beautiful day. I continued improving— have some appetite.

January 5. Mild weather. I feeling better. John Whiteside called in the forenoon.

January 6. A clear beautiful day. Bro. John here to dinner. I improving.

January 8. Somewhat colder. I continued to improve. The Doctor has not called since the forepart of the week.

January 30. Blustering morning… I settled with Doctor Kennedy. I found him in bed; he had made 26 visits charging 13 dollars. He made his bill $11.50 which I paid him and took receipt… I came home. The others made some other calls…

—*Diary of James McKie.*

Troy, Jan 13, 1858.
My dear Mother—   I should have written you before but have not been very well for two or three days— a little cold in one breast, chill from headache etc. but I am well today and we have been out riding with our Baby this aft… Father Thayer fails very gradually— has fever in the aft and sweats at night, with less appetite… Frank is well and very happy with his Boy… Write me soon and come too…   —Your *Kitty*.

 ༄ Death in the family:

February 3, 1858. Weather mild & pleasant. A very little snow & ice left. Business pretty good this month so far… Took Baby to Church & had him Christened Francis McKie. God grant that good old Dr. Berman's prayer may be around for both Parents & child.

February 8. Up to the Depot on arrival of the cars from Hoosick when I learned that my good kind Father died last eve 10 minutes past 6 o'clock. An event we have looked for daily for months almost. It is hard to give him up. I pray God that my dear Mother may find comfort & consolation. Father & Mother McKie came in morn. Went to Hoosick at eve.

February 9. At home with my afflicted Mother, brothers, & sisters. Our good Father lies cold & lifeless in the Parlor & tomorrow we are to consign him to the clods of the Valley. This is our first great affliction as a family. Mr. B— called & spoke words of comfort…

Adin Thayer, 1785–1858, is buried in the Maple Grove Cemetery in Hoosick, New York. Photograph courtesy of the Hoosick Township Historical Society.

February 10. At 11 o'clock A.M. we met to pay the last, sad offices to the memory of our departed Father. Mr. B— officiated. Would to God that the above & children could be with us in this sad hour. James, Houghton, Mary, & Porter cannot meet with us today. God grant that we may all so live as to meet in heaven. —*Diary of Francis S. Thayer.*

February 24, 1858. Colder. Mercury 12° below. Afternoon I went to the farm and engaged C. Bailey to cut some wood This is my birthday, 53 years old. Another year has gone to the records of eternity. Time flies as on Eagles wings. In many things have I offended my gracious God, and in all things come short of my duty. Who of us will be here at the next anniversary of my birthday. God only knoweth. May He prepare us for every event of his Providence and especially for a Judgment day.
—*Diary of James McKie.*

April 1, 1858. Charming day. At work all day & until after 11 o'clock at night taking inventory. Net Profits this year $16,098.09 half of which is placed to my credit making my balance $30,154.32. This year I have only 5/12 of the business & Bills pays me $225 for use of 1/12 of mill over & above repairs insurance etc.
—*Diary of Francis S. Thayer.*

Thayer family plot, Maple Grove Cemetery, Hoosick, New York.

Chicago, April 12th, 1858, Monday P.M.
Dearest Kitty—   Your thrice welcome note of Friday P.M. came to hand this morning. This is a dark rainy disagreeable day which *in Chicago* is enough to make a fellow homesick. Yes dearest, I am more than ever anxious to get home. My business here could be dispatched in time to reach home Saturday eve, but you know I have got to go to Dubuque for brother Aaron & under the circumstances I feel that it is my duty to go, for it will save Aaron a long journey & some expense. Please tell Aaron that I will leave here for D— on the 13th & do all I can for him there… And what shall I say about our darling boy. Oh how I want to kiss him & his dear Mother to my bosom. May God's blessing rest upon us and bring us together in health & strength before many days…   —Your own *Frank.*

Chicago, April 14th, 1858.
Dearest Kitty—   Your short but very welcome note of Monday came to hand this A.M. and I have only time to reply very very briefly. Well darling I have shipped about half of our wheat & it now looks as 'tho I should be able to close up my business here in one or two days after returning from Dubuque to which place I expect to go tomorrow & return Friday night or Saturday… and you may expect to see me home the last of next week. God bless you & our darling boy, Your own *Frank.*

Chicago, April 15th, 1858, Thursday P.M.
My own dearest Kitty—   When I wrote you *very hastily* yesterday P.M. I expected to have taken the cars for Dubuque this morning, but I couldn't get the wheat onboard in time so I must go tonight… This is a delightful day (the first one since I have been here) & Port is now waiting on me to take a ride about town. Last eve I went to a good Prayer meeting… Whenever the weather is pleasant you *must* order Filkins' carriage & treat yourself and friends to a ride. I expect to return from D— Saturday & hope to finish up business here about next Tuesday… You can charge a few days of my absence

to brother Aaron. Love to Mother & a thousand kisses to you all. More than ever your own *Frank*.

Dubuque, Iowa, April 17, 1858, Saturday evening.
My own dearest Kitty—   I can hardly realize that at the close of another week (when I expected to be with you) I find myself away off here in Iowa beyond the great Mississippi, farther away from the dearest ones of my heart than ever before, but so it is. Many long miles separate us, and yet you and our darling little boy are ever with me in thought. Would that I could be with you *now* all well and happy… Well darling I left Chicago Thursday eve 9 o'clock and arrived here Friday morning 8 o'clock. I found Aaron's matters here about as I expected ie, in not a very desirable shape but after two days work with good lawyers, I feel confident that all will come out right in the end. The fact is there is no money here and people cannot pay their debts at present. All have been too much engaged in speculation. Now they must go to work, and with industry and economy they will, after a few years, be able to say we are "andependent." …You may think it strange that I should go to the theater, but you will be relieved when I tell you that the theater here has been turned into a house of prayer. Yes Kitty, last eve I listened to a good sermon delivered on the stage… This is a very pleasant little city with about 10,000 inhabitants, mostly eastern people with a sprinkling of Dutch & Irish. The lead mines in this vicinity are very rich and extensive. I visited one of the mines today and got a specimen of the ore. I shall return to Chicago Monday and close up my business there just as soon as possible and leave for home. I hope to find letters from you at Chicago… A good looking man has just taken a seat at the table opposite me for the purpose of writing. I just glanced my eye over onto his sheet and what do you think I saw? Why just these words, "My dear wife & Co." I wonder who the "Co" is— perhaps a dear little boy about ten months old. Be that as it may, I know who the Co is in our firm and a lovely little number he is too… Good night my own dearest Kitty. God bless you and our dear child. More than ever your own *Frank*.

Troy, April 18, 1858, Sabbath.
My dearest Frank—   Last evening my heart was made lighter by your most welcome letter of Thursday, as yours of Wednesday did the same sweet kindness the day before. Oh, these frequent letters from you, do far more than anything else to comfort me in your absence. Mother is still here and Father, who came Friday aft. They do go home this morn… The friends in Hoosick are well. I have not said to you that Baby has shown no symptoms of hooping cough. You ask if he misses you? I know he does— I took him to your portrait just now and he said "Papa." …You say the weather has been unpleasant with you. It has been delightful here except a few days and in every degree… We have had dinner my darling and wished you here, and Father is carrying Baby around… I hope you will leave Chicago before this reaches there, but if you should not, you may be glad to hear from home. I feel that I can hardly wait for you to come…   —Your *Kitty* always.

Chicago, April 21, 1858, Wednesday P.M.
My own darling Kitty—   This morning my heart was made glad by the reception of your most excellent note of last Sabbath… Yes darling I have but

little more to do here & Friday morning I hope & trust will find me on my way to those most dear to me on earth… —Your own *Frank*.

April 22, 1858. A clear cool, frosty morning. I went to the farm and selected 46 dry sheep and put them out to grass, leaving 87 ewes to lamb…
May 4. Pleasant day. Mr. Thayer here to dinner, came up in morning and returned by afternoon train…
May 28. A clear beautiful day… I went to the farm and altered the lambs…
June 2. A beautiful day… We attended the dedication of the cemetery. Mr. Nixon made the first prayer. Mr. Smart the Dedicatory prayer. Doctor Gillett gave an address.
June 3. A warm day, getting dry. In the forenoon Almy and I went to the Cemetery. I selected two lots on Cypress Avenue, section 6 no 52 & 53 [illegible] at $24.12 & $24.75, making $48.87… —*Diary of James McKie.*

June 20, 1858. At 1/2 past 2 o'clock this morning our Mill set on fire & before daylight was a mass of ruins. Insured $14,000 on Mill & $13,000 on stock. Loss on Mill say $10,000 over insurance. Stock nearly covered. At Church in morn & heard a good sermon from Dr. Berman. My mind was not fixed on the sermon.
June 22, 1858. …All day at the ruins attending to the sale of damaged wheat which we are getting out in large quantities. Some good & more almost worthless…
—*Diary of Francis S. Thayer.*

The extensive flour mills of Bills, Thayer & Usher, in the Sixth Ward of Troy, was set on fire by incendiaries, and entirely destroyed at an early hour yesterday morning with a large quantity of flour and grain. Loss $30,000 to $40,000, insured for $27,000.
—*The New York Times*, June 21, 1858.

August 5, 1858. Pleasant. Albany in A.M… Father McKie & Aunt Almy came in P.M. Atlantic cable successfully laid. —*Diary of Francis S. Thayer.*

The Greatest Event of The Age — Success of the Atlantic Telegraph Enterprise — Landing of the Cable — The Electrical Current Perfect Throughout — The *Niagara* and the *Gorgon* arrived at Trinity Bay yesterday, and the Atlantic Cable, the working of which is perfect, is being landed today… The President, who is at Bedford, received the first information of the successful laying of the Atlantic Cable through the agency of the Associated Press… —*The New York Times,* August 6, 1858.

Troy, Aug 13, 1858.
Dear Mother—   I am happy to say that Baby is better & quite like himself again. His eyes sparkle and you would laugh to see him diving about. Old Charlie got out [of] the stable last night and got hurt in the shoulder very badly. I may have to send up after the gray mare for a few days. Yours in haste.   —*Frank.*

Troy, Aug. 17, 1858.
Dear Mother—   I know you will be glad to hear that Baby is well again, diving about and pitching into things in general as usual. Old Charlie is the only invalid in our family at present and I am happy to say that he is "rather on the mend"…   —*Francis.*

dedication of the cemetery
The Woodland Cemetery in Cambridge, New York.

Destructive Fire in the Sixth Ward   The largest fire in point of pecuniary loss that has occurred within the city limits for a long time, took place on Sunday morning and involved the total destruction of Messrs. Bills, Thayer & Usher's flour mill, storehouse and elevator, one of the oldest buildings in the city… The mill had been left at midnight on Saturday by the men, with everything safe as usual… Before water could be obtained, or an engine got to work, the entire building was in flames throughout, lighting up the city brilliantly… The mill was built by the Messrs. Witbeck, some time about the year 1790… Messrs. Bills, Thayer & Usher estimate their loss to be between $30,000 and $40,000. The mill will probably be immediately rebuilt… P. S. —We understand that a man was arrested yesterday afternoon on suspicion of having fired the building.
—*Troy Daily Whig*, June 21, 1858.

August 24, 1858. A very warm day… Clark came home this evening from his Uncle Jermain's having been there since Thursday last… —*Diary of James McKie.*

Springside, Sep. 22, 1858.
My dear Mother—   We arrived in Troy safely about 4 hours after leaving the parental roof… Baby is doing well and is pretty noisy. Frank was delighted to see Baby looking so much better. Our horse Jack is too lame to drive, more lame than when we came home. Frank has bandaged and bathed, and this morn Jack goes up to Dr. Parker for treatment, where Old Charlie is staying for the same purpose. Last Sat I went up with Frank in the aft. with the new horse, and he, to increase our perplexity, tripped on a stone and then went to limping away and Sabbath we stayed home from church with three lame horses in the stable. For our encouragement this last one is now in good condition…   —*Your affectionate daughter.*

September 22, 1858. At Hoosick. Down to Cemetery with Adin in A.M. and for the first time saw the grave of my good Father whose soul I Trust is at rest in Heaven…
—*Diary of Francis S. Thayer.*

October 5, 1858. A pleasant day. I was taken sick at 12 o'clock at night of Billious fever. I have taken oil & salts to day, but could keep nothing down. I took a sweat this morning which relieved my limbs but drove the pain to my head.
October 6. I found myself very sick. Called in Doctor Kennedy. He pronounced it Billious Fever. Continued bad through the day.
October 7. Still continued very sick. In much distress in my head. Preaching at the Church today (Fast day).
October 8. Got better through the day. Pains mostly subsided at evening. Robert Wilcox died this afternoon.
October 9. I still continue comfortable but extremely weak. Preaching at the Church this afternoon.
October 10. Continue to improve slowly. Communion at the Church today. Lucy went during the serving of one table. Mr. Campbell assisted Mr. Shortt.
October 11. I am comfortable through the day— have been somewhat excited on account of too much company. Brothers John, George, & William were here most of the day. Edwin McKie also. They attended the funeral of Robert Wilcox at 1 o'clock P.M.
October 12. Gradually improving, strength gaining. Wm. Wilcox called this morning on his way home from his Father's funeral.
October 13. I find myself steadily improving in strength.
October 14. Nothing new with me, gaining as fast as I could expect.
October 15. Still mending. David went to Schuylerville and got Almy.
October 16. I am improving. We have had most beautiful weather all the fall.
October 17. I am comfortable. Lucy, Almy, & Clark went to meeting…
October 23. A warm day, some showers through the day. Afternoon Clark went to the farm for walnuts… Edwin McKie & wife here to tea, they are about going to sail for Liverpool. Lucy & Almy out making calls. Wm. King called.
—*Diary of James McKie.*

Troy, Nov. 7, 1858.
My dear Mother—   I received your note yesterday, written you say to force a line from me… I am glad to hear that you have a girl that promises well, if

not do the best you can in a respectable quarter… We are moved to 105 First St.— almost opposite our first home in Troy… Baby's teeth *do trouble* him and *us*, but he is not sick and I am thankful… —Love to Father & Niel. Frank sends love.   —Your *Kitty*.

November 13, 1858. …Did nothing at Mill today except repair the pump. I have given up all hopes of getting up the Mill this season. Father McKie's barn & sheds burned last night.
November 14. …Wrote to Father McKie a letter of sympathy on account of his loss of about $1,000 by the burning of the barns, sheds, etc.   —*Diary of Francis S. Thayer.*

Nov. 14th, 1858, Sabbath eve.
Dear Father—   Catherine has written a note to Mother and I will write a few words to you. We were indeed very sorry to hear of your late heavy loss by fire. The paper says the loss is $2,000 and insurance $600. We hope to hear directly from you soon and that the amount is considerably overstated by the paper, as is generally the case. I need not tell you that you have our warmest sympathy under this last trouble which is light when compared with what you have passed through during the past few years. I know what it is to see property destroyed by fire, and I have sometimes thought my lot was a hard one, but a moments reflection leads me to know and feel that I should be thankful for so much of prosperity, and when I remember my losses I do not forget I have been highly favored. I hope and trust you will not let your late loss trouble you. Remember that you have much to be thankful for and that all your wants will be supplied. You will not be deprived of one comfort of life by the loss of a few hundred dollars. It is the way of the world… Anything I can do for you in regard to rebuilding I shall be most happy to do. If necessary I can raise the money to put all in good shape again. I say again don't let your thoughts dwell upon your troubles, but look to Him who will give consolation to all who are afflicted whether in body or in mind.   —Your own *Frank*.

December 1, 1858. A cold day. A great crowd of military and other citizens went to Salem to see Martin Wallace Executed for Murder. Sarah Parish came on before dinner to stay all night— her mother came after tea for the night…   —*Diary of James McKie.*

◆ Letters from Edwin McKie:

Dear Father—   We sail tomorrow [on the *Golden Fleece* from New York] at 10 A.M. if it does not storm & have fair winds. Everything is on board and the ship went out into the river yesterday. The horse (Cambridge Chief) feels well and eats well & feels quite at home in his house on the ship.
    Nette and Sophia feel anxious, but I cannot say I do. Had I any business I would not leave, but as it is, I hope it is all for the best. I think I shall be back in April or May at farthest… I bid you goodbye, E. J. McKie.   —Nette sends her Ambrotype to you and Mother by Henry.   —*November 9, 1858.*

Dear Father—   We arrived here [Liverpool] the 1st all safe and sound. Horse and all. Nette and Sophie were quite sick for a few days but got well soon. The horse came very well, not a scratch on him. He feels well and eats well. I was not sick, never any better… There is nothing of importance to

Edwin McKie had gone to England to breed his horse, Cambridge Chief, and as an agent for the Walter A. Wood Mowing & Reaping Machine Co. of Hoosick Falls, New York.

Illustration from flyer distributed in England by Edwin Mckie after he arrived in Liverpool with his horse.

write you, as I have not been here long enough to know what to write or do. They tell me times are very dull & all who are sending grain or flour here now are losing very heavily. We have just come ashore, the ship having been in the river since she arrived… Kiss Mother for me. Love to Niel, George, and all— Capt Hunt etc. and with much love for yourself, I remain Truly Yours, *E. J. McKie.*
—I will write again by next steamer — *Ed.* —December 4, 1858.

December 7, 1858. Mild & pleasant A.M. Snowy P.M. which makes fine sleighing. Kate went up home in morn & returned in P.M. She went up to see Niel whom we feared had his hand taken off by the cars as per last eves *Times*. It was another Niel McKie.
—*Diary of Francis S. Thayer.*

December 26, 1858. Still cold. This is the last Sabbath of the year 1858. God in his adorable Providence has spared our lives through another year, how many of our fellow immortals have been called during the past year to their final account. God grant that it may not prove to our greater condemnation that we have had another year added to our time of sojourning here. May he in the riches of his grace enable us, should he spare us still another year, to improve our time and our talents in such a manner that at last, when He shall call us to our final account, we may not have to take up the lamentation "the harvest is past, the summer is ended and I am not saved." Mr. Shortt lectured in the morning from Luke… Afternoon he preached from John…
December 31. A mild day, some sleet falling. The last day of the year 1858. Another year has gone to the Records of Eternity. God grant that it may not prove to our greater condemnation that we have been spared while myriads have been called to their final account. —*Diary of James McKie.*

A summary of 1858:
February 5, 1858. Frank went to Hoosick this eve for good Father is failing. Oh when he leaves may God take him to the field in heaven.

February 6. Frank came home from Hoosick this morn. His Father is going home soon we trust. May poor Mother be somewhat prepared for this separation…
February 8. Father & Mother [George & Sophia McKie] came this morn, and word that our dear good Father (Adin Thayer) died last night at 6 o'clock. It is the first bereavement in my Frank's home circle and God has kindly [illegible] to the living and the dead. Frank went to Hoosick this eve.
February 9. My Frank is at home with his mourning Friends…
February 11. Frank home this morn. He has left what he never left before— a fatherless home…   —*Excerpts from the 1858 diary of Catherine McKie Thayer.*

༄ The letters of Sophia Whiteside McKie:

Mon Morn, 7 o'clock.
My Dear Child—   I have just got up and sit here with my nightcap on to scribble you a few lines while the family are at breakfast. I am very sorry to hear that you are not as well and I fear a great worse. I knew you were suffering very much when I was there but hoped to hear you were better— I think you will have to give up walking even if you get so you feel as if you can. George feels that Dr. Gregory can perform great cures and I hope he may do as much for you as he has for anyone.

Mr. Lee has just come in and the family have all got under motion again and I must stop and help your Father get ready—

May God guide and Bless us—   S. McKie.

Sabbath eve, 5 O clock.
My Dear Child—   We arrived home safe yesterday about 11 o'clock and I feel pretty well today— but you have not been out of my mind when awake three minutes at a time since I left you— and had I fifteen minutes to think about it, I should not have left you— and I have regretted it every hour since. How I wish I could know at once how you are. I do hope you have not been sick— I do not know when I have had two as unhappy days— for I know you got your cold running about the street for me— what a shame— what did I say I wanted anything for. I wish I could be with you as quick as thought— then I could see my sweet little Franky— and if you are all well how he will shorten the days while your Francis [misspelled *Fransis* in the letters] is away.

I found Catherine here and at work feeling pretty well. Mary left Friday eve when Cath came and, with the exception of washing, this week can go on as usual. As for my going down— I can and shall go any time if you are not well and if Francis is to be gone a long time, just let me know what you would like me to do. Your Father says, "say to her he is very sorry he did not let me stay with you."

Doct Cook was here today and says he shall send you some croup medicine for he thinks every mother of an infant ought to have it by her and she can use it herself and it never fails to break it up at once.   God Bless us all Good Night— S. McKie.

Monday eve.
I thought last eve George was going today— and how are you tonight? I hope well— and my little boy? Your Father has a headache today but is better tonight— the worst he ever had, as he always thinks. Kittie left here Satur-

Sophia Whiteside McKie, 1796–1878, wrote occasional letters to her daughter, Catherine McKie Thayer, who lived in Albany with her husband. Excerpted here are some of those letters. All of the letters were written very faintly in pencil and with little punctuation, making them very difficult to read and understand. Some punctuation has been added here in order to make them easier to understand. In addition, only one of the letters is dated. An attempt has been made to put the letters "in chronological order" based upon their content— specifically by using an occasional reference to what were the births of her grandson in 1857 and her granddaughter in 1859. In any event, these letters would have been written at the farm in Cambridge, New York, between 1855 and 1860.

Sophia Whiteside McKie, 1796–1878. Minor B. King Photographic Art Gallery, Troy, New York.

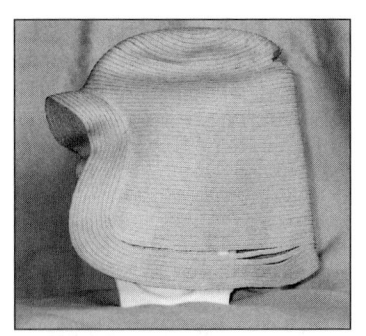

Sophia Whiteside McKie's bonnet, long stored in a trunk.

day— Sophy has been quite sick ever since she was in Troy. We have some family of men yet— but some of them will soon be gone as George can tell you. Well I have just put up the coat for George to take which I hope will not give you trouble.

I hope before this reaches you will have a letter from Francis and so good night, God Bless us all— S. McKie.

Sabbath eve, 9 o'clock.
My Dear Child—   I wonder I did not say to you I did not see how you are going to get along without Lizzie until you have a great deal more strength than you have. You are not able to take care of that baby one hour in the day and Mary, I fear, will not relieve you at all from care and you will be soon worn out and sick and what then. I think you had better keep Lizzie if you can— unless Mary is a much better nurse than I suppose she is— but do be careful and not get sick. I will say no more but hope you will think well of it before you let her go.

Sabbath afternoon, 4 o'clock.
My Dear Child—   Here I am alone in the house for the first time in my life, your Father gone to the Whiteside church. Edwin and Nettie returned from the north last eve and went down to Easton this afternoon. Niel has gone to Robert's and I have sat down to scribble to you. Francis's letter written the day you arrived home, reached here on Thursday. I am very sorry you cannot go home from here without being sick. You are worn out trying to make something easy for me— and I keep you up late at night and do a good many things that help make you tired and sick. I will try and do better when you come again which I hope will not be long for your good husband said something in his letter about coming this month. I want to see my little boy— Does he hold things in his little chubby hands? I suppose not yet but think I can see him trying. Your Aunt left here on Tuesday. I hear she intends staying in White Creek two or three weeks. I must not forget to say Nettie is much better…

I think I told you that every villainous insect felt privileged to bite or do something to me, and you will believe it when I tell you a yellow wasp stung me yesterday on the end of my little finger and although not swollen only a blotch it does not feel very comfortable but nothing to speak about. It has been a lovely afternoon and I could have wished you were here. Here comes your Father.   God Bless us— S. McKie.

Monday noon,
My dear Child—   I wish I could be there when your Father is, for I think he is uneasy enough when I am with him— but far more so without me— and I am very sorry for you, for I know just how it goes— Thurs Morn 9 o'clock. You will see I commenced this when George was here but I suppose he did not understand me when I said to him I wanted to send a letter by him. Your Father arrived safe yesterday about 2 and is about as happy as he ever is. Edwin left yesterday morning, his back much better but still very lame. I hope you will not be troubled about me when I tell you, true Ellen is gone but she has taken half the work with her. Our morning work all done in good order yesterday, our work was all done after dinner at 1 o'clock and Catherine

sat down to peeling apples and that is all I have for a girl to do, sitting work I mean. Monday the washing was done before noon and it took the two till 3 o'clock and 2 days always to iron but this week all done Tuesday before night — and I have far less vexation and take no more steps and have more time to sit down. Last week I had the carpet in the sitting room and my bedroom taken up and cleaned all while Ellen was here. You will see I wrote this 2 weeks ago and expected to send it by your Father at last but he did not have to go and I hardly know what it is and I have not time to read it. The boys are starting in such a hurry— things are going on about as usual with us and George can tell you the most interesting…

God Bless us. [illegible] grandson. How I want to see all.

Monday evening 6 o'clock— Getting better of my cold though far from being well yet as usual just finished hemming one of your handkerchiefs— and tea over and not a child about the house and do not expect to have tonight. George gone to hay and little boys gone to Saratoga and here I sit on the old black sofa with the Black pillows to my back, looking out of the north window to see I know not what. I suppose the sleeves and binding of your underclothes looked a little coarse. They did not answer my expectations after they were bleached but you must call them linen [sic] if they are half tow just as they are and some of my own spinning.

Cambridge, February 19th.
My Dear Daughter—   I received your letter last Wednesday and I have thought every day since I should write and now I shall commence…

…You Uncle James and Aunt Lucy have been here and said Mr. Crary and Mary are breaking up and going west this spring, and your Aunt Almy is almost sick at the thought of having to change her home. She is coming to your Uncle James. I think your Aunt Margaret's is the place for her if she could think so…

…I want to see my little boy and hear him say Gamma but I must stop and hope I can before long. Father sends his love to all. My love and Kisses. God Bless us. S. McKie.   —We have filled the ice-house.

Sat AM, 6 o'clock.
Your Father has gone to church and I am alone— Edwin and Nettie are in Easton. Nettie has been here since Wednesday until yesterday— there is not an article of theirs but is packed up in trunks or carried away that ever belonged to either of them except the clove basket or what remains of it— Well I will be quiet till I see you— Father has come and says cousin is more comfortable— last night and today she is kept under the influence of opium the most of the time— but is only as regards pain. She is herself perfectly— she is losing her strength. I hope you will be able to see her— she has already asked for you both the two last times I saw her and then she was too weak and too much distressed to say much— I will perhaps write more before I go to bed—

I have put a small piece of cheese up and if you think it fit to eat you shall have more when you come up. The thimble is in the basket

Mon— I have the window up and I hear the birds singing sweetly in all directions and I wish you could be here— you have birds enough I know, but I like to have someone with me that likes to speak of them. Come as

looking out of the north window to see I know not what   In 1853 and 1854, when her son Peter did not return from his trip to Australia, Sophia McKie placed a chair near a north corner window with a view down the long drive and waited for either Peter to return or others to come with news about him. After two years she removed the chair. The line in this letter, written about five years later, would be a reference to that earlier time and vigil.

soon as you can I know you will and I hope you will be able to see her living— Cousin Elsie I mean— I was thinking of her and I thought I had written her name. Father almost ready— Give a kiss to my grandson and tell him his grandmam sent it— Love and a kiss to your good husband— God Bless us all.

Friday evening, 9 o'clock.

All in bed except myself— Edwin arrived last eve about this time in good health— his sheep business rather a poor affair. He went to Easton this afternoon and fetched Nettie over— She says she was sick in bed all last week and not very well now and Phillip is very poorly— worse than ever he has been before— the cold affects him very much and she says he calls up all his food so soon that he gets no nourishment from it. Your Father's eyes has troubled him very much lately but I think they are a little better this two or three days. George has had a very lame back from a strain he got in a scuffle with his horse but is about all the time and is much better— and I am quite well for which I ought to be very thankful and now I have given you the particulars of the health of our family I shall proceed to make some other remarks—

I received your letter of Monday yesterday and I am very happy to hear you expect your good husband so soon. I hope they will arrive safe tomorrow and I wish I could be there and see the interview of the Father and his family. He must see some change in his boy. I wish I could see you all one hour. Well— worrying will do no good but I hope I shall have my wish about the work on this house— we here [sic] it will be finished tomorrow— painted, papered, and ready to move in next week—

Do not know but we wrote rather hastily about a girl— Cath was in a bl mad fit but she soon repented— George was hardly out of sight when she said she could not leave me and if there is not a pretty sure prospect of faring much better, I feel I want rather not to make a change at present. I have not mentioned this to George or Ed, for they wanted any change any way, but to think of making a change with such an irregular family is not small matter— it would vex any girl— and I hope it will be different sometime but just at present I would like a little rest— one that I think I will not have with a strange girl — how much better I could talk it over with you.

The wind is changing and the room is growing cold and I must go to bed and get up early and give your Father a dash of Salts, for Rhubarb has ceased to operate in him, and he has been in trouble four or five days.

Give my Love to Marcia and take a kiss and baby too— Goodnight— Kiss your good husband for me when he comes.

Sat morn— we are all up— your Father taken his salts— Nette says she did not sleep well and was too tired— the ride was too much— I hope she will not get sick — Edward is going to Johnsonville and I must stop. I hope you will have all your family with you tonight—

—God Bless us all S. W. McKie.

1859

January 1, 1859. A mild day. James McKie here to dinner…I mailed $2.50 dollars to *New York Times* for semi weekly paper…   —Diary of James McKie.

January 5, 1859. Very cold… Spent most of the day at the Store. Did not go up to the Mill.
February 8. Weather mild & pleasant. Sleighing very good. All day at Mill. I have little to do now save looking on. Millwrights take their own time and it is no use to hurry them.
March 12. Mild & pleasant. Office in A.M. & mill in P.M. Told several of our carpenters that we would raise their wages from 9 to 10 next week. Have made good progress this week. Bro. Port arrived here from Chicago. He started for Hoosick— cars couldn't get through a mud-slide, so he came back. —*Diary of Francis S. Thayer.*

April 12, 1859. A cloudy morning, cleared up before noon. Lucy & I went to Troy. We dined at Mr. Thayer's. Katy went with us, with their man & carriage to James Jermain's. We staid there all night.
April 13. A beautiful morning. A 10 o'clock Katy & man went to Mr. Jermain's for us with their carriage. We came over to Troy— took dinner at Mr. Thayer's, in company with Geo. Wilson. At 5 P.M. Katy & man brought us to the depot. We got home safely a little after 7… —*Diary of James McKie.*

May 21, 1859. Cloudy & a little rain in A.M. At Store in A.M. & Mill P.M… We thought of going up to Cambridge this P.M. but the weather was forbidding… Work at Mill progressing slowly, shall not get in operation before 15th July.
July 27. Up to Mill all the A.M. to witness the starting which took place about 10 o'clock on Rye. —All goes off very well and we now are assured that we have a good mill with power enough to make four to five hundred Bbls. Flour per day.
—*Diary of Francis S. Thayer.*

∽ A letter from Edwin McKie in England:

Dear Father & Mother and all the children—   I received a letter from George on last Monday by the *Persia*, and was glad to hear you were all well. I also received one from Frank a few days before. I suppose you will hear

Unsigned portrait purported to be Cambridge Chief and Edwin McKie. The horse had a distinguished pedigree and Edwin hoped to make money in England breeding it. Above, detail from the portrait.

from us by Sophia who left the 25th May by the *City of Washington*, and is no doubt home before this. We are going along slowly and both of us keep well with good appetites…

…Mother, how is your posy patch? I suppose the flowers are peeping up through the grass and weeds and occasionally see the sun. I wish you would look out for that middle cabbage. Have you had string beans? Go in mommy, give 'em beans. Mother, don't let George work too hard in the garden. He does so much when he gets a chance to, that he never thinks of his back, and makes him so bad for a long time. I am very sorry he is so desirous of keeping weeds down that he can't sleep after sunrise. Try and keep him in bed till breakfast is ready. It hurts him to be out so long before breakfast. Better set something on the table at night, for a lunch for him, when he first gets up. The days are very long here now, sun rises at 3:45 & sets 8:14, about 16 hours & 20 minutes from sunrise to sunset.

The twilight is very long. 'Tis daylight at 2 A.M. and not dark till about 10 1/2 P.M.

George, write me what you think about the bull.— Nette sends her love to you all, and says she would write if she had anything to write worthwhile. Hoping you are all well, we are affectionately yours, *Ed and Nette. —June 10, 1859 from Liverpool.*

September 8, 1859. A beautiful day. George, Sophia, Thayer, Katy & Frank here to dinner…
 —*Diary of James McKie.*

September 11, 1859. Cloudy & every appearance of rain. I am 37 years old today. How swiftly time passes away. I cannot realize that I am almost forty years old. I feel thankful that God has been so merciful to me & mine. Down to Bridge & heard Mr. Shortt preach… We had a very fine shower in P.M. —*Diary of Francis S. Thayer.*

October 17, 1859. A warm day. I cleaned cesspool under sink and dug 10 bushel potatoes across the street. Almy & I called at John Armitage's this evening.
October 18. A rainy morning, some showers & sunshine through the day. I recd a letter from Clark & Lucy… I answered them. I wrote Mr. Thayer enclosing 14 dollars for two barrels flour to be sent me. David quite sick today.
October 19. A cold day. I finished digging potatoes across the street. I attended Prayer Meeting…
October 21. A cold day. I went to Arlington and got a pair of Gate Posts for Graveyard…
 —*Diary of James McKie.*

October 21, 1859. …Mill running at the rate of over 400 Bbls per day.
 —*Diary of Francis S. Thayer.*

November 7, 1859. A beautiful day. I recd a letter from Jas. Jermain. I recd by express an Iron Gate from Troy. I paid Mr. Hawley for it 12 dols and 63 cts express charge…
November 22. A mild morning, ground covered with snow. The first steady foddering I think for sheep. Mary Barber here sewing— she went home at evening… I recd a letter from Hon. Martin Lee giving me permission to remove a fence from their family burying lot in the old yard. —*Diary of James McKie.*

December 3, 1859. About 1/2 past 4 o'clock this morning Kate woke me & I soon discovered that she was in labor. At 6 sent for Mrs. Graves who went for Dr. B— & Mrs.

Lee. After suffering intensely until just 12 o'clock we were blessed with a sweet daughter whose name shall be Catherine Sophia.

December 4. Weather cold. Four to six inches snow & some sleighs out. Stayed at home with my wife & children. John took Mrs. Lee to Lansingburgh in the buggy. P.M. attended communion. Dr. Berman officiated…   —*Diary of Francis S. Thayer.*

༄ The other news of the day:

EXECUTION OF JOHN BROWN — His Interview with his Wife — SCENES AT THE SCAFFOLD — Profound feeling throughout the Northern States. *Special Dispatch to the New York Times*
Brown was executed today at a little after 11 o'clock. There was no attempt at rescue, nor any indications of any disposition to interfere with the course of justice in any way. Indeed, there was very little excitement of any kind.

 I visited the field in which the gallows had been erected at an early hour this morning. The day was very fine and the air warm. All strangers were excluded from the town. Indeed, no railroad trains were allowed to enter during the entire day.

 The gallows was erected at 7 1/2 o'clock, and all preparations for the execution immediately completed. The reporters who had secured the privilege of being present were allowed to enter soon after. On being summoned, Brown appeared perfectly calm and collected. He took formal leave of each of his fellow prisoners, and gave each one a quarter of a dollar as a token of remembrance… He rode to the scaffold in an open wagon, seated upon his coffin. At the gallows Brown was still perfectly cool. He made no remarks. As soon as he had mounted the scaffold the cap was put on and drawn over his face. He was not standing on top of the drop. The Sheriff told him to get upon it. Brown said, "I cannot see — place me on it, and don't keep me waiting."…He suffered but little. After three minutes, there were no convulsions or indications of life. At the end of twenty minutes his body was examined, and he was reported dead.
  —*The New York Times,* December 3, 1859.

John Brown was hung at Charlestown at 11 1/4 o'clock today. The military assembled at 9 o'clock, and were posted on the field leading to the place of execution, and also at various points as laid down in the general orders. Everything was conducted under the strictest military discipline, as if the town were in a state of siege. Mounted scouts were stationed in the woods to the left of the scaffold, and picket guards were stationed out towards the Shenandoah mountains in the rear… He looked calmly on the people, was fully self possessed, and mounted the scaffold with a firm step… At half-past eleven the trap of the scaffold was pulled away, and with a few slight struggles, John Brown yielded up his spirit. The body was placed in a coffin, and is now on its way to Harper's Ferry, to be delivered to his wife, under a strong military escort.
 —*The New York Times,* December 3, 1859, *from the reporter of the Associated Press.*

PRAYER MEETINGS IN NEW YORK — The small lecture room of Dr. Cheever's Church was filled yesterday morning, it being announced that a prayer meeting for John Brown would be held… Mr. Tappan made a prayer, speaking of Brown as a Christian martyr in the hands of an infuriated mob and praying that posterity would rise up and call him blessed.   —*The New York Times,* December 3, 1859.

SYRACUSE — The City hall was densely packed with citizens, this evening, who listened for over three hours to stirring and eloquent speeches, expressing sympathy for John Brown and his family.   —*The New York Times,* December 3, 1859.

SAVANNAH — Mr. Fish, a shoe dealer, and resident of this city for several years, but born in Massachusetts, has been tarred and feathered for expressing abolition sentiments.   —*The New York Times,* December 3, 1859.

↬ Virginia newspapers:

AFFAIRS AT CHARLESTOWN — Chronological Recollections — [From our own correspondent.] Fifty-four years ago the 2d of next December, the sun of Austerlitz arose upon the great Napoleon and his army, drawn up in battle array upon the field which their valor rendered immortal. Fifty-four years later, the sun of Austerlitz rises for the last time upon old John Brown. If this communication should reach you in time, it will be laid before the public on that day so auspicious to the chief of the Bonapartes and so futile to the head of the family of Brown. The Napoleon of battles was crowned upon that day, and upon that day, one year after his coronation, he gained the greatest of all his victories. The Napoleon of horse-thieves, upon the same day, undergoes the extreme penalty of the law…

It is astonishing to see what a complete change has been produced in the feelings of all classes of people with regard to the Union. It seems no longer to have any friends in this part of the country; at least so far as I have been able to discover. The defection seems to me to be universal. All deplore the necessity, but all seem agreed that we cannot live under the same government with people who are so hostile to us— who either say nothing at all about the atrocious outrages which we have suffered, or never mention them but to turn them into ridicule…

The work of erecting the scaffold was completed yesterday on a common in the rear of the jail, and it will be finished today. It is in a position where the execution can be seen by all who may be present, but the military lines will be formed at such a distance as to preclude the possibility of hearing anything the prisoner may say…

The military arrangements for today are of the most stringent character, and those who are in the town must remain until after the execution whilst those are out must stay out until Saturday morning…

Governor Wise has issued orders that the body of the prisoner, with his clothes and all his personal effects, be conveyed immediately after the execution, to Harper's Ferry, and be delivered there to a party deputed by his wife to receive them. The body will therefore, be conveyed directly through to New York or Boston, and will doubtless be buried with all the honors of martyrdom…

A number of letters addressed to John Brown came to hand yesterday. One of them, from Ohio, stated that they, his friends, felt sure a rescue could be made and that 1,500 men had pledged themselves to the work…

Numerous reports of guns were heard last night, sentinels being as usual, extremely vigilant. A number of drunken men were brought into the guard-house during the day and night, but were discharged in a short time. One poor fellow, an idiot, was arrested and ordered to leave the town immediately…

—*Daily Dispatch,* Richmond, Virginia, December 3, 1859. (Virginia Historical Society)

The Apotheosis and Antecedents of John Brown, The Black Republican "Martyr" — Between the hours of eleven and twelve, on Friday last, the apotheosis of John Brown, the Black Republican saint, traitor, murderer, horse thief and insurrectionist, was completed. The presence of an efficient military force prevented the consummation of all plots and schemes for his rescue, and his execution went off as quietly as that of any ordinary felon… For weeks before his execution, the mails groaned beneath the weight of innumerable letters to the Executive of this Commonwealth, of a most menacing,

incendiary, and treasonable character, all aimed and designed to prevent the punishment of a traitor, a murderer, and in insurrectionist. And we are pained also to state that whilst thousands of such minatory letters were pouring in, we learn that not one was received from the "moderate, conservative men of the North," assuring an outraged and insulted State of a particle of sympathy for her wrongs… For the Pioneer State of the Revolution, for the mother of States and statesmen, for the noble old State of Virginia, the dominant party in the free States (representing as it does the prevailing public sentiment) had no words of sympathy; but for the murderer and the traitor it could not display too much affection and admiration.
—*Daily Examiner*, Richmond, Virginia, December 5, 1859. (Virginia Historical Society)

December 1, 1859. A showery day. Cornelia Howe & Fannie M— to tea. Lucy, Ann & I went to an Exhibition at the Academy.
December 2. A warm rainy day. Some snow falling at 11 o'clock P.M. I went to the Academy at evening to witness a repetition of the last nights exhibition. John Armitage & wife & Mary Barber called and went also.
December 3. A Cold day— first day of winter we have had. Mary Barber here afternoon fixing dress. Clarke took Anne S— home to stay a week.
December 4. A snowy morning. Snow had fallen 4 or 5 inches during the night. I did not go to Church. I had a lame back. David D— was ordained an elder this afternoon. The Exercises were said to be solemn. Nathan Brownell fell from his chair *dead* this afternoon. Disease— affection of the heart. It produced a deep sensation in the community. May *God* enable us to hear the voice so emphatically addressed to us "Be ye also ready, for in such an hour as ye think not, the son of man cometh."
December 5. A beautiful day. Sleighs running briskly for the first— some out yesterday…
—*Diary of James McKie.*

Troy, Dec. 5th, 1859, Monday P.M.
Dear Mother—   I wrote you Saturday A.M. and sent the letter to Buskirk's Bridge care of Mrs. Hitchcock with directions to forward the first opportunity supposing Father or some of your neighbors would be down to Church yesterday. It stormed so yesterday that I have thought my letter would not reach you before the mail will take this. Well, Mammy, as I wrote Saturday, Kitty fairly got the start of you this time. Early Saturday morning we got the Doctor & Mrs. Lee at our home and at 12 o'clock noon we had a nice little daughter Catherine Sophia and they all declare that she looks just like her Grandmother whom she is quite anxious to see. Kitty was very sick three or four hours and suffered more than when Frankie was born but the Dr. and Mrs. Lee say that she has no unfavorable symptoms. Frankie says his Mom is broken, but he loves his little sister— she is so sweet. We shall be most happy to see you any time & I know you will be delighted to see your little granddaughter. Tell Father he must come down when Kate gets smart. Yours in haste, Love to all, you son, *Francis.*

Wednesday eve. Dec. 7th, 1859.
Dear Mother—   We have been expecting you here to see your daughter & grand-daughter for two days past. I have written you twice and not a word from you. Kitty & the Baby are getting along very well. Kitty is quite anxious to see you. She feels so grand with her sweet little daughter that she can hardly wait another day before your coming. We hope to see you soon.   —Your son *Francis.*

The *Daily Examiner* had no reports of the execution of John Brown on December 3, 1859.

Catherine Sophia What's in the spelling of a name? Francis Thayer clearly spells his daughter's name *Catherine* just as her mother spelled her name. Over the years she was to be called *Kittie, Kitty,* and *Kate,* and she changed how she spelled her name, for on her grave in Troy, New York, it is spelled: *Katherine.*

Friday evening.

Dear Mother—   Kitty is sitting by my side holding the Baby. Mrs. Lee has gone downstairs after something. Frankie has just gone to sleep in "Faver's bed" Ellen is no better & we very much fear she will not recover. I will let Kitty add a word. Affectionately yours, *Francis*. —Frank says write a word. We are doing as well as can be expected. I have walked a little about the room today and am thankful that we are all so well. Have you no paper? If so write. Love to you from *Kitty*.

Troy, Dec. 16th, 1859, Friday evening.

Dear Mother—   It is with the greatest pleasure that I can write you— Kitty is better in fact. She has been on the mend every hour since you left yesterday. Mrs. Lee got her up a little while and after getting rested a little she felt much better. As for little Kitty, she is lovely and eats & sleeps like a little Kitten. A *smart* child that Mammy. Catherine Sophia the III. Frankie is well & often speaks of going to Cambridge… He wants you to come again soon. Love to all your *Francis*.

Troy, Dec. 20, 1859.

Dear Mother—   …Well Mother I am indeed happy to say that Kitty and the baby are doing well. Kitty sat up more than an hour today and I do hope she will go right straight along and get up and about soon. Frankie has a little cold but is not sick. I will write again tomorrow. Yours in haste, *Francis*.

Troy, Dec. 21st, 1859.

Dear Mother—   I am indeed rejoiced to say to you that Kitty is improving daily. This P.M. she sat up nearly two hours. Little Kitty is growing beautiful all the time and it is now confidently asserted that Catherine Sophia the III is a *nice* child, sweet and good looking as her Grandmother was in her younger days. You know Hawkins once said, "Mother was good looking *once*, I know she was." We have good sleighing and if Kitty was only well enough I would make you a visit with my wife and children. Ellen has had a relapse and is now very sick. I should not be surprised if she was never better. —Yours affectionately, *Francis*.

Ellen   an unknown person, perhaps the cook.

Troy, Dec. 30th, 1859.

Dear Mother—   …Kate had about given up the idea of hearing from you and told me not to write again until we heard from you. My wife is getting quite independent now that she has a little daughter and you must look out for her. Well Mother your daughter and grand-daughter are getting along very well. Kate is all about the upper part of the house and on Sunday we expect to have her downstairs to dinner. I am sorry to inform you that Ellen died on Monday and was buried Wednesday. All last week I went to see her every day… Our new cook does very well and we do not suffer at all in the eating department. We have had very cold weather of late— sleighing good. Suppose you come down and make us a visit…   —*Francis*.

December 31, 1859. ...We have been blessed with a sweet little daughter & have been kept in good health most of the time & have been prospered in many ways.
—*Diary of Francis S. Thayer.*

A summary of 1859:
December 3, 1859. Our Kitty was born at 12 today. Oh how thankful I feel for this gift.
—*Diary of Catherine McKie Thayer.*

VIII

1860–1861

Letters from Cambridge and Troy, Part Four

IN the fall of 1860 Abraham Lincoln was elected President with a majority of the votes in the Electoral College but only a plurality of the popular vote. Lincoln's election was an overwhelming victory for the forces opposed to slavery, but as it was a purely sectional win, it was certain that a Civil War would be fought. The Civil War seemed to have little impact on the daily lives of the extended family in Cambridge and Troy. One uncle formed a local military company and another distant cousin joined a company from Albany. Otherwise, the letters and diaries reveal that these families made few significant sacrifices during the Civil War. Life was different for another family on a farm in Virginia.

Despite the approach of war, America was growing and expanding during these years. In 1860 the Pony Express began what was described as "fast" overland mail service between St. Louis and Sacramento, a distance of 1,900 miles, but a year later the Pony Express was obsolete because of the completion of the trans-continental telegraph. By 1861 there were 30,000 miles of railroad in the United States, and the U. S. mails were for the first time carrying merchandise as well as letters.

Tragedy and family deaths had been all too frequent occurrences at the McKie farm in the past few years. Two sons, Henry and Jimie, had died, and a third son, Peter, had disappeared and was presumed to be dead. Death would again come to the family in both 1860 and 1861 and the grieving family made more trips to the cemetery behind the Whiteside Church on the ridge overlooking their farm. Despite the grim news of war and the family tragedies that brought them home to Cambridge, Francis and Catherine Thayer were enjoying their lives in Troy with their two small children.

Letters and diaries by:
Libby Beadle, a family friend in Cambridge
Sylvia Burton, a family friend
E. B. Hoyt, gravestone maker
D. M. Doub, a friend of George W. McKie
Edwin & Antoinette McKie
George W. McKie
George & Sophia McKie
James McKie
Catherine McKie Thayer
Francis S. Thayer

Letters and diaries written from: Troy and Cambridge, New York; Tennessee, Ohio and Illinois; onboard steamboats on the Mississippi; and England.

1860

Troy, January 6th, 1860.
Dear Mother—   I have just time to say that we are all very well… Why can't you come down and see us if only for a day or two? Your grand-daughter is a great child and improves every day. Kate is downstairs to dinner and tea almost every day. I carry her down and up. Frankie is well and doing about as usual…   —Your son *Francis*.

January 10, 1860. …Horrible accident at Lawrence, Pemberton mill, fell & killed over 100 human beings & large number wounded.
January 11. Weather quite mild. Everybody talking about the awful calamity at Lawrence…   —*Diary of Francis S. Thayer.*

One of the most appalling catastrophes which has ever shocked the country occurred yesterday at Lawrence, Massachusetts. About 5 o'clock in the afternoon the Pemberton Mills fell with a tremendous crash. Six or seven hundred operatives were at work in them at the time, and the lowest estimates state that the number of those buried in the ruins was at least three hundred…   —*The New York Times,* January 11, 1860.

Troy, Jan 27th, 1860.
My dearest Mother—   How strangely 1860 looks to me. The *children* are asleep, that sounds as strange as *60*, and I will write a line while I can. You know perhaps that we have all had colds— I the last and Frankie & Baby have had coughs. They are now very well, cough a little… Let me hear from you soon. I can not write any more, my eyes are not strong yet… Good-bye, God bless us all. Frankie sends a kiss. Frank sends love to all.   —*Kitty*.

Wednesday evening. (Undated, early winter 1860.)
Dear Mother—   …Well Mother we had quite an accident here last Sabbath forenoon while I was at Church. Frankie went into the back room and got hold of the matches and set his clothes on fire. He screamed and his mother was with him in a moment, threw her dress around him and smothered the flames, the right sleeve of his apron was consumed on the under side and the dear little fellow's arms burned considerably. Dr. Brimmand came in a few minutes and did all he could to "make it better" as Frankie says. We hope it will be entirely well in a few days. It was indeed a narrow escape and we tremble when we think of it. Little Kitty was vaccinated last week Monday and is doing well. Big Kitty about as usual, not very strong but I think rather on the gain. She was out riding up to Lansingburgh today. When are you coming down to make us a visit? I hope soon…   —As ever your affectionate son, *Francis*.

Troy, Wed. Aft. 4 o'clock. (1860)
My dear Mother—   …Mrs. Lee is still with me. She proposes to give up

her time tonight to stay here, wash and dress the baby and Frankie's arm— go out and spend the day and come back at eve— to do this till she is called for. She may be called any hour or not in two weeks. I have come to the conclusion that the girl I am trying, *can't learn on my baby*. I shall try again. She has been here a week and does pretty well except with Kittie and I am not going to wait for any greater development. She is one of those who can't hold a Baby… Let me hear often if but a word. I have mused and been interrupted many times, many times, and hardly know what I have written, but you can overlook my errors if anyone can. Good-bye, love to all and much to yourself, Love *Kitty*.

 Letters from Edwin McKie in Ohio and Illinois:

Dear Father—   I have got so far on my rounds all safe and sound, and leave tomorrow for Michigan and on to Illinois. This is very slow business and will keep me busy two months or more.

The farmers here feel very poor, having generally lost their wheat and corn crops last year by frost. In some sections, corn is fair, and stands in the field un-husked— corn is worth 4/— here, a low price for a poor crop. I have not made many agents yet, and shall not till I return from Michigan. I have nothing worth writing. I really hope your eyes are better, and that all are well. My best love to all, and I am yours affectionately. *E. J. McKie,* Springfield, Ohio. January 16, 1860.

Dear Father—   I am progressing slowly along, through this land of milk and honey, and in my opinion 'tis anything but milk and honey. The farmers are now putting in their spring wheat. They do not raise much winter wheat of late years. They are poorer than piss, and very reckless. Their average crops are not better than in Washington Co.

Everything at loose ends, not one in twenty has a barn. All their tools are left out from one years end to another. They will pay 150 to 160 dollars for a reaping machine— leave it where they finish cutting, and there it stands 'till another harvest. So with all their farming implements— wheat about 8/ flour 28 to 30 cts. I am in hopes to get ready to leave for home about the 1st of April. I have to go to Wisconsin after I get through here. I really hope your eyes are much better if not quite well. Douglas cannot carry his own state if he gets the nomination at Charleston. Love to all, Kiss Mother for me, and I remain yours affectionately. *E. J. McKie,* Peru, LaSalle Co. Ill. March 18th, 1860.

February 24, 1860. This day makes me 55 years old. More than half a century have I lived upon the earth: What changes have been wrought in the world since I was born. God grant that I may spend the remaining time allotted me here in such a manner that it shall not prove to my greater condemnation at last, that I am thus spared…
February 27. A fine day. Mrs. Rice & I sat up with Lucy last night. Mrs. P. Campbell & Geo. Campbell & wife here to dinner. Widow Archer came today noon to nurse Lucy. Ann Whiteside died today.
February 29. A mild day. Lucy rather comfortable, nothing of importance today. Ann Whiteside buried today. Doctor Gray called.
April 11. A chilly day. Clark down with measles…Doctor Gray called.

Ann Whiteside, 1791–1860, daughter of Thomas Whiteside, 1758–1830, was never married.

April 12. A pleasant day… Doctor Gray called.
April 13. A cool day. John Whiteside called. Clark getting better. Doctor Gray called.
April 16. A cold pleasant day, a sprinkle of rain toward night… Doctor Gray called.
April 23. A chilly day. I came down with measles. Doctor Gray called twice.
April 29. A beautiful day, very dry. Almy, Clark & David went to Church…Doctor Gray called. *37 visits to here.*
—*Diary of James McKie.*

↬ A letter from Sophia Whiteside McKie:

April 28, 1860.
My Dear Kitty Child—   Mrs. Wier has spent the afternoon with me and says her son is going to Troy tomorrow and can take anything I wish to send which is very kind. She came over because I am alone. Mrs. V— was sent for yesterday. Her son's wife was very sick. Now do not feel badly, for I did not, for I require so little to be done for me that I had very little for her to do but she made herself very useful in the housework line which was very much needed. You would be surprised to step in and see how I have improved since you saw me. (I wish I could be thankful enough) As soon as the weather is warm I shall begin to think of going downstairs. Last Monday Fanning came here to see if we depended on her coming as she had not heard from her since the first. She is very well pleased about coming and is ready, 1st of May. Niel commenced another siege last Monday going and fetching some home and making a fool of himself. I thought this morning after having a time about my alcohol and some talk after that he was going to steady down but after dinner he harnessed and was off like a flash. It is not 7 o'clock and no Niel yet. Mrs. Wier says Archy had better come over this evening. I hope he will. Now, do not think I am excitement about it for I am not. Now I must stop this and say something about your affairs. You need not think things at home here have driven you out of mind. I think of you every hour and I hope you will get well and no one gets sick and begin a long life of happy housekeeping. Well it is getting dark and now this must go.   God Bless us all. Your affectionate mother, *S. McKie.*

Niel McKie had a reputation for heavy drinking.

Someone has just drove up with Niel and he is in the house in pretty bad shape.

↬ Death in the family, Nashville, Tennessee:

Sunday, March 26, 1860. Pleasant day. Rev. Prof Vincent of the University preached a most excellent sermon for us in the morn. Dr. Roman preached in the eve to a full house or nearly so. G. W. McKie spent the day with us. I could not prevail on him to go to church, stay in the house he would & read just what he had a mind to. Bad Boy.
—*Diary of Francis S Thayer.*

Wednesday, April 25th. At noon started for Louisville on steamer. I wrote Strachan. My legs begin to trouble, pain in knees— Arrive in Louisville half past 9 P.M. Sleep on board.
Thursday, April 26th. Stopped at Galt House until 5 P.M. Saw Carter & Buchanan. At 5 o'c took Louisville & Nashville R. R. & arrived in Nashville towards morning, the most disagreeable night I ever passed with my legs.
Friday, April 27th. Arrived at Nashville 1/2 past 3 A.M. & went to bed— my knees

paining me most acutely. Get no traces of Doub. Passed a most wretched day… Isaac Smith died today. Passed an awful night. Legs pained me most excruciatingly. Doub & Cheatham appeared today to my great relief. Legs continue painful. Took sweat & emetic. Some better at night.
Sunday, April 29th. All wrong again. Took another sweat & passed a most miserable day. Doct says I have "billious & without fever" with thermatisan [illegible]
Monday, April 30th. No improvement this A.M., rather more fever. Doct came, some favorable symptoms towards night. Rained very hard this P.M. First rain since left N.Y.
Tuesday, May 1st. Cleared up during the night. Symptoms some better, but passed a wretched night. Fever continues.
— *Diary of George Wilson McKie.* [son of George & Sophia McKie]

May 1, 1860, Nashville.
Dear Father & Mother—   What would I not give if I were with you this A.M. I am down sick & have been since I got here last Friday A.M. with rheumatism, fever etc.
I felt unwell the day I left Pittsburgh & now regret that I did not then start for home instead of coming on— but I know that F. S. Thayer depended upon me & I disliked to disappoint him & then I hoped to get better daily. I have no appetite for ten days, have taken two sweats and two lobelia emetics. My knees pain me all the time but especially at night, thus depriving me of sleep. I do hope I am some better today but I am pretty weak. I seem to have a little more appetite today & indeed can say that I think I am better than when I first came. I cannot write anymore. Kindest love to Mother & self,
Affectionately yours,   —Love *George.*

Nashville, May 1, 1860.
Dear Frank & Kate— [Francis Thayer & Catherine McKie Thayer in Troy]
I write this letter "flat on my back," where I have been ever since I got here last Friday AM, confined by fever and rheumatism. I was taken sick about the time I left Pittsburgh and suffered awful torments with my legs— especially the knee joints. I am under treatment by a [illegible] and think this P.M. that I am a little better, but how glad I would be if I could put myself into Mother's care— or yours Kate dear. Kiss the babies for me and believe me.   —Yours affectionately, *G. W. McKie.*

Wednesday, May 2nd. Sick, sick, sick.
Thursday, May 3rd. The same weary round from morn till night. Think my knees are not quite as painful nor have I quite as much fever. Discharge. Doct Moredon. Pd him $14.00.   —*Diary of George W. McKie.*

May 3d, 1860, Nashville, Tenn.
George McKie Esq., South Easton, N. Y.
Dear Sir,   George W— is better, will I think be out in a few days. —Yours Truly, *D. M. Doub.*

Friday, May 4th. Called in Dr. Newman & from the moment I began to use his medicines I began to mend & how I wish I were at home with my dear mother.
Saturday, May 5th. Gaining but very slowly. Slept better last night than any night since was taken. O how dull & spiritless this is & how vastly disagreeable it is to be sick from home.

Sunday, May 6th. Clear day— Still confined to my bed. No progress perceptible. Plenty of strawberries & peas here.

Monday, May 7th. Some better today. Got out on the piazza today & feel very much better.
—*Diary of George W. McKie.*

May 7th, 1860, Nashville.
My dear Father & Mother—   I am glad to be able to write you this morning that I am a great deal better than when I wrote you last— My legs are not now very painful. I have something of an appetite— I can walk about the room a little this morning & hope to be able to get out by tomorrow. I can write you nothing of the country or people as yet as I have seen neither, only by glimpses. I should so much like to hear from home— how you are getting along with the barnyard etc. etc. Mother you must write and let Father direct it. Just as soon as I am able I shall start for the lower part of the State where I shall see more that will interest you.

The weather is very dry here and has been for a long time. Father what do you think of burning the cornstalks in the field. They do it here & in Kentucky & Ohio. Looks bad. You never saw anything equal in richness etc. the land here— a perfect garden. Write me as soon as you can & direct here.   Yours affectionately, *George.*

May 7th, 1860, Nashville.
Dear Frank & Kate—   I hasten as soon as I can to inform you of every favorable change. I am very much better this morning & am in hopes of getting up in a day or two now. My knees do not plague me very much although my right one is troublesome. The fever has left me and I am now in a very painful way. But O how I have longed for my dear old home & Mother and Sister and how much I have thought in the last 10 days of Peter, poor Peter. God knows I never meant to be sick away from home again & I sincerely hope none of my friends will be. Kiss the children & write me.   —Affectionately your bro. *George.*

P. S. I write this in bed, but I have walked around the room this A.M. Write me the news from home.

Tuesday, May 8th. Better today. Feel I am getting along now. Pd Dr. Newman $10.00. Sat up all the forenoon & got along very well.   —*Diary of George W. McKie.*

May 8th, 1860, Nashville.
Dear Father & Mother—   I am very glad to be able to write you that I am much better, so much so indeed as to be up and around again. I have been downstairs nearly all day today & if I gain as fast tomorrow shall start for Shelbyville day after.

I have been rather badly off. I'll assure you my flesh is all gone, but am thankful it is no worse. I suppose Wier has his seed all in. I don't know but I forgot to tell you that I did not intend to put any clover seed on the "back pasture." Wier had better spend a little time on the stone on the upper end of his meadow as he will mow it a great deal better. Have Tom McCune get away all the ash logs certain. It seems to me as though the black ash ought to be split this Spring. Asa Lee said he would do it for us. Get him at it. Tom McCune will have to draw some trees that are in wet places before they are split. O how I long to be home— shut up here, see nothing, hear nothing but noise. Hope it will be better in a day or two. Write me here— what is doing & how Isaac Smith is etc. etc.

Get the $10 of Norma's as soon as you can.   Yours affectionately, *George*. A kiss for Mungy.

May 8th, 1860, Nashville.
Dear Frank & Kate—   I am so much better today that I conclude I must tell you. Yesterday I dressed & went out to the Piazza and sat an hour or so and today I have been dressed all day & took my dinner at the regular table and may say that I am comfortable once more. I am anxious to hear from home— how Mother & her new girl get along together. I am also anxious to hear how they are doing about the "barn yard." I suppose you have not been up there since I left. Kiss the children for me a couple of times if you please & write me Frank— and especially if you have any news from Father & Mother.
—Affectionately your bro, *George*.

Wednesday eve. May 9th, 1860.
Dear Niel— [Francis Thayer to Niel McKie in Cambridge]   Your letter of the 6th May came to hand this morning… We are sorry to hear that Mother is not in her usual health & strength. Hope the all-healing powder will soon make her well again. You say that you can't recollect when it rained last; perhaps I can jog your memory a little on that point. You remember when we were up home last fall and that soon after we left for Troy it fairly poured down upon us so that we stopped at Elisha Giffords & borrowed a buffalo robe to protect us from the storm. I received a letter from George yesterday dated Nashville, Tuesday May 1st. He was sick but better & hoped to be out again in a day or two. We are pleased to hear that McKie is so far ahead with the spring's work & I hope he may prove a valuable man to you. Please say to Mother that her Granddaughter is getting along wonderfully. A tooth *in her hand* was discovered today by her Aunt Liz, and of course nothing else has been talked of at our home today. Kate & Frankie are pretty well, with the exception colds. After so long a time, the length of which as you say it is difficult to remember, we have a fair prospect of some rain which I hope will come soon for we are about buried in dust.

I am pretty busy nowadays getting our home started. We shall have the foundation laid this week. We can't say when we shall be able to make you a visit. Will give you due notice. Shall be with you as soon as we can. Niel— come down & make us a visit. Love to all, yours in haste,   —*Frank*.

Wednesday, May 9th. Getting along slowly. Sat up & moved around considerably today. Doub started for Lebanon this A.M. at 3 o'c. Cold & cloudy day. My leg troubles me a good deal yet.
Thursday, May 10th. Commences sunny & pleasant. Leg painful yet went out to see Col. Cheatham with G. G. Sloane. Home at noon & sick all afternoon. Diarrhea set in in evening.
Friday, May 11th. Diarrhea continues all day— makes me very weak— took teaspoon of paregoric & stayed in the d. Very weak.   —*Diary of George W. McKie.*

Residence of Francis & Catherine Thayer at 4 Washington Park, Troy, New York. Built 1860, shown here being renovated in 2004.

getting our home started   This refers to the construction of the Thayer's new home at "4 Washington Park," sometimes referred to as "4 Park Street," in Troy, New York. The house was still standing and under renovation in 2004.

d.   May mean "day."

May 12th, 1860, Nashville.
Dear Frank—   Your letter is just rec'd and right glad was I to hear from you & Kate and family. I had been doing pretty well for two or three days when day before yesterday I had a fall back, which has weakened me very much. I feel some better today. You would not know me I reckon— a mere skeleton. I don't think I weigh 120.

So poor Isaac has gone— I expected to hear it… Frank the wheat crop in this State is a total failure and also in Kentucky, although there will be a better crop in Kentucky than in Tenn. Flour is selling at Lebanon, 28 miles from here, at $7.50 per bshl. The people are disheartened and feel poor, very poor. They all write in saying that they will not get back their seed this year. The oat crop looks poorly too— Corn sells at $1.00 at Lebanon and all they use is imported, so of all this part of the State…

Accounts from the South are bad for wheat and in fact you never in all your experience heard such a universal howl as goes up from all this country in regard to the wheat crop. A man was in my room last night from Wilson Co. who has been selling threshing machinery for an Albany firm, says none can be sold this year etc. etc. The flouring mills are all idle. Hay sells for $27 to 30, wholesale— oats .65— here in Lebanon, .95. This I think will do to convince you of the inpracticability of selling mowing Machines…
It seems that Cheatham has sold the machines & that has ended it as far as he is concerned. Consequently the machines fell into the hands of ignorant niggers etc. and of course soon got out of repair and the result is that generally they are d—d. This is a most lovely country— none that I have seen equals it in general agricultural beauty… If I don't get stronger soon I shall try and come home as it will be too late to do anything by the time my strength is returned… I am glad to hear that your house is underway. Hope all will go on well. Kiss Kate & the babies & believe me affectionately,
—G. W. McKie.

May 15, 1860, Nashville.
Dear Father and Mother—   I am up again and hope to stay up this time— long enough to get strength to get home. I now think that I will not stay longer than the early part of next week— if I am able to endure the journey by that time.

The last pull back has made me much weaker than I was the first time. Diarrhea set in and had hold of me for two days. The weather here is very hot and dry. Oats are only 5 or 6 inches high— grass is looking very well. Oats are worth .75 per bushel, corn .85 and off the r. rd. [railroad] a little ways, $1.00 per bushel. Hay $30 etc. Have John knock the [illegible] in the meadow north of Mr. Wiers if he has not— & pay particular attention to the snap dragon— especially in the East field, as there is a good deal in and about the fences etc. that requires close looking to.

So I see Smith has gone, as I learn in a letter from Frank. I never expected to see him again the morning I left. It leaves his father very lonely indeed. I do hope Tom has been getting on well with the work. Mother I do hope you have got a good girl at last. If you have not, send word to Hays to get the one up at Cambridge. He knows the one that lived at Lansing's.

Good-by, hope to be with you soon,   Yours affectionately. —G. W. McKie.

Friday, May 18th.
Getting very weak. Another attack of palpitation at 4 P.M., bad. Telegraph to F. S. Thayer and get answer at 9 o'c. —*Diary of George W. McKie.*

Troy, Friday evening.
Dear Mother—   Kitty said to me when leaving the tea table, "Drop Mother a line and let her know that we are all well," which I am happy to do. I recd a letter from George dated Nashville, May 12th. He was not quite as well as he had been but hoped to be about again in a day or two. I will write you as soon as I hear from him again. He wrote me a long letter about wheat crop etc. so I judge he not as sick as he has been. Kitty finished house cleaning today and we are all nice & clean. The children are well and you know they make us very happy. The house moving forward rapidly. Cellar walls all laid and next week it will be up one story. The telegraph this P.M. from Chicago says Abe Lincoln of Ill. was nominated for Prest. on the third ballot. Mr. Seward is laid up for four years at least. Love to all.   —Your son *Francis.*

New York, Albany & Buffalo Telegraph Co.
To: F. S. Thayer. *From:* Nashville. May 18, 1860.
I am very sick & wish you to come on without delay. Answer by telegraph. *G. W. McKie,* City Hotel.

Friday, P. M. Took a short ride. At half past 7 recv'd telegraph from George at Nashville saying he was very sick & requesting me to come. I packed my carpet-bag immediately. John took me to Albany & I took Cin Express at quarter past 11 P. M.
—*Diary of Francis S. Thayer.*

Friday evening, 1/2 past 8 o'clock.
Dear Mother—   I have just recd a telegraph from George at Nashville saying "very sick & wish you to come on without delay." I leave tonight via Cincinnati and hope and pray to find the sick boy better. God grant that we may all be spared to meet him again in health & strength. [In the handwriting of Francis S. Thayer.] —— Sat morn. Frank wrote this last night to send by night and then concluded that John better go up today and I will drop a line to Johnsonville tonight and will send Mon wherever you may direct. I hope to hear today (by telegraph) that Geo is better. It seems that he had cold rheumatism in his legs and fever. He was better and then got up and out too soon. We had a letter Wed. eve written Sat. saying that he was on his back again and last eve Frank had the telegraph… I thought perhaps you would like to come down where you can hear as soon as any news are received by Tel. or letter. We wrote Aunt Almy to see if she could go over and stay a few days. Father and you could both come, only it seems too bad to leave Niel alone. You could come with John or come to the cars this aft. Drop me a line if you don't come. Let us trust God who doeth all things well. [Unsigned, in the handwriting of Catherine McKie Thayer.]

Saturday, May 19th.
Continue bad all day. Doub came back tonight.   —*Diary of George W. McKie.*

At sunrise near Newark N. Y. Fine rain last night which I hope extended all over eastern New York. Breakfast at Rochester. Left Buffalo for Cleveland about 10 o'clock. Dinner at Dunkirk. Had just time in Cleveland for call on my old friend J. R. Cobb. On for Cin at 6 o'clock, where we arrived at 4 A.M. Sabbath morn. —*Diary of Francis S. Thayer.*

Cambridge,
Dear George [in the handwriting of George McKie, writing to his son, George Wilson McKie]— We received your letter of the 8th of May and was pleased, yes and very thankful, to hear that your health was improving and we sincerely wish and hope that ere long you may be restored to a comfortable state of health. Our anxiety for you George is somewhat abated since we received your last letter dated May 8th and we hope that the next news we get from you will be still more cheering. I wrote you a long letter the fore part of this week which I hope you have received and there is very little that I can add to it in this letter. Thomas and Alex M., Gene and John have been all this week cutting wood and the tops of trees where the rail logs were taken off. Some two days more Tom thinks to finish them. It is a very slow business, then it will take some days to draw it out. Asa Lee has been splitting some three days and I hope he will continue until he finishes them. He says it is a hard job— some of them split very hard. I wrote you that there will be no time to do anything more to the barnyard till after haying. I hope the large Barn may stand up before haying, yet I don't know. The offside ox is a most miserable animal— he is now quite lame again and unless he gets better I am afraid he will not be able to go on with the business that is necessary to us. We are having pretty hard luck with our lambs… We are having a fine rain today, much needed— everything was at a standstill. My eyes are improving slowly, but far from being well. I wrote you in my first letter that Isaac Smith died the 27th of April. We have received a letter from Edwin. They arrived safely and in good health… I can write no more George. A *Father's* and *Mother's* love to you. Hurry home as soon as you can. We want to see one more [*sic*], write us when you think you will be home if you are spared—
[in the handwriting of Sophia McKie]— God Bless you my boy. How much I think about you.

Sunday, May 20th.
Very bad today. Am very weak & no appetite. Heart very sore.
—*Diary of George W. McKie.*

Sunday 20th. On arrival in Cincinnati this morn at 4 o'clock went to Spencer House where I got a good nap and breakfast after which I called on Hon. P. Mallow, at 61 McFarland Street. At 12 O'clock we took Steam Boat *Telegraph No. 3* for Louisville. Met on the boat A. J. Nutting of Troy who is traveling for a Boston House. Had a pleasant run down the Ohio & arrived at Lville 10 O'clock P.M. & stopped at Galt House.
—*Diary of Francis S. Thayer.*

Onboard Steamboat *Telegraph* — about 50 miles above Louisville, Sabbath evening.
My own dearest Kitty— Here I am a thousand miles away from you & our darling children and yet with you in thought every moment. Duty calls me another way in person and it is my constant prayer that I may find our

dear brother better and that I may soon return to you. We shall arrive in Louisville about 10 o'clock this eve & the first train from there to Nashville is at 5:10 tomorrow morning. O how my heart trembles when I think of what I may hear & see of George in the morning. God grant that it may be as we most devoutly pray for. We are all under the care of an all wise Providence & let us rely upon the goodness & mercy of Him who doeth all things well. I shall telegraph you immediately on my arrival at Nashville & keep you informed of any change that may occur. You will hear from me by the wonderful telegraph long before you receive this. I dropt' you a line from Buffalo yesterday. Arrived in Cleveland about 5 o'clock P.M… so I came to Cincinnati where we arrive at 4 this morning. I took a berth in the sleeping car as I did from Albany… It being Sabbath, no trains from Cincinnati until eve so I went to bed & slept… After breakfast called to see Patrick & Sophy whom I found had just returned (this morning on this same boat) from a four weeks journey west, returning via St. Louis & Louisville. Patrick had no news for me so at 12 o'clock I left Cincinnati for this Boat. The day has been beautiful indeed… About 150 passengers onboard, mostly southern people I judge, only one person onboard I ever saw before i.e., Mr. Netting of Troy… Everything looks new & strange to me. All is so different. I have been interested in the conversation of an old man, 71 years old, who is perfectly familiar with all that has transferred on this River since 1803, having lived in several places all along shore. He is "I reckon a fine specimen of a fine old Kentucky Gentleman."

…Cincinnati is a large & beautiful city. It looks more like our eastern cities than Chicago & other western towns of rapid growth. Patrick & Sophy are pleasantly situated in a sweet two-story house & I have no doubt they enjoy life most happily. They both said & urged strongly that if George was able to leave Nashville he must come up & stay with them until he could go on home safely. I thanked them from my heart for their kindness, and wished from my heart of hearts that it might be so… Altho' I have traveled rapidly night & day, I do not feel fatigued. On the contrary I feel perfectly well and but for the anxiety about George and my absence from you & our little ones, I should say I feel well & happy. I shall take the best possible care of myself & hope and pray that ere long that I may be returned to the bosom of my family— all as we could wish. You will my own darling be careful of yourself & not get sick. I hope Mother will soon be with you and that it may be in my power to communicate good news to you of George tomorrow before this hour. I have often thought of Frankie's being burned and of his hairbreadth escape from death. You will of course make the girls see to him when you may leave him in their care. O how I wish I could take you all, self, Frankie & sweet little Kitty in my arms. I would give you such an embrace as you have never had before. Just a word about the House— It would be well for you to go down occasionally & see that all is going on as you think best. If the Pittsfield man comes you can talk with him & find out what he can do etc. etc. Now I must say goodnight and may God bless & protect us. Many kisses for yourself & our noble boy & darling little girl. More than ever your own *Frank*.

Monday, May 21st.
About same. F. S. Thayer came at 1/2 past 4 P.M. My side about the heart very sore & cannot draw a long breath. —*Diary of George W. McKie.*

At 5 o'clock A.M. took cars at Lville for Nashville, 185 miles and a long and anxious ride it was to me for I knew not whether I should find George among the living or dead. God in His mercy and goodness permitted me to find him better & I telegraphed Kate— "George better but not out of danger." I hope and pray that the dear fellow may recover.
—*Diary of Francis S. Thayer.*

Tuesday, May 22nd.
Nashville.
Dearest Kitty—   I arrived here yesterday P.M. (May 21) about 3 o'clock and never in all my life have I approached a place with more anxiety for I had not heard a word from George since the startling dispatch we rec'd last Friday eve. How often have I thought of the beautiful and yet awful (to us) spring morning we were called home at the time poor Henry died. Was I again to hear those awful words, "too late." I knew not. You can readily imagine my feelings when I asked the young man of the Hotel who came out to receive the passengers from the omnibus— How is Mr. McKie— and how thankful and rejoiced I was when told, "He is better today." I was immediately shown to his room (on the first floor) and the meeting I will not attempt to describe on paper— the tears came thick and fast etc. etc. G— knew my step as I approached the room and if ever a poor sick fellow a thousand miles from home was glad to see a friend, George was glad to see me. I know that George was (as he wrote me) sick when he came here three weeks ago last Friday with rheumatism in his legs and confined to his room two or three days. He called a Doctor who drew the complaint from his limbs so that he felt quite comfortable, although by no means well. About ten days ago he had a pull back but Monday and Tuesday was about the city in a buggy, took a ride out to Col. Cheatham's place about two miles distant. On Wednesday after supper, of which he probably ate too much, he was taken with palpitations of the heart which continued until Saturday. The disease had gone to the heart and the Dr. was very much afraid of a [illegible] all day Friday, Saturday & Sabbath but on Sabbath eve a favorable change took place, and up to this time the Dr. says the improvement has been quite as rapid as he could expect under such a very weak state of the system.

This morn I said to George "You look better my good fellow." He said: "One thing is certain, I feel better any how." He has taken more chicken broth with a little bread, also some nice fresh buttermilk Ada Cheatham sent him… The Cheatham family have been very attentive to George, and he has also many other warm friends in the Hotel. A good woman, (a slave in the house), by the name of Sophy is very attentive & efficient, drains blisters etc. etc. Notwithstanding Geo is sick away from home, he has a Sophy to take care of him. Before I telegraphed you yesterday I visited to see the Doctor and asked him what I could say in truth. He said just what I sent. This morning he (the Dr.) said all was going on as well and in two or three days more he would have G— sitting up a little. I shall stay here until the Dr. says G— is out of danger and in a fair way of permanent recovery. G— has kind friends here and just as soon as he is able to sit up and attend to himself a little I shall set my face towards home. I want to hear from you very much and would give anything if I could be with you, and at the same time I am contented to be away from the dearest ones of my heart when I feel I know that it serves but that it should be so. However hard it may be to be away from "Kitty & Babies."

…This eve Father's letter of 14th came, in which Mother added a P.S. I read it to George. When I came to Mother's part it was too much for the tender hearted boy & the tears came and he said: "O that I could be with the dear good woman" which I hope & pray be his happiness ere long and her's too. I shall stay here just as long as it may seem best. I came here to be a comfort and help to a kind brother who would do anything in the world for me or mine and I shall stay until he may say— Frank you can go and see the loved ones at home for I can get along well without you.

I trust that you keep watch of the Home & I hope that you will not fail to express yourself freely to Jacob & Coswell. Your ideas are correct about a home as in everything else, and I shall not be satisfied if you do not stand up for Woman's rights. I feel much encouraged about George today and I do hope and pray that he will go right along getting better from day to day. Geo. said today, "Frank rub this arm." How much Geo thinks of Frankie and all of you. Tell Frankie I love you all more & more and will come home as soon as I can. And a kiss for each of you and a thousand of them. The weather here is just comfortable and I feel perfectly well. We had a fine rain here last night. Hope you have had rain in this morn.   —*Frank*.

The Doct says the "indications" are for the better today. Eat a little today.
—*Diary of George W. McKie.*

New York, Albany & Buffalo Telegraph Co.
To: *Mrs. F. S. Thayer* From: *Nashville* May 22, 1860
I find Geo better. Not yet out of danger. Has best care & attention. —*F. S. Thayer*.

Troy, Tues eve 1/2 past 6
My dear Father—   We have just received a telegraph from Frank at Nashville which says: "I find Geo better, not yet out of danger. Has best care and attention." We are relieved and hope to hear of daily improvements. Our hearts are less burdened tonight, and we hope and pray that we may not be called to bear the anxiety we have felt these four days. Love to Aunty and Neil. Mother sends love to you and all. Your aff. Daughter.   —*C. McKie T.*
—I will write when I hear.

Troy, Tues eve 8 o'clock.
My own dear Frank—   Our long suspense was broken by your telegraph at 6 o'clock this eve. Mother came yesterday morn and we are so thankful that you can say that Geo is *any better*. It lifts the burden, lights the cloud a little— our anxieties cannot cease until we hear that Geo is out of danger— 'till disease has abated. In hearing from him I heard from you and knew that you had been watched over and came safely to the bedside of the sick brother and it does seem that there must have been one healthy natural heart beat when he saw you— felt you— with him. We have hoped and prayed "Oh if thou hast not taken him away, will Thou restore him to health and we can still hope and pray. Oh it is the glorious privilege of those who trust in God though all things are taken away and no other comfort remains, the naked soul can rise to God in prayer and find peace in trusting a covenant keeping God. We are glad to learn that Geo has good care and attention. A

sister's warmest thanks to those whose hands and hearts have done aught to relieve the dear Brother when sick among strangers and a Mother's everlasting gratitude. We hope to hear of continued improvement, but feel that it must be gradual. Of course your plans for the future are not very definite. I am glad to say that the children are well… *Kittie* —Your telegram was without date but I suppose you reached Nashville this morn. Hope to hear more particulars in a few days. How I long to have you take me in your arms again. —*Kitty*.

Tuesday— At Nashville weather very warm. George still better today & I can see a little change for the better almost every hour. Telegraphed Kate the good news, also wrote to Kate, giving particulars of G's sickness etc. The people at the Hotel are all very kind towards G— & he wants for nothing to make him comfortable except the presence of his Mother. —*Diary of Francis S. Thayer.*

Wednesday, May 23rd.
Feel a little better today & eat a little chicken soup twice & at night am stronger.
—*Diary of George W. McKie.*

At Nashville weather is what we would call hot at the North. Geo continues to improve & I feel very much encouraged. Mr. Doub went to Shelbyville in P.M. Dr. Newman gave me a ride down to see Col. Cheatham at the race course. Saw some very fair race horses among them *Allindorf* valued at $20,000. Met on our return Ada & Mr. & Mrs. Smith.
—*Diary of Francis S. Thayer.*

New York, Albany & Buffalo Telegraph Co.
Nashville, May 23, 1860.
To. Mrs. F. S. Thayer— George continues to improve. He sends love. I am well.
—*Frank.*

Nashville, Wednesday P.M.
My Own Dearest Kitty—   I wrote you a long letter yesterday giving particulars of George's sickness etc. etc. Today I am happy to say George is better and I do think him fairly on the way to recovered health & strength and O how rejoiced I feel to see him look better. The Doctor was in this A.M. and said, "You are gaining all the time." This P.M. we changed the bed clothes and put some clean clothes on G. You knowing how good and grateful it is to be nice and clean after lying in soiled and sweaty clothes several days. G— said when he dropped back upon the pillows— "Frank you don't know how good this does feel." For dinner G— ate a teacup full of chicken soup with half a [illegible] slice of old bread. Ada sent him some more buttermilk this morn, also some jelly. G— says he hopes to be able to start for home in two weeks, I say three. However the Dr. says he will gain rapidly after he gets able to go to the table and eat a good meal. I feel the difficulty will not be entirely recovered in many months. The fact is G— has all his life long been imprudent and he is now paying the drafts made upon his constitution by fox hunting etc. You remember a year ago when we were up home he was laid flat on his back after one day fishing. I do hope & trust this severe lesson will make the boy more careful.

I cannot of course tell when I shall be able to leave for home but I have it in my mind that G— will be so that I can leave him about next Monday. I would like to stop over one day and visit the Mamouth Cave which is only 7 miles from the R. R. between here and Louisville. …All the Rail Roads have sleeping cars attached to the night trains so night traveling is not so objectionable as formerly… [End of letter from Francis Thayer, no second page.]

Thursday, May 24th, 1860.
At Nashville weather decidedly hot, mercury stands at 92°. Geo better today & I so telegraphed Kate. Also wrote a long letter to Kate to which Geo added a P.S. to his Mungie & Kate. G. L. Davis & Mr. Hoyt of New York stopping at the City Hotel & I feel quite at home when I can see a face that I have seen before.   —*Diary of Francis S. Thayer.*

Nashville, P.M.
My Own Dearest Kitty— I telegraphed you this A.M. the good news that George was still better… Today G— appears bright and cheerful, much like himself and if he will only be careful I shall expect to see him walking about in two or three days. He is talking about paving the cellar at home with brick so that it won't be so hard for Mother to get about on the cellar bottom which you know is now quite rough. It is decided in G's mind to use brick instead of stone & cement. G— says today that he thinks he will be able to leave for home within ten days. I shall urge upon him the absolute necessity of getting quite strong before leaving and then when he does start, take the journey as long as possible. My greatest fears are that he will be in too much of a hurry to get home. However he promises me that he will follow the Doctor's directions to the letter.

 I hope to leave here next Monday and stop at the cave Tuesday and go on homeward bound Wednesday and reach home Saturday… Last eve the Dr. gave me a pleasant ride out to Co. Cheatham's place where we made a very pleasant call and saw some of the finest race horses in the country, one horse valued at $20,000… Today as I was coming out of the telegraph office I looked across the street and what do you think I saw? — Why a slave pen. I walked over and saw men, women & children, some 20 to 30, all for sale to the highest bidder. I thought of what Dr. Baldwin said on his return from the south, when speaking of attending a slave auction, more about this when we meet.

 It is hot here today, mercury stands at about 86°. I have only been out to the tel. office and slave pen. I have just turned to G— and asked him to give me an idea. He says "Tell Kate that when I come there I want some of that good ham and warmed up potatoes." If I can get away I shall ride out to the Hermitage, 12 miles from here and see where the Old Hero lived… G— says write to Father to have the young apple trees well watered if it is dry weather. I hope for a letter from you tomorrow and that I shall hear from you often during my stay here. How does the home get along? You must give directions and have everything done as you think best. If they build the cistern before my return tell them to make it large… I hope & trust Mother is with you and will remain until my return. George says he is a little sleepy and I must excuse him from filling the balance of this page. He says he is so very comfortable that he doesn't want to move. I am glad to see him so and will not disturb him.

 Tell Frankie that Father wishes him to be a good boy, kind and affectionate to his Mother & little sister and then I shall love him more than ever. O how I want to see the dear little fellow and you and little Kitty too… But I shall leave the sunny south at the earliest possible moment to be with the darlings of my heart, my dear wife & children more than ever. Kiss the children some 1000 times. Your own *Frank*.

Friday, May 25, 1860.
At Nashville weather quite warm. Geo still improving & he begins to count the days to the time when he can start for home. Went out to the "Hermitage" with Davis & Hoyt. Saw the Tomb of the Old Hero and bot of the old slave, 76 years old, some Hickory canes. Had a very pleasant ride & the satisfaction of seeing the home & grave of a great man.
—*Diary of Francis S. Thayer.*

New York, Albany & Buffalo Telegraph Co.
Nashville, May 25, 1860.
To. Mrs. F. S. Thayer—   George still improving. Reckon he's better if don't hear otherwise. *Frank.*

On the reverse side: Troy, Friday. Dear Father— We received this today and feel much relieved and hope George will soon be out. Think I shall hear from Frank by letter tomorrow. I am up and dressed today and hope I can keep up. Mother is pretty well and sends love to you and all. I send the same. Your aff. daughter, *C. McKie T.*

[undated]
Dear Kate & "Mungie" if she is there—   I do hope to be with you in a couple of weeks. Frank will give you the size of my legs so you will know how much of a traveller I am. Good-bye & may Good Angels protect you both. *George* [letter in George McKie's handwriting]
George's legs about the size of two beanpoles. [note in Francis Thayer's handwriting]

Saturday, May 26.
At Nashville weather very hot, about 95°. Geo seems quite like himself & talks about getting up but the Dr. says he had better wait until tomorrow. (Alas the dear fellow never saw the morrow's sun) Dr. Blaikie called in P.M. & talked an hour or two with G. Walked with Dr. B. out to Mr. Cheatham's where we were invited to supper. Had a good supper and a pleasant time. Went out to General Harding's with G. L. Davis of N.Y.
—*Diary of Francis S. Thayer.*

Sunday, May 27, 1860.
A few minutes before 3 o'clock this morning Geo woke me by saying, "Frank, Frank." I was at his side in a moment He said, "Fan me. Open the windows." I did so, but it was too late, the hour of death had come & in two minutes from the time he first spoke to me the dear noble generous hearted fellow was no more. O God, give me strength in this awful hour away from home & kindred.   —*Diary of Francis S. Thayer.*

DIED   McKIE — At Nashville, Tenn, 27th inst., George W. McKie, of Easton, Washington Co., aged about 35 years — brother of Mrs. F. S. Thayer of this city.
—*Unidentified newspaper clipping.*

George Wilson McKie, 1825–1860. Photographer, F. Forshew, Hudson, New York.

City Hotel, Nashville, Tenn. May 27, 1860.
At a meeting of the Mercantile Travellers of New York held this evening for

the purpose of making arrangements to follow the remains of our deceased fellow traveller Geo. W. McKee to the station of the Louisville & Nashville R. R. on Monday morning 28th at five o'clock... Resolved: That whereas it has pleased God to remove from among us our fellow traveller Geo. W. McKee... be it therefore resolved that we do form ourselves in procession to follow his remains to the depot of the Louisville & Nashville R. R. tomorrow...

Resolved: That we deeply sympathize with his aged parents and his relations in this sudden bereavement... Resolved: That we, in behalf of his relations, do tender our thanks to the proprietors and attaches of the City Hotel for their unwearied attention to the Deceased during his short illness... (signed) *Geo. S. Davis*, Pres., *W. H. Moore*, Secty.

May 28, 1860. At 5 o'clock A.M. left Nashville for home with the remains of my dear friend & brother, George. A long and lonely journey with the dead, and O how cold the world seems. Not so at Nashville. All were kind and attentive & showed every mark of respect possible. Came to Louisville, Jeffersonville & Cin. Met P. Mallot at Cin a moment.

Tuesday 29th. On my sad journey day & night. Stopped at [illegible] for breakfast and Erie P.A. for dinner. Arrived in Buffalo 5:45 & at 6 took cars for home and O how sad will be the meeting. I pray God that He will give us all that grace and strength we so much need in this affliction. God bless in an especial manner those aged parents and only sister who have been afflicted again & again.

Wednesday, May 30, 1860. Arrived at Schenectady at 4 o'clock A.M. 46 hours from Nashville, 1,039 miles. No train to Troy until 1/4 past 8. Arrived at Troy 9 A.M. Met at depot my friends Messrs. Cowen, Howe, Heart, Strong & Graves who expressed their sympathy. At 12 1/4 o'clock took cars for J'ville. Kate, nurse & baby with me. Met at J'ville, John with carriage. Mr. Damon was there to take George's remains home. O what a house.

Thursday, May 31, 1860. A bright and beautiful day without. But O how dark to us who today commit to the grave our dear friend and brother George Wilson McKie. Many friends came to pay their respect to the dead. We buried him beside Jimmie & Henry. Rev. Peter Gordon attended the funeral. Adin & Henry were present & officiated as bearers. Just as we came home a hard shower commenced.

—*Diary of Francis S. Thayer.*

Grave of George Wilson McKie, 1825–1860, Whiteside Cemetery, Cambridge, New York.

May 29, 1860. A beautiful day. I went to Salem with James McKie. We took dinner at Williams. On arriving home I found a letter from Katy Thayer informing us of the death of Geo. Wilson [McKie]. I went to George's and back. Rev. Mr. Forsythe & wife here to dinner & tea.

May 30. A cold day, some little rain. John Whiteside here to tea. Mr. Thayer arrived at Br. Georges with the body of George Wilson who died at Nashville, Tenn. I attended Prayer Meeting...

May 31. A warm showery day. I went to the funeral of Geo. W. McKie with John & William McKie, Br. Wm & Wife were here to dinner & tea. John & William here to dinner. John & Minerva to tea. Bill McLean also. There was a large funeral. Rev. P. Gordon gave an address. —*Diary of James McKie.*

Nashville, June 4th, 1860.
F. S. Thayer Esq. Troy, NY: Dear Sir— The sad news of the death of our friend Mr. McKie reached me at Shelbyville, but I could not fully realize the

fact until my return to this place. Finding him gone, and the sadness and loneliness that oppressed me, told too plainly that I would never more meet him on earth. During the short time we were together I learned to admire & esteem him almost as a brother; I can fully sympathize in your loss. I am glad that his last moments were peaceful & that his noble and generous spirit passed so quietly and calmly to the God who gave it. May an all wise Providence comfort and sustain you in this great affliction; and may that good kind Mother, of whom he often spoke during his sickness, be enabled to feel in her heart that "The *Lord* giveth and the *Lord* taketh away; blessed be the name of the *Lord*."

The smallest trunk you took with you belongs to me and contains nearly all of my baggage. You may send it by express to Louisville Ky, care Carter & Zuchman… I found the box you sent back from the depot at the omnibus stable. You left nothing but a pair of nearly worn out boots belonging to Mr. McKie.　—Yours Truly *D. M. Doub*.

Troy, June 5, 1860, Tues morn, 1/2 past 7.
My dearest Mother—　　I intended to write you yesterday, but my time was so occupied that I had not time before 3 o'clock and the letter does not go up in the aft if it is not mailed before 3 I learn. So I write a word this morn and Frank will send up. We came home in the rain, kept dry and took no cold. We are all well. May God comfort and bless you all.　—Your *Kitty* as ever.

∾ A letter from Edwin McKie in England:

Liverpool, June 15, 1860.
My dear Father & Mother—　　Henry Mosher's letter of 28th May came giving the sad, sad, news of the death of poor Brother George at Nashville. May God have mercy and comfort and bless you both. How I do pity you, my dear good parents. How I wish I were with you to comfort you as much as I could. It seems as if your cup of sorrow had been filled before this, but it seems we are to have it overrun. Poor George has gone to meet our Brothers who went before him, and whom we shall follow ere long, and I hope where trouble and sorrow never enter. I cannot write more. I say again, God comfort & bless you. We are well and I shall go home as soon as I possibly can. Nette writes. Affectionately your children.　—*Ed & Nette*.

Brother Niel— I hope you are well. Comfort our good parents as much as you can. Be kind and good to them. They need all our kindness and tenderness. Stay with them and be their comfort.　—Your Brother *Edwin*.

∾ A handwritten receipt:

Easton, August 30, 1860. $28 Rec'd of Mr. George McKie twenty eight dollars in full payment for a set of gravestone erected to the grave of George Wilson McKie.
　　　　　　　　　　　　　　　　　　　　　　　—*E. B. Hoyt*.

∾

Fall of 1860

November 6, 1860. Rainy day... Abe Lincoln elected President...
—Diary of Francis S. Thayer.

The Presidential Election — Immediate Secession Recommended by the Governor of South Carolina — The Condition of Southern Sentiment

The Election Today — It is universally conceded that the vote of New York today decides the Presidential question. Every other Northern State is surrendered to Lincoln. The great West will pronounce for him by enormous majorities... The most remarkable feature of the canvass has been the fact that the Republicans are the only organized party in the field. Theirs is the only platform of principles and the only candidate for which any citizen has a chance to vote. The Opposition to Lincoln are united upon no candidate, nor do they agree upon any political principle. No man can tell what would follow their success, —what principles would come into the ascendant...
—*The New York Times,* November 6, 1860.

Astounding Triumph of Republicanism — Abraham Lincoln Probably Elected President by a Majority of the Entire Popular Vote
—*The New York Times,* November 7, 1860.

The result of the Presidential Election announced this forenoon created no surprise on the Stock Exchange... The first impression on the market this morning was a feeling of relief that the election was disposed of without any suspense as to the final result...
—*The New York Times,* November 8, 1860.

Friday P.M. Nov 9th, 1860.
Dear Mother—   Kitty has a sick headache today and she says I must drop you a line— 'tis not neuralgia but one of her old fashioned headaches. Hope she will be better when I go home to tea. The children are very well and as for the younger one, she is a regular little witch cat, driving about on her hands & knees wherever she had a mind to... Well, Election is over and Old Abe is elected & I have no doubt the Union will be preserved. Our County did nobly under the circumstances & Old Washington is herself again in all her glory & majesty. Woods Mowing Machine Factory was burned to the ground last Monday eve. Loss $40,000, insured for $22,000. They are going to rebuild at Hoosick as soon as possible.   —Affectionately yours, *Francis.*

Woods Mowing Machine Factory was located in Hoosick Falls, New York. Edwin McKie worked for that company on his trips to Illinois and Ohio and also while in England.

November 13, 1860. ...Business very dull & there is quite a panic in the money market in New York. Stocks declining rapidly all in consequence of the troubly south which I hope & believe will blow over ere long.
November 15. ...A little improvement in money matters in New York...
November 17. The panic continues unabated & business in paralyzed all owing to the election of Lincoln. The Southern States seem determined to kick up a [illegible] & what the end will be, no one can tell.
December 31. ...God has called from our midst our dear brother George who died at Nashville, Tenn., May 27, Sabbath morning. It was my melancholy privilege to be with him the last days of his life & to bring his body home to be laid by the side of those who

had gone before. May we all turn to our heavenly Father for comfort & consolation in the hour of affliction. My dear wife & children have been spared from severe sickness & in business I have been favored above many…   —*Diary of Francis S. Thayer.*

1861

WHAT WAS STOLEN. — The following sums were in different depositories and branch mints of the United States in the seceded States at the time those States rebelled, and were stolen from the Government:

New Orleans	$535,494
Richmond	14,095
Norfolk	11,795
Wilmington, N.C.	6,088
Savannah	4,874
Mobile	18,225
Nashville	4,880
Galveston	2,811
Norfolk	1,413
Little Rock, Ark.	58,692
Tallahassee, Fla.	679
Charlotte, N. C., (branch mint)	32,000
Dahlonega, Geo., (branch mint)	27,950
Total:	$718,998

—*Newspaper clipping folded into the 1861 diary of Edwin McKie.*

Troy, Jan 3, 1861, Thurs aft.
My dear Mother—   …I am better of my cold. Still my head aches and I have taken a sugar-coated pill and expect to feel better tomorrow… Do not hurry the stockings and do write me some particulars about yourself… Hard times down South. We hope it will all come out right. Merri Christmas and Happy New Year to you all… Good-bye. Love to all. God bless you & us.   —Your *Kitty.*

∽ Death in the family, January 1861:

Friday, January 11th.
Exciting news from South Carolina. It looks like war. God grant that not a drop of blood may be spilled.   —*Diary of Francis S. Thayer.*

Dr. Mosher here to see Mother.   —*Diary of Edwin McKie.*

Saturday, January 12th.
Rec'd a letter from Ed saying Father was quite sick. Soon after Ed Hunt came for us to go up immediately. We took the noon train and arrived home at 1/2 past 2 PM. Found Father very sick. Mother too. I am afraid that death will again very soon visit this household. How often death has visited this family since I first knew them. Four brothers have gone and now the parents are but lingering.   —*Diary of Francis S. Thayer.*

South Carolina seceded on December 20, 1860, followed by Mississippi on January 9, 1861, Florida on January 10, 1861, and Alabama on January 11, 1861.

At Home. Went to Easton at 6 A.M. for Doct. Mosher & called to get Ed Hunt & got Ed Hunt and he went to Troy & got Frank & Kate and back here at 2 P.M.
—*Diary of Edwin McKie.*

William came down and took our horse and went to see George who is sick.
—*Diary of James McKie.*

Sunday, January 13th.
Very Cold. Mercury stood at 8 o'clock A.M. at 30 below zero. Don't know as I saw the mercury as low before. Continued very cold through the day. Father and Mother very sick. Dr. Mosher attending. I am hardly satisfied with his treatment but it may be for the best. They have the best care and attention, and we must trust Providence.
—*Diary of Francis S. Thayer.*

At Home. Thermometer 30 below this A.M. Father and Mother still very sick, Doct Mosher here—
—*Diary of Edwin McKie.*

Monday, January 14th.
Weather still quite cold, but not so awful as yesterday. Mercury this morn about 18 below zero. Ed Hunt took me to Johnsonville in morn. Found the children well and happy with Mother who is perfectly devoted to them. Even heard Dr. Good lecture— subject: "Queen Elizabeth— Woman as a Sovereign."
—*Diary of Francis S. Thayer.*

At Home. Therm 8 below but mild at eve & snowing. All the neighbors in today. Father & Mother the same & Father not as well & sent for Doct M— at eve— James McKie sat up tonight.
—*Diary of Edwin McKie.*

A cold morning. Merc. 10° below... The weather moderated towards night. Some snow falling.
—*Diary of James McKie.*

Tuesday, January 15th.
Morn 10 o'clock.
My dearest Frank—   I am happy to say to you that Mother seems better, her side is somewhat relieved, her fever abating, cough very hard, but she raises and speaks more natural.

Father is very sick, had a high fever yesterday, less this morn. The Doctor does not speak decidedly. We must wait till the fever changes and while we wait let us pray.

Bring with you tomorrow some soft thin rubber cloth— say a piece half a yard square and four pieces to keep fomentations hot— I wish I had one now for poor Father.

Bring a few milk crackers. They may like them in a few days.

Kiss the dear children for me.

I am well and not over tasked.

Love to Liz and all.
—Your *Kitty*.

Eve. 7 o'clock,
My dearest Frank—   Again, dear Frank, has the angel of death folded his wings on the threshold of this dear old home.

Our dear Father gradually failed all day and quietly peacefully passed away about 4 o'clock. I went down at 10 o'clock to see him and I thought him dying, so I got someone to take care of Mother, who is really better but very weak and needs the best care, and I stayed by Father till he breathed his last. I only said one thing to him: "Mother is a little better, Father" — "I am glad she is, I am glad of it." Poor "Sophia" had his last words.

Mother bears this sorrow as well as you could expect— But oh what a house— You will be met at 1 o'clock at Johnsonville. Will you bring a blanket shawl of Liz or Mother Graves— My black dress from back closet— Bonnet, Pocket hkfs. A Change of underclothes, Crape veil in lower drawer of bureau in back chamber, Black Kid Gloves in glove box of my drawer of our room. Crape veil of Liz or Mother Graves. Kiss the dear children— I pray they are well. Love to Liz.   —Your *Kitty*.

Obituary   Deceased represented this District at one time, in the Assembly. By unceasing industry, a frugal economy and an unwavering fidelity in all that pertained to honorable dealing, deceased has ever enjoyed an abundance of this world's goods. Courteous, kind and hospitable, he enjoyed the sincere friendship of a large circle of acquaintances, and has left behind him a name and an example worthy of imitation.
—*Washington County Post.*

Weather quite mild and pleasant. —Business dull and market declining a little. —At 1/2 past 3 P.M. Father McKie passed quietly and peacefully to a better world after a week's sickness. Oh how sudden. Mother is very feeble & I am afraid she will soon follow. Mr. Allen brought the sad news at 10 o'clock P.M. Jim came from New York and stayed with us overnight.   —*Diary of Francis S. Thayer.*

At Home. Our Good Father died at half past 3 this P.M. Aged 69 years 6 months and one day. Thy children all mourn thy loss. Aunt Lucy called with H— Whiteside. Father was confined to his bed but 5 days.   —*Diary of Edwin McKie.*

A beautiful day. *Brother George Died* this afternoon. —Lucy called at George's. —I wrote William this evening.   —*Diary of James McKie.*

"Tuesday aft"
My heart is with you dearest Kate during this sad day and I wish that I might come and sympathize with you in this deep affliction.

There is one angel less on Earth but one more in Heaven, we will hope…

Your poor Mother— my heart aches for her. May she find strength from above, and be able to say, "Not my will, but thine be done." You dear Kate, I need not tell where to go for consolation in this dark hour, The God who has preserved you 'til now will not forsake you when you most need his aid. May his best blessings rest upon you, and lead you.

Libby Beadle   A letter from a close friend and neighbor in Cambridge.

Think of me as sympathizing with you all and believe me that my spirit is with you though the body is not. With a heart full of love, *Libby Beadle.*

Wednesday, January 16th.
Very stormy day. Rain and sleet. At 12 o'clock left Troy for Cambridge. Ed Hunt met me at Johnsonville. Oh what a home. I find the dead and I fear the dying. Mother is very feeble. We sent for Dr. Mosher and Dr. Kennedy. Up with Mother all night. God grant that she may be spared.   —*Diary of Francis S. Thayer.*

Ed Hunt got Frank at Lick, noon. At Home. Rained hard nearly all day. Uncle James and Aunt Almy came. Aunt Almy stayed with us. Sent for Doct Mosher by Ed McKie and for Doct Kennedy by C. Pitney at 10 PM. for Mother. I went churchyard to have grave dug for Father.   —*Diary of Edwin McKie.*

A mild morning. I took Almy to George's. James McKie here this morning. I went to Barton's with him and selected a coffin for Bro George. Mr. Shortt called. John Whiteside also. —*Diary of James McKie.*

Thursday, January 17th.
Weather mild and pleasant. At 11 o'clock we met to pay our last tribute of love to Father McKie whom we consigned to the grave. Mr. Gordon made appropriate remarks and a most excellent prayer. Poor Mother so sick she could not even take a look at the departed. I fear they will not be long separated. God grant she may be spared.
—*Diary of Francis S. Thayer.*

At Home. We buried our dear and good Father today at 12 A.M. Tis the last we can do for him here. He is with his God, and happy is he. Our loss is Christ's gain. Father how deeply we feel thy loss. Mother is no worse. —*Diary of Edwin McKie.*

A pleasant day. I went to the funeral of Bro George— Bro William came down in the Cars and got a Livery horse. There was a large funeral. Rev. P. Gordon made some remarks and prayed. —*Diary of James McKie.*

Grave of George McKie, 1791–1861, Whiteside Cemetery, Cambridge, New York.

January 18, 1861. A pleasant forenoon. Snowed hard toward night. Lucy and Mary Barber went to a private lecture this afternoon, to females. I went to see Sophia, found her a little better…
January 22. A cold morning. I went over to see Sophia. I found her a little better…
—*Diary of James McKie.*

Cambridge, Jan 27, 1861, Sabbath aft 1/2 past 3,
My dearest Frank—   I am sitting by the stove in Mother's room and *she* is sleeping sweetly. I bathed her all over, then Edwin moved her, and she soon fell into a quiet sleep. It would do you good to see her. I think Mother is doing just as well as she can and oh how thankful I am to God that He has spared our Mother to us… I hope I shall hear tomorrow that Frankie is doing *well* and that dear Baby kept so. Take care of yourself too, do not *keep* your cough. Take some flax seed tea. I feel that it has done Mother much good. Is it not a comfort in these days of tribulation to remember Him in whom we may put all our trust. His ear is ever open to our cry… Kiss the dear children. I pray they may be better. Love to Mother. God bless you and us.   —Your *Kitty.*

March 4, 1861
Weather pleasant. Abraham Lincoln inaugurated Prest. of the whole United States & I hope and trust he will show himself worthy of the high position…
—*Diary of Francis S. Thayer.*

A beautiful day. Mr. Lincoln Inaugurated President today as we suppose. Lucy had her teeth taken out preparatory to a new set. —*Diary of James McKie.*

April 13. A Cloudy day. Some little rain during the day. I have staid in today on account of going through a course of *Calomel*... *Fort Sumpter* [sic] surrendered to the *Rebels*.
—*Diary of James McKie.*

April 16, 1861. Cool & pleasant... Rec'd news that Maj. Anderson surrendered Fort Sumter after two days of bombardment. The South gains the first victory, but it will be a dear one to them...
April 17. Rainy day. Everybody talking about the state of the Country, which is in fact deplorable...
April 22. Weather warm & pleasant... Eve up town after the news which is very exciting. War & rumors of war. When & where will it end, God only knows.
—*Diary of Francis S. Thayer.*

Troy, April 22, 1861.
Dear Niel—   I send to Johnsonville today 8 bags seed (6 Timothy / 2 buck) & 2 clover, 80 lbs., as per Ed's order... Ed let me have $70 out of which I will pay for the seed & pay you the balance.

Kate & Frank arrived home safely. We are very busy getting ready to move which is quite a job.

We are all excitement here about the war which is going on in earnest. Several companies have been formed here & will march south in a day or two. It looks as tho they were going at it in earnest & before the end of this week there will be more hard fighting.

We want to hear from you often & I trust you will write & let us know particularly how Mother is doing.   —Yours in haste, *Frank.*

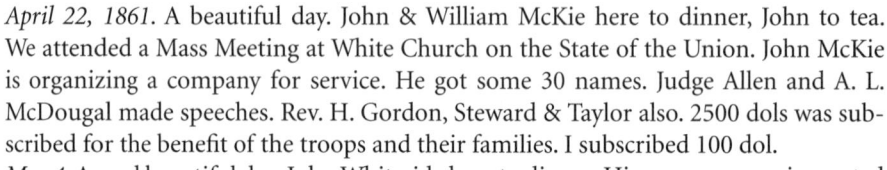

April 22, 1861. A beautiful day. John & William McKie here to dinner, John to tea. We attended a Mass Meeting at White Church on the State of the Union. John McKie is organizing a company for service. He got some 30 names. Judge Allen and A. L. McDougal made speeches. Rev. H. Gordon, Steward & Taylor also. 2500 dols was subscribed for the benefit of the troops and their families. I subscribed 100 dol.
May 4. A cool beautiful day. John Whiteside here to dinner. His company was inspected by Mr. McC— and accepted. John was elected Captain. Maggie Hunter & Fannie Warner here to tea. Scott & Jud here today. They raised the wood shed.
May 10. A beautiful day. I went toward Centre Cambridge and collected some bedding for the volunteers. At 5 o'clock Capt. John McKie left for Camp B— with his Company of about 85 or 90 men. There were some sorry partings of friends. Rev. Mr. Taylor made a short speech upon presenting a Testament to each one of the volunteers...
—*Diary of James McKie.*

The Old Home [undated, most likely 1861]
Dear Frank—   Well, I got up here very comfortably to find Mother put way back two months. She took cold with change of weather and suffered with high fever and acute pain in the right side. Her liver is affected, her skin sallow. Today she has no apparent fever, but such a coated tongue— and living on water gruel— very weak— not strong enough to talk much, but oh so glad to see me— looks a great deal brighter today they say. I have just written to see if Ruth can come back. The *nurse* they have here, highly spoken of, is *deaf*, and Mother turned her face to the wall and said "See kind Ruth now.

The Reverend Henry Gordon, Cambridge, New York. His profile in Crisfield Johnson's History of Washington County, New York, *reads: "At the opening of the war, in 1861, he took a very decided stand for the maintenance of the Union and the duty of every person to use the influence of which he was possessed to preserve its integrity, thereby making some enemies, but a far greater number of friends." He was Chaplain to the 123rd Regiment from 1862 to 1863. Photo from Crisfield Johnson's* History of Washington County, New York.

This one will wear me out." I said, "No Mother, not this week. I won't let her." The doctor said to Nettie yesterday that he thought Mother would get up from this attack but there was little to build upon.

I'll come home when I see Mother better and in better hands, if you all keep well. I hope I can come Sat. but you will hear before that time. Kiss the children.   —*Kittie.*

Cambridge, Fri. 2 o'clock,
Dear Frank—   I find Mother somewhat improved. She is bolstered up in bed once or twice a day and talks more without exhaustion and this is all the change I have to report. She seems (if raised up *quickly*) almost as if fainting, but slowly raised does not mind it much. So you see she is not very strong. She wants me to stay till Mon. aft if I can— and I have consented to if I do not leave tomorrow, or if I hear that you and the dear children are well. All the rest are well, and send love. Nette sends a kiss, & love to the children. Kiss the dear creatures for me.   —Your *Kitty*.

—I wish you could drop in tonight.

Frank— I wish you would send to the sick, two barrels of flour such as you sold us before. Send soon.   —Yours, *E. J. McKie.*

April 30, 1861. Pleasant A.M, rainy P.M. Moved from 105 1st Street to our new home on Park St. Just eleven years ago this day we were married & came to Troy. God in his good providence has given us prosperity & today we occupy a new & beautiful home with two dear children. May we ever remember that we are indebted to Thee for all these blessings…
May 6. Rainy morning… We completed our inventory & it shows a net profit of $4,221.88 on a business of about $300,000, Mill allowed nothing but expenses. The largest business & the smallest profit I have ever known…
June 16. Pleasant day at Cambridge. How changed is this house. No father here now & brother after brother we see no more. All that are left meet today— Mother, Niel, Ed & Nette, Kate & self & our two children. Did not go to church. Spent the day at home.
July 11. Weather hot. Business very dull altho' it looks a little better in New York, stocks advancing a little. War news gives them a start. Rebels are running south for their lives…
—*Diary of Francis S. Thayer.*

May 20, 1861. A cool day. I got word this morning that the Bank of the Capitol had failed, and that the stock was probably swept out. Afternoon Almy & I sent to see Sophia…
June 3. A very wet morning, cleared up about noon… News of the Death of Hon. Stephen A. Douglas today.
June 23. A beautiful day…Major John McKie came in from the Camp at Albany and took our horse & wagon and went to his Father's to take farewell of them before starting for the Seat of War. James & Neil McKie brought the horse back today.
June 28. A clear day. I went to Albany to see the 22nd Regiment leave for Washington. I staid all night at Thayer's.
July 22. A pleasant day. A great Battle fought in Virginia yesterday. Our troops defeated with great slaughter, a consternation prevails in all quarters. I wrote John McKie today, to go tomorrow. I wrote William enclosing a letter from National Bank.
July 26. A beautiful day. F. S. Thayer, Katy, Children, nurse & driver here to dinner. They went to Bro. John's for the night… —*Diary of James McKie.*

great Battle   First battle of Bull Run, near Manassas, Virginia.

◕ A letter from Edwin McKie in Liverpool:

54 Rodney Street, Liverpool, May 10, 1861.
My dear Mother,   I really hope you are doing as well as you could wish. I am anxious to hear from you…

The South are getting guns also & shipping them to the West Indies where they hope to smuggle them into the Southern states. It is very cold here & is freezing at nights. Gloomy time for the crops. I really hope Mother [that] you are gaining strength & will soon be up again. I hope you can get Ann Fonnan & that she will stay with you. If I could find a good English girl I would send her out to you. Remember me to all the family and friends and with my best love to you my dear Mother. I am affectionately yours, E. J. McKie.

Niel, I want you to write me often & let us know how you get along. Give me all the news etc. Keep your nose clean, but don't pull on it, as it is long enough now. If you want anything from here say so. I am going up to Scotland for a week or so. Leave next Monday. *Hope Bobtail is better & that Levi's dog don't lick your dog no more.* Good Morning, Sir.   Yours Truly, E. J. McKie.

Troy, July 31st, 1861, Wednesday A.M.
Dearest Kitty—   I arrived home just in time to escape the heavy shower which passed around just north of us. Everything at the house seems to be in good shape and as for the garden it reminds me of the story of Jack & the Beanstalk. We had for dinner yesterday cucumbers & squashes, shall soon have beans & tomatoes. The peas I brought down are very sweet or as Frankie says, excellent… The weather is hot & sultry. Should it continue so, perhaps you had better say where you are another week… There is nothing very new in regard to the war. All there is you can read in the papers… I hope & pray that you and the children are well and doing well. I want to see you all very much. Kiss the dear little ones for me and tell them to kiss you for Father. Love to all   —Your devoted *Frank*.
P.S. Tell Frankie to be a good boy & mind Mother.

August 8, 1861, Troy, Thursday 5 o'clock.
Dearest Kitty—   Poor Hote is quietly passing away & it is not probable that he will survive many hours. He has had no convulsing & I hope & pray that he will be spared that suffering. Rhoda has been with him all day & I shall go up after tea & remain through the night… I will write you again tomorrow eve. As ever your own *Frank*.

August 10, 1861. At one o'clock this morning my dear brother Hote quietly & peacefully breathed his last without a struggle— prayed fervently that God would bless his soul… his remains taken to Hoosick by eve train…
August 11, 1861. …Kate, Frankie & self drove over to Hoosick to attend the funeral of Brother Hote… This is indeed a solemn day for our family…
—*Diary of Francis S. Thayer.*

October 16, 1861. A beautiful day. Lucy & I went to Troy…Jas. Jermain's carriage met them at the Troy Depot. Lucy went with them to Jermain's. I went to Albany, took dinner at the Merchant's Hotel, came up to Jermain's where we staid all night.
—*Diary of James McKie.*

☙ A recipe for hair dye:

North Easton, Nov. 11th, 1861.
Mrs. Thayer—   I received a note by way of Cousin Lizzie Beadle when in Troy asking for a hair dye my sister uses. I should have sent it sooner but my Father was and is yet very sick— we have very little hope of his recovery, consequently my time is mostly taken up with him. I hope the receipt may be in time for you or your Mother.

She must sit in the sun when it is put on and until it is dry, it will be a better color. Turn out a little of the dye in a cup and take some little brush, like a tooth brush, and put it on the hair. Be careful about getting it on the face and neck— it will color. After putting it on a little while, after it begins to dry, take a little dry cloth and take your finger and rub it all off of the seams of the hair, the partings I mean. If the hair is very white you will have to put it on several times before it gets a good dark color. Let it get thoroughly dry every time you use it before applying again— To one stick of good nitrate of silver put one shillings worth of *Spirits of Heartburn* and three tablespoons of rain water and shake it well. You must have good nitrate of silver. If you don't get good the first time you can put in some more. You can tell by the way it colors. Hoping that this may be of service to you— for my sister finds it very nice for her. Believe me yours Truly, *Sylvia B. Burton.*

P.S. Anything I can tell you or you would like to know write me direct to Greenwich, Washington County.

November 25, 1861. Weather clear & cold… Kate went to Cambridge per morn train & returned at eve. She went up to talk with Uncle J. [James McKie] about buying Niel's interest in the home farm. Business very dull & prices declining…
November 29. Weather mild & a little rain. Took Kate to cars at 7 1/4 A.M. She goes home to take a deed of Niel's quarter of the Home Farm, $3,500 mortgage for whole amount payable in 10 years…   —*Diary of Francis S. Thayer.*

December 16, 1861. A mild day. I am better… Reported news of the burning of Charlestown by the free Negroes…   —*Diary of James McKie.*

December 31, 1861. Pleasant winter weather & good sleighing. Store all A.M. & out riding with Kate in P.M.… Bot Frankie a new sleigh & Kitty a rocking chair with which they seem perfectly happy. This has indeed been an eventful year. Since its beginning we have followed to the grave Father McKie & Brother Hote, and we hope and trust they are in a better world. Our Country is in a "Civil War." May God soon put an end to this calamity & bring us out of all our trials.   —*Diary of Francis S. Thayer.*

IX

1860–1865

Life in Virginia

LIFE at Eastwood was very comfortable in 1860. However, not far beyond this large farm overlooking the James River west of Richmond, Virginia, events were swirling around that would have a profound effect on the lives of everyone living at Eastwood and throughout all of America. The greatest crisis in American history, the American Civil War, was about to be fought. During this conflict, more than one battle would bring death to the Hobson and Wise families, and one northern raid would literally go through their home at Eastwood. An effort by Senator John Crittenden to amend the Constitution and create a boundary, the 36°30' parallel, between free and slave states was rejected by Abraham Lincoln, and the secession of North Carolina and ten other states followed. In 1861 Confederate ports were blockaded, and West Virginia broke away from Virginia. When West Virginia became the thirty-fifth state in 1863, Henry A. Wise described it as "the bastard of a political rape." In 1862 Congress forbade slavery in the territories but not in the states and later that year the Confederate Army invaded Maryland and met the Union army at Antietam where each army lost over 10,000 men. In September 1862 the Emancipation Proclamation was published in northern newspapers, and when it took affect on January 1, 1863, all slaves in the seceding states were considered to be free. Later in the same year Union and Confederate armies suffered over 50,000 casualties at Gettysburg. It has been written that this sometimes was a war of brother against brother and father against son. The Wise fam-

Eastwood Farm, Goochland County, residence of Plumer Hobson, 1833–1868, and Annie Jennings Wise Hobson, 1837–1914. Photograph courtesy of the Virginia Historical Society, Richmond, Virginia.

ily variation of that, brother-in-law against brother-in-law, would be apparent at the surrender of Lee's army at Appomattox in 1865. This was a war that saw new and faster means of communications. War correspondents and artists supplied newspapers and magazines with vivid illustrated accounts of the conflicts. The telegraph allowed government leaders to communicate directly and quickly with battlefield commanders. Thaddeus Lowe demonstrated how balloons could be used for visual observations of enemy lines. Mathew Brady started his photographic record of the war in 1861, and it would soon become obvious that photography, in its infancy when the war began, would become a powerful means of communications. When the Civil War ended in 1865, life at Eastwood and life in America had greatly changed.

Letters, diaries, and other writings by:
Maranda Branson Moore, *A Geographical Reader*
Rita Mae Brown, *High Hearts*
John Easten Cooke, *Wearing of the Gray*
Annie Jennings Wise Hobson
Plumer Hobson
Judith Brokenbrough McGuire
Barton Haxall Wise
Henry Alexander Wise
John S. Wise, *The End of An Era*
Mary Lyons Wise
Ellen Wise Mayo
Sallie Brock Putnam
and Edwin McKie, Francis S. Thayer, and James McKie

Letters and diaries written from: Richmond and Eastwood, Goochland County, Virginia; Charleston, South Carolina; and Troy and Cambridge, New York.

Harpers Magazine, *January 6, 1866. View of Ex-Governor Wise's Residence Near Norfolk, Virginia, sketched by J. H. Hamilton.*

The James River, Goochland County, Virginia.

◈ From *The End of An Era* by John S. Wise:

How the "Slave Drivers" Lived

Our life during the year 1860 was in strange contrast with the busy and exciting scenes of 1858 and 1859. Father's term of office expired January 1, 1860. [Henry A. Wise was Governor of Virginia 1856–1860.] He sold his plantation in Accomac [Only], and bought another in the county of Princess Anne, near Norfolk [Rolleston]. This change was due partly to domestic and partly to political considerations.

During a period of rebuilding at Rolleston, our new home, I was sent, January 1, 1860, to live with a favorite sister, and attend a private school presided over by the parish minister, a Master of Arts of the University of Virginia. The location was in the county of Goochland, about twenty miles west of Richmond, in the beautiful valley of the upper James.

From Lynchburg, which is near the foot-hills of the Blue Ridge, the James River courses eastward to Richmond, a distance of about two hundred miles, through a valley of great fertility and beauty. The width of this valley seldom exceeds a mile, and at many points it is much narrower than that. The flat lands along the course of the stream are known as the "James River low grounds," an expression which conveys to the mind of the Virginian an idea of fatness and fecundity such as others conceive in reading of the valley of the Nile. About Lynchburg, high bluffs hang over the stream, and the flat lands are narrow and small in extent; but from Howardsville in Albemarle, to Richmond, a hundred miles below, the valley broadens, and the bluffs grow less beetling as the gently rolling lands of lower Piedmont are reached. In general characteristics, the section resembles the valleys of the Genesee and the Mohawk in New York, with a greater luxuriance of woodland and more extended vistas.

Upon the swelling hills overlooking the James were built, at the time of which I write, for distance of a hundred miles or more, the homes of many of the wealthiest and most representative people of our State.

No railroad penetrated the valley. The only means provided for transporting products to market was the James River and Kanawha Canal, an enterprise projected by General Washington. It had been completed as far as Lexington, passing through the Blue Ridge Mountains at the point known as Balcony Falls, a spot suggestive of the Trossachs pass in Scotland.

Richmond 1833. Statehouse at the top of the hill, James River to the right and the James River and Kanawha Canal to the left of the river. Photo from Historic Virginia Homes and Churches *by Robert A. Lancaster, Jr.*

Kanawha Canal— The remains of the Kanawha Canal, foreground, in Richmond as seen from the Hollywood Cemetery, modern Richmond in the background, James River to the right. The nineteenth century development of the railroad, built on the tow-path for the canal, brought about the demise of the canal.

For their own transportation up and down the valley, these prosperous folk had private equipages and servants. When the distance was greater than a day's journey, the home of some friend, generally a kinsman, stood wide open for their entertainment. The canal was available upon emergency as a means of travel, but as its speed was only about four miles an hour, few of the grandees resorted to it. A fine road ran along the foot-hills, parallel with the canal and river, from Richmond to Charlottesville, often keeping companionship for a mile or two with the route of the canal. The hills were of that stiff red clay celebrated afar for its adaptability to corn and tobacco; and the soil of the low grounds, often refreshed and rejuvenated by the overflow of the James, was a deep alluvial deposit of chocolate loam, inexhaustible in richness and fertility, and producing all the cereals in marvelous abundance.

Recalling a few of the princely dwellers in this favored section, one remembers the Cabells of Nelson; the Galts of Albemarle; the Cockes of Fluvanna; the Hubards of Buckingham; the Bollings of Bolling Island and Bolling Hall; the Harrisons of Ampthill, and Clifton, and Elk Hill; the Hobsons of Howard's Neck and Snowden, and Eastwood; the Flemmings of West View; the Rutherfords of Rock Castle; General Philip St. George Cocke of Belle Mead; the Skipwiths; the Logans of Dungeness; the Seldens of Orapax and of Norwood; the Warwicks; the Michaux of Michaux's Ferry; the Morsons of Dover; the Seddons of Sabot Hill; the Stanards of Bendover; the Allens of Tuckahoe; and many others:

>"Their swords are rust,
>Their bodies dust;
>Their souls are with the saints, we trust."

Scattered along the valley, owning respectively from seven hundred to two or three thousand acres, with slaves enough to cultivate twice the lands they owned, they were the happiest and most prosperous community in all America; not rolling in wealth, like the sugar cane and cotton planters of the South, yet with a thousand advantages over them, in the variety of their productions, in the beauty of their lands, in the salubrity of their climate, in the society about them, and in their access to the outer world.

The home of my sister was on one of these fine James River estates, and her neighbors were of the most highly cultivated people of whom that region boasted. The plantation had been purchased from Colonel Trevillian, descendant of an old Huguenot family, and its name, Eastwood, had been bestowed by its former owner, Peyton Harrison. My brother-in-law, after an education in Europe, had essayed business, but ill-health compelled him to adopt a country life. The house stood in a grove of oaks of original growth, in the midst of an extensive lawn carpeted with greensward. Behind it were the stables, the inclosures, and the household servants' quarters. In front, half a mile away, were the low grounds and river; and to the left again, half a mile distant, stood the overseer's house, the quarters of the farm hands, and the farm stables. Up and down the river were visible the handsome residences of the neighbors. On remote hillsides or in the wooded points, one saw, here and there, great barns of brick or wood for storing wheat or corn, and houses where tobacco was stripped and hung, and smoked and dried, and pressed into hogsheads. Interminable lines of stone or post and oak fences, without one missing panel, showed, as few other things in farming do show, the prosperity of the owners of these lands. Great fields— this one pale green with winter wheat, this sere and brown in pasture land, this red with newly ploughed clods, and this with a thousand hillocks whence the tobacco had been gleaned— were spread out to the vision, clean of weeds and undergrowth, and cultivated until they looked like veritable maps of agriculture.

Near at hand, or far away upon the hillsides, one beheld the working-bands of slaves, well clothed, well fed, and differing from other workmen, as we see them now, chiefly in their numbers and their cheerfulness and their comfortable clothing.

Grove of oaks, Eastwood.

Remarkable as the statement may seem, those slaves, over whose sad fate so many tears have been shed, went about their work more joyously than any laboring people I ever saw.

Our school was located a mile away, in rear of the river plantations, upon a road leading to what was known as "the back country." A little church, built from the private contributions of the river planters, was used as the schoolhouse. It was near the parsonage. That point was selected, not only for its convenience to the teacher, but also because of its accessibility to the children of the smaller farmers in this "back country." It is often said that antagonism existed between this humbler class of whites and the wealthy nabobs living upon the river. Perhaps there may have been something of the inevitable envy which the less fortunate feel everywhere towards the prosperous and great, but certain it is, there was little manifestation of it there. The wealthy sought in every way to be upon good terms with the poor; and one of the best proofs that they succeeded is found in the fact that, when war came, the two stood up together side by side, and fought and slept and ate and died together, —never thinking of which was rich or which was poor, until a time when such as survived were all poor together, and those who had always been poor were in their turn the more fortunate of the two.

Our nearest neighbors were the Seddons, —one of the loveliest families of people that ever lived. The head of the house was a gentleman who, after a thorough education, had achieved distinction at the bar and in Congress, but, owing to delicate health, had retired to his plantation…

…Some of the happiest days of my childhood, some of the most elevating, purifying, and refining hours of all my life, were passed in these two households. Both Mr. and Mrs. Seddon were accomplished linguists, and demanded that their children should be as well educated as themselves. Their library was supplied with the best thought of the world, and the course of literary culture prescribed by them for their children was not only comprehensive, but was made attractive by the way in which it was pursued…

Love, intellectuality, refinement, hospitality, made that home an abode fit for the most favored of mortals; and her care for their welfare made "Mis' Sallie" the ideal, in the minds of the servants, of what an angel would be in the world to come. The children? They were numerous as the teeth in a comb. Three of the Seddon boys, ranging from a year older to two years younger than myself, were my sworn allies. Morning, noon, and night, we were together. Of course we all had horses, —everybody had a horse. Often the three Seddon boys rode to school upon the back of one filly, with a young darkey to fetch her home. Their route brought them directly past the Eastwood gate, and many a day in 1860 that blessed filly took upon her back a fifth rider, as I slipped down from the gatepost where I had awaited their coming. And many a head-punching I received from the combined forces of the Seddons because I tickled that filly in the flank, and make her kick until she tumbled the entire load, four white boys and a darkey, into the muddy road, and then, kicking at us, scampered away, leaving us to fish our Horaces and Livys and Virgils out of the mud, and walk the remainder of the way to school.

The Morson Children, first cousins of the Seddons, were also numerous; and while their residence was at a larger distance from ours, the families were frequently together. At school, during the week, plans were made for the afternoons and Saturdays, and we ranged the whole country-side, shooting, or riding, or visiting.

A favorite amusement was excursions up the canal in our own boat, drawn by our own team, to a famous fishing-place at "Maiden's Adventure" dam. Thither boys and girls repaired together, making quite a boatload, taking baskets of luncheon and spending the day.

The school-teacher, the Rev. Mr. Dudley, was an efficient man, who demanded that his pupils should study hard, and was not at all squeamish about the proper use of hickory. Notwithstanding this, he was popular, and joined in the sports at recess with genuine zest…

It was during the recess hour, on a bright May day in 1860, that a boy rode by, returning perhaps from Richmond, and gave Mr. Dudley a copy of a newspaper. No sooner had he disposed himself comfortably to read the news, leaving us boys to our diversions, than with a loud exclamation he broke forth, "Ah! that settles it. I feared as much. Abe Lincoln is nominated for President. He will be elected, and that means war."

I, who was now in my fourteenth year, and deeply interested in political matters, was anxious to know why Mr. Lincoln's election portended war any more than that of any one else.

"Well," said Mr. Dudley, perfectly sincere in every word he spoke, "Mr. Seward was the logical candidate of the Republican party, entitled to the nomination by superior ability and by long service. He is a man of very pronounced anti-slavery views, but is a gentleman by birth and association, and if elected President, would respect his constitutional obligations and the rights of the Southern States. Everybody expected him to be the nominee; but his course and utterances of late, especially utterances concerning old John Brown, are not radical enough to suit the Black Republicans. On the other hand, this man Lincoln has come to the front, venomous and vindictive enough to satisfy the most rabid abolitionist." He then proceeded to draw a picture of Lincoln horrible enough. He told how he was, in his origin, of that class of low whites who hate gentlemen because they are gentlemen; how, in personal appearance, he was more like a gorilla than a human being; how he possessed the arts and cunning of the demagogue to a degree sufficient to build himself up by appealing to the prejudices of his own class against gentlemen…

That settled Abraham Lincoln with me. I was thoroughly satisfied that no such man ought to be President; but I could not yet conceive it possible that such a monster would be the choice of a majority of the people for President. Lincoln's nomination did not, however, interfere with my happiness or appetite. In fact, I had faith in the triumph of Mr. Lincoln's opponents.

A few days after this, I accompanied my sister and brother-in-law to a breakfast at the Stanards'.

In course of conversation at table, the nomination of Lincoln was discussed. That gave rise to the inquiry, on the part of our hostess, whether her guests had read the remarkable sermon recently delivered in the city of New Orleans by the Rev. Dr. Palmer, an eminent Presbyterian divine, upon "The Divine Origin of Slavery." As none of her guests had seen it, and all expressed the desire to do so, a servant was sent to the library for the newspaper, and one of the company proceeded to read aloud the salient points of Dr. Palmer's address. Undoubtedly, from his standpoint, the great minister put the case very strongly. His arguments were, however, chiefly based upon the divine sanction of the patriarchal institutions of the Old Testament. I was not a profound Biblical scholar, but a number of very good women had spent a great deal of time, during the brief space of my life, hammering into my head portions of the Old Testament. It so happened also during breakfast that morning the Mormon doctrines of Brigham Young had come up for discussion, for Brigham was much in evidence then, and everybody, especially the ladies, had joined in denouncing him as monstrous.

The reading of Dr. Palmer's sermon occupied some time. It bored me, but I found no opportunity to escape. At its conclusion, the company agreed that it was an able and conclusive argument. Mrs. Stanard, who was a witty woman given to facetious remarks, declared a purpose to mail a copy of the sermon to Abe Lincoln. I, who was inclined to be pert as well as facetious, proposed to send another copy to Brigham Young. "For," said I, "every argument of Dr. Palmer, based on slavery of the Old Testament, is equally available for Brigham Young in support of polygamy; and I sympathize with Brigham."

It is unnecessary to add that the assembled guests, in their disgust at my "pertness," dropped the argument on slavery.

Soon after this breakfast, I witnessed the first parade of the Goochland Troop. The John Brown invasion had given a pronounced impetus to the military spirit of Virginia. In almost every county, new military organizations had sprung up. As the Goochland folk were rich, owners of fine horseflesh, and every man of them a horseman from his childhood, it was natural that they organized a command of cavalry.

…The preliminary drilling began in the early spring. And now in May, for the first time, the troop assembled in full uniform for drill and inspection. Julien Harrison, of Elk Hill was its commandant. Mr. Hobson, my brother-in-law, at whose house I lived, was the first lieutenant. The company was composed of the very flower of the aristocracy of the James River valley, and the capital invested in the arms, uniforms, and the horseflesh of the Goochland Troop would have equipped a regiment of regulars.

At their first parade and review, they were the guests of the master of Eastwood. Every man vied with every other in his mount. There were not ten horses in the company less than three quarters thoroughbred. It was indeed a gallant sight, —those spirited youngsters, men, and beasts…

The thing which most impressed itself upon me, during my residence in Goochland in 1860, was the marked difference between slavery upon these extensive plantations and slavery as it existed in the smaller establishments which I had theretofore known. It could not be truly said of these people that they were cruel to their slaves, but it was certainly true that the relations between master and slave were nothing like so close or so tender as those with which I had been theretofore familiar. The size of the plantations and the number of slaves were such that it was necessary to employ farm managers or overseers, and to have separate establishments, removed from the mansion house, where the overseers resided, surrounded by the laborers on the plantation.

As a consequence, the master and his family saw little of this class of servants, and the servants saw and knew little of the master. There was lacking that intimate acquaintance and sympathy with each other which ameliorated the condition of the slaves where the farm was small, the servants few, and no overseer came between master and servant.

Wealthy men, too, like several of those in our neighborhood, had so many slaves that they were compelled to buy other plantations on which to employ them…

The slaves upon our place presented another repulsive feature of the institution. The master and mistress were both young persons of pure, elevated Christian lives, incapable of brutality, and most ambitious to deserve and to possess the loyal love of their slaves. They could have had no country establishment without the possession of slaves; and, both being members of large families, they could not hope to acquire by gift a sufficient number of slaves to carry on their plantation. As a consequence, they were compelled to buy the essential quota. These purchases were made by families, as far as possible, but the aggregate was made up of negroes who came from different places, and were strangers to each other. Great circumspection was exercised in the effort to secure the proper kind of servants, and large prices were paid in order to secure such.

But everybody knows how little reliance is to be placed in the advance characters given to servants, and how often, when strange servants are brought together, unforeseen incompatibilities of temperament, or new conditions affect them. Thus it was that the new establishment at Eastwood, wealthy and luxurious as it seemed, had its troubles and its trials like all the rest of the world. The darkeys were jealous of each other. The ones represented as marvels of diligence and obedience turned out to be lazy and impertinent. And so it went on. The most flagrant instance of this kind was a butler named Tom, a handsome fellow, quick, intelligent, and represented as a phenomenal servant. When Tom arrived, he was a joy and a comfort to master and mistress, and they felt that he was worth the $2,500 they had paid for him. In a little while, Tom appeared, from time to time, in a condition of excitement or irritability or stupor, and his conduct was exceedingly perplexing. Suspecting liquor as the cause of his strange behavior, strict watch was kept upon the wine cellar and the sideboard, but no liquor was missed. At last, Tom developed a distinct case of *mania a potu*, and then it was discovered that he had been steadily imbibing from a large demijohn of alcohol to which he had access. As his distemper developed an inclination to knock the heads off his fellow servants, male and female, on the slightest provocation, his presence made matters very uncomfortable; and while his first offense was overlooked and forgiven, under solemn promises of reform, he soon relapsed into bad habits, and became so violent that it was necessary to have him seized and bound by Alick the gardener and Ephraim the hostler, in order to prevent murder.

Tom See reference to Tom in the letter of December 11, 1858, to H. A. Wise from A. J. W. Hobson, page 71.

Now, what would our humane and philanthropic friend, Mrs. Harriet Beecher Stowe, think of a case like this? And how would the dear old lady have disposed of it? This was one of many of the perplexing situations of slavery. There was nothing to do with Tom but to sell him with all his infirmities on his head. Of course the abolitionist will say it was awful; but to have given him away would have been imposing upon the friend to whom he was presented, and to set him free was offering a premium to drunkenness and faithlessness. Tom shed tears of repentance, and the family shed tears of regret and humiliation. But as there were young children and women all about him,—women and children of his own race as well as the white race,—and as he was liable to get drunk and violent, and to knock the heads off of any or all of them at any moment, the question recurs on the original proposition. What was to be done with Tom?

But enough of these instances. This and many others only confirmed me in the opinion, planted when I saw the sale of Martha Ann, and growing steadily thereafter, that slavery was an accursed business, and that the sooner my people were relieved of it, the better.

June came, and with it the end of the school term and my return to my father's home. I had made decided advances in knowledge. I had read the first six books of Virgil; been drilled in Racine and Moliere and Voltaire; finished Davies's Legendre; and was fairly embarked in algebra, besides a good grounding in ancient and modern history and a smattering of natural philosophy.

So I boxed my books, packed my trunk, gathered together my effects,—including my gun, with which I had become quite proficient, and a coop containing a game-cock and pullets of the choicest James River stock,—and hied myself homeward.

◈ War correspondence:

Richmond Va. June 8th, 1861.
My own dear Sweet wife—   …I expect to leave Richmond on Monday morning, taking nothing but a small supply of arms & munitions & obliged to raise men as I go on to Kanawha to take command of that Valley and to relieve Col. Tompkins who is entrenched at Charleston & beset by a large force, at last account on the other side of the Ohio & perhaps now advancing on this side. My health has improved and I hope to stand the service…
I have placed funds in Bank for you & will leave Willie Lyons a blank check for you, for all your wants. Henry can bring you up whenever you can come, and your brother talks of going down soon after you. My wife, you must not take every care upon yourself, but for yourself. I will write to you from every post… Richard will go along with me and take his chances for a commission… I hardly know what to say to you. My going as I do seems to me so like a desertion of wife & home, but you'll be safe in your brother's charge. I shall stay with him tonight and be ready tomorrow. Obe has just come to me & will try to be ordered with me. I want Henry to stay with the family and keep a look out for the protection of Mary, Néné, Mary, and the children. Tell Mary & Henry both to have my papers in my right hand-table drawers & in my mahogany writing desk secured & removed in case of need. All your friends here are well, and very kind to me. God guard & bless you— a thousand times. Kiss all for me & say I don't say farewell to any of you for I mean surely to return with my [illegible] in my hand. I will try to write again tomorrow but it is hard for me to do so at all. It has taken me near an hour to get thru with this. Your own *Henry A. Wise*

> Letter has no year but mentions grey uniforms, therefore it must be near or during the Civil War.

Washington, Sunday evening. Nov. 12th.
I am so disappointed my beloved husband, not to receive a letter from you today. I had no *right* to expect one, because you told me you would not write again for a week, but I often claim more than my *right* from you, and in the way of love, can't help it… It has been raining hard here for two days. I thought you would be glad of it for your wheat and indeed every living thing… Did you feel my presence, when you came in from the labors of the day, tired, hungry and sleepy? Ah! I trust if it is God's will, I may soon be returned to your fireside & be a comfort to you & *our* dear children. They are *mine* if they are yours— mine by adoption and affection… Néné has been a little sick today & I have with *difficulty* given her a taste of castor oil. I hope she will soon be relieved. She has been eating too much lately. I packed up your shoes and sundry other things to go by Cap. Hopkins, but he won't come. I hope you won't think me very extravagant if I tell you that I have not enough money to pay the Dentist's bill… The boys' clothes I hope they will like. Tell Richard I saw some little gentlemen of his age in the street— in grey & they looked so soldier-like that I got him a grey [illegible] about, & Johnny & himself the prettiest article for pants that I could find… I received a letter today from Annie. She was well & hard at work. I feel that God's hand is upon me— may this sickness draw me nearer to Him, prepare me better for duties here & fit me for Eternity. May God be with you my beloved husband & sanctify you & keep you. —Your devoted wife *Mary Wise*.

❧ Roanoke Island, North Carolina, January–February 1862:

There are certain names whose mere mention produces feelings of horror, or pain, or sadness from association. To me, that of Roanoke Island is one of these.
—John S. Wise, *The End of An Era.*

Attack on Roanoke Island

Captain O. Jennings Wise and Captain Coles, in command of Confederate skirmishers thrown forward on the right and left, had fallen while engaged in bravely cheering on their men. The former, though dangerously wounded in the thigh and breast, had been carried by his comrades to a boat near the head of the island and the party were endeavoring to escape to Nag's Head, on the opposite beach, when they were fired upon by the men of the Ninth New York Regiment and compelled to return. Captain Wise was twice shot while his men were carrying him from the field, and his four wounds, several of which were severe, left no hope of his recovery.

Late on the afternoon of the engagement, General Wise, who was then lying ill with pneumonia at Nag's Head, was placed in a wagon and driven fifteen miles up the beach, accompanied by a small remnant of his men who had escaped, and three companies under Colonel Richardson, who had remained at Nag's Head during the fight. From the Canal Bridge, the tug *Currituck* was dispatched under a flag of truce to Roanoke Island, to inquire for the killed and wounded, and to obtain the bodies of Captains Coles and Wise and Lieutenant Selden.

Upon the return of the boat, from her sad errand, Wise directed that the coffin containing the remains of his son be opened. "The old hero," wrote an eye-witness, "bent over the body of his son, on whose pale face the full moon threw its light, kissed the cold brow many times and exclaimed, in an agony of emotion, 'Oh, my brave boy, you have died for me, you have died for me.'"
—Barton H. Wise, *The Life of Henry A. Wise of Virginia.*

Last evening, long before the arrival of the train from Petersburg, the streets in the vicinity of the depot were thronged with soldiers and citizens who had assembled to receive the remains of Captains Wise and Coles, who had fallen at Roanoke Island. On the arrival of the cars the body of Captain Wise was taken in charge by the old honorary members of the Blues. It, with that of Captain Coles, were placed upon separate hearses and the procession formed in the manner enumerated below: The Mayor of the City, State Guard with reversed arms, Armory Band, the hearses side by side, containing the bodies, Relatives of the deceased and pall bearers… Twenty-seven carriages containing friends of the deceased… The procession moved down Main Street, and, up Ninth street entered the Capitol Square. The coffin containing the body of Captain Wise was removed and placed in the Capitol Building, in the room designated for the Confederate Senate Chamber… The funeral of Captain Wise will take place on Sunday, the 16th at 11 o'clock at St. James Church (Episcopal) and the funeral discourse will be delivered by the Rector Rev. Mr. Peterkin.
—*Richmond Daily Examiner*, February 15, 1862.

❧ A funeral in Richmond: a letter from Annie Jennings Wise Hobson:

Richmond, 16th Feb. 1862. Sunday evening.
My own dear Father—   We laid our noble hero in his last earthly resting

The Virginia Capitol, Richmond, Virginia. The Senate Chambers for the Confederacy, where Obadiah Jennings Wise lay in state before his funeral, was on the second floor, corner windows.

Rev. Joshua Peterkin, Rector at St. James' Church in Richmond.

place, at Hollywood, today. Plumer, Dr. Garnett, John & I were the only members of our own family who could follow him to the grave. On Friday, about one o'clock, we heard that ones worst fears were realized, & that the evening cars would bring his body with that of Capt. Coles to the City. This woeful intelligence came to blast hopes which had been elated to almost certainty, by previous telegrams of a far different import. The whole city was plunged in gloom. I never heard of more universal sorrow, he seems to have outlived all prejudices & all enmities; those who had been enemies in life mourn him in death; even that miserable wretch, Charles Irving grieved & said "Oh, that he could have lived! I have been looking for him for three months to ask his forgiveness for all the wrong I have done him!" Young & Old, rich & poor, vie with one another in praising him. I am told that Richmond never before saw such a procession as received his remains & escorted him to the Capital, where he was placed in the room prepared for the Senate of the C.S. (Confederate States) Yesterday morning Plumer & I, with Aunt Margaret, Cousin Sallie, Mary & Judge Lyons, Frank & James Wise went to look for the last time on our loved one's face. He appeared to be placidly sleeping, after a day of weary and *faint sufferings*, that is the idea his expression conveyed to me. He was very natural, not distorted in the least. I could only *look* upon him, for they feared to open the coffin as he had been dead so long & for the same reason G— could not take a cast of him as Plumer wished him to do. I could not kiss him, nor lay my hand upon his noble brow & clasp his well loved face! They told me you had the blessed privilege of embracing him & had cut off a great deal of his hair.

I know it was right he should be publicly laid out, & appreciated the honor intended, but it was so dreadful to leave him in that great room with no tender eyes to watch him. I would have watched beside him all the time! From the Capital, Aunt Margaret, Cousin Sallie, Mr. N. Tyler, Judge Lyons & I drove to Hollywood to make a final selection of the place of his burial. I hope you will approve our choice. The section is large enough to hold seventy-five bodies; it lies a little apart from the road in almost a direct line with the Monroe monument from the river; the ground is perfectly level, it is certainly the most desirable spot now to be obtained in the cemetery. Judge Lyons will see to its being inclosed as soon as possible. Henry & I chose Mr. Peterkin to deliver the funeral address, thinking he would have been yours & Obe's choice amongst the resident ministers; had I known Bishop Johns was in town, I would have preferred him as a warm friend of yours— a friend of longer standing than Mr. Peterkin & one who well knew & loved my Brother. Johnnie arrived this morning. I had given directions that the coffin should not be closed until he had seen him. The funeral took place at eleven o'clock at St. James. Seats were reserved for the family, Aunt Margaret, Mr. Hobson's & the Lyons' family were there. Bishop Johns was in the chancel & seemed much affected. Mr. M— read the service. Grey heads and little children bowed with us in sorrow. Mr. Peterkin's sermon was from the text "Thy will be done—" he was much affected and showed good feeling; he paid some noble tributes to the dead.

Plumer & I followed in the carriage immediately behind the hearse. The body was escorted by an unusually large procession with military honors. Owing to some delay from mismanagement I did not reach the grave in time to see the body lowered; but I was amongst the last to leave. After the services of the Church were concluded, the Masons read their impressive rituals, a military salute followed; then loving hands showered flowers upon him— among these was Addie Dean. Mrs. Tyler sent me a beautiful bouquet or rather wreath to place on his coffin. The last honor & loving tribute was paid! Dust to dust! Ashes to ashes! Our Mother earth had received him & I had to leave him alone in that dark, cold grave! yet, not forever! for in his flesh he shall see God, & O, my Father, I trust we shall see him!

I have not left my room since returning; I have felt so much prostrated even to go to see Henry [Henry A. Wise, Jr., 1834–1869] for I am not very strong just now. Henry is distressed beyond expression, but he controls himself wonderfully, considering his weak & nervous condition. I have been with him constantly ever since I arrived on Tuesday, until today. The baby has been & is quite sick. Sallie has been too much indisposed and is too broken down to nurse him & I have been aiding in tending the little boy; he is a lovely magnificent child. We heard through Colonel F— of your meeting Obe. I am so thankful he could be brought back to us. As it was God's will that he should lay down his life in the service of his country, I believe he has died and been buried just as he would have wished. It has hurt me so much that Sister, Mother, Néné, Henry & all could not have seen him— that you could not have mingled your tears with us all at his grave. Poor Henry has grieved so incessantly that he could not have *one last look*. Henry is so urgent that no one should disturb his clothes, personal effects etc. until he is able to do it, that I have determined to gratify him & have ordered everything locked up. I will see about it myself tomorrow. Johnnie left my little ones well, Virginia Lyons is with them. John is submissive & obedient to me; & I am convinced is better with me than anywhere else. He will write to you by Col. McCrae who will take this letter. John J— is in town.

And now my own precious Father I would speak to you out of the abundance of a heart heavy with sorrow for you— a heart loving & clinging to you as never before! I would speak as I believe my Mother would tell me, could she bring me a heavenly message. My Father, my Mother gave her first born son to God before his birth, she dedicated him to Him by baptism, she agonized for his salvation in prayer, & I am sure the blood of Jesus has saved him. My Mother is with her son again! Her first wish for him in this world was that he should be your chief blessing, your comfort & your pride; no one knows as well as you do, how entirely he fulfilled that desire— he lived for you! he died for you! And O Father can you not hear his mother as "Will he not be your chief blessing in death as well as life, the blessed means of bringing more closely to God than ever before, of making you One with Christ that you may be united with your loved ones in Heaven." I ask this of God in agony upon my knees! When the Lord loves he chastens. I know my Savior feels for your bereavement— that he who wept at the grave of Lazarus weeps for you; My Father in Heaven knows as no other does how much you loved him; [illegible] all the depths of your sorrow. My darling Brother made all who loved him in life happier & better, may his death be sanctified to our wounded hearts by the increase of faith, patience & chastity. I can cheerfully & patiently say by God's help- "Thy will be done—" & yet, Father, how willingly would I have given my own life to have had him spared to you— Yes, Father I would have left my husband & little ones for that!

Mrs. Tyler Probably Julia Gardiner Tyler, 1820–1889, widow of former President John Tyler, 1790–1862, who had been a close friend of Henry A. Wise. Tyler had died a month earlier on January 18, 1862.

Grave of Obadiah Jennings Wise, Hollywood Cemetery, Richmond, Virginia. "O. Jennings Wise – Born April 12, 1831. Died for his Country February 9, 1862. Blessed are the pure in heart for they shall see God."

A lock of hair. On an envelope, in the handwriting of Annie Jennings Wise Hobson, "My Dear Brother's hair." Enclosed is a lock of hair, in all probability belonging to Obadiah Jennings Wise and perhaps cut from him by his father.

This poem, in Annie Jennings Wise Hobson's handwriting, has long been preserved in the family files. It has been published in a shorter version elsewhere with the attribution, "by Accomac." Accomac, on the Eastern Shore of Virginia, was where Obadiah and Annie were born and the Wises lived for many generations.

I should feel a terrible anxiety for you could I not give you with entire trust to the keeping of a merciful God. I have been so much relieved to hear of your restoration to health & of the fortitude with which you bear your woful bereavement, & the disaster of your legion.

I have written with an unsteady hand, & feel that I have inadequately told what my heart would say. John & Plumer are in bed. They will write to you tomorrow.

I have not heard one word from Rolleston since the confirmation of Obe's death. Remember me affectly [sic] to R—, George Wise, George Bagwell, Mr. Stewart, & Peter Lyons. With tender love to Richard. I thank God they are safe! God bless you with all needed strength, save & defend you we pray. —Your own devoted child, *Annie*.

Lines on the Death of O. Jennings Wise

Mournfully the bells are tolling,
And the muffled drums are rolling
With a sad and dreary echo
Through Richmond's crowded streets.
And the dead march, slowly pealing,
On the solemn air now stealing
Hushing every lightsome feeling
Our saddened senses greet!
And a look of settled sorrow
Is on every face we meet.

To his last, long home they're bearing,
One, whose many deeds of daring,
One, whose noble, high-toned spirit
Have endeared him to us all
Now, his sleep shall know no waking
Tho his rest shall have no breaking,
And no more amid war's thunders
Shall his soldiers hear his call.
He has laid aside his armor
And his banner is his pall.

His proud heart is stilled forever
And in battle shall he never
Lead again his gallant comrades
Where the loudest cannon roar.

And the field is dark and gory
Where the bones are [illegible, *winning*] glory
Where the haughty foe is strongest
Shall he never lead them more.
Short was his career, but glorious,
Now life's warfare all is o'er.

On the dreadful field of battle
With the musket's deadly rattle
Fighting for his country's freedom
The youthful warrior fell.
And the cannon's deep-toned breathing
Bloody laurels round him wreathing,
And the huzzas of the victors
Were his funeral knell.
But the memory of his valor
In our hearts shall dwell.

And his deeds shall never slumber
For we'll ever proudly number
Wise among the ones who perished
Struggling for their liberty!
And Virginia, when she's weeping
O'er the sons that now are sleeping,
On her bosom, shall forget not
That he died to set her free
And graven on her scared tablets
Shall his name forever be!

—Dedicated to Capt. O. J. Wise

Obadiah Jennings Wise, 1831–1862. Photograph courtesy of the Valentine Richmond History Center, Richmond, Virginia.

❧ Plumer Hobson writes to General Wise:

Richmond, February 24, 1862.
My dear Mr. Wise—   You well know how my heart mourns the loss of our dear Obe. He was *very dear* to me, as to all of his family, and it is hard to realize that one so noble, so perfect and loveable can be gone from us… It is great comfort though, that he died a noble death, and that his loss is mourned by so large a circle of friends and strangers. I have just finished today packing up all his papers and personal effects, and I have determined to have them all carried up to my house as the safest place, and kept there until you shall want them. There is no safe place here, and we thought it best not to send them to Rolleston. Annie went up several days ago and I remained to see to the packing up of these things. Tyler has assisted me. Major Duffield is in town and I have had several conversations with him about you. He is very anxious that you should demand a court of enquiry and not let them put it off a day longer than necessary. I think there is some misunderstanding of your position and no full appreciation of the difficulties and injustice with which you have had to contend. Mr. Seddon, in conversation with me a few days ago, said that he had heard that although you had protested against going there with your force, that after you reached the place you had signified to the department your ability to defend it. I only mention this as a sample of the misrepresentations afloat. Mr. Seddon did not say this on his own authority, but merely said he had heard it… I shall return home (to Eastwood) this evening— Annie and the children were well when I heard from them. Love to Richard. —Yours most affectionately, *F. Plumer Hobson*. (Virginia Historical Society)

Roanoke Island   The tragedy of Roanoke Island and the death of Obadiah Jennings Wise made a profound impression upon the people of Virginia and was for many the beginning of a turning point in their opinion of the Civil War. The young Wise, known within the family as "Obie," "Obe," "Obadiah," and "Jennings," had attended college at Indiana University where Andrew Wylie, his father's mentor and friend, was the President. He studied law at The College of William & Mary from 1852–1853 and was then appointed the Secretary of the American Legation in Berlin. While working in Germany he attended lectures at the University of Heidelberg. After working in Germany for two years, Wise was transferred to Paris where he worked for another two years before returning to Virginia in 1857. Between his return to Virginia and the outbreak of the Civil War, the young Wise was involved in eight duels. In 1859 he had a duel in North Carolina with Patrick Henry Aylett, the grandson of Patrick Henry. After Aylett's shots missed, Wise fired his gun into the air. Family tradition has always been that it was on that occasion that Obadiah said to his opponent, "I make a present to your family, sir." Years later, Thomas Nelson Page wrote a short story, Marse Chan, that includes an account of a duel where the duelist fires his pistol into the air. Family tradition has always been that Page, who knew some of the Wise family, based the incident in his story on young Obadiah Wise's duel. During his father's term as Governor of Virginia, one of his assignments was to assist in the transfer of the remains of President James Monroe, a native of Virginia, from New York to the Hollywood Cemetery in Richmond— a project that was completed on July 5, 1858. Of his service in the Confederate army, one historian wrote: "In the entire Confederate army there were few junior officers as well versed in military science as Captain O. Jennings Wise, and even among the seniors there were none who, like him, had observed the armies of Europe." After Robert E. Lee expressed his admiration for a particular horse, the owner, Colonel Broun of the Wise Legion, summoned young Obadiah Wise to deliver the horse, Traveller, to Lee as a gift. Lee ultimately paid for the horse and history will record that Lee and the horse were inseparable. Writing in 1876, Henry Alexander Wise said of his first wife and his dead son: "She and Obie are above, and waiting on my case and waiting for me." Obadiah's grave-stone reads: "Died for his Country — Blessed are the pure in heart, For they shall see God." When Henry A. Wise died in 1876 his obituary included the following reference to his son: "…It is to be remembered here that these troops under O. Jennings Wise, about 450 strong, killed and wounded over 900 of the enemy, or over twice their own numbers, before they were finally surrounded and captured…" The death of Obadiah Jennings Wise would be further described by Sallie Brock Putnam, Judith Brokenbrough McGuire, and John Easten Cooke all writing in 1867, by John Sergeant Wise in 1899, and by Rita Mae Brown in 1986.   —*Editor's note.*

ᓆ   Sallie Brock Putnam:

…Our attention was now mainly directed to Roanoke Island on the coast of North Carolina… It was the key that unlocked all of the northeastern portion of North Carolina, and the rich back country in the rear of Norfolk and Portsmouth, and prevented an approach of the enemy upon those cities…

It was now threatened by a Federal fleet under General Burnside, of immense proportions and ably commanded.

Brigadier General Wise had been placed in command of the military district in which this important position was included, under the superior command of General Huger, of South Carolina…

Finding the defenses wholly inadequate, General Wise made known to the government the utter uselessness of attempting to hold the island unless efficient aid was rendered him in the improvement and perfection of the defenses, and supposed to be wholly within the means of the government to supply. Again and again he applied for help, for proper reinforcements, and it is reported he used no very measured or polite terms as to the certain fate of himself and his command, if such assistance was not secured to him. But his entreaties were cruelly neglected.

The attack on the island was made by the fleet of the enemy on the 7th of February. General Wise was at the time confined to his bed by sickness, at Nag's Head, four miles distant, and entirely unable to command in person…

…Although foreseen by him, his distress, when the tidings of the battle were borne to him, was said to have been inconceivable, and heightened by the fact that his own noble son, the gallant young captain of the Richmond Light Infantry Blues, had fallen.

The body of this amiable young officer, in whom Virginia felt all the natural pride over offspring so illustrious, had fallen into the hands of the enemy, but was treated with all the respect merited by one so worthy, and was surrendered, on application, to his broken-hearted father. On the arrival of the remains at Portsmouth, all the bells of the city tolled the requiem of the young hero,—and there his father was permitted to gaze on his placid countenance, and the still form, in the rigid beauty of death. His emotions were said to be uncontrollable, and melted all who witnessed the sight. Unable to restrain himself, he bent over the loved figure, and taking in his one of the cold hands of the departed, exclaimed: "My noble boy, you have died for me! You have died for me! You have died for your father." Large tears rolled down the cheeks of the statesman warrior, "He died for me—he died for me!" and he then fell insensible to the ground.

The devotion of Captain Wise to his father, was understood to be of a most remarkable character, and partook rather of the tender self-sacrificing nature of a daughter's love, than the less sensitive and more independent tone of a son's attachment. Ever jealous of the honor and reputation of his father, he had more than once openly resented attacks reflecting on a name dearer to him than his own life.

Never was there a sadder funeral in Richmond than that which commemorated the death of Captain O. Jennings Wise. St. James's Church was crowded to its utmost capacity, to give room to the numbers that succeeded in getting into the church, and crowds were assembled on the outside, and remained standing during the services, although the ground was saturated with mud and water from the melting snow. A long retinue of carriages, conveyed the mourning family, and the numerous friends of the deceased. The principal dignitaries of the General and State Governments attended on horseback; the Mayor and City Council, and a vast procession of citizens, the old members of the Richmond Blues, and all the military in the city, with arms reversed, and bands of music, with muffled drums, swelled the funeral cortege, and followed the hearse, in which was placed the coffin containing all that was mortal of that brave young son of Virginia, draped in the banner of his State, and the Confederate flag, in whose defence he had so gallantly lost a life so precious to his friends, his city, his country! The windows and sidewalks of Richmond were densely crowded with spectators of this mournful pageant, and tears of heart-felt sorrow flowed unrestrained, as we watched the sad train that bore the hallowed remains to their quiet resting-place, in our beautiful cemetery at Hollywood.

The gurgling, never-ceasing music of the river, and the winds as they whisper through the trees, and the birds singing amid the branches, are the endless requiem over the grave of this young patriot of Virginia, the ever-lamented O. Jennings Wise. But his memory will live in the hearts of his countrymen, until the children and grandchildren of the Southern soldier shall take up the story to tell their descendants of the deeds of daring and glory inspired by this brave young commander.

The fall of Roanoke Island produced the most profound sensation in Richmond...
—Sallie Brock Putnam, *Richmond During the War: Four Years of Personal Observation.*

～ Judith Brokenbrough McGuire:

February 1862
Tuesday—Roanoke Island has fallen—no particulars heard.

12th—The loss of Roanoke Island is a terrible blow. The loss of life not very great. The "Richmond Blues" were captured, and their Captain, the gifted and brave O. Jennings Wise, is among the fallen. My whole heart overflows towards his family; for, though impetuous in public, he was gentle and affectionate at home, and they always seemed to look upon him with peculiar tenderness. He is a severe loss to the country...

Sunday, 16th—This morning we left home early, to be present at the funeral of Captain Wise, but we could not even approach the door of St. James's Church, where it took place. The church was filled at an early hour, and the street around the door was densely crowded. The procession approached as I stood there, presenting a most melancholy *cortege*. The military, together with civil officers of every grade, were there, and every countenance was marked with sorrow. As they bore his coffin into the church, with sword, cap, and cloak resting upon it, I turned away in sickness of heart, and thought of his father and family, and of his bleeding country, which could not spare him...

—Judith Brokenbrough McGuire, "Diary of A Southern Refugee during the War, January–July 1862." Edited by James I. Robertson Jr. from *Virginia at War 1862* (edited by William C. Davis, University Press of Kentucky, 2007). McGuire's book was first published in 1867 in New York by E. J. Hale & Son.

～ John Easten Cooke:

JENNINGS WISE — CAPTAIN OF "THE BLUES"
I found in an old portfolio, the other day, the following slip from a Norfolk paper of the year 1862: "The Confederate steamer *Arrow* arrived here this morning, from Currituck, having communicated with a steamer sent down to Roanoke Island under a flag of truce. She brought up the bodies of Captain O. J. Wise, Lieutenant William Selden, and Captain Coles. Captain Wise was pierced by three balls, and Lieutenant Selden was shot through the head. The Yankees who saw Captain Wise during the fierce and unequal contest declare that he displayed a gallantry and valour never surpassed...

...Of the remarkable young man who thus poured forth his blood, and passed away, before the age of thirty, in defence of his native soil, I propose to give a few personal recollections...

Jennings Wise! How many memories that name recalls! —memories of gentleness and chivalry, and lofty honour, to those who knew him truly—of fancied arrogance and haughty pride, and bloody instincts, to those who accepted common rumour for their estimate of him...

Born in Virginia, and going in his early manhood to Europe, as Secretary of Legation, he there perfected himself in riding, fencing, and all manly exercises; studying political science, and training himself, consciously or unconsciously, for the arena upon which he was to enter soon after his return. He came to Virginia at a time when the atmosphere was stifling with the heat of contending factions in politics, and becoming the chief editor of the Richmond *Enquirer*, plunged into the struggle with all the ardour of a young and ambitious soldier who essays to test the use of those arms he has been long burnishing for battle… What the pen wrote, the pistol, unhappily, was too often called upon to support; and the young politician was ere long engaged in more than one duel, which achieved for him a widely-extended notoriety and venomous party hatred…

…He fought for secession; joined the First Virginia Regiment, and served at Charlestown, in the John Brown raid. Then war came in due time. He was elected captain of the Blues—the oldest volunteer company in Virginia—took the leadership from the first, as one born to command, and fought and fell at that bloody Roanoke fight, at the head of his company, and cheering on his men.

His body was brought back to Richmond, laid in the capital, and buried, in presence of a great concourse of mourners, in Hollywood Cemetery. That was the end of the brief young life—death in defence of his native land, and a grave in the beloved soil, by the side of the great river, and the ashes of Monroe, brought thither by himself and his associates.

Then came a revulsion. His character was better understood; his faults were forgotten; his virtues recognized. Even his old opponents hastened to express their sympathy and admiration. It was remembered that more than once he had refused to return his adversary's fire; that championship of one whom he loved more than life had inflamed his enmity—no merely selfish considerations. His sweetness of temper and kindness were recalled by many, and the eyes which had been bent upon him with horror or hatred, shed tears beside the young soldier's grave… The green grass on his grave has covered all enmity, and the love of friends has taken the place of the bitterness of foes.

Among those friends who knew and loved him living, I count myself. To know him thus was speedily to love him—for his traits and instincts were so conspicuously noble and endearing, that he irresistibly attracted the affection of all who were thrown in familiar contact with him. How gentle, modest, and unassuming those inner instincts of his heart were, those who knew him in his private life will bear witness. They will tell you of his honest and truthful nature; his unpretending simplicity; his chivalric impulses, and nobility of feeling. Indeed, you would have said that the Creator had breathed into this clay the loveliest traits of humanity, and raised up in the prosaic nineteenth century a "good knight" of old days, to show the loveliness of honour.

This was one side of the young man's character, only. With these softer traits were mingled some of the hardiest endowments of strong manhood. No man was ever braver…

He was early in the lists as the advocate of resistance to the North, and fought its opponents with persistent vehemence… At first as a private, with musket on shoulder; eager, active, untiring; inspiring all with his own brave spirit. Then, when his acknowledged capacity for leadership placed him at the head of a command, he took the post as his of right, and led his men as all who knew him expected. How he led them on that disastrous day at Roanoke—with what heroic nerve, and splendid gallantry, in the face of the deadliest fire—let his old comrades in arms declare. There, in the front of battle, he fell—giving his life without a single regret to the cause he loved.

…It would be difficult to imagine a human being more modest, kindly, and simple. His modesty amounted almost to shyness; and it was doubtless this species of reserve which led many to regard him as cold, and destitute of feeling… Self-reliance, rather than self-distrust, marked the character of his intellect—boldness to undertake, and unshrinking courage to execute. But in this there was no arrogance—no *hauteur*. In the combat he would contend with all his powers, and shrink from no odds: but the contest once over, the hot blood cool, the old modesty returned, and the kindly, gentle smile. The indulgence of his affections was evidently one of his chief happinesses. He was fond of children, and delighted to play with them, sharing their gambols and amusements with the *bonhomie* and abandon of a boy. In such scenes, the vehement young politician no doubt took refuge from the strife of the public arena, where so many hot passions met and clashed, and found in the playful antics of children the antidote to the scorns and hatreds of those grown-up children—men. It was in the society of the eminent Virginian, his father, however, that he seemed to experience his greatest happiness; and his devotion to him was the controlling sentiment of his being…

The intellect which accompanied this courageous spirit and kindly heart was eminently vigorous and original. It was rather that of the actor than the thinker—rather, ready, acute, inventive and fruitful in resources—quick to move and to strike, in debate or reasoning with the pen—than deliberate, philosophic, or reflective. It wanted the breadth and depth which result from study and meditation, but as a sharp and tempered weapon to accomplish direct tangible results, it was exceedingly forcible and effective. As a writer in the larger acceptation of the term, he was not conspicuously endowed; but his style as a journalist was fluent, eloquent, and when his nature was strongly moved, full of power and the fire of invective…

His most notable gift was unquestionably that of oratory. He possessed native endowments which entitled him to very high rank as a public speaker. In the columns of a daily journal his powers were always more or less cramped, and did not assert their full strength, but on "the stump" he was in his own element. Here all the faculties of his intellect and nature had full swing, and "ample room and verge enough" for their exercise. The spectator saw at a glance that the young man with the thin slight figure and quiet manner, was a born orator. His first words justified the opinion, and stamped him as one born to move, to sway, to direct the thoughts and the actions of men. The crowd—that unfailing critic of a public speaker's ability—always received him with acclamations, and hailed his appearance on the rostrum with loud applause. They felt that, youth as he was, and as yet untrained in the arts of the orator, he was a match for the oldest opponents, and they were content to leave the advocacy of great principles, at momentous crises, in the hands of this young man—to accept and rely on him as their champion.

…His speeches were skilful combinations of philosophic reasoning and hard-hitting illustrations. In the employment of invective, his handling was that of a master; and when his scorn of some unworthy action or character was fully aroused, his delivery of the scathing sarcasm or the passionate defiance was inexpressibly vehement and bitter…

With the termination of his speeches disappeared all the passion, vehemence, and ardour of the man. The handkerchief passed over the damp brow, seemed to wipe away all excitement; and the fiery gladiator, swaying all minds by his fierce invective, or his vivid reasoning, subsided into the quiet, almost shy young man. The old modesty and simplicity of demeanour returned, and the forces of the vigorous intellect returned to rest, until some other occasion should call them into exercise…

If enmity exist toward him in any heart, however, no answering defiance comes back. The weapon of the good knight will never more be drawn—he has fought his last battle and yielded up his soul. He sleeps now quietly, after all the turmoils of life—after heart-burnings and triumphs, and loves and hatreds—sleeps in the bosom of the land he loved, and toiled, and thought, and fought, and died for. His is not the least worthy heart which has poured out its blood for Virginia and the "South; and in the pages of our annals, among the names of our dead heroes who surrendered youth, and coming fame, and friends, and home, and life for their native land—surrendered them without a murmur or a single regret—among these great souls the Genius of History must inscribe the name of Jennings Wise. —John Easten Cooke, *Wearing of the Gray*.

John S. Wise:

When, in the Capitol of Virginia at Richmond, I gazed for the last time in the cold, calm face; when I saw the black pageant which testified to the general mourning as they bore him to his last resting-place in beautiful Hollywood, —I began to realize as never before that war is not all brilliant deeds and glory, but a gaunt, heartless wolf that comes boldly into the most sacred precincts, and snatches even the sucking babe from the mother's breast; that the most cherished treasure is its favorite object of destruction; that it ever plants its fangs in the bravest and tenderest hearts; and that that which we prize the most is surest to be seized by its insatiate rapacity.

—John S. Wise, *The End of An Era*.

Rita Mae Brown:

March 19, 1862.
…He (Henley) pinched the bridge of his nose between his thumb and forefinger. "It isn't just that. We're losing this war, Lutie. Ever since Sumner passed on, the portents and the events spell doom."
"It's always darkest before the dawn."
"This is dark indeed. I think I knew following President Tyler's funeral cortège that darkness was enveloping us. And when Captain O. Jennings Wise was carried through the town, people were distraught. I tell you I've never seen such an outpouring. You couldn't get within a block of St. James Church, even in the slush and the snow. People shivered and wept."
"He was a popular boy and a hero."
"A hero? My God, we asked him to fight off seventy-five hundred Federals at Roanoke Island with one-third that number. He was a lamb led to slaughter! So many lambs." Henley's eyes clouded.
—Rita Mae Brown, *High Hearts*, Bantam Books, 1986, reprinted with permission.

Twilight at Hollywood

> To-day our maidens gathered here to strew
> The early flowers upon the soldiers' graves,
> In their sweet custom; and at early morn
> Hither they came with blossoms, buds, and leaves
> And earnest faces fairer than the flowers.
> No grave has been forgotten—all are dressed.
> The simple soldier from the distant State

Hollywood. Illustration by W. L. Sheppard.

Is loved and honored, though perchance unknown,
And where he sleeps is beautiful with bloom.
One stayed a little, when the rest were gone,
Beside a grave. Quite motionless she stood
Until the paths grew dim, then turned away;
And twilight gathers over Hollywood.
The sun goes down behind a bank of cloud
And dashes all the stormy West with blood,
As dies a hero in a broken cause
When, pouring out his wasted life, he leaves
The land he loved to darkness and defeat.

Far down below I hear the river rush,
And standing in this city of the dead
The voice of waters seems a human cry
That rises from the breadth of all the land
Of shivered hearthstones and of broken hearts.

The city, growing sombre in the dusk,
Was lit with splendor forty months agone,
When all our best and bravest gathered there,
A nation's fortress and her capital.
The long street trembled with the tramp of men,
And rang with shouting and with martial strains;
And up the glaring river came the boom
Of mighty guns that held a fleet at bay;
But sorrow came upon her, and defeat,
She sank in ashes, and a people's hope
Sank with her; and her glory passed away.
Her arms were overthrown, her flag was torn,
Her children bent their heads beneath the yoke
In bitter silence; and her chosen chief
Was fettered in the fortress by the sea.

O rapid river with the mighty voice,
Rave through thy hills and wear away the rocks,
Even as a people wears away the heart
In thinking of their glory and their fall.

But O, the spirit of the first campaigns,
O, days of life and motion!
From Rio Grande to the Chesapeake
They gathered, sweeping joyous to the fight.
The wild yell rising from the trampling charge
Tore through the ragged rifts of battle-smoke
And rose above the thunder of the guns.
And as a great wave on the open sea,
That strikes a blow and leaves a wreck behind,
They swept along, a living surge of strength,
With tempest voice, and crest of bayonet.

God smiled at first, then turned his face aside,
And hope, that glittered like a sunlit sword,
Was quenched in gloom. And still they smote the foe
That rose with strength renewed from each defeat
Till, broken by their victories, they fell.
Forever thin and thinner grew the ranks,
The weary march, the hungry bivouac,
The scanty blanket, wet with driving sleet,
The sleepless outpost, listlessness of camp,
The longing for loved ones at home—all these,
Far more than wasting battle, wasted them
Until their strength was spent—now low they lie.
And never more upon Virginia hills
Shall thrill the onset of the southern lines.
The men that bore the bayonet and blade
Shall bear them now no more;
But oh! to think how bright and swift they were,
And now how cold and still!

O rushing river, thou at least art free
And fit to sing soldiers' requiem,
Deep-toned and tremulous—the dirge of men
That once were tameless as thy winter flood.

When once again we stand erect and free
And we may write a truthful epitaph—
A nation uttering its grief in stone
Shall pile aloft a stately monument.
Not that their fame has need of sculptured urn,
For they have lived such lives and wrought such deeds
As venal history cannot lie away;
Till then shall scattered roses deck their graves
And woman's tear shall be their epitaph.

O, river, though they moulder in the dust,
Let them not perish from our hearts—speak on,
And fill us with thy rushing energy.
That as the gathered freshets of the spring
Burst upward through the shackles of the ice,
So we at last may dash our fetters off;
For until then these men have died in vain.
        —A newspaper-clipping, author unknown,
          found in the papers of Annie Jennings Wise Hobson
         — perhaps written by her.

The Confederate Monument, built 1869, in Hollywood Cemetery, where eighteen thousand Confederate soldiers are buried. The monument reads: "To the Confederate Dead — MEMORIÂ IN ÆTERNÂ".

↬ Letters from Annie Jennings Wise Hobson:

Eastwood, 27th Feb, 1862. Thursday.
My dear Mother— Since the sad disaster at Roanoke Island I have heard only once from Rolleston, & then I received a short letter from Sister. Henry sent me upon Monday evening by Mr. Hobson a letter to him from Father & one for me & Johnnie. I am truly thankful that Father has as much physical strength and heroic fortitude as he represents; but alas! I know his heart is struck and bleeding! We are anxious to know the result of his orders to Manassas. Mr. Hobson as well as other friends have written begging him to call a court of inquiry. Certainly either Huger or Father must be to blame, & the public should be assured which is the culpable one.

I returned last Thursday (as I wrote Sister I should). The children were inexpressibly glad to see Mamma back. Since a number of the farm servants were sick, & had been during my absence, all are well now except Aggie's son Nelson who took cold with the mumps and had an attack of pneumonia; he is getting better. Plumer remained in Richmond until Monday evening when he and Pardigon came up in the Packet. Plumer packed all the things at the Legion Office except the books which Mr. Tyler will attend to. He brought up a trunk of clothes, & a box containing some trinkets, a worked chair & pair of slippers made up with some other small articles; all of which I have carefully repacked and put away myself. Henry was sitting up when Plumer left— had been in the next room. The baby was better... Ever since my return I have felt a necessity for continual exertion. *Thought* at this sad and gloomy period is too painful to be indulged in; therefore I have been exceedingly busy & have intentionally fatigued myself, that exhaustion might bring me rest & sleep at night. I am thankful to say I am unusually well. The children have gotten over their ailments, & Plumer is better than I have seen him for some time. A good part of my sorrow dear Mother has been for others— It is a small thing comparatively to suffer for one's self— a most distressing one to suffer for others & for those dear & near to us. I was much relieved to hear that calm fortitude was given you. I feared so much for you in your weak and nervous

Henry Wise Hobson. Photographer, C. R. Ress. & Co, 911 & 913 Main Street, Richmond, Virginia.

Rolleston, Princess Anne County. Home of Henry A. Wise before the Civil War. Photo from Historic Virginia Homes and Churches *by Robert A. Lancaster, Jr.*

state. I took you on my heart to my heavenly Father & asked him to give you strength & comfort... God has sent me many sweet and comforting thoughts. And after all, none of us know how short our separation from those who have found an eternal "Love, Rest & Home" may be... Oh, Mother, if this bereavement can bring Father *heart broken* from sin & self to the front of the Cross, with childlike submission to the Savior's love how greatly we shall rejoice & acknowledge that the death of our noble one was even a greater blessing than his sweet & loving life had been. I have not time to write a long letter this afternoon, as I must take a walk before sunset, & it is time my letters had been sent to the office. I wish I could see you all...   —Your truly affect daughter, *A. J. W. Hobson.*

Eastwood, 27th March 1862. Thursday.
My dear Mother—   Your letter was received on last Saturday. It seemed a long time since you had written to me, and I am always so glad to get your letters. Yet I do not expect you to write often, & always understand your long silences. I well know that you wept for yourself in grieving for our dearly loved Obe, for you must miss him very much. I wish indeed that you & all could have taken one last look at his dear face! I wonder that you stood the shock and grief of that woeful disaster as well as you did. I found that as well and strong as I am I was obliged to control myself or be sick. My nervous system will not stand any kind of pleasurable excitement, much less that of a painful nature. Your account of Father's distress touched me beyond expression. He grieves just as I knew he would, & his sorrow will be life-long. I know how your heart bleeds with and for him! God's ways are indeed mysterious, dear Mother, but I always feel assured that it is the mystery of infinite love & merciful wisdom. I could not express my feelings in regard to Father's safety! & I thank God more & more for that providential sickness which detained him from the Island. It must be agonizing for you to part with Father, & I can hardly bear to think of your anguish. Yet, I am sure in this sorrow, and terrible uncertainty you can trust "your all" —everything to God. I rejoice to learn from Mr. Hobson, who returned from Richmond on Tuesday, that Father is looking better than he almost ever saw him before. Richard came up at the same time and confirmed the statement that he is in such excellent health. God grant that he may continue so! I had hoped Father would certainly come up with Plumer; & the children were as disappointed as I was that he did not accompany him; he promises to come to see me before leaving Richmond, but I do not feel sure of the fulfillment... Mother, I have never once for one second wished him [Obadiah Wise] back; and when at the throne of Grace— & her praying for others who are yet in sin & darkness, so far from God!

I rejoice that I can never agonise in prayer for him again! Truly it is a great happiness that one of earth's dearest ones is forever safe! Yet, I never lay my head on my pillow at night that I do not see him as he lay in his last sleep; there are few hours of the day that he does not come before me in some form, in some dear association— & there are times when my heart sinks within me when I recall his fearful struggle, his last hours! As I told Sister, I have seen him seldom of late, & in all probability would never have been with him much had he been spared during a long life. And I never knew what he was to me until earth had lost him forever. Yet I grieve more for Sister's & Father's loss than for my own, and for poor Néné too— she loved him enthusiastically

& devotedly. Mr. Hobson could not have seemed more distressed for his own brother. In regard to the photographs there seems to be nothing but delays. I sent my pictures to Cousin Sallie [unknown person] requesting her to attend immediately to having it copied— to ascertain what the cost, etc. would be, whether a good colored photograph could be made in Richmond etc. She has never replied to the letter; from what I can learn, handed the matter over to Major Tyler, who has let the picture lie at some photographers all this time *not knowing whether I'd be willing to have the glass taken off* —otherwise a copy could not be taken! I don't wonder at Father's impatience over *inefficiency*! The bad weather during Mr. Hobson's short stay prevented him from attending to it personally— he directed the glass to be taken off immediately. Frank promises to see about the matter at once; & I will soon be able to let you know the result. I must tell you that I like my picture now much less than ever before. It looks as Obe did when he returned from Europe; but is not like him within the last two years; then too, it was an absurd fancy to perpetuate a likeness of him with a cigar in his hand, & the lips in the act of puffing away the smoke… The children are all quite well again & are enjoying this bright day very much. Plumer still has some cold & cough, but is better than when he went to Richmond. Johnnie continues well, & is getting on very quietly. I think he is really obedient and unusually docile with me; he is crazy to go home. I never wanted to see Spring weather more than this season; we have occasional warm days, but still so much wet cold weather, everyone is so backward in gardening. I never took a more cheerful interest in domestic affairs, & am so thankful I can do so to direct my mind from the dark storm without that is desolating our beloved land. I trust that God in good time will give us victory & peace… God bless & comfort you dear Mother—   —Your loving daughter *A. J. W. Hobson.*

◦ War correspondence:

Richmond, Va. May 17, 1862.
My own dear Wife—   I am again in the midst of overwhelming calls of duty. In an hour I shall move to Genl. Johnston's Headquarters, leaving my baggage for the time, taking only a change of clothes in my saddlebags. I send Scaggs back with a load of sugar, rice, a box containing some of my winter clothes and some of Richard's things. I particularly send you Obe's good hair mattress. It is a good one, but wants airing. My winter clothes are beginning to be too warm and I want a *few* of my summer clothes sent to me— a coat, a thicker & thinner one & some pants if I have any— two or three pair. Send me also my gray waterproof coat, the one Obe gave me. The army has fallen back to within five or six miles of Richmond. I go to camp for orders and pick up my Command. I leave every arrangement for you all to Henry, Dr. Garnett, and yourself. I heard last evening that the govt. will probably move to Lynchburg. If so, Goochland will be directly in the line of military operations. I state this that you may decide understandingly. I must remain here to do what I dare & can do for you in preventing the enemy ever forcing you to stampede again or to be cut off from you. Whatever happens, let us try to rely on God now & forever and all will be for the best… May He be ever in your heart & over you, guiding & protecting you, my wife & dear children. Your own *Henry A. Wise.*

In The Trenches. Illustration by W. L. Sheppard.

Camp on the Verina Road, New Wilton. 10 P.M. May 29th, 1862.
My Wife & Annie—   Orders upon orders have crowded upon my powers & patience today, *and* rumors of battles to come off in the morning of tomorrow rush upon me, but your letters have just come and I must drop you another line before fate reveals its goal or evil for us & ours… It is now 11 o'clock at night, all quiet. I am very weary & must stop. Don't send me anything until you have the word from me that I can get and enjoy it. We expect Genrl. J— to attack McLellan tomorrow and are all excited to watch & pray & fight. May God be over you all my dear ones whatever becomes of me. I will be prudent, but if I am taken away it will be at the post of duty & believing in Him firmly with all my sins upon me— firmly because I know His Son liveth to Save. Love & Blessings for you all. Your Own *Henry A. Wise.*

1863

Letters from Annie Jennings Wise Hobson:

Eastwood. 24th March 1863. Tuesday afternoon.
My dear Mother—   I read your letter Saturday morning very hastily, and wrote *at intervals* to Sister with Annie in my lap, with a hurried hand, and confused brain. Consequently not until night when I read your letter again did I remember the questions relative to the coffee and Caroline's dress. I'm done apologising for my crazy ways! I would like to get the coffee with you and Sister very much— 10 lbs. for my share. Mr. Hobson will go down as soon as possible and can pay for it. I will most willingly have a dress made for Caroline & clothes for John. I may need some more bale cotton to do so & will let you know if I do. As to compensation, the highest Confederate prices will be expected, especially for the honor of having me to attend to it!

I went over to see Mrs. Clark this morning taking Annie & the boys with me. Little Annie was glad to have a little change. She has almost recovered from her sore mouth, and Plumer now has the same affection, fortunately not as badly as Annie did & it does not interfere with his working; but it keeps him very fretful and feverish… But this is a bad season for gardening. I am afraid my peas will rot in the ground— the cold weather keeps them back so long. I would send you a long letter full of interesting details if I only had time, but the gas is lighted & my letter ought to be in the office… We all give in love. The children send you a kiss. I hope Sallie continues as well as can be expected. Ellen told me she had seen the baby, & he was lovely. Write as often as possible. Kiss Father for me when you see him.   —Your affect. daughter, *A. J. W. Hobson.*

Eastwood. 16th April 1863.
My dear Mother—   The mail brought me two letters from you— dates of the 13th & 15th. I have been exceedingly sorry to hear how much indisposed you have seemed to be of late, and the depressed tone of your letters shows me you are not well… I shall go to Richmond with Plumer the first of May if Anne is well enough to accompany me. I suppose you have heard through Ephraim of her having pleurisy. She has been quite sick but is decidedly better today & with care she will soon be out again… If I succeed in making my long talked of visit you must come back with me. I have arranged this plan as

a certainty in my mind, & shall tease you until you accede to it for peace sake. By that time the country will be looking so sweetly and we will have plenty of vegetables, & *we will refresh you generally*. The dusty carpet shall be removed from your room, & your own put down in my absence; —everything *cleaned & scoured*, & "spic-span nice" when you get here! and then I intend to be charming, *so amiable* that you won't believe it's me! ...Poor little Plumer is getting a whole mouth full of teeth at once, & had fever nearly every night, is fretful and evil minded beyond expression— fighting and scratching everyone. He has fallen off & is very thin— tho' he has no affection of his bowels.

Dr. Smith has prescribed for him, & hope he may be going through the worst with his teeth now, tho this may be the beginning of a weary second summer's sickness. Dr. Smith mentioned yesterday he had received a letter from you. I will ask him when he comes tomorrow whether it contained the payment of the bill. I shall not see him today. I can not tell you what I suffer daily from *hemorrhoids* accompanied by severe pain and frequent loss of blood. Dr. Smith has given me a remedy that I hope may prove beneficial for I am worn out with the suffering I have endured for nearly a month— ever since a few days after Sister left. I kept using simple remedies hoping to find relief, and finally had to consult Smith. Otherwise I am well with an unusual amount of nervous energy... Cannon says "Grandma promised to come back in March & she has not done it. It's time she'd come home." I will write to Sister soon— but hope she'll come up before I even write as she promises. May God comfort you, make your [illegible] in sickness & give you cheerfulness & peace dear Mother.   —Your affect. daughter. *A. J. W. Hobson.*

↝ A letter to Henry A. Wise:

April 28th, 1863.
My beloved Husband—   Mary has not returned. Annie's little baby died yesterday at 8 o'clock & will be brought down tonight in the boat & buried tomorrow morning from Wm. Hobson's. Annie wishes Henry to come in & conduct the funeral services— she does not wish a sermon preached. Will you & the boys come in too? Wm. Hobson will be down this evening. Annie is not coming down. Néné wrote to Henry this morning about this... I was quite sick Friday night & staid in bed yesterday. Today I have revived & am better. I would be glad to get some relief. I got your envelope yesterday enclosing Johnnie's letter. I'll write to him today... —Devotedly your wife. *M.W.*

↝ A letter from Annie Jennings Wise Hobson:

Eastwood, 22nd August 1863.
My dear Mother—   I have thought of you of late with tender sympathy— Such continued sickness as you have had for weeks is a hard trial... I feel daily that the best thing we can do for those in trouble is to pray for them... Cannon is right unwell— I am giving him medicine. Annie looks much better than she did some weeks ago. Plumer is better & Henry well. I teach the children every day & Henry is getting on easily. Cannon will soon read as well as Jimmie and is learning to write. Sarah Burns lightens my duties very much... I am always pleased to get a letter from you, but you must not exert yourself

Annie's little baby   The letter from Mary Lyons Wise to Henry A. Wise, informs him of the death of a grandson, F. Plumer Hobson, July 8, 1862–April 27, 1863. The infant is buried in the Hollywood Cemetery in Richmond.

to write. I hope this letter will find you much better, & placid & cheerful. May God's peace be with you always. The children send you a kiss. Mr. Hobson is riding out with Mr. Maben. —Your affect. daughter—*Annie J. W. Hobson.*

Mr. Maben Maben Hobson, brother of Plumer Hobson, who lived at Snowden, west of Eastwood.

◡ War correspondence:

Charleston S. C., December 7th 4 1/2 A.M. 1863.
My own dear sweet wife—   I feel very sober this morning, but not the least unhappy. Thursday last was my birthday, but *no one knew it. I did*. I could but acknowledge that time with me had taken every step but the last two times score, and then it would be a favor from Heaven if I was permitted to count with the Great Innovator the other "ten." Well! What of it?— I have been told for fifty-seven years that "Time flies," and though, in the descent of years he has but to close his wings to move more swiftly; yet the "hours lag apace" with *me without you*. What does that signify? Spell it, woman, spell it! and you will learn what spell *still* binds a [illegible]. I can't put in *old age!*— No one wished me another year or day; no one sent me a remembrance; no one prepared for me one single good thing of a feast or fair; but I was *alone* in the midst of the command of an army, and communed somewhat with myself. The next day someone found out that I was an "older if not a better" man and my quarter-master sent me a pair of *lamp snuffers*. How significant? Was it to trim my lamp of life, and to *extinguish* it without leaving a lingering spark to smoke even after the flame is out. Ah! What thoughts & signs of age contrast with images of youth, and yet the sunset is very like sunrise in life as well as in nature— they must be looked for only in different points of the compass, but there is no West and no East in pictures; the colors of Matin & vespers are the same, sometimes clear & sometimes cloudy, sometimes dark & gloomy and sometimes glowing with every tint there of gorgeous light. But Aurora *stands* in the East, with reins drawn tight on fiery, prancing studs, breathing out the mists of hot blood tinted with its saffron. Vesper goes down the steep horizon, holding & bearing back, slowly descending, in soft whispers, to quietness & rest. Morning bursts out with "light which wakes the world" to open day of noise & bustle & toil & trouble. Which ought philosophy to prefer?— Ay, which ought goodness & which ought evil to choose? There is but one answer: —To the good they are both good & glorious; to the evil they are both evil. To the good, morning is the brightness of *hope*, evening is the blessed calm of *memory*. —To the evil, the break of day is but the blaze of passion, and sunset plunges into the blackness of despair. Such was some of the imagery of my birthday reflections. You see why I am sober. And too I am away from you.

   I suppose I must have forgotten the check— but let me know when you want another. What keeps Richard still in Va? He has had time enough to be here. How is Néné? Wm. Taliaferro went on Saturday to Mr. Porchert. There is no news here. The enemy have slacked their fires. But Charleston is bare of everything & stripped for the buff or the burning. Love to all. —I'll answer whether I love you *some day home.* Your own, *Henry A. Wise*

Henry A. Wise. Photo courtesy of the Virginia Historical Society, Richmond, Virginia.

Beginning in October 1863 Annie Jennings Wise Hobson kept a diary of her life and activity at Eastwood during the Civil War. That diary is printed here along with letters and other material about that time and place.

 ꙳ The diary of Annie Jennings Wise Hobson:

October 11, 1863. Eastwood, Goochland. —9th Sunday after Trinity.
I cannot do without my journal, it proves a silent monitor and companion to me whose beneficial influence I sadly miss. I have heard men say that diarys [*sic*] and journals make us egotistical, that we are prone to dwell too much upon ourselves anyhow. How true. Alas poor human nature will think well of itself and dwell on its own perfections. But it is a different thing to examine ourselves by the light of God's word, and as miserable sinners before God. I really need something to keep me reminded of the many resolutions I made and break. God's grace has done wonders for me, yet if it should leave me one moment what would become of me. I know I am quieter than I used to be, am far less restless and ambitious, less full of self, less careful for the things of time, and more heavenly minded, but oh!— it is so sad, so sad to see how little mastery I have gained over irritability, impatience, and quickness of manner, how little endurance I have in small things. Will I ever possess my soul in patience? I have also fallen into bad habits of absentmindedness and forgetfulness about things that frequently concern others. I have gained nothing in physical endurance. May god forgive my sins and pity my infirmities.

> Go to the world, return, nor fear to cast
> Thy bread upon the waters, sure at last,
> In joy to find it after many days.
> The work be thine— the fruit thy children's part;
> Choose to believe not see; sight tempts the heart
> From sober walking in true Christian ways.

This verse encouraged me some time ago when I came upon it by chance to continue my poor efforts for the benefit of our slave dependents. I have written a great deal in it today. I leave the result to God. No church this morning. I taught my children and Sister's little boys who are with me and my colored class this afternoon— directed Sarah Burns about her Bible lessons for another Sunday. I read a while in the morning and walked in the garden. Mrs. Seddon came over and sat awhile this evening. Sister Kittie and Sister made a short visit this week. God helped me to keep from fretting over difficulties in household matters, bad bread, etc., but I have been impatient with the children. Father help me in all good endeavors and undertakings for the week to come.

October 24, 1863, Saturday.
God has led me on another week.
> New perils past, new sins forgiven—
> New thoughts of God, new hopes of Heaven.

I have carried out a resolution often made before but seldom kept of so regulating the employments of the week that Saturday evening should be a time of meditation, self-examination and preparation for the Sabbath. I have striven to do my duty and alas!— as usual have failed in much. My impatient quick manner has been little improved, and I have been far from attaining a meek and quiet spirit "to meet the hourly accidents of life." I have had to train a new cook. I had trouble with Caroline— that is she determined not to cook decently for us and to have some difficulty.

Last Sabbath was a sad trying day from vexations in household matters, and Plumer and I felt that we did not meet them as we should do, and made new resolutions in regard to dealing with our servants. How wisely St. Paul spoke when he charged masters to avoid threatening! I think we both asked God to help us, and have done better

Mrs. Seddon Sarah Seddon, wife of James A. Seddon, Secretary of War for the Confederacy, lived nearby at Sabot Hill.
Sister Kittie Martha Bland Selden, wife of John David Hobson of Howard's Neck, referred to as Brother John.
Sister Mary Elizabeth Wise Garnett.

since. Surely the dealing with our domestics impose duties that require much self-control, self-watching, unselfishness combined with common sense, and calm firmness. I ask God for wisdom in that as often as in any other duty. It is hard to find the middle ground of not imposing upon them, expecting too much of them, and yet to keep them up to proper industrious habits and respect to those above them. When I started with Louisa I asked God to help me, to keep me if it was His will from the trial of having bread and food unfit for my family to eat. All I wanted was wholesome food, no matter how simple, and my new cook has done wonderfully. I have had a trial tonight for all the bread for Sunday for want of attention is spoilt. I tried to take it patiently.

Sunday morning.
Plumer insisted upon my putting up my desk and retiring last evening; therefore I've left many things unsaid. We have a bright lovely morning. May God help me to keep His day Holy in everything. May he assist me in teaching my children and colored class and keep my mind fixed on heavenly things. No church today. God grant that Mr. Harrison may succeed in finding a minister to preach for us every alternate Sunday— an Episcopal minister for it has been no small trial to be deprived so long of the services of my own church. Mother (Mary Lyons Wise) is with me. May God help me to be unselfish in giving time to keep her from being lonely and depressed. She is sorely tried with ill health, and needs much comforting and soothing.

I feel concerned about Sister in her refugee life. I also have apprehensions for her life in her coming trial, but I try to be over-anxious in nothing, leaving all to God. I wrote to Father, Richard, and John yesterday.

December 27, 1863. Eastwood.
I little thought to record sorrow and thankfulness in such strong terms and over such events as have occurred, before seeing my journal again, when I last wrote.

Two months have passed, and in that short lapse of time Maben Hobson has been summoned to eternity!

He lay ill for six weeks, and then died a struggling painful death without uttering one word to give us hope that he had made his peace with God. Plumer and I reached Snowden about four o'clock Monday afternoon— he died at two in the night. I watched by him with Dr. Nash and Mr. Irving until he breathed his last. God grant that I may not stand again by such a deathbed. He was raving in delirium all the time, his death throes were like to a woman's in travail, his deep sepulchral voice, articulation and modulation almost gone, sounds in my ears now. His gleams of conscious intelligence were few and faint. He raved about the camp and the army. He said that he had been two long weary months on the march, that the day was almost breaking and he could go home. He issued orders, conversed with old friends and then would start

Maben Hobson Alexander Maben Hobson, 1829–1863, older brother of Plumer Hobson.

Snowden: the Valley of the James by John Linton Chapman, reprinted from Diomed: The Life Travels & Observations of a Dog *by John Sergeant Wise, The Macmillan Company, 1899.*

View across the James River from the front lawn of Snowden, October 2006.

up horror struck, imploring us to save him, crying out "Take it off, oh! take it away." Oh! God how I suffered and agonized in prayer for him. I understood the agony and bloody sweat in Gethsemane as never before! My Saviour stood in that dark room by millions of such beds! I thought he would suffocate at one time, but I entreated God that he might pass quietly away, and he heard me— a half-an-hour before he died he became quiet; all struggle ceased and he fell into the arms of death as calmly as a babe asleep. I would have given years of my life if he could have given me a sure hope that he was going to his rest after all his weary marches, and wearing soldier's life. God's will be done! He was the child of many prayers, and God's mercy is beyond our comprehension. I feel for his bereaved parents, so sorrow stricken in their old age and pray God to comfort them. The Lord did it. May he sanctify this severe trial to his wife and be a Father to the fatherless children.

Oh, that I could have some evidence that this sorrow has brought my husband nearer to God and Heaven. O my soul wait on the Lord, and He will fulfill thy hope.

Sister's troubles were over before I could get to her. She had a quick safe labor, and the little one proved to be a daughter. Oh! I felt so thankful that none of my fears were realized. She is fast getting well though the baby does not thrive as it might. I was with [her] three weeks. Plumer, little Annie, and I went down first. Anne and the boys joined us afterwards. We ran home for the troublesome business of pig killing. Néné and Mother remained at Eastwood. I was glad to be able to be of some comfort to dear Sister; and that I could send Sarah Burns to stay with her till February. The baby is named Annie. I have had a great many sick servants three or four women confined at once; and a mild form of diptheria. I trust that I am thankful enough to God that the type of this dreadful disease was so mild with us, and that my children were spared it altogether. Néné had it very lightly.

God has visited Mrs. Seddon with a heartrending affliction in taking her little Anna, (with a sudden attack of congestion of the brain), to Himself…

And now the Xmas season has come to us. None but the little children may have a merry Xmas in the war-stricken and blood deluged land. I did my best to make the little ones and servants happy and that has been for years my only happiness and amusement in the Xmas season. But surely it should always be a time for solemn thought, and chastened thankfulness. We should all echo in our hearts and lives the angel's song of peace and good will to all mankind— especially to the poor and suffering. Maria, Henry and Yelverton Garnett are with us; we had a quiet Xmas dinner. Mr. Dudley partook of it and the day was pleasant. We cannot join in the worship of the Sanctuary today; but may God bless our private prayers.

Mr. Dudley Jacob D. Dudley, pastor of Hebron and Byrd Churches between 1855 and 1867 and also the schoolteacher.

Oh! Holy Comfort, aid me in heart-searching and self knowledge, make me to know all my sinfulness, and put in my mind, and confirm in my conduct all good and needed resolutions for a more holy and consistent life. May I not be unwise but understanding the will of the Lord.

January 15, 1863, Eastwood
I close another week with a humble sense of entire dependence upon God for everything, and a more humble penitential renewal of the cry "God have mercy upon a sinner" than I have felt for a long time. I have felt for the last few weeks like one just awakening to a new perception of light, and that light showing me a clearer view of self than I had seen before. It distresses and amazes me, yet makes me approach my Father, my Savior and my Comforter with a bolder confidence, gives me a more loving nearness if possible than heretofore experienced. I am so erring and weak, so sinful and offending and yet the Comforter won't leave me, the Father forgives me every hour, and the Savior will plead for me! Amidst shortcomings and failings, amidst sins and infirmities, even when cold and dead, I have an abiding sense of this. In a troubled frame last evening the thought came to me that it was impossible to tell how much sin I could be guilty of and yet be saved by the blood of Jesus. And did it make sin any the less dreadful to me? Far from it! Sin is horrible because it is dishonor to Him who died to save me! I would avoid sin, flee from it, despise it not only because it might take away the crown from me— the crown of Salvation, but because my God wills I shall not sin. I know I feel all this in the depths of my soul and yet there is not a day that does not witness against me that flesh has dominion over me, and that the Comforter in vain instructs me. My quick tongue and irritable temper are ever testifying against me as a child of God. This is because I do not spend time enough alone with God.

Diary is clearly dated 1863, but it must have been 1864 given the sequence of the entries.

෴ A wartime schoolbook:

PREFACE
The author of this little work, having found most of the juvenile books too complex for young minds, has for some time intended making an effort to simplify the science of Geography. If she shall succeed in bringing this beautiful and useful study within the grasp of the little folks, and making it both interesting and pleasant, her purpose will be fully accomplished.

NOTE TO TEACHERS
The first part of this work is intended to be used as a reader. The second is to be studied as usual. The object of this arrangement is to make the child familiar with geographical terms before he begins to study Geography. As a pupil, the author well remembers her difficulties at this point; and as a teacher, she has been led to enquire, "Is there no easier path for the tender feet of the little ones?" Let the pupil read over and over again, the first part, and then the second will be simply a review.

Preserved with the letters and diaries is a small schoolbook, The Geographical Reader for the Dixie Children by Mrs. M. B. Moore, with a note written inside the front cover: "First geography studied by me during the Civil War— Henry W. Hobson." Henry Hobson would have been six or seven years old when he studied from this book. Portions are reprinted here.

LESSON I
What Geography Means.
1. In this book I propose to tell you about Geography. I wish you to pay good attention, and if I use a word you do not understand, you must ask your teacher to explain it to you.
2. Some people travel over the world, and see nearly every country on the globe; but as every one can not do this, it is best for every boy and girl to study Geography.

Henry Wise Hobson. George S. Cook, 913 Main Street, Richmond, Artistic Photography.

Then when they wish to travel, after they are grown up, they will know which countries are most interesting…

LESSON X

1. The men who inhabit the globe, are not all alike. Those in Europe and America are mostly white and are called the Caucasian race. This race is civilized, and is far above all the others. They have schools and churches and live in fine style. They also generally have wise and good men for rulers, and a regular form of government. The women are treated with respect and tenderness, and in many cases their wish is law among their male friends.
3. There is a class of people who inhabit most of Asia which is of a yellow color. They are a quiet, plodding race, but when educated are sensible and shrewd…
4. When the white people came to this country, they found a red or copper colored race. This people they named Indians…
5. The African or negro race is found in Africa. They are slothful and vicious, but possess little cunning. They are very cruel to catch other [sic], and when they have war they sell their prisoners to the white people for slaves. They know nothing of Jesus, and the climate in Africa is so unhealthy that white men can scarcely go there to preach to them. The slaves who are found in America are in much better condition. They are better fed, better clothed, and better instructed than in their native country…

LESSON XI

America

1. A great many years ago the people thought the earth was flat and surrounded by the ocean. Europe, Asia, and Africa, with some islands around the coast, were all the land then known. The people had ships and sailed along the coast, but never ventured out on the ocean.
2. At length some wise men began to conclude that the earth was round like a ball; and that possibly they could sail west across the ocean until they came to the East Indies…
3. Columbus then went to Spain to ask king Ferdinand and queen Isabela to fit him out…

LESSON XII

North America

1. The northern part of North America is a cold desolate region. In the extreme North west, lies Russian America. This is governed by the Emperor of Russia…
2. On the northeast we find an island called Greenland, or Danish America. This belongs to the king of Denmark. The country is cold and bleak…

British America

1. This division lies between Greenland and Russian America. It is governed by the Queen of England. The southern portion is not so cold and bleak as the polar regions. In the Canadas the people raise grain and have some fruits.

The United States

1. This was once the most prosperous country in the world. Nearly a hundred years ago it belonged to England, but the English made such hard laws that the people said they would not obey them. After a long, bloody war of seven years, they gained their independence; and for many years were prosperous and happy.

2. In the mean time both English and American ships went to Africa and brought away many of those poor heathen negroes, and sold them for slaves. Some people said it was wrong and asked the King of England to stop it. He replied that "he knew it was wrong; but that slave trade brought much money into his treasury, and it should continue." But both countries afterwards did pass laws to stop this trade. In a few years, the Northern States finding their climate too cold for the negro to be profitable, sold them to the people living farther South. Then the Northern States passed laws to forbid any person owning slaves in their borders.
3. Then the northern people began to preach, to lecture, and to write about the sin of slavery. The money for which they sold their slaves, was now partly spent trying to persuade the Southern States to send their slaves back to Africa. And when the territories were settled they were not willing for any of them to become slaveholding. This would soon have made the North much stronger than the South, and many of the men said they would vote for a law to free all the negroes in the country. The Southern men tried to show them how unfair this would be, but still they kept on.
4. In the year 1860 the Ablitionists [sic] became strong enough to elect one of their men for President. Abraham Lincoln was a weak man, and the South believed he would allow laws to be made, which would deprive them of their rights. So the southern States seceded, and elected Jefferson Davis for their President. This so enraged President Lincoln that he declared war, and has exhausted nearly all the strength of the nation, and a vain attempt to whip the South back into the Union. Thousands of lives have been lost, and the earth has been drenched with blood; but still Abraham is unable to conquer the "rebels" as he calls the South. The South only asked to be let alone, and to divide the public property equally. It would have been wise in the North to have said to her Southern sisters, "If you are not content to dwell with us longer, depart in peace. We will divide the inheritance with you, and may you be a great nation."
5. This country possesses many ships, has fine cities and towns, many railroads, steamboats, canals, manufacturers, &c. The people are ingenious, and enterprising, and are noted for their tact in "driving a bargain." They are refined, and intelligent on all subjects but that of negro slavery, on this they are mad.
6. The large lakes, the long rivers, the tall mountains, with the beautiful farms and pretty towns and villages, make this a very interesting country to travelers.

Southern Confederacy
1. These states lie south of the United States and possess a warmer climate.—The latter are mostly suited to raising grain and cattle, while the former grow more cotton, rice, tobacco, and sugar cane; with some cattle and much grain. A large portion of the country lies on the sea coast, and is level and sandy. The interior portions are hilly and mountainous.
2. This country is well watered by large rivers, and has many fine harbors. On some of these harbors, are large cities; but the Confederate States possess few ships and her cities do not grow so fast as if there was more commerce. But we have reason to hope that in a few years we shall not fall behind any nation in point of commerce, or ships to carry it on.
3. This is a great country! The Yankees thought to starve us out when they sent their ships to guard our seaport towns. But we have learned to make many things; to do without many other; and above all to trust in the smiles of the God of battles. We had few guns, little ammunition, and not much of anything but food, cotton and tobacco; but the people helped themselves and God helped the people. We

were considered an indolent, weak people, but our enemies have found us strong, because we had justice on our side.
4. The Southern people are noted for being high minded and courteous. A stranger seldom lacks friends in this country. Much of the field work is done by slaves. These are generally well used and often have as much pocket money as their mistresses. They are contented and happy, and many of them are christians [*sic*]. The sin of the South lies not in holding slaves, but they are sometimes mistreated. Let all the little boys and girls remember that slaves are human, and that God will hold them to account for treating them with injustice.
5. The Southern Confederacy is at present a sad country; but President Davis is a good and wise man, and many of the generals and other officers in the army, are pious. Then there are many good praying people in the land; so we may hope that our cause will prosper. "When the righteous are in authority, the nation rejoiceth. But when the wicked bear rule the nation mourneth." Then remember, little boys, when you are men, never to vote for a bad man to govern the country...

LESSON XIV
Virginia
1. This large State lies in the north eastern part of the Southern Confederacy. It is frequently called the "Old Dominion." The western part is mountainous, the middle hilly and the eastern level. The soil is mostly good and you will find large plantations, bearing fine crops, numbers of the finest stock. Western Virginia is one of the finest grazing sections in the South. All persons who are fond of good beef, milk, butter and cheese would do well to settle there.
2. The higher class of society is noted for hospitality and for high living. Some of these claim to be descendants of Pocahontas, which they consider a great honor. You know Pocahontas was the Indian girl who saved the life of Captain John Smith, during the early settlement of Virginia. The people used to have many wars with the Indians, and then they bore their part in the Revolution and in the war of 1812.
3. In the war for independence, this State has suffered almost as much as any. Hundreds of families were run from their homes, and lost all they had except their clothes or a little money. Many houses and farms were destroyed, and the country laid waste. Such are the effects of war.
4. This State has many fine rivers; the Potomac and the James are the largest. There are several rail roads, and canals, and one of the finest harbors in the world. Norfolk was the main sea-port town and contained a fine navy yard; but the enemy has spoiled it very much.
5. Richmond city is the capital of the State, and also of the Confederacy. This is a goodly sized city on James river. President Davis resides there and Congress meets there to make laws. Many of the large buildings are used for hospitals and there are thousands of sick and wounded soldiers constantly there. There is said to be much wickedness in the city.
6. There are a great many manufactories in this State, and almost all kinds of articles are made. But the country produces corn, wheat, tobacco, &c., in great abundance. There are many planters who own large numbers of slaves. These are generally well treated, and are as happy a people as any under the sun. If they are sick *master* sends for the doctor, if the crop is short, they are sure of enough to save life; if they are growing old, they know they will be provided for; and in time of

war, they generally remain quietly at home, while the *master* goes and spills his blood for his country.

[Review lessons at the end of the book.]
LESSON IX.
Q. How many races of men are there? A. Five. Q. What color is the Caucasian? A. White. Q. What color is the Indian? A. Red or copper colored… Q. What race is most civilized? A. The Caucasian. Q. Which is the best educated? A. The Caucasian. Q. Which are the most ferocious and savage? A. The Indian, Mongolian, Maylay and African. Q. Is the African savage in this country? A. No; they are docile and religious here. Q. How are they in Africa where they first come from? A. They are very ignorant, cruel and wretched… Q. How do the Indians live? A. By hunting and fishing… Q. What has become of them? A. The white people drove them away and took their lands. Q. Are they all gone? A. A few of them live in some places but do not seem much happy. Q. Was it not wrong to drive them away and take their lands? A. It was and God will judge the white man for it. Q. May not some of the wars we have had, have been such judgments? A. Very likely.
—*Mrs. M. B. Moore*, The Geographical Reader for the Dixie Children.

The diary of Annie Jennings Wise Hobson:

January 24, 1864, Saturday. Eastwood.
A blessed peaceful Sabbath has closed upon me! A day wherein more than usual strength has been granted me to endeavor to serve God. I taught my own children and my two colored classes and had a pleasant afternoon meeting with some of the older servants. This morning I read Jones' *Suggestions* on the training of and instructions of our servants and am highly pleased by the whole book, though I think I do not entirely agree with him in some views or rather I go farther than he does. It aroused me to prayerful thought. I walked down to the quarters before beginning the instruction of the servants to inquire how Mr. Hicks was, and to speak a few words I thought might do some good to him. I am more deeply interested than ever and I trust more effectually aroused than heretofore in regard to the condition of the negroes, and our sins as a church and a people in not doing more for their spiritual and mental condition. Oh, will God permit me to be an instrument of good in so just a cause.

I reproach myself for having been so easily discouraged in my endeavors to instruct the older ones on the place. They would not attend and I succumbed before difficulties, but I am determined by the help of God to begin again, and implore zeal and perseverance for the future. I am so sure I am fully aware of the difficulties and discouragements in the way. I know I shall often be disheartened and wearied in the work— and yet I feel a sweet trust that the Spirit will not leave me to myself— and will not suffer me to turn long to the right hand or the left in the right path.

I thank God that amidst sins, infirmities, and failures in other respects, I was enabled to control my tongue and irritable temper. It is not pleasant to think of the past week as I managed my time so badly, as to accomplish very little. I was not idle or lazy, but mismanaged precious moments that ought to have been made more of.

Plumer went to Richmond Friday. I am always *alone* (in my earthly life) without him and cannot bear to come to my room at night when he is absent. As I looked out upon the calm beautiful moonlight just now, and felt the void made by his absence, I thought so pityingly of the sad hearts that moment thinking of their absent soldiers, undergoing hardship and exposed to danger and death! God comfort them! and oh my Father have compassion upon all widows! How my heart aches for the desolations and sufferings of this war weary land. God's mercy to all in this section of Country is great, for homes and lives are yet spared; but there is so much suffering amongst the poor! and many heavy hearts! My blessing are more than I can number!

One of the saddest sorrows of my heart is my husband's lukewarm state towards God. I wish I could make him understand the bitter anguish it causes me. I pray and wait, and wait and pray! Oh! I tremble over his procrastination. God will yet speak further to him by the stern voice of sad affliction. How it will come He only knows. I wait on the Lord!

I went to Mrs. Walkers s on Friday and was glad to find her better. Néné has gone to Richmond, so Mother and I have a quiet time in Plumer s absence. Mrs. Seddon came in and took [word missing, probably refers to a meal] with us yesterday evening. Major Reeder was here a few days sick with inflammatory rheumatism. We had him brought from the Mills.

My little ones are quite well now and I am getting over my bad cold which has deterred me for three weeks from attending to my housekeeping. I have been thankful to have Eliza's efficient services. I received a long letter from Sophie yesterday. She speaks of coming to see me.

February 7, 1864. Sunday. Eastwood.
Plumer is sleeping on the sofa in front of the fire. I am all ready for bed, the little ones soundly asleep long ago. I had quite a sharp attack yesterday morning of something like cramp colic, occasioned by fresh cold getting up with Henry the night before, he had a bad ear ache. I have consequently been confined to my room for two days, and am taking medicine tonight. I have had a quiet pleasant Sabbath tho' so unwell. Could only teach my little ones today, had to give up having my colored classes with me.

I have been reading Cummin's on the Signs of the Times with deep interest— tho' one may not agree with all his views, there is much to instruct, spiritualize and exalt in his writings. We will see next year how far his interpretation of prophecy for '64 will be verified. None of us went to church today, I being sick, Plumer quite unwell, and the weather very threatening, even raining. Willie Wise came up last evening and I was glad to hear thro' him (he went to Hebron with Mrs. Seddon) that Mr. Dudley had considered my proposition and has appointed a meeting at Mrs. Seddon's to organize a society amongst us for relief of the suffering soldiers and their families. May God prosper the undertaking.

Plumer returned from Richmond Wednesday bringing Sister Kittie and Brother John. They remained with us till Friday evening when they went home. We enjoyed their visit and wished they could have stayed longer. Selden was with them and is a noble boy. I do not forget them all in my prayers.

I have at last finished Motley's *Dutch Republic*— for recreation am just finishing "Kenilworth" a story of the same times. I have been much occupied lately and devoted little time to reading, far too little to religious reading and private devotion and have suffered thereby by failing often in patience and charity. I am much interested now in finishing a cloak and hood for Sister's baby. I shall have much to do in providing clothes for the children for some time to come. Oh merciful Father in all my undertakings let not my heart be set too much on the things of this world! I had a sweet pleasant letter from Jeannie Joynes yesterday, I am always glad to hear from her. I am sorely grieved about P.W. and will certainly write to him about his habits asking God to bless my warning appeal.

February 14, 1864. Sunday evening.
Another blessed Sabbath, when amidst sinning and striving, infirmities and failures, God has given me grace and strength to do something in his great work. I taught my children, read the Bible and a lecture of Cummins to Plumer and offered up my silent prayers for God to bless it to him. I had a dull headache when I had finished and felt sleepy and wearied, was enabled to resist the strong temptation of laying down, and went on a walk with Plumer and my precious little Cannon— felt tired and badly on my return but would not lie down till dinner was over. After dinner my headache became worse, and I was not as self-denying at table as I should have been. I laid down a while and Plumer would have a cup of coffee made for me. I drank it to please him but begged him not to tempt me again with a like indulgence, for we must all learn to do without such luxuries, sick or well. It refreshed me and relieved nervous depression tho' not the pain of my neuralgic head. I was just falling asleep when Eliza came to tell me the servants were waiting for me to read a prayer with them. I taught my colored children in the morning after my walk. I was about to send them word I was too unwell to be with them, but I could not bear to miss this duty even once, and made the effort to get up and go to them— And was rewarded for doing so by a pleasant meeting. God bless it to all! Tonight I read aloud to Mother, Willie Wise, and Plumer a lecture of Hamilton and felt greatly refreshed by it. His style is so beautiful and many of his thoughts fresh and novelly presented if not original. We all retire early to our rooms tonight. Friday, the ladies of the neighborhood met at Mrs. Seddon's and formed a society for the relief of soldiers and their families. I suggested the plan to Mr. Dudley and I feel so thankful he adopted it and has been able thus far to carry it out. God grant that it may be productive of good in more ways than one!

Plumer went to Richmond Thursday and returned yesterday evening. He took the little cloak and hood to Sister. We had an amusing alarm given us by Mr. Seddon's overseer over the escaped Yankee prisoners during his absence. The servants thought we were visited by a Yankee raid and were dreadfully frightened. I have been unwell all the week, but not altogether idle nor self indulgent, tho' I have done many things that had best been left undone, and neglected some that ought to have been attended. Merciful Father, help me for the coming week.

The Dahlgren Raid:

The diary of Annie Jennings Wise Hobson:

April 3, 1864. Sunday. Eastwood.
Over six weeks have elapsed since I last made any record of my inner and outer life. I have now to speak to God's praises, to tell of his mercies and loving kindnesses in events I little anticipated when I laughed over our Yankee fright and the negroes fear of a raid.

On Tuesday, March 1st, just as I had finished dressing, and before Plumer had arisen, as he was unwell that morning, I was told that a gentleman wished to see Mr. Hobson. I sent to inquire what his business was and received the reply that the Yankees were within three miles of Dover Mills. Father had arrived the Sunday evening before,

Eastwood. The home of Frederick Plumer Hobson Esq. Photo taken in 1896. In Henry Wise Hobson's hand-writing on the original photograph: "Where Union Cavalry came" [ridge, lower left]— "Where Gen. Wise departed" [gate foreground] "Grove much thinned out & stable all gone. They were to left of house where small buildings now show." House was built by the Hobsons, sold in 1880, and destroyed by fire in 1941. In 2006 a grove of oak trees, descended from those in the photo, silently stands where the house once stood.

having driven up in Dr. Garnett's buggy. We had expected him for several weeks. My first anxiety was for him and then for Plumer. Mr. Gathright of the Goochland Troop, who was at home on furlough, brought the unwelcome tidings. We were all soon assembled in the Library, Plumer having hurried on his clothes quicker than ever before. One woman's fears however couldn't hasten the gentlemen away as quickly as we desired. As Mr. Gathright said, the report brought to him declared the Yankees had been only three miles distant the night before, and while another party had crossed river at Mannikin ferry, they even doubted whether any were near, inferring if such had been the case they would have been upon us by that time. However, in about an hour they mounted their horses and as they were riding off the servants came rushing to me exclaiming: "Mr. Morson's yard is black with men."

I looked over there and it was too true and here came the blue coats straining their horses through Mrs. Seddon's field with our fugitives in full sight and at carbine range. The two Yankees soon dashed in the yard, demanding of Moses "who was those who rode across the field? Were they Gen. Wise and Mr. Hobson and which way did they take?" and then of Ephraim, "Where is the farm stable" Néné came rushing in to me: "Oh Sister Annie, Ephraim is pointing them the way Mr. Hobson and Papa have gone! He is riding the carriage horses after them! Do speak to him!" I rushed to the Library window to see them passing, a third Yankee having just joined them. Like a dunce I exclaimed— (saying the first thing that came to me) — "Ephraim you know you have told them a lie! You know you don't know where they have gone! If you dare show them which way they've taken now, they will shoot you for having already lied to them" I don't think any of them heard what I said— of course if they had, it would have convinced them I was anxious to keep them from taking that route. My uppermost thought was to detain them if only for one moment.

Ephraim was about to take the sorrel mare and carriage horse to the wood when they came up and they made him conduct them to the stable, stopping only for a moment while I called to Ephraim, and Néné demanded if they were Yankees. "Yes, indeed I am a Yankee" was the reply. "Well you look like one," said Néné. They hadn't time to stop for a parley! They rode to the farm stable, captured Mr. Hicks, dismounted and ran in to see if they could find fresh horses. Mr. Hicks protested he did not know who Father, Plumer and Mr. Gathright were. Ephraim says he told them Gen. Wise was in Charleston and his Master in Richmond, and those were some men who had been staying here. Two dashed off in pursuit. At the edge of the wood they came up with Nelson and Pleasants who were riding two brood mares off. They asked them: "Who are those two who have just gone ahead? Where are you going?" These two juveniles say "They didn't think they was Yankees. They thought they were our men—" "so just following Master and old Gen. Wise to the woods sar." Ephraim declared to them that these boys were so frightened they didn't know what they were talking about. They went out a little further and then returned. Whereupon they made Ephraim get his clothes, ride the carriage horse and lead the sorrel mare away with them.

Meanwhile Mr. Morson's steam barn and farm stables, outhouses etc., Mrs. Seddon's barn, stable, and corn houses and Dover Mills were in flames. I expected any moment to see our building fired, and my intensest [sic] anxiety was for Father's and Plumer's safety as Dr. Smith brought the report to me that they were surrounded on all sides and would be obliged to keep to the wood. Yet I was calm and quiet outwardly. The poor little children were so alarmed that I could not induce them to eat a mouthful of breakfast until twelve o'clock when the raiders had nearly all gone on towards Richmond, leaving us with the exception of Ephraim, the two boys with the brood mares, the sorrel mare and the carriage horse unharmed. One of the two men who returned with Ephraim went to the kitchen, demanded of the maids there assembled: "Ladies have you anything to eat for a poor fellow?" and carried off a loaf of bread and the rolls remaining in the kitchen from a hasty breakfast. He said if the "d—nd women would only be quiet and nothing was disturbed, we shouldn't be harmed." He stayed around the house a while keeping a kind of guard and finally went off. Little Annie informed her Father upon his return that one Yankee was very polite and well behaved— he did not take nothing, just asked, "Ladies can you give a poor fellow something to eat and gentlemen have you any more horses about here?" Having destroyed every vestige of food for man or beast at Mr. Morson's, (they mistook Dover for Dover Mills and Mr. Slaughter for Major, the gov. agent) and burned all the corn and forage at Mr. Seddon's, burned the mills at the canal and on Mr. Stanard's place, they contented themselves with carrying off all Dr. Walker's mules, horses and able bodied negro men, (burning or destroying nothing there, they left our neighborhood.

The ill-fated Dalhgren then led them in *to the surprise* of Richmond, not making much further delay, taking time however to hang Martin, the vile free negro who absconded to them with the escaped Yankee prisoners one fortnight before the raid, and who led them upon us, to his own wife's house at Dover through hog-paths and byways. They accused him of misinforming them as to a ferry at Mannikin where they were to cross on the glorious mission to liberate the prisoners of Belle Isle, turning them loose to sack Richmond. Martin was hung four or five miles below here. I will make no comment on Dalhgren, leaving him in the hands of Him to whom vengeance belongeth; in his dishonored grave.

Father and Plumer had gotten the start of the Yankees too far to be overtaken. They reached Richmond in time to give the first alarm of the approach of Dalhgren's column, which was received by Henley's battalion on the plank road to be turned back at nightfall by one volley. Father and Peyton Wise returned on horseback Wednesday afternoon. Plumer came up in the boat.

Thursday night we had the most terrifying alarm about two o'clock by Aleck's arousing me at my window: "*Miss Annie, Miss Annie— for God's sake make Mas' Plumer and Gen' Wise get up— For God's sake make haste.*" This was all I could get out of the frightened boy. I took it for granted that the house was surrounded. I sprang up in my night clothes, and rushed upstairs in the dark to arouse Father and Plumer and then ran for the loaded carbine pistols and rifles that stood ready in the house. On my return to my room we found that the whole alarm was occasioned by Mr. Smith, one of our pickets, bringing word that a report of the Yankees being at Bowles' store, six miles distant, had been brought to him. *Our soldiers*, with Plumer, at once accompanied him on a scout and were out till breakfast-time the next morning, to find no Yankees nor any foundation for the report. Peyton Wise stayed only a day or so with us. We were glad of even that little visit. We all dined at Mr. Stanard's the Saturday following the raid.

Father paid a business visit to Richmond of a few days and then spent the rest of the time quietly with us, returning to Charleston, or rather Adam's Run the next Wednesday week. He said he had never felt so unsafe during the war as up here, after the raid. He was looking better in health, happier, more cheerful, and equable than I have seen him for a long time. In one sense it seemed sad for his visit to be made so uncomfortable, so perturbed by the raid; and on the other hand, God gave us a new evidence of His watchful providence and mercy, an earnest of His future guardianship and loving mercy. Mother stood the excitement much better than I expected but has since suffered from the effects of it. Plumer and I went to Richmond before Easter giving me the happiness of Easter Sunday at St. James'— we heard Mr. Duncan preach at night. Plumer said I was so busy bettering the sermon that I could not get to sleep that night. The sermon was on repentance— except a man be born again etc. It was simply, emphatically, and earnestly delivered— powerful and fresh in thought, yet not as thoroughly thought or as well managed as I would have liked— minor points dwelt upon too long and the most important of all, the work of the Spirit, the influence of the Holy Ghost, dwelt upon last and least. I was so much interested and impressed by the talent of the preacher that I would like much to hear him again. I am sure he was not satisfied himself with that sermon. Sister and Dr. Garnett went with me to hear him. Oh, how I prayed that the subject might be brought home to the soul of our husbands! We returned home in a pouring rain storm the next Wednesday having left Richmond in the carriage with a threatening leaden sky above us. Néné was with us. We found that Mother, the children and servants had been greatly alarmed by the report of another raid the evening before. They had even sent the horses and mules to the wood. Mother is now suffering from the severest attack she has had for along time. Poor sufferer! I feel so much for her— She has been in bed over a week.

Plumer and I have been unwell ever since my return. He is better. I am still ailing though somewhat benefited by the physick [*sic*] I have taken. Yesterday I was too unwell to teach anyone but my own children their Bible lessons. Could not read or think much myself. I was confined to my room on the 8th fast day, but joined in spirit with the great soul— cry of my country to God in our dreadful time of need. I forgot to mention Pollie Hobson's visit. She stayed a week with me just before the raid.

April 17, 1864. Sunday.
I wish to record with solemn thankfulness the nearness to God, the feeling that came over me of being in the presence of a protecting God, and guardian Angels during the excitement of the raid. While watching from the Library window the flames from

Dover Mills and Mrs. Seddon's, I sat with the Bible in my hand, reading such blessed promises as these. "The eternal God is thy refuge; and underneath are the everlasting arms." Deut 33rd. "He is the defender of all those who put their trust in Him." "The Lord is good, a stronghold in the day of trouble, and knoweth them that trust in Him." Nahum 1st 7th v.

    I was settled into a calm of trust that amidst danger and alarm gave me sublime happiness. I felt as one might do at sea amidst a fearful tempest when man could do nothing, and God alone could save. I knew that God would give me strength according to my need, that the Lord would provide no matter what happened. I endeavored to impress a lesson of solemn trust upon my little ones— tried to make them realize that God is the only sure Helper and Deliverer. There is a sweet reverence in Cannon, and a spirit of trust that is very sweet and encouraging to me. The little ones kneeled around me and prayed; but it was mid-day before I could quiet their fears and excitement enough to make them eat anything. When all the danger was past, and we were left in our comfortable home with food and buildings untouched, was it a fantastical belief in me, to feel assured my trust had been fulfilled. God had been true to his promises, and that we were spared so signally by a merciful providence. God knows it was not! I never trusted Him in vain! We have lost nothing except three horses. The negroes have returned disgusted with Yankee experiences. The dear negro lovers who came to set the captives free; robbed Ephraim of his clothes, saddle-bags and watch. This with the hanging of Martin and the occurrences of a kindred nature have taught the negroes some good lessons. How I entreat God to give wisdom to both Master and servant.

    And now in view of all that may happen in these times of desolation and trouble, I have only to say— Thou art my hiding place; thou shalt preserve me from trouble; thou shalt compass me about the songs of deliverance. Ps 33 7th v.

Prayer for family worship after the raid:
We return unto Thee, o most merciful Father, earnest and humble thanks for having delivered us from the dangers and alarms by which we have been surrounded. Through Thy merciful protection our homes, comforts and the lives of all are still spared to us. Our Father, we are not worthy of such loving kindness and watchful providence, for our sins are many and cry out daily against us! Nevertheless sinful and erring as we are, our only dependence and sure trust is in Thee! Grant us the constant assistance of thy Grace to dedicate our lives more earnestly and effectually than heretofore to Thy service, loving Thee with a supreme love, and looking to Jesus as the Alpha and Omega of our faith. Give us above all the gifts of the Holy Spirit a cheerful willingness to suffer Thy will in all things, relying upon Thy sure word of promise and instruction for light, encouragement, and strength. Hear this prayer for our Savior's sake. Amen.

Prayer for family worship in regard to the war:
We beseech Thee to continue Thy aid and compassion to our nation in our fearful struggle for liberty and national life. Thou hast sustained us in many a bloody battle and amid weakness and terrible danger teaching our enemies that the battle is not always to the strong, nor the race to the swift, and yet Thou hast laid Thy hand heavily upon us in many afflictive circumstances! While saying "Thy will be done" may we as a people learn all the lessons thy punishments are meant to teach us, with hearts and minds content and ready for amendment. Pity and secure the sick, wounded and dying, all who are afflicted in mind body or estate. Grant unto our Rulers, Generals, and Counsellors a spirit of wisdom and discretion; to our whole army courage and fortitude. Pour out Thy Spirit abundantly upon our whole land enabling us to show the

world that Thou art our Defender and Savior. Forsake us not as a nation for one single day! Put a stop to all profaneness, vice, irreligion, and impiety amongst us! Give unto our enemies better minds, and to use in Thy own good time, success and peace. We ask these blessings in the name of our Lord and Savior, Jesus Christ. Amen.

◦ *A War-Time Aurora Borealis*, by Ellen Wise Mayo:

In the winter of 1863–1864, I was in Richmond, a girl of nineteen. Our home near Norfolk [Rolleston] had been evacuated in 1862. After that, the females of our household, myself included, led a very uncertain sort of existence so far as our domicile was concerned. With our home in possession of the enemy; with father and brothers in active service; unable to foresee what a week or a month might bring forth, we had no settled plans; and I lived, first with one married sister, then another, awaiting the culmination of affairs.

Of course, the war was horrible. Horrible in so many ways that I dare not trust myself to enter upon any detail in regard to it. I cannot, however, pass the subject by without candidly confessing, that during the war there were many delightful social episodes in Richmond for young people, nothwithstanding the fact that we were half starved, utterly ragged, and from time to time racked with anxieties of all kinds.

Even as late as the time of which I write, the home (Eastwood) of my married sister in Goochland County, about twenty miles above the city, and the neighborhood thereabouts, was less changed than almost any place in the Confederacy. The people of the vicinage were wealthy, and had taken the precaution to lay in supplies of household comforts which lasted them long after the current prices of such things excluded all idea of purchasing them for daily consumption.

In January, 1864, my father, a general in the Confederate service, after a long absence, announced his coming on furlough from Charleston; and it was arranged that I should accompany him to Goochland, whither my mother had preceded us, to spend with him, among the charms of Goochland, his well-earned, brief recreation.

MRS. MAYO IN 1864.

Years after the Dahlgren Raid, Ellen Wise Mayo, Annie Jennings Wise Hobson's sister, wrote an account of that incident that was published in *Cosmopolitan* in June 1896. Portions of the article were reprinted in *The Life of Henry A. Wise of Virginia* by Barton H. Wise in 1899. The entire article and its accompanying illustrations are reprinted here.

The Packet and a low bridge, from "A War-Time Aurora Borealis" by Ellen Wise Mayo, Cosmopolitan, June 1896. Vol. XXI, No. 2. Illustrations by John Linton Chapman.

Drawn by John Linton Chapman.

The Packet along the canal.

In due time he arrived in Richmond, and our plans for the Goochland trip, which was to be accomplished by canal, were perfected at once.

It was with joyous hearts and great expectations that we started on our journey. The trip itself was so unique, and the upshot of our excursion was so contrary to anything anticipated, that the following sketch may amuse and interest the reader of today:

George Washington, besides being father of his country, was the father of the James river and Kanawha canal. He was its head; Richmond its terminus. The mode of travel on that canal was something astonishing. A ditch filled with slimy water, snakes, and bullfrogs, and fringed along its backs with lily pads and weeping willows, furnished the water-way for a boat, called The Packet, built very much upon the plan of Noah's Ark. A piece of rope, three damaged horses driven tandem, a negro, and a tin horn, were the accessories, any one of which failing, caused the trip on the Packet to be suspended or delayed until these necessary paraphernalia were provided. The general direction of the canal was parallel with the river. It wound about the base of the hills, between which and the river lay the valley of the James. The tow-path was on the embankment of the canal, on the lowland side.

At five o'clock in the afternoon, the good ship which was to bear us to Goochland, departed from the packet office in Richmond. Its speed may be calculated from the following data: starting time, already given; distance traversed twenty miles; destination reached at ten thirty P.M.

That boat was a curiosity. It was a shell divided into four main compartments. The forward and largest compartment was for passengers; behind it was a kitchen, then a compartment for servants, and lastly, the captain's room in the stern. The passenger's cabin was divided by a curtain drawn across it forward, beyond which, extending into the bows, was the ladies compartment. Where people were to sleep in such a place was the first problem presented upon entering the cabin. It was an open space, with nothing but long benches or lockers on either side, a table running down the center, a stove, and a few primitive stools. On either side of the boat were many windows. When the sleeping berths were adjusted, as hereafter described, they varied in desirability, according to their location with reference to the floor or the red-hot stove. The freight and baggage were on the deck above the heads of the passengers. The deck, even in winter, was preferable to the stuffy cabin. The terrors of such a trip were mitigated by the beautiful scenery through which the lazy outfit wound its way.

The weather, even in February, was very pleasant: and the young folk and the soldiers, of whom there were a number on board, contented themselves until darkness came on, with seats upon the trunks, bags, and barrels upon the deck, passing away the time in conversation, or in watching the ever-varying and most attractive landscape. Even this poor privilege was not without its accompanying danger, for the canal was spanned by many bridges, which were the only method of ingress and egress from the hills to the low-grounds. These bridges were so low that the passengers were constantly warned by the helmsman's cry of "Low bree-g-e!" and compelled to squat very low to avoid being scraped off the deck. The situation was always ludicrous, and the accidents resulting from these low bridges were numerous, sometimes serious, but oftener absurd. Old Aunt Dinah, servant of a friend of ours, was on one occasion caught unawares by a low bridge and deposited feet downward in the water, dressed in the latest style of the day, which was providentially a hoop-skirt. Her whoops were strong, but her hoops were stronger. The former exhausted, but the latter retained the air, and she floated gaily to the shore unharmed save from fright and foot-washing.

At bedtime stout leather straps were produced and hooked to the ceiling and the floor. Between these, by ingenious arrangements, were stretched at intervals canvass hammocks. From the lockers under the benches on each side, beds and bed-clothing were produced and placed upon the hammocks and the tables. By the time the beds were down there was scarcely space for any one to turn himself around between them. It was something not only wonderful but fearful. Fearful in every sense and to every sense. In those days boots were boots, and as each man undressed he had a distinct understanding with his neighbor as to his rights of tenure. When these boots got mixed up there was trouble. A comb and brush, fastened by chains to keep them from falling overboard, and a tin basis similarly guarded, were attached to the side of the boat on a little gangway between the kitchen and the cabin. These were the toilet facilities for the entire ship's company. Even this liberality was not always appreciated, for it was reported that, on one occasion, M. Claude Pardigon, a French knight-errant battling for the Confederacy, challenged the captain to mortal combat because he had furnished no tooth-brush for his guests.

In the female compartment there was great ceremony. The older ladies and nursing mothers were given the preference. Ladies from the Ridge country would make elaborate toilets, in order to display night-gown yokes and petticoats they had spent months in embroidering. One possessed of a vine-embroidered gown could always get a lower berth.

All things must have an end, and so after we had passed Walker's bridge and Stannard's low-bridge, the last horn blew for us; the tow-line slacked; the fiery steeds stood panting on the tow-path, and the boat sidled proudly up to the granite coping of Dover Mills, our destination. A large pole with a hook in the end caught in some well-known spot and steadied the combination sufficiently for us to make a landing.

Groping our way, by the aid of a feeble lantern, along a narrow footway on the top of the great arch where a stream passed under the canal, and gaining at last the open ground, we felt the infinite relief one always experiences upon reaching terra firma after a perilous voyage by water.

The carriage from Eastwood was awaiting us. The lights from the country store glinted on the vehicle, its harness and trappings, and the horses, chilled by the nipping air, pranced and fretted in the darkness, impatient to be off. It was but a moment's wait for the newly arrived mail, and then our host entering the carriage with us, the team, handled by 'Ephraim,' a famous driver, sprung away under his master hand, wheeling us at an exhilarating gait to the Hobson homestead. Along the public road beside the canal, through Eastwood's outer gate, up the long hill to the highlands, past the tobacco barns, we sped, until at last we caught sight of the homestead, all its windows ablaze with loving welcome, looming up in its grove of oaks, half a mile away.

One may fancy what the feelings of my father were at such a time.

For the past three years he had been in active service in the field; first in West Virginia, then at Roanoke Island, where he lost his first-born son; afterward on the Virginia Peninsula; and, finally, at Charleston, South Carolina. At last, with his furlough, the prospect of a short period of peace and domestic quiet seemed fairly to open up to him.

Mr. Plumer Hobson, our host and his son-in-law, had been prevented by ill health from entering the army. His inability to volunteer was a great mortification and distress to him. As if to make up, in another form, for the military service he could not render, he devoted himself and his means throughout the war in every way possible to charity and hospitality. It was, therefore, with peculiar satisfaction that he greeted us now, showing by every means in his power his desire to make our visit as happy as possible.

We noticed, as we drove along in the starlit night, that the northern sky was aflame with what we all supposed to be the Aurora Borealis; but our thoughts were too much concentrated upon the lights blinking at us from the Eastwood grove to pay much attention to the lights in the heavens. Wide apart flew the yard gates for us as we reached them; and wider still the great doors of the mansion house, as the wheels ceased their grinding in the gravel before the house. Joyous faces peered out into the night. Merry, happy greetings met us on the threshold. Within, the warmth of great wood fires, and the good cheer of a delicious supper, banished from our party every thought of war.

What a feast it was! Coffee from Mrs. Seddon's; sugar from Mrs. Stanard's; sorghum from somebody else. The cook had made the biscuits so light that they almost flew out of the plates; and the cow, in honor of our coming, had given down nothing but cream. The good old general, as he looked over this array of luxuries, bade good-by, for a time at least, to camp life, tin plates, canteens, Nassau bacon, sweet-potato, coffee, rice, 'Hoppin' John' and 'Hoppin'-Jinny,' 'cush,' and all the horrible makeshifts of food he had endured for months at the front.

If I enjoyed the snowy pillows awaiting, what must he have felt? For the first time in many months he tucked himself away, at midnight, in a Christian bed, with linen, lavender-scented sheets, and warm, soft blankets, to dream of days gone by, when, at his own home by the sea, in time of peace, with oysters, terrapin, and canvasbacks for the feast, judges and statesmen and even presidents had been his guests. He sank to rest, in fancy hearing the sound of the salt waves at his home, and the sighing of the winds through the seaside pines. I, happy and contented beyond expression, lost consciousness wondering what we would have for breakfast.

Before us all stretched a vista of thirty days of peace! No matter what might be beyond.

I dreamed. For a long time I glided upon smooth waters, watching ever-changing landscapes of beauty. I was not on the canal nor on the canal-boat. It was a beautiful lake, a painted boat with snowy sails, and I was accompanied by gay companions and merry music. Then of a sudden the scene changed. I was back on the miserable packet. It was dark. I was in the stuffy cabin. A fearful thumping was overhead. A drunken man on deck was trying to burst open my trunk and throw it overboard. I awoke. The pounding continued. It was some beating on the oaken doors of the house and loudly calling for the general. Dressing hurriedly, the family was soon collected in the hallway listening with bated breath. A soldier of the general's command had come up with us on furlough. His home was some miles beyond us in the back country. He had ridden thither and solved the mystery of the Aurora Borealis; for right around his home he had come upon the bivouac of the raiding party of Dahlgren. Even as he sped back to warn us he had heard 'boots and saddles' sounded. He had ridden rapidly to tell his dear old general of the danger; and, at the moment he was speaking, the enemy, according to all reasonable calculation, was coming on the same road by which he had arrived, and not over two or three miles behind him.

The news chilled every heart among us with the sense of imminent peril. The ashes on the hearth, where last night's revelry was held, lay dead. Our dream of peace and rest was over. The dogs of war were once more baying on the hot scent, and we were the quarry pursued. If the men escaped with their lives, they would be lucky. The women and children, in another hour, would be defenceless, at the mercy of ignorant slaves and hostile soldiery.

There was hurrying for the stables. In an incredibly short time 'Pulaski,' the blind war-horse of the general's dead son, and 'Lucy Washington,' Mr. Hobson's thoroughbred riding-mare, were at the door. They were not a moment too soon. But for an episode they would have been too late. The two plantations adjoining ours on the west were owned by Mr. James M. Morson and Hon. James A. Seddon, Secretary of War. Dahlgren's original purpose is said to have been to cross the James River at either Jude's Ferry, which was on the Morson place just above, or at Mannakin Ferry, three miles below us, and to approach Richmond by the south bank of the James. Whether it was or not, his force entered the Morson and Seddon plantations instead of coming straight on to Eastwood, and there lost considerable time firing buildings and appropriating horses.

Mr. Seddon's house was in full view, not a third of a mile away. It was by this time broad daylight, and from the portico where I stood, the troopers of Dahlgren were plainly visible, galloping about the stables and barns and setting fire to the buildings, the smoke from which already began to rise.

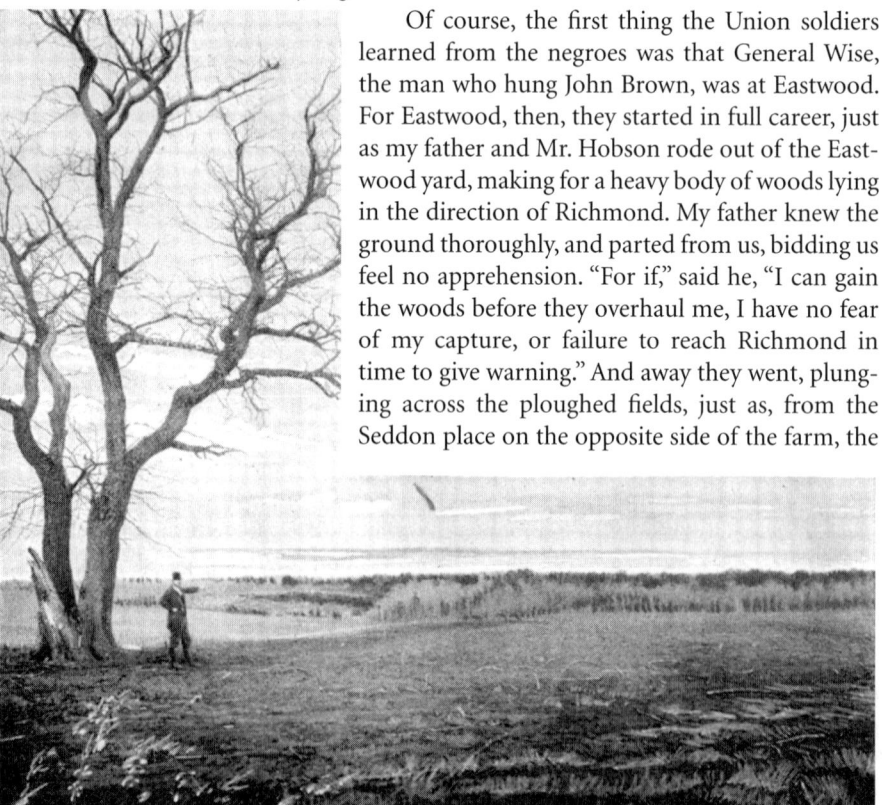

Of course, the first thing the Union soldiers learned from the negroes was that General Wise, the man who hung John Brown, was at Eastwood. For Eastwood, then, they started in full career, just as my father and Mr. Hobson rode out of the Eastwood yard, making for a heavy body of woods lying in the direction of Richmond. My father knew the ground thoroughly, and parted from us, bidding us feel no apprehension. "For if," said he, "I can gain the woods before they overhaul me, I have no fear of my capture, or failure to reach Richmond in time to give warning." And away they went, plunging across the ploughed fields, just as, from the Seddon place on the opposite side of the farm, the

Field across which Mr. Hobson and General Wise rode.

The Escape.

enemy's troopers came galloping, hundreds of them, flying like birds, it seemed to me, —fences and closed gates offering no obstacle to their headlong rush.

"Have no fear," father had said, as he rode away. Oh, no. Of course, I had none! There I stood, almost frantic, as a Union soldier dashed up, with drawn revolver, and demanded to know where the man was who hung John Brown. I can see him as plainly now as then: his flea-bitten gray horse, his McClellan saddle, his very expression as he sat there sidewise, talking so insultingly. I see the flashing eye and hear the voice commanding me to tell the truth. I clutched on the child beside me, and even as I spoke I could see out of the corner of my eye, over the trees which concealed him from the trooper, my father disappearing in the woods. I declared most solemnly (God forgive me) that my father was in Charleston, South Carolina. Anxiety and excitement excluded fear of God or man. As a reward, I was informed that I lied, the trooper adding that he would capture him if he had to chase him to ——. "Take your—— white head into the house," he said, threateningly, and I gladly accepted his invitation. From the upper windows I beheld the handsome barns of Dover and Sabot Hill in flames. About the stables the troopers were shifting saddles from their own jaded horses to Mr. Hobson's animals. Ephraim, inflamed with liquor, was marched hither and thither under cover of pistols and required to deliver everything under his care; and poor "Bob," who had been working on fortifications about Richmond, when asked about them, exclaimed, "Lawd, master! Dey is a hundred and forty-fications aroun' dat place."

An Ungentle Cavalryman.

Their stay with us was short. They took all our horses, Ephraim and several other slaves; but, on the whole, we fared much better than our neighbors. Nothing at Eastwood was burned; and after the raiding party went to pieces below Richmond, most of the horses were recovered.

Poor father, with his knowledge of the topography of the country, had no trouble in reaching Richmond, by shorter routes than and far in advance of the Dahlgren party.

Going directly to the War Department, he with great difficulty convinced Secretary Seddon of the real situation. The Department had no warning whatever of the raid, and Mr. Seddon seemed utterly incredulous at first. But once convinced, the local reserves under Colonel McAnery was called out and met and repulsed Dahlgren about five miles above Richmond. The collision took place about dusk. The cavalry charging the infantry line failed to observe an old ice-house in their front. Into this a man on a flea-bitten gray horse plunged headlong. I have never ascertained definitely whether he was the gentleman I met that morning still pursuing my father in the direction then indicated. Between our place and Richmond was Mannakintown, with an important coal-pits, ironworks, and a ferry. Opinions differ as to whether Jude's Ferry or Mannakin Ferry was the original objective point of Dahlgren. He crossed the river at neither place, but held to the north bank.

The fate of the raid is known, and I will not repeat it. The orders found on Dahlgren's body have gone into our historical archives. The bitterness of those days has passed away.

Two days after the visit of Dahlgren, father and Mr. Hobson came ambling quietly through the farm from the direction of Richmond, rising in their stirrups now and then to observe carefully what the angry little war-cloud had swept away in its passage; and, as the dear old fellow resumed the enjoyment of his interrupted furlough, with a merry allusion to his narrow escape, we all felt grateful to God that it was no worse, and that we were left unharmed.

After that we were suspicious of Northern Lights. If this story has one moral it has two, viz.:

First. Even a canal-boat can carry you fast enough toward the enemy; and,

Second. In war times, never shut both eyes when you retire, until you have solved the problem of the Aurora Borealis.

~

The diary of Annie Jennings Wise Hobson:

May 29, 1864. Sunday evening. Eastwood.
My last date was April 17th, and truly in these last five weeks "God has been my hiding place. He has preserved me from trouble." He has "Compassed me about with songs of deliverance." Terrible battles have occurred between Lee and Grant, God giving us always the balance of victory, tho' permitting no decided blow to be struck. Beauregard has driven Butler to his gunboats. Father's brigade was recalled from S. C. and covered itself with glory. Our loved ones are safe except poor Willie Wise who had his foot shot off and bore it bravely, and Aunt Margaret's George is wounded. We have been spared another raid though rumors of one reached us constantly.

October 3, 1864. Monday. Eastwood.
Four months of trial, danger, and sickness on the one hand, on the other, encouragement, strength according to the need, loving kindness, tender guiding and wonderful deliverance by the "All Father's" watchful love.

Four months since I have made even an effort to record aught in my journal! From the first of April until very recently I never knew a well day. On the 10th of July, Sunday afternoon, God gave me another little boy. [A second son named F. Plumer Hobson.]

Aunt Margaret Margaret Wise, sister of Henry Alexander Wise and widow of Tully R. Wise, a cousin. George Wise, their son, was captured and then escaped at Vicksburg and later was "desperately" wounded at Resaca, Georgia, May 15–17, 1864. He did survive the war.

The evening before Plumer had a hemorrhage. On Tuesday my baby became very ill. Plumer had a fresh spitting of blood, and the alarm consequent on both made me ill. For several days we were all in a critical condition, and from that time until the last fortnight all three have been more or less sick. During the battles of the Wilderness in May I had fearful alarms of another raid twice. Indeed we had two weeks of intense excitement, of painful anxiety, stilled only by trust in God. George Wise has passed away, having been wounded in the head shortly after the 29th of May [Battle of Petersburg]. His death has been a painful shock to me. I loved him very dearly, and it grieves me sorely that he should have died without uttering one word to show he had made his peace with God. While I was so ill God called Cousin Sallie to her rest in Columbia, S. C. I would not have her back to her suffering life, but I wish I could have seen her once more— have made her comfortable in my own home, but God knew best. His will be done! Aunt Margaret and George paid me a visit some weeks ago. George had just recovered from his dangerous wound received in Georgia. Peyton also spent many weeks with us recuperating from his wound in the arm received at the same time that George had his death blow. Ma and Pa came just after Aunt M— left, then Martha and Mildred and then Father stayed with us ten days— and now I am preparing for a trip to Richmond.

November 6, 1864. Sunday.
We have been to Richmond and returned. We stayed a little over a fortnight and reached home last Tuesday. Plumer and the baby improved greatly. Mr. Peterkin baptized the latter the Sunday after we reached town. I felt much encouraged about my precious husband and thanked God devoutly for it! Since my return Plumer has had another slight hemorrhage— the 3rd one since his first attack. It has been slight but it keeps up anxiety.

Oh! my God, have I not trusted in Thee in this trouble! Do I not wait upon Thee now! Who knoweth my heart's bitterness but my God! O Lord have mercy upon me! God is my witness that my chief anxiety is for his spiritual welfare. I know that my Father lays his Hand upon him in sickness saying "In the hour of adversity consider!" Yet, my Beloved makes no outward confession of sin and repentance, and tho' he still prays, and reads God's word, he makes no acknowledgment of greater nearness to God. O my Father may thy will be done by both of us— May we be one in Christ!

Today for the first time since my illness I taught the negro children and commenced regular duties. May God help me for the coming week and look with favor on the efforts of the day.

November 12, 1864. Saturday night. Eastwood.
The week has passed, and I review with sad heart its failures and sins. I have accomplished little or nothing in household matters or work for the children— several letters I have proposed to write are unwritten, and for two days I did not teach the children. I rise late and go to bed early— something like a torpor has taken possession of my mental and bodily energy. I know there is cause for it. My nervous system has been a good deal exhausted by months of sickness, watching, and nursing. I hardly ever get a night's rest without being much disturbed, and above all the cloud of my precious Husband's sickness hangs over me. Every and any new symptom fills me with sickening anxiety— the disease is so insidious! Yet have I the right to yield to my feelings, to lead a self-indulgent life? Ought I not to strive for the mastery "in all things relying upon God for strength and help"— Oh my Father forgive the past and lead me in the right way for the future. Henry came up very unexpectedly last evening— he looks so well and it is so

George Wise has passed away George Douglas Wise, son of John J. Wise and Harriet Wilkins Wise and cousin of Annie Jennings Wise Hobson, died at Petersburg.

pleasant to have him. May God bless the following resolutions for tomorrow—

I will rise between [originally written "*7 and 8*" but that is crossed out] 6 and 7 o'clock, be dressed at 1/2 seven, reading the scriptures and prayer, hear the children's prayers and catechism, breakfast, attend to Plumer and household matters, teach some of the colored children before breakfast, and my own little ones. Read over the service and some good sermon or religious reading. I will strive to banish all worldly thoughts and to fix my mind on things eternal and heavenly. May the Holy Spirit enable me to be charitable in thought, mind, and deed and truly self-denying. Grant me especially patience in all things.

Dear Peyton Peyton Wise, a cousin, wounded at Petersburg, captured November 1864, exchanged 1865, and later present at Appomattox.

Dear Peyton is captured! How it pains me to think of him in his prison cell each night as I lie down in my comfortable bed. Oh, God pity us in this cruel war!

November 14, 1864. Monday. Eastwood.
Two days have passed since my earnest resolution for better things, for greater striving with weakness of the flesh, greater endeavors to accomplish more. Alas! I have attained nothing! I have risen for two mornings *after seven*, and have done pretty well in the morning but I become wearied, paralyzed in mind and body so soon. I must try to do better. God help me! Plumer is better, but I am afraid to hope about him. Henry surprised us by coming up Saturday night. We had a pleasant visit from him; he left this morning; and an hour afterwards Father rode up. He is looking well and is cheerful.

December 11, 1864. Sunday.
I have been reading, with Scott's notes, 26 c. of Isaiah. All my reading of the Scriptures confirms me in my blessed trust in God as the cover from the storm of these troubled days to each individual who makes Jehovah his everlasting strength; whose mind is stayed on God. Thou wilt keep him in perfect peace whose mind is stayed on Thee because he trusteth in Thee. How strange that our Father's children are so slow in availing themselves personally of the right gift of promises He has lavished upon them. Each promise has a personal meaning and application for every follower of God who will take hold of it. Because He trusteth in God each believer is to be kept in perfect peace. What does God mean by the *trust* that brings peace? Oh! how I love that word, *trust*! I understand just this by it— I must go on day by day in the path I believe God wills me to tread striving to do and enjoy duty, to live the life of *present* endurance, fulfillment, enjoyment, or sorrow that seems assigned me by God with the loving spirit of a meek and earnest child, rejoicing to do and suffer my Father's will, and not only content but happy in leaving the future entirely in His hands as far as anxiety, foreboding, and carefulness is concerned.

I must accept each day's blessings with *enjoyment* to realize them as blessings. I must find out the *pleasure* of duties that demand my time and attention if I would do them in the best way and learn to soften or ameliorate what is unpleasant, fatiguingly [*sic*] laborious, and distasteful in them. While I provide for the future according to reason's dictates as far as I can, I must leave the result to God. I must sow many seed with cheerfulness, rake and tend them carefully, trusting God for the produce. Above all, whatever the present brings me, I must inscribe upon [it] "it is well— the best" if I feel sure it comes by God's will, by no wrong doing of my own. Even then if I learn the lesson meant it will be well— the punishment sent will "be and all the best is God's will?" Often when I realize the comforts of my luxurious home and am tempted to anxiety, lest it be taken from me, I say to anxiety— "Enjoy God's gift in the present. Use it, don't abuse it. If He sees fit to take it as thy day, so shall thy strength be." I pray most earnestly to be kept from self indulgence, to be enlightened by Holy Spirit as to what are the peculiar duties of self denial. God means that I should practice "Anxious less to please Thee much than to please Thee perfectly" I repeat often to myself— but at the same time I pray to be delivered from all the blindness of heart. God help me. I am weak! and yet I have such happiness in the Divine Son.

❦ A letter from Annie Jennings Wise Hobson:

Eastwood. March 28th, 1865.
My dear Mother—   …You may see that I have been "rampaging" since my return, & have many irons in the fire. I have given the children holiday till Anne Jones comes, (Peyton will bring her up Monday), & they are enjoying it intensely. I assure you I feel greatly relieved! Henry & Cannon have been fishing extensively in the branch & have just had a snack of fried minnows. By the by, Mrs. Walker insists that they are as good as sardines if properly dressed… Plumer has been out all the morning— but you may be sure he joins me in love. It would do you good to see how he improves… Write when you can, but I shall always understand your silence. Give my warmest love to Eliza— and tell her I shall want her often. May the Comforter abide with you always, dear Mother, imparting all needed consolation & strength. I will write as often as I can.   —Your affect. daughter, *A. J. W. Hobson.*
Anne Eliza helps in the laundry and will be very useful about sewing. She has made her clothes.

❦ The diary of Annie Jennings Wise Hobson:

April 2, 1865. Sunday. Eastwood.
I can scarcely realize that four months and a half has passed since my last record in my journal! I come again with a long story of deliverance, loving kindness, and tender love from our Heavenly Father. A few words can give the events more important to me that have occurred since my last record. I was extremely busy until we went to Richmond the last week in January, getting through the backward work with the children and servants' clothes, preparing for my intended visit to Richmond. I can say with humble thankfulness, that sickness and sorrow have been so sanctified to me that I worked industriously even these duties and household matters without my usual Martha like spirit of over-carefulness, and was greatly aided in keeping a serene temper. Plumer continued to improve till we went down. We had a quiet Xmas, my pleasure being as usual to endeavor to make the children and servants a happy season. Father was with us and Pardigan came when the holidays were about half over. Monday of Xmas week the two brides, Mrs. Wight and Mrs. Trout, with their newly found Lords, dined with us. Sophie came the last of the week. She remained with us till we left for Richmond and accompanied us there. She was most unkind in aiding me with my work for the children. She strives earnestly to be unselfish. I believe she loves me with earnest devotion, and I return it— but she tries me sorely in some things and none-the-less because I do not think it wise to tell her so fully. May God give her light and wisdom in her dark blindness.

    Mother was quite sick for some time before we left. I am sorry now I did not make a greater exertion to be with her often, but I tried to do my best, and I had so much to occupy me! I don't know either that considering all things it would have done any good. She left with Eliza for Richmond just before we did, and is now in Halifax with Henry. We stayed with Mary Lyons when we first went to town for three weeks

Mother Mary Lyons Wise, third wife of Henry Alexander Wise.
Mary Lyons Mary Hobson Lyons, sister of Plumer Hobson and wife of Judge William H. Lyons.

and were most kindly received and entertained. Plumer became decidedly worse while there owing in part to the foul state of the gas and in part to cold. I felt greatly troubled about him, and that, just at a time when a dark gloom pervaded Richmond in regard to the issues of the war. Just about the time the peace commissioners went to Fort Monroe and afterwards I spent three days of anguish of mind, and then had strength given me to "trust in the Lord with all my heart" leaving results to Him with the blessed acquiescence "Thy will be done." I really feared for some time that Plumer was becoming alarmingly worse. Thank God he became better after having a slight hemorrhage and has improved steadily ever since— is now better than he has been since his illness. We went to Pa's after our visit to Mary. All were as kind to us as possible and we had every comfort. Pollie was there and I am so glad to see more of her and to learn [illegible] her naturally excellent nature more justice than I have ever done before. She is seriously striving to walk with God— to learn His will. Poor young widow— with all her abundance and strong brave spirit, her lot is desolate! I enjoyed the Lenten services and all the privileges of the Sanctuary greatly— especially Dr. Minnegarode's happily conducted morning services, and I miss them now. I went to see many friends I had not seen in a long time.

I leave to the last the most important event of all— the Sheridan raid upon the Canal! I recorded a year ago tomorrow our signal deliverance from the Dahlgren raiders; and now blessed be God! I have another tale of wonderful protection to record. About a fortnight ago, Sheridan with some eight thousand cavalry, having routed Early, poured into the Canal from the valley, visiting nearly all the places in the Canal to General Anderson's within five miles of us. They went to Brother John's and Pollie's, taking from Kittie six men and all her mules, and some provisions from Pollie. When they came within four miles of us they became alarmed from an account of a force we had below, and turned back. This is the third deliverance of our neighborhood. Our Father grant unto us grace to let our lives and show forth Thy praise! Make me be more charitable, hospitable and unselfish than ever!

My great sorrow is that Plumer still remains in the same lukewarm state! I had hoped so sanguinely that he would unite himself with God's people before we left Richmond! My Father, hear my cry for his soul! I took my two manuscripts to Mr. Peterkin and sent him yesterday my letter to the S. C. I am waiting the result. My children were so well all during my stay in Richmond and my little baby improves daily and is a great joy to me. I am thankful to have engaged Anne Jones as a teacher for the children. I believe God directed me in this— must not decide however till results prove it. Mr. Dudley had Communion service today. I taught my smallest colored children.

my two manuscripts It is not known what this refers to.

April 9, 1865. Sunday.
This day week we went to church quietly, anxiously yet calmly with firm trust in God. We were awaiting the result of the battle pending around Richmond. How little we thought the fate of our beloved city was sealed. The battle came off, lines were broken, our men fought with desperate bravery, but we were too far outnumbered, and to save his army, Lee's men withdrew from fortifications and Richmond was evacuated. No one dreamed of such a result until after church Sunday.

Monday morning, just as we were about to get up, Major Reeder knocked at the door of the hall. He had come to tell us the dreadful news and to say goodbye. We are now left in Yankee lines. There are only four negro men on the place, and they will probably not be here long. The results of years might not have changed life as much as these six days have done. My god! What have I suffered, what do I not still suffer.

We can hear nothing from our brave army that is reliable. We hear of desertions in every direction! We were told by one who would not call himself a deserter he had been one who had given up, that Gen. Lee's forces are surrounded on all sides, that he had whipt [sic] the enemy repeatedly, cutting his way through, but I believe nothing I hear now. I have put the cause from the beginning until now into God's hands. All I ask is perfect submission to His Will, that all may be sanctified to us as a nation. I still trust that it may be God's will to give us our independence. I have always thought we might be brought to the last straits before we could obtain it— and that God would give it in such a way that we would be obliged to give him all the glory. I told those in Richmond who seemed to think that Richmond meant the South, that I feared God would permit Richmond to fall to show that He could save us without it, would vindicate His power to the faithless Southerners as well as to the proud and boastful North!

Thus far we have been most wonderfully preserved as a family and a neighborhood. The country is full of poor deluded negroes crazed by the idea of freedom and deserters; yet we sleep in peace and safety and are undisturbed all day. We have plenty to last us in the way of provisions and clothes for a long time. The enemy has not yet visited us and we hear that private property is to be respected everywhere. Every member of my own family is a sufferer by this event. My dear Sister is left in Richmond, her husband having gone to the army. Mother is in Halifax without any means of support and Henry is not able to support her. Aunt Margaret is in Richmond without any [illegible] hunger. Oh I am greatly humbled, humanly speaking greatly perplexed, but thanks be to God I do not lose my hold on Him. I trust His mercy (undeserved as it is) for us all. It seems so strange the quiet, we get on about the house doing our duty— Prayer and constant occupation keeps me from agonizing anxiety and painful thought. The agony of the thought of our brave veterans laying down their arms before our insolent enemy is the greatest trial I ever had! God help them! God helps me and mine. Oh, I know now who of my loved ones are lying cold and dead on the battlefield, or are wounded and dying. My God have mercy upon them! Above all have mercy on their souls. But I have wrestled in agony about all this till my soul has become calm and still silent before God and His will.

Monday, as soon as we heard of the evacuation, we sent for the negroes and told them that they knew the Yankees said they were free, and that anyone who wanted to go to Richmond could do so at once, but that if they chose to stay here, we would do our best by them, and stand by them to the last. Every one professed they would certainly stay here— "had no notion of going to the Yankees." But the next morning they all refused to go to work. Then Plumer called them up and told them that they must either go to work as usual, immediately, or quit the place at once. They said they did not work because they were afraid the Yankees or our men would come and catch them, but swore before God that they had no idea of leaving the place and promised to go to work the next day. After I was dressed Wednesday morning, Anne informed me that Green and Mat were the only men left on the place.

God is my witness how faithfully I have tried to do my duty by my slaves. We had nothing to do with setting them free, and are now relieved of all responsibility for their support henceforth. We will do what we can for those who may prove faithful. If we stay here we will hire labor. I have no fear (D.V) of getting on, and I feel a kind of relief to be so easily freed of the responsibility of caring for them in these times. I am less convinced than ever that it is best for them to be free, and I feel great pity for the race— but God knows I have always felt that whenever He willed that we should give up [illegible] I should not regret to part with them. With right management, I believe that in the end, we will be better off. I trust country, family life, honor, all the past, present and future to God. I fear nothing but the possibility of our murmuring at His will.

General Lee has surrendered

After four years of arduous service marked by unsurpassed courage and fortitude, the Army of Northern Virginia has been compelled to yield to overwhelming numbers and resources.

I need not tell the survivors of so many hard-fought battles who have remained steadfast to the last that I have consented to this result from no distrust of them; but feeling that valor and devotion could accomplish nothing that would compensate for the loss that must have attended the continuance of the contest, I determined to avoid the useless sacrifice of those whose past services have endeared them to their countrymen. By the terms of the agreement, officers and men can return to their homes and remain until exchanged.

You may take with you the satisfaction that proceeds from the consciousness of duty faithfully performed, and I earnestly pray that a merciful God will extend to you His blessing and protection…

—Robert E. Lee's Farewell to his Army, April 10, 1865

April 16, 1865. Sunday.
God's ways are past finding out! Even when He seems most against us, His mercies remind us of His loving kindness and tender forbearance. General Lee has surrendered! He left Richmond with 40,000 troops— he surrendered eight thousand muskets, 15,000 men altogether.

History records no event like this. An army who has fought with sublime courage for five years becoming so demoralized that they threw away their arms as they walked along, no enemy pressing in many instances. Those who stood by our noble leader to the last whipt the foe. Again and again they cut their way through, until surrounded at every point, until resistance meant annihilation and our noble Lee would not sacrifice their lives. The enemy had by their own acknowledgement 130,000 men— 12,000 in the saddle freshly mounted, while we had 3,000 broken down cavalry! With all these odds against them, Gen. Lee says, had our men fought as they once did, he could have been victorious!

Oh, I cannot write of that sad surrender without suffering! But God in His mercy so ruled the hearts of the enemy that their conduct has been nobly magnanimous. Gen. Grant not only refused to accept the sword of Lee, but would have no formal surrender. The officers of our army simply disbanded and paroled, by the Yankee authority, their men. Not one word of insult or exultation was heard from the lips of the triumphant foe, but all seemed eager to acknowledge valor, to say they knew we were over-powered by numbers and that they never had really defeated Lee. Kindness was shown to the humblest private. The officers freely offered their own money and provisions to our soldiers. This is a noble record! Their whole conduct thus far has been conciliatory and just. The most extreme journals of the North, even H. W. Beecher, advocate leniency and conciliation. They say the States are to return to the Union on the old terms excepting slavery. I for one pray God I may never see that restored! All seem to concede that the war for the present is at an end. Johnston's army is still said to be in the field. President Davis is unheard of. God guideth all! We are awaiting to see what is behind the scenes in Yankeedom that may explain their course towards us.

We have been greatly spared on the whole as a neighborhood. The Yanks did not make their appearance here until Monday last when an authorized party of 25 men, 6 whites, the rest darkies, led by our arch-rascal Ephraim came to the neighborhood and stole all the horses. The man who headed them pretended to be Gen. Draper. I had the pleasure of telling him we were not prepared to take the oath until the South had struck the last blow. To use Mrs. Puyser's expression, "I mostly found words to express myself in" to the whole party and not one gave me even an insolent look. The four men remaining here left with them. Green behaved very badly after all our kindness. Anne and Fannie, Eliza, the cook, Maria Louisa, Jeannetta and James have behaved well, been faithful. We are expecting an exodus tomorrow. Nearly all have returned being ordered out of town by the Yanks and Plumer says they shan't stay here. God have mercy on us all and especially upon these poor wretches!

April 30, 1865. Sunday.
The exodus took place, leaving us with no one on the place except Anne and Eliza, Fannie and her children and the cook Eliza with all her young ones! It was astonishing how well we got on! Now I have some servants hired about the house. Plumer has several white men and some negroes at work, and we begin to feel accustomed to the great changes of the day at once. I would not have dared to free the negroes for all of the gold of California because I knew so well that they were unfit for freemen. I am more convinced than ever that slavery for them was the fulfillment of a Divine Intention— no sin "per se" though having sins connected with it that called for reform.

The quiet and peaceful fields surrounding Appomattox Court House, Virginia. In April 1865, when the soldiers from two armies met on these fields, the Generals met in a nearby house and signed the treaty that ended the American Civil War. The soldiers, wherever they had come from, north or south, then departed these fields, returned to their homes, and started the task of rebuilding their country.

But I have long thought it best for the white race that it should be freed from the incubus of slavery. That has caused the war and our present defeat can in a great measure be attributed to it. I thank God that He has freed me from the responsibilities the institution imposed owing to faults of the South, and the canting wicked interference of the abolitionists they were heavy and wearisome beyond all endurance. I never want to see another one! I would have given up tenfold their value to be freed from those [illegible]. May God have mercy upon the poor wretches! I have prayed earnestly to be kept from all bitterness towards them; and I rejoice to have none! I feel pity for the poor misguided creatures. Freedom to them means tyranny threatens on all sides, anarchy and mobocracy promise to rule! God keep us all. May we trust in Him. I have no heart to write or think about the dreadful present. I can only wait, pray, and work as far as my strength will permit. I never feel very well. Energy and will seem to have deserted me. I feel like something worn out. Oh Father in Heaven, my only trust is in Thee.

Appomattox

General Meade, commanding the Army of the Potomac, and General Wise were brothers-in-law, the former having married Margaretta Sergeant, eldest daughter of the Hon. John Sergeant, of Philadelphia, and sister of the second Mrs. Wise. The relations existing between the two families had been of the closest sort, particularly those between Generals Meade and Wise.

The former had at one time resigned from the army, and procured through the influence of the latter a more lucrative position in the United States Coast Survey service. Afterward, through Wise's good offices, Meade was transferred to the Engineer Corps of the army, and assigned to duty at Detroit, where he lived when the war came on.

For the first time in eight years the two met at Appomattox, and their meeting was most touching and affectionate. By his tenderness and solicitude for Wise, Meade disarmed every feeling of estrangement, and after calling in person and greeting General Wise with all the warmth of old friendship, and observing that he was dismounted, he sent his young son, Colonel George Meade, with an ambulance and pair of mules, laden with every necessary and luxury, with instructions to place the outfit at the disposal of General Wise to convey him to his home, and to be turned

General George G. Meade, commander of the Army of the Potomac and brother-in-law of Henry A. Wise. Photograph courtesy Library of Congress.

over to the nearest government officer when General Wise had no further use for them. When General Meade returned to Richmond, his first care was to visit the female members of General Wise's family, and tender them all that love and courtesy could suggest. Writing to Wise in June, 1867, introducing Mr. Ropes, the historian, General Meade said: —

"I reciprocate all your kind feeling. The war never changed my good feeling for you, and never in the smallest degree diminished the gratitude I have always felt to you for the many acts of kindness received at your hands… Do believe me when I say *old* times are *present* times with me so far as you and yours are concerned, however much we may differ as to what has occurred or is occurring." The cordial feeling manifested in this letter continued between the two until the death of General Meade, which occurred shortly before that of General Wise…

…The things which most surprised General Wise at the surrender at Appomattox were the desire of the Union soldiers to see him above all others; the lack of any evidence of personal malignity shown towards him; and the large number of his foes who expressed the warmest interest and personal regard for him. Especially was this so among the New York troops, many of whom were Irishmen, who seemed to have retained for him the liveliest affection for his fight against Know-Nothingism in 1855… They sought him out, made themselves known, told him of their lifelong admiration, and begged the privilege of ministering to his wants in any way in their power. He thanked them, and protested that the only thing he needed was a good pocket-knife. Soon after their departure an orderly appeared with the finest knife to be procured, and a hamper of the choicest delicacies obtainable…

—Barton H. Wise, *The Life of Henry A. Wise of Virginia.*

☙ Three other diaries from the spring of 1865:

April 2, 1865, Sunday: Beautiful day… News of a great battle between Grant & Lee before Richmond and Petersburg in which our army was victorious. God grant that they may go on conquering and to conquer.

April 3. Weather warm & pleasant. Recd the glorious news that Grant had taken Richmond and so my loyal heart rejoices over the great victory…

April 7. Rainy am. Business begins to recover a little occasionally an order for flour… News recd that Lee & all his army captured. All the bells in town rang for an hour & then we learned that the glorious news was not true. Evening at home.

April 10. Rainy day. Recd the glorious news of the surrender of Genl. Lee & his army to Genl. Grant. The news came last night about 1/2 past 10 & such a night of rejoicing I have never seen… P.M. Attended the funeral of F—

April 15. Last night at 10 o'clock President Lincoln was shot through the head while sitting in his Presidential Box at Ford's Theatre at Washington and died at 7:22 this morning. Sec. Seward & his two sons were assassinated & it is feared they will die. A nation is in tears & mourning today.

April 19. Weather mild & pleasant. Funeral of our President Abraham Lincoln. This is indeed a day of mourning all over the land. Business suspended and meetings in all the churches. Mr. Vincent made a good address.

April 25. Charming day, warm & spring-like. Mr. Lincoln's remains recd in New York and the greatest display ever witnessed in the metropolis. Business entirely suspended.

April 28. Weather warm & pleasant… Recd the glorious news that Johnston had surrendered his army to Genl. Grant on the same terms as Lee's surrender. Up to the mill in P.M…

General Joseph Johnston's Army of Tennessee surrendered to General Sherman.

June 15. This day appointed by the President as a day of fasting & prayer on account of the death of Mr. Lincoln… Heard Prof. Lewis deliver a eulogy on Mr. Lincoln, not up to my expectations…
—*Diary of Francis Thayer, Troy, New York.*

April 3, 1865: At Cambridge… to Salem & back… Richmond fallen yesterday. Glory.
April 7. Genl. Robt. E. Lee surrendered the rebel army today to Genl. U. S. Grant. Glory. (*A note in the diary reads*: The above did not prove true.)
April 10. GLORY. At Cambridge. The rebel army under Gel. R. E. Lee surrendered to the Federal forces under Genl. U. S. Grant yesterday. Rainy day & mild.
April 15. President Lincoln was shot in Washington last night by a rebel while at the theater. Awful. Sect. Seward was stabbed in the neck three times & may not live. Seward two sons were also nearly killed by another assassin. What are we coming to.
April 19. No work today. All churches united & had funeral of our lamented President Abraham Lincoln at White Church…
April 20. Another day of fasting & prayer… Cool in A.M. Warm in P.M. & rain.
—*Diary of Edwin McKie, Cambridge, New York.*

April 3, 1865: A beautiful day. Richmond & Petersburg taken today. Jas. McKie here to dinner.
April 9. A cold morning, ground froze hard, but a pleasant day. Lucy, Almy, Kitty & I went to Church. Mr. Shortt preached from Ephesians 6th & 18 first clause, "Praying always with all Prayer." General Lee surrendered.
April 10. A rainy day… I mailed a letter to Clark. Mrs. Maynard died.
April 15. A cloudy day. The Nation is draped in mourning. Abraham Lincoln, President of the United States, died this morning from the effects of a pistol shot last night in the theatre at Washington. William H. Seward, Secretary of State, was nearly assassinated, in his bed by the same man or an accomplice. John Campbell, wife & daughter here to dinner… I deposited 500 dols for Almy and took up a due bill which she held against me for that amount…
April 19. A pleasant day. At 12 o'clock Lucy Rice & I attended the funeral services of the President at White Church…
April 23. A very chilly day. Lucy, Almy, Lucy Rice, & I went to Church. In the morning Mr. Shortt preached on the death of Abraham Lincoln…
May 6. A wet day. I planted early peas and sowed cabbage seed.
—*Diary of James McKie, Cambridge, New York.*

During this period of waiting came the news of the assassination of Mr. Lincoln. Perhaps I ought to chronicle that the announcement was received with demonstrations of sorrow. If I did, I should be lying for sentiment's sake. Among the higher officers and the most intelligent and conservative men, the assassination caused a shudder of horror at the heinousness of the act, and at the thought of its possible consequences; but among the thoughtless, the desperate, and the ignorant, it was hailed as a sort of retributive justice… For four years we had been fighting. In that struggle, all we loved had been lost. Lincoln incarnated to us the idea of oppression and conquest. We had seen his face over the coffins of our brothers and relatives and friends, and in the flames of Richmond, on the disaster at Appomattox… We were desperate and vindictive, and whosoever denies it forgets or is false. We greeted his death in a spirit of reckless hate, and hailed it as bringing agony and bitterness to those who were the cause of our own agony and bitterness… Time taught us that Lincoln was a man of marvelous humanity.
—*John S. Wise.*

There is no mention of the assassination of President Lincoln in any of the letters and diaries written by family members in Virginia. Years later John S. Wise would write about it in *The End of an Era*.

Henry A. Wise. A portrait given to the R. E. Lee Camp, No. 1, Confederate Veterans of Richmond on January 31, 1908 by his son, John Sergeant Wise. John S. Wise wrote to family members on January 6, 1908 encouraging them to be present at the ceremony where Governor William E. Cameron was to accept the portrait on behalf of the Confederate Veterans. Also presented were Henry A. Wise's uniform coat and a copy of a speech that Wise had delivered to the Veterans in 1870. John S. Wise noted that the portrait had been "painted under my own supervision, and it is, I think, unquestionably the best likeness extant of my father." Also prepared at this time was a Confederate Roster of the family of Henry A. Wise.

The diary of Annie Jennings Wise Hobson:

Undated

I wish to make note of the manner in which I spent the night of the 10th, the night the thieving party came here. None of us undressed fearing the return of the stragglers. We lay down in our clothes, making attempts to sleep soundly. Oh! How I suffered over the surrender of Gen. Lee's army. I stood in agony by the deathbed of the Confederacy, felt and saw its every throw, its desperate death struggles. The whole scene was [illegible] in the image of a dying woman. My soul became so perturbed and wild that I felt as if I should die. I took my prayer book— turned to the Psalter, and as I read precious promises in quick succession of God's mercy to those who trust and call upon Him in extremity— read the promises of His aid and sure succor, my soul became calm and submissive. I was even happy in acquiescence to the Divine Will. My worst trouble was then, God be praised.

Undated

Father has just made me a visit. He is about to leave. He has no right till pardoned by our dear rulers to make a livelihood. He has no home, and it is not in my power to offer him one. Mother is sick in Halifax having just rallied a little from a severe illness. Henry has lost his little baby. Sister will soon return to Washington to my bitter disappointment. We are all pressed for money… Tyranny threatens on all sides, anarchy and mobocracy promise to rule. God keep us all and may we trust in Him! I have no heart to write or think about the dreadful present. I can only wait, pray, and work as far as my strength will permit. I never feel very well! Energy and will seem to have deserted me. I feel like something worn out. Oh Father in Heaven, my only trust is in Thee.

Confederate Roster of the Family of Henry A. Wise

In 1908, the "surviving members of the family of General Wise" prepared a "roster" of his "personal and military family" that had served in the Confederate Army. The preparation and distribution of the roster sought to insure that all of those named would "not be forgotten by the comrades they loved so well or by the people of the South whom they served to the best of their ability, with body, heart and soul." Included on the Roster are Wise's four sons, three sons-in-law, eleven nephews and three members of his military family. Of this group, one son, Obadiah Jennings Wise, was killed during the war; one son-in-law, Alexander Yelverton Peyton Garnett, served as the personal physician to Jefferson Davis; one nephew, George Douglas Wise, was killed; and four relatives, William Carrington Mayo, a son-in-law, and James Madison Wise, Peyton Wise, and Lewis Warrington Wise, all nephews, were present at Appomattox. Frederick Plumer Hobson was rejected for military service because of a disability, but he and his wife, Annie Jennings Wise Hobson, let their home, Eastwood, be a "veritable hospital and resort of refugees throughout the war." —*Editor's note.*

X

1862–1869

Letters from Cambridge and Troy, Part Five

THE Civil War and "reconstruction" dominated America between 1862 and 1869. Antietam, Gettysburg, Chancellorsville, conscription, Vicksburg, the burning of Atlanta, the Emancipation Proclamation, Appomattox, and President Lincoln's assassination were names and events that everyone talked about. General Burnside's victory at Roanoke Island might not have concerned many in the North, but it had greatly affected one family in Virginia. The period of "reconstruction" following the war was very different for the two sections of the still united country. Victorious in the war, the industrial north prospered while the defeated and much less industrialized south struggled under greatly changed economic circumstances.

America continued to grow and change. Congress authorized "greenbacks," a new 5¢ coin, the "nickel," and *In God We Trust* to be on all coins. The newly completed transcontinental railroad network became the single most influential factor in the emergence of the new industrial age, and passenger travel was greatly improved when George Pullman built a comfortable sleeping car. Nevada and Nebraska became states in 1864 and 1867. In 1863 scarlet fever killed 30,000 people in England, and a cyclone in India in 1864 killed over 70,000. A fire in Quebec destroyed 2,500 buildings in 1866, and in 1868 an earthquake in San Francisco caused over $3 million in damages. Two other events in 1868 would soon begin to have a profound impact on the American workplace: First, Congress passed legislation providing for an eight-hour day for federal employees, and secondly, Christopher Sholes received a patent for the first practical typewriter.

Often the letters and diaries describe events and activities that are no longer a part of our lives. For example, there was "sleighing." Francis Thayer's diaries contain many such comments such as——"good sleighing," "sleighing very good," "Sleighing very good about the city," "Sleighing all gone," "About ten inches of snow this morning which makes beautiful sleighing," and "Weather mild & pleasant. No sleighing for Christmas." This is a lost tradition and pastime—America has changed.

Letters and diaries by:
Edwin McKie
James McKie
Catherine McKie Thayer
Francis S. Thayer

Letters and diaries written from: Troy and Cambridge, New York, and Chicago.

1862

January 1, 1862. New Years Day— happy to many, sad also to many… Little do we know whether we shall be spared to see the close of this year. God grant that we may be enabled so to spend our time and talents that when the Messenger of Death shall arrest us, we may be found of Christ Jesus in peace without spots and blameless, prepared to render up our account with joy and now with grief…

February 24. A soft morning, rained some, changed toward night. Major John McKie came up at 2 o'clock. I took him to William's. I had the most tedious ride home I have had this winter, or for a long time. It snowed fast, the wind blew hard and cold. I am fifty-seven years old this day. God in his Providence has spared me to see another Birthday. May he enable me so to live henceforth, that if he shall call me hence, ere another Birthday, it shall be my infinite gain.

February 25. A cold day. A great change from yesterday. I recd a letter from Katy Thayer.

March 11. A beautiful day… News today of a naval battle on Saturday last, at Hampton Roads. The rebel Ironclad steamer *Merrimac* sank our ship, *Cumberland* and took the ship *Congress*, burnt her. At that instant our iron gunboat *Monitor* came up and fought the *Merrimac* and finally compelled her to haul off. The *Cumberland* carried down 1 or 200 men with her.

March 25. A pleasant morning… Clark has gone out from home to begin his fortune in the world. May God protect him, shield him from the temptations of the world and lead him into the way of life everlasting. Enable him to fulfill well, his day and generation and finally prepare him for mansions in glory…   —*Diary of James McKie.*

January 16, 1862. At Cambridge. Weather quite cold… Kitty quite sick with croup, sent for Dr. Mosher at 10 P.M. He came at 11 & in two hours the dear creature was relieved.

January 17. Up all last night with Kitty & Oh how anxiously we watched over the dear little one. Dr. Mosher stayed all night & when he came down in the morning he assured us that she was out of danger. God grant that it may be so. In the Home most of the day.

January 19. At Cambridge. Weather stormy, nearly a foot of snow. Kitty better today & we hope the dear creature is out of danger. Our hearts have been very anxious & Oh how thankful we feel that God in His mercy & goodness has spared the little darling…
—*Diary of Francis S. Thayer.*

୧ Death in the family:

Tuesday, April 15, 1862. Weather very mild & pleasant. River rising very rapidly. There is a large body of snow up north and it is coming down in the shape of water.

Wednesday, April 16. Beautiful day… Kate took 6 o'cl. train for Johnsonville to go home to see poor sick Niel. At store until 10 o'clock.

Thursday, April 17. Charming day. River still rising, three or four feet over the docks…

Saturday, April 19. Weather pleasant but a little cooler than yesterday. Very high water up to within 7 inches of the lower floor at Mill… Kate came from home per morn cars. Niel very feeble. At 3 P.M. left for Cambridge with horse and carriage. Roads very good. Arrived at Cambridge 1/4 past 6. Dr. Cook of Troy up to see Niel.

Sunday, April 20. At Cambridge. Weather mild & pleasant. Up with poor Niel until 10 o'clock this morning. He is very feeble and I fear he is near his end. I pray God that he may be prepared for that great change which waits us all…
Monday, April 21. Weather cloudy & cooler. Up with Niel from 1 o'clock until 6. He is no better At 1/2 past 9 A.M. left for home with John, Ellen & children. Kate stays with Niel…
—*Diary of Francis S. Thayer.*

Troy. April 22nd, 1862, Tuesday.
Dearest Kitty— We arrived home safely a little after 12 o'clock. Frankie and Kitty were full of fun… I am almost afraid to hear from you— the last look I gave poor Niel went to my heart and seemed to say to me, this is the last of that noble generous hearted fellow. God grant that he may give his heart to Him who will save to the uttermost, I hope and pray that he may be spared and that his life may be useful and happy. I hope and trust that you will not expose yourself too much. Take good care of yourself and let me hear from you as often as you can. I am more than ever your own *Frank*.

Cambridge, 4 o'clock, Thurs. aft. April 24, 1862.
My Dear Frank— I found Niel more comfortable than he was on Tuesday. Today he seems weaker than yesterday. He takes very little nourishment and coughs a great deal more that a few days ago. Last two nights coughing prevented his sleeping… Poor Niel has not been willing to think that he would not get well or better but this morn he said to me the Doctor can't cure this cough. In conversation with me, he said he would try to pray and trust in the Savior. Oh let us pray for Him as we have not prayed before. If it seems best I will come home Sat morn. or the day or aft. for the Sabbath. It seems to me that Niel may live some days and still he may fail as fast as he has in a week and drop away very soon. May God spare him to give him the joy that comes from sins forgiven. Kiss the precious children for me. I want them to see N— *once more* still I think they could not stay more than come one day and go back the next. I wish you could step in and stay a few hours any time. Mother very well, and all as kind. With all the love of your *Kitty*.

Thursday, April 24, 1862. Weather continues quiet cold, ground frozen hard this morning… Recd two letters from Kate saying Niel was no better. Eve at store until 10 o'clock.
Friday, April 25. Pleasant spring-like weather. Business improving a little…
—*Diary of Francis S. Thayer.*

Sat morn. April 26th, 1862 1/2 past 11.
Dear Frank— Poor Niel is living and yet he is passing away. He may drop away any moment and he may live a few hours… We send Edward fearing that my letter sent yesterday may not reach you in time. We think your best way is to come back with Edward and come up with him from Johnsonville. Bring Frankie with you. *He never* will forget what he sees now and will make no trouble for anyone. Dear little Kitty, how I want to see her, still I do not think best for her to come. Ellen will make her just as happy as she can be… I would like you to bring— my hat in closet of silk, one with veil on it and black veil in Band box on upper drawer of same closet. My cloak. Frankie's

Niel McKie died when he was forty-seven years old and is buried in the Whiteside Church Cemetery in Cambridge, New York. The Decree of Final Settlement of his estate, dated May 27, 1895, is in the files. At that time his estate was distributed to his half-sister, Catherine McKie Thayer, 1827–1901, by then of Colorado Springs, and the two surviving daughters of his brother Edwin, 1818–1895, Florence Marguerite McKie, 1873–1959, and Katherine Whiteside McKie, 1874–1953.

low rubbers, and if he has not drawers enough clean or hose, Margaret will have them ready to send by John… The air is chilly. Let Frankie wear his fur coats and big scarf or bring his common coat— he will need it when he runs out. Ellen will put up Frankie's suits for him. I wish you would get a pair of cloth or leather slip for poor Niel, large enough and bring with you. I am writing in the parlor and hear every breath— oh this last passage, we must all make it once…   —Love *Kitty*.

Saturday, April 26, 1862. P.M. Ed Hunt came for me & Frankie. Poor Niel is almost gone. Took eve. cars and arrived Cambridge at 1/2 past 7. Niel knew me but could not speak. Up with him until 2 o'clock in the morning.

Sunday, April 27. At 7 o'clock Ed called me and said Niel was almost gone. Dressed and went down just in time to see him breathe his last at 35 minutes past 7 o'clock of one of the brightest and most beautiful mornings that ever shone upon the earth… Several came to drop a tear over the remains of the poor noble [illegible] Niel.

Tuesday, April 29. Rainy day. Niel's funeral at 10 o'clock. Mr. Gordon preached a sermon of 40 minutes… We have done all we can for poor Niel. He was a noble hearted fellow, so kind & so true. We hope that he is in a better world where there is no temptation, sin, or sorrow.   —*Diary of Francis S. Thayer.*

April 27, 1862. A beautiful day. Lucy, Almy and I went to Church. Mr. Shortt lectured upon the four last verses of 19th chapter of Luke— both services. After dinner Lucy and I went to Sophia's. Neil died this morning in the 47th year of his age…

April 28. A pleasant day, rather cool. I wrote William and John Armitage, informing them of Neil's funeral tomorrow. I selected a coffin at Barton's. I got the button-holes in my overcoat worked at Noble's. I paid Fennett 4/ for it, near the rail road track.

April 29. A rainy day. Br. William came down and got a horse and took Almy to Neil's funeral. Lucy & I went. Mr. P. Gordon made an address. At evening Lucy, Bell, Mrs. Shermand, and I went to Prayer Meeting at Mrs. Fisher's.   —*Diary of James McKie.*

May 10, 1862. At about 12 o'clock… a fire broke out in the Rail Road Bridge which was soon consumed together with nearly 700 buildings— the greatest fire ever known here. Loss of property about $3,000,000 & six or eight lives. An awful day for Troy— at one time we thought the whole city would go.

May 11. …I was out on duty with the National Guard until 3 o'clock this morning as special policeman…

May 12. Beautiful day. The City filled with people from far and from near to view the desolated part of our fair city. It is enough to make one sick to see the poor sufferers going about the street… The new firm of Bills, Thayer & Knight commenced today… Eve at store until 10 o'clock examining books.   —*Diary of Francis S. Thayer.*

Crystal Palace Mills, Bills Thayer & Knight, 1862–1866, Troy, New York.

DISASTROUS FIRE IN TROY — *The Loss Estimated at Two Millions* — A terrible fire is now raging at Troy. The bridge over the Hudson River took fire about 11 1/2 o'clock, and has been consumed. At this hour (1:30 P.M.) the fire has communicated to various parts of the city, and will destroy hundreds of thousands worth of property… The fire spreads so rapidly that but little property can be saved. One quarter of the city has already been destroyed… It is certain that some lives have been lost and rumor places the number at 10 to 15. The fire is still raging fiercely, and buildings are now being blown up.   —*The New York Times*, May 11, 1862.

THE REBELLION — The news this morning is of the most glorious and exciting character. Within the last forty-eight hours great blows have been struck against the rebellion, which make it reel and totter to its very foundation. Norfolk, Portsmouth and the Gosport Navy-yard have been captured, without bloodshed; the *Merrimac*, the "Terror of the Roads," as the rebels were pleased to style her— has been destroyed, and the triumphant march of McClellan's army has been continued almost to the threshold of the rebel Capital, while on the Mississippi, another is added to our numerous victories.
—*The New York Times*, May 12, 1862.

May 10, 1862. A cool day. Edwin McKie here to dinner. A great fire in Troy, a large part of the city destroyed. The fire commenced in the Rail Road Bridge, by a spark from an engine. The loss at 5 o'clock, was estimated at 2,000,000 dols…
May 25. A clear cold morning. Had a frost which killed cucumbers, squashes, beans and some corn… A collection was taken up for the Troy sufferers by late conflagration. 26 dollars and a little over was raised. We gave 5 dols & Almy the same.
—*Diary of James McKie.*

May 31, 1862. Warm & pleasant. Jim & wife [probably James Thayer, Francis Thayer's brother] & Ada Wood here & spent the day. Took Jim down to J. S. Grimwold's office & then up to mill. Jim says our govt never will pay its present debt. I say he is mistaken. Very good week for business…
June 15. At Hoosick, weather quite cool… Spent a very pleasant Sabbath with my near & dear friends.
July 4. In Chicago. The sad news of McClellan's repulse makes every Patriot mourn this anniversary of our country…
July 6. …The news from McClellan's army is bad enough. His loss is from 10 to 15,000. Rebel loss still more…
—*Diary of Francis S. Thayer.*

July 5, 1862. A warm day, a shower afternoon… A trial of mowers was had between Woods & Hubbard.
July 12. A fine day. Frank Thayer called this morning on his way from Hoosick to Salem to see some horses. He bought two single horses. He called at evening. Almy came home with him.
July 19. A pleasant day. Doctor Smart put into the vault today, we all attended the funeral service at Coila Church… He was a good man. I witnessed a post mortem examination of the body by Doctor Kennedy. The disease was inflammation of the spleen…
July 25. A fine hay day, the first this week. I recd a letter from Jas. B. Jermain wanting a boarding house for 2 or 3 weeks…
July 31. A clear warm morning, rained hard at 1/2 past 12. James B. Jermain called, he was looking at rooms at Doctor Coulters for his girls for a few weeks…
August 6. A warm day… Jas. B. Jermain brought his family to Doctor Coulter's. He staid with us all night…
August 7. A warm day. Mr. Jermain, daughters & Mrs. Dunlop here to tea, he all night. A heavy shower in the night.
August 9. A very warm day, a heavy shower at 3 o'clock. James Jermain staid here last night, he went home this morning…
August 11. A cool beautiful day… Jermain girls called.
August 14. A cloudy day, a little rain at evening… Katy Thayer, her Mother, Children & nurse & driver here at 11 o'clock A.M. for the night… Edwin & wife here to tea…

Bills, Thayer & Knight, store on River Street, 1862–1866, Troy, New York.

This refers to the battles around and near Richmond, Virginia.

August 27. A very warm day. James B. Jermain gave me 15 dols toward paying for Clark's military suit…

August 28. A cloudy day, a fine rain afternoon… I paid Mr. Noble for Clark's Military suit, almost 30 dols. I paid Mrs. Fuller 3/ for lining Clarks blanket and mending pants.

September 1. A cloudy day, a nice rain at evening. Clark left home this morning for the last time, for the War. God grant that his life & health may be spared, and that he may be kept in His fear and be enabled to walk in the ways of holiness and righteousness, and ere long be returned to his home in circumstances of Mercy. Lucy & I went to Salem afternoon, took tea at William's.

September 4. A fine day. Lucy quite sick of cholera morbus. Edwin here to dinner…

September 5. A warm day. I went to Troy, from there to Salem. I took farewell of Clark, perhaps forever. May God protect and preserve him, and return him to his home in due time. May he be an object of God's especial Mercy and Grace…

—*Diary of James McKie.*

War news The Battle of Antietam, where each side suffered over 10,000 casualties, was fought in September 1862.

Fredricksburg There were over 12,000 Union and over 5,000 Confederate casualties at Fredericksburg in December 1862.

September 11, 1862. …War news looks gloomy…

December 14. Weather mild… streets very muddy… Recd news of a great Battle at Fredericksburg. Loss heavy on both sides, without much advantage on either…

December 15. Weather mild… Recd news from Burnside at Fredericksburg. I fear he has been badly beaten. Eve at home…

December 17. Weather milder. Everybody talking about our shameful loss of men at Fredericksburg. O' is the man who can lead our noble army on to honor & victory. Let him come forth…

—*Diary of Francis S. Thayer.*

December 22, 1862. Not quite as cold. I went to Thos. Reed to see the situation of his farm with reference to taking a mortgage upon it. We have the account of John McKie being wounded at Fredericksburg.

—*Diary of James McKie.*

December 31, 1862. The last day of the year is upon us and the [illegible] question is, are we better than at its commencement. This year of war & bloodshed has carried mourning to many households, & now as we look ahead all seems dark & gloomy. God grant that ere long this wicked war may be brought to a close & the Union preserved. We have been blessed with health & prosperity, only two visits from the Doctor…

—*Diary of Francis S. Thayer.*

1863

January 3, 1863. …Business this week very good, selling quite as much as I desire. I have no doubt prices will be higher.

January 8. …Business very good for the season…

January 14. Weather mild & rainy. Great excitement in the Stock Market in New York…

—*Diary of Francis S. Thayer.*

January 8, 1863. A good winter day… I recd letter from Chas. Crary, also one from Jas. B. Jermain enclosing a check for 67.88 dollars for interest on two R. R. Bonds. He kept the bonds until I send for them.

January 23. A beautiful day. William came down and took our horse & Almy and went to see John McKie. John is here for the night. Some 30 or 40 gentlemen and ladies came in to see him. Mr. Mr. Taylor made an address to him…

January 24. A fine day. John left this morning for Washington. May God protect and preserve him…

—*Diary of James McKie.*

John McKie became Captain of a company of 90 men from the Cambridge, New York, area that he raised and was later part of the 22d N. Y. Regiment.

January 28, 1863. Weather mild. Our dear children are not as well. Kitty has high fever & difficult breathing. Frankie is much the same 'tho not as bad. Most of the day at home with the children…

January 31. Weather mild & pleasant, sleighing… Children very sick, particularly Frankie whose symptoms are alarming. God grant the dear creature may soon be restored to health & strength.

February 2. Weather pleasant. Frankie about the same— still very sick. May God bless & spare the dear little fellow. My whole time is with the dear one, day & night…

February 7. Pleasant & mild… Frankie better & begins to have a better appetite.
—Diary of Francis S. Thayer.

◦∾ Death in the family:

February 24, 1863. This is my Birthday. God in his goodness has spared me fifty-eight years in the Land of the Living. May he enable me by his Grace so to live henceforth, that when he shall call me hence I may be found blameless in the all seeing eye of my Lord and Savior, Jesus Christ. The day has been chilly. Capt. Hall called. Lydia McMillan here to dinner. Henry Dunham to tea.

April 12. A warm day, prospect of rain. Lucy went to Church alone in the morning. She came home at noon. I staid home alone. Mr. Shortt contrary to expectation preached two discourses. A man came from Salem (Mr. Nelson) with a letter from Almy informing us that Wm. was sick. Edwin went up with him.

April 13. A chilly day. I recd a letter from Edwin this morning saying that William showed no change. John Whiteside called.

April 14. A beautiful day. Lucy & I went to Salem and saw Br. William, we fear for the last time. He is very low of typhoid pneumonia. May God have mercy on him…

April 15. A mild day. Our dear Brother William died this morning of pneumonia after a sickness of 5 days. May God give us grace to be resigned to his holy will and enable us to give diligence to prepare for the coming of our Lord and Master. Almy & Edwin came from Salem tonight. Lucy & I went to Quasacoke this afternoon.

April 16. A chilly day, some rain during the day… Almy has gone to Salem this evening to attend the funeral of Bro. William tomorrow… I rec'd a letter from Clark today.

April 17. A mild day. Lucy & I went to Salem to attend the funeral of Brother William. I did not go to the Church where the body was taken, neither to the cemetery, on account of my weakness. Mr. Forsythe gave an address… There was a large audience and deeply affected. Mr. & Mrs. Thayer called this evening. They came down with Edwin's folks from Salem.

April 18. A mild day. I went to Salem to Julia's. I took possession of Wm's. Papers. Mr. Crary read his Will in which I am named as Executor with Brother John.
—Diary of James McKie.

William McKie, 1795–1863. Photo from Crisfield Johnson's History of Washington County, New York, 1737–1878.

May 5, 1863. Cloudy & a little rain. Business dull. News from Hooker's army is encouraging. It looks as tho' he would gain a victory. God grant that he may…

May 7. Rainy day. Recd the awful news that Hooker's Army was defeated in the great battle near Fredericksburg. It is too bad, I am almost discouraged…

May 8. Cleared off pleasantly… News from the Army don't look quite so blue…

May 20. …Paid D. Malley (unknown person) $4500 for 3 vacant lots on the east side of Washington Park… Demand for flour very good.

May 25. Delightful weather. Good news from Vicksburg. Grant will take the place if the news is reliable…

May 26. …News from Genl. Grant not fully satisfactory. I am afraid he has not taken Vicksburg…

The journal contains many comments about the settlement of William McKie's estate which was left to the "most needy" of the "heirs at law and nearest of kin" and to public charities that the executor deemed "worthy." The vague language was confusing, and the will was ultimately declared null by the Courts.

The Virginia Memorial, Gettysburg National Military Park, Gettysburg, Pennsylvania, dedicated June 6, 1917. General Robert E. Lee is mounted on his favorite horse, Traveller, with a group of soldiers representing the infantry, artillery, and cavalry of the Army of Northern Virginia at the base of the monument. Lee is looking over the open fields where Pickett's charge took place on July 3, 1863— an estimated 12,000 Confederate troops charged the Union line, over 5,000 were killed in one hour, and the Battle of Gettysburg was over.

There were over 50,000 Union and Confederate casualties at Gettysburg. On November 19, 1863, President Lincoln delivered one of the most important speeches in American history at the dedication of the military cemetery on that infamous battlefield.

May 29. …News from Genl. Grant not very encouraging. I hope & pray for the best…
June 11. Weather warm & pleasant… News from Vicksburg encouraging— I believe Grant will take the place before the 4th of July. Genl. Lee seems to be on the move— I trust Hooker will keep close watch of the fellow.
June 20. …It looks as tho' we should have a desperate battle before next Saturday night. May God grant that victory may be ours…
June 22. Cool & pleasant… War news doesn't look very good. I am afraid Lee will be too much for Hooker…
June 23. Weather cool… News from Penn. Looks bad enough. Lee is there having his own way & no one to stop him. God grant that he & his rebels may be put to flight. Where is Hooker…
June 24. Weather hot & dry… Rebels marching north. I hope they may come so far this way that they will never get back…
July 2. Weather very warm and awful dusty. News of a great battle going on near Gettysburg Pa. God grant that victory may be ours.
July 5. Rainy A.M., very few out to church… Glorious news from the army of the Potomac, Mead has gained a great victory & I thank God for it…
—*Diary of Francis S. Thayer.*

The Gettysburg Address

Fourscore and seven years ago our fathers brought forth on this continent a new nation, conceived in Liberty, and dedicated to the proposition that all men are created equal.

Now we are engaged in a great civil war, testing whether that nation or any nation so conceived and so dedicated, can long endure. We are met on a great battlefield of that war. We have come to dedicate a portion of that field, as a final resting place for those who here gave their lives that that nation might live. It is altogether fitting and proper that we should do this.

But, in a larger sense, we can not dedicate—we can not consecrate—we can not hallow—this ground. The brave men, living and dead, who struggled here, have consecrated it, far above out poor power to add or detract. The world will little note nor long remember what we say here, but it can never forget what they did here. It is for us the living, rather, to be dedicated here to the unfinished work which they who fought here have thus far so nobly advanced. It is rather for us to be here dedicated to the great task remaining before us—that from these honored dead we take increased devotion to that cause for which they gave the last full measure of devotion—that we here highly resolve that these dead shall not have died in vain—that this nation, under God, shall have a new birth of freedom—and that government of the people, by the people, for the people, shall not perish from the earth. —*Abraham Lincoln.*

Summer vacation:

August 1, 1863. …Arrived at Long Branch at 1/4 to 7 P.M.
August 2. …This is my lazy plan— nothing to do except to eat, sleep & loaf.
August 3. …Spent the day as usual eating & loafing…
August 4. Weather very warm… In bathing as usual. Poor Frankie is so timid that he don't enjoy bathing or going near the water, hardly dares wet his feet.
August 5. At Long Branch. Nothing out of the ordinary routine of affairs today— Eating, bathing & sleeping the order of the day. Nothing new in the papers from the Army. Would that we could have a little exciting news to stir us up…

August 8. At Long Branch. Weather hot & showery... Took Frankie into the water much against his will— very sorry he is so much afraid of the water...
August 12. At Long Branch, weather very hot indeed. Mercury up to about 90° & no wind. Kate packed up & is determined to leave tomorrow morning. I would like much to stay longer. Frankie mastered courage enough to go in to his neck & seems to enjoy it...
August 13. At Long Branch. Weather quite comfortable. Concluded to remain here until Saturday & then go directly home...
August 15. Weather very warm. At 11 o'clock A.M. left Long Branch for home... arrived home at 1/2 past 7 & found everything at the home in good shape. We have been gone three weeks & one day.
August 16. At home again & it seems good to be in our pleasant home after being cooped up in little 7x9 rooms...
August 30. Charming day... Ed came over from Cambridge & stayed until after dinner. It was pleasant to be at the Old Home again but O' how changed. We feel it at every step & turn. Children are perfectly happy here. Gave Frankie & Kitty a ride on the old mare. —Diary of Francis S. Thayer.

Katherine Sophia Thayer, photograph by A. Gobden, Troy, New York.

November 17, 1863. A cloudy morning, rained hard all of the afternoon. Lucy & I went to Troy, took dinner at Thayer's...went to Jermain's for the night.
November 21. A cloudy day— rained afternoon & evening... I foddered the cow for the first time this fall. —Diary of James McKie.

December 31, 1863. Weather mild... Business dull as normal at this season of the year. At the close of another year I have great reason to thank God for all his mercy & goodness towards me & mine. We have had some sickness, but life has been spared. My business has been prosperous & we have been blessed... May we indeed feel thankful & praise Him the giver of every good & perfect gift.
—Diary of Francis S. Thayer.

1864

January 2, 1864. A very cold day, merc at zero. I am much better having been unwell for a few days. I mailed a letter to Clark, enclosing silk thread, needles & 25 postage stamps.
January 21. I again commence a journal after having been sick since the 4th day of the month of Billious Fever: But through the tender mercies of my Heavenly father, I am much better and hope to be restored ere long to my accustomed health. God grant that the affliction may be sanctified to me, and that I may be more and more fitted to serve God here, and finally prepared to enjoy him in his heavenly Kingdom. I recd papers from National Bank.
January 25. A sloppy day, ice melting fast...I mailed the deeds today to Mr. Thayer asking him to forward me his check for the amount 1600 dols, being 10/acre for 1280 acres...
January 27. A beautiful day. I mailed a letter to Frank Thayer... I also rec'd a letter last night from F. S. Thayer acknowledging receipt of Deeds of Iowa lands and promising to pay for them (1600 dols) on 1 April next...
January 28. A very fine day... I rec'd a letter from Thayer enclosing a note for 1600 dols for Iowa lands.
January 29. A mild day. I mailed a letter to Mr. Thayer. —Diary of James McKie.

Due to James McKie's illness, there are no entries in his journal between January 4th and January 21st.

Iowa lands One of the assets included in William McKie's estate.

Mary Ball Thayer, 1795–1864, is buried in the Maple Grove Cemetery in Hoosick, New York.

Fence around Washington Park, Troy, New York.

March 14, 1864. Left Rochester at 7:40 with a heavy & anxious heart fearing that I may not find my good mother alive. Met Kate & children & Port [brother, Porter Thayer] at the Troy Depot. Mother was more comfortable this morning. Port & I took eve cars for Hoosick, found Mother very feeble, still she knows us & was glad to see us. I thank God that she was spared to see me again.

March 15. This bright & beautiful morning at 15 minutes past 8 o'clock our dear Mother's great spirit passed to a better & brighter world I trust. Her last words to me were— *All is bright in the future. Jesus is all sufficient. He will receive me.* So the dearest of Mothers has passed away. P.M, returned to Troy to get things for the funeral.

March 16. Weather cool & cloudy. At store all A. M. Business going along very well… at 4:45 left for Hoosick to attend the funeral of my beloved Mother…

March 17. Weather cool & pleasant. Morning down to cemetery with Ade to open the vault to receive the remains of our dear good Mother. Funeral at 11:00. Mr. D's prayers & remarks were beautiful indeed. Oh how sad to bury a good Mother. Returned to Troy in P.M. Eve at home.

March 29. …homeowners around the park agree to build a fence around it.

—Diary of Francis S. Thayer.

April 26, 1864. A showery growing day. Katy Thayer & children here to dinner & tea and for the night. I wrote Mr. Thayer this morning…

April 27. A very rainy night, rained a good deal through the day. Mr. & Mrs. Thayer & children here for the night…

April 28. A chilly day, ground white in morning. Mr. Thayer left this morning.

April 29. A chilly day. Katy Thayer & children left this morning…

—Diary of James McKie.

hard fighting The Wilderness campaign in Virginia.

May 8, 1864. Extra *Whig* this morning says Grant & Lee have had two or three days hard fighting & Grant has the best of it— six to eight thousand killed & wounded. Awful to think of. God grant that we may have a great victory…

May 9. Weather very warm. B. T. & Knight [Bills, Thayer & Knight] dissolved & Thayer

& Knight commenced business for the year. I have 2/3. Mr. K. 1/3. Up to mill in A.M. to take a/c of stock. War news is favorable for our side. Grant has gained a decided victory over Lee & I thank God for it…

May 12. Warm & spring-like. News from Grant's army looks favorable. Old Butler [Major General Benjamin Butler] is down at the gates of Richmond & I hope the Old Fellow will walk in… All the talk now is about the great Battle going on between Genl's Grant & Lee. God give us the victory.

May 13. Warm & pleasant… Glorious news from the seat of war. Genl. Grant is the man who under God I believe will give rebellion its death blow. Business very dull, markets declining.

May 14. Warm & pleasant. The news from Genl. Grant's army is good & I hope & pray he may go on… until rebellion shall be put down…

August 1. At Cambridge, sick in bed all the A.M. Bowels out of order again, took camphor & opium pills which had the desired effect…

September 3. At Cambridge. Charming day. Very little rain early in morning. Attended the funeral of cousin John McKie after which Ed took me to Eagle Bridge for 2:15 cars for Troy. Recd the glorious news that Sherman had taken Atlanta. Markets all down…

—*Diary of Francis S. Thayer.*

Francis McKie Thayer, age 6 or 7, photograph by A. Gobden, Troy, New York.

September 1, 1864. A clear pleasant day. Edwin & I went to Wm. McKie's at 6 o'clock this morning. John McKie had died at 4 A.M. His parents and friends are deeply afflicted…

September 2. A warm day. Jas. B. Jermain called. I engaged Fowler with carriage.

September 3. A pleasant day. Lucy, Almy, Mary Crary, & I went to John McKie's funeral. Mr. Shortt gave a short address… The funeral was the largest ever witnessed on a private occasion, about 100 carriages were there…

September 7. A beautiful day. Lucy & I went to Sophia's and took dinner with her and Katy. I attended Prayer Meeting…

September 8. A beautiful day. Edwin & I went to Br. John's. He is very sick— we fear unto death. I sent Doctor Gray to see him…

September 9. A fine day, a little rain early. Brother John died this morning, aged 75 years. God grant that that the dispensation may be sanctified to us all. I went there today with James McKie— he brought me back…

September 10. A clear beautiful day. Lucy, Almy, & I went to Bro. John's funeral. Mr. Shortt gave an address… John Whiteside's body was taken from the vault and buried— both bodies were in the procession from the vault to the graves. It was a solemn sight. God grant that it may be sanctified to us all— especially to Margaret, Almy, & myself, the only ones left of the eleven children of Father & Mother…

—*Diary of James McKie.*

November 6, 1864. Weather dark & cloudy. Kate seemed quite bright until she got up in P.M. and then she had a poor turn and she feels almost discouraged. I pray God she may be better soon. Now five weeks she has been sick. P.M. out with the children to see the colts & lambs.

November 8. Abraham Lincoln Re-Elected President of the United States. I gave him my vote & I thank God the great & glorious triumph. To Troy in morning & returned (to Cambridge) at noon. P.M. rainy. Kate not as well, sent for Doct. Mosher at eve. He came & said he would have her up & about the Home in a week.

November 13. Very stormy day at Cambridge, some ten or twelve inches of snow came. Took all the sheep up & gave them hay. It looks like winter indeed. Dr. Mosher did not come. Good old Dr. Morris died this morning, aged about 70.

Lt. Colonel John McKie, 1824–1864, had been honorably discharged from the Union Army in 1863 because of a physical disability. He died in an accident when he fell from a wagon that was hitched to a run-away horse.

Brother John John McKie, 1789–1864, father of the John Whiteside McKie who had died eight days earlier on September 1, 1864.

John Whiteside's body John Whiteside McKie, 1824–1864, had died on September 1, 1864 but his body had been placed in a vault at the time of the funeral service. His father, John McKie, 1789-1864, died on September 9, 1864. They were both buried on September 10, 1864. The elder John McKie had been married to Catherine Whiteside, 1793–1824, daughter of John Whiteside, 1752–1841, and Margaret Robertson, 1754–1849.

November 20. At Cambridge. Kate seems better & we all rejoice. I pray God she may go right along gaining and that we may soon be able to return to our home in Troy. The children are well & very happy. Dr. Mosher did not come today. He is very busy & can't come every day.

December 1. Winter comes in very mildly… Kate not as well… Glorious news from Genl. Thomas [George Henry Thomas] whose army has given Genl. Hood's [John Bell Hood] a good whipping…

December 19. …Glorious news from Sherman & Thomas…

December 25. Beautiful day at Cambridge. Kate feels weak & almost discouraged. The Dr. came in A.M. & said she would soon feel much better, so he has said week after week. God grant that we may soon see a change for the better. Children went to church with Mr. Pitney's folks & had a pleasant time. —*Diary of Francis S. Thayer.*

1865

February 24, 1865. A cool day. This day I attain to the age of 60 years, few live to that age. God grant that I may not have lived so long in vain. Well does it become me to live continually as they that watch for the coming of their Lord & Master. Maggie Wilcox here to dinner… —*Diary of James McKie.*

On March 4, 1865 Abraham Lincoln was sworn into office for his second term as President. His inaugural address established the groundwork for the hard work of reconciliation that lay ahead for the divided nation: "With malice toward none; with charity for all; with firmness in the right, as God gives us to see the right, let us strive on to finish the work we are in; to bind up the nation's wounds; to care for him who shall have borne the battle, and for his widow, and his orphan— to do all which may achieve and cherish a just, and lasting peace, among ourselves, and with all nations." The Civil War ended the next month. The diaries written by Francis Thayer, Edwin McKie, and James McKie for that period are on pages 316–317.

May 16, 1865. Weather warm & pleasant. Frankie a little better but still looks pale & sick. Had a long talk with Mr. Knight in regard to his ability to attend to business the coming season. He is quite confident he can do it. I am fearful he will break down again. Business very dull. Eve at home.

May 17. Weather warm & pleasant… James McKie here to settle the claim Uncle William had in Mich. He got $4,050, half of which will be divided among the poor or rather most needy relative…

June 1. This day appointed by the President as a day of fasting & prayer on account of the death of Mr. Lincoln… Heard Prof. Lewis deliver a eulogy on Mr. Lincoln, not up to my expectations…

June 2. Warm & pleasant… Kate, Mother & children went over to Movers to have the children sit for their picture for the first time. Up to mill in P.M.…

—*Diary of Francis S. Thayer.*

June 12, 1865. A warm day. I went to Albany, saw the 123rd Regiment. Saw Clark Rice, took dinner at Jermain's. Called at Thayer's etc.

June 21. A fine day. A Reception was given to the Returned Soldiers… Mr. Gordon made the Reception Speech and Adjutant Carney replied. A dinner was given to the Military Men. The Ladies in white, the Clergy & invited guests. Refreshments were provided for others at 50 cts each, to be applied to the purchase of Soldiers Monument.

June 25. A warm day. Lucy, Almy, Clark & I went to Church… God in his good Providence has returned Clark to us, in comfortable health and to attend Church for the first time in more than two years, having been in the Camp, on the march or the Battlefield, about 34 months… May we all be duly thankful to Him, from whom all Blessings flow.

June 26. A warm day, a fine rain toward night. Clark went to Albany and got his pay and final discharge from the Army. I wrote for 2 barrels flour from Thayer & Knight…

—*Diary of James McKie.*

Summer vacation:

"At my old desk in the office" Thursday eve, 7 o'clock, Aug 3rd, 1865.
My dear Kitty, Children & Mother (vacationing in Connecticut)—   After a hot and dusty ride I arrived at our delightful home about half past 5 o'clock. After occupying a 6x8 room for weeks it does seem refreshing to step into our large rooms, but the sea air is missing. It is very warm here and I long for a breeze from Old Ocean… Business since I left has been dull, still I guess they haven't lost any money— about held their own I reckon. I have thought about you all much today. Have Eva keep an eye on the children when they are near the water. If you go out sailing select a day when there is a gentle breeze & keep hold of the children & look out for the boom… It is very warm weather here now & bids fair for a hot spell. I shall go to Hoosick Saturday eve & stay until Tuesday or Wednesday. Now my dear Kitty I hope you will write me a few lines every day or as often as you have time. Be regular in your bathing & lunch & nap and by the time I get back there I hope to see you much better. Don't be afraid of the whiskey— when you get out of liquor, Jim will replenish your bottles. With a heart full of love to all of you & lots of kisses I am as ever your own *Frank*.

Katherine Sophia Thayer, daguerreotype.

Saturday P.M. Aug 5th, 1865.
My Dear Wife, Children & Mother—   We have another very hot day— mercury up above 90°. I got here just in time for the hottest weather of the summer. I shall go to Hoosick this eve, Cambridge, Monday and home Tuesday. There is very little that can be done to advantage now in the way of business and I see nothing to prevent my return to Guilford a week from today. It was quite comfortable in our room last night— windows all open in both rooms… Tell Frankie that I hope he will be the first one up and dressed in the morning and that he must be a good boy all the time. Kitty I know will be the best and dearest little girl in the house…   *Frank*.

September 22, 1865. A pleasant day. I am improving. Mr. Thayer & Family called on their way from Connecticut by way of Vermont in their own carriage. They went to the farm, their mother went with them…

McKie family plot, low stones in foreground, Woodland Cemetery, Cambridge, New York. The McKie graves were moved to this cemetery from the Turnpike cemetery, south of Cambridge village. James McKie's diary records the moving of the remains and the condition of each coffin.

View across the McKie family plot to the hills of Cambridge from the Woodland Cemetery.

buried in the Old, to the New Cemetery The "Old" cemetery refers to the Turnpike Cemetery, out South Union Street from the Village of Cambridge. The "New" cemetery is Woodland Cemetery. In the course of this move, the old grave markers were either lost or destroyed, and new markers were subsequently erected.

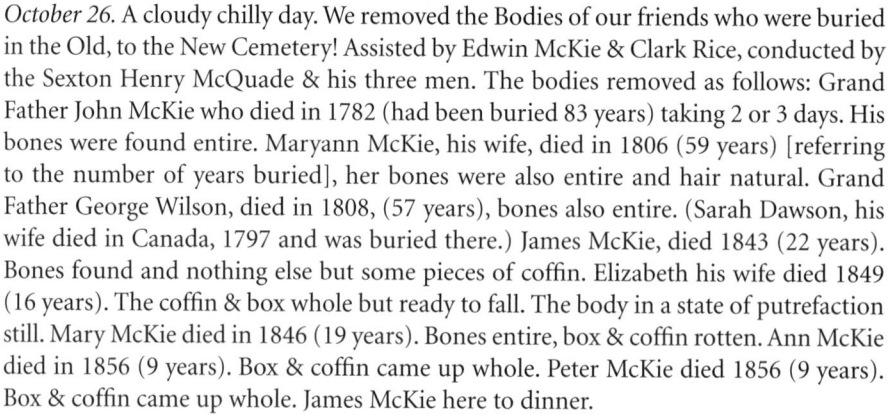

October 26. A cloudy chilly day. We removed the Bodies of our friends who were buried in the Old, to the New Cemetery! Assisted by Edwin McKie & Clark Rice, conducted by the Sexton Henry McQuade & his three men. The bodies removed as follows: Grand Father John McKie who died in 1782 (had been buried 83 years) taking 2 or 3 days. His bones were found entire. Maryann McKie, his wife, died in 1806 (59 years) [referring to the number of years buried], her bones were also entire and hair natural. Grand Father George Wilson, died in 1808, (57 years), bones also entire. (Sarah Dawson, his wife died in Canada, 1797 and was buried there.) James McKie, died 1843 (22 years). Bones found and nothing else but some pieces of coffin. Elizabeth his wife died 1849 (16 years). The coffin & box whole but ready to fall. The body in a state of putrefaction still. Mary McKie died in 1846 (19 years). Bones entire, box & coffin rotten. Ann McKie died in 1856 (9 years). Box & coffin came up whole. Peter McKie died 1856 (9 years). Box & coffin came up whole. James McKie here to dinner.

October 27. A snowy morning (the first this season), continued moderately all day… We executed a contract for the erection of a monument in the Cemetery… I paid Mial Barton 3 dols for 3 boxes used yesterday in removing bodies to the Cemetery. I paid him at the Back-yard gate…   —*Diary of James McKie.*

December 31, 1865. …Another year numbered with the past. O how thankful I am that a kind Providence has smiled upon us, preserved our lives & given us un-numbered blessings. A year ago now my dear Kate was very sick & feeble up at her Old Home in Cambridge & was obliged to stay there until 8th March. We spent three months at the seashore & enjoyed the season there very much. Kate improved almost daily & came home much better. Now she is able to walk up to Church twice this day & feels quite well… Our Children have been well most of the time and seem very happy. I pray God that He will guide & protect them always. Took upon myself the office of Elder in our Church, ordained 1st Sunday in December. I pray that I may honor the responsible office. Let my light so shine that others may be better.   —*Diary of Francis S. Thayer.*

1866

Francis S. Thayer in a photo dated 1866.

January 1, 1866. A soft day. Sophia McKie came up in the morning train to see Edwin's folks. We are spared to see the beginning of a new year. Who of us will be spared to see its close, God only knows. May he of his infinite mercy fit and prepare us for every event of his Providence and finally save us in his Heavenly Kingdom for Christ's Sake. Ada Bishop here to tea.

January 8. A very severe morning, merc 15° below zero, many things froze in the house. It continued very severe during the day. I gave Clark my check for 100 dollars to pay L. Wilson for money he borrowed of him on Saturday.

January 24. A beautiful day. Clark Rice & Anna Mary Robertson were married today at 11 o'clock by Rev. Henry Gordon. God grant them the influence of His Spirit, to guide & direct them, and an abundant measure of Grace to sustain them in all their relations in life and finally gather them to His Heavenly home for Christ's sake…

—Diary of James McKie.

March 17, 1866. At Cambridge. Very cold & windy A.M. Over to swamp with Mr. Pitney & Geddes and measured wood, 55 cords cut (on the Cambridge farm) during the winter by Geddes…

March 24. Cold & Windy. This has been the dullest week for business I ever knew in Troy…

April 5. Delightful day. Mother [Sophia Whiteside McKie] 71 years old this day…

—Diary of Francis S. Thayer.

May 31, 1866. A clear cool day. Lucy, Clark, & Kitty went to Troy & Albany to stay all night at Jermain's. I have been in bed most of the day with headache, am better this evening. Fred got some chicken feed at Blakely's. He paid him 2 dols.

June 18. A growing day… Our monument came today…

June 21. A clear warm day. Our Monument was taken to the Ground today & yesterday.

June 28. A cool day… We settled with George L. Batterson at the Bank for our Monument— 1,000 dols including Headstones for Old & young… I gave him my check for 480 dols for myself and Laetie. William & James paid 260 each making 520, all amounting to 1,000 dols. Batterson receipted the bill, which receipt William McKie took home with him. I rec'd a letter from Chas. Crary.

July 11. A very fine day. Clark & Barclay Jermain went to the ponds fishing. Mr. & Mrs. Jermain & Barclay here to tea…

July 26. A fine day. David & Warren Campbell here to dinner. Katy Thayer, children & nurse also. Catherine McKie came in to stay all night. I gave Mitchell my check for 100 dols. A circus performed this afternoon & evening. I attended Prayer Meeting at Church.

July 30. A pleasant day. Clark & Anna Mary left this morning for New York to have a bunch cut from the roof of her mouth. Mrs. Greene went with them. May God protect and support her and render their efforts successful, and return them in safety to their homes. A little shower after noon.

August 3. A cool pleasant day. Clark & Anna Mary came home today. She underwent a most painful operation…

August 8. A beautiful day. I rec'd a letter from F. S. Thayer enclosing a check for 1,000 dols, for which I am to send him his note for 1600 dols, thereby refunding 600 dols on account of Iowa lands being of less value that we anticipated, which I had sold him from Bro. William's estate…

August 9. A very fine rain today, most of the day… I mailed a letter to Thayer enclosing his note and a receipt to be signed & returned.

August 10. A pleasant day, some little showers… I rec'd a letter from Thayer, enclosing a receipt for 600 dols refunded on his purchase of Iowa lands. —*Diary of James McKie.*

Mrs. George McKie's Place and Summer Residence of Hon. F. S. Thayer of Troy, New York, Hurd's Stereoscopic Views, Greenwich, New York. Sophia Whiteside McKie, 1796–1878, in white dress, lower right. The two children are Francis McKie Thayer, 1857–1902, and Katherine Sophia Thayer (Katherine Thayer Hobson), 1859–1915.

Laetie Letitia McKie, widow of Peter McKie, 1808–1856.

Catherine McKie Thayer with her two children, Francis McKie Thayer and Katherine Sophia Thayer. Photographer and date unknown.

August 31, 1866. Weather cool & pleasant. The last day of summer. August has been a very cool month, two frosts but not enough to damage crops…
—*Diary of Francis S. Thayer.*

November 2, 1866. A beautiful day. Our Dear Anna Mary died this morning after a painful sickness of some months from Cancer in mouth, causing a swelling on the left side of neck 23 inches in circumference at the base. She died in a firm hope of Glorious Immortality— And our loss we humbly trust is her unspeakable gain. May God in his infinite Mercy sanctify the affliction, to Clark and to all connected to her…
November 3. A clear chilly day. Lucy Rice & Mrs. Jas. Jermain came up at 9 o'clock to attend the funeral of Anna Mary at 2 o'clock…
November 24. A chilly day, some snow through the day. James McKie here to dinner… I fed the cow stalks this morning for the first. Cow fodder used first time.
November 28. A fine rain commencing in the night and lasting through the day, thus filling up the springs for winter. I have kept in on account of rain.
—*Diary of James McKie.*

December 31, 1866. Weather quite cold. Streets a good deal blocked up with snow & hard getting about. Business begins to brighten up a little after a month or six weeks extreme dullness… Recd news of Aunt Sally Parsons' death— the last aunt on my beloved Mother's side. Her age was 79. It becomes us at the close of another year to thank our Heavenly Father for all His goodness & mercy towards us during the year which has been a very happy one to us as a family. May God bless us in the future.
—*Diary of Francis S. Thayer.*

1867

January 2, 1867. Weather quite cold. Went to Hoosick per morning train to attend the funeral of Aunt Sally Parsons, the last sister of my beloved Mother. Aaron & Liz intended to go but they were just too late for the cars. Returned in P.M…
—*Diary of Francis S. Thayer.*

January 20, 1867. A pleasant day. Lucy, Almy, Clark, & the girls went to Church. I staid in by indisposition. At noon Clark went to the funeral of George Law's little girl, 8 years old. Her Mother was buried on New Years Day, after being sick of typhoid fever for 8 or 10 weeks. The little Anna took the fever soon after the Mother's death and so soon followed her to the grave. How does it become us, Each one to give diligence to prepare for death, seeing we know not "what a day or an hour will bring forth."…
—*Diary of James McKie.*

February 8, 1867. Mild & pleasant. At 10:30 A.M. recd. telegram from Edwin saying "My wife is dead." Poor Nettie, her years of suffering are now over and she is in heaven…
—*Diary of Francis S. Thayer.*

February 8, 1867. A mild day. Sleighing spoiled in the street. Antoinette died this morning between 8 & 9 o'clock. I wrote Wm. Wilcox and Wm. Armitage & Julia informing them of the death.
February 11. A cold pleasant day. Edwin's wife buried today, funeral at 11 o'clock. Mr. Shortt gave a short address…
February 24. A mild day… This day I am 62 years of age. *God grant* that it may not be

said of me that I have spent the past year wholly in vain: And if it shall please Him to spare me for another year, may he of his infinite mercy, enable me so to spend it that I may make a years journey heavenward. —*Diary of James McKie.*

February 26, 1867. Mild & pleasant. Mr. Bills & I met in A.M. at our office & agreed to go on in business together under the firm of Bills & Thayer, half & half…
February 28, 1867. Very pleasant day. Up to mill in P.M. Everything in the way of business very dull. Flour, wheat, & corn declining. Mr. Knight very feeble & I am fearful he won't live a month… —*Diary of Francis S. Thayer.*

March 4, 1867. A mild day, some snow during the night…
March 5. A pleasant day…
March 6. A chilly cloudy day. I have staid in mostly…
March 7. A snowy day, sleighs running…
March 8. A clear pleasant day…
March 9. A mild day, sleighing spoiled…
March 10. A mild day…
March 11. A sloppy day, snow mostly gone…
March 12. A soft snowy day, melted as it came down… —*Diary of James McKie.*

April 10, 1867. Cloudy A.M. & raining P.M. At 9:30 A. M. rec'd telegram from Ed saying Carriage house & other building were burned last night. At 1:30 P.M. took cars for E. Bridge where Ed met me. We went over to the Old Home in the rain. We found only six buildings in ashes, loss at least $4,000, only $2,000 insurance.
—*Diary of Francis S. Thayer.*

May 9, 1867. A pleasant day…I turned our cow out across the road this morning.
May 13. A clear fine day mostly. Mitchell's' man ploughed our garden…
May 17. A mild day, a little rain at noon…Clark planted our potatoes this forenoon and went to Troy this afternoon to buy goods…
May 21. A fine day. Clark planted our sweet corn & beans… —*Diary of James McKie.*

May 20, 1867. …Thayer & Knight dissolved and Bills & Thayer commenced business again as in 1853. Up to mill & took a/c of stock there.
June 17. Weather quite warm. Up to Lansingburgh in A.M… Immediately after dinner went to Mr. Knight's and remained there until the good man died at 5 o'clock P.M. It was indeed the greatest triumph over death I ever witnessed.
June 18. Hot & sultry in A.M… Spent an hour in A.M. at Mr. Knight's… recalling and writing down some of the precious things Mr. Knight said during the last hours…
—*Diary of Francis S. Thayer.*

James McKie, 1805–1869, author of the three-volume diary that is excerpted in this book. His obituary read: "A quiet, unobtrusive gentleman of the old school has gone; another of the links which binds us to the past."

Saturday, July 27th, 1867.
City Hotel, Providence Road. Saturday eve, 10 o'clock.
My Dear ones at home—   Here I am at last and there is no way of getting to Newport until 10 o'clock Monday A.M. by Steam Boat. We came on to Springfield on time. There we waited some little time for the Presidential train [President Andrew Johnson] to arrive from New York. The Prest. arrived (sober I think) and on the steps of the [illegible] House I saw him make a few remarks— couldn't hear a word. Our train preceded the President's as far as Brookfield then our engine was disabled and we were obliged to let Mr.

Johnson pass us so at Worcester we were an hour and a half late. Providence train had gone, waited until 6 o'clock and took a freight train and arrived here safely about 9 o'clock. Have waked up and had supper and now after writing to you my dear ones I will retire with a prayer that a kind Providence may watch over us and bring us together again in peace and safety... I am sorry I didn't keep straight on to Boston and remain there over the Sabbath instead of coming here. However I must be content. Our detention is chargeable to the Prest. All along the way the people (mostly many black Republicans) were out in great numbers to get a peep at Andy. At Springfield there was a great crowd, streets full in every direction. Tomorrow I shall go to Church... I have been told this is a beautiful city. I shall look about a little in a quiet way so as to tell you of its beauties etc... Now good night. God bless you all. I am more than ever your own *Frank*.

September 14, 1867. Weather warm & pleasant... Advised with Mr. Sage & Mr. Bills about my running for Senator [New York State Senate] this fall. They both advised me to accept the nomination if I can get it...
September 17. ...County Fair commenced today. Talked with several of my friends today about taking nomination for Senator & they all say go for it...
October 5. Rainy day. Senatorial convention met at the M— House and nominated this humble individual for Senator of the 12th District. If elected it shall be my aim to discharge the duties honestly & faithfully... —*Diary of Francis S. Thayer.*

October 5, 1867. A very wet day, probably the equinoctial storm...
October 19. A fine day. I am not very well. I wrote a will today. Mrs. Judson called... Uncle William called.
November 12. A stormy day, snow from northwest all day, tedious— much like winter. I still kept in... Foddered cows first. —*Diary of James McKie.*

October 22, 1867. Cloudy A.M... Democratic conv. To nominate Senator. After talking the matter over they concluded not to nominate so I have the pleasure of running alone...
November 5. Weather very pleasant. Election day & I hope for a Republican victory. Spent the A.M. about the City at the different polls... Stayed in home most of the P.M. At the polls until 10 o'clock seeing the votes canvassed. Bad news.
November 6. Cool & pleasant. Last night was sleepless. Election news perfectly awful. Democrats carry the state... Old Washington Co. gives me about 1800 which elects me by about 1000... —*Diary of Francis S. Thayer.*

December 25, 1867. A cloudy Christmas day, some little rain and sleet falling.
December 26. A beautiful sunny day, rained smartly a part of the night...Hams salted today. —*Diary of James McKie.*

1868

January 1, 1868. A stormy day, sleet & rain, 3 inches of snow having fallen during the night. A new year has commenced. God grant that we may be enabled to make a wise improvement of our time, that we may be prepared at last to render up our accounts with joy and not with grief.
February 8. The coldest morning since we lived in Cambridge. Merc here 26° below. On north sides of building near depot 36°... —*Diary of James McKie.*

Francis S. Thayer, elected to the New York State Senate, November 1867. Denison's Photographic Parlors, Albany, New York.

April 17, 1868. I hardly know what to say here having neglected to write up this book for several days. Went to Albany in morning & returned late in the evening. I am not conscious of having done anything wrong in the way of legislation.
April 18. This has been a very busy week. My work is well advanced and I hope to get everything my constituents are particularly interested in through…
April 2. I have neglected to write up my diary for several days & I can only say here that I went to Albany in the morning & returned in the eve. Business in the Legislature is now pressing, New York Rail Road Bills up for discussion. My opinion is we shall pass no more.
April 22. This is the anniversary of the death of our dear brother Henry Mathews [McKie], 17 years. Albany in the morning…
April 30. This is the eighteenth anniversary of our wedding day and Oh how much happiness has been crowded into these years with my own dearly beloved Kate. Albany in the morning & home late in the eve. I am indeed tired of this hard work & I long for the day of adjournment.
May 2. Rainy day… Legislation is going on at a terrible rate. Bills passing without much consideration…
May 12. Warm & pleasant… Vote on impeachment postponed until Saturday…
—*Diary of Francis S. Thayer.*

May 2, 1868. A steady rain most of the day. I turned our cow to grass this morning. George Campbell here to tea… *Cow turned out.*
May 7. A cloudy, chilly day— some rain. Mr. Griffin assisted Clark in getting out manure on the garden.
May 19. A cool day. Wm. T— was killed in the steam mill— his body being sawed completely in two. I gave Clark my check for 60 dols.
June 1. A cool pleasant day. Again summer is upon us. The country looks beautiful.
—*Diary of James McKie.*

Troy. May 18th, 1868.
My dear Frank— We were all made glad of the letter to Kittie which came while at breakfast… And so Andy Johnson was not convicted and how wretchedly I did feel Sat eve, nobody to speak to about the matter. Our paper did not come— I thought I would go to the neighbors, Will Eaton would rejoice, course was not at home. Bills would say all right, So I went over to Shepherd's. "She thought they would get in a muddle." He "ya-all" acquitted I suppose." And I came home thinking that men are about as silly as women. Kittie Graves and Emma Mann were here to tea. I said, "Emma, what did your Father say bout impeachment of the President?" Kittie said, "What is impeachment, is he elected, what are you talking about?" Emma said, "Papa said he did not think the Pres would be convicted" —and so after a time our paper came and I saw what was not done. Oh these men— what unreliable stuff they are made of. It makes me think of the epitaph on the young child. "*If this was so soon to be done for, What in the world was it begun for?*" But so it goes. Edwin has just come in, going to New York tonight. Says all are well in Cambridge… —Yours as ever, *Kate.*

Troy. May 19th, 1868, Tues eve. 7 o'clock.
My dear Frank— Your most welcome letter of Sat eve came to us at breakfast and I assure you it received a most cordial welcome. We were glad and thankful that you had arrived well and safely at one end of your jour-

impeachment of the President President Andrew Johnson was impeached by the House of Representatives early in 1868 and the trial in the Senate went from March to May of that same year. Nine of the eleven articles of impeachment centered on the Tenure of Office Act and the other two related to Johnson's behavior toward Congress. Johnson was acquitted by the Senate by a margin of one vote. Whenever Francis Thayer wrote of either the impeachment or of the 1868 Republican Convention in Chicago, which he attended as a delegate, he abbreviated President, "Prest."

A dress, long stored in a trunk, belonging to Katherine Thayer as a child.

ney… Nothing new to write you. Kittie had a hard headache yesterday morn and some fever last night, but she has been out some today, but not to school, and I trust will go tomorrow. She is now at her spelling lesson and Frank sits here busy with his Geography… I must say that it has grown so dark that I cannot see the lines. I send Frankie with this to the Office— with Kittie's letter. Mother with children and myself join in tenderest love to you— with much love to Porter. —Your *Kittie.*

May 19, 1868. Rainy day. On the cars all day between Detroit & Chicago, 284 miles. Ran over an old man & killed him in Canada this morning & knocked a young man off the track in Michigan & injured him badly. President Johnson acquitted on the 11th article & this will end the matter.

May 21. In Chicago. Weather mild & spring-like. At 10 o'clock A.M. the great convention met and, after adopting a most excellent platform, Genl. Grant was nominated for President unanimously, receiving 650 votes on the 4th ballot… Left Chicago at 9:30 feeling well about the nomination. —*Diary of Francis S. Thayer*

Chicago, Sherman House, May 16th, 1868.
My dear ones at home— [Written while Francis Thayer was attending the 1868 Republican National Convention as a delegate.] …Men are here from all parts of the country to attend the convention. I have just been talking with two men from Georgia and they tell me that the news from Washington today in regard to the impeachment will embolden the disloyal people down south and that they greatly fear that it will be worse than ever down south. I hope and pray that God will deliver this Nation from evil. Perhaps He has not punished us sufficiently yet. I do pity the loyal people in the Southern States. No one is talked of for President except General Grant… It is now almost 12 o'clock and I am tired and sleepy so good night my precious ones at home, one and all. May God watch over us and bring us together again in His own good time, well and happy… —*Francis.*

Sherman House, Chicago. Monday P.M. [May 18, 1868] 4 o'clock.
My dear ones at home— This is a bright & beautiful day, rather cool however. The city is full of people from all parts of the country. Almost every state has a candidate for vice Prest… I had thought the failure to convict the Prest. would throw a damper upon the spirit of the Convention, but I find I was mistaken. The spirit of the Convention today is eminently American, ie, forgetting the past and looking forward with hope and confidence, awaiting patiently for honor & victory. We are on the side of right and altho' dark days may intervene, still I see the bow of promise— "There is a silver lining to every cloud." …I didn't think of writing a political letter when I started but you know I am now in that atmosphere and you will excuse me this time…
—I am as ever your own *Frank.*

Headquarters — Vermont Delegation. Sherman House, Parlor No. 10. Thursday evening 7 o'clock. [May 21, 1868]
Dear ones at home— Well tomorrow at 12 o'clock we all go into the convention after hard work laying our plans three or four days. Grant will be nominated without opposition. There are at least half a dozen candidates for Vice Prest. …The telegraph will inform you of the result before this reaches

you so I will not speculate upon the subject.— This A.M. I visited the Water Works and looked about the city a little. Went with Porter over to his factory where he keeps about 100 men at work making furniture of most every variety, some very handsome… The weather is cool but pleasant… Mr. Townsend is at my side and says "Stop writing to Kate and go and see my wife," so I'll go. Good night darling ones. I am more than ever your own *Frank*.

June 20, 1868. Quite warm. Recd a letter from Ed saying Aunt Almy was very low so at 2 P.M. Mother, Kate, children & self all went to Cambridge— found her very feeble but perfectly ready to go…
June 24. …Aunt Almy died at 2 o'clock this morning…

June 25. Very warm. To Cambridge per morning cars to attend Aunt Almy's funeral.…
—*Diary of Francis S. Thayer.*

Thayer & Tobey Furniture Co, Chicago. Owned by F. Porter Thayer, brother of Francis S. Thayer.

June 18, 1868. A very warm day. Equal to yesterday. Almy not much better… I sat up with Almy.
June 19. A warm day. Doctors. Gray & Kennedy operated upon Almy for strangulated hernia. She very low during the day.
June 20. A very warm day. Almy a trifle more comfortable. Wm. Wilcox, George Wilcox, wife & daughter, Thayer family here. Sophia staid with Edwin. Mary Crary came from N. York at 11 last night. Edwin & Mary Crary sat up.
June 21. A cool cloudy day… Almy a good deal relieved thanks to a kind Providence…
June 23. A cloudy day, beautiful rain during the night. Almy still lives but sinking. May God of his infinite mercy remove her gently to the Eternal World. Margaret Barkley & Clark sat up last night.
June 24. A damp morning, heavy rain in the night. Almy died at 2 o'clock this morning when her spirit we hurriedly trust winged its way to mansions on high. Mrs. Seabring left at 2 o'clock. I paid her 5 dols. I paid Sexton 3 dols…
June 25. A beautiful day. Our Dear Sister Almy was buried this afternoon. Mr. Shortt made a prayer, no other services. Friends present as follows: Mr. Thayer & family, Edwin McKie, Wm. & Margaret Wilcox, Geo. Wilcox, wife & daughter Maggie, Bell Shepherd, John & Wm. Armitage, A. Barkley & daughter Maria, Wm. McKie & wife, mother & daughter, Geo McKie, Mother & two sisters, Chas Crary & wife, Mr. Thayer's family & Crary left by 2 1/2 o'clock train. All others left but Mary Crary who stays until next week. I had three carriages from Stroud. I paid him 10 dollars on Stroud's steps. I had one carriage from Randler, paid him 4 dollars. (Clark paid 1).
August 4. A cloudy day. I went to George McKie's and settled with them the amounts left by Almy, viz 1,000 dols each. I gave Elizabeth the watch & took their receipts for all. George came and got the furniture & clothing. Lucy & I took tea at Sayles Robinson with Mr. & Mrs. Beals…
August 25. A pleasant day. Old Joshua Ripley and I went to Missiquoi Bay in Canada. I saw my cousin Almira Wilson, aged 62 years. I visited the graves of Grand Mother Sarah Wilson and her sons George, John, & James. —*Diary of James McKie.*

᠙ Summer vacation:

August 14, 1868. At Fire Island. Pleasant company here & we are having a very nice time. This sea air seems to be just the thing for my dear Kate and the children are doing well— out sailing & fishing, not much luck…

Grave of Almy McKie, 1802–1868, Woodland Cemetery, Cambridge, New York.

One of three monuments: Soldier's Monument, Woodland Cemetery, Cambridge, New York. "To the Memory of Soldiers who died in the service of their country, 1861–1865. Erected by the Citizens of the Old Town of Cambridge 1868." The monument includes the names of forty-six soldiers from the towns of Cambridge, White Creek, and Jackson who died during the Civil War, and there are twenty graves in this plot. The Woodland Cemetery contains the graves of 157 Civil War veterans. To put these numbers in perspective, the combined 1875 census figures for those three towns show the following: male population, 3,322; female population, 3,251; school age population (5–18 years), 1,743; landowners, 861; illiterates, 87; and voters, 1,744.

August 27. At home once more. Weather is delightful and really I think there is no place quite equal to our own Sweet Home. Business very dull…

August 28. Charming weather. At Store all A.M. looking over what has been done during my absence. At 1:30 P.M. left for Cambridge…

September 11. At Cambridge all day. Rained hard in A.M. and Eve. I am 46 years old & I feel truly thankful that a kind & merciful heavenly Father has watched over me another year & I pray for His blessing in future. P.M. worked with Frankie in big meadow cutting & drawing off willows.
　　　　　　　　　　　　　　　　　　　　　　　　　—*Diary of Francis S. Thayer.*

November 5, 1868. A rainy morning, cleared up at 2 o'clock, at which time I went to the meeting for the Dedication of the Soldier's Monument. Mr. Gordon gave an address in White Church. The soldiers then formed a procession and marched to the cemetery where Mr. Eaton made some remarks, and the monument was unveiled. Russell Bank gave the music…

November 18. A white ground, rained afternoon. Cow foddered first regularly. I gave Edwin 35 dols to pay for cloak in Troy. *Cow fed.*

November 21. A mild day. Clark & I put in double windows…

December 5. A snowy day, mild throughout. Clark & I washed our wagon. Lucy & Lucy Rice went to Prayer Meeting. Alfred Fassett came from N. York.

December 16. A fine day. Lucy Campbell Rice here to dinner. Lucy Rice went to Prayer Meeting… *Hams & Beef salted.*

December 21. A mild thawing day. I mailed a draft for 10 dols to *New York Tribune* for paper for 1869. Lucy & Lucy Rice gone to Prayer Meeting.

December 31. A mild day… This is the last day of 1868. Another important portion of our time is gone to the Records of Eternity. God in his adorable Providence has spared our lives, and has in his sovereign wisdom removed our dear Sister Almy to the Eternal World. We humbly trust that our loss is her infinite gain. May God enable us to follow her in so far as she followed Christ; and be prepared at last, to join those dear friends who have gone before us, in his Kingdom above.　　　　—*Diary of James McKie.*

December 31, 1868. The last day of another year has come and naturally our mind goes back over the past. The first four months of the present year were spent at Albany in the Senate and I discharged the duties devolving upon me honestly and conscientiously and I trust satisfactorily to my constituents. Our business has been very poor, all the year we have had declining markets and our losses will be quite heavy— I reckon not less than $20,000— The first year in twenty-two I have lost money. Mr. Bills, Robert & I feel pretty blue & I don't like it very much. However we are much better off than many others in the business. I have a great many things to be truly thankful for… My dear Kate's health is much improved & our dear children are well & happy… Aunt Almy has been taken to her reward in heaven & we all miss her delightful visits. Now goodbye old year. God forgive the sins of the past & help us to live nearer to Thee in the future.
　　　　　　　　　　　　　　　　　　　　　　　　　—*Diary of Francis S. Thayer.*

1869

January 25, 1869. Weather cold. Up to Mill in A.M. with Mr. Bills. We talked about business matters for another year. Concluded to go on as we are & try it one more year.
　　　　　　　　　　　　　　　　　　　　　　　　　—*Diary of Francis S. Thayer.*

February 24, 1869. A beautiful morning, snow squalls after noon. This day makes me 64 years old. God, in his adorable Providence, has spared me another year, while many have been called to The Eternal World. Should he spare me another year, may He, in his infinite goodness & mercy, enable me so to live that I may promote his Glory and the well being of my immortal soul. —*Diary of James McKie.*

April 3, 1869. At home. Talked over business matters with Mr. Bills. I told him that I would not place myself in a position so that I could not hold any political office if I chose to do so....
April 5. At home until evening & then went to Albany to attend evening session... Had a little talk with Mr. Bills about business. He hardly knows what to do or say, first one thing & then another. —*Diary of Francis S. Thayer.*

Grave of James McKie in the McKie family plot, Woodland Cemetery, Cambridge, New York.

❧ Death in the family:

April 28, 1869. A Beautiful day. I wrote Mr. Thayer by Edwin on Charter matters...
—*Diary of James McKie.*

James McKie's entry for April 28, 1869, was the last entry in his diary in his handwriting. The diary continues for a short period in an unidentified handwriting.

May 6. Uncle James McKie died yesterday at 6 P.M., aged 64 years. The last of my Father's brothers.
May 7. Uncle James buried today in A.M. Kate & children up. Very large funeral... Kate & children went down on 2:40 train. Beautiful day.
May 8. Fine, clear & beautiful day... went to prayer meeting at eve & called on Aunt Lucy in AM & PM. —*Diary of Edwin McKie.*

May 13, 1869. Charming weather. At office most of the day. Mr. Bills made a proposition to go on in business together which I shall not accept. I feel quite independent...
May 14. Delightful weather. Had some talk with Mr. Bills about business— told him I would like to rent my half of the mill for three years and I hope he will find a good customer...
May 19. Weather quite cool for the season. Troy *Times* came out with a very flattering notice of my Senatorial record. Had some talk with Mr. Bills in regard to business matters. I am not inclined to go on with him. I wish to get out for two or three years.
June 4. Weather hot in A.M... Mr. Bills & I sat down to bid for the mill but after talking a while we thought best to go on in business together, which perhaps is the better course...
June 5. Weather cool & pleasant, at store all day. Wrote a circular for the new firm & took it to the Printer's office. Mr. Bills I think feel pleased in regard to the new arrangement. Business very dull. —*Diary of Francis S. Thayer.*

❧ Summer vacation:

July 21, 1869, Troy.
My Dear Boy— [Francis Thayer to his son] I have you & your dear Mother in my minds eye, hold of hands on the dock in the full blaze of that bright light. When I could no longer see you I walked upstairs into the saloon with moist eyes and if I am not mistaken you watched the steamer with anxious eyes & heavy hearts. I hope & pray that within a few days we may meet in the full enjoyment of health & happiness. We had a pleasant passage to New York where I spent the day yesterday & came up the river on the Albany Boat last night and from Albany I came up in the cars. You cannot tell how lonely it seemed to me to walk upstairs & not find the loved ones there. It is the living presence of loved ones that makes the house joyous & happy. I hope & pray

A second monument: Goochland County, Virginia. "Erected by the Goochland Chapter United Daughters of the Confederacy, June 22, 1918 – To the Glorious Memory of the Confederate Soldiers of Goochland County, 1861–1865 – Lest We Forget."

And a third in Virginia: See page 271.

our Heavenly Father will watch over us & bring us together again in our own homes all well & happy and I trust we all look to God for His blessing… You will I am sure be a good boy, take good care of your dear Mother & darling sister. Please tell your Mother to write me what she wishes me to bring in the way of clothes etc. I trust you will answer this the day you receive it. I wish you to keep me well informed of what is going on at the *Pequot*. I have not more time to write now. With much love I am your devoted *Father*.

July 21, 1869, Troy.
My Darling little Daughter—   [Francis Thayer to his daughter]   I have written to Mother & Brother and now I will write a few lines to you. That sweet little Pink you gave me for Grandma looks quite fresh yet, and it is just as sweet as ever. I shall keep it in water until I go up to Cambridge which will be Saturday if not before. I arrived home safely this morning & you cannot tell how lonely it seemed. I hope & pray God will watch over us & keep us in health & strength to meet in our own dear home again. I think we have the sweetest home I know of. Don't you? The girls are well and everything looks nice about the House. I have no more time to write now. I hope you will answer this soon. My best love to Mother & brother and the same to you my precious one.   —*Father*.

July 27, 1869
My darling Daughter—   Your very welcome little letter of last Saturday was received yesterday afternoon and I assure you it really made my heart glad. This getting a letter from loved ones is the next thing to seeing them and I hope you will write to me very often… I tell you it is very lonely at our sweet home when you are away. No one to meet me with a loving look & sweet kiss…   —*Father*

At Home. July 28th, 1869. Wednesday evening.
My own darling Kate—   …The political cauldron in this Senatorial District is boiling a little. My friends tell me that my re-nomination is a fixed fact— in fact nothing will prevent it if I want it. The knowing ones say the course is clear for me. Fox I think would like the nomination, but he can't get it with the Whig's help. The Wash. Co. papers are out in my favor. Tell Frankie that I shall expect to see him swim very well by the time I get back there.
—Your own devoted *Frank*.

Troy, Aug 19th, 1869. Thursday P.M. 3 o'clock.
My own dear Kate—   I went to the mill this A.M. & did not find time to write a word to you before dinner. Now I am just up from dinner & will improve the few minutes before the mail closes in saying a few words to you & our darlings. Well, I hope you are in the enjoyment of health & comfort this hot day. This is the warmest day I have seen in a month. No doubt you have a cool and invigorating breeze which I wish you could send along up this way… I am going to Hoosick tonight & shall return in the morning. I know you will expect me Saturday eve and you know too that I would come if practicable. It is better that I should accommodate Mr. Bills as he has been here most of the time through the summer… Please remember me very kindly to all inquiring friends and a heart full of love to you & our dear darling children. —*Frank*.

Senator Thayer comes out with no stain on him. His record is clean. For purity of action as a legislator, no Senator stands higher than he. He has been a thorough and persistent worker, always striving most assiduously to advance all bills and measures that promised to be of benefit to the interests of his constituency. Though not speaking a great deal he has spoken often upon subjects, in which he felt a deep interest, with cogency and effect. With the experience he has acquired and the acquaintance he has gained, Mr. Thayer will make a most valuable Senator during his second term if he consents to serve again.
—*Unidentified newspaper clipping.*

Friday morn.
August twentieth and very hot— Would that I were at the Pequot with wife & children very dear… Friday morn
My own dear Kate—   Your precious letter of Wed eve was rec'd this morning… Your stay at the sea-side is drawing to a close & I hope you will make the most of every passing hour, each refreshing and invigorating breeze. I expect to spend the Sabbath with dear good Mother & Edwin. A heart full of love to you all. Your own *Fraddie*.

Troy. Aug 23rd, 1869. Monday noon.
My own dear darling Kate—   …Now I don't feel like advising you to stay until next week, but you are doing well I take it and *I am more than ever anxious that you should receive all the benefit the air and place can give you.* No doubt we shall have hot weather this week, there is every prospect of it, and I think for you to come back in the midst of a heated term it would put you back. If you have pleasant company and can enjoy it, stay another week and I will come on Saturday, stay a very few days & will come home together. Think of this my darling and act as your own good judgment may dictate. If you are *doing well*, gaining flesh & strength why stay another week. …Remember that the salt air has done much for you & that you should be perfectly contented when you are *building a foundation* for health & strength.…   —Your own *Frank*.

September 14, 1869. Very warm… At 2 P.M. we went to Hoosick to attend the funeral of Cousin Asa Thayer who died this morning. Returned at 5 o'clock, eve at home.
October 5. We are in the midst of a great flood. Terrible accident on the T&B RR [Troy & Boston Railroad] last night. Dr. & Mrs. Fowler & Mr. A— drowned in the Hoosick River. Business suspended. No mail or trains from anyplace…
October 6. Cool & pleasant. Flood subsiding. Nothing doing in the way of business. First train from New York in three days. Flour & wheat markets dull…
November 9. Cool & pleasant. I have the satisfaction of knowing that I am re-elected Senator…
December 31. Weather delightful for the season, mild & pleasant as autumn. No sleighing. A little snow to be seen off on the hills. Spent the A.M. at the office. Business very dull & I can see nothing in the future to encourage us… This has been another disastrous year for the milling business. We have, I think, lost some money & worked for nothing. Markets have been declining… God in His mercy has been pleased to smile upon us as a family… My darling Kate is better now than at any time before… In closing the record of the year I thank God for all His mercies and Pray for the health, happiness & prosperity in the coming year.   —Diary of Francis S. Thayer.

Thayer family cemetery plot, Dummerston, Vermont. The land transfer records in Dummerston, Vermont show that in the early nineteenth century several branches of the Thayer family lived there in addition to Adin Thayer and his family. The Thayer plot in the Dummerston cemetery includes this monument with the inscription, "Asa Thayer, died at Hoosick Falls September 14, 1869."

XI

1866–1876

Virginia

THE Civil War had decided two things: the Union would be preserved, and there would be no slavery in the United States. In a post-war America it was now a time of reconstruction, and there would be Constitutional amendments and federal legislation passed during this period that would try to address the problems that the entire nation faced. The wounds inflicted on the nation during the war would be slow to heal and the weakened Presidency of Andrew Johnson had no "political capital" that could be used during these difficult times. Towns in all parts of the country were erecting very similar looking war memorials honoring the soldiers who had either fought victoriously to preserve the union or in vain to preserve the institution of slavery. Alexander Gardner's *Photographic Sketch Book of the Civil War*, published in 1866, was just one of the many books that would be published about the war, and more than a century later, the American Civil War is still much written about. Near the end of his term in office, President Andrew Johnson proclaimed a general amnesty and the war, whether it was a war of secession or a war of emancipation, was over. America was still growing, and in 1867 Alaska was purchased for less than 2¢ per acre. In Virginia, the Hobson family was living on a very different farm than had previously existed.

Letters and diaries by:
Annie Jennings Wise Hobson
Frederick Plumer Hobson
Henry A. Wise
Mary Lyons Wise

Letters and diaries written from: Richmond and Eastwood, Goochland County, Virginia.

1866

∽ Letters from Annie Jennings Wise Hobson:

Eastwood, May 1st, 1866.
My dear Mother—   Although I have heard nothing from you since my return home six weeks ago, and have not so much as received a message from you since my little one week old girl came, I am still egotistical enough to attribute your silence to some other cause than indifference and I determined to write to you to tell you myself how glad I am to have your own letter. I wish to tell you candidly, that as I wrote twice to you when it cost me no little effort

my little one-week-old girl
Marianne Douglas Hobson, born April 24, 1865. The letter is incomplete and unsigned.

and pain to do so, you might at least have expressed by Néné's pen ordinary interest in my well doing, at this particular time. I have no doubt the interest was felt, but when one is sick, nervous, and suffering, it is not pleasant even to seem forgotten… even the children and servants seem to think it strange that "Grandma" and "Grandpa" Wise evince so little interest in the stranger! I know how painful writing frequently is to you and that you have many excuses, but as I said before, it would not have required much effort to have persuaded Néné to act as your amanuensis. I have nothing to say to Néné except that she knows very well how I feel about her constant acts of indifference… I have everything to be thankful for, in my own present well being, as usual with me, danger threatened and God helped me, wonderfully. I have suffered more from the consequences of the attack I had before the baby's birth than anything else and in my hours of weakness and depression I have constantly remembered you lovingly and prayerfully, and have sympathized even more than ever, with your great trial of bodily infirmity and painful suffering; so you see I have not forgotten you, even while you appeared indifferent to me. Mr. Hobson and the boys have gone up the county today to pay a visit of a week. I will resume my account of the baby for Richard's benefit as he manifests some interest in her. Give much love to Father, Néné, and Richard; I will write to the latter soon. Tell Eliza that I know *she* would write if she could, and that the baby sends love to her.

Eastwood, May 5th, 1866, Saturday.
My dear Mother—   I received your letter this morning. I cannot attempt to answer it as I wish until I am stronger— therefore won't refer to *the subject under discussion* 'till then. Tell Néné I commenced a letter to her, but found I was too tired to continue it, will write by the next mail & conclude it. I scribble you these few lines to tell you of my continued well doing and to give the promised description of the baby. I am very weak considering how little actual pain I suffered but have such a good appetite that I hope to gain strength now. I have nearly drunk a *whole bottle of brandy* since the baby's birth, & am just beginning to give some milk. Nature has dealt most kindly with me, for Dr. Smith says he never before saw me "give in" as I did after the baby was born. I didn't have a pain worth calling pain except the one that gave birth to the child, and yet lay in a fainting state for almost an hour & yet was threatened *with flooding*. I was kept quiet & slept a good deal, but had to eat very little & that of the lightest diet for three days, and to be constantly stimulated. This will account for my weakness, when you remember my bilious attack I had before the baby was born. She has been remarkably good thus far. She has a little round head beautifully shaped covered with dark hair, not too thickly for a baby— her eyes appear sometimes blue, sometimes dark hazel & are large & full— & now she begins to have a little individuality of appearance that servants are struck with her likeness to Johnny Wise. Her nose is still rather swollen to tell what it will be, but her mouth is her Father's & is very sweet. Her complexion is red enough just now to be very fair here-after. Her head is the smallest part of her, her shoulders being very broad & fat & her limbs quite long and full. Mrs. Murphy is a capital baby nurse, & a good kind old woman, & has proved a great comfort to me. Plumer & Anne have managed so well in my sickness that I've had no annoyances, & altogether have everything to be thankful for— even my very weakness & sickness since God

helped and helps me wonderfully in both. I am very sorry Henry has gone to Harrisburg before I could see him. Love to Sallie— Did she get my letters? Mr. Hobson & the boys will be home Tuesday next. Much love to all. I'm too tired for another line!   Your affect daughter, *Annie*.

Eastwood, Saturday, May 26th, 1866.
My dear Mother—   Having written a letter for the family generally, dear Mother, I put in this sheet *entre nous*. Plumer says it is time I had stopped my correspondence upon the subject that *caused us so much excitement*, but I have never fully replied to your letter as I promised and wished to do. I can't say all in a letter— nor exactly in the way I'd like best. And before I begin, let me beg you dear Mother to receive all I shall say as lovingly as it is said. To begin at the beginning— for a long time, Mother, I have wanted to have a talk with you— to tell you some things I have felt & thought & to answer some of your assertions… You have so often said to me that I did not "love you as a Mother"— as a daughter should do a Mother, while you "felt all a Mother's tenderness for me." You often made this assertion in a way that wounded me more than I admitted, for I felt my conscience acquit me of having striven as earnestly to do my duty by you as an own daughter could have done it, and for more than I saw many an own daughter do it by their mothers, and when from suffering and sickness, the extent of which you did not know because I tried to keep it from you, as you were so sick & suffering yourself, or from my natural *infirmity of temper*, I was betrayed with a more impatient, & disrespectful manner towards you than you liked, you reproached me bitterly, going so far on two different occasions without weighing the provocation as to say "no daughter with *proper feeling* could have so spoken to a Mother." It was only because you were in my own house, and because you were so nervous and unlike yourself, from suffering, that I could refrain from saying, "Mother, an own Mother would love her child too much not to excuse her more readily when she inadvertently offended, —*an own Mother* would not be so ready to take offense at the *mere manner* of a sick or impatient child, who was a woman & wife & Mother herself."

It was these occurrences between us that first led me to question seriously whether you did love me as the Mother who bore me would have done, and whether I loved you as I might have done my own Mother. And, dear Mother, you must not be offended when I tell you what conclusion I have come to. I do not believe that a woman can have exactly the same near feeling, the same tender forbearing love towards her adopted children (& such the children of a husband are to the second wife) that a good, true, unselfish Mother has to the children she herself bore. A good, true *step-Mother* may love her husband's children far more than many a *selfish* Mother loves her own children, but not as much as she would love her own children for whose life she had suffered the pangs & perils of child-birth.

My present Mother loves us all most unselfishly & tenderly, she is far more unselfish towards us than many an own Mother towards her children, but I do not think she has exactly the same love she would have had for those she *might have borne herself*. I do know, Mother that you *honestly* think you love me, & all of us, as much as you would love your own children & you love us very much, and are very unselfish in many ways towards us all; and therefore when you tell me you love me as a Mother, I do not doubt you think so; it never occurs to me to think you the least hypocritical. This is just what I meant when I said "if you had felt as lively an interest in me as you 'persuaded' yourself you did, you would have written or made Néné write a line of inquiry about me."

And I am truly sorry you so far interpreted my meaning as to say I accused you of *hypocrisy*. Mother I hope I would be at least too much of a *Christian lady* to make such an *insinuation* to my Father's wife especially as she had written most kindly & affectionately to me. No, I ventured to speak as a sick impulsive child might have done to her own Mother, and the manner in which it was received convinces me that my conclusion is right… I love you very dearly more as my Mother than I love anyone else, but I cannot feel exactly towards you, nor act exactly towards you as I might do towards my own Mother— you have certainly convinced me of that. I will not again enter upon the *discussed question* about writing to me. I did not wish you to make me any apology. —I was only perhaps *bluntly* sincere in saying what I felt that while I knew you were sick & suffering too much at times to write such a long letter, that if you had *been my own Mother* you would have felt too anxious about me not to have been compelled to *show your anxiety*— at the same time I did not doubt your true love, and anxiety in a measure, & still less did I doubt that you sincerely *believed* you felt all *you expressed*. I only meant to say you were mistaken. I wish now I had never said what I did to you… (I am so weak brained that I can't half express myself.) I want to make you fully understand me— that I do love you very much & don't doubt you in the least. I have tried to do my duty lovingly & with a daughter's willing cheerfulness by you, and where I have failed you must forgive me. I can never forget that you first showed me more tenderness than anyone else had ever done before my husband; and your love & sympathy are dear to me, and I confide in both. Plumer confides in you just as fully as I do… I believe I love you more as a Mother than I do anyone else & as much as I should do anyone in your place… but dear Mother do you not think you are at times so dark & hopeless because you *brood* so much over your sorrow, I really think no other of earth is so afflicted? There is "a best side" to everything— do you strive to find the best side of your burden? I make these remarks as suggestions not in the least as condemnatory. God knows you have my sympathy! Tell me whether you will promise to take no offense if I will write to you, as one Christian wishing to help another, just what I mean by these suggestions? I am too tired to write another line. God bless you with all needed strength, daily prays.   —Your affect daughter *Annie*.

Enclosed in the envelope, a small folded piece of paper reads: "*Miss A. W. Hobson's hair.*"

In an envelope that reads: Dover Mills, May 26.
Mrs. H. A. Wise Sr. —Richmond—   I hope you will continue better in mind and body, and you will let me hear from you, at least by the time the baby is a month old, for appearance sake, if for nothing else. God bless you all. Anne Jones sends much love to all.   —Yours affectionately, *A. J. W. Hobson*

Eastwood, May 26th, 1866.
My dear Mother—   Cannon was much gratified at the receipt of your letter and especially at your sending him the poetry & other extracts— they have had quite a mania on the subject of *newspaper poetry*… the children are constantly bringing me papers to cut *extracts from*— & very often it doesn't make much

difference what the subject is. The rain is pouring in torrents and altogether we have indeed a very gloomy Saturday (as Cannon remarked just now.) …Mrs. Stanard has been to see me twice since the baby's arrival, & was very kind in offering to do anything for me. …Mrs. Murphy went down Thursday evening— it really distressed me to part with her; she watched over me in the kindest way— she never seemed to think of herself one moment; and she managed the baby beautifully. My "dear little, fat girl" is so good that I can hardly realize I have a baby— except a little colic in the evening which is readily relieved, she gives no trouble to anyone. She generally sleeps from the time I go to bed until four o'clock, sometimes later, is very rarely restless at night, and then only a *little watchful* as Mrs. Murphy used to say, never crying. Mother, Anne was so good to me during my sickness, and has done all in her power to keep me from missing Mrs. Murphy & I have not felt the want of her attention as much as I expected… Before the little one arrived from certain reasons which *must remain secret* just now, I said if "the expected proved a girl I'd call her Marian, and the idea also occurred to me that there were already two many Marys in the family to admit of another one, Marian would be a good compromise, as we could give the young lady the pet name of "Marie"… Everyone except Néné & Mrs. Hobson have seemed to like my choice. George suggested for me to put in the *Douglas* for Aunt Margaret and I think *Marian Douglas* would be a beautiful name. I don't agree with Néné & Mrs. Hobson about the beauty of the name— I have always thought it a particularly pleasant name— fanciful & yet *good & honest*… All the children are delighted that another baby has come, but Cannon more so that "it is a little sister." Annie is pleased but not as much elated as I expected.— There is the dinner bell. My pen has quite run away with me this morning. I have said very little to have written so much. The mail brought me a letter from Johnnie today in reply to one I sent him; he complained of scarcely ever hearing from home— he was well. I am glad to hear from Dick's letter that Father got off to Northampton, as he always enjoys a visit to the Eastern Shore. I am sure you will miss Eliza— What took her to Phila. at this time? Richard also mentioned you were in town spending the day which I was glad to hear, for any little change is good for you. Mr. Hobson regrets not seeing you when he was down, the bad weather admitted only of his going out long enough to attend to his business; he & Anne join me in love to all. The children send much love & kisses. Cannon will answer his letter soon. God bless you all!   —Your affect. daughter *Annie*.

The diary of Annie Jennings Wise Hobson:

May 28, 1866, Saturday Evening, Eastwood.
Bless the Lord, O my; soul and all that is within me, bless his holy name!
My precious little daughter is nearly five weeks. She was born Tuesday, April 24th at half past four o'clock A.M. God did indeed deliver me in the perils of childbirth and the consequent sickness. He made all my bed in sickness. He caused his face to shine upon me. I have been blessed in every way: in my own well being and that of my fat fine little girl: in my husband's comparative freedom from suffering and my children's health: in the loving care and kindness of all about me. Especially my kind old nurse, Mrs. Murphy. O Holy spirit, teach me to walk softly before my God. O Savior, forgive all my past sins. O Heavenly Father, give unto me a child's true gratitude. Praise the Lord. Praise the Lord. O my Soul.

June 2, 1866, Saturday evening.
This week has passed so quickly! I have taught the children, kept house a little and directed the household generally. At times, my strength did not fully sustain me— then too, my precious husband has been more unwell of late— restless and coughing at night, and I was weak and nervous to see him suffer, and for some nights, I did not sleep at all without taking a large dose of brandy. On Thursday, my dear little baby was right sick and I became so nervous and tremulous about her that I had to give her up to Anne and went with Plumer and the children to ride. Bright sunshine, the pleasant landscape and fresh air restored me somewhat, but I really dreaded to return. Ah, how I would once have laughed at such morbid anxiety. *Sorrow and experience can alone teach us true sympathy with the weak and suffering.* I have lost two darlings and my heart will tremble over this one every time sickness touches her. In God alone, shall I have strength! I was so thankful to find she had been quietly sleeping during my absence, and I thank God that she is sleeping sweetly in her crib now.

I have had some weak suffering hours this week from various debility— especially over my Beloved's suffering. He is always so unwell at this season. His Spiritual state perplexes me and gives me the most agony. I cry unto God and he always helps me. O Lord, I wait upon Thee. My will, no Thine be done!

I have copied some of my story this week.

Ella S— joined me in sending flowers to aid in dressing the soldiers graves at Hollywood. Anne Jones is preparing to leave me. Dearest Jeannie promises to come to me.

Heavenly Father, aid me in all my resolutions for good and usefulness for the coming week for Christ's sake. *Amen*.

June 3, 1866, Sunday evening,
Couldn't attend church as the weather was too damp. The greater part of the day nursing the baby. Taught the children, read very little. But strove to learn a lesson of patience and endurance.

June 10th, Sunday.
Last week was one of varied experience. Seasons of great depression and physical weakness, when Satan tempted me to useless fears and faithless anxieties, but thanks be to God, he gave me not over unto my enemy. I strove to do my duty and failed full often. Anne Jones left me Thursday. I shall miss the child extremely, and shall have my hands more than full with no assistance with housekeeping, teaching, sewing, and last by no means, least the baby. Bless her, she has been so good during the last few days. Thanks to God who giveth me the victory over morbid fears! I can enjoy my new Darling, leaving her life and death with Him who knoweth best whether it will be well to keep her here. There are times when the little presence brings back the soreness of the bereavement of my last precious baby—boy. It is human infirmity, the infirmity of a Mother's love, God knows it and forgives it, for I close the wound and still the grief with "Thy will be done" and do not wish him back. And those two little angels bring Heaven so near to me. My precious Husband has been better of late; or is he spiritually better? Oh Lord, I wait on Thee. My sorrow over the trouble at Manchester is great. O Lord, how long. How long . I pray earnestly for light and guidance in training my little ones. Oh Father, give unto me and them Thy Holy Spirit.

June 24, 1866.
I did not get more than two hours rest last night and I have had to pass the morning sleeping. Besides, I was oppressed in heart and mind by a trouble that I mention to

two little angels The two sons, both named Plumer, who died in infancy in 1863 and 1865. Both are buried in the Hollywood Cemetery in Richmond.

none but God— will not write it where there is the least chance of an earthly eye reading. Was there ever anyone so earnestly desirous of leading a Holy Life, of living near God and for God, who failed so often in well doing? I have taught the children and read with them, and little Eliza— handed my colored class over to Isaac as I was so unwell.

My little girl is two months old today. We have determined to call her "Marian." She thrives and yet is not always perfectly well, and in spite of my hearty endeavor to overcome it, I become so nervous when there is the least thing the matter with her. Yet, I trust my heavenly Father's discerning eye does not find that I deceive myself when I say I am willing to give her up, though my heart bleed at every pore when he sees fit to call her. Jeannie Jaynes will come tomorrow. May God bless her visit to our mutual good. I miss Anne Jones very much.

My [*darling* crossed out] precious Husband told me last week that he trusted all would be well with him soon in regard to his uniting himself with God's people— "after a little…" but why any delay! He has already waited so long. And my Father, when will he conquer self and confess the Crucified?

~ Letters from Annie Jennings Wise Hobson:

Eastwood, July 8th, 1866.
My dear Mother—   The mornings mail brought me Father's welcome letter. I thank him for it and will reply soon. I hope he will indeed come up from the heat of Manchester and Richmond. I have had a trying time during the last week. Saturday evening Anne was taken with something like a nervous chill and by morning she was ill with a threatening of typhoid pneumonia… I feared Anne would be dangerously, if not fatally ill, but she is better— out of danger, but she will be unfit for any active service for some time; and she tells me that as soon as she is well enough to stand she will go to her husband and son. That means she is going to leave me. I shall write to Mary Lyons and Dr. Deane today begging them to look out for a cook and nurse for me. Meantime I must do as others have done and constantly have to do— shuffle along the best I can. I would mind nothing if I were only well and strong, but everything is an effort with me, and I cannot stand the heat of the kitchen at all. Since the servants have been sick, and Anne Jones has left— I have had to assist myself beyond my strength… I never knew until of late how ten years

The Old Marshall, the last packet boat on the James River and Kanawha Canal. The canal, with the horse-drawn boats, passed near Eastwood and family and guests could get off the packet there. Photo from Historic Virginia Homes and Churches *by Robert A. Lancaster, Jr.*

of *waiting & watching* over my precious husband, and how the war, and the giving up of my two babies has told upon me… Mr. Hobson has been more unwell since his return from Richmond than I have seen him this summer. I am anxious to have him off to the mountains or somewhere for change of air. The children are all quite well. I wish I could induce you to try Goochland air again. If you cannot ride up you could come on the packet… I am truly concerned to hear about Néné— she must go to the mountains— that would benefit her more than anything else. My little girl is taking a long nap this morning, and thereby giving her Mother a good rest. Yesterday the heat made her quite fretful… We all join in love and the children send kisses and hope to see Grandpa very soon… My love to all. God bless you with needed strength for every hour! —Your affectionate daughter, *Annie.*

Eastwood, July 8th, 1866.
My dear Mother— I wrote a sheet and a half trying to make an explanation that would make you see how you had misapprehended my letter, but so difficult do I find it to express myself as I would wish— (my brain is in a whirl this morning)— that I have just determined to wait till I see you to *talk it over,* for, dear Mother, I love you too much "*never to allude to it again.*" I have been too grieved and worried about the pain it caused you not to try to show you the motive that caused me to write it, and to try to make you read it in a different light from the one you saw it in… I beg your pardon most lovingly for causing you pain, and I beg you to trust me until you see me— Loving you as my Father's wife and my Mother's *representative* I cannot accept a mere friendship between us. I also love you dearly for the love and sympathy you have shown me from the first I knew of you. If you will let me talk to you freely and listen to me lovingly I think you will understand me as you have never done yet… I want to see you very much that all misunderstanding may be done away with. We are both sick in body and mind. I never before felt nervous weakness more… Believe me you have entirely misapprehended the matter and the meaning of my letter. Mother I must again assure you of my sympathy in all your troubles, and that your great trouble is certainly mine. May God be with you, Your loving daughter, *Annie.* —I hope my letter today will show I love you & look for your sympathy!

∾ The diary of Annie Jennings Wise Hobson:

September 30, 1866.
We returned from the mountains a week ago last Friday. *I came back to a desolated nursery with an aching heart.* The precious Darling whose short life had caused my weak Mother's heart so many nervous anxieties and agonizing fears, slept the last painless sleep in Hollywood. "*Himself My Father Savior and Friend*" *had taken her to his own blest care.* And it was His will that I should not see my dying child nor lay her to rest in Hollywood. I left here with my dear Husband about the 15th of August for the mountains, so unstrung in nerves and exhausted in health that I felt I should have brain or typhoid fever unless I had respite and change of scene. We went first to the Healing where we found excellent accommodation, food fare, and a delightful mountain locality. We improved there but the rates did not suit us. I heard regularly from my Baby. Sister had taken charge of her and my household. And though Sister wrote encouragingly, I never felt hopeful of her recovery. When I kissed the little pale face in my nursery, I felt that I saw my Baby alive

for the last time. She was just over an attack of *cholera infantum* when I left her. I was too sick to do her any good, and my husband required me with him. Duty demanded I should leave her. Duty to my husband and children. From the Healing, we went to the Sulphur. We remained there only three days, but I was decidedly benefitted. The day we left, I received a letter from Sister speaking most encouragingly about little Marian. I then determined to cast all my care upon the Lord: to have no more faithless fears, and I felt more cheerful that I had done since leaving her.

We went over to the Alum— Brother John and Pa had preceded us, and as I alighted from the stage, Brother J— handed me a letter. Fortunately, I did not open it till I reached my room. It proved to be from dear little Annie — the second line said: "I am so sorry God has taken my little sister from me." It was the last letter of family that I ought to have received telling me that my Baby girl was with the angels and that her little body rested in Hollywood. I thought I had prepared my mind for the worst but truly was mistaken! What a dark day that Thursday was! My poor bereaved heart stood cold and shivering by the three little graves of Hollywood. I wept all three of my dead babies at once. Satan tempted me sorely. The wherefore of the present and past— dark fears for the future sent clouds across my soul. I called upon God, and He gave me help— Peace and submission were restored. Strength to struggle with myself was vouchsafed. I know that my Father does not willingly afflict— that there is a need for every trial. I have questioned my own heart to know why I am thus thrice bereaved— and with humility (and I trust) contrition of soul, I discern that my sins testify against me. God calls upon me by bereavement to "consider"—and I try to obey. I consider that I am punished because— *1st* I have permitted my children and household cares to absorb me far too much. *I have not remembered the poor, suffering, and needy as I should have done* —nor striven in any way for the good of others, as I ought to have done. *2nd*, I have not contended enough with bodily infirmity and often sought my ease too much. *3rdly*, I have not cultivated loving charity as God requires. *4thly*, I have permitted various faithless fears to control me far too much— have not leant upon the Lord as I once did, casting all my care upon Him. Oh, I need to walk far more humbly with my God, far more near to my savior. I would begin the week with many resolutions for better things. May God help me.

I am greatly blessed in renewed health, and in my children's being well. Plumer is rather better but my anxiety for him never ceases. Oh Heavenly Father, thy mercies are many, and yet my griefs, trials, and cares are known to Thee. Undertake them for me, for my Savior's sake.

October 11th, Thursday.
The past week was weary and sad. Anne Jones was taken sick Sunday and was in bed 'till Friday. Poor little Charlie Seddon has been desperately ill. Thus nursing Anne, household matters, teaching the children and spending several hours trying to aid and comfort Mrs. Seddon made each day very weary and very sad. Still my heart was filled with thanks to God that my husband and children were well. Oh, it is fearful to see a child so emaciated and suffering as Charlie. May God help the poor Mother. I was inclined to yield to irritability and impatience repeatedly during the week. May God forgive me and help me to do better for the week to come.

October 29th, Monday.
Charlie Seddon died Monday, 29th October. I thank God that another of his lambs are gathered into the heavenly fold where suffering and pain are no more. May God comfort the bereaved mother.

November 18, 1866, Sunday, Eastwood.
Another Sabbath has nearly closed and what record hast thou to make my soul. God has taken me through new scenes of sorrow since I last made a long entry in my journal. I grieved with the poor suffering mother when little Charlie was taken. I love to think of him in the heavenly home with my Baby Angels. Saturday week, Plumer and I rode to Richmond on a shopping expedition expecting to return Wednesday. Sunday night Father was taken ill with Asiatic Cholera and for several days his life was in danger. I felt appalled at the idea of his dying in his present state. I cried unto God continually one long inexpressible cry, and he is still spared. He is now well enough to go to his office. O God, convert his heart. Humble him as a little child before Thee.

We left Richmond Saturday, Plumer's business and Father's illness have detained us. Plumer was quite sick and any ailment of his makes my heart sink within me. He was confined to his bed two days and was quite sick, but in God's mercy, he is better, but he looks so badly, is so dark under his eyes and is complaining this evening. Oh Father in Heaven, my agony Thou knowest that I have never asked thee to spare his life, I say about that, "Thy will be done." But, I cry out for his soul. His soul my God! Why is he so indifferent to Thy ordinances— so wavering in faith. I have spoken to him so often about this, that I doubt whether it is well to say more to him. Thank God I can believe in His promises as never before and look to the Holy Spirit as my true Helper.

Oh, when I pass one day now without some heavy anxiety of sickness I thank God. And do I not know why I need all this Chastening? My slothfulness of spirit— my refusing to strive even unto blood cries unto God and in every mercy to save me He chastens. O God, give me an enlightened judgment to discern the right and a patient spirit to fulfill it.— My soul is dark and cast down tonight because it feels so burdened by its sins and infirmities.

If I could not take them to the foot of the Cross, I would despair beneath them. Oh God the Son, Redeemer of the World, have mercy upon me, miserable Anne. Oh God, the Holy Ghost, Oh Holy Blessed and Glorious Trinity, have mercy upon me, miserable sinner.

I taught the children this morning, walked to church with Annie and loitered too much before going and got there late. In the afternoon, I again taught and read to the children and taught some of the colored children… I have been negligent in my private devotion of late, therefore have I felt spiritual depression, and gone astray in many little things— little? —great perhaps in God's sight.

I must record a sweet bright vision that came before me this evening as my thoughts turned toward my children. I thought of them as growing, expanding into full life in Heaven and joy unspeakable filled my heart as imagination pictured my redeemed mother leading my Angels to meet grown men and women— developed spirits in Heaven saying here are your loved ones, reared in the company of Heaven, educated before the Father's face. Amen.

November 25, 1866.
Keep back thy servant from presumptuous sins. A week of peace and quiet have passed. God gave me grace to try to do my duty. May he pity my infirmities and forgive all my sins and shortcomings.

November 26, 1866, Monday. Take heed therefore how ye hear, for whosoever hath, to him shall be given; and from him who hath not, from him shall be taken even that which he seemeth to have.

December 1, 1866, Saturday evening. I have indulged too much in dreaminess this week, have lacked promptness of action. I have frequently been impatient with my children. O Holy Comforter, aid me to watch myself and do better for the coming week.

1867

֍ The diary of Annie Jennings Wise Hobson:

January 8, 1867. Another year has commenced and the old year has passed silently away without note or record of its close from me. Four weeks ago last Wednesday Plumer, the children, and I went to Richmond, thinking to stay there only a week, but Mr. Hobson's business and other reasons made us determine to spend the Xmas season with Father. I anticipated a pleasant visit, especially going to church and seeing some of my town friends; and was sadly disappointed by Annie's having a severe catarrhal attack, and Plumer's having a bad cold that made him really sick; thank God they are both spared to me. Annie well, and my precious Husband, better. I had a dull Xmas, and suffered much anxiety over Annie and my Husband but God blessed it to me, I trust. I did not get to church Xmas day and only once on each Sunday I was in town. On the last Sabbath I heard a sermon from the Rev. Mr. Gilson of Petersburg on the text "*Mourn not.*" It strengthened me for all the coming year and I pray that his earnest gospel word may never be forgotten amidst any trial that may come. We returned on Friday last, thankful to get home once more. I have commenced household matters for the New Year with many petty vexations and annoyances. But I have tried to remember Mr. Gilson's words to housekeepers, over murmuring and impatience over household matters. I hope soon to get matters better organized. A dishonest faithless servant is a great trial— we should pray for them earnestly. I had a most unhappy visit to Father's. I will not— cannot write down here the dark truth that made it so. Oh Father have mercy on all! I came home weary in mind and body— partly from loss of sleep and partly from sorrow of spirit. But I have made it an excuse for too much self indulgence— must begin anew with self discipline. I have no heart to make a retrospect of the past year. May God forgive its sins, pity its infirmities, and sanctify its sorrows to me for Christ's sake.

catarrhal attack Inflammation of the membranes in the nose and air passages.

the dark truth An unknown reference.

February 3, 1867.   4th Sunday after Epiphany.
Four weeks have elapsed since our return— weeks of quiet and great blessings. Plumer has improved in health, notwithstanding his long confinement to the house by the extraordinary spell of snow and sleet and cold. My children have been well, and I, until the last few days, blessed with excellent health for the fulfillment of duties. Shame to say any indulgence in the good things of the table, at a time I could not take exercise, has given me dyspepsia. Why will I continue to tempt Providence by self-indulgence? God grant me genuine active repentance!

We have been visiting around amongst the neighbors and have entertained them for I really felt it was a duty in a quiet way to do so. I have tried to make some amends for my neglect hitherto of poor Mr. Guthrie— Cannon and Henry carried him some jelly and b.mange this afternoon. The Smith girls, Sarah Dudley and the Christians spent Friday night with me, and we organized a Society for the benefit of the Church and charitable objects. May God give us His blessing.

A pleasant Sabbath has passed— reading, devotion, and teaching the children (mine and the colored ones have occupied the hours). My soul is particularly earnest now with beseeching our heavenly Father for the influences of the Spirit to the children. They have distressed me of late by their childish quarrels— the "old Adam" betraying itself hourly. It seems to me they are so untrained in many matters in which I have tried most earnestly to train and educate them.

Oh, Heavenly Father give me wisdom and strength as a Mother, for I have been so blind, weak, and erring! Bless my humble efforts with my children. From my weakness bring strength— my darkness, light! And oh hear my prayers for my Husband for Christ's sake. Amen.

March 24, 3rd Sunday in Lent.
There is little to record of my present life, except a repetition of the past. The incessant bad weather keeps us indoors. I am too constantly occupied to be depressed by the outward lowering scene, but it tries Plumer though I think he bears the confinement with great patience on the whole. Thank God, he has suffered much less from it than I could have anticipated had I have foreseen the long continuance of snow or rain, sleet and ice, chilling winds and raw dampness that this winter has brought us.

He is sometimes better, sometimes worse. I rarely know what it is to have a night of undisturbed rest with him. Oh God sanctify to him all his bodily discomfort and sufferings. I am thankful that he is even as well and comfortable as he is. A conversation I had with him, not long ago, about his spiritual state gave me inexpressible pain. He is still dark and groping in his views.

Oh, My God, I wait on Thee with a trembling agonized heart & I know full well that I deserve the punishment his religious state brings. I know full well that my prayers have been answered. In as much as the Holy Spirit has striven with his soul, Oh Lord be patient and long-suffering with him. Leave him not to himself— draw him in Thine own way to Thee! Have mercy on him. Have mercy on me!

Anne Jones has been very ill during the last two weeks. She is now up and will resume her duties tomorrow. Having to teach, entirely in addition to my other duties, has kept me closely occupied. My heavenly Father is trying to lead me near to a higher life in patience and true Christian charity of thought and deed. How little do I profit by each day's lessons. How slow is my progress! Lord I believe help Thou mine unbelief! May this Lenten season be blessed to my soul.

I forgot to record Hallie's visit. She came up from Richmond four weeks ago, and spent a week with me, bringing her dear little boys— Little Barton just sixteen months old, running all about! What a sad pleasure it was to see him reminding me of my precious little Plumer. Oh, how I miss my Baby, but my Father knows I do not want them back from His keeping. I am not fit now to have the care of young children. My nerves are too unstrung. God Grant me strength to do my duty by those still left to me.

May 5, 1867, 2nd Sunday after Easter.
Nearly six weeks have elapsed since I have made any record in my journal. Plumer and I with the children went to Richmond the 4th April expecting to spend about ten days in town. I took the children because I thought that Anne was too feeble to teach them, and have the responsibility of their charge. Caroline Chris stayed with Anne. Plumer had been very unwell before we left, and my anxiety was more than usual for him. When we reached town a few squares walk would fatigue him greatly. Before we left he could walk 40 or 50 squares without much fatigue— he improved very decidedly. I had a delightful visit altogether— so happy and pleasant— so varied by visiting friends, the Bazaar, two nights at the Opera, the amateur opera for the benefit of the poor, that I am afraid it made me careless about the spiritual life— private devotions, etc. I thank God

deeply that I have never been exposed to the temptations of fashionable and worldly amusements— they would have tempted me sorely.

August 11, 1867, Eastwood.
Nearly three months have passed since I had either the time or inclination to record aught in my journal— tonight I feel a great desire to do so. Three months of anxiety, sorrow and care, and yet of inexpressible thankfulness and undeserved mercies. Judge Lyons died on June 18th. I wonder if I could have suffered much more for myself than I did for dear Mary— my desolated stricken sister. He died in the faith of Jesus Christ and we know he rests in God. The sad affliction brought joy to me. It was so sanctified to my precious Husband that he determined by the side of his dead friend and brother to give himself to God— to unite himself with God's people. As soon as I heard of Wm. Lyon's critical condition and that Jimmie was sick with dysentery, I went to Richmond to nurse the latter and to join Plumer who had gone down several days before. I took no rest for one week, day and night with Jimmie, and when he was most ill, his father passed to his everlasting home. My heart bled for Mary and oh! With what noble fortitude she suffered and bowed in sweet submission to our Father's will. As soon as Jimmie was better Plumer and I returned (1st July). One week later we went to Richmond and on the 1st Sunday in July he communed with me at St. James', his kind mother joining us at God's table. Oh, Heavenly Father am I as grateful for this blessing as I should be! Holy Spirit teach my life to show forth God's praise. I did not expect him to join the Episcopal Church. It was a sweet evidence of his love for me. God has given me peace in this great anxiety. Ever since we came back after this happy event, I have been harassed and wearied with preparations for the mountains and have felt far from well. Mary and her children have been with me four weeks and I have been so glad to have them. Dear Mary is so unselfish in her sorrow and yet so stricken.

Sister is in Richmond and Maria G— is with me. Sister came up Friday and staid until yesterday afternoon. I was so glad to have even so short a visit. It reminded me of this time one year ago when she came to nurse my little darling unto Death. God's will be done. Mary will go up the country tomorrow and my two precious children, Henry and Annie, will follow her tomorrow evening in the Packet to stay at their Uncle John's during our absence. Cannon will accompany us to the Springs. We propose leaving home on Wednesday and starting to the mountains Saturday or Monday.

I know not what may occur before we again are united in our sweet home. I leave all in my Father's care, asking for strength to say "Thy will be done" come what may. Plumer is and has been extremely unwell, and my heart is sickened with anxiety about him. But My Father pities my infirmities and helps me to be still in the Lord. Cannon has been extremely unwell, and I trust that the mountain air and waters may benefit him permanently. It is a sad trial to me to leave Henry and Annie, but they are in my Father's care.

Judge Lyons and *Mary— my desolated stricken sister* Mary Hobson Lyons, Plumer Hobson's sister, was married to Judge William H. Lyons of Richmond. He was related to Mary Lyons Wise, the third wife of Henry A. Wise and step-mother of Annie Jennings Wise Hobson.

January 1, 1867. Tuesday. I have been detained in Richmond by severe indisposition and bad weather. Snow is lying on the ground and the atmosphere very damp and chilly— the canal is closed by ice. Twenty dollars is to be charged to farm account of 1867 for freight on seed wheat.
January 4. Bright beautiful morning. Had my horses roughshod and go up home today, expecting to find roads good and travelling pleasant. Ordered from Oscar Gray 3 gals of fine brandy, 1 gal. cooking brandy, 1 gal. cooking wine.
January 10. Clear day. Snow still covering the ground. Hauling ice today from the canal with one wagon. Ice not very good. Three hands came from Amelia. Would not come

Frederick Plumer Hobson maintained a daily diary, a small leather-bound journal written in pencil, about farming at Eastwood from January 1, 1867, to near the time of his death in 1868. Each entry begins with a few words about the weather. Excerpts from 1867 are printed here.

for less than $10 a month. Have not engaged them. Offered them $110.00 a year. Dr. Walker will send up two wagons tomorrow to help haul ice.

January 11. …ground covered with deep snow. Clear morning. Hauling ice. Dr. Walker has sent me two wagons. The hands from Amelia went off this morning, not willing to work for less than $10 a month the year round. Had four more mules shod at Stanard's.

January 12. Hauling ice today with my two wagons. Young Goodman left yesterday for Albemarle to bring down my mare and colts. Mr. and Mrs. Seddon spent the day with us. Filled the ice-house nearly up to the sill.

January 13. …Raining and freezing this morning. A disagreeable wintry day with no prospect of the weather break up. The canal has been closed since about the 27th or 28th of December 1866. No church today.

January 18. Clear morning, *very* cold… Mr. Goodman is hauling corn from his house today. Ordered the ice-house to be filled tomorrow.

January 19. Hauling very fine ice, 4 in thick. Sent W. A. Blair check for $173.33. Sold sow at Morson's for $10.00, the boar for 8 bushels to be delivered. Mr. Goodman takes four pigs. Filled the ice-house. One wagon hauling wood in the afternoon.

January 22. Clear morning. Weather has moderated. Hands in the woods. One of the colts brought from Albemarle belonged to Mr. Monson, mare and two colts are mine. Sent Mr. Dudley a load of wood. Sold 7 sheep to Arthur Morson for 5 bls of corn and 2 bolsters for wagons. Mr. Goodman hired Knuckles for $144.00 a year and three negro men at $105 a year. We have now 10 men hired.

January 23. …Canal entirely closed to navigation…Hauling corn from Goodman's and stripping tobacco.

January 26. …A good deal warmer though snow is still covering the ground and the canal is closed. Mr. and Mrs. Stanard dined here today and Mrs. Seddon spent the evening. Cutting wood, mauling rails and hauling.

January 28. Clear morning… Olvis left my employment this morning. Sandy proposes to do so if I give my consent. Cutting wood and hauling. Told Mr. Goodman to try cleaning off plant beds and see how he could get along. Ben Green's hand carried off sorrel mare and blind horse with Goodman's wagon.

January 29. …Mr. Goodman killed three hogs this morning. Cutting wood and hauling. Sent Nelson out to look for some hands. Mr. Goodman found he could do nothing with plant bed at this time. Land frozen three or four inches.

January 31. Cloudy early in the morning… Sandy left my employment yesterday. Mr. Goodman engaged two hands from back-country to be here next Monday. Mauling and sharpening stakes, hauling. Sent six bushels of turnips to quarters. Opened kiln.

February 3. …Family being unwell, no one went to church…

February 11, Monday. Clear beautiful day. Rode out on horseback. Went to the quarters and stables for the first time this year. Wagons were hauling hay from Goodman's this morning and wood after dinner. Other hands getting wood. Weather delightful today.

February 13. Hands repairing fences and hauling. Rode over farm with Mrs. Hobson—…Nancy came here today to work (wash & iron etc).

February 18, Monday. Running four plows today, land is in good order. Hands cutting down stalks and getting rails. Agreed to let Nat Mayo put the low grounds in oats on same terms he rented from Dr. Walker.

February 19. Cloudy day though warm. Drizzling rain in the evening. All the plows are running today. Hands cutting down stalks in back field.

February 20. Too wet to plow today from rain of last night. Stripping tobacco, hauling wood and pine brush to fill gullies.

February 27. Clear day and exceedingly pleasant… Three plows running today. Cutting down stalks and repairing fences. Fixing my hot bed in the garden. Negro man Lucien commenced work this morning, wages $7 per month for three months, $8 the rest of year with the promise of more if he proves a good hand.

February 28. Very windy… All plows running today. Cutting down stalks and repairing fences. Fixing hot bed and preparing land for gardening. Warm south wind…

March 2. Rainy warm morning… Stripping tobacco. Hauling oats from Goodman's. Repairing fences. Expect to finish stripping tobacco today.

March 3. Damp rainy day. Colder than it has been for some time past. No one went to church in consequence of the weather.

March 4. It cleared off… but clouded up again. Hauling wood and stripping tobacco.

March 5. …no appearance of clearing. Packing tobacco in the hogsheads today. Sent Richard Wise check for $40.00

March 6. Damp rainy morning… Prizing tobacco. The ground was covered with snow this morning.

March 16. Heavy fall of snow last night and this morning very cold. Mr. Goodman has not been up to make any report this morning, though I suppose he can be doing little or nothing.

March 17. Clear day but quite cold… The roads are in such horrible condition that no one went to Church. Dr. Walker reported no one there but Dr. Wight and himself.

March 18. …weather moderated. Cutting down stalks on corn land. Very little to be done in this weather.

April 16. We are having a hard rain… Sent up garden seed yesterday by packet.

April 17. …cleared off.

April 21. Warm pleasant day— the atmosphere is quite hazy with some disposition to cloud up. Will probably clear up by middle of the day.

April 25. Morning cloudy and harsh, but cleared off very prettily during the day. Check expenses $50.00. Made transfer today of $3,500.00 of Va. State Stock to John Hobson as agent for Wm. P. Maben and sold $500 Va. State Stock for benefit of Wm. Maben which settles his account.

April 26. Clear beautiful morning… Paid Richard Wise $13.00. Check Geo A. Ainslie $79.00. Sold today $100 of new bonds int. of Va. State Stock for $31.75 as commission as trustee for Wm. P. Maben's children.

April 27. …Quite pleasant. Bought a bay horse from T. W. Watkins for $225 for which I gave a note payable 15th of August.

April 28, Sunday. Bright beautiful day… Took a long walk with Oscar Cranz.

April 29. Commenced raining yesterday evening, and rained all night… Did not go out of the house today.

May 1, Wednesday. Rained again…Bob came down with the horses yesterday evening. Check expenses $50.00. Bob brought home today the horse purchased from Mr. Watkins.

May 2. Clear bright morning. Quite cool early, but turned warmer during the day. Got harness etc. from Cottrell's and buggy from Ainslie… Paid Pleasants $10.00 for fixing teeth and $3.00 for the farmer.

May 5, Sunday. Clear beautiful morning. Everything in the country looking sweet and beautiful.

On May 2, 2006, 139 years after this diary was written, I visited Eastwood with my mother. It was a clear bright morning, perhaps a little cool, as we left our hotel in Richmond with Hobson Goddin, a descendant of John David Hobson of Howard's Neck, and therefore my mother's third cousin, for our trip to Goochland County and the James River Valley.

—*J. T. B. Mudge.*

May 6. Clear pleasant morning. Rode over the farm. Finished planting the field back of the house in corn. Returned to Mr. Emerson my Internal Revenue tax list. Hands grubbing clods off corn rows. Ploughing land for corn.

May 7. Commenced raining last night… Land too wet to plough. Made out the accounts of the farm hands this morning. Willie Anne has lost up to 8 days from sickness.

May 9. Bright morning… Land too wet to work. Hands in the woods getting rails. Paid Dr. Walker $170.00 in settlement of our account to date. Paid Isaac $30.00 which settles his wages in full to the 1st April.

May 12, Sunday. Cloudy morning… Settled up to 1st April, Bob $9.25, Eliza $16.50, Calistro $10.50. (Paid)… Cleared off in the afternoon.

May 13. Clear beautiful day. Ploughing for corn. Preparing land for potatoes and cutting potatoes preparatory to planting. Finished weeding plant beds. Paid Bob $3.00 additional to correct mistake. Throwing manure on heaps.

May 14. Had a thunderstorm last night… Land too wet to work today. Hauled from Dr. Walker's for use of my stable 400 lbs of hay. Sent hands down today to weed out one of Dr. Walker's plant beds. Red cow had calf today.

May 28. Cloudy morning and very sultry… Land too wet to work in the morning. Repairing roads, replanting corn. Harrowing a little of tobacco land in the evening…

May 29. Clear beautiful day… Listing and hilling tobacco land. Replanted corn a portion of the day. Planted out between 5,000 and 6,000 tobacco plants this evening. If we had the season could put out 20,000 or more.

May 30. Clear bright day, quite warm. Listing and hilling tobacco land. Planted out about 2,000 plants in the afternoon. Started for the first time sulky plow this morning, very much pleased in the manner in which it does its work.

June 2, Sunday. Cloudy morning… The carriage being broken and Bob wishing to go to church, no one but the children went to church.

June 3. Cloudy morning and quite sultry… All hands engaged in planting tobacco. Planted out cabbages and sweet potato slips. Hired two hands today. Jim Brown and Pleasants at $10.00 per month, to be paid extra in harvest.

June 14. Clear bright day… I think I shall buy a new McCormick's reaper, as it will cost about $80.00 to repair the old one. Gave Robert Williams the note at 90 days for $515.00 for account to date.

June 15. Bright clear day… Filled out memorandum list today and decided about everything except reapers. Went out to Mr. Carrington's to see Buck Eye Reaper work but it had stopped, wheat not being ripe enough.

June 16, Sunday. Rather cloudy… Heard Mr. Moore preach today.

June 17. Cloudy morning… Went out to Crenshaw's to see McCormick Reaper work. Ordered a McCormick Reaper to be sent up home immediately.

June 18. Clear day… good rain in the afternoon… At Wm. Lyons all day in consequence of his condition— He died in the afternoon at 10 minutes before 5 o'clock.

June 19. …Smith promised to ship the reaper today. Gibson's have shipped timber for barn.

June 20. Clear pleasant… The funeral of Judge Lyons took place this afternoon. One of the largest and most impressive I ever saw in Richmond.

June 22. Clear day. Boat brought up this morning the Reaper and timber for the barn… Paid $4.00 freight on the Reaper to be charged to farm account. Gleaning wheat. Will return to Richmond this evening.

June 27. …Found out that we could not finish looking over the papers so that I returned home today to return early next week. Found them harvesting and getting on pretty well considering the delays in consequence of the weather.

June 28. Clear day and very warm… Running Reaper today and farm cradles. Got up most of the wheat. Reaper works very well. Black cow had her calf this morning.

June 29. Clear morning… Running the Reaper and cradles early in the day, afterwards getting up the wheat. Gave Mr. Goodman $11.35 to pay off harvest hands.

June 30, Sunday. Clear day… Being the fifth Sunday, we had no church today. Cow with white face had her calf today.

July 4. Came from home to Richmond yesterday in my buggy, to attend to business in connection with Wm. Lyons' estate.

July 5. Clear and very warm. Looked over some of the papers of Judge Lyons.

July 16. …Cutting oats with the Reaper. Hands securing the oats. Mary Lyons came up from Richmond this morning. Mr. Powell came on yesterday to repair the machine and is at work on it.

July 21, Sunday. Clear and pleasant. Took medicine last night and feel quite unwell this morning and consequently did not go to church. Annie and children attended service. Powhatan Ellis dines with us today.

July 26. …Finished getting up oats. Hilling tobacco. Had well cleaned out today. Paid $5.00 to Mr. Nicholas for his services. Sheep got from Dr. Walker's today died a short time after getting here.

August 12. …Ploughing and hilling tobacco. Too wet to thresh wheat. Sowed rutabaga turnips this evening very late but it is the first spell that we have had in which we could sow them— using corn planter and sowing Bradley's tobacco mixture.

August 16, Friday. Clear day. Started for Richmond today with my carriage. Found the creeks so swollen could not cross and had to return home.

August 17. Clear morning. Started again this morning for Richmond and came down… Wagon brought my trunks down. Ordered today one ton of Bradley's tobacco manure for myself and one for Dr. Walker. Paid B. Watkins note $225.00.

August 18, Sunday. Clear day. Attended service today. Stephen returned with his wagon carrying a steel plow up to try.

August 20. Started to the mountains this Tuesday morning. Bright day and quite warm. Sent Mr. Goodman by Bob $140.00 which he was to use in part towards settling with hands. Sent Isaac by Bob $10.00.

August 22. We reached the Alum Tuesday night about 10 o'clock in a rain, and it has been raining often since.

September 5. Came to Calleghan's last night. Reach White Sulphur today. Weather quite warm.

September 7. Check to White Sulphur Springs & Co. $50.00. Left White Sulphur this morning for the Sweet Springs, which we reached about 12 o'clock. Had a very pleasant ride over, but after reaching here had a heavy rain.

September 8. Cloudy… In consequence of having taken medicine have not been out today.

September 20. Clear day. Very warm. Left the baths today about 12 o'clock, came to Natural Bridge stopping in Lexington to dinner. Got here after night in a heavy rain which came about 1/2 mile from here. We had a series of accidents today but thank God none were serious.

Natural Bridge. Photo from Historic Virginia Homes and Churches *by Robert A. Lancaster, Jr.*

October 4. Cloudy…Running plows today though ground is still hard. Commenced raining more in the evening.
October 5. Steady rain… Raining too much today I suppose for any outdoor work.
October 6. Clear day and quite cold. Mr. Dudley has not returned from Richmond, consequently we have no church.
October 20. Clear… Mr. Dudley gave notice today of his intention to leave here for another field of labor. The church gave its consent.
October 22. Cloudy, foggy… Sowing wheat with two drills preparing land for wheat. All negroes stopped work after dinner to vote. White hands drilled portion of the afternoon. Cleared off in the afternoon.

November 2. Paid Clarke and Dutrick on account of farm $100.00. Fallowing for corn etc. Finished dressing over the tobacco land…
November 3. Hazy warm day… Mr. Dudley absent and therefore we have no church.
November 4. Damp… Ploughing tobacco land for wheat and grubbing.
November 17, Sunday. Clear morning, turned a good deal cooler. Not feeling very well today and did not go to church.
November 18. Clear day and rather raw & cold. Running two plows, hauling up corn. Directed Moses Henly about cutting ditch for ice pond.
November 19. …Mr. Goodman has gone to Hanover today. Running two plows. Hauling up corn.
November 20. …Running two plows, hauling up corn with one wagon and hauling wood. Hauling corn with both wagons after dinner.
November 21. Hazy day… Running two plows, hauling up corn. Moses finished ditch for ice pond either yesterday evening or early this morning. Cleaning out ditch on Creek low ground.

December 20. Cloudy… Paid Moses Henly $36.00 which settles in full his bill for ditching. Killed hogs yesterday— averaged 166 lbs.
December 31. Quite a deep snow covering the ground this morning. Hailing and snowing pretty much all day. Have not been out of the house.

1868

֍ The diary of Annie Jennings Wise Hobson:

January 1, 1868. Wednesday.
We returned from the mountains the 1st of September. The whole trip was one of anxiety to me. Plumer was so extremely unwell. Several times he was really sick. We spent two week at the Alum—, thence went to the W. Sulphur and stayed three days— thence to the Old Street. This is a delightful spot, not so grand as the West Sulphur in locality, but very lovely, and enhanced by beautiful buildings and every creature comfort. We returned by way of the Rockbridge Baths and the Natural Bridge. My precious Husband, planning the whole route to give me pleasure, and it was the pleasantest part of my stay in the mountains. The Natural Bridge is even a greater curiosity— a more wonderful work of nature than I had anticipated. The children, Annie and Henry, met me in Richmond. We returned home the first week in October. Isaac had everything clean bright and comfortable for us, and never before did I return to my home with such an intense thankfulness. Plumer was certainly better than he would have been had he remained at home, but he was far from being decidedly benefited and his condition

was one calculated to fill me with apprehension. Nevertheless my heart was filled with gratitude to my heavenly Father for our safe reunion in our pleasant home, and I could cast all my care for my husband upon the great Physician. Cannon improved greatly, and has seemed better ever since. Anne Jones came to us about two weeks after my return, and the children resumed their lessons. In the mountains I engaged a Mrs. Perkins to live with me to attend to my dairy, fowls, etc. and to take charge of household matters during my frequent absences. She came in November and promises to be a great comfort to me. May the Lord enable me to do her good. I have had a quiet, happy Fall. Once I went to Richmond with Annie and spent several days— took her to the dentist's where she behaved like a heroic little woman. Two weeks before Xmas Plumer and I spent a week in town. After I came back, Anne and I busied ourselves preparing Xmas gifts for the children.

Mr. Dudley left us in November, and we now have no Presbyterian service, but Mr. Martin has been called and will take charge of the congregation the last of this month.

God has blessed my efforts to organize an Episcopal Church by enabling me to assure $400.00 as a salary, and, for the present, Rev. Horace Stringfellow has taken charge of us. He preached for us Xmas day, adding so much to the pleasure of the day. We all had a quiet, but truly happy Xmas, far more pleasant than last year. Saturday Plumer had to go to Richmond on business. He was very unwell. The children that day had their companions of the neighborhood to spend the day with them, and Anne and I exerted ourselves to make them have a happy time, and we seemed to succeed admirably. Last night Isaac and Carlista were married and we all witnessed the ceremony and looked at their supper table. The Methodist minister, the Colportueur (who has often been here) came through the snow, sleet, and rain to marry them, and he stayed all night. He is so poor— how I wished I had $25 or $30 to give him for a marriage fee.

February 8, 1868. 5th Sunday after Epiphany.
O Lord, we beseech thee to keep thy Church and household continually in thy true religion; that they who do lean upon the hope of they heavenly grace may evermore be defended by thy mighty power; through Jesus Christ our Lord. Amen.

Was there ever a time when this prayer was more needed by the church, and each individual Christian! Ritualism and Romanism, Unitarianism, Atheism— (free thinking in every form) are gathering in their victims. O Lord may indeed all true Christians who lean upon thy heavenly grace be evermore defended by thy Almighty power! Defended from thinking their own thoughts, and mistaking their own poor human judgment for the teaching of the Spirit— for they will— Deliver us from ourselves!
We have had a dreary winter outwardly— rain, sleet and snow, mud and wet. Yet I have enjoyed the indoor life intensely, and more that I can express for which to return thanks. My children have been well, my own health unusually good, and I have had far more leisure than usual for reading and recreation.

My precious Husband is very, very delicate. To our human eyes he is certainly declining, wasting day by day. I hold me still in the Lord. There are times when anguish will not be subdued, when love will weep and cry out in the agony of separation. I have no one to go to but the Lord. I take it all to the Father, Son, and Holy Ghost. Before them I pour out my sorrow. Before them I am comforted and strengthened. I feel that the Great Physician can if he chooses raise my Beloved, even from the gates of Death, and give him years of health. If it is best for us both He will do so. God knows that my every thought is a prayer for this— my whole life a pleading appeal for my Husband's life! An appeal whose "Amen" however is "Thy will be done." My prayer for myself is

Frederick Plumer Hobson, 1833–1868.

that I may have strength to live as I pray, that every iota of selfishness may be taken out of my love, that I may not one moment wish to keep him here in suffering, I may not one moment wish to detain him from the rest and joy of Heaven. Oh through Christ Jesus I would rise above all the *mere human* of my love, and in Christ Jesus I would love him as no mere human can love. I would love him here, as we shall love each other in Heaven. God first, each other afterwards. My Father grant me all needed strength! We are one in Christ! I can repeat that daily— hourly, and find present peace and foresee everlasting joy in the future.

I am so happy in the better prospects for Christ's cause in our neighborhood. Mr. Martin has come. We all like him so much, and he and his wife have my prayers and sympathy in the work before them.

◈ Excerpts from the 1868 diary of Frederick Plumer Hobson:

January 1, 1868. Cloudy morning, but cleared off very prettily during the day.
January 4. Clear fine day. Have four hands on the place. Stephen, Jordan, Davy, and Shepherd. Cutting and hauling wood and straw to the stables etc. Paid Dr. Trent $4.50 for mutton and butter.
January 22. Clear beautiful morning. Isaac sick today. Isaac came out during the morning. Shucking corn at the barn. Mauling rails and hauling.
January 23. Rainy morning. Temperature moderate. Shucking corn at the barn.
January 24. Clear day… Shucking corn at the barn. Sent Bob to Court House to have power of attorney certified to by clerk.
January 25. Clear morning. Temperature colder. Shucking corn at the barn, getting wood and rails. Barthy is sick today. Gave Mr. Goodman $5.00 to pay hands for shucking corn.

February 7. Clear… Bob has carried one of my horses to have a shoe put on. Stripping tobacco.
February 8. Clear and very cold. Hauling wood. Gave boys permission to have pony shod.
February 9, Sunday. Rainy disagreeable day. No one attended service.
February 10. Clear… Wind blustering. Cutting down stalks and hauling.
February 11. Ground covered with snow… Stripping tobacco and hauling.
February 12. Bright clear day… Calista is sick. Most of the snow disappeared yesterday. Stripping tobacco and hauling.

March 3. Clear cold… Commenced fixing hot bed today. Picking up stalks and hauling wood. Too cold and harsh to strip tobacco.
March 4. Clear cold morning. Hauling up corn stalks from field.
March 5. Clear beautiful day. Getting up stalks. Left home for a visit to Richmond.
March 6. Reached Richmond yesterday evening. Rather cloudy day though the sun is out occasionally.
March 14. Cloudy damp… They have had two more young calves since we left home.
March 25. Cloudy damp disagreeable day. Stayed in bed all day very unwell. Lewis Brock brought down 6 Hogsheads of tobacco and mower attachment with straw and corn for my horses.
March 26. Damp, disagreeable… Feel rather better today. Ordered Gwathmey and Morris to send a sack of salt up by Lewis Brock.
March 27. Rainy harsh day. I am very unwell today. Rained & froze yesterday evening and last night.

March 28. Cloudy, damp… Confined to the house still by the bad weather and indisposition.
March 29, Sunday. Cloudy, damp… indications of fair weather in the afternoon.
March 30. Indications early in the morning of clear day but clouded up and rained later in the day.

༄ Letters from Annie Jennings Wise Hobson:

Eastwood, April 23rd, 1868. Thursday.
My dear Father—   Ever since my return I have had it in my heart to write to you, but as you may suppose, there was much to occupy me after my long absence. It was well I came back for there was great need of my presence. I want to do my duty fully, and I trust, indeed, I know that God will give me strength for every hour, but oh, this house is so desolate to me. My heart aches and aches and seems made of pain. I seem to be in a "nightmare" dream from which I must awake to find him somewhere! Yet, I can rejoice that all the pain and suffering is for me alone, while he enjoys the rest of Heaven, and even in the depths of agony, I realise that our Father— God has dealt with us in tender love. I know the full meaning joy in sorrow. My precious Father you must not think me disrespectful when from out of my grief I speak to you and tell you that I have a far more bitter sorrow than this separation from my best Beloved! He is safe with God; and how is it with you my dear Father? I could endure untold suffering if it could avail me to make me know that when Death summons comes to you, it would find you as ready to fall asleep in Jesus as Plumer was. I know your intellect acknowledges and fears God. I know that you pray agonising prayers that God may grant you the Holy Spirit… Father do you wish to find God's way by the laws he has laid down whereby it is to be found? Are you sure that you have even for one day expended as much energy in endeavoring to conquer self & bring it in subjection to the law of Christ, as you have often wasted in one hour in some fruitless effort, in politics, farming or law? …I hope, Father, that you have not deemed wanting in respect because I have not consulted you in regard to my business affairs. As the property here all came through the Hobsons, I deemed it best to surrender the management of it to them; and my own plans for the future must be governed by circumstances. We are all well. The children are busy with their books, they talk a great deal about their pleasant stay in Richmond. I shall soon be busy gardening if this good weather continues; the ground is now too hot to work. We all join in much love to Mother, Richard & John, and Aunt M—. The children send you a kiss. God bless you all—   Your devoted child *A.J.W.H.*

Eastwood, April 28, 1868.
My dear Mother—   There is little of interest to tell about us… I am thankful to see this bright morning, for gardening is already so backward that we have an unusual amount of work to do. I spent nearly all day in the garden yesterday; in the afternoon I was so anxious to get in some vegetables before the threatening rain came that I dropped corn in the rows and planted snaps with my own hands. I am eager for any work that takes me out of myself… I want to be resigned, bravely, cheerfully, serenely, and to do my duty with far greater perseverance and patience than before, but I can only do so now by

Frederick Plumer Hobson died on April 4, 1868 and is buried in the Hollywood Cemetery in Richmond. Eastwood was described in his estate as follows: "Plan of East—Wood — The Estate of F. Plummer Hobson Esq. Containing 680¾ Acres 73¼ Flat land — 496½ High Land 100 woods, 14 acres yard." The probate papers incorrectly spelled his name .

God's help. There have been times lately when my spirit was crushed within me, when my bleeding heart would cry out for the presence of that tender love that had so long been the best part of my earthly life— "Oh for just one touch of his hand! One more embrace, one more look from his sweet, tender eyes!" And I could not still the pain nor silence the cry… Mrs. Walker came to see me one day last week, & her sympathy was so sincerely & naturally given that her visit did me good. Mrs. Smith and Mrs. B— sat with me awhile yesterday afternoon; the Doctor had called before and was very kind… The children are in the schoolroom. They enjoy the fine weather. We all unite in love to Father, Uncles John & Richard, and Grandma. May the Holy Comforter abide with you.   —Your affect daughter, A.J.W.H.

Eastwood, May 12th, 1868.
My dear Mother—   It is not that I have been unmindful of your affect. letter that it has not been sooner answered. I am constantly occupied indoors and out, and I have been trying to reply to the many letters of sympathizing friends which had a prior claim to yours inasmuch as they had been longer unnoticed… Our country is now so beautiful; Spring has come so gradually upon us that its charm has been greatly enhanced. Don't you think you can run up while the strawberries are ripe? They are almost beginning to turn now… I know full well dear Mother, that you feel tenderly and deeply for me in my present life— in all my sorrow. I shall always associate you sweetly with my Beloved's last illness. He was so touched by your kind thoughtfulness about him. He loved you Mother, and always spoke of you with sympathy, and affection. I know you loved him… I had such a sad sweet talk with my children last Sunday week; the dear little ones (& not so little now either) seem to miss their Father, and to feel tender sorrow for me. Annie said, "I look at his chair, and wonder if it is really so, Papa will never sit there again. Sometimes I want to see him so much." I am trying to do my duty, to have a cheerful home for my darlings— But there are times when I am so weary & heartbroken, when I feel as If my precious one wanted to have me as much in Heaven as I miss him here, and that it will only be a little while before I shall go to him. God's will be done. I know that as long as there is work and further sanctification for me here I shall not be called hence… Anne and the children are in school. May the Holy Comforter abide with you.   —Your loving daughter, A.J.W.H.

༄ The diary of Annie Jennings Wise Hobson:

May 30, 1868, Saturday evening, Eastwood.
God has answered my prayers in his own way— the best way I am sure, and I am a lone widow with a bleeding desolated heart— a heart that would be utterly crushed and broken if anguish was not stilled by "Thy will be done" and unselfish love did not whisper "his gain through your sad loss." Faith lights my darkness and whispers "just a little while," and then the perfect union in Christ in that home where there are no partings, no tears, no anxiety, no long sad days, no weary nights. Amen. Aye, Amen though to my poor human vision blinded by tears the way stretches long and dreary before me, and my bleeding heart faints by the lonely path— the desolate way. It is all needed. Though he slay me yet will I trust in him!

Annie Hobson, 1868, daughter of Plumer & Annie Jennings Wise Hobson.

October 8, 1868.
I came home. I had dreaded to return and felt as if the house belonged more to the dead than the living. But from the time I entered the house sweet peace and satisfaction came to me. Here were my duties, here my sweetest memories, here Plumer, I am sure, likes to see me best in our home, cheerfully striving to be worthy to meet him in the Home above. Henry has had two chills since my return, and is constantly complaining. I hope when the cold weather comes he may become strong, but I take him to God every day asking my Father to grant him a useful life here or an early blessed life in Heaven as He sees best. I cannot fear for myself since God treads every step of the darkest way with me. I have asked God my many years to undertake for me and mine, and he has done so.

Lord I will lay my hand in thine
Nor ever murmur nor repine
content whate'er my lot may be.
That ' til my God who leadeth me.

I have said nothing of my poor brother. He is dying rapidly of consumption— commenced to decline last Spring and has ever since been getting worse and worse. His sufferings are pitiable to see. Oh, it is sad to human vision to see one so sound and talented cut down early— the eye of Faith sees that it is the will of Him who cannot err. I pray God to give him perfect submission and sanctification in suffering. In turning over I see this book is nearly written full. What a record God's chastening it is. Lord sanctify them to thy handmaiden! Correct me in mercy, not in wrath! Amen.

my poor brother This refers to Annie's brother, Henry Alexander Wise Jr., who died February 10, 1869, and is buried in the Hollywood Cemetery in Richmond.

October 10, 1868, Eastwood.
My little Annie is with her Father. She passed to the Angels on the 16th of August. I was in Richmond.

October 16, 1868.
I could not write another line being too wearied in mind and body to dwell on the manner of my darling's death. I was in Richmond— had gone down to stay with Ma while Martha Hobson came to the country for a short respite from care and nursing. God only knew how I felt being separated from my children. Mary Lyons with her children were here, and I felt that it would be selfish not to consent to a short separation when Martha so much needed rest. When I reached Richmond I found poor Hallie bereaved of her dear little baby, who had died the evening before. A little longer than a week after I went down I heard that Annie was not well— Sunday morning— and that evening Jimmie Seddon came down to tell me that Anne Jones had killed my child by giving her a dose of TartarEmetio instead of Cream of Tartar.

Anne Jones According to the diary she was a cousin, but it is not known how she was related to the family.

November 1, 1868, Sunday.
Three times have I endeavored to write about this last bereavement— this woeful shock, and my sick heart made me give up the attempt. Sunday afternoon I had been pacing the porch at Pa's. All day I had been greatly depressed. My thoughts turned with apprehension to my children. Anxiously I recalled the delicate frame of my little Darling daughter to mind— something seemed to say to me "She will live only to suffer— She has the seeds of disease now developing." A voice seemed to ask me, "If God were to call your Darling now— at once to Himself, could you not say cheerfully Thy

will be done." I found grace to pray that if indeed my child would only live to be the victim of ill health, God would take her in His own time, away from the evil to come. My child was then with God in His home— with her Father in his happiness.

Jimmie Seddon came on horseback to Mr. Hobson's. John did not know him, told me that there was a young man at the door inquiring for Mrs. Garnett. My heart sank within me, I said to myself, "Ah, that is someone with bad news for me— news from my precious children." I sat quietly with Pa and Ma not mentioning my fears, but the few moments of suspense that intervened before my fears were confirmed were agony, but I spent them at the foot of the Cross.

Soon the doorbell rang, Richard and Sister had come around. I met them calmly saying, "What bad news from home do you bring me? Is Annie dead?"

Soon the worst was told. I was wonderfully calm. I felt like one in a trance. I went around to Father's. Oh that night of Anguish when my poor mother's soul cried out to Christ to come and stand by me, aye, in his very bodily presence, to tell if he loved me!

It seemed so terrible that the poor weak erring girl who would have died for me and my child should have killed her. Yet, I knew that God had as much right to take my child in that way as by lightning, stroke, or disease— life and death belongs to Him. I knew He would not willingly afflict us both. How much poor Anne needed the teaching the sad affliction should have taught her, I will not say here. Once the girl was comfort to me; for eighteen months morbid feeling, and a certain form of selfishness had made her a sad trial.

I am sure my faith needed fiery proof, if not God loved me too well to give me such a trial. All the human within me cried out— *wherefore, to what purpose* my carnal nature asked. I cannot recall the struggle, it sickens me. Glory be to God I have been enabled to rise out of sin, sorrow, and self, and to live the life hid with Christ alone. Had I been capable of bearing a hard feeling to poor Anne I would not have dared to go to the Communion table until it was subdued. Strange to say I had several times warned Anne against that very bottle of Tartar Emetic telling her never to touch it. Had Anne been a perfectly sane person, her conduct would have been criminal. As it is she is only to be pitied. I daily pray to God to take care of and sustain her. She is with her mother and will never live again with me.

I spent six weeks in Richmond. My daily prayer was for cheerful submission to be kept from troubling others with my sorrow, and it was answered. My tears and sighs were spent before God alone. I forgot to mention Henry's illness. I came home the Monday morning after my darling's death. That occurred Sunday about one o'clock. I found Jimmie very sick with fever, and that Henry had had fever the day before, he was then up— but Tuesday he was taken with a high fever and for two days I was taken entirely out of myself nursing him. After three days the fever was broken, but he had another attack in Richmond. Oh my anxiety by my sick children is pitiable. I am trying all the time to be willing to give him up— God pity me.

The last night of 1868:
In God's mercy I close the record of this year of chastening and bereavement, with no new trial— at least no new sorrow to record. On the 10th December, the sale of the personal property took place. It was a bitter day. I will not dwell upon it. I know the worst— I am at least three thousand dollars in debt and know not where the money to pay it is to come from. I shall try to do my best and trust to God to raise up a friend for me in His own way and good time. For a week I was much depressed and cast down. God seemed to leave me to myself to teach me my weakness. I held onto my Father's

Annie Jennings Wise Hobson, 1837–1914.

hand through all the darkness, and now in a warm sun I am treading my appointed path in peace and light.

I have had a quiet happy Xmas with my boys, Cornilia Gray and Clio— Endeavoring to make them happy has cheered me. They received presents enough to gratify their anticipation and had some little friends to dinner Xmas. We had not many good things but enjoy them and shared them with others.

Over a fortnight ago poor Mrs. Goodman was called to her long rest— a premature birth— a poor little eight months baby living, the mother paying her life for it. I trust she was ready for her Master's call! Nine motherless children, a sorrowing family. I have pledged myself to do all I can for them.

I have precious thoughts of my loved ones in Heaven celebrating the birthday of Him who was the Christ Child before the Risen Savior. Surely some angel has sung a song of peace and good will that [illegible] sorrowing spirit. I feel inexpressibly cheered and calmed, and bless God for all his mercies— for my sainted Dead, the pleasant home, a refuge of peace still spared me— my precious boys, life's duties— Above all for the gift of Jesus Christ, the Holy Comforter, for the privilege of saying Our Father in Heaven. To the everlasting keeping of the Blessed Trinity I commit myself and all near and dear to me. Amen.

The Hobson family cemetery monument describes Plumer Hobson: "Patient in Tribulation, made perfect through suffering." The monument also records the births and deaths of five of his six children: John Cannon Hobson, 1857–1890; Annie Wise Hobson, 1860–1868; F. Plumer Hobson, July 1862–April 1863; F. Plumer Hobson, July 1864–November 1865; and Marianne Douglas Hobson, April–September 1866.

1869–1876

It was a new and changed world in 1869 for Annie Jennings Wise Hobson, a widow of thirty-one. Before the Civil War she had a position of affluence on her large farm, Eastwood. At the end of 1868 she was a widow with two small children, and her life had, over the years, been saddened by the deaths of four other children. The affluence that she had previously enjoyed was in 1869 a world of debt. There are no known writings, letters or diaries, of hers for the next fifteen years. In 1869 she opened a school at Eastwood where she took in boys to board and also taught local girls from the neighborhood. In 1934, Karl

The Wythe House, Williamsburg, Virginia, 2006. Bruton Parish in background.

The College of William & Mary: Photo taken around 1875–1876 on the steps of the Wren Building, when Annie Jennings Wise Hobson was living in Williamsburg and running a boarding house in the Wythe House for students at the college. In the photo: 1. Annie Jennings Wise Hobson, second row, left of center. 2. Her son, John Cannon Hobson, left & end of second row. 3. Her son, Henry Wise Hobson, second row center– beside his mother. 4. Her nephew, John Cannon Hobson, upper right of photo. 5. Two Wise nephews, far right, front row, Yelverton Peyton Garnett and Jennings Wise Garnett (end of row). Photo courtesy of College of William & Mary.

Henry Wise Hobson, sixteen years of age, George S. Cook, 913 Main Street, Richmond, Artistic Photography. Inscribed on the back, "For My Dear Katherine– Papa's daughter, A. J. W. Hobson." Picture was obviously given years later to Henry Hobson's daughter after her father's death.

Fischer, one of the students, described the school as follows: "The conditions in this house school were ideal. The boys in her home were happy at all times; it was a well ordered household in every way and particular attention was paid to our physical and religious training as well as to the educational side." Annie Hobson moved to Richmond in 1870 when her two sons, John Cannon Hobson and Henry Wise Hobson attended Richmond College between 1870 and 1874. Both boys transferred to the College of William & Mary in Williamsburg and their mother then moved there at the suggestion of her brother, Richard Wise who was a professor at the college. Upon moving to Williamsburg Annie Hobson "took" the Wythe house and ran it as a boarding house for students at The College of William & Mary from where both of her sons graduated. One photograph survives of that time period with Mrs. Hobson and all of the boarders gathered on the steps of the Wren Building. Meanwhile Mary Lyons Wise was living in Richmond and writes to Henry A. Wise:

Richmond, May 12th, 1872.
My beloved Husband—   I have been made so happy by receiving your three letters, with the exception of the tidings that you will not be at home for two more weeks! This is my third letter to you and I am sorry to tell you that little darling Sarah was very sick yesterday & all last night with dysenteric symptoms, but is better today and very cross. Neither Annie or myself went to Church this morning, as we staid at home to nurse Sarah, who has had a short nap & wants to go out to play in the yard… I have not words to tell you how much I miss you. I repeat 'tis no home without you & I hope you'll hurry back to your wife who thinks of and prays for you all the time. Devotedly your wife, *M. Wise.*

Richmond, May 26th, 1872.
My beloved Husband—   Johnnie has just come in my room and begs me

write and ask you to come home as soon as your business will allow. He says he has "struck nil" & wants you at the Office. Sarah is relieved of dysentery, but is cutting several teeth & her bowels are very bad tho' today she seems better & not fretful... Devotedly your wife, *M. L. Wise.*

1876

DEATH OF GENERAL WISE, September 1876:

General Henry Alexander Wise died at his residence, in this city, corner of Fifth and Cary streets, yesterday morning at 11:41 o'clock, after a long and painful illness. He had a complication of diseases, and had not been to the office since the 1st of last April. During his sickness he was surrounded by living relatives and friends, who were untiring in their efforts for his relief from pain and restoration to health. His end was calm, painless, and peaceful. At his bedside stood his wife; his two sons, Dr. Richard A. Wise and Mr. John S. Wise; his three daughters, Mrs. Garnett, Mrs. Hobson, and Mrs. Mayo; two of his grandsons; an old negro attendant, and the faithful housekeeper, who has been with the family for the past thirty years.

The General was conscious up to the last, and talked clearly and distinctly to within an hour of his dissolution. Yesterday morning early he was apparently stronger than during the previous night, and in the course of conversation concerning himself said, "I never robbed the poor, and what is better, I never robbed the rich." Later in the morning, while talking to his son John, and giving him advice concerning the rearing of his children, the devoted father said: "Take hold John, of the biggest knots in life, and try to untie them— try to be worthy of man's highest estate— have high, noble, manly honor. There is but one test of anything, and that is, Is it right? If it is isn't, turn right away from it."

...In 1837 Mr. Wise acted as a second of Mr. Graves of Kentucky, in a duel with Mr. Cilley of Maine—both members of Congress—in which the latter was killed, an occurrence that created a deep feeling in the country and led to much denunciation of Mr. Wise, on whom the chief opprobrium of the affair rested for a time, although from subsequent disclosures it appears that he made efforts to prevent the hostile meeting...

President Tyler's Nomination Largely Due to Mr. Wise

The nomination of John Tyler by the Whigs in 1840 as candidate for Vice President, in conjunction with General Harrison as President, was largely due to Mr. Wise's management; and on the accession of Mr. Tyler to the Presidency, after the death of General Harrison, his influence on the policy of the Administration was very great...

As Governor

In December, 1854, he was nominated by the Democrats as their candidate for governor... The contest commenced under the most unfavorable circumstances for Mr. Wise, but was conducted by him personally with exceeding energy and crowned with brilliant success. From January to May he traversed the State in all directions, traveling more than three thousand miles... He was elected Governor by upwards of 10,000 majority.

Entered Heartily Into the War

...General Wise was warmly attached to his soldiers, and it is said that he has on repeated occasions made many and great sacrifices for them. He mingled continually with his soldiers at their campfires, and partook of their scanty faire and shared his own with comrades. He is said to have known every man in his camp by either his Christian or surname. Many pleasant and interesting reminiscences might be printed

The Wren Building. College of William & Mary, Williamsburg, Virginia, 2007.

faithful housekeeper Eliza, also Ida in some letters.

"The circulation of the Dispatch is larger than the combined circulation of all the other daily newspapers of the City." —*Daily Dispatch*, Richmond, Virginia.

In 1862 the Rev. Joshua Peterkin had conducted the funeral services for Obadiah Jennings Wise.

in this sketch of the gallant Virginia soldier… Whenever his men were in camp for any length of time he made them cultivate gardens, which supplied the soldiers with vegetables and added to their health…
—*Daily Dispatch*, Richmond, September 13, 1876. (Virginia Historical Society.)

Local Matters. General Wise's Funeral

The ceremonies incident to the funeral of the late Hon. Henry A. wise, yesterday, were of a most solemn and impressive character. Never has Richmond witnessed obsequies which more plainly demonstrated the honor and esteem in which a patriot was held by its people than did the spontaneous and profound tributes that were accorded to the memory of the noted Virginian. All through the day preparations were being made for the sad occasion, and in the evening many of those who could not gain admission to the church followed the procession as it moved away to the city of the dead…

…The beautiful burial service of the Episcopal Church was read by Rev. Dr. Peterkin, pastor of St. James Church, assisted by Rev. Charles Minnigerode, D. D., of St. Paul's Church…

At Hollywood

From St. James Church the procession moved up Marshall street to Fourth, across Fourth to Franklin, up Franklin to Monroe Park, and from thence to Hollywood Cemetery. There was a vast crowd of people assembled within the enclosure, who had gathered there to pay the last tribute of respect to the memory of the noted Virginian. The grave was dug near Monroe's tomb, and close to that of his son, Captain O. Jennings Wise, of the old Blues. The grave was bricked up handsomely and lined inside with pure-white cambric, the bed of the grave being lined of beautiful flowers.

The remainder of the burial service of the Episcopal Church as well as the Masonic service was said at the grave, the regiment fired three rounds, and the sad ceremonies were over. —*Daily Dispatch*, Richmond, Virginia, September 15, 1876. (Virginia Historical Society)

OBITUARY — Ex Gov. Henry A. Wise. Henry Alexander Wise, ex-Governor of Virginia, died at his residence in Richmond yesterday at 12:30 o'clock. Mr. Wise was born Dec. 3, 1806, at Accomac Courthouse… His father, John Wise, was son of John Wise, a Colonel in the British service, and one of the earliest immigrants to Eastern Virginia… The mother of Gov. Wise was Sarah Corbin Cropper (his father's second wife), daughter of Gen. John Cropper. Gov. Wise's father died in 1812 and the mother survived him but one year. Henry A. was taken in charge by his two paternal aunts at Clifton, and he was soon afterward sent to Margaret Academy. When in his sixteenth year he was transferred to Washington College, Pennsylvania, and with much difficulty entered the Sophomore Class, but he shortly made himself known and gave such evidence of oratorical power that he was chosen champion of the Washington Literary Society in a literary and debating contest with the sister society of Union College. Young Wise was declared the victor. He graduated in 1825 before he reached his nineteenth year. Mr. Wise left college in 1825 and commenced the study of law in the school of Henry St. George Tucker, where he remained until the Fall of 1828, when he returned home to cast his first vote for Andrew Jackson at the Presidential election of that year. While at Winchester in 1827 he became attached to Miss Ann Eliza Jennings, daughter of Rev. O. Jennings, D. D., of Washington College and was married to that lady Oct. 8, 1828 at Nashville, Tenn. Mr. Wise settled at Nashville and entered into a law co-partnership with Thomas Duncan… Mr. Wise sighed for his old home in Virginia, and after a period of indecision he left Nashville in the Fall of 1830 and departed for Accomac, where he entered upon the duties of his profession. His great abilities and legal acumen soon brought him an extensive practice which continued to him until he embarked in politics. He was superior as a criminal lawyer, and his great *forte* lay in his power over a jury. Mr. Wise, as early as 1824, when only eighteen years old, declared himself in favor of Henry W. Crawford of Georgia, the State Rights candidate for President. Owing to indisposition Mr. Crawford was withdrawn and Mr. Wise declared in favor of Gen. Jackson. In 1832 Mr. Wise was selected delegate from the York district to the Baltimore National Democratic Convention. In that convention he supported Jackson, but when Martin Van Buren received the nomination for the Vice Presidency arose and said: "Mr. President, I will not vote for your nominee to Vice President; my vote shall be cast for Philip P. Barbour, of Virginia, for that office." In the nullification mania which raged in 1832 he espoused the principles expressed in this celebrated resolution of 1798–9, as reported by James Madison, "that each State for itself is the judge of the infraction and mode and manner of redress." In 1833 he accepted the nomination for member of Congress for the York district from the Jackson party, and contested the seat with Richard Coke, of Williamsburg, a nullifier. The contest was fierce and acrimonious and resulted in the election of Wise by 400 majority and a duel with Coke… The duel was fought on the 25th of January 1835 on the Eastern Branch of the Potomac, on the road leading across the Anacostia bridge in Maryland, not far from Marlborough… Wise's ball fractured Coke's arm, but did not inflict permanent injury, and Wise escaped unharmed. In April 1833 Wise was elected to Congress and in the following October Jackson removed the public deposits. This act of the Executive deprived Jackson of many of his friends, among them Henry A. Wise. Wise was again a candidate for Congress in the Spring of 1835 and had his old rival Coke opposed to him, but Coke withdrew, and Wise was returned unopposed… In the Spring of 1837 Mr. Wise's dwelling house and all his valuable collection of books were destroyed by fire, and a house to which he then removed shared a similar fate. This so affected the nervous system of his wife that she died in the June following leaving four surviving children. The campaign of 1837 found Mr. Wise a candidate for re-election… Again Mr. Wise found himself almost a principal in a duel, this time a fatal encounter, in which Mr. Graves, of Kentucky, shot Jonathan Cilley, of Maine, Mr. Wise, acting as Graves' second. Much blame was attached to Wise for his action in this unfortunate transaction. It was said he instigated the duel, but Mr. Clay, (Henry Clay) who knew the particulars of the affair, exculpated Wise from blame in the matter… The second marriage of Mr. Wise was celebrated in November 1840, the lady being Sarah, the third daughter of Hon. John Sergeant, of Philadelphia. Mr. Wise's name was sent to the United States Senate in 1842 as the Minister to France, but it was rejected by the Whigs. The following year he was returned to Congress by a majority of 400 over Hill Carter of Shirley. Mr. Wise's health was now declining and as a relaxation from the duties of his position his friends procured him the mission to Rio de Janiero. On the 7th of February 1844 he resigned his seat in Congress and sailed from New York in the following May. He returned home in 1847, his official career having met with the entire approbation of Presidents Tyler and Polk and the Secretaries of State Calhoun and Buchanan. For some time after his return Mr. Wise retired to private life, intending to resume his professional duties, but the campaign between Case and Taylor again brought him into the political arena. In 1850 he was elected to the State Convention which revised the Constitution. During the session of the convention Mr. Wise received intelligence of the death of his second wife. (She also left four children surviving.) For the third time Mr. Wise married, this time in November 1853 to Mary Elizabeth Lyons, of Richmond, sister of James Lyons, a distinguished lawyer of that city. The Gubernatorial campaign of 1855 found Mr. Wise a

Historical marker, Accomac, Virginia.

candidate for the highest office in the State, and in May of that year he was elected Governor of the Commonwealth of Virginia for four years commencing Jan. 1, 1856, beating Mr. Flournoy, the Know-nothing candidate. In the course of his canvass, Mr. Wise traveled more than three thousand miles. He was elected by 10,000 majority. He published in 1859 an elaborate treatise, historical and constitutional, on territorial government and the admission of States into the Union, in which he upheld the doctrine of Congressional protection of slavery in all the Territories. The seizure of Harper's Ferry by John Brown occurred in the latter part of his term of office, and the execution of that enthusiastic philanthropist at Charlestown was one of the last acts of Wise's administration. The part taken by Mr. Wise in the proceedings which terminated in the breaking out of the rebellion are of too recent a date and widely known to need recapitulation. When hostilities commenced he was appointed Brigadier General in the Confederate Army, and ordered to Western Virginia. He occupied the Kanawha Valley, but was speedily driven out by Gen. J. D. Cox in a series of skirmishes. He then formed a junction with Gen. Floyd's command and served under him until he was ordered to report to Richmond. Afterward he was sent to Roanoke Island, with instructions to defend it. During the attack on the island by Gen. Burnside and Commodore Goldsborough, Wise was sick at Nags Head on the mainland, but the greater part of his brigade took part in the defense, and his son, Capt. O. Jennings Wise, was killed in the action. Making his escape after the surrender of the island, Gen. Wise was ordered to report to Manassas, after which he took no prominent part in the war. Since the war the ex-Governor has resided in Richmond, occupying the former residence of Chief Justice Marshall. Eschewing politics, he diligently devoted himself to the practice of his profession. He had been ill for several weeks, but he bore his sufferings with fortitude, and to the last his intellect remained clear and strong. A few minutes before he expired he said: "My life has been devoted to virtue. I can say that I never robbed a poor man, and what is more, and what is easier, I never robbed a rich one."

—*The New York Times*, September 13, 1876.

An unidentified newspaper clipping after the death of Henry A. Wise:

THE LATE HENRY A. WISE
An unpublished sketch of his career, written by himself.
A few years ago, a small volume containing biographical sketches of prominent Americans in public life was published in this city. Governor Wise, of Va., was included in the category. The editor, in order to insure its correctness, transmitted to him proof slips in advance of publication, and the response was the following letter, which is so characteristic of the man, that we are sure its publication will be read with interest, now that his restless and excited life has been brought to a close:

Richmond Va., Nov. 13, 1870.
Gentlemen:
In reply to yours of the 10th inst., inclosing me a proof sheet of my biography which you are about to publish, permit me to say that a much larger compass than one page could not well have contained more errors either as to number or grade.

1. I was not sent to college "by the kindness of relatives" —if by that is meant that they elected for me or furnished me the means of going to college. I elected for myself, and had a patrimony fully sufficient to pay the expenses of my education, and to start me respectably in the world.

2. During the political excitement of 1832–'33, I opposed nullification, advocated the Union, but adhered to the doctrine of States rights as expounded by Mr. Madison; as a Democrat, supported the election and administration of General Jackson, but opposed his proclamation of force, and the force bill enacted by Congress against the State of South Carolina.

3. I served in the House of Representatives of Congress until February 1844. Then I resigned my seat in Congress for the mission to Brazil.

4. I never wrote one word in my life in favor of Stephen A Douglas's nomination; to no nomination of any man was I ever more opposed. The treatise on territorial government and on the admission of new States into the Union, on the contrary, was prepared to demolish his extremely erroneous doctrine of non-intervention by Congress in territorial troubles affecting the equality and rights of the States to settle in territories. Mr. Douglas's doctrines and debates in Congress did more to bring on the Civil war which followed than any other one immediate cause.

5. I was a member of the Secession Convention of Virginia in 1860–'61, but *never* did advise "immediate secession." On the contrary, I advocated warmly adherence to the Union, and, by debate and a minority report, labored to prevail on the Convention to resolve to remain and "*fight in the Union.*" There can be no doubt or dispute about that fact here.

6. I have no recollection of advising the Southern people to "take a lesson from John Brown," though he taught them a lesson which they could not but heed; but I did advise the people of the North to take a lesson from him; "to risk the dangers themselves of war and not to send honest, but deluded, brave fanatics like John Brown to break the national peace and to endure the pains and penalties of their own felony and treason."

7. I was never driven from the valley of the Kanawha by General J. D. Cox, losing the Gauley Bridge and a large quantity of arms and stores. General Cox's forces never met my forces in the Kanawha Valley but once, and that was at Scary Creek, when 350 men under Colonel Paton, repulsed 1,350 men of Cox's command and drove them from the field, capturing Woodruff, Neff, Norton, and De Villies, the field officers of the enemy. I was ordered by General Cooper, of the Confederate War Department, twice, and by General Lee a third time, to retire from the Kanawha Valley before I did retire, and I retired burning Gauley Bridge, of my own will, perfectly unmolested, to White Sulphur Springs. There I was joined with 1,200 men by General J. B. Floyd, who was my senior. He went to Carnifax above the bridge on the Gauley, and left me on the Lewisburg turnpike to Gauley Bridge, to confront Cox. With but 900 men I met Cox's forces at the Hawk's Nest, and drove him thirteen miles back to Bee Creek, when I was met by all his forces, 2,000 men, on Gauley Bridge, and I retired with impunity again. General Floyd was driven from Carnifax by Rosecrans, whilst I was protecting his rear against Cox. He issued orders which I refused to obey, reported me to the War Department, and retreated to Meadow Bluff, twenty-five miles distant, leaving me on the east peak of Big Lewall Mountain, with only 1,619 men opposed to Rosecrans and Cox, with 7,000 men. I had fought them alone for three days until General Lee ordered Floyd back to me, and there, under fire, I was ordered to report to the War Department at Richmond, at the instance of Floyd, for disobedience. General Lee and the President decided I was right and my command, no longer a legion, but a brigade, was restored to me as soon as I rose from a

two month's illness, in the winter of 1861 and 1862, and I was ordered to the slaughter pen of Roanoke Island, where with four hundred and ten effective infantry, after a day's bombardment by thirty-seven iron-clads, an infantry force of 10,000 to 15,000 men were, on the second day of the fight, kept at bay, under close fire for five hours, before there was any surrender. I was at Nag's Head, prostrate with pleuro-neumonia, and was not even pursued on the beach in a very slow retreat to the Cunituck peninsula. I did not escape from the island, and nothing could do me more injustice or the truth more violence than to say: "General Wise afterwards took no active part in the war."

My brigade was re-organized in the spring of 1862, and I was put in command of Chaffin's Bluff, just below Drewey's on the James, and commanded all the peninsula between the York and the James; and with two regiments, without orders, on the extreme right and under General Holmes, fought in the two days' fight at Malvern Hill; afterwards scouted the enemy closely for months and made a divertissement in favor of Longstreet by getting in the rear of the seventeen redoubts at Williamsburg, and burning Whitaker's Mill and at least a quarter of a million of stores there at the headquarters of the enemy. In 1863 I was sent to the command of General Beauregard in South Carolina, and took command of the district lying between the Ashley and the Edisto, except James' Island, and with 1800 men repulsed Schiemelfinnig with 6,000, at the Haul Over on John's Island, and at the Abbepoola, nearly destroyed the Marblehead war steamer.

In May 1864, I was ordered with my command back to Petersburg. A part of it, under Colonel Tabb, on the way back, at Nottoway Bridge, repulsed two impinging forces, front and rear, of the enemy's cavalry; on the 9th of May, 1864, with but 800 men I repulsed 5,000 Kautz's cavalry on a line of six and a half miles in their attack upon Petersburg; and in six days afterwards, on the 15th of May, repulsed 22,000 men of General Meade's command under General Baldy Smith, with exactly 2,200 men, fighting all day from 3:30 A.M. to 10:30 P.M., on the same line of defenses around Petersburg; then led the two brigades, my own and Martin's of North Carolina, at Bakehouse Creek, successfully against Butler in the battle of Drewry's Bluff, and thereafter broke the lines of the enemy at Howlett's, near Ware Bottom Church, in a desperate charge, and was incessantly under fire from the 18th to the 28th of the month, on the Howlett line, where General Grant says General Butler was bottled up like a fly! I was then put in command of a dangerous portion of trenches around Petersburg, from the Crater to Reve's House, was continually under fire until March, 1865, I was entrusted with the extreme right of General Lee on Hutcher's Run. On the 29th of March, 1865, my brigade alone was pitched into the forces under General Meade, 25,000 strong, on the Military Road, and fought to check them in their advance to turn our right; and again, the 31st of March, on the White Oak Road, with McGowan's Brigade alone, attacked the same unequal force and staggered them with effect; and then followed the retreat of General Lee for ten days and nights from Hutcher's Run to Appomattox, in which I was zig-zagging at double quick from right to left and back again continuously under fire, either leading the front or bringing up the rear. I had seven pitched battles, I may say, in the ten days and nights, and at Sailor's Creek, in the retreat, saved two brigades and took them through safe, the only confederate forces which kept their organization that day in that fight. For this, when I came up with General Lee, at or near Farm-ville, I was complimented and promoted by him against my protestations. I was with him at the surrender of Appomattox, and my brigade fired the last infantry guns that day for the Confederate cause.

So now, sir, you see how unjust it would be to the United States or to me to say "General Wise afterward" (meaning after Roanoke Island) "*took no active part* in the war." If it was treason it would be unjust to the United States to say case of a prosecution for active hostilities; if it was brave, patriotic, "active" in me to do what I did, why, undoubtedly I was ten-fold more active in the last than I was in the first year of the war.

In conclusion, it is but just or due to say, that since the war I have tried to keep the peace and obey the laws, and in good faith and honor to observe the terms of my capitulation on the 9th day of April, A. D. 1865. I surrendered my arms on condition to be allowed my horses and arms, and on the parole of a soldier's honor "to go to my *home*, and to remain unmolested in all respects, as long as I obeyed the laws." I was not allowed to go to my home; but by a written order was prevented from going there lest I might offend or oust the protegées of the Freedman's Bureau. They were for years since the war in full possession of my home and almost destroyed it. I was then prohibited from practicing my profession of the law, until 1866, when for the first time I was allowed again to work for my living according to God's command, not His curse; and then I went humbly back to the calling in which alone I was trained, to earn "daily bread" for a very dependent family, stripped of everything but honor, and with no other liberty left but to live and work.

If I have been "occasionally heard from," it was not intentionally on my part. An old man, wrecked in every hope save that of heaven, not without hope in God, but without hope in the world, I may, I trust, be allowed to quietly subside in peace. That will be the best for the remnant of my days, and, I pray, may be an everlasting rest and joy for me in heaven. You have been charitable: "Henry A. Wise is entitled to the tribute of honest and earnest purpose in a "lost cause." That is true before God. My purpose was never to secede from the Union, and to fight all oppressors under the aegis of its Constitution; not for the inglorious privilege of being master of a slave; I would not have given a drop of the blood of my little finger for that curse; but for the inalienable right of domestic, State, civil, self-government, and for my own liberty, guarded by the Constitution and laws.

For these I fought and would fight again. For these I was "*honest and earnest*" and when I forsake these may "my right hand forget its cunning." I am no penitent; I *know* now what I only *thought* at the beginning— *that I was right*, "sink or swim, live or die, survive or perish," to fight for these. I am no penitent. I rather rejoice that the war occurred. It lost me every earthly comfort, but largely compensated by abolishing the curse of slavery, even though *vi concitate belli*, and by relieving my heirs forever from its responsibility and sin, and especially from it weakness for war, itself a wickedness which turned upon the masters. I make no recantations, utter no palinodes and mourn only for irreparable and inestimable losses. The United States have not money enough to bribe me, nor force enough to drive me, to take, touch or taste a test oath— that most odious instrument of tyranny; "before I would permit my forefinger and thumb to touch the pen to sign it, my right hand should be cut off at the wrist, and be nailed to a guide post to point the way to a gibbet." So Pettigrew said concerning the test oaths of nullification in South Caro-

Henry A. Wise. Photo courtesy of the Valentine Richmond History Center, Richmond, Virginia.

Wise family plot, Hollywood Cemetery, Richmond, Virginia. Buried in this plot are Henry A. Wise, his first and third wives, Anne Elizabeth Jennings Wise and Mary Lyons Wise, Obadiah Jennings Wise, Henry A. Wise Jr. and his wife Harriet Haxall Wise, their son Obadiah Jennings Wise Jr., and Richard A. Wise and his wife Maria Peachy.

lina, and so I say to the test oaths prescribed by Congress. I said all I meant and meant all I said, and tried my best to *do* all I said and meant for "the lost cause." What is "*the lost cause*?" Ah! would only that the host of voters in the United States would "do truth and come to the light." And see that the Confederacy is not the only cause lost. The Constitution is lost; the Union defined by it is lost; the liberty of States and their people, which they both at first and for half a century guarded, are lost. I am anxious only that the truth shall be told and felt. I wish to live only a little while to see the true spirit of constitutional liberty and laws under a free *republic* of States and their people revived, and I pray to be ready to go then when my only Master in the universe calls. I am willing, freely willing and more than anxious that all men of every race shall be as free as I wish or claim to be; but, whilst slaves are being made free, I protest against freemen being made slaves! Respectfully yours,

—Henry A. Wise.

On December 13, 1876, three months after the death and funeral of Henry A. Wise, the following news items appeared on pages two and three of the Richmond *Daily Dispatch*:

Trimming Down Presidential Power—
Senator Edmunds, of Vermont, spoke of the President of the Union as a man who has to "appoint postmasters and sign commissions during the next four years." What a trimming down of presidential power there is here compared with the unlimited authority Grant has exercised.

Senator Elected
Denver, Col., December 12. Henry M. Teller has been elected United States senator from Colorado for six years commencing on the 4th of next March.

It would be another eleven years before the life and work of Henry Wise Hobson, Henry A. Wise's grandson and perhaps one of the two grandsons at his bedside when he died, would intersect with the work of these two Senators. That would happen far from Virginia, in Colorado and Utah. Nobody reading the Richmond *Daily Dispatch* in 1876 could have begun to imagine those future events. During Annie Hobson's absence from Eastwood, it was leased out and then sold in 1880 for $15,500. Eastwood was destroyed by a fire in 1941. By 1880, Annie's younger son, Henry Wise Hobson, had completed law school and was working in Richmond with his uncle, John S. Wise, in the firm of Wise & Hobson, but it would not be long before Henry Hobson would leave Virginia.

XII

1870–1877

Letters from Cambridge and Troy, Part Six

ECONOMIC expansion and industrial growth were the watchwords in America between 1870 and 1877. Southern states were being readmitted to the Union and the entire nation was still in a period of "reconstruction" that would not officially end until 1877 when the last Federal troops were withdrawn from the South. The United States had a population of 39.8 million people in the 1870 census that included 4.9 million free Negroes for the first time. By one estimate, 2.3 million immigrants had come to America since the 1860 census. America was growing. Beginning in 1870, economic growth could be measured by Thomas Edison's new invention, the stock ticker. The establishment of the U. S. Department of Justice in 1870 acknowledged the growing responsibilities of the Attorney General, and in 1871 Brigham Young was arrested for practicing polygamy or what some called "that special institution." The Chicago fire of October 1871 killed an estimated 300 people, left over 90,000 homeless and caused an estimated $196 million in damages, but another fire, the "forgotten fire" of October 1871 in northern Wisconsin and the Upper Peninsula of Michigan, burned 2,400 square miles and killed between 1,200 and 2,400 people. The following year a three-day fire in Boston killed 13, destroyed over 800 buildings and did an estimated $75 million in damages. The Republican National Convention of 1872 in Philadelphia included William Henry Grey's speech seconding Grant's re-nomination for President—the first speech to a national political convention by a person of African descent. The invention of barbed wire in 1874 would forever change the western plains, and two years later Colorado became the 38th state. Penny postcards were introduced in 1873, and in that same year free delivery of mail was provided in all cities with a population of at least 20,000. One of the greatest changes in communications was about to begin transforming society when, on March 7, 1876, Alexander Graham Bell received a patent for the telephone. The prosperity in America was not being enjoyed everywhere around the world. An earthquake in Venezuela and Columbia killed 16,000 in 1875 and between 1875 and 1876 over 5 million died in a two-year famine in India.

In Troy, Francis Thayer's successes could be easily measured. He had a good business, he had been elected a State Senator, he enjoyed summer vacations at the seashore with his children, and his son was preparing to go to college. Despite all of this, illness would become a part of his daily life, and he would search in vain throughout the country for relief.

Letters and diaries by:
John Birge, Francis Thayer's business partner
E. R. Eaton, a friend in Troy

William Henry Grey (also Gray), a speech
Catherine "Mungie" McKie Thayer
Francis S. Thayer
Catherine (later, Katherine) Sophia Thayer
Francis McKie Thayer

Letters and diaries written from: Albany, Cambridge, Troy, Luzerne, and Fire Island, New York; St. Paul, Minnesota; Amherst, Massachusetts; Montpelier, Vermont; Old Orchard Beach, Maine; Philadelphia, Chicago, and the White Mountains of New Hampshire.

∽

1870

Senator Thayer astonished:

It appears from statements in the Troy *Times* that Hon. Francis S. Thayer was recently surprised by the receipt of a letter from the Assistant Adjutant-General of the United States which read as follows: *Assistant Adjutant-General's Office* Washington, Feb. 28, 1870. *Mr. Francis S. Thayer, Troy, N.Y.* Sir: Referring to your application for the remission of the sentence against your son, George E. Thayer, Second United States Cavalry, I have to inform you that the same has been presented to the Secretary of War, and that he declines to intervene therein. SAMUEL BRECK, Ass't Adjutant-General.

Three days later Mr. Thayer, having in a measure recovered from his astonishment, replied as follows: Troy, March 3, 1870. *General S. Breck, Assistant Adjutant-General, Washington D. C.* My Dear Sir: I can neither fathom nor *father* your communication of 28th alt., which I beg leave to return herewith. My only son is a lad some 12 years of age, still under the parental roof, and I am very happy to say remarkably well behaved. Regretting that any one should bring discredit on the name, I am very respectfully, your obedient servant. FRANCIS S. THAYER.

—*The New York Times*, March 8, 1870, page 1.

April 5, 1870. Stayed in Albany last night. New York Charter passed Senate today 30 to 2. Harry G— & myself voted against it. To my mind a greater mistake never was made by any party than was made by the Republicans voting for Tweed's charter.
April 6. The smoke of the battle over the New York Charter is clearing away a little. Some of the best politicians in the State congratulate me on my course…
April 7. Albany at 9:30 met my good friend Genl. Woodford… and he took me by the hand & said, "Thayer you were right on the New York Charter…"
April 26. Adjourned this morning at half past one o'clock. Had the good fortune to get my local Bills through…
April 27. Once more at home, relieved from legislative duties. This winter has been one of perplexity & dissatisfaction to the minority, and at times I have wished myself away from the halls of legislation, however I have learned something of men & politics. At office most of the day looking over business.
April 30. Beautiful day. This is the twentieth anniversary of our wedding day and our hearts should be full of thanks to our heavenly Father for all his goodness & mercy

towards us. Moved to our old store, 143 River St. where we shall feel more at home…
May 9. Weather warm & pleasant. Busy getting our office cleaned & painted…
July 7. At Cambridge. Weather very warm. Busy drawing lumber & helping the carpenters. We build a kitchen 16 x 18 on the South end of the House and use the Parlor for a dining room. Finished drawing the lumber. When night came too tired to sleep.
July 22. …Frankie (aged 13) commenced his clerkship in our office & I find him very useful…
July 29. Weather hot. Kate & Kittie took the 9:50 Express Train for Fire Island… to be absent about two weeks. I would like much to be with them but must stay at home & attend to business…
August 2. …Recd a good letter from Kate at Fire Island reporting all well & doing well… —*Diary of Francis S. Thayer.*

❧ Summer vacation:

Troy, Aug 9th, 1870, Monday noon.
My darlings—   I "broiled" in New York yesterday until 3:45 P.M., took the fast Saratoga train and arrived here at 8:15, hot & dusty. Frankie was at home reading the war news. He takes much interest in the movements of the great armies and I hope he will know more about what they are fighting for than did the Old Man "Peterkin." It seems to be quite certain that the Prussians have gained "a great victory" which I hope will be repeated in double quick succession until the proud Emperor will be humiliated if not utterly put to rout. Frankie had a pleasant visit over Sabbath at Cambridge. Mother is very well & Edwin is ditto… I don't know as there is anything new here… Frankie says he sends lots of love to Mother & Sister and I give you a great big heart full. As ever yours faithfully, *Frank.*

Troy, Aug 10th, 1870, Wednesday noon.
My own dear Kate—   Your welcome note of Monday eve came to hand this morning. Your moonlight sail must have been charming and quite in contrast with the hot dusty ride I had on that evening. Yesterday & last night we had a heavy rain storm and today it is a little cooler, but still pretty hot. Frankie & I go to Saratoga this eve. I shall return in the morning… I hardly think I shall come after you as it takes two whole days and my time now is rather precious. I wish to save all the time I can so as to spend more at the Old Home. As to the time of your coming home— I leave it *entirely* with you. You & Kittie are doing well and I think you should not hurry home but stay and get all the strength you can… It is dinner time so good bye for this time. Frankie sends much love to Mother & Sister & I too. As ever yours sincerely, *Frank.*

Aug. 11th, 1870. Troy.
My own dear Kate & darling Kittie—   Mother's letter to Frankie was recd this morning. I am very happy to know that you are passing the time so pleasantly and I trust you will leave Fire Island much improved in health & strength… Aaron has pretty much made up his mind to take his family to Watch Hill and I think that a good place for them. Lizzie is better but not strong. The War News is somewhat exciting. Prussians seem to be marching on from victory to victory and many think they can see the end. I don't

believe the French are so easily whipped. It is life or death with the proud Emperor and the tables will turn ere long. I think it will not be a war of a few days but months & perhaps years… Tis now about dinner time and after dinner I am going to Albany on business so excuse this very hasty scrawl. As ever your own *Frank*.

◦ Headlines from the *New York Times*:

WAR AT LAST, Formal Declaration by France of War Against Prussia, Acceptance of the Situation by King William, Troops Hurrying to the Frontier, and the Navies Getting in Readiness, France to Germany — She Wars Only Against Prussia. —July 16, 1870.

—THE WAR, An Actual Encounter on the Frontier at Last, The Prussians Repulsed in a Skirmish at Forbach, A French Reconnaissance Across the Prussian Boundary, Departure of the Queen of Prussia for Berlin, Her Farewell to the People of the Rhine Provinces —July 25, 1870.

—THE WAR, The First Battle—Capture of Saarbruck by the French Forces, Length of the Fight Two Hours—The Losses Light, Scenes in Berlin on the Departure of King William for the Front, Rumored Rupture Between Bismarck and Prussia's Crown Prince, Russia Denies Having Designs on the Danubian Provinces. Efforts of France to Conclude an Alliance with Denmark. —August 3, 1870.

August 18, 1870. Weather very warm. Mercury up near 90°. Hard at work all day getting settled in our new Old Home. P.M. over to Easton for stove-pipe. Kate & the girls came in P.M. & Ed brought Mother over & we are all together at the Old Home. Cooked our first meal in the new kitchen.
August 20. At Cambridge. Stayed at home. We are all so tired that we wish to rest. The weather is delightful. Expected Ed over but he did not come. Killed a chicken for dinner. We enjoy keeping house very much & the Old Home is dearer than ever.
October 19. Charming weather. At Cambridge all day, very busy fixing up things generally left for the winter. Put the plank around the cistern pump & worked hard all the

Lane and Carriage House of Hon. F. S. Thayer, Hurd's Stereoscopic Views, Greenwich, N.Y.; The Old Home, Cambridge, 1950.

day & evening. Could find plenty of work here for a month & I wish I could stay here & do it. I am getting tired of business.
October 21. Weather pleasant. Spent part of the day looking after political matters which are a good deal mixed. Business very good…
September 11. Charming day… Did not go to church. This is my birthday, 48 years old & I have great reason to be thankful to God for all his goodness & mercy to me & mine. I pray for a continuance of His loving kindness & tender mercies.
December 3. This is Kittie's birthday, 11 years old and so bright & happy. Her room is furnished with a new carpet & she has several presents from Mother, Grandmother & Brother…
—*Diary of Francis S. Thayer.*

1871

April 18, 1871. …Legislation is going on at a rate that is awful. Bills pass by the score without consideration… —*Diary of Francis S. Thayer.*

May 1871, New York.
My dear ones at home— I left home as you know yesterday 2 P.M. Had a hot & dusty ride down but did not suffer much from asthma. On arrival at 5th Avenue Hotel I went up to 26th Street and took a Turkish Bath and a luxury it was too… Well I am going to Fire Island to stay over Sunday in hopes that sea air [End of letter from Francis Thayer.]

May 18, 1871. Office of E. W. Coleman & Co., Commission Merchants.
My Darlings at home— …I have concluded to go on to Philadelphia this evening and tomorrow shall be at H. H. Mears & Son 330 & 329 South Water Street. I expect to return here tomorrow evening. I didn't have much faith in this trip but thought best to comply with the wishes of the head of the firm. It is quite desirable to have a correspondent in Philadelphia as we shall soon want to buy some new southern wheat there. I would stay at home with my dearest ones *all* the time if I could have my own way but you know I must take a short trip now & then in order to have all agreeable on River Street. With a heart full of love I am your *Frank.*

May 18th, 1871, Continental Hotel, Philadelphia, Thursday evening.
My own dear ones— I left New York at 6:30 this eve and arrived here at 10 o'clock and now, after a good supper, I'll say good night. I expect to spend the day here tomorrow and at eve go towards home or to Baltimore. Can't tell which way until I see what can be done here in the way of business. Now I am on here I might as well make the acquaintances we desire so that I shall not be obliged to make another journey. Should I go to Baltimore, I will spend Saturday there and go on to Washington Saturday eve and stay over Sunday and turn my face towards home Monday. This is a long time to stay away from you but I trust you will excuse me for it seems to be purely a necessity in order to please the head of the firm. Should I return without doing anything here, and not go to Baltimore, my journey would seem to be lost, and under the circumstances, I know you will bear my absence without saying "Frankie 'twas naughty in you to stay away so long." Rest assured I shall be with you at the earliest possible moment… Now good night. God bless you all. I do hope

Katherine Sophia Thayer, date unknown.

This letter includes the first mention of Francis Thayer being afflicted with asthma.

and pray you are feeling better this beautiful evening. More than ever your own *Frank*.

June 26, 1871. Charming day, cool & very comfortable… Eve went to Mt. Zion Lodge & then & there took my first degree in Masonry. Went home & told my dear Kate what I had done and it almost broke her loving & confiding sensitive heart.
June 30. Delightful weather. Mr. Bills at Saratoga. Came home from Cambridge this morning. Had a long & candid talk with my precious Kate & I do hope & pray that she will very soon become reconciled to my joining the Masons. Nothing new in business. Eve at prayer meeting. —*Diary of Francis S. Thayer.*

 Summer vacation:

Fire Island, July 11, 1871.
My precious Darling—   Well, I only wish I could know where are you and have been, if in Cambridge last night or in our own home and what your plans are for the coming two weeks… By the way we have moved to the bay side, have taken two connecting rooms, at the south end of the hall, one room large and one small. I found the rooms unoccupied, and without cards on them and Mr. S— said he would change if I desired, and I did because I am convinced that the air is not quite so strong on this side and thought best to try it. Hope it will be for the best…   —I am your own *Kittie*.

July 16, 1871. Metropolitan Hotel, St. Paul. Sabbath P.M.
My own precious darlings—   Here I am in this delightful city almost halfway across the continent and yet present with you in thought every moment. Another week I hope & trust will bring us together in health and strength. It seems a month to me since last Monday morning, traveling most of the time day & night, still I am not fatigued thanks be to the man who invented sleeping & Pullman cars. …All about this western country I shall give you a full description by word of mouth. My pen is not equal to the task, so wait patiently for particulars. I will write from Chicago Tuesday telling you the course of my journey. I hope you are making the most of your stay at Fire Island. Drink in the pure air, take in the good food that will give you health, strength & flesh in abundant manner. Now goodbye my own dear precious Kate, Kittie & Frankie. God bless you now and always is the prayer of your own *Frank*.

July 18th, 1871, Chicago. [On stationery of Thayer & Tobey Furniture Co, Porter Thayer's company.]
Dearest and most precious ones at Fire Island—   My heart was made glad this A.M. on my arrival here by the receipt of Kate's & Kittie's letters. I shall not go to St. Louis but leave for home tonight at 9 o'clock, spend most of the day in Toledo and tomorrow P.M. start for Troy. You may look for me on Saturday. No more time to write as Port is waiting to give me a drive about the city. Good-bye, God bless you all. Yours Always, *Frank*.

Troy, July 25th, 1871, Tuesday P.M.
My own dear Kate—   I took the 11 o'clock train from New York & arrived here at 4:45… Rec'd a letter from Edwin last eve saying Mother was "first

rate." …No more time to write. Give Frankie & Kittie a word of caution in regard to bathing & sailing… —More than ever your own *Frank*.

Surf Hotel, Fire Island, July 25, 1871, Tues. A.M.
My precious Husband— I watched long after your form disappeared, and then with Mrs. Boyd turned my back to the Bay (which I cannot bear to do when you are on it) and slowly made our way up to the house. She is most happy in her "Bob" as I am in you my darling. Saturday morning the Yacht Party authorized Mrs. Eaton to invite a Party to go out in the Yacht. The Fullers, Eatons, Mr. Livingston, and ourselves made up the company. The sail was most charming, we went up through the Bay, and after a fine lunch on board we returned about 5 o'clock having made about forty miles. We all wished you could have been with us. I forgot to say to you— How would you like to have Francis go up and spend two or three days this week at the Old Home, putting things in shape? Perhaps it is not worth while, it will not take long when we get there.
12 noon— Oh! How cold it is today. We are having a driving north-east rain storm. The Steamboat is just in and a half dozen forlorn looking passengers have hurried up through the rain— how they wish they were at home. The Bay is covered with "white caps" and as I write in our room the rain is driving against the windows with that cheerless sound… I wish you were here, but my heart is so full of thankfulness that you have been brought safely to us again and so brimming over with sweet memories of your visit here, of your pleasant readings, of our evening out-look upon the Ocean and of all our loving intercourse, that I cannot be sad or homesick. Is it not a joy to be thus fortified by the trusting love that finds fruition here? …I have just written Mother and hope you will see her… Children send love. —Your *Kittie*.

Troy, July 26th, 1871, Wednesday P.M.
My own precious Kate— I have only time to give you a thousand thanks for your sweet letter rec'd this morning full to the brim with all that makes loving hearts thrice happy. God bless you my darling and bring us together again in His own good time in peace & safety. Mr. Bills and Johnny Birge are at Saratoga and I shall run the machine with Johnny until Friday eve. Good bye Kittie, Your *Frank*.

Catherine McKie Thayer, date unknown. C. R. Clark, Photographer, Troy, New York.

July 26, 1871, Troy.
My Darling Daughter— Your very affectionate letter was recd. this morning and I thank you for it ever so much. I have only two minutes to write. Mr. Bills & Johnny Bills Jr. are away & I have all the work to do and I have been quite busy all day. It is very lonely down at our house especially when I set down at the table all alone. I hope we shall all be at home again, well & happy by & by. —Yours very affectionately, *Father*.

September 8, 1871. Perfectly delightful weather… Recd a flattering letter from C. W. G. New York suggesting my name for a high office in the State…
October 9. Terrible fire in Chicago. The whole country under great excitement. One third of the city in Ashes. Porter [Porter Thayer, brother of Francis S. Thayer, also "Port."] came from Hoosick this morning & took the first train for home [Chicago].
October 10. Hardly anything thought of or talked about save the terrible fire in Chicago.

Loss estimated $300,000,000 & 300 to 500 lives. From the accounts I think Port's street & house must be burned. Hope the factory is safe.

October 11. News in regard to the terrible fire in Chicago worse & worse & it makes me sick at heart to think of the awful calamity…

October 12. Weather pleasant. Recd a telegram from Port saying "Store & House burned. Factory & lumber found safe." We all feel truly thankful that it is no worse for the good fellow…

October 13. Recd a letter from Port in which he says we can have no conception of the terrible fire. His loss will be $30,000 over insurance. People all over the country are sending money & supplies to Chicago. Flour market dull & the demand falling off a little. 　　　　　　　　　　　　　　　　　　　　　　　　*—Diary of Francis S. Thayer.*

❧ Fires, October 1871:

A City In Ruins — The Terrible Devastation of Chicago. Three Square Miles in the Heart of the City Burned. Twelve Thousand Buildings Destroyed — Loss $50,000,000. Every Public Building, Hotel, Bank and Newspaper Swept. Appeals to Other Cities and a Noble Response. Frightful Details of the Disaster from Our Own Reporters.

　　It is impossible to give in any approach to detail the devastation of Chicago. The fire of Sunday, previously reported, began in the lumber and coal tract, along the west bank of the river, laying waste several squares, as previously reported… A violent south-west prairie wind prevailed and filled the air with fiery messengers of destruction before which the cheaper frame tenements of Market, Wells and Franklin streets melted away like wax. It is impossible now to give even an approximately correct statement of the losses, but a faint idea may be formed when it is stated that every bank in the city, except the small Savings South Division, and one on Randolph Street, in West Division, are destroyed… Men who were millionaires yesterday morning are nearly penniless today, but more terrible than all is the awful certainty that many human beings have perished in the flames—how many no one can tell… Hundred of horses and cows have been burned in stables, and on the north side numbers of animals, though released from confinement, were so bewildered and confused by the sea of fire which surrounded them… 　　　　　*—The New York Times*, October 10, 1871.

THE CHICAGO CALAMITY — I am able to commence my dispatch with the joyful intelligence that the ravages of the devouring element are checked, and the blessed rain has removed the appalling dread of total extermination that seemed at one time certain… 　　　　　　　　　　　　　　　　　　　*—The New York Times*, October 11, 1871.

DESOLATED CHICAGO — Confidence Entirely Restored and Business Reviving — Honorable Action of the Mercantile Community — No Repudiation of Debts and no Extortions from the Needs — Grocers and Coal Dealers Refuse to Raise Their Prices —The People of New York and the Whole Country Responding — Enthusiastic Meeting in London, £10,000 Subscribed. *—The New York Times*, October 13, 1871, page 1.

THE FIRE FIEND — Fires Sweeping Over Forests, Farms, Villages and Towns. Fearful Sacrifice of Human Life in Michigan and Wisconsin — One Hundred and Fifty Persons Burned in A Barn. — IN MICHIGAN — Villages and Farm-Houses Destroyed — Many Lives Lost — Fires sweeping Over the Northern Part of the State. News has just been received that the largest portion of the City of Manistee, Michigan has been destroyed by fire… IN WISCONSIN — Fearful Loss of Life at Peshtigo A dispatch has just been received from Green Bay, Wisconsin stating that a steamer had just arrived bringing a report that 325 bodies were buried at Peshtigo last night and as many more are still missing… —*The New York Times*, October 13, 1871, page 5.

LATEST GENERAL NEWS — The Burning Forests in New York and Pennsylvania — Earnest Appeal in Behalf of the Michigan Sufferers — Twelve to Fifteen Thousand People in Absolute Need — The Case Against the Arch-Polygamists in Utah — *To the People of the United States:* We need instant and plentiful aid. From 12,000 to 15,000 people, at least, in the State of Michigan have lost their homes, food, clothing, crops, horses and cattle… The number of individual farm-houses, barns and frontier dwelling which have been destroyed by the all pervading fires cannot, from want of information, be accurately calculated. The aggregate we know to be enormous. The fires are still burning, and new ones spring up. The area of ruin and devastation is daily increasing, and much suffering exists— *The Michigan State Relief Committee* — UTAH, Washington, October 24. — A petition was received at the Executive Mansion today, fifty feet long, and signed by the women of Utah, protesting against polygamy, and urging effective measures to suppress its practice in that Territory.
—*The New York Times*, October 25, 1871, page 1.

December 13, 1871. …Had some talk with Gil Robertson about my running for Congress next fall. I am inclined to go in for it if the way is clear.
December 31. …Another year gone and the great question we should ask ourselves is this— What progress have we made in the service of our kind Heavenly Father? God in His Providence has bestowed upon us many blessings, more than we can number and I pray that "each tomorrow may find us better than today." During the year our near friends & relations have generally been in the enjoyment of good health and favored with a good share of worldly prosperity, except my good brother Porter who lost half his fortune, say about $35,000, by the great fire in Chicago, Oct. 8th & 9th.
—*Diary of Francis S. Thayer.*

❧ Newspaper clippings, found in the back of the 1872 diary, but they are all dated 1871:

The following just compliment to Hon F. S. Thayer of this city we find in the *Daily Saratogian*: We hear the name of Francis S. Thayer of Troy mentioned in connection with the office of Comptroller on the state ticket. We have no hesitation in fully indorsing Mr. Thayer as a man who can be relied on every time. His position against Tammany in the Legislature of 1870, when he fought the Tweed Charter single-handed is still fresh in our memory, an evidence not only of his sagacity but his courage. Nor is his fitness for office of Comptroller any less than his ability and reliability as a legislator. With a state ticket made up of men like Thayer, the opposition will be left absolutely without cause of appeal even to Democratic voters. —September 17, 1871.

FOR SECRETARY OF STATE In several Republican journals in the state the name of Hon. Francis S. Thayer of this city has been favorably mentioned for nomination on the Republican state ticket. Some of them have suggested his candidacy for Secretary of State; others for Comptroller. To such suggestions Mr. Thayer has listened with pleasure, because they evinced the estimation among his fellow citizens of his conduct as a representative in the Legislature during the last four years. Yet he has not felt as though it would be practicable for him to accept a nomination, if tendered to him, on account

The Great Chicago Fire immediately captured the consciousness of America and is well remembered, including the legend of a cow kicking over a lantern. Peshtigo, Wisconsin, had a single horse drawn steam-pumper to combat the fire that consumed that community. Burning over 2,400 square miles in remote areas of Wisconsin and Michigan, the fire killed between 1,200 and 2,400 people, making it the most disastrous forest fire in American history.

of other engagements which seemed to require all his time and attention. With respect to these, however, it is now possible for Mr. Thayer to make arrangements which would permit his acceptance of a nomination and election, if they are made. To the solicitation, therefore, he now responds by consenting to receive the nomination for Secretary of State, if the Convention shall find it fit to give it to him.

Mr. Thayer's nomination at the present junction of our politics is one which would be well received among the Republicans in the state. His record in the Senate during a period of extraordinary temptation and amidst unusual seductions is without blemish. He constantly served the people and their interests with unswerving faithfulness. He was the only Republican Senator in 1870 who voted from first to last against the greatest piece of legislative jugglery which the Tammany Ring contrived; namely the Tweed charter. For these reasons there would seem to be a particular propriety in choosing Mr. Thayer as our standard-bearer in a campaign whose end will be a signal triumph over the misrule and corruption of the Tammanyized Democracy of the state.

—*Troy Times*, September 22, 1871.

1872

January 1, 1872. Truly thankful for the mercies & blessings of the past, I offer sincere prayer to God for His choicest blessings in the future. At 9 A.M. went to church prayer meeting…

January 4. Weather mild. A little snow but not enough for sleighing. Kate in bed most of the day with headache. Expected Dr. Mosher but he did not come…

January 10. Weather mild, south wind. Dr. Mosher came down to see Kate. I do hope & pray she may soon be better

January 20. Weather mild. Dr. Mosher came down to see Kate. Sold about 300 Bls. flour this week, very good trade today…

January 24. Weather decidedly cold. Went to Albany in A.M. to see about some Canal appointments

January 30. …P.M. went to Albany with Gil Robertson to see about canal appointments…

February 1. Pleasant winter weather. Aunt Lucy went home at 5 P.M… Rec'd a letter from Ed [Edwin McKie] saying that a little daughter was born to them this morning at 6 o'clock and both Jennie & the baby are doing "splendidly"…

February 29. Cold & unpleasant. This has been a very trying month to those who are at all sensitive to wind & weather. Kate has been obliged to stay in the house most of the time…

April 4. Bright & beautiful day. Libby Beadle here & Kate took her about town. John backed against a wagon pole & smashed in the back of his carriage which is about a $40 job…

April 5. Pleasant. Mother's birthday [Sophia Whiteside McKie], 77 years old and the light of our household. God grant that she may be spared many years.

April 30. Beautiful day. Twenty-two years ago this day we were united & Oh how much happiness we have enjoyed. God grant that we may see many more happy years…

May 19. Rainy day. In the House all day trying to get the better of a cold I have had for weeks. Took medicine and at night put a mustard paste on my chest…

June 5. Pleasant A.M. Rainy P.M. National Convention at Philadelphia to nominate candidates for Prest. & V. Prest. Grant of course will be nominated… Eve at home.

—*Diary of Francis S. Thayer.*

Edwin McKie, 1818–1895, married Jane "Jennie" I. Shortt, 1850–1930, and their baby was named Jennie Sophia McKie.

Philadelphia — Opening of the Republican National Convention — Magnificent Spectacle Presented at the Academy — All of the Old Leaders of the Party Present — Eloquent and Patriotic Speeches the Order of the Day — Addresses by Morton McMichael, Senators Morton and Logan — Fervid Utterances of the Colored Delegates

Last night was one of the most memorable in the history of this city. Blazing illuminations, great bonfires, bands of music, crowded streets everywhere…

…Finally, Mr. Borusk of California obtained the floor, and said they had all heard with delight the distinguished speakers who had spoken so eloquently in favor of the colored race, and now desired that that race now be heard through one of its representatives. [Applause.]

Loud calls were made for Gray, and Wm. H. Gray, of Arkansas, a medium-sized dark-skinned colored man, of genteel appearance and good manners, came to the platform and said: Gentlemen of the Convention: For the first time probably in the history of the American people, there stands before you in a National Convention assembled, a representative of that oppressed race that has lived among you for two hundred and fifty years, lifted by the magnanimity of this great nation, the power of God, and the laws of war, from the degradation of slavery to the proud position of American citizenship [Great applause.] Words fail me on this occasion to thank you for this evidence of your grand progress in civilization, where a people of such magnitude, the grandest and greatest nation upon the earth, not only in the recognition of the merit of the glory of the war which her noble sons waged so successfully, have in convention assembled willingly, and listened not only to the greatest of her orators, but to the humblest citizens of this great Republic. [Great applause.] I scarcely know where to begin upon an occasion like this. If I raise the curtain of the past, then I open the door of the sarcophagus from which we have but just emerged. If I go back to the primary history of my race on this continent, I would open up, perhaps the discussion of things and circumstances that would make us blush, and the blood upon our cheeks to tingle in view of the evidence of the condition of our race such as the American people have never thought of in its degradation in the shameful and humble condition from which we have just emerged. But this is scarcely necessary. We are ready to say, "Let the dead past bury its dead." While we remember these errors, while we remember all these degradations, there is no vengeance, thank God, found in our hearts; no revengeful feelings; no desire of retaliation; but God has given us a heart to thank the American people for the position in which we stand today, and we are willing, as I said before, to "Let the dead past bury its dead," and go on in our progress and fit ourselves to become what we have been made by law— American citizens in deed and in fact. [Applause.] It is the wonder of the world—the miracle of the nineteenth century—that in this great struggle, which rocked this country from centre to circumference—that amid the debris of 250 years a living people were found by this great nation, and lifted from that degradation, as it were, by the strong arm of power, and at once and without forethought placed, as I have before remarked, upon the broad plane of American citizenship. If we have failed somewhat in the sanguine expectations of our friends, yet upon the whole I think we have fairly worked out the problem, so far as we have gone. Today, for the first time, God has pleased me with a sight of that grand, noble and good old man, Gerrit Smith, [applause] who stood by us and for us when we could not stand for ourselves. [Tremendous applause.] The sight of him repays me for all the toil, all the suffering, all the pain of years. The sign of him renews my faith in that humanity which is divine.

William Henry Grey as a young man.

Gerrit Smith, 1797–1874, was an active philanthropist, abolitionist, and social reform advocate from Peterboro, New York, near Utica. Before the Civil War, he was very active in anti-slavery societies, a financial backer of John Brown, 1800–1859, in Kansas, and even sold Brown the farm in North Elba, New York, where Brown was buried. Later Smith was willing to help underwrite the $1 million bond needed to free Jefferson Davis. Working with Frederick Douglass, Smith was an early advocate of black suffrage. Smith's first cousin, Elizabeth Cady Stanton, 1815–1902, was a founder and leader of the women's suffrage movement.

There is strong circumstantial evidence that William Henry Grey, spelled "Gray" in the *New York Times* article, was the son of Henry A. Wise of Virginia. Wise had emancipated a slave, Elizabeth Gray, and her two children, Mary Jane and William Henry, in 1827. Years later, a young "mulatto boy" of that name accompanied Wise to the House of Representatives and helped him there with his paperwork. There is no evidence of any subsequent contact between Wise and the young man, and it is not known if Wise knew of Grey's speech at the 1872 Republican Convention. Grey lived in Pittsburg, Cincinnati, and Saint Louis before moving to Arkansas in 1865. He attended the 1868 Republican Convention in Chicago where, coincidentally, Francis S. Thayer from Troy, New York, was a delegate. Grey died in 1888. Some of history is incomplete and uncertain. The Virginia newspaper used the name "John A. Gray" in its brief report about the Philadelphia speech perhaps because the editor knew of Grey's relationship to Wise and wanted to minimize discussion of it in Virginia. During all of this time, there was perhaps no communication between Wise and Grey because that might have been one of the conditions of the emancipation of Grey's mother years before. Some writers in that time period might have described Grey as a "mulatto" to indicate that he was the son of a prominent white man. Descendants of Henry A. Wise and William Henry Grey today acknowledge

Continued next page

[Prolonged cheering.] We are here today, gentlemen, a part and parcel of this great people, an integral part of the great body of this country, and here for the purpose, in harmony with you, of intrusting therein of power into the hands of that hero that led us through a great bloody struggle of years; led us out to citizenship; and who, when the war ended and he was nominated for President in 1868 said: "Let us have peace." The solving of the problem of our citizenship has been the work of years. No one knew how that position was to be brought about. But few men could comprehend the situation, or the political position of affairs in the South—few men knew. I happened to be present upon that occasion in 1868 when Gen. Grant was nominated, and when I went home to my state of Arkansas I know very well, and there are men here who can attest it, that throughout that political canvas it cost the lives of three hundred black men in Arkansas to carry the State for Ulysses S. Grant. Today the problem is being worked out to further solution. The Kuklux problem is being worked out. The Kuklux situation is settled, and the peace of the country secured. But, had it not been for the law, and the men at the helm who had the nerve to execute it, that organization would be today in full venom in that section of the country; therefore, we urge upon the American people to give us Ulysses S. Grant for our candidate, for his name is a tower of strength at the South and the only name that unrepentant rebels respect. [Prolonged cheers.] He is the man to work out the great problem now being solved in this country by the great Republican Party. As has been truly said the past problem has not yet been fully solved. Its duties are not entirely fulfilled. Its organization must not yet be disintegrated. The full measure of our citizenship is not yet completed. We stand many of us in a prominent position in the Southern States, but right among the people we hold no position. The law is so weak, and the public sentiment so perverse, that the common civilities of a citizen are withheld from us. We want the Civil Rights bill [Applause.] We demand that we shall be respected as men among men—free American citizens. [Cheers.] We do not ask that for any small reason. There are always two classes of people. We have to be afraid of that class who love us too well and hate us too much. [Laughter.] All we ask is a fair share in the race of life, and give us the same privileges that are given to other men. I hope the action of this Convention will be such that we may be able to go home rejoicing. So far as the colored people of the South are concerned, they are a unit today for Ulysses S. Grant. [Cheers.] I know they told us often "niggers" can now go for the father of Republicanism. When we objected to this on the ground that he was not the Republican nominee, they said he is the father of Republicanism. Said I, "Very well; if that is so, I thank him for having been the father of such a brood of illustrious and loyal men, but I fear, like Abraham of old, he takes Hagar instead of Sarah. We cannot afford that." [Laughter.] If you do this, we do not intend to recognize any of those outside children. [Renewed laughter.] There is the inheritance of the free woman, the legitimate offspring of the old man, and we are going to keep the boys all at home. [Cheers.] I fear some of these talkers are like the Ishmaelite of old, and the old lady will have to hunt for water in the wilderness. [Great laughter.] The black people of the State of Arkansas are solid. They know who are their friends. They know very well there is no standing for the black man outside of the Republican Party. [Cheers.] They know they cannot afford to vote against their best friends, and they will not do it. They will all vote for Grant from the start, from Arkansas to the Gulf of Mexico. [Cheers.] I am happy to hear from other gentlemen of the Convention the sentiments here uttered, and for the privilege of knowing that the ranks will be kept solid together for the victory that will perch upon our banners in the coming contest. [Prolonged applause.]

—*The New York Times*, June 6, 1872.

👁 A Virginia newspaper describing the same event:

Meeting of the Republican Convention — Philadelphia
By Associated Press
The Convention Called to Order — Temporary Organization
Philadelphia, June 5. Ex-Governor Clafflin, of Massachusetts, called the Republican convention to order shortly after noon today… Committees on credentials and permanent organization were appointed… During the day speeches were made by Messrs. Morton, Logan, Gerrit Smith, Governor Oglesby, John A. Gray (colored delegate from Arkansas), and others; all of them in warm eulogy of Grant, who, it is declared, will be nominated by acclamation…
—*Daily Dispatch*, Richmond, Virginia, Thursday, June 6, 1872.

that a relationship very likely exists between them, and perhaps there will be a time when modern science will provide a definitive answer to a question that the historical record alone can not do. William Henry Grey was the first person of African descent to address a national political convention.

August 23, 1872. Weather hot & sultry. Troy in morning & back (to Cambridge) at eve as usual… Letter from Ed saying his little baby was so very poorly.
August 24. Weather hot & sultry. Kate & Kittie went to Cambridge this morn… just in time to see the sweet little baby pass away to the better land. Ed & Jennie are completely crushed by the blow. The light of their home has gone to heaven. God bless & sustain them…
August 26. Over to Cambridge with Kate & children to attend the funeral of the dear little Baby Jennie Sophia, born the 1st day of last February. Very large funeral. The whole community sympathetic with the afflicted parents. She was brought over to the old Whiteside burying ground & placed beside her Grandmother. This has indeed been a sad day to me.
November 5. Beautiful day. Election passed off very quietly. Democrats long ago made up their minds to defeat and they seem to take very little interest. At store most of the day. Business very good. Early in eve learned enough to insure a great Republican victory everywhere.
November 6. Election news comes in gloriously. Victory, victory is the watchword today… Almost every horse in the city is sick. Our horse Charley is very sick, but John takes the best care of him.
November 8. Weather cool & pleasant… My three horses sick. Charley very sick…
November 11. Weather cool & pleasant… Horse sickness better…
December 22. Cold day. Water pipes froze, burst & leaked down into the pantry & kitchen. Mr. Vincent preached in A.M. to a small audience. Cold weather kept people at home about their fires. This is the coldest day of the season…
December 28. Breakfast at 8 o'clock & soon after at Dr. Clarks where we spent an hour & a half. The Dr. examined Kate & myself thoroughly. He says there is no serious trouble with Kate's lungs, good care & good living is all she requires. To me, he said I must take the world easily which I will do…   —*Diary of Francis S. Thayer.*

her Grandmother   Catherine Whiteside McKie, 1793–1824.

A summary of 1872:
February 1, 1872. Pleasant winter day… Letter from Edwin, he has a daughter. What an event.
April 5. Mother's birthday. Pleasant day… Frank went to Albany at 5. Returned at 11

Catherine's diary has no entries describing the death of her brother's baby in August.

p.m. I rejoice in this my dear Mother's 77th birthday that she is in such comfortable health. I hope she will be spared to us many years…

April 30. Twenty-two years ago today we were married. How much I thank our dear Father in Heaven for the heart-joys of these years I cannot tell. May there be many more given us, each sweeter, better than the last.

September 11. My dear husband is fifty years old, nothing to give him but a heart-full of love and some beautiful flowers & yes a most earnest prayer that "all things may work for his best good."

December 31. This is the last day of the old year. With such feelings of gratitude and regret we write 72. —*Excerpts from the 1872 diary of Catherine McKie Thayer.*

1873

January 22, 1873. Weather cold & pleasant. Business very good. Had a talk with Mr. Bills about my selling out my interest in the business. I need for peace & rest. The fact is, Mr. B— is too fickle & unpleasant & I will sell out if I can…

February 21. The most severe storm of the season. Snowing hard from Northeast all day— 16–18 inches.
Business very dull. Had a long talk with Mr. Bills about business. We are in the opinion that it is about time for us to separate. Mill running moderately…

February 26. Beautiful day. Had a plain talk with Mr. Bills about selling out or buying out. I offered him $22,000 for half of the Mill. He offered me $20,000. Great excitement in the stock market. —*Diary of Francis S. Thayer.*

Wall Street Panic in Stocks Yesterday — Cause of the Depression — *A Heavy Operator Reported in Difficulty* — At the very latest house on 'Change, yesterday, it was rumored that Mr. A. B. Stockwell, President of the Pacific Mail Steam-ship Company and one of the heaviest operators in the street, was heavily involved, and that his failure was extremely probable… Mr. Stockwell's losses, it is generally said, are due to the course of Jay Gould, who for the last few weeks has been locking up currency, thereby forcing holders to part with their stocks. The entire stock market was terribly demoralized yesterday, especially in those lines which Mr. Stockwell deals extensively in… Jay Gould, who has kept away from the "street" for a few weeks past, and who is generally supposed to be at the bottom of this trouble was visited by a TIMES reporter, last evening. Mr. Gould said that he had heard about the trouble through his private wire… that the public did wrong to charge him with being the cause of the panic… In spite of Mr. Gould's general denial, there is but little doubt that he is at the bottom of the depression of the stock market, and that he will add a large sum to his already immense gains in the Street. —*The New York Times*, February 27, 1873.

March 3, 1873. Weather cold… Had a little talk with Bills about business matters. He asks me to give up politics & attend to business every other month for three years. I'll do as I have a mind about that…

March 19. Mild & pleasant. Business very good for the season. Mr. Bills still looking for a Partner, if he doesn't succeed soon I shall have to buy him out & run the business alone…

March 24. Very cold. Mr. Bills handed me his figures for the Mill & I put them in my pocket without looking at them. Attended the funeral of Mrs. Cumberland… At dinner I looked at Mr. Bills' figures, $22,500 & at once decided to buy…

March 26. Sleet & snow enough for sleighing again. Accepted Mr. Bills offer to sell

the Mill at $22,500 & $500 bonus I agreed to give him… Glad the vexed question is settled & I hope & trust 'tis for the best…
April 26. Cold & windy. Mr. Bills returned from the western part of the State whither he went to buy a mill. He bot one at Middleport (Niagara County).
May 24. Summer weather, at store all A.M… Markets dull and declining, stock market perfectly lifeless… eve called at Mr. Eaton's with Kate   —*Diary of Francis S. Thayer.*

That is the last entry in Francis Thayer's diary in 1873. There is no explanation for this, and there are no other diaries by him.

∽ Summer vacation:

June 18th, 1873.
My darling Kittie—   …I am inclined to get a little sea air for my asthma and don't be disappointed if I slip off to Fire Island for a day or two…*Fraddie.*

Troy, Aug. 18th, 1873, Monday, 6 o'clock P.M.
My own dear ones at Fire Island—   I arrived in New York just in time to take the 10 o'clock train, arrived in Albany just too late to take the 2 o'clock local and had to wait there nearly an hour. Rained hard most of the way. I found business matters all straight. Thought but not to go up home this eve as it rained hard and the prospect of walking or a ride on a back road seemed so good that I thought but to stay here. I will go up to Liz's for tea and after a while find my way down town.   —Yours affectionately & truly, *Francis.*

Aug 19, 1873, 2:30 P.M.
My darling wife & children—   You will look for a letter tomorrow & for the writer next day. I am afraid you will be disappointed about seeing me on Thursday for there is more to do here than Johnny Roche can attend to well. Business is good & it needs an older head than will be here when I am gone. I will certainly come at the earliest possible day… Today I feel very well and hard at work. Have just come up from dinner. A desk full of letters must be answered… Hope you are all having a pleasant time. Be careful about bathing & sailing. Yours affectionately, *Frank.*

Fire Island, Aug 20, 1873.
My dear Husband—   I have just rec'd your letter of yesterday and am glad to know that you rested well "last night." We have not seen the sun since you left us. It has rained hard every night and is raining now… Now the Eatons leave here Friday morn. What do you say to me going with them? Kittie is longing to go. Frankie is ready to do so, and I feel that you can come down here whenever you *find* or take the time…   —*Kittie.*

December 3, 1873, Troy.
My Dear Daughter—   You are fourteen years old today and O how thankful we should all feel that our home is so happy. It is my wish to make you a present not as a pledge of my love and affection for you know my darling that you have those in full measure. But it is pleasant to give and receive something on a birthday. I have not had the time today to go into the stores, and select something for you so I give you a "greenback" which will buy a token to remind you that my love is "evergreen" and constant.   —Your devoted and affectionate Father, *Francis S. Thayer.*
To— Miss Catherine Sophia Thayer, Washington Park, Troy, N.Y.

Auditorship Francis Thayer was appointed Auditor of the New York Canal Commission. An unidentified newspaper article reads: "The appointment of F. S. Thayer to the position of Canal Auditor is one of the most commendable appointments that the Governor has made during his administration. We have known him for many years, and can say without fear of contradiction, there is no higher toned, honorable gentleman in the State than F. S. Thayer, of Troy." Subsequently, political opponents accused him of certain improprieties but those were all unfounded and unproven. An unidentified newspaper column describes that: "Indeed, the Commission presented its charge to the Commissioners of the Canal Funds two weeks ago and demanded the suspension of the Auditor without having given him any opportunity whatever for a hearing. And there is every reason to believe that this report was then in type—except as some few additions have been rendered necessary by subsequent proceedings—and that the design was to consummate the suspension and publish the report all at one blow, so as to produce a public sensation. An hour was chosen for the meeting in the afternoon when it was supposed the Auditor would be away. No notice was given him. The members of the Board were clandestinely called together. The proceeding was to be entirely of a secret character, and it was expected that the suspension might be immediately accomplished before the Auditor should know it or the public hear

Continued on next page

August 11, 1873. Frank, children and myself left in the morn for Fire Island.
August 30. All home fr. Fire Island. Mother met us at the cars. Rhoda has been staying with her. House beautiful with flowers.
October 24. All came home from Cambridge. Frankie & Kittie here in school.
—*Excerpts from the 1873 diary of Catherine McKie Thayer.*

1874

Troy. April 3, 1874
My Dear Kate—   Nothing from you today. Kittie said it was too bad Mother did not write. Of course we shall hear from you tomorrow morning… I hear nothing more from Albany in regard to the Auditorship. That's a matter I shall not run after. When it presents itself in a manner that requires action on my part I shall give it due deliberation and decide wisely I hope. Of course your wishes will be consulted… I hope you are having such a good time that you will think best to stay and come up with Jim the first of next week. We will take good care of Mother & make her birthday very happy. Love to all & all love to you my darling.   —*Frank.*

April 15, 1874. Warm and sunny. Francis went to Albany as Auditor. I spent the day as best I could but do not feel that he is able to add to his labors…
April 20. Francis to Albany this rainy morn. Home to dinner… to the office and home at 1/2 past 7 or so for the eve. Raining all day and I fear my good husband has taken cold.
—*Diary of Catherine McKie Thayer*

❦ A trip to the White Mountains of New Hampshire:

July 2, 1874. …Took cars for Littleton at 8. It rained hard and we had some dinner in cars… I had sick headache. Arrived at L [Littleton, New Hampshire] at 7:30. Stopped at Thayer's Hotel, a good place. Francis and all like this house.
July 3. Francis had asthma last night. He sat too long downstairs with the door open and it was damp. Took the stagecoach… for the Profile about 9:30, distance twelve miles. It was a hard ride for Mrs. Mason, but a charming one to us, almost entire distance through woods. Reached the Profile at 1:30. It is wonderfully beautiful in situation. These grand mountains, like walls of living green, all more than I dreamed of in beauty. This aft. Mr. Mason took a short walk with me. Francis, Frankie, Kittie agree that this is the loveliest spot in nature we ever saw. The mountains are grand and start from your very feet.
July 5. Mrs. Mason and I walked to Profile Lake. She seemed a little tired.
July 6. Lovely day. Our party, except Mrs. Mason, went to the Flume and the Pool. The first is wonderful and the ride is charming. In the aft Kittie had a short horseback ride with her father.
July 7. Lovely day. This A.M. Francis & I went to Profile Lake together. Took a boat and went out fishing but did not get a nibble…
July 8. Breakfast at 7. A goodbye to our dear friends and this charming spot and with Kittie and myself on top of the coach we whirled away from the Profile down the mountain. The ride was a new variety to me but after about 10 miles I was glad to change seats with Francis. He soon found Dr. Shafton, a son of his old friend… We stayed at Fabyan.

July 9. Fabyan House. I had such a headache that I could not go on to the Crawford House. This A.M. with Dr. S— took coach for base of Mt. W[ashington]. … a pleasant ride of four miles and then took rail up the Mt. —an hour and a half took us above the world to Tip Top from which the view is indescribably grand and wonderful…

July 10. Twin Mountain House. This house is well kept and the air is very fine, the views charming, the mts not so near, and the sun rises early. Left at 8 o'clock by cars, changed five times and arrived at Burlington about 5:30…

July 11. Burlington, Vermont. This morn (cloudy) we took a carriage and drove about this beautiful town… took the boat *Vermont*, Capt Flagg, had a delightful sail to Whitehall… and then to our very sweet home.

July 13. Francis to Albany. I was busy putting away and unpacking. Kittie as useful as I could wish and Frankie lending a helping hand.

July 14. Pack, pack. Kittie and I made currant jelly this a.m.…

—*Diary of Catherine McKie Thayer.*

of it… The plan miscarried, and both the attempted suspension of the Auditor and the publication of the report were delayed. But though the Commission was thus forced against its own will into granting a hearing, it has lacked the grace to modify in important particulars, as the examination required, the report which had already been prepared." Francis Thayer resigned from that position in 1876.

1875

June 30th, 1875, Amherst.
Dear Ones at home—   We left Albany at 2:40 and came through to Springfield where we arrived at 7:30… took the cars at 8:15 for Northampton. On inquiry we learned that the Hotel accommodations were not very good at N— so we engaged a man to bring us over here (8 miles) last evening… I slept well. No asthma and this morning we are up at 7. After breakfast went to the College Hall where were assembled some slightly anxious young men awaiting the oral examination in Greek… I have engagements to meet in Albany Friday and as we shall get through with examinations by tomorrow 4 o'clock we might as well leave for home. Have done nothing about Boarding place yet. Will see to that tomorrow. Frank keeps up good courage and is as usual quiet, dignified, and retiring. There are a dozen or more boys here at the Hotel and Frank does not take to them. He says there is time enough to get acquainted. We are much pleased with the college buildings, grounds etc etc. It is a beautiful old town… It almost makes me wish I was young again. Still I'll not complain but rejoice that my humble "Alma mater" brought with it the richest treasure of my life, Old Cambridge Academy forever… All together I am much pleased with Amherst and hope and pray our dear boy will not only honor himself by coming here but add to the reputation of this old time honored institution of learning. With much love to all I am as ever yours lovingly. *Francis.*

∾ Letters to Frank at Amherst College:

Sep. 6, 1875, South Cambridge.
My dear Son—   Soon after the family party passed from sight, I went up to your room, and found razor and strap on the bureau, and queried if they should not have been put in your bag, but Grandmother and I concluded that you would be able to get a clean shave in Mass. in some way. I cannot tell you how much we have missed you all in so many ways… The remainder of the day I spent in the garden with W. McKie all weeding, pruning and clipping… That God may bless and keep you in the prayers of your loving, *Mother.*

Francis McKie Thayer, C. R. Clark, Photographer, Troy, New York.

Sep. 9th, 1875, *State of New York, Senate Chamber.*
My Dear Son—   While waiting for my dinner I'll drop you a few lines. I need not tell you that it was a "choking" time with us when we left you all alone among strangers— strangers today, but among them I trust you will now find many good friends… I pray God that you may be blessed with health and strength to bear well each day's duties. *Aim high my son*, discharge every duty faithfully & manfully, and you will succeed… With much love, I am you affectionate *Father.*

Sept. 11th, 1875. *State of New York, Canal Department.*
My dear Son—   Your welcome letter of yesterday's date came to hand this morning… We had a slight frost this morning at Cambridge. Mother & Kittie covered the flowers, tomatoes etc. in the garden last eve. I am 53 years old today. These birthdays remind me that I am growing old, so it is my son, one generation after another… —*Father.*

Sept. 15, 1875. *State of New York, Canal Department.*
My Dear Son—   Thanks for your good letter of yesterday's date. Hope you will find time to give us a few lines if not more, quite frequently. With all I have to do, I'll take the time to write you every day or two… Let us know how you are getting on in your studies and all about your introduction to College life… —*Father.*

Sep. 15, 1875, Old Home, Cambridge.
My dear dear Son—   Your good Father brought to us this evening your letter to him of the 14th and one to me written Sabbath evening. Both have been read and re-read with an interest you may understand someday but cannot now. …We trust you are in the best place for your highest good, and so trusting we have been very much pleased with the description of your rooms and hope you will enjoy yourself in them… Grandmother had a very poor day Monday. We had Dr. yesterday and she is much better today… How I would like to step in and look at you in your pleasant quarters. How do you like your slippers? I thought them beautiful, and do they fit? …GrandM says "give my love to him and tell him I wish I could see him."   —*Mungie.*

Mungie A family name for Catherine McKie Thayer.

Sept. 18, 1875. *State of New York, Canal Department.*
My Dear Son—   I suppose you have a little rest from study Saturdays. If you were at Williamstown you could come home and spend the sabbath after all. I think you made a wise choice in deciding upon Amherst… I hope you will write us frequently and keep us well informed as to yourself. Your letters are good and indeed very acceptable. Yours Truly, *Father.*

Sept. 22, 1875. *State of New York, Canal Department.*
My Dear Son—   I have nothing new or interesting to communicate… Let us know all about how you are getting on in your first weeks of college life. How about the societies etc. etc. etc. —*Father.*

September 24, 1875, Old Home, Cambridge, New York.
My dear Boy—   You letter of the 20th was brought us by Father this eve. We are glad to know that you are interested in your studies… Have you had

a touch of homesickness? I used to suffer terribly with it and know how hard it is, but you cannot miss us more than we do you. Dear Grandmother said tonight with swimming eyes, "I do so miss my good-night kiss." We all think of you with our first and last waking thoughts, and hope and pray that you are growing strong, wise and are truly happy… Kittie says who do you know in your class? You will have to tell her about the *boy*… Good night my precious boy. God bless and keep you. Loving, *Mungie.*

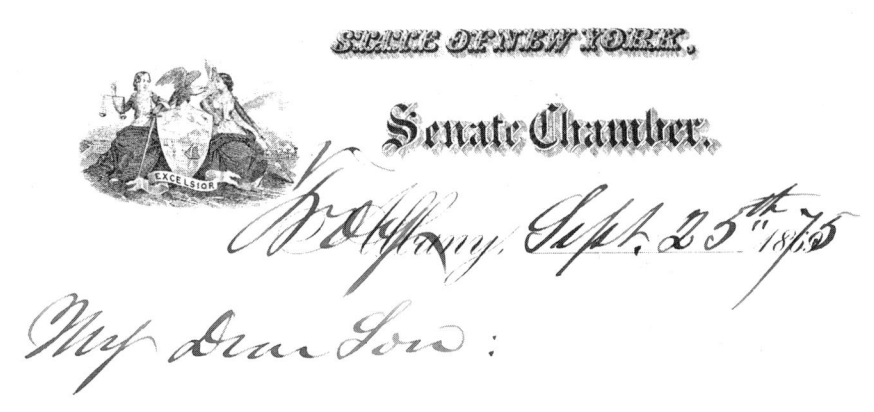

Oct. 1st., 1875. *State of New York, Senate Chamber.*
My dear Son—   Yours of 30th came duly to hand this morning. You are certainly an excellent correspondent and these frequent missives of affection are bright spots in our daily life… have no doubt your society experiences will prove pleasant and profitable. It does us good to mix with the world around us. One thing we should always keep in mind, that is, we should strive to make our associates better… I am much better of my cold & asthma. You may expect a box of grapes next week… I remain your affectionate *Father.*

Oct. 5th, 1875. *State of New York, Canal Department.*
My dear Son—   I rather expected a letter from you this morning but was disappointed. Of course I would not have you neglect your studies to write letters, but I assure you my good boy, we are all hungry for your letters and hope you will continue to write often… Write as often as you have the time… Kittie wrote you a loving letter Sunday evening, asking a good many questions etc., etc. —all of which you will no doubt answer in due time… —*Father.*

Oct. 7th., 1875. *State of New York, Canal Department.*
My dear Son—   I recd your good letter of 4th yesterday morning. With good health and hard study I have no doubt you will stand above par in all your studies at the end of your first term in college… —*Father.*

Oct. 13th, 1875. *State of New York, Senate Chamber.*
My dear Son—   Your note of 12th came to hand yesterday morning (I think you must have got ahead of time one day.) …I will send you a draft for $75, tomorrow and on receipt of it you can pay Mr. Delano. …Mother went to Hoosick yesterday to see Aunt Fanny who is very near the great change that awaits us all. Mother thought she would not survive more than two or three days… —*Father.*

Mr. Delano   The Delano House for Permanent and Transient Guests was where Frank boarded in 1875. The files include several bills from the Delano House for: board, fire, washing, and, in one instance, a "loan" of $5.00. This building was on the site of the current Mayo-Smith House, formerly the Chi Psi fraternity at Amherst College.

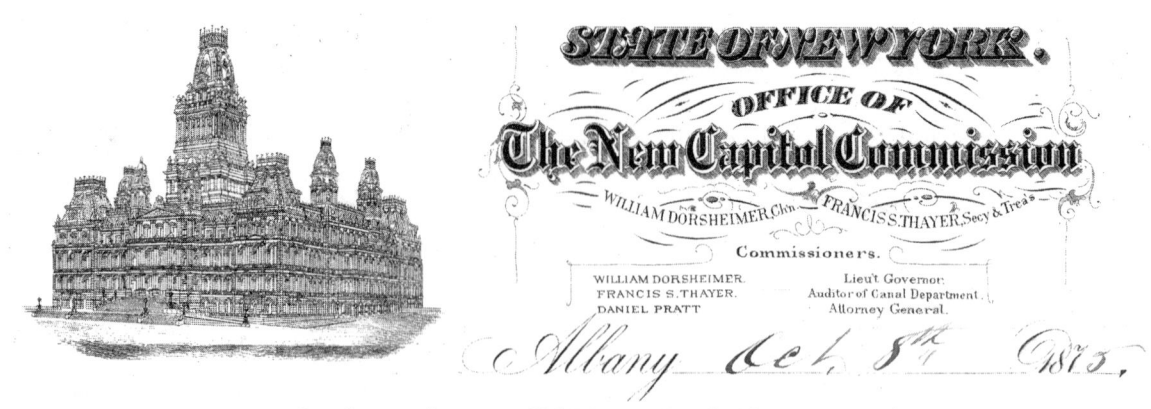

October 14th, 1875, Old Home, Cambridge, New York.
My dear Boy— We have just had prayers and Father has gone up-stairs. Kittie is embroidering. Grandmother sits by the stove, which the cold weather obliged us to resort to and Dandy lies in the rocking chair. …We now count the weeks to Thanksgiving. Father and Kittie have written so often and they write such entertaining letters that I am very tame in comparison, but if Mungie does not write often, she thinks, and well you know that, all the time of and for the dear boy. …Tuesday I went to see Aunt Fanny and I found her very feeble. Today she is still lower, but she shows great power of endurance. —Mungie.

Oct. 14th, 1875. *Office of the New Capital Commission.*
My dear Son— Enclosed I send you Troy City Ntl Bank Draft on the Third National Bank New York for $75. Made payable to your order. You can put your name on the back of the Draft right under mine and hand it to Mr. Delano. …Aunt Fanny still lingers growing more feeble every day. The Dr. said yesterday that she could not live many hours… How are you getting on in your studies? Are you making up the conditions so that you will be all right at the end of the first term?… —Father.

Oct. 16th. 1875, "Whiteside," Sabbath evening.
My dear Son— Mother says, write my dear boy and tell him how I wish I could put my arms around him and kiss him… You have been aware for two or three weeks that every letter from home might bring the sad news of the death of your Aunt Fanny —the sad reality came Saturday morning about 6 o'clock when the spirit of a noble woman peacefully took its flight to the bosom, as we trust, of our blessed Savior… —Father.

Nov. 2, 1875, Troy.
My dear Son— Your welcome letter of Sabbath evening came to hand this morning… This is election day and all the Banks are closed so in order to enable you to meet your Bill promptly I send my own Draft instead of a Bank Draft as before. You can endorse this draft and hand it to Miss Delano who can use it at the Bank. She will of course pay you the difference between the Draft & your bill. I am hopeful as to the result of the elections. However, I have room for disappointment. The Democratic party is strong still I hope & pray right and justice will prevail. Affectionately yours, —Father.

Nov. 11th, 1875, Troy.
My dear Boy—   I asked Kittie to write you yesterday about Father. He did not sleep well last night and does [not] feel as well today. His breathing is not so labored as it was the first of the week, and yet it is as difficult all the time as you ever knew it. Father just opened his eyes and said: "Writing to Frank?"— Yes, what shall I tell him?— "that I have been confined to the house since last Sat. by asthma aggravated by cold but hope the worst is over and that I can be out soon." He sat up twice yesterday, an hour or so each time, but the least movement of his hands or arms increases the difficulty of breathing. The Dr. (Bloss) told him today not to be discouraged, that the weather was bad. I do hope and pray that he will be better very soon. I am much better than I have been as you will conclude when I tell you that I sleep on the lounge and take care of Father at night. The ground is covered with snow, a light covering however… May God keep and bless you my dear boy. Write a few lines often. All send love and a Mother's heartfull   —*Mungie.*

Nov. 12, 1875, Troy.
My dear Boy—   I am happy to say that your Father is better this aft. —his breathing so much easier that he has been able to sleep some— the first relief since last Sat… He sends much love to you, and hopes you are getting on well in which we all join. We have heard nothing from you since last Fri but hope to get a letter this eve— God bless and keep you and us.   —Good by darling. *Mungie.*

Nov. 14, 1875, Troy.
My dear Frank—   I am glad to say that dear Father is more comfortable, has been sitting up an hour and a half and had a little venison for his dinner which he seemed to relish. We have not heard a word from [you] since a week ago Sat. Will you not write regularly on certain days. …Much love to you my precious boy. God bless you.   —*Mungie.*

Nov. 17th, 1875, Troy.
My dear Boy— I am rejoiced to be able to say that dear Father is decidedly better, his breathing is quite improved and he looks like a convalescent. I think your letter brightened him up a good deal, indeed we were all glad to hear from you…   —*Mungie.*

Dec. 3rd, 1875, Troy.
To Our dear Daughter—   "Sweet sixteen" today. Accept this ring from your affectionate *Father & Mother.*

Dec. 7th, 1875, Troy.
My dear Son—   I am indeed happy to inform you that the Doctor has given me permission to go out the first mild and pleasant day. During the past week I have gained considerable strength and am now able to go down to my meals. With a good appetite and good digestion I hope soon to be in the enjoyment of my usual health and strength. Four weeks last Saturday, since I gave up— it seems to me like a dream. While I have had everything in the way of care and attention that loving hearts could prompt it has been anything

but pleasant to be sick and I hope & pray that I may now be well again. All send much love.   —Affectionately Yours *Father*.

Dec. 11th, 1875, Troy.
My dear Son—   We had not heard from you this week until this morning when your letter of 9th came to hand and I assure you it met with a glad welcome. Hope you will find time to write as often as twice every week, if only a few lines. I am gaining every day. Have been out to walk a block or two twice. If the weather should be pleasant I hope to go to Albany next Monday and in the course of a few days expect to be in the enjoyment of my usual health and strength. I shall be careful and take business and official duties easily. I enclose Draft for $75 as requested. You will bring home your expense book…   —With much love from all I remain your affectionate *Father*.   P.S. I would advise you to cultivate the acquaintance of your teachers by calling frequently at their homes.

Dec. 19th, 1875, Troy.
My dear Son—   I have not written you for several days for the reason I have been engaged the whole time preparing to meet the charges made against me by the Governor's Canal Commission. You have probably seen a good deal in the papers during the past few days. I shall put in my answer tomorrow which is (I think) such as to lift the cloud thrown over my official acts by the *inquisitional* commission. I had no opportunity to explain matters or facts. They refused to hear me. Enough of this. Well, we shall look for you Wednesday. Suppose you will leave for early morning train. Mother says you had better bring your trunk & your dress suit. You can check your trunk through to Troy. Get off at Adams Street and William can take your check up to the depot and get your trunk. I am improving in health every day. All send much love.   —Affectionately your, *Father*.

1876

 Letters to Frank at Amherst College:

Jan. 7, 1876, Troy.
My precious Boy—   I have just had your very good and most welcome letter of Wed eve. which came this morning. I was out when it came, attending the funeral of Frank Plum who died Wed. aft. Christmas day he was at Mrs. Gilberts and now is he buried. He grew worse rapidly Tuesday.   —*Mungie*.

January 11th, 1876, Troy.
My dear Son—   They kept me in Buffalo until Saturday P.M., too late to reach home before early Sabbath morning. I took the sleeping train and had a comfortable nights' rest. It seems almost marvelous to go to bed in Buffalo at 10 o'clock in the evng and wake in Albany (300 miles distant) early the next morning… You will see by the *Troy Times*, which I send you, that I have resigned my office in Albany. Under all the circumstances I thought best to take this course rather than go into a long fight to regain a position which would only be a burden to me. The only unpleasant thing about giving up the office is the way and manner in which the thing was done. One thing I am sure of is I have done nothing intentionally wrong and I believe my worst

enemies do not accuse me of any crime. Violation of duty is the broadest construction they can give it. —*Father*.

January 23, 1876, Troy.
My dear Son— Your welcome letter of Friday evening came to hand this morning. I am very glad you appreciate the advice I gave you in regard to keeping a strict acct. of your expenses. These figures stare us in the face very often and no doubt with beneficial affect. Many people go on spending money without a thought until the last dollar is reached and then they wonder where in the world so much money has gone. I do not propose to give you weekly lectures on economy. You well understand my wishes and your duty, and I think I can trust you. Grandmother is still quite feeble. …Her cold is somewhat better for the past two days, but she is very frail. Her advanced age and feeble constitution are sufficient to create much solicitude when disease takes hold of her; still we hope and pray she may be spared to us years yet… She was very glad to have your letter read this morning. …Uncle Edwin was here one day this week. All well up there [Cambridge]. We shall expect a letter from you Tuesday morning. It would please Grandmother to receive a letter from you and I would suggest that you write to her. All send much love.
—Your Affectionate, *Father*.

February 1st, 1876, Troy.
My dear Son—The first of the month reminds me that you have some bills to pay and I think it is always best to be prompt in such matters, in fact promptness is one of the rare and beautiful traits of the human character. On receipt of this, please figure up and let me know the amount required to put you on a sound financial basis, keeping a sharp lookout, as it behooves us all in these times, towards economy. It is not my purpose to give you a lecture on economy every month. I think you understand and appreciate the situation and will be quite reasonable in all your expenses… —I am, as ever Your Affectionate *Father*.

February 4th, 1876, Troy.
My dear Son— It is now all of ten days since the receipt of your last letter. Much too long my son. Can not get along very well without hearing from you once or twice a week. Please write often. We do not expect long letters, but a few lines to let us now how you are if no more. Grandmother is improving slowly. Last eve she walked from the sitting room into her bedroom with a little assistance. She often inquires after you and I think it would do her good to receive a letter from your hand. Do sit down & write her one of your good full letters… I don't know as there is any news worth communicating. —I remain your loving *Father*.

Feb. 9th, 1876, Troy
My dear Son— Your very welcome letter of Sabbath eve 6th came to hand yesterday P.M. I hope you will not again allow two weeks to go by without writing to the dear ones at home. We must hear from you as often as once a week and more frequently will be very acceptable. Grandmother inquires very often, "Hear anything from Frankie?" and if your letters are not recd in due time she says, "I wonder if the dear boy is sick?" These Mothers & Grandmothers think more of the loved and absent ones than we are aware of.

Grandmother is perhaps a little stronger than when I last wrote you, but still very feeble. She sits up in the easy chair an hour or two during the day, but does not gain strength much. You must write to her. …You speak of having good sleighing. We have had very little snow… It is now clouding up and fixing for a snow storm I hope.   —I am as ever, your aff, *Father*.

April 26th, 1876, Troy.
My dear Son—   Your *long looked for* letter of Sabbath eve, mailed yesterday (Tuesday) reached me this morning. I do not like this irregularity in our correspondence. We should be regular and prompt in that delightful duty as well as in everything else appertaining to the duties and responsibilities of life. I suggest that you write to me every Sabbath eve, and I will promise to answer on the following Tuesday. What do you say to this my boy? …I am glad to hear that the interest in the revival meetings still continues, and I hope and pray you are doing your full duty as a *worker* in the vineyard of our blessed Lord & Master… —*Father*.

May 4th, 1876, Troy.
My dear Son—   I am disappointed in not receiving a letter from you today. Last Saturday I wrote you on a very important matter and while I do not doubt your answer will be all I could wish, still it would be a satisfaction to know from your own hand that you had made the wise decision I so strongly and decidedly urged you to make in regard to your studies. I will not allow myself to doubt. Now, do not fail to write very soon. I put this in with a letter from Kittie, Yours affectionately, —*Father*.

May 5th, 1876, Troy.
My dear Son—   I thought certainly I should get a letter from you today but the busy letter carrier has made his last round for the day and no letter from my dear boy. As I wrote you yesterday, I cannot for a moment think of your taking a "partial course" and I shall be grieved to the heart if you do not very soon relieve me from all anxiety on that point… It is my wish that you should be as prompt in the payment of your bills as well as in everything else. You should make your calculations and arrangements so as to have the money ready on the *very first* day of every month. Now is the time for you to form habits of regularity and promptness, which, if well established at your time of life, will be a blessing to you as long as you live… I have always noticed that the man who is on hand and prompt to meet his engagements is the one who succeeds in almost anything he undertakes. I have some customers who always send their check on the day their bills become due and those are the ones I like to deal with. Your habits of study I hope and trust are regular and systematic. It is your business to study now and the habits you form will stick to you through life, so be careful and start right. I didn't think of writing more than a line or two when I commenced, but you see the bottom of the fourth page is now at hand, so I'll stop. —Lovingly Your *Father*.

May 6th, 1876, Troy.
My dear Son—   A week ago today I wrote you a long letter on a very important matter. Of course I expected a reply without delay. You should have recd. my letter Monday P.M. and it seems to me passing strange that you did not answer it by return mail. But no, you have kept us anxiously

waiting all the week and now Saturday evening's mail brings nothing from you and we are still in doubt (No, I cannot doubt) what course you will pursue.   —*Father*.

May 9th, 1876, Troy.
My dear Son—   I was very confident, aye, was almost certain that tonight's mail would bring me a letter from you, but none came, and I was almost discouraged. You must be aware of our anxiety to hear from you and it is the strangest thing in the world that you do not write, certainly you cannot plead want of time for 'tis only a matter of a very few minutes and it was understood and agreed when you left home that you would write as often as once per week. It is not in my heart to scold or say a single unpleasant word, but really my dear boy, I do not like this long silence on your part…   —*Father*.

May 27th, 1876, Amherst.
Dear ones at home—   I arrived here at 3:30 yesterday P.M. Found Frank well and hard at work. He got behind in Mathematics, but he hopes with hard study, to come up to par at the end of the term. I have called on the Prest., Profs Mathew & White. In Latin & Greek Frank will have no difficulty in passing examinations so his teachers say. This is a delightful ["*charming*" crossed out] day. Nature is in her most charming ["*delightful*" crossed out] dress and everything in the world without bright and beautiful. Frank gave the package & letter to Miss Delano & I have no doubt she appreciated them, but she has not said so. You may look for me Monday late in the evening.   —Lovingly Yours, *Father*. Frank sends much love.

June 1st. 1876, Troy.
My dear Son—   I shall expect a letter from you tomorrow morning and hope and trust it will tell me that you are getting on bravely with mathematics under your new Prof. You will of course keep me well advised of your progress and drop a line or two as often as two or three times a week.   —*Father*.

June 2, 1876, Troy.
My dear Son—   I believe it was understood that you would write to me on Thursday, so I looked for a letter this morning but none came. Very likely you wrote, but not in time to post your letter for the P.M. mail… I trust the report in regard to your studies will be all a loving father's heart could wish to hear from his dear and only son… I trust you will give me a full letter Sabbath eve.   —*Father*.

~

Compositions:

Dame Duck's First Lecture on Education

Dame Duck lived close to the brook & every morning she took her ducklings there to swim, and as they were quite strong now, and they had seen the orchard and meadow, she thought it best to begin her course of lectures.

Catherine "Kittie" Thayer's compositions from when she studied at the Troy Female Seminary were found folded, some in envelopes, amongst the other letters. Some were labeled: "Miss Mann's Composition Class. Troy Female Seminary," today the Emma Willard School.

"Come children," she said, "it is time for our morning ramble, and I wish to talk to you all on education when we arrive at the swamp. Now children, walk behind me, one after another, and turn out your toes, look at me as a pattern of all things. Now see those young ducks fighting already. I do declare, don't let me see you doing such an ill bred thing, unless with the goslings of the old goose. She insulted me last summer. Now we have reached the swamp and we shall be free from disturbance. Take seats duckies." She soon made herself comfortable and began. "Now ducklings, the most important thing of all is to turn your toes out, and carry your head in an easy and graceful manner." She had gone no farther in her discourse when she heard a loud bark, and through the shrubs, trees, and bushes, rushed a large dog which sent the audience in every direction.

And this was the last of the duck's first lecture on Education.

Miss Mann's Composition Class. Troy Female Seminary.
A Story by the Fire — by Katherine Thayer

There may be an element of truth to this story. When writing about her Grandmother and the grandmother's sister, Kittie is describing her grandmother, Sophia Whiteside, 1796–1878, and her great-aunt, Catherine Whiteside, 1793–1824, the two daughters of Peter Whiteside, who grew up on the Cambridge, New York, farm in the late eighteenth and early nineteenth century. In the twentieth century, Eleanor Whiteside Hobson Mackenzie, Kittie's daughter, would tell her children and grandchildren a story about an Indian squaw who lived on the farm in Cambridge. The squaw had once been left there by a tribe of Indians as they passed through on their way to Canada, and for the entire time that she lived on the farm she would never come into the house except when other Indians were in the area. Eleanor Mackenzie remembered a pile of rocks as being the only remains of the hut when she visited the farm as a child in the early twentieth century. This oral history had been passed on for seven generations before the discovery of the written account of the Indian living on the farm.

A bright fire burned on the hearth. We were all waiting for Grandma to tell some quaint old story of times gone by when she was a little girl. "It was one of the favorite pastimes," said Grandma, "of my sister and myself to go through the orchard into the woods, race down the hill, and then sit under the shade of the trees. After resting we would run to the brook, clear as crystal, look at the minnows gliding over the pebbly bottom, spring from one stone to another which we used as a bridge, then follow the little path winding up the hillside on the other side until we came to a small opening where stood the hut in which the old squaw lived. She was what was called a friendly Indian, very fond of the whites, and very much afraid of the red men.

"Hearing our voices she would greet us at the door, and she was always glad to see us. During our visit she would set before us the best refreshments her hut afforded, with cool fresh water, which flowed just before her door, and we, with appetites made keen from our scramble, enjoyed our simple repast far more than the plentiful table at home. The squaw earned her livelihood combing wool and spinning for her well-to-do neighbors. After answering her numerous questions, and promising to visit her again when the nuts were ready to gather, we bade her good day and, stopping only to pick mint by the brookside and ferns from the hollows, we hastened homeward."

This was my Grandmother's story. We now go every summer to the same woods, rest under the old trees, cross the brook, climb the hill-side still kept green by the little spring, but we find only a few stones and broken bricks to mark the spot where the old hut stood.

My First and Last Day at Boarding School

I arrived at school safe and well but rather depressed in spirits, and the principal took me up four flights of stairs and down to the very end of the hall and showed me my room. It was very small and the furniture consisted of an iron bedstead, two straight back chairs, and a wash-stand with drawers. I had hardly brushed off the dust of my journey when two jolly looking girls appeared and announced dinner the next thing in order. I was guided by the joining ladies to the dining hall where I was shown a seat at the farther end of the room having to pass two hundred pairs of staring eyes, and reaching my seat I was glad enough to sink into my seat. A dish of oatmeal was set before me, which was to constitute our complete dinner. Now oatmeal in any form seemed to me more like fodder than food, and I never could eat it, and this dinner decided me. I hastened to my room, put on my wraps and took the next train for home, startling the beloved home circle around the tea table by my appearance and declaring that "This was my first & last day at Boarding School."

An Afternoon Spent with the Man in Possession of the Fountain of Perpetual Youth.

"Forty-five today and I am beginning to look quite old. A good many gray hairs scattered here and there, crow tracks very visible & I must say I am quite a spinster." This was said by a beautiful woman one morning as she sat before her mirror. "Why not go to the man in possession of the magic fountain? He will restore the beauty of youth again," said the maid. "Why what an idea, going to the ends of the earth in search of it, but I will think of the subject." The next day a friend said to the lady, "You begin to show the marks of age with your gray hairs." This decided the matter, and she resolved to take the journey and was soon on her way to the wonderful fountain. After travelling a great distance both by land & sea she arrived at a beautiful village. It was in the afternoon, and she was told to follow a well beaten path until she came to a grove where she would find the object of her search. Following the instructions, she met in her walk young girls and maidens with sparking eyes and blooming cheeks, tripping merrily along. A few minutes walk brought her in view of a crystal fountain flowing out of a rich green ground and around it were hundreds of people. Drawing near she beheld an old man take from the fountain a cup of water which he gave to a very aged man, who immediately after drinking was changed into a young and ruddy youth. As the man spied her tired face he beckoned her forward and gave her some of the water to drink. Her dimples, smiles and ruddy cheeks quickly returned, and she was the same lovely girl as of eighteen. —*Kittie T.*

This is Kittie Thayer's account of her first day at boarding school. It has been a long family tradition that that is just what happened when she was first sent to boarding school, and that in fact, she did arrive home just as the family was having dinner.

Katherine Sophia Thayer, W. Kurtz, New York, date unknown.

∼

 Letters to Frank at Amherst College:

June 3, 1876, Troy.
My dear Son—   I hope and pray that you will not neglect to write down a few lines twice each week. You will remember that you promised to write Thursday and here it is Saturday afternoon and no letter… Do turn over a new leaf in regard to your home correspondence.   —*Father*.

June 6th, 1876, Troy.
My dear Son—   I am sorely disappointed in not receiving a letter from you this morning. It is not in my heart to find fault with you but really, my dear boy, I cannot stand this want of punctuality in regard to your correspondence and again I ask you in the most loving and affectionate manner to write certainly as often as twice a week. I do not ask you to write long letters, but keep us well posted in regard to your progress etc. etc.   —*Father*.

June 6th, 1876, Troy
My dear Son—   Your very welcome letter dated 4th mailed 6th (today) is just recd. I am glad to know that you are studying hard and I trust you will come out at the end of the term fully up to the standard in Mathematics…

South College, left, dormitory where Francis McKie Thayer lived while a student at Amherst College. Johnson Chapel in background.

Ask Prof Root to write me how you are getting on. Post your letters as soon as you write them and then there will be no complaints.   —Yours lovingly, *Father.*

Sept. 23, 1876, Troy.
My dear Son—   I have no letter from you this week. Suppose you thought writing to Kittie would answer for the whole family. Not so, my son. I am selfish about this matter and cannot submit to anything short of one of your good letters quite as often as once a week. So please remember to write every Sabbath eve and be sure and mail your letter Monday…   —*Father.*

Oct. 3, 1876, Troy.
My dear Son—Your excellent letter of Sabbath eve Sept. 24th did not reach me until Wednesday morning, a day or two behind as usual. I would suggest, indeed urge upon you, the desirableness of posting your letters earlier in the week.   —*Father.*

Oct 16th, 1876, Troy.
My dear Son—   Your welcome letter dated 8th reached me Wednesday, 11th, same day it was mailed. It is really too bad to cheat us out of two or three days in the receipt of your good letters, and again I urge upon you to write every Sabbath eve so as to have your letter ready to post Monday morning. *Establish this as a rule and let there be no failures in future.* …We are again comfortably ensconced in our Troy house after passing a most delightful summer at the dear old house in Cambridge… Mother thought of writing you yesterday but she had a headache & went to bed in the P.M. She is better today and you may soon expect to hear from her… Please write me just how you are getting along in all your studies. I want to know all the particulars and hope you will keep me well posted… And now my son I wish to say a few words in closing in regard to your religious duties. Read your Bible regularly every morning and evening. Go to your Lord and master in sincere and earnest prayer often and do not shrink from the discharge of your whole duty as a professing Christian wherever you may be. "Let your light shine." Please write me on receipt of this and again next Sabbath eve.   —*Father.*

Dec 6th, 1876, Troy.
My dear Son—   Your letter of Sabbath eve giving an account of the fire came to hand yesterday P.M. John Birge who came from Boston Monday told me Tuesday morning that he saw in the *Springfield Republican* that the Delano House had been destroyed by fire. We of course were anxious until the receipt of your letter. Kittie says she thinks you must have "hurried up" a little when you saw the flames approaching. It was certainly very fortunate that you escaped as you did without much if anything. No doubt your things were stirred up and it would be strange if not damaged by hasty removal. I hope you are pleasantly fixed in your new quarters. You can remain at Mr. G—'s for the present. You may think but to take a room in the College, if so, we can send you some furniture. Grandmother is improving a little every day …All hearts are sad over the terrible calamity in Brooklyn last night. It is awful. How true in the midst of life we are in death. With much love, I am as ever you loving *Father.*

THE BROOKLYN CALAMITY — The Extent of the Disaster Underestimated. — Two Hundred and Eighty-three Bodies Recovered. — Over Three Hundred and Fifty Lives Probably Lost. — The Accounts Given By Those Who Escaped. — Two Actors Among The Victims. — Widespread Grief In The City of Churches. — THE STORY OF THE FIRE. - The Breaking Out And Progress Of The Flames. — A Terrific Scene Of Wild Despair. — The Mad Rush For The Doors. — Numbers Trampled Under Foot And Killed—The Falling Of The Walls And Galleries — Brave Acts Of Brave Men. — EXHUMING THE BODIES — The Firemen In The Smoking Ruins Of The Theatre Where Most Of The Dead Were Found — Excited Crowds Around The Building. — Early yesterday morning the people of Brooklyn realized the fact that the destruction of the Brooklyn Theatre by fire on Tuesday night had involved a considerable loss of life. Up to 6 o'clock the general public understood that the loss of life, if any, had been very small, but soon the rumor reached the public ear that the dead bodies of fifty persons had been exhumed by the firemen. When the "extras" announced this fact, the wildest excitement was created both in Brooklyn and this City, and hopes were expressed that the worst was known. Men, women, and children went rushing to the site of the ruined theatre and to the morgue in eager search for missing friends. The city put on an air of mourning, and when it was learned later in the day that over one hundred bodies had been taken from the ruins, the excitement grew more intense and sympathy for the friends and relatives of the victims was generally expressed. Again came the news that 150 bodies had been recovered, and soon that number was increased to 190. Never before in the history of Brooklyn was public feeling so much aroused... As many of the victims are working men, steps have been taken to extend relief to their families, the bodies not identified will be buried at the public expense, and on the day of the funeral business will be suspended in the City, and the day kept as a holiday.

—*The New York Times,* December 7, 1876.

THE BROOKLYN CALAMITY. TWO HUNDRED AND NINETY BODIES THUS FAR RECOVERED. — The Number Of Killed Probably Over Three Hundred and Fifty — A Thorough Search Of The Ruins Made Yesterday — Scenes At The Morgues — One Hundred and Thirty-Five Bodies Not Yet Identified — Measures For The Relief Of The Families of the Victims — Memorial Services To Be Held On Sunday — The Official Investigation. SCENE AT THE CITY MORGUE. The Crowd Outside Greater Than Those Of Wednesday — Difficulties Attending The Identification Of The Bodies. — Removal Of The Corpses On Coroners Permits. EXHUMING THE BODIES. Scenes At The Ruins — Clearing Away The Debris — The Remains of Two Women and a Child Discovered — Fragments Of The Dead Removed To The Morgue.

—*The New York Times,* December 8, 1876.

PREPARATIONS FOR THE PUBLIC FUNERAL TODAY — Two Hundred and Thirty-One Bodies Identified — Scenes At The Morgues And At The Ruins — Action Of Theatrical Companies For The Relief Of The Families Of The Victims — Subscriptions Already Received Toward The Relief Fund. — The excitement created in Brooklyn on Wednesday morning by the fire in the Brooklyn Theatre, has in part subsided, but the calamity has created an impression in the city that months will not remove. The search among the ruins were resumed yesterday morning, and one body was found reduced to a cinder, together with many small bones, and watches, keys, scraps of clothing, opera-glasses, rings, theatrical costumes and other articles. The Police were assisted and relieved by the military. The number of dead identified is now 231. Twenty-eight of the victims were buried yesterday, including the five members of the Solomon family. The Morgues still contain a number of bodies not identified, most of which are burned past recognition by features or clothing. If not identified by 10 o'clock this morning they will be buried by the city authorities. The Committee of the Common Council appointed for the purpose met and made arrangements for the funerals today and decided that the city should bear the expenses of burial where the relatives of the dead were destitute. —*The New York Times,* December 9, 1876.

1877

❧ Letters to Frank at Amherst College:

January 8th, 1877, Troy.
My dear Son— Your p/c announcing your safe arrival at Amherst came duly to hand. The day you left was stormy and blustering here and we were afraid you would meet with longer delay than occurred. …You will find Chemistry a very interesting and profitable study and I hope you will be delighted with it. …Did you find your books, especially the a/c book? You know I am particular about keeping things straight and I trust you will not disappoint me in regard to the manner of keeping acct. of your expenses… We must hear from you as often as *twice* each week and I hope you will be regular in your correspondence. —*Father.*

January 18th, 1877, Troy.
My dear Son— You welcome letter of 15th (mailed 17th) came to hand this A.M… It is no hardship for you to write to the dear ones at home as often as twice per week and once again I urge upon you to be regular in your correspondence. Just put it down as one of the duties and I hope pleasures of your College life… —*Father.*

January 22, 1877.
My precious Boy— I intended to write you a long letter last eve., but your good Father has been much troubled with asthma of late, and was in bed all day yesterday. Taking medicine, and keeping perfectly quiet, and last eve, I read to him and Mother all the eve… —*Mungie.*

January 23, 1877.
My dear Son— No letter from you today as we had a right to expect. Think you must have forgotten the promise made in your last. We hold you to all good promises my boy. —Yours lovingly, *Father.* Grandmother gaining.

January 25th, 1877, Troy.
My dear Son— My last was a protest saying your promised letters of Sabbath eve had not been recd. On going home I found your excellent letter to Grandmother and I told Kittie to send another postal taking back all I had said on the subject of delinquency. I hope you will find time to write *twice* per week, but however much your time may be occupied during the week, don't fail to write Sabbath eve. Make this a rule to be *strictly observed,* rain or shine, cold or hot. Grandmother was perfectly delighted with your letter. She read it over and over again, and I really think it "built her up." Write her often… —*Father.*

Feb 18th, 1877, Troy.
My precious Boy—   Your Father and Grandmother are sleeping and Kittie's in Sunday School, and as you are in all my thoughts I have taken a pen that we may converse a little, this will be my say, I shall expect yours very soon in reply. By the way, it seems to be so difficult for you to maintain your home correspondence with regularity that we may be obliged to resort to the new instrument, the "telephone" in order to keep up a satisfactorily frequent communication… and now I appeal to you to do everything in your power to help to lift your precious Father back to health. The first thing is, let him know you think of him, if you use only a postal card…   —*Mungie.*

Feb 20th.
My dear Brother—   Your letter we received last night and were very glad to hear from you but were sorry you made no allusion to Father's illness for he is really far from well… I hope you will write soon a little letter to him, for it cheers him up to hear from you.   —*Kittie Thayer.*

March 5th, 1877, Troy.
My dear bussard—   …Father is a little better. I should not wonder if Mother & Father will start for some warmer clime soon… *Kittie Thayer.*

bussard, also *Buzzy* Two nicknames for Francis McKie Thayer.

March 9th, 1877, Troy.
My dear Son—   Illness is my only excuse for not writing to you during the past two or three weeks. …I am indeed happy to inform you that for the past week I have gained rapidly and it seems to me now that my health will be fully restored or at least I shall soon be as well as usual… Well, Mr. Hayes is President… I am confident that we have a wise and good man at the helm and that the good Old Ship of State will ride out all storms successfully and that our whole country will grow in peace and prosperity… We hear that Mr. Mumford has taken his son from College. I am indeed sorry to hear this… What a disappointment to a parent to have a son fail in his college course… —*Father.*

May 15, 1877, Cambridge.
My precious Son—   I hasten to tell you what a comfort your letter, received this morning, was to us all… Grand Ma has not been able to sit up much this past week, but was just up, by the window with her bible in her lap, when your letter was given her. "What a sweet letter and beautiful too," she said. …Father is better, goes out now twice a day, and comes in early, does not go out evenings. Dr. B— tells me that we must go to the New Hampshire hills, perhaps to the Twin Mountain House, and see if his Asthma will be relieved there… He is so cheered by your letters… —*Mungie.*

May 27th, 1877, Troy.
My dear Brother—   After all my good advice you have again failed in writing your *weekly* letter and we are all very much hurt…   —I am your sister *Kittie.*

May 28, 1877, Troy.
My dear Son—   I am through with business for the day and now will devote a few minutes in writing to you my dear boy altho' I have nothing newsworthy of note to communicate. For several days past I have had more

asthma than usual and if I do not find relief soon shall take your mother and go off somewhere perhaps to the White Mts. for a week or two… If you are enabled to bring home a good report you will make us *indeed happy*. Make the most of your time and talents. Let this be your constant aim and if life and health are spared "Old Amherst" will give you enduring honors.   —*Father*.

June 3rd, 1877, Troy.
My dear brother—   Father and Mother are all packed and ready to start for Luzerne tomorrow morning, so I write to let you know how lonely I shall be and hope to hear from you some to help keep up my spirits… Now adieu my dear with best love and kisses from all. I am your aff. Sister…   —*Kittie*.

༄ A rare letter from Amherst College:

Amherst, June 4, 1877.
My dear Father—   I have received your letter of the 31st inclosing draft. The box of summer clothing came Saturday. Tell Mother it is very acceptable in this hot weather. The vests fit well but the Blue sack coat is too large. I can send it back if you wish and Mother can get me the next size smaller… The asthma seems to be giving you a good deal of trouble this year. But after all there is reason to be thankful that it is only the asthma and though troublesome and disturbing it is not dangerous… I have bought of the student that occupies my new room now some bedroom furniture. A bureau, washstand, and looking glass, all for $7.00. Perhaps you have some furniture at home for me. If so write me, for now is my best time to get the little furniture I need when the seniors are selling out their furniture at great bargains. Give my love to all at home. Your affectionate son, *F. McKie Thayer*.

༄ Summer vacation:

Luzerne, N.Y.
My dear Frank—   …You may return the coat by express prepaid charges, which were thirty-cents over and should be the same back. In regard to furniture, if you find what is suitable and will be satisfactory at a reasonable rate you may supply yourself with what you need. Father had a most distressing week, just passed, and he is much prostrated from it. I think his nights have been a little better here, but he is suffering today from a very severe headache… Do your best for your dear Father, for yourself and for your God in the strength He will give you.   —Your loving *Mungie*.

Rockwell House, Luzerne, June 7, 1877.
My dear Mother & Kittie—   Your most welcome letter has just been read— and I am glad to see that you are doing nicely. I do not doubt that Charlie behaves, and is a comfort to you in many ways, but do not forget that you are in school, and that unless you can practice about two hours a day, it were far better that you cease to take lessons and save the money, and let there be an understanding between you and Charlie that when you study, you study and when you play, you play, one thing at a time *well done*… And now I will tell you about your dear Father. Yesterday morning a severe headache came on which grew into a sick headache. I did all I could for him but he was not

relieved till this morning, and as he seemed to have taken a little cold we sent for a physician, and he left medicine, and direct mustard paste on the chest, so my rubber and flannel were soon brought into service. As it is raining and the air is full of moisture I presume your Father will keep quiet in bed, but I have a stove in the room, wood and kindling ready at any moment, so he may sit up a little for a change. He has just eaten a very good dinner from a table by his bedside, chicken soup, fried trout, (I wish I could give you some) and other good things. We have everything in the way of attention, the house is neat, the table faultless, and the family affectionate as well as kind in all offers of assistance to me. Perhaps God has sent us to this Doctor for something new or different and happily suited to dear Father's case I hope so. …My time is more occupied than you would think, not so much today as yesterday when I tried but failed to relieve his head… Father joins me in tender love to you and Grandma… now be a goodie girl my ting a ling. Your Loving *Mother*.
—Your Father has not written a letter since he came & say to John Birge what I have written about your father, it will save repetition.

ting a ling An occasional nickname for the younger Katherine Thayer.

Rockwell Hotel, Luzerne, June 8, 1877.
My dear Mother & Kittie—   Your Father passed a far more comfortable night than the night previous was. He says his chest is better— and now the Doctor has been in and confirmed this opinion, and says too that the tongue is much less coated, and Father quite enjoyed his breakfast. And now the clouds are breaking away and we have an occasional glimpse of sunshine, this is favorable. The mail has just been brought, and we have devoured our welcome portion with a quickness known to Fathers and Mothers away from home. I did tell you before I left home that you might have some company to tea while we were away, and supposed you would concentrate your efforts on a half dozen perhaps, when Miss E— would be in Troy. But when I read that you had company the night we left, and three or four calls from gentlemen, it struck your Father and me that our schoolgirl daughter was, or might be, a good deal occupied with society in general, perhaps *too much* for reasons less apparent to her now than ten years hence… I did not intend to say that you could invite no one but Miss E— & Mr. C— to tea next week, but that we did not wish you to invite persons frequently and so occupy all your time, as well as thoughts. As to the few favored ones I thought your own good sense must govern you. I have just got Father dressed and in our other room, and he says he has not near so much "wheezie" as yesterday, which is very apparent to me… 2 P. M. I went down to dinner at one o'clock and your Father has just about finished his dinner which he says tasted good. The air is warm, pleasantly so, and it seems to be clearing away, although we have had a shower since I commenced this… With love… Your loving *Mother*.
—I may be mistaken and have no dictionary but just look and see if an unmarried female of any age is not a girl.

Rockwell Hotel, Luzerne, June 10, 1877.
My dear ones at home—   I saw a carriage arrive a little while ago, and on inquiring find that it came from Glens Falls, and I want you to hear tomorrow, that Father is now almost free from the bronchial trouble. We chased the asthmas from the left side last night with a mustard & linseed paste, so that is better this morning, and we propose to attack the whole chest tonight, and

I think now your Father will continue to improve daily. He had a breakfast fit for a prince (as he is) sent him this a.m.— and I think he enjoyed it better than any meal since he took his room. You understand that he has not been down since Wed. a.m. Spoke of coming down to dinner but concluded to wait for *more wind*. We hope for clear weather for him— it is still cloudy and "muggy" now, but we have a good breeze from the South in our room, and could not be more comfortable at home which is saying much, and it may be cooler here among the hills. I have written this between courses at table. I wish you could be with me to eat trout. I bathed Father and got on clean clothes and left him sitting on the lounge, and now I must go up & get his table ready for his dinner, as it is going up soon. Hoping that you are all well and happy and that you will not worry about Father. We like our Doctor. Your loving *Mother*.

June 13, 1877, Lake George.
My dear boy—   We left Luzerne this morning at half past five and expect to be at Burlington tonight and The Twin Mountain House, White Mts., N.H., tomorrow. You dear Father hopes to find at the latter place the relief he sought at Luzerne, but did not receive. The asthma is present all the time, and far worse at night. So bad that he has watched the whole night through, sleeping none till after the dawn in the morning… —*Kittie*.

June 13, 1877, Lake George
My dear Mother & Kittie—   This is our dear boy's birthday and I have just written him. We left Luzerne at half past five this morning, we expect to stay in Burlington tonight and reach the "Twin Mountain House, White Mts. N.H." tomorrow where I hope and pray dear Father will find rest. He has had a little nap in the saloon and is now out enjoying the wondrous beauty of this lovely lake, set in the mountains. I wish you could enjoy it with us— I say enjoy, there cannot be much pleasure till Father can breathe better and get some sleep, but I hope to report better things very soon. Am sorry not to say something more cheerful now, but do feel that *deliverance* is near at hand, and that he will soon find great if not perfect relief… Remember me to girls and Wm. and take time to write me about everything. Father joins me in love to you and Grandmother, yes love and kisses without number. —Loving *Mother*.

New Pavilion Hotel, Montpelier, June 13, 1877, 10 o'clock p.m.
Dear Kittie—   Just arrived here and are very nicely ensconced in a beautiful Hotel. Quite different from the accommodations which were here three years ago. I am feeling better. Yours lovingly, *Father*.

◥ Letters from the White Mountains of New Hampshire:

Littleton, N. H. June 14, 1877.
Dear Kittie—M   We reached L— at 11 a.m. and leave for Twin Mountain House White Mts, N. Hampshire at 5 p.m. It is about 13 miles from here. Father much as he has been but I hope he will soon find relief. Weather warm and pleasant have had a little rain today, so that it is not dry, and there are showery looking clouds afloat. We watch the weather closely.   —*Mother*.

Pavilion, Montpelier, Vermont. A hotel in 1877 when the Thayers visited on their way to the White Mountains and used for State offices in 2007.

Twin Mountain House, White Mts. June 14, 1877, 8 p.m.
My dear K—   Here we are since 5 p.m. and now comfortably settled in two front rooms, 2nd floor. I think now Father may begin to improve very soon but it will take a little time to get him up to his usual condition. Four guests in the house and we have already rec'd much kindness. Glad to get your letter here just after we came. With love to all, *Mother*.

Twin Mountain House, White Mountains, N. H. June 15, 1877.
My dear Mother & Kittie—   Well we have passed a night here, and although I cannot say that it was a very restful night with Father, it was better than those of the past week: and at six this morning he had a cup of coffee, after which he had an hour and a half of sleep. I was never more thankful to reach a destination than when we took our seats on the piazza of this house. The front is to South. I have marked the windows of our rooms and the place on east piazza where we have been the past two hours. The air is warm & clear, and I hope brings healing on its wings. But for the mountain breeze it would be very warm here, which makes us think that it must be more heated with you, and we have been talking over the "going to Cam."   —*Mother love.*

June 16, 1877. White Mountains, N. H. Twin Mountain House.
My dear Son—   We left Luzerne Wednesday morning, passed the night at a new Hotel in Montpelier, (you will remember the old one with disgust), and arrived here Thursday P.M. We find the House & everything about it very pleasant. Your mother and I compose just half the number of guests. The journey here was about all I could stand, having been quite ill at Luzerne. Now after two days rest I feel somewhat better, but the old asthma "sticks and hangs like a dog to a root." This is not an elegant quotation especially to one just about passing into his juniorship. Well, my boy you will soon be packing up for home and summer vacation… You will have to move into your new room and get things in order so far as possible and then you will be prepared to enter at once upon your studies on your return in Sept. You will figure up the amt. of funds required to pay all bills, and $10 to $15 more for traveling expense and write John Birge care Thayer & Birge to send you a draft on New York payable to your order for the amount. You can make close connection at Millers Falls, with the train that arrives in Troy at 2:22 p.m. I notice that communication with Northampton is cut off by the destruction of the Conn River Bridge and that several lives were lost… Your dear good mother is on the opposite side of the table writing to Kittie. She has on her spectacles (I can write without such aid) and looks quite matronly and well she may for today she is half a century old and possesses in the highest degree more of all those high, noble and beautiful traits of character than are in the female, often called heavenly, than anyone I ever knew. My dear boy you are blessed, yes thrice blessed in your Mother and always let it be your highest aim to live as she would have you. You have just passed your 20th birthday. I am nearly 55. We are all growing old and I hope and pray that each added year will find us in all things better than before. Please write us here upon receipt of this. Mother sends a heart full of love and I do too. Lovingly your, *Father.*

Twin Mountain House, the White Mountains, New Hampshire. Note black dots, second floor, Francis and Catherine Thayer's rooms, and porch (lower right), where they sat.

June 19, 1877, Twin Mountain, White Mountains, N.H.
My dear Mother and Kittie—   I wrote you a few lines last night, and although I have not much in particular to say this morning, except to report dear Father's case. I will do that first and no doubt other thoughts will come. I think he slept more last night than in any one night in ten days, perhaps two hours before five in the morning. I told you that he did not close his eyes in sleep several nights till after the morning dawned. This was in Luzerne. We make up in full after coffee at six and he walks better this morning, a little faster and his breathing is not so much affected by the slightest movement, so I think the bronchial trouble had not passed away before we came here, but is now doing so, slowly and daily. We went down to breakfast about half past ten this morning, and I have left him sitting in the clear pure air, every breath of which I pray may be a blessing to him. He *looks* better, brighter and I now begin to, or rather, do feel encouraged. Care and time with the Dr's medicine, which I hope will come tonight, will bring dear Father back to a better condition than he has known in some time. I think there are many drafts in the halls here and I have to keep watch that he does not sit in an exposed position. …All the men and women about the house are New England people— and as guests are not expected here until after July fourth, the notes of preparation are to be heard and seen everywhere. Carpenters, glaziers, painting, varnishing, laying carpets, painting walls, hanging curtains, work of all kinds going on all quietly and in order…

   I have just been down to see where Father is and I found him whittling the end of his cane. This shows improvements, and as it is pretty warm I feel that I would like a lighter dress and might as well be wearing the gray one. So you may put [it] in a proper box, as small as will answer the purpose, the gray silk, my black alpaca petticoat, two undershirts (rather light) and my shetland shawl. (I thought I had it)— Two shirts for Father, eight collars, four pairs wristbands, his duster. You can put these things together and then see what size the box should be and send by Ex. I am sorry to trouble you but this gray seems rather heavy… Good bye loved ones… Father joins in love and kisses to your both.   —Your loving *Mother*.

Twin Mountain House, White Mountains, N. H. June 21, 1877.
My dear Mother & Kittie—   How my mind runs to you in these busy times, but I hope you are all better than usual in order to meet the demands for heads and hands. When this comes to you I suppose you will be at the Old Home, where we shall think of you after Friday eve. …Father was able to keep his bed last night, the second night in two weeks that he has done so. He inhales and smokes two or three times, and takes something besides, but he said this morn that he thought he had slept three or four hours before coffee, and he must have slept two after. He has just returned from the summer house in front where he has been airing and taking a sunbath nearly two hours. He lives in the open air and sunshine. It has been somewhat cloudy today, but warm and just now it is raining. I think Father is doing as well as can be expected, for he was ill indeed after leaving home.
I shall wish to know about the garden, vegetables and flowers, vines and henhouse… With a head full of love to you and Mother, regards to Wm. and girls, love to Minnie and family. In all this dear Father joins. Your loving *Mother*, my darling child.

~ Some other correspondence:

Letterhead, June 21, 1877, from John Birge, listing the different flour produced at the Crystal Palace Mills.

Crystal Palace Mills. No. 143 River Street, Troy, New York.
June 21st, 1877
Mr. F. McKie Thayer, Amherst, Mass.
Dear Sir: …I have a letter from your Father today, the tone of which is very cheerful. I sincerely trust the air of the White Mountains will prove to be just the thing to restore his vigor.   —*John T. Birge.*

154 First St. Troy. June 21, 1877.
My dear Mrs. Thayer—   Your more than welcome letter was opened with trembling fingers, but the assurance of a favorable change, the assurance that our dear friend was *breathing easier*, made us all breathe easier & strengthened me for the duties of the day. Having suffered so much myself, I can readily sympathize with suffering… As a heavy shower this morning prevented me from going over to your house, I have just sent Grandma a note & Thomas returning, says that she is very bright & strong— this is the latest bulletin…   —*E. R. Eaton.*

~ A rare letter from Amherst College:

June 22nd, 1877. Saturday night. Amherst.
My dear Father—   I have received letters from you and Mother and Kittie this week but I have been so busy preparing for my examinations that I have not found time to answer them. I am happy to inform you that I have been entirely successful in all my examinations and that I am now a "full fledged" junior. Our class celebrated the completion of the Sophomore year by a supper last night at Northampton. We left Amherst about 7 o'clock, were taken to the Round Hill House, Northampton— sat down to supper at 10 P.M. Everything was well arranged and the supper was a decided success. I had a glorious time and shall always recall the sophomore class supper as one of the happiest events in my College life. We got back to Amherst in time for breakfast. After breakfast I went to bed and slept 'til 5 P.M. and now I feel like myself again… The tone of Mother's letters is very cheerful and I sincerely trust that you will find the mountain air just the thing to restore your vigor…   —*F. McKie Thayer.*

416 THE FAMILY LETTERS

George B. Wood's *Treatise on the Practice of Medicine*, 1858, described one of the prevailing treatments for asthma as follows: "The inhalation of fumes of burning paper, previously impregnated with a saturated solution of nitre, and dried, is asserted to be sometimes very effective. It is best that the paper should have been dipped a second time into the solution and dried. It may be either burned in the chamber, or smoked by means of a pipe, or in the form of a cigar."

◦ Letters from the White Mountains:

Twin Mt. House, White Mts. N. H. June 22, 1877, Friday.
My precious Mother & darling child Kittie—   Your very good letter of yesterday (21st) came to use at three o'clock… It has rained and been very cool since two o'clock yesterday (Thurs). Of course this has shut your Father in, and if he has not made much advance, he has not taken cold. We [have] a pleasant fire in a wood stove in one of our rooms, this changes the air of both. Father's appetite is better. He comes upstairs with less difficulty, it does not affect his breathing so much and he coughs but little now. He has more trouble at night than through the day, and smokes two or three times during the night, but he is vastly more comfortable than he was when we came here… Father enjoys his *Harpers* and sends love & kisses to you… —Your loving *Mother*.

June 24th, 1877. Twin Mountain House, White Mountains, N. H. Sunday evening.
My dear Daughter—   Mother said at tea time that she would write you a few lines to send in the morning mail. But I guess she has forgotten it… Well, I suppose you are now comfortably ensconced at the Old Home. I hope so and that you will take time to rest for you have had enough for one of ripe age and experience to attest to for the past few weeks, now just take it easily. I am really on the gain today. I have walked as far as nearly out to the Twins & back. How long we shall remain here will depend upon the progress I make in gaining health and strength. I hope this week will give me a good long stride towards recovery. Love to Grandmother & yourself. Mother joins me. Yours lovingly, *Father*.

Twin Mountain House, White Mountains, N. H. June 25, 1877.
My dear Kittie—   Father wrote you last evening, and now we will say something before hearing from you. Father's night was not quiet as he was up in a chair twice, he said he slept better there than in bed, smoked twice, but this is such an improvement on a week ago, and two weeks since, that it is encouraging. I rose at 9 o'clock, he at 10, breakfast at half past 10. So you see what is lost at night is made up in part in the morning, besides he sleeps in his chair during the day. I have been with him on the piazza since breakfast, reading him to sleep, two or three times. I am glad he makes up lost time in this way. I see by the papers that the Russian troops are crossing the Danube. You know I can not help taking an interest in warlike matters, this little Hilton-Seligman affair and the St. John's fire engross all minds just now, albeit the subjects vary greatly. The "box" came last eve, everything all right, my dress has been much improved. I think Ellen a neat worker, and she may do us nicely in the house in future if we can secure her… Your Father had a letter from Aunt L— Saturday saying that "she went down to see you off, that all seemed glad to go and Grandma said she felt as strong as last year." I was glad to hear this last. And now we are thinking of you at the Old Home, have turned our thoughts from Troy to Cambridge and think we may get a letter from you sometime today. Father appreciates your cares of late and gave you some good advice in his letter to you last eve, which I pray you will heed… Of course you will all tell me how you all bore the journey… Do you remember

how prettily this house was ornamented with plants and vines and baskets? They do far more "in the season" than at that time, log cabins, canoes and all styles of hanging baskets filled with growing plants and vines fill the dining room, parlor, and entrance hall. Paint brushes and carpet hammers are in motion still but every day tells toward a final completion of the work of renovation… With love and kisses to you and dear Mother… —Your loving *Mother.*

June 28, 1877. Crawford House, White Mts. N.H.
Our dear Ones at home—   We came to this place yesterday afternoon, eight miles from the "Twin." We desired to see this wonderful mountain region of which the half may be felt but can never be told, but turned our faces thitherward hoping that the greater elevation would bring more marked and speedy relief to your dear Father. He rested more last night then he has in a week, and feels quite comfortable today. In these mountain houses, the lower rooms have no cellars underneath, and are not fit for your Father, so of course he must make the ascent of the long flight of stairs, the hardest thing for him to do, and he, of course, does it but once a day, but there being no place for him to lie down on the first floor, he finds an easy chair in the sun, and often gets several naps in the course of the day. Some mornings he has taken his breakfast in bed, and then he could turn over and have a good nap, and be quite refreshed by it, and now, after his breakfast, he is sleeping quietly and with our window wide open, although I have a shawl around me, he is receiving the benefit of this high mt. air, which I hope and pray may bring a decided and lasting change for the better. Your Father just asked me to close my letter to J. Birge by saying that should he not receive the benefit desired here, or in this region, he would try sea air, by making a short trip, perhaps to Eastport. I hope it will not be needful, and I would not dare to attempt anything but a very short voyage, say of a few hours. Indeed I must have the advice of Dr. Bloss before I would be willing to try an experiment that I could not end any hour. We will hope for the best. We missed your letter last night, as we took the train that brought the mail— it will be here soon and I can answer this aft. The train (6 p.m.) runs only to the Fabyan. Later in the season it will come here. We came in coach from Twin— …I think I answered the points in your last interesting letter. I do so hope that Grand Ma is gaining strength every day, and that everything goes smoothly with you and will do so. Frank will be with you tomorrow eve. How I should like to be with you all. Father joins in love to each and every one of the dear circle at home… Address us here till you hear of a change in our place of rest— yes *rest.* I hope for Father day and night. May God bless and keep you and us ting-a-ling.   —*Mungie.*

Crawford House, White Mts., N. H. June 29, 1877.
My dear Mother and daughter Kittie—   Your full letter of the 25th Kittie reached us yesterday aft. It was sent us by private hands last eve. from the "Twin." I felt that we were leaving home when we left there, but the wife of the Manager here just met me, inquired for Father (who has just been in to breakfast with me) and said I must ask for any and everything I wished. These New England people are brim full of kindness and it is not all dollars and cents, as we are sometimes inclined to believe before we come in contact

The Crawford House, Crawford Notch, the White Mountains, New Hampshire.

The Willey House, White Mountains, New Hampshire. Photo by N. W. Pease, North Conway, New Hampshire. In 1826, this was the site of an avalanche where nine people died as they fled from their house that was ironically saved by a boulder behind it. The house became an early place for tourists to visit and marvel at the forces of nature, and an inn, the taller building to the left, was built to accommodate them. "The Ambitious Guest," a short story by Nathaniel Hawthorne, was based on this incident.

with individuals. I think there are about thirty guests here, some permanent and others going and coming. We took a drive yesterday aft., through the "Notch" and to the Willey House, which you remember was saved by a great boulder back of it, which parted the avalanche into two streams as it were, and left the house standing firmly between while the five people who left it perished, the two who were found are buried near the places marked by piles of stones. This ride through this mountain gateway at the bases of Webster and Willard is the most awe inspiring of anything we have seen. The Port. & Og. Railroad creeps along the side of the mountain at a dizzy height above you— this will do. I thank you more than I can tell you for your letters. I knew a fresh spirit was needed about the house. I have been "played out" for some time, and made almost indifferent by more absorbing topics. "Bread is the staff of life" when good. I rejoice with you. Am glad Mother can go to the table with you… The weather yes[terday]— was pleasantly cool. Father wore overcoat all day, I a shawl. When you write me again take this letter please and answer the questions not already answered— What do you pay Thompson? Is the hen house moved? what is in the garden, of the potato bugs !! and any matter of local interest… Father slept more last night and the night previous than in several nights. A part of every night in a large easy chair, but he sleeps with less medicine and smoke, and I hope we are approaching nights of sleep without either. Now that you are all together take all the good comfort you can, keep well, and we will try and get well so as to be with you under the old "[illegible] tree" as soon as we can. God guard us all. Love and kisses to you four.   —Your loving *Mungie*.

Crawford House, White Mts. June 30th, 1877.
My dear Daughter—   While your mother is cleaning her nails and we are waiting for our breakfast at the table, I will commence this letter as it is quite late, 10:15, and the mail closes in 40 minutes. Well this is a delightful spot, one of the wildest and most charming in all the mountain range. I am improving slightly, but surely. I hope and trust. Breakfast is now being placed before us and so good morning to you all… About 7 p.m. yesterday a severe rain storm set in and it has been a howling night with wind and rain. This a.m. it is cool, the skies look full of water and we occasional glimpses of the sun. I do not know whether the storm king will have the wasting or not, on Father's account we pray for clear weather, and if he does not take cold now it is all we can expect. You answered some of my questions yesterday in your two good letters sent us last eve from the "Twin." This last place has one advantage in having stoves in many rooms and steam in halls and dining room, but fair weather will come soon… Father joins me in love to you four and regards to Wm. & E. May God keep you and us now and always,   —Your loving *Mungie*.

Crawford House, White Mts., N. H. July 1, 1877.
My dear Mother and Children—   I wish we could be with you, then we should not need the medium of pen and paper, but as it is so ordered that we must be apart for awhile, we rejoice that we can talk in this way. I have just left Father seated in a corner of the parlor, and as he seemed disposed to be quiet, I proposed coming up and writing to you, as from this time forward the cars leave here in the morn at seven, heretofore the first mail from here has been at eleven a.m; as the season advances the number of trains increase.

We have had a long south east storm. We came here Wed. eve and we have had three raining nights. Occasionally the sun has broken through for a few minutes during the day, the air has been so damp and cool that I have wished for winter clothing of all kinds: with all this, your Father has not taken cold, nor has he lost any ground. On the contrary, I think he gets more sleep from "sun till noon" and he is smoking less to reach a state favorable to sleep. I do hope that we may soon have clear weather that he may live out of doors more. He walked about two blocks and back this aft (in distance). Any ascent affects his breathing very much still, indeed there is not much change in regard to this. I do think he came upstairs easier last night than the night we came here and we hope and pray that good weather will help him steadily toward a comfortable state of health. Your letters Kittie are a great comfort to us. You answered nearly all of my questions in your last. Now that your dear Buzzy is with you, *train* him into frequent writing. He writes an excellent letter, and now he can treat us often… We have had two Epis— services in the parlor today. About forty guests here… We have every comfort. I am well and if dear Father improves rapidly, I shall feel that I arrive on the mountain top, for this let us pray. Father desired me to give love and kisses to all. In this I join most fondly dear Mother and children and to C, Wm, & E, kindness.   —Your loving *Mungie*.

Crawford House, White Mts, N. H. July 2, 1877.
My dear Mother and Children—   Still another stormy day in the mts. I think it may have rained twenty times today, and the sun has shone perhaps ten times about two or three minutes at a time. The plank walk has not been dry today so we have had no out door walk. Still with all the damp fog and rain dear Father is no worse certainly and I think when it clears up again, he will show the capacity to improve. It is quite cool and in the large parlor there is a huge fire on the hearth or rather in the fireplace in which I see three wheelbarrow full of wood placed in one day, a barrow full at a time. No mail from you today, papers from J. B. The car changed the morning time today and there is a "hitch" somewhere… Well, I trust you are all very happy together in the Old Home, or as much so as you can be, when we are away on dear Father's account. I hope everything will go along smoothly in every respect and that I can soon write you a good report when some July sunshine is placed upon our heads and softens the air. I have found your match here Kittie and more— a man who kills, skins, and eats snakes and considers them a very great luxury. (This is worse than bottling them). His soubriquet is Captain Jack. I am going to see him, he being one of the local wonders. I left Father in the parlor, he desired to join me in love and kisses to you all. I hope to hear that you are well as also Uncle Edwin. May God bless and keep us all.   —Your loving *Mungie*.

Captain Jack Jack Viles (or Vials) was an eccentric hermit who lived near the Crawford House in a "woodland shanty" where he entertained and intrigued tourists with his life and ways.

Crawford House, White Mts., N. H. July 4, 1877.
My dear Son & dear ones at Home—   Many thanks for Kittie's letter of yesterday morning. She answered all my questions and gave me several interesting items beside. I wish I could have been with the dear lamb during that awful thunderstorm… We had thunder here and it was so cool that I wondered when I heard it. One of the residents said she knew it was warm somewhere. I think dear Father is improving slowly but steadily. He walked a little farther today than before, *talks* of going up Mt. Wash., eight and a half miles.

I had a pleasant ramble up one of the hillsides, where there are a number of cascades and rocks over which the water runs similar to the flume. Have not had an opportunity to visit the many curiosities on account of the rainy days and beside I had not even a deaf companion. This eve I was invited by some ladies to join them in the future, and I may avail myself of the offer if Father can not accompany me.

"Wall" the excursionists are here, about one hundred and ninety of them, good looking people too, but some ways a crowd of this kind always seems to me like a flock of sheep settling along. This has been another lovely day, not even a fire cracker to make you sorry that the fourth of July is at hand. I said to a lady at the "Twin" that I thought there were three schools in New England that fitted boys for College (properly). There may be many more. I have since received a note from Mrs. B— asking me to give her the names of these. Please Frank write me— I had in mind, E. Hampton, Phil Academy and Andover, and enlighten me. Trusting that you young people will take good care of Grand Ma and of yourselves and have a good time and hoping that Father will improve every day, we send love and kisses to you all.   —as ever your loving *Mungie*.

Crawford House, White Mts. N. H. July 8, 1877.
My dear Mother and Children—   We started to come to our room half an hour since, but were told by Manager Merrill that "his choir" would soon sing, and so we have been sitting in the dining room listening to some most enjoyable music, party from Moody School with a few others, the Lord's Prayer, and closing with grand old Coronation, it was a sweet fitting close to a Sabbath day. The domestics here are all Vermont or New England people, the head waiter who leads the choir is to study law or medicine, our waiter is sitting for College, reads the Latin mottoes to us, and has just sent for his "English literature" because he "has time to read when he can not study." So much for this department of the Crawford. We have had two services in the parlor, Episcopal which we attended, your Father being the only gentleman present. I am happy to say that Father seems to be steadily gaining the power of walking. Yesterday we went up Mt. Willard in about two hours and a half. The distance is two miles and the road through woods the whole distance of the way. I suppose we sat down and rested forty or fifty times, *but we went up*, and had a magnificent view from the top, rested and came down. The air was clear and bracing, and cool, so that we did not get heated at all. We were surprised at ourselves, and the people at the house astonished when we reported. Today is quite warm, and cloudy, imagine "muggy" with you, but I hope you will have no more terrific thunder-storms. My Ting-a-ling does not enjoy them, and surely I would not… Father joins me in love and kisses to you all… May God bless & keep you.   —Your loving *Mungie*.

July 10, 1877, Crawford House, White Mountain Notch, N. H.
My dear Ones at Home—   The mail of this eve brought us no letter, indeed we knew that in the absence of Sunday mail, we would get none. Father's bowels are about right now, but we have not walked far today as he wishes to keep right. He keeps talking of going to the seashore to try the air and I soothe to keep still, and get the full benefit of this place… The truth is that when the mercury has ranged at 80° to 90° in the cities, it has not been

Summit of Mt. Willard, Crawford Notch State Park, the White Mountains of New Hampshire.

View from summit of Mt. Willard, Crawford Notch State Park, the White Mountains of New Hampshire.

above 75° here, to say nothing of the purity and invigorating character of the air here. I want to see him much better than he is before he leaves, and while he gains a little from day to day, the aggregate in a week, is something imperceptible. So I hope he will be content to stay a while yet. Much as I want to see you all, and see my house and all the precious ones in it, counting every hour and day away from you, and yet rejoicing that God has enabled us to make this change for dear Father's good, and beside I do feel that you will do the best at home, and J. Birge with Father's advice will do very well in Troy… Everybody sees that he is better, and I am thankful and know you are. With a heart full of loving tenderness for you all, we are your *Father and Mother*.

Crawford House, White Mts., N. H. July 10, 1877, Tues eve.
My dear ones at the Old Home—   Another Excursion from Portland here tonight and I have been listening to some good music on the piano by a young lady who played about an hour without a note, so may our daughter do one of these days. Your very pleasant letter Kittie came as usual at eve… Tonight I think of Kittie in Bennington, and I presume she will have a jolly time. We had a heavy rain last night and it has rained several times today so much, that our walk has been confined to the plank walk of about two blocks. Father came upstairs this aft. and lay down and had a nap. This is the first time he has been upstairs in the day since we left home. He takes little medicine now, has finished what Dr. B— sent him, and is now taking something sent him by a Physician in Portsmouth N. H. with whom we have corresponded. A man who has suffered many years from Asthma, and in all climes, and by every treatment, sought relief and has finally secured some measure of comfort by remedies of his own preparation, perhaps I should say inventions, so Father is trying these and attending to suggestions by the same Phy. We hope all will be beneficial. He has had that soreness of the bowels the past two days that he had in Troy. I think from cold, and it is relieved somewhat this aft… Hoping that everything will go on in the best measure with you all and

believing that you will all aim to have all things right and with hearts full of love and tenderness to you all, we are your loving *Father and Mother*.

Crawford House, White Mts., N. H. July 13 1877.
My dear ones at Home—   Your dear good letter Kittie came this eve. Also one from J. Birge saying that he had a call from Frank today (12th) and he was looking very well. By this time Charlie has left you. He has made you quite a visit and no doubt has enjoyed it. He is as you say, very kind and I think a boy of good principles and correct habits, and I hope he will do well in business. You and Frank will miss him, but then I know you and Frank can be happy with each other, your duties, your books, work of various kinds, a few good friends about, and last but not least your dear good Grand Ma to bless your every hour. As I write it seems as if I must be in a dream this being away from you so long. It is very cool tonight, there is fire in the parlor and reading and sitting rooms and it is too chilly to sit anywhere else. The great outside doors stand open till the house is closed for the night and I never leave my room without a shawl. We had a heavy rain two days since, and I think Father took a little cold, but I know he feels better tonight than last night, and I believe will rest better… There are about a hundred guests in the house now, the most of them will "tarry but a night" and others take their place tomorrow. I went alone this aft. to a rock called "Elephants head" from the very marked resemblance. I'll tell you by word o' mouth. Father joins me in love to you, Frank, and the dear good Mother. Oh how we would like to see you all… (I even saw a snake today but I did not mind.) …May God keep you and us in all our ways, "*Mungie*" —Dear K. Do show Frank how easy to write often [sic].

Elephant's Head and Gate of the Notch. Photo by Albert Bierstadt, Gems of American Scenery, Consisting of Stereoscopic Views Among the White Mountains published in 1875. The ledge known as "Elephant's Head" is to the left, just beyond the open meadow, and the Webster Cliffs are in the background. The editor of this volume has visited and hiked in the White Mountains of New Hampshire since the 1950s and has authored and edited a number of books about that region.

Crawford House, White Mts., N. H. July 15, 1877. Sab. eve 7 o'clock.
My dear Ones—   I have just come up to our room from our second service in the parlor. Father is just up after a nap, and while he is dressing I will write a few lines to you all, of whom we think so much. Kittie's letter, of Wed, was received Fri. No letter yesterday, but pleasant as it is to hear, I will think that everything is right with you when we do not hear. This has been a lovely day, just warm enough to take off all the chill that is quite common morning and evening. The mercury yesterday morning was 40°, rather low for the fourteenth of July. And this is the middle of summer. Is it possible! When it seems as if we have but just entered the summer season… —9:30 p.m. We have just come up from the dining room where we have been listening to the waiters, who sing beautifully every Sab. eve. You can understand the words they sing as if a person were reading the last piece, "What shall the harvest be?" impressed me as it never did before. We are all sowers, and what shall the harvest be to each of us, for ourselves? for our friends? Let us ponder this momentous question daily. What shall the harvest be? I think I wrote that dear Father had taken a little cold. He seems to be better of it, has breathed a little better the past two nights. He is certain a good deal stronger than when we came here. I wish he would get so that he could come up stairs without being all "wheezee," and I hope he will. He has improved in this respect and while I dressed him almost entirely for weeks, he can now dress himself, but *effort*, he cannot make much, and yet I hope and pray that he will keep on improving steadily and this will bring up anyone. It is a great comfort to hear that everything goes on smoothly in Troy and at home and helps generally to

keep Father contented. J. Birge writes very frequently and is doing as well as anyone can… I hope to hear tomorrow. Father joins in much love to you… *Mungie.*

July 18, 1877, Crawford House. Wed eve.
My dear Mother and Children—   A good long pleasant letter from Kittie this aft. with one inclosed from Uncle Will. I think you are doing very nicely, and I hope everything may be right sweet and peaceful with you all. Father and I leave at 9 o'clock in the morning for Old Orchard Beach where I hope perfect relief may be found. We can only go and see what the affect will be. Hoping, praying for the best. There are several very kind and agreeable people in the house and they say they feel sorry to have us leave, I hope they are. Weather fine today, mercury 80°, but the mountain does not prostrate like that of the valley. J. Birge writes that it is warm… Father has had a very comfortable day… I never was away from you all so long before. If you have your pictures (small ones) do send them in a letter. Father joins in love and kisses to you all. God keep you and us.   —*Mungie.*

July 20th, 1877, Old Orchard House, Old Orchard, Maine.
My dear Son—   We left the Crawford House yesterday morning and arrived here about 2 P.M. The ride down through the mountains was grand indeed. You will remember that when we visited the Mts. three years ago one of your mother's headaches compelled us to stop at the Fabyan House instead of going on to the Crawford as we expected. The Crawford is one of the gems of the Mts. —both as a point of great natural beauty and grandeur and as a Hotel. We spent three weeks there very pleasantly… I think we shall like it here (Old Orchard Beach). Last night I slept comparatively well and I have little doubt the sea air will agree with me. We shall give this place a fair trial hoping for the best results.   —With love to all I remain Yours Lovingly, *Father.*

July 22, 1877, Old Orchard House, Old Orchard, Saco, Maine.
My dear Frank—   Every time I write the date of my letters, I feel the summer passing by, and I have not seen you yet my dear boy, and I wonder when I can see you all in the dear home. Week after week has passed without the relief we hoped to find and so we have moved on and hoped on. First you know dear Father had a bronchial attack from which it has taken weeks to recover. I know the mountain air has been a source of strength to him, and he is sleeping far better nights than he did for weeks, but the shortness of breath still continues, and an ascent increases this trouble. We think there has been a little improvement in this respect since we came here, at any rate, we can not see that the air here is favorable to him. Should we do so, we must try something else. I am going to try bathing him in sea water in the evening. You understand that he cannot use his arms much. This has been a clear beautiful day, and we have not felt as "heavy as lead" as we have ever since we came here— when we have tried to walk the elasticity of the mountains all gone, but with a clear air, a better feeling has come, and oh how I hope, and let us pray most earnestly that the change may lift up your dear Father to a better state, easier breathing. I try to keep up his courage and hope for relief for him. Kittie, the dear child, has written me long interesting letters keeping us

advised about home matters and things in general for which we are thankful. Will it be too much trouble for you to write us a few lines occasionally. Try and do this to gratify Father, as it certainly would and so would give me a double pleasure. We have said that we suppose you have listened to Mr. Gordon today, we would like to have been at the Old Church— that woodchuck must be rooted out of the grave of our fore father. Father desired me to send love and kisses to you and all, and hoped we would soon come together in our home. In this I join him…   —Loving *Mungie*.

July 30, 1877, Old Orchard Beach, Saco, Maine.
Our Dear Child—   No letter since one of last Wed. rec'd last Sat. We hope all is well with you all— and naught to trouble or make afraid. The sun has not shown here since last Thurs… we had two rainy days and now we have two of dense fog, which still prevails. It does not affect Father much, but of course we cannot go out much. We had a great excitement from a theft last night. A man entered Gen. Baxton's room, took two diamonds, watch & chain and money, about $2,200 in value. Came in and went out window over piazza roof… Father has taken another bath and thinks it did him good. He is "on the gain." But the weather is bad for anyone just now. I hope we will leave tomorrow, that you are all right in every respect… I hope to see you before long… God bless you all. *Mungie*.

August 3, 1877, Portland, 5:30 P.M.
Our dear Ones at home—   Received K's letter of the 1st just as we were leaving O. O. We are now on our way to No. Conway where we may stay until Monday if pleasant there. The foggy weather at O. O. was too much for Father— it gave him the "wheezees" a little. Still he is better than when he went there… We have had a pleasant time at O. O., formed several very agreeable acquaintances, and left the place with many regrets. Hope however the mountain air will be better suited to Father's needs. You may address us at Bethlehem Maplewood House N. H. as before advised…   —Your loving *Mungie*.

August 4, 1877, North Conway, N. H.
Our dear ones at home—   I wrote you twice yesterday, and although I have nothing special to say, I thought that a few lines sent by this pm mail would reach you Tues morn. so that there would be no Sabbath gap, so I call the day that fails to bring us a letter, for want of mails on the day of rest. This House will accommodate three hundred guests and like most of the houses this year is about half full. The House and village of North Conway are situated on the upland overlooking the Saco Valley, with Mt. Washington in the distance. There are mountains in every direction, some clothed with green, some faced with a tall precipice. From my seat I see one of these perpendicular cliffs, the white figure of a horse about as large as Frank's rocker… this design is on a dark background and is much like a drawing on a blackboard. There are all sorts of resemblances pointed out to us who travel through this wonderful region. The walks and drives of this locality are said to be superior to those of any place in the "tour." There is an Echo Lake, a wonderful natural Cathedral, the ceiling of which is eighty feet from the floor, and is formed by an overarching rock, and the outer wall is formed by immense trees. I have heard about many of these places of interest. Do not know that we will ride

today, but we can take our crocheting and look. When we arrived last eve it was pretty warm, but before morning the wind blew cool, and Father has on his overcoat to keep out the wind. I hope you do not have oppressively warm weather, it is so prostrating. We have not had a day when I could not put up my hair with ease. My dear precious Mother will understand what this means. I hardly know who I am when I think that our "ten days absence" has grown into two months. I would not be willing to be put back to June 4th for Father is much stronger, has been able to take more exercise and now that we are in the dry air, I think he will keep on improving. I have just heard of a new cure for asthma— dry sulphur. We are to remain here till Mon and see the effect of this locality. I hope it will prove the best of all. Father joins in love to you three dear ones and regards to family & friends. Your loving *Mungie*.

Aug, 6th, 1877, Kearsarge House, North Conway.
Dear ones at home—   Mother says she has done most of the writing lately and now I must take my turn which I am quite willing to do altho' my poor scribble may prove a poor substitute for her lively epistles. Be that as it may, I'll just let you know that we are still here and both think it the place for us at present. We were very unfortunate in having rainy & foggy weather at Old Orchard and I think we stayed there a little too long… How long we shall remain here I cannot tell now. All this week no doubt, so you will direct your letters here for the present. I have consulted with a Homeo Physician here from Boston and he thinks he can help me— taking his medicine one day seems to have a good effect. With much love to all from Mother & self. I remain as ever your loving *Father*.   —No letter from Frank yet.

Kearsarge House, North Conway, New Hampshire.

August 14, 1877, Kearsarge House, North Conway, N. H.
Tuesday evening, 9:30 PM.
My Dear "Ting-a-ling"—   Your letter from Hoosick Falls written Sunday came to hand this P.M. —also the little package from New York. Many thanks. Hope you reached home Monday morning and found all well. Now my darling I hope you will find time to take some rest. You must by this time, with all your cares, hot weather etc. etc. etc. be pretty well "played out". Do take good care of yourself. Mother is in the parlor and by the looks of things I guess she has got hold of her match in talking and for fear she won't be ready to go to her room 'till morning I have taken it upon myself to write you a few lines just to let you know that we are doing well. Have just had a long and pleasant talk with my new Doctor. I am certainly better than when I came here and if we can have pleasant weather you may expect to hear of rapid improvement… We long to be with you and shall set our faces toward the dear Old Home and the loved ones there at the earliest possible and practicable moment… With a heart full of love to all and the same from "*Mungie*" I am as ever you loving "*Pop*."

August 17, 1877, Kearsarge House, North Conway, N. H.
My dear Daughter—   We hear nothing from Bethlehem in regard to room and as all the hotels in and about the mountains are crowded we have thought best to stay here until Monday pm and then go to Maplewood House Bethlehem N. H. You can write Tuesday at Bethlehem and in case of anything important and you wish to telegraph us you can do so at Bethlehem, and if

we have left there the message will be forwarded. I am doing very well notwithstanding the rain rain rain fog fog fog. It is clear tonight and we hope for pleasant weather. Lovingly your *Father*.

August 17, 1877, Kearsarge House, North Conway, N. H.
Our dear ones at home—   No letter today and I have nothing new to communicate except that we have had some sun today as well as a heavy rain but it does not clear off bright and certain… We will hope for a good bracing day tomorrow. Father still wishes to try the air at Bethlehem and we have written for a room on the first landing, have had no response as yet, and we may not have one, as the Mountain houses are full. A message from the Crawford to a girl here says they can offer nothing better than a table to sleep on. I am sure of one thing that Old Cambridge will look well when we do get back… I hope we shall not give our new Housekeeper any trouble, the home flavor is what we shall enjoy… Father joins in love and kisses to you three dear ones.   —*Mungie*.

August 19, 1877, Kearsarge House, North Conway, N. H. Sabbath evening.
My Dear Daughter—   Your good letter of 16th Thursday came to hand yesterday p.m. Frank seems to be going to Troy frequently. I hope he will not desert you. It makes us so happy to know that dear Grandmother is so well, "sewing today and out in the yard." …We couldn't get a room at Bethlehem and now we propose to leave here for Thayer's Hotel Littleton tomorrow p.m. 1:30 about three hours ride. Tuesday we may take a horse & buggy and drive up to Bethlehem from Littleton, some 6 or 7 miles. It has rained here almost every day this month. What I need is clear pleasant weather and I have about made up my mind that we shall have to go home to find it. Nothwithstanding the drawbacks I am better than when I came here and hope to reach home in a condition to go right along improving day after day and week after week. I hardly dare say it, but really think you may look for us the last of this week. Would that I could say tomorrow.

The President is to be up this way Tuesday. He has not sent me word to meet him on his journey but I still hold myself open to any invitation he may extend to me. I see by the papers that Mr. Hayes has lately visited the home built by his father and the one in which I was born and you can't tell what will come next. Mother is picking up things about the room and getting ready to pack so of course I had to write the letter to "Ting-a-ling" tonight. Love to all. —Your Loving *Father*.

August 20, 1877, Kearsarge House, North Conway, N. H.
My dear ones at home—   No letter today as yet. Perhaps the 10 o'clock mail may bring one— Kittie's of the 16th the last. Father wrote you last eve that we would leave for Littleton today, but this morning was bright and promised a fine day and Father thought he would try one good clear day at Conway, and I think he looks better tonight and besides, the President is coming through the notch tomorrow, probably as far as this place, and we may see him, and go on the same train with him tomorrow. The Pres. went up Mt. Washington today and stays at the Fabyan tonight… Father wrote you last eve that we hoped to be at home the last of this week, as the time draws near I count the days and how glad I shall be to see you all in the dear home

Francis Thayer was born in a house that had been owned by President Hayes' father, but it had been built before Mr. Hayes lived in Dummerston, Vermont. The Hayes family later moved to Ohio where President Hayes was born.

once more. Now, Father has just come up and says there is no letter, and the Presidential Party will be here on special train at 9:15 tomorrow am. to stay an hour and return. So good night for this time, love and kisses from both to you all… —*Mungie.*

August 21, 1877, Twin Mountain House, White Mountains, N. H.
My dear boy—   Well, here we are again in this most comfortable and pleasant place. This morning the President and Mrs. Hayes, with a large party, came to the Kearsarge for an hour where a reception was held from nine to ten. Mrs. Hayes charms everyone who comes in contact with her. We will tell you about the affair when we reach home. We left No. Conway at one-thirty expecting to spend the night at Littleton, but were detained an hour at a railroad crossing and failed to make connection, so turned in to this familiar place where we find several apparently glad to see us again. Tomorrow we hope to leave for Troy and expect to reach that home at seven in the eve. Father will look over matters Thursday with J. Birge and we hope to be with you by the five o'clock train in the aft.— and then, oh I hardly dare think I shall be so glad to see you all. Father joins in love and kisses to you all…
—Your loving *Mungie.*

∽ Colorado — planning and departing:

Sept. 8th, 1877, Troy.
My Dear Son—   …I stopped at house Thursday & Friday, came down this morning and have spent an hour at my desk looking over matters, generally an hour or two every day or two will tax my strength about all it will bear at present. Good reports from Old Amherst will strengthen and encourage me more than anything else in the world.   —*Father.*

Sept. 16, 1877, South Cambridge.
My dearest Brother—   Here I am at home again… Father did not look as well and seemed discouraged about himself, he has been taking Dr. Mosher's medicine and his (Father's) legs and fist are so very large, I had to tug to draw on his stockings. The Dr. came this morning and said he would never be better in this climate, and maybe never, and if he stayed here he would [not] live longer than spring. Is that not horrible & to think dear Father who has always done so much for us… I am so ill with the thought I can scarcely write. I suppose Mother and Father will be obliged to start for another climate soon and oh, how lonely I will be. You can see how now more than ever, you should strive more than ever to be as careful steady prudent and wise in all your ways so as to give him no trouble and if we pray, strength will be given us from above… It gave us great pleasure to see that you were a candidate for class President… —*Kittie Thayer.*

Oct. 4th. South Cambridge.
My dear Son—   …Your father is just getting his voice again, has been able to whisper only several days, and has had a very sore cough… Something has been said of our going to Denver City on Father's account, but it involves so much and separation from friends who are so dear, that we are slow to speak of it. Still I must say that I think it will come to this…   —*Mungie.*

Francis S. Thayer, 1822–1880. Photograph by Zeph F. Magill, 336 & 338 River Street, Troy, New York.

November 6th, 1877, Troy.
My dearest Brother—   No letter from you this week. How can you neglect your dear sick Father. It is beyond my comprehension. Father has not been downstairs in a week, and only walks to and from his chair. Seems weaker every day. Grandma has a cold so Mother has kept her in bed today so she may soon be better… My hair is fixed a new way on top of my head and one curl. Now good bye and all send love and kisses. —Your *Kittie*.

Nov. 18th, 1877, Troy.
My dear precious Frank—   …The probability of our going away on Father's account seems to be growing into a positive intuition and preparation. Dr. Mosher said Denver Col. was the place to winter… it seems probable that we shall go to Den— perhaps remain there long enough to try the climate and do what seems to be for the best, as we strive to now from day to day. It is the old story of nights more or less broken, and an effort to make up by naps during the day, but this is so exhausting when long continued, that it will in time wear out anyone. Dr. Hubbel expects a great relief by the right change of climate, and if months pass without a severe attack the whole condition of the chest will be improved…   *Mungie*.

Troy. Nov. 20th, 1877.
My dear Brother—   We hope to receive a letter from you this evening. Today has been quite a busy one getting odds and ends ready to go away. It is *decided* we go week after next if Father keeps as well as now. He rides out a little every day and seems some better. Mother is busy and keeps well. Grandma about the same…   —*Kittie*.

Dec. 9th, 1877, Sabbath eve, Troy.
My dear Son—   Here we are yet enjoying the comforts of our pleasant home… All the past week I gained a little strength from day to day and now I feel as tho' it would be safe to start on our long journey. Our trunks are packed and tomorrow at 2:55 P.M. we expect to leave Troy for some months. How long I cannot tell, all will depend upon the state of my health which I hope & pray may be greatly improved. We shall go through to Chicago without stopping over, arrive at C— Tuesday eve, remaining there until Wednesday noon and then off for Denver Col. where you will address us until further advised. We leave Grand Mother very well with Minnie and Mrs. T. You will be at home soon to make her thrice glad and of course you will do all in your power to make her happy in her loneliness… We shall not be here in person to enjoy your vacation but our thoughts will be continually with you and the dear ones at home. Now my dear boy, remember what you know I would say to you if I could take you by the hand and say Good Bye, God Bless you, —Affectionately yours, *Father*.

Office of Crystal Palace Mills. No. 143 River Street. Troy, New York.
December 12, 1877.
Mr. F. McKie Thayer
Dear Sir—   Your father, mother, & Kittie left Monday afternoon at 2:55 all in good spirits. A postal from Rochester says, "All well, does not tire me to ride." Your letter was sent to the house and there I re-mailed it to Denver City Col.   —Very Truly, *John T. Birge*.

XIII

1878–1880

The Thayer Family in Colorado

BY 1878, Francis and Catherine Thayer and their daughter were living in Colorado hoping that he would find relief from asthma. The growth of the United States could be easily measured by the 1880 census figures that reported a population of 50.1 million, a 25 percent increase over the 1870 census. The American people were demanding new goods and services and a nation of enterprising entrepreneurs responded to those demands. In 1879 F. W. Woolworth opened the first 5¢ and 10¢ store. The following year George Eastman patented a roll of film for cameras, and the Kampfe brothers in New York City invented the safety razor. In 1878 there was a massive yellow fever epidemic in the South—over 24,000 cases and more than 4,000 deaths were reported in New Orleans. From Colorado, Francis Thayer wrote many letters to his son at Amherst College and also a series of columns for the newspaper in Troy, New York. At the same time there was another change in communications—in 1878 the first regular telephone exchange opened in New Haven, Connecticut.

Letters and diaries are a written communication of a time and place that can be preserved. There is no similar record of a phone conversation, and the evidence of the times begins to change.

Letters and diaries by:
E. R. Eaton, a family friend
Catherine McKie Thayer
Catherine (later, Katherine) Sophia Thayer
Francis McKie Thayer
Francis S. Thayer

Letters, diaries and newspaper columns written from: Denver, Idaho Springs, Pueblo, and Colorado Springs, Colorado; Troy and Cambridge, New York; and Amherst, Massachusetts.

1878

❦ Death in the family:

Denver, Colorado. Jan 14, 1878.
My dear Mother— [to Sophia Whiteside McKie]   Owing to a snow blockade on the Kansas & Pacific road, there were no mails from the east last night, and will not be tonight, but eastern bound mails leave as usual if not by the K.P., by the Union Pacific, so I will say a word though I have very little of

Sophia Whiteside McKie remained at the Thayer home in Troy, New York, when Francis and Catherine Thayer went to Colorado in 1877.

429

Cheyenne Mountain, Colorado Springs.

My dear brother Edwin— If I could have been with you through this sad route, how thankful I would be, but "God's ways are not our ways." When I have been ill myself, I have prayed that I might live to be with our dear Mother at the last, and now, when my husband needed care, and that at a long distance from home, the loved one seems to have been snatched away in a day, as it seems. I could not have had her live to suffer, but it is very hard for me to feel that I cannot again look upon that sweetest of all, among the faces of women, to me, the soft silvery hair and the bright eyes, so full of love for us all, in every glance. Oh Edwin, our Mother was to us the sweetest most faultless of women. In a letter written the Fri before the 18th Mother asks Minnie to write me that "she is about over her cold" so that we were feeling

Continued on next page

varied news or interest. The weather, (unfailing topic), is still cold. Francis and I walked about a mile this afternoon— he is better of his cold and is able to sleep very well and has none of the exhaustion he has had at home. …we are furnished with a large basket of pine kindling wood, and the coal burns almost like wood, so that in a few moments our little stove and part of the pipe is red and the room comfortable. What a treasure this coal is here, found less than a hundred miles away and there are "mountains" of it. I trust you are warm in this extreme weather, and well and happy. Francis and Kittie join in love and kisses. Oh how I would like to spend the evening with you… Kittie is doing nicely in her music and Francis so much enjoys her practice, and as the piano is in our room, we have few interruptions. With tender love to you dear "Mungie"

Denver, Col. January 21st, 1878, Monday eve 8 o'clock.
Dear Minnie & son Frank—   Last evening our hearts were made glad by the receipt of your kind letter of last Wednesday, 16th, in which you say "Mother says she is stronger than when you went away. She goes up and down stairs three or four times a day just as she pleases." Today, Oh! how changed the news from the dear object of our deepest love and warmest affection. This A.M. we rec'd a telegram from Dr. Bloss saying Mother was dangerously ill, sudden attack plus pneumonia yesterday. At first Kate & Kittie thought they must take the first train for Troy, but on reflection it was thought best for Kittie *only* to go as Kate has, for two or three days past, been suffering somewhat from neuralgia in the side so that for a little while she could not take a long breath without sharp pain. A little medicine and free application of mustard plaster almost entirely removed the difficulty, still we did not think it *prudent* for her to undertake so long a journey. Kittie said she *must* go so we telegraphed… This evening we have Mr. Graves' telegram saying— "Doctor says don't send Kittie on any account. You need her there. Grandma cannot live until morning. Frank is covering tonight." In this trying hour it certainly will be a great comfort to have Kittie here, she is so full of tender love and sympathy I do not see how we could spare her and altho' it almost breaks her heart to think she will never see dear Grandmother again, yet she says she

will willingly stay and be a comfort to the living. Our hope and prayer is that Frank will reach home in time to receive for us all the parting and final blessing from one whose whole life has been a constant benediction to us all. Our prayer all day long has been that Mother might be spared from much suffering. We know that she is surrounded by kind sympathizing friends all striving, by every little act and look, to fill the place of those so far away. Edwin is no doubt with you and it is the great longing of our hearts that we could be there too, that we cannot be with you in this dark hour adds to this crushing sorrow. With much love to all, I remain yours as ever. —*F. S. Thayer*.

Denver, Col. Jany. 22, 1878. Tuesday evening.
Dear Minnie—   The second telegram from our dear but now desolate home, yesterday, prepared us for the dread reality of the third dispatch which was received about 11 o'clock in the evening. Early this evening we telegraphed our suggestions in regard to the funeral, burial etc. and now we have a dispatch from John Birge saying our wishes will be complied with. We hope that we suggested nothing that did not meet with Edwin's and Frank's approval. It is indeed hard for us all to bear the thought we cannot be with you to share in paying the last tribute of love and affection to dear, dear, Grandmother. This cannot be and we ask God to bless and comfort us here so far away and may God bless you all. Kate wishes Mother's little things, (lip salve etc.) on her stand, put in her bureau drawer. We have not yet thought of what it may be best to do in regard to the house etc. Hope you are well and will stay a few days at least until we can decide. You may send this to Frank. Lovingly yours. Kate & Kittie send much love. —*F. S. T.*

P.S. Kate says she knows that loving friends are doing all for our dear Mother that we could do if at home and we are thankful for all their kind and loving attentions. We shall count the hours until we hear particulars from you, and hope that the darkness of our present sorrow will not shut out from us the many blessings we still possess.

Tuesday, Jan 22, 1878. 154 First Street, Troy.
My dear Friends—   I can hardly tell you how grateful we all were for the telegram received today— everything was progressing very much as you have desired but to know that it was acceptable to you to have us act— Never was anybody so lovely— the placid expression, the sweetest look the dear Mother carries to the tomb. We all feel so much sympathy, yet can express so little & words must seem so idle to you. Your Brother Edwin's illness was unfortunate, but hopes to be down tomorrow. I know what a bitter disappointment to both you & himself not to have been able to minister to the precious one in her last hours & so tenacious am I of your rights that I almost begrudged myself the privilege of performing those tender offices your loving hands would fair have done. Your short first telegram came as a benediction in the closing hour. It was holy ground— there was every evidence that the Everlasting Arms were about her, for never for one moment since you left has there been one word of reprimand— it was always best & right, noble soul, the path of duty was ever the right one to her. What the separation cost her you alone can know but cheered by that faith which recognizes a "Father's hand in all things," she was able to comfort & strengthen all about her. Oh what precious lessons she has left us.

Thursday eve, 5 o'clock— You have been with us in spirit this solemn day, very comfortable about Mother, but the first dispatch was to me a preparation for the worst… I know I have been blessed above most children in having our dear Mother spared to us so long, and in having the light and strength of her presence in our home, for us, and our children… I know that dear Coz Minnie and other friends did all that love could do, when Mother was taken… We were asked to make suggestions and did so and trust nothing conflicted with your feelings. We have thought that the dear Mother would be taken to Cam. Fri. morn. and that last night she would be lying with the loved ones gone before, the dear old burial place grown more sacred— it is hallowed ground to us surely… Kittie is well and such a comfort to me. I am glad she did not go home… Take care of yourself, lovingly, *Sister Kate.*
—*Catherine McKie Thayer to her brother, January 26, 1878.*

Sophia Whiteside McKie, 1796–1878. Photograph by A. Cobden, Troy, New York, date of photograph unknown.

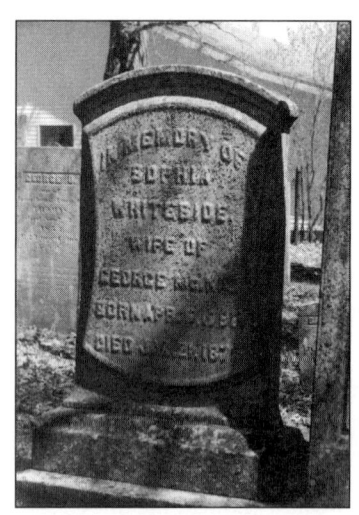

Grave of Sophia Whiteside McKie, 1796–1878, Whiteside Cemetery, Cambridge, New York.

as relatives near & more remote arrived. I never saw more heartfelt grief. The perfect quiet seemed to awe one— all felt the majesty of death & united in prayer that the balm of consolation might be poured into your hearts & that returning strength & health might be your portion. Dear Frank no longer a boy— he has come to realize the responsibilities of life & the sorrow that sometimes comes with them. He is bowed with grief for one who loved him & he loved so well, but has borne himself bravely. I gave him a few choice rose buds & asked him to put them in his dear Grandma's hand himself which he did. I placed a knot of violets on her bosom— "Being dead she yet speaketh" seemed to be the thought of each & all. Mr. Birge said to me, "Was ever one so lovely?" There was a large gathering of friends & neighbors, that is, as many as comfortably filled parlor & library. Mr. Eaton deemed it a privilege to do what he could & regrets that he cannot go to Cambridge tomorrow… Dear Grandma, for by this endearing name she permitted me to call her, I think she felt it was her last sickness but the brightness of faith never left her. When I recited, "I know that my Redeemer liveth," "Thy rod and thy staff thy comfort me," she said, "Again," & I repeated them & then the whole of the 23rd Psalm. By look & gesture she made response, especially at the last verse. I know that this letter is incoherent, but I cannot help it— pardon the detail. I know that everything that has transpired the last few days is sacred to you or I would not have dared to write in this manner. How much our thoughts are with you my dear friends— Mr. & Mrs. Thayer & dear Kittie. Accept my prayer and believe me your sympathizing friend, —E. R. Eaton.

THE SAMPLER

Small length of linen
Handspun, handwoven,
Stitched with bright silk threads
Faded now like once sharp memories
Of my Great, Great Aunt Catherine Whiteside.

The homestead where she lived,
Third of six generations,
Was it this house she tried to copy here
With trees, birds, letters, numerals,
Were these two children Catherine, Sophia?
The dead are silent.

White marble tombstones near a country church,
Catherine beside her husband,
Beloved of gods if one believe the verse,
But young Sophia lived,
Brought up her sister's children and her own,
She also lies by him who sired them all.

What will the sisters say on that last day
When waking to the trumpet sound they look
Into each other's eyes across their George?
—*Katherine Thayer Hobson*, 1889–1982

This poem was included in *I Have Seen Pegasus*, a pamphlet that was prepared on the occasion of Katherine Thayer Hobson's 90th birthday, April 11, 1979. Katherine was a great-granddaughter of Sophia Whiteside McKie, 1796–1878, and a niece of Catherine Whiteside McKie, 1793–1824, both of whom are referred to in the poem. The two sisters, Catherine and Sophia Whiteside were the two wives, first Catherine and later Sophia, of George McKie, 1791–1861.

BEEBEE HOUSE,
F. W. BEEBEE, Proprietor.

➣ Idaho Springs, Colorado:

February 19th, 1878. Beebee House, Idaho Springs, Col.
My Dear Wife & Daughter—   From Denver to Golden 14 miles, you pass through a splendid farming country, equal in appearance to the best sections of Illinois & Iowa, several places I noticed plowing had commenced. On leaving Golden you realize that you are indeed among the Rocky Mts.— the scenery is grand beyond description all the way, not a few places where the Mt. rises five to seven hundred feet perpendicularly above the track. We thought the White Mts. grand and so they are, but when you talk about lofty grandeur you will have to come west. We arrived here about 6 o'clock and found the Hotel quite pleasant. After a good supper played checkers with several and had tolerable success on the whole. Retired to a pleasant room about half past ten feeling pretty well, went to bed without smoking or taking any medicine and got through the night very well… Tomorrow, if pleasant, I expect to go to the Hot Springs, about ten minutes walk from the Hotel. I wish you could come up here, but it is not best to take the risk. If Kittie comes with Mrs. B— on Friday she will on her return give you a graphic description of the sublime scenery. All the A.M. it was warm and pleasant. Not too cool to sit out on stoop without an overcoat. I did not do it, but walked about enjoying the pure bracing air and warm sun light. I am feeling better and hope to go right along gaining health and strength every day…   —Your devoted *Francis*.

The Beebee House, circa 1899. Photo courtesy of the Historical Society of Idaho Springs.

February 21st, 1878. Beebee House, Idaho Springs, Col.
My Darling Kittie—   I passed quite a comfortable night and feel pretty well… The A.M. was bright and beautiful and I took a walk as far as I could go without getting my feet damp. I have no rubbers here. Please send them up by Kittie. The wind is east now and Mr. Beebee says we may have more snow— just now the sun is trying to shine but you cannot see the tops of the mountains. I expected a letter from you this morning, but all I got for mail was the *Troy Times* which I have read through.   —As ever your own *Frank*.

February 22nd, 1878. Beebee House, Idaho Springs, Col.

My Dear Kittie—   …I am a little more than holding my own notwithstanding the unpleasant weather. Last night I slept pretty well for me. Today it is snowing and I am under the painful necessity of lounging about the house reading the papers, playing checkers etc. Played four games, two each with two of the best players in the house. Had the good luck to beat every time… The scenery is grand and sublime beyond my power to describe. It is snowing now (1/2 past one) fast. I believe the arrangements are complete for the evening's entertainment and I expect to see a real old fashioned dance. Well— this is Washington's birthday— a national holiday… This is a very poor pen but you can guess at it if you can't read this scrawl.   —Your *Frankie*.

February 24th, 1878. Beebee House, Idaho Springs, Col.
My Dear Wife—   Yours with three other letters and paper came to hand

The Beebee House, Idaho Springs, Colorado. Photo circa 1873, during a visit to Idaho Springs by President Ulysses S. Grant, center and his entourage. Photographer unknown. Photo courtesy of the Historical Society of Idaho Springs.

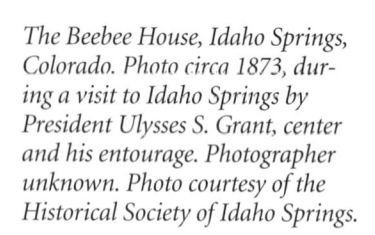

this A.M. I passed the night as usual, some wheezing and some sleep, more of the latter than I enjoyed a week ago. The weather most of the time last week was unfavorable for improvement in my case, however, I gained a little and hope that little is but the stepping stone to much. I do not know that this is a better place for me than Denver— still I think but to give it a fair trial. Today the sun is shining brightly but the air is cool and bracing. I wish I could have heard Kittie give an account of her visit to Idaho [Idaho Springs, Col.] She enjoyed every moment of the time… This is indeed a quiet Sabbath. I did not go to church for the reason I was afraid of taking cold. They have two churches here, Presbyterian and Episcopal. The Methodists are usually the pioneers in planting churches, but they are behind hand here. —I am as ever *Your loving Husband*.

February 25th, 1878. Beebee House, Idaho Springs, Col.
My Dear Wife—   …I sent you word this morning by Mrs. B— that I had a pretty good night and now I can say that I am feeling pretty well for one of my age and infirmities. It was bright and beautiful all the A.M. Now the wind is east and I shall not be surprised to see snow falling before night. The weather is a fickle jude anywhere, but here among the mountains you cannot tell what an hour will bring forth on the weather question. Unless we have better weather soon you will see me in Denver very soon. At dinner Mr. Beebee remarked that "the wind had got round in the east again." I replied, "Make out my bill and I'll leave this country the first train." On reflection I think it best to stay a little longer. Tell Kittie I sent up to the Bath House for her comb and word was sent back that they had not seen it. Mr. Beebee proposed to go up there this P.M. and inquire into the matter— said he guessed he could find it. With a heart full of love to your dear self and our darling daughter I am as ever your loving *Frank*.

∽ A rare letter from Amherst College:

Oct. 2, 1878, Amherst.
My dear Father—   Your letter of 24th Sept. has been duly received. My only excuse for not corresponding more promptly lies in the fact that if I could have written *tomorrow* I should have done so long ago but when *tomor-*

row came it was no longer *tomorrow* but *today* and hence my remissness. It is a comfort for me to feel that your health is improving so rapidly. It would seem that this fine autumn weather must give life and spirits to everyone. I am glad to learn that Kittie is up and well again after her cold. Mother has written me two beautiful letters which I really must answer. The class election came off last week. I was one of the three candidates for class President but sad to say I was defeated by a small majority. Such is the fate of those who aspire to such distinctions as class Presi. I'll never seek office again. "It's a delusion and a snare."

There has been considerable feeling between the Sophomores and Freshmen since the opening of the term and this culminated last week in a *Duel* between a Freshman and Sophomore. The duel was intended as a practical joke on the Freshman but only blank cartridges were used, but the Faculty refused to consider the matter in this playful light and the result is that the Sophomore who acted as principal in the affair and a Senior who was present to act as referee are expelled. Our class regards this penalty as unnecessarily severe and are circulating a petition to have the decision of the Faculty revoked. I am very well myself and all needed to complete my happiness is to hear that you are all well and happy at the Old Home. With much love to yourself, Mother & Kittie & kind remembrances to friends & neighbors, I remain yours affectionately, —*F. M. Thayer.*

A College Term Paper

Among the external distinctions of races the form of the skull calls for particular attention… The Caucasian race, which stands highest in the scale, is that which has produced the most civilized nations; while the Mongolian, the next in order of capacity of cranium has produced a number of nations which have remained in a fixed state of semi-civilization. The Malay is a [illegible] barbarous and the American and Ethiopian the most barbarous of all. —*F. M. Thayer.* (Special Collections, Robert Frost Library, Amherst College.)

The only surviving work of Francis McKie Thayer from his days at Amherst College is a handwritten and undated term paper in the archives at the college library, entitled: *A Study of Human Skulls.*

Oct. 11th. 1878, South Cambridge.
My dear Brother Frank—   Your letter was received this morning and delighted all our hearts. Father will send the bill to Troy and have the check sent you. Am glad the fellows were taken back, what was the name of the senior? …Your letters will be expected weekly. Do not let a week go by for Father is so sick and weak.   —*Kittie.*

Oct. 27, 1878, Troy, Sabbath eve.
My dear Frank—   We have not received letters to which we should reply, but still I remember our little arrangement for this evening, and thinking that you would miss your usual letter, I sit down for my one sided chat. Thinking and hoping that you are engaged in the same pleasing task as myself. Perhaps you do not think letter writing a very enjoyable occupation! Certainly habitual, regular, and frequent writing makes it so and the task becomes an easy pleasant pastime. Will you not try and make it enjoyable to yourself by a little wholesome discipline? …Kittie and Father join me in kindest love to you.   —*Mungie.*

Nov. 23, 1878, Troy.
My dear Son—   …We hope another winter & spring in Colorado will give us permanent relief. Pueblo, where we shall stop for a while at least, is

a small town… about 115 miles south of Denver. If we do not find it agreeable at P— we shall go still further south. In regard to your Holiday vacation we leave that to you and Aunt Rhoda to arrange just as you & she may think will be for your best good and greatest pleasure. And now my dear boy I am coming to a very delicate and important subject, one we have talked & prayed over time and again with all the love and fervor the most loving and devoted parents ever had for a child. You are so kind and affectionate in your nature that it seems strange that you should give us anxious thought. We are going far way, some two thousand miles will be between us. This may be my last appeal to you and now I pray you for your own good, for the peace, happiness and health of your loving & devoted *Father, Mother & Sister*—   [The first page of this letter is cross written and is illegible.]

1879

College Commencement:

The Hon. Francis S. Thayer, accompanied by his daughter, returned East from Colorado yesterday for the purpose of attending the commencement exercises at Amherst college, from which institution his son, Frank McK. Thayer, will graduate this year. Mrs. Thayer will remain in the West for the present. Mr. Thayer's many friends in this city will be glad to greet and welcome him home after his extended sojourn in Colorado. By frequent, excellent, and newsy letters from him, published in the *Times*, his acquaintances have been kept posted concerning his experiences among the residents of the distant state, and have been gratified to learn from time to time of his constantly improving health. —*Troy Daily Times*, June 20, 1879.

Special Correspondence   After moving to Colorado, Francis S. Thayer wrote a series of letters for the *Troy Daily Times* that were published as *Mr. Thayer's Colorado Letter*. These are excerpts from some of those "letters."

SPECIAL CORRESPONDENCE, *Troy Daily Times*
MR. THAYER'S COLORADO LETTER.
Pueblo, Col., Dec. 23, 1878. It is always a pleasure, especially when far away from home, to communicate with old friends, and I gladly embrace the present opportunity of giving you some notes of observations and facts in regard to this, the centennial state of our Union. What interests me most of all is that I find here relief from my old complaint, asthma. Soon after my arrival here, I met Gov. Pitkin, who said to me that a bounty would be paid, not for the heads of bears and wolves, but for a case of asthma this climate would not cure or greatly relieve. I replied that I hoped for the relief and cure rather than the bounty…

Colorado has obtained the reputation of being a sanitarium, where those suffering from asthma, catarrh, hay fever and consumption, if not too far gone, are greatly benefited, if not entirely cured. Why this climate is so healthful and invigorating is a prolific subject of scientific inquiry, which I do not propose to discuss without further and closer observation. On this point I will only add that the atmosphere is pure and dry, and most of the towns near the Rocky Mountains are a mile or more above sea level.

It is now nearly three weeks since our arrival here, and notwithstanding the cold and stormy weather my health is better than when I left home. The *Times*, four days old, reaches us regularly and keeps us well informed as to local events and news generally. I see you have to spread yourself to accommodate your patrons for the holidays. Wishing you the compliments of the season, I remain as ever, *Francis S. Thayer*.

Pueblo, Col., January 29, 1879. …The Colorado farmer has at least one advantage over his eastern fellow laborer, i.e., there is no danger of a wet harvest season here— when once a crop is grown it is sure to be harvested, unless, occasionally, as in the past, it is damaged by the grasshopper and the beetle. The last appearance of these pests in this locality was in 1876, since which time our New York farmers have made the acquaintance of the beetle or potato bug, greatly to their loss and sorrow. The pastoral region embraces a large portion of the state aside from the mountains. The vast plains are now dotted with immense herds of horses, cattle and sheep, where but a few years ago the buffalo and the deer roamed at will with none but the red man to molest or make them afraid. Farming, or, to use a southern phrase, ranching, is carried on here in many instances on a grand scale. The Col. Craig ranche, situated on the Huerfano River, in Pueblo county, contains 80,000 acres, and was recently sold to a company of Bridgeport, Conn., capitalists for the snug little sum of $350,000… Three of the largest towns in Rensselaer county would hardly cover this one farm.

Pueblo, Col., March 4, 1879. The Pueblo flouring mill, on the opposite side of the street, is driven by water "taken" from the Arkansas river and brought in a canal, a mile and a half in length, and at an expense of $14,000. This reminds me of the story told of the quick-witted Irish sailor. When asked why a ship was called "she," he replied, "Because the rigging costs more than the hull." Having a natural fondness for a flouring mill, I found my way hither this morning for the purpose of making some inquiries about the wheat crop of this new state. I introduced myself to the proprietor as a fellow miller from the Empire state, and told him the object of my visit. He said: "We raise the finest wheat and make the best flour in Colorado that can be produced in the whole world. Why our wheat and flour took the first premium at the centennial exhibition at Philadelphia." I doubted, within myself, this seemingly confident assertion when I remembered "Crystal Palace Mills" in Troy and the beautiful wheat we get from our own Genesee county and many of the western and southwestern states.

Colorado Springs, March 15, 1879. Ten days since, after a three months sojourn at Pueblo, we, in western parlance, pulled stakes and pitched our tent at this delightful spot, 45 miles towards the north pole and 1,575 feet higher in the air, almost under the shadow of Pike's peak, although 12 miles distant from the summit the way the crow flies, and yet so clear is the atmosphere that it appears within the limits of a morning's walk… Colorado Springs, a city of the second class, is situate at the confluence of the Fountain and Monument creeks, on the Denver and Rio Grande railroad, 75 miles

Colorado Springs, General View. F. A. Nims' Views of Rocky Mountain Scenery.

south from Denver and on the southern slope of the "divide." The town was organized and laid out in 1871, hardly eight years since the first building was erected, with the single exception of a log house built by trappers some 20 years ago. Now we see a beautiful town, containing a population of over 4,000 generally young, active, intelligent and temperate. It is not only a virtue, but a necessity to maintain temperate habits here, as the originators of the town dedicated it to temperance and every conveyance of real estate contains a chance of forfeiture, enforceable as a penalty for the sale of intoxicating liquors. Consequently you see no signs along the streets, such as "wines, liquors and cigars," "sample rooms," "Lager beer saloons," etc… The city contains 10 churches, a beautiful college building of stone in course of construction, one of the best public school buildings in the state, capable of accommodating 350 pupils, a deaf mute asylum, three banks, six hotels, one daily and two weekly newspapers, a dozen or more compact blocks of stores, shops, etc. Livery stables of which there are four or five very large ones, with splendid horses and elegant carriages, do a large and profitable business in consequence of the patronage of invalids and tourists…

Colorado Springs, April 9, 1879. …The altitude of Leadville is about two miles above sea level, and the climate anything but agreeable—as someone has described it, "much like nine months dead winter, and the other three late in the fall." Colorado Springs is one of the three bases of supplies for the new El Dorado, and I have watched with no little interest the shipments of goods, wares and merchandise of almost every description, by the more than 800 six and eight mule teams constantly employed in this service. These teams usually draw two canvas covered wagons, called "prairie schooners," and they move in fleets over the mountains and through the deep cañons and narrow passes. They carry provisions for the men and fodder for the beasts, dropping anchor wherever night overtakes them, the crew sleeping on deck or in the hold, wrapped in their coarse warm blankets, and the jaded mules hitched to a stake. The average load is 1,000 pounds per animal, loaded on two wagons… Colorado is called a sanitarium, and I have no doubt a large number of invalids come here and are greatly benefited by this health-giving climate; but it is alarming to see the hosts from all parts of the country, and old residents too, that are stricken down with that most contagious disease, which no quarantine, except absolute isolation, will prevent spreading. This disease has, at least, one peculiarity— i.e. in the selection of its victims. It fastens itself upon the strong, hardy and vigorous— the very bone and sinew of the land— while the old, poor and feeble are "never or hardly ever" attacked." 'Tis an old saying that those who are afflicted with asthma are quite sure to be free from all other diseases, and for this reason your correspondent may escape. However he has had some alarming symptoms and been obliged to go into quarantine. The name by which this disease is known to the medical profession is "*auri sacri fames*" (the accursed thirst for gold) or mining fever…

Colorado Springs, April 25, 1879. Our morning's ride of several miles over the broad plains studded with beautiful wild flowers was delightful. The weather was simply perfect, the mercury standing at 70° in the shade, with a soft and gentle breeze which made us think of the month of leaves and roses, when we hope to be at home again. In the course of our drive we saw a large flock of sheep quietly feeding on the plains near the road, and the opportunity was improved to make some further inquiries about sheep raising, and the information gained I venture to communicate to your readers, although this subject has been discussed somewhat at length by your correspondent in previous letters which have elicited particular inquiries by private letters as to this branch of industry in Colorado.

Pikes Peak Ave, Colorado Springs. F. A. Nims' Views of Rocky Mountain Scenery.

It may be asked how you can keep 1,000 or more sheep on 120 or 160 acres of land? The answer is— buy land on which there are good durable springs and you have a range of thousands of broad acres on which there is no water, and for this reason it will remain the property of the great land holder, "Uncle Sam," for generations to come, and be used in common by his children and children's children. A good sheep ranch containing 160 acres, well watered by springs or running streams, with a small frame house and sufficient corrals and sheds to accommodate 1,000 sheep, can be bought for about $1,000, or you can buy 160 acres of government lands at $1.25 per acre and make the improvements, which will cost $600 to $800. There is still another way to obtain a ranch, ie, under the homestead law, which gives to any one who will make affidavit before the proper officer that he is a citizen of the United States or has declared his intentions to become such, that he is over the age of 21, or the head of a family, and that the entry is made for exclusive use and benefit and for actual settlement and cultivation. He must reside on the premises five years, at the end of which time he will be entitled to a patent or complete title from the government. The homestead laws also provides that every soldier and officer of the army, and every seaman, marine, and officer in the navy who served not less than 90 days in the army or navy of the United Stated "during the recent rebellion," and who was honorably discharged and has remained loyal to the government, may enter, under the provisions of the homestead law, 160 acres of the public lands, and the time of his service or the whole term of his enlistment, if the party was discharged on account of wounds or disability incurred in the line of duty, shall be deducted from the period of five years during which the claimant must reside upon and cultivate the entered tract, but the party shall in every case reside upon, improve and cultivate his homestead for a period of a least one year. All lands obtained under the homestead laws are exempt from liability for debts contracted prior to the issuing of the patent therefor.

Colorado Springs, May 31, 1879. The length of my last letter was conclusive evidence that I had quite forgotten Sam Weller's idea of the great art of letter writing, "make them short, so that the reader will wish they had been longer." In future I will remember "Samuel," and pay proper respect to the value of your columns and the patience of your readers....

1880

Colorado Springs. Jan 5, 1880
My dear Brother Edwin [Edwin McKie in Cambridge, New York]—   Well,

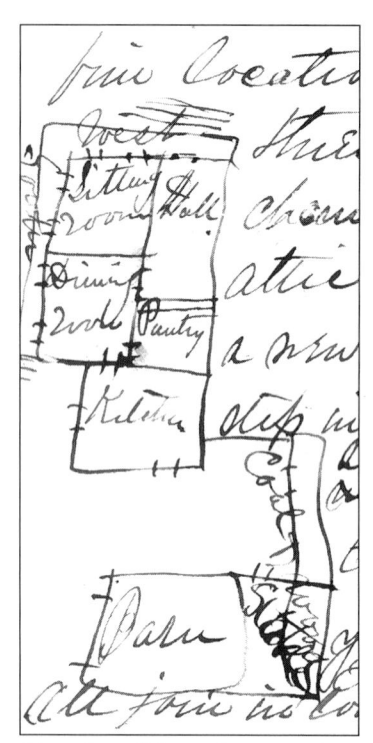

Floorplan of Thayer home on Cascade Avenue in Colorado Springs included in Catherine Thayer's letter of January 5, 1880 to Edwin McKie, her brother.

Xmas and New Years are come and gone, and it has not seemed much as it used to Edwin, when we pinned our stockings in a long row on the line in Mother's bedroom at the end of the hall— that seems, as I think of it, long, long ago, but when I ask how old I am, I cannot realize that I was born in 1827, but the years come and go, the new figures look strangely for a little time, but soon we become accustomed to the change to the eye and ear and so move on through the time allotted to each of us. Sometimes when I think that we are living where we used to see only *Indian Territory*, a few rivers, and the *Rocky Mts,* I feel I must be dreaming.

I wrote you Br. E— last summer and autumn, enclosing the letters to Troy— and after my family came out to see me, sometime after, I learned that between Francis and Kittie my letters were not forwarded, each supposing the other had taken them to you— I do not speak of them because they were worth much, but to let you know that I tried to keep up a correspondence, albeit I am a poor letter writer.

As to the health question, Francis is recovering from a cold taken about six weeks ago, he was not as ill as you have seen him in Troy, not confined to his bed or room, but very wheezy. We had the mercury 26° below zero, and the intense cold was unfavorable, but we have had for a week most delightful weather. Last Sat, Jan. 3, Frank, Kittie, and two others had a picnic in the open air about eight miles from here, and Gen. Palmer (of America) and wife have been out the past few days from eleven till four, taking a substantial lunch, building a fire and making coffee; this outdoor life is what builds up, if anything will here. We have had no rain since Sep. 1, a little snow twice, but it is absorbed by the coarse sand in a day or so. There is a sprinkling of snow on Pike's Peak and a little on some of the mt. sides but none here, as dry as summer and you can sit outdoors hours every day— such is the warmth of the sun. How I wish you could step into our cozy house and visit with us. We have a fine location, well here is the house— three rooms below, and three chambers above with one in the attic for servant. We have a new milch [sic] cow and if you could step in the pantry Edwin, you would see such cream as you used to like with jumbles when you and I were young. I am at the end of my paper. All join in love to you both and the chicks. Do write soon for I want to hear from you, am hungry to see you, as ever your loving sister.   —*Kate*. [Catherine McKie Thayer]

Kittie Thayer in Colorado before 1882.

Jan 5th, 1880
My dear Uncle Edwin—   Your nice long letter came to me some weeks ago and seemed like having a chat with you. We are all enjoying beautiful weather, so soft & warm— mercury stood 75 in shade— quite like summer. My pony is a very fine one— and for three years old shows signs of being a record pacer. Our home is very pleasant, and we enjoy ourselves much better than in boarding… Father and Mother are very well. Have a fine cow and will make some butter this week— gave the calf away. My dog is a big one, knows something will shut the doors and many other tricks. He fell down a well seventy feet deep and after working all day a man hauled him out. Give best love to all, and write me again. Do you know on the 3rd of December I was twenty? Quite the maiden lady. Now good bye.   —Your loving niece, *K. S. Thayer*.

◈ Death in the family:

"Account of dear Father's last days" —Monday, Nov 22. out sitting on the South side of the house in the warm sun. Two hours or more. Had a hyperdemic that night. Tues night I went upstairs about 11 o'clock, came down about 1 am. Dr. Strickler came with Dr. Reed, Wed. p.m. Hyperemic Wed. night.

Thurs. p.m. Mr. & Mrs. Palmer here. Dear father said he felt better than yesterday. Drs. Reed & Strickler here. Ellen drew him out to the dinner table in the next room. Kittie and I each carrying a foot, had a cheerful dinner, apparently but we were all terribly anxious at heart after dinner. Father lay down and Frank read to him a long article… and we had a pleasant chat. Dr. Reed came in, nearly 8, and sat on the bed some time, talking as if we were well. Father said he knew his condition was critical but told the Dr. he did not give up all hope of being better. Then Dr. Reed said Hart (his partner) would come up and administer the hyper after the Dr. left. Father said we will have prayers. Frank usually reads, but Kittie was near the table, she read the XCI Psalm and Father in his prayer asked most earnestly for a restoration to health & strength. Soon after Frank left to his room, and Kittie and I removed the bandages. Father said, have Ellen come and rub my legs and she was called. Mrs. T— usually bandaged the feet and legs so we said we all could do a little for him. Dr. Hart came about 10, gave the hyper— about 10:30. Father turned over to try to sleep and after a little said he would have some Apollinaris water, the hyper's made him thirsty. Dr. Hart opened the bottle and I gave it to him, and then he said "now be quiet and I will go to sleep." Kittie went to one room and soon after I went up, took off my clothes which I had kept on several nights and was robed, then put them on and came down. Father sent Ellen up to me to tell me "to have a good rest" that he "was very comfortable and expected to have a good night." I soon went down however and found him quiet and in a doze. I wished to creep in beside him for the night, but all told me to get some sleep, that I could do no good. Dr. Hart said he thought the night would be like the previous one. I finally went up for one reason only, that the more there were in the room the less pure the air would be and all his distress was in breathing, and it was so cold we could not open windows. He had Apol. water several times through the night, would call Ellen who with the

Personal check of Francis S. Thayer, with his photograph, payable to his wife. Check is dated November 25, 1880, the day before he died.

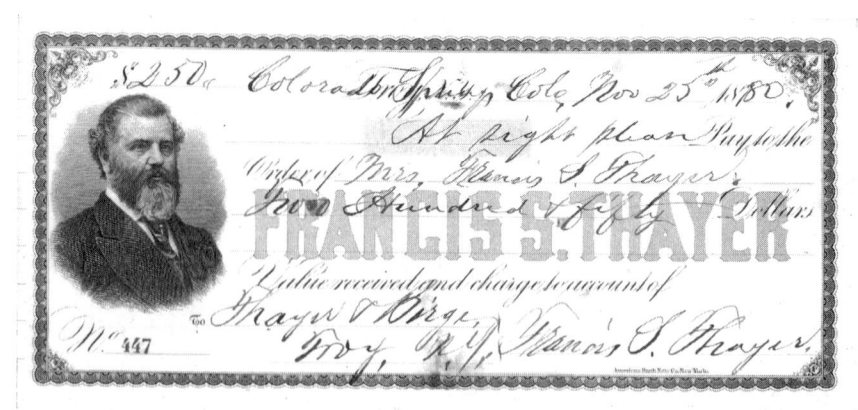

Dr. were close at hand— the Dr. in the room, E— sometimes in the room, sometimes in the next room. About five Fri. a.m. there was a little change in breathing. The Dr. gave stimulant or tried to. We were in the room in a moment, the quiet breathing soon ceased, our beloved had waked in Heaven and we to agony below. —*handwritten by Catherine McKie Thayer.*

A telegram received in Troy this afternoon announced the death this morning at Colorado Springs, Colorado, of the Hon. Francis S. Thayer of this city. The deceased was born at Dummerston, Windham County, Vt. September 11, 1822. His father was a descendant of old Puritan stock and the son Francis was one of a family of 11 children, among whom are Mrs. A. H. Graves of Troy, Mrs. William M. Cranston of London, England, the Hon. James S. Thayer of New York and the Hon. Adin Thayer, ex-canal commissioner of Hoosick Falls. In the summer of 1841 Mr. Thayer completed his education at the Cambridge Academy, in Washington county, subsequently taught school in North Bennington, Vt., and in the spring of 1842 he came to this city, where he resided ever since. Upon reaching Troy he accepted a clerkship in the flour store and milling firm of Howland & Bills. Mr. Thayer labored assiduously with marked success in his vocation until, a few years later, he was admitted into partnership with the firm named, and he had, without interruption continued his connection with the business stated up to the time of his death. The name of the firm changed at different periods, but his interest in the establishment remained. Among the partners with whom he was associated may be mentioned the late James Howland, Alfonzo Bills, the late F. H. Knight and John T. Birge, who at present is the surviving partner.

In politics Mr. Thayer was formerly a Whig, casting his first vote for Henry Clay, but joined the Republican party upon its organization. In 1867 he was elected state senator by a majority of 1,600, running more than 500 ahead of his ticket in this county. He was re-elected in 1869 by a majority of 1,196 over the Hon. Smith Strait, and during his connection with the state legislature he served in important positions on the committees of manufacturers and public expenditures and canals, commerce and navigation. In 1870 Mr. Thayer voted against the odious "Tweed charter" for the city of New York, and received the commendation and praise of the united Republican press of the state. In 1878 the deceased was nominated by the Republicans for secretary of state, but with his ticket, sustained defeat. In 1874 Mr. Thayer was appointed by Gen. Dix as canal auditor, and served one year in that capacity. Since then, owing to failing health, he took no active part in either business or politics, but resided much of the time in Colorado, where he sought relief through the climate of that locality from the disease that finally terminated his life. During his residence in the West Mr. Thayer was a frequent contributor to the columns of the *Times*. The deceased was a consistent member of the First Presbyterian church of this city, and for many years held the office of a ruling elder. He was a director at the time of his death of the Troy City National bank, and a trustee of the Troy savings bank, the Renssalaer Polytechnic Institute, the Troy and West Troy bridge company and the Troy female seminary.

In early manhood Mr. Thayer married Miss Catherine McKie of Cambridge, Washington county, who, together with a son, Francis McKie, and a daughter, Catherine S., survives him. It is believed the funeral will be held in Colorado Springs.

—*Troy Times*, Troy, New York.

The Hon. Francis S. Thayer, of Troy, died suddenly in Colorado Springs, Col., yesterday. He was descended from old Massachusetts Puritan stock. His father emigrated from the Bay State to Dummerstown, Windham County, Vt., where Francis S. was born on Sept. 11, 1822. He was one of a family of 11 brothers and sisters. Up to his nineteenth year he worked on a farm, except for a short interval while occupying the position of clerk in the village store. At 18 he was elected Captain of the local military company. In the Summer of 1841 he came to Hoosick Falls, Renssalaer County, with his father, and a few weeks later entered Cambridge Academy, in the adjoining county of Washington, where he received instruction for four months. In the winter of 1841–42 he taught school in the village of North Bennington, Vt., and "boarded around" in the families of the scholars. In the Spring in 1842 he accepted a clerkship in the flour store of Howland & Bills, in Troy, at $100 a year and his board. Five years later he was admitted to a partnership in the concern. He continued in the flour and milling business in Troy for more than 20 years, establishing a reputation for his special brands of flour that made them favorably known throughout the country, and amassing a competence.

Mr. Thayer entered manhood as a "Whig." His first vote was cast for Henry Clay for President, in 1843. When that party had outlived its usefulness he joined the Republican Party at its formation, and has ever remained its stanch and devoted adherent. He was several times a delegate to the State and local conventions, but beyond this he steadily declined political honors until, in the Fall of 1867, he accepted the nomination for State Senator from the Twelfth District, and was elected by 1,600 majority, running 532 votes ahead of his party ticket in the county. He was re-elected in the Fall of 1870. On April 8, 1874, he was appointed Canal Auditor, a position for which he was eminently qualified by his life-long interest in and advocacy of, the welfare of the canals. In 1873 he was the Republican candidate for the office of Secretary of State.

—*The New York Times*, November 27, 1880.

The Asa Knight Store, now in Old Sturbridge Village, Massachusetts. The store was built in Dummerston, Vermont, in 1838 and stocked a variety of goods from around the country and the world until it closed in 1862. In 1972 the structure was dismantled and moved to Old Sturbridge Village in Massachusetts where it stands today as an example of a New England country store, complete with the original counters behind which Francis Thayer once worked. A search of the Dummerston Town records shows that on several occasions Adin Thayer, the father of Francis S. Thayer, sold real estate to Asa Knight, the owner of the store.

Troy. December 9th, 1880.
My Dear Kittie— I enclose a letter for you that came today. Your letter written on Thanksgiving day came several days after the sad tidings that it for-shadowed. Sad as this and the letters that followed have made our hearts, yet it has brought great comfort to know how full the preparation, how perfect the trust, how sweet the calmness, of our dear Mr. Thayer during those closing days and hours of his life. To those who knew from seeing the hard fight he had to make for life, how heavy was the burden of pain that disease had imposed upon him, it is easy to rejoice that those sufferings are at an end. But the joy is for him, and I know that even that thought cannot fill the aching void in the hearts that sorrow. Long ago when I first read *Lucile* I memorized a passage that often arises in my mind now and has brought comfort in times of trouble to my heart, as it may to yours:

Grave marker for Francis S. Thayer, 1822–1880, Thayer family plot, Oakwood Cemetery, Troy, New York.

"The dial receives many shades & each points to the sun.
The shadows are many, the sunlight is one.
Life's sorrows still fluctuate: God's love does not.
And His love is unchanged, when it changes our lot.
Looking *up* to this light which is common to all,
And *down* to the shadows on each side, that fall.
In Time's silent circle, so various for each!
Is it nothing to know that they never can reach
So far, but what *light* lies beyond them forever."

That into the darkness that has clouded your life's pathway, may penetrate the divine rays of this *light beyond* and at its touch the shadows flee away, is the sincere wish of Your friend, *John Birge*.

Resolutions:

At a meeting of the directors of the Troy City National Bank, held this day to consider the sudden and unexpected death of their associate, the Hon. Francis S. Thayer, the following minute was entered on the record and a copy transmitted to the widow of the deceased: Mr. Thayer during the past eight years has been connected and identified with the interests of this bank, with a most honorable and conscientious record— having an eye single to our best interests, and always ready to aid with such advice as a long and successful business career qualified him to give. In expressing our grief to his immediate family, wherein Mr. Thayer's genial nature found its best development, we do but certify to his lovable Christian traits of character, to none so well known as they who are now under the dark shadow of affliction. We desire here to convey to the widow and children of our deceased friend assurances of heartfelt sympathy.
—Troy City National Bank, Troy, N. Y. Nov. 29, 1880. *Geo. A Stone*, Cashier.

At a meeting of the Trustees of the Troy Female Seminary, held Nov. 29, 1880, the following resolutions were adopted: *Resolved*, That by the death of the Hon. Francis S. Thayer the Troy Female Seminary is deprived of one of its truest friends and ablest advisers, and one always ready to do to the extent of his ability that which in his judgment was for the best interests of the institution. *Resolved*, That his memory will be held in high esteem by all connected with the Seminary, and that the sincere sympathy of the members of this board is hereby tendered to the family of Mr. Thayer. *Resolved*, That the Secretary be directed to transmit these resolutions to the friends of the deceased.

1880—Lives in Virginia and Colorado

As 1880 ended, there were two widows living worlds apart. One, Annie Jennings Wise Hobson was running a boarding house for college students in Williamsburg, Virginia, and the other, Catherine McKie Thayer, was living in her new home in Colorado Springs. One had a son who had finished college and law school and was beginning to set out into the world to make his name and fortune. The other had a daughter who would soon be leaving home too. It will still be seven years until all of their paths converge.

XIV

The Summer of 1882
Disease, Marriage, and Death

AS 1882 began, Chester A. Arthur, a Republican, was President and Grover Cleveland, a Democrat, was the Mayor of Buffalo, New York. Later in the year, Cleveland would be elected Governor of New York. At this same time, John D. Rockefeller was organizing the Standard Oil Trust, and Thomas Edison's steam-powered central station was beginning to supply electricity to New York enabling that city to sparkle with incandescent light. In this same year, the electric fan was invented by Schuyler S. Wheeler, silk replaced catgut thread in surgical operations, and the flooding waters of the Mississippi River left over 85,000 people homeless. The United States signed a treaty of friendship and commerce with Korea and also agreed to accept the provisions of the Geneva Convention of 1864 for improving the care of the wounded in wartime. Congress authorized pensions for the widows of Presidents Polk, Tyler, and Garfield, and, in an effort to end the Mormon practice of polygamy, passed the Edmunds Act. However, it would be another five years until the Edmunds-Tucker Act was enacted and the practice of polygamy would be ended by the courts of the Utah Territory. In the mountains of Colorado, a young Henry W. Hobson was practicing law. In Colorado Springs, Katherine Sophia Thayer, a lifelong acquaintance of Barclay Jermain of Albany, New York, was living with her widowed mother, Catherine McKie Thayer. Katherine's older brother, Francis McKie Thayer, was looking for farmland to buy in Iowa. As 1881 was ending, Katherine Thayer returned east to Albany, New York.

Architect's sketch of a house that was planned for Barclay Jermain, Esq. in White Creek, New York. Barclay's mother had come from White Creek, near Cambridge, and his father owned a large tract of land there. There is no other information about the house.

THE FAMILY LETTERS

Barclay Jermain in front of Hedge Lawn, Albany, New York. On the reverse: "Given me (Katherine Thayer Jermain, later Hobson) by Barclay, September 1881." W. Notman Photographic Co., Albany, New York.

Letters and diaries by:
Ada Thayer, the sister-in-law of Francis S. Thayer and Catherine McKie Thayer
Ada Thayer, the daughter of the above and therefore "Kittie" Thayer's first cousin. She will later be married to the Rev. C. Morris Addison.
John Birge, Francis Thayer's business partner
Barclay Jermain
James B. Jermain
Katherine "Kittie" S. Thayer, soon to be Katherine Thayer Jermain
Catherine McKie Thayer, also occasionally "Mungie"
Francis McKie Thayer, also "Buzzie"
Robert and Julie (Barclay Jermain's sister) MacCartee (also McCartee)

Letters and diaries written from: Colorado Springs, Colorado; New York City, Albany, Troy, and Cooperstown, New York; and England, Belgium, and Switzerland.

your Beloved One Barclay Jermain.

1881

❧ A letter from Catherine McKie Thayer:

Colorado Springs, December 31, 1881, Sat. 9:30 A.M.
My Darling Kittie—   None but God could know what I felt when I saw the last wave of your dear hand, and then you passed out of sight, on your long journey, with your brave, loving, great heart so full of conflicting emotions, hopes and fears. I think some Mothers would have hesitated about your going, but my child, we have had such strong tender love in our own home, such as I hope you may enjoy in yours sometime, that I could not keep you so far away from your Beloved One… Need I ask you to take *preventive* care of yourself under all circumstances? …If I only knew that he was improving and you safely going on, I could feel quite happy this lovely morning…   —Your loving *Mungie*.

Katherine Sophia Thayer, December 1881, "for Barclay's Xmas." Charles Bohm, Photographer, Denver.

1882

❧ Letters from Catherine McKie Thayer:

Colorado Springs, Jan 1, 1882, Sabbath. A.M.
My darling Kittie—   A happy New Year to you and your Beloved, and many more in the future…   —Your loving *Mungie*.

Col. Springs, Jan 5, 1882, Thurs. a.m.
My darling Kittie—   …I was in such a state that when I turned to the little clock Monday a.m., just after dear Mr. I— left, and saw the clock was stopped, not a tick, that I just screamed, you know I have laughed at every superstition, but the long suspense had so unmoved me, that I was ready for anything

dreadful… Be sure you let Barclay sleep and do not let him talk too much. Take care of yourself…   —*Mungie.*

Colorado Springs, Jan 7, 1882.
My precious Kittie—   …Everyone inquires for you and Barclay, manifesting great interest, and this eve I hope to hear from you my darling, and then we shall know particulars. I so often wish I could know just how you all are, and where you are. By wire we learn that a cold wave has struck the Hudson River valley. You *must* be very careful. I fear you left so hastily that you were not provided with flannels, as you have worn them *of late*. Take no risks dear child, of any kind, guard your feet from cold and wet and yourself from exposure as a religious duty. Do let me feel that you will keep well if possible… Love to yourself & dear Barclay…   —*Mungie.*

Colorado Springs, Jan. 8, 1882, Sab. eve 8:30.
My darling Kittie—   …I know dear child that only going to Barclay would satisfy your own heart, and I felt that you could be a comfort to him, and help the other dear ones to cheer him, and care for him. The discipline of the past has made you familiar with invalid needs early in life my darling. God grant that later years may spare you a continuance of this kind of experience, and while it is sweet to be cared for by those we love, and a precious privilege to minister to our beloved ones, still we must think of sickness and suffering as the *chastisements* flowing from sin, still as dear Father said, "We are all in God's hands, just where we would be," and if the dear Father in Heaven leads us, we will try to follow, only pray that we may ever feel the presence of His hand, ever *abide* in the Love that gave us a Savior. We will expect to hear of continuous improvement and look eagerly for letters… You can read my letter to Barclay if he consents, and I presume he will, no real secrets, only you would not let me send the first epistle. There was a little flurry of snow last eve and I did not go out…   —*Mungie.*

Colorado Springs, Jan 10, 1882.
My precious child Kittie—   …Your short letter of Fri. a.m. came this eve. A few lines saying, that dear "Barclay had had a good night and felt better," and we all rejoice. May he eat, sleep, and gain strength rapidly. We all miss you, and long to have you here again, but while you can be a special comfort to your loved one, we would have you stay with him, give him my love and sympathy, for illness calls for it… I am just about through paying the house bills, they are about twice what I thought they would be, but I will not let it trouble me— everything needful to our comfort has been done in the best manner, nothing for show, and our house is entirely comfortable, and in perfect order from bottom to top. So let us enjoy it…   —Your loving *Mungie.*

Colorado Springs, Jan 11, 1882.
My darling Kittie—   …It really seems to me that he was over-doing for some time before his illness. A man cannot go here, and hurry there, early and late, attend this meeting and that, day in and day out, for weeks and months, Sundays and all, without giving out (or in) sooner or later, and if the dear one confesses to being very tired nearly every night, the past two months, it is clearly his duty to take *better care of himself. Continual exhaustion will not do.*

let Barclay sleep   Barclay Jermain had "consumption" at this time.

My dear Barclay— Your Thanksgiving Day letter gave me much pleasure. The children of your Sainted Mother would always have been dear to me, even without a continued acquaintance, on account of the love I bore her; and the sweet memory of our girlhood days is one of the treasures I hold. But now, that I have come to love you for your own sake, as well as for the joy and peace you have given my dear child… And now, dear Barclay, if in your brief acquaintance with my dear child, you failed to read her as a bit of human nature, with a very strong sympathy for out door life and nature, taught I hope, to see the loving Father's hand in the simplest wayside flowers, as well as in the over hanging skies, then you will have to learn more of her… but did you really take in the fact, that Kittie is neither a drawing room girl, nor a most accomplished needle worker? Well, she is not… Kittie is in perfect health, we have had our colds, and Frank is still suffering from severe cold… I am rejoiced to learn from Kittie that you are all well, you will do everything for health and this includes both the positive and negative method of doing… With love to yourself and kind remembrance to your family, Your loving friend, C. McKie Thayer.
   —*Catherine Thayer to Barclay Jermain, December 13, 1881.*

Barclay Jermain. The Notman Photographic Co. Limited, Albany, New York.

How has it been? and how will it be? We have seen this suicidal work go on for years. It may be averted, it never can be remedied… —*Mungie.*

Col. Springs, Jan 17, 1882.
My precious darling Kittie—   I opened last evening's letter to add a word of thanks for your telegram of last night, which found me in bed this morning. Such glorious good news, "Barclay downstairs, much better." Thank God. I trust the long anxiety is over. You know how apprehensive I am in regard to acute chest troubles and attacks. Does dear Barclay dress his feet properly? — Wear merino stockings and heavy shoes? — Are his flannels right? You need have no *sham* delicacy about these matters, health requires attention to these important portions of dress. I have struggled with you some time, and you are just getting rational. Do your duty in this matter… —*Mungie.*

Col. Springs, Jan. 18, 1882, Wed. eve.
My darling Kittie—   … How I wish I could by a magic wand bring you two here this bright morning. The sun is fairly hot on my head… —Your loving *Mungie.*

Colorado Springs, Jan 22, 1882, Sabbath eve 8, o'clock.
My precious Ting-a-ling—   Your letter of last Wednesday rec'd this eve is the first since last Thursday a.m. and we all were hungering for news from our loved ones. I am so sorry to hear that too much attention to business has wearied Barclay. It is the old experience once again. I do not know how it can be avoided except by his leaving home; it is well to remember however, as a fixed fact, that anything that exhausts physically or mentally retards recovery. There is a weariness that brings rest and refreshment. There is an exhaustion that prevents both. The way to avoid the latter, we have seen to be impossible when at home, where business can reach one. And we have also seen that one must almost become a confirmed invalid to secure proper immunity from perplexing cares and responsibilities. I think you have seen so much suffering and known so much sorrow, from overwork, that you cannot fail to convince dear Barclay of the duty he owes himself, and his friends, in regard to his health. If money is worth anything, the *timely* use of it, in order to preserve health is one of its best uses, and if I were with dear Barclay, I think I would wish the suggestion, that if he has not the efficient help in his Office, needful to make his daily work what it should be, and *no more*, that he should secure it, if possible, and if necessary, it is possible. I trust this may be considered a case of special pleading, not interference… I see by the *Times* that the weather was very cold last Wednesday. I so hope none of you took cold. You must have provided yourself with what you failed to take with you in your hurried departure… Now if you go out in the cold, you must protect your feet and wear leggies. I feel almost as if I ought to wire you to this effect. It is so important to keep the *ankles warm* and I fear you will not care for yourself as you should. Has Barclay any cough or sensitiveness about his chest or side? Do see that he is properly dressed. I want him to get *perfectly well*, so does everyone, but there are right means to be used to aid in attaining this desired end…
—Your loving Mother, *C. McK. T.*

Katherine "Kittie" Thayer and her cousin, Ada Thayer Addison. Reproduced from an early tintype.

XIV The Summer of 1882 • Disease, Marriage, and Death

❦ A letter from Barclay:

Hedge Lawn, Albany, N.Y. Feb. 6th, 1882.
My dear Mrs. Thayer—   Your letter of the 1st reached me yesterday morning… Indeed I feel very sorry that I have taken away from you and Ada so much of the brightness and comfort that Kittie's presence gives you. And I assure great the comfort & blessing that has cheered my sickroom and made a long and tedious convalescence bright and full of sunshine. I beg you will not think I forget that what has been my gain & happiness has been to you a loss & trial. Yet I know, my dear Mrs. Thayer, that the unselfish heart speaking from the depths of your motherly love, could not rejoice as you write that you do "in the love your darling child and I have to each other." …I need hardly tell you that Kittie has endeared herself to every member of our household… But what shall I say to poor Ada. Here I am at a loss. Tell her for me, that when she becomes engaged, to select someone who is to have an attack of pleurisy nearly two months long, but beforehand to place herself at a point 2,000 miles distant from the pleurisy lover, then when he is sickest, to go him and be to him all that Kittie has been to me, and then write me that she forgives me for having taken away her "very best girl." …I believe Kittie has written you that my dear sister Marie has gone to New York to undergo surgical treatment. I feel very very anxious about her— however slight the doctors may think the danger— she is, as you know, so frail… There are so many things I would so like to say to you & talk over with you and so many kind thoughts sent in Kittie's letters for which I thank you. I wish it were possible for me to go back with Kittie, but unless it is a necessity, I know & see plainly that my duty is here. In a short time I shall make a plan but can not until I know Marie is out of danger… With much love for yourself and Ada & warm regards to all, Very affectionately yours, —*Barclay Jermain*.

❦ Letters to Francis McKie Thayer:

April 30, 1882, New York Hotel.
My darling Frank [Francis McKie Thayer]—   Well here. We are safe and not very tired. We met Ada at the door, and she handed Kittie a letter from Barclay who is ill again, with sore throat and some fever, but much better than he was the last week. John Birge came down this morning, he saw Barclay yesterday, in bed, but better, and today we have a telegram saying he "is quite comfortable and has less fever." So we hope he will soon be up again. I need not tell you that Kittie was sorely disappointed at not seeing Barclay and then to hear that he was ill was too much almost for her… Well my darling I hope you are learning what you need to, oh how lonely I feel and how I miss you all the time, my precious boy…   —*Your loving Mother*.

May 2nd, 1882, New York Hotel.
My precious darling—   …We are progressing very well with Kittie's affairs… Barclay is said to be doing very well. Kittie has a dispatch from him daily, he has less fever daily— and we hope he will soon be well… I miss you, my darling, more than I can tell, and am so anxious that you shall settle in the

Pleurisy is an inflammation of the pleura, a membrane surrounding the lungs, which makes breathing very difficult. Lung infections such as pneumonia and tuberculosis are two causes of the disease. Chest x-rays, CT scans, a biopsy of the pleura, and antibiotics would be the modern treatment. In George B. Wood's *Treatise on the Practice of Medicine*, 1858, pleurisy was identified and treated as follows: "The most frequent cause of pleurisy, as of so many other inflammations, is exposure of the body to cold, especially when previously heated or perspiring. It is said that cold drinks, under similar circumstances, sometimes produce the disease… At an early period of the disease, the lancet should be freely employed. Few diseases bear bleeding better, or call for it more strongly than acute pleurisy. The patient should be placed in a sitting posture in bed, and the blood allowed to flow until a decided impression is made upon the pulse… After the first bleeding, the bowels should be thoroughly evacuated… The bowels having been unloaded, and the febrile symptoms reduced by the lancet, opium and ipecacuanha in the dose of a grain each… may be given at bedtime… Should the inflammation continue after the pulse has been subdued by general bleeding, leeches or cups may be freely applied to the chest… The patient should be kept at rest, and should avoid speaking or coughing as much as he conveniently can…"

best way, in the best place… Kittie says tell Buzzie every revolution of the sun brings me nearer Barclay, and give him my love. God bless us all as a family. Your loving Mother, —*C. McKie Thayer.*

May 4, 1882, New York Hotel.
My darling Frank—   We are having fine weather, and getting on well with our work and expect to go up to Troy Sat. p.m. Barclay is improving slowly, but I trust surely… All send love to you…   —Your loving *Mungie.*

Troy, May 8, 1882.
My Dear Son—   Here we are in our own house… Poor Barclay is still in bed, with remittent fever, which is lessening daily, and his symptoms are all favorable…   —Your loving *Mother.*

May 16, 1882, Old Home in Troy.
My dear son Frank— I am all alone in the house. Kittie over the river as Barclay is still ill enough to be confined to one floor and his bed. The fever is much diminished but he is weak and the weather is so wet and the air so chilly that he can not convalesce rapidly, we hope for better weather and more rapid mending… You must try and write oftener if you are well, and if you are not, I still must know. I had three letters from you the first week, a splendid send off… So now my boy, buckle on your armor and let us see what you can do as an Iowa farmer…   —Your loving *Mungie.*

May 28, 1882, 4 Washington Park, Troy.
My dear son Frank—   A rainy day here and evening… I have you constantly in mind, and your efforts in the way of beginning a new home, and I hope and pray almost "without ceasing" that you may be wisely directed in all things. A telegram from Kittie after her arrival at Lakewood said that "Barclay has passed a comfortable day." It does not look very much as there would be a wedding in our family in ten or twelve days. I do not say this but keep my thoughts to myself and wait and pray, and hope that Barclay's health will be restored. With a heart full of love and thanks for your frequent letters… Your loving Mother,   —*C. McKie T.*

Troy, New York. June 2, 1882.
My dearest 'Buzzie' [Kittie Thayer to her brother]—   Mother has written you of my journey to Lakewood & I will tell you of my return Wednesday and of Barclay. He is better but not strong or well yet— and we have given up the idea of having our wedding party & a wedding at his house and will be married at Jermain Church next Wednesday which makes it much less fatiguing to Barclay, then we will go to Cooperstown to Mr. Jermain's place for a month, take two servants & Barclay's man with horses. So we can have home comforts and lead an outdoor life. I will write you tomorrow when the hour is decided upon so you will know just when to think of me as being married. Ada is here. I wish for you every day, and sometimes I feel as if you must be here. Barclay is well enough to walk about, and with care and nourishing food he will soon be much better. I have had to ask all the people not to come and it seems sad to have my dear brother so far from well & we unable to carry out our plans. Presents have commenced to arrive. I will make you a list & please write me often. We are all

the children— you & I, and must keep together. Mother is well & sends love & I give an added kiss. —*Ever your loving Sister Kittie Thayer.*

4 Washington Park, Troy, June 4, 1882.
My dear Son—   Yesterday's mail brought us yours of May 31. I had been thinking of you day after day, looking over land… As I understand it, there is not a stick, nor a building on the land… Kittie and Barclay are to be married Wednesday the 7th in the Jermain Church, in the most private manner, only his immediate family & Mr. Dunham and of ours, the Adas, & Uncle Aaron probably, & J. Birge. I wish you could be here for the little time at least, but poor Barclay improves so little, so slowly that all that we can expect is that he and his father, who has been ill, may get to the Church. There is nothing merry or bright just now, in regard to this wedding except that Barclay & Kittie are devotedly attached to each other, but we will hope and expect that the quiet Cooperstown, where the couple will be alone a month or so, with good servants, will begin, if not complete, Barclay's restoration. Should your settlement be favorably concluded, and Barclay show *very positive* signs of recovery, I may go to England with the Adas, but I cannot leave the country unless everything is moving in the right direction. God grant it may with us all. Hope you have heard a good sermon today, rain kept me in. God bless and keep you my precious son and us all.   —*Your loving Mother.*

4 Washington Park, Troy, June 6, 1882.
My dear Son—   Well my dear boy, it is two o'clock and I am tired, but I must say a word before I turn to the pillow. Cannot say how much I will sleep, for tomorrow will see Kittie united to the man of her choice and I can no longer be permitted to think of myself as entitled to her first thoughts or her time. I hope and pray that Barclay's health may be restored, and that long happy and useful lives may be their future portion. Should everything be favorable I may go with the Adas. Kittie & Barclay go to Cooperstown for a month, perhaps longer. There have been very pretty presents from B— & K's friends and B— has not seen one of them. We have had almost constant rain and B— has been able to drive but two or three times. Well, Mr. Buckley came this p.m., showed the location of your land and tomorrow J. Birge will send funds to pay for it. Mr. Buckley said… that you had written some architect for plans of house and barn: Tell me all the details my son, I love to hear them. I bought silver for Kittie in New York and *you gave her small* silver spoons, forks etc. but I did not have it sent here fearing the burglars might *scent* it and it is in New York subject to order. Kittie said she would write you tonight, but she is at work still and is very tired I know, and I will tell her to wait till the morning. Poor Barclay looked at her this p.m. (we were there) and said ("Kittie you look *so well*.") healthy. Good night, God bless us all my boy. —*Your loving Mother.*

❦ Wedding day:

THE WESTERN UNION TELEGRAPH COMPANY
Troy N.Y. June 7, 1882, 7:25 P.M.
To: F. McKie Thayer—   Kittie and Barclay married at one o'clock. They send love. All well. *C. McKie Thayer.*

Katherine Sophia Thayer, photo taken before her marriage to Barclay Jermain in 1882. Charles E. Emery, Photographer, Colorado Springs.

Send following night message from Denison Ia. To: Mrs. Barclay Jermain— Many happy days to you and Barclay. *F. McKie Thayer.*

❦ Cooperstown:

4 Washington Park, Troy, June 9th, 1882.
My dear Barclay & Kittie— We were busy at the cards last evening, and so I send you early morning greeting of affectionate thoughts and remembrance. Hoping to see you tomorrow eve, we are well and quite happy over your pleasant telegrams. What I fail to say now I can express when we meet. With tender love for you dear children, —*C. McK. Thayer.*

Delaware & Hudson Canal Company, June 12, 1882.
My dear children [Barclay and Kittie Jermain]— I am quite ashamed that I allowed the rush of farewell thoughts to crowd the dear little clock out of my mind entirely. You will forgive me, will you not? I cannot tell you in any spoken language, or in any form of speech with which I am familiar, how sweet this visit has been to me. You are so peacefully devotedly happy in each other, that it seems to add (if possible) to the unsurpassed, I almost wrote, unequal'ed, loveliness of your present home, and so, with all that you are and have at your disposal, I confidently expect you, dear Barclay, to make slow but continuous steps toward the health that brightens every other blessing. Get your tent and *live in it*. When you have fine weather, court a little fatigue, but stop short of exhaustion, rest, sleep, if you can, and then when rested, take a little more exercise, and when you get stronger, just use your arms a little, with something in your hand or hands, sitting or standing, and so adding muscular power, for with every added force you are able to acquire more. A step at a time will reach the summit of the highest hill… So my darlings, with a prayer for God's blessings on you, and on all we love, I will once more bid you Good-bye or rather, God be with you. —Your loving Mother, *C. McKie Thayer.*

Cooperstown, June 12, 1882.
My dear son Frank— I am waiting at the station "en route" for Troy, but have spent the Sabbath [with] Kittie & Barclay at Brookwood Point, 2 miles up (or down) the lake and the loveliest place I ever saw. Barclay seems to feel the influence of the change already as he slept better and has more appetite. The two people so quietly peacefully happy that I feel awed almost when with them. Their hearts are all right and everything will be done for B's health. God grant that his health may be restored. They insist *almost* that I shall go with the Adas and as you seem to have made a start in Iowa I think I will go to New York Tues p.m. 5 o'clock and we will sail on Wed at 3 p.m. by *Gallia* I have so much to finish up that I am almost bewildered. Annie & Wm. back to care for the house. You must communicate with John Birge after this in relation to money matters. I shall leave everything in his charge. I hope to find letter when I return stating plans about house, barn, breakers etc. Good-bye. God strengthen us all for our various duties and bring us together at last. Your loving Mother. —*C. McK. Thayer.*

June 13, 1882, Brookwood Point, Cooperstown, N.Y.
My darling Mother— I will try & write you just a good-bye & God bless

you from us both. Your letter came like all your loving letters. My heart is too full to write more. May the voyage strengthen you. Kiss the Adas for me. God bless you on your birthday at sea. I wish I could put my arms about you & kiss you. Your own loving little girl   —*Kittie.*

June 14, 1882.
My dear Son—   We sail this p.m. and I so wish that I could have heard something of your building plans before going. My heart protests at leaving my children. Your birthday was remembered in mind and prayer if not in gift. John Birge goes to Wisconsin this week and may… see you at Mapleton. You must write fully to him of your plans and expenditures and will draw by correspondence with him until some other arrangement is made by you… I must say adieu,   —*your loving Mother.*

June 16, 1882, Brookwood Point, Cooperstown, N.Y.
My own Darling Mother—   Today I think of you as passing your birthday at sea. I hope you are not very ill— though I think a little illness would not hurt you… Barclay seems better in some little ways— but I can not hope for rapid improvement. And if he loses no ground that in itself is encouraging. We have been to drive every day, about three miles. And Barclay has walked to the Lake and back several times. He sleeps better than when at home and eats as well… Dr. Lathrop will be here today. I will give him two weeks & if by that time Barclay is not decidedly better I shall insist upon other treatment. I do not try to do anything but nurse Barclay and keep him cheerful and encouraged. He is so sweet and tender I feel as if I were taking care of a lovely child… My nights are not disturbed, and I feel very well. So do not worry about me. I love to think of your visit here and that we three were together… Since I commenced writing I have been up to do something for Barclay seven times. So if the letter is disjointed you will know the reason…   —With a heart full of love, ever you own loving *Kittie.*

June 20, 1882, Brookwood Point, Cooperstown, N.Y.
My own Darling Mother—   I am thinking of you all constantly on the sea… Barclay is about the same and I am happy to say he sleeps well still, though has no appetite and his stomach seems to be very weak and inactive. We use a mild nasal douche. And so many many things remind me of my dear Father. You would be amused to see how well acquainted we are. I have insisted on Barclay's using a *tin cup* in the night instead of getting up— as it tired him. And a commode so that his strength is used out of doors and not tiring himself indoors… The weather is beautiful today and we are going to drive… Barclay joins me in much tender love.   —Ever your own affectionately *Kittie.*

June 30, 1882, Brookwood Point, Cooperstown, N.Y.
My own Darling Mother—   Here we sit in the pleasant sitting room. The morning is cool and we have a fire in the fireplace. Barclay has eaten his breakfast and is reading the *Argus.* Dr. Lathrop says he can see a great change for the better in Barclay's chest. He has no pain in his chest or anywhere, but his throat needs attention and treatment, and this we hope Dr. Bloss can do well. We rather expect him today but have not heard definitely. …Marie is coming tomorrow. I rather dread even Marie, for how can I hand Barclay a

tin cup... in the sitting room or have the commode here, near the fire, as I have this morning. For these reasons it would be better for us to be alone. Still *every one* must yield in case of sickness... —Ever your own *Kittie.*

Written on the envelope in Catherine McKie's handwriting: "My dear Kittie before her sorrow."

Postmarked: July 5, 1882, Cooperstown, N.Y.
[Addressed to: Mrs. Francis Thayer, 21 Holland Park, Bayswater, London.]
My darling Mother—   I am on the bed writing & my heart's darling is beside me very very ill. He may not live through the day, can not live many hours. The lungs are all filled with the germs of consumption and Dr. K— and all say there is no hope. *Please oh* please stay where you are & I will go to you. I must get away from everything when the light goes out. I think every day of Father's charge to me, "Do not let your dear Mother be troubled," & am glad you are not here. No one can bear my trouble— it is my own. I just asked Barclay if I should send you his love, he said, "Oh yes."   —*Your own Kittie.*

July 5, 1882.
My dearest Brother—   I have been so busy since my wedding day that I have not had a minute of leisure for letter writing. I have only written Mother. You are in my mind a great deal and I think of your farming & plans with keen interest. I am sorry to say that Barclay is not improving as I had hoped. His throat is in a terrible condition and Dr. Bloss is treating him. He came out & spent the night and will come again. Write me dear Buzzie. Your "Little Sister" is having a hard time. Do not write Mother about Barclay or let John Birge. I have written him but she is where she can rest & just where I would have her— "Away" from care & anxiety. If John be with you remember me to him most kindly. Write me soon please. Barclay so very weak, is carried upstairs & oh my heart is broken. Good bye Buzzie.   —Your sister *Kittie.*

Barclay Jermain, son of J.B. Jermain of Watervliet, is dangerously ill at Cooperstown. The report this morning the he was dead was untrue. A telegram today from his sister stated he was resting quietly.
—*Troy Times,* July 6, 1882.

July 6, 1882, Cooperstown, N.Y.
My dear Mrs. Thayer—   Kittie has asked me to write to you today as she cannot do it herself, being entirely occupied in her care of Barclay. She says she wrote you a few lines yesterday, but could not tell you all and I must tell you that she is going to lose her dear one— poor darling child. She cannot keep him long. We are all together here around him... Since Friday last his disease has taken an alarming form... the trouble seemed to culminate in the throat, but it seems besides to be a breakdown of the entire system at once. It has been an exceedingly rapid decline— and as you know, unexpected to all of us... Dr. Lathrop says he suffers little & will probably pass away quietly in sleep... Dear Kittie is keeping up wonderfully & is a wonder to all of us... I will not write more dear Mrs. Thayer & have written this most hurriedly that it may catch the next steamer. You will hear more from us in a day or two. With Kittie's love & love from myself, I remain yours most sincerely,   —*Julie McCartee.*

THE WESTERN UNION TELEGRAPH COMPANY
Cooperstown, N.Y. July 7, 1882.
To: Frank Mc. Thayer, Mapleton, Iowa.
Barclay can not live till night. Have written Mother. Do not telegraph. Do not telegraph her. —*Kittie T. Jermain.*

THE WESTERN UNION TELEGRAPH COMPANY
Cooperstown, N.Y. July 7, 1882.
To: Frank Mc. Thayer, Mapleton, Iowa.
Barclay died this morning. —Mrs. B. J. Germain [sic].

THE WESTERN UNION TELEGRAPH COMPANY
Marshalltown, Ia. July 8, 1882.
To: Frank Mc. Thayer, Mapleton, Iowa.
Received news here Barclay dead. Are you going on or will I find you at Mapleton tonight. Telegraph me Maple River Junction at depot three o'clock. —John T. Birge.

◦ The 1882 diary of Katherine Thayer Jermain:

JERMAIN — THAYER Wednesday, June 7, 1882 at the Jermain Memorial Church, West Troy, by the Rev. G. N. Webber, D. D., pastor of the First Presbyterian Church, Troy, Barclay Jermain of Albany, N. Y. and Katherine S., daughter of the late Hon. Francis S. Thayer of Troy.

An unidentified newspaper clipping, pasted in the diary, announcing the marriage of Barclay Jermain and Katherine Thayer.

I am going back to this sacred holy ceremony and try and tell a few little facts for my own comfort— And so we were married on the 7th of June, one of the loveliest of June days— and every breath was a prayer to our Heavenly Father to guide and keep us— His children— to feel that I was Barclay's wife meant everything and to know that our lives were one, was peace and rest to my heart and soul— and so we turned away from the beautiful church with the notes of the joyful wedding march singing in our ears.

At three o'clock we started together for Brookwood. Barclay seemed to rest during the journey and had very little fever. At eight o'clock we arrived in this lovely spot, away from all, to begin our life together. It seemed so sweet and perfect to be together— And as we said our evening prayer we both felt truly thankful for God's loving kindness. The first few days were spent in planning for the best, and wisest way to live while here. And after a few hours work, our sitting room had such a pretty home look with the little things I had brought out. The drives and little walks were less of an undertaking after a week and my darling seemed better in many ways. Less fever, he slept more and was stronger. Every day we would drive, generally on the Lake Road. And when in the air my Barclay would always seem better. Friday the 30th of June, Dr. Bloss came. He gave Barclay gargles which relieved his throat, but after his visit my dear one seemed each day to grow weaker. Marie came Saturday the 1st of July and we had our tea all together in the sitting room. It was all so bright and cheerful, but I felt that my love was not to be here long. On Sunday my Darling did not get down-stairs until almost three o'clock. He was tired and needed to rest many times during dressing. We walked downstairs together and into the sitting room, where Barclay rested on the lounge. We sat by the door looking out on the Lake and had such a sweet talk, about dear Marie. At about five o'clock the Dr. came and while he was here we went to drive. I helped Barclay to the phaeton and we drove off under the trees, down to the Fennimore Barns, and about the triangle, then home. As usual he seemed invigorated by the fresh air. And after we sat together in the sitting room, until nine o'clock when Jack carried him upstairs. Monday morning we had the usual baths and at about one o'clock Jack carried my dear one down to the piazza, where we sat for a few minutes until Barclay was sufficiently rested to take a drive. We drove up to Lake Road to Thayer's and stopped for a glass of water & a piece of ice which I cracked. And my dear one held the little bits in his mouth. On our return Barclay rested on his Father's bed, had his dinner there, and afterwards we went on the piazza where we sat for an hour or two. I had my dinner there. Jack carried him upstairs at about eight o'clock and he slept rather quietly. In the morning, it being rainy and Marie not being well, I persuaded my Darling not to go downstairs. So we three spent the day in the front room. We had prayers both morning & evening and I sang *Softly now the Light of Day.* Such a precious day. Katie and I carried my dear Barclay to our bed and that night the end began, the changes came. The memory of those next three days is mine, fresh and vivid, and it can never be taken away. The beautiful eyes spoke to me so often. When the lips were still. And the words of my Darling are all near my heart. Friday the 7th, just a month since our bright wedding morning, God called my loved one to himself. His last word & look were mine. His last kiss. And then one more Heavenly smile & my darling had gone to heaven.

∽ Obituaries:

Barclay Jermain, son of J. B. Jermain, one of the most prominent residents of Albany county, died at 11 o'clock this morning at Cooperstown of consumption. Mr. Jermain had been ill for several months but the attack was thought to be malarial, and a serious result was not anticipated. He was married four weeks ago in the Jermain Memorial Church, West Troy to a daughter of the late Hon. F. S. Thayer of this city. Dr. J. P. Bloss of Troy was summoned Wednesday to attend Mr. Jermain but before his departure received a dispatch stating that medical aid would be unavailing. The deceased was a lawyer… His office was in Albany and his residence on the Troy Road… Mr. Jermain was a cultured musician… Though wealthy and of high social position, Mr. Jermain was affable and kind to the humblest whom he met, and his death will be widely deplored. The deceased was about twenty-eight years old, but had attained influence in social, political, and business circles rarely gained at that age. His character and personal accomplishments make his death a loss which will be deeply felt in this vicinity.
—*Unidentified obituary pasted in Katherine's diary.*

The funeral of Barclay Jermain took place at 4 o'clock yesterday afternoon (July 10, 1882) from the late residence at Hedge Lawn on the Troy Road, and was very largely attended by residents of Albany, Troy and other cities, attesting in an eloquent manner the universal esteem in which the deceased was held…   —*Troy Daily Times.*

July 11, 1882, *Office of James B. Jermain,* Albany, N. Y.
[Addressed to Catherine McKie Thayer in London.]
My Dear Mrs. Thayer—   You have undoubtedly heard of the death of my dear son Barclay & its circumstances through your dear daughter Kittie. I write this to urge you not to return home earlier on that account. She will return with my family the latter part of this week to Cooperstown, where we shall all remain 'til the middle of September. She bears up bravely under this sad affliction and is a special comfort to us all. She is as dear to me as one of my very own children and is a great comfort to me & my family under this sad blow. Hoping that this may find you in improved health and that you may be sustained under this sad news.   —Yours Truly, *James B. Jermain.*

Hedge Lawn, July 11, 1882.
My dear Mrs. Thayer—   Kittie has asked me to write again for her today, as she needs all the rest she can get. I could not find time to write until all was over, but you will already have received Father's letter and know that our

Barclay Jermain. W. Kurtz Photographic Studio. Paris, Vienna, Philadelphia, & New York.

Katherine Thayer Jermain as a young widow.

Hedge Lawn, the Albany, New York, residence of the Jermain family.

dear Barclay is at rest. On Friday morning (the 7th) he passed away in sleep. For hours before & indeed all through the previous day & night, he had been unconscious with only intervals in which he came back to us, but in those he knew us all and said many things that are sweet to remember. He knew Kittie until the very end and her voice seemed almost to call him back from the other world. Not 10 minutes before he drew his last breath, he kissed her & smiled. The doctor told us that he did not suffer during the last day & night and it was a comfort to us to know that. Dear Kittie has borne it all so nobly & bravely, we cannot but love her more than ever. …During the last two nights she slept a good deal on the bed beside him while Mr. McCartee and I watched. She asks me to say to you that she is not ill— only worn & weary and that she is going to take great care of herself & you must not worry about her. Katie is most faithful & devoted & will stay with her and sleep near her. It is Kittie's desire to return with father to Cooperstown and she says she could have no peace of mind in going anywhere else but that later in the summer she will consent to go with us to the sea. …Be assured dear Mrs. Thayer that we will do all we can for her to help her bear her sorrow & to comfort and help her. We feel very much for you too, knowing how hard it is for you to be away from her at this time… We all love her so much and father clings to her & finds great comfort in being with her. He has borne up very bravely, is generally very calm, only breaking down now & then, but he will feel this loss more & more as we all will. It has been so sudden, it seems, yet like a dream to us… We all— Kittie, Marie, Will McLure, Robert & myself came home on Saturday… and it was a sad journey. We were able to have a drawing room car to ourselves and dear Barclay's coffin was placed on the floor in the center of the car— where we covered it with a soft shawl & laid on it a cross of white flowers Kittie & I made at Brookwood. We arrived at Albany safely at half-past-seven. The services at the house were yesterday (Monday) afternoon at 4… and after the crowd had dispersed, except a small number of near relatives & friends, we laid him to rest near his mother in that sweet hallowed spot in our cemetery. Some thoughtful members of the family had had the grave lined with evergreens & flowers, so that it seemed scarcely like laying him in a *grave* to leave him there. Kittie will want me to tell you too how sweetly he looked, so peaceful & calm & with a happy smile on his face. She stayed long hours by his side, as he lay in the library and it was she who, with Katie's help, did everything for him— and dressed him. Dr. Bloss has been down to see Kittie— he tells her that if Barclay had gone back with her to Colorado last winter, his life might have been spared some time longer, but after the commencement of this recent trouble in the lung, nothing could have been done for him. Dr. Bloss went out to Cooperstown once, the week before last— at Kittie's request to see Barclay. I feel that there is much more to tell, but perhaps this is enough for the present, and I want to finish this letter in time to send today. We all join with Kittie in warmest love to you & to Mrs. Ada & all. Kittie says she will write to you as soon as she feels able.   —Yours very sincerely, *Julie McCartee.*

Written on the envelope: "First letter from my poor stricken child."

July 16, 1882, Hedge Lawn.
My darling Mother—   It is very hard for me to write even to you. I have nothing to say. My all is gone. Barclay, my darling, is in Heaven & I am left. Julie wrote you so I shall not repeat. One month of the most heavenly love was given to me— it is mine still, and I can live now each hour, each minute & my heart is full of thankfulness to my Heavenly Father for those few short weeks. I find I have no need to go over the ocean. I am only at peace to be where my darling Husband was, here & in Cooperstown & where I have hold of dear Mr. Jermain's hand… I know, or I do not know, how you long to be near me and try to comfort me… But— the first ten days in Cooperstown I did believe my beloved one was better, the absence of night-sweats, fever, refreshing sleep & added strength made my heart, our hearts, glad. The Dr. told me the disease only stopped to grow with greater rapidity. I did everything for my darling from first to the last. Gave him his last bath & put on his underclothes. He knew I would & then they were all so thoughtful & let me do everything I wished. The sacred hours I spent with him— when I could be so near him & kiss the dear lips that were stilled & then his friends, whom he *honored*, bore him away & placed him in a bed of flowers & greens… Julie & Robert are at Brookwood where they will remain for the summer. Helen, Katie, Father & myself go tomorrow… We go to the cemetery, Gods Acre I love to call it, every evening— & last evening at sunset we went to the beautiful church & sat there an hour. Then we have prayers together at night & we talk together of the darling one… I have Barclay's own room in the 3rd story & am among his books & all that was most familiar to him & where we used to sit & look out on the western hills last winter & where he would talk to me of his Mother… A word about your return— You are over the ocean in safety. You are with our dearly loved Adas. You needed an entire change. I feel anxious for you to stay on the other side. Go around a little & see all you can & come back in October. I do not need you. Even you my darling, my most precious one, could not comfort my heart, no one can— & I ask you to stay where you are for my sake… You can do me a great service in looking at headstones. I wish something very beautiful at my Darling's grave & maybe you will be able to see some kind of a cross, or some design which you can get an architect to map for you… Write to your little girl— Kittie, Barclay can not call me his little girl any more. I am tired. I can not write long letters. This is an exception & has been very hard but you will make it out.   —Your own loving daughter *Kittie.*

The Last Will & Testament of Barclay Jermain, Proved and recorded December 18th, 1882… I give devise and bequeath all my property of whatsoever nature and wheresoever situated to Miss Katherine S. Thayer of Troy, and her heirs absolutely and to and for her and their sole use and benefit… executed on the second day of January in the year of our Lord one thousand eight hundred and eighty-two.   —*Barclay Jermain.*

21 Holland Park, Bayswater, London, July 18, 1882.
My dear Frank— [Catherine McKie Thayer to her son]   Out of the depths of a Mother's love and sympathy, I have just written your poor sister, the bride of one short month. As yet, we have only the cable message, sent on the 15th, delayed as I see so plainly, that I might not live through the first few days of darkness with Kittie, never forgetting to spare me even in the midst of this terrible crashing blow. I felt that I must go to her at once, but her message says "do not come, have sent letters." So for these I wait, but I feel that I cannot be long separated from my suffering child. It does seem dreadful that all her bright hopes & anticipations are buried so soon. I have not seen Dr. Churchill, but will try to see him in Paris after hearing from Kittie. I am very well and all are very kind and I shall try to be calm and self controlled, but when my own suffer, I must suffer with them. I hope to hear from you very soon. God keep you and us all. John Birge has visited you before this I suppose. Your loving Mother.   —*C. McKie Thayer*.

July 24th, 1882, Brookwood Point, Cooperstown, N.Y.
My own Darling Mother—   Another Monday. A week today since we came here. The longest week I ever spent, so so lonely— and full of longing. I would not be in any other place and my room where my darling was with me is where I am most restful. I have a large writing table and the little things on it that were down in the sitting room where we used to sit so much. It is a comfort to me to think of your little visit— how you saw us together— and you will always be glad you came… Three weeks ago today we took our last drive together. My great comfort is in knowing how perfectly happy he was in my love & how I filled his heart. The night before he went to Heaven I was beside him on the bed & he was looking at me. And all the time I was given strength to control myself & he said turning to Robert, "Those beautiful eyes, they are so lovely." So you see my eyes were not red.   —Good-bye, God bless you. Your *Kittie*.

July 25, 1882. Cooperstown, New York. [Postcard from Kittie to her brother.]
Dear Frank— Please write me. I am anxious to hear from you. Mother is well, heard yesterday. I am quite well. Hope you will get on all right and that the Puppy will be acceptable. All well here. Weather beautiful. Lake a constant pleasure to all. I can not write letters & so you will excuse postals. Much love from your sister —*Kittie*.

◞ Letters from Europe:

Dover, Kent, England, August 8, 1882.
My Darling Child—   …We left London at 12:45 and came 68 miles to Canterbury, where we stopped three hours and saw the Cathedral, a glory of the older time, Norman & Gothic, and here the Black Prince is buried. Nothing in architecture has seemed so wonderfully beautiful to me. What shall I say to you my poor stricken darling is just this— that I do feel that if we were together, I think I could do something for you. I could not bring back the "loved and gone before." I could not drive away the darkness that has settled on the future, all that is before you, as it seems to you, but perhaps we could

The Marble Arch, London.

look so steadily, so constantly, toward our Father's house, and strive so earnestly to do our duty, that something like a more peaceful resignation might sometimes come to your poor heart. We read that God promised to comfort "even as a Mother comforteth." …You must guard your health… to have you ill would kill me. God has work for you still, His work, I know you feel all this, but we must speak to each other fully.   —Your loving *Mother*.

Dover, August 8, 1882.
My dearest Kittie—   I have wished for you more than ever today for we have seen a sight that would I know appeal to you— Canterbury Cathedral. So grand & magnificent & so solemn it fairly breathes devotion into one's mind. I felt you & I could have walked about & almost lost our sorrows in the contemplation of this superb old structure that has withstood destruction so many hundred years. It is not to be described. One must see it to realize its glory & beauty… Do keep well & try & get change of air for you need it. What sweet memories you have & how truly you have been & are blessed in having the confidence & love of so true a man. He is *yours* Kittie & *forever* remember that. God bless you & spare us to meet ere long. Ever yours,   —*Ada*.

Belgium, August 13, 1882.
My darling little One—   …How is it with you my darling child today? I know how in many respects it is. "So many weeks ago today this was done." And so your weeks pass. My heart is heavy, heavy; the lightness what there was, and there was great joy for you and your beloved one, and for myself, through you two precious ones, seems to have departed, but I try to think of God's love, that he has given our loved ones victory over death through His dear son, and you are my precious child still, and my dear boy is spared, and there are so many mercies and blessings that they cannot be numbered and I try to feel resigned to God's will and pray for the same for you… Ada sends love in which my whole soul joins.   —*Mother*.

August 14, 1882, Belgium.
My dear Frank—   Yours of 26th came just as we were leaving London, and I had time to send you a p.c. only. We, the Adas and myself, left London Tuesday at 12 noon for Dover by the Sea, stopped two hours at Canterbury Cathedral, which impressed me more than any of the grand old treasures I have seen. It stands on a little green common with a few trees scattered about it… As to your arrangements for building, I am just waiting to hear what you do or have done. I know you will do your best, and if you make a mistake only *once*, you will learn constantly, experience is a thorough teacher or should be…   —Your loving *Mother*.

August 16, 1882, Cooperstown.
My dear Brother Frank—   I have had two letters from Mother within three days. She is very well and anticipates going to Switzerland and Germany… The weather is lovely but very very dry. The grass is brown and no sign of rain… Every evening we drive and I enjoy going along this lovely lake. Next week an artist is coming to paint the view from the piazza… I should so like to have you write me of your buildings and just what you are doing. I am so so lonely, and it is an effort to live day after day when the light has gone which made all so bright. I hope all is well with you dear Buzzie. We must nei-

La Staubbach à Lauterbrunnen drawing on hotel stationery used by Catherine Thayer.

ther of us give Mother any cause for trouble— and by God's grace we can do much to make her happy. With much love and praying God to bless & keep you, I am ever your affectionate sister, —*Kittie.*

Hedge Lawn, August 20, 1882.
My Dear Mrs. Thayer— Your very kind letter to me arrived a few days since, but was inadvertently left by me in Brookwood, Cooperstown… I am happy to say that (your daughter's) health has much improved and that she considers herself *well*… She is very dear to us… She is very kind and affectionate to me, and I love her as my own child. We intend to remain at Brookwood until the middle of next month… —*James B. Jermain.*

Le Staubbach à Lauterbrunnen Switzerland, August 23, 1882.
Dear Frank— We are just down 7 miles from a hotel facing the view above— glorious and beautiful. We go to Berne… Kittie has sent for a *male* St. Bernard pup… so I travel with a dog again but she wishes to preserve the breed and *you* know my self denial is a *luxury* to *myself*. God prosper you in all things. Do you go to Church? —*Your loving Mother.*

August 28th, 1882, Brookwood Point, Cooperstown, N.Y.
My dearest Mother— Another Monday has come. And I hardly know where to turn. The restless longing for my Darling is so hard to bear. And each day I see how necessary he was to me and my happiness. The others were not dependent upon him. As I was. Julie has Robert and the others were all living their lives, but my life was his. And now I feel so alone… I am going to send you a cable this week, for it must seem such a long time to wait for news. I wonder I never thought of it before… Kiss the Adas and ask Aunt Ada to write me a line. Ever your aff. Daughter, —*Kittie.*

September 1st, 1882, Brookwood Point, Cooperstown, N.Y.
My own dear Mother— Your letters do not come so often since you

Right: Brookwood, Cooperstown, New York, in 1882 the summer residence of the Jermain family and where Barclay Jermain died. Above: Lake Otsego from Brookwood.

started on your continental tour, but I know you are writing every few days, and that now you must be in Switzerland… God bless & keep you always. Ever you affectionate   —*Kittie.*

September 14th, 1882, The Old Home.
Brookwood Point, Cooperstown, N.Y.
My Dearest Mother—   One year ago today since I went to Troy and in driving to our house met dear Barclay. And he came in and took a cup of tea with me. How long ago it seems, and yes, only a year. A year tomorrow since my darling and I spent the day in the lovely country together. And then all the days following have their such sacred associations. I feel that Barclay is very near me. And I seem to think of him all the time. How kind the Heavenly Father was to let us live even for our short month together. And how much I have for which to be thankful… In a day or two I shall be away from this lovely spot. And no one can ever know the rest and peace I have experienced while here…   Ever your own —*Kittie.*

November 14, 1882, Hedge Lawn.
My dear son Frank—   I am so grieved and anxious in not hearing from you that I hardly know what I am about. Surely I feel that a letter must have gone astray as your last telegram more than two weeks ago said you had written. If I were fully able or felt that I could go I would lose no time in going to Iowa. If I feel stronger I may go, but certainly unless I hear something definite and satisfactory I must send someone soon if I cannot go myself, as I cannot bear this suspense much longer. Every night I pray for the morning mail and every morning for the night mail, hoping I may receive some intelligence. If you are ill I *should know it*, and if not I should hear from you, and so my mind and heart are rent with conflicting thoughts. Do my dear son put an end to this long suspense in some way. I am weary, weary, weary. Your sister tries to bear her sorrow alone, to carry her burden. God help her. May God keep you and us in all things. Ever your loving praying hopeful Mother.   —*C. McK. Thayer.*

XIV   The Summer of 1882 ✦ Disease, Marriage, and Death   463

◦∽ A diary:

May 27, 1882. Kittie left early for Lakewood N. Jersey to join Barclay.
May 29. Either this p.m. or tomorrow I cannot now say which, Ada and I went to Albany Cemetery after calling at Mr. Jermain's. Saw the Jermain Memorial. We read all the inscriptions & I said, "here dear B. stood when his mother was buried."
June 7. This was written in London about the 28th. Troy. Today at 1 o'clock at the Jermain Memorial Church my darling Kittie and Barclay Jermain were married. Ada & I went to Mr. Jermain's & dined & saw the bridal party leave for Cooperstown. God bless them and make Barclay well.
June 10. This p.m. I left for Cooperstown to see my dear children— found Kittie looking well, but I thought under a well disguised appearance I could almost feel a great weight of anxious responsibility in sympathy with her dear Barclay…
June 12. This a.m. rose early, breakfasted before the open fire. It does seem so strange to have my dear little girl leave me and give her presence to another, but I thank God for the love these two bear each other, and my prayer is the same, that they may enjoy each other many years…
June 24. Safely arrived at Liverpool & London by rail…
July 5. Ada and I went in p.m. to Botanical Gardens. Saw such beautiful flowers…
July 7. Friday the 7th. At Cooperstown dear Barclay died at 11 o'clock— how can my poor child bear this death of her love and all her future with him. I did not know of this until by message on Monday the 17th…
July 10. This written later. Dear Barclay buried beside his mother at 4 p.m. Little did I think when looking at the burial place of his dear Mother, that so soon, so soon, in six brief weeks, he would be buried beside her… God help the mourning ones.
  —*Excerpts from the 1882 diary of Catherine McKie Thayer, a small diary that she purchased and wrote when in London. Therefore, some of the entries are retrospective.*

Albany Rural Cemetery, Albany, New York. The grave of Barclay Jermain, Celtic cross, and his parents, James Barclay Jermain, August 13, 1809–July 12, 1897, and Catherine Rice Jermain, 1823–1873.

1883

Colorado Springs, Jan 22, 1882.
My dear darling—   …It is evident from what you say, that Mr. Jermain considered the sum invested, more or less & yours by will— *permanent investment* on the principle that it will not do to kill the goose that lays the golden egg. You see, that if you come to cut down the principal, the am't of the check you speak of every year or two, your income, would gradually diminish. When you said you had plenty of spending money, I thought of course you meant, of *income* and as you did not send me "the little book" I could not judge for myself. I really think Kittie, and I say it in all kindness, that you do not know how fast money goes and for your income you are too generous to your friends and you need not go *out* of Mr. Jermain's family to learn the lesson of careful expenditure. Now, as I should *be very sorry* that Mr. J— as you say should think you are extravagant, and as the payment of the check for $500 will leave your bk acc't "very low" (and debts to pay?) I send you New York draft for $500. If you owe when this reaches you *pay your debts* from it but do not make another one, not *actually needful* to you. Watch the little outlays and do not let the generous nature of your heart

The letter must have been written in 1883, not 1882 as it is dated, since it refers to "will" and Barclay Jermain had died in July 1882.

Katherine Thayer Jermain, J. H. Kent, Photographer, Rochester, New York.

overcome your judgment, just let your friends *learn* that you have not a large income and have not a large sum to draw from. Our expenditures as a family the last two years have been great for our means, but we did what we thought best at the time, and will not complain now… —*Mother.*

∾ James B. Jermain to Katherine Thayer Jermain:

February 9, 1883.
My Dear Daughter—   Your letter of yesterday received this morn and read with delight… You have been of great comfort to me in our sad bereavement…   —*James B. Jermain.*

February 9, 1883.
My Dear Daughter—   Yours of the 8th received this am & read with great pleasure… We miss you very much at home and regret that you are not here to enjoy the fine sleighing we have had for the last few days. There is nothing new at home…   —*James B. Jermain.*

April 30, 1883.
My Dear Daughter—   …You & Barclay are more frequently in my thoughts than any other of my children and… I long for the time when I shall again see you…   —*James B. Jermain.*

∾

In May of 1882, Robert Koch, working in his laboratory at the Imperial Health Office in Berlin, Germany, announced that his research team had isolated the germ that caused tuberculosis. Six years earlier Koch had published his pioneering work identifying the germ that caused anthrax. In 1883, as leader of the German Cholera Commission, he traveled to Egypt where he isolated the germ that caused cholera. Koch's findings ended the belief that "bad air" caused these diseases, and he was awarded the Nobel Prize for Medicine in 1905.

After the death of his only son, James B. Jermain endowed the Barclay Jermain Professorship of Natural Philosophy at Williams College, his son's Alma Mater.

XV

The 1880s

A Young Lawyer Goes West

AMERICA was growing in the 1880s and James Garfield was elected President in November of that year. In 1881 the U. S. Supreme Court ruled that income taxes were constitutional, Clara Barton organized the American Red Cross, and Kansas became the first state to prohibit all alcoholic beverages. The American west was still a place of adventure, for in 1881 outlaw William H. "Billy the Kid" Bonney, Jr., was shot and killed in Fort Sumner, New Mexico, and Sioux Indian leader Sitting Bull, a fugitive since the 1876 Battle of Little Big Horn, surrendered to federal troops. These were times of industrial expansion and natural catastrophes. After being under construction for fourteen years, the Brooklyn Bridge was opened in 1883. Built at a cost of $15 million, this was the longest, 1,595 feet, suspension bridge yet built. Only six days after the bridge was opened, twelve people were trampled to death when there was a stampede in response to a rumor that the bridge was going to collapse. The 1883 volcanic explosion on the island of Krakatoa killed an estimated 36,000 people and caused tidal waves around the world, and the dust then thrown into the atmosphere tinted sunsets for many years to come.

In 1883 Congress reduced letter postage to two cents per half ounce. The following year letter writers welcomed Lewis Waterman's new invention, a practical fountain pen. In 1884 the Supreme Court found that Congress had the legal authority to print treasury notes, then called "greenbacks," as the legal tender in the country. In that same year Mark Twain's *The Adventures of Huckleberry Finn* was published. In November 1884, Grover Cleveland was elected President. In the following year the Washington Monument was dedicated, Congress forbid the unauthorized fencing of public lands in the West by cattle and railroad companies, and letter writers welcomed a new service from the Post Office, *Special Delivery* mail. In July 1885 General, and two-term President, Ulysses Grant died and a battalion from Virginia marched in his funeral cortege. During these years exploited factory workers were being organized into unions, and in 1886 the American Federation of Labor was organized in Columbus, Ohio. The telephone, invented in 1876, was beginning to spread across America with long distance lines being established between Chicago and New York in 1883 and New York and Boston in 1884. A box camera, loaded with film, was for the first time marketed by the Eastman Company of Rochester, New York, in 1885.

In Virginia, a young Henry Wise Hobson had graduated from law school at the University of Virginia and was practicing law with his uncle, John S. Wise. However, Hobson must have been restless and anxious for a change, and he must have been planning to go out west to seek his fortune.

Letters by:
A. H. Garland, Attorney General of the United States
Annie Jennings Wise Hobson
Henry Wise Hobson
John Cannon Hobson
Thomas Nelson Page
The Stewarts— Ann, Lucy, Marion & Norma, Virginia friends of Henry Wise Hobson living at Brook Hill in Henrico County
John S. Wise

Letters written from: Buena Vista, Cañon City, and Denver, Colorado; Washington, D. C.; Alexandria, Richmond, Ashland, Petersburg, Howard's Neck, Goochland County, and Brook Hill, Henrico County, Virginia.

1881

Gone West:

In the rush and press of the Centennial, many matters of minor and of greater importance were permitted to pass unnoticed at the time. Among these was the removal to the West of one of the most talented and promising young lawyers at our bar, Henry Wise Hobson, who has gone to practice law in Buena Vista, Colorado. When any one of Virginia's sons moves away she is deprived of just so much vitality and the whole State is the loser to that extent. It is not too much to say that since the war no young man has gone forth from our borders whose loss will be more sensibly felt. Of distinguished lineage, Mr. Hobson possesses in large measure the brain, the courage, the independence, and the energy which made his grandfather Gov. Wise, the head of his party. He had immediately upon coming to the bar taken position there with the foremost of our young lawyers, and had already made his mark before he left Virginia. His many friends will be glad to hear that he has fair prospects at the start in one of the most flourishing towns in Colorado, and will unite with us in bespeaking for him a bright future and large success in his adopted State.

—*Unidentified and undated newspaper clipping from the papers of Annie Jennings Wise Hobson.*

Letters to Brook Hill:

Buena Vista, Colo. December 4, 1881.
My dear Miss Lucy—   …Miss Marion bemoans my "unhappy state" of having to write to all of the Stewart family. Well I can't agree with her, for I take them turn about and find about my only recreation is in writing to them and a few others. Then you see it serves another purpose viz: to make me remember that I am a gentleman, for I have no other intercourse with ladies. I feel like saying sometimes, as Disraeli I believe said of Palmerston, "There was a gentleman, even if he was Old Harry." You all would really laugh to see me sometimes. When I go to meals it is just as probable as not that I have negroes, Chinamen, Mexicans, washerwomen, common laborers, butchers, bar-keepers, gamblers

etc. as companions. I have had them all. Some of the miners out here call me Hobson; Henry etc. as familiarly as if we were old chums. It reminds me of Falstaff when he signed himself— "Jack Falstaff with my familiars; John with my brothers and sisters; Sir John to all the rest of Europe." But such is Western life, and you all no doubt will be charmed with my improvement in manners when I get back. But really, amongst these miners you sometimes meet with fellows roughly dressed, fearfully ungrammatical, coarsely oathed, who yet have much innate gentility of feeling, and who are honest as day and big-hearted as a bushel-basket. You can depend on these men under any circumstances. Then you see some splendid men wrecked in this country. Just across the passage is a man named Orrick, who is a perfect gentleman in his instincts and manners. This man was once a leading lawyer in Missouri, his family good and his surroundings refined. He is now a drunkard and keeps us awake half the night and bores us to death half the day. One night, when about half drunk, he gave me a history of his life and troubles, and I really felt so sorry for the poor wretch that I could hardly keep my eyes dry. The only way to keep up the hill in this country, is never to start down.

I have been annoyed lately with Rhett's indisposition. He has a chronic affection which may at some future day take a fatal turn, and yet he is seemingly indifferent to it and is very careless. Cold only makes him worse, and I have a time of it keeping him from catching cold. He and I get on so nicely, and I really believe he is becoming quite fond of me. I think it pretty well decided that we will stay permanently associated and make our fortunes jointly.

Rhett An unknown person, perhaps an employee in the law office.

As Xmas-tide draws nigh my heart begins to yearn to be with you all, and feel somewhat of home-feeling. If I am ever rich and able to found a home I am going to have such bright happy Xmas times. I intend to have a gathering of choice spirits at every Yuletide and a sacred circle of all my old friends and loved ones. You know such anticipations make my life much easier and brighter now, for I am already trying to learn heart-songs of joy for the coming times.

Antique fire engines outside the Buena Vista Courthouse. Buena Vista, Colorado.

I hear you are going to South Carolina to join Mrs. P. When do you go? I really envy you, for I have heard that So. Car. was really a Paradise of beauty during the winter months, when one can enjoy themselves outdoors. I remember hearing Mannie Rutherford describe it. Probably my impressions are due to the fact that I used to think she spoke in words of charmed music. Rhett however tells me that the winter months there are very delightful.

We had a fire the other night in the building next to us, or rather I should say shell, for such are our houses. A fire in these mountain towns does not generally stop under a quarter of the town, and so for a time we thought we would have a fine holocaust of our books and worldly possessions. But fortunately this fiend was mastered before reaching our building. You see they have very little water here and a fire is about the most serious thing to fear. Any of these people would rather face a seven-shooter than a burning house.

Tell Miss Hope and the fair housekeeper of the family that their last letters are stored away in my most valuable repository and shall be answered soon.

Indeed you know how much I value your good opinions and I do assure you it did me much real good to appreciate that I had contributed to the comfort of others in the slightest degree. Will you believe me when I say that you have a right to say anything you please at all times to me. Give much love to all my family, and be sure to kiss S— for me, and don't forget Uncle Dan. And believe me to be—   Ever as I ever was, *Henry W. Hobson.*

◦ Annie Hobson writes to Thomas Nelson Page:

1319 N. Y. Ave. Washington, December 29th, 1881.
Dear Mr. Page—   Your letter acknowledging so gracefully the small Xmas token, that was meant to show that I remembered you and would like to do better, was received this morning. Did you not get my letter inclosing a card for your Mother? I am glad that you spent Xmas day with your Mother— that was the most acceptable way of testifying your affection to her. I received a loving & very precious letter from Henry telling that his Xmas gift to me was to tell me he had not taken liquor or used tobacco in any way since in Colorado. An editor who was a Virginian said to him not long ago— "Hobson, you neither smoke, chew, drink, or cuss?" "No." "Well, just let me publish that in my paper & you can give up law & exhibit yourself at 25 cts a head out here & soon your fortune will be made." He is indeed homesick, and his last letter was so positive in asserting that I should never come to Buena Vista, that it depressed me very much… We have had a very quiet Xmas but it was pleasant… We had our plum pudding on Monday… Miss Norma S— [Stewart] sent me a lovely Xmas card with an appropriate motto or rather a motto of sweet greeting. I wish to send her a New Year's card & to write so please forward me her address at once… Henry said I would receive $150 quarterly the first quarter beginning the first of January. I have plenty of money for my present need… Any money coming to me I wish deposited in Bank & please send me some blank checks… May the New Year bring you God's best blessing… If you knew how often I have had to put my pen down & be distracted you would wonder that my letter is as decent as it is… Love to your Mother when you write. Yours truly & afftctly.   —*A. J. W. Hobson* (Rare Book, Manuscript, and Special Collections Library, Duke University.)

◦ A letter from his brother in Virginia:

Petersburg Va. 409 Washington Street. Dec. 29th, 1881.
My dear Henry—   This letter will be late in reaching you, but I hope not too late to show my love & thoughts of you at this season.

    Another year has rolled around, and is about to pass away with all its troubles and trials, triumphs, and rejoicings. It is a year which has been blessed to me in many ways. It has seen me successfully and honorably finish my course of preparation for life's work and at last started out in a course which by God's help I trust will be one of highest usefulness to my fellow men, a joy to those who love me, and one of true glory to God. That I am thus at last straightened out I owe to you, my dear brother, into whose heart God has put it to help me. No mere phrase of words can convey the deep feelings of my thankfulness to you. I feel more than thankful, I feel blessed and honored in having the love of such a brother as you have been to me. For truly it has not been on account of anything deserving in me— far otherwise. I know full well. And it is the knowledge of this, which makes your action the more precious to my heart. I thank God that He has enabled me to show my deep appreciation in some small measure by a course of which you need not feel ashamed. I pray Him at the beginning of this year that henceforth you may never have cause to regret your help to an undeserving brother. This year opens before me with fairer prospects than has many a year past. I feel again some of those anticipations of the future (mellowed it is true with experience, but all the better for that) which used to light up my hopes in the years long gone. I feel once more active impulses of a fresh life. Years long gone by flit before me, scenes of our boyhood and youth crowd upon my memory— and then darker shadows come. But I dispel them— light is before me, Thank God. And with it all there is a feeling, too deep for words, to you, my brother. And as you stand upon the threshold of another year, I trust it is one of beauty to you. The past year I know has been one of much self-denial and heavy burden, and yet even these must glow as the clouds of evening with the consciousness of duty done, of magnanimous love, and I trust too, of partial reward at least, in the knowledge that your labor has not been in vain. Then let the old year go with thankfulness, and hail the New with joy. There are hearts loving you truly praying for you daily here. There is great work and high honors before you— not merely the world's plaudits (let these come if they will) but good wishes of good men, and honorable standing among honorable men. This be your crown. And I pray God too that your life be blessed not only in this world's blessings, but in the blessings of His grace. My heart's prayer each day is that you may truly know God in Christ Jesus. May I not make one request of you? *I am not going to "preach."* It is this: In your life of business and daily harassing cares, read some in the Bible and do not forget to ask for *light*. Now I am done. God bless you through this coming year and for all time. The little ones send heaps of love to Uncle Henry. Alice joins me in much love. I send you a card, not for the beauty of the picture, but for the sweetness of the words on the back. They truly express what we would all say. So take it as from us all.   —Your affec. brother, *John C. Hobson.*
—Excuse this writing, as I write on a very bad table.

1882

◦ Letters to Brook Hill:

Buena Vista, Colo. January 29, 1882.
My dear "Sister Lucy—"   …Of course I want you to call me Henry and I am delighted to know that I have at least gained such a place in your good opinion and estimation that you will call me by my name, for I know I could have no higher evidence of your feelings towards me. And now let me thank you for your letter which was just as nice and sweet as you always are— But I am not going to pay compliments for you know what I think of you. I am so delighted that Mrs. Pinckney is so much better this winter, though that cuts me off from the hope of a possibility of her coming to Colorado with one of you. I can sympathize with her in her catarrh troubles for I suffer much with it up in these mountains. I am sorry to tell you that I have since January 1st had quite a severe attack of fever and I have not yet really recovered. The worst effects thereof are, that it seemed to open my system to rheumatism from which I suffer acutely sometimes… Do thank Mrs. Pinckney for her kind thoughtfulness in sending me the card during Xmas season. In fact I have to thank your family, one and all for the only Xmas I had. The box sent me from Brook Hill was just splendid and no school-boy was ever more delighted with a box from home than I was with the one from the Home that has adopted me. Your photograph was very good and as part of the contents of the box pleased me more than the family pictures. The girls are still very sweet about writing to me, and I assure you it does me great good. It seems so funny to think of you being in a spring-like climate. Out here we are bound in by mountains of snow that almost shut out the sky and I get so tired at times of seeing the endless dreary wastes of snow. Did I ever write to any of you that up on the top of the Continental Divide, there are places where a man can stand in summer, with one foot on the Pacific slope buried in a bed of the most exquisite wild flowers, and the other foot on the Atlantic side,

Courthouse, Buena Vista, Colorado.

Buena Vista from the Colorado Midland R. R. W. H. Jackson & Co., Rocky Mountain Scenery.

planted in a bank of snow. Now isn't that curious… I have lately been very busy in the District Court and it has sometimes almost worked me to death. Justice is more of a fiction than reality out here. Men are rarely punished for crime though many are committed. There have been no parties here lately worth mentioning so I can give you little social news except that recently the belle of the town was taken to a Hop by a bar-room keeper… I won't attempt to give you any Richmond news though my correspondents keep me pretty well informed. Then I take the *Dispatch,* that paper of magnificent nothingness. I do wish we could have such a paper in Virginia as three or four of the Denver dailies. Well I must close as my rheumatic old arm is beginning to "have a surly time" of pain. When are you going back to Virginia? …I hope to see you ere a year has come and gone. With warm and affectionate regards I am— Yours as ever, *Henry W. Hobson.*

1883

Cañon City, Colo. April 22, 1883.
My dear Miss Anne— As I laid aside your recently received letter, with its excuses for not having been written sooner, I could not help saying to myself, (for you know I have no one else to say it to), "Well she makes up for all delay by such a nice sweet letter." Don't ever think it necessary to apologize to me for not writing, for though letters from Brook Hill come to me as rays of sunshine, yet I never think I am forgotten because forsooth many days come and go without this sunlight. And with all your duties and occupations I know that it is oftentimes a sacrifice of some pleasure hour to write to me. I can truly sympathize at this moment with your sufferings from cold. As I was coming down from Buena Vista the other night there was a brute aboard who would [not] keep his window up, and I took a most fearful cold and have since been suffering a good deal with neuralgia. I thought I had come to a place where I would be free from the above bane of all enjoyment of life, but I find I have not and that my old bad habits are coming back on me… I would strike out South but for the fact that down there I would have the

Apaches and Mexicans, and it is a fair question as to which is the worse, to keep your scalp and the neuralgia or get rid of the latter at the expense of the former. I imagine I would not have such a distinguished appearance without any top to my head. But seriously I am thinking of going somewhere else next year, either to Arizona or Texas, for though one may cast [illegible] upon the rolling nature of my course, yet it makes very little difference to me, and I believe I would just as well roll as lie still. Moreover I never did think it would be becoming to a fellow to have a coating of moss all over him, he had better turn shepherd and clothe himself with sheepskin…

I have been on the go a great deal lately and oftentimes long for a little rest and quiet, for I am weary at times of perpetual motion. My two offices seem to require my constant attention in the matter of detail and system as neither of my partners ever dreamed of such a word as system and regularity. For instance, in the matter of correspondence, neither have any idea of the importance of promptness. But there is one striking difference between them. Rhett will let a letter received, lie for two or three weeks unanswered, to season; but Mr. Macon will answer a letter and then hide his answer for a couple of weeks to let the ink get well dried. The first thing I always do when I come to my Cañon office is to make a thorough search for letters, and I have been seriously considering the advisability of putting a card in the papers advertising for lost letters, for Mr. Macon has found out that I hunt for letters in the office, so he takes them to some other fellow's office to hide. A man brought me in three letters yesterday which he had run across… You guess correctly when you say that my life is not all that I could wish, but then I know full well that there are so many others who have so much more to make their lives sorrowful. My life is rather gray but there are so many that I know whose lives are black and stormy. And so I try not to complain and to hope for brighter times, for days of sunshine must come to all, sooner or later in life. I am so glad to know that both you and all the family are well… Excuse the haste of this letter but I have very little time and several other folks to write to. How I wish I were with you now. Give much love to all and yourself in particular.   —Yours affectionately, *Henry W. Hobson.*

༄ Letters from Virginia:

The letter was written on Henry Hobson's twenty-fifth birthday.

Howard's Neck A house in Goochland County owned by John David Hobson, a brother of Plumer Hobson

Howard's Neck, July 9th, 1883.
My dearest Son—   God bless you on this your 26th birthday. Surely this is the anniversary of the most blessed era of my life —the golden day that saw me given forever to your father— the day that God gave me such a son—

As I look through the twenty-six years of the past, and stand in solemn thankfulness over the mercies and blessings that are mine in the present, and then trust God for all the coming years, my heart and mind are too full for utterance— I feel overpowered by the thoughts and feelings which fill my whole soul. If I could find words to express what I would like, my letter would glow with love and gratitude, but indeed I feel too oppressed or rather too overwhelmed to speak…

You must feel that your Mother's love surrounds you— no distance can keep that away, and her prayers ever hover over you.

I do hope the birthday letters, the box and my letter all reached you in good time, and will all show how much we would like to do for our far away boy— Ah, when that word 'far away' sends a pang of pain through my heart— I hold still and say "Never far away from our Father's guidance and care"—

At last I escaped from Richmond heat on Saturday, leaving all there as usual. Mr. Page came to the train with me and was as kind and considerate as possible— Cannon met me at Pemberton, but I rode up to Cayhoes Neck and got off there— On the top of the hill stood the two little boys, Cannon and Henry, to welcome me. I do wish you could have seen how sweet the little fellows looked; both kissed me as though they knew Grandma well— Cannon looked radiant— Soon after we started Cannon said, "You see my clean dress?" Then, "I've a real nice little boy at the house for you Grandma." "Who is he?" "My little brother." "Where did he come from?" "The doctor brought him to Mamma."

My little brother   George R. Hobson born April 13, 1883.

They say he asked several times, "Can't Uncle Henry come with Grandma?" He constantly speaks of you— The little baby is a fine little fellow and seems to be very good— he does not look much like either— but is more like Cannon— There is something in his face that reminds me of your Grandma Hobson. Soon Sister Kittie and Alice came to meet me— All gave me such a warm welcome, —I feel always at home here and am always so comfortable— Already I feel better for the country air, and I can tell you it has been warm, until this morning when we have a cool rain— Alice is better looking than I have ever seen her. Bro. John is very quiet —has not been able to get liquor to spree on since Xmas— He looks silent and dejected.

I took breakfast with Lily at Mary L's Saturday morning— She will come up tomorrow or next day. She has been having a charming time in Norfolk going several times to Old Point— Mary and Josephine will go to Hampton tomorrow to board in a private boarding house, where they can get a bath— Ocean View was so crowded they could not find a room there.

Mr. Page told me on the cars that he was again more hopeful and believed he might get married next winter— Of course in strict confidence— I felt greatly relieved for him.

I sent a bunch of flowers and a few [illegible] words to Lizzie Lyons before leaving— never have seen the boy. The universal comment about Jimmie is that he does carry his head higher than ever —Lizzie Anderson's son is said to be a splendid specimen.

I hope you were able to find the connection between that last crazy letter I sent you.—

Sister Kittie receives very encouraging accounts from Selden who is charmed with Oregon— If Plumer goes on developing as at present he will be a giant.

I brought the children up a new croquet set and expect to enjoy some games very much myself.

God grant you my precious noble son many returns of your birthday and should He thus spare you to Earth, I feel that they will be years of progression —and development —years wherein you will tread upward and onward to higher attainments and greater usefulness— and above all do I pray that each passing birthday will find you nearer to God, higher in spiritual power and life. All here I know join me in love—

Think of me as finding it great pleasure to be with Cannon and his children —the baby coos and laughs to me, and seems to find Grandma very agreeable.
The peace of God keep you in heart and mind through our Lord Jesus Christ— Your loving mother— *A.J.W. Hobson*

303 E. Franklin, Richmond, Aug 22, 1883.

Dear Henry—   Your letter was duly received and would have been answered before this, but I have been in constant state of motion for the past week, and Tom Page has been as hard to get hold of as a flea. I intended writing to you before I received your letter and will write what I wanted specially to say before answering your questions.

I find upon close calculation that living as I am now doing, boarding Alice & the children & boarding myself at the Seminary, that it takes every cent of $900. You know that I have conveyed all my interest in the Eastwood notes to you in consideration of your help to me. I feel very down in the mouth sometimes & like just trying to get something to do to support myself. But I know that you & Mother are anxious for me to get my profession & I feel that it is due to you that I should. This is what makes me consent to receive your kind and loving help. I leave it to you as to what I shall do & how manage for this year. I can obtain help from some of the educational societies, but you & Mother were very much opposed to it last year. I had hoped to get the place I spoke of at the Seminary, but the fellow seems inclined to hold on and I am afraid I shall not get. That would have paid me $300. I owe a little over $100 which I have to pay by the 10th of September and would like to get that amount by that time.

Now as to your questions— 1st. The loan is $1164 & is due on the 30th of October. 2nd. I should like the money to come in installments every 3 months. I should like very much to have $250 now, which would include the $100 I spoke of above, and the rest you can arrange to suit yourself, as I can make my arrangements accord with yours without any trouble. 3rd. Mother is very much in favor of going to Ashland and I think it is a very good plan in many respects. I think she needs to go off from here where she is always mixed with Aunt Néné & her affairs, and I think the children would brighten her life for her. I made the calculation of expenses with her the other day and I think $75 for house rent & all expenses, except clothes, a full allowance per month. It costs me from $250 to $275 at the Seminary for nine months. I allow $150 for clothes for us all & a little extra expenses. What remains over from these two amounts goes for living expenses. From this you can see what it costs me to live & what I can give towards defraying expenses at Ashland, on a basis of $900. This is a horrid pen & you must excuse the writing. 4th. I leave the whole management of the finances in your hands and perfectly willing that you do whatever you think best. Tom says he does not think there will be any trouble in disposing of the notes, and that he has already seen Hill on the subject.

Now about another point— I have told Mother, my dear old fellow, that I desired that she leave all her possessions to you. To you they ought to go & to you they must go. I am not only willing, but glad that it should be so.

Now I have written as fully as I believe necessary on the above points and am willing to do whatever you think best & want you to give me your exact ideas on the subject of what I wrote in the first part of the letter.

I have taken a great interest in your contemplated change of location and have thought much over it. But I have not written to you to give any advice on the subject because I thought you were far more able to determine what is best than I could possibly be here. I saw Henry Coke when here & talked with him on the subject. There certainly seems to be an excellent opening in Texas.

At the same time, as far as I am able to judge, I think it would be risky in you to go there now, and that you would be much safer in going to Denver than to Texas. You have made a name & reputation for yourself in Colorado which will follow you to Denver. In Texas you would have to start entirely fresh as when you first went to Colo. I have no doubt that you would succeed in Texas, but it seems to me a more immediate success awaits you in Denver. But, as I said before, you are better able to judge for yourself than we can here. You know that my prayers go with you wherever you decide to go.

I have already written you a longer letter than you will care to read, I expect, & so will close up. I like the work here very much, but hate to have to be separated so from Alice & the children after being away from them so long. I shall enjoy my stay at home very much next month. The session does not begin until Oct. 1st. I believe I have given general satisfaction at the church & much gratified at times by the kind remarks which are made to me. Mother has been in an upset condition, and I don't think I ever saw her in more depressed state of mind. I have been doing my best to get her away from here, and thought I had her off this morning, but she changed here mind. She will certainly go off to the Blue Ridge in the morning however, and I think the change will do her good. Let me hear from you soon. Alice & the boys would send love I know. —Your affec. bro. *John C. Hobson.*

August 27, 1883, Richmond.
Dear Henry— …I have sold Woodlawn for $8,500 & everything is ready… 1/3 to Wise heirs to wit $2,476.16. Of this Sister Annie gets 1/3, Mrs. Garnett 1/3— H. A. Wise's children 1/3 = $826.38… Your cash will be diminished probably by $10 to $15 by expenses of Judge Hewes & myself… From the above you can easily see what to expect…

— Now as to other business… I am sorry to hear you contemplate a change. I hoped you had been so fortunate as to strike a place where you could make money & after a while save enough to come home, but Sister Annie tells me you have no idea of returning to Virginia in any event at any time. You & I doubtless feel differently about such matters for while I "cuss" the infernal old hole— sometimes I think I will rest my [illegible] here for it is about as good as anywhere else. Of course if the Colorado climate affects your health you ought not to stay, but independent of that I think it unwise to shift from place to place. You are young now but every year is precious in that it, passed in one spot, identifies you with the people, enables you to understand their laws, wants & woes & ensures you their employment, whereas changing, the time past is lost, the time to come must be consumed in reaching anew the point abandoned at your present location. I only throw out these suggestions which have doubtless occurred to you often & over, because you know my dear Henry, that I want you to succeed & realize all your hopes. I was much amused at your criticisms of the Bourbon Convention. I always told you Henry that you were too Utopian in your search for a political party with which to affiliate. You want men to be better than they are & are vainly searching for some political paradise in which you can rest your delicate sensibilities. You will live & die in that vain search. For myself I did not affiliate with the Re-adjusters because I believe them to be perfect. On the contrary they are far from it & both in man & measure fall far short of the perfection I can imagine I would like to see; but with all their sins of omission & com-

---

Woodlawn was a plantation in Louisiana that belonged to Thomas R. Jennings the brother of Ann Elizabeth Jennings Wise, 1808–1837. Thomas Jennings died intestate and his assets were divided between his sister's children. Though not an heir, John S. Wise assisted with some of the required legal work.

During the 1870s groups of conservative Southern Democrats reclaimed control of their state governments from what were considered to be carpetbag Republican politicians. Though this group called themselves "Redeemers," another, somewhat derogatory term, "Bourbons," a reference to the reactionary Bourbon kings of France, has been more lasting. The "Bourbons" in the American south sought minimal government and did not include traditional southern values of agrarianism and states' rights in their brand of conservatism.

John S. Wise, 1846–1913, as a young lawyer. Photograph courtesy of the Virginia Historical Society, Richmond, Virginia.

mission I think them so superior & preferable to the miserable shams, liars, & imposters, imbeciles, false pretenders, & idiots who guide the Bourbons that I do not see how any sensible or progressive man can hesitate one instant in opposing the Bourbons. You ought to have thrown yourself heart & soul in with us here & today you would be a bigger man that you ever will be in that cussed Canyon country, but you would not. I have always thought that Tom Page with his piddling *laudi da* notions and constant intercourse with you, emasculated your political manhood & kept you from dashing in where you belonged. That & the disagreeable society results flowing from your taking your sword out & throwing the scabbard away, destroyed all the defiance of Bourbonism which I tried to put into you & I saw my pupil drift away from me with feelings of distress & regret. Now Sir, you have had a long lecture but alas too late. I have a thousand times wished I could have foreseen what has come & infused you with the intense loathing I feel for the Bourbon crew, so that we might have had in you a new champion & you might have been a leader. But it is all gone & idle to discuss. To every affectionate sentiment of your letter of several months ago I return a heartfelt amen. Dear Henry— I feel towards you as if you were peculiarly mine & in all your future believe me my heart is with you. What I have said above is only to express what has a thousand times sprung from my love for you since you left. It was just that feeling that a fellow had in battle, which made him fight with more spirit when his favorite regiment came in sight. We are bound to whip the Bourbons & will do it. Our fellows are well in hand this fall & hungry for them… We are all well here & unite in much love. —Your affectionate uncle *John S. Wise*.

The letters *from* Thomas Nelson Page have been long preserved in the boxes of papers. However, no letters *from* Henry Hobson *to* Page have ever been found. Those letters may have been destroyed when Oakland, the Page family plantation near Richmond, burned. The Thomas Nelson Page Papers at Duke University contain letters from other family members to Page.

Richmond, Virginia, October 11, 1883.
My dear Old Henry—   It is not without good reason that you complain of my silence. I have for a full month complained of it myself, but what between sickness, depression, and work I have not had any time at all… I am exceedingly sorry that you have been so harassed & disturbed about money matters & what is worse by the unsettled condition of the plans of those here who are dependent on you. I don't know how the Ashland plan will eventuate; but it will cost a heap of money. I am afraid, for your mother is one of the most extravagant, as she is one of the most generous people in the universe. She thinks that because she spends no large sums that therefore she is economical; but a greater mistake she never made. She helps everybody, contributes to everything & is in the unfortunate condition of having very expensive and high-toned tastes & very low and empty pockets. I know where of I speak, for I am in [illegible] but I do hope she will do well and be happy in Ashland. (end of letter)   —*Thomas Nelson Page.*

1884

The letter begins with much about the business affairs of Henry Wise Hobson.

January 14, 1884, Richmond, Virginia.
My dear Henry—
…We have had a rough spell of weather. It has put a stop to all business pretty much. All weathers are about the same to me now. I hope you find Texas more congenial and agreeable than Colorado was. I saw your mother today. She was in town and dined at our house; was looking well and seemed

in good spirits. I hope from what you told me that your stay in Colorado was at least pecuniarily profitable. I think you did marvelously well; to get to a new place, make a good reputation and money enough to keep so many people going as you did. Keep going, and leave with a considerable balance in your pocket. Business is so dull here, it is a scratch to make a living… [end of letter]   —*Thomas Nelson Page.*

☙ Letters from Virginia:

Ashland, Sunday night, February 3rd 1884.
[Addressed to: Henry Wise Hobson esq. Attorney at Law, Dallas, Texas.]
My dearest Son—   Yours of the 30th Jan. was waiting here for me when I came from Church today… Many thanks for the check & your promptness in sending it. It is certainly an inexpressible blessing to hear you are so well… I took little Cannon this afternoon, his first experience at Church & he behaved with the decorum & propriety of a grown gentleman. He is certainly one of the most attractive little fellows I ever saw, & I think Alice is getting almost jealous of his devotion to me. Did I tell you that I have taught him to speak of me as "My young grandmother." I believe he thinks all that is charming & agreeable centres in me. Little Henry has become such a sweet bright little fellow, very chatty and lively, & is also becoming very fond of me. George is just the nicest baby I know. Everybody pronounces them such pretty children & they are…How old & settled you are getting. Don't you fall in love with a "mere child." Alice with all her willingness & desire to do right is child enough for me… I hear of John as constantly passing through Ashland. I do not suppose it would ever occur to him to give me a call. It is getting late & you must have already discerned that I am far from brilliant this evening. May the love of God the Father, the sympathy & aid of God the Son, & the guidance of God the Holy Ghost be always yours.   —Your devoted mother. *A. J. W. Hobson*

Ashland, March 5, 1884.
My dearest Son—   I sent you a p.c. yesterday promising a letter today and here I am this evening seated pen in hand to carry out my promise or perhaps I should say to have the pleasure of a chat. Your letter telling of young Patten's having reached Dallas at last was received today. I am sure that you will find that he is a thorough gentleman despite the comment of the clerk of the hotel; everyone seemed to like him so much. He lingered in New Orleans to witness the Mardi Gras.
    March 6th—   My hope of a quiet evening with you was disappointed by several interruptions until it was too late and I was too tired to write. I have the baby [George R. Hobson] in my room now trying to break him into good habits— his mother had spoiled him so, and she looks so badly and seems so utterly tired and good for nothing all the time. I have improved the youngster very much, but he is still restless enough to make it necessary for me to take a long rest every day. Remember that young Patten is a great-nephew of Mr. Slaughter's.
    Having already expressed my opinion about Denver and Dallas there is little left for me to say on that subject. I have always thought Denver more desirable than Dallas in many respects. Yet it was well to have your Texas craving fully satisfied. You speak of those Western places as permanent residences.

I have not the least fear but that ultimately you will return East somewhere—though I may not live to see it.

I am very guarded about expressing my opinion about John— and I can again say with all sincerity that I feel no resentment against him and that my indignation and grief is more against the *selfish crookedness* that makes him act so than the deed itself. You may be sure that Sister speaks to no one of it as she does to me. You should need no assurance my dear kind son of my appreciation of your efforts in trying to provide for me, but I have no fears as to the future for myself, and it gives me great concern to think that it troubles you so much to deny yourself & work to make a provision for me, and I may never need it. I am so afraid that you stint yourself often far too much.

We have again had a bitter spell of weather though night before last it cleared so beautifully that Alice and I went to see the Shacklefords after tea. It was a lovely moonlight night, and yet we woke yesterday to find snow on the ground. I have been vainly hoping that our expenses in fuel would grow less. This leads me by the by to say that I can just as well give you a statement of what my pecuniary status will be on the 1st of April now as then. You may remember that I told you it was possible that I might find it difficult these first three months to live within your allowance for *everything*. Everyone says that this has been the most expensive winter known for years for fuel, meat, eggs, & vegetables— these months have also been the ones that are most expensive for fuel. Two persons have lately told me that they have burnt double the amount of fuel this winter than they ever did before. One fire has been obliged to be kept up all night for the baby. I have put my fuel under lock and key. We take breakfast in the little kitchen, and have no fire in our semi parlor and sitting room until eleven o'clock. When Alice and the children are with me very little fuel has been consumed in her room, and yet the fuel bills have appalled me. Had I been able to lay up a larger supply in October I could have bought it much cheaper. Soon our requirement for fuel will be very little. Eggs, butter, and vegetables are already becoming cheaper, and I have learned how to gage the family wants exactly. So that after this I can easily live within the limit allowed.

I can figure you our average since the last of December when I commenced here and had to have large fires through the house to dry it: Meats, $16.00— Eggs, Butter & vegetables, $13.00— Milk, $5.00— Grains including flour, meal, lard, soap and starch, $17.00— House rent, $16.00— Servant wages, $10.00— Light, $2.00— Fuel includin**g** [illegible] & dry wood, $18.00 Total: $97.00. Deduct $6.00 put in by Cannon for milk and servant— $91.00. So there will be an average of about $11.00 per month over your remittance for regular expenses. In addition I have had to spend about $7.00 on various things connected with the house such as cleaning out the well, stripping doors and windows where the air poured in so much and various necessary etcs not included in repairs. Then my own personal expenditures on stamps, small things generally yet needed articles will average about $8.00 per month. I shall need about $24.00 for myself. In other words it will take in April about $65.00 to set me square with the expenses incurred since we started here, personal and household, and I trust that I will not again at the end of any quarter have to make such a statement of debt. I have entered into details to show you how we have fared exactly. I have done my best, and must say that if Alice were only more efficient, would take over proper care of her own children, I might do better. She has not the power, mental, moral, or physical, to do better with my good *intentions* about it, I really fear she is getting into bad health. [end of letter from A.*J.W.Hobson*]

Brook Hill, April 17th, 1884.
My dear boy—   If anybody had told me that your last letter should or could have remained so long unanswered by me I think I should have retorted quite sharply that *it was simply impossible,* …I have wanted to write, and lately could have done so, but that you were moving so constantly between Dallas & Denver that I could not make out where to direct a letter. Now however, that you have written to say that Denver is the permanent abode, I am going to inflict this on you, and fortunately for me (in one way) I am so far away I can't hear your yawns over its stupidity. I do trust that your latest move will prove of real benefit both physically and financially, that neuralgia will leave you now forever and good health and prosperity attend you. You certainly are entitled to both if ever anybody was. I do wish so much you could come in by June as I flatter myself you would like to be at my marriage as much as I would like to have you— of course though if you can't come, you can't, and it is just another instance of how cranky life is. Those who can be with us are often those who feel least interest in us… Everything looks as lovely as it can look at Brook Hill in April and every day there are new beauties— the lilacs, hyacinths and daffodils, and then the woods are full, the dogwood, red bud etc. You know how it looks. I only wish you were here to sit on the front steps and enjoy it, for I doubt if even Denver can boast of such a lovely spring landscape! …Good-bye, write whenever you can, and you can be sure of one thing and that is that by whatever name I may be called, I am now and always,
—Yours affectionately, *Marion M. Stewart.*

Theological Seminary, Alexandria Va. May 10, 1884.
My dear Henry—   Your short note with enclosed check was duly received two or three days since, and would have been acknowledged at once; but I desired to arrive at a definite arrangement which I had in hand at the time before writing to you. In fact I have delayed writing for some time because I wanted to know certainly about the matter before I wrote to you. You asked me to let you know how I was getting on with the amount of money I received & whether I was free from debt. In regard to the first, I have managed, by economy, to get on very well with it and can so continue to do. But I find that I shall have to ask you if you can let me have the July installment by the last of June, say the 25th, before I leave here. I ask this so as to enable me to leave clear of all debt here. If this is not convenient to you, say so, & let me know at once, so that I can make my arrangements accordingly. In regard to debts I have not contracted any this year which I shall not be able to pay off, with the July installment, as suggested above. Much to my surprise, however, I find that I owe a dry good's bill of about $60, much of which was made by Mother for the children & on Aunt Kittie's account. This was done last year. I have made arrangements to take Christ Church (the same I had last summer) for the months of July & August for $100. This will enable me to clear myself of this debt, without having to call on you for more than the regular allowance. It is because I have been waiting for a definite settlement in regard to this that I have delayed writing to you. So with this hundred dollars this summer & the regular allowance from

you I shall be able to start square next session & keep out of debt. Do not say anything to Mother about the aforesaid bill, as I have said all that was necessary, and there is a clear understanding now, that no bills are to be made in my name without my knowledge & consent.

I am making arrangements for some work here next session which I shall write you about when I have fully completed them. I made a short visit a few days, home, on my birthday, which gave me a rest, besides the pleasure of being with them all. So I did not receive your letter of kind wishes until after my return… You know that I expected nothing in the way of a present. You give me enough already and your love & esteem are worth more than anything else to me. I am glad that you are finally settled & your mind at rest on that point; for uncertainty is one of the most wearing things upon a man's constitution & mind. It is with me, I know. I pray God that you may be blessed & prospered in your work at Denver. I shall be very busy until the end of the session but that is not far distant. Write to me when you can. It is very late & I must close. I sent you the *Seminarian* for last month. It contained a notice of an address which I delivered on Easter Sunday for which I received many compliments from all sides.   —Your affec. bro. *John C. Hobson.*

May 22, 1884, Ashland.
My dearest Son—   It is nearly ten o'clock and I am alone, seated in my small hall, the door opening into the porch being open giving me the cool night air fragrant with the odor of honey suckle, & a glimpse of the high stars & there is no moon tonight. Your "Mamma" has always said that it would never do for her to have too much at a time in this life because she could enjoy all that is enjoyable too intensely & I am really amused at myself— the way in which I am so delighted with my changes in this small domicile— in my plain little dining room, all clean & white with the clean coats of whitewash, and that the old kitchen can be made habitable by a few batches of whitewash. I am so glad to be so much more comfortable for housekeeping purposes… Yesterday I went down at eight o'clock, having collected all the flowers I could find around the neighborhood, & with two boxes of lovely green house flowers bought by Mother & myself from Gordon's (Ashland florist), Mother having written & asked me to get some for her… I went first to Father's section, where I found Ben Harris, the man who attends the sections for me, already there with his watering pot. I covered Father's, Obe's, & George's graves with lovely roses & other flowers…

This describes a trip to Hollywood Cemetery and visits to the graves of Henry A. Wise, Obadiah Jennings Wise, and George Wise.

Friday afternoon, May 23rd, 1884, (a second page)
Sleepy eyes threatening to close prevented me from writing another line last evening. Alice will go in a little while to the station to meet her sisters and two young friends who are going to come up and spend tonight and tomorrow with her. I asked her to take this to the office… I was so full of Hollywood that I did not tell you Annie G— came up Monday evening and spent the next day with me. I left here at eight o'clock & she went to Washington at eleven… I have only time to scribble this before Alice leaves. You shall have a long letter soon. All send love & kisses.   —Your devoted Mother, *A. J. W. Hobson.*

June 1st, 1884, Ashland.
My dearest Son—   Half past nine o'clock this quiet Sunday evening. At last

I can shut the door of my room, bolt myself in, and hope for an undisturbed hour to write you the letter I have been trying to get off for two days.

I wrote you of Cannon Jr.'s sickness— he had a chill and quinine has now kept it off… and he is brighter and better than before he was sick, but meantime little Henry has had an attack of fever that looks much like a chill, & George has been cutting a tooth or rather is trying to get a large tooth and he has been feverish and fretful and very aching. I have just been trying to get him to sleep, he has so worn out his poor little Mother. The Doctor here thinks these children and Alice are still affected by the malaria brought from the upper country, for all Ashland contends that no resident of this *healthy* area ever has chills unless they brought them from some malarious other place. We have been giving Henry quinine today and he has had no return of fever but has been up playing about this afternoon and evening. There is still so much measles all around us that I feel they may be taken with it any day. …Monday morning. It is almost useless for me to undertake to do anything at night. Sleep overcomes me at once… You ought to have seen me out early this morning setting out a lot of plants, brought me by Mr. Finsley, a colored gentleman who is my man of all work, coming to my aid at all times. The plants were a present. My little flower garden is promising. I am sure it will be source of health & joy to me as well as great pleasure… I am sure you have been busy in Cannon City [Cañon City] & therefore my usual Sunday letter did not come. In regard to your feelings about an addition to Cannon's family, I think it is perfectly natural that you should feel that your burden so unselfishly & kindly borne had already been heavy enough.

I have felt it most sadly for you being tempted almost to despond. I have felt it keenly for myself & most depressingly in view of the poor helpless inefficient little Mother, for whom I have far more pity and sympathy than blame. She is really a sick woman— if her health was better she would be very different I am sure & she does try to do her best & God expects nothing more of any of us. Now our part is to receive the children of this marriage as God sends them, asking that we may have the ability to do our part by them, and that they may prove a blessing to all despite the care, anxiety & expense that must come with them. Certainly these three little boys are promising children— except the little George seems to be delicate. I sometimes feel that he may not live to get through with his teeth. I am so sorry that you have not known him in his lovely babyhood. He has made a great deal of sunshine for my life— compensating for all the care I have had with him treble fold. The other day, just after the two little boys had been sick, on the first day that they were both out together, I found them two little rush-bottomed arm chairs that I had made for them here at the extravagant price of 30 cts each (& nice little chairs they are) out in the yard by a little flower bed I have given them for their own, they were side by side with their little tools scattered around, and it came over with a sickening feeling, how bereft I would feel if those little chairs were suddenly left empty forever by some blasting stroke of disease. They are never sick that I do not feel I will let nothing else trouble me if they can get well.

Cannon & Henry are very bright & well today… You will be pleased to find your namesake such a talkative, sociable little man. He minds all strangers. George is still pained with a tooth & has little appetite. When you take his tea and food to him he shakes his head in the most pathetic sort of way as

an addition to Cannon's family Alice Hobson, wife of John Cannon Hobson, was expecting her fourth child.

if to say— "I can't." Hearing Henry crying I went in the yard to see what was the matter. Each of the boys had one of my small garden hoes digging some weeds up & Henry had hurt his finger.

I look around my sweet little home with such content & thankfulness, and wonder if you will ever see it. Such strangely cool weather as we are having. It is so unseasonable and by no means healthy. Ashland certainly agrees with me. I have been better this spring than any spring before in years… I wish I could give little Cannon a change that would eradicate malaria from his system… Alice sends love. The little boys, kisses. They talk incessantly of Uncle Henry. Cannon is very busy with his examinations— says he has several irons in the fire towards helping himself next session. I have heard nothing from Richmond lately. God bless you & make your truly His own. —Your devoted Mother— *A.J.W. Hobson.*

Ashland, June 12th, 1884.
My dearest Son—   I have tried to get a letter off to you by the two o'clock mail but just as I took my pen the last preventive came in the way of a visit from Dr. F— who came to see the baby.

the baby George Hobson born 1883.

The little fellow had a high fever yesterday evening & he has been having a hard time with his teeth of late. I fear he is very delicate, and it comes over me often that he will not live the summer out. He is more like little Marianne than anyone else. Yesterday afternoon as he was lying in my lap, so sick and feverish, a ray of sunshine fell all over his head and it looked like burnished gold. It was more like my conception of angel hair than anything I ever saw. It occurred to me that I must send you a little curl to see— hold it in the sunlight & see how golden it is. He has no fever today but is fretful and miserable… do hope you are not tormented with flies in Colorado— they are dreadful here and I am waging war on them all the time…

—After dinner— I would like to write more & be more agreeable but I am just too sleepy & this must go off by the seven o'clock mail. The little boys send kisses and Alice love. Cannon is in the midst of examinations & I am sorry it is turning so warm again. God bless you ever—   —Your devoted mother— *A. J. W. Hobson.*

Ashland, July 3, 1884.
My dearest Son—   For two days have I tried to write you without accomplishing it (as you have found out). I am resolved that nothing shall prevent my getting a letter off to you by the seven o'clock mail… Mr. Shackelford came early Sunday morning & insisted that one should read the service Sunday morning & one in the evening. Cannon read in the morning & he did it very well indeed— with a little improvement he could do it very well. I wished you could have heard him. His tones of voice reminded me of Henry, my brother. Mr. Shackelford wanted him to lecture in the evening but he said he felt too tired & run down to do so… He [John Cannon Hobson] went to Richmond today expecting to return this evening.— Monday morning I awoke to find it pouring rain with every promise of a most inclement day… Yesterday I was very tired & took a rest in my room (after three days of guests) & just as I was about to write to you, little George was taken really ill for a while & I was nursing him until eleven o'clock, when I consigned him to Alice— he is much better today but feverish… I received your dear let-

ter in the morning and it seemed a quick answer to my heart out-pouring. It comforted me something in the same way that your putting your arms lovingly around me might have done… But for these little children I should feel tempted to take your offer of going to you next winter into most serious consideration. My heart just yearns over it on your account, but I feel that I must consider my real duty in the matter & certainly until the next confinement is over I should take care of this helpless family, & one prime reason for my staying here, & trusting to God for strength to go through is that Alice could do nothing but board— & for the respectability of the family we ought not to let her do that, & I do not think really decent people would stand her careless, slovenly ways, which I just insist upon being different. She learns less from being with others than anyone I ever saw. I think Cannon is sad & depressed about this family now, & sees plainly what is before him… At the same time I must say I do not think he appreciates the sacrifice & efforts I am making for him and his— he should do so. He & Alice are in many respects like two big, selfish, untrained children immersed in themselves; but he does make her stir around & take more trouble than she would otherwise do. One important reason why you may think that this arrangement should end sooner is that it may be the establishment will prove too expensive for you… God the Father, Son & Holy Ghost be ever with you— Your devoted Mother —*A.J.W. Hobson.*

◦᪲ Letters from friends in Virginia:

Brook Hill, June 9th, 1884.
My dear Henry—   How shall I thank you for your share in that lovely ice cream set that Tom Page and yourself have sent me? I am so gratified and delighted with it, and much more with the affection and interest which prompted you to get it. I can't say what I feel, but I thank you for it most heartily and only wish you were here to hear from my lips how I will always value & use it with such sweet memories of "auld lang syne". Goodbye dear Henry and forget that though I am going to change my name, I am not really going to be different, and will always be,   —Yours affectionately, *Marion M. Stewart.*

Brook Hill, July 3rd, 1884.
My dearest friend—   I am in hopes that this letter and the little cigar cutter will reach you on your birthday & though neither are of any intrinsic value I [illegible] they will serve to remind you that you have a friend in far away Virginia who only loves you the more as the years go by. Ah! dear, I have but few virtues, but of them is loyalty to my friends & I am getting to an age now when I feel that the old friends are the best indeed. I cannot feel in the same intense way for the friends of today as I do for those who have laughed & cried with me through most of my life. I often wonder how many years it will be before I see your face again & the thought of long years of separation makes me very sad, but this I do know, that if your age should be 52 instead of 28 when next we meet, that you will still be my friend, the friend of my life. …Marion received your sweet letter just a few days before her marriage and she was gratified by it. It is so nice to feel that we are dear to those we care for. I suppose that she has written you long ago to thank you for the ice cream set that you and Mr. Page sent. It is a perfect beauty and fortunately

she got nothing that conflicted with it. What do you think of her getting two hundred presents? And most of them such handsome ones... This letter has been almost entirely taken up with the wedding so that I will ensure enough old gossip for another epistle. Till then goodbye with the heartfelt prayer that God's blessing may rest upon you now & always. —Ever your affectionate *Norma Stewart.*

➤ Letters from Annie Jennings Wise Hobson:

Ashland, July 5, 1884.
My dearest Son— Sitting on our little porch tonight enjoying a most delicious breeze & the loveliest moonlight, wishing you could see how really lovely our little yard looks in the moonlight. My heart & mind were filled with recollections of the past connected with your birthday which will be next Wednesday, July 9th. I have been thinking of it constantly all day & trying hard to get through the "must be done duties" of Saturday to write you... I can say you have proved to your Mother the next best blessing after your Father's devotion & tender care— And here tonight do I thank God devoutly for the gift of such a loyal, loving son, endowed with so many qualities of heart & mind, with a just and noble satisfaction. (I do not like the word *pride*.) & I pray God to bless him abundantly in all things, to prolong his usefulness for many years... As I write this my eyes are almost blind with tears— they run down my cheeks and I seem to stretch my arms over the great distance that intervenes between us & in spirit to span it and to take you in. You are not really as far from me as the other son of mine, who has placed insuperable barriers between us, that can never be passed on earth.

I had hoped to make you a birthday present, something for your office or room, with my own hands, but while I have this helpless family on my hands & the incompetent Ashland servants to deal with, I fear I will never find time for aught but plain work & household duties. I feel sure you have more books now than you can take care of, & indeed anything I should buy for you would be like making you pay for your own present as I have nothing of my own & we are all like leeches on you now.—

Sunday— Tired nature could stand it no longer last evening— it was nearly eleven o'clock, & I had been going & working incessantly from half past five in the morning. Saturday & Monday are my hardest, busy days, but I thank God so intensely for the strength & physical ability to go through with it all... I have thought long and seriously of your proposition, but am convinced my duty 'till Cannon is ordained, is with his family— it is what your Father and my Father would wish me to do & above all it is what I believe God indicates as the present duty for me... Mr. Shackelford gave us a very good sermon this morning. He looks very badly & will I hope soon have a holiday... Cannon went to Richmond yesterday evening to officiate for the Christ Church people today— will be back tomorrow evening... It is time this scrawl was in the office. I shall write to you on your birthday. (I hope you will awake with a sense of your Mother's loving presence being with you in spirit, wishing you every birthday greeting and tender blessing on your 26th birthday.) Little Mary is very anxious to send you a card & Annie too— both send you love and many happy returns. I called little Henry & said, what must I send Uncle Henry for you on his birthday which is almost here— "Send him my love," the little fellow said. Cannon comes in too and says, "Send him my love too." Annie Mayo says I wish I had something to send him. Alice of course sends love. A Sabbath greeting to my far off boy. Replete with love & tenderness… —Your fondly devoted mother— A. J. W. H.

Ashland, September 2nd, 1884.
    Your letter written last Wednesday was received on Sunday, my dearest son, and read with the eager interest every line from your dear hand receives. By the by, a curious feeling came over me when opening the last pamphlet you sent. I felt like caressing the wrapper as I realized how your hand had held it and so neatly sealed it up to send your Mother… I gave a long deep heavy sigh as I read that you again had to move— hunt up another abiding place. God grant that the pilgrim state may not last much longer. My precious noble boy I do not think that even you realise [sic] how constantly your Mother's heart and mind lingers around you with tender sympathy entering into all your cares, anxieties, and deprecations. So constantly it comes over me that it seems so hard that you, the bread winner for all, the one who is toiling and denying yourself for us all, should have no home, no real resting place by the wayside while we have such a pleasant little nest. Sometimes the temptation will almost overcome me to have hard feelings against Cannon… because I sometimes feel that his unfortunate marriage has fixed such a burden on you and kept me longer away from you than I ought to be. Yet poor fellow I realise more fully every day that his evil time is ahead of him, & he fears & foresees it too, and is often a sad man over the deficiencies… of his poor feeble characterless little wife. She is much disgusted at his sustaining me in my discipline of the children and condemning her. Mother has been so sweet to Alice trying to draw her out, and she now says that she is convinced there is nothing in her, and that I might as well let her alone, & she has taken no pains to conceal from Mother her disagreeable temper and indolence… it would be a merciful kindness if God took the poor helpless little woman to another [illegible, *place*] where what is good in her might develop into *something*, but I think that will not be His way with Cannon… Otherwise if they can get on without us I would rather they should be apart from us where we would not be mortified and grieved over the home that awaits Cannon— or that I fear awaits him— He is much better, returned from Richmond yesterday saying that he felt better now than he had done this summer… Now I can assure you that my experience here has given me a training that will be highly beneficial towards our living together in Colorado. You & I could get three living rooms, & a little place— if only a closet for a kerosene cooking stove, and with one servant I would show you what nice housekeeping we could have. My life here has been one of service and yet, my dear son, I never regret it one moment. When I undertook it here, to carry on the present work, I earnestly asked God not to let me begin here unless I could go through with it— and give me the needed strength and patience… I have kept Mother here with all needed delicacies & Cannon too… She wanted to make me accept $25 from her, & I would not do it, told her you would never forgive me if I did such a thing. She is better but still very feeble. I think she is just gently going down the hill of life… Grandma sends love & an earnest God bless you. Your mother sends you her heart's most loving greeting. —Your devoted mother— *A.J.W. Hobson.*

Mother Most likely a reference to Mary Lyons Wise.

baby girl Mary M. Hobson, born December 2, 1884.

Ashland, December 10th, 1884.
My dearest Son—   …As to the Louisiana lands, little have we left. Didn't you receive the papers stating that we were having an amicable suit with the D—'s to sell the other lands? My share will be very small… But indeed my son, once out of this Ashland dilemma & your Mother will make it the aim of her life to be as little expense to you as possible… I must tell you something that will make you more partial to your nephew Cannon than ever before. He stood gravely by his mother's side this afternoon looking at her as the baby girl took some of her many meals. Directly in the most *oracular* way he said— "I don't know what you wanted to bring that baby here for. You had one baby already— George was enough!" I wrote to Cannon this afternoon telling him you offered congratulations or condolence whichever he preferred. This scrawl must go at once to the office. The little boys send love & kisses. Alice also. May God ever bless & protect my precious, absent boy—   —your devoted mother. *A.J.W. Hobson*

Ashland, Dec 21st, 1884.
The little ones are nestled all snugly in bed this Sunday night before Xmas. I have let the nurse go out, and hope for a quiet hour to write my Xmas letter to my far off boy— My loved and loving son… Even as I write this do you not know that your Mother's heart is sad & weary as she thinks of you so far away and homeless… Through you, your Mother has a home that she has so long been without, and her heart is gladdened by the dear loving little children that she can gather around her, and tell of the Babe in Bethlehem… Cannon can come to a home and family life and ask God to bless you for your goodness to him. Your liberality enables your Mother to do something towards the pleasure and happiness of others. My good, noble son, there should be great peace & joy in your heart as you think of all this, and I know you will thank God for giving you the brains & heart & will to do all this. Thank Him my son as your Heavenly Father who gave His only Son as your Savior & Guide. I thank God for such a son. I have gone to Him upon whom I cast all my care & to whom I carry all my sorrow, and asked that we may be together another Xmas… Peace, good-will to all My son; & shall we not extend it to poor little ignorant weak Alice & her mother? Mrs. Pettit was sick and did not come. It would be very hypocritical in me not to say that I was greatly *relieved*. Yesterday as I was as busy as possible straightening up my pantry and getting things all right for Sunday & the coming week, a message came from Alice saying her Mother would be here on the 5 o'clock… As she had twice put me to the trouble of fixing her room I though she might have asked if it would be convenient for me to have her now. It was hard to receive her politely and as a lady in my own house, but I did so… I had a cry and a struggle before I could overcome all the miserable rebellion I felt against this visit. Yet my conscience as a Christian and a Mother told me that there would be something inhuman in not being willing for Mother & child to meet under such circumstances. I knew Alice longed for her Mother. On my knees I determined to conquer all my ill-feeling & I have done so. Mrs. Pettit herself is so much more of a lady, quiet & refined, than I expected to find her. She is a weak woman doubtless & my hardest feeling against her is the way in which she spoiled and indulged Alice. I did not invite her as a guest to my house, but as a Mother to see her daughter under existing circumstances. I think she understood this. All of Alice's

relatives by her Mother's side that I have seen are not people to be ashamed of. Her Uncle, Mr. George Richardson, is a quiet refined gentleman, and I have no doubt but that they deplored (the brothers) their sister's marriage to John Pettit. Of course, Mr. & Mrs. Pettit were to blame for the marriage, but I cannot hold anyone as responsible as I do the *son* that I *reared* marrying as he did… I have been so much happier & brighter today for conquering all my ill will & *natural human rebellion*, and being glad that Mother & child could be together. Mrs. Pettit has a very hard [illegible] life with her drunken, improvident husband… When you wake Xmas morning there must be some instinct that will make you feel as if your Mother's greeting of kiss & loving embrace & prayerful blessing was with you— truly in spirit I shall be. It is such a blessing to hear your health is better. God grant that it may steadily improve.

I must tell you that you would be exceedingly gratified if you could have heard Cannon inform Mrs. Pettit this evening that I was his "charming young grandmother & he was my boy & he loved me better than all his grandmothers & was never going to leave me." He has been trying to be a very good boy today. He is a bright observing child & can be very fascinating when he chooses. His last demonstration with me is to come up & say, "bless your heart, I certainly love you." …All are asleep, so take all love messages for granted. God's own peace be yours.   —Your devoted Mother— *A.J.W.Hobson.*

A letter from an uncle in Virginia:

Richmond, Va. December 27th, 1884.
Dear Henry—   …I have no time nor inclination to talk politics. Am now up to my eyes in better paying work & the past election seems a long way back. I was very much disappointed. I think a great calamity has befallen the country. I strove loyally to avert it & deplore it from the bottom of my heart. The combination of negro killers & free traders gained an ephemeral triumph. The country already sees & feels the mistake. The little knob of men who carried New York, New Jersey, Connecticut, & Indiana already find that they have struck down the party of loyalty & progress and enthroned a coalition between the lagging & disloyal and bloodthirsty Southern & the greedy Britain. The next election will correct all this & with sublime faith I await it… I sent you the papers, documents, you wished. I have not yet been to Congress except one day. Have been too busy in law to bother with it. An effort will be made January 8th to resuscitate the Massey case, but I do not think it will amount to much & even if they should turn me out & him in, the term is almost expired & it would be a great relief to me for I am heartily sick of Congress & want to go home again. I wish very much you could have been with us this Xmas. All the children are well & happy & unite with Eva in much love to you. Eva says that if you come to Cannon's ordination you must be sure to make our house your home… Have had little opportunity for sport this fall altho' I have the best dog I have owned since old Henry & scooped 236 birds before I was caught & brought back from the woods to which I took after the election. I must close now. I sincerely hope, my dear Henry, that this has been a Merry Xmas to you & that the New Year will bring you abundant store of health, happiness & prosperity— & in this wish your Aunt Eva & all the six little ones unite in hearty chorus under the wreaths of cedar & holly. My home is yours as long as you live.   —Your affec. uncle, *John S. Wise.*

the past election   Grover Cleveland was elected to his first term as President in November 1884.

been to Congress   John Wise was a Member of Congress from 1883 to 1885.

1885

~ The United States Attorney in Colorado:

Washington, April 18th, 1885. Department of Justice.
My Dear Sir—   After carefully considering all the endorsements… I concluded to send your name to the President for Dist. Atty of Col. He has approved it & appointed you. You now enter upon a theatre of no little importance. It will afford you full opportunity to do great good for the country & to help yourself forward in life… You will have to be cautious and fair enforcing the law whatever it may be… I have written this frankly to you in part for this consideration & also for the friendship & regard I have long had for many of your relatives… I hope & trust you will be successful there in your public duties & always be prosperous. —Very Truly Yours, *A. H. Garland*.

H. W. Hobson esq. Denver, Col.
[In another handwriting a postscript has been added to the above letter—]
Dear Henry—   This letter was handed to me by the secretary with the request that I would add a word to it & forward it to you. I will only say that I hope you will recognize the importance of the position & its responsibility as well as the opportunity it affords for you to make a reputation for yourself and show your appreciation of the Secretary's confidence in you by reflecting credit upon the Dept and adding strength to the Administration. We are all well & heartily congratulate you… P.S. Regards to Judge H— [Judge Moses Hallett]

~ A letter from a friend in Virginia:

Richmond, Virginia, April 18, 1885.
My dear old boy: Accept my warmest congratulations on your appointment. The first thing which greeted my eyes in the paper this morning on reaching my office was your appointment as U. S. Dist Attorney. Now this looks something like business. That you, a boy of twenty-three or four, should go out from your people and seize the prize from all the bar of the Great State of your adoption is an honor indeed. And the manner of your appointment, as the candidate not of the Ring nor even of the politicians, but of the honest people, the Reform element, gives it additional lustre. I have always bet on you from my earliest intimacy with you, and unless I am mistaken this will be but the prelude to far higher honors. I bespeak a large measure of honor for you old man and a life of great usefulness. And God knows I wish you them. Nothing that I can think of would just now have given me more pleasure than the recognition of your value by this public appointment. You deserved it in Virginia and you deserved it in Colorado. And now I begin to have hope of your coming on again this summer. Willy Christian is to be married on the 2nd of June to Julia Jackson and has written to ask you to come in and wait on him. I will be Best man unless Carter thinks he ought to be. So if you can come you must. And we'll all renew the old days. I reckon you'll have your hands full.

   Again wishing you all success and every blessing. I am ever, your old crony, *T.N.P.* [Thomas Nelson Page]

Henry W. Hobson has been appointed United States District Attorney for Colorado and as it is the initial appointment of President Cleveland in this state, some comment upon it may not be out of the way. Mr. Hobson is a grandson of the late Hon. Henry A. Wise of Virginia and has inherited the ability of that good old stock of people. As a lawyer he is considered one of the hardest working and painstaking in the state and while he is young in years and practice, his ability and position at the bar has been recognized by the profession. Morally and socially his position is well secured and guaranteed by a strict code of morals and a rigid adherence to the amenities of social and professional life. If the Federal appointments in this state are to partake of the character foreshadowed by the appointments of Mr. Hobson the vitality of the democratic party in this state will receive new life from this transfusion of clean blood.
—*Unidentified and undated newspaper clipping.*

Henry Wise Hobson, Charles Bohm, Photographer, 284 Fifteenth St., Denver. Writing on September 13, 1898, his mother said that he had a beard in the mid-1880s.

∾ A controversy:

PATTERSON CROWD DOWNED
Henry W. Hobson is Appointed District Attorney for Colorado
Mr. Henry W. Hobson of this city was yesterday appointed United States District Attorney in place of Judge Brazee. There were five or six applicants for this position, and it is one of the offices for which the Patterson-Sullivan combination earnestly strove to control the appointment. Mr. Hobson was supported by General Bela M. Hughes, and the appointment therefore is a strong indication as to what influence will control in the Federal appointments in this State.

Mr. Hobson is about 28 years old… He is recognized as a gentleman of high character and culture. He is a lawyer of superior ability, and by his energy and studious habits he gives promise of attaining a high rank in his profession. The appointment of Mr. Hobson is looked upon with favor by the better class of Democrats in Denver, and it is considered as a clear declaration that the Patterson faction will not be very influential with the Cleveland administration… They who, a few weeks ago, were so confident of controlling public patronage in Colorado that they called a caucus in Mr. Patterson's office to agree among themselves as to how the offices should be divided up, find now that they have no offices to divide. They thought that they verily were the people and that wisdom would die with them, but now their house is left unto them desolate and there is none to comfort them and none to pity.
—*Denver Tribune Republican, undated.*

THE PATTERSON CROWD SQUELCHED
The procession of Republican office-holders in Colorado has begun to move. A few weeks ago President Cleveland appointed a couple of Democrats to small postoffices, but the first big sweet plum was taken from the Federal basket yesterday and given to Henry W. Hobson, Esq., of Denver, who is to be United States District Attorney for Colorado… So far as we can learn the appointment is a good one, and will give satisfaction to the bar and the people generally, though of course Patterson, Sullivan and Arkins will tear their hair and make the atmosphere blue because Rising was not appointed.
—*Unidentified newspaper clipping.*

The appointment of Henry W. Hobson, Esq., as United States District Attorney is the very best that could have been made… The University of Virginia is his Alma Mater. The law course there is very thorough and difficult. Probably the best Professor of Law (John B. Miner, esq.) in the country heads the Faculty of that department. Henry

Hobson took the whole course in one year, and although the youngest of twenty-six, graduated fourth in the class, most of whom had studied for two or three years… In politics a liberal Democrat, Mr. Hobson belongs to those young men who recognize the wisdom of submitting cheerfully to the past, and, by wiping out sectional narrowness, promoting the welfare of the whole people… No young man in the State gives greater promise, none is more honorable. Pleasing in appearance and manner, he wins friends readily. To those whom he has tried he remains fast and true, independent of policy. His courage is remarkable; and his convictions are always expressed fearlessly.

—Unidentified newspaper clipping.

"A new and extraordinary phase of Northern Bourbonism has been developed in Colorado. Some Democratic politicians from that State, who called upon the President to protest against certain recent selections for Federal offices, complained that the appointees are "ex-Confederate boys." The country is familiar with the ancient complaint against giving any office— except of course a United States Senatorship from Virginia or something of that sort— to "ex-Confederate soldiers," but what these people complain of is the appointment of "ex-Confederate striplings," young fellows of twenty-seven and thirty, who were babies when the war broke out. At this rate one shudders to imagine what will be the obloguy heaped upon the next generation, the grandsons of the men who fought in the rebel army. Exile is the mildest fate which can be expected for these unborn victims of Northern Bourbonism."

—Unidentified newspaper clipping.

༄ Letters from Virginia:

Richmond, Sunday, Oct. 11th, 1885.
My dearest Son—   Day before yesterday in Western parlance might have been called a boom day for me inasmuch as I felt so much brighter and better in every respect and I wanted to write to you and let some of the warm glow & brightness of the October sun shining in my pleasant little sitting room get into my letter…

right to the house from the depot Annie Hobson writes of going to visit Cannon and Alice Hobson who were living in Petersburg, Virginia.

…The street car took me right to the house from the depot. No one saw me coming and I walked in on them all in the dining room. The first sound I heard was my dear little George fretting & his father coaxing him to take some medicine. Cannon & Alice were sitting with their backs to the door & did not even see me when I walked in. George has a kind of malarial fever that comes & goes and he has not been actively enough treated. He looks so pale & changed, and we all fear also suppressed whooping cough as there has been so much of it in Ashland. Yesterday his fever scarcely rose at all & Cannon thought him better. If he does not improve during the next week I will get a room at a boarding house near them and take him in charge during the day. That dear little fellow has loved and been to me what no other has been since little Annie was taken. All say it was pitiable to hear him beg for me when he first went to Petersburg, he insisted that Grandma was down the street— "take me to Grandma" his constant cry. Yesterday he held out his little arms at once & seemed perfectly satisfied as long as I had him. I have never felt that the child would live, and while I should miss him a long time, I could not ask to keep him should it be God's will to take the precious baby to heaven. Do not understand that at present the child is desperately ill, but there are symptoms about him that I do not like and seem to indicate to me serious trouble. The little girl has improved very much, and Cannon & Henry look very well. The house is a very comfortable one… two large rooms on the first floor, two & a half rooms on the second, and a very comfortable servants room & kitchen in the yard. Cannon has fixed the front room as a study with his book-shelves, the large desk (yours), the mahogany table… my parlor table that I took from Néné & the large rug that was in the room you slept in when in Ashland… In the dining room they have the [illegible], the yellow sideboard, the dinner table I had in Williamsburg with two ends for side tables, my dining room chairs & two of the arm-chairs— he also has your Father's arm chair. They are comfortably fixed upstairs… I thought it best to let them get their own china, & they have a very nice looking dinner set— like the old blue china your Grandpa Hobson, and that cost only $16.00. I selected it for them & it included tea & coffee cups & tea & breakfast plates… Considering how sick George has been I think they have gotten fixed speedily. Cannon looks worn & tired & was not well yesterday— just needs a little rest. —Everyone has been very kind to him he says. Alice seems to be actively stirring herself about household matters. They have a nurse & cook, & the washing is done at home… Cannon was so delighted to see me and little Mary stretched out her arms to come to me at once. Henry was very quiet but said he was glad. When I left in the evening, and Cannon & I got on the car, little Cannon ran right after us— his Father told him, "Go back— you are too dirty boy to come." We thought he had gone back, & after the car started [I] looked & there was Cannon clinging to the back railing as he stood on the step. I ran & brought him in; he said he must go with Grandma to the train & wanted to come back with me to Ashland… Your devoted mother, *A. J. W. Hobson.*

Petersburg, Dec. 26th, 1885, Saturday.
This morning when I went to breakfast I found lying on my plate your letter written last Sunday. My dear noble son— Surely no sweeter and more precious message of Peace and Good Will could have come to me this Xmas season… I went up to Cannon's immediately after reading it & I found him in his little vestry room— that is after seeing him at the house when he had to hurry off to see his Sunday School teachers about a tree they are getting up for the Sunday School children & poor families (& the majority of his people are so poor) and I put the letter in his hands saying "read this my son, & feel that your Mother responds fully to every word…" …I attended to my poor folks in Ashland & came here Thursday morning. Cannon met me at the cars but had to leave me early on account of having a funeral & wedding both the same evening. Alice & I took the three little boys at once down the street to see the stores, but such a poor old display as can be had here, but they enjoyed it. George was in a gale of excitement. I took Cannon & Henry separately & let them get things for each other. I had seven dollars given me by John, Néné, Mother Hallie, and Mr. Richardson besides your $5.00. I bought some toys for everybody. Cannon bought a very nice book from you to all the boys— one that will be good for them for several years… A spirit of great kindness has been evinced by all. The children had their stockings & a few toys before I got to Cannon's for I am again staying with Mrs. Lee & glad to help her out a little this Xmas but the main gifts were kept 'till Grandma came & they were very happy. Nothing has given more pleasure than a tremendous express wagon sent to Cannon by Mrs. M— —large enough to put either George

or Henry in. She also sent Henry a large wheel-barrow & George a very big trumpet. Little Mary came in for her share of toys, & I am so delighted to find her so improved in every way, & she is really a little beauty & has lost her woe-begone look entirely. After distributing the presents, we all went to the Church close by. Cannon did not preach, as the former rector was to administer Communion for him. It is a plain little chapel & with a half dozen exceptions the congregation were poor, very poor people and the music just what you'd expect under such circumstances, but I had deep peace and thankfulness in my heart & asked nothing more… We had a luxurious dinner & everything on the table except a sponge cake had not cost one person one copper. You may be sure your name was often on our lips and that we felt your presence was needed to complete our happiness… My Xmas prayer for my noble beloved son is "Give him spiritual strength, the whole armor of God for the battle with life he has to fight, the guard of Angels & finding influence of the Holy Spirit in all hours of danger, peril & difficulty."   —Your devoted mother. *A. J. W. Hobson.*

1886

Petersburg, May 4th, 1886.
My dearest Son—   Your short letter of remembrance that my birthday was approaching was received just before I left Ashland or rather the evening before I came over here (last Saturday morning). Yesterday your long pencilled letter written from Leadville came here forwarded from Ashland. I thought very lovely & loving in you to remember my birthday by even a few lines amidst your pressing business engagements… The drawback to my happiness over your letter was to hear you are sick, & I don't like the symptoms you talk about— nausea & headache like that often precede fever, & it also shows not only a spring attack, but that you are broken down, just worked to exhaustion. Such attacks are just what I have now whenever my nervous system is run-down. I had a dreadful one in Washington that I would not tell you about, & another last month in Ashland. I get into a state of congestion that is only broken up by repeated doses of warm water to make me throw up. Mustard plasters in between times & then when I have conquered the nausea to a degree I take a big dose of bromide of potash & get some sleep… It was also an intense blessing to realise that you & I stood nearer in sympathy & *human friendship*, & I do believe there will never again be a cloud between us. Then too I was unnaturally grateful to feel that I owed my independence & freedom from pecuniary care to the noble generosity & unselfish care of my loving son— and that through him by God's blessing my heart & mind were at rest about Cannon's future as well as present. Never did a birthday bring such a sense of mercy & blessing to me personally… I tell you Cannon's marriage, with the woman he has, inevitably puts great hindrances & drawbacks in his way. I feel deeply sorry for him in his domestic life & he tries to bear it patiently, & I believe she tries to do her duty in her way, but she is no help [illegible] practically nor intellectually to a poor minister… I must tell you at once that you do Mr. Wharton great injustice in regard to his estimate of you. While you were at Wm & Mary & repeatedly since you left, he told me that there was not a boy at College, not excepting Jennings, that he thought had more talent than yourself, that even in your Greek class, lazy as you were,

Jennings Obadiah Jennings Wise, 1831–1862.

when you did apply yourself, you astonished him— that he thought you would be the most successful of all the young men of those ten years. Col. E— said the same. Mr. Wharton thought you had the finest talent for speaking. When in after years I told him of your stand at the University, & then late of your success at the bar in Colorado & your standing as a man amongst men, he reminded me of his prophecy concerning you. Whenever I see him he always asks for you with warm interest & normally sends his love… Here are Cannon & little Henry come to dinner. I want this to go off this evening & will finish my reply to your letter *next time*… Love from us all in Petersburg. I am sure you will come out victorious over all your enemies. God preserve & bless you.   —Your devoted mother, *A. J. W. Hobson*

❧ And meanwhile in Colorado:

United States Attorney's Office, District of Colorado
Henry W. Hobson, U. S. Attorney
May 7, 1886
Hon. George F. Edmunds, Chairman Judiciary Committee, U. S. Senate:
Sir:

I have today received copies of the affidavits of Henry Stevens and J. H. Hammond, together with certain protest of T. M. Patterson and C. S. Thomas, referred to in your letter of April 30th, and I respectfully submit the following answer.

I will say however generally that I cannot enter into any discussion concerning matters transpiring before the Grand Jury further than to deny the truth of what is charged against me. Such a course, upon my part, would be manifestly improper, and with all respect for you and the Judiciary Committee I must decline to follow it. If such were proper I could file a dozen affidavits of the Grand Jury controverting Mr. Hammond's and Mr. Stevens' statements. Mr. Stevens has come as near violating his oath as a Grand Juror as it was possible for him to do. I would submit that he has in spirit violated it. It is certainly a matter of comment and one affecting a man's credibility that, having taken a solemn oath to preserve secret what transpires before the Grand Jury, he should be so manifestly anxious as Mr. Stevens seems to be to disclose such things.

Mr. Hammond has also in effect violated his oath taken before the Grand Jury in disclosing what he claims happened in the Jury room. Again Mr. Hammond's and Mr. Stevens' affidavits were drawn in the office of Messrs. Patterson & Thomas, and are sworn to before a clerk in their office who is a notary.
Mr. Stevens' Affidavit:

Mr. Stevens makes no charge against me except by insinuation. Suffice it to say that the investigation he claims was made by the Grand Jury of which he was foreman was such as rendered the proceedings a farce and was a travesty upon justice. I am credibly informed, though I cannot vouch for the truth thereof, that Henry Stevens went from the Grand Jury room direct to the Denver Post-office and told Mr. Speer of what had been done in his case…

In so far as his affidavit reflects upon my action it is absolutely false.
Mr. Hammond's Affidavit:

After several months of criticism and controversy surrounding his nomination, Henry Hobson wrote to Senator George Edmunds of the Senate Judiciary Committee. One faction of the Democratic Party in Colorado was opposed to his appointment and was trying to defeat it in the Senate.

I will not discuss the facts or evidence in the case against Mr. Speer with Mr. Hammond except to say that the statements of a man who stands indicted for perjury should be at least taken with some grains of allowance when made against the man prosecuting him, and concerning the matters for which he is indicted…

I would respectfully submit that a man who would make an affidavit with such a manifestly false purpose and with such a clear intention of misleading you and your Committee deserves little credit. No rational man in reading Mr. Hammond's affidavit and Mr. Patterson's protest can draw any other conclusion than that they wish to produce the impression that I, knowing that Hammond's entry was all right and in fact having stated so, had him indicted concerning the same out of revenge.

Mr. Patterson's Protest:

I now come to the protest of Messrs. Patterson and Thomas and would here say that in all that follows Mr. Patterson is alone referred to. I am credibly informed that Mr. Thomas accepted Mr. Patterson's word for the statements of the protest and signed it accordingly. Be that as it may, I am under obligations to Mr. C. S. Thomas for kindnesses in the past before he became my enemy through the influence of Mr. Patterson and the fact that he now tries, together with Mr. Patterson, to do me a serious wrong, can not make me forget my obligations. With regard to Mr. Thomas I prefer to rest with the simple remark that he was mis-informed when he signed the protest. But so far as the matter of the protest is concerned, it is a tissue of falsehood from beginning to end. Let me take the charges up categorically. It is charged:

First: That I have shown myself unfit for the position.

I am not the person to bear testimony concerning that, but I can say with propriety that only a few weeks before he made this protest, Mr. Patterson found out by actual interviews with the President and the Attorney General that my services for the past year had been so satisfactory that they laughed at his attacks upon me.

Second: That I have had innocent men indicted through malice and then refused them speedy trials to gratify my malevolence.

Mr. Patterson knows that statement to be false, for with the exception of the Speer case, I have never in any case refused as speedy a trail as the defendants wished…

Third: I am charged with malicious prosecution in the case of Hammond. Mr. Patterson was present in Court when the indictment against Mr. Hammond was returned, is, as I am informed, his attorney, and knows that no such indictment as is alleged in his protest was ever returned against Mr. Hammond.

Fourth: In reference to the Hallack matter, I have only this to say. I received from the Department instructions to begin criminal and civil actions against E. F. Hallack for timber trespass. In the exercise of a discretion given me by the Attorney General, I wrote a letter to Mr. Hallack, a copy of which I enclose. This letter I do not think Mr. Patterson exhibits. After waiting nearly ten days I wrote a second letter, a copy of which is enclosed, and in answer to this I received the very discourteous letter, copy of which is enclosed. Upon the impulse of the moment I wrote an endorsement thereupon and returned the letter. To the folly of such action I plead guilty, but there is nothing more in the matter. The case was a simple misdemeanor, and I chose for good and sufficient reasons to file an information instead of proceeding by indictment and presented sufficient ground for filing the information to the Court to be allowed to do so. Surely this does not prove me guilty of corrupt action…

I now come to the Speer case and will answer some of the statements of the protest specifically, but will state generally that the protest is false in every material particular and being mostly of a general nature, not supported by evidence of any kind, and not even sworn to, my simple denial should be sufficient. I however wish to point out its falsity in some respects.

With the exception of the *Rocky Mountain News* and a few insignificant country newspapers followers of the *News*, and with the further exception perhaps of one or two side hits from the *Denver Times*, a paper whose editor is unfriendly to me, the press of the State *has not condemned my course*, but, on the contrary, I have received a most gratifying support from the vast majority of the newspapers. Senators Teller and Bowen I imagine receive our principal papers, and they can state whether I speak truly or Mr. Patterson. The *Rocky Mountain News* is notoriously the personal organ of Mr. Patterson, and it is a matter of common notoriety and belief that he writes as much for the editorial columns of the *News* as its regular editor, and particularly in those matters concerning which he is personally interested, either as attorney or otherwise. I believe that he wrote most of the editorials appearing against me as I am satisfied that he prompted them, and with regard to the dispatches which he files as exhibits, I can state of my own personal knowledge that the correspondent of the *News* who sent those dispatches was in close conference with Mr. Patterson in Pueblo before the same were sent to the *News*. The editorials and telegrams exhibited by Mr. Patterson are maliciously false and the style thereof should alone condemn them. One thing is curious and that is that in no other paper published in this State did any telegrams or any communications similar to the one exhibited appear. And on the contrary, if Mr. Patterson had the fairness to do so, he could file telegrams and communications in other papers directly and incontestibly controverting the statements in the *News*.

With regard to my conduct in the Speer case before and after the first investigation before the Grand Jury, I respectfully submit without comment a letter which I published in the *News* in answer to a fierce attack upon me, and will furthermore state what I did not say in this published letter that from the very inception of this case, I kept the Attorney General advised of my action and was proceeding with his approval and under his orders.

After a careful consideration of the case, and being fully informed of the manner in which the November Grand Jury had acted, I reported the case to the Attorney General and received from him positive instructions in the premises. Again when in Washington in January I had a conversation with the Attorney General and received further instructions…

I am not at liberty to give your Committee any correspondence which I may have had with he Attorney General, but if you wish for the same, I would respectfully refer you to him. Suffice it to say that he has assured me that I have his entire approval of my course in the premises, and I have no objection to the entire correspondence going before your Committee if he deems such proper.

As I stated in the beginning of the communication I cannot enter into a discussion of matters transpiring before the Grand Jury, but I would offer

the Speer case R. W. Speer, the Denver Postmaster, was indicted in a land fraud case and acquitted in 1885.

this suggestion. How does Mr. Patterson know so well what took place in the Grand Jury room? The means of his knowledge are apparent to any man, or he must have made up all he states, and the source of his knowledge being corrupt, can any charges based thereupon be fairly urged against me?

Mr. Patterson's statements of what took place after the indictment against Mr. Speer was returned are false, and I will ask the endorsement of the District Judge with regard to the truth of what I now say.

First: Mr. Patterson and Mr. Speer were on the ground before the indictment was reported, and were fully advised of what was going on before the Grand Jury. Moreover the indictment was telegraphed to the *Denver News* nearly twenty-four hours before it was returned into Court and was published in said paper nearly twelve hours before the Grand Jury made its report.

Second: When the matter came up on Friday the 5th of March, I did not open my lips concerning the motion for a speedy trial, and the Court of its own motion refused to hear the application and continued the case until Monday the 8th of March.

Third: The Court was near the end of the term and Mr. Patterson knew that if a trial were to be had at all at that term, that it must have been within a week from the time that he made his application. He also knew that my witnesses were scattered, some across a mountain range which could not be crossed on account of the snow, and over which Mr. Hammond says, he had to snow-shoe twenty-five miles. Mr. Patterson knew, as every lawyer does, that the evidence needed before the Grand Jury is not half of that needed before a petit jury, and he also knew that it was impossible for me to be properly ready for trial without several weeks preparation. Consequently he was very anxious for a trial at the Pueblo term, hoping to catch me unawares and defeat me through lack of preparation.

Fourth: When the motion for a speedy trial came up for hearing on March 8th, it was near the end of the term as I have stated before, and in fact Court adjourned on the 13th.

Fifth: It is untrue that I showed in Court vehemence or feeling in opposing motion, but I stated the grounds of my position fully, fairly and dispassionately.

Sixth: Mr. Patterson denied the justice of my position or questioned the truth of my statements and demanded an affidavit from me. So reasonable and satisfactory however were my statement and my position that the Court refused to require any affidavit and over-ruled Mr. Patterson's motion without hesitation. And the statement that I "induced the Court" so to do is untrue.

Seventh: It is also untrue that Mr. Patterson asked for the transfer of the case to Denver. I voluntarily made the offer from the very start, stating that I was willing to give Mr. Speer as speedy a trial as possible and that I would give him a trial at the May term to be held in Denver. Under the rules of the Court this transfer could not have been had except by my consent, and when the Court stated my offer to Mr. Patterson, after it had decided to continue the case, and asked whether he would consent to the transfer, he took twenty-four hours to consider the question, and upon the following day came in and consented thereto.

In conclusion I would say that I have written the foregoing letter expecting to submit it to the Honorable Moses Hallett, District Judge, and to ask him for his endorsement concerning certain matters therein stated. He is advised concerning many of the facts of the case, and he knows something of what transpired in the Grand Jury room. He is also aware of the manner in which I have discharged my duties and what my stand is in the community. He also knows the character and position of Mr. Patterson, and certainly if anything in my letter were untrue or unworthy of belief, I would not show this letter to the Judge of the Court of which I am an officer.

Again, Mr. Patterson and Mr. Thomas are law partners and are the attorneys for Mr. Speer and Mr. Hammond. Mr. Patterson is my bitter personal enemy, and both he and Mr. Thomas have lately taken every opportunity of doing me an injury. Moreover I would respectfully submit to your Committee the fact that I have been in office over twelve months, having been appointed on the 23d of April 1885 that from the time of my appointment to the time that the Senate met, Messrs. Patterson & Thomas never raised their voices against my appointment, so far as the President and the Attorney General are concerned, and never directly or indirectly made any charges against me in the Department. The Senate met in December, and from that time until Mr. Patterson was employed as attorney for Mr. R. W. Speer, Mr. Patterson never made a charge against me, never filed a protest against my confirmation, and allowed five months nearly to pass without a word to my detriment. So soon however as Mr. Patterson became Mr. Speer's attorney he commenced a fierce assault upon me, making charges that no one ever heard of before, and which he would not dare give publicity to in this community. Again, Mr. Patterson, claiming that he can prove his charges by incontrovertible evidence, has never filed a charge against me in the Department of Justice although he knows full well that if he could sustain one tenth of what he alleges against me before your Committee, that I would be summarily removed by the President. Again, although Mr. Patterson claims that I am notoriously unfit for my office and that I have conducted myself in a manner notoriously disreputable, yet out of nearly three hundred members of the Denver Bar, and out of the entire Bar of the State, he was unable to get any one to sign the protest which he has filed against me, except his law partner. Again, Mr. Patterson files general and sweeping charges against me with but few specifications, and in the particulars wherein he has been specific, I submit that I have shown his statements to be entirely untrue.

Finally I will again say to you and to your Committee that I should be extremely glad to have my correspondence with the Attorney General before your Committee if you now have any doubts concerning my action in the Speer case. I have no doubt that, upon a request from you, the Attorney General will submit all letters and correspondence to your Committee for inspection. I can say in that correspondence I tried to do full justice to Mr. Speer at the same time that I did my duty as a public officer.

Respectfully, *Henry W. Hobson.*

State of Colorado, County of Arapahoe

Henry W. Hobson being first duly sworn deposes and says that he has read carefully the foregoing letter and that the statements therein are true and correct. [signed] *Henry W. Hobson.*

Subscribed and sworn to before me, *Milton G. Cage,* Notary Public

In so far as the foregoing letter related to matters of which I have knowledge, I believe it to be a correct statement of them. As to what took place in the Speer case at Pueblo it is entirely so. The charge that Mr. Hobson has been prosecuting that case with malice toward Speer or any one is absurd. From the first hour of the Speer investigation he and his numerous friends have exerted themselves to the utmost to stifle it. At times they have been very near success and all the outcry about malice, false testimony &c. is the usual clamor of people who suspect that they are in danger. In my judgment Mr. Hobson's conduct in that case has been open, fair, and honorable and in view of the aspersions directed against him it may be due to him to say that in his conduct of the office of District Attorney I have seen nothing to condemn. I regard him as an honorable young man and wholly incapable of the things alleged against him.   —*Moses Hallett,* District Judge.

Denver, Colorado, May 7th, 1886.
To the Hon. George F. Edmunds, Chairman Judiciary Committee, U. S. Senate:
Sir: We, the undersigned members of the Bar of Colorado, practicing in the Circuit and District Courts of the United States for the District of Colorado, being well acquainted with Henry W. Hobson, Esq., United States Attorney for the District of Colorado and familiar with his course and conduct in said office for more than a year past, take pleasure in bearing witness to his ability, efficiency, honesty and integrity, both in private life and in his official conduct. We think Mr. Hobson is in every way qualified for the position, and assure you that his confirmation will be in the interest of good Government, to the advantage of the public, and thoroughly acceptable to the Bar of this State and to all good citizens. Respectfully —

A note reads that this letter was signed by 20 attorneys from Denver.

The National Archives, in Denver, Colorado, contains Henry Hobson's papers for the period that he was the United States Attorney for the District of Colorado. While perhaps his most famous case was the Mormon Church case that he argued and won in Salt Lake City in 1887, the archives show the nature of the other cases that he was responsible for prosecuting including, perjury, timber trespass, counterfeiting and one case of prosecuting a man for sending obscene letters in the mail.

The 1886 indictment of Walter W. Clary for counterfeiting quotes a letter from Clary: "These 'goods' are printed from the finest engraved steel plates on paper equal in texture to that used in the manufacture of the genuine U. S. Bills. And are guaranteed A—1 goods in every respect. Three of the bills of our issue are struck from original plates stolen from the Treasury Department in 1871 and are consequently genuine except the signature… Our price is in every case ten percent of the face value of the goods— whatever the denominations… Discounts— We wish to state concisely that it is not our practice to make any reduction from our established rate. The small discount of 10% off which we have sometimes given on bills of the larger denominations fifties & hundreds, will no longer be allowed… Shipments will be made by ordinary mail…" Clary reportedly sent one letter to a prospective customer saying: "Your name has been sent me by a confidential agent, as a man with whom I could safely deal. My business is not a legitimate one. I cannot be very plain, but if you have any need of the green articles I deal in— Sizes, ones, twos, fives, tens, twenties,—

Write and I will send terms and sample if desired."

Found in Henry Hobson's personal files was a letter addressed to him on August 7, 1888: "Dr. Sir: Send you enclosed a letter in the Spanish language and a translation of the same in English. The District Attorney here said it would be well to state the Case to you. We do not know the exact nature of the offence. If it is not a Case for the U. S. Court please return the original letter and please inform us if we can proceed under the State Law. We have conclusive evidence to prove the sender and writer of the letter to be one Manuel Sandoval, a resident of Pueblo… We have another letter of the same Nature in our possession send by the same person. Awaiting your reply we remain respectfully yours, Salvador Gonzales."

In November 1888 Manuel Sandoval was indicted for sending a "certain lewd and indecent writing" through the mail. The indictment, entirely in Hobson's handwriting, reads as follows: "Manuel Sandoval did deposit and cause to be deposited in the Post Office of the United States… certain obscene lewd and indecent writing in the form of and purporting to be a letter… enclosed in an envelope, sealed and stamped… addressed to Antonia Lujan… a female person residing in said city of Pueblo, Colorado. And which said writing, purporting to be a letter, was written in the Mexican language, sometimes called the Spanish language… and in and by which said writing purporting to be a letter, various and numerous indecent lewd and filthy names, epithets, and words were applied to the person to whom said letter was sent… and numerous indecent, lewd, and filthy charges and insinuations were made against the character, chastity, virtue, person, and actions of the person to whom said letter was sent… And near the end of which said letter were the words in Mexican… which in the English language mean as said Jurors show in substance and effect, 'Maria Antonia Lujan the pimp of Salvador Gonzalez be of the cut finger.' The language, contents, and purport of which said writing, purporting to be a letter, are not more fully sent out and shown according to their tenor and effect because of the great difficulty of translating said writing into the English language and also because the contents, language, terms, and purport of said writing are so obscene, lewd, indecent, and filthy that said jurors [the Grand Jury] consider it improper to spread the same upon the records of this Court as the same would be offensive to the Court, contrary to its dignity and against public morals… And said jurors do further present that he the said Manual Sandoval well knew the contents, purport, and effect of said writing, purporting to be a letter, at the time he deposited it… in the mail, and he well knew that said writing was non-mailable matter under the laws of the United States…"

The National Archives also contains the records of a large number of timber trespass cases where individuals and corporations were accused of unlawfully cutting large amounts of timber on public property. The indictment of Levi Spracher and Charles Ireland on March 1, 1889 reads that they: "…did unlawfully cut and did cause and procure to be cut and did aid and assist in cutting on certain public lands of the United States in said Saguache County… a large amount of pine and other timber belonging to the United States, to wit, timber sufficient to make four thousand mine props such as are used in timbering coal mines, of various sizes and dimensions…" Other frequent issues of the time concerned fraudulent land claims under the Homestead Act.

The indictments are all signed: "Henry W. Hobson, U. S. Attty. for Colo."

—All the work of a young United States Attorney.   —*Editor's note.*

◡ And years later:

There are two honest democrats to Colorado at least. This number is not large, but it is important. Both are lawyers, a good deal above the average of the profession. One is Senator C. C. Parsons, the author of the glass ballot-box law. The other is United States District Attorney Hobson, who is making land stealing odious. He secured the indictment of nine Bent county land thieves yesterday. One or the other of these gentlemen is liable to be the next governor of Colorado. Both represent the best— and, alas, the rarest—element in their party. Both have done good service in the suppression of scallawaggery in Colorado. —*Unidentified newspaper clipping.*

On Monday the Honorable John B. Fleming qualified as United States district attorney for Colorado. This is the first important change in the federal offices in Colorado. Hon. H. W. Hobson sent in his resignation as district attorney directly after the fourth of March (1889). Mr. Fleming is a young man like Mr. Hobson and we trust he will make an equally strong record. The appointment of Mr. Hobson as district attorney was very severely criticized by the party; first, because Mr. Hobson had not been for many years identified with the democratic party in this state, and secondly, because he was a young man without great experience. But the fears that were expressed as to his ability to discharge the duties of his office have proved groundless. He has been, take him all in all, the most successful district attorney the state has ever had. His success in Colorado led the government to have him employed as special counsel in important cases in the territories. He has managed several cases where the opposing counsel have been men of national reputation, like ex-Senator McDonald and the Hon. B. F. Butler. All of these cases he has managed successfully, and he leaves his office with a reputation as a lawyer that few men in Colorado have. It has always been supposed that political influence had more or less power in controlling the prosecution of certain kinds of land or timber frauds. But Mr. Hobson's personal character is so high and the management of his office has been so clean that he never has been even suspected of being controlled by any improper influence in the conduct of his cases. He goes out of his office with a record as a very able lawyer, and as an honest, honorable man.
—*Unidentified newspaper clipping.*

◡ A letter to a Senator:

United States Attorney's Office, District of Colorado
Henry W. Hobson, U. S. Attorney
January 3d, 1887.
Hon. Thomas M. Bowen, U. S. Senate, Washington, D. C.—
Dear Sir: I am informed that some action will be taken at the present session of Congress with regard to changing the system of paying officers of the Department of Justice in various Districts by salaries instead of fees.

I would most earnestly suggest to you the advisability of such legislation. The reasons therefore will address themselves to your mind at once. After nearly two years of experience I find that a system of paying salaries would promote the good of the service in every way. As an abstract proposition, I would suggest that under the present system every inducement is offered to

District Attorneys to bring all the suits and create all the litigation they possibly can without regard to the justice of the cause or the prospect of success…

I would also beg leave to suggest that in case such a bill as above referred to comes before the Senate, that sufficient salary should be paid to the officers of this District to justify good and competent men in taking the position. I understand that formerly a bill was introduced paying the District Attorney and Marshall $3500 a year. This amount in entirely inadequate… This District is one of the largest in the United States, territorially speaking, and the work is very heavy, and under the present system of paying District Attorneys, I am not paid for more than about one third of the work I do…

I do not write so much for myself inasmuch as I do not contemplate holding office longer than four years, of which two have almost elapsed, but in justice to those who will have to act under this bill in the future, I take the liberty of writing to you upon this subject.

I have a written a similar letter to Senator Teller and Representative Symes.

Very Respectfully, *Henry W. Hobson.*

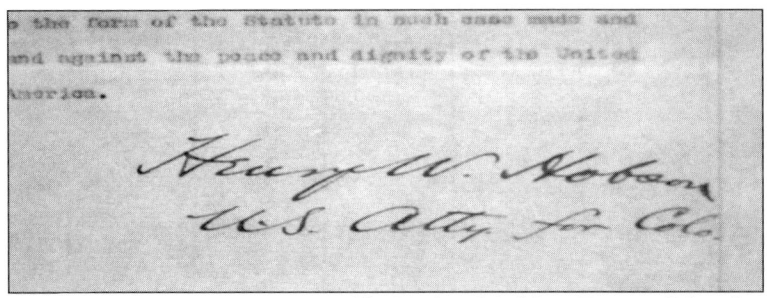

The National Archives, Denver, Colorado

And an unidentified and undated newspaper clipping from the papers of Annie Jennings Wise Hobson:

"The following poem appeared forty years ago in a paper, the name of which we don't know. We trust things have improved since that time."

> The Devil came up to the earth one day,
> And into a courthouse he wended his way,
> Just as an attorney, with very grave face,
> Was proceeding to argue the "points in the case."
> Now, a lawyer his Majesty never had seen,
> For to his dominions none ever had been.
> And he felt very anxious the reason to know
> Why none had been sent to the regions below.
> 'Twas the fault of his agents, his Majesty thought,
> That none of these lawyers had ever been caught,
> And for his own pleasure he felt a desire
> To come to the earth and the reason inquire.

Well, the lawyer, who rose with vision so grave,
Made out his opponent a consummate knave,
And the Devil was really greatly amused
To hear the attorney so grossly abused.
But as soon as the speaker had come to a close,
The counsel opposing them fiercely arose.
And he heaped such abuse on the head of the first,
That made him a villain of all men the worst.
Thus they quarreled, contended and argued so long,
'Twas hard to determine which of them was wrong,
And concluding he'd heard quite enough of the "fuss,"
Old Nick turned away and soliloquized thus:
"If all they have said of each other be true,
The Devil has surely been robbed of his due;
But I'm satisfied now it's all very well—
For these villains would ruin the morals of hell.
They have puzzled the court with their villainous cavil,
And I'm free to confess they have puzzled the Devil;
My agents are right to let lawyers alone—
If I had them they'd swindle me out of my throne!"

XVI

1887, Part One

A Very Busy Year

As 1887 began, Henry W. Hobson was very busy as the United States Attorney for Colorado and Katherine Thayer Jermain, a young widow, was dividing her time between visits with her mother in Colorado Springs and her in-laws in Albany, New York. Things would be different at the end of the year. Elsewhere, after fifty years of being on the throne of England, Queen Victoria celebrated her Golden Jubilee, a flood on the Yellow River in China left over 900,000 people dead, and the Post Office adopted a policy of delivering mail for free to all communities with a population of at least 10,000. In Richmond, Virginia, Frank Sprague built the first successful electric trolley line with forty cars operating on twelve miles of track.

Letters, telegrams, and writings by:
Ada Addison, Kittie's cousin
Samuel Fisk, a friend of Henry Hobson's in Denver
Annie Jennings Wise Hobson
Henry Wise Hobson
James B. Jermain
Katherine Thayer Jermain
James "Fitz-Mac" Philip MacCarthy, a newspaper columnist
Katherine, Katie, Savage
Catherine McKie Thayer
Francis McKie Thayer
Mary Lyons Wise

Letters written from: Denver and Colorado Springs, Colorado; Richmond and Ashland, Virginia; Seattle and Tacoma, Washington Territory; Portland, Oregon Territory; Utah Territory; St. Louis, Missouri; Hot Springs, Arkansas; New York City, Cambridge, White Creek, Albany, and Hoosick, New York; Philadelphia; Washington, D. C.; Fitchburg, Massachusetts; and aboard trains.

∽

1887—Henry & Kittie

Monday morning. [Undated, early 1887.]
My dear Mrs. Jermain—   I hardly think I shall be able to get down to say goodbye to you at the train, so I shall send a word in this way. I am somewhat puzzled to know why I should be so anxious to say goodbye to you for a few

Katherine Thayer Jermain, taken between 1882 and 1887.

days. I suppose it is because you are very pleasant to me, and I like to show my appreciation of the same. I thought something of going down to see you last evening but I felt so supremely stupid that I did not feel justified in imposing myself upon anyone. I saw no-one at the Springs, not making an effort to pay a visit. I need not say I missed you very much. I shall see you Saturday, will I not? Until then goodbye—   Very Sincerely, *Henry W. Hobson.*

February 9, 1887, The Denver Club.
Dear Mrs. Jermain—   I had hoped up to the last moment to get down to the Springs to your german but the fates are against me. I am obliged to go East tomorrow evening and I will be busy in Court every hour until then. It is absolutely impossible for me to leave and so you must forgive me. As an evidence of my earnest desires in this respect, I will say that every difference between us is forgotten on my part and henceforth I will think of you only as the charming Mrs. Jermain of whom I heard so much before I met you.
— Very Sincerely, *Henry W. Hobson.*

April 12, 1887, The Denver Club.
My Dear Mrs. Jermain—   Do you know I think you are a most charming woman to have written me that note of today, and since you so rewarded my one essay at "pencilings," I will be bold enough to try another. I am much better today and unless the Doctor takes a very decided stand I am going to reappear in the world tomorrow. If so, I will try and call tomorrow evening… Believe me I can write better than this ordinarily. Thank you so much for your sympathy—   Sincerely, *Henry W. Hobson.*

Henry W. Hobson, United States Attorney
April 15, 1887.
My dear Mrs. Jermain—   You will pardon office paper, will you not, when I say that I have none other at hand. I cannot go down, I fear, tomorrow morning, so will not impose on you to the extent of asking you to go by the 8 o'clk train, though really I never thought you had any such intention. I may go by the mid-day train but about that I will tell you this evening. Where, do you ask! Why at the Windsor, provided you are going to see me when I call. If not, send your refusal back by the bearer of this and I will stay at home. I am making the fact that I wish to persuade you into an engagement for next week an excuse for calling again this evening, but to be very frank, I think the true cause is, that I had a charming visit last evening and hope for another such this evening. And after all, is not that a sufficient reason for a man to give to a woman? If not, you must be free from some qualities of sympathy (how much better that word is than vanity or weakness) which I should not like to think you lacking in. But I have written a *letter*, and alas for *good form*, on business paper.   —Yours Sincerely, *Henry W. Hobson.*

May eighth. Sunday Morning.
Dear Mrs. Jermain—   I must be in Pueblo next Thursday on business and I thought I would leave here by the mid-day train on Wednesday and stop at the Springs for the evening. Don't you remember you said we would have our drive the next time I went down? I am not certain I can get through Court on Wednesday in time to take the train I wish, so don't count certainly upon me

until I arrive. If I do not see you Wednesday however I hope to do so soon. I returned yesterday from Leadville after a week of hard work and today I am loafing. I remember my day at the Springs very pleasantly. That was a day when you were pleased to be charming in every respect, although in good faith you seem that always to me, and I am inclined to think to others too. Goodbye for the present, Sincerely, *Henry W. Hobson.*

May 17th.
Dear Mrs. Jermain—   I am so disappointed I cannot possibly get down to the Springs today, for I have a case which will detain me in Court over the day and then I must hurry to Pueblo. I am afraid you will not care a bit, for you have not even written saying you would take me to drive and that too after I had invited myself. I do care however, and as I need a holiday, I am going to spend Saturday evening and Sunday at the Springs provided I can get off. I have bored you so with notes, however, that you will hear from me no more until you see me in proper person. I send you some flowers this morning, paying you the compliment of taking them personally to the depot. When sent from the florists this morning they seemed badly put up, but I did not have time to examine them so I must trust to your telling me whether they reach you in good condition. I do trust they will and that they will be pretty, for you should have only the prettiest of flowers—   Very Sincerely, *Henry W. Hobson.*

Henry Wise Hobson, Charles Bohm, Photographer, 284 Fifteenth St., Denver.

Wednesday Afternoon.
My dear Mrs. Jermain—   How disappointed I am. I had set my heart on seeing you here this week and from the number of times I have asked Ralph (the black-haired boy) whether any telegram had come, he was beginning to suspect that something serious was up… Do you know I think I would give up almost any amount of pleasure for myself, if I could thereby give you any pleasure. Yet I am a selfish fellow as a rule. I am looking forward to Saturday with much eagerness, for I am going down for another "quiet Sunday" at the Springs, unless something more important than "Court duties" comes up to prevent… You will not forget our engagement for Saturday afternoon will you, and there will be no more headache, will there! How much of my "quiet Sunday" are you going to let me spend with you? In this connection I must thank you very much for the pleasure you gave me last Sunday…   Yours Very Sincerely, *Henry W. Hobson.* P.S. You signed yourself very properly in your note.

June 1887, Colorado Springs.
My dear Mr. Hobson—   The little pin attached I have selected for you— thinking you might be willing to accept it in payment of my debt… I am glad I have met you. And always please remember I will be glad to see you. With kindest remembrances and hoping you are well, Very Sincerely Yours   — *Katherine T. Jermain.* P.S. If this sharp point is likely to break friendship do send me a penny— though for my part, the superstition does not hold good.

With this letter is an envelope containing dried flowers that reads: "Probably the leaves from the roses given Mother by Father when he went to see her in Col Springs."

June 20th The Denver Club, 6:30 P. M.
Dear Mrs. Jermain—   I have just come into the Club and received your note and have only time before the mail to acknowledge the same. It was very nice in you to let me know about your movements, but then you are always nice. If you

Katherine Thayer Jermain, probably taken in Colorado Springs between 1882 and 1887.

will permit me I will meet you at the train on Wednesday, which I take it will be the mid-day train. I am sure you will not object to having a man look after your baggage etc. I will then arrange about seeing you. Excuse this hasty scrawl for I am hurried and have an execrable pen. Sincerely, *Henry W. Hobson.*

June 29th, 1887.
My dear Mrs. Jermain—   Though it is very late, almost ten o'clock, and I have done a hard days work, I will give myself the very pleasant recreation of writing to you. It was most thoughtful and kind in you to send me that little note from the River, and when I saw your handwriting on the envelope, I was puzzled, for I did not expect to hear from you until you were at your journey's end. But it is the unexpected pleasure which ever causes the greatest delight. Really, Mrs. Jermain you show more appreciation of what little I do for you than I deserve… Behold the photograph! The day after you left I went down and ordered it. I did not sit for it, but ordered from an old negative. I am entirely aware that the photograph is better looking than I am and therefore am afraid to abandon this I know, for another that may be too just. Now bear in mind Madame, that you have promised to send me yours in return… Don't delay too long about sending your photograph, or I shall begin to— well I won't begin anything for I know you will be prompt in performing your promise… I now know definitely that I must be in St. Louis to argue a case before Judge Brown on September the 19th. I had expected to go to St. Paul and from there I hoped to run over to York State [New York]. I cannot now say whether I shall be able to go from St. Louis. Moreover I may go East as far as Washington sometime during the summer… It is just a week ago tonight that I said good-bye to you at the train and yet it has seemed much longer. Last Saturday I was really in a bad humor that I did not have the pleasure of a trip to the Springs. But of course I could have gone, but where would have been the "pony express," and where would have been the driver of the same… I have lived my usual quiet life since you left, being at my office almost every night, and indeed it has been very warm for hard work. How glad you must be that it is eleven o'clk— that I am very tired— that I know nothing which will interest you and that I have not been able to talk with Dr. Fisk in order to get any items of news to detail! Well goodnight! I trust sincerely you reached your journey's end in safety and that your visit East will be charming in every respect… Again good-night. I shall sleep better for this epistolary chat with you.   —Yours Sincerely, *Henry W. Hobson.*

July 9th & 11th 1887. Denver.
My dear Mrs. Jermain—   Your nice note telling of your arrival at your journey's end should not have remained so long unnoticed. I have however been so occupied during the last ten days, being worked day and night that it has been impossible for me to write. I now have only a moment, for you will appreciate how busy I am when I say that all last week I was, and this week I am in Court from 9 to 6 and obliged to do a great deal of office work at night. It was very nice in you to write so soon after you got settled and truly I longed for the beautiful quiet scenery you gave a sketch of, and I thought how delightful 'twould be to lie lazily with you, spinning out the afternoon with you along the river, in the woods, careless of the humans about us, except ourselves… I suppose ere this you have received my photograph and letter.

Don't feel called upon to say you "like the photograph because it is such a good likeness of me." I directed it to Albany… All Denver is now excited over a very unfortunate tragedy. John A. Witter died last week in a very curious way and it is now definitely settled that he was poisoned with arsenic, the poisoning having extended through weeks. The evidence is very strong against his wife and the case will lead to [a] most disgraceful scandal affecting some people somewhat prominent in Denver Society… Well I must really close as I have not another moment. In your pleasant little home you must think of how much I wish I could be on hand… If your Mother and Brother are with you, please present my regards. Goodbye! Yours Sincerely, *Henry W. Hobson.*
July 23rd, Denver, Colo.

My Dear Mrs. Jermain—   I wish I could make you appreciate the pleasure I felt in receiving your photograph. It brought to mind so many pleasant things and especially the pleasantest of things— yourself. It is a good photograph, and yet, shall I say frankly what I miss about it! I miss the expression of Mrs. J's face— an expression which no photograph could show or give. I cannot say more without becoming complimentary and such would be I fear too much like a 21-year old boy. Whenever I look at the photograph, I am at first greatly pleased and then there steals over my pleasure the shadow of a regret that I have to be looking at a photograph instead of the only true original. Can you not understand what I mean? I am sure you do, for you understand me in so many things and ways… Well I must say goodbye for I have a vast pile of work to do before going away and I am almost in despair as to how I am to get through with it. I don't know and have not known where to direct my letters to you except to your place at White Creek, so I expect you will find quite a packet of letters there from me. My sincere advice is to note on the envelopes the one posted last, read that and destroy the balance. Thus you will save yourself much burning. But as an Irishman would say, when you have read all the letters through you will find this bit of advice and doubtless act upon it. Goodbye. Again many thanks for the photograph—
    Yours Sincerely, as ever, *Henry W. Hobson.*
P.S. By-the-way, shall I interpret the "Yrs. Etc" on the back as meaning anything I wish? How charming that would be.

July 24, 1887, Sunday, Denver.
You have doubtless discovered by this time, my dear Mrs. Jermain what a very poor correspondent I am. To the charge I plead guilty at once… It has been so long since any woman, except one or two tried friends inherited from my boyhood, has cared to be troubled with a correspondence with me that I have gotten out of the habit of writing social letters. Even my friends aforesaid have become accustomed to hearing from me at irregular intervals of one, two, or three months… How I wish I could have been with you in your wanderings "over the hills and far away." Did you find anyone whose company you could stand better for a three or four hours drive, than your Colorado driving companion… I had a pleasant surprise this morning when I received from my mother a large photograph, half-life size, of my father who was a very handsome man. We have never had aught than a photograph of him and for years I have looked forward to the time when I could afford to have a fine oil portrait painted by a first class artist. I was

devoted to my father as a child and have the sweetest tenderest memories and recollections about him and of him…

Yours ever Sincerely, *Henry W. Hobson.*

August 8, 1887, Denver.
My dear Mrs. Jermain— …Do you know, I must thank you again for your photograph. I like it better now than I did at first and I liked it very much then. I have had many pleasant thoughts arise, as I looked at it. Goodbye! I shall not write another word. If you don't withdraw your invitation you may yet see me at Hill Farm.   Sincerely, *Henry W. Hobson.*

⁊ An undated letter to Henry Wise Hobson from his mother that begins on page 9, probably written in August 1887:

I had to drop the housekeeping plan all together for I found that she [Alice, wife of John Cannon Hobson] forgot half of everything, got into snarls with the servants, each trying to lay the blame of carelessness and inefficiency on the other. Now to speak of Alice for the last time. She is either incapacitated by debility and ill health (yet I never saw a better appetite, she eats twice as much as I do and now sleeps every night till half past seven in the morning) or she is the most inefficient woman of her age I ever met. Her idea of usefulness is to work herself to death now and then at the machine at some sewing (in which she has improved, but still sews far from neatly) & to write to Cannon. She does not deny that she despises the care of her children. She neither knows how to amuse, entertain or instruct them, and can neither take proper care of them or herself. She has a certain kind of capacity of loving and bestows that chiefly on Cannon. She is both opinionated and self-willed despite her protestations of willingness to be taught etc. I have never succeeded in getting her to make an improvement of any kind without a struggle and firm persistency. She is much more willing for me to take the children and govern them, than most women would be, but that is in the part due to Cannon's influence. We will have a cross in her as long as she lives, and Cannon has tied himself to one who can certainly never be a "helpmate" to a minister. But we must make the best of her. I have given up the effort to teach her, what she does not learn from example she will not learn at all, and I have determined that I will try to be kind to her and let her alone. It may be ill health, and I try to think it is, but I assure you that whenever she has to make any extra exertion she is utterly wretched, and the minute anything is troublesome she frets over it or wants to give it up.

I have told her positively that as Cannon's mother I claim and shall exercise the right to see that the children are trained in habits of health and cleanliness— and to that she passively submits, glad to have any trouble taken off her hands.

She and Cannon are both like children themselves in many regards. Nevertheless, the three bright sweet little boys, handsome and attractive and so easily managed, are a great compensation and delight to me. I am so glad to have them, and the only shadow over them is that just as they have grown into my life, I may have to give them up. I do not mind any trouble with them and their presence is sunshine and warmth to my life from which the *earthly presence* of little ones went so early.

I believe Alice to be truthful and to have good principles. Had she been trained to some higher standard of life and duty something more might have

been made of her… Now do not fear that I shall live in hot water with her, indeed I shall not. I have tested her fully and I shall be as kind to her as possible but let her alone; hoping and praying that she may see more clearly and learn something from example after a while—
Ten o'clock at night—

I did not begin with the intention of giving you such a dissertation. I had to stop to go to church. I took little Cannon with me, and he behaved with the gravity and decorum of a Judge. I asked him after church if he understood what was said, "Yes." "Well tell me something he said." "I understood it, all but I cannot tell you anything."

Do not think for one moment that I regret having come here with Alice and the children. It was full time that the children should have come to me, and it is a great mercy that she will let me regulate them. My burden is far from being heavier than I can bear, and I have been in remarkably good health. My new cook is getting well in the traces, & seems anxious to please and stay with me. The first would have done very well but from the effort to increase the family minus a husband, she had to retire from active life. This new girl knows much more about cooking than Kate did when she came, and is a better subject to work on if she is not ambitious in the same way.

Really I will not bore you with any more length of letter, though I have not said half I would like to say. I am sure the little boys send kisses and Alice her love. If she does not improve soon I am going to send her to her mother to pay a visit, and have entire relief from the children. She has had a right trying time and peculiarly to try her with the little ones so nearly all babies. I could get on just as well without as with her I assure you, and if I had a sensible efficient nurse in the place of a poor little weak Alice, I should have a much easier time. You may think I am exaggerating, but indeed it is so that she cannot put the baby to sleep without such a row that I have been forced to take all such things in my own hands. I have now so trained him that he will often go to sleep with a little gentle rocking in his crib. Now we must remember that Minnie G— is just as inefficient in these things as Alice, but in such a different way, she is so humble about it & has so many other lovely qualities to make up for such defects. I have heard very little from Richard of late.
—God bless you ever, Your devoted Mother, *A. J. W. Hobson.*

August 26, 1887, Denver.
My dear Mrs. Jermain—   I have been back two days from a trip which lasted two weeks. I find both of your late letters awaiting me. You are very nice! I suppose a good many people have told you this before and I have thought of it often before, but the fact was much emphasized in my mind by your writing the two letters to me. I really have no time for correspondence as I am pushing to get straightened up for another absence next week, during which I will probably be one day at the Springs.— Alas! you will not be there. Notwithstanding my hurry however, I am going to scribble you a line… I am so sorry your Mother has been unwell this summer. I know what a strain you must have been under to be absent from her whilst sick. I suppose she will be with you by the time this reaches you, and how much do I wish that she will be entirely restored to health… Goodbye! I must close for there are two men in the outer office waiting for me.   —Yours Sincerely as Ever, *Henry W. Hobson.*

September 2nd, 1887, Hill Farm, White Creek, N. Y.
My dear Mr. Hobson—   A few days since I received your letter and I was glad you made those "two men wait in the outer office" long enough to send me a line. I did not before know that gentlemen were in the habit of looking over letters not addressed to them… My Mother writes of you calling on her. I expect her here next week, and I will be very happy… I wish to tell you how to reach this out-of-the way spot. You can leave Albany for Troy, at the even & half hours… Arriving at Troy you can leave Troy, Fitchburg R. R. for Hoosick Falls… where I will meet you. The distance from here is eight miles— an hour's drive. Will you kindly let me know when you will be likely to come as many days in advance as convenient… Last week I had 4 fresh-air children from the city for a week— it was delightful to see their pleasure over every flower & blade of grass. I gave them a picnic on my summer-house hill. Today is rainy, despite it I have driven several miles. I often laugh when I think of our drives in snow & hail storms— and the time we turned our back to the storm. There is *no time* in my house. No ticking of clocks. Next week though the old one on the stairs will be set… With my very kindest regard and hoping to hear of the "visit" & its time or date— I am yours very sincerely,
Katherine T. Jermain.

↬ A letter from Annie Jennings Wise Hobson:

Ashland, Sept. 4th, 1887, Sunday afternoon.
Yours of Aug 27th was received on Friday, my dear son, welcomed as is every missive of yours & read with even more than usual interest & pleasure, for it gave me an insight into your heart and mind that I have long wished to have… There is always one aspect in your regrets that is very painful to me. You so constantly speak as if held back & kept down by the necessity of working for others & with such chafing about being in debt.

In regard to the last I have something to say later, and now let me speak to you very sincerely— read & think of what I say not merely as from the mother who has the right to counsel you, but as the best friend, who has studied your mind & character from the cradle, ever alive to your highest interests & never blinded by love to your imperfections & faults. From your childhood you showed what I term brain power— & by that I mean more than intellectual. You evinced intellectual capacity combined with great will power & keen inquisitiveness that asked the why of everything; but there was always a lack of what I term *spiritual apprehension*. You were always loving & generous & yet exacting & selfish in some things— small things— a great deal of self assertion in demanding your rights combined with impulses that often made you secretly thoughtful & unselfish & at times, with a morbid irritability and sensitiveness that made your Mother's heart ache, in view of the suffering it would bring to you in the future. I always said you have much to suffer in this life. You always rebelled against authority— and yet gave up in love. I was always glad that before you were 10 years old I perceived that you could master knowledge rapidly when you chose and then know how to use it— that you have inherited from my father. You never gave the least evidence of precocity nor the slightest tendency to *bookishness* or a student's genuine characteristics. I never saw the least evidence of "genius," as it is usually meant, in you or Cannon. I did in little Annie, but for you, your father,

Grandfather, and I early predicted intellectual power & force of character to succeed in life's battle. You have many of the characteristics and inconsistencies, mental & moral, of the Wises, combined with certain harmonizing & equalizing qualities from the Hobson's, which give you your individuality & form you a man to take a front rank amongst men & to do good & noble service in your generation.

The sketch given of you by Fitz-Mac is on the whole a fair one and yet superficial. He did not take in the whole man and I doubt if he is of the kind to appreciate you at your best. He did not know enough of the circumstances of your life to make a just estimate & due allowance for your position as a very young man to have taken the *strides* you have done in your position politically & as a lawyer. Ten years hence, if Fitz-Mac is capable of judging & you are alive, I am sure he will speak very differently of the "impact" of your mind. I doubt if he is a mind capable of discovering the *real man* in you.

Yours is a mind and heart to be taught far more by contact with mankind and developed by the circumstances & conditions of life than through books. The written thoughts of other minds will teach and enlighten you only as they aid your own *original* thoughts & develop the latent feelings & better impulses of your nature.

What I mean is that you have no sponge-like capacity of *absorbing knowledge* from others, and must think *with them* as well as *by them*— think for yourself… Can you question that the impelling necessity of working for others has brought out some of the noblest characteristics of your nature? Had you married a woman of means & settled down to an easier life would you be the man you are now? Had you have made more money more rapidly with only yourself to spend it on, would you have altered your present status as a lawyer & would not politics have come in your life as a dangerous & doubtful game for soul & body— for purse & mental development? I will tell you what you need to make you the man you ought to be— you need the *impact* and heart contact of the Savior, God, Christ Jesus. You need to go to Him as he shows Himself in his written life, to go to Him by spiritual communion as a little child asking to know Him and to have the power given you to take Him unto your heart & mind as He reveals Himself only to the childlike… In a short time I feel that the heavy burden of supporting others will be greatly lightened. You can give up the District Attorney's place… I am going to Richmond tomorrow for the day & want to mail this letter this evening. Do you know that your Mama could be a help & power in your life if you would let her, & I hope ere long you will. I am very well… My first waking thoughts Sunday morning go out in prayers for you & Cannon. I wonder how you have spent the day & if you have once thought that your mother's prayers are following you. —Your devoted mother, *A.J.W. Hobson.*

—I have also received the photo views of Denver & enjoyed them and appreciated your thoughtfulness in sending them.

This letter refers to a sketch of Henry Wise Hobson that was written for the *Gazette* by James "Fitz-Mac" Philip Mac-Carthy, 1869–1920. A copy of the column must have been sent to Henry's mother soon after it appeared. *Political Portraits*, a collection of MacCarthy's profiles of prominent Colorado residents, was published in 1888 by The Gazette Printing Co. of Colorado Springs. The column is reprinted below.

THE GAZETTE
Sunday, August 21, 1887.

Men are formed not less by the forces that oppose them than by those which support. This is to say our lives are shaped not less by our antipathies than by our sympathies.

Life is a pendulum swinging between that we dread and that we hope for. Ambition is the impelling force and there is no repose but death.

Mr. Henry Wise Hobson, United States district attorney for Colorado, is a man of whom it may fairly be said that his enemies not less than his friends have made him. He is one of the most capable and promising young men in political life in the west. To abilities considerably above the average he unites high resolve, unflinching steadiness of purpose, great industry, correct moral equipoise and a force and simplicity of character which make him at once a strong and admirable young man.

He has a fresh, virile, lovable nature.

He is thirty years of age. When appointed district attorney he was twenty-eight. That appointment launched him suddenly into one of the most memorable political struggles of Colorado— a struggle marked by every phase of political indecency and every resort of personal acrimony, but out of which he came, in spite of some indiscretions of judgment, stainless and victorious; and today he enjoys the confidence of the national administration in a greater degree than any other man in Colorado. That confidence the high and sterling integrity of his character entirely justifies. All things considered, it could not be reposed in a safer man.

His intellectual status cannot be indicated by a word— unless that word be courage. He is not a genius, though men no abler than him who get into the gutter twice a week are called geniuses. The estimate of a respectable life is not illuminated by that sort of a contrast. He is not small enough to be described as merely clever, and there is not that impact from his mind which makes the distinct impression of mental powerfulness.

I first met Mr. Hobson in '84 on the political platform at Salida. He there gave a resumé of the political situation which struck me as singularly fair, forcible and candid, and I said to myself, "There is the man for the long pull." He was followed by Judge Felker, the inimitable farceur, and by the Hon. Charles Thomas, whose scintillating wit kept the audience in a roar, yet Mr. Hobson was the only speaker who left impression on my mind. He said nothing very striking; and his remarks ranged along the upper level of the commonplace, but they were uttered with a logical clearness and with a presence of moral candor which interested me at once in the character of his intellect. I have come to know him rather intimately since and acquaintance has only confirmed the impression of that night. That impression is the clearest indication I can give of his intellectual status. I think that his mind is bright, clear, strong and candid but not powerful. It is a very well balanced and round mental organization. One less symmetrical would make a more distinct impression because the weak points would illuminate the strong by contrast just as the human figure in perfect proportion looks smaller than it actually is while the eye unconsciously magnifies the ungainly one.

To estimate a man correctly we must look before and after—whence he has come not less than whither he is tending. Mr. Hobson has the blood of a race of politicians in his veins and forces within his nature are almost certain to impel him toward a political career.

Politicians, like poets, exist in all degrees, and while Mr. Hobson lacks the powers that carry a public by storm, he has those better elements that gradually inspire a confidence which once founded is not easy to overthrow.

I know plenty of men, young men, and not very big men, either, who, to use a colloquial phrase, can "walk all round" Mr. Hobson in politics. Thousands of little, clever, scheming politicians are admirable in their proper sphere and worthless beyond it. The weakness of such men is that they fail to recognize their own limitations. They are blind to the patent fact that simplicity wins not less than cunning in politics, and that the broader the field the better its chances. They forget that while they are "walking all round" such a man as Mr. Hobson he is forging ahead with an earnest and definite purpose.

He has not, indeed, developed any marked capacity yet for leadership, but he has achieved a position of singular independence and of considerable personal power, and without any special genius the character of his mind seems to compass fairly and intelligently the whole diapason of political force.

He is on the broad track. If he sticks to it he is bound to become a great influence and a good influence in politics. If he leave it the fault is in himself, not in his circumstances.

No one of course can predict at what point the judgment of a young man will give out and Mr. Hobson may be lured into the labyrinth, but looking backward as well as forward I think not. His character, his record, his blood, give a good warrant to confidence. His nature is essentially simple, candid, independent and fearless. Honor is the beacon of his ambition, courage the watchword.

The most substantial encouragement to virtue in public life is the spectacle of virtue triumphant.

On that account Mr. Hobson's success over his enemies has a certain aspect of moral value toward political life. There are many evidences that the patriotic instincts of the country are just now, after a long lethargy, gathering a fresh and healthy impulse.

Mr. Hobson had the luck, or the sagacity to take the new tide at its flood and he has become the representative of a better state of public sentiment. In this regard the villainous and indecent onslaught of his enemies has only served to emphasize his position. The opposition to him was not, I think, at first of a personal nature, though under his stout and manful resistance it soon assumed a very personal character. It came entirely from a faction of his own party. His enemies were bitter, indecent, and remorseless, but they mistook their man. They expected to overwhelm him, and their cruel conduct only developed his inherent strength. They attacked a boy and found themselves confronted with an earnest, virile, fearless young man. They assailed his honor and fixed public attention on the fact that his honor was invulnerable. They exhausted every resource of scurrilous epithet and villainous cunning against him and forgot that he drew constantly on the exhaustless resources of candor. They advertised him as a fool, and the public began to notice with interest that he was an unusually capable young man. They called him a stuck-up aristocratic ass, and the public being put upon inquiry learned with satisfaction (as the public always does) that he is not only a charmingly modest mannered young fellow but that he has indeed an illustrious strain of blood in his veins—honest blood, fighting blood, the pugnacious blood of that Henry A. Wise, who was governor of Virginia for the four years preceding the rebellion.

Governor Wise, the grandfather of Mr. Hobson, was one of the most sagacious and influential politicians of his day. For fifty years he was one of the prominent characters in the public life of Virginia and he was at times a powerful national figure. He was a man after the pugnacious type of Andrew Jackson—ambitious, capable, fearless, independent, defiant, a fine lawyer, an able debater, the author of some controversial literature on the scope of the constitution, he made his way to the front rank of political power while almost a boy and held it for half a century, by the side of Webster, Clay, and Calhoun in congress and among a galaxy of able lawyers and statesmen in Virginia, not by any favor of fortune, for he was always poor, but by sheer force of personal character and a genius for public life. He had that magical power of political oratory which in these days we call magnetism and the basis of which is conviction and courage.

His son is that enlightened and progressive republican John S. Wise, considered by many the ablest lawyer and statesman of the south today, who ran against Fitz Hugh Lee for governor of Virginia in 1885.

The American people are always proud of good blood when it runs with good brains and modest manners; and there is not a more modest mannered young man in Colorado than Mr. Hobson.

He is, no doubt, justly proud of the illustrious grandfather after whom he is named, and perhaps a little boastfully proud, with fervid admiration of idolatrous youth, of the able and distinguished uncle who has been a father to him.

It is a generous pride, a worthy pride, a pride which not to feel would indicate a mean and ignoble mind.

But the Wises do not at all belong to the senseless and boastful social aristocracy of Virginia any more than Henry Clay did, though like him they have always maintained a high position among the peerless aristocracy of brains. They have not the "Norman blood." They are not descended from lord anybody. They are without "family" in the Virginia sense. They are plain, poor people who made their way to the front by sheer force of personal character, and the social aristocracy of Virginia have always been against them. They are solid against the uncle to-day, and they were solid against the grandfather in 1854. Against every odds the grandfather had the magic to win; but the voiceless eloquence of an empty saddle was invoked against the uncle, and he lost.

The people of Colorado were far from displeased to learn that Mr. Hobson came of such able and respectable stock and the gibe of his enemies promptly redounded to his advantage.

One mind always to some extent reflects the sentiment of most minds and as for me I am free to say it increased my interest and confidence in the young man.

Next to good personal character I value good blood, because though we breed children with less care of selection than we breed domestic animals the chances always are that the good strain will tell. Pride of ancestry is the noblest pride of the human heart. That sort of tradition is a hostage to the future. Only mean and ignoble minds resent it. I have no doubt that it inspires the ambition of Mr. Hobson, that it holds him up to the best that is in him. It is no idle sentiment that feeds a weak and superficial vanity, for his manners are the acme of modest and unaffected simplicity. It is a generous and noble impulse that crowds the spirit on to high and clean endeavor, and it always commands respect when it is earnest and constant to itself. I shall forgive Mr. Hobson the honorable desire to be thought a gentleman as long as he preserves the character of a gentleman, and so I think will all the people of Colorado.

He beggared himself to pay his dead father's debts with a little inheritance which came to him in his own right, and worked his way through college by teaching. That shows the character of his family pride to my satisfaction.

I can forgive him his boyish and boastful admiration of his distinguished uncle because I happen to know that uncle is an unusually able and admirable man, and I should be glad to see the republican party recognize the regenerated patriotism of the south by nominating John S. Wise of Virginia for vice president next year. I think it might prove the salvation of the party.

In personal appearance Mr. Hobson is a tall, thin, raw-boned, flat chested, yellow-haired, young fellow with a delicate manly-boyish face and a pleasant blue eye. His features are radiant with intelligence though there is no distinct impress of power upon them. His instincts are alert, nervous and sympathetic.

Any judge of physical types would say at a glance that Hobson is a man of strong racial traits. That is something which altogether eludes the common eye but is always a study to those have the instinct for it.

He looks like a puritan but for the provincial southern twang in his voice he might be taken anywhere for a Yankee of Yankees. Of his type he is rather a handsome fellow, but it is not the type that school girls languish over. It is the type that discloses to the eye of the connoisseur distinct and estimable race marks—marks that indicate not high breeding nor low breeding but the successful reproduction of a strong ancestral stamp.

Though his disposition is naturally sweet and cheerful, there is beneath the suggestion of a temper that will rasp the edge of adversity if that edge be turned too constantly toward him. He has courage, and a good deal of patience of will, but he has a delicate physical organization that is sure to break down into fretfulness and peevishness if the world go too hard with him.

In the fullest and best sense of the word he is a self made man, and he is a fine example of that strong spirit of intellectual mastership in the south which no misfortune could crush and which impelled her young men whose fortunes were broken by the war to grasp eagerly all the poor advantages of their impoverished schools when their disheartened fathers laid down the sword in despair. Education alone could preserve their dignity and they flew to it, under every privation, as the sound resource of hope.

Mr. Hobson's father had been rich, but he died leaving his family in poverty.

After making his way by hook and crook through William-and-Mary college the young man took the law course at the university and at twenty-one entered the law office of his uncle in Richmond, where he had at least the advantage of the highest legal associations until he came to Colorado in 1881 and settled at Buena Vista. In the spring of '84 he removed to Denver and in 1885 was appointed United States attorney for the district of Colorado.

I speak with reserve in saying he has the reputation of a very good lawyer. His political enemies had not a leg to stand on when they attacked his professional capacity for the place.

Though he had taken the stump in the preceding campaign, it cannot be fairly said that he had earned any claim to such distinguished political recognition as he received, and it has always remained a mystery to the general public why and how he came to receive it. I cannot go into details, but he showed a good deal of political sagacity in managing the matter.

The situation in Colorado was extraordinary. The democrats were divided into bitter factions. One of these rather arrogated to itself the title of "the better elements" of the party, and the other was supposed to contain "the scum."

As a plain matter of fact "the scum" was (as the scum commonly is) the real working arm of the party. If it did not contain the virtue, it at least contained the brains and the muscle, and under all considerations of political justice it would ordinarily be entitled to control and patronage. But in their determination to do this at any cost the leaders of the scum had over-reached their purpose. During the winter preceding the inauguration of President Cleveland they had entered into a conspiracy with Senator Teller, then in President Arthur's cabinet as Secretary of the Interior, to whom they had been useful in his election to the senate, to procure the resignation of the republicans holding federal offices in the state and the immediate appointment of democrats agreeable to the contracting parties. It was an adroit scheme to rob the new president—in every way a shameless and indecent scheme to all concerned.

It was, however, far under the surface, a conspiracy of more than political significance. The most substantial reasons existed why Mr. Teller and some of the other conspirators should wish to have the new corps of federal officers under friendly obligations to themselves.

But the scheme failed. President Arthur refused to co-operate in the infamy and the plotters fell upon their adversaries, "the better elements," with the ferocious rage of humiliated intriguers. The president learned the situation and naturally took the side of his friends. Mr. Hobson had secured the endorsement of the better elements at home, and availing himself of some influence in the east he secured the nomination. This was reason enough for the antagonistic faction to fall upon him with tooth and nail. As he could not be confirmed till the meeting of the Senate in December, they had time to concentrate all the devilish acrimony of impotent villainy against him.

The real motive of the special and personal opposition to Mr. Hobson lies too far beneath the surface to be completely uncovered in so brief a sketch as this—it lies in fact so deep that he has never completely discovered it himself. He is not a man of much insight into the remoter springs of human design. He attributes the opposition he encountered mainly to the personal animosity of Mr. Patterson. I feel warranted in asserting that he is mistaken. Mr. Patterson is not a fool. He has one of those peculiarly strong, logical and rational minds through which an action may be traced to its impelling cause. Like Senator Teller, he has the mind if not of a patriot at least of a diplomat. He does nothing, like impulsive and inconsequential men, without a motive. He is called a cunning man. The word does not describe him. Nature has endowed his mind with a faculty to perceive how other minds operate. Therefore he reads the motives of other men and conceals his own. That is the quality of his cunning. He is not half so sharp in this regard as Governor Eaton, but he is a great deal more comprehensive.

It is true he headed the opposition to Mr. Hobson but I venture to say that (in the beginning at least) he had not a particle of personal feeling in the matter.

The faculty to divine the motive from the action is not one with which Mr. Hobson is largely endowed, and the real motive in this case was both remote and obscure. The key to the riddle is the word "land-frauds." As for the rest, Mr. Patterson is a lawyer and has a great many clients.

If General Sparks had not been appointed commissioner of the United States land office Mr. Hobson would never have been attacked.

Through the wisdom and firmness of an administration which, whatever its faults, every candid man must concede to be both courageous and patriotic, Mr. Hobson has triumphed, and public opinion in regard to land frauds in Colorado has undergone a great change. Of that change he happens to be, and not without considerable personal merit, the representative figure. Land stealing has become in Colorado a matter of more than questionable respectability, and everything has worked together for his good. He may be considered an established young man, and the forces that opposed him have contributed to his establishment.

Speaking comprehensively of his character and abilities, the honorable judge of the United States court said to me the other day, "Hobson is the best district attorney the government has ever had in Colorado." —*Fitz-Mac.*

Sept. 23, 1887, Philadelphia.
My dear Mrs. Jermain— I am just passing through Philadelphia on my way to Washington from St. Louis. Will you not write me at 1319 New York Ave. Washington, how long you expect to be at your place in Washington County. I would like very much to avail myself of the opportunity of taking advantage of your invitation, and yet I may not be able to get away from

Washington before week after next… I may get off for a day or two next week. I probably seem very uncertain but I have business in Washington of a very important character, and I cannot now tell how long or when I will have to be at it. Excuse this hasty scrawl for I am writing between trains with an execrable pen… Sincerely, *Henry W. Hobson.*

September 26, 1887, Hill Farm, White Creek, N. Y.
My dear Mr. Hobson— Your letter of the 23rd from Philadelphia reached me today. The first word I have had since my guide to White Creek was sent… My Mother & Brother are the only ones here at present— tomorrow they go to our "old home" in Cambridge— thirteen miles from here— over the hills & while they are there I will be here & there. Now, I hope you will gratify me by coming here for a few days— if you could come this Friday it would be perfectly convenient— and if the coming Monday or Tuesday, it would be equally convenient. Is it asking too much for you to telegraph me on Thursday or Friday whether you are able to come this week— that I may arrange my plans for your pleasure. Mother is sorry to be away when you come, but I have promised if you will not be over-tired to take you over for a call… I hope all you wish for & are working for in Washington may be realized… Mother sends her kindest regards & I write with her in the hope to see you soon. —Yours Sincerely, *Katherine T. Jermain.* P.S. I do hope you will come but remember my place is in the real country and a kind of camp— but I promise you quiet & a welcome. *K.T.J.*

SEPT 29, 1887.
THE WESTERN UNION TELEGRAPH COMPANY
TO: Mrs. Katherine T. Jermain— Will leave this morning eleven thirty to catch train leaving Troy at five. You must not come out if it is raining. *Henry W. Hobson.*

Oct. 3, 1887, New York.
My own Darling Kittie— I am going to scribble you a line whilst waiting for a friend to come. You don't know dearest how I hated to leave you last night and all the way to the station I was thinking the sweetest dearest things of you and then my thoughts kept pace with the R.R. train until sleep came and dreams about you came in rapid succession. Ah Kittie! You are very very dear to me and I look forward impatiently to the time when I can call you my wife. Aunt Ada (I suppose she spells her name that way) said last night that I must do all I could to raise and elevate myself to be worthy of you. Thank her for the advice and tell her that I know full well I am not now worthy of you, but that you my darling have undertaken to make me better, higher, purer and that I shall be a willing and apt pupil… Do you know Kittie, that when I think of you, and go over in my mind all that you are, I feel almost awed at the goodness of Providence which has given you to me. I do not know why I deserve you, but I do know that you love me, and I simply bow my head and heart in grateful thankfulness. My thoughts are with you every moment and sometimes I shut my eyes and see you standing before me with your love-lit eyes and smiling happy face and I almost hold out my arm to clasp you to my heart. Do you know sweet love that one of the happiest memories I have of my visit to you is the change which came over you after I arrived and the great happiness you showed in having me with you. I trust we will have many,

Henry W. Hobson visited Katherine Thayer Jermain at Hill Farm in White Creek, New York, at the end of September 1887.

very many as happy days sweetheart as we had last week and yesterday… I am going to Wilmington tonight or rather today to join my Mother and early tomorrow I will be in Washington. After thinking the matter over I have concluded to tell my Mother of our engagement, but under a solemn promise of keeping it to herself for the present. I don't care to have any long announced engagement or to have you discussed by my family. They will all love you dear. I know full well and I will be so proud of you. Who can help loving you? My friend has come in and I must suspend— I will finish this at the hotel. …I have just five minutes dearest to finish this. I have had Tiffany send you today a necklace. I am afraid you will not like it. If not I have arranged for it to be changed. I send you the card of the salesman so you can either write to him or see him. Do not hesitate to say so if you do not like it. I sent it by express to Hoosick Falls so look out for it… God care and protect you sweetheart. Love to your dear Mother and Aunt Ada. Pardon this disgraceful scrawl. Yours devotedly forever, *HWH*.

Monday Morning Hoosick, N.Y. [Postmarked October 3, 1887, mailed to Washington, D. C.]
My Darling Henry—   I smile as I see what I have written but it is all true & much more. Only a few hours since you left me— and a great loneliness has taken hold of me. Still dear I am so entirely happy in your love. And the future, our life together. That— now though you have gone. I am content and so full of thankfulness for the love that has been given me. Yes, I love you my dearest one. And sometime you may realize something of the love I bear you. You have no idea how sorry I was when ten o'clock came and I discovered your valise. It was too late then— & this morning I am, with Aunt Ada, taking it to Hoosick. I went into your room & found your slippers, which I place in the pocket of the valise. I took out *Marriage as a Venture* as I wished room and it is not appropriate for the occasion. Aunt Ada says she had "to kiss him because he was from the South, not because he was a man." I tell her I *know* you have met him before. I never saw two people embrace thus the first time. I will keep the umbrella for you. Excuse this scribble. I must stop writing to take your valise. How I miss you, my own, my Sweet Heart. Will write tomorrow & whenever I feel the need of you.   —Your loving *Kittie*.

Monday evening, Hill Farm, White Creek. [Mailed to Denver.]
My darling Henry—   Aunt Ada and I drove over to Hoosick in the buggy and there I posted your letter. It rained and rained. I put the mare in Uncle Adin's barn and then, as there was no one else to do the thing, carried your valise to the train myself— in time to put it on the mid-day train. It weighed 33 pounds. I actually was delighted to do it all myself & felt lonely to leave your belongings to the Express man… I want to say Good night to you my dear love. I am more & more happy in your love & the thought of our life together fills me with gratitude to God. Good night— my darling. Lord bless & keep you always in my prayer   —Your own living *Kittie*.

October 4th, 1887, Washington.
My dearest Sweetheart—   I know I could not receive any letter from you this morning and yet I had a hope, that by some unaccountable means, I would get one. I wrote you such a hurried kind of a scrawl upon yesterday

that I felt almost ashamed to send it and yet dearest you knew when you received it that it was a little outpouring of my love for you. What would I not give to see you and kiss your sweet lips. Did any two lovers ever enjoy each other with more purity and sanctity that we do? I believe not, for when I am with you the world seems full of goodness and purity and you my love seem to be the center of it all… I came on to Washington this morning and am now writing from the Department whilst I am waiting to see the Attorney General, my chief. I have been so afraid you would not like the necklace I sent you. If you do not, will you please take it back and get something more. I send you the name of the salesman… Do not think me silly to write so much about my love for you, for remember Kittie I have dealt so long with the stern hand, non-beautiful side of life that my love for you and your love for me comes to me with all the freshness and building character, that belong to the love of a school-boy. I do not know how long I shall be in Washington, but just as soon as possible I will leave for Denver for my work requires my attention… I did not tell my Mother last night of our engagement, though I had a chance. Your name is so sacred and dear to me that I shrink from anything that will make it a subject for common comment even by my family and even though all they should say could be said in your presence. I am still hesitating about telling her, not because of any lack of confidence in her, but for reasons which you understand. By the way, I find Tiffany & Co. did not put in any charge for expressage, and it at once struck me that perhaps they sent the package collect.— Wouldn't that be funny? You will tell me however if they did, won't you dear? I was in a great hurry when I rushed in to get the necklace and have it sent off. The Attorney General has sent for me and I must go to him. I will have no more chance to write today so I must say goodbye…   —Devotedly Yours My Love, *Henry W. Hobson.*

Oct 5, 1887. Department of Justice, Washington, D. C.
Darling Kittie—   I must write to you hurriedly for I have very little time. I want especially to tell you that I told my Mother last night about our engagement under a promise that she would not tell anyone. She was perfectly delighted dear at my description of you, and I believe she is really glad I am to be married. She said she would write to you today and tell you what she thinks about it all. My cousin Mary Gannett who along with the others are after me a good deal about you, says she met you several years ago at Mrs. Rigg's reception, and last night she said, "Why she was just perfectly lovely Henry." Dearest love I only wish they knew as I do how good and lovely you are. But they will all know it someday and love you. Do you know Kittie, I have thought that it might be the correct and respectful thing for me to do, to write to Mr. Jermain. I think he would appreciate it, and as he has been so good and sweet to you Dear, I would not like to run the risk of wounding him. What do you think of it? You have so much sense about everything that I am willing always to defer to you… As matters look now I will not get away from here before Friday night. But I will wire you… Tell Aunt Ada I don't care why the kiss was given, so I got it, still I know it was for your sake. Love to her and tell her I really am very fond of her…   —Yours devotedly, *Henry W. Hobson.*
P.S. Valise not yet received but I suppose it will be in tonight. That was not my valise and I know nothing of *Marriage as a Venture.* I never saw it, but I think

dear you had better read it carefully for, in marrying me, you are certainly indulging in a good deal of a venture. *H.W.H.*

Hoosick Falls, at Uncle Adin's. Tuesday evening. October 2nd. [Postmarked October 6, 1887.]
My own Darling Henry—   This morning the mail-bag was brought in and in it I found my precious letter. It was sweeter than any letter has ever been to me. This I say Sweetheart for I wish you to know what your loving words are to me. And such a long letter to write during those few hours in New York. I read Aunt Ada wee bits and she says, "Well he won my heart,"…Darling, Darling, my heart is so full of thankfulness for your love & I will pray to be given strength to be the wife you deserve, the wife I would be— for no one but the Heavenly Father knows the depth of my love for you. You are the light of my eyes— and my heart is over-flowing with love for you… I am glad that you will tell your Mother, and trust she will be impressed with the wish we have for nothing to be said at present. Will you, if she is with you, give her my tender love, and tell her I hope she will try & love me sometime, not for myself, but because I love her son with all my heart and try & have her feel that she is always *first*. I never wish you to think of me before your Mother. I know I will love your Mother… After you left I went into your room, washed my hands in the water in the bowl and used your towel which you threw on the bed. And it was a comfort, for you had touched them. Oh Love, how precious you are. God keep and bless my darling… Good Night dear Love. You will let me hear what you think best to do in regard to New York.   —My heart's love to you—   Your own loving *Kittie*.
P.S. I can't write you how perfectly happy I am. And how proud I am of you my love. I am glad you are so handsome. Aunt Ada says you have such a sweet mouth. I am shocked my Darling Love. My Sweet Heart.

October 6, 1887, Thursday evening, Hill Farm, White Creek.
My precious Darling—   Where do you think I am? —in bed! Aunt Ada & I came back, (I can't say home for you make my home now) from Hoosick this afternoon about five o'clock, after a very trying day… 'twas peaceful & restful to drive towards these hills & dwell on you my Darling & your love for me. I say every day over & over, it is ever present, 'How God has blessed me' & I hope & pray I may be to you all that you need, all your heart longs for. When I was ready to say my prayers I went into your room, & knelt by the bed, and said my prayers there. I am so full of longing & if I could only feel your arms about me & kiss you— I would be so satisfied… When we came to the village store I found your letter— Darling you have no idea what your loving words are to me— and I read them over & over & over… And no woman I know could ever have been, or will ever be, more happy & satisfied than I. When you received those telegrams I half knew you were troubled and wished so much to help you, for I saw you were anxious— I wish to know all about your worries— and I trust these vexatious matters can be righted or mended, when you return to Denver. Dear one, please remember to take lunch every day— & not work so long without food. I hear my dear Mother is well & enjoying a visit from some cousins she has not seen for years. It is very funny to hear Aunt Ada talk of you and she says she wonders she didn't get a letter instead of me— says that you would have kissed her again if there had been time. Do

Katherine "Kittie" Thayer and her cousin, Ada Thayer Addison.

tell me your number & street in Denver, *no more* letters to the Denver Club. Still the name of the salesman did not come and when it does I will return it— the necklace. You know I wish something I can always wear, night and day and those beautiful blue stones would be discolored, turn green. I do think this circlet lovely, but not simple enough to be worn as I wish to wear what my darling gives me— and what I wish is a string of gold beads— they I can wear constantly, and they will be put on by you… And I long so to see you. My dear dear love. You told me once of your Grandmother showing you her love letters. I know I could show her yours & she would be proud of you… I breathe a prayer for you my own Darling— Always.   —Your ever-loving *Kittie*.

A letter from Catherine McKie Thayer:

Cambridge, October 6, 1887.
My darling Kittie—   Your letter of Mon p.m. came Tues eve. So sweet to hear the bird singing in your heart— may the song be as sweet and strong and gladsome a way on into the future— many many years… I shall expect to see you and Ada— am so glad she was with you for your sake. Give my best love to her… Everything comfortable here…   —*Mother*.

New York, Tuesday evening 1887, Brevoort House near Washington Square. New York. [Postmarked October 6, 1887.]
My own Precious Darling—   Aunt Ada & I sit here alone, in the dear little sitting room. You know what I say 'dear' for anything connected with you is dear. And you my Love are going farther away from me each second. And then in another way we are coming nearer to each other. The ten weeks we counted will be passing. You can never go away from me again while we are engaged… I *must* see Mother very soon— and talk with her… Can't you see my darling that until I have talked with my Mother about many things I do not wish any announcement made. My idea is to have her announce it when she returns to Colorado. It is right that she should have this privilege. And then at the same time our marriage at an early date can be spoken of… Now I have to think of Mr. Jermain, who, as I told you, always has been all that a father could be to me, and then there are three of the sweetest of women, all devoted to me… I have been thinking and thinking of you— all the time and our life. Would you be willing to be married in Fitchburg and I could go to Ada, who is like a sister to me, and we could be married in Morris' church and have a breakfast at the Rectory. If I am away from Mother I wish a very quiet wedding and if it were in Washington you would have to ask all your relatives and I would then wish to ask mine— and the talk and preparation would be more than I could endure… I have talked with Aunt Ada and she thinks the Fitchburg plan lovely… Now Sweetheart I will stop. You must forgive this scribble. You ruined my pen, it was lovely before. My own Darling good night. All my heart is yours, and I am your own *Kittie*. —You have made me so happy.

October 6, 1887, Washington.
My own Darling—   …Two of my friends have come from Richmond to spend a day with me— Tom Page (he is the one you are to kiss) and Carter

Branch. I however must tell you how I love you… I wish you would send me my Mother's letter. I would like to see what she wrote you. In replying, address her letter to Ashland, Hanover Co, Va. I am detained here rather longer than I anticipated. I may wire you tomorrow to meet me in New York on Saturday… Pardon my haste… Yours loving and devotedly, *Henry W. Hobson.*

October 11th, 1887, Windsor Hotel, New York.
My own Sweetheart—   Last evening your message reached me… I am very anxious to reach the cottage and receive your Mother's letter and yours, Darling, you are the dearest love… We reach the cottage tomorrow at five if all be well. Do be careful in every way for you belong to me. Your head, I hope is through aching… This darling takes a heart full of love. My own sweetheart, I love you more and more dearly if possible. Your own *Kittie.*

Oct. 12, 1887, Denver.
My darling Sweetheart—   Here goes for a lightning express letter, for I am over-head in work and hardly have time to groan. But I have a few moments to say I love you Dear one, and a thought of you creeps in (audacious trespasser!) very often between the joints of heavy business cogitations. I have you, *own* you! Yes you are mine and I am just going to be a tyrant in the way I assert my rights. You can't get away now, for I have you bound solemnly and so I will hold you. I wrote to your Mother today, a very shabby and sorry kind of a letter, but then Dearest I was and am so busy. I meant it to be sweet and affectionate and I hope she will think it such. Don't forget to send me my Mother's letter as I wish to see it. Do not forget either to write to me about Mr. Jermain, giving me his full name and address. I really think Darling, that proper respect demands that I should write to him before our engagement is announced. I would not for the world have the good old man's feelings hurt… You don't know Kittie *cherie*, how I enjoyed your letters received when I got to Denver this morning. Oh! how sweet they were and what a darling you were to write them. Of course I would have kissed Aunt Ada again and I may as well say right now, so that there will be no future disagreement on the subject, that I propose to kiss Aunt Ada whenever she will permit me to do so… I expect to go to Salt Lake tomorrow or Friday. You write to Denver however. A thousand blessings and a world of love— A kiss and love for Aunt A—   —Devotedly Yours, *Henry W. Hobson.*

A letter from Catherine McKie Thayer:

October 12, 1887.
My dear Child—   …It seems to me that I must have missed a letter, or you must forget that I know nothing of the *why*, or *when* or *how* as to your future— more than the few brief words spoken when you were here, and these gave me no hint as to the *desired* future— and when you say you do not wish a wed [wedding] dress you make me sit down at once— and wonder what you and Mr. H— and Ada are talking over, as to time, place etc. Do you not see that I am wholly in the dark. I am glad of your happiness, for I think Mr. H— can be trusted, if he loves you, and I heard him say that he learned some time ago that you *were not* an heiress as had been said. So I see but one reason for his coming to you, indeed I entirely believe that he loves you.

He added to me, that he "was a poor man"… Neither of you can marry for money but I judge you can be happy & comfortable in a worldly sense if you are governed by your judgment— and this, I think you will be… I see diphtheria in W. C. [Washington County, N.Y.] …   —*Mother*.

October 13, 1887, Hill Farm, White Creek.
My own Darling Henry—   …Your Mother's letter, it was the most lovely unselfish loving letter. I knew I should love her, and when I had read her tender words I went to my room & thanked God for this added blessing. I have sent Mother your Mother's letter, and when she returns it I will copy it & send it to you, for I can't let it go so far away. Last evening I wrote your Mother a long scribble & told her I loved you and wished to be all to you that she could wish me & that she must help me— for I know she can. Don't write her for my letter, for it is only to her… Now Sweetheart I will not write longer. Two weeks tonight since you asked me to trust you. How all the world is changed… Oh Henry I will try to be all I can be as your wife.   —My own Darling Love— Your loving *Kittie*.

October 13, 1887, Denver.
My own Darling Kittie—   I could not get off to Salt Lake today owing to press of business, but I shall go tomorrow… Remember darling, you promised not to be hurt by not writing long letters. I love you just as much as though I wrote twenty pages a day. I will be unable to write tomorrow but will drop you a line from the train Saturday… God bless you sweet one… Your devoted Lover, *Henry W. Hobson*.

Union Pacific Train, Utah. October 15, 1887.
My own Darling—   I know you would rather have a badly written letter in pencil than none at all and so here goes… My darling Kittie you have so much sense, a great deal more than I have. That Fitchburg plan is just the thing if it suits you. I would marry you with perfect satisfaction anywhere and I wish you to consult your own wishes entirely about the plans and time… As you say, if we are married in Washington there will be a great bustle and gathering of people and many incidents that I do not think would be pleasant. In Fitchburg we could be married as quietly as we please in Morris' church and he and my Brother could officiate together. Do you know love I have always thought I would like to be married by the Episcopal ceremony. It is so chaste and beautiful, a fitting ceremony to join our loves into one sweet life. Still if you wish any other ceremony it shall be just as you wish… Well darling I have written as much as I think you can read at one sitting. Indeed I doubt if you can read what I have written at all. My paper has gotten soiled, my pencil is soft… and altogether this is a poor letter. But then sweetheart it carries a world of love to you and along with it also goes such great longings to see you…   —Yours devotedly, *H.W.H.*

October 15th, 1887. Hill Farm, White Creek. [Mailed from Hoosick Falls, N.Y.]
My own Darling Henry—   Now I am off to Hoosick to meet my dear Mother… You are in my thoughts constantly. —And every hour I would be near you— my sweetheart. I am with you in your work. And you must feel you have all my sympathy & love in your work. In fact, in all which con-

cerns you my Darling. Will write a longer letter as soon as I have talked with Mother. This tells you I love you— more & more, my precious love. Your letter from Lincoln received. So glad to hear you will have a plentiful supply of paper & envelopes when you leave me again, which I trust will never be…

—Your Love, *Kittie*. (What are you signing yourself as in business letters, *Henry W. Hobson*?)

Sunday Evening, Hoosick, N.Y. [Postmarked October 17, 1887]
My own darling Henry—   Mother and Aunt Ada are sitting here talking and I have turned away to send you a few words of love. Today I have written your Mother again. I think I will write her regularly, on Sunday, for I like to feel I write a few moments to her that way. Yesterday I went over to Hoosick in the buggy. Arrived there about 10 which gave Mother a little time to visit at Uncle Adin's. We came home very slowly, (but this is not home now)… She has decided that it will be best for us to be married in the East, and thinks Fitchburg, Ada's home, her husband's church will be the most suitable place. It is only an hour from Boston. So you know darling that Ada has always been more to me than any other woman and the thought of being with her, at this time, is very sweet to me— for if I am to be away from Mother, I feel that to be with Ada would be much better than to be married from Washington. There are only nine weeks now, oh, my sweetheart— how I have lived on the sweet hours we have spent together. And how happy and content I am in resting in your love. Yes, my Darling I do love you with all my heart. This week I am packing here. And will go to the Jermains next week and tell Mr. Jermain of my engagement. Will you write the letter to him, and send it *to me*— As I should like to hand it to him when I speak to him. You know he is almost eighty and I wish to tell him of my love as gently & quietly as possible. This will be the last of next week, or as soon as the letter comes. My mother will go back to Colorado the first week in November & after a few days, or in fact as soon as she returns, she would like to announce herself, our engagement. And the same day you will tell your Denver friends and your Mother can tell her family in Richmond. Mother thinks this is the dignified means of making our engagement known. Now my Darling I hope you will write me what you don't like. And any suggestions you will make will be very gratefully received for your wishes will be mine. Mother sends her best love to you & Aunt Ada sends nothing less than a kiss. Will you please write me what your new duties are. I simply listened to all you told me and now feel there is so much I wish I had asked but our time was so short, and I am sorry I did not kiss you more than I did. You are the sweetest dearest one in the world and I am so lonely for your dear presence. You are everything to me and I long to do something for your comfort. How long will you be on that trip to Salt Lake etc. for if we go to the first of February there would be very little time between our return from the East to get any house in order before we would be off again & maybe we had better wait until our return from the far west before we settle our house. I have to ask this on account of my furniture. Excuse the crossing. I promise never to do it again, but I expected never to go on as I have. Good night, my own Darling. Kisses & all my love to you Sweetheart.   —Your own *Kittie*.

October 17, 1887, Hill Farm, White Creek. [Postmarked October 19, 1887.]
My own Precious Darling—   Today has been rather lonely. I woke with

the crossing Kittie is apologizing for cross-writing, the practice of writing first on stationery in a regular fashion and then turning the paper sideways and writing across what has already been written. This was a common practice and is very difficult to read.

a headache— most unusual for me. And when Mother & Aunt Ada left I was on the lounge, feeling very miserable… My darling never think I wish you to write me long letters, for I appreciate how busy you are… You have no idea what your letters were to me today when I felt so lonely, and I was comforted immediately. All day I have been keeping quiet. And I like to think you took your nap here. Now my head is quite better. And tomorrow I will be quite well. I think of you in Salt Lake and trust you will be very successful in every way… My eyes ache & I will stop. Two boys have spent Sunday, leave tomorrow, aged fourteen, one Mr. Jermain's grandson, both with guns and rifles— such a noise all day. I took dinner on the sofa & after they have asked me questions about the west, ranches, bears, Mt. Lions, horse & cattle thieves, until I am tired out. Excuse this rambling letter. If only I could kiss you Good night, and put my arms about your neck. You are so sweet. God bless you & keep us until we meet in safety.   —Your own loving & devoted *Kittie*.

A letter from Annie Jennings Wise Hobson:

Washington, D. C. October 5, 1887.   Last evening my dear boy told me that you had promised to be his wife, and from my very Mother's heart I write to say, "God bless you both" my dear Kittie. From all that he has told me I know that you would not have me approach you formally, even by letter, but that your true woman's heart would wish me to follow the spontaneous impulse that bids me speak just as I feel. Henry has been a very noble and devoted son, and a self sacrificing friend to his Mother. It would be a poor return not to love him as unselfishly and devotedly as he deserves. I have long prayed to our Heavenly Father to lead him to a Good, true, Christian wife; the most intense desire I have long had for him (next to my prayers that God's spirit would teach him to be a true child of God) was, that he should marry a *woman* who would indeed be a "better half," helping and guiding him to a higher and more spiritual life; that he should have the blessing of a wife who could make a *real home* for him, giving my long homeless boy, just the loving, womanly care and noble influence, for body and soul, without which every man must suffer mentally, morally, and physically. No one can do that like a true & devoted wife. No, not even a mother, when the time has come that a man *ought* to have a wife. I have great confidence in Henry's judgment of women. Therefore I do not doubt one statement that he makes in praise of your pure & lovely character, and many attractions, but believe that you will prove the answer to my prayers for my intensely beloved son. So I am ready to welcome you not only as a daughter but as God's gift to us both. Can I say more than that? I hope that we may meet at no distant day. Henry has spoken so often of your Mother, and in such warm terms of friendship that I feel as if she and I were already friends. If the life of a devoted son can be an earnest of your future happiness with my Boy, you can surely trust, implicitly & confidingly, in his love and care. May God grant you a long and blessed life together. Believe me most sincerely yours with a heart all ready to love. —*A.J.W. Hobson*.

October 18, 1887, Tuesday evening, Hill Farm, White Creek.
My hearts Darling—   If our dates hold good we will be married two months from now… I love you so dearly that this separation is more hard

than I could have believed… Have been packing linen and thinking where I would use it. And now it is very late. I have been writing some business letters and one to my Mother. I know she will be glad to receive your letter… It is rather lonely here… The fire is delightful. I love to dream over it— "of what may be." An open fire is the only comfort which is companionable. I hope we will be fortunate enough to have an open fire, a grate. And then I wish you to sit in front of it & be comfortable in our home, with your books & papers & be willing to put the book down to hold me & let me kiss you. How entirely sweet you are. You have no idea how I admire & honor you, my precious Love, and how much I wish to be in your life… And now my love I must stop writing. It is twelve o'clock. And I must do a great deal tomorrow, that I may go to Mother this week. Good night. I wish I could kiss your lips my Darling. —Your own loving *Kittie.*

✎ A letter from Catherine McKie Thayer:

South Cambridge, Oct. 18, 1887.
My dear Henry—   On my return from White Creek, where I spent Sunday, I found your letter of Wed. last. There is no cause for regret, as to the manner of introducing a subject, that must, of necessity, be far apart from all other topics… My little visit was given up almost entirely to the past, present, and future of you two people. We only wished you with us. I find that Kittie has the highest respect and the deepest tenderest love for you and the most implicit trust in you, and surely if I understand you both, you must be happy with each other… I have always liked you, as I told you, and you are dear to me now. And when I say that I entrust the future of my darling child to your care and love, with the restful assurance of happiness to you both, can I say more… May God guard and keep you and Kittie always. *C. McKie Thayer.*

October 19, 1887, Hill Farm, White Creek.
My own Darling Henry—   It is always so restful to turn to you… I hope to drive over to Mother's Friday afternoon or Saturday. She writes that she has received a lovely satisfactory letter from you… You will be quite frank & tell me if it is convenient for you to come for me at the 17th of December— if the 10th would better suit you, it will be equally well for me & you decide. This is only a little letter. It takes you more love than I can express. I feel so content & happy in your love. And I take perfect satisfaction in knowing Henry Hobson is *my very own*. You are so precious my Love. Last night I dreamed of you my love, & then awoke to find it quite untrue. Only I knew you were mine to love, honor & obey. I love you so tenderly my darling. You are so much in all ways—   —Your own loving *Kittie.*

✎ A letter from Annie Jennings Wise Hobson:

Ashland, Hanover Co. Va. Oct. 19th, 1887.
I think that some Heavenly influence must have led you Dearest, to write me that loving missive of the 16th, which reached me to today, for I so needed words of love and tenderness; and did not yours promise for the future as well as bring a cheering sweetness for the present. I address you by the above terms of endearment from my very heart, because I feel that you are to be and have

already *begun* to be amongst the dearest ones of life to me. No need to beg me to love you for Henry's sake, for my whole heart has gone out to the sweet womanly nature that speaks in your letters… I am so glad that I am not *too old* to be a real friend & companion to you… I do love to read of your devotion to Henry, and I am so thankful that he has chosen a *woman*, not a mere inexperienced girl… My preacher Boy has written me a most alarming and discouraging letter about his health, though an examination of his lungs by an experienced physician proved them sound; but his throat is so much affected that he has been ordered not to preach for a while. I hope it is only an aggravated attack of catarrh and am going on to see about him and to question the Doctor for myself. He has been spitting blood for days, though his physician says that this is a relief to some congestion about his throat. I shall go to Amherst tomorrow. I have long been very anxious about Cannon's health, and I felt very bowed down & desolate last evening, and so grieved lest a trouble might be coming to shadow & darken your's and Henry's joy. I laid it all at the foot of the Cross. I cannot one moment distrust the love that has sustained me in all these years of trial. —I fell asleep with the last thought. God is always kinder and better than our fears. Today I feel brave and trustful… Kittie dear, are we treating Cannon, Henry's only brother rightly, not to give him our confidence? He will be so glad for Henry & be more than ready to welcome you as a sister. He is the most prudent person, & if you desired it, would not even tell his little wife. But do as you prefer about it… You must indeed be an exceptional woman, Kittie, to give your lover's Mother such a place, right beside him in your thoughts, and I think I can respond without conceit, that no woman could appreciate it more than his Mother does. I too thought of him in Salt Lake… I am going to send you by express a Gold Medal which Henry received at the University as the best debater. I have another given him at William & Mary— he brought both to his *Mama* and I put the University one away carefully saying, "*his wife shall have this—*" & now I send it to the noble, sweet woman who has promised to be his wife, as a pledge of my trust and confidence, my Mother'slove for herself and my faithful friendship… Remember me most warmly to your Mother, and tell her that I shall surely in every gratitude be compelled to love her for having reared so sweet a daughter for my son, thereby giving me a daughter, even as I will give her a son of whom she need not be ashamed. I shall be glad to know your brother also. Tell him that 'the boys' have always been my charge & vocation. God bless you ever.   —Yours lovingly, *A.J.W. Hobson.*

Hill Farm, October 21, 1887.
My own darling Henry—   I was so distressed to hear of Cannon's illness and hope it is not as serious as your Mother fears. I am going to write her to tell your brother, for I would like him to know of my perfect happiness. Darling you must know and feel that in all your anxieties and sorrows I am present and I wish to help you bear them— And always feel I wish to hear all that worries you, for if you conceal your anxieties, I am no help, but a burden… Henry, Henry, you are everything my heart longs for… Oh my darling I do so long for you…   Your own *Kittie.*

Oct. 23, 1887, Denver.
My darling love Kittie—   I am just back late this afternoon from Salt Lake. Ah Dearest, how my heart yearned and hungered for your letters and when I

got here and found them, six in all, I wanted to read them all at once and do you know, I was so foolish in my delight that I broke open every one, glanced at them, kissed them, before reading any one. What a lovely sweetheart you are to me my own love. Would anyone write dearer, sweeter letters than you do? But do you know Kittie my love, my time for unalloyed joy has not yet come. I feel I must tell you of my new trouble, for I am so depressed about it and so unhappy and I feel so much for my poor Mother. I know it is selfish and weak for me to impose this upon you and yet my darling are you not now almost my wife and have we not promised to have nothing from each other? Do you remember Kittie my telling you of my Brother, of how delicate he has been and that I feared lung trouble. I also told you, as I thought it proper and just, of the possibility of his whole family being dependent upon me? Well my fears have, I am afraid, been too soon realized. The enclosed sheet from a letter received from my Mother explains the trouble. I took the letter over and read it to Dr. Fisk and he very frankly told me he thought the indications were very grave and that from this letter he could scarcely think my Brother was troubled from the throat. Ah Kittie my darling what shall I do? I have not the courage to say that you should give me up, with this new cloud hanging over me, but Dearest I know I am not dealing justly with you, not to say that you should not marry a man situated as I am Kittie. Kittie, you are so dear to me. You are all I dream of as a wife, a loving help-mate and companion in life, and I don't know what I should do if I were to lose you.

This afternoon Dr. Fisk said carelessly that S— told him you were not coming back to Colorado any more and my heart was cold for an instant, and then glowed with the sudden consciousness that I knew so much more than they did. God knows I have not one selfish thought about this thing except the dread of how it may affect you. I can say truly for myself, God's will be done. I think it my duty to tell you of this Dearest, so that you may know all and so that your Mother may know it too. I feel like a man with a great weight hanging over his head by a thread and I hardly know what to say. Kittie I cannot give you up and yet Dearest if you do not think or if you Mother does not think you should marry me until this thing is more definitely settled, I will bow with submission to the justice of your course. If on the other hand you are still firm in your willingness to share all my sorrow, all my misfortunes, my darling, I would and will be so proud of you and will face everything with a cheerful brave heart. Dearest, Darling, Do not misunderstand me. For your sake and for you I would go down into the lowest depths of misfortune, and all that I write, is only because of my feeling that it is but justice to you. I don't know what to say or what to do— I have told you all— I feel absolutely confident of your love. Write me what you think about it all. In my own distress and perplexity, I do also, so feel for my Mother. She is so proud of my Brother and has formed such bright hopes for his future. Poor woman, her cup of sorrow has overflowed so often. I feel tonight as though I could go down on my knees to you, and yet I know that it is a time for me not to think of myself, but to face the situation manfully and say do what you think right. Kittie, my life, my hope for life, if you do not wish under the circumstances to marry me, do not throw me off entirely. Let me still hope that you will marry me if the cloud passes away. I have but one wish in the matters and that is to marry you as soon as possible. God knows I wish it with all my heart and mind. I know that I have written in a weak and foolish way, but there are times in the life even of the bravest man, when he tumbles before some evil that he cannot thoroughly see. Forgive me darling and write to me at once. I so need your sympathy and words of love. I enclose a letter to Mr. Jermain as you wish. If it is not as you wish it send it back. My darling I cannot think you will turn back,— but— ah! I cannot say more. I must write to my poor Mother and it is getting very late. Write me my own that you will marry me despite all things and I will be so happy. And yet how selfish that is. —My love, my own, my life. Yours devotedly, *Henry*. —Darling— I would give almost anything to be with you tonight! I love you— I love you— I love you— *H*.

Home Farm, Sunday evening, October 23rd, 1887.
My own precious darling—   Yesterday after a busy morning I went up in the room where you slept, knelt and prayed God to bless & keep us and then left the little cottage in my buggy, driving "Molly" and travelled the dear road over the hill to Cambridge… I do long for you and feel as if I can't wait a *minute*… I was so happy in receiving your letter from Salt Lake. I know you are more busy than words can express and I do wish you to feel I am not exacting. Never write when you can close your dear eyes and rest for a few minutes. I only wish to know you are well… Your life and very breath are so pure and sweet. Darling we must help each other to be better, truer, more Christ-like and I feel you are going to be such a strength to me… I found Mother & Frank delighted and happy to see me. And we have had lovely *Mother talks* and a sweet drive today, to the Old Church-yard where our kindred lie. Tomorrow I go to Hedge Lawn, the Jermain's… to keep house— letting Marie (the unmarried daughter) go to NY for a few days. Mother & Frank will come there Tuesday and spend a few days and as soon as your letter to Mr. Jermain comes I wish to tell him of my engagement… Your Mother is sending me by Express a medal you received at the University and I intend wearing it about my neck. Is it not dear of her— Oh, Henry she is lovely to me. And I am so thankful you are bringing me the joy of such love as your Mother will feel for me… My love good night…Your own *Kittie*.

Oct. 24, 1887, Denver.
My darling, darling Kittie—   I wrote you a letter last night that I am thoroughly ashamed of, and you ought to be ashamed of me for writing it. But my love you cannot understand what I felt and how wave after wave of fear swept over me. And above all was the fear that I was not acting justly towards you. It is all over now however and I am a man again. My forebodings may turn out ill-founded and untrue. I sincerely pray that they may, but come what shall, I am ready to receive it bravely… My sweetheart I must again thank you for your sweet loving letters. I was so disappointed however not to receive one this morning, though I of course know that there is good reason for the failure. My Mother sent me your last letter to her and she is as delighted as a child over your writing so sweetly to her. You are the dearest sweetest, best girl in the world. Of course my Mother will love you. Who could help it? …I am a good deal perplexed because certain business complications in the way of cases to try and so on, are arising which may make it necessary for us to be married a little later in December, or about January 1st. I am worried to death, for we ought to have been married long ago and I am very impatient… I cannot decide about our house arrangements until I see your Mother and

talk with her. I have a strong antipathy to going anywhere except to our own house and I think it would be charming to have it all ready for us when we get from the East and your dear Mother here to receive us… The fact is my Darling, I don't know anymore about going to work preparing to keep house than a child and I am going to do just what your Mother thinks best… If my letter to Mr. Jermain does not suit you, just sketch out your ideas and I will write accordingly. I have wired my Brother to go to Richmond at once and consult with the best specialist and I trust the result may be better than I fear. I must now close sweetheart, for I have so much to do… Devotedly and forever, *Henry*.

Hedge Lawn, Albany, N.Y. Wednesday afternoon.
My own Darling Henry—   …I am going to see about a dress for Katie Savage (the little grand-daughter of Mr. Jermain) who must have a new dress because she "is going to a party." I see that on last Friday the Mormon Church case was concluded but some decision given on the 5th— So I can't be certain how long you will stay in Utah. Indeed about all I feel certain about is that I love you more & more. I long for you Darling… Your own *Kittie*.

༄ A letter from Annie Jennings Wise Hobson:

Oct. 27, 1887. Amherst, Virginia.
My dearest Son—   The first pleasure & duty of the day is to write to you & first of all to tell of the lovely letter received from Kittie yesterday, in which she gives me permission to tell Cannon & his wife of your engagement. I have read the dear letter over three times, and daily feel that your love & anticipated marriage had indeed brought a new joy and happiness in my life. It was dated from South Cambridge. I had written to Kittie yesterday. I have sent her your University gold medal. You may remember that I always said your sweetheart and wife should have it. I told her that I had been keeping it for her all these years. It does my whole heart good to discern how she loves you, and my precious son in her sweet way— out of the fullness of her womanly sympathy she told me that which indeed filled my Mother-heart with joy. Of how you had thanked God for the promised gift of her love and life, and asked to be made a better man. I have written her that the chief desire of my soul was to know you were one in Christ… She tells me that about the middle of November she wished me to announce her engagement to all your relatives & friends. Of course to Mother, your Aunt Mary Garnett, and your Aunt Mary Lyons you will write yourself. How Mother will delight in Kittie's sweet letters to me. I shall show them to her. One thing I wish you to consider— Kittie says— "did you know we are Presbyterians? But when we are married (*I love to write that*) Henry & I mean to attend Church regularly, and I think we will go to his own Church— and that church will be mine." This is very lovely, but my son, if your wife is devoted to her Church & finds she can there worship God more after her own heart, you ought to go with her, as she is a communicant & you are not. It was thus your Father acted towards me… Dr. Thompson came in to see a patient in the house. I had a long interview with him. He seems to be a good & intelligent man. He apprises me that he can detect nothing wrong about Cannon's lungs and sees no reason why he should not gain strength & health by proper care & has promised me to insist upon Cannon's

beginning a system of physical education, chest exercises, proper diet, giving up tobac, regular hours & for a while light work. He also promises to inform me at any time that he discovers organic disease & to watch him carefully. He seems to be very fond of Cannon. I spent the day at the Rectory yesterday— I never saw Alice look so well and seem so energetic. She is really rather pretty now and her figure has improved. It does one good to look at the children. You would delight to see little Cannon's handsome ruddy face and clear complexion and his limbs are developing, gaining flesh & muscle. George and Henry look handsome and robust for them. All three are really handsome boys now, and real boys… I received your letter from Salt Lake City & read it with intense interest. I pray God to give you power & wisdom to do His work well & faithfully in warring against that Mormon heresy & wickedness, for such I hear it is… Feel that your Mother's prayers will ask help & wisdom for you. These mails here are so irregular but I do trust my letters telling of Cannon's improved condition reached you speedily & that your heart & mind are thus relieved…

The end of this letter from A. J. W. Hobson has been lost.

Oct. 28, 1877, Denver.
My own Darling Kittie—   Yesterday I was busy all day taking depositions and last night I had to go to the Charity Ball at the Windsor with Mrs. Edson. Consequently I did not write to you, but Dearest I thought of you a good deal, in fact a great deal. I had intended to stay away from the Ball but the day before yesterday Mrs. Edson asked me to escort her saying Tracy could not go. I tried to get out of it but failed and after I consented to go, she invited a Miss Loyd to go along with us. I had rather a stupid time and stood it as long as I could, until finally about a quarter after two I went to Mrs. E. and told her I had ordered my carriage and would like for her to go home. I did not go to bed until after three o'clk. Imagine my disgust! That is the last time however I will ever do that. My principal pleasure at the Ball was in thinking of you and wishing you were with me… I have been ordered to start for Washington Territory on Monday next. I will be away two weeks perhaps and therefore will not be in Colorado when your Mother arrives. In view of that Kittie I am going to tell Dr. Fisk and my friend Hill of our engagement before I go. I wish them to learn of it from me on account of our intimacy and they will keep it entirely secret until your Mother arrives and announces it in Colorado Springs. When she does I would like for her to write a line to Dr. Fisk and ask him to announce it quietly here to my friends. I have some warm friends here and I do not wish to wound their feelings by appearing to neglect them… I am also going to write to my Mother to make the announcement about the 10th of November. I always speak frankly to you and so I am going to say that I have not been entirely satisfied with the delay in the announcement until so shortly before our wedding. Still your reasons were good ones and I am willing my love to do anything to please you— I wish you would tell me how I should dress for our wedding and at once, for I must order some clothes. I have no more idea about what is correct in such matters than a child and you always know everything… I hear encouraging news about my Brother and I have also, I think, arranged so that if he has to leave that climate I can get him a Parish out here. There is a nice little Parish at Cañon City open, and though the salary will not be a living one for him yet, I will have to help him out. I am amused at the medal my Mother sent you. Such things now seem so trivial,

such successes I mean. I made rather a bright course at College however for a lazy non-studying fellow… The more I think about Fitchburg the better I like our plan for being married there. I laughed at your conjectures with regard to yourself and my Mother. You are both very dear to me but in different ways. She is my dear Mother. You are to be my loving wife. There should never be any question of first or second between you. Remember that my darling. I must now close. You are so sweet and loving, so dear in every way to me. Bless you sweetheart—   —Yours Devotedly, *Henry*.

October 28, 1887, Hedge Lawn, Albany.
My own Darling Henry—   Today I am richly rewarded by the arrival of two of your dear letters. I do not believe any woman ever received such letters. I love them & I read over the sweet words of love again & again. And I think if you continue to write such tender letters daily I must change them for postals! Do you know I have put them under my pillow & in my dress & pocket & then Darling, every chance I find, I take out the precious sheets & read over all my Sweetheart says to me… I think the 17th is the *better day*, if convenient to you my Darling… You have little idea how I will pet you. And how patient you will need to be. Indeed you are fresh & sweet. You are naturally so… This morning we went to my Father's grave, in the Cemetery above Troy. A lovely day & all so peaceful. I never have told you how much my Father was to me. We were companions— and so necessary to each other. I wish you to write me about your brother. I wrote your Mother to tell Cannon of our love. Then I have been thinking— I wonder if you will laugh that there is no use of our having an extravagant wedding trip. Why should we begin our lives as we would never live afterwards? …And I do wish to see your Mother & spend Christmas with her— as it will be sweet to remember all our lives. I think I would talk about anything with you— Are you not my very own? I love to think of my love, so handsome, so manly, so noble. You have the highest kind of beauty. I am so glad you are so good to look upon. I wish I could put my arms about your neck & kiss you, long & tenderly— & look into your face & stroke your hair— & put my lips to your neck, oh, love, Darling, how I long for you now Sweetheart. 'Good night—' God bless & keep you Darling. Three weeks from tomorrow…   —Your own Sweetheart, *Kittie*.

THE WESTERN UNION TELEGRAPH COMPANY
Oct. 29— 1887.
To: HENRY W. HOBSON
Letters from Denver recd. Your Brother's illness nor anything else could change plans. Mother and I send much love.   —*K.S.J.*

K.S.J. The use of these initials, instead of "K.T.J." is a little confusing. "K.S.J." would stand for Katherine Sophia Jermain as "Sophia" was her middle name as a child, see page 227. Normally she would have used the initials "K.T.J.," Katherine Thayer Jermain, at this time.

October 29, 1887. On the train.
My own Darling Henry—   Your three letters, last from Salt Lake & two from Denver reached me this morning. Your loving words are everything to me Darling. Your letter telling me of your brother's condition made me very sad. Why my love, what would my love be worth if I would let anything save Death separate us. It makes my heart stand still. Your sorrows & joys are mine— & all your responsibilities mine too. If now you had ten children dependent upon you, you would have to let me share your lot… Mother has spoken of wishing to buy a little home for us, even though it might not suit us

for long— it might be a good investment instead of renting. You know Darling I have everything in the way of furniture we would need & silver, china & linen. (Table & bed) and we would need to buy very little… I love your letters and where you wrote "almost my wife" my heart yearned to be near you…
My darling when I see you again I will be too happy. This is a scribble but the train shakes & pencil bad. Still never did I love you more and long for you as now. God bless & keep my Darling. You are more than heart could desire my sweetheart. Good night my love   —Your own devoted *Kittie*.

The Farm, October 29th, 1887, Saturday evening.
My own Precious Darling— Since my arrival I have read your letters again. I am so glad I telegraphed, for tonight you know that I am loving you and that nothing can change our plans. My sweetheart, how could you *dream* for an instant that I would give you up? …Tonight I find a letter from Cannon, which I enclose and a note from your Mother, saying Cannon is better. I believe the bleeding is from the acute inflammation, caused by catarrh… Your letter to Mr. Jermain satisfies me entirely— it is perfect, dignified, respectful, and natural. I return it to you that you may copy it (keep this please) and date it, *Nov.* for it will be November when I go to see him and I do not like him to feel I have kept the letter. His initials are *James B*. Now I wish to say that though I am very very fond of all of this Jermain family and I expect them to continue to regard me with affection, that whatever their course may be, my happiness can not be, in the slightest degree, made less for my Love. I am perfectly happy and oh so thankful for your love… Your own Loving & Devoted *Kittie*.

⁕ A letter from Annie Jennings Wise Hobson:

Amherst, Va. October 26, 1887.
Dearest Kittie— Just a moment have I to scribble you a line. I am so glad that I can tell you that Cannon is better. I thank God that no cloud from his sickness will darken your & Henry's present happiness. I feel so concerned lest the letter I wrote you from Ashland, & the medal should not reach you— especially the last after *keeping it for you all these years*… I think of you every day and with such sympathy in having "Your Boy" so far away. Be married as soon as your can (if your Mother thinks it best.) …Life has taken my son from me in a way marriage could not do. I have tried to accept it as God's will, bravely & cheerfully. The tie between you and your Mother must be very close. God bless you. Yours lovingly, *A.J.W.Hobson*.
—I had a letter from Henry from Salt Lake. Of course you did too & feel the same interest I do in the case there. I shall deem it an honor from God for my son to fight in any way the Mormon enormity.

October 31, 1887. The Farm, South Cambridge.
My Darling Love Henry— Today is lovely and I have been over on the adjoining farm planning a barn with a carpenter… Yesterday we went to Service in our little church and enjoyed it very much. It is sweet to be in the home of ones Father. Before I was dressed this morning, that distressing letter from you had to be read. Why Sweetheart how terrible for you to feel so afflicted & I not near to comfort you… I long for you. I would give anything in the world to feel your arms about me & kiss your sweet lips. Here is a bit

Enclosed with the letter was a piece of the material for her wedding dress.

of my wedding dress. I am such a baby about including you in everything… I will write at length tonight or tomorrow. This goes to station for evening mail. You are my own precious love. God bless & keep you…   —Your Devoted & loving *Kittie*.

November 1st, South Cambridge.
My darling Henry—   This morning I have your letter of Friday last, the 28th. I am so thankful to hear with no delay of forwarding. I should expect you to take Mrs. Edson to a ball. She definitely enjoyed herself to stay so late. And it is very nice for you to be her escort. It is quite right your telling Dr. Fisk and Mr. Hill. I am glad you have done so. And it is far from my heart to have any friends of yours slighted. Remember when I gave you my promise, Darling, that I told you I had my duties to Mother & various matters to arrange with my Mother… I have talked over everything. We decided that it was best on all accounts not to speak of our engagement until we had made some definite plans as to the present and future. And that after Mother's return to her Colorado home was the time to announce our engagement. To have done so earlier would have caused Mother to be much tried by an army of friends here and then the questions to be answered… And now by the time Mother returns we will have our plans in a manner formed & when she announces her daughter's engagement, she can, at the same time, say we are to be married in a few weeks. I am very sorry my Darling if you have been dissatisfied that there has been delay in announcing our engagement & a great lump came in my throat for I have tried to do with Mother all that seemed right… Mother is not strong. She is delicate and feels very keenly my leaving her, though is perfectly happy in the thought that you are my husband and I your wife… Every night she puts her arms about me and kisses me, and says "I hope & pray your Beloved one is well, Darling." She puts herself completely aside… It is so hard to be away from you and not be able to talk over so many many things. You had to leave me so soon, and in so many ways it would be so much better to talk over our plans than to write. I will see the Jermains & talk with them all this week… I have decided to be credited with the amount for the necklace & when we are in N.Y. together we will select something together. Now my darling love, this is a shabby letter but scribbled while those two old ladies (whom you saw in that little house) are here for the day & are asking me questions. Mother is due in Colorado the 12th & will, if all is well, announce the engagement the 14th. This I will write your Mother, that she may do so at the same time. Best love Darling & I hope my precious love is well… Love & kisses Sweetheart   — Your own *Kittie*.

Green River, U. P. Railroad, Nov. 1, 1887.
My darling Kittie—   Oct. has at last gone and Nov. come. Now let that speed away, like this train which is moving about 40 miles an hour over a rough track… My darling how I miss you every hour and long for your presence. I must close now as we are almost at the station. With devoted love, Your own *Henry*.

Occidental Hotel, Nov. 4, 1887. Seattle, W. T. [Washington Territory]
My darling Kittie—   I have a few moments at this hour (lunch time) and I must send you a word of love. I arrived here last night about 10 1/2 o'clk and for the first time was glad you were not with me. All the Hotels were full and

only after wheedling and coaxing the Clerk did I get him to give me a bed in a room with another man. I put up with it all however, very uncomfortably, but my dear you would indeed have been out in the street… Seattle is a bustling irregularly built and rather striking Western Town— the principal one in the Territory. It contains about 16,000 people and bids fair to be an important place. I have been very nicely received here and expect I will enjoy my stay if I get a room which, by the way, I have not yet succeeded in doing… I am not going to write you much about my trip for I have not time in the first place and secondly I wish you someday to see it all yourself… Pardon this dirty— blotted paper. I am writing at a filthy table and I think I have ink up to my elbows. Ah dear love! How far I seem to be from you and how much I wish to see your loved face and kiss your loved lips a hundred times. Never mind our separation is not to be for long. Goodbye! A thousand measures of love I send. —Yours devotedly, *Henry*.

◦ A letter from Annie Jennings Wise Hobson:

Amherst Co. Va. 1887.
Dear Kittie—   I just have a moment to tell you that Cannon is better and is improving. The physician here assures me that he finds nothing wrong about his lungs; but after a while he will consult a specialist about his throat & the catarrh from which he suffers. He preached & read the service yesterday & stood it very well… —Yours lovingly, *A.J.W.H.*

Nov. 5, 1887, Seattle, Wash. Ter.
Office of the Clerk of the District Court — Third Judicial District of Washington Territory, King County
My own darling Kittie—   I will scribble you a few lines in the Court Room and whilst another fellow is talking, for if I don't get this letter into the mail by 2 o'clk you will miss for a day hearing from me and I know cherie that would distress you. As I write I am quite sure there is a fellow sitting across the table who is straining his eyes to see what I am writing. But I do not care, for if he were to succeed sweetheart, I think he would come to the conclusion that I am writing to someone I love very much and who I think is the sweetest woman in the world. It seems so hard that day after day passes and I do not hear a word from you. Never mind, for I am going to start towards the East in a few days and expect to find a package of letters at Boise City. I did not forget your photographs this time and they are a great comfort to me… —Yours Devotedly, *Henry*.

The Tacoma, Nov. 6, 1887, Tacoma, Wash. Ter.
My darling Love—   I am over in Tacoma spending Sunday and seeing the place. I received your telegram about the Jermains and it was just like your dear thoughtful self to send it. I am truly delighted to know that everything in that quarter is as you say "entirely satisfactory." I suppose you have seen by the papers that the Supreme Court of Utah unanimously decided in my favor that case I was in Salt Lake about. This dearest is another stroke of good luck which I am sure you have brought me. I am perhaps prouder of winning that case than any I ever won before, for not only was it the most important case I ever won, but I had against me two of the most distinguished lawyers in the

that case Fully described in the next chapter.

United States. Would I think the winning of this case will mean a great deal to me professionally—Ah Kittie, as I stood a little while ago, looking at Mount Tacoma as it stood out grand, serene, and towering above the Cascade Range, with my pride and ambition stirred up by the news of my success in this case, I can hardly describe my intense longings to rise and tower like this mountain over other men. And then came the ever depressing fear that I did not have the capacity so to do. I sometimes wonder whether my intense ambition is wrong and foolish and yet I cannot think so as long as I am ambitious to rise for good and in a good way.— Ah my sweet one, you must help me to rise and be great… I will finish at Seattle tomorrow and hope to win my case. I will start for Portland where I will stop a day and leave for Denver. Goodbye Darling…   Yours Devotedly *Henry*.

❧ Three letters:

Fitchburg, Nov. 6th, 1887.
Dear Mr. Hobson—   My cousin has told me of her engagement & I want to offer you my hearty congratulations, for you have won a woman who will make your life all your fancy paints it. My "little sister," as I call her, is *very* dear to me & I have hoped & prayed this happiness might come to her. I rejoice with her that you have done so much to brighten her life & can but hope all the good things I hear of you are true. I guard my Kittie's happiness very jealously & shall expect a great deal of you. I am ready to believe anyone, who really knows her cannot fail to be the devoted husband she deserves & so I am ready to welcome you & do all in my power to let you see how near my heart Kittie's welfare and happiness is. I hear there is a prospect of your being married here & if anything could add to the joy I feel it would be *that*. To be near her & with you both would make me feel I really had a share in your happiness. We have a beautiful church & a cozy little home where everything could be sacred & quiet. My husband adds his congratulations & hopes he may welcome you here before very long. I am looking forward to a visit from Kittie as she has never been here & I hope you won't come too soon, only because I know that means you will take her away. After the [illegible] I will always be enchanted to welcome you both & the oftener the better.
—Yours sincerely, *Ada Addison*.

November 6, 1887, Sunday eve.
Dear Mrs. Jermain—   Though I have had Mr. Hobson's consent to my writing you, for over a week now, yet I have been so absorbed with some serious cases that I have been treating, that I have not taken time for the writing. I know that you will not misinterpret this frank statement, but will believe me when I say that it has given me great pleasure to learn that we are to have you in Denver. I look forward with eagerness to the pleasant times that I anticipate when my pleasant associations with Mr. Hobson will be rendered still pleasanter by the presence of her for whom I have so high a regard. You know you will have to learn to like Denver, despite your strong Colorado Springs proclivities and the light esteem in which we are held by the Springs people. You will like it I know, and the warm friends that Mr. Hobson has gathered around him here. We have especially delighted at the honors heaped upon

him by the Administration and now comes the news of the success of his mission to Salt Lake. The case has been decided in favor of the Government. Really Henry seems to be in luck all around. If I have said more or less than I should have or that I have intended, in this letter, I shall look for an opportunity of rectifying it after Dec. 17th … Very sincerely, *Samuel A. Fisk.*

Colorado Springs, November 7, 1887.
[Catherine McKie Thayer to her daughter.] …This a.m. Dr. Reed called, just lovely. When he was about to go I said, sit a moment, I wish to tell you something. K— is going to be married. "I am glad to hear it." "But," I said, "you don't know to whom, the man is Mr. Hobson." "I am glad of it more. I like him. I like all I hear of him and hear he is a rising man. I am sorry she has got to live in Denver." "Well," I said, "that is better than the Hudson River Valley."… —*Mother.*

South Cambridge, Sunday evening, November 6th.
My own Precious Darling—   For two days I have not written you preferring to send two dispatches from Troy, that you might have at once the latest news of me. Now I must tell you of the Jermains. Marie was in her room and bed, not very well, and I went in to see her and tell her of my Love yesterday morning. I told her and then answered her questions about you and she asked to see your photograph, admired it very much— was as sweet as anyone could possibly be, told me I would always be inexpressibly dear to her and nothing could change her love… You would admire her very much. She asked if she might have your photograph, so I gave her the one I had intended for Aunt Ada… I can't tell you what a comfort it was to have Marie so happy with me in my *fullness* of joy. Mr. Jermain listened to all I told him and said very little, though every word he said was to the point and showed he wished me to accept what would make me happy. I think you might write directly to him… and please do not say anything of your desiring me to retain their love and the same interest as heretofore— that is for them to offer first. If your letter to Mr. Jermain comes before you receive this I will hand, or rather send it, to him at once… The medal has come & such a *beauty*. I am going to wear it on a fine chain about my neck, under my dress— and your Mother says she has "kept it for me all these years." What a lovely one she is… My heart's entire love, from your ever-devoted *Kittie.*   I love you, I love you, I love you, more & more & more, my own precious darling.

Nov. 8, 1887, Portland, Oregon.
My dear Mrs. Thayer— [Henry Hobson to Catherine McKie Thayer]
I start homeward tomorrow but have to stop over in Idaho. I hope to get back to Denver Sunday next. I am afraid I will be unable to go down to see you until the following Sunday as my Court is running in Denver and I have a Grand Jury next week. I will go down however sooner if I can. Will you kindly write as soon as you receive this what you have done about announcing Kittie's and my engagement. I have written to my relatives and my letters will reach them about the 15th next. I am very impatient to get some letters from Kittie as I have had none since I left Denver. I want to see her very very much but I suppose I will have to wait until I go east in December to bring her back

Samuel Fisk was a Denver physician and friend of Henry Hobson.

The engagement is announced of Mrs. Katherine Thayer Jermain, formerly of this city, to Henry Wise Hobson, United States attorney for Colorado, residing at Denver. The marriage will take place some time this month at the Episcopal rectory in Fitchburg, Mass.
—*Unidentified newspaper clipping.*

with me… It seems to me a year since I saw Kittie. She is certainly the sweetest woman in the world— at least to me, and I believe also to you.   —With much love, Yours Sincerely, *Henry W. Hobson.*

Many of the letters written onboard trains are in pencil.

Nov. 8, 1887, Northern Pacific R. R. Bet. Tacoma & Portland
My darling Kittie—   I am going to try and write you a letter on the train so it will go off tomorrow morning from Portland. I think so much and so often of you that I feel like writing constantly. You may be thankful that every Post does not bring you several letters… This abominable train is beginning to jolt like a farm wagon… Tomorrow I take it you will start for the Hot Springs with Frank. I sincerely trust he will find that they do him much good. I am so glad you do not need any kind of treatment but are strong and healthy. Stay so dearest for me and for my sake. I laugh to myself sometimes when I think of how astonished the Richmond people will be at my marriage. They of course assumed that I would eventually marry a Virginia girl and indeed, I have been most positively assigned to at least four or five. But my love, I will show them that my New York—Colorado link is better than any of them— sweeter, lovelier, more lovable. Tom Page, I have of course told Tom, for you could not have expected me to keep this matter from Tom. Well he is just charmed and writes charmingly about you. I of course told him he could kiss you, just as I kiss his wife and he says— *"Kiss her— Well I rather think I will."* So you see my dear that Tom and I have settled that matter. You do not mind a kiss so much, do you Kittie? I know you have a liking for them when I am the other party. Ah me! That just makes me think how much I would like to kiss you now… The rain is pouring— pouring, pouring and everything looks gloomy. In fact I have hardly seen the sun since coming out here. With all this surrounding gloom it is very cheering and comforting to have you and your love to turn to and to have a subject to think about that dispels all gloom in my mind. Well I am going to close for I can hardly read my own writing. Good-bye my darling. Warm regards to Frank. —Yours Devotedly as ever, *Henry.*

Albany Depot, Tuesday 8th, November. 7:30 P.M.
My own Darling Henry—   Have just come in from N.Y. Left at 3:30 PM. Saw my two sisters-in-law… They have always been perfect in their devotion and kindness to me… I enclose Katie's letter received today. She has been an idol of mine…   —Your own *Kittie.*

❧ Katie's letter:

Hedge Lawn, Nov. 6, 1887.
My own darling Kittie Cat—   After you left yesterday I tore upstairs and threw myself on the bed and I cried as though my heart would brake. I could not help it, I felt as though I would never see you again. It's lovely for you I know, and I love you always the same, but— but— we won't see half so much of you. Oh Kittie you don't know *how I love you*, more— more than I can tell. Aunt Marie asked me if you had told me. So she showed me his picture. He *is* handsome, so brave and noble looking, I am sure he *must* be lovely. But he isn't good enough for you. In fact no one could be, no one! I don't blame him for loving you. In fact, how could I when I would do just the same thing

if I were he. Poor Kittie Cat, it must have been hard for you to tell us all, but you knew that we would love you just the same. Didn't you? It's a perfect day, today, and Sophie and I have just come home from a walk. We went to our lot, in the cemetery, to see the new cross on dear Auntie's grave. It is lovely— I wish you could see it. We stopped at the station on our way home, to watch the *"Micky"* lovers from Albany. It was great fun. There was one couple, that we caught in the act of embracing, when we appeared on the scene— it was highly embarrassing for all parties, but they wouldn't say anything but love when we were by— queer wasn't it!!

As we were coming down from church we met Kittie & Sophie, and I got out and walked with them. We were walking along and talking, when suddenly Sophie said those men have got "Teddy" in that buggy. Just then the buggy drew up in front of a tavern, and saying, "Stay there and be quiet you cur," to a dog, turned to go into the saloon. We were prepared to rush up to the men and say *"What are you doing with my dog?"* — when out jumped a wretched little cur, with a head of a terrier, and a body of— goodness knows *what*. If we'd been dogs we would have gone off with our tails between our leg; but as it was, we turned away with a decidedly "left" feeling in our hearts. Dear little Keefro has missed you so, he looks so disconsolate. I will always have him to make me think of you, though I need nothing to keep *you* in memory; for my own dearest, I could never, never forget you who are almost the dearest person in the world to me. I wish I was in New York with you! Do you remember the first time I went to New York with you. Didn't we have a lovely time together. And the doll you gave me, what a beauty it was. Oh, to think that you are going out to Denver to live, and I— I— won't see you for so long. I can hardly bear to think of it. But I must say good night as I have written 12 full pages, so my dear Kittie cat, good-night. From your best lover, a kite full of love, *Katie*.

Office of James B. Jermain, No. 2 James Street, Albany, N. Y.
November 9, 1887.
My Dear Daughter—   As we shall not probably meet again & to avoid any exhibition of feeling on my part in the affair, perhaps in the presence of a stranger, I hope you will excuse my absence this morning. Without finding any fault & acknowledging that you are at perfect liberty to change your condition in life, it is a great trial to me that it must be so, bringing up as it does so many sad memories & blasted hopes. May God bless you.   —Yours affectionately, *James. B. Jermain*.

November 11, 1887, St. Louis, Missouri.
My own Precious Darling Henry—   It does not seem as if I ever could say enough loving words to you my heart is so full of love & tenderness… Mr. Jermain feels my going very much, is overcome with feeling, & so quiet. I will probably not go to the Jermain's at present for it makes it so hard for the old man to see me… Your mother has written me such a lovely letter. It is very precious & she approves of all our plans. Now my Love, my Life, my Darling, Good Night. God bless & keep you sweetheart. I think of you constantly & wish for you every hour. Oh, if I could only feel your arms about me…
—Your own Devoted *Kittie*.

Katie The letter is from Katherine Savage, the granddaughter of James B. Jermain, to her aunt, Katherine Thayer Jermain, widow of Barclay Jermain, before the latter's marriage to Henry Wise Hobson.

The letter is from James B. Jermain to his daughter-in-law, Katherine Thayer Jermain, after he heard of her engagement to Henry Hobson.

∽ The letter to Mr. Jermain:

Nov. 13, 1887, Denver Colo.
My dear Sir—   I suppose Mrs. Jermain, your daughter-in-law, has told you of our engagement and of my wish to make her my wife at an early date. I however feel that I must write to you personally and ask your permission and consent, for I know from what she has told me that you have stood so truly in the position of a Father to her, and I can not but pay you the respect, that I would to her own Father if he were living.

 I should perhaps have written before but my necessary absence and almost continual travelling for the past month must be my excuse for my delay.

 I feel the delicacy of my position and request for Mrs. Jermain must be a very tender tie between you and your son's memory. I have always respected and admired, without a shadow of jealousy, the sweet love she evinced to her husband and his memory, and I would indeed be an unworthy man if I could wish her to be different. I may further say that I have never for an instant thought of having her change her feelings of affection for you and your family if you and they are willing for her to continue her love. I trust you will give your willing consent to my request and I promise that I will try to be a good true husband to her— one worthy of her love and of the respect of her relatives and friends. She is young still, not only in years but in sweetness and purity of soul and capable of making a man very happy. May I not ask that you will consent to my being the favored man.

 If not too presuming, I would also ask for the approbation of your family, whom I have learned to respect highly from what Mrs. Jermain has told me of them.

 We wish to be married on December 17th as I am a very busy man, and my business will need close attention after January 1st. Trusting that you will receive my request with consideration, I am Sir, with great respect, Yours very Respectfully,   —*Henry W. Hobson.*
To— Jas. B. Jermain Esq. Albany, N.Y.

November 1887, Hot Springs, Arkansas.
My own Darling Henry—   Two precious letters reached me. One I found at the Post office on my arrival— written in Court at Seattle. The 2nd received yesterday, Sunday morning, written Tacoma. I am so rejoiced to hear of your gaining the suit in Utah. And I am so proud of you and your ambitions and I am so ambitious for you. I wish to be a help to you in all ways. For Darling you are my very own. You must take me way off to Washington Territory. I should love to see that wonderful country & you need not plan to leave me in Denver, for I could not be left. And after all this long separation I am not going to be left for a single day, unless you think it absolutely necessary… As soon as you can fix the date of your coming east I am sure you will tell me, for it will be a relief & make me more content when I know exactly what your plans are as to the date of your coming… I do value the daily expressions of love— it bridges the distance. Then tell me how you like my samples and if we are likely to be entertained in Richmond— or go to any parties, so I may pack my clothes accordingly. I want to send by freight all my belongings not necessary, that you may not be burdened by trunks, but I always have a great

number of packages— so prepare yourself… I will write daily.   —My Pride you are. My Joy & Your own Loving *Kittie*.

Nov. 13, 1887, Denver.
My own Darling Love—   A few hurried words tonight sweet. I have just returned this afternoon and though very tired, I am perfectly well and happy Darling. I enjoyed your dear letters so much, only there were not enough of them, only three. You don't write to me nearly so often as I do to you. There! I am showing jealousy already… I am glad you went to the Hot Springs with Frank and I wish you to feel when you are my wife that you are in every way as near to your family as before… I received a sweet note from Aunt Ada thanking me for a book I sent her. She says she will not commit herself absolutely until after we have been married five years, but that she must confess she likes me very much at present… Now sweetheart I must know about your wedding ring. Take a careful measurement and send to me. Isn't it funny— I never thought of a wedding ring until today on the train. I wish you would also make any suggestions you think proper about the kind of ring you wish. I wish I could ask you and get a correct answer, what you wish for a wedding present. I am the poorest fellow in the world to select such things and I wish so much to please you. Couldn't you drop just a hint— just say what you think would be a nice present for a friend of yours to give his bride— I am afraid I have not a bit of romance in my composition, or I would never ask such a question… I hope to hear from your Mother tomorrow and will follow her directions in all things. I would not put off our marriage for a day for any consideration. We ought to have been married a month ago… I will be head over heels in work the rest of this month, so you must put up with short letters and fewer of them. Still my dear one you will be constantly present to my heart and mind. Warm regards to Frank. And Goodnight— I send a thousand kisses.   Yours devotedly & forever, *Henry*.

The pictures received! I am just charmed with them. I thank you so much. Dearest, darling, love— goodnight!

～ A letter from Annie Jennings Wise Hobson:

The Highlands, Mitchell's Station, Culpeper Co. Virginia, Nov. 7th. 1887.

The blessing of another dear sweet letter from you has come to me this morning, my darling Kittie, and with it two other letters which seemed like direct answers to prayer, from friends whose sorrows and temptations have long been on my heart and mind… I should love to see our dear Boy's letters to you. You will yet show them to me? Kittie darling, it just delights me to see you *so much in love*. What you term your "outbursts" are charming. I have always said that if Henry was not my son & I a young female, I should fall desperately in love with him. And then it is so loving and confiding in you to come to me— his Mother— with it all! God bless you for loving him so devotedly & enthusiastically! …It is lovely in you and your Mother, dear child, to come to me with them at all. I am really so concerned that your own dear Mother cannot be with you… Your whole vision being married at your cousins in Fitchburg met my fullest accord and the "quiet wedding" without "display or criticism" shows that my daughter has just the fine refinement and reverence of nature that I would find in my son's wife. If possible it is the desire of Cannon & myself to be present. I desire so earnestly that he should marry you, and he performs the service so solemnly and beautifully. I do hope that I can yet arrange it for you to spend two or three days in Ashland with me. I would love you to know the dear friends with whom I live and who are so kind to me, but we have not been able to get the house we proposed renting together, where I could make you so comfortable… I will carry out your wishes about announcing the engagement to Henry's relatives and friends. I think your Mother is very wise to wish you to keep house. Has Henry told you that I shall have a service of silver that was my Uncle's, Dr. Jennings & a set of china— very pretty old fashioned French china— (also his), to send you? Now I must reply to the other items which as yet have had no response. Of course I expect you to call me by some name that tells I have a Mother's love for you and that you freely give the daughter's love to me— but Dear, what you call your own Mother must be a sacred one name to you, so I shall not expect you to give me the same endearing term of Motherness that has always been yours for your own Mother. It was the votive of a truly noble Christian woman that led you to say you should go to Henry's Church if he desired it— that is you meant I am sure if it was for his highest good. My own Mother & all her people were Presbyterians. My husband's family were & are Presbyterians. Plumer loved his own Church devotedly, but joined the Episcopal Church because I was a communicant when we were married and he was not. Now Kittie, I have reminded Henry of this— I pray God to guide you to do what is best for you both, and yet I would not have you leave your own Church if it hindered & grieved you, or it distressed your Mother. Now I must stop. I shall endeavor to write to you once a week hereafter… My thoughts and prayers will follow you continually. My love to your Mother and regards to your brother. Send me your Mother's address in Colorado & I will write to her myself.   —Yours most lovingly, *A.J.W. Hobson.*

A letter from Cannon tells that he has improved so much but he is going on this week to Wilmington, Del. to consult a specialist & if necessary will go to Phila.

Denver, Colorado, Nov. 15, 1887.
My own Darling—   I could not possibly write to you yesterday— what a pile of work I had to do. Today I can only scratch a line to say I love you and every thought of you, God bless you my own love… Tomorrow our engagement will be announced by your Mother and me. How proud I will be to have the world know I have won you, that you are mine alone. Oh sweetheart, I wish you were near for me to kiss… I am bewildered with work here and am at my office night and day… You see I treat you just as though we were married, write to you on office paper and very hurriedly.   —Yours devotedly, *Henry W. Hobson.* —Then a business signature again. That was a slip. I meant *"Henry."*

Denver, Colorado, November 16, 1887.
My darling Kittie—   Why don't you write to me? I have only received four letters from you written within the last two weeks. I was not in a good humor when I got up this morning and when I got to the breakfast I found Dr. Fisk had perpetrated one of his very silly jokes, which aggravate me very much sometimes, and this morning I was put into a worse humor by it. Then

when I came to my office and found for the third morning no letter from you I became savage and have continued so all day— as my clerks have unfortunately found out… But I am not going to say anything more for enough of my bad humor is already in this letter. Four weeks from Saturday Dearest I hope you will become my wife and my greatest blessing in life. Yet four weeks seems a long time and the weeks seem to pass by with leaden heels… I fear I have done some swearing today which would have shocked you. I now snatch a moment to write to you and find fault with and growl at you, but still to send a great deal of my deep love. I will tell you sometime about Dr. Fisk's joke. I fear I was not good tempered about it… Goodbye and don't feel badly over my growling. I am now showing one of the bad sides of my character of which I told you. Yrs. devotedly, *Henry*.

◦∕ A second letter from Katie:

Hedge Lawn, Nov. 17th, 1887.
My dearest Kittie Cat—   Oh! You dear one, how I love you! I received your dearest letter today, and I read & re-read it. It was so dear to me. When the train whizzed you out of sight I immediately turned my attention to all the funny things I could possibly see for I can tell you I felt pretty "down at heart." …Oh, how I wish I were at Hot Springs with you, would it not be lovely. Kittie Cat, I suppose you will think it a very foolish thing to say, but it's true, if I were a man I would fall in love with you and marry you, see if I wouldn't. But as it is, you are my *dearest* friend in the world. Really everything here goes on just the same; we are all well and happy, with the exception of me and I am not as *happy* as I can be without you. "Are you the dearest little woman in the world?" Why of course, and you just tell Mr. Hobson for me that he has the best choice of any man I know of. Grandpapa and Aunt Marie are going to N. Y. for a few days… Now Kittie Cat I will own up that I am writing this letter at 11 o'clock, and I don't think Aunt Marie will exactly approve, do you? …Now you are *not* to send *this* letter to Mr. H— on any account… Good-night my own dearest, with love to Mr. Thayer, I am you own little *Katie*.

Nov. 18, 1887.
My darling, my Sweetheart Kittie—   You don't know how relieved I was to get a letter from you this morning. Just to think five days since I had heard. Oh Kittie! How could you treat me so? But I am so delighted to hear from you again that I am not going to quarrel a bit, but devote all the little time I have to saying sweet things to you… I expect to get to Fitchburg either the night of the 15th or the morning of the 16th. Then Sweetheart, darling mine, I will be with you. You don't know how warmly everybody has congratulated me, and I think there is genuine delight… My dearest, I will at all times be tender, affectionate and respectful towards your Mother— Not only because she occupies that relationship to you but also because she herself commands it. I admire your Mother greatly and hope to merit her admiration… I am fearfully pressed now with my Court running and my Grand Jury in session. I have to be with it all day and then every night I am working until eleven o'clk preparing indictments. But the Grand Jury adjourns tomorrow and I will then have a short respite…   —Goodbye my love, my own— Don't treat me so badly again about writing— Yours Devotedly, *Henry*.

Nov. 19, 1887, Denver.
My darling Love—   I am very tired, having just finished with my Grand Jury, and it is very late, but I must send you a line to say I think of and love you. Two sweet letters from you, yesterday one and one today. Dr. Fisk says my action and choice meet with universal approbation, and if anyone knows, Dr. F— does. He is a splendid fellow but very fond of a little harmless gossip. He was almost bursting until he had permission to tell of our engagement…
—Yours devotedly, *Henry*.

November 19, 1887, Saturday morning. Hot Springs, Arkansas.
My own Precious Darling—   A few minutes ago the office boy brought me your "growling" letter of last Wednesday. [November 16th above.] It seems as if I must be near you now & put my arms closely about my Darling & tell you again how entirely and wholly I love you. Four weeks from today you will be my Husband. Oh, the joy and peace that thought brings to me… Now Henry, we are not going to begin in a Hotel. I would rather have *anything* in the way of a house, than that. There will be something, don't be too particular. However tiny, let us be in our own home. Sitting room, dining room, pantry and kitchen, that would answer… What does it matter how simply we begin? It can all be charmingly pretty. We can be alone. Why think how people live in smaller quarters in N.Y. and Paris… There must be some little cottage, and I fear you are not looking for this style of house. I do hate the idea of a Hotel drawing room, three times a day— no privacy at table. I'd rather be in a boarding house, much rather, or have a house of four rooms. Darling I want to feel we are in a home, and all by ourselves, with no restraint. A hotel life would be so constrained and unnatural… My heart's fondest love— my arms would go out to you. Kisses innumerable are yours & myself & whole heart & life   —Your own loving & devoted *Kittie*.

Your letter to Mr. Jermain was entirely satisfactory & I am very grateful in my heart for all your sweetness. Remember you are *much more now* than anything has ever been in my life. —*Kittie*.

THE WESTERN UNION TELEGRAPH COMPANY
Nov. 20, 1887, Denver Col.
To: Mrs. Katherine Jermain, Hot Springs Ark.
Am here well much love. I go to Springs Tuesday. —*H.W.H.*

Henry W. Hobson, United States Attorney.
Nov. 20, 1887. Denver.
My own Darling Kittie—   Here I go writing a letter to you from my office, for I can write more quietly here than at the Club… Tracy Edson telephoned down to me last evening and asked that I would go up to see his wife for a few moments which I did and had a chat alone with her for about twenty minutes. Do you know dear, she looked so worn and weak and thin I could not but feel a great pity for her. She spoke as sweetly and nicely about our marriage as possible and what she said of you really made me feel more warmly towards her… When I was leaving she said "Henry the only objection I have to your marrying is that your wife will not like me as

well as I could wish, and that thus you will be drawn somewhat away from me"— ...And when I shook hands with her, she looked up and said "lean over my Dear fellow and let me kiss you, just once for joy at your approaching marriage to a good true woman."

I hear today from my Brother that after consultation with a specialist he is confident that his trouble is catarrhal, and that whilst his lungs are weak, they are free from disease. I feel much relieved and hope that he will soon be entirely well. I have not yet been able to see your mother, though I propose doing so tomorrow evening... And now another day of our period of waiting to become one has gone by. I wonder how many times a day I think of this and every night I feel great joy that we are one day nearer each other...
—Yours devotedly, *Henry*.

❧ A letter from Catherine McKie Thayer:

November 20, 1887.
...Your letter with copy of Henry's came this a.m... I trust Mr. Jermain will answer it in a good spirit— how can he do otherwise? ...I cannot look for a house until I have seen H— in Colorado— and talked with him. Perhaps he may have something in view. I do not see that you have very much to do in N.Y. You have plenty of time to think it over, to concentrate your thoughts and plan wisely. I do wish you to have a good rest before the 17th... —*Mother*.

❧ A letter from Annie Jennings Wise Hobson:

Richmond, November 21st, 1887.
My dear Kittie—   Seated by my side, my daughter is going to write my greeting to you. It gives me pain to use my pen, and I write even with a pencil with great difficulty. Like my dear Annie, it has for some time been the desire of my heart to see my dear, noble Henry married to a good, true Christian woman. I have great confidence in the judgment of my grandson, and if she whom he has chosen is only half what Henry represents, she must be one to him and keep my love. I call you Kittie, for Annie tells me that is your wish. I shall not be satisfied 'till I hear that you can induce Henry to return East to live. You need make no plans for the future that will take my dear Annie away from me. Give my kindest regards to your Mother, and tell her that I know she may safely trust her daughter to the keeping of my Grandson. I have prayed through many years for my dear Henry, and now you shall be beside him in my prayers. May God make you one in Christ. Yours Affectionately, *Mary Lyons Wise*.

Mary Lyons Wise   The third wife and widow of Henry Alexander Wise and Henry Hobson's grandmother.

November 22, 1887. Hot Springs, Arkansas.
My own Darling Henry—   Today brought me your letter after the grand jury was finished. I do hope you will have a few hours in which to rest. I now tell you I am not going to allow you to work as you do now. You are too precious and I will not have you a victim of overwork. You will be my sweetheart— ...I think of you always... Henry Darling I love you so dearly. God bless & keep my dear love.   —Your loving *Kittie*.

Colorado Springs, Nov. 22, 1887.
My darling Kittie—   I am writing to you from the sitting room in your own house at Colorado Springs with your sweet Mother to see that I am behaving… Just a moment ago she came in and said that as I always claimed I found a storm at the Springs, she supposed you had sent me an umbrella… Just to think of it— I Henry Hobson, who for years has laughed at sentiment and love, defied the claims of women and proclaimed my determination to remain unmarried, am now writing, calling a woman sweetest of sweethearts, and thanking her as my darling for an umbrella… Just to think that I will never spend a moment in your own house with you as your accepted lover. But then, what two people could have sweeter hours than those we have spent together since our engagement. Goodbye for today. With the biggest lot of love you ever had sent you.   —Yours devotedly, *Henry*.

◦ A letter from Catherine McKie Thayer:

November 22, 1887.
My dear Kittie darling—   …Henry tells me that there is not a house to be had, so far as he has been able to learn, and he fears you ("we") will have to go to a Hotel, thought the Albany preferable to the Windsor for some reasons— does not like either for you, or himself, —but thinks there may be no other way— for the present… H— says he was talking with a friend who has just put up a house and what has cost $10,000 would now cost $15 thousand. Masons asking $5.50 a day— the opinion is that sooner or later the prices must drop in real estate, and for wages, and building be less expensive— so much for house… H— has just had a letter from his Grand mere, "sweet" she is, "ready to love his wife." "Said his Mother and brother's wife were not congenial." He asked me about the Jermains— had not heard from anyone yet. I said all were sweet to you. He then asked about Mr. J. I said he felt it very much as his daughter said and I tried to tell H— how Mr. J— could depend on you as he could not on his delicate daughter… I spoke about the 17th, he said alluding to my reference to his Mother's letter as to that date, that his Mother & Brother could stay in Fitchburg or go to N.Y.—he did not propose to have them "chaperone us on our bridal trip." He seems very happy, radiantly so, and I believe is a high minded honorable man— and *if you grow*, you can satisfy him and make him happy— but he would not long be *content* with a companionship that was not a steady, if not a rapid development. Will give him the umbrella when he returns… Speaking of the 17th Sat. "My Mother would not travel on Sunday. I think she would stop anywhere on the plains etc." Henry spoke of you as not wearing flannels, he really thought them necessary for a protection. I said we had talked it over, and you had talked with an old physician in the East, and I thought you were fortified in your opinion by what he told you— "but, H— said, "I think she needs something for protection." I said I thought flannel made you restless & uncomfortable. "Well," he said, "then she can wear silk." I really think Kittie, that he feels exactly as I do, that you *should* wear some kind of high necked undervest to keep you well— now will you not get some silk vests— they need not be heavy— pray do— but they will be a covering. I will gladly buy them for you. I wish to tell you all that I can that Henry has said but I do not now think of anything else… A heart full of love, *Mother*.

November 24th, 1887. Hill Farm, White Creek. [Mailed from Hot Springs, Arkansas.]
My own Darling Henry—   Last evening I wrote you a long letter in bed— but this morning was dissatisfied with it & so did not send it. However yesterday's mail took a letter & a photo I found for you which you may like… Today your dear note & your Grandmother's letter came. Darling love, I do know what a true, noble, pure man is to be my husband & every day I thank God many, many times, for your love— and pray to be the wife your heart longs for. Today is Thanksgiving— and it always is so closely associated with my dear Father. I feel so keenly his not having lived to know you Darling & to see my joy and perfect happiness… When this letter reaches you, you will be able to say "Week after next." I think Henry of our marriage with perfect content & joy… I return your Grandmother's letter. I only hope they will think me half worthy of you. Then I will be fully satisfied. Before you leave Denver I wish you would have several photographs taken, but better still, go in N.Y. Now remember, several positions, full and side face…   —Always your own Loving & Devoted *Kittie*. You are so handsome & I am so consumed with delight!

Hot Springs, Arkansas, November 25th, 1887.
My own Darling Henry—   No letter from you today— And knowing I will soon have one I am content & happy. If five days go by you may expect fifty telegrams. I enclose your Mother's and Grandmother's letters. Henry, you must not praise me to your friends. Why it makes me faint hearted— they will expect so much. Darling, won't you try to take as long as you possibly can in the East. I think considering it is our wedding journey you might take a little vacation & not be "hurried & flurried" as your Mother thinks you will be… We have been separated all these weeks of our engagement & I had hoped we could have several weeks together in the East. The rain has come & dust laid, which makes walking possible to our delight. Oh, Love, I am thinking of you always. Don't think I am exacting about our stay in the East. I think you will understand that the time we are together after we are married, before our return to Denver & our home, is more precious than I can in any way describe to you. And to be "hurried" & rush to Richmond & be every moment trying to do more than is possible would take away much of the sweet rest, peace & quiet I so longed for. I think you should make a special appeal to the Attorney General & not have him give you any orders for three or four weeks! & don't let those hateful telegrams, making you uneasy, come pouring in. You Darling— see how jealous I am. I do wish you to have a long rest and I have so much to talk with you about. I can't wait long to see you. Be sure & come the evening of the 15th. I will remind you of this often. In a little over a week I will be gone… Three weeks from tomorrow, what a little time Darling but how the days drag. Now my Sweetheart, goodnight. You are my very own & I love you more & more. You are all in all to me. My hearts deepest tenderest love to you my love.   —God keep my Darling, Your devoted & loving *Kittie*.

☙ Letters from Catherine McKie Thayer:

November 25th, 1887.
…I just wrote Henry that you would like a home, but said you prefer'd a Hotel to a large house. "Larger than you need," quoting your words, that I

supposed he knew that your house must be within luncheon distance of his office…

November 26, 1887.
…you have heard me say often, that I have loved the Jermains from their cradles, and loved their dear Mother as I love no other friend. I hope before this can reach you, that you will have had such letters, as will quiet the little unrest that the rather long silence may have caused— but you are so anchored in your love for Henry, and his for you, that all other matters will seem only ripples on the surface that cannot disturb the quiet depths of such an abiding love…

November 27th, 1887.
…I see in the papers and hear from people, that many houses have been built, but entirely fail to meet the demand. So when you receive this you must feel still more the difficulty in finding what you wish…

Henry W. Hobson, United States Attorney. November 25, 1887.
My Darling Love—   I send you some more letters which I think perhaps you may wish to read. If they bore you Dear, don't hesitate to skip them… I received a very nice letter this morning from Your Uncle Adin which I answered at once. This morning I also received a letter from your Mother on the house question, saying that if I had no objection she would come up for a few days and see what she could do. I wrote her that I would be delighted if she would do so. Your dear loving letter telling of your Brother Frank's keeping my letters in his pocket made me feel much sympathy with him. I have done likewise many times… Oh Kittie! What a darling speller you are— you write "tell me when you will stop so I may *no* when to reach you." Never mind sweetheart I will give you lots of lessons in spelling when we are married. Do you know I am almost tempted to give up our trip to Richmond. If it were not for my Mother I certainly should. We will be bothered to death about where to stop and stay. I think I shall go to a Hotel, though the Richmond Hotels are simply beastly. There are reasons why I do not care to stay at my Uncle's, Mr. John Wise, and yet he is the first relative who has invited me to his house. There are also reasons why I cannot stay at Tom Page's, but I am most inclined to his house. I am so truly rejoiced my loved one to hear that you are again well. I have been so anxious about you. Don't be imprudent anymore. Suppose something serious had resulted from this cold! My darling it is too terrible to think about. I note what you say about the roses and you shall have them if they can be gotten, and of course they can. And are the roses to be all I shall give you on your wedding day? Ah no! My dear one. I will give you myself, my all, and I will tie the roses and also myself in bonds of sacred love. A friend in Washington sent me a very nice notice of our engagement from a Washington Sunday paper. Well I must close for I have only time to run for a little lunch and get to Court. By the way Kittie are you going to have your piano sent out? I do so love a piano in a house… Goodbye my darling love. All my heart is yours—   Yours devotedly, *Henry*.

your piano   Kittie purchased a Steinway grand piano soon after the death of Barclay Jermain in 1882. It was subsequently shipped to Denver in 1887 when she married Henry Hobson. In 2008 it is in the home of Henry and Kittie's granddaughter.

November 26, 1887, Hot Springs, Arkansas, Avenue Hotel.
My own Darling Henry—   This morning I have received your letter from the Springs & the following from Denver… And indeed, all you say goes to

prove that [it] is best we should begin at the Albany. And as it is best, I am very happy in it… All the letters from Virginia I read with great interest— especially Tom's [Thomas Nelson Page]. I love him now and have accepted him with you and you with him. Indeed I hope he will write me. Why, how many invitations. The Stewart's, Mrs. Wise, Tom's. Won't we go to see your Aunt Mrs. Lyons? …My Sweetheart how can I ask Mr. Jackson to our wedding when I am not inviting anyone? …And then I do feel, as my Mother will be absent, I wish as few present as possible. Your Mother will be a comfort & Cannon & Tom Page, Ada, Aunt Ada, Morris, his Mother. However I will send a note to Mr. Jackson & tell him there are to be no invitations but if he should happen to come we would be very glad… I must not in any way make the least excitement or trouble for Ada, for she expects to be confined in March, and she is not over strong. I think she is very very sweet to accept my desire to be married from her home, so willingly. She is the dearest girl in the world… I think you ought to write Morris Addison & tell him of your gratification regarding Fitchburg, & our wish to be married in his church— *Your* brother performing the ceremony— & with Morris to assist. This is the way to make it all smooth & easy. Tell him it has always been your and your Mother's hearts desire. This should come from you…   —Then I will be your loving & devoted wife. You are my own darling sweetheart. Kisses.   —Your *Kittie*.

November 27, 1887, Hill Farm, White Creek. [Mailed from Hot Springs, Arkansas.]
My own Precious Henry— This morning your letter written on last Thursday, Thanksgiving, came to me. It is such a luxury to lie in bed and read your soul & heart… I remember a friend of mine married & went with her husband to Virginia— & she said the women met her as if she were not a lady, & were suspicious of her until she had lived among them some time. Not that they were rude or discourteous, only they were surprised & could not accept the fact, that a New Yorker was a true *gentlewoman*. I am going to keep close hold of your Mother & Tom… I think Darling that Mother would like to see you before you leave for the East. It would be a comfort to her— she is so alone. Please write her to come to Denver— show her the rooms in the Albany— & have a talk with her before you go. Dear soul she is so brave & sweet… I have written your Mother to ask Cousin Mary Lyons to accompany her to Fitchburg. Your Mother needs some sweet, sympathetic woman with her…
—Your Loving *Kittie*.

Denver, Colo. November 27, 1887.
My Darling Kittie—   I had intended to write you a nice long letter today but this morning, just as I got to my office, Dr. Fisk called for me to go out into the country with him. The morning was superb, the view grand, and the atmosphere perfect. I could not resist the temptation and so I went. Fisk now has a horse and buggy, a very nice outfit. The afternoon was well on the wane when I returned and after going through with my letter writing, some that had to be sent off, and straightening the office up, I find that I have only time for a hasty letter to you… You will have numerous friends in the Department (of Justice) where I am very popular. Robinson says the Department people are very much pleased and gratified at my winning the first two big cases I was assigned to as Special Counsel— the one in Utah and the one in Wash.

Territory... I have received no letter from you today, but I know my own true love that the mails are at fault. Goodbye. God bless and keep you. Yours devotedly & forever, *Henry*.

Monday Evening, November 28th, 1887, Hot Springs.
My Darling Sweetheart— This morning no letter from you came to me... and I could have cried. As the days go by I seem more and more impatient... I send you a letter from John Birge— he was in my Father's Bible class for years, as a boy, then Father gave him a position in his office— and finally made him a partner. He is true as steel, good as gold and manages my Mother's affairs in the East. He has known me since I was a wee thing— and all he says is from his heart... You are the dearest sweetest love in the whole world. Much tender love & kisses Henry Darling. —Your own *Kittie*.

◦∾ A letter from Catherine McKie Thayer:

November 29th, 1887.
...Henry said he had a dispatch from you as to his health, and he read one to me in which you said "do not take the Ward House, will be satisfied at the Albany, get sunny exposure etc." This he cannot do at the Albany. The Proprietor would do anything possible for him but the best rooms are taken first, naturally. Then Henry came here where he can get the same rooms (or corresponding ones) that Mrs. W— had. Said he did want you to have a good deal of sun and these rooms would give it. That a deduction would be made when you were away for any length of time— and he thought you quite agreed with him that it was best not to go into a large house, or make a splurge for a little time... He said many men whose homes were out on the hill took luncheon in town, and really were at home very little. He said sometimes it was necessary for him to work evenings, and if his home were not too far he could take books and papers and work there. Dear dear child how I wish you could decide this matter... Now dear I think I have told you about all I am thinking of, only he said he could store *anything* that was sent here without trouble. I said as to house, Henry perhaps you better postpone your marriage till spring. His face lighted with that beaming radiant look & smile and said we have gone too far now. He said to me the other day in a letter that he should feel so relieved when you were his wife... —*Mother*.

Hot Springs, Arkansas, November 30th, 1887.
My own Darling Henry— This morning I received your letter of Sunday and I was so glad you had the opportunity of some hours in the fresh air... I do hope you have given up trying to get a house. I don't want one if we are to be away so much. Let us be as free as possible. With no servants... Home is where the heart is— so we will have a home, though not a house... I am so pleased with Mary Lyons' letter. Two months yesterday since you asked me to trust you, and it seems years... I can't believe it is such a little time... Your loving and devoted *Kittie*   —or Katherine as you like.

Nov. 30, 1887, Denver.
My darling Love— I am going to write you a hasty letter because I did not write yesterday as it was impossible, and next Saturday is your birth-

day. First as to a few matters referred to in your letters— I will write to Mr. Addison at once as you suggest, and will say I wish my Brother to assist. Let the Preachers arrange their parts between themselves. Nobody is going with us to Boston after our wedding if I can help it… Your Mother came up yesterday afternoon and she and I have been conferring together about quarters and going to see sound houses. I will not enter details as I am so hurried and I doubt not she will write fully about it. I fear we can get no rooms at the Albany and if we go to the Windsor we will have to take the rooms furnished— although of course we can use many of our own things. Depend upon it my darling Kittie I am going to do everything to make you most comfortable and contented, and if we have to go to a Hotel at first, I know dear you will be content. It will not last very long… And now dearest a few words with regard to your birthday. It cannot but be a very sacred and precious day to me since it is that upon which you were born to be in after life my love and loving one. The three days that shall always be most near and dear to me are your birthday, Sept 29th and our wedding day— All together in a group… Pardon the hasty and unsatisfactory way I have written to you about your birthday, for I am so very busy in Court and with a string of people waiting to see me whenever I have a moment in my office— I am now keeping some parties waiting whilst I dash off a kind of letter to you. But though I write so hastily, you must feel assured dearest that I have a thousand loving and different thoughts about your birthday. I can't write more. Goodbye. God bless you loved one. In a little more than two weeks I will take you in my arms as my wife. —Yours devotedly, *Henry*.

Dec. 1, 1887, Denver.
My darling Katherine—   I have but a moment to write. Your mother went down this afternoon. She and I agreed after fully looking around and consulting that the best thing I could do would be to engage rooms at the Windsor. I am going to do that despite your telegram. It is the best I can do dear and so you must try and be content. If after we have tried it you find you do not like it, we will change. I could not secure decent rooms at the Albany— it is full to overflowing with people who are going to stay the winter… Don't fear about my Mother going on our trip with us. She will not do so. Leave all that to me. We will be alone darling for at least a few days… Only think, this is the first day of the month that is to be our wedding month. Two weeks from tomorrow I will be with you. Bless you my heart, my life. I think I shall call you Katherine. Goodbye. I am pretty hard worked. —Devotedly, *Henry*.

❧ A letter from Catherine McKie Thayer:

December 1, 1887.
My precious Darling Kittie—   Have just finished reading the letters I found, yours of Nov. 27th with Marie's inclosed, yours of 28th also, and Marie's and Mrs. Hobson's. I too had a letter from John Birge, chiefly about you…

Now as to Marie's letter, we must expect and it is right, that she should shield her tired, shrinking father from *all trials*, neutral or otherwise. I pity the poor old man, he loses all in losing you, as he now feels, and it is almost insupportable to him. I have no doubt that you entered largely into many of his future plans— "you and I like Hedge Lawn" and in many ways you were like a right arm to him. And now he feels even as he did not when his son was taken, for you were left to *comfort him* in ways in which his own delicate daughters, however loving, could not. So now he is trying to accustom himself to the thought of looking forward to life without your "comings and stayings" in the household to which you gave a new life and interest. He can not feel to trust himself to meet you, until he is stronger, until time has done the blessed work of healing the wound… for as you are concerned, it is an awful blow to such an old man. He cannot feel as I do, that I rejoice in the love that has given life new meaning and purpose to you; and then I know Henry and already love him dearly— it is all lost to Mr. Jermain, from *his* standpoint and think how lonely the outlook.

I am to have you near me, I trust. I think of your happiness with Henry, as well built upon his, with you. We know it must be mutual. I hope Henry will really love me sometime, but to very few women is given the love your father bore my mother, but then they had most intimate relations, many years, and she was one in a lifetime to know. But all this is an aside—

To return to Marie and her father, she must cheer and support him through this great trial, and in time, I have no doubt, he will be truly *glad* to see you. Now, as to your course: first let me speak of Marie, her letter shows tender love for you and you know she loves you dearly. You will accept it as always. Write her as you have done, express yourself naturally, speak frankly of your love for the dear father, whom you are grieved to pain, ask her to tell you when you may write to him, tell her, as you may truly, that it is the only real sorrow of the present time, but you need not say that you feel that you are doing wrong in causing this trial, as you could not. I wish some of the family would meet Henry— he would win them, if they could see him… I hope for the sake of the family they will answer H's letters… I cannot see, deari [*sic.*], how you can help telling Henry how Mr. J— feels and how he shelters himself and is protected by his friends in every way, that he may not suffer from a necessary parting…

Only a word, and then my precious reading, and to God in prayer for all my loved ones, and to my pillow— dear Mrs. Hobson, her endearing terms, her confidence and frankness, are indeed rare. One would think she had known you years. I think you must call her Mamma Hobson— it will give her such happiness, and *I will be so glad to have you*, it is not my name, and if you commence at once, will be easy & natural— her dear Mother's heart has had such sore trials. Good night. —December 2nd. My dear darling I wish I could talk of everything to you… Now I must write to the J's [Jermains]— they are trying to make "things" comfortable by keeping things in the distance. Well I mean to preserve a visible link in some way, and through this, will hope that in time you may again be a delight to the father's heart just as it should be… As to Richmond, Henry will attend to these, as he should, and I trust all carrying out of any suggestions made by you, as to dress or forms of attire, will meet with his approval. How I would like to be an invisible bird in the air, with eye and ear to follow you, in your southern trip, but you will tell me all about it.

Now as to Ada— She has written me and of her "expectations"… and of her delight that you are coming to her. I hardly know just how to manage as to Ada's expenses. Think I will write her, that I wish her to have *all* the

Katherine Thayer and her cousin, Ada Addison. Date unknown, from an early tintype.

assistance she wishes to make the occasion comfortable for her, not one of fatigue and that when it is over, she must let me know the outlay it has been to her— then of course I would add to this sum a present of money and send check for all. I would like a bit of cake… Will you have the new piano sent up? …I did enjoy listening to his [Henry Hobson's] account of his life, and of the "fight" into which he was forced, and out of which he came in such good condition. I knew of the latter as to results, but did not know any of the details… I trust you will send me word *in particular* as to how much money I should send you, or have you done so already? For you may count eight days or *more* in the snow season— to here and reply— think I will write John Birge to give you what you ask for in N.Y.— and I will send check in this. Now you do not wish to be extravagant— but you can have some money *on hand*— you do not wish to be short… I take it for granted, that you have fixed upon prices— or will do so, for I cannot be prepared to know if bills are right, perhaps you should look them over *first* and send them to me… I think I will write Marie that I have just put away the last of the flowers we bought and say that you write, or I hear through you of her visit with her father to N.Y…—*Mother*.

December 2, 1887, Hot Springs, Arkansas.
My Darling Sweetheart—   No letter from you today, but several others from Ada, Aunt Ada, Mother & Mr. I—, he is an intimate friend of ours… Your mother has sent me a lovely basket for balls of wool— knitting basket. So dainty & pretty. It was so kind of her to remember me. Oh, how grateful I am that you have such a lovely Christian Mother. She will be so helpful to me— & she is so young. I wrote her I feared she would make the bride look quite middle aged. I wrote Mrs. Wise, a hurried letter and I send you your mother's letter… Two weeks from today I will be with you my love, if all is well, Ada writes a box has arrived from Philadelphia & awaiting me in my room. Mother writes so sweetly of you, she thinks you are worthy of my heart's best love— and she thinks you are very fine looking. Only thirteen days before I will meet you love. Mother sent me a birthday present of a check for $100 and I am going to spend it for what I may wish most— something I can always keep. I am so thankful you are feeling and looking well. Oh, Darling don't let any ill befall you. It would kill me. My heart stands still. You are my own Henry, to be my husband, loved more than you know now. God keep & bless my darling love. My sweetheart. Fondest love & kisses.   —Your devoted & loving *Kittie*

December 3, 1887, Saturday, Hot Springs, Arkansas.
My own Darling Henry—   I woke this birthday morning to find your dear letter containing your loving tender birthday wishes and of course you know, they are more, far more precious to me than anything else on this day. You wrote hurriedly, but your letter was so entirely satisfying to my heart— and I feel so perfectly satisfied & happy. As I was dressing the box came & I did not wait a moment to open it— but was I now looking at this exquisite mirror. It will be so useful & is exactly what I needed. The size perfect & *such a beauty*. The combination of copper with the brass. I arranged my hair before it and it will be a welcome addition to my toilet-table… "Two weeks from today—" Oh, my love. How much those four simple words convey to us. Darling I will be such a thankful grateful happy wife. And you are more to me than words

can ever tell you… Less than two weeks and I will be your darling wife— it seems too good to be true— It seems a year since you kissed my Good-bye… You are so sweet to write every day.   —Your own darling *Kittie*.

WESTERN UNION TELEGRAPH COMPANY
Dec 3, 1887, Denver Col.
To: Mrs. Katherine Jermain, Hot Springs Ark.
Congratulations & love many happy returns for you and me. —H.W.H.

Dec. 4, 1887, Denver.
Darling Katherine—   Just a few lines to send my love… I hope you will be contented about the Windsor. I think we can arrange to use much of our furniture and things and thus be surrounded by familiar effects. Everything shall be done to suit you and you shall have the upright or grand piano as you think best… I will leave possibly next Wednesday. Katherine darling, where did you get the term "Lamb" for me— only think of such a word as applied to a great grown man who rather makes a point of his dignity. Don't think I mean to complain dear, for I do not. I only mention it to let you have a little glimpse of one of my peculiarities. I have always had a peculiar prejudice against two things— "petting" in public, i.e. before other people and the use of diminutive and childish terms of endearment. So Sweetheart, you shall pet me all you wish when we are alone together and you shall call me all the dear names you wish so they are not diminutive and childish… After thinking the matter over, I fear we cannot go to a Hotel in Richmond. It would be misunderstood. The people there are fearfully provincial in some things. I have almost concluded that we will divide our time between my Uncle Mr. Wise and Tom Page, spending one night with the Stewarts and one with Joe Bryan. About my Uncle, you about express my feelings when you say "it is a good time to begin anew." He and I have always been devoted to each other and very congenial. The feeling I have had all arose on account of his wife. That was years ago however and she and I have been excellent friends for a long time. I will write a nice letter to my Mother about accompanying us to Boston and will advise her of our wishes in a way that will not wound her feelings. I wish I could be with you on Saturday at your birthday "lark"— Oh sweetheart! How glad I will be to enfold you once more in my arms. You did not send the letter you mentioned. I must close. Goodbye my darling one. Yours devotedly, *Henry*.

༶ A letter from Annie Jennings Wise Hobson:

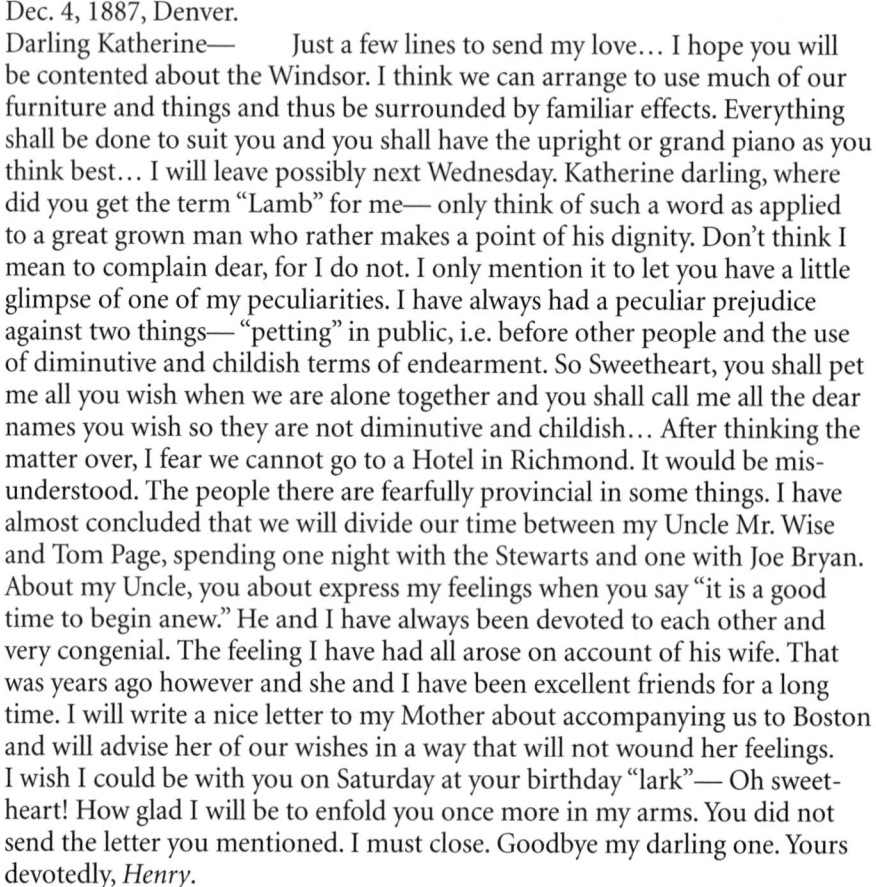

Ashland, Sunday afternoon, December 4th, 1887.
Seated quietly in my own room I hope, Dearest [illegible] to have an uninterrupted hour to commune with you. It is hard to realise that only one more Sunday will pass before I meet my dear Boy's chosen wife— the daughter given in answer to my prayers. Your two letters respecting the all *important matter of dress* were received just before I started to Richmond on Friday. I read each one over twice… You are right about *wine*— Henry comes of a race on both sides of the family, to whom stimulant in any form means temptation. This is all I would say now. We will talk this over— You may be sure that I did not forget that the 3rd, yesterday, was your birthday— and it was my

December 3, 1887, was Kittie's 28th birthday.

The Windsor, Denver, Colorado.

dear Father's birthday also; he would be 82 years old if alive… I inclose a letter for you to forward to your lovely Mother, because I am not certain of her initials— you did not tell me. I like all the arrangements for your quiet wedding. I think you will like my dress when you see it & say I was *right* the way I have arranged it. I have a *short skirt* & a train skirt… Mary Lyons is exceedingly gratified at your [illegible] invitation for her to accompany me, but she says it will be impossible for her to do so. She told me to say nothing would give her more pleasure in every way & to give you her most appreciative love & acknowledgment. I will explain all about it to you… Yes dear Kittie you will be much in my life because of the [illegible] blessing you will bring my boy, but if you expect us to be much together you will have to come East. My post of duty is now in Virginia near Cannon and my dear old Mother. I hope some day to see your sweet Colorado home, but when will it be! …Now this is our confidence letter— Henry is never to see or hear of it. He wrote me that he was mortified over Cannon's very poorly inscribed letter to you. Cannon has not the pen of the ready writer for letters as our boy has, & in his [illegible] life he has contracted careless habits. The day he wrote to you he was feeling nervous & sick, & he had to vacate his study as it was to be plastered, & the noisy children were all around him. I shall stay closely by you in Richmond, and you shall certainly spend at least one day & night in my simple little home in Ashland, & know my surroundings, & appreciate my present life's work. Hallie wrote me that she and Barton had such a charming day with your lovely Mother, who was by far "the most elegant woman she had seen in Colorado."

And now Dear dearest I must close. Just take an imaginative kiss & squeeze, & I think I was delighted at being called Mother— no I mean 'Mamma'— The tea bell. Peace & joy be with you, Your loving Mamma— *A.J.W.H.* —I am very much afraid that you will be greatly disappointed in the beauty & attractions of the Mother Henry has described, unless you have a great deal of ideality— *A.J.W.H.*

❧ A letter from Catherine McKie Thayer:

December 5th, 1887.
…It is so hard to get things right, when people are so far apart and accommodations limited— each anxious to suit and satisfy the other. But do be satisfied with the best we can do— you can better yourself as soon as you please. I know you will be darling…

Dear Darling— The sheet I have written should be burned but I did not see this and kept on and you will be muddled I fear, but you must burn these last letters, They have so much personal in them. I think Henry must feel wounded that Mr. J— does not write and I am going to speak to him of Mr. J's tender love for you, his shrinking nature and the way in which he is sheltered by all his family. I can't bear to have H— feel hurt through you. His letter was most respectful, honorable, manly and sweet. And *decency* required an answer but I fear H— will not get it. There may have been a "conclave" but Marie or someone should write and say that writing would agitate Papa— silence is so discourteous to H. —so disgraceful to them. I feel ashamed, mortified, but dearie, I can not unsettle you in your love. I'll not say much to H— but I think I may say a word. I begin to feel like asking if the J's feel that they are above complying with the commonest form of propriety, answering a civil letter. I hope you will not think I do wrong but I must show H— that the family is one of peculiarly timid character, *shhh shhh*— all in a whisper… I dare say H— was asked to dine tonight & think of my saying that "I would like to see him fifteen or twenty minutes any time before 7 this eve." I dared not put it later as bus leaves here at 8 and if he were a few minutes late I would be cut short… I have four subjects and they are written out on paper before me. H— said he feared he could not possibly get away tonight, he has to stop in Omaha and Chicago, I think, see about his clothes in NY, and reach you the 15th… —Love & kisses, God keep you always my darling, *Mother*.

Denver, Col. Dec. 7, 1887.
My darling Katherine—   I have only a moment to write for I am packing to get off tonight. Am not certain I can do so. I could not write yesterday for I had no time. Your mother was up yesterday. I was so puzzled to know what to do for you, that I wired her to come up and she kindly did so. It was very sweet of her. She said I had done the best thing and so it is now settled that rooms at the Windsor will be ready for us… After our marriage however sweetheart, you will not have any more men calling you "Kittie," will you, unless I ask for it to be done. There is not the least jealousy in what I say, for I am above that, but I do not like too much familiarity on the part of men with women… I am so glad you liked the mirror! I was really perplexed to know what to get for you. Goodbye, I am so busy I can't write more now—
—Yours devotedly, *Henry*.

Dec. 8, 1887. U.P.R.R. Neb.
My own darling—   Here I am on the train speeding towards the East and towards my wife to be. It seems so funny to me that in less than ten days I will have been metamorphosed from a fellow leading the careless, free, irresponsible life of a bachelor, with all its lack of comfort, real pleasure, and zest, into a sober, responsible married man with a charming wife to care for and to look after me… I am sure you will understand my feelings of last evening when I had packed my trunks, stripped my rooms and stood amongst the relics of many years of bachelor life. Then I had to say goodbye to my friend and room-mate Hill, to my land-lady and my rooms. I did not feel sad exactly, but just a trifle regretful, such as you must and will feel over leaving your home, your family, your familiar old surroundings. However I said farewell with a laugh and a jest, delivered up my latch key, and so ended my bachelor life. No note, just then, for I went to the club and then I met quite a party of friends, by accident entirely, and I called upon them to drink a last bachelor bumper with me. Dr. Fisk went to the depot with me and said goodbye to his bachelor friend. And so Dearest, I have turned my back upon my old self, my old life. I will see in New York a few old friends, will spend a day or two with them and then I will bid a last farewell to the bachelor Henry Hobson— then will I say, "*le roi est mort, vive le roi.*"

   Then will I enter upon a new field, hand in hand with the woman I love and to her will fall much of the responsibility of my future life… In dealing with your future husband don't make any to-do over little things, the non-essentials, and don't be over-sensitive. Don't be too exacting in wishing him to conform to your standard and ideas but try to meet him on a middle ground where your and his standards, ideas, and characters can become harmoniously blended. Shall I tell you why I give this advice: First, because your happiness is the first thing in all the world to me— Secondly, because if you pursue a course contrary to what I advise, the most devoted love cannot prevent constant friction and irritation. Do you know dear, and I speak to you as though you were my wife already, I do not believe any Mother and son are more genuinely devoted to each other than my Mother and I and yet she has never been able to adopt and follow the course I suggest to you and so there has been in the past much of needless heart-burning. We are both learning better now where the safe middle ground is but unfortunately instead of starting, years ago, both in the same direction, we went in opposite directions and so our courses have been very circuitous ones... The rest of our youth will be devoted to helping, each the other; our middle age will we pass in trying to do good, and may I not add, in gaining fame, for you know dear I am very ambitious. Our old age will we devote to enjoying whatever of fame may have been rightly won, and one in sympathy, love, and life will we go down the hill of years, in a glow of content and happiness as soft and sweet as the light of a parting May day. Such is my dream sweetheart, as I approach the day when you are to become my wife, my all—

Your mother came up to Denver again yesterday. Why, I do not exactly know, for I only saw her a few moments. She was as sweet as possible. Indeed she is always that. She asked me if I had heard from Mr. Jermain and seemed to think it necessary to explain something about the old man and his condition, by way of excuse for his not writing. I have hardly thought of his not writing. Of course I wish he had acted differently, but then I would be contemptible to have any feelings— even a shadow of resentment, towards an old man because unwillingly he sees a woman go out of his life, whose value to him, I of all men can fully appreciate. I have written to my Mother & Brother to meet me in N.Y. on Wednesday morning. I will have them go to Boston for a day or so before our marriage and go to Fitchburg from Boston. That will better enable me to have them return to New York, when we go to Boston. Let me say now that upon this subject you must use all your tact— let me manage things and I am sure I can do so without a furor. My Mother knows me well enough to know that when I make arrangements I generally mean what I do... Well I am going to close this scrawl, for I am sure your eyes hurt you as much as mine do. We are running through a snow-covered country and in bright sunshine. Consequently the glare is fearful. Goodbye dearest. Take good care of yourself.   —Yours devotedly, *Henry*.

A letter from Annie Jennings Wise Hobson:

Richmond, Dec 9th 1887.
"Katherine's Mamma" sweetest & dearest, your p.c. was received this morning... My first thought this morning was— Only one more week before Kittie & I meet! All my arrangements will be completed tomorrow & I return to Ashland. Wednesday I shall go to Washington, Thursday to New York— Friday evening to Fitchburg. You have never told me your plans in this way. Do you propose leaving Saturday & for where? I must have a peep at Boston. Cannon writes he is so much better. I know you will love my preacher boy. Kittie I shall feel so sorry for him at your bright marriage. It will be such a

contrast to his own folly & weakness of the past… I have rejoiced over the lovely weather— May it continue with bright sunshine for the *bonny bride.* Mary Lyons grieves that she cannot go. Mother was really happy over your letter to her, & Mary Lyons so appreciated hers. You will love your Aunt Mary Lyons— (Plumer's only sister)… I scribble this against time— hope you can read it. I am quite as much in love with Henry as you are, only my love is not as blind! God watch between us & bring us safely face to face.   —Your loving Mamma, *A.J.W.H.*

∽ A letter from Catherine McKie Thayer:

December 10, 1887.
My Darling Child—   By the time you read this your beloved one will be very near you, if not with you, and when you do come together I feel you will be very happy, and think this long absence ended—   —*Mother.*

Dec. 12, 1887, Hoffman House, Broadway, Madison Square, New York.
My darling Girl—   I arrived in N.Y. this morning and before I was dressed I sent you a telegram. About 10 o'clk I went over to my Club and found your several letters which I of course enjoyed. I have not only a few moments to write for I must go to Tiffany's, my tailor, several other places and then get downtown to meet a business appointment… I have also considered what you say about our paying a round of visits in Richmond and think you are right about that and as much as I dislike to run the risk of offending my relatives and friends, you of course are the one I wish to please. I shall therefore decline all invitations to stay at any private houses and shall wire my friend Branch in a few moments asking him whether he can secure us a suite of rooms at the Hotel. This will give us more freedom in every way… I will reach Fitchburg Thursday night if I possibly can my darling, and if not I will be there Friday morning. I have made arrangements to have my Mother & Brother go to Boston before Saturday.   —Yours devotedly, *Henry.*

Dec. 14, 1887, Hoffman House, Broadway, Madison Square, New York.
My darling Girl—   All day long I have tried to write to you. You can't understand the whirl I am in. My Mother & Brother came this morning and after a hurried trip downtown on business and eating lunch, I had to go out with my Mother. I returned at 5 o'clk. and just as I was about to write, cards came up from friends. They have just left & I have time only to say I love you and then rush to dress for a dinner. Bless you my dear love. I love you just as much as though I wrote fifty pages.   —Yours devotedly, *Henry.*

∽ A letter from Catherine McKie Thayer:

December 13, 1887.
… Of one more thing I wish to speak in regard to the new life just about to open upon you— of your devotions in your own room. I want you to begin in the right way, seeking the strength and guidance you will most surely need, reading and prayer at night, and prayer, before you leave your room in the morning… and I trust that you will not misunderstand me. I know that in all the haste that comes with change of place, sometimes, and the rather

unsettled conditions, and new relations, one may feel that *when* they get settled, they will return to old ways, or rearrange to suit the new conditions and the tendency is to drop away from old habits, even, and defer for a more convenient season the performance of a well admitted duty or privilege. So dear one, I know you will wish to commence the new life, asking every blessing on you and yours and trusting the Father's love and care. My thoughts are with you always, and I hope someone will not think the task too great to tell me every detail of which I cannot be witness. I think Ada will, and I sincerely hope she will not be fatigued in any way. May the dear Heavenly Father give to you and Henry all that is for your highest good. He knows what this is— we do not. And with this goes a Mother's prayers and the faith that "all things will work together for our good" for may I not hope that we are all His children? —With abounding Mother Love, *C. McKie Thayer.*

❦ A letter from Arkansas:

Hot Springs, Ark. December 17, 1887.
Dear Kitty—   By this time you have changed your name again.
Was much interested in the description of the preparations for the wedding heretofore. I earnestly pray that your new life may be all sunshine, what more could I say!
    I see much of the Darts— Hope Miss D. won't get too fond of me for her own peace of mind. Am civil spoken to the other people and will try and rub them the right way… I am looking and feeling first rate and taking very good care of myself. Begin my second course tomorrow. You can think of me around the Merry Christmas Tree at the Hot Springs— for the Doctor is going to keep me here thro' the holidays —Goodbye & Good luck to you and Henry.—   *F.M.T.* [Francis McKie Thayer]

❦ Three letters from Catherine McKie Thayer:

December 17, 1887.
My dear Son & Daughter—   Only time to say God bless you my children for this mail. With a heart full of love. Am well. Your loving Mother.
—*C. McKie Thayer.*

December 19, 1887.
… As to the people of Hedge Lawn, I am ashamed of them all— humiliated because they are old friends— Discourtesy, like wrong doing, really can harm no one but those who show it. We know it never can give happiness or pleasure, but let us remember, that any man on earth who would or could take you *out* of that family, by a stronger claim than the one that held you there, must for a time be looked upon as having taken their own… Thank Mrs. Hobson for her several letters. Will write but I have so many to see. My time is very much occupied. Tender love to you & Henry… —*Mother.*

December 22, 1887.
This a.m. mail brings me yours of the day before your marriage, two letters and inclosures… I trust you are feeling quite well after your headache at Fitchburg… It strikes me, that you and Henry are on a tour of inspection, first he,

then you. Well, when it is over, come to me, and I will take you just as you are, only you must be all to each other to satisfy me… As to dear Mr. Jermain, I really feel very sorry for him. He tries to preserve his dignified silence because you have crept out from under his parental wing and found a mate. Poor lonely heart, this change is a real death to so many hopes, expectations and joys. To him, he would rather feel your arms about his neck this moment than any one thing that can come to him. He looks upon marriage as the evil of this world because it has taken (did it not give?) so much out of his future and hopes for re-union where marriage cannot come. Poor old man, how I pity him. So I said, "answer from your heart, not your head" and sometime, not in the distant future, I think he may find joy in you still… The readjustment will come. I return some letters, as you may wish them… —*Mother.*

∼

Henry Wise Hobson and Katherine Thayer Jermain were married in Fitchburg, Massachusetts, on December 17, 1887. Henry's brother, Reverend John Cannon Hobson, and Reverend Charles M. Addison, who was married to Kittie's cousin Ada, jointly performed the ceremony.

Chapter XVII

1887, Part Two

Henry Wise Hobson and the Mormon Church

THE Republican Party platform of 1856 described slavery and polygamy as the "twin relics of barbarism." Henry Wise Hobson was born two years later at Eastwood, a farm in Goochland County, Virginia, where his family owned slaves. John S. Wise, Henry Hobson's uncle, visited Eastwood in 1860 and recounted in *The End of an Era* an episode when a sermon by a Dr. Palmer, entitled the "Divine Origin of Slavery," was read aloud and after which one of the guests suggested sending a copy to Abraham Lincoln. John Wise responded and proposed that a copy should also be sent to Brigham Young, for, as he quipped, "For every argument of Dr. Palmer, based on slavery of the Old Testament, is equally available for Brigham Young in support of polygamy; and I sympathize with Brigham." Soon after this, the young Henry Wise Hobson would be a witness to the Civil War and the end of slavery, and then, years later, as Special United States Attorney, he would be the principal attorney in the effort that ended polygamy.

Within the Mormon community polygamy was sometimes referred to as patriarchal marriage or plural marriage, but throughout the rest of the nation, it was referred to as the "Utah situation." The first legislation to outlaw polygamy was introduced in Congress in 1854, but it would be another eight years before any law was passed. A very important section of the 1862 act prohibited religious and charitable organizations in any Territory from acquiring real property worth more than $50,000, but this law proved difficult to enforce in Utah since Mormons always controlled the juries. Another piece of legislation, the Edmunds Act, was enacted in 1882, and then the Edmunds-Tucker Act was passed into law in 1887. Throughout this time there were numerous successful prosecutions of individuals for polygamy, but its practice was not condemned by the Mormon Church. The 1887 legislation specifically directed the Attorney General to initiate proceedings to forfeit and escheat to the United States all property held by the Mormon Church in violation of the law of 1862—all property in excess of $50,000 in value. In 1887 Henry Wise Hobson was the U. S. Attorney for the District of Colorado, but he was to be called upon to argue the case against the Church of Jesus Christ of Latter-day Saints, the Mormons, in Salt Lake City. At the same time, he became engaged to Katherine Thayer Jermain, a young widow, who was living in Colorado Springs, and they were planning a December wedding. Throughout this period he kept an extensive file of newspaper clippings, correspondence, telegrams, and some of his legal notes about the Mormon case.

Letters, notes, telegrams, and newspaper reports by:
A. H. Garland, Attorney General of the United States
Henry Wise Hobson
G. A. Jenks, Solicitor General of the United States
George S. Peters, U. S. Attorney in Utah
Justice Zane of the Supreme Court of the Territory of Utah
Others involved in the case were: Colonel J. O. Broadhead, attorney for the Mormon Church and President of the American Bar Association, and J. E. McDonald, a former Senator from Indiana and another attorney for the Mormon Church

Letters written from: Denver, Colorado; Salt Lake City, Utah Territory; Washington, D. C; and aboard trains.

∼

1887

GOVERNMENT WANTS CHURCH PROPERTY — TWO SUITS PLANTED—
In Which the Modest little Sum of $4,000,000 is all that is asked for.—
One Million from the P. E. [Perpetual Emigrating] Fund, and $3,000,000, Excess in Church Property.
Our readers will remember the recent visit of Solicitor-General Jenks and the peculiar air of mystery that shrouded his movements at that time… When pressed for information in regard to the purpose of his visit he said: "Oh, it will all be made public in about two weeks time." This was on the 10th, and yesterday, just twenty days afterwards, the object of his mission was disclosed in the planting of suit in the Supreme Court against the Mormon Church to recover, under the Edmunds-Tucker law, all property in excess of the $50,000 held by the church or by its Trustee-in-Trust.
—*The Salt Lake Herald*, July 31, 1887.

Henry Hobson was appointed Special United States Attorney immediately after he had become engaged to be married. The letter from the Attorney General specifies cases in Washington, Montana, Wyoming, and Utah in which Henry Hobson was to be involved. Many years later his daughter would describe her father's position as being "Special U. S. Attorney for all the States and Territories West of the Mississippi."

Department of Justice October 5, 1887 File No. 4320.
Henry W. Hobson, Esq., Denver, Col.
Sir: *You are hereby appointed a Special United States Attorney for the following purposes*:   To assist the United States Attorney for the Territory of Washington in the conduct of the case of the *United States vs. The Northern Pacific Railroad Company, et al*, now pending in the District Court of the 3rd Judicial District of said Territory.

Also, to assist the United States Attorney for the Territory of Montana in the conduct of the several cases brought by the United States against The Northern Pacific Railroad Company, the Montana Improvement Company, or either of them, their officers, agents, and employees and also against their co-defendants, and which cases are now pending in the different Courts of the different Judicial Districts of said Territory of Montana.

Also, to assist the United States Attorney for the Territory of Idaho in the conduct of the several cases of the United States against the Northern Pacific Railroad Company, the Montana Improvement Company, their officers, agents and employees and their co-defendants, now pending in the several

District Courts of the respective Judicial Districts of said Territory.

Also, to assist the United States Attorney for the Territory of Wyoming in the conduct of the case or cases brought by the United States against Isaac Coe and Levi Carter, and which cases are now pending in the several Courts of the respective Judicial Districts of said Territory.

Also, to assist the United States Attorney for the Territory of Utah in the conduct of the cases of the United States against The Perpetual Emigrating Fund Company, and the *United States vs. The Church of Jesus Christ of Latter Day Saints, et al*, now pending in the Courts of said Territory.

You are hereby directed and authorized to enter your appearance in the above named cases without delay, to make such investigation of the same as may be necessary, to confer about them with the respective United States Attorneys above referred to, and in conjunction with them to take such steps and proceedings in said cases as may be deemed advisable and for the public service, subject to the direction and control of this Department.

Your compensation as Special Attorney herein, is fixed at the sum of Five thousand dollars ($5,000) a year or at that rate, to commence from the date of your qualification as such Special Attorney, and in addition thereto you will be allowed your actual and necessary traveling expenses whilst away from your domicile and whilst engaged in the conduct of business connected with said cases and the discharge of your duties hereunder, said expenses to be stated and reported in the usual manner required by law and the Rules and Regulations of this Department.

Under this appointment you will also be expected, without additional compensation, to appear and act as Special United States Attorney in any Judicial District outside of that of Colorado in such cases of the United States as may be from time to time designated by the Attorney General and concerning which you will receive special instructions. The said appointment is to be taken subject to any change that the Department may make. —*A. H. Garland*, Attorney General.

MR. HOBSON'S NEW OFFICE
He Is Appointed Special Government Attorney for the Entire West

H. W. Hobson, Esq., United States District Attorney for Colorado, returned yesterday from a three weeks visit to the National Capital. While there Mr. Hobson passed much of his time with Attorney-General Garland. It has been learned that Mr. Hobson was highly complimented upon the enviable record which he has made in Colorado. In recognition of the esteem with which he is regarded by the Administration, Mr. Hobson has received the appointment as Special United States District Attorney for all of the Western Districts extending to the Pacific Coast. Mr. Hobson will hold this office in addition to the one he already occupies, and his duties thereunder will consist in his appearing and assisting in conjunction with the regular District Attorneys of other districts of such important Government cases as the Attorney-General may designate. This gives, in a measure, jurisdiction to Mr. Hobson as District Attorney throughout the entire West. He has already been assigned to duty in important land cases in Utah. He will leave for Salt Lake City on Friday for the purpose of appearing with the District Attorney of Utah in the important cases recently instigated by Solicitor-General Jenks, to confiscate the entire property of the Mormon Church, valued at nearly $5,000,000. Notwithstanding that Mr. Hobson's duties outside of his district will require much of his time, he will continue to devote special attention to Colorado Affairs. This will necessitate the employment of an additional assistant, who will be commissioned upon Mr. Hobson's return from Salt Lake.

This new appointment, in conjunction with his position of United States District Attorney for Colorado, insures Mr. Hobson a salary which is most gratifying.

—*Unidentified newspaper clipping, 1887.*

The Republican congratulates Henry W. Hobson, Esq., upon his appointment as Special United States Attorney for the Western Districts of the United States. This is in addition to his office as District Attorney for Colorado. The appointment is a recognition of his services to the Government in this State. Though Mr. Hobson is a Democrat, yet *The Republican* can frankly say that he is an excellent official, and it is glad to see his good qualities appreciated. —*Denver Republican,* undated.

Letters to Kittie:

Marshall & Royle, Attorneys-At-Law, Salt Lake City, Utah, October 16, 1887.
My own darling Love—   Whilst waiting for a gentleman I must send you my love. I think I treat you right shabbily about writing to you, but indeed my dearest I am so crowded that my writing at all is a great big piece of evidence that my thoughts are always with you. I have to confess that I am working today, Sunday, but it is a kind of pulling of the ox out of the mud. Tomorrow I have to go into the trial of an immense case and one concerning which I knew nothing until this morning... Goodbye dear, for Mr. Marshall has come in and I must go to work... Don't be impatient about another letter for I will be heels over head in work for several days.   Ever yours devotedly, —*Henry W. Hobson.*

Oct. 18, 1887, Salt Lake City, Utah.
The Cullen. S. C. Ewing, Proprietor — Daily Rates $3 per day.
My Dearest Love—   How much I wish to see you and how I long to get your letters for I know there are a number in Denver. Ah sweetheart, how nice it will be for us to be together for all life. One week of our time of waiting has passed and by the time you get this, a second one will be gone. Do you know Kittie I have not yet gotten over my daze about this thing. I have always had a lot of conceit about most things, but I never had any personal vanity about women, and I have never been accustomed to thinking they were in love with me. When I read your letters darling, and I do read and re-read them, and see

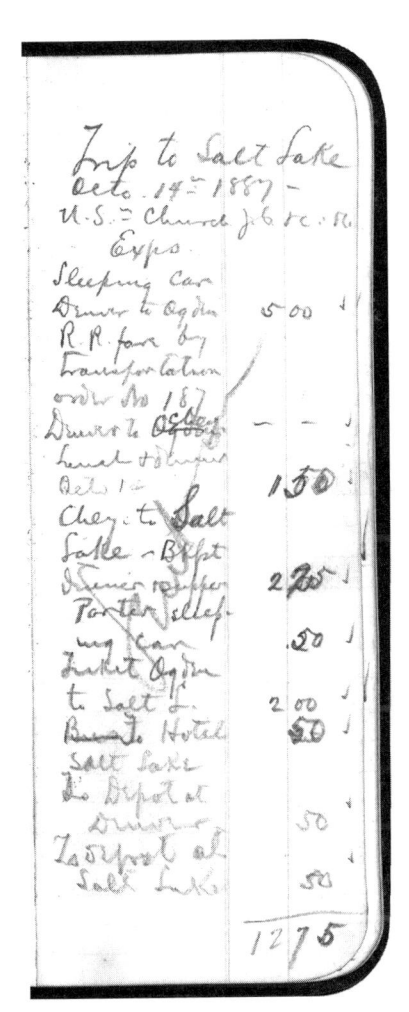

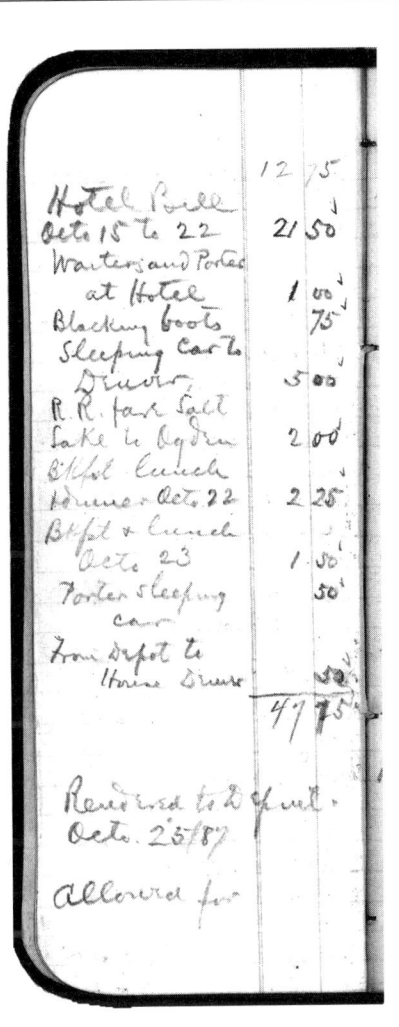

Detail from Henry Hobson's expense account book for his trip to Salt Lake City, October 15–22, 1887. Expenses included: Ticket from Ogden to Salt Lake, $2.00; seven days in the hotel, $21.50; and waiters and porters at the hotel, $1.00. Total expenses for a week: $47.75.

what you say about loving me, how that your love for me is more to you than anything else and much more of the same sort of loving sweet confidences, I cannot understand it, and I ask whether this is all for me. Dearest girl how I appreciate your love and confidence and believe me I will always try to deserve the same… Goodbye my love— my sweetheart— You are very very dear to me, Devotedly Yours, —*H.W.H.*

Oct. 18, 1887, Salt Lake City, Utah.
The Cullen. S. C. Ewing, Proprietor — Daily Rates $3 per day.
My sweetest Darling— Only a word, but that I must send you… I am right in the middle of my case and am having a stiff fight against distinguished and able lawyers from the East. I cannot say when I will get away. Possibly I may be here all the week. Sweetheart, darling, my own dearest Kittie what would I not give for one look at you and one long sweet kiss. God bless you dear and pardon this hasty note. —Yours devotedly forever, *H.W.H.*

MORMON CHURCH SUITS — A new Tack taken by the Imported Attorneys — Old Answer and Demurrer Drawn. — A new demurrer filed instead of them. — Constitutionality of the Law Denied — Other Supreme Court proceedings.

The Supreme Court of the territory of Utah convened in the Federal courtrooms at 10 O'clock yesterday morning, Chief Justice Zane and Associate Justices Boreman and Henderson being present. The clerk read the proceedings of the last day. On motion of Ben Sheaks, Colonel J. O. Broadhead of Missouri and ex-Senator J. E. McDonald of Indiana were admitted to the bar. District Attorney Peters moved the admission of United States District Attorney Henry W. Hobson of Colorado. The iron-clad oath was administered to all three gentlemen, each one swallowing it without a quiver: more than that, Colonel Broadhead and Senator McDonald seemed to regard the thing somewhat as a joke…

Ex-Senator McDonald, of Indiana, one of the imported attorneys of the Mormon Church, here arose and asked leave to withdraw the former answer and demurrer in the suits of the *United States vs. the Church of Jesus Christ of Latter-Day Saints* and the Perpetual Emigrating fund company; and the further privilege of filing a new demurrer. He also desired the postponement of the case till today at 10 o'clock. There being no objection raised by the District Attorney, the Court granted the requests.

DEMURRER The above named defendants, by protestation not confessing all or any of the matters and things in the plaintiff's bill of complaint contained to be true in such manner and form as the same is therein set forth and alleged, do demur to the said bill of complaint and for cause of demurrer show and allege:

First: That said Supreme Court of the Territory of Utah has no jurisdiction of, or over said defendants, or either of them, or of the subject matter of said action.

Second: That the acts of Congress of July 1st, 1862 and of March 3rd, 1887, referred to in plaintiff's bill of complaint… are unconstitutional and void.

Third: That said complaint does not state fact sufficient to constitute a cause of action.

Fourth: That the plaintiff has not, in and by its said bill of complaint, made or stated such a case as entitles it, in the court of equity, to any discovery from these defendants… or to any relief against them or either of them, as to the matters contained in the said bill of complaint, or any of such matters.

Wherefore, and for divers other good causes of demurrer appearing in said bill of complaint, the defendants do demur thereto, and humbly demand the judgment of this court whether they shall be compelled to make any further or other answer to the said bill of complaint; and pray to be hence dismissed with their costs and charges in this behalf most wrongfully sustained. —James O. Broadhead, J. E. McDonald, Franklin S. Richards, LeGrand Young, Attorneys for the defendants.

…It is a curious fact that notwithstanding the interest that one would naturally think every Mormon would have in these suits, coupled with the fact that, for counsel, there were present two distinguished gentlemen "from the States," there were not more than a dozen spectators in the court-room, and half of them were Gentiles. Inside the bar were nearly forty gentlemen, mostly lawyers.

—*The Daily Tribune*, Oct. 18, 1887.

Gentiles non-Mormons

❧ A letter to Kittie:

The Cullen, Salt Lake City, Utah. October 19, 1887.
My darling, my Darling—   How I long to see you! It seems to me that each day I am away from you it is harder to bear… I enclose an extract from this morning's paper about my speech. Of course you don't want to read the legal arguments but I know you will enjoy seeing the complimentary part, for are not my successes now yours my darling. With every step upward that I

take, you go with me and do you know Kittie that I hope some day to put you in high places. I am ambitious and earnest and it remains to be seen whether I have sufficient ability to rise as I wish. I certainly have not done badly for my years and not many men of my age occupy such positions of responsibility as I do, or have to such an extent the confidence of the entire administration. There is a piece of conceit for you! Did I write you that just before I left Denver I had received a proposition from one of the best firms of Denver… I must now close for I have only a short time and I must write one or two business letters… Ah love— Kittie, how I long to take you in my arms and kiss you.   —Devotedly & forever, *H.W.H.* —I write with a horrid pen. Excuse all blots etc.

THEY GO OVER AGAIN. Suggestion to avoid the taking of Testimony. Priority of Receivership Motion. Solicitor Jenks to be here to take charge of the Government's Case. Threes U. S. Commissioners Appointed.

There are no other references in the newspaper accounts to Solicitor General Jenks being in Salt Lake City to participate in the case.

The Supreme Court opened again at the usual hour yesterday morning. The prospects of the arguments on the church suits drew out a much larger crowd than is generally seen in the court room, and inside the railing there was a big showing of legal ability…

Mr. McDonald, of the defense, said that in all cases the plaintiff is supposed to be prepared to defend their complaint, and that the defendant is always allowed to interpose legal objections. He said that if the points set down in the demurrer should be held by the court to be well taken, there would be no necessity of appointing a receiver.

THE COURTS RULING on this point was that the matter of appointing a receiver should be proceeded with at once.

…TO OBVIATE TAKING TESTIMONY Attorney Richards, of the defense, stated that he would like to have time for a meeting of counsel of the two sides, as he thought that they might come to an agreement whereby, on the admission of the facts in the case, the taking of testimony might be obviated. On this suggestion the court again adjourned until this morning at 10 o'clock.   —*The Daily Tribune*, October 19, 1887.

THAT CHURCH PROPERTY — Arguing the Motion for Appointment of a Receiver. — An Agreed Statement of Facts…

The Church cases were again the attraction of the day yesterday when the Courtroom was filled with those who are interested in the important proceedings. After the opening of the court Mr. Peters stated that counsel for the two sides were about to agree upon a statement of facts and asked for a continuance until 2 p.m. in order that the arrangement might be completed. The Court granted the request and the adjournment was taken.

IN THE AFTERNOON there was the same crowd present and the interest was quite as great. Mr. Hobson, of the Government counsel, began by stating to the Court that counsel for the two sides had agreed upon a statement of facts by which the motion for the appointment of a Receiver might be argued without testimony…

The complaint which has already been published in full by *The Tribune* was read by Mr. Hobson…

…The Order of Argument. Mr. Peters announced that it had been agreed that counsel for Government should open the case; the other side should then reply; Government should have another turn; the defense should then close their argument, and the Government counsel should close the case. Mr. Clarke opened for the Government, beginning with a brief statement of the case. He said that Congress had annulled the act incorporating the church, and there is no one now legally entitled to the care of the property, and it became the duty of the Court to appoint a receiver… He quoted the United States statute which limits the holding of real estate by the church to the value of $50,000 up to the time of the disincorporation. He termed the government of a Territory a "limited democracy," having a Legislature, whose acts, however, can at any time be annulled by Congress, and claimed that Congress has a right to legislate over a Territory on any subject whatever… In conclusion, Mr. Clarke said that they would contend that Congress had the right to repeal the act under which the church was incorporated, and thereby disincorporate the church; that the property of the church is now a trust without a trustee; that it remains only for the Court to appoint a receiver to take care of the property until it is finally decided to whom it rightfully belongs. The court adjourned. — *The Daily Tribune,* October 20, 1887.

ARGUMENTS OF COUNSEL

Col. Broadhead's Masterly Talk Against the Law — Mr. Hobson's Conclusive Rejoinder — The Day Consumed in a Tournament of Words that Afforded a Treat to the Large Assemblage in Court —

The second day of the arguments in the great church cases attracted a crowd of spectators, which included nearly every member of the Bar Association of this city, and outside of these was a large assemblage, including many more intelligent persons than it is usual to see on the spectator's benches. In fact, it is seldom that a mere discussion will hold a crowd together as that of yesterday did; but, on the other hand, it is not often that such legal ability is heard in our courts, and to this fact, as well as to the importance of the case, may be attributed the interest so plainly shown…

COLONEL BROADHEAD'S SPEECH

Colonel Broadhead then arose and began his speech in opposition to the appointment of a receiver.

He began by characterizing the move for a receiver as extraordinary under the existing circumstance. He said that a remedy like this should only be applied in a case where it could be shown that the property was in danger of being wasted or destroyed or where it could be shown that the defendant was insolvent or dishonest… He claimed that no fraud had been shown and that it had not been shown that the defendants were insolvent… Colonel Broadhead then dwelt at some length upon the power of the court in the premises… Colonel Broadhead closed by stating that if the decision of this court should be against the defense they would appeal it to the highest tribunal in the land…

The Impression made by Colonel Broadhead's speech was at first profound, and many opinions verging upon extravagance, were expressed by different parties. The quiet manner and speech, and the seemingly logical deductions of the gentleman did much to produce this impression, and it is a question as to how far it is justified. Legal minds were at first struck by the argument and were unstinted in their praises, but in talking the matter over many of them agree that while the deductions were perfectly logical from the hypotheses used, the fault lay in the assumption of false premises as a basis for the conclusions, and in a failure to properly consider the difference between the Territorial condition and that of Statehood. Of course, but little can be judged on these points from the synopsis given above, as the details of the speech must necessarily be passed over…

MR. HOBSON

Mr. Hobson began by stating that he had not expected to enter into the argument of the case and was, therefore, at a disadvantage, but he showed before the close of his address that he was not to be handicapped much by this fact.

Mr. Hobson said that the object of the suit was to dissolve the church incorporation, giving the surplus property to the school fund, and distributing that which remained among those who were entitled to it. Congress had placed the matter in the hands of this Court and the government now asked that a receiver be appointed to take care of the property and to see that it was not allowed to go to waste or be destroyed. Congress has vested this Court with this exclusive right to administer on the church property, and there is no alternative but to appoint a receiver. Although the complaint in the case might be defective, yet the Court has a right to take the matter in hand and make the appointment requested. In any case where there is an equitable proceeding with a view to the distribution of property, if that property is in danger of being destroyed, the Court has a right to take it in custody. Mr. Hobson said that in this case the property is in danger, and all who know anything of the ways of the Church of Jesus Christ of Latter-day Saints, must recognize the fact. Should the Court allow the personalty to remain in the hands of the church trustees until the case is finally settled, it might be scattered to the four winds, and it would be impossible to collect it again. Pandora might as well attempt to bring back the evil spirits escaped from her box.

Mr. Hobson argued, first, the reserved right in the organic act, whereby Congress may revoke or annul enactments of the Territorial Legislature; that the incorporation of the church, and the resulting accumulations of the church conferred no vested rights, but such incorporation was simply a license, subject to the reserved supervision of Congress. Further, Congress provided in 1862, together with the limitation of church holdings to $50,000, that property so held should not be used to encourage polygamy or immorality, whereas it is notorious that the Mormon Church property has been used strenuously and continually for this forbidden purpose. That church acquisitions have been in contempt of this statute and its use of them in defiance of it. Its real estate has also been acquired since the passage of the law of 1862, for it was not till 1868 that any of these land titles passed from the Government. Therefore, both because the titles had been acquired subsequent to the passage of the limiting law and because the use made of the property is contrary to law, it is the duty of Congress to intervene and enforce the escheat.

Second, even though no express reservation had been made in the Organic Act, it follows from the nature of the fundamental supremacy of Congress in Territorial affairs, and in the exercise of its supreme police powers, (undisputed instances of which were given) that the National Legislature necessarily has the right to intervene to protect the Nation from the gross and treasonable evil attacking it. And in the exercise of this intervention it designates this Court as the tribunal in equity whereby the remedy may be made effectual. And the power of Congress to fix and amend the jurisdiction of its Territorial Courts cannot be questioned.

That this property would be used to help the fight for the supremacy of polygamy, Mr. Hobson said was a well-known fact, and therein it would be used against the Government of the United States.

That portion of Mr. Hobson's speech referring to the polygamy evil was to the point and must have told with the court.

"How long," the speaker asked, "must the finger of scorn be pointed at us from foreign lands because we are powerless to suppress this shame which we all recognize and which we all abhor?" He argued that in refusing to appoint a receiver the Court would perpetuate the power of the church, and would thereby cripple the efforts of Congress to down the monster.

In regard to the legality of the acquisition of the church personalty, Mr. Hobson said that over $250,000 worth of property had been acquired since the passage of the

Henry Wise Hobson. Photo by J. E. Beebe, 1716 Arapahoe Street, Denver.

law of 1862, which placed the limit at $50,000. He knew that at least $250,000 worth had been accumulated since that time, and he wanted a receiver to find out how much more. In a charitable trust the property does not go back to the donors in the case of the dissolution of that trust, as they have no further interest in their gifts after they are once made.

Mr. Hobson called attention to the fact that certain stocks and bonds had not been included in the conveyances, and asked what had become of these stocks and bonds? Mr. Hobson closed his address with another eloquent appeal for the appointment of a receiver.

THE SPEECH was a striking contrast to that of Colonel Broadhead (attorney for the church), a contrast as striking as that between the two men themselves. Hobson's was full of the fire, spirit and eloquence of youth, and his logic was sound and conclusive. Many high compliments were paid the gentleman on his great effort, and none will say that they were not deserved.

The Court adjourned until 10 a. m. today.

—*The Daily Tribune*, October 21, 1887.

 Legal notes:

Included in the files with the newspaper clippings, letters, and telegrams are ten pages of what appear to be Henry Hobson's notes used in the oral arguments. The notes, all in his handwriting, are excerpted here.

…With regard to vested rights — A vested right is one which vests upon substantial equities and it must have its reasonable limits and restrictions, it must have regard to the general welfare and public policy. A party cannot have a vested right to do wrong, to violate the law. A vested right cannot be a mere expectation. Rights are not vested in a charter, but in the power to be exercised thereunder etc…

…As to reservation of power of Congress to disapprove Territorial rights…

…Difference between repeal and disapproval…

…True if rights become vested under a power given by Congress prior to revocation of that power vested rights cannot be impaired, but as soon as that power is revoked or restricted, no rights thereunder can be acquired…

…Examine Act of Incorporation together with Organic Act… In the first place the right to hold property is not an unlimited right… The legislature in many respects legislated on questions which were beyond their control and was in excess of its powers…

…The Act of 1862. (a) The circumstances under which it was passed & the object to be attained, (b) The title of the Act., (c) The law was intended to revoke the Act of Incorporation., (d) An act can be repealed or changed either expressly or by implication… (e) Corporations in taking corporate franchises are subject to any future legislation… (f) The Act of 1862— if it meant anything, means that after that date restriction was placed on the Church of J. C. of L.D.S. as to its acquisition of property. And that said property could not be used either directly or indirectly for purposes of encouraging polygamy…

…The Act of 1887. (a) It dissolved the Corporation & vested its estate entirely in the Court for administration. (b) The Trustee was officially defunct and had no further powers. (c) The Act was constitutional…

…Congress could pass Acts of 1862 and 1887 by virtue of its police powers… Discuss general nature of Police Powers… Discuss the Church & the bearings of this doctrine thereupon…

…Take up statement of facts and discuss some…

…All of the Real Estate has been acquired since 1862. The Church authorities prior to that time were only squatters. The public lands in Utah prior to 1862 were not open to entry. No right whatsoever could have become vested… After the passage of the Act of 1887 control and authority over the Real Estate was absolutely taken away from the Church and Trustee and it was absolutely under the control of this Court to dispose of according to said Act and the principles of Equity…

…The action of the Church was that of a dead defunct body. It pretended to still have existence. As well might the stockholders of a defunct business corporation attempt to act… The action of the Trustee was manifestly to defeat the operation of this law and to deprive this Court of its jurisdiction. The whole transaction bears the impress of fraud… This court sitting as a Court of Equity must take steps to recover it…

CLOSE OF THE ARGUMENT
Senator McDonald Considered to Have Done Poorly—

The great speeches of Thursday were a big advertisement for the Supreme Court as a place to pass away a few hours to advantage and the crowd of spectators was, therefore, again a very large one yesterday morning when the tribunal assembled to proceed with the church cases.

The arguments were resumed immediately upon the opening of the court, the first speaker being Ex-Senator McDonald of the defense. To the surprise of many, the Senator did not attempt to refute the masterly argument of Mr. Hobson; but, with a little slur at that gentleman's speech he passed to the points that had already been presented by Colonel Broadhead and proceeded to argue upon those grounds…

…After consulting briefly, the Court announced that the opinion would be delivered two weeks from tonight, Nov. 5th, at 7:30 o'clock.
—*The Daily Tribune*, October 22, 1887.

◈ A letter to Kittie:

Oct. 26th, 1887. Denver.
My darling Love—   …I have about decided not to go into that firm I wrote you of. There are many considerations which lead to this course and which I cannot explain in a letter… Yours devotedly,   —*Henry*.

THE RECEIVER GRANTED

Exhaustive Opinion by Chief Justice Zane, for the Court. Boreman and Henderson Concur.

The Whole Question Examined in Every Light and the Law Fully Expounded—a Very Able Document.

At 7:30 o'clock last evening the Territorial Supreme Court met in the Federal Court Room, for the purpose of rendering a decision in relation to the motion to appoint a receiver in the case of the Government vs. the Mormon Church Corporation.

Special U. S. Attorney Henry W. Hobson was in Tacoma, Washington Territory, arguing another case on behalf of the United States Government.

All of the Judges were present, as were District Attorney Peters and Assistant District Attorney Clarke, on behalf of the Government, and J. O. Broadhead and F. C. Richards on behalf of the Church.

OPINION OF THE COURT

On the opening of the Court the clerk read the minutes of the previous session and then Chief Justice Zane delivered the following decision: *In the Supreme Court of the Territory of Utah, June term 1887, United States of America, plaintiff vs. The Church of Jesus Christ of Latter-day Saints, et al., defendants:*

Zane, C.J.— The complainant filed in this court its bill in chancery under an act of Congress in force March 3d, 1887. The bill prayed that a decree be made by this court forfeiting the charter and dissolving the corporation known as the Church of Jesus Christ of Latter-day Saints, as well as for the appointment of a receiver for the assets of the corporation, until disposition could be made thereof according to law, and for other relief. The motion for the appointment of a receiver is now submitted for our decision, on the bill and the facts as stated in a stipulation entered into by the parties and filed in the case.

On the 8th day of February, 1851, the Assembly of the so-called State of Deseret, afterwards organized as the Territory of Utah, passed an ordinance incorporating the Church of Jesus Christ of Latter-day Saints. After the organization of the Territory of Utah, this ordinance was re-enacted January 19th, 1855, by the Legislature and approved by the Governor of the Territory…

SCOPE OF THE INCORPORATION.

The purposes of the corporation as indicated by the powers conferred upon it by this charter are numerous and varied. Some of them, it is true, are expressed in vague terms; but the capacity is granted to act in various ways and to make laws and regulations with respect to very many subjects. The corporation is confined to no particular purpose. No precedent can be found for conferring upon a private corporation such a variety of capacities; some of them, it is believed, are above the reach of human laws…

The charter of a corporation should always specify the purposes for which the corporation is organized, and powers adapted to that purpose should be granted. If the corporation is to be a public one, powers adapted to the regulation of conduct and to public purposes should be given, with such incidental capacity to do business as may be essential to such an organization, and no more…

EXTRAORDINARY POWERS CONFERRED

The charter of the Church of Jesus Christ of Latter-day Saints is most extraordinary in the extent of the authority it assumes to confer upon, and in the number, the variety and the scope of the powers it places in the hands of a religious body. It declares in effect, that all the Mormon people, who at the time of its enactment were, or who might afterward become residents of the Territory, are a body corporate with perpetual succession…

THE RIGHTS GAINED

In this charter, the respondent insists the church gained a vested right upon its acceptance, and that Congress has no power to disapprove, or to annul it. We know of no precedent for holding that a corporation could obtain a vested right in a charter like this… The case of *Dartmouth College vs. Woodward* has been regarded as settling the question that the charter of a private corporation constitutes a contract between a State and a corporation… But we find no case holding that a charter granted by the Legislature of a Territory gives such a vested right…

…Such are some of the powers conferred upon this church corporation by this remarkable act. To such a charter it is claimed the church has acquired a vested right. If this proposition is sound the corporate body known as the Church of Jesus Christ of Latter Day Saints may endure under this charter to distant ages. But we are of the opinion that a vested right could not be acquired in such a charter.

THE POWER OF CONGRESS

Further, Congress possesses the power to enact laws for the government of the Territories. It may make provision for territorial governments and extend the authority of Territorial Legislatures to all rightful subjects of legislation…

In the case under decision the Territory was organized under the Organic Act approved September 9th, 1850. Among other provisions is the following: "That the legislative power of said Territory shall extend to all rightful subjects of legislation consistent with the Constitution of the United States and the provisions of this act… All the laws passed by the Legislative Assembly and Governor shall be submitted to the Congress of the United States and if disapproved shall be null and of no effect."

THE CHARTER IN QUESTION

The charter in question was a law passed by the legislative assembly, and the right to disapprove it was expressly reserved, and the church must be held to have accepted it with the knowledge of the reserved right of disapproval. That being so the church will not be heard to say that it was accepted without conditions…

We are of the opinion therefore, from a view of the whole subject both from the nature of the powers granted by the charter itself, and from the form of the grant and of the acceptance that the acceptance did not give the corporation a vested right in it…

…From the provisions of the act of 1862 it is clear the Congress did not regard the charter as a contract, otherwise it would not have changed its provisions. We may assume that Congress changed the charter according to its conceptions of duty in the time with the understanding that it might be changed further or altogether disapproved, whenever in the opinion of Congress the good of society required such change or disapproval.

THE SEVENTEENTH SECTION

The seventeenth section of the act of March 3rd, 1887, under which this bill is filed, is as follows: Sec. 17. That the acts of the legislative assembly of the Territory of Utah incorporating, continuing, or providing for the corporation known as the Church of Jesus Christ of Latter-day Saints, and the ordinance of the so-called general assembly of the State of Deseret incorporating the Church of Jesus Christ of Latter-day Saints, so far as the same may now have legal force and validity, are hereby disapproved and annulled, and the said corporation, in so far as it may not have, or pretend to have, any legal existence, is hereby dissolved. That it shall be the duty of the Attorney General of the United States to cause such proceedings to be taken in the Supreme Court of the Territory of Utah as shall be proper to execute the foregoing provisions of this section and to wind up the affairs of said corporation conformably to law; and in such proceedings the court shall have power, and it shall be its duty, to make such decree or decrees as be its duty, to make such decree or decrees as shall be proper to effectuate the transfer of the title to real property now held and used by said corporation for places of worship, and parsonages connected therewith, and burial grounds, and of the description mentioned in the proviso to section thirteen of this act, to the respective trustees mentioned in section twenty six of this act; and for the purposes of this section said court shall have all the power of a court of equity.

The power of Congress to dissolve the corporation styled the Church of Jesus Christ of Latter-day Saints necessarily follows the right to annul its charter, which we have held could be done. This disposes of the question raised upon the first clause of the seventeenth section of the act…

The second clause of the seventeenth section quoted makes it the duty of the Attorney General of the United States to institute proceedings in this court to wind up the affairs of the corporation dissolved by the first clause of the same section, and gives the Court power to make such decree as may be proper to transfer the title to real property held and used by the corporation for places of worship and parsonages connected therewith and burial grounds, as mentioned in the proviso to section thirteen and in section twenty-six of the same Act. For the purpose of such proceeding the Court is given all the powers of a court of equity… The property so forfeited and escheated to the United States and the proceeds thereof are to be applied to the use and benefit of the common schools in the Territory in which such property may be.

THE ACT OF 1862

Section three of the Act of 1862 is as follows: Sec. e. *And be it further enacted,* that it shall not be lawful for any corporation or association for religious or charitable purposes to acquire or hold real estate in any Territory of the United Stated during the existence of the Territorial government of a greater value than fifty thousand dollars; and all real estate acquired or held by any such corporation or association contrary to the provisions of this Act shall be forfeited and escheat to the United States…

It will be seen that section thirteen of the Act of March 3, 1887 authorizes the forfeiture only of the property obtained or held in violation of section three of the Act which took effect July 1st 1862—that is to say, property acquired after the Act took effect and in violation of it. And we here remark that the policy of limiting the amount of land which religious corporations may hold is not new; but it is a practice that has obtained for ages. It was announced in Magna Charta more than six hundred years ago and continued by many enactments of Parliament designed to meet the evasions and contrivances of the church for escaping the laws. It has been the settled policy in this country as shown by the statutes of various States and a quarter of a century ago Congress limited the amount of real estate that any church might hold in any of the Territories. It has been the settled design of such statutes to confine church holdings to the amount necessary simply for church purposes; and the observance of such laws has been secured by forfeiture, which seems the most appropriate and effectual method.

VESTED RIGHTS NOT DISTURBED

We are unable to discover that any of the provisions of the Act of Congress of March 3rd, 1887, relating to the corporation of the Church of Jesus Christ of Latter-day Saints interferes with vested rights or is in conflict with any provision of the Constitution of the United States…

That since the 19th day of February, 1887, there has been and is no person lawfully authorized to take charge of, manage, preserve or control the property, real and personal, which on or before the day and year last aforesaid was held, owned, possessed and used by the corporation of the Church of Jesus Christ of Latter-day Saints and by reason thereof all the said property as referred to in the third paragraph of this bill is subject to irreparable and immediate loss and destruction.

The reasons for the statement of facts in terms so general are sufficiently apparent. When the corporation was dissolved its officers and agents no longer had any legal right to the possession of its property, to its use or to the rents and profits thereof.

It further appears from the allegations of the bill that the respondents are receiving and applying to their own use the rents and profits of the property and claiming the right to sell, use and dispose of it.

Assuming the facts to be as alleged in the bill, a portion of the property must be forfeited and must escheat to the United States to be applied to the use and benefit of the common schools of the Territory of Utah…

We are of the opinion that the facts alleged in the bill are sufficient to authorize the appointment of a receiver according to the prayer…

…From these facts it sufficiently appears that the defunct corporation has in its possession real property in value exceeding fifty thousand dollars, the limit fixed by the act of Congress of 1862 and that a portion of it is not a building or the grounds appurtenant thereto held for the purpose of the worship of God or parsonages connected therewith or burial ground, and that title to a large portion of the same property was acquired subsequently to the time the act of 1862 took effect…

Boreman, Justice, concurs.
Henderson, Justice, concurs.
Filed Nov. 5, 1887.

—*The Daily Tribune*, November 6, 1887.

THE MORMON CHURCH CASE

Salt Lake, Utah. The Supreme Court tonight, by unanimous decision, decided to appoint a Receiver for the Mormon Church property in excess of the limit fixed by Congress in 1862, Judge Zane writing the decision. A review is made of the Territorial act incorporating the church and the power of Congress to annul it is affirmed…

—*The New York Times*, Sunday, November 6, 1887.

The *News* recently drew public attention so emphatically to the unfitness of Mr. Henry Hobson to appear for the government in the Mormon church case at Salt Lake against Ex-Senator McDonald and other distinguished lawyers of national reputation who appeared for the Mormons, that the friends of our talented young townsman will be peculiarly gratified to learn that he has beaten Senator McDonald and the whole brilliant array of legal talent employed for the defense out of their boots— routed them horse and foot. The Supreme Court of Utah has sustained him at every point and placed the Mormon Church property and the perpetual emigration funds in the hands of a receiver. Mr. Hobson is among the brightest young men of the west and the spiteful attacks of the *News* can only serve to fix public attention on his superior talents. He is not yet thirty and he is already launched upon a brilliant career. It would satisfy most men to close their lives with as much distinction as his is opening. He is one of the courageous young leaders of the clean democracy of Colorado, and he has since his appointment to the government service evinced such a clear, and fearless sense of duty that his honor not less than his ability commands the confidence and respect of even his political opponents. His success in this Mormon case will give him a national reputation as a lawyer. —*The Denver Republican*, undated, 1887.

Geo. S. Peters, U. S. Attorney, Sale Lake City, Utah.
Nov. 10th, 1887.
Henry W. Hobson Esq., Denver, Col.
Dear Sir: The Court sustained us in all of our points in the church case. Yesterday evening the Court overruled the demurrer filed by the Defendants and there-upon they filed answers. The copies which they furnished me I sent to the department in order that the Attorney General might be fully advised of the exact condition of the case.

It will be necessary for us to file a replication within the next twenty days. When and where can we get together and consult further in the case?

I have mailed you newspapers containing full accounts of the proceedings from day to day. The Court has been in session every night since Saturday night and I have been kept quite busy, preparing entries, settling differences with the other side, etc. etc. In my judgment the answer does not raise any question that has not been already settled by the Court in passing on the motion and demurrer. Thanks for the copies you sent me of complaints in timber cases. I have the decision to which you refer so you need not trouble yourself further by sending me another.   —Very Truly Yours, *Geo. S. Peters*.

↬ A letter to Kittie:

Nov. 12, 1887, *U. P. Ry. between Pocatello & Cheyenne*.
My own sweetest Kittie—   How I was rewarded for my *impatient* waiting, when I got to Pocatello and found a nice packet of five letters from your own darling self. And do you know love, as I read your letters (four times since receiving them) I felt that my letters must be so cold and commonplace as compared with yours, rich in the burst of love, confidence, and joy that form a mosaic of most delicious sentiment.

Dearest, sweetest I thank you so for all your letters and if mine seem cold remember that I am not much learned in the art of saying nice things and that my epistolary practice has been for years in the field of business correspondence… Ah sweet you are my honor, my pride, my hope and with you and about you are gathered my day-dreams and ambitions. I always thought my Mother flattered and praised me too much, but you, why you are an Arch-flatterer and you say such things as were never said before to me by anyone. But I am glad you say them dear! …As matters now stand I think we can stick to 17th of Dec. as our wedding day, and I do not anticipate anything arising to change my plans… I will be in Fitchburg a day before our wedding and end our short engagement in the sweetest mellowest glow of our lover's twilight. The next day *cherie* we will begin the long day of our married love and happiness… I am glad you liked my letter to Mr. Jermain. I will, as you suggest, copy it and make such changes as may be necessary on account of the lapse of time etc. and then send it to you to be forwarded… Of course my love, we will be asked to entertainments in Richmond for the city is usually very gay during Xmas season. I used to be quite a favorite socially in Richmond and had many warm friends, socially speaking and I hope I have many true friends still there. I am sure we will be warmly received and yet we must remember that I have been away eight years nearly, and things have changed much since then and I have not been back a great deal. Still I think as an original proposition, you can count on going out a good deal.

So you think I was a pleasing mixture of indifference and boldness in the days of my courtship! Why you sweet love. You would not have cared for me nearly so much or so quickly if I had been otherwise. You did not start out with the idea of loving me but of having me love you. I started out with both ideas and confess Dearest that my way and my success are the nicest… I spent yesterday at Blackfoot Idaho, right up amongst the Shoshone and Bannock Indians. I saw a lot of them and such funny looking creatures they are with their freshly painted faces and in their fantastic dresses and costumes. Everywhere I go I am recognized as the man who argued and won the big Mormon Church case at Salt Lake. It is quite a *cause celebre* in the West and I have many nice things said to me. I have been investigating a terrible tangle of important cases, which the Attorney General has instructed me to clean up. Well my darling I have written you quite a long scribble in pencil, and I am going to close. Goodbye my own, my darling. Ah sweetheart, your very name is precious to me.   —Your Devoted *Henry*.

1888

Legal matters:

Geo. S. Peters, U. S. Attorney, Salt Lake City, Utah.
January 19, 1888.
Henry W. Hobson Esq., Denver Col.
Dear Sir—   Yours of the 11th was received a few days since. I have been quite busy in the Supreme Court for the past ten days. Have had another contest in the church case. They made an application to the Court for the allowance of an appeal to the Supreme Court of the U. S. from the order appointing a receiver, which after a somewhat protracted discussion, was on yesterday by the Court denied. I enclose herewith a newspaper clipping containing the decision of the Court. They will probably review their application at Washington.

The cases are at issue and we expect to begin the taking of testimony at an early day. In my judgment the testimony should be very full, and show clearly the kind and quantity of the Defendants property, the uses it has been put to etc. There is a vast amount of property in the Territory which belongs to the church, if we are able to research it and bring it to light.

Hope you may find time to impart to me from time to time such suggestions as may occur to you respecting the conduct of this important litigation. I shall keep you advised of the progress. Mr. Clarke has not yet returned from the East.   —Very Truly, *Geo S. Peters*, U. S. Atty.

January 27, 1888.
Henry W. Hobson Esq., Denver Col.
Dear Sir: In reply to yours of the 23rd, I will say that if you can find the time to do so I would be pleased to have a conference with you respecting the future management of the Church case. Suit your own convenience as to time.
—Yours truly, *Geo. S. Peters*.

February 24, 1888.
Henry W. Hobson, Esq. U. S. Attorney, Denver, Colorado.
Sir: …the bringing of suits by the Receiver against the parties holding the property in trust seems to be the proper one to pursue.   —Very respectfully, *A. H. Garland*, Attorney General.

Department of Justice, Washington, March 13, 1888.
Henry W. Hobson, Esq. Special U. S. Attorney, Denver, Colorado.
Sir: If, from your knowledge of the facts and circumstances surrounding the cases to which you refer, you believe your presence is necessary at Salt Lake City, you are authorized to go there to make the necessary examination, consult, and prepare paper.   —Very respectfully, *A. H. Garland*, Attorney General.

April 12, 1888.
Henry W. Hobson, Esq. U. S. Attorney, Denver, Colorado.
My Dear Sir: …The Attorney General has written to Mr. Peters communicating to him the propriety of acting in conformity to your suggestion, if it can be done in view of all the circumstances of the case.   —Yours Truly, *G. A. Jenks*, Solicitor General.

July 10, 1888.
Henry W. Hobson, Esq., U. S. Attorney, Denver, Colorado.
My Dear Sir: I regret that the probable absence of the Attorney General during the month of which you speak will render it impossible that I should enjoy the pleasure of accepting your invitation. The case to which you refer, I feel confident, is in good and competent hands. The work seems, from what I learned from reports of the United States Attorney and yourself, to be progressing as favorably as we could hope… With sincere regards and kind wishes to Mrs. Hobson and yourself, I am,   —Yours truly, *G. A. Jenks*.

Department of Justice, Washington. July 16, 1888.
H. W. Hobson, Esq., U. S. Attorney, Denver, Colorado.
Sir: I just received yours of the 11th instant, with reference to the property turned over by the Mormon Church to the Receiver. The amount aggregates about $780,000, exclusive of the temple, and the buildings appurtenant to it. Mr. Peters was here this morning, but I have not had full conference with him, and cannot speak with precision. I will have him call on you at Denver on his return, and explain all to you, so that you may act in conformity with your joint judgment. This turning over of property, if it be all that can be recovered, will, of course, lead to a final decree. With reference to that, you will want to examine with care, and see that it conforms to the full justice of the case. We will not consent to, nor finally formulate the decree, until it shall have been submitted to you, and you shall have joined in a report thereon.   —Very respectfully, *G. A. Jenks*, Acting Attorney General.

August 6th, 1888.
Henry W. Hobson, Esq., U. S. Attorney, Denver, Colorado.
My Dear Sir: …I think it quite important that we have a conference soon with respect to the entering of a final decree and the filing of an information

to escheat the property in the Church cases. Would it be possible for you to come over the last of this or the first of next week?   —Very Respectfully, *Geo. A. Peters.*

THE WESTERN UNION TELEGRAPH COMPANY
Night Message. Sept. 8, 1888.
To: H. W. Hobson, U. S. Atty Denver, Col. — Case set for fifteenth. Come at once. *Geo. S. Peters.*

September 24, 1888.
Henry W. Hobson, Esq., Special U. S. Attorney, Denver, Colorado.
Sir: Your report of the 18th instant just reached me. The cases at Salt Lake City are so important that, if Mr. Peters desires you to go back on the 6th of October, comply with his request, if possible. Your letter, to which you refer, concerning the Northern Pacific cases, has been referred to the Secretary of the Interior for his consideration and recommendation. I saw him personally a day or two ago, and suggested to him the propriety of speedy action, and stated my approval of the course suggested by you. I trust I will soon have his reply, when I will communicate with you further. Very respectfully, *G. A. Jenks*, Acting Attorney General.

A VICTORY FOR THE GOVERNMENT
The Church Sat Down Upon by the Supreme Court—Salt Lake City, Utah.

In the case of the United States Government against the Mormon Church, the Government today scored a complete and final triumph, so far as the Supreme Court of the Territory is concerned. About a year ago, shortly after the case was instituted, the Supreme Court unanimously decided the main law point of the case upon a demurrer to the bill and in the fight made against the appointment of a receiver. All the points were decided in favor of the Government.

During the last year the receiver has collected about one million and half dollars worth of property belonging to the church. On Saturday last the case came up for final hearing and determination as to whether the church corporation should be declared dissolved and with regard to disposition of its property.

There has been a bitter fight all through. Much testimony has been taken and some agreed statements of facts entered into. Today the Supreme Court disposed of the case, deciding all points in favor of the Government. It judicially declares the dissolution of the Mormon church as a corporation and the substance of the decrees is that all the property, real and personal, becomes escheated to the Government for the purpose of public schools, although the real property is held pending the completion of formal proceedings for forfeiture brought by the Government.

One of the most determined efforts on the part of the defensive was to get the property of the dissolved corporation for the unincorporated church, on the ground that it was composed of the members of the Mormon Church, who were legal successors in interest to the corporation, and on the ground that the property was acquired upon trusts, which are an item of existence. The court denied the rights of the individuals and declared, emphatically that any trusts in existence in said property which could be so devoted, were in whole or in part connected with the upholding of polygamy, and were, therefore, unlawful. The Court declared that the present church still upheld and taught the doctrine of polygamy.

The attorneys for the church at once perfected an appeal to the United States Supreme Court. The receiver meanwhile will hold the funds in his possession and should the United States Supreme Court affirm the decree of the Utah Supreme Court he will distribute the funds among the schools of the Territory.

United States District Attorney Hobson of Denver made quite a record for himself in the Church cases. He had to cope with the ablest legal talent of the country, the Mormons, in addition to able local counsel, having employed Colonel Broadhead of St. Louis, President of the American Bar Association, and Ex-Senator Joe McDonald of Indiana. —*The Denver Republican*, Tuesday, October 9, 1888.

October 16, 1888.
Henry W. Hobson, Esq., Denver, Colorado.
My Dear Sir: I received yours of the 10th instant, and will file it among my semi-official letters, as you request. I think you and Mr. Peters have done your parts well, and am exceedingly glad you have brought the business in the lower court to so favorable a result. I am not disposed to throw any obstacle in the way of an advancement of the cause. If you have any authorities or briefs in the case, I wish you would send them now. When the case comes to argument in the Supreme Court, I will consult with the Attorney General as to the necessity of having you participate therein. Personally I certainly would be very glad of your assistance. I am, Yours Truly, *G. A. Jenks*, Solicitor General.

THE WESTERN UNION TELEGRAPH COMPANY
Washington, D. C. Nov. 13, 1888.
Spcl. U. S. Atty. Hobson, Denver, Colo.—
District Atty Peters deems it very necessary you should be in Salt on seventeenth inst. In Church case. You had better make your arrangements and go. —*A. H. Garland*, Atty. Genl.

THE WESTERN UNION TELEGRAPH COMPANY
Salt Lake City. 16 November 1888.
To: U. S. Attny Hobson, Denver. Can you be here twenty-fourth. Important that you should be. Answer. —*Peters*, U. S. Attorney.

THE WESTERN UNION TELEGRAPH COMPANY
Salt Lake City. 17 November 1888.
To: U. S. Attny Hobson, Denver. Court adjourned till twenty eighth. Best could do. Do not fail to come. Have written. —*Peters*, U. S. Attorney.

THE WESTERN UNION TELEGRAPH COMPANY
Washington, D. C. November 21, 1888.
To: U. S. Atty Hobson, Denver.
Be at Salt Lake City by the twenty-eighth to look after the Mormon Church matter there. A letter from me will meet you there. —*A. H. Garland*, Atty Genl.

THE WESTERN UNION TELEGRAPH COMPANY
Washington, D. C. November 28, 1888.
To. U. S. Attorney Hobson, Salt Lake City, Utah. — I have not data sufficient to advise or instruct you certainly upon the facts there. The court should be able to deter-

mine the matter justly. You must exercise your best discretion on all the facts of the case in view of my letter to you of the twenty-second instant. The amounts do appear to me very unreasonable.   —*A. H. Garland*, Atty Genl.

Department of Justice, Washington. December 8, 1888.
Henry W. Hobson, Esq., U. S. Attorney, Denver, Colorado.
Sir: I received yours of the 30th of November last, containing newspaper slip, and reporting your action with reference to the adjustment of the fees of the Receiver and his attorneys in the case of the United States vs. The Church of Jesus Christ of Latter-day Saints. Your action meets with my approval. You will continue to guard the interests of the Government in the matter with diligence, as the emergencies of the case from time to time demand.   —Very respectfully, *A. H. Garland*, Attorney General.

∾

Despite all of its efforts, the Mormon Church was unsuccessful in its appeals, including before the U. S. Supreme Court. That court agreed that Congress could both repeal the Church's charter and seize its property. In August 1889 there were local elections in Salt Lake City that the Gentiles, the non-Mormons, won for the first time. The *Sacramento Bee* reported: "The effect of the election cannot but be salutary as far as Utah's interests are concerned. The Mormons, who styled themselves as the People's Party, were opposed to any internal improvements, such as waterworks, sewage, etc, while the Liberals, or the Gentiles, were strongly in favor of such. It will result in Salt Lake City becoming the principal point between Denver and San Francisco, and will be the greatest thing for Utah that ever happened." Of this same election the *Chicago Tribune* wrote: "The result of the recent election in Salt Lake City for Territorial, Legislative and County officers is the beginning of the end so far as Mormonism is concerned. The revolution will grow and spread until the whole Territory is redeemed from the political domination of Mormon priest-craft." Both in the courts and at the polls, the Mormon Church was losing. A year later, in September 1890, Church President Wilford Woodruff issued what would be called the "Woodruff Manifesto" in which he urged the members of the Church "to refrain from contracting any marriage forbidden by the law of the land." The following year Church leaders requested amnesty for many of the individuals convicted and imprisoned for practicing polygamy. In January 1893 President Harrison granted amnesty to a limited number of persons and the following year President Cleveland granted a broader amnesty. By 1893 Henry Hobson was in private practice but was thinking about returning to government service in the new Cleveland administration. In February 1893 he wrote to his uncle, John S. Wise: "For four years I had throughout the West charge of most important Government work—the great fight with the land rings of several States and territories, sole charge of the great Mormon Church fight, of the great Mexican Land Grant cases and of all the extensive litigation between the Government and the Northern Pacific RR." He remained in private practice. In October

1893, recognizing that the Mormon Church had officially rejected polygamy, Congress voted to return to the Church some of the property that had been previously seized. A constitutional convention in Utah in 1895 included a declaration that "polygamous or plural marriages are forever prohibited," and Utah became the forty-fifth state on January 4th, 1896. During all of this time Henry Wise Hobson was undoubtedly aware of all of the changes that had come to Utah in part because of his work. —*Editor's note.*

XVIII

1888–1889

Colorado

AFTER their marriage in December 1887, Henry and Katherine Hobson traveled to Richmond where they met and visited with his family and friends before returning to Denver and their rooms at the Windsor Hotel. Their lives had changed and change was coming to America at this same time. The Oklahoma Indian Territory was opened to white settlers, and four territories, North and South Dakota, Montana, and Washington, would become states. The adding machine was invented, the sewing machine was first marketed, and amateur photography became more possible when George Eastman improved and marketed the Kodak hand camera. The Great Blizzard of 1888 paralyzed the east coast and killed an estimated 400 people; there was a six-month epidemic of Yellow fever in Florida; and an unknown number of people were killed when a dam broke in Johnstown, Pennsylvania, and that city was covered with over thirty feet of water. In the 1888 elections Benjamin Harrison defeated Grover Cleveland in the electoral college vote though Cleveland won the popular vote, and Harrison became President in March 1889. Jefferson Davis, the President of the Confederacy, died in New Orleans in December 1889. During this time Henry Hobson would be very busy as the United States Attorney in Colorado and Katherine would have her first child, Katherine Thayer Hobson.

Letters by:
Annie Jennings Wise Hobson
Henry Wise Hobson
John Cannon Hobson
Katherine Thayer Hobson
Thomas Nelson Page
Catherine McKie Thayer
John S. Wise
Mary Lyons Wise
and the first of *Papa's Letters*

Letters written from: Colorado Springs, Denver, and Pueblo, Colorado; Amherst, Ashland, Richmond, and Mount Vernon, Virginia; Salt Lake City and Ogden, Utah Territory; St. Paul, Minnesota; Laramie, Wyoming, Territory; Boise City, Idaho, Territory; Butte City, Nebraska; Philadelphia, Washington, D. C., New York City, London, Paris, and aboard trains.

1888

◈ Letters from Catherine McKie Thayer:

January 9, 1888.
With all the mail trains that are between here and Denver, I think no one receives a letter the day it is written— a letter leaving here by the 10:20 will be until the next day reaching its destination, so I suppose we may make up our minds to this. Dr. Reed, who was just here and asked for you, said a friend put two letters in the Office, with his own hand, in Denver, and the Dr. received one the next day, and the other the second day after... I hope to hear from you tomorrow, and to see you before long, and most of all that you and Henry keep well. With a heart full of tenderest love to both   — *Mother*.

January 10, 1888.
This a.m. at eleven, came your letter of Sun. eve— also one from Dr. Fisk written "Sun" and the Denver stamp on both is "Jan 9 1 P.M." I hope we may be able to count on the delivery of a letter before day after tomorrow. I am so glad you like your rooms generally— and I would like to feel that Henry is satisfied... —*Mother*

505 Cascade Avenue, Colorado Springs, January 12th, 1888.
My Darling Husband—   Yesterday I felt very forlorn, and heart-sick, to have you walk off— & leave me. And all the way down I was missing your dear presence and longing for you. On my arrival the man met me— and soon drove me here. No one to meet me but a servant at the door— ran upstairs & found Mother on the sofa in her room, looking so weak. Dr. Reed was with her but he left us alone... Mother coughs badly and has no appetite, but is better. She has been quite ill and is far from well yet... Frank will be here next week. I think it best, Sweetheart, to remain until tomorrow. It will do Mother so much good. But Darling I want to go to you today, this minute. I woke in the night & missed you. I feel as if I were only half living— Mother loves to have me talk about you— and I know I have the most loving tender of Husbands. And I thank God from my heart for the greatest of all earthly blessings. I don't think I half show you how devotedly I love you & you must help smooth out my roughness. My cold is better & this morning I can *taste* & distinguish quail from potatoe [sic]. Such a delicious breakfast up in Mother's room so not to miss one moment with her. She is so delighted, like a child. And we are talking over our wedding & some business matters. I see my coming has been of real value to her. I wish I were less lonely & I feel so badly leaving you for two days— And Darling I hope you will think me right to stay until tomorrow. Take every care of yourself. Tomorrow I will leave at 3— PM— *Santa Fe*— and if you are at the gymnasium don't neglect your exercise to come to the train... I hope & pray my Husband is well this morning. The day is lovely— no umbrella needed. My whole heart's love to you. I am so so full of longing to see you. Excuse haste. I put special stamp on envelope. Mother sends her love. Your own loving devoted wife *Katherine*.

❧ A letter from Annie Jennings Wise Hobson:

January 14, 1888.
It will be a week tomorrow dear Katherine since you must have arrived in Denver. I have not received one line from you or Henry… It is the first time Henry ever failed to write to me promptly & I try to hope it is the fault of the mails… I left all well in Washington. A letter from Cannon said all were well there. Kiss Henry for me, and tell him I shall expect a letter once a week at least, if only three lines or even three words. God bless you both with a plenitude of happiness & a full life. —My love to your Mother. Your loving Mamma, *A.J.W.H.*

February 10, 1888, The Union Pacific R. R.
My own Darling Wife—   How I have missed you since I left you yesterday at the depot and I have wished a hundred times I had brought you along. I did not know before how you have become a part of my life since we were married. I don't believe I shall ever leave you behind again. I am writing my first letter to you as your husband. Doesn't it seem funny— we have gotten to know each other so well and become so well fitted into each other that it is hard to realize we have only been married, not quite 2 mos. I know I have the sweetest loveliest wife in the world and I do pray that I may be all to you as your husband that you deserve. I am perfectly well, only I long to see you. I am writing this hurriedly before breakfast so I can mail it to you at the breakfast station. Kiss Mother for me & God bless you my darling—   Your devoted husband, *Henry*.

❧ A letter from Annie Jennings Wise Hobson:

February 10, 1888.
How I wish I could make you feel dearest Katherine, the great happiness your letter, received a short while ago, gave me… The first days of matrimony are trying enough, and yours have been especially so. I feel greatly with you in your separation from Henry… I am glad to think that "mother & Frank" will have you all to themselves a little while. I know how happy both will be, and you are just the one to be comforted in the anxiety of separation from "our Boy," by knowing that it is good for them to have you… Katherine, from the second night of our marriage, Plumer and I never retired until he had read a chapter in the Bible with me, and hand-in-hand we knelt together in prayer. You are indeed right in saying, that it would be good tidings to my Motherheart, to hear that you read God's word nightly together, & especially was I gratified to know that he had proposed it… I should love to think of his kneeling in prayer with you, as his Father & I did.
    February 11, 1888. Dinner interrupted me… Henry writes that you have made the rooms so lovely— & this was the conclusion of his last letter— "You admire my wife very much I know, but you do not begin to appreciate what a fine woman your daughter is. She is one in ten thousand." Now be happy over that! Of course my son will be tender and devoted to you. I would disown him if he did not be more of a lover and more devoted twenty years hence than now. —I hope he is "ever so good" to your Mother also… We are again in gloomy

winter weather— so piercing cold, gloomy skies… I have a batch of letters to get off this morning. If my precious boy has returned kiss him many times for his Mother… Write as you can without taxing yourself. I stand constantly in spirit beside you & my dear son & my prayers ever follow you—   Your loving Mamma— *A.J.W.H.*

[Postscript on another piece of paper] Henry has mentioned several times that you were not well, dear Katherine. Will you not understand me if I say to you that we are so much alike that I can enter into every feeling you have in the first sacred experience of married life. I can surmise that you would keep from your Mother when she is not well all your ailments and troubles. Now if there is ought you would like to ask my advice about as to your physical health will you not do so unhesitatingly, as if I was your second self. I might put you on your guard & give some helpful advice— Your Mamma— *A.J.W.H.*

February 11, 1888, Salt Lake City, Utah. The Cullen, S. D. Ewing, Proprietor. *Rates $3.00 Per Day. Special Rates To Tourists.*
My darling wife Katherine—   I got in last night and wished to write to you but got into the hands of the District Attorney soon after my arrival and then I was "done for." I telegraphed you however and suppose you will get the message this morning… I wonder my dearest all the time whether you are so lonesome and blue as you thought you would be or I might say as I am. I long for you every moment almost and feel that somehow the world is out of joint with you away. But it will only be for a few days— a week from today we will be together again… I appreciate every day how much of my life you are and are going to be… —Your devoted husband, *Henry.*

February 12, 1888, Salt Lake City, Utah. The Cullen.
My own darling Wife— It seems to me I want to write you every hour or send

The Cullen Hotel, Salt Lake City. "The modern hotel of the west, steam elevator, incandescent lights, steam heating, hot and cold water throughout 128 rooms, including 30 suites with bath rooms attached, sample room 20x25 feet, on ground floor, specially lit and supplied with all comforts and conveniences."

you a telegram. This morning in going through my pockets I found a letter I had written you on Friday afternoon on the train, in order to mail it at Ogden and have it reach you Sunday. How I failed to mail it I cannot say, except that I am the most careless man alive about letters. Never mind sweetheart, I was thinking about you all the time. I wish for you always but then it is well you did not come for this usually pleasant city is about as disagreeable as any place you could imagine. The streets are simply impassable without going to your shoe tops in mud… I find Salt Lake just on the verge of a Real Estate boom. Property has already gone up here greatly and the more conservative men tell me that there is going to be a big increase this Spring and Summer. They will begin here this Spring what they most need— the putting in of a good sewer system, the supplying of the City with better water and the paving of the Streets. From what I can see and hear I am confident that money can be made here. I went out yesterday afternoon with a Real Estate man, an old Colorado friend of mine, and he showed me around… I let the Denver boom go without making a dollar, whereas if I had done like Cuthbert and Fisk and others I know I could have made 10 or 15 thousand dollars. The trouble with me is that I am too conservative by half and am afraid to risk money upon almost certain ventures… What a beggar you are anyhow. It is "Mother I want this" and "Mother I must have that" etc. etc. It is a wonder to me that your Mother does not have to go into bankruptcy. I will wire to Cage to notify Mrs. Whittaker that we will be absent somewhat longer than we intended. You must however my dear, make up your mind, by the time you return to Denver whether you wish that house, for we cannot keep her waiting any longer. I have no wish except that you shall be pleased. I must now close my darling for I wish this to go in the mail today, so that you will get it Tuesday morning. My first thought in the morning and my last thought at night are with you my love, my wife, and no distance can separate us in love and sympathy. With much love for your Mother and Frank, believe that I send you a world of love and a thousand kisses—   Your devoted husband, *Henry*.

February 13, 1888, Salt Lake City, Utah. The Cullen.
My darling Katherine—   I have not received a line from you since I came here and I am half way out of humor about it… The weather here still remains cloudy and disagreeable and perhaps that has something to do with my spirits for nothing so easily affects me as the weather. I can't tell you Dearest in words how much I wish to see you. I am always imagining that you are unwell or that something is happening to you which I could avert if I were with you. When we meet, my joy and my petting shall show you how much I have missed you and what a trial our separation has been to me… Fortunately I am very busy here and do not have much time for being blue. When not occupied with my duties which brought me to Salt Lake, I am busy studying up a very important question relating to Water Rights which I have to argue soon. I have put in a long night in a law office and most of yesterday, Sunday. I have a constitutional aversion to loafing and wasting time though I do not like hard work either… Are you entirely well my dearest wife and do you sleep enough? I am afraid no one takes quite as good care of you as I would like, for until I married you everyone seems to have looked to you for care and to have let you scuffle for yourself. Give my best love to your Mother and also a kiss. I think she is the nicest sweetest Mother-in-law any man ever

had and I *know* she is the best I ever had. This must go to the mail. A hundred kisses my darling and a whole heart-full of love— Yours devotedly, *Henry*.

February 14, 1888, Salt Lake City, Utah. The Cullen.
My Darling Wife Katherine— Your letter of Friday finally came yesterday morning and I now know the fault lay with the mails for another letter came last night… I laughed at myself when I found myself kissing your letters and calling you all manner of sweet names. You are my first thought always now and surely no man could have a sweeter and more ennobling thought…
—Your loving husband, *Henry*.

Denver, The Windsor, March 9, 1888.
My Dear Uncle Johnnie— [Katherine Hobson to John S. Wise] When Henry goes off on business trips I spend the time at my Mothers. She lives only three hours by train from Denver, and frequently she comes to see us. She & Henry are a joy to behold. They are so congenial & devoted to each other. I wish you to meet her & she to know your family… he [Henry] is so busy, works very hard. I often go to the office with him at evening— take my books & work. And you will be surprised to know that I sit *speechless* for two hours, while Henry works away on his briefs… —Your devoted niece, *Katherine*. (Virginia Historical Society)

Colorado Springs, March 13th, 1888.
My Darling Husband— I feel like quoting the verse "not that I've anything to say, but only that it comes from me." I have been so lonely at night and through the day it is hard to be separated. Frank met me & Mother was at the door. I had supper & a talk, and to bed. I heard the train pass which I trust has carried you safely to your destination— Sweetheart, do be careful & prudent and meet me on your return well, and yourself. I have decided to let the Jermain matter, as to Bank Stock, rest until you return. I want to know what you think on certain points before I decide & Mother thinks it will be as well. And it will do those two old gentlemen good to wait. Mother says you can count on the money $5,500 any day. She can arrange it with El Paso Bank for friends. You can telegraph me if you wish this money $5,500, & where to send it before your return. Also if you see any property you consider a paying investment to hold & sell later, Mother would be willing to invest money there & you could telegraph terms etc. to her. She would only wish to invest $10,000, not over that amount. Maybe she could join Dr. Fisk in his scheme— What do you think of that? …Mother is quite well & sends love. Also Frank. We are talking over the Range (stove) question & will be able to decide wisely. Weather lovely. Do not be discouraged & dissatisfied with the little house— it is going to be charming when we are settled— And we will forget the disagreeables— dwelling on faults often magnifies them… You Darling— how I wish I could see you for a little while. I can't express half how much I miss & long for you. I must tell you of the travelling companions on the Pullman you transferred me to. I never heard such profanity— Every breath, then plenty of whiskey— and finally an old fellow got out of his berth & went to the dressing room in his drawers & shirt— & one man lit his cigarette and got into his berth. I would have done better in the ordinary car. Now my Darling Husband I must stop with tenderest love & kisses to my own love. Keep well & be careful & come to your loving *Katherine*.

Colorado Springs, March 15th, 1888.
My own Darling Husband— This hour the postman brings your letter from Gunnison— it takes a long long time for letters to come less than 300 miles, but how precious your loving words are to my heart. The days are passing which bring us nearer each other— together. I have thought over the Jermain request, and have concluded to ascertain from Mr. H—, the executor with me & the lawyer who had the making of the will, whether the estate has been closed & we discharged as Executor & Executrix. For how could I comply with Mr. Jermain's request if I have become the owner of the property & have been discharged... I am so sorry to have all of these unnecessary matters to bother you with darling, but you are so kind & patient. That it is another reason I have for loving you more & soon I trust all these disagreeables will be over & then we will forget them. I am busy picking up some of my things here, linen etc. & packing to ship to Denver... I see by papers that the U. P. R. R. has *struck*. Don't get tied up where you can't get away— and do keep well my Darling Husband. How glad I will be to see you again. You are more necessary & dear every day of my life. With my hearts tenderest love & many kisses, Your Devoted & Loving Wife, *Katherine*.   —Nearly 3 months married on Saturday & how entirely happy.

the estate The estate of Barclay Jermain, Kittie's first husband.

March 15, 1888, Salt Lake City, Utah. The Cullen.
My darling Girl— I got in this morning and wired you to that effect. I am all right and free from rheumatism. I feel a little tired but that is natural considering the fact that I have been on the go for several days. I got your letter written on the train the night you left me. My sweet wife I cannot tell you how I enjoy and prize all your loving words... Don't worry yourself on my account about the Jermain complications. He (Mr. J—) has shown a littleness and meanness of spirit towards you, that I should hate to think could ever belong to me. All the feelings I have, are some of indignation and resentment on your account and at your being treated so unworthily. Old Mr. Jermain, my darling, is a man who is just big enough to make and keep money. He could never be equal to doing anything else in life. I have no feelings against him on my account except those of pity and some contempt... I expect to leave here tomorrow at 4:10 P.M. and get to Boise at 1 oclk the next day. I am indeed glad I did not bring you. I have to go from 4 to 2 oclk that night on a narrow gauge— mixed train without a sleeper... I must now close my darling for I have an appointment. Give best love to Mother and Frank, and give the first a good round kiss for me. I was about to say the "dear old lady," but I know you would tell her. A thousand kisses and a world of love for your own dearest self.   —Your loving & devoted *Henry*.

Colorado Springs, March 16th, 1888.
My Dearest Husband— Your letter from Montrose is received. In answer to your telegram Mother arranged to send $5,500 for you to use as you thought best, and added $10,000 for herself. This you know by wire. The El Paso Bank telegraphed First National of Denver that "Fifteen thousand, five hundred dollars were this day sent you to deposit to Henry W. Hobson's credit."...I send you a proof of my photos & I have ordered a half dozen of another kind. I won't go again soon— it has proved *too expensive a luxury*... but on reflection I won't send you a proof, for it's in the dress you despise. You

will have to reconcile yourself to my best gown for it is very handsome & suitable & will be my best for at least 3 years… Oh, my own Darling, how I long to see you. I dreamed last night we had just met & I wished to kiss you & you sat down with a lot of papers at a big table and said, "don't bother me" & put on your spectacles. You are dearer every day & mean so much— Everything in my life. Now I will stop. My heart's love & many kisses to you my Darling Husband. Your Loving Devoted Wife, *Katherine*.

Boise City, Idaho, March 18, 1888.
My darling wife—   I wrote you a letter this morning & sent it off. I will write a line now just before going to bed thinking it may go East on the morning train and reach you Wednesday at Colo. Springs. I sent you a telegram tonight which ought to reach you early tomorrow, Monday… I long for a time when with my wife and a home I can spend the Sabbath as a decent Christian. Let us try dearest hereafter to make Sunday a real day of rest and also of loving companionship with each other. I think of you at all times and even long for your flattery and compliments…   —Your devoted *Henry*.

⁓ Letters from Annie Jennings Wise Hobson:

All of Annie J.W. Hobson's letters from March 6, 1888–May 6, 1888 were written when she was staying in Washington with her sister, Mary, who was married to Dr. Alexander Yelverton Peyton Garnett.

1319 N. Y. Ave. Washington, March 22nd, 1888.
My dear Katherine—   A letter was received from Henry yesterday dated 16th from Salt Lake & saying that he hoped, unless deterred by the R. R. strike, to get back to you today. The strike has been over some days so I shall think of you as being made happy by having your errant boy with you today. Such a comfort to know your Mother had you during his absence… Will you understand me if I say something to you Dearest. I am sure you will not misunderstand. If in looking over your summer wardrobe you find any dresses that are too shabby for Denver & yet might be remodeled for a person in Alice's position in Ashland— & she is much smaller than you, do not feel any hesitation as a matter of delicacy about sending such to Alice. Minnie often does it, & so do the Lyons & she is very thankful to get them, & has no false pride about it. She writes that she needs house dresses. The poor, tired woman has been sick (I fear what it is) and has constant neuralgia. The last letter said Cannon was suffering very much with catarrh again, & the weather has been much against him… Dr. Garnett is trying to write his speech to be delivered in Cincinnati at the opening of the American Medical Association of which he is President. I am helping him all I can with it, for he has to write by snatches.

I do hope your furniture will reach you in time. I shall be beside you in thought fixing and arranging the *little home*. I know how sweetly and deftly all will be done. I shall stand in each room in spirit.   —Your loving Mamma, *A.J.W.H.*

March 22, 1888.
I am always in thoughtful loving you in your hardships, my dear son. It was a relief to hear from you yesterday & to know when you expected to get back to Katherine today. Ah, my boy, as you find unhappiness in such separation, do you think with deeper sympathy of your Mother's separation from you, & with no one to fill the gap. I feel very much for you & Katherine in this aspect of your life… I sent them [John Cannon Hobson and his wife Alice] $10.00 of

the money you inclosed, keeping the other $15 to get the material for spring clothes. Alice replied with warm thanks saying it came just in time for many needed things— doubtless shoes etc. for the children. I am troubled to hear of a return of Cannon's catarrh but he must expect that... Ever devotedly your mother, *A.J.W.H.*

1319 N. Y. Ave. Washington, March 29th, 1888.
Your dear letter was received yesterday my beloved son, and read twice over with interest and pleasure. It is indeed good to think of your having a sweet, loving home of your own, with such a wife as Katherine to be the light and "genius" of its most blessed influences. Even if I never see it, I can picture it with colors bright & lovely from imagination, and love's tender touches, and your being happy in it and blessed by its comfort and sweetness, it will be as a *home of peace*, for my heart... I had a very manly letter from Cannon the other day, begging me not to let you know of his pecuniary straits— saying he was determined to get on without your being burdened any more, and he thought he could now do so. I shall tell him the two boxes are from us both— that is all. I know all about their affairs & way of management, and I am sure you will best serve them by sending me smaller sums at stated times, and it puts me in far better relations with them to be the apparent donor. I intend to conquer, (God helping), all the difficulties between us by love and forbearance. All I ask for life now is to forget myself and live each day as God appoints it. All here I know join me in love, but no one knows I am writing. —Your devoted mother— *A.J.W. Hobson.*

In the news:

There is a vacancy on the supreme bench of the United States. As the recognized organ in the West of the Democratic party, and having a natural and uncontrollable desire to serve the state when opportunity presents, we are determined that this one shall not be lost. *The News* very seldom interferes with other states in the matter of appointments, but from a sense of duty a departure must be made in this one instance. Our candidate for the exalted position of chief justice is a citizen of Virginia temporarily sojourning in Colorado. Although young in years he has succeeded in climbing ambition's ladder, looking complacently over the topmost round with the self-reliant and self-confident air of a man of fifty instead of one whose beard just speaks him growing toward a man. Henry W. Hobson might not accept the position, but this alarming doubt shall not interfere with our good intentions in putting him forward. The well known yielding and shrinking modesty of the man cannot interfere with our sense of duty in as modestly placing him in the field. That mercy which droppeth like the gentle dew from heaven upon the place beneath might temper his decisions to the shorn lamb. Our candidate is a stranger to prejudice. As a lawyer he acknowledges few equals and no superiors. He does not believe with the sad but pensive poet "that there is no law so tainted and corrupt but some sober brow will bless it and approve it with a text." Calm, deliberate and self-possessed, he would bring to the position numberless qualifications which he knows himself to possess and which he modestly confesses are not resident in other men of equal birth and breadth. He would not brook the law's delay or suffer the insolence of associates, and would be so clear in his great office that the injured people of the State of Colorado, where he is now a visitor, might plead "like angels trumpet-tongued, against the deep darnation of his taking off." "We are not mad, but bring us to the text, and we will the matter reword which madness would gambol from."

—Unidentified newspaper clipping, probably published after the death of Chief Justice Morrison Waite on March 23, 1888.

❧ A letter from Henry's brother in Virginia:

Amherst, May 30th, 1888.
My dear Henry— You must not think my delay in answering your letter any indication of my lack of appreciation of your love & thoughts towards me at that time.

I did not answer at once as you wrote that you and Katherine were about to start on a trip. About the time you returned home I was away at the Council of the Diocese in Stanton, and I take the first opportunity since my return to write & thank you for your letter. Indeed I trust that as the years roll by with us we will both ever remember one another at such seasons & keep unbroken the bond of love which such occasions more especially call forth in expressions of kindly thoughts & deeds. I have a great deal to be thankful for as I enter upon my 32nd year. Indeed my heart has been filled to overflowing in thankful recognition of all the goodness of God to me at this time. I look forward with hope and joy, and am cheered by the love and sympathy of those who are dear to me. That you, my dear old fellow, are not least in that number, you well know.

Do you know, I was looking over the old Academic Dictionary we used as boys at school & college, the other day, and happened to be glancing over the "Signification of Christian Names" in the back of it. My eye fell on the name "Henry." The signification given was "uncertain." But that was scratched out & you had written in place of it— "Head of the house." That carried me back to the time when we were little fellows & how you used to say that, "Brother was going to marry & have a family and you were going to make money & support him." And then all the memories of our childhood came clustering around me. Truly, old fellow, you have been "Head of the House" and your childhood's prophecy has been fulfilled much more literally than was dreamed of when it was made. God bless you abundantly for it all. I rejoice to know that you have now a home of your own, a sweet, loving woman for your wife, and a bright future of usefulness and honor. As the years go by, may nothing ever come between us or any that are dear to us to cause the least jar, but may we be drawn closer & closer in love & sympathy. I am glad to say my health is very good now & I think my catarrh is improving gradually. I have been very much interested in my garden this spring & have done right much work in it myself. Alice has been greatly interested in chickens & now has about 100 young chickens. So with our garden & chickens we expect to live quite royally this summer. We are expecting Mother to come up soon and spend a good part of the summer with us. I am glad to say that I think she & Alice understand each other better, and have wiped out old scores and made a fresh start. It is indeed a matter of rejoicing to me, as it has been a trial & pain to feel that Mother and Alice could not get along together. When the overtures were made and everything smoothed over I wrote Mother a very plain letter and also gave Alice a good talking to, & so I hope that there will be no further trouble.

 The chicks & Alice are asleep and I must be getting to bed. I know the chicks all send love & kisses to Uncle Henry and Aunt Katherine. Alice, I know, joins me in much love to you both. Give my best love to Katherine. Tell her she owes me a letter, and when she has nothing better to do, she will greatly delight her bother C— if she will write me a nice long letter & tell him something about yourself. Please excuse this scrawl. I am quite tired & sleepy. God bless you now and always. —Your affec. bro. *John C. Hobson.*

Rev. John Cannon Hobson, 1857–1890. Photograph courtesy of George Hobson.

June 10, 1888, Butte City.
My Darling Wife— I don't believe there is any ink in this house, for I have been unable to get any and so I write in pencil. I have been feeling badly all day— nothing serious except a headache which I think was brought on by travel and having my rest broken several nights in succession. I have been lying down most of the day and as it usually does, my headache goes right to my eyes. I tried to read the magazines but found I could not. I think I will be well tomorrow… In looking forward and forming pictures of the future it is a great comfort to me as well as a great pleasure to have you always in the foreground of the picture as my constant companion and helper— always loving, patient and sympathetic. If you were not superior in sweetness to most other women you could not stand your cranky, dictatorial bad tempered husband. My faults of temper are a sore trial and mortification to me and when I wound you my darling, you must remember that I suffer afterwards a great deal more that you do. Have you heard from Mother yet? I am beginning to feel a little anxious about her though as a rule I never imagine ill because people do not write. I will try and write her a line today… Well I will close for I want to write to Mother and my eyes hurt me a good deal. Love for your Mother. —Your devoted husband who wants to see you awfully, *Henry.*

July 23, 1888, Philadelphia.
My Dearest Katherine— I have but a moment to write you as I am very busy. I got in all safely last evening and Dr. K— met us at the depot and brought us up to his house. I sent you a telegram telling of my safe arrival. I have been working all day trying to get up some enthusiasm in these cold Philadelphians about business. I think it very likely I will go to Washington in a day or so and then come back to Philadelphia to finish up. By the way, you did not put any socks in my valise, and not being able to get at my trunk, I had to wear the same pair of socks from Denver to Phila. Just think of that for me and with only one chance to bathe on the way… My darling girl you don't know how I miss you every hour and long for you… I would give much to give you one big hug my darling. Love to Mother & Frank. —Your devoted husband, *Henry.*

◆ A letter from John S. Wise:

Aug 22, 1888.
Dear Henry— Replying to yours of 14th, I am going to make New York my residence. The bargain is closed and settled. I am going into the biggest

thing in America, and this is not bragging but the fact. I begin work there September 1st but will come back here in October, wind up my affairs here and move the family to New York City. I start on the terms mentioned to you, but with the prospect of a large increase and employment from other parties. I enjoyed seeing you in New York very much and look forward now with peculiar pleasure to the time when you and Katherine will come and stay with me there. Tell Katherine I hope the powder puff and powder suited— Yours Truly, *John S. Wise.*

༄ A letter from Annie Jennings Wise Hobson:

Sept. 7th, 1888, Amherst Co.
My dear Katherine— Your letter of the 2nd & Henry's of the 1st were received yesterday and read with great pleasure… I understand all you meant in regard to his anxieties and fears about Cannon. The earnest desire of my life is that neither Cannon nor I should cloud your happiness— disturb the serenity of yours and Henry's life… duty requires that I should be near Cannon's children if not with them. Through love I have conquered Alice's prejudice, & I am sure there will be no more heart-burnings between us… I believe she tries to do her duty as far as she is capable of conceiving it, but she is in all things the most inefficient person I ever saw. She & Cannon are little better than untrained children in all practical affairs. They will never be any better, and by God's help I propose to try to make the best of them… Cannon is compelled to be so much away from home; when here his time must be spent either studying, visiting or taking the rest his delicate frame requires, & Alice is utterly incapable of being the true Mother to them, to say nothing of taking both father's and mother's place… I shall endeavor to bear all my cares, anxieties & self denials without casting a shadow of them all to darken yours or Henry's life, which has trials enough of your own at present… Such a dreary North-Easterly spell as we are having. This morning I have had the stove put up in my room, and the wood fire feels delightfully comfortable… Cannon & Alice are in the parlor by an open fire and do not know I am writing. I gave the children Henry's messages & they were much gratified… God bless you both— Your loving Mamma— *A.J.W.H.*

Sept. 16, 1888, Odgen.
My Darling Katherine— Just a line to say where I am. I am at Odgen thanks to the Utah Central which brought me here and to the bad management of the Union Pacific which keeps me here. Without qualification or exception the U. P. Road is the most abominably managed Road in the U. S. or on the face of the globe. We have been lying 3 hours at the depot beyond our starting time and except for one hours waiting for the Cen. Pac. Train to arrive, no mortal man can give any reason for the delay except bad management. If I had my way I would discharge every man around the place to let him feel the pangs of being without a situation. I would then hang him up by his thumb for 24 hours to let him experience what it is to wait. I would then broil him slowly on a big grille so that he could truly feel what it is to be kept waiting for 3 hours in a red hot station. The Scoundrels! My cruelty would just then have commenced… I hope to arrive at Cheyenne sometime before the end of the week but when I cannot say. I should arrive there tomorrow

morning. I had intended to stay there a day and go on to Denver on Tuesday, but alas my dearest the present prospects are that you will see me about Oct. 1st. I am in a perfect rage with this R. R. and that is the end of the matter. Love to Mother & your own self. I am in no fit humor for a letter. In order that this letter may reach you as soon as possible I will not mail it on this train which runs across the country once in a lifetime, but will send it to San Francisco, then by way of the Cape around to London by sea, then to N.Y. and to you from the East. When you finally get it you may know that you will see me someday if I live long enough to reach you. Your devoted husband, *Henry*.

❧ Letters from Annie Jennings Wise Hobson:

Amherst, September 17, 1888.
Another sweet letter from you… Alice is so indisposed, looks very badly seems utterly wearied out, therefore I have relieved her of all household care, and thoughts about the children, so you can imagine that my present position does not admit of much leisure for letter writing. The pile of mending here is something appalling! However we are fortunate in a good-natured white girl of seventeen who can greatly assist in that. Cannon found her in Petersburg, & took her to rescue the girl from most adverse influences at home. Her father forsook her Mother, & she "took up" with another man. The cook here, though a darkey verily, is better than the majority we find in Amherst & tries to do all I tell her. The dear children are not as well trained in prompt obedience as I would like, but they are manageable & devoted to Grandma, though they occasionally get insulted over stringent measures. Little George is my shadow. He has the softest, sweetest voice, & there is something very winning about him… Sister has written to me twice of late, the first letters since Dr. G's death… So you had again seen our boy go off carpet-bag in hand for Buena Vista. These constant separations are very wearing & trying, & I hope the day is not far distant when Henry can give up the Govt. Positions. You have my tender sympathy. All your loving words about my visit were fully appreciated, but I do not think I can go this fall to Colorado if I ever do. You & Henry will have to come to see me. Kiss my dear Boy for me… —Your loving Mamma, *A. J. W. Hobson.*

Amherst, October 1, 1888.
While Cannon & Alice are playing backgammon I must write out some of my heart's fullness to you… I note with sympathy and deep interest all you said regarding Henry & politics— I agree with you that he is too ambitious— is wearing his life away too fast. Yet I can understand that just now he might be urged to pursue the course he has done as a duty— but I should dislike to see him concern with politics for any length of time. I feel deeply for you in the unrest such constant separations must bring, and in your anxiety for Henry's too busy life… —Lovingly your Mamma, *A.J.W.H.*

October 5, 1888. U.P. Ry. [Union Pacific Railway] Near Laramie.
My darling Wife—   Here I am on the U.P and late of course. We ought to have left Cheyenne this morning at 2:30 oclk. and we did not leave until 9:30 — 7 hours late. The train from Omaha was 6 hours late in getting into Omaha & then to get the spirits of the engineers up, the train coolly laid at

the depot an even hour or evil hour whichever you like. I will get to Salt Lake tomorrow morning instead of tonight. You don't know how lonesome & disconsolate I was when you left me yesterday. One would think I had never been accustomed to being alone. But my darling I am daily becoming so dependent upon you for comfort, pleasure & company that I hate to feel that you are not within a few moments walk… It is very chilly this morning and we have fire in the car. Take care of yourself my dearest one and be ready to meet me upon my return in good health. I will wire you when I get to Salt Lake as I know you are always anxious to hear of my whereabouts and howabouts… I would give much to be with you and hug you. Love to Mother & Frank. Your devoted husband, *Henry.*

October 6, 1888, Salt Lake.
My Darling Wife— I am in my room for a few moments and not having pen & ink here I am going to scribble you a line in pencil… I never had a more tedious trip than that of yesterday. The Engineers seemed bent upon lousy time and when we got into Salt Lake this morning we were 13 1/2 hours behind. I was however busy all day yesterday for I had a very important official brief to get up and I spent the entire day at it. My being busy did not however prevent my slipping in many loving thoughts of you my dear one. I am so lonesome when away from you and feel rather lost. As has been usually the case, I found things not ready out here and so instead of getting through today & starting home tomorrow I will now have to stay over until Monday night… I have the same room at the Cullen that we had when you were here with me and it is full of sweet pleasant memories. What a charming trip that was… Well, goodbye for I must go to work. I think of you all the time… Your devoted husband, *Henry.*

Oct. 7, 1888. Salt Lake City, Utah. The Cullen.
My Darling Wife— I received your telegram this morning and I can't tell you how glad I was to get it and to feel perfectly assured that last evening you were entirely well. I am getting, as I usually do, very impatient to get back to you and the time passes very slowly… On the train out I struck one of these obtrusive aggressive kind of fellows who push themselves on you whether you wish it or not. Rather oddly this fellow said he was sure he had seen my face before, and that he believed it was in Richmond Va. Doubtless he did. He claimed to be a New Yorker and put on a lot of style about it, and sneered at everything western. I thought to myself that if he were a New Yorker, he was an underbred common one who had seen little of the world. Lo and behold, when after getting here I found out from things that he said that he is nothing but a poor provincial half tar-heel and half-Virginian named Cole. His family is a very respectable and good one and on his native heath he is doubtless a very good well-behaved fellow but in his efforts to conceal his provincialism and to pass off as a New York swell he runs into vulgarity. This morning the Southern flavor came out strongly. He came into breakfast and bored me greatly with his talk about the South and its people, their superiority over everything, everybody etc. etc. I stood it pretty well until he got on the subject of women and was lying egregiously about the virtues of Southern women and classifying all Northern women by the vulgar low types he had met in New York, probably variety actresses etc. He finally asked me, "Did you ever

meet a Northern woman who could hold a light to our Southern *ladies*?" The deed was done and you would have laughed to see the way I turned on him and answered, "Yes Sir, I married a Northern *woman*, (emphasis on the woman), who stands so far above most of the southern *ladies*, in all that to my mind constitutes gentle womanhood, that I would not insult her by drawing comparisons, and I have never known any Southern *lady* to stand above her. She is a type of Northern gentility among the women of the North who are her friends and associates." That settled him and he immediately tried to switch off on Western women and attacked Chicago. I did not intend to let him go, so I "fetched him another flower," as a pugilist would say, by remarking that, "I had met as refined and cultivated people in Chicago, as I had ever met in the South, but that perhaps he had not met that class of people whilst there." Breakfast was then over and we parted. I don't know that I have anything more to write you unless I indulge in a few pages of love making, which I could do with the greatest ease. I don't know but that you would enjoy that more than anything else, you are such a sentimental, silly, darling if you are a *Yankee*. Give my best love to dear Mother and tell her the only thing I have against her is that she is a *Northern Woman* instead of being a sticky heeled Carolina lady. Goodbye darling my wife— Your devoted husband, *Henry*, "A Southern *Gentleman* by God Sir."

Catherine McKie Thayer and her daughter, Katherine, date unknown. Studio of C. L. Gillingham, No. 15 South Tejon Street, Colorado Springs.

◌ Letters from Catherine McKie Thayer:

November 8, 1888.
Came up from down street an hour ago and since then have been doing the last things in your old room. Have had matting taken up and trimmed. By the bulletin board… I conclude that Harrison is elected. I am grieved for any trial or disappointment that this may bring to Henry and on the other hand, I have really suffered over his hard never ending *pressure* of work, feeling that sooner or later it would tell upon him… Let us all try and believe that all will be for the best, and for his good and yours… God bless you my dear children. With tender love and kisses, *Mother* —Your dear letter this a.m. was a comfort.

December 2, 1888.
Your train just passed and I stood on chair on the porch to see the last of you… I try and remember that you are happy with your dear Henry, and I know he will take good care of you, and when I think of you both, dear children, my strongest desire and prayer is, that you shall daily, hourly, recognize God's love for you, and that your hearts may be filled with grateful love for all He hath blessed you with, up to the present hour. I would like to see you tomorrow, but I could not ask you to stay away from Henry & he could not stay, but you will know that your Mother's heart is just by yours, and that I am asking our Heavenly Father to guide you in *all* things, that you may do all your duty, above all, that He may help you to be His child, living very near Him, by prayer, leaning on Him always… these are the guides and safeguards and supports in life…

like to see you tomorrow "tomorrow" would be Katherine Hobson's 29th birthday.

Dear Mrs. Hobson, with her morning hour of reading and devotion by her lamplight, seeking strength to meet her trials, to do her duty, and asking all that is good and best for her dearest loved ones. I feel rebuked for my lack of outward devotional attention to all that is best. I think "our Father" knows

my heart and what it most craves— for us all— and for His dear children…
—*Mother*.

❦ Letters from Annie Jennings Wise Hobson:

Washington, December 5, 1888.
My dearest Son—   …I have made a perfect business arrangement with Cannon & Alice. I pay rent for my room whether there or not— so much board when there, and the privilege of using the parlor as my sitting room, I furnishing fuel. Thus I can always have a decent place to receive my friends who call. I do not propose to come any more in contact with Alice that I can avoid, nor do I intend to work myself to death for either. Cannon and I have a clear understanding and are more in accord than we have ever been, and it shall be my happiness and privilege to help him and influence his children, and their love is such to me, and they are all promising. I think that if you will let all the help you propose giving him come through me it will place me in a very different position with Alice… God Keep you both, Devotedly your Mother —*A. J. W. Hobson*.

Ashland, December 12, 1888.
My dearest Son—   Here in Mrs. Brown's dining room I am having the box nailed to send you containing the four decanters and the celery stand that matches them. I shall love to think that you and Katherine will use them… I spent yesterday straightening up my receipts etc. and last evening I looked over a box of letters— One of the first I placed my hands upon was from my precious Minnie— next there almost fell into lap a letter from Dr. Moore written soon after your Father's death, just before he went to Nashville— & right by it, was such a characteristic letter, written by dear old Dr. Plumer to Cannon just after your sister's death. Then next I took up the first letter from Father after my return to Eastwood the spring of '68 after my Beloved had departed, released from suffering to eternal bliss… Indeed they came to me not only as voices of love and friendship from the past, but as spirit voices from the dear ones in Paradise— tears, blessed tears flowed freely! This morning I feel lifted up, comforted and so thankful to God for the undeserved blessings of the past and present. Later I read letters written by you and Cannon that same spring. I shall send yours to Katherine to read, & some of mine too. I wish also to send your Grandfather's letter— so exactly like him. I wish Katherine to see that also. Then I picked up letters of mine written to Obie when I was only eleven and twelve years old, two or three when I was thirteen. Mrs. Brown to whom I read them was as much amused as I was… This day one year ago I left Ashland for Washington to meet Cannon en route for New York to attend your marriage. Ah! How long ago it seems now & how all lifes aspects have changed. I have such hearts ease about you and such sorrow for my dear Henry Garnett. It makes me thankful to hear of Katherine's good health…   Your devoted mother, *A.J.W.H.*

Amherst, December 28th, 1888.
Ever since Xmas day have I tried to write to you both dearest Katherine and my kind precious boy, but I had to get my room comfortable, as all my goods & chattels had arrived. I did not reach here until Saturday evening

between six and seven. Alice had left nearly all the little she had to do for Xmas to be accomplished Monday. Xmas day the children just demanded my whole time, and each day has seemed so incomplete because I could not express some of the thoughts & feelings going out to you both. Ah, the sad, dreadful news from Thom Page cast such a gloom over this Xmas, & I would have so loved to talk to you both about it! Yet I must first tell you how happy and delighted that box made these children & gave joy to all. When I returned I found the box safely deposited in Cannon's closet. It was not opened until Xmas eve when we put out all the toys & presents in the parlor. Several others had given me money for the children, part of which I expended for books and simple toys and nothing proved a duplicate of yours. Little Mary had to have one table all to herself so rich was she. The stockings here also hung in the parlor and for their stomach's sake, and in view of getting to Church, we did not let them go in the parlor until after breakfast. We had prayers and then took them in. Such delighted faces. The tables were piled up with toys and useful presents. They seemed to think that Aunt Katherine and Uncle Henry must have had a gold mine at command. Cannon had let them spend the money you sent Henry in their own way & for each other. I was gratified to see how judiciously they did it… Uncle Henry is like a fairy God-Father to them…

—Dec. 29th. I could not finish my letter yesterday— the inevitable interruptions came and I was too tired to hold a pen or think a thought yesterday evening… Poor Cannon Sr. has had a season of constant work. He had to eat his Xmas dinner hurriedly & go right to New Glasgow to hold another service. He came back Wednesday &, as Henry said, had to attend a Xmas festival for the Sunday School that evening, and after they all came home we sent off some fireworks, those I brought from Richmond were pretty and delighted the children… And now for myself I must speak. The photographs reached me Monday & I cannot tell you how I prize them Katherine… Cannon's present was having a grate fixed in my room. Mine to him was a delightful open Franklin stove for the study, which he so enjoys. Best of all, the dear letters from you both, here received the day before Xmas. I read each with streaming eyes & three times over. I folded them back in the envelopes. I sent my Heavenly Father a speech-less prayer— just turned to Him my heart & mind overflowing with gratitude for the love of my dear, devoted children… Since then my pleasure has been with the children & I have kept them happy & made them careful with their toys. Alice takes no more interest in their pleasures or gifts than if they were a hundred miles away. She misses so much in this life, poor little thing! My room now looks so cozy & comfortable. I will write & describe it to Katherine… I have scribbled this amidst every kind of distraction. God keep you both in all safety of soul & body.   —Your devoted mother, *A.J. W. Hobson*.   —I shall write to Thom Page today. I am so distressed for him & I know how Henry grieves.

 A letter from Catherine McKie Thayer:

December 20, 1888.
After reading dear Mrs. Hobson's letters this a.m., I concluded that my scrawls are the most empty as to expressions of interest and poor in form, that child can receive from parent…   —*Mother*.

> Three Christmas letters:

All of these Christmas letters are in the handwriting of Annie Jennings Wise Hobson.

Amherst, Dec. 29th, 1888.
My dear Uncle Henry & Aunt Katherine— Having recovered my temper, I will now write my letter. I thank you so much for your presents and money. We could not have had half so nice a time without your gifts. I bought a tool chest for myself and building blocks… You are certainly good to us. Mary is so delighted with her tea set. Papa bought Mary a baby carriage & a big doll in it & you ought to have seen how happy she was. I forgot to say that Henry & I have each a drum & George a gun… Grandma expects to have a nice time reading the books she received & playing games. She showed us all the beautiful pictures that came with the Xmas magazines & she is going to have some framed for the nursery… Uncle Henry kiss & hug Aunt Katherine for us and tell her we wish you would bring her to see us… I hope to write a letter soon all myself. Your loving nephew. *J. C. Hobson.*

Amherst, Dec. 29th, 1888.
Dear Uncle Henry & Aunt Katherine— We are learning to write but we cannot write well enough to write a letter, so Grandma will be our scribe. I have had such a happy Xmas and I thank you so much for all you sent me. Yours were the nicest presents we got. I did not spend all my money, Uncle Henry, but kept some for hard times. I bought a tool chest and a school bag, a [illegible] for Jennings and a rattle for the baby, a book for Mary & George and a little hatchet for Cannon. Grandma & Papa bought some fire works and we shot them off Wednesday night instead of Xmas night because Papa was away at New Glasgow, & I tell you they were fine… —Your loving nephew, *Henry W. Hobson.*

December 1888.
Dear Aunt Katherine & Uncle Henry— George & Mary want to write to you too. Grandma showed us how to build the pictures on the blocks last evening & it is the nicest game, & the books are so nice. Aunt Katherine we would love to hug you & kiss Uncle Henry for sending us all these things. Aunt Katherine, Mary thinks her tea set very "beauful." Uncle Henry, I [George] ought to be your boy 'cause I love my Grandma so. She says I am her sweetheart. We want to go to play now. Goodbye. Your loving niece & nephew, *George & Mary.*

1889

> A letter from Catherine McKie Thayer:

January 6, 1889.
This a.m. as we were at breakfast your letter of yesterday with inclosures, bearing special stamp was delv'd. Today we have the usual postal delivery because of changes being made at the Post Office. I so much enjoyed dear Mrs. Hobson's letter— one thing is certain, you and your dear Henry are ever in her prayers and the coming one is already consecrated— by prayer and hope and faith… —*Mother.*

∽ A grieving friend:

Richmond, January 7, 1889.
My Dearest Henry & Katherine— I can not attempt to write much, but I must tell you how grateful I am for all your kindness. Your letters have gone to my heart. The beautiful Christmas card book came the day before my Darling was taken sick, and she was so gratified. "We must send them a card," she said, expressing regret that we had not already done so for she was sincerely attached to you both, and you were constantly in our thoughts. The next afternoon she came home from her downtown preparation for a Christmas visit home, with a headache. We thought nothing of it as she was quite subject to them and after she retired was taken sick. I had no idea she was ill even when I sent for the Doctor next morning before day, or indeed when another physician was called in, and she sank to sleep like a little girl and had passed away before I realized her danger. A blood vessel had been ruptured and internal hemorrhage had been going on for eighteen hours. This is what the Doctors say, and I have no reason to suppose they are mistaken. I thank God that she did not suffer much, and that she had no terror. I have given you the particulars because I know you will want to be told them and perhaps you cannot otherwise learn them. It is harder than I ever dreamt it could be. I could not bear it but for the blessed hope that I shall meet her again. I know now that the soul is immortal, and I pray God to keep her and let her spirit be with me until He shall see fit to let me go to her which He will be merciful and let me do sometime— maybe before long. He knows how she loved me, and He knows how pure and good she was. I know well that she will intercede for me, and I intend with His help to try and live so that I may be with her hereafter. I was not as good to her as I ought to have been, but her pure and trusting heart never knew my shortcomings. I was all the world to her as she was to me, and her nature was so joyous that even with such a clod as I am, she lived in absolute content. No one knows but I how true and faithful she was to both God and man. Her last act on earth was one of divine charity in filling a poor old negro woman's apron with good things for Christmas, and I think that never was there a fitter preparation for the entrance into God's kingdom. I have come back and am trying to work. They tell me this will help me to "get over" it. I am not expecting this for I know that I can never get over the loss— the want— the hunger that consumes by heart, but it will at least be doing what I recognize to be my duty and what I know she wishes me to do if as I must and dimly believe she is given the power to know still that I love her. I cannot therefore go away at this time; but it is very sweet to me to feel that you two still think of me and have your home and your hearts open to me. Nothing could give me greater pleasure than your sympathy, and if I found it right to go away I should go to you, for I know that I should find love and sympathy with you, and you must not feel that your invitation is wasted because I do not accept it at this time. Someday maybe I will come for I feel my dears that I have a place in your hearts as you both have in mine and as you had in that of my Darling. Ever since I was a man, Henry has been as my twin brother, and his wife, even before I knew her, was my sister— after I came to know her, she was doubly dear to me. It may not be worth very much, but I pray the God who has my Beloved to keep you both safe, and to

Thomas Nelson Page, Henry Hobson's very close friend, was married to Anne Seddon Bruce on July 26, 1886. In this letter, to Henry and Kittie, Page describes Anne's death just before Christmas 1888. Her grave in the Hollywood Cemetery reads: "Here lies all that is mortal of an angel."

preserve you to each other through a long a happy life and then to bring us all to his home where she now waits for us. My dearest love goes with this letter to you both. Your devoted Brother, *Thomas Nelson Page.*

—Write to me when you have time. It will be a charity for which I will love you and God will bless you. I have not told you half of what your sweet letters have brought to me. God help me!

❧ A letter from Annie Jennings Wise Hobson:

Amherst, January 10th, 1889.
Each day of this week Katherine darling, have I thought to send you a long chatty letter… When I endeavor to work or write I realise fully the sad experience of the old woman who lived in a shoe, without the power of getting rid of the troublesome ones by putting them to bed. I do feel very sorry for poor Alice. She certainly endeavors to do better, and has taken a much more industrious turn for the new year… How do you think we have occupied all yesterday morning? —Unpacking a large box sent from All Saints Missionary Association, Worcester, Mass. You know how these boxes are sent out by the Missionary Association to country clergymen with large families and small salaries. They had written asking the names & measures of all the family. Each child had their presents beautifully put up, the white clothes all tied with ribbons and carefully labeled… It gives everyone such a good supply in clothes, and will make it easier for me to keep the children in clothes. Cannon especially needed the shirts as, except the two you sent, all of his are in a bad way… I have made my first pair of socks for the expected son, & a second is nearly done. Tell me how many small socks you have. I never make many very small ones. Next I wish to make him a silk & [illegible] cap. I thought of making him four night flannel skirts. I never used those kind you wrote about— because they are needed such a short time, & I never saw the especial good of them. I shall also send a large flannel shawl for his bathing shawl, as I always put a baby in flannel right from the bath— wrap them up while wiping the upper part of the body… I find myself constantly picturing your home. I think how sweet & clean that baby boy will be… Mary picked up one of the little socks I was making & asked who it was for. I said, "I expect God will send Uncle Henry a little baby & these will be for him." She was the most delighted creature, & just after Cannon came in she rushed & told him— "God is going to send Uncle Henry a baby & Grandma said so." In the most excited way he demanded "how I know— & whether Uncle Henry wanted a baby." I answered in general principles. He then rushed to Henry— "Oh, Henry, Grandma says God can send Uncle Henry a baby— & that he too may have a little girl soon." This last was his own interpretation of the sex, not mine. Is it prophetic, I pray.   —A.J.W.H.

Amherst, Va. Jan. 28th, 1889.
My dear Mother— [John Cannon Hobson to his mother]   As I expect to go six or seven miles in the morning to see a dying man, I write you a few lines tonight before going to bed. Your letter was received this evening & was very glad to get it; but am sorry to hear of your trouble with cold. Colds, however, seem to be all the fashion here. I thought I had gotten Cannon & Henry all

straight, & in fact they were almost well, but Cannon has come home from school today barking worse than ever, and I shall keep him at home until he gets better. George has been sick today, & I made Alice give him broken doses of calomel through the day & hope he will be better in the morning. I have kept him in bed all day. Jennings has a slight cold. He is as bright & bad as ever. I ask him where Grandma is, and he puts on a solemn air & wistful look, but will not say a word. The baby & Mary are quite well. I know you miss the children very much & they miss you. I see that Cannon & Henry clean their teeth & nails every morning & say their prayers to me. I have not been able to see about Ogden's bill yet, as, until today, we have had incessant rain & I have been afraid to venture out any more than I could possibly help. Today it has turned quite cold & I hope for a freeze. I had service here Sunday morning, but it was such a wretched day I did not attempt to go to New Glasgow or to have service here at night. I cannot tell whether I can go down to Richmond to see the S. S. Institute or not. If the children are well & I feel that I can leave them a few days and can make arrangements I want to make about services— I may go down. Otherwise I can not do so. Many thanks for your kind offer about expenses. If I decide to go, will accept the offer, only I will regard it as an advance.

I think the compound oxygen is doing me decided good. I regard my catarrh now as better than it has been for the last two years. Still I am right far yet from a cure, but hope the oxygen will work it out. Aunt Martha was here today to see me about cooking. I told her I could not afford to pay more than $4.00 a month. She then said that you were to give her $1.00 to help about the children. I told I knew nothing about it, but would write you & let you say for yourself, so that there could be no misunderstanding.

I see Doctor Minnegerode has at last resigned St. Paul's. Poor old man. I know it was a hard struggle with him to give up & lay down his harness. He has done a noble work for the Master. I want Alice to go over to Lynchburg Friday to have her teeth fixed— they have been aching right much lately & the sooner she has them fixed, the better. I hope with change of weather, your cold will break up & you will be able to go about in comfort & health.

The children are all in bed, but I know each one sends Grandma a good hug & kiss. Jennings sends two each. Love to all at Aunt Mary's & to Grandma & all there. Alice sends love. God bless you & be with you. With much love, Your affec. son, *John C. Hobson.*

❦ A letter from Annie Jennings Wise Hobson:

Mount Vernon, March 4, 1889.
Your Boy left me this morning for Amherst. As he could only stay one day there and one in Washington I did [not] see the least use in my letting him spend so much money for my travelling expenses… but he will write to you about Cannon & the necessity of his going West for change, rest & in God's mercy recuperation… I took the little cap I made in Washington to pieces & arranged it over again much more prettily & it is now ready to send to you… It has really grieved me that Henry had to leave you at this time, and I shall feel glad and relieved when I know he is back with you. What you write of your suffering with catarrh also distresses me, & I also feel for your Mother's

Your Boy This is a reference to Henry W. Hobson in this letter from Annie Jennings Wise Hobson to Katherine Thayer Hobson.

anxiety… I am glad you liked the little socks, & I see them on the darling little feet… Henry will reach Amherst this afternoon & he will write you all about it & his plans for Cannon. Dr. Thompson recommends a long rest & change of climate, especially wishing Cannon to avoid our changeable spring, & Henry hopes to induce him to go to Denver for a while where he can get Cannon a room near your house… We all think that Henry looks so well— as if he had been so cared for & loved. Tell your Mother I am very grateful for all her kindness to him. I am afraid she spoils him. This is a poor letter, dearest, but the best I could do today. No one knows I am writing, but I am sure all join me in love…   —Your loving Mamma— *A.J.W.H.*

Katherine Thayer Hobson, the eldest child of Henry Wise and Katherine Thayer Hobson, was born in Denver on April 11, 1889. Henry Hobson, when traveling in future years, frequently wrote home to his children, first to Katherine and in later years to the other three children. In 1900 a collection of these letters, entitled *Papa's Letters*, was privately printed by Charles Scribner's & Sons. The original letters are in the files which also contain a few other letters to the children that were not included in the book. The four children referred to in the letters are: Katherine "Sweetheart" (born 1889), Henry "Henny Penny" (born 1891), Eleanor "Piggy Blue" (born 1893), and Thayer "Little Man Child" (born 1897). The book is dedicated: "To 'Sweetheart', 'Henny Penny,' 'Piggy Blue' and 'Little Man Child' — In Memory of 'The One They Loved Best'." Upon receiving a copy of the book, Thomas Nelson Page wrote to Katherine Thayer Hobson from Egypt: "Only a few days before we reached Aswan coming up, the mail had brought me the little volume of Henry's letters and I had sat up on deck and read them alone and felt that it must all have been a dream and he must be living after all… I have not told you how tasteful I think the little volume is. I shall always keep it." All of the letters are reprinted here, interspersed with other family letters.

When Katherine was four days old:

Pueblo, Col., April 16th, 1889.
My Darling little Cupid-mouthed Daughter: Your Papa had hoped to go home to see you and your dear Mother to-day, but is afraid he cannot do so. He will, however, be home to-morrow.

I am just as well as I can be, except that I am awfully homesick and want to see you and your dearest Mother awfully. You must just put your arms around her neck and squeeze her until she grunts for me and give her a hundred kisses. If you grow up to be half as lovely and sweet as your Mother your Papa will just worship you.

Don't eat so much that the fat of your cheeks will cover up your two bright little eyes. Kiss dear Grandma for me and take a whole heart full of love for your own little darling self.   —Your Devoted Papa.

This is to be read to my little Daughter. She will understand every word of it, I know.   *H. W. H.*

◈ A letter from Annie Jennings Wise Hobson:

April 29th, 1889.
Your Father gives such accounts of your precocity, my darling little new Grand daughter that I have no doubt but that you can fully appreciate all I write, especially if interpreted by your sweet Mamma. That Easter cross was very lovely and especially precious because it was the only Easter greeting I had from Denver & I have always loved that poem… It is impossible for you to want to see me as much as I do you— how much I long to take you in my arms no one knows! Your Mamma must give you just one hundred kisses for me. Being my Granddaughter of course you appreciate poetry & will not refuse the offerings of my muse. God bless you my darling. According to your Father's account of your appetite you will appreciate my saying, *I must go to dinner.* —Your devoted Grandmother, *A.J.W.H.*

This letter is addressed to "Miss Hobson, Katherine Thayer Hobson, born, April 11, 1889, c/o H. W. Hobson."

◈ A letter from Catherine McKie Thayer:

…As to the Virginia Hobson family, I hope they will find comfortable economical quarters. I would hardly think that Henry would consent to that large family coming to Col.— where living is so much more expensive. Certainly he can draw the line on this subject. How can his Mother think of the family moving to Col. unless Cannon can aid very largely in their support. I suppose she hopes that Cannon may take a church in the fall. I hope he may but everything costs so here, and they would need so much help… Looking over your letter, I hardly think you will put the baby on a bottle and leave her. I think, as they say, that as little K— is so well it would be a mistake to make a change for a few days only… —*Mother.*

May 26, 1889, Denver.
My darling wife—   I felt awfully lonesome when I left you and our baby today and if I had followed my inclinations I would have thrown over going East and stayed with my loved ones. I always enjoy a trip with you so much and I have gotten so that I don't enjoy going anywhere without you. My thoughts will be constantly with you and baby and may a kind Providence protect and care for you… Write me all about baby every day and how she grows and improves in body and mind and about her little triumphs and the admiration of those who see her…   —Your devoted husband, *Henry.*

From May to June 1889, Henry Hobson was in New York on business.

◈ A letter from Annie Jennings Wise Hobson:

Amherst, June 25th, 1889.
I scribbled a scrawl to Katherine last evening and commenced a letter to you which I added to this morning… Yesterday was just one month since Cannon was injured and to my great relief & enjoyment he and I took a ride in a very comfortable buggy & good, safe well-gaited old gray horse, and a right good traveller he is too. Thanks to Henry Garnett's gift I felt I could afford to make a month's bargain for rides three times a month. We are to have the horse and buggy twice weekly & two horses once a week so that the children can go for five dollars for the four weeks. Folks are poor enough up here, money a scarce article and a little is well esteemed in these parts. When I told little Cannon

Katherine Thayer Hobson and her daughter, Katherine. Taken when Katherine was eight weeks old, June 1889, Gillingham, Colorado Springs.

your message about sending him something nice as a reward for being patient & brave, he said, "Well riding out would be the best thing as Dr. Thompson says I must not walk much for some time." Grandma thinks this too, & I need it as much as he does. Stooping over him so much & lifting has brought my ailment on severely & I feel incapacitated for walking. Indeed I am run down physically just in the way that means need of rest. Some pleasant drives out from this confined little house, where ears, eyes & nose are often sadly tried, where the whole soul is put out of harmony by the want of the rule of duty and law, will benefit me greatly. Cannon will soon be out of Dr. Thompson's hands as he expects to take the splints off in ten days. Dr. Thompson says that great care & watchfulness will be required for several months to keep him from running, jumping or being too much on his feet. He will therefore be my especial charge. My loving care over him has brought us very near to one another. It is very gratifying to me to think that my constant devotion night & day bringing around him that kind of motherhood his life so much lacks will ever be a pleasant dear memory to the child— aye to his latest years.

I trust I have sown some seed for time and eternity in heart & mind. He is a boy of brains & character, & if developed in the right direction will make a most attractive noble man. Yet there are characteristics which if not restrained— weeded out, will bring him & others to grief. Neither Cannon nor Alice know how to deal with him. I wish I could have charge of him 'till he is almost fifteen. He reminds me of you very in his long-headed ways and remarks.

I was talking to him about Grandpa Wise— told him of his three marriages about which he made many queries. After a long pause he gravely remarked— "Grandpa Wise was certainly unfortunate with his wives. It seems to me that as the last Grandma Wise lived so long with him and has lived so long since he died, it is a pity he did not marry her first." What think you of such deductions?

The morning of the day that the photographs of the dear little granddaughter came I woke from a vivid dream. I had been holding your baby girl in my arms, with fervent caresses & you were watching us. She was a star eyed little one, with the most peculiar way of opening her little mouth giving the impression of jolly good humor… I have kissed & kissed the little face, & Katherine's (so full of loving motherhood) & almost cried over all. It is a sweet picture of Mrs. Thayer, full of tender pride over the lovely big baby of eight weeks. You have reason my son to be proud of such a baby— & with the mother she has, she must ever be a blessing. I was so delighted to read in Katherine's letter how sensibly she was training her not to be troublesome. Ah, truly the thought of you & your happiness, & God's good gift to you of such a wife is a strong consolation amidst my present trials…   —Your loving Mother, *A.J.W. Hobson.*

July 22, 1889, Denver.
My Darling Wife—   I am back all well & safe and will go just as soon as possible to Central City. I am up to my eyes in work so can only send my love and kisses. I only find these bills sent to me my love. You had better attend to them. Just read the enclosed letter from Mother— Did you ever hear of such a crazy idea. Don't say anything about it. The money from Salt Lake property has come and you can tell your mother about it. You made $4,000 clear &

letter from Mother It is not possible to identify that letter from Annie Hobson, or it may be lost.

clear above all expenses interest etc. etc. You are getting to be too rich anyhow. I have not heard a word from you since I left but know you have written. I am hungry for a line from my darling wife & baby. Bless you dearest ones all. Love to Mother & Frank,   —Your devoted husband, *Henry W. Hobson.*

❧ A letter from Annie Jennings Wise Hobson:

Amherst, August 10th, 1889.
My dear Son—   You will be glad to know that we are all moved and most comfortably settled with Mrs. Taliaferro who is a sweet Christian lady, and has been exceedingly kind. I had a business talk with Mrs. Taliaferro. I knew that she had offered the rooms to Alice with various perquisites at a much lower rate than to anyone else because Cannon is a clergyman. It was just one of those arrangements to breed the familiarity of contempt. I found she could give me a large comfortable room & porch with the use of her old fashioned hall, equivalent to a room with a fire place… Alice is *beneath* my comprehension and is not even a good and reliable woman as I believed her to be. She has a cat nature in every way, and not even a cat's instinct of gratitude. Cannon is her God and she is as selfish for him as she is for herself. She is going to move Heaven & Earth to try to go to Colorado in the fall— and if she cannot accomplish this, he is to come & visit her this fall.

    Cannon is in a measure as unreasonable & selfishly inconsiderate as she is. In one sentence he writes he is too anxious to get to work to relieve you of your burdens etc. In the next he says, "Certainly I expect to come in the fall if you cannot come out here. My ticket— return ticket— is good as far as Chicago, from there I shall have to pay." That means you will have to pay, and it makes me so indignant that he should one minute consider taxing you in this way. I say most emphatically and with a protest of righteous indignation, that for the sake of these poor little children, in defense of unborn humanity, and in justice, to say nothing of gratitude to you & me, Cannon has no right to come on to his wife, and run the risk of another child in his state of health. A protest from you made with tack [*sic*] will do more good than from any one else. I think you can manage by getting Dr. Fisk to forbid it. When she does first go out it seems to me it would be far better only to take Mary & Alice & to leave the boys with me till they get settled & a little ahead— I have so arranged matters with Alice that there is no necessity of her having any servant except Annie, the white girl, as she puts all her washing out. I even pay for Cannon's washing… You say you do not see why I should stay here all the summer— In the first place, I have no money, in view of the dentist bill before me, to go to a watering place… In the second place, Cannon will for months require all the watchfulness I can give him. Dr. Thompson has forbidden any climbing and warns against over-exercise & Cannon is by no means as obedient as he might be. The trouble now is not to overtax the limb. There is more shortening than he at first thought and any weakness overtaxed in the limb will insure a halting gait… Eliza has returned from her visit to Williamsburg. I would love to have Mother here but there are reasons why I cannot. I do not know that she would come. She speaks of being very feeble. Sister does not write very cheerfully from the Baths & does not seem to find it comfortable. Mollie is ready to go to the mail. I have my own servant who cleans my room— comes every morning & evening, & altogether I am fixed according

John Cannon Hobson briefly went to Colorado in 1889 in search of a better climate for his illness, but neither his wife nor his children accompanied him on that trip.

to my mind… —Your devoted Mother, *A.J.W.H.*   —Please destroy this as soon as read— *do not leave it around in your office.*

༄ A trip to Europe:

August 15, 1889. U. P. train.
My darling wife—   My mind has hardly been without a thought of you and our darling baby for 5 minutes at a time since I left you. I did feel so sorry for you as I told you good by and saw how hard you were struggling to keep up and not cry. I never in my life started off on a trip with so much inclination to stay for it is hard for me to leave you and baby… I love you more and more every day… At breakfast I got something into my eye which I cannot get out and it has been worrying me all day— disabling me from using my eyes to any extent. I will have 3 hours in Omaha and I am going to an occulist and have the trouble removed… Well I cannot write anymore for my eyes hurt me. Give my dearest love to Mother Thayer and a big hug and many kisses and as for you & baby darling, you have my ever present thoughts and tender love. Lovingly, *Henry.*

August 16, 1889, St. Paul, Minnesota.
My darling wife—   I write a line to let you know I am all right… I went to see a Doctor about my eye. He examined it carefully with a microscope & said that there was a cut on the under side of the upper lid made by some sharp edged matter getting under the lid. There was however nothing there & he gave me a wash which I have used, and this morning the eye is almost well. Well I must close as I have to meet some gentleman… I go to Chicago tonight. Goodbye with a world of love. Devotedly your husband, *Henry.*

Colorado Springs, August 17th, 1889.
My Darling Husband—   Will write you a line in care steamer, so you may hear from us after you sail. You could not be going & leaving us better. Katherine has slept under the trees for three hours & is blooming as a rose— her cheeks so pink & "eyes of the sky" as you say. I am feeling very well. Your telegram from Chicago has arrived & to know you are well today is a joy… Katherine sends you, with her Mother, all the love possible & many kisses. Next time you go you will have to take us with you… Now sweetheart, enjoy yourself every hour, don't over-tire yourself & think of me as happy & full of delight in your opportunities. God bless & keep you my love. I love you so dearly & long to feel your dear arms about me. Your own Loving Devoted Wife, *Katherine.*

Aug 19, 1889, New York.
My Darling Wife—   I got in last evening at 7:30 and got a room at the Southern Society for the night though today I move over to the University Club. After washing up a little I went up to Uncle John's, thinking he might be in town… They all asked most affectionately after you and the baby and expressed a great desire to see you. Aunt Néné was as funny as ever. She said she almost threw Grandma into a swoon when that little picture of you and the baby came. She says Grandma came up & presenting the picture said, "Who do you think that is?" "Well," said Mrs. Mayo, "it looks something like

Katherine but from the picture I should think it was one of your darky friends and her baby." She said Grandma went off in great indignation… You are always with me darling and with you is your beautiful baby…   —Lovingly your husband, *Henry.*

Colorado Springs, August 20th, 1889.
My Darling Husband—   Yesterday I received your two letters, one from St. Paul the other from Chicago, both so welcome. Then your telegram from New York… She (the baby) is asleep in her carriage out of doors— so fair & lovely. She kicks *furiously* in her bath now, rests a half minute & begins again. Everyone admires her & says "What a beautiful child." …I am splendidly well & Katherine could not be better. Tomorrow you sail— I told the Baby this morning, "Papa is going away," & funny to say she then cried out, but I comforted her, told her, "Papa will soon be coming back," & she was soon smiling… I told Cannon I would keep him posted about you & he said you would not have time to write him. I will also write your Mother frequently & send K's photographs, as soon as I receive them, to all you mentioned. I shall think of you continually & wish I could enjoy everything with you but I know it is best for us to be here… Even should Mother fail to go East I think I will have to go— though she has not said a word to indicate failure. Dr. Reed came to make a social call, said the Baby looked wonderfully well, he let her stand on her feet "to try her strength" he said. I can't believe that if all goes well you will read this scribble in England. Doctor said the Jackson baby has a regular *Banker's grip,* never opens hand always tight shut. I miss you darling more than I can tell & still am glad, glad, glad you are able to go… And now I will stop writing until Friday & take our heart's love & every tender loving wish, from your devoted wife, *Katherine.*

August 21, 1889, University Club, Madison Square.
My darling wife—   Just before starting for the steamer I must send you a line. I will also write a few lines to send by pilot… Good bye darling ones all… I shall look forward to our reunion as the pleasantest happiest result of my trip. Blessings be yours. Devotedly your husband, *Henry.*

August 21, 1889. Steamer *City.*
My darling wife— Just a line to say I am off and am thinking of you all. The steamer is not very full— passengers rather scant… Your letter just recd as I got on boat and your telegram this morning. Now darling I am not going to write any more for two reasons— one that I want to see the harbor, the other that if I write more I will get into a vein of blues… Again goodbye to you all with dearest love. Yr. Devoted husband, *Henry.*

Colorado Springs, August 23rd, 1889.
My Darling Husband—   This morning your letter from New York came, of last Monday, after lunch, and it was so welcome. I felt quite jealous of William as he had a lette*r yesterday* from New York. John Birge telegraphed that you sailed & were in good spirits. I will be so thankful when I hear of your safe arrival on the other side & know you are safely over the sea Darling. You don't know what a comfort your letters are to me. After this week I shall expect a weekly one, but not oftener for I know how hard it is to write when

In the late summer of 1889 Henry Wise Hobson made a trip to Europe while his wife and new daughter remained in Colorado Springs with Catherine McKie Thayer.

travelling & that will satisfy me... I did not make this sacrifice of separation to have you attend to other peoples affairs. You have been working for others *all* your life & this is *your* outing & remember it Darling one. I want you to think of yourself *first* every time. Now sweetheart I have had my say & you must not think me selfish & unkind, but I know these people better than you do & there is always something asked for, twenty times a day... This morning spent an hour at Dentist's having my teeth nicely cleaned and one little filling put in... My heart's best love & kisses Darling one. Your own loving wife *Katherine.*

Colorado Springs, August 1889.
My Darling Husband—   Your precious letter from the Club, written just before starting for the steamer, was received since my last letter to you. It is such a comfort to me to feel that your life now has more peace and content in it than before we were married. If I have brought joy & content to you Dearest, you know you have made my life full & rich [torn page] ...This darling Baby girl of ours is in her carriage near me. She is as well as she possibly can be & this morning early gave me a message for Papa. It is, "Tell my Darling Papa that one of my chief delights now is to tear up paper and Mamma gives me envelopes. Well won't you write me two letters while you are away— one from London & one from Paris. Mamma will let me tear up the envelopes [torn page]" ...How I wish you could see her this minute in her carriage by me, her little hands moving about and she *squealing*, that is her latest accomplishment. Her cheeks are rosy, her hair in little rings, and certainly she is as lovely a Baby as one could possibly see. She has her rubber rattle in her hand, biting the ring... I wrote your Mother a long letter & also to Cannon. And as soon as the photographs come from Beebe's I will send them to all I think you would wish them sent to... Mother and I talk of you constantly, and today I trust you are nearing land & that I will hear tomorrow of your safe arrival & maybe have a cable on Thursday or Friday... You have no idea how I delight in thinking the day coming will bring all you have read of England & its history into a reality & it makes reading so much more interesting— after ones *eyes* have seen & not be relying on *others* who have seen. Remember & try to see the effigies in Westminster... [end of letter].

Colorado Springs, August 30th, 1889.
My Darling Husband—   Two great causes for happiness regarding you are mine— first the telegram announcing safe arrival of the steamer at Queenstown, reached me Tuesday afternoon about five o'clock— then yesterday, Thursday, the cable "Echo, Bank Lakes" —I can see your smile... you are going into that charming Lake Country— how I loved it... & then I fancy you will continue to Scotland— this is my plan for you. Just four years ago I was there. Well my Darling one, I am very happy to know you are safe & well. It was in my mind constantly & I said over & over to Katherine, "Your Papa is well & gone to the Lakes." She is as well as can be & so pretty & sweet... I write Cannon & your Mother of your arrival... Heard from your Mother this morning. She is evidently delighted with her quarters. Alice must try her fearfully. Says Cannon writes he is going East in November & Alice tells everyone so. I am sure you will be firm & hold your ground on this point but time enough when you come back. Cannon writes me he liked his quar-

ters exceedingly at the club & that he was a great deal happier to be where he could attend the services at the cathedral— so you see your family are all happy & content. You know Darling I think of you all the time. Every thought seems to have *Henry* in it & that I love you with my whole heart my dearest one. What would I not give to have you with me for a little while, not that I would take you from your trip either. No one knows how delighted I am to have you off for an outing & only your precious self to think of. I do not plan or talk much of my trip East. We are so well and it is some time before the proposed start. The only pleasure, free from fatigue, that I see in going is meeting you Darling— visiting & nursing a baby is certainly very tiring and distressing to Mother & child. Well we will see. Now I will stop & get ready for our drive. Katherine is the picture of health & beauty as Thompson walks up & down the piazza with her. Mother joins in much love & *a kiss too* she says. My heart's love & kisses to you Darling. Every good wish. God bless you ever is my prayer, many times in the day & night. Your own devoted & loving wife, *Katherine.*

Sept. 2, 1889, Tavistock Hotel, London.
My darling Wife—   I cabled this morning my arrival in London and now I write a line. I got here last night from Liverpool… Tell my darling little daughter I think of her all the time— aye every hour frequently… Goodbye my life. Love to all at home. Yr. Devoted husband, *Henry.*

Colorado Springs, September 3rd, 1889
My Darling Husband—   The many days that must elapse before hearing from you by letter are made happy by hearing by cable. Yesterday, Monday "Boot-Echo" reached me. Indeed it is a joy to know just where you are & how. And Darling I thank you from my heart. You are always so considerate on my account. Your Baby girl is in her carriage by me, her hands & feet flying *faster* than ever. She is as well as can be and each day does some new sweet thing, puts out her hands to come to me & today as she lay on the bed she made a sound so like "Papa" that I was startled. "Bapa, Bapa Bapa" for I was thinking of you & she looked up in my face & repeated the sounds again & again. Mrs. Thompson sings to her "Papa's coming pretty soon, pretty soon" and I sing to her when she goes to sleep that she is "Papa's little lamb." …Next week at five months old I will have her weighed. It is so aggravating Beebe's photos have not been sent us, have written him twice & today a postal saying "the photographs will be sent you in a few days." Mother so anxious to see them, will pay for them *all*. She is well & sends you her best love & a kiss. Says she thinks of you as her own dear son. Two or three nights ago as I was tucking the blanket around Katherine, after nursing her, & happened to tuck it with my finger ends next to her side & in her sleep she gurgled out a *ticklish* laugh just in your sensitive place, when you say, "Now Katherine don't you touch me," & I say, "I promise." It was so funny & made me laugh. Now she is holding her rubber rattle and biting the ring… I wrote your Mother a long letter & told her of hearing you were in London & well. She writes very cheerfully & Cannon also. Your Mother wrote that Cannon wrote Alice he was surely going home in November, but that won't be possible as it is the very worst season of the year. Dr. Fisk will settle that for you… The weather is perfect & we are out the whole day. Katherine's color is lovely & everyone says she is the "picture of

health." …Take my heart's best love & kisses my Darling Precious Henry & be sure & take the best care of yourself. Your own devoted & loving *Katherine.*

Sept. 5, 1889. Tavistock Hotel, London.
My own darling wife—   I am going to write you a line this morning before I go out for this afternoon I am going down with your Uncle William to Ascot. I wrote you he came for me at 11 on Monday & we went to the City together where I got some letters from you and which entirely delighted me. I read them eagerly & slyly kissed the place where my darling baby had put her little mouth. Whilst I was standing there… reading my letter, someone came behind me… It was Tom Page, and with him were Rosewell, his brother, & Bob Hanson of N. Y. (Bald Bob). Could I have had better luck? Well at 4 o'clk I went to their lodging and was with Tom most of the time until he went to the Isle of Wight… He will be back by Monday & promises to devote next week to me & to showing me London… I am not going to try to explain what I have seen & done in London for I have done & seen a great deal & it would take me too long… Tell Mother Thayer I thank her more every day for this charming trip. God bless you all. Your devoted husband, *Henry.*

Colorado Springs. September 6th, 1889.
My Darling Husband—   The days pass & another Friday comes, and my day to write to you. Now I am counting the hours until next week for then I look forward to receiving your first letter from Queenstown. Katherine is by me, sleeping peacefully in her carriage. She is rosy & so well… Every morning I look for the photos & still they do not come…it seems absurd to wait a full month to get 3 dozen photographs, but they shall go to you the hour they arrive here. Katherine says, "Ask Papa to bring me two white Shetland veils… I want the real Shetland wool, so soft." My darling, you don't half know how happy & content I am with my sweet little one near me & the assurance that you are well. And I do so hope the visit & sea voyage will be of great benefit to you. I think & wonder about you so much of the time… Have had sweet letters from the Jermains. Mr. J— celebrated his 80th birthday last week. He is a little stronger… My heart full of love, Darling precious & many kisses. Your own loving devoted *Katherine.*

Colorado Springs, September 10th, 1889.
My Precious Darling Henry—   This has been a rich full day to me. Your letter from Queenstown, such a treasure it is. I shall read it over & over & Katherine nursed while I read it aloud to her. Darling it seemed to bring you so near & I felt almost as if you were nearby. I could almost hear the tone of your dear voice… All you told me of the Steamer, the passengers, the crew, was of interest & told so delightfully. I was overjoyed to know you were hungry & slept well & no sea sickness. Indeed I have everything to be thankful for. I was so glad to hear you say the Beautiful, beautiful ocean, for I feel just so about it. But when I look into our child's eyes & see her beautiful smiling face I have no regrets, and am so happy here, caring for her instead of a trip abroad. I am enjoying and thanking God for the privilege of staying home to care for *our* "Baby child" as you call her. Sometime we will be taking a trip together & planning & enjoying everything side by side, and the enjoyment will be all the more after having a trial trip, as this has been. Every day sweet-

heart I love you more & no one could be prouder or more happy with their Husband's love than I. Katherine is very well, indeed no child could be better & she is shown Papa's picture more than once daily & don't think she will be strange with you Darling. I always say "Papa" the first thing in the morning and kiss her for you many times a day & the last thing at night— & say "God bless Papa" …It is very warm indeed in the East, I should hate being there now. Have no definite plans yet, but will write you as soon as we are able to plan with any certainty. Certainly this is the best place for Katherine now… Mother sends her tender love & a kiss to her "dear son." …Stay just as long as you possibly can, for every hour will do you good. I have cried bitterly & many times over your tired weary self, working so hard for everyone & so bravely. Think of me as entirely happy in your pleasuring— delighted in the rest it must be to you. With more love & kisses from *Katherine*, your own devoted wife.

London, September 11th, 1889.
My Darling little Daughter with "Eyes of the Sky":   Your Papa is going to write you a letter, though you cannot now read it. But your sweet Mother will read it for you, at this time, and will keep it for you, so that in the future you can see how your Papa loved and thought of you in this far-away country. I think of you and Mamma all the time, and everything I see I say to myself, "My two darlings, the two Katherines, will see this with me some day." All over England, my little one, I have looked at the beautiful rosy children, so healthy and merry, and full of life, and I would think "My little Katherine is going to be just like these, for her Mother will bring her up sensibly and well." But, my precious, you don't know, and can never know, perhaps, how my heart longs for you when I see the other people I meet with their children.

   To-day, Mr. Rosewell Page, who is a friend of your Papa and will be a friend of yours, and I went out in the morning to Hampton Court. The sun was shining beautifully all day and we did so enjoy the old Court and grounds. Your Papa saw pictures of beautiful little boys and girls in the Art Rooms, and felt like going up and kissing them all for the sake of his little girl,

Thames Embankment, postcard from London.

only if I had done so, the big policemen, in scarlet coats with yellow gilt bands around their hats, would have put me in jail.

And what do you think I got for you? Well, I went out under the great big chestnut trees that have been growing hundreds of years, and under which you are going to play some day, and I picked up a lot of beautiful chestnuts, and all for you, and Mamma.

And what else do you think I did? Why, I walked right into the midst of about thirty or forty beautiful deer, with spotted skins, and big branching antlers, and some of them came up and licked my hands. Just think of that! And won't you love to pat the heads of the beautiful deer when you see them?

After staying around Hampton Palace as long as I could, but not seeing half enough of it, for it is a famous old place, we walked through the beautiful "Bushy Park" and to Teddington, a little town on the river, and there we got an old waterman who rowed us down the river to Richmond. My, My! Little Daughter, what a beautiful place Richmond is, and how I did want to take you in my arms and roll right down the soft green banks.

I am going to tell you all about these places when you are big enough and I am going to teach you their histories, and all about the things that make them very dear to all English people and those of English blood.

I wanted to stay to dinner at the Star and Garter Inn, but Mr. Page wished to come home, and so we took a little steamboat and came down the beautiful Thames River. Tell your Mamma that I am laying out plans every hour for *our* trip, that is, *you*, first of all, because you have never seen these things, and then Grandma, Mamma, and me.

I reckon your Mamma will think when she reads this letter that it is not the kind of a letter to send such a little girl, but you just tell her that Papa is writing this letter to last a long time, and so you can read it when you are a big girl. I say tell Mamma lots of things because I just know you are clever enough to understand lots of things, and though you can't talk quite as well as some folks, yet your dearest Mamma understands everything you say, for you whisper right into her heart, and it understands when the head cannot.

And now I am going to say good-night, for I am tired. I hope to hear from Mamma to-morrow, and I write to you tonight because I will be busy all day and will not have time.

Put your fat darling little arms around your Grandma's neck, and around your Mamma's neck, and hug them hard for Papa, and tell them how I love them; and also tell them that you are the very idol of your Papa's heart, and one of his chief joys in life.

Keep well, my little one, for your Papa's happiness is much wrapped up in you.   Your devoted Papa, *Henry W. Hobson.*

505 North Cascade Ave., Colorado Springs, September 13th, 1889.
My Darling Husband—   I read your two letters over & over and think of you so constantly. Especially do I long for you to see our Darling Baby. She is so attractive & cunning in her short dresses & looks much older. Every day she does some new thing… How I shall love to hear you talk about your trip, and how much you will have to tell me & I shall live it all with you. [torn page] …No pictures yet from Denver… hope those will come soon from Beebe's. Take my heart's love & kisses from Your own loving wife, *Katherine.*

1889 — [on the European trip]
My darling wife—   Just a line to you with the enclosed to my little daughter. I am very well and very busy... How I miss you darling mine and long for you. Today I received a letter (forwarded) notifying me that my resignation as Special Attorney would go into effect on Sept. 30th. I am rather glad for the office was one of grave responsibilities. I had made a good reputation and I think my successor will fail for there are some tough cases unfinished. Still the loss of the salary is something. But I don't worry over such matters...
—Devotedly, *Henry W. Hobson.*

Paris, September 18th, 1889.
My own Darling little Daughter: The last time Papa wrote to you he was in London, and now he is going to write you a French letter—that is, from Paris, for I would make but a poor show if I attempted to write in French.

Just as soon as you are old enough Papa is going to see that you are taught French, and by that time he will be able to speak it also.

All this week I have been spending in shopping and seeing the Exposition;—and, oh! what a beautiful, bright city Paris is, for by day it is all in a whirl, and between the bright-looking people, and the pretty stores, and the sunshine, I think it the prettiest city I know of. And at night, little Daughter! Why, at night, the beautiful lights of all kinds sparkle and shine in the streets and stores, and if you were here you would have to wink and blink your dear little blue eyes because of the lights.

I wish you could understand and enjoy toys and doll babies, for I have seen more of them, and they are the most beautiful I ever saw in my life. At the Exposition there is case after case of the most lovely dollies, dressed in the richest way and according to the latest fashion. I spent several hours in the dolls' department, looking at them. And then, too, there are all kinds of toys, and some of them are so pretty that I am sure a little wee girl like you are now would enjoy them.

Yesterday Papa went up on the highest tower in the world and it took him three hours, and was very tiresome. Going up is all humbug, and you can't see much after you get up there on account of the smoke and fog.

highest tower in the world
The Eiffel Tower, 984 feet tall, was opened at the Paris Exposition in 1889.

Paris – L'Eglise Notre Dame de Paris, *postcard from Paris.*

Henry Wise Hobson and daughter, Katherine. Photograph by Beebe, Denver.

You must be a very good little girl and not cry or worry Mamma, or Grandma, and then Papa will love you more than he can tell. I got all the sweet cooing messages you have sent, and also the little flowers you kissed with your darling lips. They are very dear to your Papa, for you are the idol of his heart.

I am not going to write any more now, for I must go off. Hug and kiss both Mamma and Grandma for me. Your devoted Papa, *Henry W. Hobson.*

Colorado Springs, September 17th, 1889.
My Darling Husband— Another precious letter from you— it came Sunday from London, dated the 2nd. It has comforted me very much to hear of your wanderings. I laughed again & again over your first walk in London & I think you will soon be "*on you feet*" as you say. How delighted I will be to hear you tell of it on your return my Dearest one. Katherine is sitting up in her carriage, as I write, & looking all about… I wrote Beebe a note requesting him to send the photographs at once & hope they will come. There is no excuse for such behavior— and if I did not care so *much* for those pictures of Katherine I would refuse to accept or pay for any of them… The more I think of it the more impossible a trip East seems. First it would have to be made without you. Second my chief pleasure in going would be to meet you & after meeting you I know we would be hurried & tired by two days in NY & then the trip out. There are none but tiresome pleasures connected with visiting of a Mother & nursing baby & it's too much to undertake, too much of a risk in your absence Darling… Now I have calculated the expense & find to take a nurse & stay at a hotel in N.Y. & Richmond, that it would not be less than $450— & that will go a great way towards some of the necessary expenses & I don't feel justified (as I should if either Katherine or I needed the change) in spending that amount of money. I would much rather, and shall stay here, as long as I can, then go to my beautiful little home & get it in order, then be ready to greet you my Precious one & how entirely happy I will be. At this distance I am sure you will think me the better judge. [torn page] …My tender love & many kisses, *your devoted wife.*

Colorado Springs, September 20th, 1889.
My Darling Husband— Your second letter from London was received this week— telling of your meeting with Uncle William & the Pages & Mrs. Harrison. It delighted me to hear all about your shopping & the "buses" & the thought that you have been free from your work these few weeks has been such a joy & comfort. I knew it would be exactly what you needed & that each day would be a delight. You are one of the happy individuals who see everything & I am *so so* glad you have been in England… I get very lonely & feel of longing, but of course I would for I love you with my whole heart but I am able to keep my mind dwelling on the bright side, with this Darling child to cheer me & most loving Mother. Of course you will be disappointed not to have me meet you, but *all* considered I do feel I am doing quite right in staying here— and still I am disappointed too… I hear good accounts from Alice of family. Your Mother writes me often. Cannon thinks himself wonderfully better & Dr. Fisk wrote me "Cannon is doing well." So you have everything to comfort you regarding the health & well being of your large family. I will go back to Denver in time to get all in perfect order

before you come & hope Mother will be with me when you arrive. It will be such a pleasure to her… It is almost two years since you were in White Creek. I shall live it all over sweetheart & my happiness has increased every hour since. You are my idol & you know it. Katherine sends her dearest love to her Darling Papa— and you should see her look at your picture & smile & put her lips on it to kiss, mouth *wide open*. Now I must stop & assist Mother for a little while… You are in my heart constantly & thoughts are full of you. With hearts tenderest love & kisses to you my Darling. Your devoted & loving wife, *Katherine*.

∾ A letter from Annie Jennings Wise Hobson:

Amherst, September 7th, 1889.
[to Katherine Hobson in Denver]

Your letter telling of the cable dispatch was received this afternoon, dearest Katherine… I wish to have a full, free yet confidential talk with you about Alice. Let me first say that I meant not the least allusion to her pecuniary affairs. She boasts of her wonderful management in that, & I believe conscientiously tries to be economical & saving as far as she can in her own selfish way. I know she has paid some small back debts of Cannon's, and she ought to have done so. She has had no house rent to pay, no milk to buy, except for the little baby & tea as a friend gives it to her. She has been buying butter at 12 1/2 & fifteen cents a pound & all provisions are in a like proportion as to price. The white girl who nurses for her was bound to Cannon 'till twenty-one, he agreeing to give her only food and clothes, and she has not given her one cents worth since the first of January, making it as an excuse that her mother sends her clothes & money. She has not had one cent to spend for the children's clothes on her own. Here I have made her house rent and expense for cooking and fuel a *nominal* sum— $6.00 per month for both & I bear all expense for little Cannon. Her income from her sister's board & what I have paid with what Henry sent has been between eighty and ninety dollars monthly for nearly three months, and that sum here is equivalent to three hundred in Denver. I give her full credit for an earnest endeavor and desire to avoid debt and make her money hold out, though she has spoken of her allowance in very contemptuous terms.

Now dearest, I wish to write you feeling that God knows every word I shall tell— You know the circumstance of Alice's marriage. I have always thought that Cannon was far more to blame than she was. In all that I have ever done for her, in all my intercourse, I have had but one desire and that was to do her the greatest kindness and to make her see life in its true aspects of duty and unselfishness.

Perhaps someone of quieter manner and with more diplomacy might have availed more with her. Yet I may well say "perhaps" for you see what a gentle man Cannon is, and he could not prevail upon her to be otherwise than slovenly, careless, and indolent. I have seen her show him as much temper as anyone else. He has said to me when I have spoken about most deplorable neglect— "Mother I have to submit to what I cannot have corrected or live in a perpetual row." I think though that he has been weak in not being more firm & persistent in insisting upon reforms really necessary to health and common decency.

Sept. 13th— It is hard to realise that so many days have past since I commenced my letter to you, Dearest. Between the children and the household my time is not my own… To continue and end about poor Alice, I wish you to understand that in saying you would be more indignant than if you knew all, I meant that if you could witness her disrespectful, unlady-like conduct to me, her utter want of appreciation of my efforts for the good of herself and children, you would be indignant that Henry's mother could be treated in the way she does. You would scarcely credit the statement I could make of the utter carelessness and neglect of duty I *have* to speak about for health & decency's sake. From her servants I have to submit to humiliating insolence if I attempt to do my duty by the children. Let me give you an illustration. Last week I found her after dinner seated in the front porch with the baby so wet that she stained the porch when she sat and with a greasy bone in her hand. She was on the floor & would soon have been pelting the planks with the bone. Jennings ran in from the nursery with a piece of sweet potato he was eating. I took him by the hand & said: "Come darling, you must not eat your potato here & drop it about." —and then to Alice I said, "Alice it is not right for you to have this dirt made at the front door and by Mrs. Taliaferro's parlor unless you have it cleaned. I have the right to speak because I have to clean this part of the house. For four afternoons have I had to call my servant to sweep & wipe up the trash & mud left by the children, & as you have two long porches of your own, I think you might be more considerate." She sprang up in a rage, and I would not have had you witness the scene she made. I do not think you would have wished to speak to her again. Her common method is to sneer at my Christianity. I said— "Alice I cannot imagine what there is to excite this vituperation and disrespect." —"No Madam of course not! You persecute me on all occasions & then you are a Saint ready to ascend to Heaven."

Imagine how I feel when at eight o'clock I see little Jennings handed over to an untidy untrained negro girl to be given his breakfast while the Mother is not up. Last week, when the white girl (who does nothing but clean the nursery & give attention to the baby as she chooses & to Jennings— who is waited on by the little darkey as if she was the Mother) was sick, little Alice was handed over to this little darkey to be washed & dressed. The little darkey is up every morning betimes & does more work than Alice & the nurse put together all day. When I go to my breakfast at half past seven, Annie Mason is just getting out of her bed, and Alice is about turning over. The little darkey constantly gives the children their breakfast. The contrast between Mrs. Gray's sweet clean baby & little Alice was very great. Alice constantly smells so sour and neglected that I cannot kiss her & now she is so handed over to the darkey nurse that *l'odeur d'Afrique* adds to the other bad odors. Oh Katherine I cannot tell you what a Cross it is to me.

Since writing to you, a friend gave me a clue by which I found out everything about the proposed trip to Colorado to be taken this fall at the expense of a friend. I went to see Mrs. Allen, a good kind-hearted woman literally from the plainest class, whose husband had made some money shop-keeping in this little village. I told her plainly, with courteous thanks for her kind intentions, but that I scarcely thought she understood the true condition of affairs. I told her that I understood that she had proposed making an effort to take up a subscription to raise a sum to send Alice to Colorado this fall. She explained the whole circumstances.

Alice goes around so lamenting her separation from her husband and telling of his homesickness & depression of spirits from missing her & represents that only poverty keeps them apart. Mrs. Allen asked how much it would take to pay her expenses to Colorado. Alice said fifty dollars would be enough to take her & two children to Denver. Mrs. Allen proposed raising the fifty dollars amongst her friends, & some others of Alice's spoke of adding to it. Yet Alice told me that a friend from affection for Cannon, and one to whom she preferred to be under obligation than Henry, was going to give her the means to go to Denver and to help pay her board for a year, stating that she presumed the amount would be about $300. I asked Mrs. Allen if she was aware that Cannon's brother gave them an income quite as good as any Church Cannon could expect to get would pay, and much more than the majority of people in Amherst had. She was not. I told her about Henry's nobility, and assured her that whenever the Doctor thought it was for Cannon's welfare that his wife should go, she need not be on charity for her travelling expenses. Alice speaks to people of "private means of their own," but if she has ever given Henry credit to this for his full generosity, I've never heard of it. I told Mrs. Allen that I had written to Dr. Fisk asking his opinion of Alice's proposed plan, and that when the reply came I would tell her what the Doctor said. Mrs. Allen thanked me for making her understand the true state of things with Alice, and agreed with me that good sense dictates that Alice should submit to the Doctor's and Henry's wishes.

The very next day Mrs. More, the wife of the Methodist minister, a good natured, well-meaning but very long-tongued woman, was here, & with all the Taliaferros around in reply to an inquiry whether Cannon would come to Virginia this fall, she (Alice) said, "No, he cannot come. I want to go to him; a friend would the means for me to get there, but the question is who would support me after I reached there." She seemed oblivious of her statement about the $300 & was trying to provoke me to say something. I seemed not to hear her, but I requested my friend Mrs. Taliaferro to explain the true state of the case to Mrs. More.

Katherine— does anyone suppose that I am so above human nature that I am not tempted to query why I, who have given up my life so devotedly to my only two sons, am cut off from them. I would give more than I can express to be able to nurse and look after my poor sick son. It grieves me to think that he has to be alone without someone to nurse him— but it is all God's appointment for the many mercies connected with the trial if I did not cheerfully and submissively say "*Thy will be done*" and trust Him for the result. It never seems to occur to Alice that there is any trial or sacrifice except for herself. She *despises* me and her feeling towards Henry is far more rankling offended pride because she has to be dependent on him than gratitude.

Yet I do not attempt to judge such as she does. I leave that to God. She is an undeveloped child in character and conceit is her disease & selfish egotism her bane. She has some good qualities, —who hasn't, but all are brought out for herself and her husband.

Now what object have I in telling this to you? Because the time may come when an utterly different story may be told to you, I wish you to know the truth. This is only for you. I would not have Henry & Cannon to know the whole truth— especially Cannon.

She is so much the creature of impulse & passion that I do not think she realises what she does, & no one can talk more plausibly or put herself up more in a martyr light.

In a certain way she tries to do what she conceives to be her duty, but a narrower vision of duty never was.

Sometimes I feel as if the strain is more than I can bear, & feel as if my heart would break for a little loving sympathy— but the children's love consoles me in human need & God gives me needed strength. Please read & burn this & do not tell Henry one word to trouble him.

I think it would be well for you to write yourself & tell Alice your view of her plan of going west.

Kiss the darling baby for me. Send me the size of her head that I may make her another silk cap. Pray for me & love me. My love to your mother & kind regards to your brother— I hope to get a letter from you by the five o'clock mail & perhaps one from Henry… (end of letter missing)
—A.J.W.H.

September 21, 1889, Paris.
My darling Wife—   A few lines to go to you by Wednesday's Steamer. I am as well as I can be in body and mind except that I am beginning to get pretty homesick for wife and baby. I have been very busy running around although for two days we have had rain. Yesterday I spent the entire day in the Louvre picture galleries. Ah me! What a world of art there is there and yet I fear I am not sufficiently cultivated in art to appreciate the Old Masters according to the merits ascribed to them. I have also been to the Notre Dame… I stopped writing here to go to breakfast and then received a dear letter from you and one from Mother. Again nothing from you about your plans but Mother wrote that you had written her your abandonment of your trip East. Why don't you write me your plans darling? I have been worried a good deal over my uncertainty as to where you and baby were… Perhaps your not coming East may be wise for it is a long trip for a short while but you should have written to me as soon as you changed your mind… You don't know how much comfort & pleasure I derive from your letters my dearest and I yearn from day to day for them. Kiss my darling baby many times a day for me. Goodbye for the present. A world of love for all. Your devoted husband, *Henry.*

Colorado Springs, September 24th, 1889.
My Darling Husband—   Today brings your letter written from Ascot & it delighted me exceedingly… & you will tell me all the *rest* when we meet & what a glad day that will be… It has been such a comfort to feel you have been well all the time & I pray God to keep & bless you my Darling one. Here comes Katherine, she has kissed the opposite page… & blurred the writing & rumpled the sheet, you won't mind. She is *whooping* as you say & her latest trick is to say "Hey, hey, hey." Her body is the plumpest prettiest thing you ever saw & you should see her kiss your photograph, her mouth opens & she bends her face down. She is a darling… I miss you more & more & long for you hourly. God keep & bless you… Your own devoted & loving wife, *Katherine.*

Colorado Springs, September 27th, 1889.
My Darling Husband—   I will write you a few lines hoping they will reach you at Queenstown & now I feel the next letter I will write will be to New York. Your entirely charming letter to the Baby came yesterday and was so welcome. She was nursing as I read it, and it was like a fairy tale & will always be a treasure for our Darling to read what her Father wrote her from Old England. I trust every day has brought you keen enjoyment & that you are returning well content with the trip & willing to go again & take me. I see by your letter to Katherine that you mean to take her sometime. I notice what you say of your Special Attorneyship ending. Well I think that I can manage more economically than last winter. I feel so well & strong & I don't need a new thing & you can use every cent of the money you call mine (which is ours). Don't worry. I have a letter from Cannon & he says he is feeling quite well & thinks the improvement is permanent. Katherine is certainly as sweet as can be… We go up (to Denver) Monday 30th & I shall send you a cable, so you may hear as late as possible. I have not cabled before for writing so regularly & being perfectly well it did not seem worth while. Mother sends much love, we have been out driving for 3 hours with Katherine. Hope to find a few rooms near us where Mother will be comfortable & free from care & where she can see Katherine daily… I shall think of you Darling one constantly on the sea & pray you may have a prosperous voyage. Let me hear every day as you did going over & mail it in New York… Your own loving & devoted wife, *Katherine.*

෴ A letter from Annie Jennings Wise Hobson:

Amherst, Sept. 27, 1889.
My dear Son—   Doubtless you and Katherine are surmising what has become of me. For three days I have tried to write— Cannon was away in Pulaski City, S. W. Va., Alice exceedingly unwell, and I was running the house and children. The very day I was about to write I was seized suddenly with aches and pains and from a sore throat. I was really very suffering for four or five days and could not leave my room until Thursday when I took a pleasant ride. —Since then the weather has been too windy and uncertain for me to venture out and I have had a great deal to do and have again taken charge of the *menage* and children, for Alice is in no condition to attend to anything. I had to take so much quinine and D— powder that my brain felt very muddled. The duct of an ear became very involved and neuralgia seemed to attack the throat. I had certainly a painful heavy time being my own nurse and Doctor, but I hope soon to be all right and that after the cool snap we will have some pleasant weather.

I was taken sick the day after your letter telling of your politicating came, and then there was one from dear Katherine and I've had another lovely letter from her beside. She shall have an answer from my heart very soon.

Cannon returned from Pulaski city last Saturday looking much better. Bishop Randolph came that evening and preached here Sunday morning and at New Glasgow in the afternoon, returning here to tea. I was too sick to see him at all.

Cannon had only five candidates (for confirmation). His class last year was a large one— (fifteen), for a small church, and few are now left to be confirmed. I can enter fully into your feelings in regard to the part you have taken in politics and can see how you might regard it as a duty, and from my very heart and mind commend your course, yet I also agree with Katherine that you are overworking yourself, and that it is a great pity that you have entered a firm where the senior partner is to go into politics which means that the work of the firm will fall on you… I must send this at once to the office. All here join me in love to Uncle Henry & Aunt Katherine. I have much to tell you but must defer…   —Your loving Mother, *A. J. W. H.*

Sept. 27, 1889, London.
My darling Wife—   I must write very hurriedly as I have to catch Tom Page before he leaves for Liverpool (he sails tomorrow.) I not only want to say goodbye but he owes me 50 pounds and I want it…   —Devotedly your Husband, *Henry.*

Home, October 10th, 1889.
My Darling Husband—   Today I am twice made glad, two precious letters from you— one from Paris 21st, London the 27th. I am so proud & glad to receive your dear letters & all these summer days they have been my great comfort & joy. The two to Katherine are treasures. And now I am writing to you in New York, thank God and soon I shall see you… It seems too good to be true. I feel exactly as if you were my love & had been years & years away, but instead you are the dearest & most noble & best Husband & have been away two months. (You see only superlatives apply to you.) Sweetheart, if you were here now I would, well I am wild, almost, to see your dear face again. Do take every care of yourself & come home to me well. Don't stay up late & eat rich food in N.Y. You will lose all the good of your trip. Take all the time you need in N.Y. & Philadelphia & Washington & then come home to us. Your Baby Girl is anxious to see you I know. She is six months old tomorrow. My thoughts & prayers are with you on the sea Darling. We have been up here a week, & Mother is with me. [end of letter missing]

Home, October 17th, 1889.
My Darling Husband—   Tomorrow I hope for news of your safe arrival. Last night I woke & thought, as I always do, instantly of you, and prayed for your safety & then cried fearing some ill might come to you, my *life*, but I feel that soon you will come home well. You will let me know by telegram what time you are to arrive… Dr. Fisk will see you & tell you that he left us splendidly well. I almost *hated* him seeing you before I do— felt really jealous… The work in the little house is nearly completed & will be most comfortable & it is perfect to have Mother so near. I don't think she is as strong this autumn…   —Your own loving wife, *Katherine.*

Home, October 18th, 1889.
My Darling Husband—   This minute your telegram was received. Oh the relief & joy I feel to know you, my own Dearest, are perfectly well. You have been so constantly in my mind and as I sat nursing our Baby at 12:30 your dispatch was brought me. I shall look anxiously for your letter, and be so

thankful to welcome you home. I sent a telegram to you last evening. I knew you would wish to know the minute you reached land. Katherine is now flat on her back biting her rattle & kicking— the picture of health. She sends love & kisses to you I know. I will send Cannon word of your safe arrival & write your Mother. Mother is in bed today, had a pain in her chest, from cold, she is better & will be all right in a few hours… Have only time for this line, but it takes you my tenderest heart's love… You don't know how I love you. You are my idol. Take every care of yourself. Your devoted & loving wife, *Katherine*.

Home, Saturday eve. October 19th, 1889.
My Darling Husband—   This note will probably not find you in N.Y., for from your second dispatch I think you will have started by next Wednesday… We are very well and anxiously awaiting your coming, but don't feel I am wishing you to come before you have quite finished all you need to accomplish… Mother is better, up today. Her home will be sweet I think— such a blessing to have her so near. Wrote your Mother a long letter last night. Cannon tells me that Alice writes [that] your Mother is going to Washington with Cannon 2nd, the last week October. Cannon has the hope of getting the place of Chaplain at Wolf Hall. I can't think of anything but your coming. I try to imagine how you will look & what time I will be going to the station to meet you. Take my whole heart full of love & many kisses from Katherine & me. You are the most precious Husband heart could desire & I love you more every day & hour. Your devoted loving wife, *Katherine*.

    A letter from Virginia:

Richmond, October 24th, 1889.
I am so thankful my dearest darling Henry that you've been across the ocean, had a delightful, successful trip & have returned home in revived health & have now your lovely wife & babe clasped to your heart… I've enjoyed your letters to your Mother so much— especially the last about the Cathedrals & I would like so much to have seen Edinburgh. My honored Father drank deeply from the fountain… more than 100 years ago! …Your loving GrandMa, *M. L. Wise*.

December 25, 1889. Denver.
My Dearest Grandma Hobson—   Papa is going to write a letter to you for me this Xmas day because I want to send you my love and one of my new photographs. Don't you think it is jolly? I had a fine time when it was taken and the old man who took me could hardly keep me in the chair, for I was trying to crawl over the back. Now you never got a letter from an eight months old grand-daughter, did you, and one written on Xmas day, so I am going to tell you all about my Xmas. Well I have been sick for two days with a bad cold and had to stay in the house, but I made up my mind to be all right today and I am. I hung up my stocking last night and this morning when Papa came stealing into Mamma's & my room thinking he would catch me asleep, I sat right up in bed and said "High" to him… I have been just as jolly as possible all day and I believe I like Xmas. I wish I could be with my little cousins, Uncle Cannon's children, but they might not like me for I want to have my way always. Tell dear Uncle Cannon from me that I miss him a whole

Catherine McKie Thayer and her granddaughter, Katherine Thayer Hobson, 1889. Studio of C. L. Gillingham, Colorado Springs.

lot and wish he were here. But I know how glad his children are to have him at home, for I love to have my Papa come home every day… Mamma says to tell you she has been sick several days with a cold but she is better now. Papa is well. Don't you bother about sending me anything for I know you have been awfully busy. Show my picture to Grandma Wise and the rest of our folks and tell them I say "High"— That is what I always say when anything pleases me. Well I must play some and I want Papa to play with me. He belongs to me today. Mamma & Papa send much love and so do I.   —Your loving little Granddaughter, *Katherine*.

XIX

1890

The Robert E. Lee Memorial

On May 26, 1890 Annie Jennings Wise Hobson wrote to her son about an upcoming event in Richmond:

I wish I could find words to make you feel, my dear loving son, how those short letters written in Court go right to my heart. They show that my far off boy is never too busy, too occupied in mind and heart to think of his mother… You are fast approaching that grand climatic life— 35, when so many people who inherit disease show weakness & often die. If I could only impress upon you the importance of taking care of yourself in every way till you had safely passed that period. After that all of our family grow stronger & more capable of enduring… On Saturday I took a hansom cab & with little Annie M— went to Hollywood to inspect our sections there to see if they would be in order for the Memorial Day Friday… The turf is growing beautifully on Cannon's grave & our corner looks as if love took care of it. Alice & I joined together in putting it in order. I do hope that after this year we can begin to put by something to erect a central monument there. My idea is a large rustic cross on rock where the names of all can be engraved. Hollywood looked so lovely, & was [illegible] with the perfume of flowers. I felt it would be so restful to be there when life's work is done… Alice will come down with the dear children & here with me the dear boys shall see the reunion of our Confederate soldiers… I want the boys to remember that they saw the scene of the procession by my side. I shall not attempt to take them to the statue till tomorrow for the crowd will be too great. I asked Mr. Williams today to send you a Saturday eve's *State*. Notice the tribute to General Lee from an Englishman soon after the war— at the time he was paralyzed. Keep it to read to our Baby someday & read it to Katherine now… We are going to decorate the front porch… A confederate flag & shield, the St. Andrews Cross flag, a Virginia flag & drape the red & white of our bars, but no U. S. stars & stripes— this is our funeral! …I cannot see how Richmond can accommodate the crowd that is coming. I wrote to Katherine last week. I shall look eagerly to hear you are safely back from your trip… Everyone sends love to you and our darlings… I sent you some verses about the first series of the pictures & there will be some more about the others. My love to Mrs. Thayer & God bless you all. Your devoted mother, *A.J.W.H.*

In 1890 Annie published a pamphlet about the dedication of the Lee Memorial that is reprinted here. Robert E. Lee had died twenty years earlier, on October 12, 1870, at his home in Lexington, Virginia.

The front cover of Annie Hobson's memorial pamphlet with the artwork, signed "A. W." in the lower right, and otherwise described as a "youthful artist," a "debutante in art."

"Memorial of the Unveiling of Lee's Statue"
Richmond, Virginia. May 29th, 1890
Wm. Ellis Jones, Book and Job Printer —1890

Preface to the second edition:

The first edition of this unpretending memorial was hastily sent out as a venture. The friendly appreciation which it has received, warrants a second edition. The first met with the impartial criticism of a true friend and competent critic. He insisted that the "Memorial Ode" and "Address to the Battle Flag," could be expanded and made more worthy of the theme. Like the fugitive attempts of even true genius, these humble emanations, required more thought and labor, than the first impulse of strong emotion had bestowed. Therefore, both have been revised and expanded.

The Ode, describing the bringing home of the statue, and conducting it to the site where the pedestal awaited it, seemed an appropriate addition. This Ode can claim the merit of being historically true, from the first verse, invoking the "Trusted Bark" that bore the precious freight, and telling the eager expectation of a people's heart, to the last stanza, which left the veiled statue upon the pedestal.

The beautiful design on the cover, which illustrates the prologue of two sonnets, is the first attempt at original illustration, by a youthful artist. This *debutante* in art, whose rare powers of exquisite delineation give promise of a bright future, is a faithful art student. Virginia should be proud to claim her as a daughter, and can feel assured, that if cherished and encouraged by her own people, she will be an honor to the State.

The address to the "Editor of the Mail and Express" is left out, as unworthy a place in this memorial. From the first, it was only a *jeu d'esprit*, intended for all fanatics, who objected to the display of the Confederate flag, and for every narrow soul who misrepresented our motives in bringing out our war banners, as memorial tributes on the day of the unveiling of the beloved Hero of the "lost Cause."

Two critics, who did not witness the extraordinary scenes of May 29th, thought that the dedication was overdrawn, too highly colored. It came spontaneously from the writer's very soul, and has found a response from so many hearts and minds, that it must be an unexaggerated sketch and true to the spirit of the day. Therefore only a few verbal changes have been made in this dedication, and General Lee's own declaration inserted where one sentence was omitted.

Robert E. Lee

Another objected to the sentiment which declared, that "our Chieftain was more sublime and heroic in defeat than the victors in their triumph," etc. He said that it was invidious to Grant's deserved reputation as a general and ungrateful to his magnanimity as a victor. No such meaning was intended, nor is it necessarily implied. Lee is spoken of as "the *man* divine from God," not merely as a military leader.

To the tribute there given to him, we are glad of an opportunity to add another. We claim that the history of mankind can show no manhood, excelling in harmonious proportions and rare combinations Robert E. Lee, our "Stonewall" Jackson, and our earliest martyr leader, Albert Sydney Johnston.

These representative leaders of the South were men of high mental endowments, strong in moral virtue and Christian excellence, cultured gentlemen and chivalrous knights. We say with gratitude unspeakable and noble pride, these men are the outcome of a civilization so often maligned, as being barbaric in cruelty, contemptibly ignorant and sinfully voluptuous. The whole life of the South denies this charge, and History will do justice to a long suffering people.

Again the word "martyr" has been criticised as used in the dedication and poems. The North has its martyrs as well as the South. The fanaticism and prejudices of the extremest of the extreme led North and South to contest, war and death.

The South fought for self-preservation against unwarranted interference and the tyranny of compulsion; and our martyrs fell by thousands. The Northern martyr gave his life for what he deemed essential to self-preservation—the Union.

There will be more martyrs arising from strife in some form, unless there is a Union of "just men" "through all the land," who will view the responsibilities of the hour, and the difficulties of the political situation with the eye of truth, and who will establish not only a rule of justice, but a higher law of "peace and good will," which shall rise above sectional prejudice and party faction. God grant us the harmony which must result from such a rule, and a peace which shall insure a free government.
October 15th, 1890. *Annie J. W. Hobson.*

THE PROLOGUE

> The Lost Cause buried lies, its winding sheet
> By Glory made and wrapped by Liberty;
> Grief placed the flag of its Confederacy
> Beside its grave, where Love and Honor meet—
> The Sun of its brief day, which ne'er shall greet
> Another dawn sinking to fateful night,

A covenant of freedom writes in light
Behind disaster's clouds—the last rays feat—
A Bow of promise, that new life shall rise
From Martyrs' graves, and battle wage
Against oppression, born from section's rage,
Against hypocrisy's bland cant and lies,
When Truth's own starlit standard shall unite
Just men, through all the land, in wisdom's might.

The Wraith of that Lost Cause now soars in flight
To bear on high our blood-stained Southern Cross,
Our hallowed Oriflamme of Valor's loss,
Amidst the constellations of God's night;
Reflecting deeds of proved, heroic might,
The glorious radiance of the righteous fame
Inscribed by Virtue's hand around each name
Of Leaders brave, who battled for the right,
Of dauntless Chiefs, who 'neath this banner fought,
Defending sacred homes and Sovereign State
From Tyranny, which claimed to be the mate
Of Liberty, in freedom's mail, truth wrought.
Now there its stars shall guide to heights sublime
Tried souls, who climb the adverse steeps of Time.

ODE

O trusted Bark, with sure speed bring
   The precious freight consigned to thee,
While winds of heaven blow warily
   Across a tranquil, solemn sea;
For on towards the setting sun,
   Expectant throbs a people's heart,
To welcome that grand form you bear,
   By woman's love evoked from art.

The magic spark the tidings flashed,
   The ship has reached the Western shore;
Ah! earnest praise uplifted hearts
   To Him who safely brought it o'er.
That freight transferred was borne right on—
   As clouds pass swiftly overhead—
Towards the site which rightly lies
   Between the living and the dead

Hollywood Cemetery and the City.

Virginia, noblest mother, stood
   With wreaths of Amaranth in hand,
And called her children to come forth
   As love's devoted, reverent band;

She bade them meet with homage due
    The image of that filial son,
Who fought the fight for her dear sake,
    Where glory, if not triumph, won.

In silence waits the sacred charge
    On threshold of Lee's city fair,
When through the golden, pulsing light
    Low murmurs stirred his native air.
Hark! How the sound swells fast and far!
    Now echoing footsteps throng each street,
While woman's voice and childhood's words,
    And manhood's tones each other greet.

Around each decked, triumphal car
    A strong, tense cord—ne'er used before—
Was bound and tied by loving hearts;
    That cord, now sacred evermore,
No hireling touch could desecrate,
    For baby clasp and maiden's hand,
Manhood and youth by hoary age
    Made strong the strength of love's command.

There one was drawn by boyhood's throng,
    Who shouted out with youth's own glee,
The privilege and glory great
    Of bearing on our Chieftain Lee!
The next was drawn by maidens fair,
    And tiny girls with gladsome smile,
While right in front a tottering babe
    Was borne aloft or walked a while.

Now women grave and gray bent heads
    Commingle in another line,
Where hearts were filled with sobs suppressed,
    While many a tear unshed did shine
In eyes, which had our hero seen
    In all the glory of the past,
From hearts, which ne'er the woes he felt
    Could cease to feel while life shall last.

The ways were lined with every age
    Afoot, on horse, in densest rows,
All saw, with solemn joy, the sight,
    While e'en to some fond memory shows
Another scene of long ago;
    A hero passes through the streets
A Chieftain in adversity;
    Oh! sad the woe his coming greets!

He rode through this same city when
    She mourned in ashes o'er her dead,
And bowed her every grief to share
    His noble and uncovered head.
"The paling fires" gleamed on his face
    "The death lights of Confederacy";
And e'en to foes revealed the man
    In all his calm sublimity.

For generous Federals gave three cheers
    To greet him as he passed along,
The tribute of their soldier hearts
    To him, who in defeat was strong
With honor's strength and valor's might,
    In duty's deeds so bravely done,
Who leading on a hope forlorn
    His greatest trophies nobly won.

Today in triumph he is borne,
    For love and glory here unite,
While memory nerves the feeblest arm
    To help conduct him to the site
Where Lee upon his faithful steed,
    Shall stand fore'er beneath God's sky,
The highest type of noble life
    While heroes live and martyrs die.

Now, there Virginia's tender care
    Shall gently raise him to the place
Where all will be close-veiled from sight,
    Till from our leader's noble face,
A living hero's honored hand
    Removed the veil, revealing Lee
Before an eager, waiting host
    In all his calm, grand majesty.

DEDICATION

my grandchildren   At the time this was written, Annie Hobson had seven grandchildren— the six living children of John Cannon Hobson, her oldest son, and Katherine Thayer Hobson, Henry Wise Hobson's oldest child.

To my grandchildren— the great-grandchildren of General Henry A. Wise, whose brigade covered the last of the retreat of the Army of Virginia, until the surrender at Appomattox, and whose enduring veterans claim that they fired the last Confederate muskets which flashed their protest on Virginia soil—I dedicate these verses. They were fugitive from heart and brain when the soul was deeply stirred by the memories of the past revivified by the surroundings of the present. They are bound to gather as "In Memoriam" leaflets of a day, which witnessed one of the most remarkable pageants, and the most exceptional, which mankind has ever seen. On that day a vast assemblage— youth and maturity, childhood and old age— were called together by love and reverence; and they met to form a mighty retinue, whose martial grandeur was evoked from the dead years under the banner of "A lost Cause;" whose civic display was a tribute from memory; whose notes of triumph were only echoes from an irrevocable past, where the end was defeat; whose lights of glory were reflected from the heroes of fruitless victories, and from the haloes of Martyred souls who passed through the fires of battles lost. Let these verses prolong the echoes of that day through the chambers of your souls. I would that you should never forget the shout which ascended to the translucent dome of God, when the hand of love and homage unveiled the form majestic—a shout echoing the universal verdict—that our chieftain was more sublime and heroic in defeat than the victors in their triumph, and grander in adversity than their greatest in prosperity. By the side of Lee, you should ever honor the living hero, General Joseph E. Johnston, who was the last to surrender before the inevitable, in the face of disparities which only a miracle could counteract.

I enjoin upon you never to forget that, while there were tears amidst our smiles and great sobs from our hearts, as the battle worn and bullet torn war-banners were unfolded before our eyes, and while hands were clasped in pathetic grief over the old veterans marching their last round upon Time's history, there was not a cheek which blushed to own the "Lost Cause," and every head was proudly lifted to see the "Starlet Banner" waving in new glory, exultant, because it was the flag unfurled by Lee in defence "of the inalienable rights sacred to freemen."

In the name of honor and valor, of liberty and morality, I adjure you, amidst the vicissitudes of life, and the changes of political creeds and human governments, never fail to do justice to the integrity of motives, and to recognize the inspiration of duty and honor, which led the heroes of the "Lost Cause" to do and dare, to risk defeat in opposition to a compulsion, which was clothed in the hypocrisy of freedom, and claimed a Divine Right which contradicted the very laws of God. Write upon your memories, in golden letters, the declaration of Robert E. Lee: *"We had sacred principles to maintain and rights to defend, for which we were in duty bound to do our best, even if we perished in the endeavor."*

Robert E. Lee Memorial, Monument Avenue, Richmond, Virginia. Dedicated 1890.

The Southern Confederacy belongs to the dead who rest with God; whatever power of resurrection it has in the cause of liberty and right, we leave to Him. Southern principles and fidelity, Southern honor and valor should live with the living to accomplish God's purposes in the grand march of progress and civilization for a nation's highest good and the enlightenment of the dark places of the earth.

June 6th, 1890. *Annie J. W. Hobson.*

ADDRESS TO THE BATTLE FLAG

St. Andrew's Cross on Crimson Ground —
The Cross Studded with Stars,
the Same in Number as the Confederate States.

O scared Stars, O hallowed Cross,
   On banner dyed in blood red hue;
To-day, no emblem of our loss,
   Unfurl thy glories to our view.
Now, wave exultant e'er each head,
No longer prone beside our dead.

Love calls on memory to display
   The record of thy glorious past,
Love brings a chrism here to-day
   To consecrate while time shall last
Anew the meaning of thy fame,
Enwrapped around our hero's name.

Above the Chieftain loved the best,
   Proclaim the praise our hearts would tell,
To North and South, to East and West—
   "This man his birthright would not sell."
Wave out, "Beneath this Cross our Lee
Won honor's immortality."

Wave out, how every Southern heart,
   In love for our Confederate Lee,
Perpetuates by highest art
   The story of that loyalty,
Which, through defeat and country's loss,
Ne'er blushed to own thy Stars and Cross.

Beside Virginia's standard tell
   The contest of unequal might,
While Southern flags the echoes swell
   Of every deed of Valor's fight.
Recall each grand war bugle blast
When Victory crowned thy noble past.

Yet other flags to-day should droop
   Beneath thy Cross all hallowed there,
Above the man who ne'er did stoop
   Beneath his burden of despair—
Who kept, through every direful ill,
A blood red Cross, his emblem still.

Some day, upon the crystal walls
   Where time records its history,
Thou shalt be hung—e'en in those halls
   Where heroes dwell eternally,
This shall be writ: "Beneath this Cross
Men fought and died, nor counted loss."

AN EPIC

UNVEILING OF THE STATUE OF GENERAL ROBERT E. LEE.

May 29th, 1890.

With tender hand and reverent mien unveil
That form of Majesty! Let heaven's own light
Reveal the man sublime who bore aloft
A banner, whose device—a Cross starlit—
Meant this to his great soul, from first to last,
That duty's voice bade honor's hand unfurl
That flag—a sign for men to dare and die
Protesting 'gainst compulsion's tyranny.

Immortal love invoked the Muse of Art,
To show to all posterity the grand
Calm man of fortitude divine, who bore
A country's loss in meek humility
Before Christ's Cross—the Hero of Defeat!
Bid Music come, with anthems toned like chaunt
Of winds that sweep around our martyred dead,
To join in unison with this high theme.

Behold our Chieftain! That uncovered head
Ne'er bowed before dishonor's shrine, but faced
The will of God with brave, uplifted front.
O'erpowered by disaster's cruel might,
He met inevitable loss, which came
By dire, disparate force, unconquered still;
To him a world admiring gave applause,
Yet to his dying cause could give no aid.

Where is the Poet Seer, with wings to soar
To that high peak serene, above the clouds
Of black adversity, whose towering height
Was never scaled by triumph's heroes in
Prosperity, above the dissonance
Of strife, where Glory stands in robes of light,
To crown the heroes of true valor's might
With wreaths unfading from th' eternal hills?

Ah! when this Bard inspired shall here descend
With Lyre, whose strings of gold were drawn through fire
From Heaven, eyes dim shall full, clear vision have
To see our Chief upon his own lone height.
Then summon here the Muse of History,
With torch lit from the altar fires of Truth,
Illumed to show the things concealed now
By faction's hand or silent by our graves.

Bid Clio seek Minerva's shield, which can
Reflect the Gorgon head of prejudice
By error's serpent locks encoiled, and then
Reveal where fettered liberty was chained;
Thus seeing, write: "This Chief a phalanx led
To victory oft—always to valiant deeds—
Against a mighty host, whose ranks could be
Replenished by the myriads of the world."

Behold those lines attenuate by Death!
Those men, with souls alive and iron will,
In bodies starved, half clad and worn as were
Their rifles and their blood-stained, unsheathed swords,
Encompassed by the burnished bayonets
Of vigorous, serried legions, numbered five
To one. They never faltered in the fight
And victory won while human strength held out.

Whene'er she would record the rightful praise
Of our loved Chief, her pen of gold should dip
Into the life blood of a people's heart, and write—
"The Lost Cause furled its flag and found a grave
Beside our sacred dead. The Leader who
Had held the pass of its Thermopylæ
Ne'er quailed, until he heard the widow's wail,
The orphan's call, and mother's cry bereft."

'Twas then he asked the shield of power to guard
Their rifled homes, all desolate and dark,
From more calamity. On his great height
He proved his saintly life, in very truth
The martyr yielding up himself without

One thought of his own loss. In woman's heart
He finds a shrine fore'er! Aye, she will crown
Him as King Arthur's peer through every age.

True, knightly men in every land shall bring
The homage due to our immortal Lee,
And recognize a man from out God's own
Divinity, who great in war, was grand
In peace, as there he stood, a sentinel
At Duty's post, until a messenger
From God the solemn summons brought, to meet
The final contest and the last great foe.

O paradox divine! That foe, e'en Death
Upon his "pale horse," blew the bugle blast
Which bore him on to certain victory!
This summons brought commission sure for life—
Triumphant life attained by mortal life
Laid down! Our Lee shall live forevermore
By Glory wreathed on his own height serene,
With Aureole crowned amidst the saints of God.

The back cover of the memorial pamphlet with a drawing of the Lee statue.

XX

1890–1897

A Growing Family in Denver

IN 1890 Henry Hobson, by then a former U. S. Attorney, was turning his attention to his family and to the private practice of law where his successful work for the railroads would both keep him very busy and make him financially secure. He and his wife already had one child and three more children would be born during these seven years. The Virginia family, his mother and his brother's family, would continue to require his financial support during all of this time. However, living in Colorado gave him some distance between those worries and his personal life.

America continued to grow and change. During these seven years three territories, Idaho, Wyoming, and Utah became states—Wyoming being the first state with women's suffrage. The west was still being settled, and in 1890 there was the massacre at Wounded Knee where 200 Indians were killed. In that same year Congress created Yosemite Park and also provided for the forfeiture of unused land grants that had been previously made to the railroads. In 1890 Emily Dickinson's poetry was first published, and two years later Joel Chandler Harris published *Nights With Uncle Remus*. In 1893 The World's Columbian Exposition opened in Chicago and in October the Hobsons visited it with their new daughter, Eleanor. In that same year a hurricane killed 1,000 people in Charlestown, South Carolina, and Savannah, Georgia. The Chicago fairgrounds burned in 1894. In 1894 Congress passed the first graduated income tax, but that was declared unconstitutional in 1895. In 1896 the Supreme Court, in *Plessy v. Ferguson*, ruled that "separate but equal" was constitutional, thereby legalizing the practice of racial segregation which would last until the middle of the twentieth century. In 1897 President Cleveland vetoed legislation requiring literacy tests for immigrants. During these seven years there were other successes and failures. Elsewhere, the attempt to convert the United States to the metric system was defeated by Congress in 1893; successful off-shore oil wells were drilled near Santa Barbara, California, in 1896; and the first subway was completed in Boston in 1897. In 1896 gold was discovered in northwest Canada near Klondike Creek, and within two years over 100,000 prospectors had gone to Alaska and Canada to search for gold. In 1896 Rural Free Delivery was established throughout the country—letter writers would be very happy. On September 21, 1897, the *New York Sun* ran its now famous editorial by newsman Francis Pharcellus Church that declared, "Yes, VIRGINIA, there is a Santa Claus. He exists as certainly as love and generosity and devotion exist, and you know that they abound and give to your life its highest beauty and joy. Alas! How dreary would be the world if there were no Santa Claus. It would be as dreary as if there were no VIRGINIAS." During these years, Henry Hobson, his children, and Santa Claus would all exchange letters.

Letters, telegrams, and diaries by:
Alice Pettit Hobson
Annie Jennings Wise Hobson
Henry W. Hobson, (son of John Cannon Hobson)
Henry W. Hobson
Katherine Thayer Hobson
Katherine, Henry, Eleanor, and Thayer Hobson
Fred Horsbrugh
Ella Miller, the nurse
George W. Richardson
Catherine McKie Thayer
John S. Wise, Uncle John
Papa's Letters
and Santa Claus

Letters written from: Denver, Colorado Springs, and Pueblo, Colorado; Boston and Fitchburg, Massachusetts; South Cambridge, Johnsonville, Albany, Manhattan Beach, and New York, New York; Richmond, Ashland, and Norfolk, Virginia; Chicago, Washington, D. C., Texas, Quebec, London, and Belgium; from aboard trains and steamships, at railroad stations, and from Santa Clausville.

1890

Home. Sunday, January 14th, 1890.
My Darling Husband—   There is very little to write you, only I wish to send my daily line of love to you who are so constantly in my mind… You should see Mother manage Katherine, has her *sit down*, it is so gentle & yet *firm* and brings back her way with me. As I said when a child, "When Mother says *No*, she means *No*." …Mother sends you tender love. She has spoken several times of the good it does her to hear "his dear voice" in the morning. My heart full of love to you & Katherine sends a kiss. *Your devoted wife.*

Home, January 15th, Monday morning.
My Darling Husband—   Yesterday afternoon I received your Sunday letter and hope you did not take cold from the extreme cold of the car— it is dangerous to *sit* in such a low temperature… Mother sends you her best love & my whole heart full goes to you my precious one. Katherine dreams of you for she smiles. Your own loving wife *Katherine.*

January 17, 1890, Boston, Young's Hotel.
My darling wife—   Yesterday afternoon I received two very welcome letters from you which did my soul and heart good for they told me of the well-being of my dear ones… My business is progressing slowly but I am encouraged to think I will be successful. I will probably have to return to Boston before I go West for this is a slow place and you cannot rush business. I have been most pleasantly and courteously received and the people here remind me strongly of the English people in their customs and manners. …I

think it likely I will go to New York tomorrow and to Richmond Monday. I must now say goodbye for the day as I have an engagement in a few moments. Blessings upon you all and how I wish I could hug my darling little one.
—Your darling husband *Henry*.

Home, Saturday evening, January 18th, 1890.
My Darling Husband—   The week of your absence has passed away, and I trust each may pass & find you well at the end and that all you hope for in a business way may be accomplished. Your daughter has had a sweet happy day. She calls out when she is in her carriage to almost every man she sees appearing & says "Papa" and "Dada." …I took Katherine [to the photographer] yesterday and she crept all over the floor and kept saying "Hi" at everything… And now my darling One Good night. Take my heart's love & many kisses. Your own loving wife, *Katherine*.

Home, January 19th.
My Darling Husband—   This afternoon Mr. Cage brought me your first letter from Boston, and I am so glad to have it, for you seem nearer. I sincerely trust you were able to see Ada— it will be so pleasant to hear of her… Not one word from your Mother since you left. I trust you may find an adjustment easier between her & Alice than you anticipate. If any suggestions or hints are made regarding *our* taking one or more children say that Katherine would not accept such a responsibility & be positive. I can't help what they think… Oh how I long to see you, my precious one… —Your own devoted & loving Wife, *Katherine*.

Home, Tuesday evening, January 21st, 1890
My Darling Husband—   This morning your letter recd… Do be careful of yourself every minute… Give my love to all in Richmond, the family & friends, specially the dear Stewarts, Tom & Carter… With a heart full of love & love from Mother who sits near, I am your own Devoted Wife, *Katherine*.

January 21st, 1890, University Club, Madison Square.
My Darling Wife—   I have just finished my work for the day and stop at the Club on my way up town to get a letter from you and to answer some letters. I am quite tired but sitting still for a while will rest me. I am much pleased with the result of my work here and in Boston. I see no reason why we cannot put our Trust Co. scheme on a successful basis. Strange to say I have only had one short letter from Richmond. They are funny people about some things… tomorrow night I go to Richmond… Love to Mother Thayer, baby, and your darling self. Yr. Devoted husband, *Henry*.

January 22, 1890, Richmond. Page & Carter, Attorneys and Counsellors at Law, 911 Main Street, Richmond, Virginia.
My darling Wife—   Like an odor of brine from the ocean comes the thought of the day, some two years and more ago, when we spent some happy days together in Richmond. This morning upon getting here I went to the Exchange and had my breakfast and a wash and then went up to hunt up my people. Since then Tom Page has insisted upon my going up to stay with him and I shall do so. At the hotel this morning the same old "tacky" crowd

A few of the letters are dated 1889 but that is crossed-out as it is an obvious error. The daughter, Katherine Thayer Hobson, was born in April 11, 1889, so letters dated "January" and mentioning her must be 1890.

was there— women looking as if they had not washed themselves for a week and had fallen into their clothes by accident. Men whose clothes were spotted, their linen soiled, and who talked in low tones and looked around to see whether people were listening to them. These forsooth monopolize in their opinion the aristocracy of America, all the virtues, all the beauty and all the talent and above all, the same black-faced greasy fingered, dirty aproned waiters of the days when we staid at the Hotel.

    I spent an hour with Mother and had a "full report." You know what that means. I saw Grandma for a few moments and John [brother, John Cannon Hobson] a moment as I was coming down to see if I had any mail. Alice looks uglier than ever and has a wicked light or rather glitter in her eye. I think she would like to choke us all… I am just as well as I can be but am beginning to be bored already and everything looks like Sunday here and a dull Sunday at that. I have just shown Tom the baby's pictures and he was perfectly delighted and says you must send him a picture at once— one of the last. I wish you would. Love to dear Mother Thayer and for my darling baby, her Papa's whole heart.   —Your devoted husband *Henry*.

January 25, 1890, Richmond.
My darling wife—   I am scribbling a line before breakfast as it is hard down here to get a moment during the day to write. I spend as much time as possible with John. I can see a great change in him since he left Colo. He is much weaker and looks much worse. He could no more pretend to do now what he did then than he could fly. He eats almost nothing and hardly says anything, and yet he seems to feel hope. His wife is a perfect burden and it would be better if she were away. His children are nice little ones but are allowed to over-run his room and make a good deal of noise. I am enjoying staying with Tom very much. He seems in better spirits than I have seen him since his wife's death. I want you to know his sister-in-law Mrs. Baylor, an old sweetheart of mine by the way. She is a very lovely sweet woman with two very sweet little girls. Tom seems really glad to have me. I saw Anne Garnett yesterday who asked with great interest after you… Yesterday afternoon I went out to Brook Hill with Mary Lyons and saw Mrs. S— [Stewart], Mrs. Bryan, & Hope. …Grandma looks better than I have seen her look for years and seems stronger. The dear old lady talks all the time about her "two darling Katherines." To undertake to tell you all that is said and asked about you would take me a week. The Lyons are in a great stew— Cannot tell you about it before I return but I think it is all a tempest in a tea-pot…   —Your devoted husband *Henry*.

Home, January 27th, 1890.
My Darling Husband—   Today I have your letters, one from NY and the one from Richmond written just after you arrived, but better than all the telegrams saying you were well & would leave for NY last night. It seems to bring you so much nearer. I hope your stay in Richmond has been less trying than I felt it would be. I lived through the days with you & you have my heart's entire love and sympathy in this great sorrow & trial. Katherine has had a long day out of doors, hours. She is so interested & engrossed in all that goes on… —I am your own loving *Katherine*. Oh, my own love how precious you are to me.

❧ A letter from Annie Jennings Wise Hobson:

404 E. Main. Jan 31, 1890.
My dear Son—   …I have been quite sick but a prescription of Dr. Oppenheimer's has benefited me… Your sweet tenderness & gentle kindnesses were a great comfort to me while here & I shall ever remember that visit… I have not been able to see Cannon for ten days, as I have had to keep in my room, but I hear he is very feeble & miserable… Kiss Katherine & the darling for me. I've been looking at her dear little face taken with yours tonight… *A.J.W.H.*

❧ Family matters:

#404 E. Main Street, Richmond, VA. March 3, 1890.
My dear Henry—   I received your dear kind letters and I cannot tell you how my heart goes out in gratitude and love for all you have been and are to me and mine. Our children shall be taught to know that they owe you far more than they can possibly ever repay, no matter how much they may be able and fortunate enough to do for you. And there is nothing that I would not do to help or oblige you. I shall certainly regard what you said about Mother and try with all my heart for it to be as you wish… It will give me real pleasure to be any help and comfort to my darling husband's mother. Mother has always given me the credit of doing and feeling many things against her than I have done or thought of doing. But I am willing to let the past be buried and with God's help make the future far different. Her life has been full of trials and sorrows, as well as my own— and I will stand beside her in love and true sympathy if she will let me… I only want you to understand that I wish to help myself, thereby helping you, in every way I can. I fully appreciate what you are doing for us. I wish you to take what money I have and invest it as you think best. I have $700 in hand, having received a little more since I wrote you. Out of this, Mother advises me to keep $100 for general expenses… And in regard to getting settled, I went up to Ashland this morning by Mother's advice, as well as by my own judgment rented a very comfortable house at $12.50 or $150 per year… So, I shall get my furniture down from Amherst as soon as possible. You advised me to do this— get settled somewhere, you remember… One thing in regard to money matters I think I forgot to mention. I will receive annually from the Widow's and Orphan's Fund, between $100 and $200. When I will receive the Brotherhood Fund, I can not tell. It depends entirely on when it can be collected. Mother and the children are well. I feel my loss more and more as the days go by & sometimes I feel as if I can not bear my sorrow! God help me! …Give tenderest love to Katherine and the little Katherine. Please excuse bad writing as my hand is aching so badly, I can scarcely see. With dear love, and deep appreciation for all the sympathy and tenderness shown me in my distress. Your affect. sister, *A. P. Hobson.* [Alice Pettit Hobson, widow of John Cannon Hobson]

John Cannon Hobson, Henry Hobson's older brother, died on February 15, 1890. Henry then assumed an even greater responsibility for the welfare and education of his brother's children in addition to providing financial support for his mother and grandmother. A stained glass window in Cannon's memory was installed in the Ascension Church of Amherst, Virginia, where he had served as rector from November 1886 to March 1889. A historical sketch of the church reads: "Mr. Hobson was said to have been of lovable and gentle personality and deeply consecrated." John Cannon Hobson is buried in the Hollywood Cemetery in Richmond, Virginia.

❧ A letter from Annie Jennings Wise Hobson:

404 E. Main, March 18th, 1890.
I have only a few moments to write, My dear Son, before going to dinner, but I must tell you how lovely I feel it was for you to write me that letter about

the darling little granddaughter. I appreciate that you wished to cheer and brighten me, and it did come like a sunbeam… A letter from Mrs. Brown said that the house is all ready for Alice. I shall write to Mrs. Brown today about getting fuel for her. Mrs. Brown cordially invited her to stay there until she is comfortably fixed— ready for the children who will remain in Richmond till she has arranged the house. I have just heard for the first time that my dear old library desk was burnt up in the Petersburg fire… Oh! I wish I could get all my dear hallowed things, the little I have left, together in some resting place! Yet, yet this may be wrong! It is God's will. I shall indeed be a pilgrim literally on this side & I may cling too much to mere things! …Mrs. Howard is willing to rent me one room here— in the hall & front room, for a month, and I must have some place to be quiet & rest when undergoing that ordeal at the dentist's. I think I will stay till May 7th. A place to myself where I can do just as I please would give me a rest I could get in no one else's house. All here are as usual & Mother read your letter with great enjoyment… Kiss Katherine & the baby for me and give much love to Mrs. Thayer. God keep you all— Devotedly your Mother, *A. J. W. Hobson.*

Denver, July 9, 1890.
My Dearest Mother Thayer—   I don't know how I can thank you for your sweet letter and your more than generous gift. Indeed it is too much for you to give me and I wish you would let me make it $100 instead of $500. Above all however do I value the love and confidence you give me and it is a most comforting thought to me that I have in any way been able to cheer and brighten your life… If I owed you gratitude and love for nothing else, I would owe a big debt for my lovely sweet wife. I cannot write much dear Mother Thayer but believe me my heart is always full of tenderness for you.
—Your loving son, *Henry W. Hobson.*

Fitchburg, Saturday Oct 11th, 1890.
My Darling Husband—   …Yesterday I went to Boston to search for a cook—went to eight places and am on the track of a splendid Swede who has excellent relations & character, so I stay over today to see her… and do be *careful* of your precious self. Address So. Cambridge… —Fondest love, Your own devoted Wife, *Katherine.*

☙ A letter from Annie Jennings Wise Hobson:

Ashland, October 22nd, 1890.
My dear Son—   Last Saturday evening I came up to spend Sunday with the children— to see Miss Mayo, their teacher, about their studies etc. & to look over their clothes and find out what they would really need at present. As usual, quantities of old things required being made new and I gave the "remaining" to a good woman here to whom the work is a kindness, and she will do it in a way to save clothes & money. If ever Alice undertook to do the work (which she hadn't the remotest idea of doing) it would be a botch, time wasted & clothes thrown away… I send you the boys' reports. I wish you could write to them about them and urge them now to study & work in earnest. A letter from you would do great good. I wrote to Katherine yesterday. Now I must write to Sister. I have scribbled this before breakfast, with the

interruptions of the little ones coming in to say "good morning" & to say their prayers. All join me in love to Uncle Henry & wish they could see him, Aunt Katherine & little Katherine. God guide & bless you. Devotedly your Mother, *A. J. W. Hobson.*

South Cambridge, Oct 28th, 1890.
My Darling Husband—   Yesterday your telegram of 23rd was received, so glad to hear and to know "case goes so smoothly." In the evening telegram of yesterday, rec'd, asking for news of Katherine, but it was too late to answer until this A.M. I had sent you a message Wed. P.M. that you might know K— was all right and not be worried by my letter. I can't understand its not reaching you and relieving you of any worry… Katherine is on my lap as I write, she is the sweetest baby in the world & Frank says so too. She is so affectionate & high spirited too… My heart full of love & devotion. —Your own loving *Katherine.*

∽ A letter from Catherine McKie Thayer:

Colorado Springs, Dining room, Wed. 12 a.m., Nov. 12, 1890.
My precious daughter—   Your letter in pencil of Mon A.M. came by *this* a.m. delivery. I shall show envelope to the Postman & make him explain. I am silent under many delays, but will not submit to postal delinquencies between you and me without protest…

Colorado Springs, December 27th, 1890.
My Darling Husband—   Will send a line for you to receive tomorrow. I feel so lonely to be away from you… Mrs. Jackson congratulated me on *my prospects*, and if I only can give Katherine a dear little sister for a companion. I intended asking you to write your Mother, so she would hear by the New Year— please do & remember she and Alice sent you the pickle— and the boys (3) the tray. Now I will stop and only add my heart's best love & kisses to you my Darling Husband, Your own loving wife, *Katherine.* —Katherine is running after Toodles & calling "Toodley"— she is so lovely & like you.

∽ In other news, Wounded Knee:

THE HOSTILES SURRENDER — *Returning in Droves from the Bad Lands* — Big Foot and His Braves in Charge of the Seventh Cavalry — The Indian Trouble Rapidly Nearing Its End. — A Courier has just arrived with the report that Big Foot has surrendered to the Seventh Cavalry…   —*The New York Times,* December 29, 1890.

A FIGHT WITH THE HOSTILES — *Big Foot's Treachery Precipitates a Battle* — Big Foot's braves turned upon their captors this morning and a bloody fight ensued…
—*The New York Times,* December 30, 1890.

ANOTHER INDIAN BATTLE — *Thirty-Three of the Hostiles Bite The Dust* — Early this morning another bloody battle took place between the Indians in Two Strikes' band and soldiers near this agency… The attack was sudden and unexpected, but the cavalry men returned a brisk fire and succeeded in keeping the savages in check until the arrival of a company of infantry…   —*The New York Times,* December 31, 1890.

1891

∾ A letter from Annie Jennings Wise Hobson:

Ashland, Jan 22nd, 1891.
Your letter my dear son telling of the darling's illness reached me yesterday evening. I am really glad I did not know of it until you could say she was really out of danger. I hoped to hear again today. As for myself, I feel as if I had been imprisoned amidst care and drudgery. As I wrote you, I insisted upon Alice's going to Richmond. Soon after she left the whooping cough fully developed with the three younger ones, and the boys are coughing more or less. It was a blessed relief to have Alice away. I could then control the children and watch over them as they needed. With the coughing & the cascading & restless nights it has been a severe ordeal and then there was so much chaos to restore to order. I felt I had a special mission, & the worst is over for the younger ones if Alice will take care of them & try to keep them from taking cold. Complications with lungs or liver is the thing to be dreaded in whooping cough especially with delicate children under seven years of age. A white woman who has been helping me with the mountain of mending & neglected clothes said, "Mrs. Hobson, God sent you at the right time to these children." I am glad I have been able to do it. I awoke this morning with a longing to know how little Katherine is. How I should have loved to have helped Katherine nurse her. God grant that she is really getting well. I know how you have both suffered to see her suffer & all the anxiety you felt. I looked at her picture (the Xmas one) last night & *pictured* all the darling had gone through. I hope you will let me hear very soon from her.

As I write, your inclosure of the money order was received in the letter forwarded to me from Richmond. I appreciated your sweet thoughtfulness in sending it, but I wish you had not, for you had already, & Katherine likewise, contributed too liberally towards my nurture. I have had to put aside all thoughts of the Memorial… I must tell you that I was a little "downed" by your criticism that found the poems "pleasing & touching—" was that all? Is there no strength in the epic… I am going to induce Adele W— to work that illustration of my sonnet up as she could do, & we will have that well lithographed & see if we cannot do something on shares with the Confederate Memorial Association…

After a few remarks in regard to your version of my speeches that wounded Katherine & mortified you I too prefer to let the matter drop. But I must tell you that I would give more than you will ever understand if this painful & most mortifying incident had not occurred and yet on the whole I see that it is well, even if one more of life's pleasant delusions is dispelled. I shall never again allude to it to Katherine, but in justice to myself I must reiterate my surprise and dazed feeling at the words attributed to me. I do remember saying to Mrs. Thayer that not only had you the burden of Cannon's family but your own generous impulses in helping others, and that you were a Wise like myself and one that disdained aught but the best if you could have it. All I said was really an indirect compliment to a generous nature. This conversation occurred *after dinner*— & I most emphatically deny, and in *pained astonishment*, the assertion that I said aught that could be contorted into the sentence you put in quotation marks— "that K— & H— should be

the poems This is a reference to the poems that A. J. W. Hobson wrote about the Lee Monument, reprinted in the previous chapter.

content to live in a simpler and less extravagant way & that then Henry would not have to work so hard." I could not utter a thought that had never been in heart & mind. I have some indistinct recollections of some remarks about the extravagance of young married women which was meant as a jest following something between H— & myself said in undertone. It would have been indelicate & ill-bred indeed to have entertained Mrs. Thayer & Katherine at my brother's table with such innuendo bits & criticisms. I must be candid & say that while the first heat of pained excitement is over, my mortification is intensified & I am perplexed to explain how either Mrs. Thayer or Katherine could have so misconstrued or contorted anything I said. I am very quick in my perceptions & I think it very probable that I can trace influences behind this that made them think one of my faults was the tendency to do this kind of thing. It is so evident that you & Katherine are fully persuaded that I did & said all I was accused of. You certainly do not accept my denial, & like some others say, "I talk so much that I do not know what I say." I am silenced towards Mrs. Thayer & Katherine. They are certainly very magnanimous & sweet tempered to forgive such intrusive, ill-bred remarks, but I must tell you that I feel as innocent of the spirit & words attributed to me as a proud, truthful well-bred woman should do, and that remarks made in so different a spirit should have been so contested & exaggerated perplexes, grieves & mortifies me. I shall never allude to them to either your wife or yourself again. If I ever meet Mrs. Thayer again I shall be strictly on my guard, and I cannot feel as unconstrained with Katherine. It is natural that you should look only at your wife's side & that her testimony should stand against mine. I again repeat I would give more than words can express if it had not occurred, & by God's help I will endeavor to forget it— as a woman & Mother I am wounded and humiliated as any true lady would be— You were right to tell me, because I had a right to defend myself, & it was best for me to be guarded in future in my intercourse with your wife's family. It is nonsense to say Katherine was not wounded & mortified by it. Now let it drop. My previous intercourse with your lovely wife was a great solace to my desolate life, & I trust that nothing will henceforth occur to mar that harmony between us. Perhaps at some future day she may know me well enough to wonder how she or her mother could have thus misunderstood me.

    I feel just what your anxiety is about your wife in the trial before her. If anything happened to her it would be a great blow to me on your account— but I believe God will carry her safely through and there will be another darling to add to the sunshine Katherine has brought to your life.

    God grant you every blessing you so rightly deserve & may the coming years lighten all the burdens of the past. I direct this to Symes Block & will write a letter to Katherine to the house. Kiss the darling baby for me & my letters will give my message to Katherine. Alice will be at home on Saturday. All the boys send love. I enclose Henry's letter which I forgot to do before.
—Your devoted mother, *A.J.W.H.*

    A letter from Catherine McKie Thayer:

My darling daughter—   This a.m. your p.c. came… Dr. Reed sat a half hour with me and, in some incidental way, spoke of a worthless fellow here, a husband & a father of four children, the wife a good woman & not well. The husband's father, through his attorney, had offered to take the four children, rear & educate them— and the communications come through Dr. Reed. He said he replied, "*No*" most emphatically— "if the offer were to take the Mother & children he would not say no" etc. The Dr. said that nothing but gross immorality should separate a mother from her children or some "*dire necessity*." I have no idea who Dr. R— refers to but the subject was so much on my mind, and I have thought so much of all that Henry did, that I wish you would read what I am about to say to him. I know that if he feels that my judgment is faulty, my love & interest are wholly sincere & tender. Ask Henry if it would not be wise to talk alone with Alice and get her views— draw her out in his kind way. He may influence her more than all others in this way— by advice, suggestion, may help her. She is young, unusually well, and the natural & rightful protector and companion of her children. She had the love of their father and while she may not be a woman of great executive ability, she undoubtedly loves her children and they love each other — and where *love is,* with what there must be in those children, they are more likely to do more than less, than one would expect— besides Alice will be satisfied with a modest home & way of living & this is much to Henry. Then, as to Mrs. Hobson assuming the entire care and responsibility of those children, I fear she would break down in a short time. Since I have known Henry she has had no housekeeping responsibilities, except during poor Cannon's last illness, and yet she is rarely well, always writes of weariness & overwork and still she has been at liberty to go & come as suited her feelings and wishes. I really feel that to assume such a load of care at her age and with her nervous temperament is what no friend of hers should permit her to do for her own sake. It does seem to me that one should think long and purposefully as to this subject. I know dear Henry wishes to do right— do his duty— and do justly, and I do not think he will take any hasty *action*— indeed I think he will hesitate long before he will separate a mother [end of letter]

Chicago, April 8th, 1891.
My Darling little "Dauda": Papa has not much time to write you a birthday letter, but he must send you the million gallons of love he feels for you. You are just like a little star for your Papa, which follows his every step, twinkling and laughing brightness and happiness into his life. You can't understand that now, but your still dearer Mamma will keep this letter for you, and some day when you are able to understand, and your Papa will be getting old and foolish, you will like to read the letter he writes you now.

Since I can't give you a birthday present on your birthday I must tell you about the doll that I am going to carry you from New York. She will have the most beautiful hair, with a big piece of real ribbon tied around it to keep it out of her eyes, and those eyes shall be just as nearly like yours as I can find, and they will open when she wakes up and shut when she goes bye-bye and you sing "rock-a-bye baby" to her as you sing it to Papa. Her ears will be little pink-tipped ones, and big enough for you to put your little finger into them, and make her deaf, as you try to do with Papa. Her nose will be so big and nice that you can blow it, and she shall have a handkerchief of her own. Her mouth and cheeks will look so much like cherries, you will bite a piece out for breakfast, as Papa bites yours. She will cry, too, and have such a lot of beautiful dresses, and, in a word, be such a doll as you have never seen at all.

doll that I am going to carry you from New York While in New York, Henry Hobson bought a doll for his daughter that would be forever known as "New Yorky."

You must let Charlotte, and Helen, and Gladys, and *Mildred even* play with it, and tell them to be gentle with dolly and not to pull her hair, because she will cry. But there is one little girl who must never play with your doll and that is "Lucy." (Selfish spirit.) When Lucy comes you must run to Mamma, or Mary, and say, "Hurry up, put dolly away; Lucy is coming."

And what do you think Papa saw yesterday as the "too-too" cars were bumping along, taking me to "York"? Why, Johnnie Bunnie! I heard something say "Hi"! I looked around and there sat Johnnie Bunnie, on his hind legs, with a gray coat and a white cravat. His ears were standing straight up, and his hands and feet were all black, where the tar baby had caught him. "Hello! Mr. Hobsing," he said, "where's Kaky?" I replied, "Why, Johnnie Bunnie, is that you, how did you get loose from the Tar baby, and away from Mr. Fox, and Mr. Dog?" "Easy enough," he said; "tar baby couldn't hold me long, I was so strong, and Mr. Fox and Mr. Dog were both afraid of me when I got loose." "Why, Johnnie Bunnie," I said, "you are telling a story; didn't Kaky and I see Mr. Fox have you the other day, and you were begging him to let you go?" "Oh, no," he said; "Mr. Fox was down on his knees, begging me not to hurt him, and I was just lying on my back laughing at him."

What do you think Papa did then just to fool Johnnie Bunnie? He hollered right quick: "There's Mr. Fox coming, and Mr. Dog is mighty close behind him!" Johnnie Bunnie jumped up and he said, "Humph, I certainly am sorry I have not the time to stay and see them, but dinner must be ready by this time, and my Papa doesn't like to wait for dinner." Away he went "plunkety, plunkety, plunkety," "plunk, plunk, plunk." But just as he was getting over the fence he turned around and hollered back, "Tell Kaky I heard she was two years old and was going to have a 'bufuller' doll. I want to see it and am coming again soon."

Away he went through the corn-fields, and there wasn't any fox at all, because Papa was just fooling.

And now, my precious little Easter lily, Papa must say good-by, and send you more love than he has for all the other little girls in the world put together. Papa thinks about you and Mama all the time. Take good care of her and Grandma, for not many little girls have such a Mamma and Grandma as my little "Kaky."

You must say your prayers when you go to bed, on your birthday, and ask God to bless your Papa, who loves you as much as though you were as big as an elephant.

Give Mamma her letter, and as for you, my little angel, your Papa showers wishes for all blessings upon you. —Your Sweetheart Papa, "*Henry*."

Johnnie Bunnie, Mr. Fox, Mr. Dog, and the Tar Baby are all characters that appear to have been borrowed from Joel Chandler Harris' Tales of Uncle Remus.

Colorado Springs, Monday afternoon, April 13, 1891.
My Dearest Husband—   Today no letter from you, but I did not expect one. Have just come in from a walk with Frank and Katherine, she in her carriage… I have no news from Denver but a letter from Mr. Jermain, enclosing $2.00 fee for [illegible] fee. I returned $1.00 as the charge was only $1.00—thought it best to be as particular as the old gentleman desired. I hope you are prospering in every way, my darling Henry and that your business may prosper. …Your own devoted wife, *Katherine*.

China made by William Ellis Tucker of Philadelphia and given to Sarah Sergeant when she married Henry Wise in 1840 and then used at the Executive Mansion during his term as Governor.

Katherine Hobson and Henry W. Hobson, born May 16, 1891.

the boy Henry Wise Hobson born May 16, 1891.

A letter from Annie Jennings Wise Hobson:

28 College Place, April 21st, 1891.
My dear Son— I was delighted to get the telegrams from Richmond which told that you were safely back with Katherine & the dear baby… I would prefer sending you the china because I have no place to keep it. Yet if you would rather it should stay as it is till the new house is built, it can be done. The silver you can take out if you wish it sometime on your return… I have given up all expectation of having more than a temporary abiding place for myself. I have had my part of the enjoyment of these things my dear son & if it will give you pleasure to have them, I undoubtedly wish you to enjoy them. I feel sure that when Cannon's children grow up you will let them have a share of them if they are worthy to do so. Remember the bedstead at Mrs. Taliaferro's. She has that stored in an outhouse. I think it will be well to have that sent to you as soon as you have a place for it. I know how Katherine will value all we had as sacred to the past of our lives… God bless you all. Kiss your darlings for me. —Your devoted mother, *A.J.W.H.*

28 College Place, April 1891.
My dear Katherine— Just a line to thank you for your sweet letter telling about the Easter cards being received & the details about the preparations for the darling's birthday that I so loved to know… This is another month of anniversaries for me. Yesterday was the day of my betrothal to my noble, devoted love, 24th was my little Marianne's birthday, 25th Cannon's, 28th, mine. April 4th my precious husband entered into his rest 24 years ago this April. My first baby Plumer died on the 27th. Around them all I shed no bitter tears & with the tears are tender smiles & gratitude [illegible] God for all the blessings for earth & heaven that they brought me & above all for the wonderful spiritual experience that has brought me into closer fellowship with the Divine & proved that our [illegible] God keeps every promise… Every day I pray God to bring you safely through the trial before you & to bless you with a lovely babe. I am thankful that you are so brave & well. I appreciate all your love & appreciation of Henry. God will give him the strength to do the work & bear the trial he has appointed in connection with the many he has to work for… Alice writes that all with her are well. Kiss my darlings. God bless you all. —Devotedly, *A.J.W.H.*

Family matters:

Denver, May 20, 1891.
Dear Mother Thayer— All are well at our house, except that the boy is a "howler." He disturbs his Mother a good deal and if he continues it tonight I am going to make a fight to have him put in the back room. I think it very important that K— should not have her rest broken… Give many hugs and kisses to my darling little daughter. I can't tell you how much I miss her. Tell her that Papa thinks of her all the time and loves her ten times as much as the boy. —Yours affectionately, *Henry W. Hobson.*

Denver, May 22, 1891.
Dear Mother Thayer— All are well at our house. The baby seems to be

getting better, sleeps better at night and gives his mother more rest. Your note duly received this morning. I note how you rise in arms in defense of my past attacks upon Katherine. I suppose she has been a remarkably good child. By the way your telegram about the express package did not reach me until yesterday, for two causes, one is that it is never safe to send telegraphic messages between here and the Springs and expect them to be delivered under twenty-four hours; the second is, that you sent the message by the *Postal Telegraph Company*, a new Company, which may possibly account for its not being delivered. It costs 15 cents more to send a message by telephone, but it is no more trouble and is always quick and safe. I have several times called your and Katherine's attention to this fact, and it may be well to remember it, in case you are anxious to have a message reach me promptly. All join in love, —Yours affectionately, *Henry W. Hobson.*

—Give my dearest love & a thousand kisses to my darling little "dauda" —Katherine said today that the way I treat the boy and the way I treated "dauda" when a little baby are noticeably different.   H.

Catherine McKie Thayer to her brother:

May 22nd, 1891.
Dear Brother Edwin—   You will appreciate my relief and pleasure when I tell you that Kittie had a fine perfect boy Sat am the 16th. K— & the baby are doing as well as possible so far. Little Katherine is with us and is a great comfort. She is very active as you know…

…We had to order Dodds to shingle the old home house and lay porch floor— paid $117. He was ordered to put on the best shingles, and he writes that "the roof ought to last twenty-five years." I hope it will, but it won't. Now with love to wife… and a great deal from Frank & me to you, as always your loving sister.   —*Catherine Mck. Thayer.*

Denver, May 23, 1891.
Dear Mother Thayer—   All well here. The youngster is getting to be quite an orderly & well behaved young man. He does not feed as often at night as K— and is not so wakeful. When he is asleep, he is pretty good looking, but when awake, you never saw such scowls and faces and he is far from good looking. Love and a thousand kisses to my little "dauda" —I sometimes am right heart-sick to see her. Next week I think if it suits your convenience I will have Thompson bring her up for a day— about Thursday or Friday. With love—   —Yours affectionately, *Henry W. Hobson.*

Edwin J. McKie, 1818–1895.

Denver, June 14, 1891.
Dear Mother Thayer—   I will scribble you a line and at the same time try some new paper my stationer wishes me to buy. K— will probably not get a letter downtown before afternoon. Yesterday she had a bilious attack and some trouble with her bowels attended by a headache. The Doctor said it was nothing serious and was caused by something she had eaten and the warm weather. I am quite sure a day or two before we had new potatoes which she ate. They upset me, or something did, and I attribute K's trouble to same course. She was much better last night and Miss Miller told me she had a good night and when I left the house this morning K— was still asleep. The

Henry W. Hobson, left, and Katherine Thayer Hobson, center, at their first house in Denver with children Katherine and Henry and a nurse.

most serious result is that it throws her back a day or two in getting out and I think she needs exercise badly. The boy is splendid and was as good as possible all day yesterday.

But what I wish to say especially today is tell you how much love I send you for your birthday. Surely no one has ever come more gratefully and graciously into my life than you have done and I feel assured that you enter fully into my feelings and life both in sympathy and with love. Your birthday is therefore an especially glad day for me as indeed it is to all your family and friends. I wish I could have had the time to go out and hunt up some nice testimonial of my love & affection, but as it is, and on account of great press of work, I have to content myself with a box of flowers which will be sent you tomorrow. K— and I were speaking yesterday of what a disappointment it is to us that we cannot spend your birthday with you. But in any event be assured that we will be with you in spirit and that throughout the day we will turn in mind & thoughts very frequently towards you with much love & tenderness.

I have been talking to K— lately about how pleasant it would be if instead of building a big expensive house in Denver, we were all to go back to your sweet old place to live, and to the old house and farm the place. Six months of the year at least you could be there and two or three months we could be out here with you. Thus we could be more together than now. I could establish myself in Albany, not so much in law work exclusively as in a line of work which would not confine me so much and would reach out to this country— as for instance, representing and looking after the western investments of companies & individuals. She says I could go to Albany every day as Mr. Thayer used to do. I am tired of this country and people. I am wearing out here and getting very little out of life for what I give and I would like to go back to live amongst people with whom I can sympathize more. We were talking about how pleasant and sweet it would be for you to go back to the old home of your childhood and see your grandchildren growing up around you as you grew up amidst healthy & pure surroundings and associations, physical, religious, and mental. Such things and plans may be all dreams but still it is pleasant even to think of them. I cannot think that I will remain permanently in Denver and yet a change must necessarily be a serious thing. As my children are born, I find I have not so much of the ambition for show and fame as I once had but long more for real quiet family life and look forward to raising and training my dear little ones to make good men and women.

But I must close with dearest love and with wishes that the Good Father will bless all of us by sparing you for many years to come.   —Your loving son, *Henry W. Hobson.*

to build a house   This refers to the plans to construct a new house at 933 Pennsylvania Avenue in Denver, years later described as one of the "handsomest and most substantial residences in the city."

June 30th, 1891.
My Darling Husband—   This morning your letter came & Katherine would have it "read & kiss Papa's letter." …We are going to drive this afternoon— a lovely day. I am more and more relieved that we are going to build a house more moderate in price. It would be such a mistake to be burdened by too much expense— especially with all the *burdens* you have of necessity. Carriage here so will stop. Much tender love & kisses. Will answer my letters while here though writing makes my eyes ache & I feel

as if pins were "sticking me" as Katherine says. But a few notes will not matter. With more love always, your devoted wife *Katherine*.

Col Springs, July 6th, 1891.
My Darling Husband—   Have been thinking of you all day and of the plans and wondering if you are not quite worn out today, after figuring and bending over the "pictures" as Katherine calls the house plans. Katherine was quite expressive after you left. She cried and insisted "Papa *is* coming back." We will decide on mantels as soon as the plans arrive. Mother & the babies have been for a drive and Frank took me to circus, which was *poor*, except for three baby lions… Be sure to occupy *my* room if anyone stays at house. I never like anyone to sleep in my bed & room. Hope we can get satisfactory bids on plans very soon. Katherine asks to "go to telephone & speak to Papa." With heart's best love, your devoted wife, *Katherine*.

Colorado Springs, July 8th, 1891.
My Darling Husband—   …Am quite excited to feel that excavations for our house commence tomorrow on your birthday which will be such a pleasant association. Will go to the telephone this afternoon & hear your plans and speak of stone. Wish I could be with you tomorrow. I know you do not like birthdays of your own— still I must always remember them, and think of and pray for your best good & our happiness together & with our children. Mary sent a letter of *yours* here, which I return. Hope there is nothing important in it… —My heart's best love, *Katherine*.

Colorado Springs, July 9th, 1891.
My Darling Husband—   All day long I have thought of and longed to be with you. My token will be a little delayed, but something you will prize I know. Certainly my whole heart's love is yours my Darling, and dearest prayers for every good to come to you… I wrote Dr. Stedman & told him of Katherine's condition. She is not ill, but "my bowels are not right" —took her to Dr. Reed yesterday, he said, "No medicine," but she is losing flesh & this irregularity has gone on long enough. I told Stedman the whole story & expect medicine tomorrow. The little darling is all about, but does not eat as well as she ought & is a little pale… Fondest love & many kisses. Your own devoted *Kittie*.

Colorado Springs, July 13th, 1891.
My Darling Husband—   The day is deliciously cool and your son is in the hammock asleep by me as I write, Katherine in her crib. The first thing she said this morning was "I have no pain" & she is decidedly better… I think Stedman's remedies have acted like a charm. It is a great thing to have such a good Doctor for our children. Katherine sat on my lap at breakfast & ate some oatmeal and I read her your letter from Las Vegas which had just arrived & she told Margaret, "*Papa sends Dauda hundred kisses and wants to eat me up.*" … I will be so glad to see you again my Darling One… *Katherine*.

Colorado Springs, July 14, 1891.
My Darling Husband—   This morning I received your telegram and am glad you will be in Denver tomorrow. Will go to the telephone in afternoon to let

Katherine Thayer Hobson with Henry Wise Hobson on porch of the first Denver house. Photographer, John A. Trendel, 1420 Larimer St. Denver.

you know how we all are & to hear of you. Katherine is decidedly better. Poor little creature has suffered with retention of the urine. She would draw up her knees & scream with pain and say, "Something hurts." "Wipe my tears." But Doctor Stedman sent medicine which has acted like a charm. The diarrhea has ceased and this morning she ate with relish… Yesterday morning we all took a long drive— the little baby slept all the way. It was a cool delicious air… If there is a thunderstorm I will not go to telephone… —Your devoted wife *Katherine*.

Denver, July 24th, 1891.
Dear Mother Thayer—   The men have commenced work upon the house, and we will soon have to commence making payments. Under the contract we pay every month about 80%. I wish you would write me, at once, about money arrangements. You had better write me fully so that I will know just how matters stand, and what arrangements you wish to make about payments. Of course, if it is necessary, I can arrange to raise what I owe you and pay it first, but will say frankly that if you have money on hand that you are holding for the purpose of putting into the house, it would be a material assistance to me if you would pay that out first, and let me make the last payments… Our boy is splendid, and I am rapidly developing quite an interest in him. —Yours affectionately, *Henry W. Hobson*.
  —Tell my darling little one that Papa thinks of her every hour. I think her Mother was quite wounded that K— did not "howl" when she came away. —H.

⁌ Family matters:

922 Broad Street, Richmond, September 9th, 1891.
Mr. Hobson.   My dear Sir—   Your letter duly received, and I can assure you that I appreciate all you say. Indeed her [Alice Hobson, widow of John Cannon Hobson] future has pressed with much anxiety on my heart and brain, and I feel unable to cope with the grave question of what she can do, and what can she get to do, that will afford an honest support for her and her little ones. There is really so little open to a woman with so few available gifts and such a large family. Whenever I see her, she talks the matter over with the greatest anxiety and looks upon her future as we do, and feels the importance of and is ever on the lookout for employment. The last suggestion from her, (and I expect you will agree with us in thinking it the best,) is that she commence at once to prepare herself to teach. She says that Mr. Brown of Petersburg, Virginia, was a good friend of her husbands and has told her that he would do all he can to have her appointed teacher as soon as she is ready to accept the position. He is Supt. of the public schools of that city. When she gets the appointment she can feel that it is a permanent one, and she will receive from thirty to fifty dollars per month. This amount added to the amount the church allows her (the widows & orphans fund) and the little interest she receives from her investment, will go far in defraying her expenses. I trust she may be able to carry out this plan, for to me it looks like the most feasible one. I think it best to keep her in ignorance of our correspondence. You are daily performing your Christian duty in providing for the fatherless and widow in their affliction, and great will be your reward. Wish-

ing you every success in fighting the battle of life, I am most truly your friend.
Geo. Wm. Richardson.

❧ A letter from Catherine McKie Thayer:

Oct. 22, 1891.
My darling One— You see I have taken a large sheet like you. Your letter of Tues eve *came* this a.m.— such a comfort… I wish I could see *you all* for a day, but I cannot "run up" as some can you know— but it is a joy to hear of you so often & fully… Henry talked to me of his "very strong desire" (not to get rich) but to feel that he had enough to provide for the dependent people in Va. & feel too that you had enough for yourself & children and not be burdened by those in Va. He said ever since J's death [John Cannon Hobson] this thought had passed upon him— that his health was good, but life was uncertain & he wished to see you & the babies provided for first of course and then the others…

Colorado Springs, December 2nd, 1891.
My Darling Husband—   Had a letter from you yesterday & suppose you were too busy to write. I look for the postman every minute to bring me a line. Mother is better daily. We got her up in a chaise for a few minutes last evening. She was soon in a dripping perspiration, so weak, but day after tomorrow I hope to leave for home— Friday, morning train. I have felt so badly to be away from you all these days, and the only compensation is that I have done Mother great good… Your letter of yesterday just here, and thankful you are well, how glad I will be to see you my Darling one. Always your loving devoted *Katherine.*

Colorado Springs, December 3rd, 1891.
My Darling Husband—   Your letter received this morning… Both children are very well, and I have them both at night with no trouble and you will not need to have broken nights rest, it is all wrong and you must have your rest unbroken hereafter. I trust you have good news from Alice and your Mother. What a delighted woman she will be to have you for Xmas & those children— for you are an ideal to them… I hope you can run down here for a few hours before you go East. Mother does love & enjoy you so much. Your daily letters have been such a comfort to me & each morning I have felt strengthened by them… Take fondest love & kisses from your own devoted Wife, *Katherine.*

New York, December 19th, 1891.
My Darling little "Dauda":   Papa promised to write you a Xmas letter, and though it is late and I am tired, I am going to send you a little letter all for yourself.
   When old Kris Kringle comes around, —for that is what Papa used to call Santa Claus, —you must steal up on him, whilst he is putting pretty things in your stocking, and say "Booh"! and then when he is scared you must grab his bag of toys, and run away with it. But when you have gotten it you must be sure and divide the toys with your sweet little Brudder.
   I do wish you were with your Papa in "York." You never saw such beautiful toys and dolls and all kinds of things. What do you think happened to Papa at

a toy store the other day? He was trying to see how a spring gun went off, and he got his finger caught in a spring, and he squealed like a pig. Just think of your Papa squealing in a big toy store: "Wee! Wee! Wee!" People thought I was such a funny Papa.

I bought a gun for your little cousin Cannon, a ball and bat for Henry, a paint-box for George, a set of ten-pins for Jennings, and some pretty things for Mary and the baby. And all the time Papa was thinking, "I wish my darling Kaky were here."

My little darling, your Papa loves you, oh so much! You must always love Papa better than anybody except Mamma; and when people say, "Kaky, who is your lover?" you must always say, "My darling Papa." Papa does wish so much to be with you.

Good-night, you little light of my heart. You won't understand much of this letter, but Mamma must keep it for you, and some of these days you will read it and think, "How my Papa loved me."

Kiss Mamma and Grandma and little Brudder for me. —Your devoted Papa, *Henry*.

My Darling little "Dauda":   Papa must send you a little letter because he wishes to see you so much "he could eat you up." Papa can't tell you how he longs to take you in his arms and play bum-bum-bum, swing, horse-back and everything else you like. You are getting so big now that soon Papa will have to swing and bum-bum-bum "ittle brudder" and let you look on. Tell Grandma that "ittle brudder" already likes to be jumped, and whenever Papa comes around he begins to fuss until he is jumped.

Papa sends you a little piece of poetry about kittens and babies. Give it to Grandma and tell her she must never drown your kittens.

Mamma and "ittle brudder" both wish to see you dreadfully and so does your Papa. God bless you my little one.   —Your devoted Papa, "*Henry*."

This poem was attached to the original copy of this letter but was not included with the published letters

Which One Was Kept

There were two little kittens, a black and a gray,
   And grandmamma said, with a frown;
"It never will do to keep them both,
   The black one we'd better drown."

"Don't cry, my dear," to tiny Bess,
   "One kitten's enough to keep;
Now run to nurse, for 'tis growing late
   And time you were fast asleep."

The morrow dawned, and rosy and sweet
   Came little Bess from her nap;
The nurse said, "Go into mamma's room
   And look in grandma's lap."

"Come here," said grandmamma, with a smile,
   From the rocking chair where she sat;
"God has sent you two little sisters,
   Now, what do you think of that!"

> Bess looked at the babies a moment,
>   With their wee heads, yellow and brown,
> And then to grandmamma soberly said,
>   "Which one are you going to drown?"

Richmond, Virginia, December 26, 1891.
My Dearest Mother Thayer—   This morning I got your sweet letter with your generous present. My dear good Mother, it is not gracious to protest against presents received, but you are too generous to me. I think you are giving me and mine a royal present. Still I know it gives you pleasure and I therefore am grateful for all you do. Dear Mother Thayer one of the greatest pleasures of my life is the fact that I have been able to carry any light and joy into your life— that I can give you an assurance that your dear Daughter has a protector and husband to care for her all her life and that I have given you dear little ones to comfort your older years and make the "homeward path of life" bright and happy for you… God bless you and preserve you to us all for many years to come.   —Your loving son, *Henry W. Hobson*.

1892

A letter from Catherine McKie Thayer:

January 16th, 1892.
My darling Kittie—   No letters from anywhere today— it is dull, looks like snow and is snowing on the mountains now. We have had so many dull days looking like snow but none coming, but as Frank said yesterday, it is such a relief to have it milder. I trust you are well and your little ones— bless their dear hearts, and Henry too. Frank has been to get tax list, $380.70. The assessment is low on this place, only $5,600, but the rate is high, almost 4%— so many improvements at once— water extension, school building budget etc. We will pay half, $190.35, before Feb 1 and leave the other half until July or before July 1st any time…

Colorado Springs, February 18th, 1892.
My Darling Husband—   I have your letters written on the train and they are such a comfort to me. Katherine says over & over, "Papa sent love & kisses to me." She talks about you very often & wants "to go to New York." I shall send a telegram so you may hear in New York on your arrival. The weather is perfect here— and the children out all the time… Next week I expect to go to Denver to see about the house… So Darling I will try & not neglect our house. How I wish I might be with you in Albany today and in New York, but with such a big elegant boy to consider I can only be thankful, and more grateful than words can express, for my home— which means my Husband & Babies…   —Your own loving *Katherine*.

Colorado Springs, February 20th, 1892.
My Darling Husband—   Two letters from Cleveland received today. I quite felt as if I had been there and have always heard that Euclid Avenue, in early summer, was most lovely. The more you see of other cities the more you appreciate Denver, but I think you will like old Albany. Katherine suddenly got feverish & hoarse yesterday afternoon & when I came up at eight

Katherine Thayer Hobson and her daughter, Katherine. A. E. Rinehart, Denver.

in the evening her hands were still warm. So I gave up going to the Club Ball though I had intended going with the Jacksons for a little while. About nine Katherine gave a croupy cough and Frank went off for Dr. Reed. He sent a prescription which seemed to relieve her. She did not have a bad attack at all— only I feel so badly to have the slightest thing come to the darling in the way of pain. Doctor here this morning said K— could be dressed. She does not feel her usual bright self, but much better in every way— she so enjoyed hearing me read your messages to her & repeated them over & over… I trust you have heard from your Mother. No letter here yet from her, but I will write again. By the way, suppose you do not send for your Mahogany bed just yet. It might hurt your Mother's feelings to have your Father's bed taken away and we will have plenty of furniture without it. We will have a mahogany set for your room, cherry for blue room, ash for red room, and for the present I wish to keep yellow room for a convenient storeroom. Next week I am going up to Denver to see about several matters. Much love & many kisses… Take the best care of yourself. Your own loving *Katherine*.

Wednesday A.M. [undated, most likely February 1892]
My Darling Husband—   Your letter received with your Mother's. I never seem to do the right thing regarding her. I purposely did not allude to February 15th & Cannon's death, though wrote her and now she feels hurt… My plan is to leave here tomorrow P.M. Mother better, and no reason why I should stay longer. We hoped for plans so we might look them over & decide on *details* together, as one can not by writing— if they would only come tomorrow A.M. Mother intends to supply *funds* and wishes us to build this Spring and I wish her to have her wishes and ideas adopted in the house. It will be a great comfort in the future to feel her hand and eye overlooked the minute details of my house & will sweeten life— but there is one thing you and I will insist upon, that a house must be finished by autumn. I don't care to build unless that can be assured, would rather wait a year. Good bye Darling, God bless you & bring us all safely home again. I never loved you as much as I do now. Katherine sends a kiss. Your own devoted *Katherine*.

February 22, 1892, University Club, New York.
My darling wife—   I received a letter from you this morning dated the 18th. You don't write very often but your letters are always so welcome & cheer me up so that I shall not quarrel with you… Tonight the Southern Society Dinner comes off but I shall not go. Any assemblage of Southern men always bores and provokes me, for I have to submit to an overflow of arrogance, self satisfaction, narrowness and self-exaltation that is very galling. I fear I should never have been born in the South… By-the-way, I had a long letter from Mother this morning. It was one of her characteristic epistles and except that it assured me she was not sick, I should have preferred not getting it. Oh well! I don't mind her letters… —Love & Kisses for all. Your devoted husband *Henry*.

Denver, March 10th, 1892.
My Darling Husband—   Your telegram from Chicago came yesterday and your letter, en-route, just brought to me. Sorry to hear you had to spend eight extra hours with such a *set* as you describe in your car… Now I think of you with Uncle Johnnie and one always has such a good time with him… I beg of

you not to buy any expensive dolls for Katherine. Some of those little, 3,4, & 6 inch affairs, which she can use in her doll house... Take our heart's best love & kisses, from your children & Devoted wife, *Katherine*. P.S. Always give my best love to dear Uncle Johnnie.

◦∽ A letter from Annie Jennings Wise Hobson:

Ashland, April 9th, 1892.
My dear Katherine—   ...Alice Sr. went to Richmond on Tuesday to gather up her belongings. I can assure you that the new plan works beautifully. It is certainly far better for me & the children & she seems very much happier & more agreeable. I could be very happy if I did not constantly feel how much Henry disapproved of my undertaking & that the present arrangement only taxes him more. God grant I may see some way to stop that... I am often thinking how entertained you would be to see my life with these children. The three older boys sleep in the room Henry slept in. I have to wake them up every morning and you would smile to see the sleepy Cannon & George coming to put their arms around my neck... George has had a very bad cough lately & I let him sleep late. Mary has had a slight bilious attack during the last week but is benefited by a little dosing. Jennings, my heart's delight, is very self-willed and often disobedient... I arose this morning at five o'clock. Saturday morning means extra baths for all the children. I make them wash & sponge off every day, but twice a week get in big bath tubs. I am now writing before breakfast so as to send this off by the ten o'clock mail... I enjoyed your last letter so much. Kiss our darlings & Henry. God bless you all.   —Yours lovingly, *A.J.W.H.*

Denver Club, Denver.
April 10th, 1892
My Darling little three-year-old Dauda: Papa is so grieved that you will not be with him on your birthday. What a big girl you are, and you will soon be wearing a long dress like Mamma. How did you like that plaything I sent you? Just think! Papa used to have an old black nurse who jumped him just like that nurse in the toy.

To-day we are in the beautiful new house Grandma gave you and we do want darling little Kaky so much. Your doll-house is all ready, and dolls in it too; and your room is the most "bufuller" room in the house. All your dolls are crying for their Mamma Kaky to come back, and give them their dinner and undress them.

What do you think? Last night Papa and Mamma took your dear little kitty out to your new house, and she went all about hunting for you, and crying, "Kaky, Kaky, Kaky."

You are my sweet, precious little three-year-old rosebud to-morrow, and you must think about Papa, and love him, I want you to be a great comfort always. Papa loves you more than tongue can tell.

You must be a very good girl and mind your good Grandma, who loves you very much. Everybody loves Kaky, and so you must not do anything to make people sorry they love you.

Papa is going to bring you home very soon.

A thousand kisses for you, my little jewel.   —Your devoted Papa, *Henry W. Hobson.*

THE FAMILY LETTERS

❦ Family matters:

Young's Hotel, Boston, June 20, 1892.
Dearest Mother Thayer—   I was a brute to forget your birthday, but I did and there is no use of whipping the devil around the stump. Still, you may pardon me when, for remember that I forget my own Mother's, wife's, babe's, sometimes my own. But it does not need a birthday dear Mother Thayer to fill my heart with affection for you. Every day is the anniversary of some day in the past when you did something loving and good for me and so each day makes me care more and more for you… I shall take you back some bit of a momento, not much, only an earnest of love and heart-felt wishes that you may be spared many years to me and mine. I have only a moment to write. Much love—   —Your loving son, *Henry W. Hobson*.

Denver, July 11, 1892.
Dearest Mother Thayer—   Many thanks for your sweet birthday letter. Do you know that the first thought I had of my birthday was today when your letter came. I had forgotten it entirely but that is not surprising for I had a thousand things to think of. Yesterday, Saturday, I had a telegram sent from K— sending love & kisses from all and I never connected it with my birthday. I write hurriedly at 10:30 o'clk. I shall surely see you this week. Much love   —Yours lovingly, *Henry W. Hobson*.

❦ The Summer of 1892:

In the summer of 1892, Katherine Thayer Hobson vacationed at Manhattan Beach on Long Island with her two children and wrote frequently to her husband in Denver. Vacationing with her was Katherine "Katie" Savage, the granddaughter of James Jermain and the niece of Katherine's Hobson's first husband, Barclay Jermain. Also visiting was Thomas Nelson Page, Henry Hobson's close friend from Virginia, who was courting Katherine Savage. The letters were written from the Oriental Hotel on Manhattan Beach (see letterhead at right). Excerpts are printed here.

July 10, 1892.
Katie is anxious Tom should come down & made me say whether she would like to have him come or whether she would best enjoy herself without him. And she said, "Oh, I want him to come."

July 13th, 1892.
Katie & Tom are on the piazza and I have asked to join them presently… They have been out in a row-boat this afternoon… We went bathing this morning & Tom is teaching Katie to swim, the chief feature seems to be not holding her up for Katie would disappear. And then a kind of water-spout and tremendous spouting and then Katie would gradually appear. She said she was full of salt-water but smiling all the time. I have talked to Tom as you advised, and I think he means to be very careful & let Katie have an opportunity of knowing

him thoroughly. I should say that she is pleased with his attentions, but can't say anything more. Her father comes down this week, and he can see Tom and make friends with him.

July 15th.
Tom & Katie are enjoying each other most of the time. She told me yesterday she liked him better than any man whom she knew and wondered why she were not madly in love with him and she wishes to see him and know him thoroughly and decide *how much* he means to her— that she feels it the greatest honor to have *such* a man devoted to her. Tom behaves beautifully— and is lovely and attentive to me & the children. He wishes there were other girls here to devote himself to, but *she* is the only one.

July 16th.
Tom is in at dinner with some friends— men who heard he was here & came down to spend the afternoon with him & evening. He is not in a very happy state of mind. At his time of lifetime, even moments lost are very trying, but he has Katie to himself much of the time. Her father will come Monday & he and Tom can make friends. Katie tells me she likes Tom better than any man she knows. (Tom of the private opinion the others are all boys.) I really believe if he progresses slowly & gives her time he would win, but he may go too fast. I am busy cautioning him… I am writing now so that one of Tom's friends will post this in town tonight— no Sunday mails from here.

July 19th.
Tom left us this morning at eleven o'clock. Kate went upstairs for a book to return to him, suddenly the porter came & told Tom he would have to run for his train, which he did— without a good-bye to Katie— she looked blank and when she came— you should have heard her expressions of surprise. She sank in a chaise and said she did not believe he had gone— of course he told me he adhered to his promise but she knows he is interested in her and wonders she "is not desperately in love with him." Thinks she began thinking of him as an older man, not a possible beau, and that is the reason Mr. Savage is coming here today & he takes Katie up on Lake Champlain camping in August & she says if she makes up her mind that she is in love with Tom, she is going to ask him up there & he says if he is asked he will go. She likes & admires him more than any man whom she knows & says she would not endure seeing him attentive to any other girl. They have both talked to me and talked again, and I truly could not help admiring Tom & the stand he took. He has gone to visit at Monmouth Beach and has many invitations for the summer, but he said he thought it time to leave here before things went too far. Marie writes most discouragingly of her Father [James Jermain] and that she is very anxious. I feel Katie may be called home any hour.

July 24th.
Tom is back, came about two o'clock and he & Katie are on Piazza talking it out. Miss King took Tom into her care all the afternoon & he came home from a walk with a daisy in his button-hole which we made him take out before we would go to dinner with him. Katie said he might love Miss King to his hearts content, but to see a daisy in a man's button-hole was sickening.

July 26th.
Yesterday the hottest day of the season and I had to go N.Y. and over to Jersey City with Katie, though Tom offered to do it all for me. However I went at once to a hair shampooing parlor & had my hair attended to. I sat there quietly until it was time to meet Tom & Katie at Delmonico's for lunch… She confided in me that if she were to see much more of Tom she should be desperately in love with him, that she almost loved him now, that he was the dearest fellow in the world and I truly think if Tom takes his time, and goes very carefully, he will win… I was much amused when Tom told me that he was telling Katie that she would marry young Carter of Cooperstown & she turned and said, "Oh no I won't! There is hereditary deafness in the family." …She told Tom, so he says, that she liked him much better than any man whom she knows and he went off feeling greatly encouraged. I was getting a little tired of *both* of them…

Oriental Hotel, Manhattan Beach, Long Island, July 28th, 1892.
My Darling Husband—   Last evening I received your letter of Sunday. It was such a comfort to read all of your long, big sheets of papers— to hear about the speech etc. I know you did well. The idea of a *Butler* is so new to me that I will have to take a few hours in which to think it over. I know we need a man for certain things, but it seems to me that our house & our demands are not as large as many who keep a waitress and chambermaid combined. Indeed I know this is a fact and if Belle can't do the work we must get some abler bodied servant. In many ways I should dislike a man very much— and I do not think it would be possible to adjust our family to such an arrangement. It is all very well for you to desire it, who are away all day & when you are home have a man to wait upon you— & then you go away so often too, but the inconveniences would be mine and I think we are able, & I should adapt our living to what a cook & waitress can do for us— with a third person as nurse. Anyway I wish to try it before I believe it can not be done… Marie writes me that Katie arrived, & her Grandfather [James Jermain] so glad to see her. I think she takes a more serious view of life & Tom has done her no end of good. Your own devoted & loving wife, *Katherine.*

The Farm, Cambridge, August 9th, 1892.
My Darling Husband—   … I am so glad you have a good man— and if you think it best to hire him permanently, why do so. Would be glad if he could get another half-day place— it seems too bad to have to feed a man. They eat like wolves generally, but if you feel it is the better, may I agree with you and we can try it. I know Annie will not wish to give up her room— she has so many things & it is larger and I think so convenient for a cook and the n. west room will be quite large enough for a man, but you can decide that if you think best either way… Tomorrow I expect the cook & very glad I shall be. I wish you could eat one of my breakfasts… We see our dear old Whiteside cousins and it is a great pleasure to see them & hear of the old times… I think of you all the time & hope you are well. How glad I shall be to see you my darling. My heart's best love, your own loving wife, *Katherine.*

The Farm, Friday morning. August 12th, 1892.
My Darling Husband—   Yesterday I had three letters from you— one from the Springs was such a special comfort & joy to me… Katherine has on her flannel dress and plays on the porch until the grass dries… She said this morning "I am growing so fat that Papa will say when he sees me, why who is this big girl?" … Henry is rolling a little wagon about the floor & hall— he is such a mischief— one has to watch him every minute. Yesterday a big fat letter came to Tom [Thomas Nelson Page], addressed to my care from Katie. I did so wish to know its contents & know Tom will inform me quickly… Tenderest love & kisses, Your own devoted & loving wife, *Katherine*.

Johnsonville, Aug. 13th, 1892. Saturday.
My Darling Husband—   Yesterday brought me your letter saying you were not feeling well. It worried me so to think of your midnight work at the office. Am waiting for my train for Troy and will scribble a line as I may not have another chance today… Katherine was up & ate breakfast with me at 1/4 past seven. She confessed to a very naughty act while I was away yesterday. I had shown her a little angel with wings & tiny flaxen curls and let her hold it in her hand until she was satisfied, then took her & showed her where we would keep it— that Grandpa gave it to Mamma, when I was a little girl and that I would feel so badly if it were broken and to be sure not to touch it— that when she wished it I would be glad to show it to her. Well, when I was away she went and got it "and bited off the little angel's feet and broke one of its wings," so she told me, and so it is. I was distressed for I took time to explain to her why I wished to keep the little toy & did not do as many would, take it away before she had enjoyed it… I did not whip her, but I told her the lovely lilies I had brought from Cambridge she could not have, nor the little frosted cakes (she calls pies). I was foolish enough to cry for she disappointed me so… This is the first naughty act she has done in a long long time… I found out in N.Y. two of your Grandfather's favorite dishes— fried apples & bacon for breakfast and baked pears and we will have them. Do try and not work so late at night— it will wear you surely and you will not be as well and able to work the next day. I am going to get some little token for Mr. Jermain's birthday— it is today and send it to him… I expect to have a great visit with Nellie, for it is five years since we met & as she says "Engaged, married & two children since we parted." … Next week we are going to take some drives to Bennington & White Creek… the golden-rod lines the roads and I have never seen the country as beautifully green in August. It is like June. Now my darling one, take my tenderest love & a heartful of longing to see and be with you. Always your own loving wife, *Katherine*.

South Cambridge, August 14th, 1892.
My Darling Husband—   Yesterday I went to Troy for the day and accepted Mr. Jermains's invitation and took dinner with him on his birthday. Marie telephoned me that *he* wished me to come and I went down at one o'clock. He was very sweet and glad to see me and asked me to come again and said, "I thank you for coming." He was helped to the table and is much better than three weeks ago… I took him a little china cream jug & sugar bowl which he seemed to like and said it is very pleasant to be remembered. Marie said, "It is the loveliest thing that ever happened— your coming today." And of course to

feel that I have seen the old man and that the strained position of nearly five years regarding them is removed is a relief.

Darling do you know I never loved you as much as when I walked away, down the path to the cars, from the house, after my visit, or as fully realized what your love means to me and how happy I am and blessed, and you are more and more to me every day of my life… Marie Jermain spoke to me about Mr. Page, said he was following up Katie now with letters… that she felt sorry to have anyone come between Katie and her last year of school, that Mr. Savage had written her about Mr. Page's "attentions" and she had replied that she thought he might stand his chances among the many others— but if Mr. Page & Katie were interested in each other she thought all attentions should cease, all meetings, for a time until Katie is twenty. Then Katie would have had the benefit of the advantages of this fine school in Boston and sufficient time would have passed for Katie to test her regard for Mr. Page. *Anyway*, Marie does not wish Mr. Page to press his suit *now* that Katie is *a child*. Mr. Page has a great advantage and his age, position & personal charm are great etc. I told her frankly that I thought Tom very much interested in Katie, that I felt sure his actions could be governed by her wishes and Katie's father's… And I mean to write Tom and tell him to let the girl alone for a time. He said he will not make love to her and then tells her that he cares more for her than for any woman who he knows and asks her how much she likes him. This seems to be as nearly like love making & speaking as can be, but maybe not to a Southerner. Anyway, I am not going to have Katie troubled now… Katherine sent you love & kisses earlier in the day. She is a darling… Take my tenderest love & heart's longing for you, your own devoted wife, *Katherine*.

The International Trust Company, Denver, August 16, 1892.
My darling Kate—   I have your letter written in pencil from the train. I am again all right and have not been working at night for a week though I must go at it again tonight. I was quite delighted with your account of Kathleen and the wax angel— not with her action but with the cuteness of her way of doing things and her honesty in telling of it. You must be very careful about punishing her when she comes and tells you about any misdeed. I would rather have her do a hundred naughty things and go unpunished than to ever think of concealing anything or telling a falsehood. I was also much tickled over my boys spirit in asserting himself and fighting for his rights. What a sweet little action that was of Kathleen's when he bit her. Dear gentle spirited little thing how lovable she is— But we must not let the boy get into the habit of biting… —Devotedly, *Henry*.

South Cambridge, Thursday, August 18th, 1892.
My Darling Husband—   …Today I have a letter from Marie asking me if it would be too much to ask me to come to dinner next Saturday, that her Father wished to have that pleasure to look forward to. I shall try to go… Katherine is as happy as a Queen… Henry has one more tooth!! Now a double one— it is so delightful and I am so thankful that he gets them with so little difficulty… We are going for a walk now and the children for a drive to the station. Take tender love & many kisses from the children. God bless and keep you my darling husband. I hope you are feeling better & less over worked. Your own devoted wife *Katherine*.

August 21st, 1892, South Cambridge.
My Darling Husband—   …Have heard nothing from Tom & Katie and wonder if they are writing and planning to meet…   *Katherine.*

South Cambridge, August 23rd, 1892.
My Darling Husband—   Your letter received yesterday was such a comfort to me. I always do know I have your love & sympathy and strength, but with all your responsibilities, I did feel so regretful & I felt also that all the expressions of the past, taken as a whole, might have more earnestness than jest, and I have made up my mind not to be depressed & dwell upon the six Virginia children & let the sweetness and joy of anticipation be marred by anything. There is one thing I do think and feel sure of— that it is far better to have our children come near enough together to be companions than to have years elapse and no playtime between them, or school days or congeniality. Katherine and Henry are more to each other every day and she is very patient and gentle, generally. My darling husband I would not be happier than I am with your love and devotion… Much tender love & many kisses to our most precious one. Your own devoted wife, *Katherine.*

Denver, August 28th, 1892
My Darling little Kathleen, Papa's little Joy and Idol: Your dear Papa is going to write you a great big letter, all to yourself, just as he writes to Mamma. I am going to whisper all kinds of sweet and loving things to this letter, and when you get it you will hear lots of sweet things. You will hear your Papa calling, "Kathleen, little darling, why don't you come home to comfort me?" and "Kathleen, little sweetheart, I am awfully lonesome without you," and "Kathleen, you rascal, I want to have you ride on my back, and pull my hair," and "Kathleen, Mrs. Smith, why don't you bring your little girl to see us?"

I am down to-day with your sweet Grandma, who talks all the time about you, and tells me all the cunning things you do. She says she does not think Papa will ever let you come to Colorado Springs, when he gets you home— he will be so glad to see you. I think you and I will stay together a little while anyhow, and I expect we will have to let Grandma have "little Brudder."

How your Papa does wish he could chase chickens with you, and hold you way up in the trees, to knock apples off, and milk the cows, and make the old pig squeal, and lots of other things we do at Cambridge.

Hug and kiss your darling Mother, and your precious little "boy blue," for me every day. Your Papa loves you more than tongue can tell. —Your devoted Papa, *Henry.*

South Cambridge, August 28th, 1892.
My Darling Husband—   Well, Tom came Wednesday, late in the afternoon, and I was glad to welcome him. He seemed to enjoy being here though yesterday was rainy all day. He never was *more* charming. Read a new story to us, recited poetry and was a delight generally. We had a long talk about Katie and he said he made up his mind he would find out if Katie were at all interested in him before getting in too deeply himself & says he is satisfied she is not. He told her father everything— he quite agrees with the family generally that Mr. Savage is "more of a fool than anything else" and has influenced

Katie & made her feel that to be interested in anyone would be a great mistake. I don't think Tom is suffering, but I know he is disappointed… I took him to Johnsonville, six miles off, to catch the Saratoga train where he had duties today at the National Bar Association and was obliged to leave here so soon on that account. Katherine was overjoyed to see him and a box of peppermints & he was jubilant over the boy. Today is rainy and stops our hoped for trip to Bennington… Your letter from the Springs I received yesterday and one I could read to Tom, for his pleasure. I am glad Mother & Frank had the comfort of your presence for Sunday… —My hearts best love & many kisses. Your devoted *Katherine.*

South Cambridge, Wash County, Sept. 12, 1892.
My Dearest Husband—   Your letter to me and one to Katherine has just reached us. I think your letters to Katherine are perfectly wonderful and I mean to put them all together, to have them bound in parchment for her. They are the sweetest, most ideal letters a child ever had. I read the letter aloud to Nellie & Ada and they never heard "anything as beautiful." I was glad to hear that you went to the Springs and glad too that Mother did buy the rug… Edward took me to the auction and the crowd over on the lawn, bidding on the furniture, auctioned from the piazza. I got for $6.70 a beautiful pair of silver candlesticks, which belonged to my Great Grandmother McKie… and will take them out to Mother as a *present.* Of course she will value them more than anything else I could buy. I got two mahogany footstools and one cherry… a high post bedstead. I could not endure seeing the family pieces being carried off by people who live like pigs. There was sadness and amusement combined in the quaint auction & mostly country folk… I feel relieved about Tom Page, for Katie is very young and might have worried his life out. However if she had been fond of him how glad I should have been. Devoted & tenderest love and many kisses. Your own devoted wife, *Katherine.*

In 1893 Thomas Nelson Page married Florence Field of Chicago.

◦ Ever interested in politics:

Aroused at Silver Cliff — Silver Cliff, Oct. 17 [1892]— The grandest political demonstration in numbers of attendance, elegance of preparation and in the appreciation of the speeches by the multitude, has just closed at 10:30 p.m. At 5:30 a large concourse of carriages containing prominent citizens, and headed by the Silver Cliff cornet band, met Hon. Charles S. Thomas, Democratic candidate for Congress, and H. W. Hobson, at the Denver and Rio Grande depot, from whence they were escorted to the St. Cloud. A special table was spread in honor of the distinguished visitors… The hall was packed, and crowds thronged the doors and windows. The crowd is estimated from 1,200 to 1,500, fully twice the number that attended the meeting of Felker and Eaton the night before last. Hobson spoke first, and the audience was captivated by the pleasant, forcible and telling delivery of this brightest of Colorado's young orators. His style wins the hearer by its manifest cander [*sic*], and he made many votes for the Democratic ticket… The town has been illuminated and is ablaze with light and enthusiasm. Count on a victory for the Democratic state and county ticket in this Republican county this fall.   —*Unidentified newspaper clipping.*

Denver, October 27, 1892.
My Darling Kate—   …I am very lonesome without you and the children, but think it better if I go to St. Paul that you should not make the hurried trip up here. Tell K— I dreamed last night I saw her in a great big room full of dolls and they were chasing her around falling over her, hugging her, jumping on her shoulders etc. At last she saw me and came running, crying out, "Oh Papa, Papa help your dauda." And I grabbed her in my arms with one doll swinging to her hair. Kisses for my beautiful chicks. Much Love.   —Devotedly, *Henry*.

◊ Letters from Catherine McKie Thayer:

October 4, 1892.
…I told Frank just now of your expectations. "Well," he said, "if people knowing the pains & penalties of bearing children, will go on having them, it must be borne." I think he felt *sorry for you chiefly*, but he said very little. He thinks child bearing breaks down women & they look so worn. He will feel better when he has seen & talked with you…

Dec. 17, 1892.
My precious One—   …I know mails are not regular although our writing is. *I complained* in Denver and have here, and I know no other way to have neglect corrected. Send your envelope to your Postmaster or show it to your postman and ask the cause of delay. Call it what it is, bad service…   —devoted *Mother*.

Denver, December 18th, 1892.
My Dearest little Sweetheart: Papa has been thinking so much about you, ever since you ran away from him and went to see Grandma, and wants to see you so badly, that he must write and tell you about his love. Are you forgetting Papa, and is he getting away from his place of being loved "best of all"? That would break Papa's heart right in two pieces, just as you break a ginger-snap. That little rascal of a Brother has just come in, hunting for a piece of candy, and I asked him what Sister sent him. What do you think he did? He made a smack with his lips, which means that you sent him a kiss. He is such a funny boy, and can't talk a bit yet, and keeps saying "hau"! What do you think he did the other day? Why, Papa brought home a box of candy for Mamma, and gave "Brudder" one little piece. He saw the box, and knew what it looked like. Well, the next day he ran into the little library alone, and saw the box of candy up on the shelves. So he pushed up a chair, and got it down. In a little while he ran out to Mamma with his mouth stuffed full of candy, and his cheeks looking like balloons. He also had both hands full of candy. Mamma went into the library, and what do you think she saw? Why, the empty candy-box, and every bit of the candy scattered around on the floor. Brudder had emptied it all out, and then picked out the biggest and prettiest pieces. Now, wasn't that cute?

   Papa dreamed last night that he saw you in a great big room full of dolls, and they were chasing you around and falling over you, hugging you and jumping on your shoulders. At last you saw Papa and came running, crying out, "Oh, Papa, Papa, help your Dauda," and Papa grabbed you in his arms with one doll swinging to your hair.

Tell Grandma Papa will want you home for Xmas, for you were away from him last Xmas. We are going to have Santa Claus here too.

Mamma and Little Brother send lots of love and kisses to you. You are Papa's idol, and he thinks of you every hour. Don't forget Papa and love him just as much as ever, when you come home. Love to everybody. —Your devoted Papa, *Henry*.

Denver, December 23rd, 1892.
My Darling little "Dauda":   Papa found out to-day that you could not come home for Christmas, but must stay with Grandma. It pretty nearly broke Papa's heart, and will spoil his Xmas. You are your Papa's idol, and he had planned to have such a happy Xmas. Santa Claus had promised to come and bring you lots of things and maybe let you have a sly glimpse of his tiny reindeer. Now, however, I will have to write him to go to Grandma's, and as her "chimblys" are not big enough for reindeer to get down them, I am afraid you will not see them. If you had come home you would have had a beautiful Xmas-tree, with lights, and pretty shiny things, and lots of pigs, and deer, and cats, and dogs, all in candy. Papa would have played with you all day, and at night read to you, out of some of your nice books. We will have to let it go now until next Xmas. Papa has a splendid big real wagon for you, —a buckboard, —one big enough for you and Brudder both to ride in, and Helen can pull you all over Denver. It is too big to send down to Grandma's, so I will keep it for you until you come home. You must be a very good girl on Xmas, and get Grandma to tell you all about how Jesus was born, and how the stars shone, and the "Herald Angels" sang with joy. You must always remember that Xmas is the day for little girls to say very sweet prayers, and to try and be very obedient and good-tempered. Don't lose your temper, or say a naughty word all day, and think about your darling Papa a great deal. If you see any poor little girls you must be sure and give them something nice. On Christmas morning you must crawl into Grandma's bed, and say, "Xmas-gift Grandma," and then you must put your arms around her neck, and say, "God bless you, darling Grandma, for being so good to me and all of us." Your Papa can almost cry to think you will be away from him.   —Your devoted Papa, *Henry*.

A letter from Annie Jennings Wise Hobson:

Ashland, Dec. 19th, 1892.
My dear Children—   I must send you my Xmas greeting together. Everything seems to have conspired to keep me from sending my Xmas letter. Last Thursday I sent our few offerings and, some days before, the pickle, Alice's & my Xmas present to you… The stores are not very brilliant and varied this season. Bettie Ambler constantly does work to help on their slender income and I knew Katherine would value the bureau scarf as made by her. Mother had told me to get something for her that Katherine could use in her confinement, & I thought that the blue mantle would be pretty and useful… I am really giving no presents this season for I need all I can get to stock my little farm with chickens, ducks etc. & meet other expenses in getting a start & I encourage the children in their humor for saving this Christmas— They are to go down tomorrow (if rain does not prevent) to make some purchases & see the stores…

We have all agreed to spend very little on Xmas good things— to have no plum pudding or plum cake, just a simple dessert & fruit… I know Henry will miss his bright darling but it is best she should be with Grandma Thayer. Every day I hope for a letter telling me the expected has come. How I should love to put my arms around you both and try to express the unspeakable happiness I feel over the changed status of my life. I never expected again to have a place so much like a home to spend a Xmas season. Despite all the care and responsibility that is upon me I find a full deep compensation in the love and companionship of these dear children. It seems dear Henry, as if God had given me back the six that death and life took from me. So many have told me that I look ten years younger since coming here. Do I not owe all this to you both. I really feel too that by the end of another year Henry's burden will be lighter. Alice seems bent now on getting something to do. Steady *inevitable* work might be the saving of her. I do hope to help much in the living expenses of this family after I get a good start. May this Xmastide be a very blessed one with you both— Some day I trust we may all spend one together… I will write you all about our Xmas & what the children bought. They are already very delighted over a pair of white rabbits bought with their own money. We shall celebrate Xmas day Saturday & give the servants Xmas day as their own.

This is a poor, inadequate letter & I feel as if I had so much to say. I am really too tired & sleepy to add another word.

—Thursday morning 6 o'clock— And I did not add another word, for I could not but just had sense enough to get to bed. Nature takes very good care of me in sending straight to the arms of Morpheus when rest is needed. The rain is pouring so that the children will have to defer their day of shopping— a real Northeaster. I am very sorry for it on their account & because it will also interfere with the dressing of the Church preventing the evergreens being procured & sent…

So often when I get up in the early morning & the mornings lately have been very beautiful, when the moon and daystar shone in the glow of the early day-break light— I stand beside you all, Katherine & the sleeping babes, & think perhaps Henry is up also, and I ask God's blessing on my far off dear ones. Now again a blessed Xmas when the Emmanuel may indeed be with you all, Kiss the lovely little Henry for me, & I know you will give the new comer a kiss for Papa's Mamma… We will all be near each other in heart & spirit & my place is here while the dear Lord watches between us. The children will send a joint letter, & all send love & Xmas greeting & fully appreciate, even the little Alice, that Uncle Henry and Aunt Katherine are their Santa Claus.

—Devotedly with tender lover, your mother, *A.J.W. Hobson.*

—Alice is at her Mother's— I know she went to Richmond to meet her friend Mr. McSparrin— a sort of *ne'er do well* that she met in Norfolk last summer.

Xmas day 1892.
Dearest Mother Thayer—   If I don't write you a line tonight I don't know when I will. It was so good and thoughtful of you to send me the check and nothing could have pleased me so much. The only drawback is that I sometimes fear you do too much for me and mine and that I am a burden on you. When you gave me my wife you did all that one person should be called on to do in a lifetime. Perhaps you have noticed a peculiarity of mine at the table,

of never liking anyone to serve me, but preferring to pick things for myself. I think I have that peculiarity in all the affairs of life. I have rarely seen anyone who could even by accident select a present for me, which I really wanted and so the most sensible thing anyone can do is to let me pick myself. You must have learned that trait of my character for you always so acceptably and so sensibly tell me to do my own selecting… I have thought a great many many times today of my darling little girl and were she with anyone else than you, who have almost as much of a charm to her as we have, I should feel quite jealous. I was much touched with her messages in your letter today, and I trust she has been a good little girl. Tell her Papa is going to see her pretty soon and has a lot of beautiful things for her. K— will write you about our Xmas and little boy blue's Xmas-tree (a little one.) We have had a quiet but happy and peaceful day. K— is about the same though more comfortable today. Goodnight dearest Mother Thayer and believe me I always appreciate your love and thought. —Your loving son, *Henry W. Hobson.*

1893

A letter from Annie Jennings Wise Hobson:

Ashland, Jan 11th, 1893.
My Dear Son— I had so hoped for a letter today telling me all about the new girl and the well-doing lovely Mother. Yet I ought to make allowance for the severe weather that has interrupted the mails and your busy life. We have the severest weather we have known here for many years, & most thankful was I when it moderated today enabling me to get out with Alice & Jennings… I had the pleasure of getting yours of the 8th yesterday & rejoiced over the good news from Katherine… Last night I was dreaming of Katherine & the baby off & on through the night, and that new girl was the biggest funniest new baby I ever saw & she seemed particularly pleased with me. As I awoke the last time I was saying, "Well, Katherine is Papa's girl, Henry is Mamma's and you are mine." …I am sure you would love to name her for me & appreciate that, but really, since the fate of my own little darling, named so lovingly for me by your father, I often feel that I do not wish another child to bear the name… I wrote part of this before breakfast & now am scribbling while the servants get their breakfast. The children have just gotten off to school. Henry has commenced this quarter. I am glad to say that they are improving steadily under Miss Scott. Cannon has especially improved in his arithmetic. I have commenced teaching Jennings. I am sure that boy has brains. His beautiful face is such a pleasure to me… Mary is bright at her books, but, really Henry, that child gives me great concern… I have been horrified to find how corrupted all their minds have been by being given up to negroes. Cannon's less than any & through him I have found out the whole truth about them. Mary had actually been teaching Jennings the most *vicious* things & she is such a story-teller. They were being trained in vice like children of the slums. God grant I may bring out the good to put down the evil.

Now I wish to let you [know] my final conclusion about Alice. We have given her another year of trial with endearment to bring out good if there is any in her. What is her life? She gets up generally about eight o'clock, often later— Alice sleeps in her room and she pretends to bathe & dress her & I

the new girl Henry and Katherine Hobson's third child, Eleanor Whiteside Hobson, was born on January 7, 1893, in the new home at 933 Pennsylvania Avenue in Denver.

constantly have to take the child and give her a bath because she has every evidence of being un-bathed— she *dusts* her own room. *Sometimes* she comes to me "if you have any mending send it to me & I will do it." I don't send it because I should have it to do over. Through every kind of weather she trots to the Post Office— thrice & thrice a day. On Sunday, the same, although she rarely ever goes to Church. She write, writes, writes! —her sole occupation. She keeps her room in a disgracefully untidy state. I am obliged to keep Alice away from her as much as possible because in her Mother's room she gets so filthy & is so spoiled & incessantly allowed to eat candy & trash that keep her stomach disordered. When her Mother is here she is like a different child. Conversations are repeated to me by the children that show me that her influence is pernicious over them. Her last man craze is a Mr. McSparrin, the son of a Methodist preacher, "who has no faith himself." She met him in Norfolk as Secretary of the Norfolk Club. Since then he has had several *situations.* My belief is that he is an adventurer. The children tell me— & Cannon verifies it that she informed them she had had three opportunities to marry 'since Papa's death' & but for them would be married. She told them Mr. McSparrin had addressed her. He is only 28 years old. She paints black her eyelids, more vulgarly than ever. She told Bettie A— that Mr. McSparrin's poverty was all that kept her from marrying him. I do not believe he *intends* marrying her. I think he is getting everything *out of her he can*. I know she lent him money. This is in strict confidence. She does not know that I know this.

Now it is injustice first to yourself & then to me and Katherine that she should be leading the life of a wealthy woman of ease at yours & my expense. She only pays me $8.00 a month for food, lights, extra milk & to help with the rent. What her food costs me would pay for my extra mending & sewing.

Now, for my conclusion. I was dreadfully opposed to the idea of her getting an office. Like Katherine I revolted at the idea of separating Mother & children. I am sure she will not get the Post Office here, especially as I hear from good authority that the whole community, having already found dissatisfaction from one woman's (Mrs. Mayo's) having it two years, are opposed to a woman's having it again. Many of Mr. Brown's friends are urging him to take it, which, with the real estate business, would be a good thing as he could give up his clerkship at the C. H. I do not know whether he intends even trying for it. If Alice [were to get] into it I doubt whether she would have the perseverance in getting up early & staying late to keep it. She seems to have some ability for writing & a more mechanical work of copying would be work she might do. She is hankering after a place in Washington, and if you could get her a clerkship, it would be the best move for all. It is a dreadful thing to say, but the best good of the children requires her to be separated from them. I let her go her own gait. We do not clash, but it is a constant irritation to witness the life she leads, & a constant self-restraint to avoid collision. It is time she was learning what work means.

I write all this for you alone— burn when read.

If you are coming on in February you can see about it. George Wise told me he would aid in getting her work in Washington if she could not get the Post Office… I must send a line to Katherine & I am sure you are tired of this scrawl.

You have my sympathy having all those letters to write & so much business on hand… Your mother's thoughts and prayers are ever with you   Most lovingly, your Mamma— *A.J.W.H.*

◌ Ever interested in politics:

Denver, February 18, 1893.
Dear Uncle John— [to John S. Wise]   You know that I have for years been talking in an indefinite way of quitting this country and going East to live. I don't like the country in the first place and secondly I am slowly wearing out and getting old under the nervous strain I am always subject to here. I have a fine business, a handsome income and unnecessary work. Looking ahead ten years I may have a few hundred thousand dollars, but no spirit, no life, perhaps no health. Now it has occurred to me that there is possibly in the near future an opportune chance of my quitting this life and preparing a way for successes in the East.

under Cleveland   Grover Cleveland defeated Benjamin Harrison in November 1892 and was elected to a second term. Cleveland was inaugurated on March 4, 1893.

If I could get an office under Cleveland to suit me, and one in which I could make some reputation, it would give me a chance I might not otherwise have. Men of brain and vigor who can show capacity to men of influence of affairs do not as a rule have much difficulty in getting a foothold. The idea of trying for an office is only of the vaguest kind with me, in fact hardly more than a dream. Indeed even if I were inclined to make the effort and could succeed, I am not sure I could arrange to leave this place or that my wife would consent to my going into public life. Moreover, I have a great dislike to "office seeking" and "legging" around for the favor of office dispensers. Again I fear that my ambition, or rather self opinion, would over-vault itself, for I would not consider any low office. For four years I had throughout the West charge of most important Government work— the great fight with the land rings of several States and territories, sole charge of the great Mormon Church fight, of the great Mexican Land Grant cases, and of all the extensive litigation between the Government and the Northern Pacific R.R.

I never lost an important case for the Government and would have completed successfully all my work if I had not resigned as soon as Mr. Harrison took office. Consequently I think I am qualified to handle important affairs and would most assuredly not accept any position that was not dignified and which would give me a chance to make some reputation. If I wished any office, I would like the position of Assistant Secretary of the Interior which has peculiar charge, I believe, of Public Land questions and with which questions I think I am qualified to deal. I would also like to be Solicitor General or have one of the good Assistant Attorney Generalships…

If he would appoint me at all, he would do so without any undignified efforts on my part, for he knows me well enough to know whether I would suit him. Of one thing he could rest assured— he would never have any officer more loyal to him and his future.

What do you think of all this? Write me frankly your views and advice and understand that I have not a single definite idea in regard to the matter. I am but speculating… I know that you would do anything for me you could, but in the meantime give me your views. I have a high stand in the community both as a man and a lawyer and I am growing everyday, but also I am growing old and worn too. I do not know that I could afford to give up my excellent practice and good income, and yet I long to get away from this country. At the bottom of it all perhaps may be the thirst for public life which runs in my blood. Many of our family have been cursed with it and I suppose it would be better if we were as slothful in ambition as cows. I have always had a longing for politics and only poverty and sense of duty to others have kept me out of the [illegible]. Whether now or in the future I feel sure I shall drift into public life whether for weal or woe no one can say. If I had a half million dollars I would not hesitate now. As it is I have some property and could afford office for a few years, if I could have an office that would give me a chance to make an opening for myself.

But I have bored you enough. Write me your thoughts and what you can do. Of one thing you can rest assured that if I finally go in, no backer of mine will ever be ashamed of me. Please let this letter be confidential. I am only dreaming now as I said before and would prefer that you keep this entirely to yourself. —Your affect. nephew, *Henry W. Hobson*.

I may be East next month. I am tired and want to rest. (Virginia Historical Society)

◆ Letters from Catherine McKie Thayer:

March 10, 1893.
…I have no one *in view* as cook now— one from Boston has been "companion" —would like to come, has been at cooking school, but cannot wash. Why cannot we sit in our skins & then we would not need washing done…

March 13, 1893.
My dear daughter Kittie— …Joanna, Mrs. Metcalf's old cook, has engaged to come Wed. eve the 22nd. All call her an excellent cook. She looks like a woman with a head on her…

March 10, 1893. Palmer House, Chicago.
My darling Wife— I wired you yesterday of my arrival, we having been detained 8 hours by a washout… You will doubtless be glad to hear that I have about concluded to give up the idea of any Government position. I think it wiser for the present. It is a sore trial to me to be compelled again to lay aside my ambitions and longings but I feel that my duties and obligations to others are such that I have no right to take any risks. It is not for the purpose of making money that I do this, for I have a contempt for the mere desire to make money. I should now dislike to have any honorable position offered me for it would sorely tempt me. I shall however do my duty and perhaps all will come right in the end and in a few years I may be in a financial position to gratify my love for political life. I fear you do not sympathize with my ambitions for public life, and I can't say I blame you, still that love is in my blood and no one knows how many bitter moments the necessity of putting down my ambitions and tastes have given me. I feel that I am fitted for public station and believe I could do honor to myself… —Lord bless & keep you all. With a world of love & many kisses, Your devoted husband *Henry*.

Denver, Sunday March 12th, 1893.
My Darling Husband— Today I am wondering if you are in Chicago or New York. Your second letter came yesterday and gave us all much joy… By the way you have another daughter! No mention of her *existence* in your letters. And though you may not confess it, you know you forget her most of the time. Sometime you will think her the greatest pet of the three. I have

Eleanor Whiteside Hobson, A. E. Rinehart, Landoner Block, Denver.

been having Frank look at our coal bills and calculate how much coal we use a month and he says there is something wrong with Thomas' management or with the furnace & he is going to the furnace men to see what such an enormous use of fuel means… With a heart full of love & kisses and longing to see your dear self. Always your devoted wife *Katherine.*

Denver, March 14, 1893.
My Dearest Henry—   …Your letter from Chicago received yesterday— and so welcome Darling. I can indeed sympathize with you in your desire to enter a Political Sphere, but I do feel that after four years spent in office you would feel you had sacrificed much— and what would you have gained. I can see on the other side how a public position would open many congenial avenues for you socially… then I think of our children and feel anxious that they should spend the first few years of their lives in this climate in order that their chests may be developed and if they have inherited any tendency to lung trouble it may be irradicated [sic]. Your health & theirs is my first thought, and indeed my happiness in life. I think so often of your dislike for this place & the life you lead here, and am sorry from my heart that it is so— and that we let Mother build this house. Indeed if I could go back I can see how differently I should act. Less thought for my own happiness and a proper recognition of your burdens and cares would have made you able today to embrace a life which appeals most to you— one can't see clearly always blinded by self… Take my heart's best love and many kisses from your devoted wife *Katherine.*

March 15, 1893, Washington, Department of Justice.
My darling Kittie—   I am waiting to see the new Attorney General and will write you a line. It would have amused you to see me waiting & chafing yesterday "at the portals of the great." Whilst formerly I had the entrée everywhere, I did not succeed yesterday in seeing anyone, for Senators & Representatives have precedence and they are over-running everything. They go around from Department to Dep. with trains of followers. I saw one Senator yesterday take in 15 at one crack to see the President. I shall make one more trial today & shall then quit. I have little to accomplish and shall not waste time. I shall probably go down this afternoon to see Mother and then go to N.Y. I can't help feeling that when I am so busy it is most inconsiderate in her to refuse to meet me. But then my darling one you are the only one of my family who has ever had any consideration of any kind for me. Poor Aunt Mary is very badly off. She is scarcely able to raise herself in bed. Saw R— Last night. He is as cordial & affectionate as ever. Well I must see the Atty. General if I can slip past some member of Congress. Love & kisses for my darlings. —Your devoted husband *Henry.*

March 17, 1893, Virginia.
My Darling Wife—   I scribble a line from Grandma's room. I came down to Ashland last night and spent the night and today. Mother & I have come down for a few hours. Yesterday I saw the President and several cabinet officers. Will tell you all about it when I return… I found all well in Ashland and here. Poor dear old Grandma is just as sweet as ever but her mind is failing— no memory. She is nearly 79, quite old… Grandma talks about you

and the chicks all the time and has made me read one of your letters twice. I had a sweet letter from you yesterday. Of course I remember I have another daughter but I do not wish to spoil her by making too much fuss over her before she is three months old. Bless my little tots, all three. I do so long to hear the music of their voices, to greet their pattering footsteps, and to feel the heaven of their little loves. Tell K— that Papa brags about her all the time... I will tell you all about the children here when I return. I never feel so proud of you my beloved one or more lovingly appreciate your tenderness and sweet character than when I leave you and see other women and compare you to them. You are the sweetest most lovely wife that ever man had. I hope to see you next week and long for the hour. We will, I hope, get off to California by the 1st if the Doctor lets us. Goodbye my sweetheart & love & kisses for our babies.   —Devotedly *Henry*.

August 22, 1893,
My darling Kate—   I felt like a brute after leaving you that I should have become impatient over your being a little late and that I should not have even thanked you for bringing in my heavy satchel. The fact is, I was so afraid and worried lest I should have to leave without saying goodbye to you and my precious children and after a perfect whirl all the morning that I was not in the best of humors. You always forgive and excuse my bad humors my darling one, and no matter how disagreeable I may be at times you can always be happy in the assurance that I love you better than all else in the world, that you are the sweetest wife a man ever had, and that you have brought me more happiness and comfort in our few years of married life than I had ever dreamed of having... Devoted love & kisses for yourself and all the chicks. I write this hastily before getting to the Springs as I feel I shall not have time there. We are now almost at the depot. I shall think of you every hour and long for your sweet company and companionship. Yr. devoted husband, *Henry*.

Chicago, October 6th, 1893.
My Darling little Kathleen, "Papa's Idol and Chum":   Yesterday when I went to ask "the man" for letters, my heart went pit-a-pat with joy when a cunning little letter marked "For Papa, Chicago," came slipping out. I have read and kissed it many times, and I am now going to write a short letter to you.

   How do you suppose that little letter marked just "For Papa" found its way to Chicago, and to me? Do you think it was a good fairy that guided it on its way to rejoice your Papa's heart? What makes you think I am going to stay away from you for a long time? I am going back to Denver in a little while, and this letter is just to tell you that I have not forgotten that thing you wanted me to bring you from the World's Fair.

   Every day I say to Mamma, "How I wish my little Sweetheart Kathleen were here, and how she would enjoy all the beautiful things." Never mind, I will tell you and Brother all about *everything*.

   I must write a little letter to Brother, too, so I am going to tack a lot of kisses to this letter for my heart's precious. Little Sister Eleanor is a jolly little sprite and is enjoying the Fair.   —Your devoted Papa, *Henry*.

Henry W. Hobson, 1893. Pike's Peak Photographers, Colorado Springs. At this point in time there were three people named "Henry Wise Hobson." First there is the lawyer, born in 1858. Secondly, he had a son born in 1891. Lastly, there was the son of John Cannon Hobson, another Henry Wise Hobson, born in 1880. Neither of the younger Henrys ever used "II" or "Jr."

Chicago, October 6th, 1893.
My own Pride and Joy, Henny Penny: You have not written Papa a letter, but then you are a little boy, and do not know how to write like your big Sister. Papa loves you so much, however, that he is going to write you a little letter, and send you some kisses too.

Are you a good boy, and do you mind your dear Grandma who is staying with you and taking such good care of you?

I know you are, for you are Papa's little man. Do you know that little Sister Eleanor can almost stand up by herself now? Well, she can, and is as cunning as a little white mouse!

You must dream about what Papa is going to take you from the Fair, and you will get whatever you dream of.

Good-by, my sweet boy.   —Your devoted Papa, *Henry.*
Kisses for Henny Penny.

1894

Family matters:

Denver, February 18, 1894.
Dear Uncle John—   I have not heard from you for so long that you almost seem to be a stranger. What are you doing that you do not drop your Colorado kin a line or two occasionally. I have been going East for two months but one thing and another has prevented. I now expect to go to New York in March or April on business for my Railroad company… Katherine and I had planned a nice trip to Florida via New Orleans for March and then home by New York, but I have had to give it up on account of work. Mother wrote me of your trip to St. Louis and I was much in hopes that you would run out to Denver to see us… I hear little from Richmond and that little is generally somber and sad. All of our people back there seem to be under a cloud of misfortune, death, poverty, and melancholia. But I have not told you anything of Katherine and the chicks and indeed there is little to say except that they are all as well as possible. Little K— still retains her pre-eminence for beauty and grace, but my boy Henry is a fine manly little chap. Little Eleanor is not as good looking as the other two children were at their age and is quite backward in walking and talking but she is a dear little mite and quite the pet of the family. Katherine, when she wants to be particularly complimentary to the children, always compares them to "Uncle Johnnie's children." We both believe that the most important elements in a child's life are happiness and sunshine. The first ten years of life are apt to fix the shades of color to character tastes, disposition, and heart. Consequently we are trying to make our little ones entirely happy. There are no rules or precepts to harness their spirits and actions, and we only punish when obliged to do so. Obedience and truthfulness are I think the two cardinal child virtues and my children are very obedient and we have tried to keep them from knowing what falsehood is… Do you ever see Tom Page when you go to Washington? He has feathered his nest with the softest of down. Katherine is asleep or she would send some nice message. We often think and speak of you and possibly K— may go to New York with me when you can see her. Much love to your family and all the children.   —Your affect. nephew, *Henry W. Hobson.*
(Virginia Historical Society)

Denver, April 9th, 1894.
My Darling little Sweetheart—   Papa is in bed with a cold to-day, and he has had time to think a great deal about you. You are most five years old, and getting to be such a big girl, but it does not seem very long since you were a little wee girl, smaller than Piggy-wiggy Eleanor, and Papa used to take you on a pillow, and walk with you to put you to sleep. Pretty soon you will be big enough to dress, and take care of yourself, and then you will become Papa's little companion, and travel about with him. We will go to New York, and England, and lots of places. Papa and Mamma have sent you some birthday presents to-day, and because we wanted Boy Blue to feel he was not forgotten, we sent something for him too. You will get a good many things maybe, and you must remember that Brother is a little boy, and won't understand that just the folks who have birthdays get presents, and that his birthday will come in May. So you must be generous with him, and let him have some of your things, for he is always generous to you.

Papa misses you more than six tongues could tell, if he had that many. Did you ever hear of a man having six tongues? Women sometimes do, but you must be like Grandma and Mamma, and just have one tongue.

I miss my darling little Kathleen every minute of the day, and think of her sweet little arms around my neck and her kisses on my mouth. Next year maybe you will be with me when your birthday comes, and we will have such a jolly time. What will we do? I am not going to tell, but let you wait and find out. Good-by, little darling, and ask Grandma to give you a thousand kisses for Papa, on your birthday.   —Devotedly, your Papa, *Henry.*

Denver, April 9th, 1894.
My Darling Little Henny Penny—   Next month you will have your birthday, and then you will get lots of beautiful things, and everybody will be kissing you. So on Sister's birthday you must think about yours, that is to come pretty quickly.

What a cunning little letter that was you wrote to Papa, when he was away in Omaha. And do you know where it is? Papa folded it up, and put it in his pocket-book, and he will keep it always.

You must be a nice boy with Grandma, or we will have to bring you home to have the measles. And you will look like such a funny boy with little red bumps all over you.

When Sister's birthday comes you must kiss her, when you wake up in the morning, and be good to her all day. Papa wants to see you very very much, and some day I am just going to steal down to see you.   —Your devoted Papa, *Henry.*

Washington, D. C., May 14th, 1894.
My Sweetheart and Idol—

Do you sometimes think of your Papa who loves every bit of you, even down to your wee little piggy toes? Well, I think of you, and every time I see anything that is very beautiful I say to Mamma, "How Katherine would enjoy that!" To-day we went to see a lot of lovely birds in a museum. And there we saw the lyre bird, we will tell you all about it when we get back; and the butcher bird, and the red flamingo, and the sheep bird, and so many other curious kinds of birds.

You just ought to see that piggy-wiggy girl Eleanor. She thinks she owns everything she sees, and she wants it. Everybody here says she is very sweet, and I think they are right— Don't you?

You have not written your Papa any letter since he came away, and you had better do so quickly, and let me know what you want me to carry you, when I go home.

Good-by, my heart's idol. Be a good girl and don't give Grandma any trouble.   —Your devoted Papa, *Henry*.

Washington, D. C., May 14th, 1894.
My Darling little Boy Blue—   Papa has thought about you most all the time since he came away, and now you are most three years old, and soon will be my Big Boy Blue. I saw lots of things in New York, but nothing half as sweet as my "Pride and Joy."

What do you think Papa is going to carry you when he comes home? Why, a beautiful lot of tin soldiers, and a real cannon that will shoot, and you can play fighting with them. I hope you have been a really good boy since we left you.

When your birthday comes you must tell Grandma to give you two or three big kisses for your darling Papa.

Good-by now, and write Papa a letter very soon.   —Your darling old Dad, *Henry*.

Santa Clausville, Near the North Pole, July 2nd 1894.
Dear little Katherine and Henny Penny: I received your sweet letter and am glad you have not forgotten me. There are some children who do not believe in me, and I am sorry for them, as I will not take any trouble about children who do not think there is any Santa Claus. So when you hear people say there is no Santa Claus, you just laugh, and say you have received a letter from him and know there is.

I have written down in my book all that Katherine said about the doll, and her dresses, and I have cut out the dresses and will make them just as you say. I think the pink and blue dresses are very nice for balls, and the purple dress for evenings, only I believe I would have the purple dress trimmed with velvet instead of lace. I am afraid the red dress is not quite suitable for street use, and think a brown dress would be better. Still if you insist on a red dress, I will make it. I will also make the canary yellow dress for the phaëton, but you will have to be very careful not to allow it to get wet.

Henny Penny shall have that horse he wishes, and it will be a lovely pink horse, with big yellow spots on him, and he will prance and run just like horses in the streets.

If you dear little children want anything more you must write to me. If anyone tells you there is no Santa Claus you go to your Papa and ask him, for he knows all about it. Your loving friend, *Santa Claus*.

Be careful in addressing your letters.

Katherine & Eleanor Hobson, 1893. Rinehart, Denver.

◈ Family matters:

The Southwestern Limited — Wagner Vestibule Train, May 29th, 1894.
Dear Uncle John—   I scribble a line on the train though I can hardly do so legibly. I enclose a check for $100.00 to be sent to Grandma as my contribution for three mos: from June 1st (June, July & Aug). I wrote to Henry Garnett I would do so and suggested his paying $100, on July 1st, leaving your payment for August 1st. There is one thing that I think we should all be careful about and that is to be prompt in our payments. I shall try to be up to the day, and as I have many things to cause me to forget, I wish you would, before my payments are due, drop me a line. I leave you to make the permanent arrangements about the handling of the money, Henry G—and I insisting only upon what I discussed with you, viz; that the money shall be used exclusively for Grandma (and of course old Ida) and not to be subject to demands from other sources.

Another thing, I would ask of you. If any question is ever made as to why we do not use mother as our disbursing Agent, you will avoid saying anything which, if it were repeated to her, would wound her feelings. It is easy enough to say we adopt any particular course as a matter of convenience or perhaps to avoid any chance of family complications or rows. Confound the train I can scarcely hold my pen. I am sorry not to have seen more of you.   —Yours affectionately, *Henry W. Hobson.* (Virginia Historical Society)

June 2, 1894.
Dear Henry—   Your letter with the check was duly received. I sent the money at once to Mother and to Néné. I send you copy of the letter I wrote to Boulware, also the letters I wrote to Mother and to Néné. These place the matter fully before you.

Thinking it over, I concluded not to enter into any side talk about the matter with Néné. In regard to Sister Annie, of course, we ought never to mention our discussion. There was no reason why she should be disburser, and therefore there was no reason for discussing why she should not. I have not yet heard from Boulware, but dropped him a line telling him that you had paid and I had sent the money for June…

…Kiss Katherine and the babies for me.   —Yours affectionately, *John S. Wise.* (Virginia Historical Society)

Denver, June 4, 1894. Law Offices of Pattison, Edsall & Hobson.
Darling Kate—   Just a line to say I am well but dreadfully pushed. The chicks in splendid shape and crazy to see Mamma. The weather very pleasant. Love & kisses for all. I felt sure you would not leave N.Y. before Friday. Devotedly, *Henry.*

Denver, June 16, 1894.
My darling Kate—   Today I have the first letter from you since Wednesday and the second in a week. I suppose it is useless to complain, but somehow your letters do not reach me. Yesterday was your Mother's birthday— I arranged for an outing with her and the children… I had a letter from Cannon yesterday telling me of his Mother's marriage last week. Thank God for that relief… —Love & Kisses, Devotedly, *Henry.*

At this time Kittie was traveling in the east and letters to her were addressed "c/o" James Jermain in Albany and then forwarded to White Creek, N.Y. Some were forwarded again to the Equinox Hotel in Manchester, Vermont.

his Mother's marriage   This is a reference to the marriage between Alice P. Hobson, widow of John Cannon Hobson, and Mr. McSparrin.

Denver, June 27, 1894. Law Offices of Pattison, Edsall & Hobson, Denver. Darling Kate— A nice letter from you today, first since Monday. This letter is dated Thursday. I am fairly well but anxious to get away. Can't say what I shall do. Hate to think of going away without you. Love & kisses to Eleanor. Devotedly, *Henry.*

Denver, July 4, 1894. Law Offices of Pattison, Edsall & Hobson, Denver. Darling Kate— All day long I have been in the thick of the fight against strikers, directors telegraphing etc. We are beginning to break it I hope, unless it *breaks* out in a fresh place. Have had a large number of men arrested in Trinidad & Pueblo. I am thoroughly disgusted & tired. The children are well and enjoying the 4th though it has rained a good portion of the day. I bought them a whole lot of fire works and all the children of the neighborhood have been at our house most of the day *helping*… No letter from you today but I expect you get tired of reading that. Love & kisses to baby Eleanor. Sorry I can't write more but they are waiting for me at the R.R. office. Devotedly, *Henry.*

Denver, July 5, 1894. Law Offices of Pattison, Edsall & Hobson, Denver. Darling Kate— The chicks had a nice 4th and I gave them a lot of fireworks… I was working all day on the strike. I am loaded with that and I fear that the worst is to come yet. Not on the Railroad but in the Courts… I will probably be broken down after this fight and think now there is more chance of my going to Europe than before. I am glad you are safe in N.Y. and not tied up at some place between here & there. Love & kisses to baby Eleanor. Had a letter today.   —Devotedly *Henry W. Hobson.*

Denver, July 8, 1894, Law Offices of Pattison, Edsall & Hobson, Denver. Darling Kate— I am so worn out today I shall not write much. Everything quieter here and I think we have the strike broken in this State but Chicago seems to be in an eruptive condition. We have been very near to a great upheaval and civil war and matters could not have gone any much farther without producing most serious results… I send you a letter from Barton Wise. I wish I could go East for my *rest* without being under the necessity of going South. It may sound strangely but I dread seeing *any* of my Eastern relatives. As it is I must either give up taking a rest or go abroad. I would like to do as Barton is doing— select some great place in New England or Colorado on a lake where I could boat, fish, hunt & walk etc. etc. I would rather do that than go abroad and I could then have you with me. The chicks are well, but I really long to have them under your management again, especially Henry. He has developed some bad habits since you went away. Say nothing of that however to your dear good Mother. Love & kisses for my darling Eleanor… Devotedly, *Henry.*

Katherine Thayer Hobson with her daughter, Eleanor Whiteside Hobson, 1894.

∾ In the news:

STRIKE IN COLORADO IS OVER *Men Have Returned to Work and Trains Are Moving.* Pueblo, Colorado, July 11. — The firemen and brakemen on the Rio Grande have voted to return to work. Places of striking switchmen and shop men will be filled and all business was resumed today. Strikers at Gunnison returned to work last night. The strike in Colorado is at an end so far as its impairment of services in concerned.

Salida, Colorado, July 11. — The Denver and Rio Grande strikers at this point have reported for duty. The company will have no further trouble in running its through trains. At Grand Junction the presence of 150 regulars has had a very good effect. The strikers and soldiers had a friendly ball game yesterday. Regular trains were sent out by the Denver and Rio Grande, the Midland, and the Rio Grande Western. At La Junta the strike is ended. Many of the strikers are leaving the city in despair of getting their places again. The Companies of Federal troops who have been on duty at Trinidad for a week have returned to Fort Logan being replaced by a company of colored troops from Wyoming. Five more American Railway Union men have been arrested for participating in the disturbance June 24. Trains are running regularly.
—*The New York Times*, July 12, 1894.

July 13, 1894. The International Trust Company, Denver.
Darling Kate—   Yesterday Judge Hallett kept us in Court until 1 o'clock and then until after 6 o'clock in order to finish some "striker cases." I have succeeded in holding nearly 40 of them in jail and at the same time have won their good opinion. Judge H— seems much pleased with the way I have handled the business and I have had the burden of the fight for all the railroads. Henry Rogers… yesterday congratulated me warmly on what they were pleased to call "the vigor and ability" with which I had managed the business. Trumbull and some officials are very much delighted and finally this morning the attorneys for the strikers thanked me on their behalf for "the great fairness and decency" with which I had treated the prisoners. They said the men recognized the fact that whilst I proposed to punish the guilty ones, I was anxious to avoid doing injustice and that I also showed a courtesy towards the defendants which they appreciated. I tell you all these things because I know you will be glad to hear them. I think myself that the course I have pursued has met with signal success. I have had almost the entire direction of matters on our Road and largely upon other Roads. I have made it a point to act quickly, with vigor and firmness and at the same time with fairness. In matters of this kind, expedition, courage, and fairness are the true qualities which tell. So far as the State is concerned the strike is over and everything is as quiet as possible. Moreover, all the Roads to Chicago are running, but I think it safer for you to wait a short time. In coming home you will have to pass through a very dangerous belt, that comprising Chicago. I have another batch of strikers to prosecute tomorrow and then I hope my work is over for the present. I do not see much chance of my going abroad. Matters are in such shape and so many things seem to demand my attention that I have about given up the idea of going away. I am sorry but still I can manage to get along. I now look forward to a trip with you next spring. Henny Penny said this morning— "Papa I seed Mamma 'ass night, and she say baby Eleanor nuttin but a 'ittle mistif (mischief)" —Poor little K— has been getting into lots of mischief and trouble and seems to have had a spree of bad temper and imprudence which has worried me. She needs you badly. I am writing from the Trust Co. during the noon hour. Everything is very quiet here. The Palmers go East next week and sail between the 25th & 30th… Love & kisses to my darling baby and do not let her forget me. I wish to see you more than I can express in words.
—Devotedly your husband *Henry*.

∽   Family matters:

Denver, Colorado, July 16th, 1894.
My dear Mrs. McSparrin—   Pressure of business has prevented my sooner answering your late letter, and I am now compelled to dictate a reply. After consideration I have determined not to interfere in the matter of accounts between you and my Mother. Aside from the fact that for years my Mother has freely spent her money upon your children, it is to be remembered that the funds given by the Church belong as much to your children as to you, and now that you have married again, they belong entirely to them. Notwithstanding that, you have had the exclusive use of the annual payments and have also received from me the greater portion of the original amount given by the Church. Even if the amount claimed by you is in fact due, I do not just see why it should not be kept and used for the children.

At the present time it is perhaps better for me to express myself frankly, so as to save misunderstandings. It is unnecessary for me to discuss the history of my brother's marriage. Suffice it to say that although it was against my desires, it was an occurrence which has very gravely affected my life. During his lifetime I tried to the best of my ability to hold up his hands and since his death I have tried to do my duty, as I understood it, towards you as his widow and towards his children. So far as the children are concerned, I shall, under certain conditions, continue to care for them. As for yourself, you having remarried, and though I wish you every joy in your new life, it is my wish that henceforth our paths should run apart. So far as your children by my brother are concerned, the question of their future must be soon determined. In no sense is it my wish to alienate them from you as their mother, or to prevent free intercourse between them and you; still, I wish it to be determined at no distant day, whether they are to be brought up as members of my family or as members of Mr. McSparrin's family. If you determine upon the former course, then their control and direction must be given up to us, in which event I shall charge myself with their continued support. If, however, you determine upon the latter course, you and Mr. McSparrin must take them and provide for their support and I shall feel myself absolved from all responsibility in the promises.

Without intending the least disrespect, I may say that your husband and his family are strangers to me and to my family, and his friends are other than the friends of my family. Since these facts will probably be permanent ones, your decision as to your children will be the determination of their permanent family relations, friends and associates, as well as the question of the responsibility for their support and rearing.

The disposition to be made of the personal effects left by my brother also demands some expression of my views. Legally speaking, if his estate were settled it would not begin to pay the debts which I could prefer against it. The larger portion of the personal property which was used by my brother during his lifetime did not belong to him, but to my Mother, and it is now hers. So far as the balance is concerned, I leave it to my Mother to determine what shall be kept for his children and what shall be turned over to you. From any point of view, it seems to me that my brother's personal effects should belong to those who now represent him. These effects are of little pecuniary value, but they should be of value to his children as having belonged to their father.

Of course, if you insist upon it, I will have the necessary steps taken to have administration upon my brother's estate, but I do not think such a course wise or necessary. I think the above is all that it is necessary for me to say.

I am glad to hear that you are happy in the new relations, and trust that they may prove all that you wish. We came, however to the parting of the roads the day you married Mr. McSparrin, and it would be hypocrisy for me to pretend that I desire those roads ever to come together again throughout the balance of our lives.   —Yours very truly, *Henry W. Hobson.*

October 1, 1894.
Darling Kate—   Two letters from you this morning when I got back to N.Y. and of course I was perfectly delighted. I had a pleasant visit in Wash yesterday with the Garnetts and they all sent much love to you and the children… I long to see my darling chicks, but it is worth leaving them to appreciate how much more lovable & beautiful they are than other children. I send them all different kinds of kisses below. A big round kiss for Katherine because she is as sweet as a big round peach. A big square kiss for Boy-blue because he is a big solid boy and can stand square. A big squeaky kind of kiss for Eleanor because she is my squeaking piggy-wiggy.   —Devotedly *Henry W. Hobson.*

October 19, 1894, Southern Pacific.
Darling Kate—   This from the Nevada desert where sage brush and alkali regale the eye. The "old Master" had someone in view for punishment when he created this country. We get to San Fran tomorrow morning if we are on time. One sees the most miserable people on Western trains. We have a combination in our car who could run a freak exhibition. One man is the image of an old dignified ape. Another is exactly like an old mongrel dog with dirty grey whiskers and bleared eyes. The latter has a family of four besides himself and, as far as I can make out, they all slept in two berths. I sometimes wonder what some women have in their heads. There are six women aboard of various ages and during the entire day yesterday not one of them looked at a book. One old lady opposite me, who looks just like a parrot, has four bags, and she spent her entire day rummaging in them. Another fat one in front alternated between groaning and grunting.   —Devotedly *Henry.*

1895

New York, January 20th, 1895.
My Darling little Sweetheart—   Papa was so glad to get your letter. This is a valentine for you. Mama will tell you what the letters spell if you will tell her what the letters are. Now, here is my valentine:
"If" — No, that is Henry's. This is yours:

> Roses are red,
> Violets are blue,
> Sugar is sweet
> And so are you.

Papa thinks about you, and Mamma, and Henry, and Eleanor, all the time.
   —Your devoted Papa, *Henry.*

The letter has incorrect dates, for Eleanor Whiteside Hobson was born on January 7th, 1893

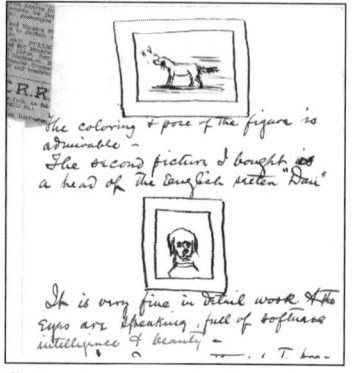

❧ A letter from Annie Jennings Wise Hobson:

1319 New York Ave. January 31st, 1895.
My darling little Katherine—   Papa's Mamma will think that the dear little sister Eleanor came to us the 12th of February while you know that her birthday is the 12th of January. Now I am so glad that Eleanor is yet too little to think I forgot her birthday. I send some books to her today that you must give her and say, "Eleanor, Papa's Mamma sends you these books because you had a birthday last month. She sends you three books that Henry and I can enjoy telling you about, and Sister will show them to you." …I was so glad to see your Papa for two days and so sorry to say "Goodbye" to him. Now I want you and Henry to do something for me every night. When you kiss Papa "goodnight," say "and now here is another *goodnight kiss* from Papa's Mamma," and Henry can kiss Mamma a goodnight kiss for Papa's Mamma. Will you remember to do it? If Henry forgets won't you whisper in his ear, "Kiss Mamma 'good night' and say 'God bless you' for Papa's Mamma." You must too say 'God bless you' to Papa for me. Papa & Mamma must kiss you each once for me and you darling can kiss little Eleanor for me. Now you must give her two birthday kisses for me, two for Grandma Wise and two for her little cousins. Now I must close for in a short time I am going back to my darlings in Ashland. No one knows I am writing. Give my love to Grandma Thayer, Papa & Mamma & the darling brother and sister. Don't I wish I could see the big baby-house, play with you in it and tell you stories. Tell Henry my next letter shall be to him. Give Eleanor and Henry a real hard hug for me. God bless and keep you all 'under the everlasting arms.' Ask Mamma what that means.   —Your devoted Papa's Mamma. A. J. W. Hobson.
Tell Eleanor a little pair of pink dressing shoes will come to her also from me.

❧ Family matters:

February 22, 1895, Union League Club, New York.
My dear Katherine—   Your sweet and most gratifying letter came duly to hand and although I sent you word I would answer it in person I am going to write because I can render you a good account of my stewardship for you… I bought you two lovely specimens of Tracy's art at prices which will surprise you. The attached slip will show you that the public appreciated his genius more highly even than I anticipated when Henry & I talked on the subject. What surprised me most was the lack of discrimination & knowledge of art in the bidders. Some of the most indifferent pictures sold well while the two I picked up are full of character, especially *Tracy* character & are the cheapest pictures I ever saw. I paid $75 each for them & you will never get two others like them for the same money. A bit of color or a little finish in the background of a picture would make it sell for $150 to $200 regardless of the merit of the animal portrayed, whereas Tracy's talent lay in his lifelike painting of the dog & any tyro could put in his surroundings.

Observing this I bided my time and when it came to the sale of Champion of Gloster I found an exquisite dog, full of the artist's best power of expression, but very rough & crude in its background. It was a perfect likeness & I thought it might add to your appreciation to know that he was a Rich-

"I bought you two lovely specimens of Tracy's art… The sketch on the opposite side gives you an idea of what it is like," John S. Wise. John Martin Tracy, 1843–1893, was a friend of John S. Wise's and is described in Wise's book Diomed, Lamson, Wolffe & Company, 1897. The two paintings purchased at Tracy's estate auction are still owned by a member of the family.

"Dan." Oil on canvas, 15 x 12½ inches. The Durand Press. All rights reserved.

"Gloster." Oil on canvas, 11½ x 17½ inches. The Durand Press. All rights reserved.

The sale of paintings by the late J. M. Tracy was begun at the Fifth Avenue Auction Rooms, no. 238 Fifth-ave., last night. There was a fair attendance, and many of the paintings brought good prices… Mr. Tracy was pre-eminently a painter of dogs… The total obtained for sixty-three canvasses was $5,777.50, an average of about $92. The sale will be ended tonight.

—*Unidentified newspaper clipping*

mond dog bred by Theo. T. Taylor, and that I knew him from a puppy. The sketch on the opposite side gives you an idea of what it is like. The coloring and pose of the figure is admirable. The second picture I bought is a head of the English setter Dan. It is very fine in detail work & the eyes are speaking, full of softness, intelligence & beauty… he [Tracy] is known as a dog painter pre-eminently & his dog pictures will be more valuable when his rather inferior attempts at general painting will decline… The pictures are both in frames of excellent taste, covered with glass & I am sure you will feel you have been fortunate in securing them. They will probably start by express tomorrow. I propose that my daughter Eva shall go with me this time to Denver & she is wild with the anticipation. My wife Eva is in Washington now struggling with the Daughters of the American Revolution … Goodbye dear Katherine— Kiss those dear little babies for me, give my kindest regards to your Mother & hug yourself for —Yr. affec. uncle —*John S. Wise*.

March 3, 1895.
My dear Katherine—   …I had yesterday a lovely letter from dear old Sister Annie & I know it would have done Henry's heart good to read her allusion to him "woman never had a better son than Henry"— The rascal pretends he does not care particularly for demonstrations of affection. To me they are the best of life. The love & flattery of my own dear old Mother are the sweetest thing in life. Henry is a humbug about this. He is just coy— "Playing for more of the same…"   —*John S. Wise*.

 Summer of 1895 — The Cambridge Farm and A Trip to Europe:

May 10, 1895, Denver.
Darling Kate—   Your telegram from Troy this morning was joyfully welcomed as it told of your safe arrival. By-the-way you sent it collect. Whenever you send an answer to a D. H. message, tell the operator so and if necessary show the message you answer… I know that I miss you and the chicks dreadfully and I do wish I were with you at dear old Cambridge… Keep me posted as to all the children say and do, for I think of them hourly.   —Devotedly, *Henry*.

D.H. Dead Head. As Henry Hobson indicates, the recipient of a telegram marked "D.H." could send a reply without being charged. The term "dead head" originated in the early part of the nineteenth century referring to the members of a theatre audience who had been admitted without charge. Later "dead head" referred to travelers who went by ship or train without being charged. Hence, the recipient of a telegram could reply without being charged.

Enclosed newspaper clipping: "Mrs. Henry Hobson has gone to New York where her husband will soon join her for a European trip."

May 13, 1895, Denver.
Darling Kate—   Before going home I must send you a line. You will be glad to hear that Fawny-paws is again found but from the circumstances I do not know how long he will "stay found."…He was in good condition and as Clinton tells me, not hungry… You must have left full data with the newspapers. The morning after you left there was quite an article about "Mr. & Mrs. H. W. H. family, servants etc, leaving in a special car for New York etc. etc. and from there to go to England." Nothing direct was said about a special steamer but there was a strong intimation that we would have one. Yesterday the enclosed appeared… Give dearest love & kisses to my chicks. I should have had a line from Troy this morning but did not. Suppose you were busy.
—Devotedly, *Henry.*

Denver, Col., May 15th, 1895.
My Darling Boy Blue— To-morrow is your birthday, and Papa feels very much ashamed that he did not write you a letter in time to reach you before the day came. Never mind, I told Mamma to get you the nicest tricycle she could find as my present to you, and if she has not done so you write and tell your old Papa partner.

What a big boy you are getting to be! Four years old! You will soon be trying to throw your old dad down, and be thinking you can whip him in a fair fight.

Did Mamma tell you that someone had stolen Fawny-paws, twice in the same week, and the last time the thief took his collar off, and kept it. Lucius found Fawny-paws once, and brought him home, I expect I will have to bring you home to take care of him.

How is that little rascal Eleanor? Has she gotten into lots of trouble with the pigs, and cows, and sheep? I suppose you and Katherine punch the fat pigs, until they grunt, feel the pretty little calves, and run after the lambs.

Tell "Little Sweetheart" that her dear Papa is going to write her a letter very soon, but that this is your birthday letter.

You must be a good sweet boy and obey Mamma when she speaks. Papa is very proud that he has a fine, manly boy, to take care of his little sisters, and if anything tries to hurt either of them you must stand up like a hero, and fight for them. Now that you are four years old, you ought to be a good fighter.

Tell Katherine that I went out to Glen Eyrie last Sunday and saw the little ponies that Miss Elsie and Dorothy used to ride when they were wee tiny girls. I saw the big dogs too.

I want you to come home and sleep with me, for I feel awfully lonesome at nights. God bless you, my sweet boy, and make you good and brave, so that you will be a great big comfort to Mamma and Papa. Kiss your dear sweet Mamma a hundred times for Papa.   —Your devoted Papa, *Henry.*

Glen Eyrie General William Palmer's home in Colorado Springs.

Denver, May 17th, 1895.
My Darling little Sweetheart—   When I opened Mamma's letter this morning, out popped six little violets, and I said, "They are as sweet as my little idol's six little years." Now, wasn't that funny when you sent them to me. I suppose you feel very old, being six when Henry is only four. I know you were as sweet as possible to him on his birthday, and made him feel glad that he had a sister six years old. When I was at *Glen Eyrie* the other day every-

body asked, "Where is dear little Katherine?" and when I saw the ponies, and rubbed their noses, they seemed to ask, "Where is Katherine?" Old Leo went hunting around behind logs, and rocks, as if he thought you were hiding.

Naughty Fawny-paws ran away again yesterday, and Clinton told me when I went home to dinner that he was lost. After dinner, however, I heard a little noise at the dining-room door, which opens on the porch, and going there, Fawny-paws slipped in, wagging his tail.

Whenever I think of your being at Cambridge and of my not being there, I just feel like howling and jumping up and down. You must get everything in shape by the time I come. Harry and Nelson both want to know about you every time I see them, and Nelson says you will cook better than he does if you travel on the car with a kitchen very much more.

Now I have written you a nice long letter and you must write me one, and send me lots of love and kisses. Kiss Henny Penny and Eleanor for me.
—Your devoted Papa, *Henry*.

Henry Wise Hobson and Fawny-paws.

Boston & Chicago — Special Train, May 25th, 1895.
My Darling little Piggy Blue—   Papa can hardly write straight, the car is shaking so, and you will think what a funny old man Papa is, to write just like a hen scratching in the sand.

Who do you think I rode down-town with the day before I left Denver. Why, with little Margaret, in her Papa's buggy, and when she heard I was Katherine's and Henry's and Eleanor's Papa, she asked all about you, and I told her about Katherine's chickens, and Henry's bicycle, and your everything. Do you know that she wears spectacles just like you and Papa do when we read our newspaper.

Old Fawny-paws misses you, and the rest of the children, so much that he is crying all the time, and sometimes he is naughty and runs away. But he was at home this morning.

This morning Mr. Thorn said he wanted to buy "Eleanor," and I said, "All right, ten millions of dollars," and as he did not have that with him, I could not sell you. Ask Mamma if she thinks that is enough for you.

Kiss Mama and Katherine and Boy Blue for me, and then kiss yourself, right on your sweet little mouth.   —Your devoted Papa, *Henry*.

May 25, 1895. Boston and Chicago Special — Wagner Vestibule Train via Boston & Albany, N. Y. Central and Lake Shore
Darling Kate—   Here I am hurrying towards where you are and I cannot tell you how disappointed I am that I cannot spend tomorrow with you and the chicks. I have counted on ever since leaving Denver but after getting your telegram and examining the time tables I had to give it up… I cannot say when I can go up to see you but possibly not before the last of the week… We had a fearful day yesterday in the eating line with not a morsel of food fit to eat. The dining car between Denver and Omaha has been taken off. I am enjoying greatly the beautiful green trees and fields and long to live among them. I do not like the West very much. Do you know I still have my winter flannels on. It has been cold enough for fire in Denver and I do not find my flannels uncomfortable even today… It seems hard that I should pass so close to you and not see you, but I must be in N.Y. tomorrow morning.
—Devotedly, *Henry*.

June 7, 1895, Penn R. R. train.
Darling Kate—   This is the same old story of railroad letter written as I am leaving you and as an exception I am going homeward leaving you East. I hated dreadfully to have you leave me the other day and felt a little like crying myself. Somehow our little trip had not been a "howling success" and yet I felt it should have been. I fear I am selfish where you are concerned and wish a monopoly of your time and attention… I do so long to see my darling chicks and I am going to do so as soon as possible. I shall try & reach you before July 4th. I do not see much chance of our sailing before July 10th. …Kiss my darling children many times a day for me…   —Devotedly, *Henry*.

❧ A letter from Catherine McKie Thayer:

June 9, 1895.
My darling Child—   How I wish I could have been at the Old Home to surprise you when you reached there Wed eve— as I trust you did… So glad to hear that you are safely home with children again after all the heat you have passed through. So, a week from tomorrow Mrs. H— will be with you— how strange it all seems, but how sweet for her to see *all* your children— and have a glimpse of northern country life. Hope it will be *cool* summer weather. Have you any screens for door & windows, and how are the window fastenings?—Do not wish them to fall on heads or hands… Just think of all the dear little ones going to the dear old church and being "quiet & good." Tell them I love to think of it…

June 9, 1895, Denver.
Darling Kate—   All safe at home again and miss you dreadfully… I enclose some bills I know nothing of. If they are correct return them and I will pay them. I would like to clean up all bills before going away for the summer.   —Your devoted husband, *Henry*.

June 19, 1895, Denver.
Darling Kate—   You must have a "dandy" postmaster at So. Cambridge. No letter has come since Sunday from you and the excuse of Sunday is not good… I think you had better write these ladies who wrote asking your views on the subject of woman's suffrage in Colorado, "that you prefer not to express any views at the present time, that the experiment has hardly been in operation long enough to have produced any practical results which can be relied upon as true indications of effects for the future; that being an accomplished fact and not a question or abstract consideration, Woman's suffrage in Colorado must be now judged by practical results and not by any theories on the subject or prejudices which one might have for or against it; that being a bitter opponent of the idea of woman suffrage and it having been in operation in Colo so short a time I hardly think it fair or proper for you to pass judgment upon its effect, especially as any expression from you (me) would possibly be used." The fact is I do not want to get mixed up in the thing and yet courtesy demands that you should answer the letters of enquiry… I hope Mother is with you by this time. I wrote her a letter yesterday. Hug and kiss the old woman for me. I do so long to see my

chicks and I become very mournful when I think of being away from them for a long time… —Devotedly *Henry*.

June 23, 1895, Denver.
Darling Kate— No letter today from you. It is pretty hard to be both lonesome and without any word from those who make up everything in life for me. I am at my office today, working, as I have had to be in Court several days and I am making great efforts not to let my work become "balled up" on me as to interfere with my getting away… Do remind me to tell you of my correspondence with Col B— on the subject of Fleece stock. We shall not stop paying dividends because of the robbery. I hope Mother is now with you. Lover & kisses— Devotedly, *Henry*.

Henry Wise Hobson. W. Kurtz, New York.

Denver, June 23rd, 1895.
My Darling Boy Blue: Have you been taking care of Mamma and the girls for me as you promised to do? I was at Grandma's the other day, and she wanted to know "what is Henny Penny doing," and I told her you were helping to fix the ice-house, were washing the sheep, were attending to the chickens and ducks, were keeping folks from robbing the orchard, were catching fish, and doing lots of other things that our dear little man should be doing to help folks. That is what I have a big fine boy for, and when you get to be larger you will have to come down to the office, and help me. I tell you I need you pretty badly every day.

I want to know who is going to drive over to meet me when I go to Cambridge again? Is your dear Grandma Hobson with you now? You and Katherine and Eleanor must be mighty good and sweet to her, and love her "lots," for she is your Papa's only Mamma, and if it had not been for her, you would not have had any Papa at all.

Be a good boy. I am very proud of you. —Your devoted Papa, *Henry*.

Denver, June 23rd, 1895.
Hello Piggy Blue! Hello! How are you? Pretty well, thank you! Well, so am I. Don't forget to come down to the station to meet me when I go to see you, for I am going to put my head out of the window of the car when I get near the stopping place to see if you are waiting for me, and if you are not there, maybe I will go right on, and see if I can find some other little girl.

I am afraid you will have to punish old Fawny-paws when you come home, for he is a great run-away. He ran off last week and lost his collar, and now Clinton has put a piece of brown ribbon around his throat and embroidered "933 Penn. Ave." on it. What will you do to him— pinch his ears, or pull his tail? —or get a little switch and whip him a little bit?

You must keep one little place in you heart always for Papa and don't let anybody else get into it, for I shall cry if you do. —Your devoted Papa, *Henry*.

Denver, June 23rd, 1895.
My Darling little Sweetheart: What a forgetful girl you are! You promised Papa to write to him and I have been to the Post-office every day, thinking I would get a letter, but none has come. The other day I thought that the

Postmaster had been stealing my letters from me because he did not have as nice a girl to write to him, and so I made up my mind to take a big club and beat him until he gave me my letters, but he said he did not have any, and so I could not pound him. I am afraid you have not written.

Last night I was sitting, after dinner, reading my paper on the front porch, and the nicest little girl riding in a seat fixed to a bicycle came to see me, and I gave her a big plump kiss.

Your dear Papa loves you more than tongue can tell, and wants to see you *very very* much. Kiss all the chicks and Mamma and Grandma Hobson.
—Your devoted Papa, *Henry*.

June 25, 1895, Denver.
Darling Kate—   Just a line. Two letters from you today. I enclose your slip about Mrs. Sheedy. She died Saturday. I have one of the worst colds I have had in years. Cannot imagine how I caught it but am sick with it and obliged to work like a dog. Tell Mother I appreciated her letters and will surely join you all as soon as I can. Two letters today from you. I go to Colo. Springs tomorrow afternoon. I have taken a quart, at least, of turpentine pills but they do not seem to do much good. I am feeling too badly to write more. Bless your darling heart. I shall see you next week if all goes well. Love & Kisses.
—Devotedly, *Henry*.

June 26, 1895, Denver.
Darling Kate—   This evening I go to Colo. Springs to say goodbye to your Mother. I am already beginning to feel like a boy out of school. My cold is much better. The second quart of pills did some good. I took about 60 in 36 hours… I want all the children to come to the station to meet me. I will not have a trunk but my coat case. By-the-way, if Edward Whiteside is laying out any plans to drive me all over the county, you put a veto on them. Say I must spend the few days I have with Mother & children. One day I want to get a team & all go to White Creek. The rest of the time I wish to stay at the Farm… Everything is crowding in on me but I am working night & day & cleaning up work in great "gobs" —I keep three stenographers busy all the time. I have only two important matters unfinished and I hope to get them in shape on Friday. Goodbye & many kisses for all.   —Devotedly, *Henry*.

June 27, 1895, Denver.
Darling Kate—   It is treating you rather meanly to put off writing to you always until the last hour of the day, but I can't help it, for every minute of my day is taken up… I trust you will enjoy Mother's visit. I am sure you will have tact enough to avoid any friction, especially over the children. Be careful to avoid inviting anything which might lead her to try to manage the children, for her system is different from yours and I do not think the chicks would quite understand her… Goodnight. Love & Kisses to the Darlings,   —Devotedly *Henry*.

Letters from Catherine McKie Thayer:

July 5, 1895.
…When I came home found your dispatch telling me that all was well, Henry with you, that you would leave Tues. a.m. and expected to sail by *Paris* Wed

11 a.m. So much that I wished to know. Oh, these last hours how I long to be with you but it cannot be… I do not think Mrs. Hobson will care to stay after you leave— such a lack of companionship for her… Will be interested to hear how Henry passed his time in the country— wonder if you went to Whitecreek…

July 6, 1895.
My darling Children—   This a.m. I had p.c. of Tuesday telling of Henry's unexpected arrival, and yours of Monday giving description of going to Church. So glad Mrs. Hobson could go the little family Church on the hillside and hear Mr. Gordon's unusual Christian teaching. I think Marie must have taken Mrs. B— and sent you her cook— I hope there will be no more trouble with stove— if this should continue to give trouble, Miss Miller better get a suitable one for the kitchen… sufficiently large with a *good draught*. I will write her… It is plainly to be seen that you and Henry are a real stay and support to him. He is not a person who carries his heart or his trials "on his sleeve," he does not continually call for one's sympathies. This might, does grow tiresome, but it is out of the very burden of trial and perplexity that he speaks. Poor soul, may the "ray of hope" you seem to have revealed to him, grow into a broad beam of light to cheer his future steps. It is good to hear that you are better of your cold. I hope quite well of it— and that Henry seemed well when he came in and called "Chicky blues" —what a screaming and scampering there was to be sure, —such a joyful surprise— and to find his Mother there too— Just the ones he wished most to see. I know you must have had a sweet time then— all of you. Suppose Marie did not get up, nor you to see her again. When I think how much that Old Man [James B. Jermain] would enjoy dear Henry and the little ones. I cannot but feel what a pity it is that the sweet memories they would leave with him, cannot be a part of his life… Thank you my dear daughter for all your sweet pleasant letters

unexpected arrival   Henry Hobson had taken an early train to Johnsonville and then walked from there to the farm— approximately six miles. Upon his arrival, there was great excitement.

The Old Home, Cambridge, New York. Built by Peter Whiteside, 1755–1835, owned by four generations of his descendants, and not sold until the late 1920s. Photograph probably taken about 1895.

from the Old Home. I have been living with you in spirit and wished I could assist you in the work of repairs… Now I must close and take this— May God guard you always… God bless and keep you again my dear children, with tenderest love and earnest prayer of your Mother, *C. McKie Thayer.*

❧ Annie Jennings Wise Hobson writes from Cambridge:

The letter is addressed, "Henry W. Hobson— On Board The Paris. *On God's High Sea"*

July 9th, 1895, Home Farm, South Cambridge, N. Y.
My dear Son—   Another anniversary of my marriage and your birthday is here— I sent you a letter to greet the day on yesterday. Surely this anniversary should always come to me as the first "red letter" day of my human life— the day which gave me such a husband and such a son. Your Father's love and devotion stands next to the Divine Love in my life in every human and spiritual sense. Almost from boyhood you have endeavored to do for me as your Father would have wished. God has blessed you for it, and He will bless you through all the coming years… Now, goodbye and God grant you a prosperous out-bound & homecoming voyage, and a most delightful and revivifying holiday time for both you and dear Katherine. You could have given me no greater pleasure than this happy time with your sweet wife and lovely children. It will always be lovely to remember. God grant we may all meet here again under as happy auspices— happier indeed, for then you may not be going away. "Mizpah"   —Your devoted Mother, *A. J. W. Hobson.*
—I love to remind myself that I write this in Katherine's old home— It is so pleasant to have had our blessed reunion in this beautiful country.

Mizpah   A Hebrew word meaning "watchtower," there are several places in Palestine that bear this name.

Home Farm, Tuesday afternoon, July 9th, 1895.
Just a line my dear Henry & Katherine hoping it will reach you in time to give a last glimpse and final goodbye before the gangway has been drawn up. Miss Miller tells me that you saw us waving. How touching & graphic was the scene. Little Katherine was inclined to be very excited & lament loudly, but I said, "Come, Mamma must see us waving to her till out of sight," so the darling put her hands over her face, & with such fervent tones *cried out*, "Dear Jesus keep my Mamma & Papa safe & bring them back safe!" Then in a moment she was waving my handkerchief, while Henry *took my apron* and I shouted, "lets give them a brave send off." In a moment they had no thoughts but for the waving & watching to see Mamma wave. Frank too stood by helping— holding up Henry… Eleanor was fast asleep when we came in… Eleanor had a long nap— did not come down till we were nearly done, & we heard her say as she came down the steps, "Miss Mill eatin up my dinner." Miss Miller soon convinced her differently, & she ate a hearty dinner. I have been entertaining them ever since & they have been very good and happy… A.J.W.H.

*you saw us waving   My precious Darlings, Katherine, Henry & Eleanor— Mama is thinking of you all the time & of how you waved to me. I saw you until the woods hid you & I waved too. I hope you have had a happy afternoon… —Your own Mama.
—Kittie Hobson writing to her children as she left on her trip to Europe, July 9, 1895.*

University Club, New York, July 9th, 1895.
My Darling Chicks—   When I left you the other day I most cried I was so sorry to run away from you. Wouldn't it have been funny to see your big tall Papa standing on the back end of the car boo-hooing, and all the folks laughing at him? Well, I didn't care, for I was leaving the sweetest chicks in the world and they were not. I want to know what sweetest Piggy Blue said when she found out that Papa had gone away from her.

I want Katherine and Henny Penny to be very good and gentle with Eleanor, for she is nothing but a baby and her Father's darling pet.

I suppose when I get back, Henny Penny will be driving all the wild horses around the country.

My darling little Katherine, you are the oldest, and you must obey Miss Miller, and be as sweet and good as possible and Papa will bring you the Canterbury violet and purple dress and anything else you wish. I want to have letters from all of you, and to know just what you wish me to bring you.

I expect Mamma to-night, and I suppose there was great lamentation when she left you.

Good-by, my sweet precious darlings. Don't forget Papa, and he will be back to see you before very long.   —Your precious Papa, *Henry*.

Tell Miss Miller and Katie good-by.

July 9th, 1895.
My dear darling Mamma—   Henry has written to Papa and I must write to you. We were all delighted to get Papa's letter, but tell Papa he don't know everything. He thinks Henry will be driving wild horses, when he will be in Virginia fishing, for he says he is going to steal off with Grandma Hobson and go home with her, and go fishing with her boys. What do you think of that! We were all so glad to get your dear letter Mamma. I love Uncle William for going to meet you. Grandma was looking at her watch a little after eleven o'clock, and I knew your heart was so heavy when the gang-way plank was pulled in and the shore went back and you were leaving us all. Miss Miller, Grandma, Henry, Eleanor, and your Weanie Baby [went] to see Cousin Nellie and Aunt Katie today. We are going to Saratoga tomorrow and Cousin Nellie will send us word this evening whether she can go with us. Aunt Katie is well and sends her love. —

The letter from Katherine to her mother is in the handwriting of her grandmother Annie J. W. Hobson.

Sailed from NY on *City of Paris*— American line at eleven A.M... My heart so full of longing for my three darlings & Mother... Letters from all & wrote to them by Pilot. Cabin most comfortable— large & airy.
—*Diary of Katherine Thayer Hobson, July 10, 1895.*

Henry & Katherine Hobson traveled to Europe in the summer of 1895. On July 10, 1895 they sailed from New York to Southampton aboard the S. S. Paris, and they returned on the S. S. New York, leaving Southampton on September 21, 1895. The children, Katherine, Henry, and Eleanor, spent the summer on the farm in Cambridge, New York.

❦ A letter from Catherine McKie Thayer:

July 10, 1895.   My dear Grandson Henry: Now that Papa is gone, and you are the gentleman of the house, I suppose you will try to be like Papa, and take care of everybody. I just have a post card from Mamma written just as you were all starting for Whitecreek. You must have had a beautiful drive that day & sometime you will tell me what you think of the White Creek cottage. Give kisses to your sisters   —*Grandma*.

❦ Annie Jennings Wise Hobson writes from Cambridge:

Home Farm, July 11, 1895.
My dear Katherine & Henry—   Here I am writing in the sweet parlor, in the big rocking chair... I hope my letter reached you in time to give the home pictures up to Wednesday morning— or rather till bed-time Tuesday night... We all rejoiced that you had such a bright day to sail. We all looked at the

clock about eleven yesterday & I stood in spirit by you both as the last scene of parting was enacted & saw the gang-way drawn back too. Now I cannot say another word. Messages of love from us all and our prayers following you for a pleasant voyage to England.   —Your devoted Mother, *A.J.W.H.*

Home Farm, South Cambridge, July 12, 1895.
My dear Henry—   All your letters have reached us. As we came from Saratoga, I found your letter to Miss Miller & Katherine's to the children when I got out for the mail. Miss M— and I understand about the cablegram business. I have just written to Mrs. Adams that I will be here until Monday & in New York at John's [John S. Wise's home in New York City] till Saturday… I ought to be at home now.

—Monday. Mrs. Whiteside met us at South Cambridge with Henry to go with us. Ida was so womanly she insisted upon staying home to do the household work. I mailed a letter to you inclosing letters from the children. We had a lovely day for our outing and we all enjoyed it… We then visited the Park, drank some water from each spring there. Katherine was delighted with the deer. We took the children to the so called *Indian camp* and they, the *pretended Indians*, were scarcely half-breeds. One man pretending to be an Indian looked like an Italian. We bought some trifles for Henry & Eleanor and then sauntered around… Mrs. Whiteside took us to a restaurant to get our dinner where the prices were within the limit of our purses… As it was we saw nearly everything to be seen and I shall always recall the day with pleasure and thank Katherine for the delightful jaunt. Frank met us at S. Cambridge and we had a pleasant ride home. Henry & Eleanor were waving to us in the yard as we drove up, just as the sun went down. Henry & Eleanor were all ready for bed & it was not long before Katherine followed… Katie and I took the children to the wood this morning and they had a happy time. Little Eleanor clings to me & Henry is as good as he can be, so lovely & obedient. This morning Eleanor was inclined to be rebellious about something. I said, "Well I must go right away." She clung to me, "No no! Stay with me."…We have all tried to keep up bravely & cheerfully & found great consolation in the children. Yet it seems so long since you both went away, that it is impossible you should have gone only a few days ago. Katherine had another p.c. from Mrs. Thayer yesterday and Katherine will send her a postal today.

—After Dinner— The children all took a nap before dinner. Eleanor is still asleep… Kisses from all the children. Katherine will write a letter the next time. Katherine has just come up and sends love to Papa & Mamma & says she is so much obliged to Mamma for the happy trip to Saratoga… Here is little Eleanor all ready for dinner. I hope you are both "aisy in mind" about the children and having a pleasant time. God watch between us.
—Your devoted Mother, *A. J. W. Hobson.*

South Cambridge, July 12, 1895.
My dear Mrs. Hobson—   Mrs. Hobson [A.J.W. Hobson] is writing to you and I will only send line. Mrs. Whiteside went with us to Saratoga yesterday, day was cool, we had a very pleasant time… Henry & Eleanor just up from their nap and are playing so sweetly in the north room… H— wants me to tell you and Papa that "I are a good boy" and E— says, "I good girl." I hear K— at piano. Mrs. Hobson will take tea with Mrs. W— this evening. This

leaves all good happy and well… Kind regards to Mr. H— Love and best wishes. Yours sincerely, *Ella Miller.*

Ella Miller was the nurse.

U. S. M. S. "PARIS," July 12th, 1895.
My Darling "Chicky Blues"—   Here we are, a long ways out on the big blue ocean with nothing in sight to drink except water, and that is not very good except for fish. You don't know how many people are on board the ship, nor do I, but I expect there must be a thousand, and a lot of little children. Maybe you will go down to the seashore this summer and see what a big ship is, but I send you a picture of one so that you can tell what kind of machine we are on. Right where I have marked a cross is about where Mamma and Papa sit on deck. We have three big black funnels, out of which black smoke pours, and two masts and a flag at the mast-head.

We have not seen very many things since we left New York, but yesterday five or six, or maybe more, big whales came close to the ship, and everybody was very much excited and calling out: "Look at the whales!" Well, Papa had seen whales before and he thought if he could get one pretty close to the ship he might catch him to send to you chicks to put in the pond down in the woods. So he called out to the whale: "Mr. Whale, come up here close, and maybe I will give you a little child for your breakfast." Of course I was fooling about that, but I wanted to offer something nice to the whale. Well, they all just laughed, and roached, and humped themselves, and spouted water way up in the air, so that the other fish all around thought it was raining and ran for their umbrellas and water-proofs. So then I said, "Mr. Whale, Mr. Whale, I have a nice piece of chocolate cream here, that the Chicky Blues sent you." When they heard that, one big old whale put up his head and winked his eyes very solemnly at me and said, "I'm afraid you will play that Jonah game on me." "What is that?" said I. "Don't you know?" said he. "No," said I. "Humph," said he, "I will sing it to you," and so he began in a voice that sounded like a thousand big bass bull-frogs:

> "Mars Jonah he jumped down a whale
> And cotched his innards nigh the tail.
> De whale he spout; de whale he roar
> Till he spit Mars Jonah on the shore;
> And den he asked, 'What is you about,
> I thought the earthquake had got out.'"

Everybody on the ship laughed at that funny song, and the old whale made a bow so deep it carried him out of sight in the water and with a shake of his tail went to chasing little fish around.

Now, Mamma says that is all a fairy story, but I tell her that maybe it is but I got a part of it from the Bible, and that ought not to tell fairy stories.

We have only seen one other steamship since we left New York, and that was not a very big one. Maybe we will have a race with some other ship before we get to England, and then you will almost be able to hear the people shout and see them wave their hats and handkerchiefs. You ought to see our bedroom (only they call them cabins on board a ship). It is the cunningest little place, with one berth or bed right above the other, and one little round window and a sofa. Then there is a wash-stand, and just enough floor for one person to dress in. It is not a great deal bigger than Katherine's doll-house at home. So Mamma lies in bed while I dress, and then I go on deck and she dresses. If you children were along we would have to hang you up on hooks to sleep.

Now I am not gong to write you all the news but leave some for Mamma. Good-by, my precious chicks. I think about you all the time. We will swim if the ship tips over.   —Your devoted Papa, *Henry*.

◦ Letters from Cambridge:

Home Farm, July 14th, 1895.
It is late dearest Katherine, all are in bed except myself & I must write a few lines before I lay me down to sleep. We have had a bright, peaceful Sunday, after a day of incessant rain which the thirsty earth must have drank eagerly and all nature seemed rejoicing over it… We had tea early, and after tea I read to the children a short time & then they had a little play and went to bed early. I asked Eleanor "What I should say to Mamma & Papa." "—Tell Mamma & Papa I are been a dood dirl." I read to Katherine & Henry also this morning… The children were very good and happy yesterday despite their confinement to the house. Henry got an old valise & packed it with all sorts of things preparing to go home with me. I have persuaded him to wait till he hears whether Papa says he can go. Katherine tried very hard to keep from outbreaks all day, but it was beyond endurance when Eleanor dressed herself in the red skirt "Mamma made just for me," but I soon restored peace… My first thought as I awoke this morning was of you & my dear Henry on the sea & how we were all together last Sunday. I prayed that "God's day" might bring some spiritual blessing to you both. Now my heart says a loving "good night—" sleep well "rocked in the cradle of the Deep" & sleep safely.
—July 15th. Just a line to say that I will leave in about two hours for South Cambridge… Well my happy visit ends & I expect to return with heart & mind refreshed by all the love & kindness shown me and filled with such pleasant pictures of the lovely old homestead and beautiful country. Miss Miller has been a delightful hostess and I hope we will meet again for I feel a warm friendship for her, as if I had always known her… The children send love and kisses to Papa & Mamma… Here I am dear Henry in Troy *en route* for New York… Eleanor & Henry seemed really grieved at my coming away. Eleanor said, "Where are goin' Gram— I go wid you." Henry had set his heart upon going with me & I could only pacify him by saying that he must write to you in England & ask to go. —My heart was really heavy leaving the darlings & aches when I think how long it may be and how much may occur before I can see them and you & Katherine again. Yet I ought to be so grateful for this past month, and I am glad to think I have my dear Virginia children to make my life full & such a pleasant home to return to… All the Whitesides begged me to come back another year… Kiss Katherine for me…   —Your devoted Mamma, *A.J.W.H.*

South Cambridge, July 18, 1895.
My dear Mrs. Hobson—   We have not heard from you yet but hope to soon. Mrs. Hobson left us Tuesday and we all miss her very much. She enjoyed being with the children. The chicks are very well, eat and sleep

Shakespeare's Birthplace as it appeared in 1769. Card purchased by Katherine Hobson in 1895, Shakespeare View Store, 1 High Street, Stratford-on-Avon– "The largest, cheapest & best collection of Shakespearean goods in Stratford."

well. The children, Katie & myself went to the creek today, had a lovely time through the woods and over the hills, gone three hours, ran into four of the Burton children wading in creek. K— thought she could too. Last Tuesday she enjoyed the birthday party very much, when she came home said she did not eat any of the birthday cake, she said it was very rich and would make her sick. I told her before she went not to eat anything that would make her sick. Tomorrow we all go to Mrs. Whitesides for the afternoon… Hope you and Mr. Hobson will have a pleasant and restful time and come home looking so well. Nothing more I can think of now. With much love— *E. Miller.*

July 19, 1895. London, England. Henry went to the City for mail & on business after going to tailors. I went too & we were blessed by finding mail & cables saying all were well in Cambridge.
July 20. Saturday. Packed in morning… Arrived in Stratford about 3 P.M. & went to Shakespeare's birthplace. I found my interest centered in the visitors who have been there… the Church was most interesting where Shakespeare is buried & we saw the register where his death & birth is entered…   —*Diary of Katherine Thayer Hobson.*

❧ Postcards from Catherine McKie Thayer in Colorado Springs:

July 20, 1895. My darlings all— K—, H—, & E— Is it not lovely to know that dear Papa & Mama are all safely landed in England. Well, we will try to be good & keep well so as to greet them with happy faces on their return. I trust you all do as Miss M— and K— wish you to. —Love & kisses from *Grandma Thayer.*

August 6, 1895. My darling Henry— Was it not fun to take a ride in the wheel-barrow with Sister E—. Grandma is so happy to hear of all the pleasant things you do in the dear Old Home. You and your sisters, give them much love from me & take much to your dear little manself. So thankful that you & Papa & Mama all well. Love & kisses — *Grandma*

◦   Reports from the nurse:

South Cambridge, July 23, 1895.
My dear Mrs. Hobson—   Will tell your first that the children are well, as this is what you will want to hear most. Last Friday Mrs. Whiteside invited the children to spend the afternoon, so Katie, children and myself went. When there we learned it was John's birthday— had supper and the children had a lovely happy time, the six on the lawn looked so lovely and played so sweetly together. They were all glad to hear of the well & safe arrival of Mr. & Mrs. Hobson… Yesterday we had our supper out in the woods, little ones thought it very much fun, everything tasted so good to them, they went to the brook & threw pebbles in water. They were very much afraid the cows would find the basket and eat what was left… I often hear from Mrs. Thayer and [she] is well, and from Mrs. Hobson too. I believe she leaves N. Y. today or tomorrow… Your trio sends hugs & kisses to Mama & Papa. K— thinks England is not very far way now. Regards to Mr. Hobson with much love & very best wishes. Yours sincerely, *E. M.*

South Cambridge, July 28, 1895.
My dear Mrs. Hobson—   The children are well & happy. This is what you will want to know first and they eat and sleep well…We had another lovely rain in the night. Today is so fresh & cool, it is just right. We have not had any warm nights, that is to be uncomfortable— our room is so lovely & cool. Two bats flew in the room last night. K— was sleeping, I got up and put a towel over her hair to be sure they would not light on it, and then I got them out… Katie, the children & myself went to Church— the little church was full as it could be— I did not think it could hold so many people. The sermon was so good, as it always is, plenty for everyone to take away and a great quantity left. I wish I could hear him every Sunday the whole year round. So many asked if I had heard from you since you left— I said we hoped to get a letter soon… Mrs. Hobson will leave N.Y. tomorrow to go home, she wrote me— said she is well— she writes often… Mrs. Thayer writes often too and I try to write as often as I can to both mothers on both sides. —Mon. July 29th. The greater part of this letter I wrote on the north window until it got too dark to see. Then stopped to write to Mrs. Thayer and Mrs. Hobson their letters… I am trying to answer K's questions and write to you at same time and I do not think you will be able to read what I am writing… K— says she has a letter to put in with this to you if she can find it, she wrote it yesterday. H— prays God to bring Papa & Mama safely back over land and sea. E— will always say, when I ask her what I will say to you— "Say turn home," then she will laugh as if it is so much fun…With much love and best wishes, Most Sincerely, *Eleanor Miller.*   —The garden looks very nice and clean now. We have peas, beans, turnips, cucumbers, very soon corn. Will have some this week. Katie said to tell you she is getting fat, and the children are too. Tuesday and all are well.   —*E.M.*

Ghent, Belgium, July 29th, 1895.
My Darling Chicky Blues—   How are you, I wonder, to-night? Papa and Mamma think about you all the time, and every hour we wish you were with us to see the funny and queer things we see. Wouldn't you have liked to have

been with us the other night in London at the theatre, and seen a lot of dolls and play men, as big as some folks, and bigger than any of you, talking like real folks, and saying the funniest things and singing real songs? They seemed to be doing so because there was a man called a ventriloquist, who made them seem to be talking. Then right on the stage was the most beautiful little gray donkey and a jolly little monkey. The monkey rode the donkey, standing up on his back, and dancing and turning summersaults. Every time the monkey would stop, a man would give it and the donkey some candy, and then they would go on and do something else. Sometimes the monkey would fall off and then he would grab the donkey's tail and jump up again.

Yesterday we were at a place called Ostend, on the seashore in Belgium, where there was a most beautiful sandy beach where hundreds of people were, and the queerest kinds of little houses on wheels, for people to get into, and go out into the water to bathe. A great many lovely little children were playing on the sands, with their dresses tied up around their waists, and their legs bare, running into the water and paddling around. Some were making castles out of sand, with spades, and putting the gayest kind of flags all around on the castle walls. How we longed to have you there, and Mamma would say every now and then, "That little girl looks like Katherine," or, "That little boy is just about as big as Henry," or, "Look at that lovely little tot, just the size of Piggy blue."

Do you know what kind of shoes many of the children of this country wear? Why, the funniest little wooden shoes that they stick their feet into and go clattering about in them, making a big lot of noise, and chattering away so gayly, and seeming to be having such a nice time. If you were here you could not understand a word they say, for they all speak French, and for all you would know they might be a lot of monkeys. But they are not monkeys, and if you were to stay here long enough you would speak French, and then, when you would go back to America, the little boys and girls there would not understand you. Then there were at Ostend a lot of the nicest little donkeys on the sands, that people ride, and I know that if you were there you would be riding all day.

To-day in Bruges, a very very old place, we saw a lot of very queer old things, and there were big dogs hitched up to real carts, full of all kinds of things, and the dogs pulled the carts instead of men. Mamma did not like to see that very much, for she thought the big lazy men ought to pull the carts, and let the dogs trot alongside.

I am afraid you are not old enough to understand about lots of things, but there are very old and beautiful churches and the quaintest old houses, and the oddest looking men and women.

You do not know how glad Papa and Mamma are to hear that you are such good children. My darling precious chicks, we want to hug and kiss you, all the time, and we don't think we can ever leave you again for so long a time. You are more precious to us every day we stay away from you, and I think sometimes Mamma has a little cry all to herself because she is far away from you.

If Katherine were here she could see lots of places where kings and queens are buried, and have beautiful tombs, and she might sometimes see real princes and princesses. We have been where there are palaces most gorgeously furnished, and the other day in London we went to see a whole big building full of pictures of princes and princesses, lords and dukes, etc. We also saw the splendid golden cradle in which the children of the Queen of England were rocked when they were little babies, with the most beautiful clothes of lace that they wore.

We are having a beautiful time, and Mamma has bought Eleanor to-day the prettiest little Belgian hat, and we have also a lot of things for Katherine, and Henny Penny. I wonder if my man-boy is taking care of his sisters for Papa whilst he is away? We send a thousand kisses and hugs for each of our own darlings. Good-night.   —Your precious Papa, *Henry W. Hobson.*

Carlsbad, August 15th, 1895.
My Darling Chicks—   Papa has not written to you for almost two weeks, because Mamma is writing all the time. We think and talk about you all the time, and everywhere we go we get something for our darling chicks, so that you will have things from all over Europe. How I wish you could see the little donkeys here pulling around the bath-chairs, just like that one that Grandma has at Colorado Springs. I know you would be wanting to ride all the time, which would send me to the poor-house.

Tell Miss Miller that we are going to-night to Vienna, and from there we will probably go direct to Paris and then stay somewhere steadily for several weeks.

It has been raining hard all day, but that does not keep the little donkeys with their carriages in the house. Mamma does not like Germany, because the old women have to carry heavy loads on their backs, and the men do not work very hard. I think that is very cruel, don't you?

I wish you were close enough to me to give you all a thousand hugs and kisses. The next time we come to Europe all of you shall come, and maybe Katie and Miss Miller. Wouldn't that be fun alive? Tell Grandma, when you write next, that we wish her to be at Cambridge to meet us when we get back. It is getting to be so near the time to go back that I am already beginning to feel good.

I am so proud of you all that you have been such good children, and you will be so glad when we get back and see all the things we are going to carry you. Give Miss Miller and Katie lots of regards and good wishes, and be sure and love them for taking such good care of you. Mamma and Papa both send heaps of love.   —Your devoted Papa, *Henry W. Hobson.*

Oatlands Park Hotel, Walton-On-The-Thames, Surrey, September 3d, 1895.
My Darling Chicks—   My stars! How Papa wants to see you. It will not be very long before we start home and then we will make things crack with joy. I know you will be glad to see me when I haul out of the big trunks all of the beautiful things we have for you. Let me see, we have bought you, —well, I am not going to tell you, but surprise you all, but they are just beautiful, and when you see them you will just bubble, bubble, bubble, until folks will think there are three little kettles of water boiling around somewheres.

Mamma and I are now in the most lovely place, not far from London, and near the River. There is a nice lake right back of the Hotel, beautiful flowers around, the grandest old trees, grass and everything. There are a lot of little children here, and if you chicks were with us you would be so happy and we would be so happy that I expect the Angels would say: "We are not half as happy up here in Heaven as those Hobson chicks are down by the Thames; we

Oatlands Park Hotel.

will just go down and join them." Then we would have cherubs playing tennis and boating and running around hiding behind the big trees. Never mind; the next time Papa and Mamma come to Europe you shall come, too, and then you shall come down here.

I suppose Grandma Thayer will be going to Cambridge pretty soon, and will be there when we get home. You must be very good to her and make her wish to go back to Cambridge with her Grand-chicks.

Miss Miller writes such nice letters about you that I feel very proud. You must watch Miss Miller and Katie very closely and not let them fall in love with anybody around there and be getting married before we get home. From what I hear, however, Katherine will be marrying, and what will the Major-General do then?

Mamma sends you each a thousand hugs and kisses, and I send you so many that I cannot count them. Regards to everybody, and especially Miss Miller and Katie. Kiss each other for me.   —Your devoted Papa, *Henry W. Hobson.*

༄ A letter from Catherine McKie Thayer:

August 12, 1895.
My darling precious Child—   How I wish I could put my arms around you my dear child. This p.m. I had your letter from Brussels… It seems to me that Henry is taking a *flying* trip— unless you stay away longer than I thought he intended. I am often asked how long you are to be away and of course do not know yet, if you do. I think such rapid travel and sight seeing tends to confuse the mind— much like newspaper reading as compared with a few solid books— however one may get some general ideas. I do hope you will not expose yourselves to great heat… I am so glad if Mrs. Hobson enjoyed her stay in Cambridge. I wrote her in N.Y. & hope she rec'd my letter… she asked me *when* you would be back in Cambridge & how long you would probably stay there etc. So we concluded that in any case I could not be there long. If I go, there is some sentiment about our being there together with your

darlings— pleasant for all to think of in years to come and I would like to see the dear old place and a few people and *you all* there but I think Henry will wish you all in Denver before very long, and then you know it gets cold… in Colorado …Of course I will be anxious to take you in my arms as soon as you get on this side, but if I know you are all well, I can wait awhile till you come home… Now you can tell me what you think…

❧ Reports from the nurse:

Sunday, Aug. 1895.
My dear Mrs. Thayer—   The children are well and enjoy everything… This afternoon we went to the woods and down the creek. I wish you could have seen them, they all looked so lovely. I wish so often I could take their picture. Eleanor walking on a log, the sun shining on her here and there through the branches, her hair so curly and soft around her face and her eyes full of mischief. She looked a perfect picture. At the same time Katherine stood in the brook with two wet feet— slipped in the water. You should have seen the surprise look on her face. Henry sitting in the middle of the brook on a very large stone— not saying one word but looked so happy. He was pleased to get his Uncle's postal— [rest of letter torn]

South Cambridge, Aug 9, 1895.
My dear Mrs. Hobson—   The children are so well and happy, and so full of play that I cannot get them to write. I do not worry them about it. Eleanor would like to write every day. She will say "I want to write to Mama and Papa, can I have ink?" …The children are delighted with their Papa's letter. I hope you can read this. K— has come to me several times for something and you know I have not learned to write and talk at the same time as you have. Sunday is our day at Church again. Kind regards to Mr. Hobson. Hope Mr. H— and yourself are well and having a lovely restful time. With much love. Your sincere friend.   —*Ella Miller*.

Henry, Katherine, and Eleanor Hobson playing in Whiteside Creek behind the Old Home, Cambridge, New York. Photo circa 1895.

Whiteside Creek, Cambridge, New York, 2004.

South Cambridge, Tuesday, August 13, 1895.
My dear Mrs. Hobson—   The children are all as well as they can be and I think they are just as happy as they can be too. They never fret or worry for anything… Katie and the chicks went down the road— I called to her and asked her to bring me some goldenrod if they would see any. Eleanor is coming over the bridge with a big armful. I wish you could see her, she looks like a picture— she has put it in my lap, on ink, paper & everything & said, "This is for you." I am so sorry that I haven't something to take the children's pictures when they look so sweet. Mrs. Thayer always writes she is well, we hear from her almost every day…The children send love & kisses to Papa & Mama. All send love… With much love, sincerely, *E.M.*

South Cambridge, Tuesday, Sept 10, 1895.
My dear Mrs. Hobson—   This is a lovely morning after yesterday's rain. The children are well— they are playing very happily on the porch. A letter from Mrs. Thayer last eve— she wrote she is well. Have not heard from Mrs. Hobson for some time but she is busy with her six children since Miss L— left her for vacation. Aunt Katie is well and always pleased to hear any news from you…We will all be glad to see you and Mr. H— home. Hope you have had a lovely time and are well. Mr. Whiteside said to me that you would sail on the *New York* Sept 21st. After today I will send my next cable Friday before you sail… I have not said anything to children yet about your coming, they would tire themselves thinking and talking about it… Remember me kindly to Mr. H— Children send love, hugs, & kisses to Papa & Mama. Pray our dear Heavenly Father may keep us all well and from all harm as in the past and bring us all safely together again. Yours with much love. Hope to see you soon.   —*Ella Miller.*

 ~ Letters from Annie Jennings Wise Hobson:

Ashland, Sept. 28th, 1895.
My dear Children—   As it is not possible for me to take wings & fly to New York, to give you a loving greeting of welcome, I am up long before six

to write you a line or so in time for the early mail. It would be an unspeakable pleasure to give you both many kisses & old fashioned hugs & to see the darlings meet you and to give them & you both farewell kisses before you go to Colorado, but duty all around forbids... I am waiting early for the intelligence that you are safely landed in New York... We have had no storms, no rain here... My garden dried up long ago. Nevertheless I have so much to be thankful for. Scarlet fever in a mild form has been very near me & yet the children have escaped that and any serious sickness. Cannon left on Thursday for the High School. He wanted to go back and yet his eyes were full of tears as he told me "good-bye." ...Your, or rather Henry's letter of the 14th reached me day before yesterday. It is so blessed to hear of your delightful stay at the Oatlands Hotel... I love to think dear Katherine of your joy at being with the children...   —A.J.W.H.

Sept 28th, 1895.
Dearest Darlings—   Don't I wish I had been with you to have Papa & Mamma back & say with you "Thank our Heavenly Father that He heard our prayers!" You must each kiss Mamma & Papa for me & give Miss Miller my love, a shake-hand for joy & a *squeeze* — old fashioned hug Eleanor! Do not forget to thank God!   —Your devoted Grandma, *A.J.W. Hobson.*

༄ A letter from Catherine McKie Thayer:

September 29, 1895.
...Judge Paterson's stenographer came down with him yesterday— said "The Fleece pd $1,000 last month & div for $2,000 came in this a.m." Good news for Mr. Hobson...

༄ Back home and back to work:

Sept 30, 1895. N.Y.
Darling Kate—   Just a line to say I am safely here... I felt very blue at leaving you and the chicks and after getting on the train I felt badly over having left you without telling you how I have enjoyed our long trip together and thanking you for your goodness & sweetness to me. I am not much given to talking about my feelings and I sometimes fear that you will think me lacking in appreciation. Still Sweetheart I do appreciate you and your lovely conduct to me. I want you to forget and forgive all the disagreeable actions I have been guilty of this summer for the sake of the tender love I bear you. I fear at times I behave very brutally to you and yet you are always good, forbearing, and considerate. I cannot tell you how sweetly and lovingly I will remember & cherish the trip we have had during which you have been my loving companion and comforter... Take my heart full of love and gratitude for the pleasure you have given me. Tell my darlings that I never knew how much I loved them until I came back to them the other day... By-the-way, whilst I think of, be sure some days before you start to arrange for your sleeping car accommodations to Chicago— I will arrange for them West of that in case I cannot send on a car for you. Goodnight my darling one and know always that your happiness is my principal aim in life—   —Devotedly, *Henry.*

October 4, 1895. N. Y. Central Train.
Darling Kate—   Here I am west of Buffalo and with good luck will be tonight on Rock Is. train for Denver. As I got near Albany last night I had a great big longing to get off, see you and the chicks and if I could have gotten out last night I think I should have taken a day… I lunched yesterday with Tom Page down in the City and enjoyed it very much. He is now anxious to get Rosewell away from Richmond and broached the question of my taking him in Denver… Poor old John S. [John S. Wise] is in rather bad spirits. He is not doing much in his business and I believe he has "lost his grip." I managed without any specially disagreeable features to explain Trumbull's letter to him, as I had previously arranged with General Dodge to retain J.S.W. for his reorganization committee, upon no regular salary, but to be paid after reorganization. This will give him a good show if he will only take advantage of it. I do not of course *know*, but I think that if I had had J. S. W.'s chances & openings in N. Y, I would now have an *assured* position. But the trouble with him has been too much pleasure, too much dining & speaking, too much of dogs and hunting men, too much dabbling in politics, too much of Clubs, too much of fighting and newspaper notoriety, too much of running around to gratify his vanity and also but not least, too much of story telling and joking, dirty stories, swearing and offenses to the sensibilities of others. The above qualities and habits… do not make a lawyer successful nor make his income large. He has a great deal more ability intellectually than I have. He has a touch of genius in fact whilst I have not a suspicion of the same, yet he lacks some qualities which are necessary to inspire the confidence of men of substance who have important interests to be cared for and who are willing to pay others to give this care.

I wish to train our boy to be earnest, conscientious, thorough and pertinacious in the performance of anything he undertakes, to take note first of the duties of life and to give his pleasures a fullness and roundness because of his duties well performed. In that way I will make him a good man and the measure of his worldly success will be fixed by chance and his internal abilities. I have come to believe that success may be defined as the result of chances, opportunities properly taken advantage of. But I have moralized enough for one letter… Give much love and many many kisses to my chicks and tell Eleanor that Papa will be at the station to meet her in Denver & hug her tightly… Yr. devoted husband, *Henry*.

October 5, 1895, University Club, Madison Square, New York.
Darling Kate—   Another day gone and I am that much nearer Denver though I am quite tired of the trip. I find that I do not stand the trip so well as I used to and in fact, despite my young looks and big boasting, I am not as young as I used to be. Hard work and continued strain have taken a good deal of spring away. I must now begin to get it back and grow young again… On the train with me are several Denver women stenographers who know me but for the life of me I do not know their names. One of them has her Mother with her, a poor old lady, very frail and apparently very sick and in pain as she is constantly moaning and giving expression to her suffering. They all seem to know I have been abroad and I cannot imagine how my movements have become so much the property of the public. I dislike that kind of notoriety

so much. No man would more keenly enjoy real prominence and fame than I would, but I despise even conspicuousness and empty notoriety… I only wish you will have as cool pleasant weather for your trip as I am having, though I see no reason why you should not. Be sure however to have drawing rooms so that you can control the air. Last night the air in the car was awful and I slept all night with an open window. Most people smell so when undressed… The faces and figures of the little ones are always racing before me and I almost stretch out my arms every now and then to catch them. Hug & Kiss the darlings for me every day. Tomorrow I will send you a telegram.   —Yours devotedly, *Henry.*

October 13, 1895, Denver.
Darling Kate—   You had better be glad my conscience got hold of me after I had written a page of genuine *growl* and *kick* about the way your letters come. I tore it up because I became ashamed, but I do wish you enjoyed writing to me as much as you do to your mother. I have been working at my office all day trying to straighten up my desk and poor Miss Fallon has to suffer by reason of the same. I have been straightening out several accounts for the year ending June 30th, 1895 and also for period since, as they were in a sad state of mix and puzzle. From July 1st / 94 to July 1st /95 we collected in cash (gross) over $52,000 in the two offices. Of this about $16,000 was on account of disbursements, leaving our gross income from fees, about $46,500. Our expenses were about $13,000 leaving about $33,000 net for distribution. I and E— Gall got in round figures $12,000 each and Pattison about $9,500. Of the gross collection, the Denver office collected almost $40,000, the Colo. Springs office about $13,000. Of the $33,000 net divided, the Colorado Springs office only collected about $9,000 leaving $24,000 to the credit of Denver office being net income for year. Of the amount of $40,000 gross collected in Denver, the business brought into the office directly by Judge Pattison brought only about $1,300. Deducting income from R.R. as a joint *viz* $18,000 it would leave the amount realized from *my* business at nearly $30,000. At the same time credit must be given Judge P— [Pattison] for a great deal of work done on business which came into the office through me. I thought you would be interested in the above details. I am amused at it and wonder how long the above condition will last. I think we must do the largest cash business of any firm in Denver, with the exception perhaps of Walcott & Vaile. What bothers me is to know where my money has gone— how it has been spent and what I have to represent it. My income for the year from July 1 /94 to July 2, /95 was—

Law office	$12,000
Inter. Trust Co.	3,500
Fleece Co. (about)	8,500
Misc sources	2,000
Total (Estimated)	$26,000

Where oh where is it? Well we must try and save something this year.
   I had a long letter this morning from Mother. She seemed much pleased with the little things you sent her. She tells me that Aunt N— had finally closed up— which is a good thing. Mother seems to have swooped down on poor old Grandma [Mary Lyons Wise] and carried her off bodily including

all her belongings (especially the $100 a month allowance we provide). Well I cannot help it and I shall not worry. I know it means additional expense in some way to me, but they have gotten so used to my help that they long for more & more all the time. I suppose it is mean for me to feel that way, but I do and I need not pretend to have other feelings. Mother writes me that in accordance with my directions she has had my handsome mahogany bedstead put in thorough order, also a handsome old mahogany claw footed table that used to be my Father's library table. She also says that she has our old mahogany dining room table (now that Aunt N— has broken up) the one my Father bought when he went to housekeeping. It is not the dark black beautiful mahogany but the light reddish mahogany. The question is what shall we do about this furniture. Perhaps we had better wait until you get here and we have then discussed the matter.

 I shall not to go St. Paul for I am not in the best of form and I wish to straighten up my business. Mrs. Mechling has rented her house to a man named G— and is, I hear, going to N.Y. for a time. I am told there has been a good deal of attempted blackmailing here this summer by disreputable women. They have one going now in jail. They always strike prominent citizens with families. Friday a well-known man, a friend of ours, came to me in great trouble because a girl had accused him of having put her in a family way, and her mother had demanded money or she would expose him. The woman even went so far as to bring a suit for support on account of seduction. After satisfying myself that the man was innocent I told him to go and tell his wife at once and I proceeded to jump on the women with both feet. I had them arrested and in the station house in a few hours, and the girl then broke down and admitted the whole game. After giving abundant evidence by her own confession, the detectives let them go upon promise that they would leave town. I was in favor of prosecuting them but my client dreaded scandal, and having downed the blackmailers, he let them go. I am now waiting to see how soon some woman will try her hand with me. She will meet a tough customer if she does. Do not say anything about the above matter, for of course it is a professional secret and we managed to keep the entire matter quiet. The detectives tell me that there have been a dozen attempts this summer to blackmail prominent men… Tell Henny-penny he must be ready to ride with me next summer when we go to Cambridge and I get him a pony. Of course K— will ride *anything* from a steer to a puppy. Hug and kiss my darling little Eleanor and tell her she shall ride with Papa on a big horse whilst K— and H— ride a little pony. Everybody asks about you and the children and wish to see you… Well, I must write a line to Mother and the afternoon shadows are getting to be very long. Much love to dear Mother Thayer and a basket full of kisses for my chicks. As for yourself of course you have my whole heart. Devotedly, *Henry*.

October 15, 1895, Denver.
Darling Kate— A fine letter came from you this morning and I was delighted to read about the children and their doings. I do not like to think much about them for I get so lonesome and they have been away from me for such a long time except for a few snatches. Someday I am going to take all the children and go away for a week to let you see how the house seems without them… Love & kisses. Devotedly, *Henry*.

∽ A letter from Annie Jennings Wise Hobson:

Ashland, Va. Dec. 18th, 1895.
Dear Uncle Henry—   I hardly know how to thank you for again remembering us so generously this Christmas and Aunt Katherine's letter has just come sending money from our little cousins. You make us so happy. May you and Aunt Katherine and my little cousins be three times as happy as we are because you are so good to us. I hope some day to show my gratitude to you in more than words. The three boys want to save money enough to get a Bysicle [sic]. I may go on a hunt Xmas week with Mr. McSparrin up in Goochland where his Father lives. Cannon will be with us Xmas. Kiss Aunt Katherine and my little cousins for me. I will write to Aunt Katherine to thank her for her present. Give my love to Mrs. Thayer. She was so kind to my Papa. Tell Aunt Katherine I will buy a pair of fleece-lined kid gloves with part of the money sent me. Kiss Aunt Katherine & my cousins for me.   —Your loving nephew, *Henry W. Hobson.* [Letter is in the handwriting of A. J. W. Hobson.]

1896

∽ Family matters:

January 3, 1896.
My dear Henry—   …The picture of those three little darlings came, & how well they look & how beautiful they are. Were ever there sweeter healthier faces grouped into one focus of the camera? And how old it makes me feel to see *your* children. But I remember you from the day you were born and when Bangs came to see me yesterday & said he was going to ask Cleveland to tender you the U. S. District Judgeship for Utah, I not only felt very old but very proud. Don't quote me about it, but it is so. Do you want it? Let me know. Maybe I can pull a string for it. I had a glimpse of Henry Garnett when he was visiting Annie. He stayed with me overnight. He is by no means a well man. He looks very waxen & is horribly depressed. From the bottom of my heart I trust he is not seriously sick & that he may soon be restored, for Henry is a very fine man & while he has saved something, it would be a great hardship on his family if he was disabled. The restoration of good feeling between him & Annie seems to be complete & I am very glad of it.

I have had one or two sweet letters from Sister Annie of late. The old girl seems to be very happy. She has now a sort of cross between an old woman's home & a kindergarten & Henry it would make you laugh to see the show. I went there for a day & it was equal to a circus. When I left, somebody in Richmond asked how Mother was getting on & I said, "Splendidly. If she doesn't get trod on." There was Sister Annie, all Cannon's children, Mother, Idie [Eliza], Mother's servant, Cook, serving girl, a white woman with a bastard child (best looking one in the house), washer woman, man with a load of wood, two niggers turfing in the front yard & everything going sizzling. And dear Old Sister Annie was in her glory. She gave me a delicious breakfast & did everything in the world she could to show her love & appreciation of my visit. But it was more a New York ferry-boat landing than anything else. I wonder what K— and Mrs. Thayer would have thought of it all. …Good-bye old boy. A Happy & prosperous New Year to you & hug & kiss your dear wife

Three children of Henry W. Hobson and Katherine Thayer Hobson. Eleanor, left, Katherine, middle and Henry, right.

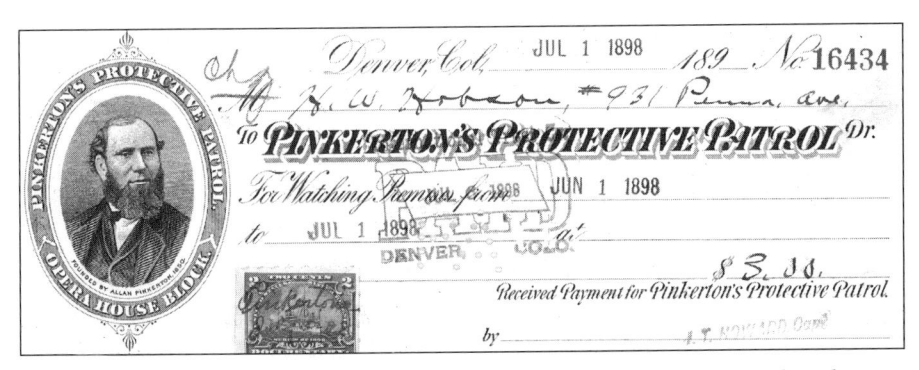

Home Security in 1898. Cancelled check for security at 931 Pennsylvania Avenue residence in Denver.

& the children for me. Tell K— her dog is simply splendid. He is as handsome as a picture & smart. There are no flies on this one. I sent him to Cape Charles. By the way, I have received no notice of the arrival of your picture. How shall I proceed to find it? You kept the man's letter & I have no memorandum of ship or anything else. You must return the letter & tell me where to look.   —Your affec. uncle, *John S. Wise.*

U.P. Train, January 25, 1896.
Darling Kate—   If anyone should ever take the trouble to investigate our married life they will find a large part of our relations existing in letters written by me from RR trains. I wonder how many letters I have sent you from way stations? I had a very comfortable night and feel very well this morning. This train now has a dining car so that I got up at a comfortable hour and had a fairly good breakfast. Be sure to send me those prescriptions, or rather copies of the same from the Shelly's drug store, for I have only a small quantity of powder which I find very beneficial… I think you had better tell Johnson to sleep in the house whilst I am away especially if you take Clinton to the Springs for I hardly trust poor little Mary alone in the house. Also arrange so that either Mary or Johnson shall be on the premises all the time— especially at night. There are a good many thieves now in Denver and a good many burglaries have occurred. I think it would be well to send your silver & jewelry to the Safety Deposit Co. before you leave. …Tell dearest little Eleanor that Papa kissed her three or four times whilst she was asleep and is going to return to her very soon. I kissed the others just as often. You forgot to give me directions about buying Henny Penny's trousers for him. Perhaps, as I shall be coming East again before he is five, it may be as well to wait until the Spring. He shall go into trousers when he is five & be a boy all over. Kiss the darling chicks a thousand times for me and take many kisses & much love for yourself.   —Devotedly *Henry.*

◦ Missing legal papers and dinner instructions:

March 9, 1896, Santa Fe Route Eating House & Dining Car System.
Darling Kate—   Here I am at La Junta until tomorrow morning and in consequence of a nice job on the part of Eddie at my office— Thursday I took the Pecos bundle of papers on my desk, the Bill of Complaint which I had gotten prepared and sworn to in N.Y., and the *one indispensable paper* at the hearing in New Mex. and without which I cannot move a peg. I told Eddie to copy it, explaining to him that it must be done by Saturday, as I had to take the original

with me. Yesterday morning I asked him if he had copied that Bill and he said he had. I presumed of course that he had filed the original in the only proper place in the office where it should have been filed— the bundle of papers on my desk. I prepared and had made a lot of other papers and yesterday had Eddie and Miss Fallon pack all my papers in my travelling case. This morning I awoke early and thought I would check up everything, and to my disgust I found that everything was in the box except the Bill of Complaint. What the boy has done with it, I don't know, and I can only wait here for it. I of course am very disgusted and were it not for my own neglect I should be inclined to deal quite severely with the boy. There is no excuse for him not returning the paper to the proper bundle, yet if I had checked up the papers before leaving my office, this delay would not have occurred. I should have done so but I was pushed right to the last moment and was completely worn out and my mind was too tired to go much into detail when I left. I am partially to blame however and yet it shows the burden upon me of watching not only the important matters at the office but every detail— even to the filing of papers. I have been keeping the wires hot this morning trying to catch someone in Denver (it being Sunday everyone is out of the way) and I hope to have the paper sent to Pueblo this afternoon where I will have Campbell to meet it.

This delay may throw me into Thursday getting home. Now note the following about the dinner. If I cannot get home in time I will wire you Wednesday morning. I cannot in any event get back before 6 o'clock Wednesday. If I am not on hand get anyone you please to preside. General W— is a nice old fellow and perhaps would enjoy it. Be sure to engage a good waiter to help Clinton. Better get Owens or that other fellow (Trip is it?)

If you run short of a man write a note to Rhodes and at the same time have Mosby see him and arrange matters. On Wednesday morning get from cellar 2 quarts of sherry. I think they are there— if not send Johnson to the Denver Club for it and tell them to send a good dry sherry. I think they call it "Den-Club Sherry"— this will be more than enough with what is on the sideboard.

Also two qts. of Claret Chateau Palmer which have Clinton put in place to get chill off.

Also 2 qts. and one pint of Champagne. I don't think there are any quarts left in rack, but there are some in a box open on floor if I remember. If not, there is some champagne in a box Otis Spencer sent me at Xmas. Have this iced *in the morning. Don't use* any of the Claret in the decanters for it is sour. Use the sherry however.

Have one bottle of claret decanted and only have the other opened when needed. One bottle may be enough. One bottle of sherry with what is in the decanters should suffice, but you can have another bottle in reserve. You will have to watch the wine service to see that it is not awkwardly done. I have always had to direct it from my end of the table. Sherry should be served with soup. Claret should be served after the fish with the entree. Champagne after the entree with the roast or game as you may have it. If you do not watch the wine, the fool waiter will serve sherry two courses too late and so on, getting in his champagne with the coffee. Moreover they serve too rapidly if you do not watch them and also let all the decanters get empty and fail to fill them. It may sound paradoxical to say all these mistakes can be made, but the capacity of waiters for being fools is unlimited. Now do watch things if I am not there and don't delude yourself with the idea that not much wine will be or ought to be drunk. Army men and several other of the men we have are good drinkers and a dinner (at least at my house) is not the place to reform morals.

Now for after dinner— You had better let the men smoke and lie in the dining room as it is much more comfortable than the hall. Have my box of cigars put upon the table and as soon as you get this letter wet the sponge in the box so as to have the cigars in good condition. My bunch of keys with box key is in one of my bureau drawers. When the cigars are put on the table have a box of matches put on also, you will probably think as an ornament as all women in my house seem to think cigars can be lighted from the electric lights. When the cigars and coffee are served, have the decanter of brandy and the green mint decanter and the decanter of Scotch Whiskey put on the table with a pitcher of water. Remember to suggest to the waiter that brandy and green mint are not taken in tumblers but in cordial glasses and Scotch Whiskey in tumblers and not cordial glasses— so there should be both kinds put upon the table. As you cannot stay in to drink with the men, make Clinton understand very clearly what is wanted and you *SEE* that she does it by asking in the parlor. Don't trust her, for there is no trust to be placed in anyone. Before leaving, speak to General W— or whoever takes my place and extend the freedom of the house to him and ask him to see that everything goes straight and to order the servants to bring whatever is not on hand. Now do like a good girl, see that everything goes well and don't presume it will as a matter of course. I always have to attend a good deal to details and I have always taken pride in the smooth and correct way our dinners have gone off. Remember that wine badly served or a go-as-you-please after dinner scramble for cigars will spoil a whole dinner. Moreover don't trust to Clinton about the lights. If you do not give the orders, the hall lights will be dim, the porch light out, the parlor dark etc. When the guests arrive and when you go into dinner you will find the lights entirely bad.

You perhaps do not know how much attention I give to the details of your dinners, but I do— For instance let me relate—

When I get home I see that the porch and vestibule electric lights are on, that the hall lights including one by coat closet are all in shape with no lamps burned out, that the halls do not look like junk shops or lumber rooms with everything thrown about, that the parlor and dining rooms lights are right etc. I then give specific orders about the lights and a little before seven I see that the lights are turned on.

I then go to the table and see that the glass is all right, and clean, and frequently I have to rearrange all the glasses and wipe some.

I then decant the wine, give specific orders about its service and see that the decanters are properly placed on the table— During dinner I follow the service and give orders from time to time to the waiter in an undertone— After dinner I see that everything is properly served— Last I see that the guests do not run away with anything, that the doors are locked especially in the dining room, and that everybody gets to bed.

With all the above duties upon me, you will understand that I feel somewhat timid about letting you have a dinner of 14 without me, especially as you pride yourself upon not pandering to the vices of men.

I believe I have about written myself out upon this subject, and as the train goes shortly I will close.

I had an awful time last night— did not get here until 1 o'clk. Found the hotel without a bed, had to hunt all over town to get one, finally found one worse than the one we had at that place in Montana, simply rolled around all night trying to find a soft place and escaped this morning at 7 o'clk. Love and kisses to the darlings. —Your devoted husband *Henry*.

March 9, 1896, Santa Fe Route Eating House & Dining Car System.
Darling Kate—   Again I am off having gotten my paper. I kept the wires hot yesterday morning until I caught Whitted and had him send the paper to Pueblo where Campbell (who is with me) kindly met it and he got back last night. I put in a day of work yesterday and so my time will not be entirely lost though I don't know how my stenographer will enjoy it. I suppose you have gotten my long homily on the subject of dinner. I had nothing to do but work off a bad humor and I thought dining was a fair subject for that. I am very well. Love and kisses to all. This is the worst hole you ever saw though the hotel is good.   —Devotedly *Henry*.

March 1896, On the Train, 9 o'clock.
My Darling Husband—   I am so so desolate & lonely without "my better half" & still I know it is all right & it is best you should take your trip without me this time. Even now I am looking forward to our reunion. Henry, I am so proud of my Husband. You please & delight my eye. And as you stood there outside the car I felt so thankful & full of joy to feel you were mine. I don't think I ever make you appreciate how fully & entirely I love you. You comfort & strengthen me & are so patient. You do behave so beautifully in regard to all these miserable Jermain complications & I do love you for your patient generous actions & advice & think that I was "mean" to you last night. That is all a dream of yours. I know I never moved away from your dear self. This takes you my heart's love & kisses. My love, my all—   Your own loving wife, *Katherine*.

◦᳁ Family matters:

Denver, March 16, 1896.
Dear Uncle John—   Your letter of March 13th, with enclosures, duly received. I had already gotten a letter from Henry Garnett. I expect to be East in the course of a few weeks and will take up myself the matter of Grandma and adjust it. I will send on the first of April the $100 that Henry Garnett may owe.

I am inclined to think that you are wrong about taking old Ida from Grandma. Whilst she is of no physical service, yet she is a good deal of mental comfort. Grandma has become thoroughly accustomed to her and she is too old to re-adjust herself to new associates. The same is true of old Ida. You had better let the matter rest until I go East and see what can be done…
—Yours affectionately, *Henry W. Hobson*. (Virginia Historical Society)

April 16, 1896, New York.
Darling Kate—   Tomorrow I hope to go down to Virginia. I wrote to the Stewarts asking whether they wished to have me for a day or two but I have heard nothing from them. I may hear today. I am going to indulge in strategy

to keep from staying in Ashland. I would rather be in a lunatic club for the same length of time. I noted what you said about my "whining" over myself and I think you are right— I make a great fuss over little things and am especially inconsiderate of you when I am sick. I care little what other people think about my health but I will try to correct my fault hereafter so far as you are concerned… I am better I think as far as my cold is concerned but I am still troubled and hope the rest in Virginia will do me good… I will close now but will keep this letter open until I get uptown and add a line if I can. No time to write now. Love and Kisses. I am so *tired* of this work.   —Devotedly *Henry*.

New York, April 23rd, 1896.
Dear old Chum Henny Penny—   Papa received your letter and was so pleased with it. I did not have a bathroom at Saratoga and had to wash in the basin, but here I have a good bath every morning. I saw a little boy to-day, only three and a half years old, who says he wants to shoot Indians and bears. When I told him about you and your hunting and pony, he said he wanted to go home with me, and took hold of my hand and wanted me to take him along. I think he would be a very nice little playmate for you, and you could teach him how to ride and shoot. You must not forget how to ride while you are away from the pony for so long a time.
     Good-by for now.   —Your devoted old "*Pop*."
Master Henny Penny, care of Mamma.

❧ Katherine Hobson to her Mother:

July 17, 1896.
…Waiting for Henry to go to see a cart for the pony— I think driving for the children such better exercise than riding, this hot weather. How the "Fleece" is going down. Henry says it is worth as much as when it was $170, but I do not feel so…

July 19, 1896.
…Henry heard from his Mother the other day. She does not think Cannon had better return to the High School that he prepared for… I do not know what Henry will do— suppose yield to his Mother as usual…

Tuesday, July 21, 1896.
My Dearest Mother—   Henry told me on Sunday evening as he was writing at desk, to his Mother, most of what I enclose. I read his reply— H— seemed so depressed, told me not to write her any more about him & his work… then he tore letter up, 135 pieces or more & I thought I would like to read for myself and worked the puzzle out today— quite a task. It is just as well you and I were one on these matters & could *talk them over*. We are well, children out on pony this P.M.

❧ A letter from Annie Jennings Wise Hobson:

My Dear Son—   …as I write I feel faint & far from clear-headed because only a stern sense of duty to myself & others induces me in any way to add to your

This letter from A. J. W. Hobson to her son is dated July 15, 1896, and is the only letter from her in that year. According to Katherine Hobson in the July 21st letter to her mother, Henry Hobson tore up the letter from his mother and put it in the trash after he had read it. Katherine recovered it from the trash, pieced it together, copied it, and sent it to her mother in Colorado Springs.

care & anxieties. Past experience has taught me that it is so much better when one has strength & life to speak & be understood than to leave life-long regrets behind... I am now fully convinced there is something organically wrong with my heart. There have been so many sudden deaths around me that I feel as if I should heed the warning & be prepared for any emergency, & it is best you should know the truth. I do not mean to alarm you to say that I am in any immediate danger... but I do appreciate that my life must have less of anxiety & care, more rest & recreation if I am to last. The symptoms that convince me of this are such as I never had before, breathlessness when I walk any distance, especially when I walk upstairs... I am fatigued and a faintly sickness comes over me. And if I am the least alarmed, a telegram will make me feel faint. I do not believe I would stand any sudden shock. After sound sleep I will wake up finding the action of the heart faint & often this is followed by a profuse perspiration, especially early in the morning. Now this may be only because my nervous system is run down & in need of rest... There is also a certain congestion of the kidneys. Now my dear good son I wish to say this— If aught should happen and I should be called suddenly, know that I have faced it & fear nothing, casting myself on the infinite mercy of the God man, who as Father said, Know my nature & pities my infirmities— in whom in my poor halting way I have tried to serve, trust, & feebly love.

You would find a letter stating my wishes & telling about my affairs. You may be assured that your Mother's last loving blessing was with the son who had tried to make her life brighter & lighten her responsibilities & ever show her a loving devotion. My last thought, I am sure, if I had time to think, would be a prayer that you would be united with me & our loved ones in Heaven. I have felt such terrible depression of late... and to put it in the mildest way I do not wish you to have a broken down Mother in your hands. I really feel that the best solution of the Life's burden to the problem of your life's burden would be my release by death.

What I have would support the children without taxing you. Do all you ought to be expected to do and Alice & her husband would have no alternative about doing their duty by them. I cannot tell you how it depressed me to hear you speak, as you did at Old Point, as if the very iron had entered your soul from the fetters these poor children have long put upon you. It has constantly rung in my ears & repeated itself in my heart. I can assure you that if I am still spared to life & can do any work, that if Mother goes first, I shall break up, insist upon Alice taking her children & get some position where I can live comfortably & do less work, have far more rest that I have now.

I have been so discouraged about these children during the past year— my efforts seem to be unavailing to develop them morally & mentally. I seem to have little influence for good on them. Do you know that my conscience & judgment seem to arraign me of late, in having been very blind & selfish in considering the children more that I did you, that I did not consider your welfare as I ought to have done, that I should have made their Mother take them & my punishment has come upon me as I deserve. Katherine has written me about her depression, really feeling appalled by the responsibilities upon you. My heart has ached for her & I have felt so powerless to help in the matter. If you were to break down, it would kill me.

Yet I must add now to your burdens by three requests which, if you can grant, are the last of the kind I shall ever ask. Of that you may rest assured.

1st. I feel sure that rest of body & mind would be very beneficial. Now I can not leave home for any time but I could take it here. I would much rather you should make me a present now than at Xmas. Send me a $100 to do as I please with and I am going to stop my sewing, darning & mending and take some rest & recuperate in my own way… I would especially like to have it before the 1st of August for some reasons (I will not tell you just now)— indeed as soon as you can send it. One I will mention is that having to buy Cannon about $25.00 of clothes, he has just about [illegible] out his summer suit, lost & outgrown his underclothes & came home shoeless and my having a Doctor's bill of $18 & this being the quarter of my rent which I had advanced. I barely have enough to run me through the month. Next month I would be much obliged if you could advance me $50.00 to get my coal & part of my winter wood, both will be much cheaper if purchased now. It will be one worry less to know they are secured. If I die there will no trouble in disposing of them. Send me the $50 next month & deduct $10 each month from monthly allowance. I do not wish you to give me this. Lately my mind has been *exercised in every way* & my responsibilities have come upon me with a weight never felt before. *Fears haunt me.* I do most emphatically ask this of you as an act that will insure me much peace of mind. If you were suddenly taken off and I left with my present responsibilities, I should not have $10 to call my own, no means if necessary to raise one dollar with except through the kindness of friends. All I ask is for you to give me $1,000… and this shall be the last request for money… you will ever have from me. I have been haunted lately by a nightmare of being left as I was when your Father died, without a right to anything in the world. I know you lovingly desire… to make my last years as happy & peaceful as you can & this act would conduce greatly to my peace of mind.

 Now Henry if you feel I ought not to have written this letter and if you can not accede to my request please say so quietly without a reproach for the past. You reproached me once in Richmond about my course. (*Where she wanted $500 or $800 & would not tell for what —*)… I could not stand any reproach no matter how much I deserve it just now. One thing I do know, that no matter how you feel that & what you may express, you have done your part nobly & fully & with an upright sense of duty & integrity which excites my admiration & increases my love.

 I wish to add one thing while I think of it. If anything comes from the Texas lands, it is yours not mine. I never intended otherwise.

 Now, about Cannon, I send you a pamphlet & letter from Rev. J. Green Shackelford who was Rector here when I first came to Ashland & who was a warm friend of Cannon Senior's & whom I count as life friend. He is a gentleman & scholar, a man who understands men & has been most happy in bringing up his only son. You may remember that his first wife died when Green Shackelford Jr. was with Cannon the first year at the High School & had an excellent influence over him… I am convinced that such a school as the Episcopal Male Academy, which is more like a home school, would be far better for Cannon… he could not go to the High School for less than 350 or 400 for board, washing & tuition. I know of no one to whose care I would more gladly commit Cannon than to Green Shackelford's— he would have with him the influences of a home life and care far more that at the High School… I do request that you write to Cannon & require him the 1st of

August to persue [sic] some instructive reading with me & to give 2 hours daily with Mrs. Walter to Latin & Math… and if he refuses to study he ought to be put to work… I am free to confess that I try to hope better things as he grows more manly, but I have never seen a more careless indolent boy of 16— though Henry Garnett & Johnnie were about as bad at his age. The boy has no very dreadful fault except his indolence & has improved upon last year in some respects. If I could only arouse some steadfast earnestness in him. I do not believe he has any propensity to be vicious. If you will send me the money I will tell you how I mainly propose to enjoy it. I have been trying to make up my mind for a week to write this, and no one will believe the effort of will it has cost me (*Then a lot about Grandma Wise & the Garnetts — the end I copy, K.T.H.*) God grant that this letter may bring you no great addition to your burdens & make you realize that only sense of duty made me write it.

➢ Katherine Hobson to her Mother:

July 22, 1896.
My Dearest Mother—   …It is as I feared. Mrs. Hobson is tired of her life with the children and would break up when her Mother dies & feels now she should have left the children to Alice's care. I did feel so sorry for Henry with his Mother's varied appeals & his pathetic answer, sending the $150 as though I can not afford it, but refusing the money as a bond for her own use…

July 24, 1896.
… Henry wrote his Mother, if he died she would be provided for, but he would not give her the $1,000 he thought she meant…

July 24, 1896.
… I feel just as you do about the condition of Mrs. Hobson & her surroundings. This A.M. I have been on piazza with K— She is really improving in her reading… Henry has a law case sent from N.Y. which he worked over all last evening. I take my tonic & feel better & am trying to be quiet & patient & restful & good, but it is hard work. Love & Many Kisses. Your own devoted *Kittie*.

July 25, 1896.
… Judge Hallett came over last evening— he had lunched with Henry & Judge Brewer yesterday. I think the Judge's friendliness a great gratification to Henry…

July 31, 1896.
… As for the Fleece, I am perfectly disheartened about it. I told Henry I felt so badly about & perfectly discouraged. He said that he was not, that he thought the future of the mine depended on the openings & development in the lower workings. Well we must wait & see, but I do mourn the loss, as I told Henry, it was such a restful condition to feel such a monthly dividend was coming in. I can not see *why* Henry does not say more about it. He said another expert has been down and reported favorably on the property— some French expert… Henry reads a while in evening & then gets sleepy & takes a nap. He says he is too tired to work or read. I think it is chronic, his talk about being tired, "dead tired." I do not know that he has had any response from his Mother since his letter. At least he said nothing of it. Love & many kisses, your loving *Kittie*.

August 11, 1896
…The day is much cooler than yesterday— a freshness in the air… I now think so much of the heat in the East & wonder if old Mr. Jermain will be prostrated. I can't help but think they could get him into a cooler atmosphere, even in a bed in Special Car, but Marie evidently dreads such a move…

August 13th, 1896, Denver.
My Dearest Mother—   Here is a letter from Marie which will show you she has the electric fan. I was intending telegraphing her suggesting a fan— they certainly cool the atmosphere in a room very much…

N. P. Railroad, August 20th, 1896.
Do you know, chicks, I went all around last night and stole a little honey from each one to take with me to keep my mouth and lips sweet while away. If it were not for that, I am afraid my mouth would be very bitter and naughty sometimes.

I have Katherine's honey chucked away in one cheek, and Henny Penny's in the other, and Piggy Wiggy's smeared on my lips and on the tip of my tongue; so there is no place for bad tastes to get it at. [unsigned]

University Club, New York, August 23rd, 1896.
My Darling little Sweetheart—   You let Henry and Eleanor get ahead of you in writing to your Papa, and Eleanor even sent me a present. I wish you were with me in New York, for it is so cool and pleasant and we could go out to Manhattan Beach, and see the beautiful fireworks. To-morrow I am going to see if I can find a little girl's side-saddle, and maybe some day soon I will buy it for you. If you are going to ride my big horse, however, you will have to ride a larger saddle than would do for the pony.

Good-by. Your Papa sends you a hundred kisses.   —Your devoted Father, *Henry.*

Denver, July 12, 1896.
Dearest Mother Thayer—   Your sweet birthday letter and more than generous gift came safely to hand upon the morning of the 9th. I cannot thank you too much for your sweet remembrance and loving words… I had hoped to have accomplished more at 38 than to have acquired only the ability to earn honestly a few thousand dollars more or less a year. Perhaps however that ability reaches the limits of the sphere cut out for me and it is but brave to recognize such a fact. I fear I am to be only a money-maker in life and as compensation for my buried hopes, to have a loving wife, the sweetest of children, and a most comforting second Mother. Perhaps Henney-penney will do something in life and then will I not have borne the cross in vain. With a heart full of love & gratitude.   —Your loving son, *Henry W. Hobson.*

◦৹ Family matters:

Sept. 23, 1896.
Dear Henry—   …I had quite a lively time with a horse last Saturday at the Cape. He kicked the whole front out of the wagon, then kicked me three times on my legs & finally, when I jumped on the buggy seat, kicked my posterior & sent me head over heels over the wagon, landing on my head in a potato

patch. God knows why the brute did not kill me & I must be the toughest citizen living. My leg is as black as tar but nary bone could he break. I believe he was thoroughly disgusted at the futility of his efforts. My folk will be home soon, I am glad to say— Fall is here & it is getting lonesome... Kiss K— & the children for me.   —Your affec. uncle, *John S. Wise.*

 Letters from Catherine McKie Thayer to her daughter:

October 6, 1896.
...I am wondering if you will go to Ada's or Hedge Lawn first. Mr. Jermain so feeble— poor Marie— what a blank life will be to her without her Father— so empty. He & she have walked together so many years— others have come & gone— they alone remained. I feel very sorry for her...

October 23, 1896.
...I think much of Mr. Jermain in his feebleness— and of poor Marie— if the end must come soon, I am glad you are near...

November 13, 1896.
...Will be interested to hear from you at Mr. Jermain's— just how he is & Marie. I hope K's portrait will be satisfactory to you & Henry...

November 19, 1896.
...I feel almost anxious as to K's portrait— so almost impossible to get what satisfies *all* ones' own family— and K's face varies with every thought and emotion. I trust you & H— will be entirely pleased with results— as to others it will not matter... Poor old Mr. Jermain, to tip over in his chair— it seems that no one can be guarded against bad nurses & accidents if he is not. I am glad only a "little lameness" was the result...

October 18, 1896, Colorado Springs.
Darling Kate—   Here I am at the Springs with the darling Chicks. I arrived a little after eleven and found them both out on the carriage block waiting for me with their little faces wreathed in swirls of delight. Now that they have gone up to bed I have gotten the first opportunity of the day to write to you and my letter will not go off until tomorrow. I know however you will be reconciled to that on account of the cause of the delay. They have both clung closely to me all day. They went up to see me undress & shave— then escorted me to the bathroom, where, their sleeves having been rolled to their shoulders, they helped soap my head & wash my back— then they stayed with me whilst I was dressing— then I had to read with them until lunch— after which we went off to Roswell for an outing and they played an hour in the Grandstand from which they saw the Wild West show. We got home in time for dinner and after dinner to bed they went, both insisting upon sleeping in the crib by my bed. Henry wishes to go home with me in the morning and so does Eleanor of course. He of course gave up however when I asked him if he were going to leave Eleanor when you confided her to his care and he had promised to take care of her. He also wants to go to Texas and Eleanor does too, she telling her Grandmother, when objection was made, with a fine show of indignation— *"Why I have never been to Tekis and I must go."* I never

Katherine Hobson was on a trip east at this time with her daughter Katherine. The other two children, Henry and Eleanor, had been left in Colorado Springs. On this trip they visited Fitchburg, Massachusetts, Albany, New York, and Virginia where they met Henry.

saw them look better and darling little Eleanor is as rosy as a carnation. They both talk a great deal about you and Katherine… I wish you could have seen Eleanor leaving Church today with Henry as her little boy and Grandma, Miss Miller, and me as the congregation. She got a long stick from the yard, then a hymn book, a Bible, and a catechism. She would take her stick and lead the choir with most frantic waves of her baton, shouting a jargon at the top of her voice. Then she preached a very earnest sermon in a loud tone of voice, having the Bible open before her and gesticulating vigorously with her little fat arms. Then patient little Henny-penny would be put through a course of catechism, she explaining to him that he could not go to Heaven and see "Dod" unless he was good… She would not let him stir from his seat whilst this performance was going on. Finally Henry in desperation suggested to her that it was time to play the organ and he dashed for the piano. His Grandmother however objected and the services were adjourned. I found out today that he and Eleanor amused themselves one day cutting off the ends of my box of cigars and breaking a good many— Henry explaining that he "*sought I would 'ike that.*" They have been very good, their Grandmother says, and they seem happy though their little faces look rather pathetic and long when they speak of Mamma in tender tones… I had a nice hunt yesterday afternoon killing 18 duck which is a very good bag for me.

I left at 6 o'clk this morning on the train and caught the early train from Colorado Springs. There has been a vast improvement in the arrangements at the lake since I was there some weeks ago. The old crowd in charge have been turned off— the buildings have been painted— all the old furniture sent away and now we have nice iron bedsteads, new blankets, clean sheets, a good cook, decent food, and three very good men as servants and boatmen. The Club arrangements are now very comfortable. I sent 1/2 doz duck to Mrs. Trumbull by Johnson and brought a dozen beautiful duck to your Mother who promptly sent some of them to Mrs. L— …Goodnight sweetheart mine. I shall be so happy when I join you East. A 100 kisses for Katy. —Devotedly *Henry.*

Denver, October 21st, 1896.
My Darling little Chicks—   How much I do want to see you, and I think about you a hundred times a day. I am going to Colorado Springs on Friday night, to see you before I go to Texas, and I will spend all Saturday morning with you. I get letters from Mamma, and she tells about how Katherine is playing with the Boughton children and Aleck and Aaron and having a fine time. Don't you wish you could be with them? Katherine has been to Sunday-school, too, in Troy where Mamma used to go when she was a little girl. Give much love to Grandma, and take a thousand kisses for yourself.
—Devotedly, *Papa.*

November 1, 1896, Colorado Springs.
Darling Kate—   Whilst waiting for the chicks to take them to Church I will write to you. I am going up at 1:40 but come down again next Saturday to see the little ones. Yesterday afternoon they went downtown with me and had quite a frolic in the barber shop whilst I was having my hair-cut. Then came soda water of course. Henry slept in my room last night and woke me at about 5 this morning… Henry this morning wished to know when dear

Mamma was coming home to take him back to Denver. He said he thought about it all the time. Your telegram to your Mother came this morning and from it I infer you reached Fitchburg Friday. I look forward eagerly to your letters in Denver. Your Mother read your long letter of last Sunday and by accident read that you said Mrs. J. S. W. was a "bore" —She has not stopped apologizing yet for what she calls her bad manners which amuses me for no one thinks Mrs. W— so much of a bore as I do. I must go now. Give a big big hug to my darling little Kate— Love & kisses—   Devotedly *Henry*.

Chicago, November 11th, 1896.
My Darling little Chicks—   You will, I know, be glad to get a little letter from Papa. I went from Denver sooner than I expected and I expect you and Grandma were surprised to get my message. We have had snow all the way, and yesterday you two chicks could have slided up hill and down hill on your sleds if you had been with me and had hitched your sleds on to the rear of the train. Wouldn't that be funny, having a sled hitched to a train and going "whiz" through the country? I have been thinking about you two little darlings all the time, and I hated so very much to leave you, but then Grandma and Miss Miller will take good care of you (and when I go home I expect we will have most [of] a trunkful of things for you). Tell Grandma I have Henry's suit, or rather the one that isn't Henry's, in my trunk. I don't know yet where I will meet Mamma and Katherine; maybe in New York and maybe in Boston. Everything is kind of mixed up. Give much love to Grandma and Miss Miller, and you two kiss each other a hundred times for Papa.   —Your devoted Papa, *Henry*.

◦ A trip east—1896:

Fitchburg, November 3, 1896, Election Day.
My Darling Mother—   This morning brought me your letters of Thurs. & Friday, and such comfort they gave me. I am so glad your cold is better— be very very careful. Katherine has just been out, & came in radiant with a large picture of *Bryan,* she paid ten cents for. She says she found one man in Troy for Bryan. Oh dear will he get in. I bought & read the *World* yesterday & there seems such uncertainty— there is a great Bryan tidal wave. And whether it will overwhelm the McKinley boat is hard to tell… I hope there will be such a defeat that the Bryanites will feel discouraged to proceed. I can think of nothing else. Today we have been at Mrs. Addison's to dinner, with Ada & children. Morris off on some work. I enclose Marie's & Katie's letters. Have written Marie I would stop at Hedge Lawn…   —Love & many kisses. Your own Devoted *Kittie*.

◦ A letter from Catherine McKie Thayer:

My darling One— … I think Henry looks better than he did when last here. I think better than any time since his illness. Miss M— been talking about Henry's Mother (did not know until told I her that you were going to Virginia.) Henry said he dreaded going, spoke of the complaints he rec'd & of the disobedience of the older boys & said that he disapproved of her taking all that family & the old people etc. & I said I think you should talk plainly with the boys, and

Bryan William Jennings Bryan, defeated by William McKinley in the November 1896 elections.

as their uncle it is from duty to do so. He did not seem to feel as if he should do much *talking*— take care of them 'till they were 17 …he will talk to them though & give them good advice. My darling one, you will need wisdom & strength and grace & the gift of gentle speech for this Southern trip & you may feel that I ask God that you may have it. Henry said you thought you might go to our old Church today. I hope the day is as lovely there as here… H— says he does not expect to be in N. Y. before Nov. 15th —you may know this. He said a little stay East would do you & K— good— both of you…

◈ From Kittie in Virginia:

November 18, 1896— The Jefferson, Richmond, Virginia. Ainslie & Webster, Managers.
My Darling Mother—   We left last evening at 9— had dinner with the Hagermans— they both well & like Manhattan very much. Mrs. H— sent love to you. We had a sweet call with Pages & Stewarts yesterday P.M. Mrs. Page was perfectly delighted with Katherine & the Stewarts just as appreciative though less demonstrative… all asked for you & wished to be remembered. I always feel they are genuinely good, true Xtian [*sic*] women. Had a very comfortable night on train. All slept well… We reached Ashland about 8:30 this A.M. Henry Jr., Mary, & Jennings met us with a note from Grandma Hobson & saying she would be here at 2:30 today. Henry is asleep on the bed now, getting a nap. Everyone says he is "looking splendidly—" Katherine playing about the interior court, where there are palms, Banana trees, a fountain, & bed of grass, marble walks between. Very lovely. She has been playing fairy land— had her dolls there. I am trying to be a *good girl* and not have a slight thing mar our stay here. *It takes 2 to make a row*. Henry & Katherine going to meet Grandma. She returns at 7 o'clock… Your telegram a delightful welcome— and such a comfort to know all are well. Will send to Boston for letters. Had one from University Club Monday evening… Now must stop & dress— very mild day… Love & many kisses to all— especially my Darling little ones.   —Your own *Kittie*.

Will write as I can. We make our headquarters here and go to Ashland for the day to see Grandma Wise.

Henry Jr.   Henry Wise Hobson, born 1880, son of John Cannon Hobson.

Henry is asleep   Kittie's husband, Henry Wise Hobson, born 1858.

◈ Letters from Catherine McKie Thayer:

Nov. 18, 1896.
My darlings all—   …If you have not heard from the chicks [Henry and Eleanor Hobson] as constantly as you could wish, it has been because I did not know whether you would remain in Boston or go South until last eve— but the chicks are & have been well, now painting on my floor… Will you, Kittie, order the Virginia pickles for me, a good quantity & of more than one kind. I have no pickles & do not care for what we buy here. Give love to Mrs. Hobson. I know you will have a pleasant reunion. Remember me to Grandma Wise also. Although I have not seen her, I know she is lovely. Eleanor has just kissed me for you all & "sends love to Grandma Hobson & all my little cousins." Henry sends "love & kisses." And I send Mother's love to you & Henry & sweet love to Katherine. —*Mother*

November 22, 1896.
Today I have your first letter from Richmond— glad you are in what Uncle William thinks the most beautiful, best hotel in the country [The Jefferson]. K— may well play fairyland— so pleased that you had a sweet time with Mrs. Page & the Stewarts. I would like to see K— with the dear young girl, a picture indeed… Henry says "I send love to Grandma Hobson & my cousins" & E— says "tell Grandma Hobson I am folding my towel & send her & my little cousins my love." Miss Miller joins me in desire to be remembered to Mrs. Hobson. I trust all will be well and that you will have a lovely time in every respect. There is much love sent in this sheet, but I think it will still hold dear tender love from me to you & K— also to dear Henry…

Colorado Springs. Nov. 24, 1896.
My dear Daughter— …I can say that chicks all well as they have been & send love & kisses… I think by the time this reaches Richmond you will be away from Virginia. I seem to be writing many times to the place you have been in. The weather mild… *Mother.*

 ∽ From Kittie:

Postcard: Richmond, Nov. 25, 1896.
My Dearest Mother— Henry, Katherine & I are ready to have breakfast & to go to Eastwood at 8:40 to spend the day & return 7 this eve. No mid-day train. Day lovely. All well. K— quite over her cold attack. I have not written for I have had not a moment of time. Will write today from country. Love Kisses & hugs for you & Babies. Your own Loving *Kittie.*

November 28, 1896, The Jefferson, Richmond, Virginia. Ainslie & Webster, Managers.
My Darling Mother— We are waiting, Henry & I, for Katherine to finish dressing— did not wake her and she slept until 8. My first thought at waking & on going to sleep was of dear Father & living over our last day with him. You and I know it *all*, and there is no word expression needed. It has worried me so not writing frequently since I have been here. I had your letter last night— after you had received my letter written on my arrival here, and felt we were nearer each other.

This is Friday the 27th Nov. Yesterday could not get farther than above… Mrs. Hobson has been with us almost constantly here & we in Ashland twice & will give you an idea of how much time we have spent there.

Arrived Wed. A.M. 18. Mrs. H— came from Ashland at 2. returned 9 P.M.
Thurs. 19. Mrs. H— came 8 A.M. Ret. 12 taking Katherine & Katie.
Friday 20 H— & I went Ashland 7. We returned 7 P.M.
Sat. 21 Mrs. H— was to come. Wired she could not.
Sun. 22 Mrs. H— came Sunday A.M. and remained overnight here.
Mon. 23 Mrs. H—, Henry & I went 40 miles up James River to see Uncle John Hobson.
Tues. 24 Mrs. Hobson came noon train and spent night.
Wed. 25 Henry & I went Eastwood, took K.
Thurs. 26 H—, K— & I went Ashland for day.

Katherine's father, Francis S. Thayer, had died on this date in 1880.

Friday Today Henry on to NY & I returned here. Mrs. Hobson came P.M. train & stopped until we left. This is a little mixed but you will see how it has been.

So, from the account by dates, you can see we have devoted our time to her but she says we have not made her any visit, (as we did not stay in Ashland). Yesterday we went up at 12. Expected to go on 7 A.M.— but Katie told us she had been all day with Mrs. Hobson while we were at Eastwood— that she thought Mrs. H— would prefer us to go at noon & we gladly stopped in bed until half past seven. Henry, K— & I went to Eastwood, where H— was born, on Thursday at 8:40 A.M.— hired a buggy & drove all about that beautiful James River Country all day— the fine residences situated on the hills above the river— a perfect day & Henry as happy as a boy going all over the house & grounds & to the negro quarters— found 2 old slaves delighted to see "*young Marse.*" "*He's a gentleman chure nuff.*" Is interesting. Went to the neighbors houses, and at mid day lunched & drove until 5:45 P.M. train. Left at 6. K— was so responsive and charming, saying, "Good bye dear Eastwood, good bye." … We had a delicious dinner at Mrs. Hobson's on Thanksgiving. Henry sent the 3 older boys off to the ball game in Richmond & K— had a lovely play with Alice, Mary, & Jennings. The weather has been perfect— no rain, constant sunshine. I have tried to be a good girl & there has not been a single disagreeable occurrence. Grandma Wise so glad to see us & very sweet. I have a letter of Henry Clay's, Grandma gave me for Henry Jr. & Pres. James Monroe's also. We have been entertained by everyone almost in Richmond who is kin to Henry. Aunt Mary Lyons, tea twice, Cousin Frank Wise, tea, Barton Wise (who is married & has a baby,) tea… Mrs. Hobson has no easy life— 6 children. Grandma Wise's mind goes around in a circle… A woman over eighty, Scotch. Warm hearted & loving & an old colored woman, Aunt Betsy, who sleeps in room with Grandma & cares for her. Such a household & all calling Grandma *Annie*, & "Miss Annie" all the time. Grandma's room opens on the piazza & she sits out, walks up & down and plays with her one hand (other all drawn up) on the piano, hymns & Scotch airs. She is very sweet. I wish you could see her. She is so distressed about being a burden on Uncle Johnnie & Henry. Tells very clearly of her fortune & giving everything to "my dear Husband" & "now Johnnie says my money is lost & I hope it may be recovered for I do not wish to be dependent" for I refused to marry my dear Husband, sent him away, never expected to see him again for I did not wish to interfere with the prospects of the motherless children… Henry went to N.Y. Thanksgiving night & joins me in Washington tonight. Important R.R. conference yesterday in N.Y. He will go Monday to N.Y. or Boston, do not know which… We are all well. I never saw K— more lovely, as she sits before me. Love kisses to all.   —Your own devoted *Kittie*.

Henry Jr. Henry Wise Hobson, born 1891.

◆ A letter from Catherine McKie Thayer:

Colorado Springs, Nov. 28th, 1896.
My dear darling one: This p.m. I have your p.c. written before breakfast Wednesday a.m. last.— the day you went to Eastwood —what a day that was for you all.

Hedge Lawn, December 17, 1896.
My Dearest Mother—   Katherine & I with Katie left N. Y. at 1 o'clock yesterday. Arrived here at 5:30. Left a furious snowstorm in N. Y. but none north

of Poughkeepsie. All glad to have us. K— sweet & natural with old Mr. Jermain. Knelt down by his chair, as he talked with her. She thinks this the loveliest place, the grounds, greenhouse, little & big dog. I went to Troy this morning. Saw Uncle Aaron, Kittie & Lizzie. All well. Uncle A— just over a head-cold but new remedy of Dr. Bloss cured him quickly & had Doctor see me & he told me not to take a sleeping car before Monday night— that my cold was in just such state I might add to it. So I had to telegraph Henry in N. Y. that the Doctor said my leaving tonight would be a great risk & he had answered to stay here until I can travel with safety. He will stop over a train tomorrow… I am so disappointed & my wedding day too, but so glad it is not serious & all are well. Now supper is ready & I must go down. The delay means only a few days longer separation my Dearest. All so glad to have us here. All send you much love.   —Ever your own loving *Kittie*— Hugs & kisses to my precious Babies.

1897

༄ A letter from Annie Jennings Wise Hobson:

Jan 1st, 1897.
Last night, or rather evening, I set apart to write my New Year's letter. At the time I might have done it, Mother wished me to sit with her. When I took up my pen on going to my room I really went to sleep over it. Therefore I must wish you a blessed New Year and truest happiness on this first day of 1897. I have been through so much & feel so wearied physically that my hair is torpid in sympathy. So I do no more than put my arms in spirit around you and with a heart too full for utterance say God bless you as your Mother feels you deserve it, and carry you through all the troubles, trials & perplexities of the year before us which seems to come in with a gloomy presage of increasing troubles in the political & money world.

—Later— Just as I had scribbled this a neighbor came in, a very bright pleasant woman, & while I really enjoyed her visit and it took me out of the ruts of "domestic infelicities," I heartily wished she had deferred it until another day giving me time to get my letter off by the one o'clock mail. Now I have only a short time left before dinner to conclude. Your letter written on Sunday reached me yesterday afternoon. I think it was very lovely in you to find time amidst such a pleasure to tell me of your Xmas day & send a New Year's greeting…

—Again an interruption. I must now conclude at once as I have an opportunity of mailing my letter for the evening mail. Mother joins me in an earnest New Year's greeting & Eliza also. The three younger children have been with their mother since Wednesday & the boys do not know I am writing. Poor little Bessie has had a dull Xmas between waiting on her Mother & helping me. Today I had Susie Butler to aid me, & I sent Bessie to spend the day with some children. Kiss my darlings for me & my dear sweet Katherine… A blessed New Year to all… God watch over you all! Your devoted Mother,   —*A. J. W. Hobson*.

༄ Katherine Hobson to her Mother:

March 14, 1897.
My Dearest Mother—   Henry brought your letter home from the Post Office an hour ago. Was glad to hear but sorry you did not say how your cold

was— hope you cough less. It is too bad you should be alone this Sunday & not here... H— will have to go East about March 25th he says— R.R. business. Henry was in a talkative mood last evening. At dinner, I said he had been making an inventory of our property & a very conservative one— not counting Fleece as assay value, leaving it out... & we reached $150M. Nine years ago, "I had nothing, you had about $23,700"... considering the amount of money he spent in roving... our trips & the *load* in Virginia, he has done pretty well. Said February (last month) collections in his law business largest he had ever made ($7,000) clear. After paying about $2,000 to old firm accounts (P&E and all office expenses.) He said he sent [Henry] Coke $600 a year to send his Mother. Coke had a loan of $5,000 at 8% which gives $400 and H's sending $600 gives his Mother, for herself, $1,000. Henry pays $75 every other month for Grandma [Mary Lyons Wise] & Uncle J— the $75 the alternative month. So. Mrs. H— has $900 for Grandma & Eliza and H— sends $75 for the children each month... This gives Mrs. H— over $3,000 and H— is determined to find out who she owes and how much. He wrote Tom Page and asked him, as he did Carter, but he has not yet heard from him. He has said several times "he feels so humiliated to have his Mother around borrowing, that people would not understand, thinking he was treating his Mother closely." I feel very sorry for him & *mad at her*. Henry has written her he was *in debt* & can not send her the $1,000 she asked for. Her answer shows he wrote of his debts & inability to save enough to pay those debts, (including the $10,000 he owed you, he says, which makes a good excuse he says in this case for refusing). Now good bye, Henry back. Love & kisses, dinner ready— Your devoted *Kittie*. Children send love & kisses. All well & happy.

◈ A letter from Annie Jennings Wise Hobson:

April 1897.
Dear Katherine—   ...I am so thankful that the trying ordeal of taking the children through the measles is over. Everyone except George has been sick several days & Rosa Brooks was ill. Cannon had it when a baby. I had quite a sharp little attack myself but am better. God Bless you all.   —Your loving Mamma, A. J. W. Hobson.
—I hope you are daily growing stronger. April 6, 1897. Last Sunday Plumer had been in Paradise 29 years. [letter is in fragments]

April 11, 1897, New York.
Darling Kate—   Eleanor's letter has taken your time today. I sent K— a telegram [this was her eighth birthday] today and had her answer just now. Darling little soul! This morning I started to attend Grace Church with your Uncle W—. I never saw his English training more distinctively shown. When we got there the aisle was packed about half way up with people waiting. He said "my goodness we shall have to fight for a seat" and away he went pushing and fighting his way through until he got to the *very head* and I watched him attack the usher until he got a seat, *first of all*, and ahead of women, men & children. It was the most extraordinary performance I ever saw and *so English*. I did not attempt to follow him but stood near the door until 11:15 when the rain was so uncomfortable and the draught so bad I quit and came to the Club. He came up after Church and to his expressions of surprise that I had left him, I dryly said he "showed more *vigor* in getting through a crowd than I

Uncle W— William Whiteside, who lived in England but was visiting New York.

was capable of." I worked until 11:30 last night upon Mr. Hagerman's papers and two hours this morning. I sent them to the Hotel with a note saying I would meet him tomorrow morning. I have just had a note that he will be here in ten minutes to see me upon an important matter. You see how much rest I have. I am just crazy to see you and the chicks and feel almost like running out to Denver & coming back to finish my business. Best love & kisses. I am glad Nellie is staying longer. —Devotedly *Henry*.

June 1st, 1897, Nearing Omaha.
My Darling Husband—   Eleanor went quietly to sleep in my berth and then Katie stole her & they slept in the lower berth of the section. Henry was asleep before we were out of Denver— and he likes the upper berth & wants to sleep there always. We all had a most comfortable night thanks to your loving generous care. Diomed is quiet & well & ate his breakfast. He is to have a good run in Omaha. He whined with joy to see us this morning. Henry said I am going to write Papa the first letter on my new pad. Katherine is coloring pictures with her box of Faber pencils you bought her… I think this is the best time for our trip, for it is warm even now. Poor Katherine was so homesick leaving— she cried & sobbed at the house & when I went in the State-room she was crying & saying, "Oh, I want my dear Papa & am so lonely without him." She has more affection & tender feeling than both the others… All the chicks send love & kisses to you, in which I join.   —Your own devoted & loving wife *Katherine*.

My Dear Papa, We miss you very much. Come soon. Love and kisses from *Henry*. June First 1897.

June 2nd, 1897, Chicago.
My Darling Husband—   Sent you a dispatch. You never saw Diomed feel better. She is now in baggage car in care of a man until six P.M. She had a fine run in Chicago. We have all had a walk— fine cool morning… There is nothing to add except we all wish you were here, but you will be coming next week and that fact braces me up… Will you please find out if I have any interest from the ten thousand you gave me in State Trust Co. I wish to pay a bill with it— be sure & find out at once & let me know… Love & kisses from all. Your own Devoted *Katherine*.

༄ Katherine Hobson to her Mother:

Sunday P. M.
My Darling Mother—   …So I go down tomorrow [to Troy] for day & hope to find a cook & bring her back. The mosquitoes thicker here than you ever saw them. There has been so much rain. The children perfectly happy running about— picking ferns and flowers & K's favorite Birch to chew bark. Mike Varley is coming Tuesday to put flower garden in good order. We will have a quantity of roses, but a lot of old wood to cut off & I shall put some fertilizer on & about them… Am writing in Sophia's bedroom— 3 chicks in beds. H— just wakes to ask if I will send Grandma the pink geranium he found in the woods & I say 'yes', & K— the violets, & E— the fern. Woman will do our washing living next to Ruth & Clara's… Have read Bible to chicks & heard prayers. I have gone to bed at 9 P.M. & ready to go… Will try to see the Jermains tomorrow but my *first* attention given to a cook. Marie writes

Diomed was a dog owned by the Hobsons in 1897. *Diomed — The Life, Travels, and Observations of a Dog* by John Sergeant Wise, Henry Hobson's uncle, was first published in 1897 by Lamson, Wolffe & Co. Wise's book includes a description of John M. Tracy, whose paintings are described in these letters, February 22, 1895. There are photos of a dog, labeled "Diomed," in the Wise family papers at the Virginia Historical Society.

of a white woman married to *colored man*, whom Maggie speaks well of who would come— but can not take such a woman unless I can not find another. Hope Henry's coming will be deferred for I can not see my way to get off now & I feel very well. Kate's just as good as can be. Kitchen clean & fresh.
—Love & kisses, your own loving *Kittie*.

Home Farm, South Cambridge, N. Y., June 4th 1897.
My Dearest Husband—   Yesterday was glad to receive your telegram & answered it at once. I had Uncle Aaron meet us, which was very kind in him… Had a very busy day in Troy and found the cook who had promised to come had been taken ill. So I had a search for another & failed to find one & came up without one. Must go down tomorrow & continue the hunt. The house is clean but in entire disorder & we had a terrific thunder-storm last evening & it has rained every other day for a month… Tomorrow I will send you word about West Shore trains. I hope I will not have to go from here before Friday, as I am the only one who can attend to various matters here. Expect to see you soon. Mrs. Knapp writes she will come & stay with the children… Children join in love & kisses to Darling Papa & I do the same.
—Your own devoted wife *Katherine*.

June 5, 1897, Denver.
Darling Kate—   Do you know I was much shocked to find a few days ago a lot of snow white hairs in my mustache. It made me feel older than anything that has happened, but you will be perfectly delighted as my mustache will be an offset to your hair… I have just gotten a lot of new information about the Jennings family which seems to trace them back to New England and the early settlers. If the connection is made, it will establish my Yankee blood in great shape…   —Devotedly *Henry*.

June 6, 1897, Denver.
Darling Kate—   If I do not go crazy over the worry and annoyance I have to submit to from my relatives it will be a wonder. I sometimes feel like cursing the whole lot, excepting Mother, and absolutely cutting off communications with them. But even then she would assume the load of the batch and draw upon me to pay expenses. God may love them all but he lets other people enjoy their company and carry the burden. I have just written a letter absolutely declining to take Cannon out here, absolutely declining to endorse a note etc. etc. Will it end someday— When I die perhaps— if not before… To add to my bother came an invitation from the Trumbulls insisting upon my dining with them at 1:30 which will break right in on my work. I wish people would let me alone. Love & kisses to the darlings. They and you are the only ones from whom I get real comfort.   —Devotedly *Henry*.

❧ Katherine Hobson to her Mother:

8:45 A. M., June 9th, 1897, Johnsonville.
My Dearest Mother—   On my way to Troy to see a cook if there is one to be seen. There is little to write since yesterday p.m., but I wish you to hear often. This is a rainy day. So much water on ground… Katie & I have concluded that even the white woman with a colored husband, if she is a

Henry Wise Hobson, (aged 40). Pack Brothers, 935 Broadway, New York.

good cook, can come for a temporary at least. The old Maggie at Jermain's says she is respectable & well spoken of & said to be a good cook. There is something repulsive in a white woman marrying a colored man but I think we will not dwell upon *morals*. 4:45 P.M.— Have had 3 applicants, now sitting with one of them, "Anna" who has good recommendations from Mrs. George Gould who says she is "good cook, neat & capable," only hope she will prove so. She is young, say 25 & says she is strong & is somebody anyway… I have had to buy a new stove— old one would not draw well or bake on bottom. Uncle Aaron told me of a place & I have bought one for $34.00, which is said to be a fine "Baker"— holds 3 gal. water in reservoir, has 6 griddles… All the chicks were asleep when I left this A.M— Katie deploring my going out. I told her I had found the only way to accomplish anything was to persevere. Of course you would expect Katie to be helpful, but she has been as kind, considerate & done everything so well & so interested, no *sighing* over what was to be done. You do know what a contrast these rains are to our Colorado weather— such a downpour… I do hope you can come later on & be in the old home with us. Love & many many kisses my Darling Mother— —Your own *Kittie*.

Home Farm, South Cambridge, Thursday June 10th, 1897.
My Darling Husband— Yesterday, (Wed.) I went to Troy by 8 A. M. train. At Johnsonville asked if there were any telegrams, and was assured there were none. I spent day in Troy, cook hunting, & came home in pouring rain to find your telegram of the 8th. Where it was all day yesterday, I do not know, but there was no way of answering until early this morning which I did… The rain has been almost incessant since we came. The Brook would be called a River in England… And I found a cook who began her work today. She is well recommended & young & I think interested to please & be generally useful, but I must teach her our ways… The house was not cleaned. Woman had to attend funeral for 3 days when she should have been here & a cleaner is a rare quantity here. Ed Whiteside of course, like all men, (you excepted), thinks if a house is swept, it is clean. I have gotten *a man of 20*. I don't call him a boy. Think he will be excellent. I had him when we were here the fall we returned from Europe… & liked him then. He is older & steady & gentle. He is used to the care of horses & not in the least afraid of them… We have been here a week tonight & every minute has seemed *full*. The children are as free & happy as birds. Eleanor full of her tricks to sleep with me more frequently than the other children… Diomed is the happiest dog, sleeps in the lower hall & is always affectionate & we all love him— if he does track the mud— he has perfect habits… I can hardly wait for you to come— or rather to meet you my Darling One— and count the days. All send you love & kisses. —Your own Devoted *Katherine*.

South Cambridge, July 3, 1897.
Dear Mother Thayer— The other day in Troy I had a full talk with John Birge about the mill matter. From the first I advised strongly that the sale of the mill be made absolute and that the proposition of $10,000 cash and bal. upon mortgage be accepted… In addition to this matter I think you should be here personally about the farm. I have been examining things quite carefully and unless you are willing to let things go down much more, it is neces-

sary for you to do considerable work at once… all fences about the house are in bad shape. The barns also need considerable work both upon the sides & roofs and painting is badly needed. My idea is that if you come here & get some good man to go over the place he could determine just what should be done to preserve the building & fences… I will be here for at least two weeks longer and I wish you could be here whilst I am. Within a few days I am going over the entire place.   —Yours lovingly, *H. W. Hobson.*

෴ A letter from Annie Jennings Wise Hobson:

Ashland, July 4, 1897.
My dear Son—   I have been recalling this day two years ago when we were together with your darlings and sweet wife at the Home Farm. I presume that you are certainly with them today, and I am sure the fire-works are all provided for a grand display tonight and shall picture you all with the Whiteside cousins enjoying the children's pleasure. The memory of that summer will be always very sweet, though in all human probability I shall never be with you all there again, & it may be the only time I shall ever see our lovely precious darlings all together. Therefore the one time will be all the more dear to recall… My boys have gone on a church picnic not far from Ashland except Jennings. He & the girls prefer a treat of ice cream to fireworks. The servants are going off on a picnic excursion this afternoon. So if we are not patriotic in fire-works, all are determined to spend the 4th in some way as a holiday time. [end of letter]

Ashland, July 9th, 1897.
My dearest Son—   I arose very early today and hoped to have a quiet half hour to devote to you on this your birthday & the anniversary of my marriage, but the inevitable "must be done" work came up & now I am too weary after dinner to collect my thoughts. I have been thinking of you in the sweet old homestead & the pleasure you will try to give the children and they will give you in celebrating Papa's birthday and pray for the blessing of God the Father, God the Son & God the Holy Ghost upon you… I have just come from Mother's room. She was quite sick last evening, had an attack of bowels in the night. She is liable to have her liver out of order at this season & I had been trying to persuade her for a week to take a little medicine. I had to send for the Doctor early this morning… I wish especially to tell you of an interview I had with Mr. Edward Bissell. He says that he is sure Cannon could learn as readily as his brother did to "herd cattle." Cannon rides very well now. He has ridden a good deal in Ashland. George Bissell went to the work as unfitted as Cannon is. He is sure that in a few months Cannon can earn good wages. The climate is fine for consumptive tendency… Cannon said the day before yesterday, "I wish to go to the Ranch as soon as possible. If Uncle Henry will help me go there & till I get a start I will bind myself to pay him back. If I succeed in life I hope to pay back to him or his children all he has spent on me. I intend to go to work in earnest." As soon as I hear from you I will write to Mr. Whitcomb if you prefer me to do it… Mr. Bissell also told me that if I would write a formal request to him regarding Henry, he had a friend in New York to whom he would apply & he thought it more than probable he could get Henry a place on some ship about to make a long cruise… I

am so glad you like the monument. Will answer the dear letter rec'd yesterday more fully another time. I enjoyed your account of the 4th. —Your devoted Mother, *A. J. W. Hobson.*

From an undated letter:
Now about Henry— He returned last week having had I think a delightful pleasure trip. I find Mr. Curtis sent him really more as a guest. The Captain, who seems to be a good excellent man, said he had little for Henry to do but that his conduct was excellent. Henry is more infatuated with the sea than ever... He (Mr. Curtis) advises that he should be put on some sailing vessel from New York— an American vessel on a regular long cruise. He told Henry that the cabin boys place was about the only work he could get, that he had not the physique required in regular ship work. He advised me to write to Johnnie & ask him if he knew anyone connected with the sailing vessels of the New York merchant service. I have done so & Johnnie has promised to make inquiries for me. He then told Henry that if he still wished to try sea life he would have to be examined by the Board for Physical Examinations of a training ship and if he could pass, be trained there for the life he has chosen. Dr. McSparrin, Alice's husband, has told him to try one voyage as beneficial to him physically & then to consider studying medicine & trying to get in the Navy. This idea seems to please him & I believe he would make a fine Doctor. He has as much education as many who have become good physicians & he likes natural history etc. These boys have taxed your purse & disappointed your natural pride in family & hope of better things. They have taxed my means, made my heart bleed & embittered life with disappointment & mortification. Yet many have done worse & ultimately developed into useful good men. So I shall try on with them praying, hoping. They are Plumer's grandchildren, they bear his name & that alone is an incentive to me. Mr. Curtis has offered Henry a free passage on one of his sailing ships if a place can be found for him in New York. It is time this was mailed. I will write again day after tomorrow. Kiss the darlings for me and give the inclosed to Katherine. —Your devoted Mother, *A. J. W. Hobson.*

Home Farm, South Cambridge, Monday P.M., July 12th, 1897.
My Darling Husband—   Your telegram received this noon, and I am just going to answer it. I have thought of you every minute it seems since you left & worried lest you should be prostrated by the heat. A letter from Marie says that Saturday night they thought her father could not live through the night, so prostrated by the heat. I do not think I could go to N. Y. & face such heat... The children keep asking "When Papa is coming home" & it seems desolate without you & they feel it. We all went to Church yesterday, but the service is very different without Mr. Gordon... —Always your own loving wife, *Katherine.*

༄ Two deaths:

July 12, 1897, *Home Farm*, South Cambridge.
My Dearest Mother—   Last Saturday I wrote you of Henry's going off at 5:27 P.M. to meet Uncle Johnnie in Albany. We all went to the station to see him off & I felt so sorry for him for the loss and then to have to have him take the trip in the intense heat— just as he was beginning to get a real rest

and free from pain in his ear— to see him sitting, reading under the trees or going to the woods with the children or striking the golf balls for practice— delightful… I had a telegram today from Henry, he said *"Funeral Monday, will be in NY Tuesday…"* He wired his Mother to meet him in Washington at Shoreham Hotel. I do not see how poor Aunt Mary Garnett will endure this loss & having to know he took a drug to end his life & the four children, two young women & two young boys, 13 & 15 …This death of Henry G— is the fourth grown child Aunt Mary has lost… Tomorrow I shall go down to Jermain's. I feel Marie would appreciate the old man's last words to me there when I said I would come again, "The oftener the better." If any changes come at Hedge Lawn I will telegraph you… *Kittie.*

4 P. M., Wednesday, July 14th, 1897.
My Darling Husband—   Yesterday I was in such a hurry sending you the telegram from Johnsonville I did not realize I had sent it to the Club instead of to the Hotel. I hope it did not make you any serious trouble. I arrived here about seven & found Mrs. McCartee with Marie. They were so glad to see me and said they thought I would come but did not wish to ask me to do so fearing I might come if I were not feeling just well. It is still & calm here & Marie as brave as can be, feels so thankful her Father was saved suffering. The service is at 4 P. M. tomorrow from the house… My heart-full of tender love. Always your own devoted wife *Katherine.*

Hedge Lawn, July 14, Wednesday.
My Dearest Mother—   I arrived here in a pouring rain at about 7 PM last evening… On Monday Mr. J— failed rapidly, just breathed more & more slowly until he breathed his last. The intense heat was too much for his feeble strength… Marie, Cousin Nellie, Archie & a Doctor were with him at the last. Fred Townsend came this A.M. at breakfast time… I do not know whether Henry will get here to funeral service or not— he need not go to Cemetery— but go up on the 6 P.M. train if he wishes & horses will be at Johnsonville. When I know of any *future* opening of Last Will & Testament will let you know. Cousin Nellie says, "What do you suppose Cousin James did?" —and I suppose others wonder also…   —Your own devoted *Kittie.*

Hedge Lawn, Friday A.M., 9:30
My Dearest Mother—   Yesterday I did not write. I spent all day doing many little necessary things up to hour of service. Mr. J— was laid before mantel in parlor, plain black casket, silver handles, as simple as could be. He looked calm and full of strength and restful… A very large attendance of course… 32 carriages were necessary to take family & relatives & friends… At grave Marie turned to Julie & said, "Where is Kittie Hobson?" I stood just behind her… & she turned & said, "Oh you darling." She told me yesterday, "You are an angel"… so I know I have been a comfort to her… Your *Kittie.*

July 20, 1897, Hotel Manhattan.
Darling Kate—   This morning I saw Mr. Jermain's death announced and wired you at once. I cannot leave here before tomorrow night but can be in Albany by 11:30 at night. I am sorry, for many people will be grieved… Love & kisses to my darling chicks.   —Devotedly, *Henry.*

Henry Hobson was going to one funeral and his wife was preparing for another. The letter refers to the death of Henry Garnett, "Henry G—," the son of Mary Elizabeth Wise Garnett and Alexander Yelverton Peyton Garnett. Henry Garnett was therefore Henry Wise Hobson's cousin. The letter also refers to James Jermain, "the old man," Katherine Hobson's father-in-law by her first marriage to Barclay Jermain, who was gravely ill at Hedge Lawn, the Jermain family home in Albany, New York.

Albany Rural Cemetery, the cemetery plot of the Jermain Family.

South Cambridge, July 22, 1897, Thursday evening.
My Dearest Mother—   Henry started home this evening 5:27 P.M. Leaving Albany 9:30. I think he rather wanted me to go down with him & stay overnight at Jermain's, but I felt so blue at having him go… So I stopped at home with the children & waved H— off from S. Cambridge. I feel so sorry his trip should not have been more of a success— his ear & the going to & from Albany in the heat to say nothing of the pain… & then the week spent in going to Henry Garnett's funeral & keeping his Mother from tearing everyone to pieces— She saying she was "Sister's representative" & wishing to arrange everything before any orders were rec'd from Aunt Mary. I think no one ever had a harder time than Henry… I think if Henry could have been here as he wished & lived as we were living, so naturally, he would have gone home greatly refreshed & benefited. As it is, he is *disgusted* when he packs the clothes he has not worn & books he has not read…   —Your own devoted *Kittie*.

Home Farm, South Cambridge, July 23rd, 1897.
My Darling Husband—   We are as lonely as possible without you. It is really sad to me to think how your vacation was ruined & all the quiet times & rest & reading you planned for here was not possible— and I wish I had not let you go to Washington to have all that trying ordeal in the heat. It delighted me to see you eat & get such a good color— & I try to feel that you have had some rest from your office & hard work which so constantly besets you… There is a great deal that is sweet & precious to remember during the past six weeks and I have been with you in a quiet restful way which makes me value & love you more than ever, if possible.   —Love & many kisses from us all to the dearest Papa & husband in the world. Your own devoted wife, *Katherine*.

Johnsonville, July 27th, 1897.
My Dearest Husband—   I am going to scribble you a line on my way to Albany to spend night with Marie & have my visit there over… The chicks came to station with me & went on to Center Cambridge to get some raspberries the Dodds offered us… Fred Townsend has been sent for to talk over matters with Mr. H's partner, & straighten out any complications if possible regarding Katie's share in the estate— so Marie wrote me… There is nothing like having a husband one adores & three children— & you have given me every luxury heart could wish for always & perfect satisfaction in your devotion. I am on that express from Johnsonville to Troy & it is rather shaky to write [letter written in pencil]… Love & kisses always from your own devoted *Katherine*.

~ A letter from Annie Jennings Wise Hobson:

Ashland, July 30th, 1897.
My dear Son—   Your letter written on the train reached me day before yesterday. I am truly sorry your holiday was at end & that Katherine had to give you up, & that you have to go hard to work again. We are having now the most delightfully cool weather like the fall, but like all unseasonable weather I fear it is not healthy. I have never felt well since my return from Washington, & again my old enemy malaria has been asserting itself showing a slight tendency to fever every night & in the middle of the day. I shall attack the enemy vigorously…

Our children have kept unusually well. Mother & Eliza are as usual, the dear old lady becoming more clouded in mind each day. The other day to test her I said, "Mother, who was Plumer Hobson?" She replied, "I have heard the name, but I have forgotten about him." When I explained he was my husband she looked a little confused but did not mind not knowing.

—Later. I commenced my letter this morning hoping to get it off by the mid-day train, but some household duties interrupted, & now I must try to conclude. I cannot feel very clear headed for I have again had something like a dumb chill and have considerable fever and aching all over. Your letter inclosing check & Henry Coke's was received by the last northern mail. Many thanks for your prompt remittance. God will bless the son who never forgets his Mother. I have read the letter from the Texan Ranchman carefully. As I have sent an application to the man who is foreman on the Wyoming Ranch, I feel I had best wait to hear what he has to say. As I wrote you, Mr. Addison is a stockholder to a considerable amount in that Ranch Co. I consulted him as to his opinion of the relative advantages of Texas & Wyoming. He told me that he would greatly prefer Wyoming being well informed on the matter. He said that the ranchmen as a class were better than the Texas cow-boys and there was more opening in other directions in Wyoming than Texas. Just as George Bissell did, the other young men have started as herders of cattle and had risen to better places on the Ranch & now had places. He said if Cannon would work faithfully & was willing to begin at the beginning he would use his influence to get him promoted. Cannon read the letter, and said very sensibly, that as the foreman of the Ranch wrote in such a discouraging strain and seemed unwilling to try him except as a personal favor to Mr. Coke, he would prefer hearing from Wyoming before making a decision. I am expecting a letter daily. Now I must close as writing makes me feel nervous…

Mother tells me daily messages & blessings to send you & Eliza always adds an "Amen." I know how busy you are & how you have to write to Katherine. Just a line weekly to say how you are will satisfy me now. *E. W. Whitcomb, Cheynene Wyoming* is the address of the foreman of the Ranch to whom I wrote. You can leave all the responsibility to me in this case & need not come forward if you do not choose. I will forward his letter as soon as I receive it… May you & yours keep well & the time fly quickly till you are reunited. No one knows I am writing. Your devoted Mother.   A. J. W. Hobson.

—Mr. Bissell has written to his friend Mr. Taylor in New York to see if he can get Henry a place on a ship.

August 7, 1897, Legal Department of the Union Pacific, Denver & Gulf Railway Company. Denver.
Darling Kate—   Your letter with Tom's came today. I am sorry for Tom in a way and yet I really think it will be a relief to the family to have his Father pass away & not hang on as a burden to everybody… Your Mother was very pronounced in her views the other day and I agree with them. I have arranged for the car [a private railroad car] from the 14th to the 18th and shall if possible go on with it for I cannot reconcile myself to letting you come alone. By that time you will have been able to make all arrangements. I shall go to the Farm when I go East. I am very happy at the thought of having you and the chicks at home again… Love & kisses to the darlings. Devotedly *Henry*.

Home Farm, South Cambridge, August 8th, 1897, Sunday A.M.
My Darling Husband—   We drove to Cambridge yesterday afternoon and stopped for tea at James & Annie McKie's— drove home by South Cambridge & reached there about eight-thirty and among the mail were your two telegrams— the first as to the car & second as to my time for coming home. Of course I wish to be home in good time, but there is no reason for me to start a week from tomorrow and cut short the children's time here— where they are getting rosier & stronger every day. And I feel better than I ever have before at this time— my feet & limbs, always before bloated & puffed, but here not so. And it is a relief to get about so easily. It was 8 months the 29th July since I was ill & 9 months Aug. 29th and so my time can not be before the second week in Sept, or after the first week. Miss Miller and Mother have gotten together and imagine all kinds of ills & chances. And I am going to write them both today. Miss Miller must have forgotten my dates. We are all out on the N. side of the house in lovely air & this afternoon go to the Whiteside Church… Tuesday the 24th would be two weeks from the coming Tuesday and I think it would be a good day for me to start, bring me on the 25th to Chicago & 27th Home, Friday. I like to get back before the end of the week. This leaves me two weeks here, to attend to the water & settle matters & leave, pack etc. I will send dispatch tomorrow & you will receive this my Darling Thursday morning. Eleanor has written you a letter all herself. She & Henry went to Cambridge with me. The horses drive very well, more evenly. We all send much love, and many kisses. Your devoted Wife, *Katherine*.

Home Farm, South Cambridge, August 10th, 1897.
My Darling Husband—   Two weeks from today I shall be starting home to you. That was my first waking thought. Yesterday brought me your two letters, one from Springs, one from Denver… Have just come in from the well, the engine is still working away. They have driven 90 feet & no water. The gravel struck the other day was a vein & now "hard-pan." They must be near water… Samples of paint to Mother… The plumber came yesterday & I went all over with him… 90 feet — my whole mind seems to be on well & water. I hope I will act wisely, but wish I had your head or Mother's. Love & Kisses, *Katherine*.

Home Farm, South Cambridge, August 12th, 1897.
My Darling Husband—   Yesterday at three o'clock I received your telegram. I was perfectly distressed you should not have heard from me & went right down in the rain & telephoned a message to Johnsonville. It seems strange when I write so constantly you should be three days without a letter. There is no reason for going into detail of the Jermain will, for I am convinced I have no part in it… My whole mind is full of starting week after next to you my Darling one… Well now 100 feet & in rock, which is more encouraging— & a little more water found— a little vein I think… I will write daily, whether you hear, or not…   —Your own devoted wife *Katherine*.

Home Farm, South Cambridge, August 16th, 1897.
My Darling Husband—   No mail went yesterday, Sunday, so I write today. Water running over the pipe… Mr. G— coming to make thorough test of supply today & I will add report later. The two men are drilling now, think

best to make it still deeper in order to open up any additional veins there may be. There is nothing more to be said regarding the Jermain estate & I have put the subject aside. The old man had a perfect right to leave his money as he did & I am only disappointed he did not feel inclined to remember me, which would have shown thought… We are all very well, & next week hope to be with you… Ada & her children seem to be enjoying themselves & they pair off so pleasantly— Julia & Katherine, Henry & Medora, Thayer taking a big brother's care of Eleanor— and no disagreements which is remarkable. I will add our tenderest, best love to the dearest Husband & papa in the world. There can be nothing regarding settling the Jermain Estate to make your coming to Albany at all necessary. —Supply of water in well 120 Gal per hour. There is about, (when pipe is full) 225 gal standing in well. Men have drilled 135 feet, depth from surface 12 feet, to bottom of well, 147 feet. —I am going to let the men drill on today & tomorrow as I think it wise to try & increase supply [letter incomplete]

Ada Thayer Addison, Kittie Hobson's first cousin and the wife of Rev. Morris Addison, must have visiting in Cambridge with her three children, Julia, Medora, and Thayer. Therefore, the Hobson and Addison children were second cousins, and they remained close for the rest of their lives.

Home Farm, South Cambridge, August 17th, 1897.
My Darling Husband— Your letter from 'Lake City' here this morning. We drove to Cambridge last evening & left samples of paint for barns with painter, yellow & white trimmings… The engine has broken, last evening, 141 feet has been bored. They are expecting Mr. Mc— & get orders as to having it repaired— of course they can not get it away until it is repaired… I am quite interested over what Dr. Fisk says happened in our early married life. I sent you a night message from Cambridge— poor Mother has gotten herself so worried over what I might have had from the old man [James B. Jermain]… Love & many kisses from us all. —Your own devoted wife, *Katherine.*

Any letter from Lake City would be about the Golden Fleece mine, but there is no such letter in the files for this time.

Home Farm, South Cambridge, August 18th, 1897.
My Darling Husband— …The water is running over, pipe full. And the men will have engine mended by tomorrow & test supply again & then will decide if it best to add nine feet to 141, to give 150 foot depth & provide a greater supply. I shall be busy closing up & not try to write much, except a scribble & postal to Mother… "*next week*" I keep saying. Much tender love & many kisses to you from us all— —Your Devoted Wife, *Katherine.*

❧ Katherine Hobson to her Mother:

Home Farm, S. Cambridge, August 23rd, 1897.
My Dearest Mother— This A.M. brings letter & postal… He [Henry] went to Albany on morning train, comes back to Schaghticoke to see a man about cistern, or reservoir, on hill… Henry arrived very unexpectedly, wired he w'd be here at evening train & finished his business and left Troy at 2:30 & *walked* from Johnsonville just as we were in carriage to drive to Johnsonville to meet him as I had telegraphed, but he was *through* & came. I think H— feels there is a chance of the 150 thousand codicil being for me but I do not think it can be proved. Katie Savage has a daughter doing well. H— saw Judge Learned in Albany & said the Judge was inclined to think legacy for me. H— saw will, all in Mr. Jermain's writing, except the 4000 annuity to me— that in a woman's hand. Marie told me "Auntie Cummings was present" when I was last at Hedge Lawn so I presume she wrote it. There is no use of thinking this is a

The will of James B. Jermain included a confusing reference to "Katherine." It was unclear whether that referred to his former daughter-in-law, by 1897 Katherine Hobson, or to his granddaughter, Katherine Savage, by 1897 Katherine Townsend. After considering the issue, Katherine Hobson did not contest it.

possibility for me. The name was not *mine at the time* & Granddaughter too. The will full of inaccuracies H— says… —Your devoted *Kittie*.

➢ Family matters:

Denver, September 7, 1897.
Dear Uncle John—   After much "backing and filling" I have finally gotten Cannon placed on a ranch in Texas, where he is to go to work, and I suppose he is off by this time.

I am very anxious to get Henry to work now, not only because he is worrying his Grandmother pretty nearly to death, but also because he is trifling and idling away his time in Ashland, forming bad habits with reference to work and running the risk of acquiring bad moral habits. He seems very anxious to go to sea, and I think the idea a good one. You will remember that his father shipped on-board a vessel, for a trip around the world, as an apprentice, and it occurs to me that there must be ship companies who would take a boy, especially if I were willing to pay something to get him a place. I should think that New York or Baltimore would be the best points. Do not such large firms as that of W. R. Grace & Company run a lot of ships engaged in traffic.

I don't want you to put yourself to any personal trouble, but thought you might employ a man for me to hunt up this matter and see what the openings are for a boy like Henry. I should be very much obliged if you would give it your attention.

Jack seems to be getting along nicely. Katherine and the new boy are first class.   —Yours affectionately, *Henry W. Hobson*. (Virginia Historical Society)

the new boy Francis Thayer Hobson, Henry and Katherine Hobson's fourth child, born on September 4, 1897.

➢ A letter from Annie Jennings Wise Hobson:

Ashland, Sept. 10th. 1897.
My dear Son—   It was a great treat & pleasure to read your letter so bright & happy over the fine new boy & so full of gratitude for the safety of the good true Mother and devoted wife. Mother also enjoyed it exceedingly. I am very thankful for anything bright in my sad life so darkened by the curse of these boys. I inclose an itemized account of what I had to expend on his ticket. The weather is so extremely warm that everyone agrees that we should wait till the hot spell is over before letting Cannon start South. The sultry heat is sickening. He will of course go by Memphis & Louisville, not by New Orleans as the yellow fever is there. He seems much pleased at the prospect of going and says he will prove there is something in him… I did not receive your letter giving directions about Cannon's going till Sunday afternoon. Everything is ready for him to go when the heat abates. We are now having the worst heat of the summer. I feel it very depressingly.   —Your letter of the 7th just received and read. Yes I am over all bad effects of my fall & my good horse has been doing beautifully. I spent two days— or rather Monday till twelve o'clock & yesterday till four— getting Cannon's clothes etc. I dined at Dr. Oppenheimer's. Néné & the girls are there & Mr. Mayo is paying a short visit there. Mary Mayo has just returned from Raleigh Springs. The "on dit" that is now a great excitement in Richmond is that Mary Lyons is engaged to a wealthy Jew— a Mr. Millisher, said to be handsome, highly educated, a gentleman & very rich. She is now at the Hot Springs with him. What are we coming to if this is true!

I only hope it is, for Mary would be happier & more useful as a wife.

—Later. I had much more I wished to say but have been interrupted. Kiss the four "grands" for me & dear Katherine and God's blessings on you all. Love to Miss Miller if with you. Kind regards to all. Your devoted Mother, *A. J. W. Hobson.*

Enclosed with the above letter:

Cannon's acct.
Tickets to Dallas— $37.80. Could have gotten a second class for $30.80 but that did not give him admission to the dining room. He can buy a berth on train, much cheaper than in Richmond, for about $6.00. I thus propose giving him $9.00 to get meals & for a little surplus, in all $15.00

This makes traveling expenses, $52.80.

1 suit of clothes	$10.00 (and a very good one)
3 white shirt	$2.50
6 negligee	$3.00
shoes	$3.50
8 handkerchiefs	.80
cap & hat	1.00
comb, brush etc.	1.50
	$22.30

…Please send check at once as it will bring me too low in funds to advance this… I made him a present of a very inexpensive but good silver watch. It was second hand— left in an old jewelers hands for a debt of $3.00 & he let Cannon have it for that & he says it was a $20.00 watch and a good one.

Sept. 13th, Monday P.M.
My Darling Husband—   There is nothing to write of except we are all getting on well, & beginning to believe you have really gone. I feel it is right you should have gone & would have been unhappy if you had stopped here on my account. How thankful & grateful we should be that I am getting on so well, no complications, & this lovely healthful Baby Boy of ours, to cuddle to my breast & console me, in my loneliness for you my Darling. I never have told you how I appreciated all your tender thoughts & acts towards me. Your coming home early to read to me. Every act has been so full of loving thoughts for my comfort & happiness. The children send love & kisses… Do be careful of yourself. I feel the distance between us because I am not able to travel. Should you be ill, God bless & keep you my own Darling one. Your own Devoted & Loving Wife *Katherine.*

Tuesday P.M., Sept. 14th, 1897.
My Darling Husband—   This A.M. I have your dear precious letter from the train. You say so much that comforted me and I felt stronger & happier. Also received telegram from Chicago. Ever thankful you arrived safely & will have an answer to greet you in New York. Miss Miller tells me of women in my condition who have tired their eyes & become stone blind by writing &

reading. So as I do not wish to have glasses added to my gray hairs, I can only send a scribble. Katherine has a little stomach disorder today & fever is better than this morning… Henry sleeps in your room & has on one of your cravats & says he will take care of the family… The children join me in love & kisses to you, our Darling Husband & Papa. The baby eats, sleeps & then repeats it.
—Always your own Devoted wife, *Katherine*.

Wednesday P.M., Sept. 15th, 1897.
My Darling Husband— Another day has come, & we are all well. The Baby Boy asleep by me as I write. Sent you a dispatch to N.Y. this A.M. Katherine is as lively as can be today, compared with her feverish condition of yesterday & Doctor says she is all right. Johnson took Katie & children out for a good drive this A.M. By the way, all your winter underwear are in perfect condition, not a button out of place. This is a delightful cool day. Such a relief not to have to be here in heat. I trust you will escape the intense heat of last week in the East, 102° Mother read— the highest temperature of the season. Eleanor insists on helping Henry take care of your room & the two little creatures are in their cribs there, alone & run up to Katie to the blue room, in the morning. This is a poor scribble, but I wish to send a daily line of love my Darling Husband. I miss you so much, but feel thankful you were able to go.
—Always your devoted *Katherine*.

Thursday P.M., Sept. 16th, 1897.
My Darling Husband— Our little son is twelve days old today— he seems to have more plumpness and sweetness every day. I have a hope he will have your Mother's beautiful brown eyes— they look dark, but as the other children disappointed me as to their eyes, not being brown, I have no faith now… This mornings mail brought yours from Chicago & so thankful for the dispatch from N.Y. In these days of R. R. accidents I feel so thankful of knowing you are safely at your journeys end. Today is a raw, gray one— rained all night. Three children just gone for a brisk walk— they all send love & kisses & Mother sends her best love. & my whole heart full & kisses goes to you. Your own Devoted *Katherine*.

༄ A letter from Annie Jennings Wise Hobson:

Ashland, Sept. 16th. 1897.
My dear Son— From your letter received yesterday in all probability you are in New York and therefore I will write there for I am sure the letter sent to Colorado regarding Cannon was not received. The weather has been so sultry and the heat so extreme that I could not think of letting Cannon start South till the heat had abated somewhat. Today it is decidedly cooler and I wish to get him off next Tuesday. I do not presume that a week or ten days can make any difference and I did not wish to run the least risk of making him sick. I wrote asking Henry Coke to send me his number. He has not even the number of his house upon his envelopes. I inclose a list of Cannon's actual needs & you can determine how much he may require in case of emergency. Let it all be charged to his $300 for the sooner he finds out just how little $1.00 can do the better for him. The less he feels at his command in Texas the better for him. As I wrote in my Colorado letter I would not consent to letting him have

his father's watch, but I gave him a very good second hand silver watch...
While I think of it I must tell you a singular coincidence; it proves to be made by Cooper, in London, the same maker as your father's watch...

—Later. I could not conclude before breakfast & must do so hurriedly now. We all send love. I enjoy your letters about the new boy so much. I hope he will have dark eyes as both Katherines were so anxious to have one brown-eyed baby. I wish I could run up & see you & Johnnie, but it would be impossible for me to leave home. All join me in love. Our children have been so well this summer but the heat has affected little Alice & she has a bilious attack, & my enemy has been trying to assail me again... I hope you will have a successful trip. Much love to John & Henry. Your devoted Mother. *A. J. W. Hobson.*

WESTERN UNION TELEGRAPH COMPANY
Telegram to Henry Wise Hobson in New York City.
Agree better to defer plumbing until spring. All well. Love *K. T. Hobson.* September 17, 1897.

September 18th, 1897.
My Darling Husband—   Your daily letters from the train are a great joy to me... I never saw the three children look more healthful. They are as pink & white & sweet to the eye as heart could wish. The Baby has been asleep over four hours— he is settling down into a quiet little soul. He thinks he is hungry all the time he is awake. It is well I have such an abundant supply of food for him. My greatest comfort now you are away is nestling up our new Boy to me & feeling how grateful I should be for you, & him, to say nothing of all my other joys. Take every care of yourself.   —Always your devoted loving *Katherine.*

WESTERN UNION TELEGRAPH COMPANY
Telegram to Henry Wise Hobson in New York City.
Hope you keep well. Katherine and all well. Much love. —K. T. Hobson. September 18, 1897.

WESTERN UNION TELEGRAPH COMPANY
Telegram to Henry Wise Hobson in New York City.
Daily messages a comfort. All doing well. All send much love. Answer 18 D.H. —*K. T. Hobson.* September 19, 1897.

WESTERN UNION TELEGRAPH COMPANY
Telegram to Henry Wise Hobson in New York City.
We are doing well. Glad to hear you are well. All send much love. Answer to 16 D.H. —*K. T. Hobson.* September 20, 1897.

Tuesday, Sept. 21st, 1897.
My Darling Husband—   This morning your letter from N.Y. of 18th & telegram from Boston this morning too. Mother went down at once to office & saw Miss Fallon who sends you everything relative to Farm by tonight's mail... I am glad Henry has a place on a ship as that seems to be the life he prefers and a boy will probably do better in a life he has a taste for. Love & many kisses from all, Darling one. Your own Devoted *Katherine.*

WESTERN UNION TELEGRAPH COMPANY
Telegram to Henry Wise Hobson in Boston.
All doing well. Farm papers to Hotel Manhattan today. Ans. D.H. 18   —*K. T. Hobson*, September 21, 1897.

Denver, Wednesday, Sept. 22nd, 1897.
My Darling Husband—   This morning I had no letter from you but yesterday two. As soon as one mail has come, I long for the next. We were all upset this morning hearing by your telegram from Troy, that you did not receive our telegram sent yesterday to Boston. Immediately on receipt of yours, Mother went down herself, and I do not think the operators pay any attention to either end of our messages. A kind of fate seems to overtake them & delay them. I trust Mr. Hagermann is getting his matters into an improved condition and will get enough money to make him feel able to pay you all he owes you, & interest. No one has a right to accept your services when they can not pay for them. Still the only way now is for you to *work* to put Mr. Hagermann on his feet again for that will mean your getting what he owes you & his failure means no payment of fees to you. I could not get to sleep the other night counting over the number of people dependent upon you. There are only 15! I should think Aunt Mary Garnett would like to do something now. Henry Garnett can not object to maintain her Mother. As I think of life there always is one person who is called upon to help everyone. I have plenty of time for thought as I lie here in bed— and you, your patient, brave course in life & so unselfish. I am glad I have the capability to appreciate you, as well as love you. Baby is nursing so excuse this scribble. All send love & kisses.
—Your devoted *Katherine*.

There are only 15! Katherine and the four children, A.J.W. Hobson and Cannon Hobson's six children, Mary Lyons Wise, Eliza, and servants in Denver and Virginia would be fifteen or more people dependent on Henry Wise Hobson.

WESTERN UNION TELEGRAPH COMPANY
Telegram to Henry Wise Hobson in New York City.
Yesterday wired Young's Hotel immediately. All doing well. Papers went to Hotel Manhattan. Love Answer 18 D. H. —*K. T. Hobson*. September 22, 1897.

A letter from Annie Jennings Wise Hobson:

Ashland, Sept. 22nd, 1897.
My dear Son—   I said goodbye to Cannon last evening with a very aching heart. Yet I had much to comfort me in the way he went off. He sobered down for several days and showed much feeling, yet I believe he has firmly and manfully made up his mind to do his best and to begin life in earnest. He had a long comforting talk with me the night before. I know he loves me as he does no one else. We parted in my room and we were both sobbing. The boys saw him off at the train. George and Jennings came back with sad faces & little Jennings cried himself to sleep. I do believe, I certainly trust, that we will both yet be glad and proud of him. He has brains enough to do much if he chooses. He has an especial talent for mathematics. He has left two as fine "Drop puppies" (that is what John calls them in his book— cross between setter & pointer) as I ever saw. He was offered $25.00 for one a month ago. We have promised to try to get them out to him as his Xmas present. He said, "Once I hope yet to pay back to Uncle Henry all I have ever cost him." I drew a draft for $100, but I gave him only $85 altogether— $25 after getting his

ticket he had for travelling expenses. I knew if I gave him more than necessary he would not be careful. I wrote to Henry Coke to give him $15 in Dallas & charge to my October account. He went by the Chesapeake & Ohio via Louisville, thus not going near Atlanta. Mr. Hull here told him to buy his sleeping berths as he needed them as the cheapest way to get them. I gave him nearly a days provisions. I believe God is guiding all and that this may be the surest way of enabling him early to lift your burdens.

Now about Henry— What position do you propose getting for him? I think Mr. Curtis' advice about Henry was good. He said get him some place like a cabin boy's where he can sleep in the cabin & not with the common sailors. He said he would have plenty of time to learn about true sailor's life if he chose, & it would strengthen him physically to stand an examination for a training ship when he came back. He is intensely pleased at the prospect. I have to go out on business & must conclude hurriedly. I hope you will not be too worn out by your hard work. I am so truly glad to hear that your boy & Katherine are doing so well. We all have many trials but more blessings. Tomorrow is Sister's sixty-8th birthday [Mary Wise Garnett]. Much love from Mother & Eliza & from the children. Your Mother's devoted love is ever beside you. God bless & guide you— Your devoted Mother,   —A. J. W. Hobson.

John Cannon Hobson Sr., 1880–1960, at the Espuela Land and Cattle Co. in Colorado, Texas, 1899. Just to be confusing, "John Cannon Hobson Sr.," 1880–1960, was the son of "Rev. John Cannon Hobson," 1857–1890. The son, John Cannon Hobson Sr., had a son, John Cannon Hobson, Jr. Photograph courtesy of George Hobson.

Ticket vis Memphis, Louisville etc. (thus avoiding yellow fever in New Orleans) from Ashland.	$37.80
1 pr. of shoes	3.50
1 suit of clothes	10.00
1 white shirt	.50
6 colored shirt	3.00
6 handkerchief	.80
2 cravats	1.00
Night drawers & shirts	2.00
1 razor (which he would get)	1.50
	$60.10
6 pr socks	.75
	$60.85

You will know best what to allow for emergencies. Mr. Hull, the agent here, says he can get a sleeper on the train for about $2.00 a night & he will be on three nights. He will need money for food. He says he prefers that all should be charged to his account. I make him pay for all his clothes because he has abused & lost so many that I have bought for him. He has had five suits of clothes since April counting 2 nice suits sent by Sister & one made from your clothes & all not fit to wear.

Thursday, Sept. 23rd, 1897.
My Darling Husband—   Today brings me your beautiful long letter of Sunday with so much of interest. I am afraid you will have all your trouble on Uncle Johnnie's account for nothing. He would have to be born again to make him tactful… I always look on the Trust Co. as a child of yours. I remember one evening we were walking home on Grant Ave. years ago, & you told me of your hope to establish such a Company & then your list of names for subscribers for its stock. It has been a source of pride & gratification to me

to watch your success in establishing the Co & influence with men regarding it… A letter from Katie Townsend— she says Fred hopes you will stop in Buffalo, or if not, he will see you in Albany. They remain quiet about the will by Mr. Milburn's advice… We are all well. Love & kisses. Baby crying for me so must stop. Your own Devoted wife *Katherine.*

WESTERN UNION TELEGRAPH COMPANY
Telegram to Henry Wise Hobson in New York City.
Wired Young's Hotel Tuesday that farm papers went Tuesday night to Hotel Manhattan. Well. Love. *K. T. Hobson.* September 23, 1897.

Denver, Friday, Sept. 24th, 1897.
My Darling Husband— …I have been sitting up in a chair a little while today. The Doctor says to keep still for four weeks in order to put organs in a normal condition & have contraction sufficient & no enlargement of abdomen which so many women have by getting up too soon. My head aches & I am not going to write any more. Two precious letters from you today… The baby well & chicks also. Love & Many kisses from your children & devoted wife *Katherine.* —I wrote your mother a few lines the other day— thought she would like to hear directly from us.

WESTERN UNION TELEGRAPH COMPANY
Telegram to Henry Wise Hobson in New York City.
All doing well. Etc. *K. T. Hobson.* September 24, 1897.

Denver, Saturday, Sept. 25th, 1897.
My Darling Husband— As I write am sitting up, and feel stronger than I have yet. My headache has gone. Our boy is three weeks old today and next Saturday I am going to have him weighed. Henry brought me in a large bunch of sweet-peas from our vines this AM… I wondered you said nothing of Albany matters, but perhaps you had heard nothing from Mr. Peltz… You can well imagine I am anxious to hear what the verdict is & that my mind dwells much on the subject… I hope you will get somewhere to church tomorrow. You have not been to church in nearly four months. I feel so grateful for my blessings that I think we should be mindful of our Father who has given us all to each other. Love & kisses from us all to the most precious Papa in the world. —Your own Devoted Wife, *Katherine.*

WESTERN UNION TELEGRAPH COMPANY
Telegram to Henry Wise Hobson in New York City.
Glad to hear you are well and doing well. Love. —*K. T. H.* September 25, 1897.

WESTERN UNION TELEGRAPH COMPANY
Telegram to Henry Wise Hobson in New York City.
Glad to know you are well as all are here. Love —*K. T. Hobson.* September 26, 1897.

WESTERN UNION TELEGRAPH COMPANY
Telegram to Henry Wise Hobson in New York City.
All doing well. Will notify office you may leave any day. Much love. —*K. T. Hobson.* September 27, 1897.

WESTERN UNION TELEGRAPH COMPANY
Telegram to Henry Wise Hobson in Albany, New York.
Glad to hear when you leave for home. All well. Much love. Answer 17 D.H. —*K. T. Hobson.* September 29, 1897.

༄ A letter from Annie Jennings Wise Hobson:

Ashland, October 7th, 1897.
My dear Son—   I am in one of my restless states tonight. Something has disagreed with me so in the small hours I will scribble a few lines to you. I wish to inclose Mr. Horsbrugh's letter telling of Cannon's safe arrival. I hope every day to hear from him. I am very glad to hear what he said about the character of the cow-boys, Cannon's associates… I saw Mr. Curtis who so kindly offered Henry a place on one of his schooners to New York & he told me one would start in about two weeks & would arrive there in four or five days & he would let Henry know in time. I will write John about it. I hope you are now safe in Denver enjoying home, wife & children…   —Your devoted Mother, *A. J. W. H.*

༄ A letter from Texas:

Espuela A Land and Cattle Company, Limited, Espulea, Dickens Co., Texas
30 Septr. 1897.
Madam [to Mrs. A. J. W. Hobson]:   I am in receipt of your favor of the 22nd inst, and have carefully noted the contents. Your grandson arrived here the day before yesterday, and today is out riding, along with another, looking after some fence. I think he will do very well, so far as I can judge; but of course this will, in a measure, depend upon himself. The outfit of men here at present happens to be rather above the ordinarily accepted type of "cowboy;" and he will be treated very kindly, and have every opportunity afforded him of learning the work, and making himself useful. This is a very healthy life, and very rare are the sick spells, especially among the younger hands.
    I shall take pleasure in letting you know, from time to time, how he gets on. Respectfully. *Fred Horsbrugh.*

༄ Family matters:

October 14, 1897.
Dear Henry—   …The good ship *Kenilworth* sails on Wednesday, October 20th. I have written for your brevet cub to report here ready for shipment. Sister Annie is very hot on the trail. She has opened a lively correspondence with the sea-captain in regard to his clothing apparel, begged him not to let the boy chew tobacco, thrown in an incidental allusion to her own seafaring on the ship *Constitution*, and I expect will wind up by finally requesting the captain to have family prayers on the ship daily. The old fellow was in to see me this morning, and I think he is rather tickled at having a female correspondent. He seems to be a fine old chap and I expect he will make that boy dance Juba with a rope end in the horse latitudes.
    Hugh is today making a fool of himself by riding from Washington to New York to break the record. He left Washington at 5 A. M., and should be

here tomorrow morning at the same hour, distance 240. He has a lovely day for the business, but I am just sitting here ready to hear that his bicycle has busted, or the cars have run over him, or he has broken a blood vessel, or something else terrible has happened.

I was down in Washington yesterday, and dined with dear old sister. She has shrunk away to a little bit of a dried-up woman who looks as if a breath would blow out her life. She talked with me about Henry, and it seemed to cheer her to have me there. Poor little Maria was ill in bed in the morning with cold, but was up at night. A good strong man in the house seemed to do them all good, and it is pitiful enough. I was as cheerful as I knew how to be, but I felt more like crying than laughing. That household reminds me of a tree that has been struck by lightning.

Your aunt Eva has gone back to the Eastern Shore, and I think I will run down tomorrow night. When I come back I will speak to you definitely about what arrangement I can make for the horse. If you want a horse you ought to buy him.

Enclosed are two bills which were sent in by the stenographer, one of which is yours and one is mine. If you choose you can pay both. They all relate to the old General's matter, and as I have no funds in hand, you can take them all, if you like. If you are only going to pay your own bill, I think it is so small you had better let me pay it.   —Yours affectionately, *John S. Wise*. (Virginia Historical Society)

THE WESTERN UNION TELEGRAPH COMPANY
Denver, October 19
To: Hon John S. Wise   —Tell Henry didn't have time to write him after hearing ship sailing. Give him some money. Tell him goodbye. If going San Francisco give him letter to John Henry and tell him to enquire for letters there. Safe Voyage. —*Henry W. Hobson*. (Virginia Historical Society)

Denver, October 21, 1897.
Dear Uncle John—   Your letter of October 18th received. If you can arrange with Hugh about the horse, I will take him and would be very glad to have him keep him and use him during the winter. Ask Hugh to be careful about his mouth, as I want him for his Cousin Katherine and wish to keep his mouth in good shape… Tell Hugh that I shall probably not need the horse until June or July of next year, so he will have him for some time.

I am glad that Henry Hobson has gotten off all right. I feel sorry for the boy, but it is the best thing for him, to let him strike out and make a man of himself. I sent Mother a check for his expenses and told her that she must settle with you for any advances that you have made.

Many thanks for your kindness about the horse and also about Henry. Jack was at the house last night. He seems to be getting on all right. Katherine is better, but still somewhat under the weather with neuralgic attacks.
—Yours affectionately, *Henry W. Hobson*. (Virginia Historical Society)

October 25, 1897.
Dear Henry—   …You need not feel sorry for little Henry. He is as happy as a clam at high tide. In my opinion he will take care of himself. From what I could see of him he does not care a chew of tobacco for anybody else in this

world. I am sorry to hear Catherine is troubled with neuralgia, and trust she will soon be in perfect health. Give my tenderest love to her. I took tea with Annie Garnett last night, and spent a very pleasant evening. —Yours affectionately, *John S. Wise.* (Virginia Historical Society)

Denver, November 22, Monday [1897]
My Dearest Henry—   There is very little to write of except a 'hold-up' last night, the cook at the Pearce's, at seven o'clock— and her purse taken. This is a decent community— before long it will not be safe to go out by day. Katie is going home tomorrow night— & is delighted. Eleanor's feeling is deep & many tears at the idea of Katie's going away. John seems to have had such a delightful visit and certainly appreciates all you did for him in every way— and he leaves tonight. We are going to send Diomed off Wednesday night. I asked Miss Fallon to write to Nebraska two days in advance, so there would be no mistake… Please do not bring toys home for the children. They have so many & they have about forty Xmas experiences a year that Dec. 25th has not the importance it should have… Much tender love & kisses from your children & devoted wife.   —*Katherine.*

Denver, November 24th, 1897.
My Dearest Husband—   Tomorrow will be Thanksgiving. I hope you will have some chance of a pleasant day. All the celebration we will have will be in our hearts for your absence makes any effort seem useless. Your letter from Chicago came this morning. I think you are quite right as to the Cambridge Farms and agree with you, under the present circumstances, it would be very unwise to encumber yourself with added indebtedness. Another year you may be in a very different condition and the same opportunity will be open… Jack Wise is getting fatter & better looking every time I see him. I really think the fellow is better *fed* & nourished than at home— but this is not an opinion to be circulated. I am sure Diomed will enjoy a hunt, for some birds. He goes off with a pass tonight, and Johnson will take him down. The children all send with me best love & kisses to Papa. Always your own devoted wife, *Katherine.*

❧ A letter from Annie Jennings Wise Hobson:

Ashland, November 24th, 1897.
My dear Son—   Your letter en route for Chicago reached me today. I am indeed very sorry that you are compelled to leave home at this time… You ask the ages of the children. George was fourteen last April. He is small and backward, but becoming more manly & seems to be trying to study. Mary will be thirteen Dec. 3rd. I am impressing upon her that she too will have to depend upon her own exertions as soon as she is old enough. Jennings was ten years old in August & Alice nine in September. I take what you say as you meant it about not sending your children anything much at Xmas, & I feel that you are right— & especially that I have not the right to do so. I suppose we agree that there will be no Xmas gifts all around? You have been already too sorely taxed by me & times are too hard for such luxuries. Your children will miss nothing from me amidst the many & better gifts they have, & I necessarily have only a small share in their full, happy lives. It is a sad, humiliating thought that I shall always be to them the dependent, poor grandmother. Yet I take the trial

along with the other inevitables of life… It is time this was mailed. All join me in love. I have a birthday present for Katherine & something for the fine, new boy which I will send at once with a letter to Katherine. God bless & take care of you. —Your devoted Mother, *A. J. W. Hobson.*

Denver, Thanksgiving 1897.
My Darling Husband— We are just through our dinner and I have promised the children to go up in the play-room for a romp. We are having quite a heavy snow-storm from the north. Johnson came in for money to buy a snow shovel. He got "Di" off all right last night. Maybe the man who hunts him will cure him of that bad habit of jumping… There was to be a big football game this afternoon, but the Denver team & Boulder University will be disappointed with such an amount of snow. Your telegram came this morning, which I answered at once. I am thankful you are safely in New York and my heart goes out to you in love & tenderness on this day of Thanksgiving… All your chicks send love & kisses & a heart full of love to you from your own devoted wife *Katherine.*

WESTERN UNION TELEGRAPH COMPANY
Telegram to Henry Wise Hobson in New York City.
We are all well and send much love on Thanksgiving. Answer to 15 D.H. —*K. T. Hobson.* November 25, 1897.

Denver, Nov. 27th, 1897.
My Darling Husband— You have been gone a week tonight and I look soon for a letter from New York. None has come today… Henry has gone out with Johnson to exercise the horse— it is a raw chill day & I did not care to go out— Have been doing the interesting work of regulating the linen closet & taking everything out of the nursery closet— toys & casting away broken playthings. Got rid of a great clothes-basket full. I think it is positively wrong to continue as we have in giving the children toys in such number. They enjoy them far less than if they had fewer. Let us begin on a different basis. Katherine & her Grandmother are playing a game & the former delighted at having beaten. Eleanor is sewing on her machine. I am going to read *The Deer Slayer* to Katherine. She is trying so hard to read well by herself… We all send you love & kisses. Always your own Devoted Wife, *Katherine.*

Denver, Nov. 29th, 1897.
My Darling Husband— This morning I have three letters from you, which makes up for several days— and so much interesting matter to think of. Mother will write John what you say regarding Farms. I rather hope Donovan will be the tenant, but anyway we will know if he does, what kind of man he would be for the future, as Supt. or leaser of both farms. The Whitesides look upon your visits as great events in their quiet lives. I have always thought if you could get under Albert Whiteside's outer rudeness & talk with him on subjects, you would find him far more interesting than you imagine… Jack was up yesterday for dinner & spent the afternoon. He was very well & is spending all his evenings studying, preparing for the exams which come off the 15th. Katherine & Eleanor were both heavy with colds on Thanksgiving. I went to the office, and saw Jack, and asked him to come up to dinner, or any meal he felt like coming to. Jack told me yesterday he stayed in all day as it was

so stormy. The affairs in Austria are quite stormy & interesting… I had your letters & telegrams this morning. I wonder how you got to St. Louis. I replied at once. It is good to feel you are well today. Love & many kisses to you from the chicks & your devoted wife *Katherine.*

WESTERN UNION TELEGRAPH COMPANY
Telegram to Henry Wise Hobson in New York City.
We are all well and send much love. —*K. T. Hobson.* November 29, 1897.

Denver, Nov. 30th, 1897.
My Darling Husband—   Katherine, Henry, & Eleanor are out playing— and have good appetites & fine spirits today. I looked out the nursery door, sitting in a chair, & saw Henry in a tree as high as I was. I opened the window & asked him if he were having a good climb, & he smiled & said "I wish I could get higher" —one inch either way & down he would have gone— but boys will climb I suppose… You will see your Baby much grown on your return— he is as jolly & sweet as can be… Your own Devoted & Loving wife *Katherine.*

Denver, December 1st, 1897.
My Darling Husband—   This morning your letter just before starting for Washington came, and Tom's warm invitation. I am so glad you had the opportunity of seeing him, Florence and Maj. & Mrs. Page… Katherine & Eleanor & Henry are writing you letters. I do not know when they will be posted. I wrote the Stewarts last night & your Mother. I told her I had saved some of her pretty Xmas remembrances of last year, for the children, and not to send toys this year, that I was going to do very little in the way of presents… Another snow-storm today. We miss you all the time and will be thankful to have you home again. Dearest one, God bless & keep you & us in my prayer. I joined the "Dames" in the State of Mass. only because I thought in our being East together there might be, as before, some occasions where we would both enjoy being & my not being a member would make my going impossible, but I have taken no part here, nor talked with anyone. And my name was sent the chapter here I suppose. There are too many home duties for me to run in Societies & Clubs. Henry has come to finish his letter, so I must give him a little attention. Mother expects to go home next week. She has so enjoyed being here— And it has been such a happiness to me to have her in our beautiful home. And she appreciates all your sweetness to her. Love & many kisses from us all to you our Darling Papa. Your own Devoted wife *Katherine.*

[undated, pre Christmas 1897.]
Dear Santa Claus—   I want a doll with long curly hair of yellow and Brown eyes. Eleanor wants a work basket. Henry wants a sled. I want a trunk for the Big doll and lots of cloths in it. I want a prety [sic] Bible and a box of candy. The Big Doll I want to be 3 feet tall. I want a purple Silk dress for the Big doll. Eleanor and Henry want some dolls too. Henry wood [sic] like a doll dress in pink Silk and have Brown eyes and yellow hair. He wants it to be 1 foot high. Eleanor wode [sic] like a baby doll in white. Henry wants a [illegible] and real horse. We are going to leave the playroom door open and we want the Xmas tree in the Red Room. Baby Brother wants a doll with a blue dress.   —from *Thayer, Henry, Eleanor,* and *Katherine Hobson.*

the Stewarts   These are Henry Hobson's friends who lived at Brook Hill in Virginia. Henry wrote letters to them in 1881 when he was practicing law in Buena Vista, Colorado.

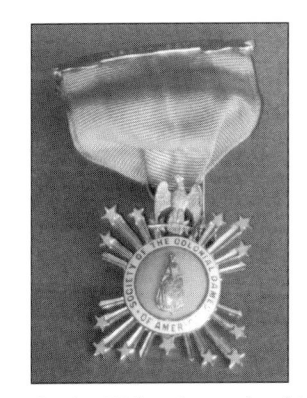

Katherine Hobson's membership medal in the Society of Colonial Dames to which she was admitted in November 1897. The records show that she was ninth in descent from Ralph Wheelock, 1637–1684, and that she was member number 138 in Massachusetts. Henry Hobson was a member of the Society of Colonial Wars.

Florence Florence Page, the wife of Thomas Nelson Page.

The Chinese vase. It has always been the family tradition that one of Henry Hobson's last gifts to his wife was this Chinese vase that was always kept on the piano. One day the children accidentally knocked it off of the piano and then told their mother that the "most dreadful thing" had happened. She was relieved to find out that it was only the broken vase, which was subsequently repaired.

This letter was written on Katherine's thirty-eighth birthday and is incomplete.

Denver, December 2nd, 1897.
My Darling Husband— Today there are two letters from you— one with Florence's enclosed from Washington, and the one written the evening of your arrival in New York. The prophecy of Tom's friends as to his never doing any more work has turned out just as I thought & said it would— Florence & the ease & luxury of the past four years have been an incentive to possibly the best work of Tom's life. What an awful pity that Tom has no child of his own. They are wretchedly poor in that respect, for I know Florence longs for a child… Do not try to write when you are so pushed for time. I know I have your thoughts & love and can be content until you come back to us and I feel your dear arms about me. Another snow-storm… Please see in N.Y. what you can buy a child's bicycle for— Katherine's size, 9 years. I am not sure it is best for her to have one & shall say nothing to her… Poor Aunt Mary Garnett— how the lights in her life have gone out. I am sure it was a comfort to her to have you there— wonder how you settled with your Mother, not going to Ashland. The children send love & kisses always & my whole heart of love goes to you. Always your own Devoted wife, *Katherine*.

December 2, 1897.
Darling Kate— In a hurry as usual, and you have to suffer in the way of poor letter. I had John Birge over to lunch & talked over farm matters fully with him. I would enjoy John more if he would talk less, not so loudly and keep shaved. He had at least two days growth of beard on today… I had a letter from Ada today begging me to go out & spend Saturday night with her & shall try to do so. I don't know what to do with the elk head. Maybe we can send it to the Univ. Club for storage. I can't tell you how lonesome and depressed I am without you and I wish I never had to leave you. Love & kisses for the chicks. —Devotedly *Henry*.

WESTERN UNION TELEGRAPH COMPANY
Telegram to Henry Wise Hobson in New York City.
Lovely letter and presents received add happiness today. Much love from all to you. Well. —*K. T. Hobson*. December 3, 1897.

Denver, Dec. 3rd, 1897.
My Darling Husband— My heart has been full of love & tenderness for you today especially as I have realized, from the beginning of the day, your loving care, that I should be remembered as thoughtfully as if you were here & not two thousand miles away. The "blue piece of paer" (as the children call it) was under my plate and I am so grateful for all your generous remembrances. But it was too much. The children, girls, gave me lovely flowers. The boys (plural you see) a pretty pearl handled knife for my desk which I needed— and Katherine & Eleanor, a beautiful pair of blankets for my bed. Mother a check for $100. Your Mother sent me a handsome frame and to "Thayer" a jacket & three pairs of socks. Just see what a celebration I have had & your absence has been the only thing lacking. The children were perfectly delighted with your letter & the fairy tale— and I read it several times, but the whole letter was a joy to me— and I only wish I were deserving of the half you say, but I do love you with all my heart. And long to help you to make the most of…

Denver, Dec. 4th, 1897.
My Darling Husband—   Your letter telling of your possible start for home next week Tuesday just received. We will be overjoyed to have you back with us once more. Have only time for this line before the mail. We are all well & send love & kisses to the dearest Papa & most precious Husband in the world.
—Your loving devoted wife *Katherine*.

WESTERN UNION TELEGRAPH COMPANY
Telegram to Henry Wise Hobson in New York City.
Better defer wheel purchase for present. All well. Much love. Answer to D.H. —*K. T. Hobson*. December 7, 1897.

❧ A letter from Annie Jennings Wise Hobson:

[Fragment of a letter, December 1897, to Henry W. Hobson in Denver.]
…The Church received the profits [from a local church sale] & small as it was, it helped considerably. This will be my Xmas pleasure to feel I have assured Mr. W— of his salary which is pitifully small. I do not propose to make any presents. I shall get me a much-needed bonnet and wrap with your present to me and the rest will enable me to do other needed things.

   Later— I scribbled this in Mother's room. The dear old soul is sitting up again, but she is so deaf & mentally bewildered that it is painful to be with her. She forgets everything as fast as she hears it. I shall get her a few presents to send to Mrs. Taliaferro & Mary H— which always delights her & the rest I shall use to get her a nice wrapper &, if she can be induced to use it, a nice ear trumpet which will cost five dollars… These children are going to spend Xmas day with their Mother, & look eagerly forward to spending part of the week there, two at a time. I shall make no good things except a little jelly and simple cake for Mother. I shall send Katherine a center-piece bought from the sale, which was done by one who had no other offering to make in the cause. I will go down on Wednesday and look for a book for you. It is a sad Xmastide for me for many reasons. The two boys so far away with such an uncertain future, & at present my life seeming such a failure with them. Henry Garnett gone. Mother in such a half-dead state. You so harassed by care & now pecuniarily strained, & I feeling each year more unbearably that if these children are weights on our life, your very goodness to me giving me pain, & yet amidst it all I'd not forget the many mercies which encompass my life.

   —Later. This is not my real Xmas letter though I wish you & yours a blessed Xmastide. I scribble under difficulties wishing to thank you for us all for your kind & generous presents & may God ever bless you for your goodness to your Mother. Best love to the darlings & a kiss to Katherine—
—Most lovingly, *A. J. W. H.*   —No one knows I am writing.

❧ Katherine Hobson to her Mother:

December 24, 1897.
My Darling Mother—   The baby is looking with the greatest attention to my moving hand over the basket. He has just nursed, & I will scribble a line, so you will hear tomorrow… Henry at lunch and took Henry downtown

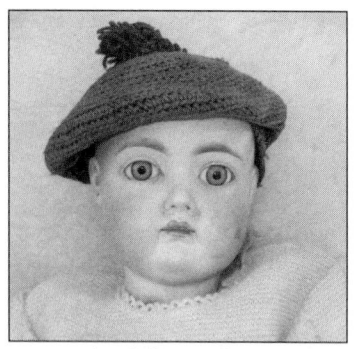

New Yorky, doll given by Henry W. Hobson to his daughter Katherine.

after. The tree up in red room. All trimmings by it & gifts on bed so think we can make quick work of it— with Jack's help... Mrs. Fowler has sent some things here, 2 plates for K— & a book for Henry... *New Yorky* had her hair curled last evening & is fine... Your letter came by P.M. mail. Glad your night was comfortable— don't get cold... God bless & keep you my precious Darling one. I have all your little bags ready for the stockings...   —Devotedly *Kittie.*

◦ A letter from Annie Jennings Wise Hobson:

Ashland, Dec. 28th, 1897.
My dear and loving Katherine and Henry—   I must write you a joint letter... Xmas day I had not a moment... I looked after Mother. The dear old soul is sitting, even walking around some again, but her deafness is much worse and I do not think she will ever be as well as before... Alice wrote that the children had best come on Monday as Dr. McSparrin would go on a visit to his father's and she would have more room for them... My memory went back over the Xmastides spent with my darlings & devoted husband at Eastwood, as it has not done for years. I would shut my eyes & go over the scenes & how my loving bright-eyed little Annie with her quaint, sweet ways, seemed right by me. Do you remember Henry the little baby house where the presents were mysteriously covered? I could only think of Henry & Cannon with a prayer... I enjoyed so much dear Henry your letter about the children & I so loved to hear about little Henry, God bless him. I would give anything to hear Eleanor talk, & to think the little Thayer's babyhood will pass without my knowing it. I enjoy intensely your accounts of him. It was lovely in you Henry to write about the Xmas day when you were so busy. Your dear letter awhile back was a great pleasure to me, dear Katherine. I must now bring this often interrupted letter to a close & mail it... God's best blessings be with you & yours during the coming year.   —Your devoted Mother, *A. J. W. Hobson.*

◦ Family matters:

December 28, 1897.
My Dear Henry—   ...I hope you have all had a Merry Christmas, and are well and happy. All of our household is at home, except Jack, whom we miss dreadfully.

I was 51 years old yesterday, and feel as spry as a cricket—not half dead yet. We had a lively home gathering, diversified by the presence of a red-headed Irish cook, who made it as lively as a fighting Tom cat slung through the window could have done. She came for a week, but after three days of war, pestilence, and famine I gave her her week's wages to leave. That woman, bred to Fitzimmons, would produce an offspring that could whip out the entire City of New York on a fair and square fight. Your aunt Eva looked like a dying gladiator. She was gentle, subdued, and appalled.

I went down a week ago to try to get three days of shooting with Dick. It rained cats and dogs the whole time I was there, and I only got out one day.
  —Good-by. With love to all, Yours affectionately, *John S. Wise.*

XXI

1898, Part One
Henry W. Hobson and the Practice of Law

BY 1898, Henry Wise Hobson was very successfully established in his private law practice. Unfortunately, he was spending much of his time in New York working for the railroads and was separated from his family. During this year, the Spanish-American War dominated the newspaper headlines and was a part of daily conversation. The U. S. Supreme Court, in *United States v. Wong Kim Ark*, found that American citizenship was to be considered without respect to race or color, but the State of Louisiana adopted a new constitution allowing the disenfranchisement of black citizens through the use of property and literacy tests. Also in this year: the term "radioactivity" was first used when Marie Curie discovered the elements polonium and radium; an English bacteriologist determined that malaria was transmitted by mosquitoes; and the first Food and Drug Act in the United States was passed in response to the poor quality of the meat that was supplied to the American soldiers fighting in Cuba.

Letters, diaries, and telegrams from:
Annie Jennings Wise Hobson
Katherine, Henry, Eleanor, and Thayer Hobson— the four children of Henry & Kittie Hobson
Henry Wise Hobson, son of John Cannon Hobson
Henry Wise Hobson
Katherine Thayer Hobson
J. G. Shackelford
Catherine McKie Thayer
John Sergeant Wise
John "Jack" S. Wise, Jr.
and Papa's Letters

Letters written from: Denver and Colorado Springs, Colorado; New York City and Cambridge, New York; Ashland and Fredericksburg ,Virginia; Washington, D. C., San Francisco, Boston, Chicago, Houston, and aboard trains.

∼

1898

Denver, January 5th, 1898.
My Darling Husband—   Today your letter came & telegram and it was a comfort to know you were well. And I am going to send a line to Sapinero

Francis Thayer Hobson, born in 1897.

Katherine Townsend was the married name of Katherine Savage, the granddaughter of James Jermain.

to let you know your wife, & four Babies, are well. The Baby is fine & evidently expects rubbings he does not get… I had a letter from Florence Page today. They have had a big reception, and a house full of visitors & Roswell is engaged, to a cousin Ruth, and everybody is enchanted and *superlatively* happy. In some way or other Henry, Eleanor, & Katherine are having a delightful play with the Parkers by the swing. I have sent Johnson out to drive the horses for three hours… Eleanor is very excited about her birthday— and thinks Papa will surely be home… I like Tom's new chapters— there is a purity in his writing, which is an unusual thing these days… he does not think it necessary to interest one to have the heroine a prostitute, & every woman untrue to her husband— & the men running away with some married woman. I must write Florence tonight. We shall be over-joyed to see you back my Darling one… Love & kisses from us all. Your own *Katherine*.

◦∽ Letters to Catherine McKie Thayer:

Denver, January 17th, 1898.
My Darling Mother—   …That Mayo fellow was found gambling with R. R. funds in Pueblo and has lost his position & Henry got him & his wife passes to Omaha to get them away from here. H— says he is not going in future to burden himself with those who have no possible claim upon him. He sent in his resignation to Denver Athletic Club and Chamber of Commerce on January 1st— trying to cut down expenses. I think H— means to try to cut down living expenses in every way in order to pay what he owes… There is nothing to write of & I will get ready for lunch. I promised the children I would play the piano for them to sing… With love always & kisses, your own *Kittie*.

Denver, January 27th, 1898.
My Darling Mother—   Henry told me last evening when he came home that he would "have to start East tonight. Gen. Dodge had telegraphed that he was needed there. I had done a great deal of work for the Gulf R. R. and now when the fruit is almost ready to pick I wish to be on hand." (Meaning getting his fee.) I have just been brushing and cleaning a coat & vest. Ordered his trunk up. The new bath-tub just been brought up by *six men* & they to take cracked one out. I should greatly prefer one like yours but this is paid for, and we wish to get rid of the cracked one. I have your letter regarding Katherine Townsend. How sad to hear her throat is so affected, one tonsil "eaten away" —dreadful! …The children are at their lessons but going out at twelve with Katie in pony car. The plumbers are making a riot in the hall, but Thayer sleeps on…   —Yours devotedly, *Kittie*.

Denver, January 28th, 1898.
My Darling Husband—   The night & morning has passed without you. Katherine woke about one o'clock to call out "Is Papa here? Has he gone? Did he kiss me?" All on her mind. Your son Henry was a full hour bathing this A.M. He came into my bed at six o'clock, and said "I do miss Papa." Eleanor informed me this morning, "I was just fooling Papa— I did not want any money for brushing his hair." I went to the Trust Co. & took my *gems* & left them in Box 984… I saw Mr. Mallon— he was in town for the day, asked me if you went on to attend to Mr. Hagerman's business? And if you were his law-

yer, and if you had said if he were likely to raise the money for his schemes? You can be sure I was very careful in reply… Went to your office… Miss Fallon was cheerful— said the office did not seem to have a head when you were away… The children are out, afternoon lovely. I am going to pay some visits. All send love & kisses. Your own devoted wife, *Katherine.*

Denver, Saturday, January 29th, 1898.
My Darling Husband—   Your telegram from Chicago came and I answered it. Your first letter also. You are always so thoughtful about writing and I fully appreciate my daily letter from you. The three children each with a pair of cheap skates have gone out to City Park… Your Baby boy is in my arms as I write— just waked from his afternoon nap. I think he misses your rubbings and jumpings. Dear little soul, what a pet he is & will be. There is nothing as lovely in this world as a dear baby. I hope and pray all may go well with you & your business affairs… Write me about Mr. Hagerman's affairs. I do hope he may succeed in his efforts to raise the money for it means your being paid— but I have said this a hundred times. All send the dearest Husband & Papa in the world love & kisses. Always your Devoted Wife, *Katherine.*

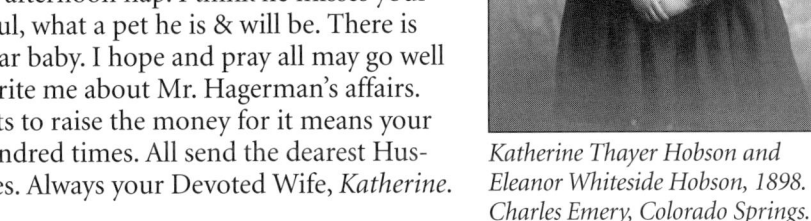

Katherine Thayer Hobson and Eleanor Whiteside Hobson, 1898. Charles Emery, Colorado Springs.

Sunday, January 30th, 1898.
My Darling Husband—   This is a most lovely day— a true Colorado day— clear sky and bright sun. The children had a fine time skating. Henry & Eleanor declare they had no tumbles and Katherine one. They say they are going to surprise you by all being able to skate when you come home— So you must be surprised. Jack is coming to lunch or dinner today, and we are to have Quail— 2 for him. The children have gone to Sunday School… I think so much of your plans, and of what you are trying to achieve— and the future, but have resolved to try and live well each day, as it comes, and trust— and not act carelessly & say "it is only for a little while." …I often think of your saying if you were a bachelor you would not hesitate a moment as to your plans. And hope & pray your not being free from family ties will interfere with your best development & you must feel that I am in perfect sympathy with you in the plans for the future. Dr. Fisk & Mrs. Rogers just stopped to say "Good Morning," she looking very frail & plain. The Dr. said, "Poor girl she suffers terribly."   —A heart full of love. Ever your own Devoted wife, *Katherine.*

Jack   John S. Wise Jr.

Colorado Springs, Sunday, February 6th, 1898.
My Darling Husband—   Today I think of you as spending Sunday with your Mother & Aunt Mary. As your letter indicates I hope all will be pleasant and happy… All children well & happy, been to Sunday School & out all day… The Baby grows sweeter every day— it is pretty to see Mother with him. The children send love & kisses with mine to the dearest Papa in the World. Mother says "Give my love to dear Henry—"   —Always your own Devoted wife, *Katherine.*

Colorado Springs, February 7th, 1898.
My Darling Husband—   This has been a perfect day and all the afternoon I have been out skating with the three chicks. I went out to the storeroom & got my skates and found to my surprise I could move about, greatly to the

children's delight. This morning I had a sitting at the dentists and three teeth filled and tomorrow go again. I have not been able to go for some time with the Baby's coming. We hope to have his photograph taken this next day for though I tried in Denver at Rheinhart's last week, but they were dreadful & every proof poor… It was pleasant to think of you with your mother yesterday & Aunt Mary would be comforted to see you also. I so often think of Henry Garnett & his untimely end. Love & many kisses from us all to you our dearest one—   —Your own Devoted *Katherine*.

Colorado Springs, February 9th, 1898.
My Darling Husband—   This morning brings me your letter of Saturday from Washington— poor dear Aunt Mary. I hope she will not suffer. How natural your Mother should wish to be near her… You seem dearest to be so often surrounded by depressing sorrows. I hope & pray you may keep well. Katherine sends you the enclosed valentine, selected it herself. She so often talks of you, "Dear Papa." I will have her write your Mother, but I can not have her write in detail…but she will say enough to be satisfactory. We are going to the photographers this afternoon to try Thayer's photo again. He is on Mother's lap now, after a long nap. Glad you saw the Pages. Your Mother will appreciate your being with her. What a son you are! —Always have been to her. Love & Many kisses to you from us all. Your own Devoted Wife, *Katherine*.

∽ In the news:

THE MAINE BLOWN UP —Terrible Explosion on Board the United States Battleship — Many persons Killed and Sounded — None of the Wounded Men Able to Give Any Explanation of the Cause of the Disaster.   —*The New York Times,* February 16, 1898.

THE MAINE DISASTER — Capt. Sigsbee Reports the Number of Dead as 253 and of Survivors as 96 — Only Theory as to the Cause of the Disaster — All the information at Hand Tends to Indicate That the Loss was Due to an Accident.
—*The New York Times,* February 17, 1898.

Friday evening, February 18th, 1898.
My Darling Husband—   Every time you leave me it seems harder. I do not get used to it, for every day I certainly love and appreciate you more thoroughly and my entire happiness is when we are together, and after ten years & four of the dearest children my love has never lost anything of its first freshness & interest. There is no old story about it. I am writing with Thayer in my arms, who is as lively as a cricket… Have been devouring the news from Havana. I do hope the loss of the *Maine* may be an accident. The children all asked if you kissed them in their sleep— and I told them you gave them more than one kiss. The snow of last night is almost gone, but it is a cold uncertain day. Eleanor never moved in her little bed last night, and she seems to have made up her mind to sleep there regularly, so of course she will… Love & many kisses from us all. Your own Devoted wife, *Katherine*.

Denver, February 19th, 1898.
My Darling Husband— Such a lovely day— birds singing, and three children out— Thayer sleeping. He went to the breakfast table this morning, very

much propped up by pillows, in a high chair. The children were delighted… Reports seem to show the Captain & officers of *Maine* who were saved were chiefly away from their ship, when accident happened. I trust the war clouds will soon break, but the papers are certainly interesting and diverting… Your telegram from Chicago was very welcome. I always feel so thankful that these numberless journeys have been made in safety… Love & kisses from us all to you who we all love so & long for.   —Your wife *Katherine.*

Denver, Thursday Morning, February 20th, 1898.
My Darling Husband—   Have just answered your Chicago telegram, so you may know today of your family. The children have gone to Sunday School. I celebrated yesterday afternoon & all night with a headache and am staying at home. I saw on your bureau the buttons you wear so much, not links, & will send them if you wish them… Some of Katherine's little photographs are very amusing— she says "This one of Papa in his riding costume is beautiful," and certainly it is good. I wish you would try to go to Church in New York. It would be better in every way, a recognition of the day, and comfort to us both, when so much separated. Then Darling, there is another thing I would like you to do for me, go to some good photographer & have a photograph taken for me. I have only the one taken twelve years ago. Another lovely day— and a week ago you had just arrived. I appreciate so thoroughly your coming home for those four precious days. I am going to get Thayer's short clothes ready at once, he is growing so fast he will soon need them. Eleanor is trying to teach him to say "Papa" by the time you come home. She said last night— "I always feel I must cry when Papa goes away." They all send love & kisses whenever they see me writing. Be very careful of your precious self for you are everything to me. I am counting the days as they pass bringing you nearer to me.   —Your Devoted Wife, *Katherine.*

February 21, 1898, New York, The Waldorf-Astoria.
Darling Kate—   Before going downtown I must write you a little letter for fear I shall not have another chance before mail time for the afternoon trains… I have quite a good-sized room @$4 a day which is far and away better furnished than anything at the Manhattan. My wall-paper would delight your heart being covered with running wild roses. In the bathroom is an electric heater for curling irons and that also I know will please you, for I have seen you so often burning your fingers whilst attempting to get your pet vanities into shape. The service is excellent… Whilst it is a vulgar place in its ostentation & noise, I must bring you here at some time just to see the building and the luxurious appointments…   —Best love to the chicks. Devotedly *Henry.*

Denver, February 22nd, 1898.
My Darling Husband—   The snow is falling heavily and Washington's Birthday rather a failure as far as an outing for the children though Henry has retired to the Turner's house with his flag… Henry sang himself to sleep last night with "My Country 'tis of thee—" …so you can see we are trying to be patriotic… I was in the Trust Co. yesterday— how elegant it is & complete with the additions. Love & kisses from us all.   Your Devoted Wife, *Katherine.*

Henry Wise Hobson, Davis & Sanford, New York.

The Astoria, New York City.

◈ In the news:

EXAMINING THE MAINE —Naval Court of Inquiry Arrives at Havana and Starts Upon Its Investigation — Its Proceedings to be Strictly Secret — Report that the Officers of the *Maine* Think the Battleship Was Not Destroyed by Accident — Extraordinary Activity in the War and Navy Departments Causes Comment in Washington.
—*The New York Times*, February 22, 1898.

Denver, February 23rd, 1898.
My Darling Husband—   Our truly ideal Colorado weather seems to have arrived today. There is nothing to write of except our constant love for "the dearest Papa in the world—" as Katherine says. Henry has said his table of fours today, an event in his life. Johnson has built a cunning little birdhouse for Henry, who came in with more paint on him than on the house… This being Ash Wednesday I suppose the Parkers are starved & kept in a dark room. I asked Jack up for dinner last night, but he had an engagement & gone to Pueblo today— he was quite important telling me. Now I am going to take Thayer for a drive. Love & kisses.   —Your Always Devoted *Katherine.*

Denver, February 24th, 1898.
My Darling Husband—   Your letter of Monday has just arrived. I love to hear of all that is said about "the young red headed lawyer" …You are so much away from me I need all these compliments made to you, to keep my spirits up. This morning comes *The Washington Star*. I have subscribed for it until the middle of April. The *Maine* & Spanish question so interesting. I felt I should like to know just what was said at the Capital. I read what Pres. Harrison said as to the *Maine*. Everything he says reads so well. Indeed you shall never be a soldier. I have had enough discipline in your absences without the terrors of war added. There is nothing patriotic about war… The *Rock Island* is going to put on a fast train between here & Chicago April 1st. Love & kisses from us all. God bless & keep you always. Your devoted wife, *Katherine.*   —Hurrah! You have been gone one week. One less until you are back to us.

Denver, Friday, February 25th, 1898.
My Dearest Husband—   Your letter of Tuesday received this morning. I hope the "tangle" of your business will be less troublesome when this reaches you. And that Mr. T's spirit of the lion will not be so easily transformed to a dove by the presence of moneyed men. How tired you must be of it all… Katherine just brings me a letter for you. The dear little creatures they talk about you often. As I bathed Thayer this morning I wondered if I half appreciated the privilege I have of handling & mothering such a lovely Baby. And you should receive a hundred dollars a day extra for being away from him in the very prime of his Babyhood… I read everything I can find about the *Maine*, and the cause of her destruction is still a mystery. It gives me a most uncomfortable feeling to read of our insufficient coast defenses and even the suggestion of war is terrible enough. [end of letter]

◦ In the news:

THE LOSS OF THE MAINE — No Information Has Been Made Public as to the Cause of the Disaster — Court of Inquiry Makes No Disclosures — Congressmen and Naval Officers in Favor of War if Justified by the Findings of the Court of Inquiry.
—*The New York Times,* February 25, 1898.

Denver, Saturday, February 26th, 1898.
My Darling Husband—   …Your delightful letter of 23rd received this morning. To hear of your success is in a measure compensating and a great happiness to me. Only my pride is such that I wish all the praise given you, which is your due, and I believe all these men know & recognize *who* "is at the helm—" and Mr. Trumbull just talks to comfort himself. We are having lovely weather… Your dear Mother's letter was very sad and she will be lonely indeed without the love & devotion of the Mother.   Later— It really means more to her life than you or I can know. I read all the news about the *Maine*… for it seems to me it would be far better for our Government to give up the *Maine* & two or three other Battle ships, than have any approach of war. I am all for peace & concessions. The three children are popping corn, over a fire on the lot and I can see a popper half full of white corn. Mother's three lots have been a fine playground. I let Katherine drive the pony about two blocks, again & again, with two little girls who play in the orchestra. She came in so delighted. Tomorrow is Sunday & a lonely day without you… Our whole hearts full of love my Darling One—   —Your Devoted Wife, *Katherine*.

Mother's three lots   the three open lots adjoining the property at 933 Penn Ave. in Denver that were owned by Catherine McKie Thayer.

◦ An earache:

Feb. 27th Dear Papa—   Eleanor is screaming with a earache. I have gotten her a cup of tea. Mama is rocking her and sends love and kisses to. Love from *Katherine*.

"My dear Papa I send you a letter. I have an earache & a stiff neck & a headache. from Eleanor" [in her mother's handwriting]

Dear Papa—   I don't know what to say to you but I would like you to come home. from *Eleanor*. [letter is in a child's handwriting]

Denver, February 28th, 1898.
My Darling Husband—   Two letters from you this morning… Eleanor has written you a "funny letter." She says Katherine has an idea you must know everything that is going on. And yesterday, when Eleanor had an earache, went to the library desk and wrote the enclosed. The little girl had several hours of pain & rested through the night, but seems all right today. I kept her in this morning… The news seems less inflammable. What awful calamities by sea… I see Katherine & Henry driving the pony— they can't drive by the Ballens' as the boys there stone the pony— Good Manners. Jack did not come yesterday to dinner. I believe he has gone to Pueblo, at least the office boy said so when he brought my stand-by, *The N. Y. Times*. Thayer is on the bed, crowing & making

the sweetest sounds. I will send their photographs when they come from the Springs. My whole heart goes out to you in longing & constant love… Do write about your work. I am so intensely absorbed & interested in it & I like to know from day to day. Chicks send love & kisses. Your own loving wife, *Katherine.*

In the news:

THE MAINE DISASTER —Information as to Its Cause Has Not Yet Been Received at Washington — No Evidence that the Ship Was Destroyed by Design — Warlike Feeling in Spain Finds Expression in Predictions of Hostilities with This Country — Spaniards Predict War. —*The New York Times,* February 28, 1898.

University Club, New York, March 1st, 1898.
My Darling Ducky Lucky and Henny Penny—   As I write I can almost hear you piping away in your hen-yard, and I think it was very nice for two little animals to write their Papa such sweet letters as I received yesterday. Some of these fine days I am going to give the policemen who watch me the slip, and run out to Colorado to see my chicks, and then there will be a great to-do.

My goodness! —how I wish you could see the beautiful store-windows. I never saw them prettier. There are windows full of the most beautiful silks and satins and all kinds of gay-colored things for spring, and also of the most beautiful scarfs and sashes, stockings and bonnets. Then comes a window full of lovely dolls, another full of soldiers and all kinds of toys. So they go, and if I were to try and tell you about the things I see, I would be writing for a week. You must tell Eleanor that I am going to write next time to her and Thayer, although she has not written to me yet.

Mamma writes that she told you about George Washington on his birthday, and when I get back I shall expect you to tell me lots about him.

I am going to send you a colored picture of the *Battle-ship Maine,* that the Spaniards blew up, and maybe we may have an awful time and war over it. I hope you have felt very great pity for the poor little children of the men who were killed.

I think about you lots and lots of times every day, and I love you better the longer I am away from you.   —Your devoted Papa, *Henry.*

Denver, March 1st, 1898.
My Darling Husband—   The first day of spring is a lovely one, and I hear birds singing. No letter from you today, but the going to the Farm would make your letter a day longer in coming. Eleanor seems quite better of her earache, but a little tired. She keeps asking, "Why Papa don't write something about her ear." As if you would know at once. Thayer is having his morning naps in your room now and seems to enjoy it. He is a very determined little fellow and when he wishes anything, he wishes with all his heart. And he is such a good baby I never feel he ought to cry a minute. There is a certain amount of depression about the first of the month, and bills coming in. Certainly we are living very simply but I do not seem able to cut down the expenses very much, and I wish so much to help you to pay that indebtedness by making our demands less… Driving the pony by themselves seems to be a great delight to the chicks, Katherine & Henry. I discovered the latter stand-

ing on the step of the cart with one foot, and the pony trotting briskly, kind of military maneuver, for he was dressed in his soldier suit. Henry says, tell Papa I have only one more lesson in my first reader, he stands by me now & Katherine holding Thayer. All send you love & kisses with mine. Your Always Devoted Wife, *Katherine*.

March 1, 1898. University Club, Madison Square. New York.
Darling Kate—   No time for a letter today downtown and I am writing to K— & H— now, so you must not expect very much of a letter. My cold is practically cured and I feel very well again… My R.R. matters are progressing slowly but on the whole well. It requires great patience and great control of temper. I am learning valuable lessons in these regards. You must not get too exaggerated an idea of my importance here. Much of my work has to be necessarily quiet and secret and I cannot get full credit for it. Frequently I have to work through another person… Today I had a letter from Mother enclosing letters from the old sea-captain with whom Henry sailed and also from Henry. The old skipper wrote in the most commendatory way of Henry's conduct and behavior and said he was obedient, willing, and industrious. Henry's letter was disgraceful in spelling, composition, and handwriting but was a manly letter. He told of some rather "nasty" weather experiences he had gone through with. In one storm they lost a mast and several boats. I think they will go to Liverpool from San Fran… The weather is very pleasant now. I am afraid we will sooner or later have trouble with Spain but I hope not. Love & kisses without numbers.   —Devotedly *Henry*.

Thursday, Denver, March 2nd, 1898.
My Darling Husband—   Have your letter of Monday today. So thankful your cold is better. Wish you would send me a telegram when this reaches you, telling me if you are really better of your cold… You can be on the lookout for investment for the Albany Bank Stock but do have it in something equally safe in these times of war cries & unsettled conditions— a low rate of interest which is *sure* is much to be desired. Certainly you & I do not wish anything speculative, and have enough non-productive property… Have sent off the letters thanking for the U. P. pass & send photos to you at Hotel today. Always your own Devoted & loving wife, *Katherine*.

∽ In the news:

MYSTERY OF THE MAINE — No Information From the Court of Inquiry as to the Cause of the Disaster — Not Likely to Lead to War.
                              —*The New York Times*, March 2, 1898.

Denver, March 5th, 1898.
My Darling Husband—   Your letter of 2nd received this morning. . .You must do exactly as you think best regarding investments. You know what seems best, only I would say, be sure what money you have as principal be put in something safe. You have worked too hard to take any chances of it being lost. Mother writes me that Mr. Peltz is in the Springs. I quote from her letter— "Mr. Peltz said 'I never saw such delicacy shown by any man, in regard to anything, as shown by Mr. Hobson, in regard to Mr. Jermain's family before

Henry Wise Hobson, in an unidentified newspaper clipping from his mother's desk, shown arguing a case in court. The headline notes that "Union Pacific Counsel Appeals to Justices Hallett and Riner…" Hallett was a close friend of Henry W. Hobson. The articles begins, "Couched in the polished language of an advocate and embellished with protestations of respect for the other side, Attorney Hobson conveyed plainly in…"

& after Mr. Jermain's death. I consider Mr. Hobson the most perfect gentleman I ever met, & you Mrs. Thayer have reason to be proud of such a son.'" Mother replied, "I am very thankful to have such a man as the husband of my daughter." You can imagine Mother enjoying his call, loving you as she does… The Buckleys have a case of measles— Isabelle, but light form, taken today. And I am going to try to protect our children by keeping them away. We all send love & kisses. You ought to make a turn in the stock market these days for your profit… —Your Own Devoted *Katherine.*

March 5, 1898, New York.
Darling Kate—   You will be glad to hear I made a master stroke today and drove home to the extent of making sure that I have been working to accomplish unless some unforeseen obstacle arises. I have been working and pushing, waiting for my opportunity, and today it came. I availed myself of it assuming a good deal of responsibility in forming the issue and succeeded beyond even my own expectations. In a word, I have now gotten all parties so committed that within 2 weeks we should be in a position to go ahead with a clean re-organization… The result to me personally which will please you most is the fact that I have so conducted this matter that I have not only won the respect of my own people but I have strengthened the confidence which the opposing people had in me as a fair, honorable, and honest man. That to me is more than any pecuniary reward which I may receive, and it should be so to my wife as I have no doubt it is. The success does not mean an early return home for many details remain to be worked out and I shall have to stay with these people until everything is cleaned up… I am too tired to write more now and have an execrable pen. I can almost cry, I want to see you so much but I comfort myself with thinking it is all for the best… A thousand kisses for you and the darling chicks.   —Devotedly *Henry.*

Denver, March 7th, 1898.
My Daring Husband—   …It comforts me to know your work is progressing to your satisfaction and really the closing of the Receivership & Reorganization is not to be of long duration. And if you bring your interests to a successful termination we will rejoice and trust you will receive a just reward… Katherine had her turn at earache yesterday, and it was very severe. The Doctor gave her morphine and cocaine in her ear and hot poultices. I am glad to say she is all right today, but tired. Henry has gone off to afternoon school with Paul— some flag ceremonies. The boy was so anxious he could hardly eat his dinner. The Baby is on the bed kicking & talking— he is growing sweeter every day… Eleanor just going out, as lively as a cricket. They all send love & kisses with mine… Katherine cried so for you when she had earache— "Oh I want Papa, I want Papa so badly." God bless you dearest.
—Your Devoted Wife, *Katherine.*

New York, March 7, 1898.
Darling Kate—   Whilst waiting for a conference to go ahead, I will scribble to you. I take advantage of my opportunities for a line to you as they arise… The photographs came this morning and I was perfectly delighted to get them. My heart gave a big jump of joy and especially as they are so good… Kiss them all for looking so beautiful and sweet although I do not like

the idea of having my man-boy holding a doll in his arms. I am truly grateful for them. Goodbye for today and take a heart full of love for yourself and the chicks. The picture of Mother T— is beautiful. —Your devoted husband, *Henry.*

New York, March 8th, 1898.
My Darling Boy Blue—   Such a lovely letter that was which I received yesterday from you, and I write you a letter in answer all to yourself. I am very proud to hear of your driving the pony by yourself and that you drive children to school and back. Remember you must never get scared when you are driving and lose your head. If the pony goes a little fast, just put your feet against the dash-board and pull hard and he will stop soon. I kissed those kisses you sent me and every morning I kiss each of those pictures of you chicks that Mamma sent me. Be a good boy and take care of the things in our room. Tell that little rascal Eleanor that if she bothers our things we will cut her hands right off. You do not know how much I want to see you, and I think I will bring you to New York the next time I come and make an office-boy of you.
    Give many kisses to Katherine, Eleanor, and Thayer, and a lot of love to Mamma.   —Your devoted Papa, *Henry W. Hobson.*

Denver, Wednesday, March 9th, 1898.
My Darling Husband—   No letter today but two yesterday… When Mary came in this morning she found all of us in my bed and said, "How happy Mr. Hobson would feel if he could see that bed." Henry replied, "We could make room for Papa too." He always thinks of you. The day is lovely and I hope by tomorrow I can go out as my cold is better. I think of you and dream of you my Dearest one and pray you may be kept in peace and safety and prosperous in all which you undertake. Love & kisses from all your loving ones.   —Your own Devoted Wife, *Katherine.*

Denver, Friday, March 11th, 1898.
My Darling Husband—   Your letter of 8th just here. Everything encouraging as to your business is a joy to me. I think you are very wise to keep out of Wall St. To borrow for speculation, with the chances of stocks dropping, would be an awful calamity to us just as you are creeping out from indebtedness. And the worry it would give you… Take every care of yourself and not get another cold… God bless & keep you my Dearest one. Love & kisses from us all, Your devoted Wife, *Katherine.*

March 10, 1898, New York.
Darling Kate—   Congratulate me upon closing day— all references to settle up all our U.P. controversies and all that now remains is to get in the Master's Report and an order confirming it. I have really done some fine work and feel proud of it. I had a very amusing episode with Parker. He came all the way from Denver to testify, brought a trunk full of papers and then found that he had left all the necessary papers in Denver and he could not turn a wheel. You will be amused when I tell you how I extricated him from his dilemma and made it appear he was a splendid witness. He was wild this morning and perspiration rolled off of him as he dashed wildly through his papers to find what he

did not have. It was a great blow to his vanity, and if I had not helped him out I think he would have resigned his position. I am sorry to say my chances of getting to Denver next week have gone… I am so distressed about darling little Katherine's ear and when I hear of their suffering I feel like crying. Tell her I am going to try and write her a nice letter tomorrow and tell her all about the splendid show I went to see last night. I wish the children could see it— except the last act. That was a very pretty woman (French) who went up a trapeze completely dressed and undressed upon the trapeze. It was very improper and I am afraid you would have been awfully shocked but it was one of the cleverest bits of work I ever saw. The woman had on flesh colored tights, but as she took off dress, underskirts, shoes, stockings, garters, and chemise, it looked, for all the world, like a woman getting down to naked flesh. When she finally finished, she had on a very pretty blue silk bodice and trunks and performed beautifully upon the trapeze… Dearest love & kisses to all. I shall hope to spend Sunday with Ada. Goodbye sweetheart mine—   Devotedly *Henry*.

New York, March 11th, 1898.
My Darling little Sweetheart—   Papa was so distressed the other day to hear about your ear, and when I read about your crying for me I almost cried, too, for you. I know it is all right now and that is a great comfort. I went to the theatre the other night and saw such an amusing show. If you were here I would let you go to the matinee. There were a lot of cockatoos that were so smart they could do almost anything but talk, and they chattered enough to make up for not talking. There were two or three old fellows who were evidently very jealous of each other, and every time the show-woman's back was turned they would have a free fight. The show-woman was a very pretty Italian girl, dressed in pink. Then there were six sisters, all dressed in silk of the colors of the rainbow. They had on long skirts and looked as though they were dressed for a ball. They did some wonderful things and performed more acrobatic feats than I ever saw women perform before. All the time I thought

Catherine McKie Thayer and her four grandchildren, Eleanor & Katherine Hobson, Henry Hobson (standing) and Francis Thayer Hobson in her arms.

that if you were watching them you would be taking notes and saying you would learn to do their tricks. There were two such handsome young fellows who did splendidly upon the trapeze, rings, etc., and some of their acts were very startling. Then there were two funny clowns with a real donkey right on the stage. He was about as big as Jean and he was the "out-kickingest" donkey you ever saw. He kept everybody roaring with his funny kicking, and sometimes he would pretty nearly split the clowns open, he would throw them so hard. You must remind me to tell you chicks all about this donkey. There was a man in evening suit and silk hat who did some very remarkable things upon a wire rope. It was wonderful. There were lots of other things about which I have not time to write, but tell Mamma there was a woman with a splendid contralto voice, who sang a song about the *Maine* which set everybody to cheering tremendously.

Tell Mamma I send her a note from Aunt Nellie, which I have answered. I do not see very much to write you children about, for I am very busy all the time. I am going home just as soon as possible, and you chicks must not stop loving me very hard. Talk to Thayer about me lots, so he will not forget me. Good-by, my darling little one, and give lots of love and kisses to Mamma and the other chicks. —Your devoted Papa, *Henry*.

New York, March 12, 1898.
My Darling little Peek-a-boo— How nice it was to write me that lovely little letter on Bunny-rabbit paper and tell me how much you want to see me. Why that was writing me *more* than if you had told me lots and lots of other things. Then, too, how much you have improved in your writing. I did not know you could make such nice letters, and you have been learning very fast since I came away. Maybe you will be able to read to me when I get back. Do you know I was going out to Stamford to see Thayer to-day and talk with him about you, but Aunt Ada wrote me that her house was full and if I went I would have to sleep with the children. Now I think Thayer is a nice boy for your sweetheart, but I do not want to sleep with him, and so I did not go to Stamford. Do you sleep in my room now? I wonder where you all are every morning, and I expect I guess right when I guess you are in Mamma's bed. Give a great deal of love to all our family. —Your devoted Papa, *Henry*.

Aunt Ada Henry Hobson refers to Ada Addison, his wife's cousin, as "Aunt Ada" when he writes to his family in Denver.

Union League Club, New York, March 13th, 1898.
Darling Henny Penny— You owe me a letter, but I am going to have you owe me two, because I want to tell you how much I love you and think of you. This morning, just as I was going to church, I saw some children in the hotel who made me think so longingly of my chicks, and I did want so much to have you with me. But you must stay at home when I am away and learn to take care of Mamma, for that is what my man-child is to do all his life. It is so warm that, if my chicks were here, we could all go the Park and have a play. There are lots of children out to-day.

Love and Kisses to mamma and the other chicks. —Your devoted Papa, *Henry*.

Denver, March 13th, 1898.
My Darling Henry— This is a windy day… Three children gone to Sunday School. Spring is coming for I see blue birds from my window… The

three (Parker) children came yesterday, just as I had the Baby undressed for his bath. I told Mary to ask them to come up, "to see the Baby in his bath" & Eleanor came back & said the Parkers were not coming in the house. After, when I said to Annie, "I am sorry you could not come in to see the Baby bathed," she replied, "Mother would not let us because he is a boy." I think it is immoral to suggest any idea of that kind in connection with anything as pure & innocent as a Baby. I am trying to be amused over it, but don't you tell Mr. Parker. I suppose they will cover up the objectionable features of the Christ child's form. You see I am roused on the subject. Jack is in New Mexico, so we missed him today… —We all send you Darling one our hearts full of love & kisses. Your own Devoted wife, *Katherine.*

March 13, 1898, Union League Club, New York.
Darling Kate—   Church going is a difficult proposition for me in N.Y. This morning I started out not because I wished to go very much for I would have preferred loafing a bit around the hotel. I thought you would be pleased however and so on your account I put the "loaf" aside. I first tried Grace— The entrances were crowded out to the front door and the ushers were calmly letting the people stand, until 11:30 I suppose or perhaps until Church should be over. I could not stand that so I struck out for Trinity. I got to the church about 11:15 and found it only about 2/3 full but the confounded usher, instead of putting me in a pew, insisted upon my taking a seat upon a very uncomfortable bench in the center aisle and right in the line of draught. I do not believe I caught cold but it was pure chance whether I would or not, but I was very uncomfortable. They have no decent Church hospitality in N.Y.— Still I went to Church and you can take it as a tribute to you. The sermon was poor, but the text was good— "This is a true saying etc. that Christ came upon Earth to save sinners"— It was treated in a very conventional & commonplace way but I could not but think how, right at the entrance of that maelstrom of greed, avarice, fraud, robbery, & ignoble aspirations, Wall Street, the text could have been made the starting point for a fine discourse upon higher, nobler, sweeter objects and aspirations, could have been given as a motive to some men in the congregation for making their lives tend to some better purpose than mere money making. Ah Kate I am so tired of it all— I mean the struggle for money which I see about me every day and what makes me the sadder is that I am in it and engaged in the fight. But as God is my witness I am making the struggle not from love of money but from a sense of duty to those I love and who are dependent upon me to provide for— wife, children, Mother— and also to gain a position where I can devote my energies to better things and cultivate higher aims and ambitions. With me, the question is not when I have enough to satisfy my greed but when I have enough to entitle me honestly and conscientiously to retire from the fight for money. Not from life's work or battle, for I shall never retire from that whilst I live… I want to influence men by character, intellect, superior accomplishments. That is the career I long to enter upon or at least long to try and then abide the result. If I fail it will be from lack of capacity not from lack of spirit. I am beginning to be very impatient sweetheart to rejoin you and my children and I am very depressed at times… Love & kisses Sweetheart mine. You are all the world to me.   —Devotedly *Henry.*

March 14th, 1898.
My Dear Papa—   I know how to dress myself and bathe myself and comb my hair. I could go to New York with you now. If I did go I have to take *New Yorky* with me. I want a wheel now. Your letter was very nice… I hope you will come home soon. Henry and Eleanor are writing to you. All my dolls send you their love. Today is very windy but we had a beautiful weather before that. Love and kisses from all. From *Katherine*.

Monday, Denver, March 14th, 1898.
My Darling Husband—   Two letters from you this morning… Honorable success is your reward for all the devotion you have given your work. How funny for Mr. Parker to leave his important papers— if a woman had done it, everyone would say, "how exactly like a woman." I am glad you could pull him out of the mire. Eleanor has brought me a letter to send you— of course she has help, but the sentiments are her own. You will recognize it… Will you let me know as soon as you have any idea as to your movements, the probable dates of your return, if not before April 10th or 15th. I wish to go to the Springs when this months lessons are over and have a change & rest… Love & kisses from us all. Your own Devoted wife, *Katherine*.

March 14, 1898. The Union Pacific System — Office of the Receivers
Darling Kate—   We have just signed final papers in our Gulf settlement with U.P. and are sending off papers to Judge Sanborn for approval. If he approves, that chapter will be closed, the most complicated and tangled of all we have had to wade through. All our other maters are in process of adjustment and will be in time… The news has just come that we have bought two battle ships abroad which makes I think for peace. The stronger we become and the better prepared for war, the less probability of war or if we have war, the shorter it will be… Goodbye. Love for all— Devotedly *Henry*.

Denver, March 15th, 1898.
My Darling Husband—   Your letter of Saturday just here. I could cry with disgust when I read how Henderson tangled & upset everyone and delayed you. I hope by Monday everything went smoothly… Long letter from your Mother, which I will answer. She seems to have some "hidden sorrow" to judge from the tone of her letter. I wonder if Rosa Brooks could have gotten young Cannon into trouble. I always thought harboring such a known, bad woman, was very dangerous to the morals of those two boys. Katherine delighted with your letter & all the lovely things you told her of the play. We talk of you so much my darling one. Your own Devoted & Loving Wife, Katherine. —When we say to Thayer, "Do you wish to see Papa" and say "Papa, Papa," he always smiles, never fails. I want to be a part of you my Darling one… I live with you in your work & trust you may have no disappointments. Mr. Hagerman seems always to be getting into a hole & needing you to extricate him— and I am glad you can. Here the darlings come with their letters. Henry & K— so anxious to be writing a letter each week to Papa. And all so anxious to go to New York the next time you go. Katherine's ear is quite better… how soon she will be nine years old. Thayer is my greatest comfort. When I feel all full of cry & loneliness for you I cuddle him up close to me….
[end of letter, page missing]

March 15, 1898.

Darling Kate—   Another beautiful day! Really New York is doing itself proud in the matter of weather. Your letter, another dear one, came today and I take great comfort in the regularity with which the letters come… I am beginning to see my way clear at least to cleaning up my debts. That will indeed be a God-send. I told Parker what you said about the Wolfe Hall matter… Of course I shall not tell him what you wrote about the baby, but I agree fully with your views, and I feel some indignation mixed with a great deal of amusement. What [illegible] and nonsense and it all arises from the false standards these people have. I wonder if Mrs. Parker does feel that our little girls are not as pure minded and as chaste in thought as her girls because they see their little baby brother in the bath. It is the same kind of sentiment which makes fools cover up nude statues. However the Parker children are sweet little companions for our children and I suppose we will have to put up with Mrs. P's peculiarities. The thing that makes me indignant is the suggestion to *our* children that there is anything improper in their seeing a boy baby naked… Goodbye sweetheart. It is such a comfort to me that you are so pure minded and lead such a pure life. Our children cannot but be chaste with you as their Mother. Love & kisses.   —Devotedly *Henry*.

Denver, March 16th, 1898.

My Darling Husband—   Your long interesting letter of Sunday came this morning. I do appreciate your going to church, and I am sure we are united in the wish to recognize the day… You are always so considerate of my wishes Darling. Your letters to Henry & Eleanor have come today. I just read Henry's to him. I wish you could have seen the three about me— listening, their faces beaming. Henry, Eleanor, Thayer, and I started for a drive but the wind came up, and we had to return home. We drove to Mrs. Trumbull's and asked her to let me know if I could do anything to help her for her reception which comes off tomorrow. I go to pour chocolate at four o'clock until six. I could not go to church too & leave Thayer dinnerless. I wrote your Mother a long letter last evening & told her all the pleasant things I could think of about the children. Dear soul I think she feels Aunt Mary's loss terribly and I feel great sympathy for her. Mother writes me Jack took dinner with her last Sunday on his way South. Could you buy me a few little things in New York if I send you minute details? The spring is coming on and I feel so helpless in buying here… I am sending your Mother a photograph of children. Everything is going on well here— except Fawny Paws who is having her ear treated at the Doctors… Love & Kisses from all. Your own Devoted Wife, *Katherine*.

Denver, March 17th, 1898.

My Darling Husband—   It seems as if visitors had a special spite against me— they will come just as I sit down to write you & today Mrs. Prince, who lives so far out of town. I felt I must see her. Especially as she has "expectations" for April. She had been at the Trumbull's at lunch & someone had spoken to her as having a Baby in the "Autumn of life—" which made her indignant. She is a sweet, enthusiastic, kind woman and Miss Miller is to take care of her. And speaking of Babies, the Jackson's have another, a girl, born yesterday & named Margaret. How proud & thankful Mr. Jackson is of his wife & children.

Well the festivities waged at the Trumbulls & I poured chocolate for two hours— Mrs. Kountze, coffee. She spent the day there, or from twelve & retired upstairs to rest for an hour between times. I suppose they will show "the bed Mrs. Kountze rested on" later on in life. Mrs. Trumbull had decorated the house very profusely— vines all over the parlor walls & green & white shamrocks in peppermints to honor St. Patrick. Mrs. Trumbull was very well dressed & a splendid crescent of diamonds! Mrs. H— of Chicago (& the head of the Woman's Clubs in America) should begin again & be taught a lesson in modesty. Her square cut dress was so low that it was disgusting. I never saw anything more vulgar. Mrs. Trumbull's sister was dressed in a lady-like way. I think Mrs. MacBeth was the best dressed & finest looking woman there. Mrs. I— and Mrs. Wallace seemed to be running everything and there was a fortune-teller!!— before whom people kneeled or knelt (I read kneeled is preferred) & had their fortunes told. But as I listened to Mrs. Cherry being told she was musical, I had no tact. Where Mrs. Cherry has never been able to hum a tune, I turned away & replied, when asked to try my luck, that my fortune was told. By the way, tell Mr. Trumbull his wife's day was a success, in every way (from their standpoint it was) and he sent her a very lurid telegram which she showed me. It was so business like in tone. Now you have certainly had nonsense enough to rest your mind. Who do you suppose said, "How do you do sweetheart" to me? Mrs. Thatcher— it really pleased me for she says so little, as a rule, and is one of the entirely proper people. The Van Schaacks sent you an invitation to meet Judge & Mrs. Gabbert & the members of the Denver Bar Association— and I am declining for you— "Mr. Hobson's absence from the city prevents etc." You should have seen that little Mrs. Skinner at the reception, covered with gilt jewelry and talking of Mary Kountze & Mary won't go to her house. I had fun all by myself, to see Mrs. Skinner's attack on the Kountze family. Mrs. K— so polite & distant… Mrs. Trumbull said Mr. Trumbull wrote "Mr. Hobson was the best man in the world" & I never disputed it. You should have been around to hear Mrs. H— enlarging to Mrs. Trumbull & to me on the excessive vulgarity of the Waldorf Astoria— and I had too much sympathy for Mrs. T— to say, as I wished to, "Why that is where our husbands are stopping."

Mary Lyons knows very little about you since you have matured & a man who learns to control himself can be the best & most able peace-maker & understand how to be tactful & an able conciliator. The chicks are asleep & I am writing in my room… I shall not miss a day in sending a letter, only one since you left & that on ear-ache Sunday. Four weeks tonight since you left me & each day brings us a day nearer each other Dearest One. The children are loving & longing for you with me.   Your own Devoted Wife, *Katherine.*

March 17, 1898, New York.
Darling Kate—   Congratulations are in order for last night we had a telegram from Judge Sanborn that he had signed orders in our settlement matter, and it is now an accomplished fact. This has been the most troublesome and delicate matter we have had to handle and our people are very much delighted with its successful outcome and so am I… I shall try to go to see Ada Saturday but shall probably have to go to Boston Sunday night. Love & kisses to the darlings.   —Devotedly *Henry.*

The Waldorf, New York City.

Denver, Friday, March 18th, 1898.
My Darling Husband—   Your letter of 15th received this morning. I am glad everything goes well with your business & that your cold is better. There is nothing new to write you after my volume of last night and we expect to go to the Springs for Sunday… The children send you "heaps & piles" of love. Mr. Trumbull's attitude towards the lawyers always provokes me but life is too short to let it be more than amusing. How I wish for you. Dearest Love & kisses form us all. Your own Devoted Wife, *Katherine.*

March 18, 1898.
Darling Kate—   I can only send a line— Two sweet letters from you today. I am so pressed & harassed today not by reason of any real troubles but because of the "cussedness" of people I can't turn loose upon. Mr. Hagerman is in another snarl. I was working for him last night, all this morning and will be all tonight. He will not do what I advise. I gave him some plain talk this morning. I will try to write a nice letter tomorrow. I did enjoy so immensely the 3 letters from the chicks. Bless their darling little hearts. —Devotedly *Henry.*

Colorado Springs, March 19th, 1898.
My Darling Husband—   This is a lovely day, and we had a safe trip on the Gulf down here— though of course Eleanor got sick on the curves as usual… Mother seems quite well and so glad to see us all— five weeks today since she went home & she thinks the Baby has grown sweeter & prettier if possible… One of Mrs. Trumbull's guests came on the train, a Mrs. Hatch from Dallas. We had a pleasant chat together and says Mrs. Coke is one of the most beautiful women in Dallas and everything so highly of Henry Coke… The chicks send much love & many kisses with mine to you. Always your own Devoted Wife, *Katherine.*

March 19, 1898, New York.
Darling Kate—   Today I thought I would surely get time to write to you in a leisurely manner, but I have been kept here so late by Mr. Hagerman's work that I must write hurriedly if I am to get out to Ada's for dinner as I promised… I hope to be home before April 1st but I cannot tell certainly. I will of course wire you as soon as I know. I may go at any time after next Wednesday. I am so glad dear little Thayer is such a comfort to you and I feel he will be to both of us in after life. However, we have that idea about all of our children. I shall try to write to the chicks soon… What would you think of coming on in April, staying here for a while and then going to the Farm? I may have to be East a great deal during May & June. Don't worry about Mother. There is nothing in that suggestion you made I think. The trouble is she has gotten tired of her jobs of caring for the children and Grandma, has gotten into debt, has become absorbed with the idea of working out some "career" for Henry, and has some wild ideas of what she is going to do. I have been having a most hysterical kind of correspondence with her ever since I have been East (another pleasant pastime of my trip) and am slowly drawing out the facts. I don't care what her plans are as she will probably in the end do as I wish, but her indebtedness is what worries me. I have absolutely and positively refused to advance her a dollar until she makes a full and frank disclosure and she,

swearing she will never do so, is gradually doing it. Of course I am going to help the old woman and straighten her up, but I will not until she tells me all and then I will try and do so in a way to guard against a re-occurrence of the trouble. I fear that may be impossible, for improvidence and capacity to get into debt run in our veins. She says she has been foolish and erred (probably speculated) but I do not reproach her very much for that, for I too have often been foolish in such matters. What I blame her for is her concealing the matter from me… I have written [a six page letter] until I have cut my time very short for getting to Ada's. I am glad to go out there and have a quiet day. I have, I fear, written a very ill natured letter but if you felt as cross as I do you could as least excuse it. Love & kisses to the darlings. Of course I always include Mother T— in sending love.   —Devotedly *Henry*.

Colorado Springs, March 21st, 1898.
My Darling Husband—   Your letter telling of your possible home-coming after the 23rd has delighted us very much, and I trust we may soon hear it is a fact. Then you will have been gone nearly six weeks. I have a letter from Florence Page— she says Tom is having many compliments for his novel… How splendid to see a prospect of your feeling relieved regarding your debts. I believe I am as much relieved, at the prospect, as you, for I hate to feel you burdened and pressed my Dearest one… Thayer is sitting in his little chair by me as I write, playing with his rattle & trying to choke himself. I think you will think him very sweet & bright & very good looking. There seems to be but one opinion on that subject. All send best & tenderest love to Papa. We all long to see you. Always your devoted & loving wife, *Katherine*.

Colorado Spring, March 22nd, 1898.
My Darling Husband—   Two letters today, the announcement that Judge Sanborn signed the papers is splendid and I feel light-hearted. It is only a very big man mentally who could stand Trumbull's *stealing* your ideas & advancing them as his own. Sometime you can show him up and make him see what he is stealing— it is a kind of theft of intellect I can scarcely endure. The next time you go away I am going to do as Mrs. Parker does, pin notes on your clothes, only I can not rise to poetry. How funny that was, but I think Parker needs such a stimulant… Aunt Ada made Thayer two lovely bathe robes. She says he is her dear Baby— his name means so much to her. Maybe you saw them all Sunday. Mother sends you her tenderest love, & my whole heart full of love & longing go out to you my Dearest one. Always your devoted wife, *Katherine*.

March 22, 1898, New York.
Darling Kate—   This is a wet weeping day but I have kept well wrapped up & worn overshoes. If nothing new comes up and I have good luck I will start for home by tonight week… I had such a [illegible] manly letter today from Henry Hobson which I will return to you as soon as I get it back from Mother to whom I wish to send it. I will also send you my reply. I enclose a slip which may interest you. I am convinced we will have War and that is the opinion which is growing here even amongst the most conservative men… I must go say goodbye as it is nearly 6 o'clk. Love & Kisses to the darlings.
—Devotedly *Henry*.

Henry W. Hobson, the son of John Cannon Hobson, was working as a cabin boy aboard the Kenilworth *and wrote this to his uncle.*

◦ A nephew goes to sea:

San Francisco Cal
March 14, 1898
Dear Uncle—   I received your kind letter today. I had written to you before, intending to send it inclosed in a letter to Grandma to send you as I did not know your address, but somehow failed to put it in. I am glad to hear I have another little cousin. I must refuse your generous offer to send me money. I am sixteen; and it is high-time some of the burden was taken off of you. I went on this trip with the intention of making my own way after this. I did not realize until now how kind and generous you are, and how ungrateful I have been. The help you will be so kind to give me after this will be considered a loan. It would be no use in my trying to fit myself for some profession, I have lost too much valuble [sic] time to make up. My only course is to go to a navigation school and work hard for promotion. I have a raise of five dollars on my wages, and hope to save a little money. I hope George and Jennings will fulfill your hopes and pay you as much as is in their power by studying hard and doing honor to Father's memory and his name. I have thrown away opportunities that can never be recovered. I am glad to hear brother is getting on finely on the ranch. I have written to him twice but have received no answers. Give my best love to my Aunt Katherine and my little cousins, and take a heart full of love and gratitude for yourself. Your affectionate nephew, *Henry W. Hobson.*

March 22nd, 1898.
My dear Henry—   I was very much pleased to get your letter of March 14th. It is in the right spirit and I am glad to see that you have started out with a determination to make your own way. If you keep up that spirit and maintain a high standard of honesty and integrity, you will succeed. One thing you can rest assured, that as long as you strive earnestly and faithfully to do honor to your name and to your father, you will have a sympathizer and backer in me. I will cheerfully help you in any way possible to enable you to get a good start in life, and if you need any money I am willing to let you have it on the terms you mention as a loan. If, after your trip is finished you are still determined to follow the seas as a calling, we will talk about the navigation school, etc. My advice to you is, to stay with your ship like a man until she comes back to New York. I have not heard from Cannon for some time. I have only a moment to write and dictate an answer because I want you to get it before you sail. Remember one thing, my boy, and that is that you can be a gentleman and an honest man under all conditions and circumstances of life, and that is what your father would have wished you to be. Hoping that you have a good voyage, I am, Your affectionate uncle, *H.W.H.*

Colorado Springs, March 23rd, 1898.
My Darling Henry—   Your letter of last Saturday received today. I am so sorry dearest for all your worries on Mr. Hagerman's account— and try and look at the end where you will receive the money compensation which will help you to rid yourself of debt. I do not wonder your temper is sorely tried, and that you are worn out, but you can extricate the old man & do for him what no one else can at present, and it is for your personal advantage to

do all you can and keep straightening out matters. I know in his heart Mr. H— feels you are a great comfort & stay to him… Dearest I think it is better you should realize that your Mother may be quite deeply in debt. You know for several years she has asked for large sums of money at one time for ten thousand dollars, and later two thousand. And when you refused those sums asked for a smaller sum, and that I believe she applied to interest on debt. I feel you are right in saying that until you have an entirely frank statement you will not advance any money. Why if this were to continue, you will be in debt to a very large extent, & the most of it to the people who lend your Mother money. I know you will be responsible and will pay— and if you clear up the present indebtedness how can you be sure it will not be repeated, as it has been before. When I think of the income your Mother has, of your monthly allowance to the children & Grandma's fund, all coming from you, and see you working as you do, I think your Mother should strive to make your burdens less & not heavier as she does. Certainly I never saw a Mother who, adores a son, from every standpoint, more devoted love than your Mother owes you— and how does she show it? Well there are some things one can not understand in this world and this is one of them. I am willing and anxious to relieve you in every way possible and make our expenses as little as possible, and in doing this I have a right to ask you to insist that your Mother should not go into any speculations & borrow money— the debts to hang over our heads. You dearest, most precious one, I wish I could put my arms around you & tell you how deeply I feel everything which troubles & annoys you… Love & many kisses my Darling One. God bless & keep you safely. You are all in all to me. Your Devoted Wife, *Katherine*.

March 23, 1898, New York.
Darling Kate—   Here is another emergency letter to be written whilst waiting for some gentlemen. It is the same old story of wait wait wait… By the way, did I write you that Uncle J— [John S. Wise] has moved into his new offices? He has, and they are palatial as compared with his old ones and he is fixing them up… He has moved in, somewhat as we moved into our house, and there is now a combination of carpenters shop, paint shop, upholstering and law business… One of the amusing things is that upon the door leading into my room which connects with Uncle J's room by a hall, he has had painted "Mr. Hobson." That in a N. Y. law office means that I am a clerk. I have laughed at Uncle J— a good deal about it and told him he was a great fellow to work me first for the office and then pass me off on the public as a clerk. I don't care however and sometime I will have it taken off. It is still cloudy and threatening though not actually raining… I will keep the letter open until I get your letter today.

   Later— Here I was stopped and had a splendid meeting with the U.P. people— settled the only outstanding Gulf controversy on a very satisfactory basis… I must close for my time is short. Love & kisses to the darling chicks. Devotedly *Henry*.

Colorado Springs, March 24th, 1898.
My Darling Husband—   This is a perfect day… We are all in a state of expectancy wondering what will be outcome of affairs in Washington, during the next few days. Your older son has been to the barber's, taken there &

left with money to pay & come up *alone*. He was very proud to be trusted to "come up like Papa" and said, "Now remember not to send for me." Clinton has just been to see us. She thinks the Baby "almost grown, not a baby at all" and Henry, "so like Mr. Hobson." Of course Katherine rode Clinton's wheel all the time, and has just been in to tell me how lovely it was… I hope for a line from you tomorrow written in Stamford. Eleanor sits in my lap, and is very anxious to hear about Thayer. He wrote her a sweet letter the other day. There is nothing especial to write of. Love & many kisses always to you our dearest one. How gladly we shall welcome you home. Take every care of your dearest self for my sake.   —Always your devoted *Katherine*.

Colorado Springs, March 25th, 1898.
My Darling Husband—   Two dear loving letters from you today which have been such a comfort. I am glad you had a little time at Stamford but hardly think it was not what one would call restful. You will always have a warm welcome from Ada & Morris. You must never think or speak of your not being considerate of me in any way. No woman ever had a more loving devoted husband than I have, and I thank God every day of my life for my numberless blessings. The children have just been to the Creek to pick flowers— all three stand by me as I write and send you love & kisses. We hope you will be with us by April 1st…I am going to hire a bicycle for them to enjoy tomorrow… Mother sends love & kisses & love from Your Devoted Wife, *Katherine*.

March 27, 1898, New York.
Darling Kate—   Today is a dreary one, for not only is the rain pouring on the outside but I have a headache and feel very depressed and blue— There is nothing especially the matter— only a little let-down after a hard week's work and depression over my long continued absence from you and the chicks. I am staying quietly in my room and trying to rest, for I need it… Everybody here is in a state of suspense over the Spanish troubles. The "classes" of N.Y. are quaking over their dollars and the "masses" are babbling over with enthusiasm. I greatly admire McKinley's course and especially the tact and real strength with which he has managed Congress, though I suspect that whilst the tact is his, the strength has been supplied by his advisers. Poor old General Dodge is very much worked up over the matter and seems determined that there shall be no war in any event. I fear the old man is pretty well loaded up with speculative overtures and that the War (if it should come) would mean serious financial troubles for him. There is no real cause for any business depression but it will inevitably come owing to the timidity of people of business. I am counting upon spending next Sunday with you and the chicks, but I am almost afraid to think of it as it will be just my luck to be detained. Still I get much pleasure out of the anticipation… I cannot write more for my eyes are hurting. Goodbye my dear sweetheart. My whole heart is yours.
—Devotedly *Henry*.

The Waldorf-Astoria. New York, March 27th, 1898.
My Darling little Chicks:
Papa was so much pleased with your three little letters that he read them over and over again and laughed with joy every time he read them. Now you see

how much good your letters have done me way off here in this wilderness of work and business. Some of these days you will understand how one can be in a wilderness even amongst so many people and in such a big city as New York. Mamma has told you, I expect, about going up to see all the Addison children last week. Monday was Thayer's birthday and I thought to myself, "Eleanor certainly wants me to send something to her beau," so I got Uncle Tom's book that you have enjoyed so much. It is that one about the two little Confederate boys. Then I learned that next Tuesday would be Julia's birthday, and so on yesterday, thinking Katherine would like to have me send her little chum something, I selected three beautiful little silk handkerchiefs for Julia. Now I thought, there is dear little Medora, who has no birthday at hand and who is Henny Penny's "best girl," and I know he will not like to have her feel lonesome and not get anything, so I just picked out three silk handkerchiefs for her, just as pretty as Julia's. So you see I have been looking after your love affairs as well as my business.

This will probably be the last time I shall write to you before I go home to see you, and you can all be guessing whether I got "A little time" for my chicks before leaving New York. Henny Penny knows about our confidential talk on that subject. Papa sends you a big heartful of love and a basketful of kisses.
—Devotedly, *Papa*.

Colorado Springs, March 28th, 1898.
My Darling Husband—   Your letter which came yesterday gives me hope you may be starting home by tomorrow night. Still, as it is not certain and you will be glad to get a line before you leave saying we are all well and send you our entire love & many kisses… It will be such a joy to see you home again. Always Your Own Loving Wife, *Katherine*.

March 28, 1898, New York.
Darling Kate—   Two letters from you today and both from Colo Springs. I am very busy and do not know just when I will be anything else… It looks less likely that we will have war. The President's message is admirable and White winged Peace seems to hover over the land. Tell Henny Penny I am very proud to hear of his going to the barber's alone and that I shall be expecting him to do all kinds of things alone after this. Any boy who is old enough to be at a barber-shop alone can travel without a nurse. I have not had a line from Mother for ten days or in response to my demand for a statement from her. I do not know just how this matter will work out but I hope for the best. I wish I could feel differently about her but I do resent her constant demands upon me as being inconsiderate and unjust. It is one of the troubles however which I have to bear… Love & kisses for all including dear Mother T. I send my letter to Denver as I suppose you are back.   —Devotedly *Henry*.

Colorado Springs, March 29th, 1898.
My Darling Henry—   Three letters from you this morning and I am so thankful for all the good news they bring— First always that you are well & having success in your affairs. Indeed you do well to tell me all the complimentary things said of you. To have men appreciate your talent and attainments is the greatest satisfaction to me who loves you so devotedly. "*Mr. Hobson*" on your door! That is a blow. I should have thought you might have

been consulted. It is good deal like the lame horse and "Di" and many other experiences with Uncle Johnnie. You need not worry about Mary Lyons. Aunt Mary and her family have had the larger part of your Grandfather's property— and after spending it, Mary must turn to you— for whom the family never held out a helping hand when you were a student & working to finish your education. And then when you were so poor in Richmond & a few hundred dollars would have meant so much and now let them care for themselves. You have enough burden as it is & you will do well to think more of yourself. Mr. Trumbull I know appreciates you, but I am jealous of his taking any of the results of your efforts & calling them his own instead of saying & writing, "Mr. Hobson, our council [sic], advises." I feel *so so* keenly in everything which touches you… We all send our tenderest love & many kisses to you. Oh, how glad we will be to have you home again… Always your own Devoted Wife, *Katherine*.

From the letters it appears that Henry Hobson was able to return to Denver for a very brief visit. The next letters start with him leaving Denver on April 15, 1898.

April 1, 1898, New York.
Darling Kate—   This is April Fools day and I hope that it will not be for me, for I hope tonight to close up my matters in such shape that I can leave for home tomorrow night, arriving on Tuesday morning. The War clouds are hanging very low and the alarms are almost ringing. I am glad matters are coming to an acute state, for this suspense is very trying to the country. I feel sure that with all its ills admitted, the war if it does come, will result in great good to the country in many ways. Above all it will nationalize the country more and that is my great hobby in politics. I have been quite excited all the afternoon over the prospects of getting home and I can hardly contain myself… Poor old Mother. I received a "scorcher" from her today, very hysterical and very defiant. I want to help the old woman & pay her debts and propose to do so but I am determined if possible to have a full disclosure of her debts once (and) for all. I have paid her out (as I thought) too often and she does not seem to appreciate that my work earnings mean provision for her under all circumstances & provision for you and my chicks. I shall write her a gentle affectionate letter but I will be firm… I am very very happy at the prospect of starting Westward tomorrow and am so afraid something will prevent. I wired you this morning but have gotten no answer. I will wire you tomorrow, but the fact is I don't know where you are. Love & kisses to the darlings.   —Devotedly *Henry*.

∼ In the news:

WHITE HOUSE WAR COUNCIL — Naval Experts Discuss with Cabinet Officers the Ways of Fighting Spain — Aggressive Operations for the Army and Navy Talked over — Both Departments Fully Prepared to Strike Decisive Blows — Naval Officers Impatient. — DIPLOMACY AT AN END — The President and His Cabinet to Submit the Controversy with Spain to Congress — The Issue Regarded as Made Up — Both Governments Convinced that Nothing Can Be Accomplished by Continuing Negotiations.
     —*The New York Times*, April 2, 1898.

Denver, April 10th, 1898.
My Dearest Henry—   All day I have wondered if you are better… Henry had a croupy attack last night & evidently a combination of smoke, fire &

water & [illegible] — I am keeping him in my bed today and he is lively & will be all right tomorrow. Eleanor cried for you as if her heart would break. I had to take her in my arms & we all used our powers to divert her. Mother went down to the Trust Co. on her way to Station & Mr. Gibson showed her the Safety Deposit. There were some army officers there putting away their treasures prior to going to war!— which seems sure now… I did hate to have you go off so soon again— it seems like a dream you being here. If you can accomplish all you wish to do there will be compensation. Love & kisses from us all to you our dearest one. Henry printed the enclosed. [enclosure missing] Your own loving wife, *Katherine*.

Denver-Chicago Special, April 16, 1898.
Darling Kate—   Something unfriendly certainly got into my inner parts yesterday for I was completely knocked out. I was quite sick after leaving Denver and finally had to go to bed, but did not succeed in getting to sleep until very late— 2 o'clk perhaps… I feel very sluggish and dull now but trust I will be all right by tomorrow. I can't imagine what the trouble is as I have been very careful about my eating. I always leave something behind. This time it is my slippers. I wish you would do them up in a package together with two sets of pajamas and send to me at the Astoria… It was oppressively warm last night until after midnight and I longed for cooler night garments. Today is a beautiful sunny day but quite warm… You do not know how disconsolate I felt yesterday at having to start off on this trip… I see by the papers this morning that the orders have been issued for mobilizing the troops in the East or rather for gathering them along the Atlantic sea-coast… Love & kisses for the darlings. Devotedly *Henry*.

Lake Shore Train, April 17, 1898.
Darling Kate—   Gradually I am approaching New York. I say gradually because I am on a very slow train. We reached Chicago on time and caught the 9:30 train… We have no dining car and only reached Cleveland at 8 o'clk this morning when we had a very poor breakfast, dinner at Buffalo, supper at Rochester. Albany 11:30 tonight. But I had a splendid sleep last night and this morning I feel very much better— in fact almost myself and I have no doubt that by the time I get to N.Y. (in the far away future) I will be all right again. The country is beginning to look very fresh and pretty. The grass is quite green and the trees show a ripple of fresh color which will soon burst forth into real green… I have a lot of work to finish up and I feel quite lazy and good for nothing— Still after I have gotten to work I will become interested. The Senate has passed its foolish and unlawful resolution recognizing a government which has no existence… Hugh Wise I suppose, is already killing Spaniards. Notwithstanding all of my theories I wish sincerely there were some way that war could be honorably avoided. But I do not see how it can be and we will soon be in the midst of it when I believe this Republic will show foreign nations how a government of Democracy can fight… Love and kisses for the darlings and a heart full of love for your own darling self, Devotedly *Henry*.

Denver, April 18th, 1898.
My Darling Husband—   Your letters received this morning. I knew you felt wretchedly when you left. There must have been something at the ban-

Katherine Thayer Hobson, artist and date of portrait unknown.

quet Wednesday night to upset you. It was a relief to receive the telegram saying you had arrived safely in New York & well. I replied at once. Will go down with your slippers & 1 1/2 sets of pajamas this afternoon. The other new jacket not quite finished but will mail it in a day or two, so you will receive it before you need it… I will write you as to Frank's present— it is a rather difficult question. Henry is quite better & out. All look rosy & well. How much we have to be thankful for in the health of our children. I am entirely absorbed in my family & the expected war. The Ft. Logan officers were given a supper at the Denver Club Saturday night… Campion's laundress was held up last night at ten o'clock— Katie heard the cries from her room & Mr. Parker went out to the rescue, of course the man escaped. Love & many kisses from us all. Always your own Devoted Wife, *Katherine*.

Denver, Tuesday, April 19th 1898.
My Darling Husband—   Another letter from you this morning written from the slow train— but maybe you had a more restful trip than if on one of the "*flyers*" Your package went off last evening. I am so glad I had a telegram from you yesterday, for I felt quite worried lest you should be really in for an illness. These horrible reports for war and the Resolutions by Senate & House make me so worried… All the children are out, this beautiful day. They talk of you so much, and Katherine is pathetic about your being away so much, but I try to keep in mind that these protracted absences mean a united home life later on. Mrs. Hallett has a tea this afternoon and I must get dressed & go pour tea for her. So take every care of yourself… Through Mother I have been trying to get at what would be a suitable present for Frank & will let you know later the result. Love & many kisses from us all. Your own Devoted Wife, *Katherine*.

Denver, April 21st, 1898.
My Darling Husband—   Your first letter from New York today. It relieves me to hear you are feeling very well. Henry has his flag flying & wishes he had a Cuban one. He spends most of his time crawling in & out of that box they call a house. I thought I would pull up Eleanor's garters today and found she was wearing your metal trouser clasps— you wear when you ride your bicycle, & refused to remove them, saying "they are the best elastics I ever had." They are all on Mother's lots— What a blessing that ground has been to them, for a play ground. Austria is reported as having tendered her protection to Spain— enabling all the Spanish to engage in war… I see Hugh Wise is off too. The old & the young. Jack sent a note he would come for tea tonight & he will know all about it. Mrs. Hallett's tea was very pleasant, and the house charming with flowers, or rather ferns. The Judge is in Pueblo… Love & kisses from us all, Your own Devoted *Katherine*.

∽ Two letters from the children:

[undated]
Dear Papa—   Your letter was very very nice and I was so glad to get it. As you said you were going to take me next time you have to go to New York and make of me an office boy— I won't forget it. Eleanor has not yet meddled with our bureau so I hope you won't have to cut her hands when you come

back. Katherine lent me her stand in the nursery. Now I can manage the pony. Lots of Kisses, *Henry*.

Dear Papa— I want a bicycle and I want to be your office boy too, and dress up in pants so you can take me to New York. Good bye, your *Eleanor*.

April 21, 1898. N.Y. N.H. & H. R.R.
Darling Kate— Since reaching N.Y. I have been in such a whirl that I have had no time to write you a decent letter— I have however thought about you all the time. I am now writing on a very rough train as I had no time to write in Boston today. What have I been doing? The Lord only knows beyond trying all the resources of my diplomacy to get discordant elements together upon definite line actions and keeping my temper. The shuffling, shifting, and timidity of some of the men I have been dealing with are truly astounding, and they represent enormous moneyed interests…

Henry went over the other day to see Hugh on his way to the war and waited from noon until 2 o'clk at night. He says Hugh was the trimmest cockiest looking officer in the Regiment and seemed assured of eating up Spaniards by the dozen. Poor little fellow, he will be as game as possible but he may never come back. My expectations for months have now come true and war is upon us. I hope and pray for the speedy success of my Country. I am above all things a patriot, and I look for much glory and good to come from this war. As the fighting approaches I feel my blood begin to course faster and faster and I would give a great deal if I could take a hand. I have always believed I would make a good soldier. If my judgment however is correct the war will be a short one. Now, mind my prediction— We will take Cuba and Havana with very little trouble. There will be one or two sea fights in which we will signally defeat Spain. There will then be friendly mediation by neutral powers, an armistice and peace, followed by the establishment of some form of government in Cuba under our protection. From all the information I can get, I can not but think that the Spanish Army & Navy are both rotten at the core and will go down quietly before the dash, courage, and steadfastness of our American soldiers.

Remember there will be a temporary prostration of business and some financial pressure but this will be followed by an era of great prosperity. All this I predict upon the supposition that Spain will not back down without any serious struggle which I think improbable. See whether I am a prophet or not! …Did I write you that I had ordered a lot of photographs for you. I did, and you will have enough to give everybody. I never expect to have another taken and so you had better make the most of these. I bought a new silk hat the other day also… Do write me at once suggesting a wedding present for Frank. I would like to give him a nice present from us jointly and one from the children. If you do not help me out I will probably get some conventional silver. Also send me address of the woman he is marrying so I can it send to there… Kiss all my darling chicks for me many times a day. I am having another but very mild correspondence with poor old Mother but I am keeping firm.
—Devoted love, Your Husband *Henry*.

Henry and *Hugh Wise*   Two brothers, sons of John S. Wise.

Denver, April 22nd, 1898.
My Darling Husband— Your second letter from New York received. I

wish you would not feel you must write me every day while you are in such a hurry. I am sure of your constant love & thoughts. It is delightful to me to feel you have been the means of helping Mr. Hagerman for I have known them so long and I should have been sorry to see them reduced to nothing financially, and then I have hopes now of your receiving what you have worked so hard for. It seems as if I thought so much about money these days— and the gaining of it— but only as the means of giving you the rest you need… Some awful report comes by the boys… that some Spanish ship has been blown up but I fancy it is talk. I feel always as if I would rather be ignorant of the conditions than upset all the time by reading these reports. Capt. Savage left today and there is nothing but war in the air. Frank's plans— Mother wishes to write off to the friends in the East. They will be married very quietly— only her family & Mother. I have Mother's Xmas check to me— $100, and I am going to use that for a present and let them buy what they wish & suit themselves. So do not think of buying anything for Frank. I am so glad I have the money & need not draw any of our funds. Take our heart's best love always. Your Devoted & Loving *Katherine.*

April 22, 1898, New York.
Darling Kate—   You can imagine the feeling of relief to me when I tell you that today we finally closed all our settlement… Well the fleets have sailed and the God of Battles must now preside over our destinies for a while. I feel confident of very rapid success but no one can tell and we may have to win success through bitter adversity. Henry Wise is trying to get an appointment as an officer and wants to go to the War. I almost wish I were 25 and in a position to go. I may run down to Ashland tomorrow night and try to straighten poor old Mother out. I have finally gotten out of her that $1,050 will pay every dollar she owes. I, of course, must fix her up, but I want to do so in a manner that will keep her from getting into debt again. Poor old woman she seems to be a great mess and is now worrying for fear that Cannon will enlist and be killed or die of yellow fever or that Henry's ship may be caught by the Spaniards and he lie in a Spanish prison… I cannot write more now for I have a long letter to write to Mother and I also want to write little letters to the chicks. I am longing to go home.   —Your devoted husband *Henry.*

In the news:

THE WAR HAS COME — Spain Refuses to Receive our Ultimatum and Gives Passports to Woodford — Our Fleets Expecting Orders to Move — President to Issue a Call for 100,000 Men to Form the Volunteer Army — Fleets to Move at Once.
—*The New York Times,* April 22, 1898.

April 23, 1898, New York.
Darling Kate—   Tonight I am going to run down to Ashland and spend Sunday with Mother. I dread the experience but I do not see how I can get out of it and so had better face the music… There is a good deal of excitement here and much lack of patriotism on the part of those I come into contact with… I had a letter from you this morning at the Hotel but no pkge. yet. Your letters are always so welcome and prized. I will be here until Wednesday night when I go to Boston. On my way back I shall try to spend a day at the

farm. By the end of next week I will, I trust, be on my way home. I must now close for I have an appointment and will be busy for the rest of the day. Love & kisses to yourself & the darling chicks.   —Your devoted husband *Henry*.

April 24, 1898, R.J. & P. R.R.
Darling Kate—   As I wrote you I came down to Ashland [Virginia] last night and am going back tonight not only because I want to be in N.Y. tomorrow but because one day is about as much as I can stand here. I can't undertake to write you all about my trip for it would take hours, but it was not as bad in some ways as I anticipated. The fact is that on Friday I wrote the old lady that I would help her and when I got here she was so much pleased with that promise that she did not have an Iliad of woe to pour into my ears. All her trouble has been on account of her debts. I wrote you that I had finally gotten a statement of her indebtedness and after thinking the matter over by concluding to advance the money under the guise of a loan from the American Loan & Trust (Jordan's Co) with me as an endorser and at 5% interest. I want her to think she is still in debt and with the obligation to pay it off and at the same time relieve her of debts pressure and put the interest low. I will find of course some way to relieve her of the interest. As long as I can keep this over her she will probably not go deeper in though I believe she is entirely serious in protesting her intention never to again get into debt… I had a full talk with her about her plans and she has nothing definite in view except to make a literary career for herself. Just think of it, 61 and starting over that thorny path. I never had a more perplexing question presented to me than the one here.

   Dr. Fox tells me that Grandma [Mary Lyons Wise] may live for years and I thoroughly believe she will— Old Lady a cripple. Mother unfit to continue care of them and every other member of her family positively refusing to undertake the job. Then these children who impress me more favorably every time I see them so far as personal attractiveness is concerned— especially the two little girls. They are very well bred and nice looking , and after talking the matter over today, I do not think they are backward as compared with other children… Poor old Mother is physically and mentally unfit to care for them and yet who else is to do it. I have some ideas in my mind of which I will talk to you when I get home. Grandma is very very infirm mentally. Her mind seems now to be confined to a very few lines and she goes over & over the same matter. It took a good while this morning for her to appreciate who I was and then her ideas were very hazy. Spoke of how I had grown— thought I was quite a young man etc. She asked me 50 times today, if she asked me once, how old I was & would then protest I could not be over 25 etc. She asked me an equal number of times whether I had any children— how many, sex, ages, names etc. She had a dim idea that I was married but insisted she had never seen you. She does not remember my Father at all— although she lived years in his house and yet babbles about people she has seen little of and who have been very ungrateful to her. It is pathetic to hear her talk of Néné (who owes her a great deal) as like daughters to her, when they have neglected her shamefully and some of them paid her no more attention in her old age and affliction than if she were a dog. Her own relatives too. You would be amused to hear her talk about dear Johnnie providing so comfortably for her and then thank *me* because she had heard that when Aunt N— broke up & she had to move, *I* had sent some money to help her. Poor old woman, she does not seem to appreciate *at all* that it is I who have put up thousands of dollars during the past ten years for her comfort & support, whilst her own relatives and those nearer to her have treated her as a piece of worn out baggage. As usual, Dear old Mother got out a few of her treasures to send you— Trifles in value, but priceless because of the sentiment, the pathos, and the tenderness connected with them and their donation.

You are an ideal to her, and she loves to talk of you and the children, and yet she feels very keenly what she thinks is the necessity of her living apart from my wife & children. The 28th is her birthday and I wired you tonight to have K— write to her and to send some trifle. I have urged her to go off somewhere this summer for a rest and she has promised to do so, and now that I have relieved her of the pressure of her debts she seems quite gay in anticipation of a trip. The pleasure of seeing her so much brightened repaid me for my trip though it was depressing enough in other respects.

But I have written you such a gloomy kind of a letter. I wired you to send me the name of the plumber in Hoosick. I will try & have him meet me at the farm this week and see about the plumbing. It is very hot tonight— almost like a summer night and I am suffering from heat. My package had not come last night— at least they said at the Waldorf it had not, and I need the thin night-clothes badly. I pretty nearly melted last night. I cannot imagine what has become of it. Tell Henny-penny I heard about a boy seven years old who still sucks a bottle and smokes cigarettes. He also swears like a trooper. I was much disturbed to hear about those occasions in our neighborhood. How shocking such a state of things is and how disagreeable to live in a community where they occur. I must say goodnight for I am very tired. How glad I will be to be back with you my precious one. You are indeed the light of my life and heart. Love and kisses to the chicks.   —Devotedly *Henry*.

THE WESTERN UNION TELEGRAPH COMPANY
New York, April 26, 1898.
Mrs. Henry W. Hobson, 933 Pennsylvania Ave. Denver.
Johnsonville tomorrow. Boston Thursday. Probably leave about middle next week but cannot say positively. Am well. Much love. *Henry W. Hobson.*

Denver, April 26th, 1898.
My Darling Henry—   Your several precious letters I have received and I am so thankful you have closed up those complicated matters and their success assured. I do not wonder you felt "let down" now the pressure is over. We sent your sleeping jacket today— you will maybe need it for a change. I trust you are a correct war prophet, but I have a feeling the Spaniards will take Washington & the whole country. I believe the foreign powers will join Spain to defeat us. The newspapers are enough to drive one wild— first saying one thing & the next *Extra* contradicting their statements. Poor little Hugh, I hate to think of him off in that fever stricken country. You were so wise going to Ashland, and it will be such a relief to you & your Mother to have her matters settled between you & I hope she will receive receipts in full, up to date, from her creditors, so there will not be any complications later on for you to face. I have gotten from Tiffany's a very pretty pin, brooch, for the children to give

Miss Harriet Jones… It seems so strange for Frank to be married. I have no intention of taking a nursing baby two nights on the train, to be at the wedding as I have not been east with you… it was lovely & kind of you to suggest my going & I appreciate it. Both Katherine & Henry have written sweet letters to your Mother for her birthday & she will have a present from them. A heart full of love. Your own Devoted wife, *Katherine*.

Denver, April 27th, 1898.
My Darling Henry—   Yesterday was very glad to receive your telegrams giving me a definite idea as to your plans. I think of you as at the farm today— hope you will find everything to your satisfaction. Mrs. Hallett's second reception came off yesterday afternoon & I went over to help her in any way I could… Mrs. Hallett & her friend take dinner with me tonight, no one else, so we shall have a good visit & no formalities. We are going down to the Springs for Sunday. Maybe I can be helpful to Mother before she leaves. She will go a week from Saturday. We will be here for the Orchestra Concert. These war rumors are most distressing and I should be happier not to read the papers. No letter from you today. It worries me to have you write when you are so busy. The children send love & kisses for your letter… Your Own Devoted Wife, *Katherine*.

Denver, April 28th, 1898.
My Darling Husband—   Mrs. Hallett, Mrs. Long, and I had a pleasant quiet dinner last evening— and then Mr. Parker came & spent the evening & took the timid ladies home. Col. Woodhull & Mr. Malburn were *held up* the other evening. The Col. having his arms held, his silver watch taken, & pushed back into his pocket— he scolding all the time & was told to stop, or he would have a knife run in him… Your letter from train from Ashland received. What a terrible condition of affairs. I think a literary career the most absurd thing I ever heard of for your Mother to think of— & why the care of those four children of Cannon's is too much for her, I can not see… Your Mother has her own plans & will carry them out. I know Darling one how worried and troubled you have been and you have my most tender loving sympathy. I do wish we could wipe out Spain & trust soon she will be so defeated that she will give up Cuba. It is too bad you have not received the package. It was sent to your Hotel the same day I knew you had left your slippers. (You wrote from the train.) I had a telegram sent today asking if package was received. Love & Kisses many from us all. Your own Devoted wife *Katherine*.

April 28, 1898, Hotel Touraine, Boston.
Darling Kate—   This morning a letter from you was received here forwarded from N.Y. What comforts your letters are, especially as I am so depressed and blue about being away from home and having to be on the run so much. I am glad Henry is so patriotic. Tell him he must keep his flag flying until we whip the Spaniards…   —Devotedly *Henry*.

April 29, 1898, New York.
Darling Kate—   …I enclose you a letter from Mother. You see she is happy now that her debts are paid.   —Devotedly *Henry*.

∽ A letter from Annie Jennings Wise Hobson:

Ashland, April 27, 1898.
My dear Son—   Surely there could never have been a more dutiful & loving son than you are. Your coming down Sunday stirred my soul to the very depths & I wanted all day to put my arms around you & tell you how I felt about it but I feared to break down entirely & make a scene that would be trying to you as well as myself… [letter incomplete]

∽ A letter about family matters:

The Episcopal Male Academy, Houston, Virginia.
Rev. J. G. Shackelford, B. L., U. VA., President and Rector, St. Johns Church.
April 29th, 1898.
Mr. Henry W. Hobson, Denver.
My dear Sir—   Your favor of the 26th from New York City has been received. It will give me pleasure to have your two nephews in our school. I remember their father & Grandmother with pleasure, and also recall meeting you on one of your trips to Ashland. Owing to the increased cost of living, produced by political causes and the Spanish War scare, I am compelled to add something to my charges of last session, which were $200. They will be published in the forthcoming catalogue as $225 for Board, tuition, lodging, fuel, lights, washing, and mending. It will give me pleasure to offer you for the two sons of a brother clergyman, these advantages for $400, making a reduction of $25 each on the regular charge. I do not furnish books, paper, pen, ink & pencils but they can be secured at the usual prices in our town book store.

The ages of the boys is not against their entering here, as I can provide for boys of all ages.

If your mother needs a quiet place among nice people, at which to board, it can be secured in our village at very moderate charges; but I would desire, under this plan, sole charge of the boys in order to relieve her of any responsibility. Hoping to hear from you favorably, I am, Faithfully yours, *J. G. Shackelford.*

A nice school for *girls* is conducted in our village also. It is more a day school.

Gulf Train, Saturday, April 30th, 1898.
My Darling Henry—   Here we are going to the Springs. Katie, Henry, Eleanor & Thayer. Katherine comes with Mary this P.M. as I did not wish her to miss the Orchestra drill this A.M. Mrs. Hatch has gone away & Mother suggested I should bring Mary for a few days & have her help with the children. This morning I put Thayer into his short clothes. He is very cunning, but I feel lonely for my long clothes Baby— it is the first step in advancing towards manhood & after the first is taken, the others follow so closely. This is Mother's wedding anniversary and it is pleasant to take the chicks there today… Mother & Frank go a week from today. I do hope this marriage will give Frank great happiness & bring the best & most satisfying life to Mother. Whatever she has done & will do, will be because she believes it right & her duty… When Spain's navy begins to show itself & "*Capture Florida*"— last nights paper said it was the plan, we may be glad we live in Colorado… The

children send Love & kisses & their Mother a heart full of love. Always your own Devoted Wife, *Katherine*.

—Please do not bring a *bit* of candy or anything. The candy upsets the children's stomachs.

April 30, 1898, New York.
Darling Kate—   …Today is a lovely day and I am feeling well except for being *very very* tired. I want to see you my darling sweetheart more than I can express in words. When I am away from you a big cloud seems to hang constantly over my heart and mind. But it will come out all right in time and then we can take matters more quietly. Love & kisses to the darlings.
—Devotedly *Henry*.

Colorado Springs, May 1st, 1898.
My Darling Husband—   Your letter from Johnsonville received. I was very glad to hear of your day in Cambridge— how painstaking you are in all matters, so thorough— never anything half done. We came here just in time for lunch yesterday and Katherine & Mary arrived safely later in the afternoon. I left my letter to find Mother's glasses, & now on my return find Eleanor rubbing it over, & saying in reply, "Papa will not mind." [letter is smudged] What a child she is. Instead of May Day being sunny, warm & bright, we have a snow storm all day & now four o'clock the sun is shining— & chicks all off for a walk… Mother is writing John & her friends about Frank's intended marriage. Neither he or Miss Jones wished anything said until just before the wedding— and all people wish to manage those affairs to suit themselves… All join me in love & kisses to the dearest Papa in the World. Always your own Devoted Wife, *Katherine*.

May 1, 1898, New York.
Darling Kate—   April has gone and I am still here longing to get home and today very blue, because of my absence as indeed I always am on Sundays… Last night I went out to the Wise's to dine and had a very good dinner and a very pleasant evening… We [Henry Hobson & John S. Wise] had a good talk. We went over all the experiences in regard to dueling etc. from 1878 to 1881 with which I was quite intimately connected… Everyone is awaiting with much interest the news from Manila and expecting a complete victory for the American ships. The incessant newspaper excitement is becoming very tiresome. I do not pay any attention to it expect to be bored. Half the dispatches are manufactured in this country and the other half are ground out by correspondents who have to justify their employment. They have made more fuss over a 15 minutes bombardment of a half finished fort in Cuba than the English would make over a great victory… I have nothing in the world of interest to write you except that I love you more every day and long for your dear presence. Love & kisses to the darlings.   —Devotedly *Henry*.

In the news:

A WEEK OF VICTORIES — Washington Authorities Think Decisive Successes at Manila and Cuba Are Near — Dewey Is Relied On To Take The Philippines — Complaint that There Are Too Many Officers and Too Few Privates in the Army Now Assembling. —*The New York Times*, May 1, 1898.

Colorado Springs, May 2nd, 1898.
My Darling Husband—   Today brings us an account of terrible loss & destruction of the Spanish fleet at the Philippines. I wish I could hear the latest reports as you are hearing— if this could be the beginning & end of war. What a blessing. Another snow today… Thayer is enjoying creeping in his short clothes. He is sweeter & more precious, if possible, every day. The other day Mary found Henry climbing *out* of the windows at home & when she told him that I had told him not to do so, he turned and said, "Mary, now you heard her say not to climb *in* but did you hear her say not to climb *out*?" Mary said, "that he make a splendid lawyer Mrs. Hobson." I was much amused. Hope I shall hear something definite soon about your return… I miss you terribly. Love & many kisses. May God bless & keep you. Always your own *Katherine*.

May 2, 1898, New York.
Darling Kate—   No letter from you today or yesterday and it is such a loss to me when I do not hear. I can't imagine why two days should pass… Today came the news of our sweeping victory over the Spanish. As far as one can learn, we simply annihilated the Spanish fleet and without serious injury to our ships. It was a very gallant and fine piece of work. Dewey dashing into Manila bay in defiance of torpedoes, forts or anything. Whilst our fleet was superior in force yet the Spanish were supported by land forts and had the choice of positions. If we can not meet and crush the Atlantic fleet we will have very little more war. I enclose these little flag emblems for the children to wear on their fronts. I want them to learn to love the flag… Yesterday I went out to Grant's Tomb. It was a perfect day. Love & kisses immeasurable.
—Devotedly *Henry*.

Colorado Springs, May 3rd, 1898.
My Darling Husband—   Two letters from you this morning— one from Boston & 2nd written on your return to New York… Your Mother's letter shows, from its tone, that she feels entirely relieved of pressure. I wish she would not buy presents for me & the children. It is one of the ways in which she uses her income and then has to borrow. I am glad Mary Lyons is to have such a pleasant outing. It will be such a pleasure to her… No war news today… Henry Wise will go off & be killed probably. I shall tie Jack in Denver, but I think he is too sensible. Love & many kisses… Your own devoted & loving wife, *Katherine*.

May 3, 1898, New York.
Darling Kate—   All day I have been trying to read two letters from you in a satisfactory way but have just succeeded at 5:30 and I am too tired to write much. I have been very busy today closing up Mr. Hagerman's matters and have finally forced out of him fees on one account to the amount of $4,750. He is beginning to kick, and tomorrow I am to meet him and have it out on account of general services. It is a disagreeable task but I suppose it is unavoidable… The news came today that we had captured Manila. I am look-

ing for a big sea fight in the Atlantic in a few days and when it comes and we win it will end the war quickly. I feel confident we will win. I have no patience with General Palmer's views and position on the Cuban question… Tomorrow is a holiday and I am not sure whether I will come down-town or not. Love & kisses to the darling chicks. I send this to Denver as I suppose you will be there by Friday. Devotedly, *Henry.*

Colorado Springs, May 4th, 1898,
My Darling Henry—   Your letter of Saturday came today. No message yet announces your home coming… It was funny hearing about Mr. Hagerman & Uncle Johnnie haggling as to payments. From all I have heard of Uncle J's work from Mr. Hagerman, I think $5,000 a big sum, for he has been from the first careless and negligent. If Uncle J— can get $5,000, you, with your work & devotion should receive 50… Don't you do one thing for Aunt Néné, she has children grown & let them take care of her as you do of your Mother… If you lived East you would be lived with by half your relatives & supporting them. And Aunt Néné earns a good living herself. It makes me so indignant to see how you are bled— and have to work & demands to help an older generation who should have too much pride to ask. Frank is getting his trunk & clothes in order. And I am glad to be here to help Mother. She will feel his being absent… Miss Jones wrote me, "We know each other's faults & are neither of us young & will not expect too much." This reads sensibly. Well I will hear all about her from Mother… Our precious baby is eight months old today & so sweet & lovely. He sends kisses to Papa & all the rest of us love & kisses. Your own Devoted Wife, *Katherine.*

❧ In the news:

WAITING FOR NEWS — Details of Commodore Dewey's Victory Over the Spaniards at Manila Still Unknown — Word Expected Soon — Europe in Sullen Mood — Emperors of Germany and Russia Greatly Exercised Concerning the Future of the Philippines.   —*The New York Times*, May 5, 1898.

May 7, 1898, New York.
Darling Kate—   The news (authentic) of Dewey's great victory has just come. Eleven ships sunk or burned, 300 killed, 400 wounded for the Spanish and not a ship of ours lost, not a man killed and only six wounded. There is nothing like it in naval annals, and it is a magnificent evidence of the skill and bravery of our naval men. I feel great pity for the poor Spaniards who seem to have fought bravely… I had a letter from Mother telling me about having spent a day in Richmond going to the Alms House Hospital to see Rosa Brooks & her baby, to another Hospital to see old Mrs. Taliafero and to another place to see an old invalid named Mrs. Sully. Bless the old woman's heart— she is always running around after some poor or decrepit person but I wish she would not feel it necessary to give money to them all… I cannot write any more today. Love & kisses to the chicks and my heart's dearest missive to you my sweet loving wife. You do not know how I want to see you, now how comforting your letters are. One came this morning.   —Your devoted husband *Henry.*

Rio Grande R. R. from Colorado Springs, May 9th, 1898.
My Darling Husband—   We are just on our way from the Springs... Frank had pleasant letters from John Birge, and Lizzie Alexander. I wrote Frank today, the last time I can write him with just the same feeling, though I can honestly say I am glad if he will be happier and find a larger, fuller life, but I think I had gotten used to feeling I was first in his affection. I think I wrote you how delighted he was with our present. Mother gave Miss Jones one hundred dollars to use as she liked— and Frank gave her a plain watch, gold with her monogram... We all are so glad to welcome you home my Dearest one. Another month of separation. I can hardly wait to hear how you came out with Mr. Hagerman. Certainly he ought to pay you handsomely for all you have done. I hope you remembered to put in your bill the trip you made to N. Y. three days after you had returned to Denver two years ago. You are too apt to forget what you do for others. We expect Mother & Katherine Wednesday afternoon— how interested Katherine was in going— a trip to her is the joy of life & going to a hotel. The chicks send love & kisses & I a heartful. I took Henry & Eleanor to the Dentist to be sure nothing was neglected. There seems to be a necessity now days of filling first teeth— the dentist said both Henry & Eleanor's teeth were well formed... Always your own Devoted Wife, *Katherine.*

May 9, 1898, New York.
Darling Kate—   Today is a beautiful one after a week or ten days of rain & clouds. We hear nothing from Sampson's fleet... I am sending some little war things, with directions for use, for the children. They will amuse them on Henny-penny's birthday. Be careful not to have them hold the things close to their faces. In setting fire to the flags do so with a lighted match. With the other things however you must use a piece of *cord* just as you use punk. Light the cord, then blow out flame and touch at point indicated with the live end. The man who invented these things is making money hand-over-fist... Love & kisses for all of my darling ones.   —Devotedly *Henry.*

Denver, May 10th, 1898.
My Dearest Husband—   Here we are again in our beautiful home— and a lovely day it is. I have your letter of Saturday when you had heard of Dewey's magnificent victory. The account in the *Republican* from *N. Y. Herald's* eyewitness was wonderful. It seems impossible to believe not one of our men were killed. This morning I heard from Mother from Kansas City, they had just reached there, all safe & Katherine was as happy as could be... Four or five times I have seen a look like you, in his [Thayer's] dear face & then I tell him he is Papa's Baby & give him an especially hard hug... Love & kisses from us all. You dear soul having to work so hard to get a compensation for all your work. Maybe it is better you stayed on & had the matter out. Always your own Devoted *Katherine.*

Denver, May 11th, 1898.
My Dearest Henry—   Mother & Katherine arrived here this morning at 11:20— *The Flyer* from Kansas City. Mother liked Miss Jones & says she has a low toned soft-southern voice and everything she saw about her was agreeable... Mother says Frank had a very kind telegram from you which he

appreciated… Johnson is cutting grass. He took Henry out to see the soldiers in camp this morning… We miss & long for you all the time and shall be so thankful when we have you home. Be very careful of your dearest self. I shall be glad to see the *Herald* & will save Henry's letter for him. I give him his reading lessons as Miss Rollier is ill & Eleanor goes to the kindergarten with Dorothy— *perfect bliss*. All join to Papa in love & kisses & my whole heart is full of love & longing. Your own Devoted *Katherine*.

Miss Rollier   A Swiss governess who went daily to the Hobson home in Denver and gave lessons to the children.

Denver, May 12th, 1898.
My Darling Husband—   Katherine has written you a letter, and Henry has been having his reading lesson to me. He seems quite anxious to have you think he has improved, when you return… The day is lovely. I started by having your dear letter. I was sorry to hear you had tooth-ache. This you told me several days ago. You take such care of your teeth they should be perfect. By this time maybe the Hagerman war is settled, for you seem to have been having one at least on rates. I tell the chicks that your being away so much now will make you able to stay at home more by & by— And I comfort myself & live in that hope. Mother sends you her best love. The envelope proved to contain *not* a plumbers estimate, but a fine map of Cuba. Where oh where are those Spanish ships? Their movements seem shrouded in mystery… Love & A heartful from Your Devoted Wife, *Katherine*.

Denver, Col. May 12th, 1898.
My Dear Papa—   We reached home yesterday at noon. We saw Uncle Frank married to Miss Jones and she is now my Aunt Harriet, and I like her very much. They left for Chicago at 6 P.M. and we left at 7 P.M. Miss Rollier is ill. She will be able to teach Monday. When you bow to Baby he will bow to you. He is very cunning in short clothes. Henry hopes you will be home for his birthday. Henry wants to go to war. We wear our pins. I and all thank you for sending them. Love & kisses from all.   —from your baby *Katherine*.

The Waldorf-Astoria, New York, May 12th, 1898.
My Darling Boy Blue:
What a sad thing it is for Papa to have to write you upon your birthday, when he had counted on being with you! But you must have the best time you can, and tell Mamma to give you that present I got for you, which I hope you will like as much as you did the typewriting machine. I am also going to send you a lot of War things, which you will like and which you can show people. I know you are a good American, for you love the flag and like to have it unfurled. When you get to be seven years old people will expect a good deal of you, and I want to feel very proud of you. You would feel very much amused if you were here and could see the newspaper boys going wild in the streets over the "Extras." Maybe you would turn newspaper boy yourself. Did Mamma give you that buttonhole flag I sent you? Well, do you know that the streets are just full of men selling War buttons and flags? If I cannot be with you I shall expect you to tell me all about your birthday.

   Be a good boy and take care of Mamma, the girls and Thayer, for you are my big man-boy. Your Papa sends you a whole heartful of love. —Your loving "*Dad*," *Henry*.

Denver, May 13th, 1898.
My Darling Husband—   This morning I have your letter telling of the interview with Mr. Hagerman… I saw a telegram to Miss Fallon, asking for papers, which show you are still working away on Mr. H's business. This morning tells me of Sampson bombarding San Juan & the Cape Verde fleet in the vicinity. And we are anxiously awaiting to hear of a battle. One can never tell if a report has any resemblance of truth until several days have passed. Henry will enjoy the soldiers very much… This morning I have been out for two or three hours, sowing the flower seeds & making a garden with the children & now I see Eleanor watering hers— the chief pleasure. Judge Hallet is in Salt Lake. Mr. Barber has offered his services to the Navy but having but one eye he will probably be rejected. He retired when he married his rich wife. Love & kisses from us all my dearest one. You have my tenderest most heart-felt sympathy in all your struggles and pray your devotion to all of us may be rewarded. Your own loving Wife, *Katherine*.

Denver, Saturday, May 14th, 1898.
My Darling Husband—   We are down at the Trust Co., three children & Paul waiting for the soldiers & parade celebrating Dewey's Day— City gay with bunting & crowds out, fire crackers & popping all about. The more noise the greater the success I suppose. Your letter telling of the Hagerman settlement received this morning. I am thoroughly disgusted with both he & Mr. Otis after all your work to try & *beat* you down & so much of the payment dependent upon the success of their schemes… Everyone is most anxious to hear of Sampson's next move on the Cape Verde Fleet— or where? I am going to buy the *Herald* for a few days. The *N. Y. Times* is too quiet & I am like the chicks— I like the pictures. Mr. Todd says everything is going on well here. He has been up with the Daughters of the American Revolution cheering the soldiers, they were presented with colors by the Sons of the Revolution & made a fine show. Love & Many kisses from us all. Always your own Devoted, *Katherine*.

Denver, May 16th, 1898.
My Darling Husband—   This is our boy's birthday and very happy he seems. We woke at five-thirty, he sleeping in my room as a "great treat" he said— and had your letter to him to read. Then Eleanor made her appearance & gave Henry a gun which shoots small rubber balls. And we had a game in bed— we were Cubans & Henry playing the foot-board was a fort & defending us. Katherine joined us & we had a merry time. Little Eleanor said "Oh I do wish my Papa would come home." …We are to have our cake at tea with eight candles & a drive this P.M… Jack was here yesterday— he is well & I think will go to war in Hugh's regiment. When you come home he will talk with you. Your two letters received 12th & 13th. Finish up everything you need to. I know you will come when you can. My dearest one. Our hearts best love to you & kisses. Your own Devoted Wife, *Katherine*.

THE WESTERN UNION TELEGRAPH COMPANY
New York, May 16, 1898.
Henry W. Hobson, Jr. 933 Penna. Ave. Denver. Col.
Much love and congratulations on your birthday. Give Mama and other chicks love and say I am well. *Henry W. Hobson*.

Denver.
Dear Papa—   I was delighted to receive your presents and I thank you so much for them. The Cuban flag will be lots of fun. Eleanor gave me a nice gun. Last Saturday I went to see the parade with Mama, Katherine, and Eleanor, and we saw the fire department. Good bye my dear Papa with much love from *Henry.*

May 16, 1898, New York.
Darling Kate—   Today I came up-town at noon both because I had nothing to do down in the City and because I did not feel very well. I am awfully blue and feel as though I must go home in spite of everything. I almost cried when I read in your letter that you had to explain to the children why I was away from home so much. I should think they would imagine that I had just quit for good. I feel quite as sorry for you as I do for myself for I know it must be awfully hard on you darling one… Everything here is in a state of suspense on the subject of the Spanish fleet and practically no business is being done. Those Spaniards seem to be too much for us in the matter of cunning and dodging though we may surpass them in fighting qualities. I am uneasy lest they spring some surprise on us and take a fair advantage though I suppose everything is fair in war…   —Devotedly *Henry.*

Denver, May 17th, 1898.
My Darling Husband—   Mother had your letter forwarded from the Springs… Yesterday afternoon we drove, Katherine, Henry & I, way out on Broadway. The weather changed very much before we returned and I felt chilly. A swelling came in one of my breasts & I have had the fever… but after the night I feel better, but I shall stay in today. Have come into your room and Thayer is asleep by me, on your bed. He crept into the bathroom after Katie this morning. He sits on the floor alone and you will think him much changed. Henry enjoys his fire-works, was very generous & gave Johnson's boys one of each kind. When you come home we must make our plans for the summer. If you are to be here the greater part of the season I shall not go to Cambridge & separate myself from you, but we can talk it all over. Miss Rollier is back again. I shall have the children keep up their lessons, for two hours is not too much at any season. And Katherine is doing very well with the violin. I follow you all through your many & difficult complications & hope & pray your faithful following of duty may be amply rewarded. Katie has been with us six years today. The chicks send love & kisses. Could you find out if the U. S. Express has passed dividend or not. I do not see it in *N. Y. Times.* Your own Devoted Wife, *Katherine.*

May 18, 1898, New York.
Darling Kate—   Last night I slipped away from the Hotel again and spent a pleasant evening reading at the club… Now about the summer— It looks to me as though I should have to be back East by the 15th of June and be here off and on for some time. I want a good rest and I am going to take it. Had you not better arrange to come on in June and we can make our headquarters at Cambridge farm and I can come to N.Y. as I may be needed… I hope your Mother will go to the farm with you this summer.   —Devotedly *Henry.*

Denver, May 20th, 1898.
My Precious Darling Husband— The telegram has just come saying you are detained until next week and I am so disappointed… I know you are as disappointed as I… but before many days you will see your way clear to start and I think we should both dwell on the fact that we are all well… I feel we have so much to be thankful for only I long for your presence more than I can tell. It must have been a great satisfaction that the Syndicate recognized your services & gave you a substantial proof of it— that check was a comfort to think of because it did not represent such an amount of hard work as your earnings usually do. I often see your tired face between me and every bill I spend. The news of the terms from the Syndicate must be the means of relieving you from some Trust Co. indebtedness you felt you wished to pay… Jack was here to tea last evening. I love him very much & it makes me sad to hear of his strong desire to go to war. The thought of the fleets & Dewey & *everything* is most unsettling. We have had the great pleasure of reading Hugh's letters. He shows a fine noble nature. I pray God to guard & keep him. On Wednesday the servants rooms were broken into & a dollar & a half taken from Lena's purse, her bed pulled to pieces, her trunk. Mary had $15 under her pillow, he did not get that, but lifted up her mattress. Henry was in the 3rd story of Buckley's & looking out & saw a man sitting on servant's bathroom window sill. He said to Paul that might be a robber & came home to tell & of course he had escaped. The City Detective came up & as Mary, & Henry, & Dora (a woman cleaning) had all seen the same man they got a good description… Of course the robber will never be caught. The children were so excited & woke crying all through the last 2 nights but are quieting down today. The boys said when he saw them "he jumped back in the room quick" but when they disappeared to come home & tell, he made off. So you see I did not write Wednesday with this excitement & the telegram came saying you were to start. My whole heart is full of love & longing my Darling one. Ever your own, *Katherine*.

May 20, 1898, New York.
Darling Kate— This morning I was pretty nearly at the breaking down point when I found that I cannot get away tomorrow but must stay here until next week. I say I cannot— I mean that I cannot without leaving a matter unfinished that I have undertaken to carry through. My home-going would not be entirely happy if I abandoned the task and failed to accomplish my purpose. Therefore I must stay with the matter until I carry it through or find out that it is beyond my power. The trouble all arises through the vacillation and perhaps bad faith of some of the Union Pacific people and I must play the game out with them… Yesterday for the first time in the long strain I lost my temper for a little while and did some plain straight talking— I don't mean profanity or vituperation — but just plain language. I was very much mortified over it and yet I am not sure but that the occasion had arisen for some display of temper. I know sweetheart that this continuing absence must be very hard on you but I can't help it… I am so disgusted with the way the Spanish fleet has outwitted ours I don't know what to do. Sampson seems to have accomplished nothing except to burn coal, waste ammunition and get his ships found. It seems that the *Oregon* is safe which is a great thing… Uncle John has this morning gotten a letter from Henry who is with his Mother

saying he had accidentally shot a hole through his foot. This comes just as his Father thinks he has gotten him an appointment of Captain in the Army. Poor Henry is heartbroken. I can't write more now for I must go off to keep an engagement. I can't think of my disappointment sweetheart without almost crying. Kiss and hug all the chicks for me and love to your dear Mother.
—Devotedly, *Henry*.

Denver, May 21st, 1898.
My Darling Husband—   All day I have been handling your library, dusting & putting back in exactly the same order. Johnson has no head as to returning the book to the same shelf. I hope you will be home before the dust has a chance to settle on them… I have let Henry's hair grow until he looks like a foot-ball player because he says, "Oh I want to wait until Papa comes & go with him." It seems to be the height of a small boys ambition to go to the barber's with their father, but we are to go this afternoon & Katherine & Eleanor with us. Mother and I are going over to the Hallett's for dinner tonight… Eleanor has written you the enclosed [not found] with very dirty hands and brings it— "send it to my dear Papa." The dirt is a part of the sweetness. I think of you all the time my own precious husband and long for your coming. I had your letter of 18th May. It must be restful for you to run away to the Club for evening reading. Glad you saw Tom & Florence. They are always so genuinely glad to see one. Chicks send love & kisses to you. My Darling how I long to see you. Ever your own devoted wife, *Katherine*.

May 21, 1898, New York.
Darling Kate—   Two letters came from you yesterday which I have read several times with much joy… Tell Henny Penny I enjoyed his letter very much and am so glad he had a happy birthday… My business looks much brighter today. The little row I had the other day did a good deal to clear up the atmosphere despite my mortification over losing my temper. I hope to get things settled in a few days so I can go to St. Paul on my way home… Nothing definite from the fleets today and I was so anxious. Last night about 1 o'clk a perfect bedlam broke loose at the Home Office, just a block from the Hotel, from the newsboys crying "*EXTRA*". It woke me up, and I was quite sure news of a battle had come and it kept me awake an hour. This morning I found it was all about a report that the Spanish fleet had left Santiago. I suppose our people are doing the best they can but the delays are very exasperating. Three weeks tomorrow since Dewey's victory and no relief sent him yet. Well I suppose we all think we can run things better than those who are in charge… Goodbye for today. I am not very busy pending action by U.P. [Union Pacific Railroad] people. Give love & kisses without measure to all the chicks and your Mother. For yourself sweetheart you have my whole life.   —Devotedly, *Henry*.

Denver, May 22nd, 1898.
My Darling Husband—   This is a perfect day. We have been to church & Sunday School. Henry having had a birthday since last Sunday had the pleasure of dropping seven pennies in the birthday box. Jack is downstairs chatting with Mother & I have come up to nurse Thayer, who looks at your portrait and bows. Now all are out at the swing. Mr. Buckley brought Henry

home two pretty specimens from the mine today & Henry wishes, "Papa would sometime bring Paul some little thing"— he does not wish it to be one sided. Last evening at about eleven a boy was about, calling an *Extra*. Of course I got one & the report was 11 Spanish ships sunk, and I went to bed feeling another victory like Dewey's had come maybe, but this morning a false report! The City Detectives think that they have caught the "robber"—a jockey from San Francisco. I trust it is so. Tomorrow will investigate. We are to make abdominal bands of gray flannel for our volunteers going to Manila & send on by Dr. Parkhill. My share is 12 of the 600. It is hoped wearing them may prevent chill & bowel trouble. Love & kisses many my darling. Your own Devoted Wife, *Katherine.*

May 22, 1898, New York.
Darling Kate—   Another Sunday has come and caught me here and with no better prospects of fixing a definite day for departure than I had last Sunday. I at times feel like giving way to screaming and unrestrained rage but that would do little good. I must stay with the plough to the end of the furrow. But I will not dwell on the matter for I get too much worked up. Yesterday I sent out by Harry some articles, books etc. Amongst others you will find three little caps and flags I got at the dinner the other night for the children. There is also some soap which is splendid for shampoo and I want you to try it on the children's hair. It leaves my hair much softer than ordinary soap…
—Devotedly *Henry.*

Denver, May 23rd, 1898.
My Darling Henry—   Monday always brings two letters from you… Jack tells me today that the report from the Detectives office is that our thief has not been caught, but I am not going to tell the children, for they seemed to feel so relieved that he was caught… Poor Henry Wise. I am perfectly discouraged to hear of his accident and Jack is distressed. I only hope it was with a revolver & a clean wound. A shotgun would mangle his foot. Maybe Jack could be the Captain— he is very anxious to be something… The baby is rather out of order today, but oil is working its cure. He is such a darling. Eleanor's letter I enclose now. Work our your schemes & do not come before you can come feeling you have done *all* you can. There could be little pleasure for you gained if duties were neglected. Mother heard from her daughter-in-law today. She seems a sensible woman… A heart full of love. Your own, *Katherine.*

Denver, May 25th, 1898.
My Darling Husband—   Will send a line to St. Paul, so you may hear from us there. I was writing you yesterday when your telegram came telling you would probably get off Thursday night. I hope it is true, but I always feel something may come up. I took my flannel bands down to Unity Church where they were being collected & counted. A thousand I saw there taken to Daniels & Fisher's to be packed… The children are perfectly delighted with their cups & flags— & Katherine's is of course on her bureau. Henry's and Eleanor's in the dining room. I have your letter of Sunday telling of your theatre party— am glad they all seemed to enjoy themselves… The Baby seems much better & jolly. A few hours of bowel trouble will give a Baby a sick look.

I shall say nothing more to Jack as to not going to war. We shall be so glad & thankful to see you home again & can but talk over our plans then for the summer. With devoted love always & kisses from all, Your own, *Katherine.*

May 26, 1898. En Route Wagner Vestibuled Train
Darling Kate—   *A dozen times hurrah.* I am on my way west and Monday morning, if all goes well, I will be with you my sweetheart and the darling chicks. I have had a hand-full and up to the last moment I thought I would be detained for several days… Tell my precious children that for the summer I am going to devote lots and lots of time to them and that we will do all kinds of things that are nice. I cannot contemplate ever leaving you and them again. I do not know just when you will get this letter but maybe before I get back. In any event it does me lots of good to write. A mountain of love thousands of feet high.   —Your devoted husband *Henry*.

◆ In the news:

SPAIN'S LAST OPPORTUNITY — Henry Norman of the London Daily Chronicle Says She Must Sue for Peace or Lose All.   —*The New York Times*, June, 3, 1898.

SPAIN ANXIOUS FOR PEACE — Politicians and Financiers Are Desirous of Ending the War Without Delay — The Voice of the Military Men is Still for War.
—*The New York Times*, June 4, 1898.

SHARP FIGHTING AT GUANTANAMO — Marines and Cubans Capture A Spanish Camp — Huts and Well Destroyed — Two Cubans Killed, One American and Four Cubans Wounded — Enemy Lost 40 Men — Attack Made After Exhausting March Up and Down Steep Hillsides in Glaring Sun.   —*The New York Times*, June 16, 1898.

ROUGH RIDERS PROVE HEROES — Their First Battle Marked by Many Acts of Bravery — Lured Into An Ambuscade — Trying Fight Lasting Two Hours with the Concealed Enemy — Spanish Loss Heavy — Bodies of Thirty-nine Spaniards Found on the Battlefield — Burial of Our Dead Soldiers.
—*The New York Times*, June 27, 1898.

◆ Going East for the summer:

June 28, 1898. Left Denver at 4 p.m. with Kittie & family for Cambridge in D & G private car, very warm. Dear Henry waived us off at station.
June 29. Very warm last night, never knew a warmer night— baby feels heat very much…   —*Diary of Catherine McKie Thayer.*

Henry Wise Hobson returned to Denver and a month later the family headed east to the farm in Cambridge, New York.

Chicago, R. R., June 29th, 1898.
My Dearest Henry—   Have come to the little desk to write a line to you. The car is so unsteady I can barely write. We are very well this morning & Thayer had a good night. Fortunately it cooled off about ten o'clock. The dust was awful & I don't know what we should do unless we could keep undressed with cool wrappers, as we can in this lovely roomy car. The children's drawers & gingham aprons are their costumes. The meals have been excellent…
All the time I am reminded of the work & devotion which assures us all these

Dear Henry, providing all these comforts Given his position with the railroad company, Henry Hobson was able to arrange for his family to travel in a private railroad car when they went east.

comforts & luxuries. My Darling One— and I fully appreciate your loving care. Mother has said several times, "Dear Henry, providing all these comforts for us." The children are interested & good as they can be. Eleanor cried for you & said "it is so lonely leaving Papa standing there all alone," but I tell her you will come soon & we will welcome you— oh, so gladly. All send much love. This is a poor scrawl, but it takes my heart full of love to you my precious one. Your own, *Kittie.*

June 29, 1898, Denver.
Darling Kate—   Yesterday, as I saw you all off, I felt very down hearted and came up-town feeling reluctant to go home… It was cool here but I felt very worried about the effect of heat on dear little Thayer. Today it is very cool & pleasant and I trust the change will reach you… Devoted love to all.   —Your devoted husband *Henry.*

July 1. Cambridge. Once more in the Old Home & the hot journey over.
                    —*Diary of Catherine McKie Thayer.*

Home Farm, Sunday July 3rd, 1898.
My Darling Henry—   Your letter & telegram were brought up last evening when we went for the mail and it was too late to send an answer then, so I am going to send Arthur to Johnsonville today, Sunday, and you may know today your little boy is better. The heat upset him very much on the way & he cut a tooth the day we were broiling in Nebraska. But for the car & the chance to find a cool spot & any little breeze, I think he might have been in a critical condition. The dust & smoke were thick & they made Thayer's eyes sore, & it was a pitiful sight to see him cry, the tears pouring down his cheeks. It was a great thing our stopping in Chicago, for there was a lovely breeze & we all got baths. The weather is warm but quiet & fresh air have made Thayer better, but it will be some days before he regains his rosy cheeks & bright ways… Broker [a horse] is a classical failure. He threw Arthur twice between West Troy & here— Won't hold back going down hill, rears, and not at all safe for the children to ride after. And I am not going to be unsettled & made anxious by having them. Maybe Uncle Johnnie would like to buy him— you might ask him… The water runs well & seems cool… The plumbers are coming back this week to put in baths & sink… Yesterday was full of putting away trunks, getting settled generally. I should like to be in Troy for a morning but it is too warm. The children are as happy as can be, running all over & catching fish. All have pails with fish & Eleanor says she has a kindergarten, a big fish for teacher & a lot of little ones… We are hoping to have you with us another Sunday. Hope you will win your case. A heart full of love & kisses from your own Devoted *Katherine.*

July 3, 1898, Denver.
Darling Kate—   Today I am at the office working hard upon my case which is indeed the case of pulling an ox as well as an ass out of the pit. I expect to be here tonight and tomorrow working… I am quite anxious about Thayer. I have had no letter since the one written west of Chicago and no telegram since Friday. I cannot think there is anything seriously the matter with him or else you would have wired me but I cannot help feeling stirred

up… Tell Henny Penny that when I go bed at night or get up in the morning I almost cry at the sight of his empty little bed… Did you notice that Shafter commenced the attack upon Santiago as soon as Maj. Daniel reached the front? …Give a great deal of love to all.   —Your devoted husband *Henry*.

Home Farm, July 4th 1898.
My Dearest Husband—   Today is not as warm as yesterday, but we would all be more comfortable if it were cooler. Arthur, working in the garden, came stumbling in, overcome with heat & now I suppose will be laid up for a few days… I told Henry he would have some fireworks later on, but with Thayer needing quiet & rest, I felt it would be wrong to make a noisy day of today. With such fearful reports of Santiago's wars, there will be many mourning on this day of celebration. Thayer slept more quietly last night and his eyes were not glued together this morning. Arthur has painted the woodwork in dining room bright yellow instead of cream white & it has to be done over this afternoon. Thayer nodded his head this morning when we asked if he loved Papa. All send love & kisses, your own devoted wife, *Katherine*.   —Arthur just came about. Looks as good as new.

July 4, 1898, Denver.
Darling Kate—   …This is a most glorious Fourth. The most glorious since the "original." Today all sections of a United Country can rejoice over the splendid feats of our Army & Navy. History does not show a more brilliant record for an untrained inexperienced Army than that which the Santiago Army has been making, nor do naval annals contain such remarkable histories as those of Manila & Santiago in some of their features… I cannot but regret that you will not hear of the splendid victory until tomorrow for I would on this National birthday like to know that your heart was throbbing with patriotic fervor as mine is… Tonight they will have a big celebration at the Denver Club, and if I can get through with my work, I will go to see the fireworks… Give much love & a great many kisses to all and especially my darling little baby.   —Your devoted husband *Henry*.

July 5, 1898, Denver.
Darling Kate—   Just home for a bite and then off to the office to work on this confounded case. I read the riot act in a quiet way to the Colorado Springs people last night. I never was so tired of a case… I hope to get away Thursday night & reach you Sunday morning but I cannot tell. I am pretty worn out but otherwise well. Love & kisses for all.   —Devotedly *Henry*.

July 6th, 1898.
My Darling Husband—   Your Baby boy is better today than since we left home. It is lovely & cool, about seventy… The children are all at the woods— except Thayer, with the Boughtons. Poor little Carrie B— has heart trouble, her body is bloated, and they have to drive down to the woods with her. Katherine has taken down some little treasures to give her. It is so sad to see a child ill & suffering. Edward & his wife were here this morning to call. They always come when one is unsettled… fresh coat of paint on dining room. Love & kisses many from us all. Your letters are a comfort. Your own Devoted *Kittie*.

◦ Letters from Annie Jennings Wise Hobson:

Ashland, June 27th, 1898.
My dear Son—   Your letter was received yesterday when I was quite sick. As I wrote you yesterday, I mean Saturday, I was in Richmond to see about Rosa Brooks— I have succeeded in getting her back with the baby in the Magdalene home on the condition that I will try to get or give her sewing to help support the baby. In the fall she will have to put it out with someone. And, my dear good son, I wish you to weigh well what I say. Everything seems to point towards my not breaking up this fall. I have in crops of oats for my horse & cow, a full supply of winter vegetables, for all of which I would not receive their worth to me if the place is rented, & I am sure Col. Patton would find great difficulty in renting it in the fall. Having to get ready, George & Mary, for school is enough for me to do before October, and I should have to prepare to move during the heat of September— one of the most trying months to me. I am now having a restful sort of time & enjoying it, and if I thought I had all this before me, it would upset me very much. This I can do, rent from Col. Patton by the quarter instead of the year. I am sure the place could be easily rented in the spring… The expense of moving would be considerable… It would be more than I could stand to have to part from Little Alice & Jennings now. They are not the kind of children to be put off from home influence and these two children have become especially near & dear to me, & they both seem inexpressibly distressed at the idea of parting from me. This year would test what George & Mary will do at school, and I shall send them both with the understanding that unless they apply themselves, the advantage will not be repeated.

   I do not believe that Mother [Mary Lyons Wise] will last very much longer. Not only does her mind grow worse but she is physically far more feeble, & she is beginning some trouble with kidneys and liver. She has been very prostrated this morning. Just now she said, "Dear Annie, I feel I cannot be here much longer. I pray God to take me. It will be a relief to you all!" I clearly foresee that she will require hospital treatment if she lives on, and then I shall try to arrange to be near her. God grant she may go before the last physical ailment of paralysis & old age attack her… If she is here another spring, I will find a way to provide for her if we break up, and I will take all the children to Mrs. Taliafero in Amherst C. H. where they will receive every attention & kindness & can be boarded on very low terms… She it was, who took us in when Cannon's family had to give up the Rectory, and who kept the children before they were brought to Richmond after their father returned from Colorado. Mrs. Taliafero would be so glad to have the benefit of our board… Bettie Ambler says that she will come & take charge here at any time in the fall that I may wish to take a trip or rest. Or I might also make an arrangement to take a house in Williamsburg where she could have a room, & take charge of Mother & the children when I desired it… [end of letter]

Ashland, June 27th, 1898.
My dear Katherine—   Your note announcing your arrival in South Cambridge and being domiciled in the Old Home reached me today. I had been expecting such tidings as Henry wrote you expected to come East this month. We are rejoicing also in a rain for all growing things were suffering & all humanity seemed parched. I never suffered from heat as I did for two weeks this summer.

It completely prostrated Mother and I thought for a while, one night when I called to her, that she was going to have another paralytic stroke… George passed his examinations… Mary received excellent reports and has improved in every respect, but she is very delicate… Bro. John [John S. Wise] has had several paralytic strokes & is in a very bad way… Now I must take up lifes burden & work as never before. Through Johnnie's liberality I have been able to keep my comfortable home, but even if Mother lives I must leave it in October. As long as she lives and Johnnie enables me to do so, my first duty will be to her. When she goes, if God will give me the health and strength, I will place my poor children, who are regarded as the "Pariahs" of the family, in some school homes and find employment for myself, that will enable me to educate & give them a start in life & if possible to leave them a little something. Mary is very frail and seems very grave & sad. I hope your limb gains strength. It distresses me to think of you on crutches. I am sure it will do you all good to come East & hope you may find comfort & peace in the old home & restoration to strength that will benefit your knee & bring it back to its normal condition…

Life seems more & more a dream— everything so unreal. My garden work will be accomplished by the middle of July. I must then sell my horse & carriage & probably my cow. I will think of you & the children in your pleasant rides around your beautiful country… Tell dear Henry I received his letter & will answer it soon… I believe that John's family are at Cape Charles. My prayers ever follow Hugh in that wicked contest in the Philippines. Everyone is in bed & I am almost too tired to write coherently… Again God the comforter be with you. Yours in sympathy & affection. *A. J. W. H.*

Ashland, July 6th, 1898.
My dearest Son—   Your letter of [blank space] was received today and it grieves me to hear you are still detained by plodding work in Denver. I am glad that you heard all had arrived safely at the Old Home. I hope that the change will soon tell upon little Thayer. Nothing is more beneficial to a teething baby than a decided change. Little Katherine will soon be herself in that healthy invigorating climate, & the change will be good for all… I have been thinking all day that your anniversary of life, your 40th birthday will so soon be here. I wish you to write me the title of some book you would like to have for your summer reading. I like the thought of the books handed down to your children— (if only one here and there amongst them) being associated with "Papa's Mamma" as a birthday gift.

It is hard to realise that you have passed through forty years of life, for you are still "My Boy" to me and always seem so young. I am glad & proud my son, of the record of those years. It has not been given you to stand a hero upon any battle field before the world, or to perform any brilliant deed, yet I feel assured that you have fought a fight on the side of right and duty that has been noble and good in the sight of man and God; you have trod a steadfast path of integrity and earnest endeavors unselfishly and manfully for others, and you have proved yourself every inch a man and have helped other lives by the use you have made of God-given ability and the manifestation of high character.

I would have rejoiced to see your spiritual development on a higher plane, and it is a deep sorrow that you have not yet declared yourself a "Soldier of the Cross" before the world; yet I do believe you have sought and had divine help in your aspirations and endeavors as a son, a brother, a citizen, and a man unusually blessed as a husband & father. Surely no Mother ever had more reason to thank God for a noble son than I have, and to pray that he may be spared to a vigorous and happy old age, & that all the latter days of life may be far better than the first here, and that your own children and loving wife may fully compensate for all the yoke borne in youth and early manhood. May you reap richly in the love & devotion of your children as the most blessed reward for your life of filial devotion to your Mother. Sometimes I have had the hope that while enough life and vigor was left to me to do so, I might come into your life before I died in some way that would be a joy & pleasure to you as well as to myself, but I feel now it will never be & I do not deserve it. I do ask God if possible to grant that my dear Father's prophecy may prove true, that I may die sitting in my chair at work. The children all join me in love and wishes that you may have many happy returns of your birthday. As usual my three anniversaries come together, and many are the memories and blessed thoughts that cluster around them…

We have had the most prostrating weather I have ever felt in Ashland. Even poor old Mother succumbed to it & she generally does not feel the heat. This dreadful war keeps me in a state of excitement all the time… It is so terrible to read of the dead & wounded amongst our brave men. It seems to me such an unnecessary sacrifice of life… I have dreaded to look amongst the list of the dead fearing Hugh's name might be there. I feel for so keenly for Johnnie. He is so devoted to his boys & he must especially miss Henry. Not one word from Cannon or Henry. I can only trust to God's care & His answers to my unworthy prayers. When you get settled down in New York we will discuss my plans. I do wish you could have a real rest. It makes me uneasy to hear of your weariness. I shall write to Katherine tonight. God bless & keep you through many years of happy life—   —Your devoted Mother, *A. J. W. H.*

—I forgot to say that I gave the children a few fire-works for the fourth. George & Jennings went to a picnic… We had a cold dinner & I treated to ice-cream. The little girls went black-berrying. We came near having a very serious ending. About seven o'clock, no nearly eight, I went to the back porch and smelt something burning. I hastened to examine [illegible] found in the oil-closet (so called because it was made to keep kerosene & all pertaining to the lamps), a table on fire. The law I lay down is that no match or light must be taken there, especially no lamps lit there. It was evident that someone had lighted a lamp there and thrown the match carelessly down. In ten minutes the whole closet would have been in a blaze. Two buckets of water extinguished it. I thanked God for the narrow escape we all had. Mother & Eliza send you ever so much love & would have birthday messages if I had told them about the 9th, but in self-defense I did not, because Mother would have asked so many questions… [end of letter]

∽ In the news:

A DAY OF THANKSGIVING — President McKinley Asks the People to Praise God for the Success of our Arms — And Offer Prayer for Peace — He Fixes the Next Assembling for Divine Worship for the Observance in All the Churches of the Land

LA BOURGOGNE SINKS AT SEA —Five Hundred and Sixty-two Persons Lost with Her — Wreck Off Island Sable — French Liner Collides with British Ship *Cromar-*

tyshire — In Heavy Fog At Dawn — Out of 725 Passengers and Crew Only 163 Saved — Fierce Fight for Life — It is Charged by Survivors that the Crew Beat Passengers from Lifeboats. —*The New York Times*, July 7, 1898.

July 9, 1898, B. & W. Train.
My Dearest Mother—   When I woke up this morning and was thinking that I must write you a line, all at once I thought "why this is my birthday" —I have been under a strain for the past two weeks. I have been, until yesterday noon, ten days engaged in a very important trial and at my office until 11 o'clk every night working upon the case. I left the jury hung which means either a compromise verdict against me or a mistrial. The judge took a most outrageous partisan course against me and I fear the other side tampered with some of the Jury. I am now late in getting East but it cannot be helped. I am going to stop for a day at the Farm to see my wife and children and will reach N.Y. on Tuesday night if all goes well. As soon as I can do so, I wish to run down and settle about Grandma and the children. K— writes that they got through all safely and that all were well except little Thayer. He cut a tooth on the way and suffered very much from the heat and was quite sick… I do not know what to write you in the way of a birthday letter, for I do not feel very lively or cheerful. The fact is, I am utterly worn out and whilst my general health is better than ever before, I am very very tired mentally and physically… I cannot help feeling a little impressed over the fact that today I pass the line dividing youth and early manhood from middle-aged manhood. Forty years of my life have gone and so many disappointments have come. Ah! Watchman— What of the hour! …I do not forget this is also the anniversary of your wedding day and I wish you many pleasant and happy thoughts and memories. If you can for a time forget the sorrow laden years and go back to your earlier life, surely much joy and pleasure must come. I fear you are having a very hot spell if the newspaper accounts are correct and that you are all suffering with heat. Poor old Grandma, it must be hard on her and yet she has passed into the lotus period of forget and after all, physical discomfort is not much if the mind is free of care. Our poor soldiers in Cuba must be suffering dreadfully and what gallant men they are… I am one of those who believe that achievements such as those of the past two months, though dashed with savagery and blood, go to make a Nation strong, a People Great. I think the war will be over before Henry & Jack get to the front though they both seem to be very enthusiastic about fighting… You will remember that I predicted that at every meeting under fair conditions, the Spaniard would go down before our Navy and Army and the results have been so complete that they have almost seemed like *Opera Bouffe*… There are many things in our environment and institutions I would like to see improved but on the whole I am a pronounced optimist and expect great things of our nation for the future. I hardly know what my plans for the summer are. My work in connection with our RR reorganization will be the controlling factor, and I will have to come and go as that demands. I shall be so glad when it is all over and I can once more follow a quiet steady life. There is not even about this kind of work the gratification arising from good intellectual work, gratified ambition, reputation made. It is the work of the money-changers in the Temple and I feel I am worthy to do better work. Ah well! We shall see. I have written you a poor kind of a birthday letter but as I said in the start, I am not in the mood for pleasant writing and then the car is so full of dust and dirt. My loving greet-

This is the only surviving letter from Henry Hobson to his mother.

ing however goes forth to you upon this my 40th birthday. —With much love, Your loving son *Henry W. Hobson.*

~ Correspondence with John S. Wise:

South Cambridge, July 8th, 1898.
My Dearest Uncle Johnnie— You are in my heart & mind all the time. As I think of Hugh in the thick of the fight. At, Santiago, his pure, manly, noble, face in all that fearful scene. May God keep, & bless the dear fellow. You have my tender, loving sympathy in all your anxieties… I am all for peace and think it is a mistake to have gone into this war. We had a hot trip on from Colo. Thayer is now eight months old and he was made quite ill by the fearful heat… We are all resting in the delicious, cool, quiet country… Mother is here & enjoying seeing her four grandchildren (the sixth generation to live here) in her old house… *Katherine.* (Virginia Historical Society)

July 8th/98.
Dearest Katherine— For that sweet darling letter I will open mine by a present for Henry's birthday— Trumbull & I have just resolved to give him an extension of his furlough— Say to him that we held a meeting of the Committee today & adjourned *until Wednesday next* so that he may remain with you until next Tuesday evening. Now there is a present of 4 days & I call it a nice one.

I do not know how to thank you dear K— not only for your words but for the love & solicitude breathed in every line of your letter. I will confess it that dear little Hugh is my very heart's core & I never knew what agony of waiting was in store for me until the bloody work at San Juan heights began. First I heard of the battle— Then that Kent's Division was bearing the brunt of it— Then that the Spaniards were offering a stout resistance— Then that our troops had stormed & won the hill— Then that our losses had been very heavy, first 1,000, then 2,000, & finally 3,000. That was Saturday night. I was in the country & Sunday we could learn no more. I'll never forget the pain of that night & day. Eva bears up bravely under such circumstances. I was so agitated I walked three miles from the Depot. The full moon lit the way & I looked at it time and again & wondered whether it was shining down on his dead face at Santiago. It was after midnight when Eva & I sat in our room & talked about it. I didn't tell her that Kent's Division had fought and suffered most, but she saw how troubled I was and at last said, "Oh! John, it's *terrible*. When the other two died I at least had the consolation of sitting by them & cooling their foreheads or placing ice to their lips, but now we can do *nothing, nothing*." But we both agreed that nothing would have kept him away.

He had been twice ordered to leave his regiment and report to General Douglas for staff duty. Both times he replied that he would not consent to leave until after the fight. It was eleven o'clock Sunday night before we heard a word— Then came a telegram telling us Hugh was safe. Dear old Dick who loves him almost as much as I do, went to the War Dept. & stayed there until he heard the returns from every regiment, & then he telegraphed me. I cannot describe the relief it gave me. Monday the 4th came the news of our great victory over Cervara, & the towns-folk turned out that afternoon & made me deliver a Fourth of July address. The agony was over. On my return I found

the other two died John S. Wise and Evelyn Douglas Wise had nine children, two of whom died when small children.

Wise family cemetery, near Chesconessex Creek, Onancock, Virginia, where, "eight generations of your children's ancestors have lived, died & been buried" –John S. Wise.

letters from him describing his life on the transport, & now I am waiting to hear the little monkey's account of the battle. I suppose the next trouble will be with Henry & Jack whose command will go off in a day or two. I am going down to spend Sunday with them.

Truth is I am deeper into this business than I intended & sincerely hope that the indications of coming peace may soon fructify. I find it much harder to watch & wait for my boys than it was to do a little fighting on my own account. Jack sent me your letter to him & I was glad to see it. He is very proud of it. It is a great joy to me that you & Henry found Jack congenial. I love Henry, & trust him, I am proud of him as a boy of my raising, & want my boys to know & feel it.

It is too bad about the baby being sick— *Of course* he chose the very time you traveled to cut a tooth. I hope the new place will speedily revive him. Take him out to drive— By the way you never said a word about how you like Broker— I hope you do like him for he has cost enough to be good. Katherine can't you bring little K— sometime & go down with me to Accomac? They are crazy to have you— Tell K— that Néné has a beautiful black pony & pony-cart and Bossy a St. Lawrence skiff. She can ride & sail & have a glorious time. Bossy caught 30 crabs on one tide. Now do come & I [will] show you where eight generations of your children's ancestors have lived, died & been buried. Our folks have been there since 1635.

I am not half done which I wanted to say but must close.

—Good-bye affect, *John S. Wise*.

July 8. Henry left Denver this p.m. —*Diary of Catherine McKie Thayer*.

∽ In the news:

SPAIN REALIZES WAR IS HOPELESS —Cabinet Said to Be Dominated by the Peace Idea — Inclined to Early Action — European Powers Advising Madrid Government to Yield — Expectation of Help from Other Countries Abandoned.

—*The New York Times*, July 11, 1898.

July 11. Henry came today from Denver. —*Diary of Catherine McKie Thayer.*

July 19, 1898, Old Home.
My Darling Husband— The rain came about ten last evening & rained all night. The brook is broader than the Bridge. We had a thunder-storm too— a great deal of flaring, heat lightning. Today is muggy and cloudy... I am going to telegraph those plumbers, they are too trying. And no tub could be on the way since June 29th! I forwarded a letter from your mother & Dr. Fisk. I shall write your mother at once. Yesterday I had a bad headache all day and through the night. Eleanor stepped on one of her chickens this morning & she was so distressed, but I gave it 2 drops of whiskey and brought it out of its stupor. Mother is downstairs again & feels much better... —Love to Uncle Johnnie. *Always your devoted Wife.*

July 20th, 1898. Old Home
My Darling Husband— This is a warm day & the general appearance of the country is much improved by the rain... The plumber is putting in the sink. The tub was shipped on the 13th & will "come over any day now." So the plumber says in his leisurely way... The Baby crept up the porch steps today & cut another tooth... —With a heart full of love— *Katherine.* —All chicks send love.

July 21, 1898, Hotel Touraine, Boston.
Darling Kate— Only a moment to write. I am just off for N.Y. I hope to be with you tomorrow night. Much love & many kisses. —Devotedly *Henry.*

July 25, 1898, New York.
Darling Kate— A short letter to say I am all right. I got in this morning at 6:30 after a fair night only... I am afraid I was very cross and edgewise on this trip, but I am beginning to believe that is my chronic condition. I am so testy and unstable and it takes very little to upset me... Uncle J. has a splendid letter from Hugh describing the fighting and I am trying to get him to publish it. Capt Anderson of Hugh's regiment & one or two privates who are in hospital tell Uncle J— that he showed splendid courage. One of the papers in describing his photographic exploit speaks of it as a fine piece of gallantry, coolness, and audacity combined. I have nothing more to write and it is late. Love & kisses to the darlings. —Devotedly *Henry.*

A letter from Annie Jennings Wise Hobson:

Ashland, July 15th, 1898.
My dear Son— Each day lately I have hoped to hear of your arrival at the Farm, & that you had spent at least a few days with your dear ones... Your letter written on the 9th *enroute* to New York has been read with pleasure more than once... I do indeed believe that you are worthy of a better life than the drudgery for the mighty dollar. Yet yours has been a consecrated life of toil because of the noble motives that impelled you. It has always been a cherished hope of mine that your latter days might be given to higher and more congenial work & vocation. I have asked God that if possible such might be the case. I feel that it will come to you after an experience that will lead to higher

spiritual development when all life will stand on a grand noble plane. I understand all you express about the realization that you have passed the dividing line of life…

—July 16th. I am writing at six o'clock on the front porch. We have the most exhausting spell of heat I ever felt… Thursday it commenced to be hot again, but the boys & I were given half tickets that we might go to Fredericksburg & visit Camp Cobb— taking Henry & Jack a good supply of edibles… Therefore we carried a good supply of fried chicken, a ham, vegetables, cake, delicious home-made bread, pickles, and sweetmeats. Henry was to have met us at the depot to take us to the camp. He did not get to the depot on time but met us on the way. A carriage offered to take the two boys and myself to the camp & all our boxes & bags for fifty cents. Henry jumped in the carriage with us & he speedily had the various packages put away in the tent… He told me that his Mother and sister & Tim had arrived from Accomac that morning, and that he must ride immediately to the hotel to see them. I must confess that I did not feel happy over this information. I knew Eva would want her boys to herself during the short stay & our day with them was spoiled as I had hoped to spend it. I went with them to the hotel and did not receive a very warm welcome from either of the Eva's… As soon as possible I left them with their boys and went to find the residence of my friend… Henry then invited us to come out in the afternoon and see the camp fully, the drilling & target practice. He came for me to join his Mother & Eva in a hack. The camp-ground is beautiful but lacks shade, but they have excellent running water from a cold spring… The boys seemed most gratified at my coming & contribution in edibles. They look so well… Eva looks very worn and has evidently suffered much over Hugh. She told me what a trying ordeal she & John went through when, for several days, Hugh was reported missing. When we parted Eva was much more cordial & gracious and expressed quite warmly her appreciation of my going to see the boys…

I do hope you have received my various letters— some addressed to Cambridge & some to the Cable Commercial Building. I told you in one the arrival, after a long delay, of your two photographs which gave me such pleasure. I think both are excellent, & I wish to make the frames for them myself. You could have sent me nothing that gave me the same pleasure. I enjoy looking at the children & then your dear self; & what I wish to make it complete is a picture, a good photo, of the lovely Mother… I will send this letter to South Cambridge as I feel sure you will spend Sunday there. I wish to write to both Mrs. Thayer and Katherine. I am so relieved by the surrender of Santiago. The report of yellow fever amongst the troops made me feel ill. I pray daily for peace. I hope John's two boys now in camp will never get to the front before peace comes. I felt heart-sick with anxiety about Hugh… Do inquire at the Sewall line office as nothing has been heard from the *Kenilworth*. There is no reason why it should not return now. It is dreadful not hearing oftener from my boys. All join me in love. I must close at once in time for the mail. Kiss the darlings and Katherine for me… I hope the dear little Thayer has revived. God bless you all & may you all have a happy September. —Your devoted Mother, *A. J. W. Hobson*. —The boys enjoy their camping out in New Hampshire with their teacher, though they say their fare is atrocious & scanty. The girls are so lovely to me. I do hope to hear from you today. Cannon will be 18 the 31st.

Eva   Eveyln Byrd Douglas Wise, wife of John S. Wise.

⁓ Letters from Camp Cobb:

Camp Cobb, Fredericksburg Va. [undated]
My Dear Cousin Henry—   Throckmorton has just told me that you say you have not had a line from me since I left Denver. I did write you from New York…

Mustered in Norfolk Wednesday. Thursday we left by boat for Washington. Friday we arrived here and pitched "Co L" in camp with the 4th U.S. Vols.

This is Sunday. The men are getting some rest. Yesterday Henry went to Washington to see about his uniform. Our second lieutenant is a man named Peyton: He's from Staunton and a nice fellow. He was at the V.M.I. [Virginia Military Institute] with us. Belonged to the Class of '93. Was a sub-professor there when I was in the first class. We have a V.M.I. man for our first sergeant and another for another sergeant. We have seven or eight old soldiers in our company. Yesterday we started squad drill and I have never seen a company make as good a start as we made.

While in Norfolk Henry picked up a negro. We picked him up in the street. He is the most utterly worthless coon I ever saw. Henry spends half his leisure hunting for his negro and the rest of his time damning the negro and making him do what he wants done. Yesterday I gave the negro the hot end of a rope. That made him work about an hour. Now Henry carries a rope for his man.

Peyton has a lot of business to wind up in Staunton so I let him off first. When he comes back he'll bring his man-servant for himself and me. Col. Pettit is a very fine man. He has his regiment in very good condition considering they are all green soldiers. I am going to send a button to Eleanor. It is the first military button I got into my hand upon entering the service. I had my hair cut short several days ago. You should see it. It sets like the quills of a porcupine.

In Onancock I found the family all well and very nicely fixed. I have not had time to write to them yet. Bridget whelped three very handsome pups several days before I got home. Two of them are dogs. She has never allowed anybody to go near them yet but I claimed first dog pick for you. If you want it, you should write and get a positive promise of it before it is given away. My company has a very handsome collie dog. They stole him in Norfolk. They stole a kitten in Washington.

While I have been writing Henry's negro went to sleep in Henry's bed. Henry has just thrown him on the floor. The guard is now after him for bringing liquor into camp. Sad to relate he is not guilty… I got a sweet letter from Cousin K— several days ago but I haven't had time to answer it yet.

Before I mustered my men I was working and traveling day and night. Fighting will be a picnic for us. We never had time to change our clothes half the time.

When you've time, write me. Give my love to Cousin K. and the children—   With best love —Yrs affectionately, *John S. Wise Jr.*

Camp Cobb, Fredericksburg VA June 28/98.
My Dear Cousin K—   As I was about to write to you a day or two ago, Throckmorton told me to write to Cousin H— so I missed writing as early as I intended to write. Now I can write only a few words. But I will write what I can to show you I am always thinking of you.

I went to Washington yesterday and purchased my equipment. Our camp is settled now. Our men are beginning to look like soldiers. They are all uniformed and equipped in full. Our regiment has more equipment and is in better condition than a great many that are much older.

The V.M.I. is coming out in fine colors in this war. In this regiment it has three captains, two 1st. Lieutenants, two first sergeants, and several privates. In the list of second lieutenants appointed last week there are about twenty-five V.M.I. men. They have gone from almost every state in all offices from Colonels down and as privates too.

Uncle Dick is in Washington. I stayed with him last night. He is in very good health. He is very busy now. I have not seen him as well in a long time. His nerves are better than I ever knew them to be.

Little Hugh is with Shafton at Santiago or Cuba— He's in the thick of it. We hope to be there before many moons. I hope to be Battalion adjutant as soon as one is appointed for our third battalion.

This a pretty country down here but it is as hot as the mischief. It was one hundred and seven in the shade Sunday. We have had a little rain but not much.

Give my love to the "chicks" and Cousin Henry and Mrs. Thayer.

—With best love for yourself, Affectionately, *John. S. Wise Jr.*

◦∾ Death in the family:

July 26, 1898. New York.
Darling Kate—   Today we heard sad news about poor little Henry. We saw the enclosed in newspaper, and it is confirmed by cablegram to the agents here. We can get no further details. I feel very much distressed over the matter. I have written Mother hurriedly… I wish you would write a nice letter to Mother at once. I am very hard worked here and it is pretty hot. I hope to get up to The Farm on Friday. Let me know about new horses.   —Love & kisses for all. Devotedly *Henry*.

Kenilworth Afire at Sea — Clipper ship from Hawaii for New York puts into Valparaiso with Captain and Two Men Dead. The American clipper ship *Kenilworth*, according to a cablegram, put into Valparaiso yesterday with her cargo on fire. The captain, first-mate and cabin boy were dead. Just how they lost their lives is not known, but it is supposed they were suffocated. The *Kenilworth* is a four-masted steel vessel of 2,293 tons, owned by Arthur W. Sewall of Maine. This was her second experience with fire. The *Kenilworth* is loaded with sugar and sailed form Hilo, Hawaii, May 22 for New York. She was commanded by Capt. John G. Baker of Searsport, Me. The mate, John Piper, lived somewhere in New Jersey. The home of Hobson, the cabin boy, is not known. The vessel was built at Glasgow, Scotland, in 1887. She is 300 feet 2 inches long, 43 feet beam and 24 feet deep. She was badly damaged by fire in 1890 and was purchased by Arthur W. Sewall, who obtained for her American registry.   —*Unidentified newspaper clipping.*

July 27th, 1898, Old Home.
My Darling Husband—   Arthur went to Troy yesterday, taking one pair of horses & returning with the other pair from H—'s. He says they drive much more freely than the other pair. We are going to try them tomorrow. Have been to Beadle Hill this morning. Took Harriet. She calls me by my name very naturally. Eleanor & Henry went too. Katherine had a very happy day yester-

day at the Boughtons… You had better take the best care of yourself this hot weather… —Much love & many kisses, from your devoted wife. *Katherine.* —The children send love always to Papa.

July 27, 1898, New York.
Darling Kate—   I am writing whilst listening to testimony with my good ear. I am very very busy and will have to write as I can. We have been able to get no further details about poor little Henry but Uncle J— is going to Washington this afternoon and he will get the Secretary of State to wire the Consul at Valparaiso…   —Devotedly *Henry.*

July 28th, 1898, The Old Home.
My Dearest Henry—   Your letter received last evening. I am heart-sick over Little Henry's awful end. I saw in the *Herald* that the Capt. & 1st Mate were dead, but no mention of Cabin Boy. That boy was a manly fine fellow. I liked him & his eyes were so beautiful & his gaze. And he seemed so grateful for the little affection I gave him. I have written your Mother & suppose of course, you will write Alice. I shall. When that boy was given money to go to the Base Ball game, he went to see his Mother instead. And I liked him for it. The morning is raining and we hope our cisterns will be filled… We will hope for your coming Friday, but I fancy you will wish to be with your Mother possibly & much as I long for you here, you will, I know, do what you feel would give her the greatest comfort. Tenderest love my Darling one. I feel so anxious to have you working away in the heat. God Bless & keep you.   —Always your own loving wife— *Katherine.*

New York, July 29, 1898.
Darling Kate—   My how busy I am and have no time for letters. I was working again until 11 o'clk last night… I had a pitiful kind of a letter from Mother today. Poor old woman she seems to be hard hit. She will enjoy hearing from you. If I have good luck I will leave tomorrow at 1 o'clk and reach you before 7. I am almost worn out. Love & kisses. Devotedly, *Henry.*

 ~ A letter from Annie Jennings Wise Hobson:

Ashland, July 27th, 1898.
My dear Son— Your letter and John's came this morning. I had sent the phaeton to the Depot thinking it possible that you or John might come, but not expecting either, knowing how busy you both are. I saw a notice in the *Baltimore Sun* which said that the Captain, First Officer & Boy Hobson were reported dead. It was a fearful shock! As my dear Sister said one year ago when Henry Garnett died, "I have never had a sorrow like this before." I was completely unnerved for a while. Now I feel that no human sympathy can help me. As a second notice said, that the death of the Captain and Mate have been corroborated and no mention of Henry, I seized upon a feeble hope, & wired the Sewall Company in Maine, & received the reply that "their advisers reported Hobson as dead."

    I thank God for the letter he wrote me from San Francisco telling me he now knew how good & kind I had been, & that a fool he had been, & his letter to you was brave & manly.

I have wept sorrowful tears for the good Captain who wrote me such a kind letter about Henry. It is blessed to repeat myself, "his conduct has been excellent & he is a great favorite with sailors, officers and the Captain." He said in his letter to me, "Grandma, I shall be so glad to be back with you." If I could not trust that God had so answered my prayers that His grace had made my poor Boy ready for the dark passage— could not trust to the infinite mercy of a God— man who knows our infirmities, I could not face this bitter grief. If I did not know how I tried in every way to dissuade Henry from persevering in trying a sea-faring life I should reproach myself bitterly, and I know that both you & John were acting for the best.

Mr. John Addison came to see me last evening. It was he who secured Henry's trip for him to Charleston & he seemed really fond of the boy. He has much to do with the shipping of chemicals etc. When he heard all the circumstances, he at once said what I had thought probable— "From all accounts the cargo caught fire, sugar burns slowly but makes a dense smoke, & they must have been suffocated before the fire was discovered." This death was far preferable to me from fire & agony of pain. I can only say, "Out of the depths have I called unto you. I am dumb before this."

I would not have had you come, for I wish you to get through your work and take some recreation. I inclose you a letter returned to me from the Dead letter office. I would rewrite & condense it but am not equal to any exertion I can avoid.

I slept very little last night. This letter will give you my reasons for not breaking up 'til the spring. I think George & Mary's going to school had best be deferred till next year. George himself says he would prefer to study with Miss Lowe another year and be better prepared for school, & she is capable of preparing him.

It seems doubtful now about Mary's getting the scholarship at Sophie's & there are reasons, I cannot tell you why, it would be better for her not to leave my care for another year. I could not give up Jennings or Alice, especially since one is gone. I trust my boy is with his father at rest forever— only to be praised for and not to be prayed for, as Cannon is. I wrote to Cannon today telling the sad story & I know he will suffer for he loved Henry devotedly. I enclosed the letter to Mr. Horsbrugh asking him to break the news & be kind to the boy so far from home & sympathy.

It was a great relief to hear that Cannon had done nothing really unprincipled. I was so afraid he had given way to temptation or had some difficulty that had involved him in serious trouble. Mr. Horsbrugh depicts Cannon as I know him to be, but though it may be weak to do so, I still try to hope his soul will yet develop, & he will be his best.

I had a letter from him the other day saying, "I am in fine health, & have a pleasant time but I have worked very hard during the last month, & Mr. Horsbrugh told me the other day that he was going to put my name on the payroll the first of next month." So it seems as if Mr. Horsbrugh was thinking better of him. I do not mean to be conceited about my judgment as to Mother, and though I do deserve any reproach you can give me about my failure in life & the burden it has entailed on you, it hurts none the less when given. One consoling thought about poor little Henry is that I hope he is free from sin, temptation, & suffering & there is one less to burden you in the future. The strongest incentive I have to live is to try in a few years to free you of care about these children. I would be glad to think that in a few years we would all be where Henry is, leaving you without any incumbrance from us.

The distress of the children is very pitiful. Yesterday it was almost more than I could stand, & I had to ask God to give me the strength to comfort them. Mr. Ware, as I wrote you, has been taking his meals here as a boarder & I cannot tell you how good and lovely, even as a son, he has been to me, & he has been almost made sick by sympathy.

Poor Alice wrote in agony— Henry is her favorite child & she expects to be confined in two months. I pity her deeply.

Mother's failure is evident. Mr. Ware yesterday noticed the changed expression of her face. She scarcely recollected who Henry was & did not take in the trouble when Mr. Ware told her about it.

Your loving sympathy is a solace, but a wound like mine only God can heal. I have grieved that such a trouble should come upon you when so burdened with work.

George is like one who has received a nervous shock. Is there any chance of recovering Henry's body— Could it not be embalmed & brought home— unless he has been buried at sea. If my letter seems incoherent, do not wonder, I feel so dazed. I had a telegram of sympathy from Barton Wise. All Ashland friends have been very kind & sympathetic. I try to realize amidst the darkness that God's light is behind the thick cloud & my many mercies.

God bless you my noble, good son & bless all yours and save you from such heart agonies as I have endured, rewarding you for your goodness & faithfulness to me & these children as you deserve. Henry will tell his father about it. Love to all at the Home Farm. I had a lovely letter from Katherine which I will try to answer soon. Do not attempt to come here while it is so hot. I would not have you come, & it would trouble Katherine as it did last summer when you did your duty in coming to Henry Garnett. I mean she was so concerned lest you be made sick. The children send love. Do not trouble to write long letters when you are so busy.   —Your devoted Mother, *A. J. W. Hobson*.

THE WESTERN UNION TELEGRAPH COMPANY
July 29th, 1898, Washington, D. C.
TO: John S. Wise   Following reply just received from Valpariso: "*Kenilworth* put into Valpariso twenty fourth instant. Investigation made cargo of sugar on fire eighth instant. Captain, Mate and Hobson, died same night by inhaling gas from burned cargo. Buried at sea. Measures to extinguish fire taken." *Wm. R. Day* 10:37 a.m. (Virginia Historical Society)

August 1st, 1898, The Old Home.
My Darling Husband—   …Your visit was such a joy & our walk yesterday was so lovely to me… Going over this lovely country & wandering about with my *best beloved*. You do not know that every day you are more & more precious & I am more & more in love with you.   —Love & kisses, many, to you from your own devoted Wife, *Katherine*.

August 2nd, 1898, The Old Home.
My Darling Henry—   The enclosed letter came for you this morning & I send it, having read it, as your Mother so directed on her envelope. We had a

beautiful rain last night & water in both cisterns— clear & fresh. Hope to hear by tomorrow you are safely in N.Y. It is such a pleasure to have had you here. I am leaving that sweet love story for you to finish. I have a letter from Jack today— his company is the best and finest in the Army… Mother is enjoying her old home so much & it will always be a comfort to me to have seen her here with the children. She said to me last night— "I would not stay here ten minutes without you & the children." Think of her memories! Parents, Husband & six brothers, all gone. Then though it is a pleasure to her to have Frank & his wife here & see them happy. And she is to talk over Farm matters with him this week. If you are to going to Virginia I wish you would go when I am not able to take walks & go browsing around in the hot sun… Much tender love & kisses from us all. —Your own Devoted wife, *Katherine.*

August 2, 1898, New York.
Darling Kate— Only time for a line. I had your sweet letter today and it is worth more than money can buy to get such dear loving words from you upon whom I am so dependent for everything in life. Of course it is all right your keeping what you please out of your money, and if you wish more, say so. I enjoyed my Sunday immensely. I am so busy, and it is so hot. Love & kisses. I cannot write more. —Devotedly *Henry.*

The Old Home, South Cambridge, Thursday, August 4th, 1898.
My Dearest Uncle Johnnie— We all thank you for the two letters of Hugh's. What a splendid fellow he is. I feel so proud of him & his record if he must face the foe & death, as he did. I am glad he was in that charge up San Juan Hill. His letters show his heart has been sorely tried. God bless & keep him… I hope time will show there is no truth in the report of mutiny on the *Kenilworth.* Poor little Henry. Oh, Uncle Johnnie, how it tries ones faith to live & accept all these terrible afflictions. Much love to all. The Baby is eleven months old today & such a Darling… —Always loving, *Katherine.* My brother asks to be remembered— he & his wife are here. (Virginia Historical Society)

August 5. Henry came.
August 7. Henry and Little H— walked over to the Whiteside's— came back & all walked over to the Boughton's. In p.m. all went to Church. After H— & I walked about, talked over plans. In p.m. all went to church… H— read to chicks.
August 8. Henry left early for Johnsonville. —*Diary of Catherine McKie Thayer.*

XXII

1898, Part Two

August

AFTER spending the weekend at the farm in Cambridge, Henry Hobson returned to New York City on August 8th while Katherine and the children remained at the Old Home.

Letters, diaries, and telegrams by:
Henry C. Coke
L. M. Cuthbert
Annie Jennings Wise Hobson
Henry Wise Hobson
Katherine Thayer Hobson
Katherine Thayer Hobson (II)
Raleigh C. Minor
Rosewell Page
A. E. Pattison
Annie Stewart
Lucy Stewart
Francis McKie Thayer
John S. Wise
Catherine McKie Thayer

Letters and telegrams written from: New York City and Cambridge, New York; Sapinero, Colorado Springs, and Denver, Colorado; Brook Hill, Henrico County, Charlottesville, and Ashland, Virginia; Dallas, Texas; and Jacksonville, Florida.

~

August 1898

August 9, 1898, South Cambridge.
My Darling Henry—   It is lovely here this afternoon. So charming to see Eleanor washing under the pine tree, using the tub & wash-board she purchased the other day in Cambridge. She wishes you to know what she is doing. Mother, Harriet & Katherine went to Troy for the day. It is always interesting to me to see how Mother enjoys taking Katherine off with her. Old Cousin Robert has been reading Hugh's letter & told me today "it was a fine account & agreed with the *Tribune*" which is his chief delight in life. I do hope if we are to go to the Pages it will be cool to stay, for I should hate to take my precious baby off in intense heat. Eleanor has a yellow kitten & has named it "Buttercup." Mr. F— came yesterday with the horses & I took Mother out

after them. They drove very well and we are just going again. They are somewhat afraid of cars Arthur says. Not fast, but drive along well. We are going to Greenwich tomorrow. Much tender love & kisses.   —Your own loving devoted wife *Katherine.*

Tuesday, August 9, 1898, New York.
My darling Kate—   Here I am flat on my back and one of the most dilapidated specimens you ever saw. You and Mary pretty nearly killed me with your food. About half-way to the station yesterday a sharp pain came on and by the time I reached Albany it had become very acute… From Johnsonville to N.Y. I was vomiting and suffering intensely. Great clots of bonny clabber, peaches, eggs, everything came up but with no results so far as relief went. I was fortunate in getting a sofa to lie on as I could not have stood it. By the time I reached N.Y. I was in such pain that it was with difficulty I could get to the hotel and my bed. I sent for Dr. Lincoln but he was away and they sent me a young man named Miller that I think very poorly of… He says I was simply poisoned by the bonny clabber, having eaten it at the wrong state of fermentation. My intestines were like balls of iron. I spent all yesterday & last night trying to get quick action, but with no results except more suffering. I did not sleep 15 minutes the entire night. The Doctor was here at 8 o'clk this morning (twice yesterday) and says the danger point is passed, that the appendix is perfectly clear and all fever has subsided, so that now it is the clabber and tied up condition which have to be overcome… This attack is a good deal worse than my Old Point attack and I have never eaten soft shell crabs since. Parker insisted on coming down & staying at the hotel last night to be with me. It was most kind in him although for some reason I should have preferred not to have him around. I am still feeling awfully though I have not much pain. This morning for the first time I retained some milk toast & tea in my stomach. I cannot write more now. Don't worry over me as I am getting along all right and will probably be out tomorrow. I sent for Uncle Johnny & asked him to bring his Doctor but he is away… Love & Kisses   —Devotedly *Henry.*

bonny clabber   Naturally soured, curdled milk, popular before pasteurization.

Wednesday, August 10, 1898, New York.
Darling Kate—   I am still in bed— been there ever since Monday. I have suffered a great deal of pain and had to take a good deal of morphine. I hope to be out tomorrow but think I will certainly be around by Friday. Today I have a man nurse (an inefficient fellow) and am applying poultices to my stomach to relieve the bowels. I have not heard a word from Tom [Thomas Nelson Page] and so do not know whether we can go up there or not. If they want me, I have made up my mind to take a week off— especially in view of this attack. Trumbull comes on next week but he can wait a few days for me. I am feeling too badly to write much so you must do with this poor letter. Love & kisses for all.   —Devotedly *Henry.*

August 10. Kittie had letter from Henry that he was ill of Chol. Mor.
                                                —Diary of Catherine McKie Thayer.

Chol. Mor.   Cholera Morbus, acute gastroenteritis.

Holland House, Fifth Avenue & Thirteenth Street, New York.
August 10, 1898.
F. B. Gibson Esq., c/o International Trust Company, Denver, Col.
My dear Gibson—   Yesterday, when your telegrams came about those Rio

Grand Southern bonds, I was suffering intensely, and was too sick to give any attention to the matter. Moreover, I think the bonds are too high at the price offered. Of course you will do no harm by soliciting business under the new Bankruptcy Law, but I don't believe that you will make very much.

    Mr. Trumbull wrote me in reference to the talk he had with you on Colorado Central matters. What he says is all a bluff, but, of course, this is confidential.   —Yours Truly, *Henry W. Hobson.*

Thursday, August 11, 1898. 20 Broad Street.
Dear Katherine—   You are such a sensible level headed woman I do not fear to alarm you & I know you love & trust me too much to think I am holding anything back. Therefore I write to tell you that Henry is sick & just how he is. The poor old boy ate some peaches & some bonny clabber before he left you & they made him very sick on the train… When I returned yesterday morning I found a note from him asking the name of my family physician. That was written Monday & I did not get back until Tuesday. I went down & found he had a Dr. Miller who is attending to Dr. Lincoln's practice in his absence… Henry was weak & had suffered great pain in the abdomen & had been otherwise most uncomfortable… I went back last night & found him sleeping very quietly. I wanted to write to you yesterday but he objected saying that you would want to come down & that it would be hard on the baby etc. etc. This morning I went down early & found his temperature good & his pulse normal & his skin cool & moist but he complained of great weakness, which was natural after his vomiting & purging. To satisfy myself, I then went to see the doctor & had a long talk with him. He says Henry threw himself back by several imprudences, which I need not enumerate, but that he thinks he will now be all right in a day or two. I told him, that unless he was satisfied at his afternoon visit of Henry's thorough convalescence, I wanted him to call Dr. Dew into consultation & this he cheerfully agreed to… I know you have sense enough not to get into a needless excitement or to imagine things are worse than they are. If you were foot-loose I would rather have you here— not that he really needs you but because nobody can minister to a sick man as acceptably as a wife— but there is no necessity for your coming, & considering the baby, I would not do so if I were in your place. If he had been well enough I would have recommended that he let me remove him to my house where he would have a lovely cool floor all to himself & a drug store nearby, but Henry is a stubborn fellow about staying at a Hotel & I was in no condition to remove him. If he does not improve, as I think he should, I will write or telegraph you to come down, but don't expect to do so. Now you have the whole situation just as it is…
—Yours affectionately, *John S. Wise.*

THE WESTERN UNION TELEGRAPH COMPANY
To: Mrs. Henry W. Hobson
Aug. 11, 1898.
Am better but still in bed. Seem quite sick but nothing serious. —*Henry W. Hobson.*

THE WESTERN UNION TELEGRAPH COMPANY
To: Henry W. Hobson — Holland House NY NY
Distressed to hear you are ill. Are you better and up. Arthur waits Johnsonville for answer. Well, love.   —*K. T. Hobson.*

THE WESTERN UNION TELEGRAPH COMPANY
To: Henry W. Hobson — Holland House NY NY Aug. 11, 1898.
Day cool. I shall try to go to New York today, or tomorrow morning. Baby well. Much love. —*K. T. Hobson.*

THE WESTERN UNION TELEGRAPH COMPANY
To: Dr. Samuel Fisk   Aug. 11, 1898
Ileocolitis worst stages. Now passed. Do not worry over me. —*Henry W. Hobson.*

ileocolitis Inflamation of the small intestine.

THE WESTERN UNION TELEGRAPH COMPANY
To: Mrs. Henry W. Hobson
Aug. 11, 1898.
There is no need of your coming to NY. The worst of my attack is over. —*Henry W. Hobson.*

THE WESTERN UNION TELEGRAPH COMPANY
To: Mrs. Henry W. Hobson
Aug. 12, 1898. Thursday.
Come on first train. Answer to house & office. —*John S. Wise.*

Miss Fallon was Henry Hobson's private secretary in Denver.

THE WESTERN UNION TELEGRAPH COMPANY
To: Miss M. E. Fallon 725 Ernest & Cranmer Building, Denver.
Aug. 12, 1898.
Take to-day all securities in my box standing on book in name of Mrs. Hobson and make special trust deposit in her name of such securities. Are all premiums on my life insurance paid— if not pay immediately. You need not worry over this telegram I take this course as I will be operated on today for appendicitis— do not speak of this to anyone outside of Mr. Whitted and Gibson.   —*Henry W. Hobson.*

THE WESTERN UNION TELEGRAPH COMPANY
To: Mrs. Henry W. Hobson
Aug. 12, 1898.
Wired you last night & think you had better come down. Answer to house & office where to meet you.   —*John S. Wise.*

THE WESTERN UNION TELEGRAPH COMPANY
To: Dr. Samuel A. Fisk
Aug. 12, 1898.
Hobson has appendieites [*sic*] I believe. Consultation this evening at nine o'clock with Abby and other physicians   —*Arthur L. Fisk.*

THE WESTERN UNION TELEGRAPH COMPANY
To: Jno. S. Wise.   Commercial Cable Bldg., Broad St., New York. Aug 12, 1898. — Arrive New York nine thirty.   —*Mrs. K. T. Hobson.* 4:23 p.m. (Virginia Historical Society)

THE WESTERN UNION TELEGRAPH COMPANY
To: Mrs. Thayer
Aug. 12, 1898
Leave five five arrive New York about nine. Lets hope & pray for the best.   —*Kittie.*

THE WESTERN UNION TELEGRAPH COMPANY
To: Mrs. F. McKie Thayer — Johnsonville, New York   Aug. 12, 1898.
Katherine wishes you to come at once with children and Mary. Henry operated on for appendicitis. Resting well now.   —*John S. Wise.*

August 12. Kittie, Henry & Baby went to N.Y. to see dear Henry— summoned by wire.
—*Diary of Catherine McKie Thayer.*

❧ In the news:

WAR SUSPENDED, PEACE ASSURED — President Proclaims a Cessation of Hostilities — Protocol is Now in Force — Concessions Made by Spain — Yields Cuba and Puerto Rico and Occupation of Manila.   —*The New York Times*, Saturday, August 13, 1898.

THE WESTERN UNION TELEGRAPH COMPANY
To: F. M. Thayer, Johnsonville
Aug. 13, 1898.
Find Henry very ill at Rosevelt [*sic*] hospital. Kitty children well. —*C. M. Thayer.*

August 13. I took K—, E—, & Mary & went to Johnsonville & to N.Y. —summoned by wire. Reached Roosevelt Hosp. At 6. All saw our darling & at 8:20 the Angels took him.
—*Diary of Catherine McKie Thayer.*

THE WESTERN UNION TELEGRAPH COMPANY
To: Frank Thayer, Johnsonville. Aug. 13, 1898
Henry Hobson died here tonight. Appendicitis. Funeral Troy Monday afternoon. —*John S. Wise.*

THE WESTERN UNION TELEGRAPH COMPANY
To: Frank Thayer, Johnsonville. Aug, 14, 1898
Henry's funeral changed to Tuesday afternoon Troy instead of Monday. —*John S. Wise.*

❧ In the news:

PEACE ENVOYS NOT YET NAMED — Manila Occupation Delayed — Warship Hit By A Shell — Havana Forts Fired on the *San Francisco*, *Miantonomoh*, and Yacht *Sylvia* — Tore A Hole in the Flagship.   —*The New York Times*, August 14, 1898.

August 14. I at Plaza with children. K— at Hospital. Down at Roosevelt to see poor child at 7 o'clock. The children came at 9 to hear the dreadful fact that Papa was gone.
August 15. Out all day till 5 p.m. with Miss Vincent— then went to Chapel where H, E, & Thayer were christened by their dear Father.   —*Diary of Catherine McKie Thayer.*

❧ Obituaries:

DEATH OF HENRY W. HOBSON
Denver Attorney, Well Known in Virginia, Dies in New York
New York, Aug 13. — Henry W. Hobson, forty years old, a lawyer of Denver, Col., died tonight in Roosevelt Hospital from the shock of an operation for appendicitis. He was

Henry Wise Hobson, 1858–1898. Pack Brothers, 935 Broadway, New York.

brought to the hospital from the Holland House a few days ago at the suggestion of his physician. Lawyer Hobson was born in James River, Va., and his father was the late P. Hobson, one of Virginia's best-known men. The son graduated from the University of Virginia. —*Washington Post*, Washington, D.C., August 14, 1898.

HENRY WISE HOBSON DEAD
Henry Wise Hobson, a well-known lawyer of Denver, Col., died at Roosevelt Hospital last night. He was attacked with what was at first supposed to be cholera morbus, Monday night. The case developed into appendicitis, and Drs. Abbe, Dew, Miller, and Fiske [also Fisk] were called in. An operation was performed on Friday, but it was too late, and Mr. Hobson died at 8:25 p.m. yesterday.

Mr. Hobson was born in Virginia. He was a grandson of the late Governor and General Henry A. Wise, and a nephew of John S. Wise of this city. The latter was in constant attendance on him during his illness. Mr. Hobson moved to the West about 1881, without patronage or fortune. He rose steadily and rapidly, until, at the time of his death he was one of the most prominent lawyers in the Western States. He was United States Attorney for Colorado in President Cleveland's first Administration, and afterward was appointed to conduct important Government cases. Among these were the suits against the timber plunderers in Wyoming, Montana and elsewhere, and the suits involving the Mormon Church property. After handling these successfully he became counsel for several important railroads.

Mr. Hobson was in New York as leading counsel for the receiver and Reorganization Committee of the Union Pacific, Denver and Gulf Railroad. Mr. Hobson's acquaintance and business connection with members of the bar in New York, Boston, Philadelphia and the eastern cities was large, and he held the highest place in their respect, confidence, and affection. His death will be mourned by a large circle as a severe personal as well as business loss. He was only forty years old, and his career as a successful and prosperous lawyer was at its zenith when he was stricken down. He leaves a widow and four little children.

Recently Mr. Hobson had been honored by the alumni of the University of Virginia, of which he was a graduate, by being selected to deliver the annual address at the next commencement of the University. —*New York Tribune*, August 14, 1898.

H. W. HOBSON DIES OF APPENDICITIS — Brilliant Denver Lawyer Succumbed to Shock After Operation Had Been Performed
Henry Wise Hobson, a prominent lawyer of Denver, Col, died last night in the Roosevelt Hospital from the shock of an operation for appendicitis. He was brought to the hospital from the Holland House a few days ago at the suggestion of his physician, Dr. Robert Abbe, of No. 11 West Fiftieth Street. Dr. Abbe performed the operation.

Mr. Hobson had come to this city in connection with the reorganization of the Union Pacific, Denver and Gulf Railroad, of which he was leading counsel.

He was seized with the disease on Monday, and it made such rapid headway that his family was scarcely able to reach him before he died.

Mr. Hobson was born in Virginia and was a graduate of William and Mary's College... He went out West when less than twenty years old, was admitted to the Bar and made rapid progress in his profession. He was United States District Attorney for Colorado under Cleveland. He had a lucrative practice and had acquired a large fortune...
—*New York Herald*, August 14, 1898.

DEATH OF HENRY W. HOBSON
The Denver Attorney succumbed to the effects of an operation in New York City — A Brilliant Career Suddenly Terminated.

A telegram received at 9:30 last night by Elmer E. Whitted, the attorney, announced the death of Henry W. Hobson in Roosevelt Hospital, New York, at 8:25 o'clock. The Telegram was quite brief and ran as follows:

"New York, Aug 13. — Mr. Hobson died at 8:25 of septic peritonitis. Funeral at Troy Monday afternoon. Notify All. Mrs. Hobson standing up bravely. —A. D. Parker."

A. D. Parker was one of the closest of Mr. Hobson's friends.

A little later the following was received from Frank Trumbull, who left Denver Thursday to join Mr. Hobson and arrived in New York at 6:30 p. m. yesterday. "New York, Aug 13. Mr. Hobson died at 8:25 tonight. Sick since Monday. Operation yesterday at Roosevelt Hospital for appendicitis. Please wire me Judge Hallett's cable address; also please notify McBeth and Gibson. Have wired Wilde. —Frank Trumbull."

These terse particulars are all that the many friends of this prominent citizen and able lawyer have at hand to inform them of his sudden taking away. It was not known in Denver that Mr. Hobson was ill and the news of his death comes with stunning force to those to whom he was dear.

On the 8th day of July Mr. Hobson left Denver for New York to continue the work of reorganizing the Gulf road, an undertaking which has occupied his time and energy for the past year. Receiver Trumbull went to join him in the labor and it was the intention of both to continue together in the metropolis for some time to come.

The family was at Mr. Hobson's fine farm in Washington county, New York, near Troy. The Denver residence, 933 Pennsylvania avenue, was closed and left in charge of servants.

From what has been learned through private telegrams, Mr. Hobson's illness was not considered serious until Monday. At that time he showed symptoms of appendicitis, which gradually developed until Friday, when Dr. Robert Abbe, one of the most eminent surgeons in New York, decided that an operation would be necessary. Dr. Arthur Fiske [Fisk] of Denver was present and witnessed the operation.

For a time it seemed that the best results would follow. The patient rested comfortably during the succeeding night and had apparently lost but little of his vitality yesterday morning. Later in the day, however, it was discovered that peritonitis had set in and the greatest alarm was felt.

As the afternoon wore on, Mr. Hobson sank rapidly and the end came early in the evening as above stated. Around the bedside were grouped Mrs. Hobson, her mother and Mr. Hobson's mother, the latter having come with all speed from her home in Virginia.

The death of Henry W. Hobson at the present time cuts short a life already brilliant with many successes and rich with promise for the future. Mr. Hobson was a young man, barely 40, and his physical make-up was apparently that of one who was proof against the erosion of years.

Virginia was Mr. Hobson's native state and there he received his growth, education, and training. When quite a young man he was graduated from the William and Mary College. Afterward he took up the study of law in Richmond.

In 1881 Mr. Hobson came to Colorado and made his home in Buena Vista. There he practiced law until 1884, when he removed to Denver. He had scarcely been in this city a year when President Cleveland appointed him United States district attorney. While occupying that position, Mr. Hobson was put in charge of a number of important government cases, special cases that required in their management the exercise of the nicest judgment as well as the most persistent effort.

The great success which attended him in all that he did while in office was the subject of much admiring comment on the part of the oldest and most distinguished attorneys of the state, and it has been said of him many times since he relinquished the office that he was one of the best district attorneys that ever performed the functions of that important office in Colorado.

Mr. Hobson came by his abilities honestly. He was a scion of a famous stock. He was a grandson of Governor Henry A. Wise of Virginia and a nephew of John S. Wise of New York.

Mr. Hobson's wife is a daughter of Mrs. Catherine McK. Thayer of Colorado Springs and a most estimable lady. There were four children born of this union, two boys and two girls. The youngest child is but little more than a year old and the eldest, Catherine, is not yet 10.

At the time of his death, Mr. Hobson was counsel for the Union Pacific, Denver & Gulf road and also for the Denver, Leadville & Gunnison, which positions he had held for some time past. The institution in which he took the most pride was the International Trust Company, which he organized in 1891. The welfare of this corporation lay near his heart and he devoted a great deal of his time and energy to the accomplishment of his plans in this regard. His success is well known. It was an achievement of which he had good reason to be proud. He saw the company grow and prosper in response to his efforts and he was ever alert to discover new influences which would in any way effect its development.

Mr. Hobson was a man of extraordinary energy and all-around ability. Though young at the time of his death, he had earned for himself a high position not only at the bar, but in the business world, and men in all walks of life looked to him for advice and guidance. He was a member of the University and Denver clubs, and though a man much given to study and meditation, he was ever affable and entertaining and took rank in a quiet way as one of the social leaders... —*The Denver News.*

The death of Henry Wise Hobson, a leading lawyer of Denver, Col., who has friends in this city and in Cambridge, occurred at the Roosevelt Hospital in New York Saturday evening. Mr. Hobson went to New York on business in relation to the reorganization of the Union Pacific, Denver and Gulf Railroad and suffered from illness thought to be cholera morbus. Appendicitis developed, however, and he was taken from the Holland House to the hospital, where an operation was performed, and death resulted from the shock. The deceased was a native of Virginia, being a grandson of the late Governor Henry A. Wise of Virginia, and he was a nephew of John S. Wise of New York. He went west before he reached his majority and made his fortune largely from the Golden Fleece mine at Lake City, Col. A wife and four children survive. Mrs. Hobson's maiden name was Thayer and prior to her marriage to Mr. Hobson she was the widow of a son of the late James B. Jermain. She was a daughter of Mr. Thayer of the firm of Bills & Thayer, who were proprietors of the Crystal Palace Mills in this city. Mrs. Thayer has a summer home at South Cambridge and her daughter and husband were frequent visitors. The funeral will be held at the Earl Chapel, Oakwood cemetery at 2 o'clock tomorrow afternoon. —*The Troy Daily Times,* Monday, August 15, 1898.

Hotchkiss Mountain, Lake City, Colorado, site of the Golden Fleece Mine. Lake San Cristobal at base of the mountain.

༄ The Golden Fleece:

Within the letters there are a number of references to the Golden Fleece mine located in Lake City, Colorado. There are Henry Hobson's letters of June 16, 1895 and October 13, 1895, there is his obituary from the Troy Daily Times, August 15, 1898, and there are papers from the settlement of his estate showing his interest in this mine. Founded in 1874 as the Hotchkiss Mine which was then abandoned by the late 1870s, the Golden Fleece was one of the richest gold mines in the history of Colorado. The Golden Fleece Mining Co. was formed in 1891 by a group of investors from Denver and the largest discoveries were made in the mid–1890s. From newspapers and newspapers we know the following about the mine:

The Golden Fleece owners are perhaps the only mine operators in the state who have not made a cut in wages. They are now paying and always have paid the old price of $3.50 per day for miners. —*Lake City Times*, February 22, 1894.

Seventy-five men are employed on the Golden Fleece, only six of whom are engaged in taking ore out, the remainder doing development work. Notwithstanding the few taking out pay mineral, over $20,000 worth of ore was shipped out last month.
—*Lake City Times*, May 30, 1895.

June 13, 1895, Sapinero, Colo.

Darling Kate—   Whilst waiting for the train for Lake City I will scribble you a line. We came down last night on the narrow gauge train, there being no other, and truly I never had a more uncomfortable night. In the first place the train was crowded, the car stuffy, and the berths too short… I do not feel very "peart" as the darkies say. In fact I always dread this trip. We have along an Ex-Governor of Rhode Island who is going up to see a property near Lake City in which he has been swindled… By-the-way, you will be disgusted, I have no doubt. when I tell you that I have taken to smoking a pipe. But I do not intend to do so regularly but only when off on trips, when cigars are hard to get and on steamers or when little comfort is to be gotten out of smoking a cigar. I can't say that I have yet become enamored of the pipe, and the first time I tried it, it rather made me sick, and I had to give it up. But then it is "so English you know." I suppose by the time this reaches you, Mother will be with you, as she said she would start next Monday. I am delighted that the dear old woman is with you and the chicks… If Mother is with you give her a heart full of love and take for yourself my sweetheart what you always have—my whole self, heart, soul, and mind.   —Devotedly *Henry*.

June 16, 1895, Colorado Springs.

Darling Kate—   Yesterday's letter exhausted the news for a time so you will only get a line today. By-the-way I intended to say to you not to say anything to Mother about the Fleece. She does not know I have any interest in a mine. If she did, the family would soon know it, and I would be asked then to turn my interest over to the thieves. I have had a nice pleasant day with your Mother. She liked all the presents. She looks very well. Love & kisses to the darlings.   —Devotedly *Henry*.

GOLDEN FLEECE FLEECED. *Some Startling Discoveries Made at Lake City Last Week.* Recent discoveries and developments at Lake City have brought to light the fact that for months past systematic robberies have taken place in the Golden Fleece mine and the loss is the owners and is said to aggregate $160,000. The Golden Fleece is one of the richest and most productive in that vicinity and the ore was very high grade. For several months the company has been shipping one car of very high-grade ore to the smelters for treatment and the average returns from this car have been from $12,000 to $17,000. However, during the last eight months the returns from this car of ore have begun to decrease and Superintendent David Acres has been at a loss to account for this as the assays showed the ore to be of the same value as before…There are three tunnels in the mine, and in order to find where the leak occurred the mine was closed down and the three tunnels protected so that nothing could be taken out of either… The result of the investigation has proven conclusively that for many months the mine has been systematically plundered, and the owners believe that every man working in the mine has been implicated in the steal. There were three shifts of men employed and one left every night at 12 o'clock. It is at this time that it is believed most of the stealing was done. It is supposed that the ore was removed in sacks and then taken in wagon to Lake City, and then shipped to the smelter or sampling works. Messrs. Pierce and Lee of the Colorado Ore Sampling Co., part owners of the mine, went to Lake City last week to satisfy themselves of the truth of the reports that reached them, and they decided that the mine must remain closed down until the tunnels could be provided with iron doors to prevent the repetition of such thefts in the future. The Golden Fleece mine is capitalized at $600,000 and made all its owners wealthy. Twenty-five percent per annum has been paid in dividends in addition to expenditure of large sums for development and improvements. There are about seventy-five employees whose payroll aggregate about $10,000 a month. The output has averaged from $20,000 to $40,000 per month. It is thought that the robberies in the Golden Fleece mine have been done by a gang who have systematically been plundering the mines of the West for years. In all probability efforts will be made to break-up the gang but who the leaders are it is impossible to determine. The owners of the mine have determined to offer a reward of $1,000 for the arrest and conviction of each and every person implicated in the theft of ore. Messrs. Pierce, Lee and Hobson returned yesterday from Lake City and state that they have determined to close down the mine until they are satisfied that they can operate it in safety. They believe that it will be impossible to obtain justice in Hinsdale County as many people who were cognizant with the facts and have political influence in the county have been mixed up in it. —*Denver Times,* June 17, 1895.

June 18, 1895, Denver.
Darling Kate—   Last night I had a line from Mother saying that on the account of the death of her friend Mrs. Brown she would have to postpone her trip. It is just like the dear old woman— still there is no earthly reason why she should do so… I cannot write any more tonight as I am very busy. Love & Kisses to the darlings—   —Devotedly *Henry.*

The legitimate output of the Golden Fleece last month is estimated to be $40,000. If reports are true the illegitimate output was about $20,000. These two sums added together make the total production of this great tellurium producer. But just who got the benefit of the latter sum is not known. And perhaps never will be. Then again there is much doubt as to the correctness of the figures.   —*Lake City Times,* June 20, 1895.

The Golden Fleece people are building a new bunk-house large enough to comfortably accommodate about thirty men. About seventy-five men are now at work on the mine, and as soon as the bunk-house is completed the force will be increased to over one hundred men.   —*Lake City Times,* July 4, 1895.

A CRACKAJACK The richest shipment ever made from this camp. A car of Golden Fleece ore worth $60,000 sent out Tuesday morning. — Two men sent along with the car to guard it to its destination. William Lippitt and Harry Vaughn were the shot gun messengers sent with the car to Denver. — A car of ore was sent out this week that for richness eclipses any shipment ever made from the Golden Fleece. The car contained seven tons of first class ore, the balance being second grade mineral, and it is safe to say the value of the care of ore is $60,000. The Fleece is fast becoming the wonder of the state. Last month the net earnings were $53,000. In October they paid an extra dividend of $15,000, will do the same this month, and in December will pay the lucky stock holders two extra dividends of $15,000 each. The mine is owned by seven men, two of whom have small holdings, and is capitalized for $600,000. The percent of dividends of capitol stock is the largest of any mine in the United States. This world beater is located near Lake City in Hinsdale County, and mining men and capitalists are fast getting on to the fact that for a place for profitable investment Lake City is the headquarters.
—*Lake City Times,* November 21, 1895.

Another car worth $60,000 was sent out from the Golden Fleece this week.
—*Lake City Times,* December 19, 1895.

❧ Personal papers:

A certificate for 47,958 share of the Golden Fleece Mining & Milling Company's stock is held by us as Trustees, which stock is owned by the following parties:

Henry W. Hobson	8,494
Samuel A. Fisk	9,494
Maria V. Reeves	1,994
Geo. W. Peirce [sic]	13,988
David K. Lee	13,988

—From the papers of Henry Wise Hobson, January 3, 1896.

"Memoranda Concerning Matters In My Safety Deposit Box And Among My Other Papers:

...3rd. There stand in my name 51,500 shares of stock of the Golden Fleece Mining & Milling Company. Of this amount 50,000 shares belong to my wife, and 1,500 to me. In addition to this, I own four and one half fortieths (4 1/2-40) of the stock bought from S. S. Kennedy under a Declaration of Trust, dated April 14th, 1895, signed by Biddle Reeves, which Declaration of Trust is in my safety deposit box. I also have a similar interest in a syndicate of which Geo Peirce [sic] & Biddle Reeves are managers for purchase on sale of Fleece stock." —undated papers of Henry Wise Hobson.

Death of Former Golden Fleece President — David K. Lee, at one time president of the Colorado Ore Sampling Company, and later for a number of years and during the mine's richest and most productive period, president of the Golden Fleece Mining company, died a few days ago at his home, 1763 Williams Street, Denver, at the age of 68 years. —*Silver World*, November 22, 1917.

It is not known what happened to the stock in the Golden Fleece that Henry Hobson owned when he died in 1898. By the early twentieth century the ore had been depleted and the mine was closed.

❧

❧ The funeral:

The remains of Henry Wise Hobson, the prominent attorney of Denver, Col., whose death occurred in New York Saturday night, arrived in this city [Troy, New York] this afternoon for interment. The remains came from New York in the special car *Aladdin* on the regular train which reaches this city at 1:50 o'clock. In the funeral party were the wife and four children of the deceased, Mrs. Hobson's mother, Mrs. Catherine McKie Thayer; Mr. Hobson's mother from Virginia, John S. Wise of New York, an uncle of the deceased, and Mrs. Wise, Miss Wise, Mr. Mayo, Thomas Nelson Page, the author, Carter Branch of Richmond, Va.; Judge Vail of Omaha, Neb.; J. Kennedy Todd and Henry Budge, of New York, and Judge Hoyt of Denver, and the pall bearers— Frank Trumbull of Denver, Col.; Elmer P. Howe of Boston, E. C. Henderson and R. L. Harrison of New York, Heth Lorton of Virginia and New York, Dr. A. C. Fisk of Denver,

Joseph Bryan of Richmond, Va., and William H. Lyons of New York. The remains were taken directly from Union depot to the Earl Memorial chapel, where a service was held. The officiating clergyman was Rev. C. M. Addison, rector of St. John's Episcopal Church of Stamford, Conn., an intimate friend of the family, Mrs. Addison and Mrs. Hobson being cousins. The interment was in the Thayer plot in Oakwood. The floral tributes were of remarkable beauty and elaborateness and were the gifts of warm personal friends and business associates of the deceased. The floral pieces included a choice tribute from the officials connected with the Union Pacific, Denver and Gulf Railroad. The arrangements for the funeral were in charge of A. D. Parker of Denver, a close friend of the deceased, and J. Crawford Green of this city. Mr. Parker is the auditor of the Union Pacific, Denver and Gulf Railroad, of which Mr. Hobson was the general counsel, and he was with Mr. Hobson in New York on business connected with the reorganization of the railroad company when Mr. Hobson was taken ill, remaining with his friend until the end came. Frank Trumbull of Denver, the receiver of the railroad company, who was in the funeral party today, arrived in New York Saturday night shortly after Mr. Hobson's death.

—*The Troy Daily Times,* Troy, N. Y., Tuesday Afternoon, August 16, 1898.

August 16. All came to Troy from chapel with the dear one and at 3 p.m. saw him laid beside my dear Husband. Our car filled with friends & flowers. Awful thunder storm going up. Ada with us at Cambridge. Oh these awful days, how can they be borne.

—*Diary of Catherine McKie Thayer.*

An obituary by a close friend:

HENRY WISE HOBSON

Henry Wise Hobson died last Saturday evening in New York after a short illness, as reported briefly in *The Times* of Sunday. But yesterday he was a member of our Bar, taking part in the daily life of our people, going in and out among them, respected and beloved by them. Bearing a distinguished name, he inherited, along with the appearance, many of the rare gifts of his ancestor, Governor Wise. Reared in the school of gentle manners, so often found in the old Virginia country life, he early learned the necessity of ruling completely a spirit that had been else ungovernable.

He graduated at William and Mary College and entered the University well equipped for the work he undertook, and left it with the good opinion of all who knew him. He had made his B. L. in one year, but he had not won the "Jeff" Medal, though he had tried for it. To the University he ever turned as to a fostering mother, and in his last hours expressed his deep appreciation of the honor done him by his fellows who had elected him alumni orator for next year. He had hoped to be able to show himself worthy of the occasion and the honor.

From the University he came to this Bar, and was a partner of his kinsman, John S. Wise, Esq. He was recognized as a good lawyer, a fearless advocate and a faithful counsellor. The Bar honored him. The bench trusted him. He fought hard, but it was a fair fight. His appearance at the time was striking. Tall and spare he stood, weighing perhaps a hundred and thirty pounds. His face, at first sight, so refined as to appear almost womanly, fully satisfied the requirements of force. In any company, one would have asked who is that man. If to some he appeared self-absorbed or indifferent, it was because he felt that one equally intimate with all, can hardly be sincere with any. Those that knew him well knew that he had in a marked degree the quality of sincerity.

Such was the young lawyer that went West some eighteen years ago. Settling in the mountains of Colorado, in an out-of-the-way place, he at once made an impression in his new home. Denver, the capital of the State, with it business interests, soon attracted him. There he established himself, and took a position which he has since held as one of the first men of the West. His appointment as District Attorney by Mr. Cleveland was a merited honor. The administration of that office brought him in contact with the leading men of his adopted State, and gave him opportunity to show what was in him. But even at this time his thoughts were ever with his friends in Virginia. To one he offered a partnership, to all his unchanged affection. Here dwelt his mother. Here was the home of his ancestors. Fortunate was he in marriage. His domestic life was very happy. His wife, who had been Miss Catherine Thayer, came of old New England stock. His people were hers, and hers were his. Four children survive him.

Large interests came to be represented by him. I recall a striking incident perhaps unknown to any other now living on this side of the Atlantic. At a dinner given him in London by certain English gentlemen, who were his clients, he was called upon unexpectedly to respond to a toast. Before he recovered himself he mentioned that he had been that evening at the "Empire." His hosts showed much amusement, as they shouted almost derisively "The Empire, ha, ha!" But the young American was equal to the emergency, and those who thought the Empire Theatre a trivial place for a lawyer entrusted with large interests of English investors, were soon overwhelmed by his splendid apostrophe to the Empire of Great Britain. Beaconsfield at a Primrose dinner could not have received a more cordial reception.

His business increased, and each year saw the effect of additional burden upon him. His visits East, which had formerly been for pleasure alone, soon became full of business, and the work he was doing when the great Taskmaster called him was as important as a lawyer is often called upon to perform.

Devoted friends rushed to his bedside when the news of his illness came. Loving hands ministered to him. Prayers rose to Heaven for his recovery. Death came, but it came to one who though but forty years old had fought a good fight, and who laid down his armor, having done his duty as a faithful servant.

A pathetic scene was that when the mother brought her youngest children to the font to be baptized in the presence of the father's body.

Buried away from the scenes of his childhood, he rests where those who knew and loved him wished him to be. His memory shall abide with us as long as we wish to remember a faithful friend and a noble-hearted gentleman.

—Rosewell Page, *The Richmond Times*, Richmond, Virginia, August 19, 1898.

to the font to be baptized Rosewell Page, the brother of Henry Hobson's life-long friend Thomas Nelson Page, is referring to the baptism of three of the children, Henry Wise Hobson, Eleanor Whiteside Hobson, and Francis Thayer Hobson. After their father's death, the body was taken to a church in New York City where the three children were baptized beside the open coffin. From there the funeral proceeded to Troy, New York. This incident is also referred to in the August 15th diary of Catherine McKie Thayer.

The Undelivered Speech:

In July 1898, Henry Wise Hobson was invited to give the 1899 annual address to the Alumni Association of the University of Virginia Law School. In the weeks that followed he began making notes and outlining the speech that he planned to give the following year. Those notes are on several pads in an envelope marked: "Notes — probably for lecture he was to hold at University of Virginia." The notes, all written in pencil, are difficult to read and contain references to books and quotes that he must have been planning to further research.

The note pads are not numbered so it is not possible to say in what order these comments might have been intended.

The invitation to speak & a few of the notes for the undelivered speech:

University of Virginia, Law Department, Prof. Raleigh C. Minor, July 8, 1898.
Hon Henry W. Hobson,
    Dear Sir—   As the Secretary of the General Society of the Alumni of the University of Virginia, I have the honor to inform you that at the meeting of the Society held in June last, you were chosen the Alumni Orator to address the Society at its next annual meeting to be held next June during the final celebrations of the University of Virginia.
    Trusting that you will find it possible to accept the invitation of the Society, and with very kind regards, I am   Very Sincerely, *Raleigh C. Minor*, General Secretary.

Law Offices of Coke & Coke, Dallas, Texas.
June 30, 1898.
My Dear Henry—   …This trust matter has given me no trouble, and, in fact, I have received more benefit from it than I have suffered trouble or inconvenience; but, aside from any question of benefit, you will understand that I am always ready to serve you in any way within my power. I am much pleased at the honor conferred upon you by the Alumni of the University of Virginia and, without being posted in such matters, I should consider it a high compliment. The misgivings you express about your ability to come up to what may be expected of you, are not altogether in keeping with your usual cheek, for if there is one quality which you do possess it is cheek and assurance. I do not believe that you feel the misgivings you express, but if you do, I do not. I heard you make a number of addresses and speeches in your younger days, and you know as a matter of fact that you possess much capacity in that line. Knowing that you are not easily scared and over-diffident, I have no doubt that the result will be entirely satisfactory both to yourself and your friends. If circumstances will permit, I should like to be on hand on the occasion.
    I received the picture you sent me, for which please accept my thanks. My wife, who is something of an artist, says that the picture is beautifully executed, and they all agreed that it was a striking likeness. I hope you will note the accurate use of the word "beautiful," and be careful to see the thing qualified by it. I do not want you to think we are so "fallen from grace" and have so little regard for the truth as to speak of the original as being beautiful.
    —With best love to all at home, I remain, very truly your friend, *Henry C. Coke.*

∾ Excerpts from the notes:

Twenty-one years ago I left the University of Virginia to take my place in the ranks of active, working citizenship. A year ago, upon the recommendations of a friend and the kindly indulgence of the main body of Alumni here assembled, I was selected to deliver this address. The honor is one which I most highly prize, and yet I cannot but recognize that it was an offering to that great section of our common country in which I reside in

Henry Hobson had a great interest in American political history. Another reference to "nationalism," the topic of his planned speech at the University of Virginia, appeared in his letter of April 1, 1898, when he wrote: "Above all it [the Spanish–American war] will nationalize the country more and that is my great hobby in politics."

the west and to the whole body of our western alumni with whom I stand upon a parity in the matter of individual destinations and importance. With that in mind I have thought it not inappropriate to select for my address a subject connected with the west, that west extending from the Allegheny mountains to the Pacific Ocean…

…Thus Jefferson, the great apostle of State Rights, by his Louisiana Purchase and Tyler and Polk by their Mexican acquisitions, probably did more to Nationalize this country, strengthen the hands of the central government and destroy the prestige of the States Rights school of men than any other men who ever held power in this country with the exception perhaps of John Marshall. Marshall announced the principles and sowed the seed. The Louisiana Purchase and Mexican acquisitions supplied the territory for the fruition of these principles, for the growth of these seed. The balance of power against the State Rights school came gradually but truly from the West, and it was the power of the West which forced the issue of Nationality to their arbitrament of war, which supplied Lincoln the means of destroying slavery and which carried to a successful conclusion in favor of a National Supreme Government— the Great Civil War…

…The tide of emigration from Virginia and other southern states united with that from New England in the broad prairies of the west but did not carry with it the old southern political ideas and principles. The development was distinctly nationalistic in character and results. Even the veto of Madison of the legislation for internal improvements in 1817, based upon a nation in Madison's mind toward the early Virginia constitutional ideas, had a powerful influence upon the future. If that measure had been successful, the connection by canals and post-roads between Virginia and other southern states with the new country of the west must have kept pace with the connections of New York and Pennsylvania but the action of the President resulted in the Northern States establishing such connections themselves whilst the Southern States did nothing. Thus the great Northwest became inevitably connected with and allied to the north in sympathy, socially, commercially and otherwise… —Henry W. Hobson.

Memorial tributes:

PLEAS IN THE CIRCUIT COURT OF THE UNITED STATES FOR THE DISTRICT OF COLORADO SITTING AT DENVER.

5TH Day Tuesday, November 8th, A. D. 1898.
Present: The honorable Moses Hallet, District Judge and other officers as noted on the first instant.

In the matter of the death of Henry W. Hobson, a member of the Bar of this Court. : At this day comes L. M. Cuthbert, Esq. an attorney of this Court and presents to the Court now here certain resolutions upon the death of Henry W. Hobson.

And thereupon it is ordered by the Court that the said resolutions and the address of Mr. Cuthbert and the reply of the presiding Judge of the Court be spread upon the records which is accordingly done, in words and figures as follows, to wit:

The undersigned, appointed a Committee by the Bar Association of Arapahoe County, to draft and present to the various Courts resolutions upon the death of our late friend and brother, Henry W. Hobson, met on Wednesday the 19th day of October, 1898, and adopted the following:

ADDRESS OF MR. CUTHBERT

There have been few careers among the members of the Bar of this Circuit, more eminently successful than that of Henry W. Hobson. With a singleness of purpose and a devotion to his life-work that would alone ensure success, he bent his every effort toward the attainment of professional efficiency in the highest and truest sense. And his efforts were not in vain. Gifted with unusual natural abilities, his earlier years were devoted to the training and development of his best faculties, in intercourse with leaders in the profession: so that he was peculiarly well fitted to grapple with its difficulties and to carve out for himself a name and career of honor.

Law has been truly called a jealous mistress. And those who have received her highest favors have been obliged to give her their undivided devotion.

Too often do we find in the history of one thus blessed by inheritance and fortune, the absence of some quality essential to a successful professional career, that dilettantism which is the natural result of a brilliant but misguided mind seeking intellectual energy, the scattering and diffusion of ideas and abilities, or the want of perseverance and devotion.

In the character of him to whom our thoughts are now directed there was no such break, no such wanting link in the chain of a life which he made strong and enduring. He threw aside all that encumbered him in his race of life, and pressed forward, with splendid ability turning neither to the right nor left, unaffected by the phantom whispers of political ambition and undisturbed by the criticisms of professional adversaries, until his race was run and his victory won.

To him all honor is due, and we, his associates, meet here today for the purpose of giving expression to that sentiment of admiration and approbation which it is ever fitting we should give to one who has so well earned it.

The Records of this Court, the chief arena of his career, abound with testimonials of his struggle and victories. The esteem in which he was held by the Judges of the Court and the members of this Bar, is the best evidence of the respect he commanded and the standing he secured.

Incapacitated at times by ill-health, he worked far beyond his capacity: generous in his dealing with his fellow men, he never allowed his inclinations to overcome his sense of duty: charitable in all things, he was eminently just: and devoted to his profession he cultivated the gentle arts of literature, so that there was no narrowness in a mind which he had broadened by extensive reading and intellectual converse.

It may be well said of him that "tho' he be dead he yet speaketh." And it is to us, his associates and co-workers, that his silent language appeals most strongly.

I take it that the completed life of every man has in it a lesson, either of good or evil, for those of us who are left, And it seems to me that the life of Henry Hobson teaches, above all things, the lesson of Labor. Fancy may conceive: Talent may design: but labor rears the structure, whether it be the perishable edifice of the undying character of man, by which alone the builder is to be measured.

THE ANNUAL REPORT OF THE AMERICAN BAR ASSOCIATION, FOR 1898:

Henry Wise Hobson, Colorado.

Henry Wise Hobson, of Denver, Colorado, died on August 13th, 1898, from appendicitis, after an illness of two or three days.

He was born on his father's plantation on the James River, in Virginia, on July 9th,

1858. He was a scion of a famous stock being a grandson of Governor Henry A. Wise, of Virginia, and a nephew of John S. Wise, of New York City.

After taking a course at William and Mary College, Mr. Hobson entered the University of Virginia, where he graduated in the law class of 1878. At the last meeting of the Alumni Association, in June 1898, he was chosen to deliver the address before the Association at its annual meeting in June, 1899.

After taking his degree, Mr. Hobson practiced law with his uncle, Mr. John S. Wise, at Richmond, for a short time. He turned his footsteps westward and settled in Colorado in 1881 and in 1885 was appointed United States District Attorney by President Cleveland. He was afterwards placed in charge of all timber and land litigation west of the Missouri River, as Special Attorney for the Government, and was counsel in many cases of great importance, among which were the suits growing out of the sequestration of the lands of the Mormon Church.

In December, 1887, he married Katherine Thayer Jermain, daughter of Francis S. and Catherine McKie Thayer, of Troy, New York, who, with their four children, survives him.

After the inauguration of President Harrison, Mr. Hobson resigned his position as United States Attorney and took up the practice of law in the city of Denver which he continued up to the time of his death. He was General Counsel of the Union Pacific, Denver & Gulf Railway Company and also for the International Trust Company of Denver, of which latter institution he was the promoter and active moving spirit.

Mr. Hobson was an accomplished lawyer, original and acute in argument, with a keen, penetrating mind. He was tactful and resourceful; never at a loss in any emergency. In the most difficult cases in which he was engaged and in the most important crises of his life he never seemed to doubt or hesitate— if he did, he gave no sign. He seemed intuitively to see the right thing to do and to do it. Firm in his opinion and courageous in the expression of it, he was wholly free from intolerance and prejudice. He was a useful citizen, as in addition to his legal acumen and learning, he was possessed of rare executive ability and was a perfect master of details.

He seemed almost to delight in difficulties and in taking burdens upon himself. Men came to him bowed down with trouble which seemed almost greater than they could bear, and departed with light hearts, having left their burdens upon stronger shoulders. He was a man of strong personality, inspiring liking and confidence, and, although but a young man himself, men in all walks of life looked to him for counsel and guidance. The initial quality of greatness was born in him. Born in him also was that marvelous initial force and tireless energy which never failed and which marked him as no common man. Any judge of physical types could see at a glance that he was a man of strong racial traits.

To his personal character the highest tribute of personal praise can be accorded. Courteous and considerate in his social and business intercourse, temperate in controversy, generous to the shortcomings of others though exacting the highest degree of personal integrity from himself, exceptionally fortunate and happy in his domestic relations, he perhaps realized that greatest glory of all— the consciousness of a life well lived.

On Tuesday, November 8th, 1898, the members of the bench and bar of the United States Circuit Court for Colorado met in the city of Denver to pay their tribute of respect to the memory of Mr. Hobson. In response to resolutions expressing their sense of loss and appreciation of the high qualities of Mr. Hobson's character and abilities, the Hon. Moses Hallett, Circuit Judge, said:

"The Court unites with the bar in expressions of sorrow for the death of Mr. Hobson and directs that the resolutions now presented be entered of record. We cannot fully express the sentiments by which we are moved by the death of a man of Mr. Hobson's worth. He was our friend, made such by the candor, sincerity, generosity, sympathy, and truthfulness of his nature. He was an able upright lawyer; earnest and forcible in every just cause; helpful to the Court; courteous to his opponents and true to the principles of justice. He had taken at the bar and in social life the position which these qualities are sure to command. One may say of him, as was said of another:

'Honor and fortune crowned him with its wreath;
Justly the world to him adjudged its prize,
But simple, heedless of its flattering breath,
His path was onward with uplooking eyes.'

We sincerely mourn his untimely death and we shall always keep in sorrowful remembrance his nobility of character and the manly qualities for which he was greatly distinguished."

Letters of condolence:

Brook Hill, Aug 17th, 1898.
Oh! My poor dear Katherine— May God in his great mercy help you to bear the grievous sorrow He has laid upon you for vain indeed is any help of man. It seems too terrible to be true… Oh! The loyal heart, the loyal nature which gave so plenteously of its best and was *always* the same— how much richer are our lives for having known him. And how poor the world seems without him! If he was so much to us— What was he not to you, his very own, the heart of his life, his perfect wife. How can you live without him? God alone knows, but surely he will give you strength to live for the sake of his precious children. Your grief is too sacred for even words of love to reach it now. I dare not enter into a shrine so holy. Somewhere in God's universe this day he prays for you & your love cannot die & that strength may be yours and he loves you forever more & more. It may be that he is very near you and that your cry for help mingles into his supplications for you. At all events he has been called up higher… In God's great universe he is working this day, learning lessons of his Master which perhaps he could not have learned here— "in the hard streaming tide" of the much of what we call life… Kiss these blessed children for me. In deepest sorrow… I am faithfully and lovingly yours, —*Annie C. Stewart.*

Brook Hill, Aug 18th, 1898.
My poor dear Katherine, dearer to us now than ever for the sake of him who has gone, whom we both loved— I write only to give you my heartfelt sympathy, to mingle my tears with yours. Henry was the most loyal loving soul I ever knew and he is now "Where Loyal hearts and true stand ever in the light." On his photograph is written, in his own dear hand, "For my home folks at

Brook Hill—" And I believe there are none in this your hour of dark despair that are more one with you in grief than "his home folks at Brook Hill." May the God of the widow and the fatherless have you all in his Holy keeping is the prayer of yours in loving sympathy, —*Lucy Stewart.*

August 17, 1898.
My dear Katherine—   On Henry's desk I found two volumes which I have sent you. They were sad reminders of one of our last interviews here. A bookstore sent me sixteen volumes of my father's book & Henry, seeing them, asked me to inscribe one to little Henry & one to you, which I did. He intended to take them home with him but overlooked them.

   I hope, dear Katherine, that you all had a comfortable trip home & are rested & refreshed.

   We reached here safely about 9:30.

   God bless you & temper your great sorrow. I cannot say more. Nobody mourns Henry's loss more truly than myself.   —*John S. Wise.*

126 W. 86th Street, New York, August 17th, 1898.
My dearest Katherine—   My first waking thought just after dawn was of you and your mother. I realised with an agony of tears what the first awaking in the home would be. I took all your surroundings in mind and heart, and all my weak human helplessness could do was to ask Divine help for you. It would have added much to the pain of these dark days to have gone back to the lovely Home Farm where I went so happily before. I never expect to see it again. If I had thought I could really comfort and help you I would have made any sacrifice to have gone, but I know you asked me because you thought that it might be refreshing to me. You had your own dear, good Mother & did not need me. I hoped to ride with you to the depot & from the Chapel to the last resting place, but was told that it was arranged that Eva was to go… I have had very little real part in your life except in the respect and affection you have ever shown "Henry's Mother," & the many sweet, considerate attentions which made my life so much the richer & sweeter. No one could have been such a congenial mother and devoted a wife to Henry as you were. You were an answer to my prayers and a benediction to his life. I have been thanking God this morning for the happiness you gave him and the sweet influence of your devotion and I felt really glad today as I thought he had never known one agony of bereavement & that all the care & perplexity and uncertainties were now on my side, not on his. How I did plead for his precious life for yours and his children's sake! For myself only saying, "Thy will be done" because I know God doth not willingly afflict & chasten us." I never before asked for one of my loved ones to be spared, but oh, that Friday night I passed through my Gethsemane, & I know what the Savior's cry meant as never before, "If it be possible!" Had it been possible for his & our best earthly good, my Heavenly Father would have answered my prayer. Tell Henry's precious little Katherine that Grandma feels the touch of her clinging little arms— that would comfort her now. I am grateful to God that I have seen the children. I shudder as I think what it might have been had it occurred in Denver.

   I dared not look at him again in the Chapel lest I should break down completely. You have laid Henry in a lovely spot, & I know you love to think of him as by your father. I tried to fix the place upon my memory, for it may be I will never see it again.

    I intended leaving tomorrow but I feel so sick & weak today that I had best wait, & besides I have some business with John. I will leave Saturday… Kiss the darlings for me & my love & heartfelt sympathy for Mrs. Thayer. My love to Katie. Send me a p.c. to say how you all are. You have so many letters to write. May God give you hourly grace & consolation. Kiss the precious baby again & again.   —Your devoted Mamma, *A. J. W. Hobson.*

Camp Cuba Libra, Jacksonville, Fla., Aug. 21, 1898.
My Dear Cousin K—   I arrived in Fredericksburg Tuesday afternoon. Then I found that we were preparing to leave for this place. The first and second battalions of my regiment left Thursday afternoon but owing to the railroads failing to supply cars in time, my battalion, the third, didn't get off until Friday morning at seven. We had a very nice trip. Our men behaved well. They gave us no trouble. We are camped on the St. John's River. We are nicely camped. We are on a sand hill in pine woods. Florida may be pretty in the eyes of some but it doesn't strike me that way. I think it is the least attractive place I ever stopped. It is not as hot as Virginia and we have a nice breeze all the time. It is very humid and damp and we have rain two or three times a day. The vegetation is not pretty but rather scarce and thirsty looking. Hugh is here. He looks very much fagged out. I wanted to be with you and by you at your worst time but I could not. I was ordered away and had to go. I love you dearly Cousin K— and have always known you to be a fine woman but the strength and the character you showed in your trying situation last week showed me that you were even better than I ever gave you credit for being. Give my love to Mrs. Thayer and the children and remember me to the servants. With my very best love I am affectionately yours,   —*John S. Wise Jr.*

The Old Home
My poor Sister—   Our hearts ache with you and for you in this shocking and terrible bereavement, and for the fatherless little ones. I know there is no comfort in words at such a time as this, and yet it would seem heartless not to tell you that we mourn with you. If you can find consolation in anything, it will be in the thought that you have been true and kind and devoted as a wife and mother. Harriet joins me in loving sympathy to you and mother.
—*Brother Frank.*

August 22, 1898. Law Offices— Pattison, Waldron & Devine, Denver, Colo.
Dear Mrs. Hobson—   I gravely doubt whether any word which I might dictate or thought which I may express can afford either strength or comfort to you in this time of trial. I have long hesitated, thinking it might be best for me to remain entirely silent, but it has seemed to me that I should at least attempt to express my sympathy with you, and to assure that I am not unmindful of your sorrow. Your dear husband was with me for a long time upon the evening of the day before he left Denver. He was cheerful, full of hope and anticipated much pleasure from the trip before him. He was worn and tired as he had been a great part of the summer, but it never

occurred to me that any calamity could overtake him for many years to come. He was a man possessed of singular fortitude and almost perfect courage, as you well know. He was in the midst of his career; his life imperfect and incomplete. His achievements had been great for one so young, but all of us believe that had he been spared, he would have accomplished great things in this life. But I must not detain you by these expressions of my admiration and esteem, for you cannot well be patient with them now. I have stood by the open graves of all my brothers and sisters save one; of my father and mother— of my first born child, and of many kindred, and with that experience I desire to say to you, that I have no more doubt that your dear husband is still a living being than I have of my own existence. I do not need to say this to you, because I am satisfied that you have long cherished this hope, and that it is now one of the convictions that supports and makes life tolerable to you and the future years that are to come more easy to be borne. I have often in years gone by used the language of one of the most beautiful characters whom I have known in this country when endeavoring to give some slight comfort to those suffering such a bereavement as yours. There are more beautiful discourses on death, but none more beautiful than the one before me. This is the closing paragraph:

"Soft as an infant's sleep shall be the coming of death to you and to me. Sweet shall be the rest which falls on the soul, wearied with work and the body exhausted by years. Tenderly shall the death cloud envelope us, and hide all familiar things from our failing sight, and when we awake again, with no abrupt transition, with no punishment, we shall find ourselves gently led into new beings, in the midst of old and new friends. We shall be in the presence of a more divine beauty than that of this earth, and with faculties opening into greater power to meet the new knowledge and the new work of that next world— that vast beyond."

Believing this, death is robbed of its terrors. I shall hope to see you upon your return to Denver, in the meantime I pray that you may have strength to bear the present and courage to look without flinching into the future. With kindest regards, and tenderest sympathy, I am,   —Very respectfully yours, A. E. Pattison.

❧ Letters from Annie Jennings Wise Hobson:

Ashland, August 26th, 1898.
My dearest Katherine—   Why do I not hear from you— Two weeks today since we were with our precious one together watching [him] leave us— crossing the dark river. Two weeks since we parted in Troy next Tuesday & not one line from anyone with you. I am filled with apprehension lest you are sick or your dear good Mother. For myself, I scarcely know how the days go by. I am waking & dreaming all night… God gives me strength to take up each day's duties & go on with them, & to try to help my poor old Mother on. As each evening comes the shadows darken & I can only cry to my Heavenly Father, "God be merciful & give me all needed strength." Oh! How my heart bleeds for you, & I must be so far apart & not be able to have the privilege of doing one little service to help & sustain you… Can you not bring the precious children to see me before you go West? It seems a great deal to ask but in the uncertainties

of life I may never see them again… I also inclose a letter from Captain Baker's wife which will speak for itself. I wrote to her from New York. A letter from Eva tells me that Hugh has again had fever, & will be given a furlough.

Dear old Mother talks of you and our dear Henry all the time & sends tenderest love & sympathy. Eliza says, "Words can not tell her how sorry I feel for her— tell her so with my love." …I do not forget all the mercies and blessings that surrounded us in those last days. I am thinking of his not going to the Home Farm this afternoon & your desolation tomorrow when he cannot be with you, yet I believe he will be very near you. If my letters are incoherent, it is because my brain feels *addled*. If you cannot write, get someone to send me a few lines telling how you all are. Kiss all the darlings for me, & take little Henry in your arms & press him to your heart for me. All the children send love. Not one word from Cannon. He may not yet have heard the sad loss— the irreparable earthly loss he has sustained. God the Comforter be with you & impart all the courage & faith you so sorely need.   —Your loving Mamma, *Anne J. W. Hobson.*

Ashland, August 28th, 1898.
My dear Mrs. Thayer—   On next Tuesday it will have been two weeks since I parted from you in suppressed agony. I left my last child with you all in strange scenes: sleeping the last sleep where his Mother might never again stand beside his resting place. I did it willingly & unselfishly for Katherine's sake especially as he had desired it. It was the end of the long years of earthly parting and being apart. Thank God, my dear Henry never knew the full distress of those years of separation to me, & how I felt that the years were putting our lives further apart, despite his love & loyalty & faithful devoted letters. Now he is to be praised for & not prayed for. Now I shall be going nearer & nearer to him. I can sincerely say, that my darkest sorrow is not for myself but for his wife & children and their sacred earthly ties— for what they have lost in him. I also feel deeply for you, dear Mrs. Thayer. He has indeed been as a son to you, and you will miss the sweet privilege of being a Mother to him & rendering the sweet services & aid that were denied to me. You and your lovely daughter were indeed the benediction of his earthly life. It is so lovely to recall how he loved & enjoyed his sweet attractive children. I know my loving, all merciful Heavenly Father would have spared him to them could it have been possible. It tried me sadly to hear nothing from you all, & I again intreat that if no one else can do so, Katie may tell me if anyone is sick & how all are. This is the last letter I shall write till I hear from someone. Please give the inclosed to Katherine, & I hope you too may find comfort in the little leaflet inclosed. Kiss the darlings for me. I determined to inclose this letter to you, in case Katherine was sick. God the Comforter be with you all.
—Very affectionately, *Annie J. W. Hobson.*

Dear Mrs. Hobson—   I know how dark and sad the future seems to you; how hard it will be for you to bear the loneliness of your life, and my heart aches for you when I think of your home-coming. We miss him in the office more and more every day and cannot see how we are going to hold together without his clear brain and steady purpose, and I do not wonder when you say, that but for your children and the duties you must perform, it would be easier for you to give up. I can understand you too when you say you have memories that few possess. Your life together was a beautiful one, and it must be the greatest comfort to you to know that you have nothing to regret and that you and Mr. Hobson's children were the most beautiful things in his life. He was like a different man when he spoke to or of you, and I have often noticed how the tone of his voice and the expression of his face would change when you or one of the children came into the office. And in the seven years I worked for him I could not help but remark from year to year how his character seemed to change from quick nervous irritability to a more tranquil, thoughtful, considerate, and kindly disposition. He had many beautiful attributes of character himself, but he also took many of his wife's with him into the next world.

Thank you for the kind message about the flowers. I wish I could have seen Mr. Hobson before he was laid away.

Please thank Little Henry for his message and tell him the green stars are on the window yet.

With love to all of the little ones and to Mrs. Thayer, I am Yours most faithfully, *M. E. Fallon.*

The Last Will And Testament of Henry W. Hobson:

FIRST. I do appoint my wife, Katherine T. Hobson, if she be living at the time of my death, Executrix of my Estate...

SECOND. The International Trust Company holds, as Trustee, certain policies of insurance, under a Declaration of Trust. Fifteen thousand dollar ($15,000) is held for the benefit of my Mother, in case she survive me.

Henry C. Coke, of Dallas, Texas, holds in Trust five thousand dollars ($5,000). This amount I direct to be paid to the International Trust Company, as Trustee, to be held upon the same trusts as were created with reference to the $15,000 insurance money to be held by said Trust Company. The condition, however, of this bequest is, that my note for $5,000 held by said Coke, shall be cancelled and surrendered.

I desire that my mother's income during her lifetime shall be at least twelve hundred dollars ($1,200) a year, and if, for any reason the twenty thousand dollars provided for with said life insurance, and the $5,000 due by Henry C. Coke shall not produce the sum of $1,200 a year, I request my wife to make up any deficiency, in case she can do so without injustice to herself and children.

THIRD. If my Mother survive me, I direct that all of the personal effects belonging to me, in the possession of my Mother shall remain in her possession until her death. If she does not survive me (or, surviving me, after her death) I bequeath all of said personalty to my wife; or in case she be dead, to my children share and share alike. I desire all personal effects which have especial association with my Father and Mother to belong to my Wife and children.

Signed and witnessed, June 9, 1897. [The files include both a handwritten draft and a typed copy of the will.]

◈ A letter with the will:

June 25, 1895, Law Offices of Henry W. Hobson, Ernest & Cranmer Bldg, Denver, Colo.
My Darling Wife and Children:
   This letter accompanies my will and is to be delivered to you.
   I am sure you will appreciate the motives which have led to my providing for my Mother. To her I owe a debt which can never be repaid in this life or in the life to come.
   I do not leave you much. To my Wife, however, I leave the memory of a devotion and love which were always constant and intense. Since our marriage she has been my companion, my life, my love. All that is brightest in my life I owe to her and the children she has borne to me.
   To my children I leave that which I inherited and derived from my dear Father and Mother. From my Father I inherited an unsullied name, which I have tried to carry without reproach among men and in the world. From my Mother I learned that the performance of the duties of life, as they are presented day by day, should be the highest and noblest ambition of a man's life. I have tried to follow the training of my Mother and when I have failed it has been through my weakness and not from lack of proper teaching.
   In my will I have made no especial provision as a testimony of my love for my dear Mother Thayer. My sincere love she has had in life and I now bear testimony to her goodness and sweetness to me. No man ever had a sweeter or more considerate friend, Mother, or counsellor.
   I have not been in life what is *called* a religious man, but I now declare my firm faith and belief in God, the Father and in Christ, the Son. May this Father and Savior bless and preserve you, comforting my Wife and inspiring my children to be earnest, true and faithful men and women.
            Your devoted Husband and Father, *Henry W. Hobson.*

Henry Wise Hobson, from a hand painted miniature, photographer unknown— a number of his descendants have inherited his red hair.

◈ Handwritten by Katherine Thayer Hobson and reproduced photographically after the death of her father:

> Dedicated to Mama in memory of
> Henry Wise Hobson
> who went to sleep August 13th, 1898.
>
> Thou art gone, Our Precious Darling
>   But thy loved ones left behind
> Know that you have seen The Savior
>   In his beautiful, beautiful land.
>
> Our minds are often haunted
>   With the lovely words you've said

And I dream that you stand smiling
 Right beside my bed.

When the glorious trumpet soundeth
Then thy loved ones left behind
Will cross the river to thee
 And live in the beautiful Celestial land.

from Katherine Thayer Hobson.

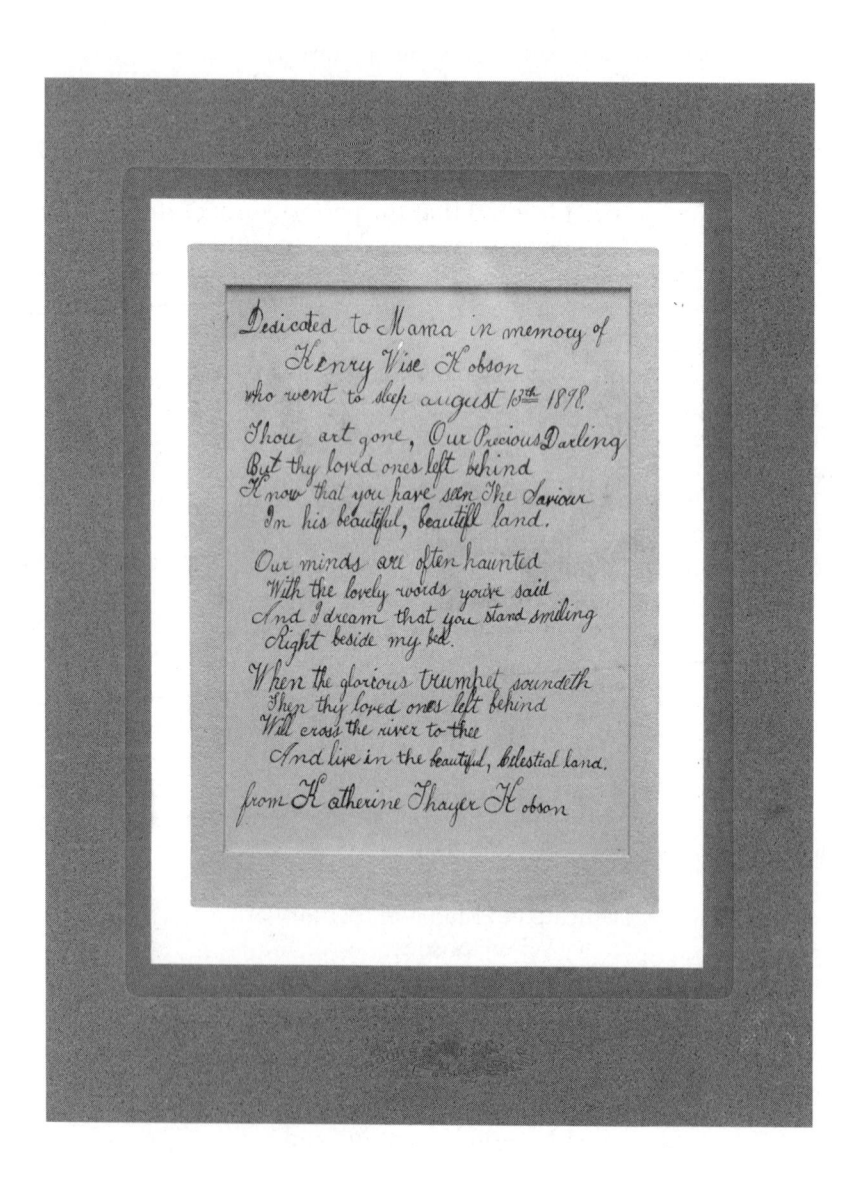

Poem by Katherine Thayer Hobson, 1889–1982, for her mother.

XXIII

1898–1916

A Widow and Her Children

IN August 1898, Katherine Thayer Hobson, not yet thirty-nine years old, was a widow for the second time in her life. Her grief was great, yet she had four small children to educate and raise, and that would be her major task and responsibility in the years ahead. With all of that to do alone, without the assistance and companionship of her husband, she may not have paid too much attention to the national and world events that surrounded her during these years. The Spanish-America War ended in December 1898 with the Treaty of Paris. "Consumption," by 1898 called Tuberculosis, had taken the lives of many of her family, including her first husband, but in 1899 the first Tuberculosis center in America opened in Denver. In that same year, President McKinley became the first President to ride in a car— a Stanley Steamer. In the years ahead the automobile would transform America. Henry Ford organized the Ford Motor Company in 1903, introduced the Model T at a cost of $850 in 1908, adopted the conveyor belt for his assembly line in 1913, produced his millionth car in 1915, and sold the mass-produced Model T for $310 in 1926. At some point during these years a young Henry Hobson went to get his drivers' license. As he was leaving he turned to the Sheriff and said, "I want one for my sister too." Upon being told that Eleanor Hobson, age thirteen, could drive a car, the Sheriff gave him a license for her. Eleanor Hobson never took a drivers' exam, and at that time the Hobson family had license plate #25 in Colorado.

America was growing during all of these years. The census of 1900 showed a total population of 75.9 million, with 3.4 million people living in New York, and by 1910 there were 91.9 million Americans. In the 1910 census less than half of those over twenty-five years old had completed high school and only 4% had attended college. The success of the Singer Sewing Machine enabled that company to build the first skyscraper in New York City—a 47-story building completed in 1908. In that same year General Electric received patents for both the electric iron and the toaster, and in 1911 Willis Carrier invented the air conditioner. Life in America was changing. Natural disasters and fires ravaged some American cities during these years. A September 1900 hurricane killed over 6,000 in Galveston, Texas; a Chicago theatre fire in 1903 killed 588; a 1904 fire in Baltimore destroyed 2,600 buildings; the 1906 San Francisco earthquake and fire killed nearly 700 people; and a West Virginia mine explosion in 1907 killed 361 miners. The "Lower 48" states became complete in 1912 when New Mexico and Arizona became the 47th and 48th states. The assassination of Austrian Archduke Ferdinand and his wife in June 1914 in Sarajevo was cause for many declarations of war amongst the nations of Europe, but until April 1917, the United States remained neutral in this European conflict that eventually became World War I. Between 1914 and 1917 Germany tried to create an alliance between itself, Mexico, and Japan, and this was cause for suspicions and tense relations between the United States and Mexico. In 1914 American troops occupied the Mexican city of Veracruz, and in 1916 Francisco, "Pancho," Villa attacked settlements in New Mexico and Texas killing seventeen Americans. The 1916 incursions by Mexican guerilla forces resulted in the call-up of different National Guard units throughout the country.

In the fall of 1898 Katherine Hobson returned to Denver with her children and lived there until 1903 when she moved to Colorado Springs. She would also spend time living in Dresden, make a trip around the world with her daughter Eleanor, and live in hotels in the East where her children attended school and college. However, before August 1898 was over, there would be yet another crisis for the family.

Letters, diaries, and telegrams by:
Annie Jennings Wise Hobson
Eleanor Whiteside Hobson — Mackenzie
F. Thayer Hobson
George Hobson
Henry Wise Hobson
Katherine Thayer Hobson
Katherine Thayer Hobson — Kraus
George M. Mackenzie
Dr. H. D. McQuade
Thomas Nelson Page
Catherine McKie Thayer
Harriet Thayer
Edward Whiteside
Eva Wise
John S. Wise

Letters written from: New York City, Cambridge, Troy, Albany, Buffalo, and Cooperstown, New York; Ashland, Cape Charles, Williamsburg, and Brook Hill, Henrico County, Virginia; Stamford and New Haven, Connecticut; Denver and Colorado Springs, Colorado; Watch Hill, Rhode Island; Washington, D. C.; Kansas City and Excelsior Springs, Missouri; Santa Barbara, California; Baltimore and Catonsville, Maryland; Andover and Boston, Massachusetts; Trenton, South Carolina; Bryn Mawr, Pennsylvania; Aswan, Egypt; Maine, Dresden, Paris, and aboard trains.

The End of August 1898

From Catherine McKie Thayer:

WESTERN UNION TELEGRAPH COMPANY
August 21, 1898.
To: Telegraph Operator, Johnsonville NY for Mrs. Henry Hobson, So. Cambridge, N.Y.
Have seen best surgeon. Knee not serious but needs a little attention. Will stay till tomorrow. Will send Dr. Bloss medicines by evening train —*Mother*.

knee not serious Less than 10 days after the death of Henry Wise Hobson, his older son fell on a rusty nail and had to have knee surgery in Troy. He was taken there by his grandmother while his mother remained in Cambridge with the other children.

August 22, 1898, Troy House.
My darling child—   Mary has gone out to wire you that we stay tonight… Dr. B— said it was the wisest thing to put Henry in the care of a good surgeon at once— "an ounce of prevention etc." "You need have no apprehensionness," he said. "He will be all right in a few days." Dr. H— [Houston] has a little boy about H's age… After we see Dr. H— tomorrow we will decide about going to you. Henry said, "Tell her I send love & kisses and I'll be back as soon as I can." Dear child, so like his precious Father…

The Old Home, Thursday evening. [August 25, 1898]
My Darling Mother—   Your package & letter enclosed received & on the box was marked "From Hospital, Troy, N. Y." To feel you have taken Henry there, it would have been better to have told me, for though I have read & read your letter, I can not see anything in it to cause anxiety but then you withhold taking Henry to Hospital & so there must be something to do to his knee besides cleansing, for that could be done at Troy House. I have lost so much. I just feel I can not endure it but I wish to know all & everything about it. That dearest little fellow. I knew he was suffering and yesterday that poultice, that was hardly more than as warm as my hand, made the tears fall like rain. A whole week, nearly, since it happened. Tell Henny Penny that Mama has missed her big boy all day so much & he must hurry and get well & come home to her & I send him hundreds of kisses & hugs & love— More than this letter will hold. Many kind letters today. I love to read what is said of dear Henry. I am so glad Dr. Bloss is home… I am so thankful you are with Henry… tell me everything… A heart full of love. God bless & keep us all. Katherine much better & baby too, medicine given… your *Kittie*.

St. Mary's Hospital, Troy, August 26, 1898.
My darling child—   The Dr. has just left having undone & dressed Henry's knee— found it in good condition, swelling down, cool, not sore, full movement of knee joint… He said "tell the Mother, Henry is doing excellently well, the joint right, the wound drained clean, pulse & temperature about normal" (there has been a little fever…) …"by the last of next week I feel that he can go to his Mother." I know this time may seem long to you, but his present condition is such a relief to me that I feel a great burden lifted from me, soul & body & thank God all the time. I said to the Dr. now that it is cooler his Mother may think of coming down to see him… The Dr. said, "I see how anxious the Mother is to see her boy— but he is perfectly happy now & I fear it would break him up to *part with her,* I'd not advise her coming." I feel so too & so does Mary… Henry now has a little visitor. I left his room to have floors wiped, bed changed and so on. This visitor is a foundling left at foot of Hospital steps & he has been reared here. All are kind to him. He came on St. Andrews of the Cross day— so he is named Andrew Cross…

Sunday PM August 28, 1898.
My Dearest Mother—   Sent you a postal the other day & Henry a daily message. On Friday eveng [sic] expected a letter from you— none came. Arthur has been sick, but is better, so Katie went over to the Boughton's at 8 p.m. to hear if Mr. B— had seen Henry & came back with a very satisfying

report of a visit to Henry at noon Friday. Yes, Saty. a.m. your letter came of Friday. I was to have taken 11:18 train from Johnsonville, but after reading your most satisfactory report of H's condition & that Dr. Houston could not advise my coming, I gave up because I felt he knew best, and I would not take the responsibility of disregarding his opinions, but I was so disappointed— no letter last night. You do not mail them early enough, but Friday's report most satisfactory & H's letter & rose. I think you had better stay right on at Jermain's, every reason why you should & Marie so glad to have you, & be near Henry until it is safe for him to come home. I wish him to stay in the hospital until his knee is quite well— he might come maybe a few days earlier & hurt his knee & have a relapse— do not wish any *chances* taken, a week more of absence may mean a stronger condition & less liability to hurt it. The samples received. I think better not get girls any black wool dress just now— their sailor suits will soon be back & new materials will soon be on market... Thayer's cold is very slight— he is lively and bright. Katherine has gotten much better of her cold & eats with more relish— she is so tender & sweet with me. Eleanor is into any & everything— sunshine & clouds near together in her nature. Harriet entirely lovely & Frank quiet & pleasant... Miss Fallon has sent me Henry's letters & one has the statement of what Henry expected to receive from the R. R. matters. I shall copy & send to Mr. Trumbull... I feel so much easier to have you near Henry— poor little man. I am glad he was brave. All send much love to you & him... Tender love, your own *Kittie*.

The Old Home, South Cambridge, August 29th, 1898.
My Dearest Uncle Johnnie—   I know you felt for me in having Henry go to the Hospital, & have an operation, under ether— he is doing finely. I send you his letter, not because it is from Santiago & describes a battle, but because that Little fellow never faltered & has "been brave like Papa," when his wound is dressed. And by him stood my dear Mother, holding the little hand, until he went to sleep, & he was taken into the operating room. These have been trying days. I try to feel courage when I feel the Baby's hands & realize his entire dependence. Three weeks ago Henry left me. Oh, only did he not come under the eye of some physician who could see the trouble? It seems so cruel that Henry who was always doing for everyone, should not have had everything done for him— but for Him who rules, & guides us, and promises to sustain, I could not go on. Henry must be away another week— he fell & punctured the synovial gland, the opening so small it could not heal from outside and had to be opened & scraped. He wrote this with his typewriter for you because he loved you so much he said... Katherine's cold is better. Eleanor happy all the time, as is Thayer. I love to hear their happy voices. I have too many blessings, and I keep them, or try to, at the front of my mind. And such memories of nearly eleven years married life. He was my lover always— and such devotion— and such companionship. Every year we grew nearer & dearer, if possible. I have had much taken— but our children left me— and he told me that last day, smiling, he loved to think of my character... Always your devoted, *Katherine*. (Virginia Historical Society)

He wrote this with his typewriter An unfound letter from the younger Henry W. Hobson.

Saturday afternoon. [undated, sometime in August 1898]
My Darling boy, —Henry—   Today I have your lovely letter & rose, the first you made— it is pretty & Mama loves it. We are well & think of you all

the time. Mama is going down soon to bring you home. I hope you will thank your kind Dr. for being so good to my little Boy who is so precious… Thayer has only a tiny little cold. He keeps looking around. I say, "Where is Henry?" Katherine is taking good care of your turtles— her little one is dead. Eleanor & Katherine & Thayer send love & kisses with mine. Love to Mary. Aunt Harriet sends you love. —Your *Mama.*

South Cambridge, Sept 1st, 1898.
My dearest Boy—   …I wish you to stay until your leg is in a condition not to be hurt by the slightest touch & the wound healing well. If you come before that you might be worse for it. Let us try & be patient and in a few days you will be home. Take Mama's love & kisses & Thayer's. He is asleep by me as I write… Love to Grandma & kisses. Always think how good she is to you & all of us. Love to Mary. Your loving *Mother.*

Sept. 3rd., New York.
Dear Katherine—   You must pardon this paper. It was so hot I could not remain at the office & brought sundry letters home to answer but can find no other paper but this pad left by Dick on his last visit. I was absent Friday 26th to Friday 2nd moving my family effects to N.Y. & to Cape Charles. Mrs. Thayer's letter about Henry was forwarded to me in Accomac just as I started on a drive of 55 miles & so I only had a chance to answer it yesterday. Indeed I did feel for you about little Henry. I rejoice with you that the little chap is doing well & his little letter shows it. I send it back to you. Keep it & put it away. I have all the letters my boys have ever written me from the first & someday they will be interesting to my *grandchildren* I know. He had better not play much with loaded bullets from Cuba. His remembrance of me was very sweet & I want him always taught to cherish me as a near & dear friend, for his Papa was very dear to me.

this paper Written on stationery from the House of Representatives, Washington, D.C. The letter suggests that a pad of Congressional stationery had been left at John Wise's house by his brother, Richard Alsop Wise, who was then a Member of Congress from Virginia.

his little letter The unfound typewritten letter referred to in letter of August 29, 1898.

You and yours have been constantly in my mind. In the long drive down the Eastern Shore I though of you constantly. I feel just as you do concerning Henry's death. The thought that even I might have detected his peril & forestalled the danger has cost me many an anxious pang, & yet I have consoled myself by the assurance that in what I failed in, it was from no lack of love or interest or solicitude, but from ignorance & hope. As for the poor doctor, we cannot hold him responsible for an error of the head. I do not doubt that he did his best. The result, sad as it is, we must accept dear Katherine, & we cannot relieve the sorrow by reflections on what might have been. There is a wonderful amount of philosophy as well as comfort in those lines of Burns—

> Then at the balance, let's be mute,
>   We never can adjust it;
> What's *done* we partly may compute,
>   But know not what's *resisted.*

The last lines from Robert Burns' *Address to the Unco Guid,* or *the Rigidly Righteous.*

I have letters from all the boys & they report themselves well. Hugh greatly improved since his return from Cuba. They expect to be ordered to Havana in Oct. I pray that it may not be until the sickly season is over. Am writing to Jack today & will deliver your message.

Eva Evelyn Byrd Douglas Wise, wife of John S. Wise.

Have no fear of my tenderness for Eva, dear Katherine. I love her very much. She is a girl of very fine points & high character & her faults are due not so much to herself as to causes outside herself. Still I know her worth & am sure that each year we will grow nearer and dearer to each other.

…Well this is a most unsatisfactory letter, but I am glad to know I had brains enough left to write at all. With love to Mrs. Thayer & the little ones. —Yours affect. *John S. Wise.*

September 6th, 1898, John S. Wise, Attorney at Law. 44 Broad Street. New York.

My Dear Katherine— I enclose you a bill, just received, from Drs. Abbe and Fisk. I consider it a rascally demand. There is no other term by which to characterize a claim of this amount for services of that character. Dr. Abbe saw Henry for the first time about 8:30 P. M. Thursday, and you know that he died within forty-eight hours. This demand is for less than four hours actual service. I enclose you a copy of the letter which I have written them. You will see that I have simply informed them that I referred the matter to the executor. Mr. Whitted is here, and, unless you instruct the executor to pay it, he will most assuredly submit the question to the County Judge, who passes on such claims, and the Judge will, in all probability, decline to approve the account for more than one-half the claim. I hope you will not have any false delicacy about letting this matter take its proper course. Certainly these men have shown no delicacy towards you. They are a pair of hogs. I do not know whether your relations to Dr. S. A. Fisk justify it, but, if they do, if I were in your place, I would send the bill to him, and I think he might bring proper influence to bear, by which it can be reduced to honest limits. If he does not, my cool advice to you is to let the executor handle the matter entirely, and not to hesitate about permitting him to defend the estate from this robbery… I send you herewith my receipt for the money expended on Henry's funeral expenses. You will need it in settling the account. —Yours affect. *John S. Wise.*

Bill from the Roosevelt Hospital following the death of Henry Wise Hobson. Note the charge on August 12th for "1 Btl champagne 1.50." Total hospital bill for three days was $96.71.

September 8th, 1898, John S. Wise, Attorney at Law. 44 Broad Street. New York.
My Dear Katherine—   I have all your letters. Of course, I will not quarrel with you about the payment of the bill of Dr. Abbe. I only say it was unconscionable, and if I had been in your place, I would have allowed it to be settled by the administrator according to law.

I was suddenly called to Washington yesterday to get Hugh his Captaincy. He is now a Captain, which is quite an honor for a youngster of 27…
—Yours affectionately, *John S. Wise.*

◦ A letter from Annie Jennings Wise Hobson:

Ashland, Sept. 13, 1898.
My dear Katherine—   I have been living over the scene of a month ago. In spirit I have been beside you and the dear children. It still seems like a heartless fearful dream. Sometimes I query was it really Henry, my son, my last child, my hope, and dependence, I saw laying there, dying on that bed in the hospital… I have tried to make this a day of thanksgiving— for Henry's noble and devoted life and for his peaceful transition to a higher sphere without long, protracted illness & suffering. I feel the blessed comfort of knowing that all human skill and foresight could do was done, and that he had the luxury & comfort of that lovely hospital & the kind care of those good nurses. It was so blessed that we could all be with him. Oh! the legacy of love meant by that last embrace & those last fervent kisses… I inclose you the birthday letter Henry wrote me on the cars, thinking you would like to read it. I send you today two photographs of Henry that I like much better than the last he sent me. One (the one with the beard) was taken the fourth year he was in Colorado— the last before he was married. I thought you might not have copies of these & would like to have them… Last but not least it is an inexplicable relief to hear such good accounts about my little Henry— how precious he is. My love to Mrs. Thayer, & also to Kate. Kisses for the darlings. Did Mrs. Thayer get my letter? God the comforter be with you—   —Your loving Mamma, ever with tender sympathy, *Annie J. W. Hobson.*
—Did you go to Oakwood on the 13th?

The Old Home, South Cambridge, Sept. 25th, 1898.
My Dearest Uncle Johnnie—   Your letter from the Cape was most interesting and I am very grateful & appreciative of your taking Katherine. You are next their Father to them & me and I shall hope they may all have the benefit of your companionship & interests to help form their characters. What you said of Katherine pleased & made my heart glad… Tell Eva she *must* come— that Eleanor says "her God Mother must come to see her." Send a postal what day & train. The Baby is nursing, which accounts for this scribble— he & his entire dependence keep me more than anything else. Henry left me these darlings to live for— And I know he would say "Katherine will do her duty for my sake & theirs" —but seven weeks ago he was here. Every place always seemed beautied where he was… Henny Penny made his final visit to the surgeon Thursday & he said the knee was perfect… I shall see you before I return to Colorado. We remain here until Oct 17th… —Yours, *Katherine.*
(Virginia Historical Society)

appreciative of your taking Katherine Letters indicate that the younger Katherine Hobson had gone to visit John S. Wise's family at the end of September— Eva Wise writes: "My dear Cousin Katherine— Katherine seems perfectly happy. We went in bathing yesterday and she was delighted. I got her a nice little suit… Our program for today is to go down and play in the sand until dinner time… I have never seen a child love the sea more… Devotedly, *Eva.*"

Kittie writes to her daughter on September 10, 1898— "My darling Katherine— Mama recd your letter yesterday. I hope you will try and be a very thoughtful girl… I should like to see you bathing & playing in the sand… Henry's knee is improving. I want you to stay at the sea & enjoy yourself & get rosy & fat. Tell Cousin Eva to take you on any excursions she likes… Your loving Devoted *Mama Kittie.*"

༄ A letter from Annie Jennings Wise Hobson:

Ashland, Oct. 13th, 1898.
My dearest Katherine—   I have had a letter in heart and mind for you for days. Your dear letter has been repeatedly read. Yes, yes I know, I feel all the time how the dear Papa is sorely needed. My sorrow is for you and the dear children. Let us cling to the thought that God is our Father and try to feel that He loves us and those children far more than human love can imagine… I am so glad to tell you that I have had a lovely letter from Cannon. I was so distressed that I had not heard from him since Henry's death that I wrote to Mr. Horsbrugh. The letter was dated Oct 2nd. He said— "I am surprised indeed that you did not receive my letter. As I came back to Camp the 23rd of August I received the dreadful tidings of Uncle Henry's illness & death. I was so shocked that I could scarcely write, but I did so at once, and the next day I returned to Camp, & until yesterday I have not been within ten miles of a P. Office. I feel still too dazed to write about Uncle Henry, but feel assured you have the tender sympathy of my whole heart, and I am going to work manfully and will do everything I can [to] help you. I am now receiving $300 a year as wages. I cannot save very much of that, but as I do save it I am going to invest in cattle. Men have come here without a cent and in five or six years are worth at least ten or fifteen thousand dollars. I give up all idea of a profession or other business until I can make money ahead." —He will write to you as soon as I send him your address… A letter from Mr. Horsbrugh has followed, saying he thought I no longer had cause for anxiety about Cannon, that the life there would make a man of him, and that he would do all in his power to help and encourage him…   —Ever your devoted *Mamma, A. J. W. Hobson.*

The Old Home, October 15th, 1898.
My dear uncle Johnnie—   …I went to Troy yesterday & to our lot in Oakwood. Our grave is beautifully green, having been sodded and I covered it with branches of bright maple and sumach. All was lovely, and peace there, and I am so thankful for that most beautiful lot. Two months tomorrow since you comforted me so by your dear presence after doing everything for Henry in life & death. I sometimes think I have said too little of this which has been ever present, but dear Uncle Johnnie, you know I feel deeply all your kindnesses. Much love to you all.   —Always your devoted *Katherine.* (Virginia Historical Society)

October 17, 1898.
My dear Katherine—   Your two letters of 12th & 15th were on my table this morning and you do not know how it distresses me to see you so dejected. I love you very dearly and want you to be happy and to realize that happiness after all is within ourselves. Repining or mourning dear Katherine does nothing for us. Far be it from me to counsel you to forget dear Henry or to abate one jot of that tenderness which I know you feel & which the dear fellow so richly deserved. But Katherine it is our duty not to be dejected & to accept life's fate, determined to defy its hard blows. Life & death seem to me so material. Were I to know that I shall die tomorrow I would only say— "Well! My time has come!" Were my wife, who is dearest of all to me, to be taken tomorrow I would say with a great sob no doubt; "Well, her time has come." I have tried to school

myself to the philosophy of death. To realizing that the oldest & strongest of us are here for but a brief span— a span so infinitesimal in the ages, that we are as nothing & that if one of us goes before the other, it is simply the inevitable & we who linger a little while yet, must not vainly rapine, but await our turn and seek to be happy as we can, not only for our own sakes but for the sake of those about us… Think of what you have left. Your sweet Mother and your dear children. If Henry could draw near to you and put his arm about you as of old, he would tell you just what I say. I want you to try to place dear Henry's memory in the tenderest shrine of your heart but at the same time to know & realize that when you are happy, and content, and accept the inevitable, you do what he would have you do— for he had his sorrows & his losses and his disappointments and always bore them bravely… You little know how it grieves me that I am so powerless to soothe and comfort you, or how much you & yours are in my thoughts.   —*John S. Wise.*

St. John's Rectory, Stamford, Conn., October 25th, 1898.
My Dear Uncle Johnnie—   …Henry & I loved each other so dearly, & wholly, that we never longed for outside elements, and he told me over & over, and showed me that he was more my lover after nearly eleven years of married life than ever. Maybe "his day had come," as you say, but my heart is so full of longing for his presence that I feel lost…   —Yours, *Katherine.*
(Virginia Historical Society)

1899

January 26, 1899. Children visited Papa's office last time.
—*Diary of Katherine T. Hobson*

THE WESTERN UNION TELEGRAPH COMPANY
March 21, 1899.
Capt. John S. Wise—Eliza died ten minutes ago apoplexy wire Richard. *A. J. W. Hobson.*

April 27th, 1899.
My dear Katherine—   How are you? How is your knee? Please answer these two questions first and foremost. It is nearly May 1. When are you coming East? The house is rapidly rushing forward to completion. I hope it will be ready by June 1. Remember you buy your ticket to Old Point… Dear Hugh is gone. He wrote from San Francisco that his train stopped only thirty minutes in Denver. He sailed March 20th for Manila & I feel as if the darling little chap had settled in the fading light of sunset. But I have faith & hope that he will come back. It is a sad business in which he is engaged— Shooting niggers to make them love liberty— Inviting them to become Americans to be burned after being bound to trees & drenched with kerosene oil. What a charming picture our civilization must present to these Malays & cannibals. The War Department advises me that Henry & Jack will be at Camp Meade Pennsylvania May 10th when their Regiment will be mustered out… I have a letter from Sister Annie— She tells me about "the children." Well you know I am not crazy about that. I told her, "Now about Cannon's children, I wish you would not press me on that subject. Cannon's conduct was so selfish & so stubborn & the woman so repulsive that these children represent it all

Eliza was the white nurse who moved to Virginia from Philadelphia when Henry A. Wise married Sarah Sergeant in 1840 and then remained with the family for fifty-nine years.

your knee Katherine Hobson had torn ligaments in her knee.

Atlantic Monthly   John Wise's book, *The End of An Era*, was serialized in the April and May 1899 issues of the Atlantic Monthly and was published by Houghton, Mifflin & Company that same year. A few years ago the editor of this book obtained a copy in which an unknown previous owner had written, "Absorbing! Filled with unusual information of the Civil War Era. Well written too."

to me." I know the answer. But I do not want to argue about it. I know how bitterly Henry felt about it & there was much to exasperate him concerning the children themselves. God knows I could not harbor bitterness against the little things, but you cannot expect me to feel towards them as I do— either the interest or the affection. I would not for the world repel any affection they may feel for me, but I do not want to profess for them more than I feel. This is almost brutally blunt but I hope you will not be offended at my speaking to you honestly. I hope I may not hereafter hear so much about Mary's bellyache or George's bruise. I have plenty of people to love already without having this lot dumped on me. You must get the *Atlantic Monthly* for April & May and read my articles. They'll interest you. Eva likes them because I gave her the money they yielded to buy a dress. Eva is better. Cuba nearly knocked her out. It is beautifully bright & warm here now. Tomorrow I'll plant some roses & one will be named "Old Katherine," one "Young Katherine" and one "Little Katherine" & one for Eleanor, for Mrs. Thayer, Mrs. Hobson & "the yaller har'd gal" & the monkey. Well, here I've written myself to death. Good bye, Yours, affec. *John S. Wise*.

Back to Cambridge, 1899:

The Old Home, South Cambridge, June 23rd, 1899.
My Dear Uncle Johnnie—   We arrived late this afternoon & your letter was so grateful to me for Henry & I loved this place so dearly and the coming back is so sad & dreary… The children are of course over-joyed, & explored all they could before dark. We are in dire confusion as carpenters & painters are not through yet. We had a very comfortable trip & no extreme heat for which I was especially grateful for our Baby… May God help your dear boy Hugh— My heart aches dear Uncle Johnnie for your anxiety…   —Your devoted niece, *Katherine*. (Virginia Historical Society)

Katherine Hobson to her mother:

June 29, 1899.
The Old Home
…I have a letter from Mrs. Hobson which makes me very angry & you will see why— & giving Uncle Johnnie the credit, as if H's [Henry's] position was nothing, of her home, but I shall not reply *one word* to her. I wrote her from Denver & she never answered or speaks of the letter and I am not going to ask her here. I wish you would read this letter to Mrs. Hatch & hear her quiet sentiments regarding these expressions of Mrs. Hobson… Henry has just been in the meadow & picked one of the loveliest groups of grasses, yellow & white daisies & buttercups & I have it by me on porch— wish I could hand it to you…

July 1st, 1899.
… The paperer went off yesterday, we have curtains up in Grandmother's room— they make it fresh & clean and Mary put up curtains in sitting room this morning— all fresh & clean and dining room going up this P.M. So gradually we will be getting like a settled people. Thayer is putting a little two wheel cart on porch & then pulling it off the three steps… Katherine has her pet chicken… Eleanor is mixing chicken food— meal & water…

The Old Home, South Cambridge, July 3rd, 1899.
This is a very hot day. I have no thermometer— think it better not to know…
Tomorrow is fourth of July & I have a few fire works crackers & how small they look compared with the good times their Father gave them & his provision, but they will have to learn to be satisfied & happy with less & they can connect their best times with the dear Papa…

July 9th, 1899. The Old Home, South Cambridge
…This is dear Henry's birthday which we celebrated the 11th last year when he arrived. Sometimes I feel I should not have tried to come here— the place cries for him at every turn.

The Old Home

Leave the road, and follow a shady lane,
Cross the brook, and high on a rise of ground
The old house stands, watches and waits in vain

For the clan to return, descendants now scattered wide,
The elms brought home in a wild flower bunch by a child
Are dying giants, and all the rooms inside

Once filled with babel of voices and childish glee,
The borning, the dying, dusty and empty gape
Like old dry shells that echo the sound of sea

While the small paned windows look down the meadow's sweep
And the pillared porch invites to the cool long hall,
I think I can hear the heart of the old house weep

For the young, for the aged, for all who have passed the door,
Vibrating still to the sound of departing feet
Like the strings of a harp which will never be played on more.
　　　　—*Katherine Thayer Hobson, 1889—1982.*

This poem about the farm in Cambridge, New York, was included in *I have seen Pegasus*, a pamphlet of poems that Katherine Thayer Hobson prepared on the occasion of her 90th birthday, April 11, 1979. It is not known when the poem was written.

The Old Home, Cambridge, New York. "The elms brought home" have died.

❧ A letter from John S. Wise:

July 7, 1899.
My dear Katherine—   ...Poor sister Annie! She reminds me of a loose sail on a stranded boat. She flaps & flops & frats & frazzles herself out whether anybody notices her or not. If one gets too mean he may get a crack over the head with a splintered speech so the best way is to steer clear of it all. I am glad to hear her investments will pay her so well. Concerning myself, I only continued the payment of $75 per month until she should begin to get her income. Mrs. Stone sends Mother $25 a month, and since Idie's [Eliza's] death it does seem to me $100 per month for Mother is more than liberal. I shall tell Sister Annie I think $50 from me is enough hereafter. If with her income she must sell cows & horses, it is extravagance that causes it. When Mother dies I shall, so long as I am able, continue to give Sister A— $25 per month for her goodness to me when I was a child & for the love I bear to Henry's memory. I feel no obligation to care for or interest myself in Cannon's children. Maybe it is wrong but I cannot help it. They are not Pariahs as far as I am concerned. Poor little devils. They are simply nothing to me & I do not propose, with all my other burdens, to have them saddled onto me. About the Golden Fleece matter, I fear I can be of no service. I could not afford to undertake to place the stock with others... I shall look forward with great pleasure to your visit to me & try to make you have a nice time. Am so glad your knee is improving...   —*John S. Wise.*

Mother Mary Lyons Wise, the third wife and widow of Henry Alexander Wise and stepmother to his children.

❧ Katherine Hobson and her mother:

July 15th, 1899, Saturday afternoon.
My Dearest Mother—   [after visiting Troy]... Then we went to Cemetery & florists. Henry took a pail of water so we could put our flowers in water on the dear one's grave. We sat at that Sacred Spot a little while. The Cemetery looks and is well kept...

August 13, 1899.
My darling One—   How can I ever write this date without agitation. Harriet & Mrs. Parker & I have been talking of a year "ago" since luncheon... Mrs. P— so full of tender feeling for the dear one gone & for those who are left. I cannot put on paper what we have said... I can only ask our dear Heavenly Father to help you & give you the peace that can come only from Him. Yes— the eighteen years seem "short & long," as you say. I raise my eyes to dear Barclay's beautiful face & see those deep dark expectant eyes, so beautiful. I wonder what *all* our beloved ones are doing & do they meet or know each other in any way. We cannot know here for theirs is a higher happiness than we can understand *now*... I feel an irrepressible longing to be with you & the dear children, to hear your voices. It is very well here, but my heart is with you & your family... God comfort you...   *Mother.*

❧ Family matters in Virginia:

The Old Home, South Cambridge, September 22nd, 1899.
My Dear Uncle Johnnie—   ...Mrs. Hobson wrote me for $100.00. I enclose her letter, which please return. It seems better you and I should know

exactly our standing regarding her affairs. I sent her the money by return mail, because she was Henry's Mother. Henry bought all the furniture of her years ago, and wished his children to have certain pieces— the portraits etc. As she seemed to wish me not to tell of this request for money, you will know how to treat the knowledge… [incomplete letter from Katherine Hobson] (Virginia Historical Society)

Ashland, Sept. 13, 1899.
My dear Katherine—   Circumstances have come to pass that compel me most reluctantly to ask a kindness at your hands. Col. Patton is recovering from a desperate illness, and it is necessary that he should be moved here as early as possible in October. I must move somewhere in a very short time. I have had the use of his furniture all these years. I do not know what I should have done otherwise when Alice left taking (with Henry's consent) all she claimed. With what she took and what she destroyed of mine, she left me no common chairs, except some arm chairs & a few rockers. I have nothing to sit on in dining room or bed-room. She also took the stove & I have used Col. Patton's— so another must be purchased. In the house I have in view & I think I will be able to get for a much lower rent than this, I can make Mother comfortable and cut down expenses everywhere. I shall keep only a cook and a small boy. I can make Mother very comfortable there. After October 1st Johnnie will send $25 less a month for Mother in view of Eliza's death. I have not yet parted from my horse & little carriage nor my cow as it paid me to keep both till I moved. By hauling my own wood I save 75¢ a cord, and I wish to haul a supply to the new place while I can get it. Wood is going up in Ashland at an alarming rate so many are cutting wood to send away. Having the horse to help move my furniture will also save me much expense. As soon as moved, I will sell the horse, carriage and cow… parties have already engaged to take the horse & cow.

Mary leaves for school next week. Her outfit for the winter, travelling expenses and money needed to take for incidental expenses will amount to at least $30. As yet Johnnie has sent me no money & it often does not reach me till the twentieth of the month. Under the present [illegible] could you let me have $100 until I can get a little ahead. Cannon writes that he is trying to save money to help me. Now Katherine, I come to you to ask this in a distinctly business way as a business transaction. Not as having any claim on you as Henry's wife, but as the one to whom the money will revert in case of my death… Mr. Gibson emphatically says that I have no right to ask again any advance from the Trust Co. I will not accept it except as a business transaction, giving you a note with interest. I believe you will do this if you can. If not, candidly say so. God knows if our positions were reversed how gladly I would do it for you. John speaks of what he does for Mother as if only in a great measure done for me. If it did not help my personal income I could not keep Mother, & I certainly work for what I get and when Mother is taken (if I outlive her) I believe God will give me strength to find employment and get ahead before the days come when work is impossible, especially to put by something for my poor little girls if they are alive. Both are as delicate as possible. Two other matters demand immediate attention. Henry & I promised either an enlarged photograph or a crayon picture to St. John's Church library in Petersburg. He said he would help me give it, when the vestry wrote asking for a picture of him. The care of the section at Hollywood must also be paid for— $10. I make all these statements to show you that there is a need for ready money that I have not in hand now. If you cannot oblige me I will sell my watch, the old clock & that beautiful card table that came from the Government house with the claw feet. With the history attached to it, I can get a handsome price, but I did want your little Henry Wise to have it. While I think of it, I would like to have your wishes about the bedstead— the one Plumer died upon. Henry had said he should have it packed and sent to you last summer. I have no spring to match it, and in the smaller rooms of the house, to which we will move, it would be much in the way. I have little storage room there. …I think I wrote you that I was for some hours a very sick woman three weeks ago last Saturday. For fifteen hours I could not lie on my left side, the heart was so involved & I have not yet felt like myself. When the warm weather is over and my move made I hope to have a little rest which I sorely need. George & Jennings will go to the Free School. Next year George must go to work. Poor Mary is very delicate, very common-place & will never make her living by her brains. I see little prospect of her getting any educational advantages after this year. I have greater hopes for George & Alice than any of the others, yet poor little Alice is very frail… I am sorry to shadow you amidst your own distress & bereavement with my cares & troubles, but I have never felt so weak, so in need of a little loving sympathy as now. Kiss the dear children for me, and give my love to your Mother and also to Kate. Remember me to all my South Cambridge friends very cordially. The country must look very beautiful now. When will you return to Denver? Mother sometimes appreciates your messages & then again cannot understand who you are. The other day she insisted I was Gen. Wise's niece, never his daughter. I want little Henry to have the likeness of my father that Mother gave Henry. All join in love. God the comforter be with you.… Yours most lovingly, *A. J. W. Hobson.*

Sept. 27th, 1899.
My dear K—   Yours 22nd found me when I came home this A.M. I left here [New York] Wednesday night & spent Thursday, Friday & part of Saturday at the Cape… OH! Katherine what a world it is— and here is this letter of Sister Annie to you. To me she writes of her appreciation of my kindness & how she hates to think of my burdens— To you, as if I helped her tardily & ungraciously, & to Néné, she talks as if I owed her more that I grudgingly give. Thank God I do not do whatever I do with the hope of thanks or appreciation… I send you a copy of my letter to Sister Annie in reply to two I found here. You see I did nothing about what she wrote to you or said to Néné, God help her. She is a hopeless spendthrift & cannot resist her role of martyr in playing which she often appears an ingrate without really meaning it. To me Sister Annie is a constant irritation… Still, you did right. She is my sister, & to you she is Henry's Mother. On his death-bed, between gasps of pain, he said "I have provided $25,000 for Mother." — "You know her Uncle John, I fear it is not enough." I interrupted him & said "Henry don't let that trouble you. As long as I live & am able I'll do what I can to help." "Yes," said he "I know you will, but I want you to talk with Katherine & tell her how I feel about it & ask her, for my sake, if she can, sometimes, without depriving herself & the children, help her along a little. You know how it has always been & I know it

always will be so, as long as she lives. I know how K— feels too, but deliver my message and she'll understand. And tell her…" —here his voice broke— "…I could not speak to you of what I feel about her, or of what she has been to me. God bless her everything." I held his hand & stroked it & turned away to conceal my tears & strengthening his voice he added, "Old Kate will do right— She needs no telling." Oh! Katherine, I am crying as I write it & I write it because I know that dying thought of you is more precious than anything else he could have left you, & remembrance of it will make you forget all else but that you've had the opportunity to do as he knew you would. This will atone for the annoyance & distress from other standpoints… It distresses me to hear Mrs. Thayer is to be an invalid for several weeks. Give her my love & best wishes. If you'll ship Henry down to me by Express, I'll give him a good time & return him in like good condition as received. …Our new house is #154 W. 76th St. …Goodbye dear K. I feel better for writing all this. Kisses for Katherine, Henry, Eleanor, Thayer.   Yours affectionately, *John S. Wise.*

❧ Two letters to Thomas Nelson Page:

Denver, 1899.
Dear Uncle Tom—   I was so disappointed not to get a wheel the other day, one that had been promised to me for a long time and I don't know who to ask now for it. Will you give me one? I'll send you kisses for it, if you will. —Your little *Eleanor.*

Denver, 1899.
My dear Uncle Tom—   I don't believe I can find words big enough to thank you for your nice telegram. It is a bicycle I would like so much to have. When I see you I will give you a big kiss and a hug.   —From your little *Eleanor.* (Rare Book, Manuscript, and Special Collections Library, Duke University.)

1900

❧ A letter from Virginia:

Ashland, Va. June 6, 1900.
Dear Aunt Katherine—   I don't know how to thank you for your kind offer to send me to the V.M.I. but I don't think I am in any physical condition to go there for I have not been the same since I had the mumps. But I would be ever so much obliged to you if you would send me to the Business College of Richmond on the condition that I should pay back the money when I am able to do so. And if anything should happen so that I could not do so, you are to take it out of the legacy left me. Your offer is a very noble one and I will try to show you how much I appreciate it by making the best of my opportunities. Grandma will write to you the terms of the college and the advantages it affords. The expenses will be far less than that of any other college. Grandma will also explain fully about this. God bless you for your goodness to me. I am sorry to hear that Henry and Eleanor have the measles & hope Henry will soon be up. Love to all my little cousins.   —Your devoted nephew, *George R. Hobson.*

This letter is from the son of Rev. John Cannon Hobson.

850   THE FAMILY LETTERS

Summer 1900

Letterhead from the Larkin House, August 1900.

→ Three letters to Grandmother:

Postmarked: July 27, 1900.
Larkin House, Watch Hill, Rhode Island
Dear Grandma—   We have a very rainy day but now has stop. This afternoon a lady had a pin show… We have to little friends Stewart and Add. Stewart is a very prety boy and Add prety to but not as prety. Stewart has bear legs and fluffy trousers. Love to Jennie and all my friends.   Good bye from *Eleanor*.

The letters are addressed to Mrs. Francis S. Thayer in Denver. Eleanor was seven years old at the time, and the family was vacationing in Watch Hill, Rhode Island, where Katherine Hobson had invested in real estate.

Postmarked: August 24, 1900.
Larkin House, Watch Hill, Rhode Island
My Dear Grandma—   I thank you so much for your letter. Stewart and Add have gone away and I have no playmates. Katherine is having her violin lesson now and I have nothing to do so I am writing you. Henry has a grate [*sic*] big kite… It rained this morning but clear now. We are all well, and send love and kisses.   —Good bye from *Eleanor H*.

Postmarked: October 29, 1900.
Stamford, Connecticut.
My Dear Grandma—   I miss you very much. Medora is not dressed yet. Mama is not home yet. I like to get up and dress fast. Henry is going to school and thinks it is easy. Love to all from *Eleanor*.

August 2, 1900, Larkin House, Watch Hill, Rhode Island.
My Dearest Mother—   This is another lovely day, only one rainy day in

Katherine Thayer Hobson and her four children, Katherine (left), Henry behind, Francis Thayer, in his mother's lap, and Eleanor, standing, right. Photo may have been taken in Watch Hill, Rhode Island.

two weeks... I found a cross in stone cutters shed about 9 feet high & was so pleased with it that I asked if they could set it up for me to see this morning. They said yes & I was there at eleven & was delighted... The cross is so strong & beautiful in form & a wreath of *Holly* unites the four arms. This delighted the children, as K— said, Papa picked holly in Virginia at Eastwood & it grew there. I am perfectly satisfied & so relieved it will be finished & set between Sept 22 & 29th. The one I saw was on order. I will send you a sketch... I feel this is a great thing to accomplish to ones satisfaction... Jack [John S. Wise Jr.] writes his father has taken cold, pain in his back & if he is not better, Jack will not leave him— So unusual to hear of Uncle Johnnie ill. I feel anxious to hear again. Not a *line* from Mrs. Hobson yet. She is a compound of irregularities...   —Much tender love, your own *Kittie*.

Larkin Square, Watch Hill, Rhode Island, 2005.

Sept 4th, 1900, Larkin House, Watch Hill, Rhode Island.
My Dearest Mother—   K— at her violin, playing a very pretty selection which she is going to play with her teacher for Marie [Marie Jermain] before the latter leaves next Monday. I think the month's lessons have done K— the greatest good & the firm teacher who will not let K— go on to another bar until she has mastered the last one. We have to leave here Friday & will go to the Plimpton House, which keeps open several weeks longer... Henry playing boat & Eleanor also. I think I shall let Mary go home this week Saty. for a visit of a few days. She is a very excellent woman & servant & devoted to us in her way. There are only a few people left here and Mr. Howe told me he could not afford to run the hotel after Friday... I took Aunt Ada to Westerly to see the cross & decided on lettering. The base is all cut & cross in stonecutter's hands. Wreath to be of Holly & the best workman put on it— height 8 ft. 5 in. You will be glad to know all very satisfactory & to be set Monday Oct. 1st & I to be in Troy— hope I can stay at Hedge Lawn a few days at that time... Much love from all... Always your own *Kittie*.

Diagram of the proposed stone for Henry Wise Hobson's grave as drawn in Katherine Hobson's letter of September 4, 1900 to her mother.

Sept 10th, 1900, Plimpton House, Watch Hill, Rhode Island.
My Dearest Mother— Yesterday the four children went to church with me— all in white... At 4 took all children to Light House south of Larkin House. Marie joined us there & we had a pleasant visit. She goes today or tomorrow— may not get *the seat she wishes* on train from Hartford, oh me! how helpless town people are... I am so enjoying the children. K's day to take care of Thayer. I send you the drawing of cross, 8 ft 5 in... Marie thinks it very beautiful— & it not at all like the one I ordered for Barclay which is pleasant to her. Marie has good news from Katie— all going well but the hot weather *awful* in Albany & Katie there... Tenderest love & kisses my Dearest one, your devoted *Kittie*.

Sept 14th, 1900, Plimpton House, Watch Hill, Rhode Island.
My Dearest Mother—   ...Went to Westerly yesterday. Ada & I saw cross— the carving of wreath on cross being done. Holly— an Italian, doing the work & beautiful— the base finished & lettering polished, completed—

    Henry Wise Hobson
    Born in Goochland County Virginia
    July 9th, 1858
    Died August 13th, 1898

Detail of Henry W. Hobson's gravestone showing the holly that he had "picked" in Virginia at Eastwood.

Most satisfactory. The foundation laid Tuesday Oct. 2nd, cross set on foundation Oct. 3 …the wreath needs 2 whole weeks work. I shall be in Troy Monday 1st to see foundation— Henry put where it will not interfere with monument & if best have Henry's body moved— it will not be hard— if another position will be best… I shall be at Hedge Lawn. Shall say nothing to *anyone* but you about moving remains so there can be no talk or suggestions… Tenderest love & kisses my Dearest one, your devoted *Kittie*.

Hedge Lawn, October 3rd, Wednesday P.M.
My Dearest Mother—   Your letter sent here, recd yesterday at breakfast… Katherine and I were met by William Johnston in Albany & came up by Electric car. William looks well & not as fat— and happy here. He took me to his house in Watervliet yesterday on my way from Troy & I saw his wife— not a year older, fair, rosy, not a gray hair— so glad to see me. 22 years in Nov. next since Wm. left us… Yesterday a.m. I went to Troy, Wm. Johnston taking me & Katherine. Henry picked me a great armful of rose geranium branches at Watch Hill & it was beautiful & fresh to take to Oakwood. Everything was peace there, a lovely soft Oct. day & today the same. I have to have a change made & it is so. You see the monument would be injured & the Cross have its arms seen against monument from some points. The grave to be opened & casket removed today— other grave dug & to be there alone (because I wish to be alone) at four o'clock to see the dear body buried. Henry would have been near me had he been alive & such work done. I have a large piece of white tarlatan, 2 yds long & 1 1/2 wide, & am covering it with white carnations… to lay over the casket, a tender loving covering. William took me from cemetery to Uncle Aaron's— I saw him, Kittie & boys. All well. I have your several letters & so thankful to hear. Am just off to Troy now… Tenderest love & kisses, your devoted *Kittie*.

Friday morning, Oct. 5th, 1900.
My Darling Precious Mother—   Yesterday as I had no time to write I telegraphed you… The new grave was in rock & blasting necessary, this I found out when I went up with Uncle Aaron Wed at 4 p.m. The workmen had taken dear Henry's body up & the case was on lot & covered with Katherine's soft white blanket of flowers, impossible to have a new grave ready until yesterday (Thursday) p.m. I sat for an hour near our dear one, Uncle Aaron going to his lot, & made our appointment for yesterday at three, ordered a Cross of ivy & a few white carnations. Katherine & I went up to lot yesterday & Uncle Aaron there. Katherine placed the Cross on the casket & we saw the dear one's grave made again. Such a perfect day. The dear little baby's grave moved east 18 inches, the box still there after all these 46 years. The foundation for Cross at head of grave laid on solid rock. Katherine & I feel alike. She said, "I know Papa's spirit is in Heaven but I love to be near his dear body again." She is the most beautiful, loving, rare child… I went to Uncle Aaron's to dinner… Mary takes children to Ada's Saturday. Ada glad to have them… Love & kisses & God bless & keep us all.   Your own *Kittie*.

Hedge Lawn, Troy Road, Nov 7th, 1900.
My dearest Mother—   It is early and I have picked up my pad to write you a line. Don't know *how badly* Bryan is beaten yet… Servants bring word,

22 years in Nov since Wm. left us   This refers to 1878 when Francis and Catherine Thayer moved from Troy to Colorado. William Johnston had worked for them prior to their move. He was now working for the Jermain family, and he would again help the family in December 1915.

"McKinley elected." …I never expected anything else… I expect to stop in Washington from Monday to Wed & ask Mrs. Hobson there to see us. It seems better to let her see the children but *I will not* go to Virginia to visit & it will be a little outing for her. I shall write her to stay. I wish the estate would transfer a little money to my account for the Cross…   —Your own *Kittie*.

◌ A letter from Catherine McKie Thayer:

Nov. 22, 1900.
My darling Child—   This p.m. yours of Monday the 19th came with several inclosed— dear little Henry's too & a copy of one sent Mrs. Hobson. I am so very sorry that she will not join you in W— to see you & *all* of the children— it would seem to me that she would be so glad to see Henry's children— but I never understood Mrs. H's dealings with her only son & only child & I cannot expect to comprehend her now. I honor her for having had such a son…

It is not known why the letter refers to Henry Hobson as the "only son & only child" of Annie Jennings Wise Hobson.

The Raleigh, European Plan, Washington, D. C., Nov. 26, 1900.
My Dear Old Santa Claus—   I am going to write you what I want for Xmas. I want a camera with plates about 4x6 and a purse and a plain gold ring. And will you please give Thayer a horse and cart that he can get in and give me a watch and fill my stocking too.   Love you to Santa from *Eleanor Hobson.*   —We will be in Denver, Colorado.

◌ A letter from Catherine McKie Thayer:

December 3, 1900, Colorado Springs.
My darling Kittie—   This is your birthday, my dear child, and how strangely I feel looking over the past— so near the Thanksgiving season which is all reminiscence when away from my children. You know my heart is full of thankfulness that God gave you to *us* and now the dear children are added, as a joy & a blessing to our circle. You must remember hearing dear Henry say to me, "you would not have these children but for me." Not such sweet ones I am sure. We have much to thank God for— our sweet memories & sad ones blend… I think the best wish I can make for you is that all whom you love may keep well and be truly good and this is my prayer for you— that you may have health & strength for every duty & a clear vision of what that duty is— and that you may have that constant peace that God can give His children when they can say & feel "He leadeth me," & so may He & you, with His help, lead your little ones. A heart full of Mother-love to you & to all the dear ones from me, on this one of the sacred days—   Your devoted *Mother.*

◌ In Sparta, Georgia:

Sparta, Georgia. Tuesday, Dec 11th.
My dearest Mother—   Your telegram to Frank recd last evening— which he answered at once. I have only had a cold & being where I could stay in bed a day, did so. We are driving out daily & all well. Sorry you had any worry. I did have quite a feverish attack in Troy and will tell you *all about it* when

I return the 20th. You know there was much typhoid, but I escaped that & am deeply grateful & I am all well now & the "Grands" never knew I had any indisposition… Your own loving *Kittie*.

❦ A letter from John S. Wise:

New York, December 27, 1900.
My dear Katherine— Your prompt & loving telegram reached us at Williamsburg & we all appreciated it. There was such a wealth of flowers I made no attempt to carry out your request as I could only have procured them by wiring to Richmond, so I took the liberty of omitting them & your sweet thoughtfulness was fully appreciated by us all.

Poor old fellow. As he lay there he looked younger, and more at rest than I had seen him for years— and so so peaceful— He looked like our Grandfather Sergeant. A likeness I had never before seen so strong. He did not seem to be dead. Sunday morning I went in early and said "Good-Morning Dick." We were alone a long time together.

When I last saw him in Washington Friday 14th he told me he was dying, but I could not believe him. I begged him to go home & he promised to do so. His condition disturbed me so I wrote to Speaker Henderson & told him my brother was remaining there from a sense of duty & at the peril of his life & begged him to send for him & make him go home. Before his answer reached me, Dick was dead.

We walked together from the Capitol to my train & on the way I told him to cheer up. That will-power had much to do with the cure of disease— "Ah!" said he, "That's all well enough. You know your business & I know mine. I am a physician & know my case. I am not afraid to recognize a truth that would be apparent to me in the case of any patient— I am a dead man. The wear & tear of these contests has killed me. But," he added, straightening up, "they have made me kill myself fighting them & I shall die on top— My only regret is I am not strong enough to fight any more & whip them again as I would—"

Finding himself worse he paired with a democrat & left Washington Wednesday. He reached home Thursday & found Henry absent in Hampton on business & Virginia about to go to Richmond to do some Xmas shopping. At first he begged Virginia not to go, but she said she had some little things to buy that she must have & would be back next day without fail, so he accompanied her to the train bidding her hurry home before he died. Then he ordered his buggy & rode out to the country & cut some sprays of holly which he took home & with which he decorated the picture of his dead wife & of the little boy named after him, whose deaths nearly killed him. As evening came on he grew lonesome & went down for companionship to the Colonial Inn & sat with Mr. Spencer expressing anxiety for Henry's return. Henry found him at the drug store where his first words were "I certainly am glad you're back. I did not want to die in that house alone." Then Henry asked him how he was & they procured some medicine which he intended to use & went home. Henry says he had not for years seen him so at peace & so cheerful. He had a large box filled with the Xmas presents he had brought home & laughing said he had been too weak to open it & had to call in Hillman, a servant, to help him. Henry said he talked of every-

---

he told me he was dying The letter is describing the death of Richard Alsop Wise, the oldest child of Henry A. Wise and his second wife Sarah Sergeant Wise, who was a physician and lived in Williamsburg, Virginia, and was a member of Congress at the time of his death. Henry A. Wise had once said of Williamsburg: "Five hundred lazy watching six hundred crazy." Writing in *Diomed*, John S. Wise said of Williamsburg, "…a Virginian who does not know Williamsburg argues himself unknown." He continued, "Williamsburg of to-day is but an insignificant village. Williamsburg of the past is an immortal and glorious spot, around which the affections of every lover of our early history linger with unspeakable veneration."

thing especially about "Johnnie." Then, about eleven o'clock after addressing some seeds & some Xmas presents they prepared to retire. On reaching the room he said that walking upstairs made his heart pump very hard & sat on the bed. Henry was arranging to shave— Suddenly he said *"Henry— I don't know what has happened. I think a blood-vessel has burst. I can see your body by not your head—"* Henry sprung towards him felt his pulse & forehead & started out to call a servant. He said *"Hurry back. Don't let me die alone."* —Henry was back in a few moments. Dick was lying on the bed. In response to enquiries he said, *"I'm glad you are back. Have you arranged. Have you—"* —but the aphasia rendered him incapable of saying more & after peacefully breathing for an hour he passed away without a struggle or any of the repulsive horrors of the disease which took him off.

On Sunday morning we had services at his home. The same minister who married him, Rev. Dr. Wharton, laid him to rest. I wish he had been buried in old Bruton Parish Church, but he said he wanted to be laid beside his wife & his child & our father in Hollywood. Everyone was very good & sympathetic & he was honored as became his position. Many people who had been his opponents politically came forward and spoke admiring of him and so he sleeps in Hollywood.

Today is my fifty-fourth birthday— I feel as if I am a hundred years old. My brother's death, after over fifty years of sunshine & sorrow, always filled with love & loyalty, has seemed to take more out of my life than ever went at one time before. I realize how lonely old age must be if we linger.

It is not belittling what is left to say so. I know how much is left to me— More than to many many others, and for it I am thankful. And between the sobs which no philosophy can stifle I try to be a philosopher.

Your sweet little book came this morning & I shall keep it & prize it.

Kiss the dear little ones for me & believe me as ever dear Katherine—

Yr: affec. Uncle, *Jno S. Wise.*

Richard Alsop Wise, 1843–1900. Anderson & Co, Richmond. Date of photo unknown.

your sweet little book   Papa's Letters

∽

A Story —My Hospital Chum

By Katherine Thayer Hobson, (under the pen name of Sophie Errington.)

Chapter I

Lying in my bed, in the half-dreamy state that comes after an operation when one has first waked, and looking at the rays of an October sun, as it sank in the valley of the Hudson, I was roused to the present by a racking cough, close by. Something prompted me to call out, "You have a bad cough." (I am always interfering, my children say, whenever I see anyone ill. They say, "Mama, you can't let anyone enjoy their pains without trying to be one with them.")

The response came in a choked, old-child voice.

"It's only Rosy—" and at the same instant a golden mass of hair of glowing red was gleaming in the sunshine of the hall window set around the thinnest, most pathetic little face, above a child-figure, worn by wasting disease.

Again I was interfering and inquisitive, and said, "Come in and see me, and rest. I am so homesick to speak to a child— for I have four at home."

The child slowly advanced, saying, "And does ye be wanting me?" and I said, "Yes, wanting you— child."

By my hospital bed was a little chair, and in this my grave faced visitor seated herself, sighing and straightening the ugly, dull brown folds of her plain, neat dress. She was small for nine or ten, but she looked one hundred years old out of those big yearning blue eyes— and I saw I was to be under a ruthless cross-examination at no distant date. I waited. The sun touched her hair, and I thought of four other little heads with their glow of gold and wondered and wondered. Finally after a full two minutes gaze, my visitor spoke gravely.

"Ye looks bad?"

I had not seen my face for four days, and had gone deep down into the valley of the shadow, but God's hand had brought me out into His blessed sunlight and my Doctor, who, I am sure, will have a crown for every day in the year, when he goes to his reward, had been telling me, "Mrs. Errington, you look fine." Well, one hears the truth from a child; and it never hurts, for the source is pure— I said,

"Oh, I am fine, the Doctor says," and the reply came—

"They bee's always a saying that."

"Well," I said, "I am tired of myself, and I wish to hear about you, for I shall be here several weeks, and I should like to have a friend to pay me visits, every day."

My would-be friend answered, "Ye'll be lonely here Christmas, it's then ye'll want yir mither."

I interrupted hastily— "Christmas here! Why I will be two thousand miles away from here, with my mother—"

My caller replied, "Don't set yer heart on it— it's safer not to—"

Here was a wise woman, but I grew restless. Christmas in the City Hospital! Even with Angel-faced sisters, and another Angel as nurse, all my own, and Gabriel let down in the shape of my Doctor, and the Hospital Priest, who had prayed for me during my dark lonely hours, and who was coming to talk of Mr. Dooley to me, No! Never! And I said changing the subject— "What do you wish for Christmas?"

The blue eyes met mine, and she said, "I be wishing for a doll to keep me company o' nights while the cough bees with me. Queen Elizabeth dropped my doll, but I keep her pieces by me, for I had her company for three years, and she always is awake, when I bees coughing."

"Of course, keep her pieces always," I said, "for her feelings would be hurt, if you threw them away, and bring her pieces to see me. I am acquainted with many invalid dolls and find them most interesting."

Rosy brightened and spoke quickly— "Mary will be here tomorrow, Lady, and I never told of her pieces before."

Confidence was established, but my curiosity was aroused— "And who is Queen Elizabeth?"

"Oh she bees the old one in the old woman's ward, where I live. I used to live with the children, but for a year I bees taking care of the old ones. The Queen walks at night, and she sat on Mary, who was in her bed on my chair."

I said, "What an awful Queen."

"On no, she bees harmless," said Rosy, "she just sat down to rest and never knew Mary was there. The Queen has asked every day since for the Princess, as she named my Mary. She bees good."

A righteous Judge was my companion. "Well," I said, "let us talk, Rosy, about the new doll, and plan what it will look like, how big will it be? and the color of her hair? and eyes? and then how old is she to be? and how is she to be dressed?"

The look I received was one of rebuke—

"It's better not to think ahead, and wish— and just be thankful if I get any one."

"No," I said, "I don't play that way. I like to think ahead, and all about the size and colors."

"You bees grown Lady; but you talk like the children in the ward, who is new there."

"Now Rosy, you have said such a nice kind thing to me, for if I make you think of the children we are sure to be friends."

"No, Lady, they were not all my friends. Some of them are bad."

"Well," I replied, "I am not going to be bad. How old are you, anyway, Rosy?"

"Noine come May," said my guest.

"I am forty," said I.

The answer was immediate— "Looks is deceiving, Father Mulligan says— I thought you bees fifty sure."

Alas, ten years older, in four long days of suffering. It was too much, and I asked, "Rosy, now how big is she to be?"

"Not too big, for my arms is tired mostly," she said, "and I should like to take her in the garden—"

"About so long?" (measuring on the sheet).

"Yes, and not thin. I be tired o' lookin' at bones."

"No," I said, "she shall be so long, and quite fat, and three years old?"

"No, two; at three they runs off."

"Well, two then, and her cheeks shall be pink?"

"Not red with the hectic, please," said Rosy.

Heavens! This sage in wisdom.

"No— a pink like that— there in the sky—"

She turned and after a few minutes said, "That will do."

"And her eyes, Rosy— blue or brown?"

"Well, if they could be the color of yours, though they looks green, with yellow—" (peering in my face) "and I never favored green except in grass and leaves."

I had not lived in vain, to have my visitor constitute herself my chum, and wished to duplicate my poor tired eyes. My heart was full.

"Now Rosy, my eyes would not look well in any doll's head. How could you put eyes fifty years old in the face of a girl doll baby of two years?"

The reply came slowly, still looking at my eyes— "They are not— pretty, but it's the look of them, I bees thinking of."

"But— you are lazy," I said, "here the sun has gone down and we have only gotten her size, and her eyes— must they be blue or brown?"

"Not blue— brown please. Most people has blue eyes."

"And her hair?— brown or golden?"

the hectic Often an afternoon increase in temperature, accompanied by a flush on the cheeks, occurring in active tuberculosis, consumption, patients.

"Golden, and curly, please."

"Yes, and a pretty nose? and two little pearly teeth, and tiny mouth and red lips—"

Here Rosy broke in, "Oh don't say anither word, please or I shall dream of her, and then waking, I'll be that lonely!"

"But," I said, "you have the pieces close by."

"Yes," she said, "but they are not aisy to handle."

"And now," I interrupted, "Rosy about her dress? Of course, all her underclothes are white, and trimmed with lace, and stockings, and tiny, bronze slippers with heels, and the dress, now think what color?"

The answer was instantly given— "What ye will have it— blue, or rose, or white, or red, but please not black."

"Two dresses then," I said, "one for winter of wool, and one for summer of muslin; and coat and hat for winter, and a sun hat with a blue ribbon and white daisies for summer. And now we have settled about the doll, let us eat a banana," and I took one from a plate and gave it to her.

"That's good and goes down aisy. Thank yez," she said.

A bell rang, and Rosy started up. "That's for the vespers, and I will pray for yez, for ye needs prayers. Good by."

And I replied, "Come tomorrow afternoon at four o'clock surely, and I will show you my little girl of eleven. Good by, Rosy, don't forget to pray for me."

"No, I will mind ye,— good by, and thank ye kindly for all your talk, for you talks more than Queen Elizabeth, and I heard the Doctor say, 'Poor fool, her tongue is hung in the middle and wags both ways,' and it may be the same with you. Good by," and Rosy slowly walked away with the faintest shadow of a smile.

At this minute my sweet nurse, "Nibby," came in, and said, "Did I see Rosy coming from here, and has she been talking to you?"

And I answered, "No, it seems I have been talking to her."

"Well," Nibby said, "I left you to rest and sleep and I thought you would not talk, for you only know the Doctor and the two sisters and the Priest, and I knew they would not come here, and now you have been tired out by Rosy."

"Stop," I almost screamed, "she is my life-saving station— I woke wondering if I cared much to make the effort to get well, and now Rosy has showed me that even her life in a City Hospital ward for 'old ones' is worth while, and made me ashamed of myself; so get me beef tea, and egg-nog, and get me up soon to play dolls with Rosy."

Nibby looked down at me and said, "Forever more! You need your stimulant, and then I will go to Vespers and pray for you." and she vanished.

Chapter II — Another Day

Monday broke bright, clear and crisp in October glory— like a Monarch who returns to his country to claim the glory that is his by right.

Time flies in a hospital, with its routine of nursing, Doctor's visits and stuffing processes, and one gets soon to have an active interest in the inmates. So during my toilet, I attacked the long-suffering patient Nibby and questioned her about Rosy. I found the child was an orphan. She was nine years old. Her mother had died in the hospital of consumption, a few weeks after the child's birth. Rosy had inherited the disease; her eyes had been affected, and she had lost the sight of one. Until the year before she was in the children's ward, when it was thought best to have her moved to the ward for old women and there she had lived, putting "Queen Elizabeth" back in bed several times each night, and having the beloved "Princess Mary" crushed by the Queen in the wee small hours of a winter night. Every Sunday morning up at five past five for Mass in the Chapel, and finding "the Old women not as tiresome as the noisy children, who always were unaisy."

I said, "Now Nibby, dear, I wish you to go into the town for me when I sleep after dinner." She said, "I will not be allowed to leave you on any account."

"Well," I said, "Are you by any possible chance allowed to telephone?"

She answered, "I might get permission."

"Well, do, at once," I answered, "And now, write for me— 'a little girl doll, 16 inches long, not longer. Golden, curly hair, brown eyes, teeth to show, stockings, bronze slippers, underwear that will come off, and night gown— light blue wool dress, and coat; and hat for winter wear— flowered muslin dress, white straw hat, with blue ribbon and daisies— to be selected by "Maggie" at Fair's— and send at once to Mrs. Errington, at the City Hospital."

By this time Nibby was looking agitated, and began, "The Doctor will say—" when at the moment the Doctor walked in, and I said, "Can't I please send a telephone message for something I wish at Fair's, by "Maggie"? (for everyone knew Maggie), and he said, "Why certainly, go on, Miss Nibby and do it."

So I was satisfied, and later dear Maggie came herself, and everything was right, only the doll's mouth showed eight teeth, instead of two. And I settled to rest.

At five minutes to four I had Nibby playing "Sister Anne" at my west window, and looking down the hill, overhung by arches of giant elms, their leaves making glowing yellow atmosphere in the Western sunlight. I said, "Tell me the minute you see her, Nibby."

Silence. Then, "Here she comes, running up the hill, in the middle of the street, and waving, and behind her the faithful Billy, bearing her coat and a basket."

Nibby said, "She is kissing her hand now, and her long curls are flying out from her head, like sunbeams."

"Nibby," I cried, "Now— where is my little sweetheart?"

And she says, "She is climbing the steps, and is now out of sight—"

Three minutes more, and out of the blaze of a sun lit corridor stepped my child, quietly with her hands full of roses. She enters, kneels by my bed, and buries her head and when she kisses me, she says, "My ownliest mother— here is your Weanie baby to comfort you—" and then we begin to talk and I tell her of Rosy, and the doll, which my child is to give her, for Weanie hears what a good lesson the little Rosy gave me, and how when I was thinking it would be easier to die, than try to get well, Rosy had shown me how in her sad life, life was sweet and worth living, and made up of kind acts, and I must wish to live for the sake of my four children.

Just then there was a gentle tap at the door, and I said, "Come in, Rosy— you are in time to see my little girl Weanie."

Rosy stepped into the room and the pity and motherhood in my child woke as she went to meet her, and there they stood hand in hand, until

Weanie said, "Oh, did you bring Mary? I want so much to see her face—"

Rosy carefully drew a box from under her little black cape, and seating herself, removed the cover, and displayed Mary's remains. The body was covered with a little sheet of cheesecloth, snowy white, but the poor head was broken badly, a piece actually gone, letting one look into that hollow chamber of mystery where the once blue eyes were faintly seen. Not a smile, not a word was said, and then Weanie covered Mary with the box lid, and said, "Poor thing, she is very dear, and like some of my children, and now Rosy, I wish to see Queen Elizabeth" —and off the two children went to the old woman's ward— where the Queen's pleasure was great on seeing a new child's face, and invited her to stay in her castle always, and rather frightened Weanie, by telling her that her hair was too long, and it took her strength and ought to be cut off; so the children wandered back to me, stopping to see the Chapel, whose Altar was being decorated with flowers by the Sisters. Nibby had put the new doll on the table in her box and I said, "Now Rosy, there are some new pieces for you to care for," and Weanie led her to the table. The box was opened, and silence reigned for some time. Then whisperings, and then louder murmurs as the wardrobe was displayed. The hat with the blue ribbon and daisies was the greatest joy, and when it was put on and the full effect given, Rosy exclaimed, "It's not to be believed such a sight is true."

Suddenly the child's face quivered and she said, "Sure, I was forgettin' the pieces."

And I said quietly, "Mary is tired, she needs quiet and rest, and she must have long days and nights of quiet, and this lively, noisy little girl must have your constant care, and I think she is naughty too—"

Rosy caught her up, and looked long into her face and said, "Is it naughty you say? No, she is good, but a bit light."

Just then Nibby came in with decision to banish my visitors. Weanie kissed me, and we spoke our parting words; "God bless you and keep you."

Rosy slowly approached the bed, and touching my finger-tips, as if they were the petals of some delicate flower, she softly said, "Thank you kindly. It's as if me mither had come back. Good night," and Rosy vanished with her baby girl of two, but the pieces were held close to her heart.

Chapter III

The last week of October had come, and I was sitting in the sunshine trying to fashion some doll-clothes and for the first time wished I knew more about the use of a needle. I remembered my Mother once saying, "Oh, child, everything pinned instead of sewed!" and I answering, "I can't do much with a needle, but there's nothing I can't do with a pin," and my blessed Grandmother coming nobly to my rescue and saying, "Have patience, Kate. What Sophie sews will never come out."

Rosy sat near me and I said, "I never did care much to sew, one of my friends 'Molly' made all my dolls' clothes, while I played Ball and Prisoners Base" —and visions of my childhood, and the Park and the two giant Elm tree homes came crowding upon me, and even the dread of Mary's voice calling through the palings, "Sophie, Sophie, time to come in."

I was motionless and speechless, and way, way off, when Rosy brought me back saying, "And what was her name?"

"Whose name?" I said.

"Why yer doll's name."

"Eugenie, named after the most beautiful woman, who was Empress of the French— and now is an old lady and lives in England, where she was given a home by the good Queen Victoria, who was her friend when "Eugenie" was an exile— and every day she prays, kneeling on blood red velvet cushions at the side of her Husband and Son's tombs."

"And is this Queen beautiful now, Lady?"

"More beautiful than ever, when I saw her she had the face of a saint and she has had to part with and give up everything— her country, her throne, and flee in the night, and I am proud to tell you than an American helped her to escape to Paris. The Empress had one beautiful Boy, who besides being manly and beautiful to look at, had a beautiful soul and God watched over him and guided him in all ways and he grew up to be a man and the English Queen was his friend and earthly Patron Saint and the Princes and Princesses his friends. This French Prince was an officer in the English Army, and he went away from England with his heart full of love and happiness, for a lovely Princess had showed him her heart was his, and then the poor, patient, beautiful Empress thanked God and felt He had given her the greatest joy a Mother heart can know, in making her Boy a true, honorable, Christian Soldier."

"Is that the end?" said Rosy, "Did the Prince come back and marry the Princess?"

"Yes," I said, "he came back after a very brave, manly noble service in his regiment and for his country, but he was murdered by savages, and the poor Empress Mother had only her Boy's body brought to her to bury."

"And the Princess died then, Lady?" asked Rosy.

"No, she could not die, but she mourned with his Mother for her lover, and even now, years and years after, this same Princess often visits the lonely Empress Eugenie."

"Oh dear, oh dear, why did he die, and the Mother still lives?" said Rosy.

"Yes, she lives and is now very old, and her life is filled with kind acts for those who suffer and she goes daily to the Chapel where her husband, Napoleon, the III, and her Boy's bodies lie in beautiful Tombs."

"I am sorry for the French Mother and shall pray for her— but she's *had* her own to love, and bein' old she's not long to wait to meet them."

I said, "Yes, that is a great comfort, and suppose we talk of Christmas, Rosy. Of course you are going to hang up your stocking at the foot of your bed?"

"No, Lady, I could not, for it would go to my heart to wake and find it empty."

"Empty!" I cried, "Empty, who every heard of a good child's stocking being empty. I only hope that little Sparrow out there has not heard you for they all carry tales to Santa Claus, and if he hears you have said this awful thing, he won't come at all— but let us throw out some bits of crackers, and maybe if the Sparrow over-eats and drinks water, his stomach will be too heavy for him to fly too far— Get two crackers from my stand."

Rosy gazed sadly at me and slowly spoke in tones of rebuke.

"Animals speaking, Lady! Whoever heard of the like?"

"Now I have you caught, Rosy. The Bible tells of it— so— and you ask Father Mulligan."

The Empress Eugenie, *a doll belonging to Katherine Thayer Hobson, 1859–1915, as a child and described in her story about Rosy.*

Empress Eugenie, engraving by W. Wellstood from The Ladies Repository, *November 1866. The young Katherine Thayer Hobson may have been given her doll on her seventh birthday in December 1866, and she may have named her doll when she saw this illustration in the magazine that her parents subscribed to. The magazine described itself as "a general literary and religious magazine for the family."*

"Well it's not in me to go agin the Holy Word of God, but Lord forgive me— it sounds looney for a bird to be flying to the North Pole and speak to Santa Claus, and I bees heerin' he's no real person."

I spoke with decision and firmness, "Well, believe what you 'bees heerin' but Weanie and I hang up our stockings and they are always full."

"But Lady, Weanie has you and you has Weanie and the three other kids, and it's a change when ye thinks of me."

"Yes," I said, "but Love is the same wherever one finds it and can't you trust old Santa Claus for this year?"

"As it's you, Lady, who bees mothering me so handy-like and bein' used to kids, I'll give in this year and hang up my stocking but think of me when I bees feelin in the dark of Christmas morning, and finds the stocking empty —" but, clasping her little hands, "If it's empty, I'll believe Queen Elizabeth has helped herself to the inside and be thankful she did not take the stocking and all, as she did last year— and it was not found until the snow melted on the north roof in the spring."

"Was it empty?" I asked.

"No, the cakes and sugar sticks were gone, and of course she had been having feasts with some men in her mind, named Sir Walter and two Earls and a man who writes verses, and he must be loving too, for the Queen keeps saying, William, my friend, the Player and Poet, says 'This World's a Stage and that all the grown-ups are players, and Lady, that's only from a poor fool's head, like the Queen's."

I said, "I just hate Queen Elizabeth, Rosy."

"Hate her! Don't say that, Lady, for you may be the same as her some day."

"Now, Rosy, I am going to show you two letters," taking up a little book, this first one is to Santa Claus, because Weanie and the three other kids had been told there was no Santa Claus, so they wrote a letter to Santa Claus, asking him and this is the letter:"

Dear Santa Claus—   It is my mother that is writing this time for me. I want that little bureau with one little shelf at the side, and I want the blue little necklace with that little bag, and the pink one with the little looking-glass to it. And I want the one with the little comb to put around your head. And then bring the biggest horse that rocks to me, and the next biggest to Henry, and the little black one to Eleanor. I want that big doll at the Singer Sewing Machine store in the window, and be sure to bring a Christmas-tree. Bring Henry a horse, a cart with ladders hanging on it, and an engine, and some hose, and some horses, and the things that goes round, men on horses; there is music about it.

Santa Claus, please bring Sugar Plum Baby a white stove, a blue doll house, a little wagon, a little dolly; why, bring me a little yellow bureau, and a glass to look in— not anything else.

Bring Henry a little book, please. Please bring Katherine a living canary bird— a mother-bird— and please bring Henry a live feather-bird, and Eleanor a mamma bird, and Katherine a purple dress for a doll.

I love you very much, you are so kind to me at Xmas time, and I would like to see you, so would Henry. We are trying to be gentle and loving and kind, and we send you kisses and hugs, and here are the kisses; Kisses from Henry, kiss from Eleanor, kiss from Katherine.   —Your little friends, *Katherine*, *Henry*, and *Eleanor*.

"Oh," said Rosy, "I would not be so bold-like."

"It was not bold," I said, "for he is all love and the children's best friend and now hear his letter:"

Santa Clausville, North Pole, December 11th, 1895.
To Katherine, Henry, and Eleanor Hobson c/o Papa and Momma Hobson, Denver, Col., U.S.A.
My Dear Katherine, Henry, and Eleanor—   I received your nice letter and I am so busy making things for Christmas that I have not time to write you myself, and so have to dictate a letter. The last time I was in the United States I got a typewriter and stenographer, and now I can answer all my letters.

I do not know how many of the things that you want I can bring you. I will try and bring you all that I can, but there are lots of little girls and boys in Denver who want some Christmas things, too, and we must make them go around.

If you are not good children I will have to pass by your house and not give you anything at all.   —Yours affectionately, *Santa Claus.*

"Why he *must be someone* if he wrote that letter, and I will hang up me stocking and trust him for sure."

"And now what are you going to ask Santa Claus for, for he likes to know what one most wishes for."

"Well, I'd be asking for a banana for every day; they goes down aisy and no hurt to me throat. Would that be askin for too much, Lady?"

"No, not too much, Rosy, but bananas grow at the South Pole instead of where there is snow and ice near Santa Claus' Home, and what do you think? Sister Annie has a whole bunch of bananas, which are yours, and she said you were to have them any time of the day— or night."

The tears came in Rosy's eyes and she said, "Me dreams true, Lady, for I dreamed I had a bunch all my own and Queen Elizabeth and I were having what she calls a Banquet in the Banqueting Hall, and she says our night-gowns are robes of satin of state, and she says her lovers are a great bother to a Virgin Queen."

"What will you like to have Santa Claus put in your stocking, Rosy, —tell your heart's wishes."

"It's a comb for my hair and a brush all my own for it is sometimes a long time I bees waiting for the ones on the chains in the washroom, and some handkerchiefs with bright borders and a glass to the full of milk by my bed at nights and 25¢ and a pipe and tobacco."

"What in the wide world will you do with a pipe and tobacco, Rosy?"

"Why," said Rosy, "the Queen says she wishes to smoke a pipe, as she is used to pipes in Ireland, and I should like to see her settin aisy, smoking, but, oh, I must go, as the supper will be ready. Thank ye for a good time, Lady."

"Here, take this little Red Riding Hood and tomorrow I will tell you about the awful, great big Wolf that most ate her up."

"I've heard tales of that, Lady, in the children's ward, and we used to cover our heads at night with the bed-clothes and would almost choke. Good-bye, Lady, "My Eugenie" will be grand in her red cloak, and thank ye, and goodbye."

Chapter IV — Good Bye

"What shall we put in the toe, Mama," said Weanie, for we sat behind locked doors, and a huge white stocking was hanging limp from Weanie's hand.

"I think the little picture of you, Weanie, for it would be sweet to have the face of a friend to greet you."

So Weanie wrapped and tied with bright red ribbon a tiny little frame, and plunged her arm way down the stocking leg and out through the foot, to the toe, remarking, "What kind of a lady wears these stockings, Mama, a giant lady?"

"I think they are made for children to hang up on Christmas Eve."

"Oh, may I have the mate to this for my stocking?"

"Yes, dearest, only I thought we would take it to Grandma. That would be splendid for she never has room enough for all her presents in her stocking. And now shall we put in the pipe and tobacco (for Sister Annie had given her consent for the Queen to have a Christmas smoke.) Be very careful not to break the pipe stem."

"Oh," cried Weanie, "it has so much paper around it Rosy will think it's a pin cushion— and now the foot will be full when my little thimble is cuddled in, and the silver and blue motto with the lines on it."

"And now, Weanie, fill that exquisite cut glass— ten cent glass, with the Ridley's candy and put a bit in my mouth for it is, you know, my favorite kind— as you chicks say. Now I will tie this little cap of silver paper over the top with the red ribbon and you wrap it— and now where are the brush and comb?"

"Oh, Mama, do you think they are nice for a stocking, they are something everybody has."

And I said, "Everybody ought to but dear Rosy has none and I think they will appear pretty to her."

"Now where are you going to put the dollar Aunt Marie gave me for Rosy?" "See," taking the dollar out of her blouse pocket, "how shiny bright I have made it and it is a holy dollar for God's name is on it."

"Aunt Marie is always doing beautiful things. She is taking care of hundreds of children who have no fathers or mothers or friends. 'Homeless' they are called— and here goes the dollar. Weanie, this is the twenty-five cents, for Rosy wishes to do something specially with it, or she would not have asked for it, and it would be hard to part with that beautiful shiny dollar— and now can you help fold this little red flannel wrapper, or shall I call Nibby?"

"No, that is easy, for it is not much bigger than New Yorky's long coat. Mother you have missed saying today, 'and how is my sweetest grand-daughter?'"

"But I would have asked for her, for this is only the second time you have come without her."

"But I left her asleep, and it took all Billy's arms and mine to carry these things, with your mutton-broth, and he dropped the rolls twice in the mud."

"Never mind, they were not hurt, one little bit, for they had three or four coverings of paper. Now put the wrapper in the long way, and here are the little blue slippers I crocheted."

"And," cried Weanie, "the box of dishes for Eugenie's tea-party."

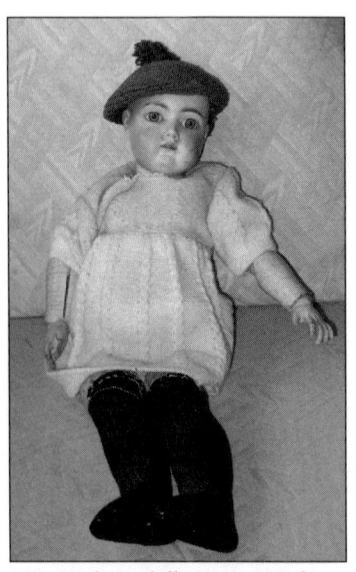

New Yorky, a doll given to Katherine Thayer Hobson, 1859–1982, by her father.

"Just see these little spoons and here is the little prayer-book and the rosary from you, Weanie, for Rosy only told you she wished for these, and a little purse to hold the rosary."

"Now, Mama, please put this funny Jumping Jack in to stick out of the top and it will make Rosy laugh."

"I do hope so, dearest, but I notice Rosy seldom laughs now— but if she feels she is loved and remembered [at] Christmas, she will be less sad."

"Oh, Mama, can't we take her away with us and maybe she would get well."

"No, Weanie, the doctors say Rosy will very soon go to her mother, and that is better for she has no one here and everybody there."

"But Mother dear, Rosy is happy and never complains."

"Yes, she is happy because she is doing something 'Kind Like' as she says to help the 'Old Ones,' think of that little girl putting Queen Elizabeth back to bed half a dozen times a night."

Weanie spoke slowly, "And Rosy says she likes the Queen! I don't. She said my hair ought to be cut off at once, and I ran away."

"Well, Lambie, you see Rosy lies awake coughing many hours in the night, and to have the Queen awake and wandering about the ward, and talking, makes it less lonely, and the Queen is devoted to Rosy and always minds her— except when she found the whiskey bottle, the doctor had accidentally laid down, and went into a room and locked herself in, and drank and drank, and then went to sleep on the bed, and everyone thought the Queen had gotten out of the Hospital, and only at three the next morning did Elizabeth walk into the ward singing *The Wearing of the Green*, and woke everyone up, and it was Rosy who got her to bed and kept her quiet. You see Rosy has employment, work to do, and that makes one happy."

"Put in this little baby doll, in long clothes. See Weanie, the cunning little socks Nibby made her— and leave the head sticking out. Why she has as much hair as you had the day you were born, for I curled it in little rings."

"Now, Mama, I will pin this rosette and streamers on the very edge of the stocking and the red ribbon will look very gay. Oh, how happy Rosy will be. Weanie we must put it in the closet for Rosy is sure to come at four and the carriage will be here at five to take us and Nibby away to 'The Haven of Rest.' Oh, if we could only take Rosy, but the doctor says she is far better here. We will write her often, and she has her bunch of bananas, which seem a comfort."

There was a tap at the door and Weanie unlocked the door. "And were ye locking me out yer last day here, Miss Weanie?"

"No, Rosy, but we were packing and did not wish to have people coming in."

"And it's unaisy I am to have ye go and when I told the Queen me best friends were lavin' she said 'put not yer faith in Princesses' and it's no Princess you are, Lady— but just like the best of mothers."

"Yes, Rosy, just a mother but I think that is the best thing in the world to be."

"Well as I've niver known aither mother or fathers I won't be passin' judgment, as Father Mulligan says."

"Rosy are you going to write me?"

"It's poor scratchin' on paper I'd be makin' but the Queen writes fine, and I'll be coaxing her to write."

"And tell me everything about yourself and the Hospital, and think about the stocking, and Santa Claus."

"Well betimes I will, but it's unaisy yer goin' is makin' me, and I hold you in respect for not hollerin' when the stitches were being plucked. I was listenin' at the door, and prayin for yees."

"Why it's your prayer, Rosy, that helped me, for I was crazy to scream, but the Doctor looked so sorry and has been such an angel, I felt I would try to be quiet."

"Anyways I bees proud of ye, for you beats the men for they make cries and groans, which sends me off quick."

"But Rosy maybe they are worse off than I was."

"No, Lady, it's been said often ye were that near dead it was hard to bring ye back."

"Well, Rosy and Weanie, I am back now and a very happy hungry person," as Nibby came in with a bowl of broth.

"The carriage will be here in fifteen minutes, so drink this," said Nibby.

"And where is my party for the children, Nibby?"

"Coming, you can't have everything the same minute," and she went out.

In a minute in the nurse came with a tray and two plates, with ice cream of three kinds and a third plate of lady-fingers.

"Oh," cried Rosy, "pink ice cream. I'd heard of such but never thought of seein' and atin' it. I think, Lady, I should like to take a bit to the Queen. She sat by me bed the whole o' last night trying to help me and gave me her pillow and said, 'Unaisy is the head that wears the crown' and she told me I was all she had in this life, and she was lost like thinkin' of my goin' on the long journey, and cried soft-like, but I told her I was here for all me life, and then she said, 'Yes, all yer life, but thanks be to God I'll be takin' the same long journey soon, and follerin' after yez there, where our mithers is.'"

The lovely face of Sister Annie was seen in the door followed by Sister Ursula and I had Nibby bring more ice cream and they quite enjoyed it, only Sister Annie said, "This is a good-bye feast, Mrs. Errington," and I said, "Oh no, I will always be coming back," and she smiled and said, "Not for treatment we hope, but to see us."

Nibby brought my coat and bonnet, and Rosy gave me two lady-fingers to 'aise my hunger' and put on my gloves and tied the strings to my bonnet, and we all went out to the elevator, and down to the entrance, and I found myself amid all the Sisters and we said "Good-bye" again and again and Father Mulligan had been called to a sick man. The sisters were sweet to follow me to the door and I told them I wished I could take them all with me for they had been so good and sweet and dear to me, and Sister Annie said, "Miss Nibby, take the best care of Mrs. Errington. I trust you." Then I stooped and putting my arms around Rosy I kissed her many times, and her face was pale and she smiled and said, "I'm never greeting for me mither, now," and I put the child's hand in Sister Annie's and went out of the door, followed by Nibby and Weanie, and through dim eyes saw Rosy, waving her little hand as we passed out of sight.

Christmas

A month later, I was returning from a walk in the Georgia woods with my brother and Weanie and the "three other kids" came running to meet me and said, "A lot of letters," so we hurried on and soon were sitting before an open fire and the promise of a cup of tea. I looked over my letters and found one which I knew was from Sister Annie. I had received several wandering letters from the Queen, with sentences about Rosy, but she was chiefly issuing commands.

I opened the Sister's Letter, she began by telling me they were all so glad I was better and after a sentence or two said, "Poor Little Rosy can't live but a week, or so— she never leaves her bed now— is sweet and patient, and speaks of you, and Weanie often— Rosy is so anxious for Christmas to come."

I said, "Frank do write me a telegram to send at once—"

He rose, and went to his methodical desk and replied— "Well—"

"Sparta, Ga., Dec. 3 1900.
To Sister Annie, City Hospital, Albany, N.Y.
Do not wait. Hang up Rosy's stocking tonight. —*Sophie Errington*."

Weanie said, "Why the stocking won't be half so nice before Christmas," but I insisted it would be "much nicer," and Brother went to the office, and I sat in the fire-light, with the four chicks, and Mamie read to them and I dreamed of that little girl in the "Old Ones" ward.

A week later a letter reached me, it read—

"To Rosy's Friend dear Mrs. Errington— The telegram came safely, and that night, after Rosy was asleep, I stole into the ward and tied the stocking to the iron foot-board of her bed— just where you showed me. The night-light was burning, and the child's face was as an angel's. I stooped and kissed her for you, covered her more closely, and left the ward. At five o'clock I returned. Rosy was lying with the stocking clasped in her arms, the Baby Doll lay close to her face. The smile on her face was the smile given in Heaven, of Peace and Rest, and Joy. The Long Journey being over, and her mother found at last."

• The End •

Epilogue:

It is known that in the fall of 1900 Katherine Thayer Hobson, when she was forty, had a mastectomy at the St. Mary's Hospital in Troy, New York. There are a number of empty envelopes addressed to her at the hospital, all postmarked in October. There is one letter, dated October 5th, from her mother in Colorado Springs: "My darling Child— Today I have yours of Wednesday eve, going to the Cemetery— dear child how I wish I could be with you all those trying days. I know you are doing your best for the loved one gone, the loved ones living. Yes, dear Henry would have helped you do some painful duty— & the love he bore you will help you more…" It is also known that Katherine Hobson and her children spent Christmas 1900 in Sparta, Georgia, with her brother and his wife. They returned to Colorado soon after that.

After leaving the hospital in Troy, Katherine received a letter from her physician:

D. W. Houston, M. D., 44 Second Street, Troy, N.Y., November 13, 1900.
My dear Mrs. Hobson—   You have no idea how I miss you. It was always a pleasure to see you daily and to watch the progress of your case from day

to day until your days of convalescence came and I felt that your recovery was assured. Your operation was a very severe one, but your good sense and strong backbone were mighty pillars for me to rest upon in carrying out my work. I am sure that your troubles are now at an end and you will now go on for years without aches or pains. I saw dear General Kent and he told me that he had seen you off on the cars and he spoke so sweetly and tenderly about you.

Tomorrow I shall send my picture to Henry and one will follow later for you. Loving regards to dear Henry and his charming sister Katherine whose well-balanced mind, with her sweetness and gracefulness, fairly captivates me. And now Mrs. Hobson let me thank you for the cheque and again and again I thank you for the many kind things you said in your splendid letter. Tell Miss Niblock she must look after your every want as I shall expect a report from her when she returns. Mrs. Houston sends her love to you and I send my love to you. —Ever yours most sincerely, *David W. Houston.*

One question remains unanswered: Was there such a child as "Rosy" at the St. Mary's Hospital in 1900, or is this a work of fiction? St. Mary's Hospital, in 2006 a part of Seton Health System, no longer has patient records or registers for that time period so those can not be examined. However, there are a number of other facts that should be considered. Dr. Houston's letter refers to a "Miss Niblock," and the story refers to a nurse named "Nibby." Those must be references to the same person. The story refers to "Aunt Marie" who "takes care of hundreds of children." This is a reference to Marie Jermain, the sister of Katherine Hobson's first husband, who was still living nearby in Albany at the time. In 1882, Barclay Jermain had died of "consumption" just like "Rosy." Marie Jermain and her father, the late James Barclay Jermain, were the primary benefactors of the Fairview Home for Friendless Children, an orphanage, in Watervliet, New York. Therefore, the comment about her taking care of "hundreds of children" can be explained. There is another mention of a "foundling left at foot of Hospital steps" in Catherine Thayer's letter of August 26, 1898, when she was in Troy with her grandson for his knee surgery. The story mentions a store named "Fairs" which may be a fictionalization of "Frear's Department Store," one of the first big stores to have different "departments" all in one building and that operated in Troy from the mid-19th century to the 1960s.

Katherine Hobson's oldest daughter is identified as "Katherine" in the typed manuscript, but that is crossed out, and "Weanie" is substituted. This reference to the younger Katherine Hobson is unfamiliar to her surviving nieces and nephews. However, that must have been an old and long forgotten nickname, for she refers to herself as "Weanie Baby" in a letter of July 9, 1895, page 691, and a June 1913 card, not published here, from Katherine to her mother and her sister, is signed "Your own Weanie."

It is a fact that Katherine Thayer Hobson had a doll named "Empress Eugenie" that had been given to her by her parents and that her daughter had a doll named "New Yorky,"—the names given to the dolls mentioned in this story. The story names both Katherine Thayer Hobson's Grandmother and her brother by their real names, Sophie and Frank. The telegram is sent from Sparta, Georgia, which is where Katherine went after leaving the hospital. Is it coincidence that the telegram is dated, December 3rd, Katherine's forty-first birthday? Assuming that Rosy is speaking with an Irish accent, she would perhaps have been descended from one of the many Irish immigrants who went to Troy in the middle of the 19th century. The "little book" including the correspondence with Santa Claus would be *Papa's Letters*, a collection of letters from Henry Wise Hobson to his children that Katherine Thayer Hobson had printed in 1900. *Papa's Letters* included three letters with Santa Claus. However, only two are referred to in this story. For the record, the third letter is as follows: "My Dear Santa Claus— I have changed my mind. I saw a doll at the doll show with a blue velvet cap and a little white bird in it. I want that doll. Henry wants the house with firemen and engines that he saw at the doll show. Eleanor wants a doll dressed in blue. —Your affectionate little girl, *Katherine*."

This story may be the only record of Rosy, a poor orphaned girl who lived out her life at the St. Mary's Hospital, dying there of tuberculosis at a very young age.

After her surgery and recovery, Katherine Hobson endowed a bed at the hospital. —*Editor's note.*

1901

A letter from Egypt:

January 2, 1901.
My dear Kitty—   Though we are very far off, you and the chicks have been much in our thoughts all this holiday season… Christmastime always brings Henry very near to me. He and I used to go Christmas shopping together, getting our little Christmas gifts for our friends, and I can even now see him as we went in and out of the little shops in Richmond in the glow of the lights picking out what we thought suitable and counting up our money to see what we could buy. I have thought of you a great deal, my dear Kitty. Christmas is rather a sad time with us when we are in middle life. But though the memories are sad there are some that are very, very sweet…

Our visit here has been very interesting— of course it must be when one is wandering among a people who come either out of Genesis or the Arabian Nights… The life about here is simply vivid with color… No picture gives the faintest idea of what it looks like; for the natives who are about, ten-to-one are clad in all sorts of curious garbs, blue, yellow, black, white (very dirty) and their heads are either be-turbaned, or are be-fuzzed… they wrap their head up and leave their feet and legs bare. The climate here at this time is not in the least what I imagined. We have had three days of almost continuous rain. It was about a week ago. I go around in the same clothes I would wear in Washington today. The natives however go barelegged, and with only a cotton gown garment; and two days ago I saw a little child lying on its mother's lap stark naked. I was then in my overcoat. How they stand it, I do not know. Next to the color one sees, the most obvious thing is the dirt. I thought our negroes were dirty, but they can't hold a candle to the low-class Egyptian. They are simply caked with it. I had an idea that the Mohammadans were clean— they are not. I also had an idea that I should hear the muezzin three times a day, and that at the call every Moslem would fall down on his knees and go to praying. I have heard it just once— at the university the other day, and I have seen perhaps a dozen men praying outside of the mosques… We have found the bazaars here disappointing— very dirty, and not very inviting. The life in them is of course interesting simply because it is so different from ours. "The Streets of Cairo" that you remember at the Worlds Fair in Chicago were almost as interesting, and were very much cleaner. The real sight here, after the people on the streets with their color and dirt, is to stand on the desert and look across the Nile Valley with its wonderful green to the brown desert again. Then to think what that little ribbon of green has been to the world…

I trust you and the children have had a lovely Christmas. If your mother is with you please give her my love or send it to her if she is not…

Give my very best, my bestest love to my nephews and nieces. I think of them, every one, and would love dearly to see them. I am afraid they are growing very big.

Ever, my dear Kitty, your faithful and affectionate friend
—*Thos Nelson Page.*

╰ Death in the family:

THE WESTERN UNION TELEGRAPH COMPANY
Denver, Colo., Jan 4, 1901.
To: John S. Wise, Try 154 West 76 St. N. Y.
Mother died peacefully today services here, interment in Troy later, notify Ashland. Insert notice in Troy papers.   —*Katherine T. Hobson.*

THE WESTERN UNION TELEGRAPH COMPANY
Denver, January 5, 1901.
To: F. McKie Thayer, C/O Ticket Office Union Depot, St. Louis, Mo.
Most rapid pneumonia developed. Recovery hopeless. Has spoken of you with devoted love. —*Kittie.*

THE WESTERN UNION TELEGRAPH COMPANY
Denver, January 5, 1901.
To: F. M. Thayer, C/O Pullman Conductor Denver Sleeper,
Burlington Train No. 13, (Sunday) St. Joseph, Mo.
Our dear mother has passed peacefully away. Carriage will meet you on arrival. —*Kittie.*

THE WESTERN UNION TELEGRAPH COMPANY
Denver, Colo., Jan 5 1901.
To: John S. Wise: I appreciate deeply your words. Services at house Tuesday. Interment in spring at Troy. —*Katherine T. Hobson.*

╰ Obituary:

A beautiful life has ended in the passing away of Catherine McKie Thayer, which occurred on January 4th at the home of her daughter in Denver, Colorado.
"When softly, from that hushed and darkened room,
Two angels issued, where but one went in."

Thus has death closed the roll-call of one of the most remarkable families ever reared in Washington county—a family noted for high intellectual endowments—keen and brilliant wit, courtesy and kindliness of manner and unbounded hospitality.

In 1814 George McKie married Catherine, daughter of Peter Whiteside. In 1815 their first child, Niel W., was born. Soon after Mr. McKie removed from the adjoining town of White Creek to Cambridge, and at the homestead in the west part of the town, Edwin J. was born in 1818.

After the death of his wife, which occurred in 1824, Mr. McKie married her sister Sophia. In 1825 George Wilson was born, followed by Catherine, Henry Matthews, James and Peter.

For thirty-five years fortune smiled upon the McKie family, then it seemed as though "misfortune's cauld nor' west mustered up" not one, but many "bitter blasts for them."

In 1851 Henry died. In 1853 Peter accompanied Rev. Peter Gordon to Australia whence he never returned, and to this day no one knows his fate. In 1855 occurred the death of James, the youngest of the family save Peter, and about this time Mr. McKie saw the accumulated savings of a life of thrift and industry swept from him by unwise indorsements.

In 1860 George Wilson, and one year later his father, broken by his afflictions, also passed away. Niel's death occurred in 1862, and Edwin J., the last surviving son died in 1895.

Mrs. Thayer's character was a combination of those elements which go to form one of the noblest types of manhood or womanhood. Her parents both came of an honored ancestry, her father of Scotch and her mother of Irish descent.

She was born at her father's home in Cambridge, June 16, 1827, where she passed her childhood and girlhood, attending the old Cambridge Academy, then under the charge of Dr. Bullions, of blessed memory, and the Poultney, Vt., Seminary. While at the former school she became acquainted with Francis S. Thayer, whom she married in her early womanhood, and made the city of Troy her home until 1877, when Mr. Thayer's failing health made imperative a change of residence.

Leaving her aged mother, to whom she was devotedly attached, Mrs. Thayer, following the dictates of both her duty and her affection, accompanied her husband to Colorado, in the vain pursuit of health for him, Mr. Thayer dying there in the autumn of 1880.

Previous to his death, Mrs. McKie [Sophia Whiteside McKie, 1796–1878] died in Troy, Mrs. Thayer's attendance upon her husband preventing the solace which would have come in being with, and ministering to her mother in the last days.

All these grief-laden years, which would have crushed many a one, Mrs. Thayer endured with a Christian fortitude, though much of the time in feeble health.

Her last visit to the beloved Cambridge home was in the summer of 1898, returning to Colorado in the autumn of that year.

Mrs. Thayer possessed that indescribable charm of manner—that stately, though kindly dignity—which gives to woman her highest grace.

This charm of manner won all hearts to her—with strangers—even before a word was spoken. What has been said of another may be truly said of her, "To know her was a liberal education."

Her life in Cambridge as a girl and as a woman, in Troy and in Colorado, was one of helpfulness and pleasure—giving to all with whom she came in contact. In society, in the church and in the family she was always a devoted Christian friend, daughter, wife and mother.

Catherine McKie Thayer, 1827–1901. A. E. Rinehart, photographer, 413 Larimer St., Denver, date of photo unknown.

Memorial urn for flowers over grave of Catherine McKie Thayer, 1827–1901 inscribed: "Dearest Grandma from Katherine, Henry, Eleanor & Thayer." Thayer family plot, Oakwood Cemetery.

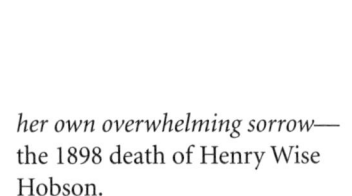

her own overwhelming sorrow— the 1898 death of Henry Wise Hobson.

"None knew thee but to love thee,
Nor named thee but to praise."

Two children are left to mourn the loss, Frank McKie Thayer and Katherine Thayer Hobson, who were devoted to their mother. No parent was ever blessed with a more devoted daughter than hers has always been. While passing, as she recently has, through her own overwhelming sorrow, her first thought has always been how best to spare and shield her mother from what would cause her trouble or annoyance.

The world is richer and brighter for lives like this just ended, and poorer and more desolate when they go out. But their influence will be long and gratefully felt, and their memory fondly and tenderly cherished.

We deeply feel our loss in this sad bereavement and our hearts go out in the deepest sympathy to those most closely related, and upon whom this sorrow must fall with crushing weight.

"Yet love will dream and faith will trust,
(Since He who knows our need is just);
That somehow, somewhere, meet we must.
Alas for him who never sees
The stars shine through his cypress trees,
Who hopeless lay his dead away,
Nor looks to see the breaking day
Across the mournful marbles play!
Who hath not learned in hours of faith
The truth to sense and flesh unknown,
That life is every Lord of Death,
And love can never lose its own."

—Edward Whiteside, *The Washington County Post*, Cambridge, New York, January 18, 1901.

Edward Whiteside was Catherine Thayer's cousin in Cambridge.

The probate papers for Catherine McKie Thayer's estate show that she had an estate of $144,839.36 most of which was left to her daughter. One provision of her will reads as follows: "Eighth: I do give and bequeath to Albert Whiteside, of Washington County, New York, as Trustee, and to his successors in trust,

The Whiteside Church and Views in the Whiteside Cemetery, Hurd's Stereoscopic Views, Greenwich, New York. At one time, Thomas Whiteside's infant son had been buried on a slope east of his home, and afterwards, in 1793, Phineas Whiteside had been buried nearby. A bequest of one hundred pounds from Ann Whiteside in 1800, lumber cut from the surrounding woods, and labor contributed by members of the community resulted in the building of the church in 1800 beside the burial ground. The church was destroyed by fire on July 30, 1983, but soon afterwards the community constructed a new church that was dedicated in December 1984.

forever, the sum of Five Hundred Dollars, which sum shall be invested and held in trust for the following purposes: The income from said sum shall be used for the purpose of keeping in good order the fence around the graveyard connected with the Whiteside Church, near West Cambridge, Washington County, New York, and to keep the grounds of said graveyard in good order. Any surplus of such income, over and above what may be necessary for the above purposes, shall be devoted to the support of said church."

☙ Letters of condolence:

The International Trust Company
Denver, January 5, 1901.
Dear Mr. Wise—   I have just come from Mrs. Hobson's, and she wishes me to express her appreciation of your message of sympathy.

Mrs. Thayer's death seems to be very sudden. She had a slight cold on Saturday, which appeared to develop into an attack of *la grippe*, which is quite prevalent here now. Not until Thursday night was she taken seriously ill, the disease then developing into bronchial pneumonia, from which she died a little before 11 o'clock yesterday (Friday).

Katherine has been quite dangerously ill with *la grippe*, her temperature being 104 and above for the last four days. This morning the fever is under control and the Doctor thinks there is every indication of a favorable turn in her condition. Temperature 100 1/2, pulse 100, this morning.

Everything is being done for the family that is possible, and they have ample help at the house. The services take place at the house at 2 o'clock on Tuesday, with temporary interment in the vault here. Mrs. Hobson expects to remove the remains to Oakwood Cemetery at Troy in the Spring.

She will write you as soon as she is able to do so.   —Yours sincerely, *F. B. Gibson*, Vice President.

Denver, Colorado, January 5, 1901.
Dearest Uncle Johnnie—   Your two messages received. I know you and Henry and Jack would do anything for me you could. You know what this loss must be to me.

Mother was taken with grippe Saturday evening, the 29th. We were not alarmed until Thursday evening, the 3rd, when pneumonia developed, and it

Catherine McKie Thayer's headstone in the Oakwood Cemetery, in Troy, New York, reads: "God's love runs faster than our human feet— to meet us coming back to Him and rest."

was so rapid that God took her away at eleven o'clock Friday morning.

Katherine has been very very ill with grippe, but is out of danger today. We do not dare to tell her of her Grandmother's going.

Services at the house on Tuesday, the 8th at two o'clock. Afterwards Mother will be placed in the receiving vault here and in the early summer we will take her to Troy.

Your dear letter of the 2nd and I have read over and over. It is such a comfort to me to feel how you loved and appreciated my darling Mother, for it was mutual. The last day she lived she spoke of you saying, "Dear Uncle Johnnie, how he has suffered in the loss of his brother. My heart aches for him, and I think of him so often. Always give him my love."

Dr. Fisk very fortunately was in Denver when Mother's condition became alarming and watched her constantly, —never leaving the house. Our own dear Doctor Stedman was the attending physician.

Tell Jack, Mother said, "Be sure and give my love to dear Jack when you write. I do not think he will ever disappoint me. I grew so fond of him the winter he was here."   [end of incomplete letter from Katherine Hobson to John S. Wise] (Virginia Historical Society)

Troy, January 7, 1901.
My dear Niece—   Your telegram reached us about 9 A.M. Friday and my first thought was Uncle William!! I thought Aunt Kate was so well! —and hence the shock was all the greater, and sad as it is. I am so glad that you had arrived and were all united once more, and that she died surrounded by those she loved most, and which undoubtedly contributed to her peaceful end… She saw the dawn of a new century only to be ushered into the dawn of a glorious immortality where no pain or sorrow ever comes.
—*Uncle Aaron.*

Denver, January 24th, 1901.
Dear Uncle Johnnie—   Your several letters, with those of Jack and Henry, have been received and I thank you from my heart for all your kind and sympathetic expressions. My mother was in such an excellent state of health and in such fine flesh and color and showed a lively interest in and keen appreciation of the great and little things of life that I feel as if she had been taken away in the prime of life… Her going was so sudden that it is almost as if she had gone out from full health and of course I must feel the loneliness and longing that would follow the absence of such a presence from my life. I am much stronger and go out daily into the sunshine. Katherine was seized with grippe the next day after the beginning of my mother's illness and for ten days was very ill. She is now, however, recovering her strength and goes out every day…   —Your always affectionate *Katherine T. Hobson.* (Virginia Historical Society)

Aswan, February 8, 1901.
My dear Kitty—   Your letter with its sad announcement of your dear Mother's death met us on our return… and I cannot tell you how my heart goes out to you. Only a few days before we reached Aswan coming up, the mail had brought me the little volume of Henry's letters and I had sat up on deck and read them alone and felt that it must all have been a dream and he must be living after all, and even now as I write, I have the pang of the sad

the little volume   Papa's Letters

realization of the fact as if I had awakened to it but here.

Words have no power to say what I have in my heart to say to you. I can only sorrow with you. I know what your love was for your mother and how worthy she was of it. Henry too idealized her and always spoke of the affection and sympathy he had from her with the deepest feelings. I am glad to have known her. She made a great impression on me. I would have loved anyone who loved Henry, and helped him, but this was for her own sake and yours. She has left you only sweet memories. But when our dear ones go we want them, and memory is a poor comforter. We who have had our Mothers left to us have been very blessed, but this makes it all the harder to face the inevitable separation when it comes. I can only think of your loss. Your little ones too will miss her. They were a great happiness to her and her love and care will always have been a benediction to them.

Henry's letters brought me very near to the past. They had so much of his cleverness and of his sweetness which always came out when he spoke or thought of his children. He never was with me that he did not tell me of them. I remember his telling me once of going into Huyler's to get a box of candy just as he was to start for home. He had just stopped in somewhere and bought a little cap for Katherine and it was wrapped in a bit of tissue paper as he did not have time to wait for a box. The girl in Huyler's who was waiting on him began to flirt with him by asking about his sweet-heart for whom he was getting candy, and he said it was for his baby. "You have not any baby," she said. "You are not married." "I haven't?" said Henry. "See here." And he unwrapt his frilled cap then and there. You must give my dear love to the children… I trust Katherine is again well and strong, and that all the others Henry, Eleanor, and Thayer are as well as can be. Give them all my love and say that Uncle Tom thinks of them a great deal. I have not told you how tasteful I think the little volume is. I shall always keep it. Your devoted old friend,
—*Thos. Nelson Page.*

Denver, February 10th, 1901.
My Dear Uncle Johnnie—   …For forty years the Mother love & devotion has surrounded me and there is a great loneliness in being deprived of it. I thank God for all I have had & hope for health & strength to do still for Mother & Henry what they would have wished for these dear children…
—*Katherine* (Virginia Historical Society)

New York, N.Y., March 5, 1901.
My dear Katherine—   …I know what a blow your dear mother's death was. It was hard to give her up. But, remember, it marked a distinctly new era in your life. Theretofore she was the head. By her death you have moved up. When disposed to mourn, remember how bravely & sweetly & strong she assumed her position as leader & realized her duty to be bright and loving, for the happiness of those in her flock.   —*John S. Wise.*

◦ Death in the family:

Mrs. M. E. Wise Died in Ashland Yesterday
Mrs. Mary Elizabeth Lyons Wise, wife of the late Governor Henry A. Wise, died between the hours of 7 and 8 o'clock P.M. yesterday, at the home of her step-daughter,

When Mrs. Wise was first united in marriage This obituary is reprinted, with its poor syntax, mistakes, and contradictions, just as it was published in both the *Richmond Times* and the *Richmond Dispatch* on July 18, 1901. The obituary incorrectly states that Sarah Sergeant was Henry Wise's first wife and then correctly states that she was the second wife. The obituary incorrectly states, but never corrects, that Annie Jennings Wise Hobson was Sarah Sergeant's daughter. In fact she was the daughter of Anne Jennings Wise, the first wife. Such errors and contradictions cause nightmares for modern researchers.

Grave of Mary Lyons Wise, died July 17, 1901, third wife of Henry A. Wise, Hollywood Cemetery, Richmond. A second nearby stone reads: "A tribute of love from her nieces and nephews and Mayo Grandchildren," a reference to the children of Margaretta Ellen "Néné" Wise, 1844–1909, who married William Carrington Mayo.

Mrs. A. J. W. Hobson, at Ashland, Va. Mrs. Wise was in the 86th year of her age, and had been an invalid for the past ten or fifteen years. Her death, while a shock and a source of great sorrow to her friends and relatives, was not wholly unexpected, owing to her advanced age and long years of suffering. Captain John S. Wise, of New York, her stepson, is expected to arrive in Virginia today. He will immediately make all arrangements for the funeral, which will take place from the chapel at Hollywood tomorrow at some hour yet to be decided upon.

Mrs. Wise was the third wife of the late Governor Henry A. Wise. Her maiden name was Mary Elizabeth Lyons, the daughter of Dr. Peter Lyons… Mrs. Wise was one of a family of four children, three daughters and one son… It is said that Mrs. Wise, then Miss Elizabeth Lyons, a mere child, climbed into the lap of LaFayette, when he visited Richmond, and kissed the great French commander. It is said also, that when Henry Clay was introduced to the Misses Lyons, he was heard to exclaim: "Miss Lyons! I should like to be thrown into a den of such!"

Miss Lyons met General Robert E. Lee, then Colonel Lee, immediately after his return from Mexico. She met him at Arlington and immediately recognized him from his portraits which she had seen. She was afterwards a frequent visitor to General and Mrs. Lee at Arlington…

Besides being a great belle before her marriage and a favorite in society after that event, Mrs. Wise was a woman of the highest Christian character and was a member of St. James Protestant Episcopal Church. She was beloved by all who knew her, and her death will cause great regret among all who have known her.

When Mrs. Wise was first united in marriage to Governor Wise, in 1853, there were in the household of the governor. The fruit of his first marriage to Sarah Sergeant, of Philadelphia, a number of small children, whom Mrs. Wise loved tenderly and acted towards as a devoted parent. Those of these children who survive are Hon. John S. Wise of New York; Mrs. William C. Mayo of Richmond, and Mrs. A. J. W. Hobson, of Ashland, Va.

…Early in his [Henry A. Wise] life he removed to Nashville, Tenn. where he engaged in the practice of his profession. Here his first marriage to Miss Ann Jennings took place. Later he was married to Sarah Sergeant of Philadelphia, and still later, as known, to the late Mrs. Wise.

…He [Henry A. Wise] died here [Richmond] September 12, 1876 and was buried in Hollywood Cemetery. Mrs. Wise will be buried by his side tomorrow. —*Richmond Dispatch*, July 18, 1901. (Virginia Historical Society)

Denver, August 12, 1901.
My dear Uncle Johnnie—   Ever since the news of Grandma Wise's death reached me I have intended writing you… Your Mother's going is a blessed release to her— being so infirm in body & mind— but the severing of another link with the precious past brings the sorrows, & heart-aches freshly upon us— and I know your heart has been heavy with sadness— here was one of the most gentle, sweet natures, I ever met— and she loved you beyond words to express. I think her voice as she talked of "Johnnie" was so full of intense love, trust, and admiration. In everything which comes to you of joy & sorrow, you know I feel for you & with you. This time of year brings back the going out of this life of our Dear Henry— God bless him— how he loved you & us all. Three years are gone. I am trying to work out this problem of loneliness. My Mother was so a part of everything in my life. It is hard to feel I have not her to turn to at all times… I had a good letter from Jack as to George

Hobson's future— & advising the V.M.I. I have decided to offer him a year there & shall write him today though I am almost sure he will not be allowed to go. Still I will have done what I can... Katherine is enjoying Colo. Springs for a few days— Henry building a train of cars... he is growing every minute and is a great comfort to me. Eleanor the same little "fat girl" —as Jack called her. I think Thayer is more like his Father in his bright quick mind and rare sweetness... Remember I am always loving you & wish so often you were nearby & not all those miles away. Banshee is by me, on the porch as I write— he is a dear & we are all fond of him & so good-natured. Thayer almost hugs the life out of him. The old Dandy is growing very fat & life rather a labor. Excuse this scribble— I write out of doors & a pad is convenient. When you have a leisure five minutes send me a line but never feel you must write. —Always your devoted niece, *Katherine*. (Virginia Historical Society)

Banshee and *Dandy*   two family dogs

👉 A letter from a friend:

Nov. 11th, 1901, 1759 R Street, Corner New Hampshire Avenue, Washington. My dear Kitty—   I am glad to know you are still on this side of the country. Your sweet letter gave me a great deal of comfort; for the sympathy of friends do good, and no one has had sadder occasion to know it than you... My father had been very feeble for several years, and had failed a good deal in the last months, though except for a cold, from which he had almost recovered, he appeared about as well as usual. He died one morning suddenly and quite painlessly just after he had been playing with Rosewell's little girl, who was his great pet. Well, that is the best way to die. His work was done and well done... There seems to me to have been a moral fibre in the past generation which does not often exist in our own. The simplicity of life counted for a great deal. Ours is so rapid and so complex, we do not have time or opportunity to ponder on the serious questions of life. We get our conclusions from what others say or write... I am going to deliver an address at Ashland, Virginia, soon, and shall have a word to say of Henry. He always stands to me as an inspiring type of the young Virginian who by a combination of forces overcame all obstacles and forged to the front as if by a law of Nature. Give my love to the children. My wife joins me in devoted love to you always. —Ever yours most affectionately, *Thomas Nelson Page*.

The Raleigh, Washington, D. C., Nov. 24th, 1901. My dearest Uncle Johnnie—   I thank God for the lovely comforting meetings I had with you in New York & to have our children know & love you is one of my ambitions & they feel you belong to them. Aunt Eva was as sweet & lovely to me as possible & please give her my love... You did so much for me in every way. The only failure was getting your Sister Annie here. I think of her stretched on the martyr's bed she has created for herself & writing to every friend she has of her bitter disappointment. Not a word from her & it is just as well...   —Your devoted *Katherine*. (Virginia Historical Society)

The Raleigh, Washington, D. C., Nov. 27th, 1901. My Dear Uncle Johnnie—   ...Your Sister Annie had her valises packed from the *first* & never intended staying away. She came Saturday evening. I have done all I can for her & paid her board on here until Saturday— corner room on Penn & 12th… God she has worn me out & said mean things of the people Henry loved best— it is a great thing to live 2000 miles from her. I have done my duty I hope & Henry would have wished his Mother to see the children. The atmosphere I live in is full of peace & love, and our creed is not to wound the feelings of others and how Mrs. Hobson can indulge in such heart threats & call herself Xtian, is beyond my [illegible]. Henry said after our visit to Virginia & his Mother, four years ago, "I never shall take you there again, or go myself except from necessity." You are good & patient… but I am weak & tired & I have been awake all night as a result of her talk— And am so glad I will soon be out of her atmosphere for one needs to be strong to meet the blasts…   —Love to you all, *Katherine*. (Virginia Historical Society)

1902

∽ Death in Missouri:

The Newton, Excelsior Springs, Missouri.

Excerpted from lengthy letters from Dr. McQuade to Katherine Hobson about her brother, Francis McKie Thayer.

Dr. H. D. McQuade, Kansas City, Mo., March 25th, 1902.
My Dear Madam—   I am just returned from Excelsior after a two days visit with Mr. & Mrs. Thayer. I am very much pleased the way Mr. Thayer has improved not only in appearance, but mentally & physically…
—Yours resp. *Dr. H. D. McQuade.*

Dr. H. D. McQuade, Kansas City, Mo., April 4th, 1902.
My Dear Mrs. Hobson—   Your letter of the 3/31 at hand. Have still the same reports from Mr. Thayer & must say am well pleased with the results we are obtaining. Mr. Faxon called last evening & remarked that he could see such a remarkable change mentally & physically…   —Yours resp. *Dr. H. D. McQuade.*

The Newton, Excelsior Springs, Mo., May 21st, 1902.
My Dear Mrs. Hobson—   Mr. Thayer is now resting very quietly, mind is perfectly clear, but is very weak & exhausted… I am compelled to return to the City today, will leave here at 1:15PM returning about 7 PM & will stay over the next day. As soon as he is able I shall insist on his going to Colorado Springs, whether it will have the desired result or not I cannot say, but the extreme heat here is so prostrating, that as soon as he is able to be moved, I will suggest the change. The rooms are similar to a bake oven, hardly a breath of fresh air stirring. I will advise you from time to time as to conditions. Have not had the time to write Mrs. Thayer, will do so today or tomorrow.
—Yours resp. *Dr. H. D. McQuade.*

Dr. H. D. McQuade, Kansas City, Mo., May 22nd, 1902.
My Dear Mrs. Hobson— I wired Mrs. Thayer this a.m. "Your presence needed at Excelsior. Mr. Thayer ill." There was a remarkable change for the worse took place last night. Could not stimulate the heart action, & did not respond to usual methods. I left there at 1:15 PM & will return this evening with oxygen & a trained nurse. I left Dr. G— in charge until my return. Will advise you later. —Yours resp. *Dr. H. D. McQuade.*
P.S. Heavy storms have caused a break in the telephone lines.

The Newton, Excelsior Springs, Mo., May 22nd, 1902.
My Dear Mrs. Hobson— Mr. T— temp 95, pulse 96… Have started to give him oxygen & brought trained nurse from the city. The radial pulse is more perceptible this evening. I am in hopes by morning there will be a marked change for the better. Have not heard from Mrs. Thayer as yet. Sent her a wire at 1 P.M. —Yours resp. *Dr. H. D. McQuade.*

Francis McKie Thayer, 1857–1902, date of photograph unknown.

THE WESTERN UNION TELEGRAPH COMPANY
Excelsior Springs, Mo.
To: Mrs. Katherine Thayer Hobson
Mr. Thayer quite ill. Advisable for you to come. Answer. —Yours resp. *Dr. H. D. McQuade.*

THE WESTERN UNION TELEGRAPH COMPANY — May 24, 1902.
Excelsior Springs, Mo.
To: Mrs. Katherine Thayer Hobson
Pulse one sixty, respiration forty. No rallying as expected. *Dr. H. D. McQuade.*

THE WESTERN UNION TELEGRAPH COMPANY— May 24, 1902.
Excelsior Springs, Mo.
To: Mrs. Katherine Thayer Hobson
Your brother passed away at four-ten today. Everything was done to save him. Mrs. Thayer is here. Body will go to Kansas City tomorrow morning. Go to Midland Hotel if you come through. Answer if coming. *A. R. Newton.*

◦ Obituary:

Francis McKie Thayer, son of the late Senator Francis S. Thayer of this city, died Saturday at Excelsior Springs, Mo. Mr. Thayer had for a number of years resided at the family residence in Colorado Springs, but was in ill health for some months, and had been at Excelsior Springs, where he died quite suddenly Saturday. Mr. Thayer was a graduate of the Troy Academy and of Amherst College. He is survived by a wife, who was a Miss Jones, an accomplished Southern lady, to whom he was married some years ago; also one sister, Mrs. Katherine T. Hobson. Mr. Thayer was a nephew of Aaron H. Graves of this city. The funeral services will be held tomorrow morning at 10:30 o'clock at the Earl Memorial Chapel, Oakwood Cemetery. Carriages for friends will be at the Union Depot on the arrival of the train at 9:30 o'clock.
—*From an unidentified newspaper in Troy, New York.*

Grave marker for Francis McKie Thayer, 1857–1902, Thayer family plot, Oakwood Cemetery, Troy, New York.

Eleanor Whiteside Hobson, right, and her brother, Francis Thayer Hobson, in Dresden.

Dresden, 1902–1905

Savoy Hotel, Dresden, 1902.
My Dear Grandma Hobson— We arrived in Dresden at 1 A.M. Sunday morning & we are not settled yet. For a day or two we were undecided which hotel to go to but think we shall stay here. From the little I have seen, I think Dresden delightful, & I am looking forward with the greatest anticipation to the day when we will go to the art galleries… We have very pleasant rooms here, & a little balcony overlooking the lovely little court here, in which are flowers, trees & a fountain. Eleanor & Thayer are out there now singing in the sunshine. I think I shall soon be able to understand & speak German as I am trying to learn it. Mother sends love & says she will write as soon as she gets a chance. As it is half-past-eleven I am going out to get a little air, so I will close. With the tenderest love to Papa's Mama & my cousins I remain your loving Granddaughter, *Katherine*.

July 9, 1902.
Dear Katherine— Yours 8th to hand. Yes, today is Henry's birthday. How well I remember it forty-four years ago. The season is much the same as it was then. The packet boat arrived in Richmond about 6 A. M. each day. Old Idie had gone up to be with Sister Annie. The morning of July 10th I was playing in the Capital Square in front of the Governor's house, just about the age of your Henry now. I can see the old woman show up, returning, & hear her tell us it was a boy, born the day before, & Mother & child doing well. Then I knew & loved him through his infancy & childhood, & after his father's death was almost father. Taught him lots of things he ought not to have known & some, I hope, that did him good. And so the old story went through storm & sunshine, in sorrow & joy, but always with love, until it was my sad lot to aid in stretching out his dead limbs & closing his eyes and laying him to rest. God be praised for this sad privilege. Sad beyond anything I can express for there was so much of good in Henry in mind & heart, & character, & the pride I felt in him and love I bore him was second only to that I cherished for my own sons and daughters. He sleeps well. After all that is all we can hope. Life

Left, Henry Hobson residence at 933 Pennsylvania Avenue, Denver. Right, 505 Cascade, Colorado Springs, built by Francis and Catherine Thayer. Katherine Thayer Hobson moved here after the death of her mother.

and death are only things of a few years. The grave holds an array of my loved ones; those left are growing fewer and fewer. Let us who are left cling only the closer to each other by the memory of our lost loved ones. We have much still to be thankful for. You, with your dear little ones, and I with mine, now almost all grown, should thank God every day for such blessings, & rejoice to see that they love us just as we loved the dear old ones who were to us what we are to them…   —*John S. Wise.*

◈ Moving:

Junius F. Brown… received the deeds to two purchases which make him owner of the house and seven lots at 933 Pennsylvania. This is the old and well-known Mrs. Henry Hobson home, one of the handsomest and most substantial residences in the city… The house stands on four lots… Adjoining this are three lots, till yesterday the property of Catherine McKie Thayer…   —*Denver News*, February 20, 1903.

After the death of Catherine McKie Thayer in 1901, Katherine Thayer Hobson moved to the family home in Colorado Springs and sold her home in Denver.

◈ A letter to Virginia:

Savoy Hotel, Dresden, February 6, 1904.
My dear Mama—   It seems a long long time since we have heard directly from you. I hope you & the children are very well. I had a letter from George sending me a little photograph of himself. It is a great comfort to hear he is doing so well— and it must be such a comfort— as no one but you can understand to your loving heart— who have done so much for him always. Is Cannon quite well again? —and no bad results from his accident? We are all very well. The children are working diligently in school and interested. It seems strange to think Katherine will be, on eleventh of April, fifteen! She is very tall and seems strong. This age of a girls maturing is often a critical point in their lives. Henry is tall and strong too— very fair, and a great comfort. He is now decorating his room with some paper flags about a foot long of different countries put on twine and strung from corner to corner— and Thayer in delightful conversation with his big brother. Eleanor is the same dear little womanly creature, always thinking of my comfort & so steadfast— the other day she wrote you. Caroline Wise has been in town four months… She has several old friends here and has enjoyed it. It has been pleasant for Eleanor & Thayer to have this little cousin here. She has dark brown curly hair, & brown eyes. Henry and Eleanor go to afternoon service Sunday and sing in the choir— and also attended Sunday School before church. We like the Rector, and his wife. Miss Jermain had a very severe attack of typhoid fever in the autumn, but is beginning to drive out. I sent Xmas wreaths to Oakwood for our precious Papa & my loved ones and thought you would like to know… The symphony concerts I enjoy here very much and I keep busy with my lessons in the Berlitz School. The Gallery is always a delight. Do you continue to have some of the students in your family? I told Caroline last Sunday I would rather sit down to one of your delicious meals than any cooking I knew of. How much Henry used to enjoy the scrambled eggs and [illegible] hash. Try as we would, they were never quite right at home. The children send you love & kisses. They always ask God to bless "dear Grandma Hobson"   —Always with love your devoted, *Katherine.* Uncle Johnnie sent me a fruit-cake for Xmas. It was eleven weeks on the way.

Katherine Thayer Hobson in Dresden.

Eleanor Whiteside Hobson in Dresden.

Envelope addressed: Mrs. Henry Wise Hobson, Savoy Hotel, Dresden, Austria.

THE INTERNATIONAL TRUST COMPANY, Denver, Colo., March 22, 1904. Mrs. A. J. W. Hobson, Ashland, Virginia.

My dear Mrs. Hobson— I am much pained to learn of the difficulties with which you have had to contend for some time past. It must be hard for you to understand and be reconciled to these hardships and responsibilities. If you can one day see the grandchildren educated and settled in life, or at least in a position to care for themselves, it will be some recompense, especially if they come to appreciate fully, all that they owe to you.

I am very glad under the circumstances, to take the responsibility of advancing $100.00 out of the income due you next July, and send you, herewith, a draft for that sum; also a receipt for you to sign.

I hear only occasionally from Mrs. Hobson in Dresden. She appears to keep herself wholly occupied, which, of course, is the best thing possible; but as yet, she has made no mention of her intention to return to this country.

With very kind regards, Sincerely, yours, *F. B. Gibson*, Vice President.

March 25th, 1904, Santa Barbara, Cal.

My dear Kitty— To hear from you was indeed a refreshment and a pleasure… I think of Henry very often. The years make no difference in my affection for him. He always remains in my memory and in my heart as he was so long ago when he and I lived together in Shafer's building and ranged together over the whole field of literature, politics, philosophy, and life. Others grow old and gray and wrinkled and crabbed but he stays always young and fresh. Give my dear love to every one of the youngsters, Katherine, Henry, Eleanor, and Thayer. Bring them up to love me and look on me as I was to their father… —Your devoted and faithful friend. *Thomas Nelson Page.*

Savoy Hotel, Dresden, June 5th 1904.

My dearest Uncle Johnnie— The children are all in bed, and as I sit here will write a line to you. Your letter was recd. I knew Henry Wise's death would pain you much— "Dick's boy," as I have heard you say, "was next your own." I wrote Virginia. I feel deeply for her & can truly sympathize. A little while ago I was talking to all the children of their father. Thayer discovered tears on my cheeks & not finding a handkerchief, reached for a piece of blotting paper, and applied that to my face— not a word was said… Poor Mamma [Annie Jennings Wise Hobson], she will not write me, or the children, but it makes no difference. She is my Henry's Mother & I will write her & remember her always. Little Henry asked me the other day, "I did not think Grandma Hobson would forget my birthday" & I told him he might be sure she did not & that the moment she woke his birthday she prayed for him. I am so glad George Hobson has a place for the summer. Next year he will graduate & then I will try to help Jennings, the youngest boy… I feel coming over here has done me great good. I had much to tax me physically & mentally— and I needed to be helped, to adjust myself to my new condition. I expect to spend the summer on an island in the North Sea— "Sylt" —a half-day from Hamburg— where there is fine bracing air & good bathing… I kissed the children for you— they are all devoted to you, & we must have much happiness together in the future— life can not be the same but we have much left, and I wish to live to do my best for these precious children. My dear love to every one of you, especially my Néné, God bless & keep you, Devotedly, *Katherine*. (Virginia Historical Society)

Hôtel de l'Europe Place Royale, Bruxelles, August 31st, 1904.
My Dearest Uncle Johnnie—   August's last day has come, during the month I have thought much of you, and our dear Henry. And six years ago. Thank God for the loves which are gone and the loves which remain to bless our lives... We have had fine weather, and are all well. Naturally we all drove on a coach to Waterloo & spent the day. Thayer remarked, "Napoleon was beaten and he is the one I hear most about..." Henry is a fine boy, and I can depend upon him. They all have their faults but thank God I have their love and confidence... Eleanor is half head & half heart and such a comfort... All join in best love, and a kiss to dear Uncle Johnnie   —Your devoted *Katherine*. (Virginia Historical Society)

Katherine Thayer Hobson with her daughter Eleanor Whiteside Hobson in Dresden, 1904.

Savoy Hotel, Dresden, March 20th, 1905.
Dearest Uncle Johnnie—   When I read in your letter "Well old woman," it seemed as if I heard Henry's voice for that was his tenderest most loving form of calling me... I wrote Mrs. Hobson I would probably return sometime in June, but might not, my plans uncertain. She has *lately* made me more enraged— says George Hobson says he wished he had taken her advice in his education & will study medicine after he finishes at V.M.I. with his earnings & *her help*. I do not believe he said anything of the kind & that "all he has when he graduates is the U. S. Army & Engineering" & that those boys Jennings & George must be true to the South & not under *Northern influences* & that Henry was weaned away & "his lack of loyalty to south was a great grief to me." Think of her saying this where but for northern influences & money from 2 northerner sources, where would she & those children be today. I am not going one step to Virginia. Henry said before his death "I shall never go to Va. again, have made my last visit there." I have for nearly seven years done my best, it may be a poor best, but God knows I have tried— and I am through, except in sending money to help her out & I do not believe George said any of the things she reports. He is a good boy & appreciates what I have done. I do not want thanks. Everything I have done has been from a selfish motive to please myself & my love for Henry... —Your devoted *Katherine*.   (Virginia Historical Society)

505 Cascade Avenue, Colorado Springs, November 15th, 1905.
My Dearest Uncle Johnnie—   It was most kind and loving in you to write me that splendid letter I received yesterday... I have just written Mamma & sent her fifty dollars— poor soul. She has had many heartaches and I hope this winter, when she is free from care of the children, she may have peace & comfort. When I told my three children I was writing they all said, "Send her love & kisses." ...Katherine writes me happy letters. She is settled down to her winter's work & has three people taking care of her. I feel content knowing she is better placed than she could be here. Henry is in the Cutter Academy and works hard... he is so tall, 5 ft—11 in. I hope he will not outgrow his things— of course he has joined a debating Society which meets Friday evenings. Eleanor & Thayer go off happily to school every morning and at dusk each evening Thayer and I study our spelling lesson. The Irish Terrier Banshee

is a constant companion. —Always your devoted niece, *Katherine*. (Virginia Historical Society)

1906

505 Cascade Avenue, Colorado Springs, January 22, 1906.
My Dearest Uncle Johnnie— …I had a sweet letter from Mamma at Xmas, which is as it should be. Cannon & George Hobson & Mary seem to be self-supporting which is a comfort. Take a heart full of love & a kiss from your loving niece *Katherine*. (Virginia Historical Society)

1907

Postmarked: October 11, 1907, Colorado Springs. [letter addressed to Geneseo, New York]
Dear Mother— We are all well & missing you very much. I have been up at the gym this afternoon. I got A+ in my history test. It works to be on the good side of a teacher. Palmers were here yesterday. Mary is busy housecleaning. I think I will take the cook's salt & pepper, she flavors to highly for my taste. Much love from all, *Eleanor*.

Postmarked: November 7, 1907, Colorado Springs. [addressed to New York]
Dear Mother— Your telegram came this morning and was quite a surprise as we had been writing all the time but had sent our letters to New York

Palmers General William Palmer and his family were the founders of Colorado Springs and friends of the Thayer and Hobson families.

Katherine Thayer Hobson (center) and her four children, around 1907. Eleanor, lower left, Henry standing, Francis Thayer beside his mother and Katherine standing, right.

Pony cart in front of Thayer–Hobson residence at 505 Cascade, Colorado Springs. Referred to within the family as the "pony cart," this "trap," a light pleasure vehicle, was made at the Troy Carriage Works in Troy, New York, circa 1895 and was used by the family for many years. For more storage, the rear seat could be folded under the front seat. In 1953 Katherine Thayer Hobson, 1889–1982, gave this carriage to The Long Island Museum at Stony Brook, New York, which houses the finest collection of horse-drawn carriages in the United States.

thinking you would be there. I suppose, as you have lengthened your stay in Albany, you will not be home the eighteenth… Mary went Monday afternoon and we have someone now who seems very satisfactory. Mary is paying her 30 dollars a month but she says that you must make your own arrangements… I suppose you are having a grand time… Much love from us all from *Eleanor Hobson.*

Dec. 7, 1907.
Dear K—   I forgot, in writing yesterday, to tell you I have mailed to you a copy of the book for General Palmer, which I commission you to deliver before Xmas with my kindest regards… The Cape is fine. The railroad has given notice to clear the right-of-way, as it is about to begin building. I send plat showing how it goes… Don't forget, when I die, to ask for the letters from Henry & you & your children, to me. I keep them all in a nice box & they'll be easy to find.   —*John S. Wise.*

the letters from Henry & you
John S. Wise refers to the letters from Henry and Kitty Hobson to him that are now in the collection of the Virginia Historical Society.

1908

February 5, 1908, New York.
Dear K—   …Oh! Katherine if you could but have seen that beautiful tribute to Papa. It was one of the simplest & most touching things I ever saw. Stonewall Jackson's little Cadet Aide-de-camp, now an old gray minister, was master of ceremonies. Henry Wise, our dear old "Dobbin" who led the cadets at New Market, spoke for us. He the oldest of our five survivors, except poor old George who was dying at that very time. The Governor received the things in a beautiful speech. Half a dozen bent survivors of the Old Brigade, & the "Blues" —Col. Edwin Harvie came down from Washington & Armistead Fayton from Amelia… Dear old Sister Annie was there too— & Katherine she behaved like an angel. Next day the Governor entertained Eva & myself at luncheon. We had a glorious success of it. We came back by way of Washington where John C. Wise & his wife Agnes gave us a pretty lunch. Then we reached home Monday night & Tuesday morning came the telegram announcing the death of poor old George. I would go straight back to attend his funeral but am in no fit condition to travel… I saw Sister Annie

Written after the dedication ceremonies of a portrait of Henry Alexander Wise, see photo, page 318.

three times & was very affectionate with her, making no allusions to anything & permitting none. She looks very old & pitiful & is strikingly like Papa…
—*John S. Wise*…

❧ John Brown:

Home, February 1908.
My Dearest Uncle Johnnie—   *Important*. I am given the subject for our Tuesday Club "John Brown was he a fanatic, a hero, or both" —And I wish to know if you will be so very kind as to write a few items on the subject. It is supposed to be a little talk (perfect foolishness & utter waste of time) on the subject, lasting fifteen minutes, not more. Can't you express me the tokens he gave your Father to pass about among the meeting. I will return it at once. At any rate do help me to read something on the subject which will not disgrace my family, as I should do if I wrote it myself without your help.   —*Katherine*. (Virginia Historical Society)

February 7, 1908.
Dear K—   …I am writing your John Brown speech for you & will send it tomorrow. It is a daisy. Get Rhoades' History & read up on it. You can find it in your public library… —*John S. Wise*.

❧ A letter between cousins on getting an education:

May 28, 1908.
Cadet Jennings W. Hobson, V. M. I., Lexington, Va.
Dear Jennings—   I have your letter of the 25th. Of course, you may have ideas of your own on where you want to go to school. Maybe it is best to let boys follow their own inclinations, but it is my opinion, that more young men are ruined by following their own inclinations, based on premature and immature consideration, than are by any other course known.

Your Aunt Katherine, you say, has written you she will pay your expenses to the Cambridge Seminary, and nowhere else. It is her desire and her ambition that you boys shall be something and amount to something, and while I do not doubt that she would ultimately come around and do what under the circumstances seem to be the best, I should think that such a strong expression of her desire would about determine your course.

I am not surprised that some of the local ministers advise you to go to the Alexandria Seminary. Without knowing, I assume that I am correct that at least the majority, if not all of them, are Virginia ministers who graduated from the Alexandria Seminary. Probably the breadth and scope of their information is just that size. They are probably, as most of them, thoroughly imbued with the virtues of "old Virginia," and in total ignorance of the values of "the world." Alexandria is the next thing to Pompeii on the face of the earth. I understand the garbage of the houses is there dumped in the gutters, and the sewerage is so inadequate that the neighbors have to consult each other before dumping in them. I understand they probably have almost a mile of paving in the city, and an infinite supply of legends and traditions of the extinct past, with nothing progressive in the present, and thorough indifference to the future. For pan-theological artists and ancient catholicism, I sup-

---

a little talk "It has been said the John Brown is one of those characters in history which has become prominent by apparently touching a spark to a train already laid… His case was dealt with by the State authorities. He was convicted, sentenced & hung. John Brown refused to plead insanity and forbade his lawyers to make such a plea— he was defended by able counsel & his conviction was certain. He declared he had a fair trial & had been treated humanely. My Grandfather [Henry A. Wise, grandfather of Kittie's late husband, Henry Wise Hobson] who had several interviews with him in prison was impressed by his courage & apparent truthfulness. He spoke of him as one of the most fearless human beings he had ever seen. Brown would talk freely of his plans, movements & purpose of attacks, but was silent concerning his associates … Brown refused to admit that he had been guilty of treason & held he had been justified in all he had done by a 'Higher Law.'"
—*Excerpts from Kittie Hobson's eleven pages of notes for her speech about John Brown.*

pose it would be an ideal spot for a student, but for a live human up to date minister, Alexandria does not appeal to me as a place of instruction.

I suppose most of the ministers around Virginia are on a salary ranging from $125 to $250 a year, and are walking advertisements of its fitness. And the blue laws of Virginia which prohibit children playing games on Sundays, and make little country boys put on their shoes and burn their feet to go to Church Sundays, are good demonstrations of their efficiency, while the degeneration of the community and its industrial and agricultural condition is attributable to the "damned Yankees."

I think if you will look over the United States, you would probably find that Alexandria is the quietest place you could study in, but that Cambridge Theological Seminary ranks considerably higher than Alexandria. You have at Cambridge the advantage of the Harvard University. You have the advantage of being brought into intimate association with the progressive and successful people of the country. Your Aunt Katherine has spent her life amongst the progressive and successful elements of society, and none of them came from Virginia. I have traveled over the United States and a good part of other foreign countries. I am "from Virginia," and glad of it, and there is no power on the face of the earth can make me "to Virginia." It is the only place on the face of the earth that I can positively say that I would not live under any conditions. Virginia, as it styles itself, meaning the tide-water part, and excluding the infamous valley which the eastern people say is not Virginia, is today the most abandoned spot in the United States. It has no agricultural, commercial or manufacturing interests. East of Richmond, excluding the port of Norfolk, its population is largely of black majority— indolent, worthless, bankrupt, and poverty stricken. All who want to do anything have to leave there. Compared with it, the Sahara Desert and the Mohave [sic] Desert are surging booms.

Alexandria, from all accounts, is the Mecca of this enlightened condition. Boston is commercially, financially, and industrially, one of the centers of the globe; socially and professionally, it is unmatched in the United States, and the Harvard University, of which the Cambridge Theological Seminary is substantially a part, holds the globe over a position alongside of Oxford, Heidelberg, Leipsic, Cambridge, and the leading universities of the world. For you to talk about taking Alexandria in preference to Cambridge is perfectly childish. You might as well take the Virginia Military Institute in preference to West Point, or Randolph-Macon College in preference to Harvard.

If to be a minister is, in your opinion, to be one of the things you see creeping around the small villages of Virginia, then the sooner you go out to some other community and learn your mistake, the better off you will be, and the better secure will be your future. I say this in all kindness, but I am obliged to say that if you go to Alexandria, and your Aunt Katherine consults with me, and is in any way controlled by my advice in the future, as she has been in the past, and in the case of George, while I should like to help you, I do not expect to be able to give her much encouragement.

You have spent almost you entire life within Virginia, and if I am not mistaken, have never been far out of it. Now don't you attempt to predicate your life and future on your knowledge of things against the advice of people who have been around and seen and know more than all Virginia will ever hear of. Yours very Truly, *John S. Wise Jr.*

Jennings Hobson became an Episcopal minister and at one time had a church in Bluefield, Virginia.

Eleanor Whiteside Hobson attended the St. Timothy's School in Catonsville, Maryland, from 1909 to 1912. During those years she wrote to her Mother and her siblings on a very regular basis about her activities at school. Being at school in Maryland, she was able to visit relatives and friends in Virginia, including her Grandmother, Annie Jennings Wise "Grandma" Hobson, in Williamsburg, Virginia, and Thomas Nelson Page in Washington, D. C.

Eleanor Whiteside Hobson fishing in Colorado, date unknown.

1909

September 27, 1909, Rock Island Lines.
My dearest Family—   So far, safe as can be. At the beginning of this letter I will say that according to many, this writing will be highly *characccactterisstic*. It is now about 3:30 P.M. and I have shaken all my adoring friends in order to write to you… Mr. McIntyre is making himself very interesting, if that were possible, by coming up whenever I am reading and talking about the University of Iowa, which he attended, or some subject quite as interesting. Miss Barnes & I lunched together on grapes, bouillon, crackers & caramels… Since our repast we have been playing cards… After we left Colorado Springs, Miss Barnes suggested looking at the mountains from the back platform, and I stayed out there 'til I nearly dropped. I know every nook & cranny of that range. The flowers are by me on the seat but are getting rather faded. Will write again tomorrow. With best love to all I remain your very affec. *E.W.H.*

September 28, 1909, Englewood.
My dearest Mother—   Here I am with my suitcase on my lap preparing to occupy the 4 hours of my stay here. I could not write on a bag so the suitcase is extremely useful. I have just arrived on time after a very pleasant journey. Yesterday Mr. McIntyre took Miss Barnes & me into the observation car for the Victor concert, and afterwards invited us to dinner in the dining car. After our meal we went back to some more music & then I went to bed. I did not sleep particularly well as there were frequent stops, and new passengers coming in the car most all night. I arose quite early, and after I had waited some time to get in to the washroom, I finally finished my "toilette." We had the same porter on the train that we had when we went to Virginia so he took a kindly interest in me. Miss Barnes provided me with some breakfast she had brought along with her so it was unnecessary to go to the dining car… I invited Miss Barnes into lunch and we had broiled whitefish, gingerale & cheese & crackers. Ah, yes my shoe-strings are still in good condition. I still have your umbrella also. Will write you a line from Catonsville tomorrow explaining my condition. Best love to K—, T—, Mary & yourself. I can imagine you & K— in Denver today. I hope you will be moderate in your use of the liquid refreshments. Best love again from your affec daughter. *E. Hobson.*

Postmarked: October 1, 1909, Baltimore, MD.
Dearest Mother—   Arrived safely yesterday and was met by the French teacher who had already collected about ten girls. We then came out here and went to the school to meet, meet, meet everyone. I next went down to the club-house and found my roommate, a very attractive girl of fourteen. We have a very nice room with two beds, one closet, one wardrobe, 1 washstand, 1 dresser, one desk and about three chairs. We have breakfast at 8, lunch at quarter of two and supper at quarter of seven. Last night we had some kind of codfish dish. This morning we had oatmeal, scrambled eggs & coffee. Last evening after supper we came up to the school & we all went up to the gymnasium and danced and sang 'till nine. We have almost absolute freedom at the Club-house except for attending the study hours at the school. About the only rule is that we have to be in bed at quarter of ten. I am waiting to arrange my schedule and took this time to write to you… I had a fine trip east and got along splendidly. I have enough to pay my music for the half-year and about

twenty-five dollars over. You can not have more than two-fifty in your room so I will deposit the rest… The girls are lovely and are very cordial toward the new girls. Everyone kisses everyone else good-night which I think might be omitted. I take my bath at night. We have from after lunch till quarter-of-five recreation but we have to be dressed for tea & be at the study hall then. After dinner we go to the school again to study… I will write more when I get settled. I telegraphed you yesterday. Hope you got it. Love *E. W. Hobson.*

October 4, 1909, Catonsville, MD.
My dearest Mother—   Here your blessed angel is with a bad cold in her chest, shut up in the house to get well with carbonic vasoline smeared all over her chest. This vasoline gives the same warmth as a mustard plaster but does not burn. They are going to make a fire in the dining room in a few moments and I am going in there to roast this miserable cold out of me. They have rules and rules which make me feel as if I were in a convent. We can't go out of the yard without a chaperone. We can't write to any male except brothers and fathers, and I shall have to get special permission to write Mr. Parker. I have slam banged my clothes into the one small wardrobe, two dresser drawers and one washstand drawer they have given us. I keep the tray of my steamer trunk on top of the wardrobe, also a suitcase with my summer coat in… They took all my money away and allow me an allowance of fifty cents a week, of which I spend 30 cents for church & Sunday school. I can have 10 cents worth of candy a week. What I shall do with the other ten cents I can not say. It is very true that we never appreciate home till one gets away. They work you very hard and I worry and worry most the time about some lesson or other. I have begun my music… I have been here since Wednesday and have not yet had word from any of you… I sleep with four blankets over me and am cold even then… You are allowed to go away every six weeks from Friday to Sunday but as I have no place to go I shall have to stay here… The girls play basketball a whole lot and are trying to get up the spirit of the new girls. As soon as I get well, I will see if I can do anything in that line. I have had this horrible cold ever since Thursday. It first began in my head and gradually descended. My roommate is very amusing. She evidently is allowed to read or do almost anything she likes and of the 300 and some books she has read in the last year, a good many are far from proper for a girl of fourteen. She uses two expressions most of the time, either "I nearly died" or "I never did that in all my life."… We have to go to church and Bible class on Sundays, and I tell you I would get out of the latter if I could. Don't be surprised if they do bring me home on a bed before long. Oh I tell you I am in a splendid state of mind… Give my fondest love to everybody & everything in Colorado… Keep lots of love for yourself and believe me ever your fond and affec daughter. *E.W.H.*

October 9, 1909.
Dearest Mother—   I have fifteen minutes between now and the time we start to study hour so I thought I would write a line to you. They allow us to stay down here for evening study hour which is a great relief as it was not at all agreeable to go up to the school every night from 7:30-9:00. I played basketball today for the first time and tennis yesterday. I am getting on pretty well in my studies but they are hard as the dickens! I am starting German & French to get the grammar and hope to pick up and remember the language later. I am taking an English course which is very interesting… I received a

letter from Henry yesterday, but he did not say very much— so do write me everything he says. I suppose he is too busy to write so many people. Every six weeks the girls are allowed to go to Baltimore for Saturday night and Sunday. This is a great event and all the girls go. As I have no family in Baltimore, or friends, I have thought up a plan for what I shall do. Will write it in detail later. I get 50 cents a week allowance and this does not go very far. It is such a bother to get anything here as I can't go into the village, so would you send me several yards of bright red worsted to mend my sweater with. Also some stamps. 30 cents of my allowance goes to church leaving me 20 cents to meet any little expenses for things I may need… Best love from *your devoted daughter* in a dreadful hurry.

St. Timothy's School, November 5th, 1909.
My Dear Mother—   How long ago it seems since I waved good-bye to you from the east-bound "Rock Island" train which bore me here. When I think that it is only a little over a month I could almost think I had lost track of the days as they went by. I have been having some exceedingly interesting work in school in the last week… I have not yet finished my preparation for tomorrow's studies so I will close. With very dearest love believe me to be as always, —Your very affectionate daughter, *Eleanor Whiteside Hobson.*

November 27th, 1909, Epsilon Theta Psi, St. Timothy's School.
Dearest Mother [addressed General Delivery, Andover, Massachusetts]—
No words can describe my feelings when I received a postal from someone in Andover yesterday saying Henry had Diphtheria. This morning your letter came. I could not in the least control myself and wept till my eyes were sore. Miss T— and Miss A— were so lovely and sympathetic… You poor dear angel having this terrible trouble come to you. God give you strength to go through with it all. I felt from the first moment you would come east, and it is a great relief to know you are with him. I could not bear to think of him all by himself so far away from home. I have just received a message from Mr. Stearns saying you had arrived and he was doing splendidly. Oh! how glad I am. I enclose a letter from Katherine which I thought you might like to see. I wrote H— a long letter yesterday and tried to be cheery while I was weeping hard. I will write dear little "chix" in Colorado as soon as I finish this letter. I got my second report card yesterday… Give my best and dearest love to Henry… Always your very affectionate daughter   —*E. W. Hobson.*

November 30th, 1909, St. Timothy's School.
Dearest Mother [addressed to General Delivery, Andover, Massachusetts]—
Your postals have been received and you cannot imagine how relieved I am to hear of Henry's improved condition… Everyone has been lovely about Henry's sickness. I had spoken of it before I got your letter. Miss S— asks regularly twice a day as do also the other teachers… If it is possible, do plan to come down and see your own pet lamb while you are east. I should so dearly love to see you. I send you a little birthday present tomorrow and in case I do not get a chance to write you again before your birthday let this serve as a birthday letter, and let it bear you my dearest love and many happy returns of the day. Give little brother dearest love and best hopes for a speedy recovery. Ever your devoted daughter with very dearest love, *Eleanor W. Hobson.*

Andover, Mass., November 30, 1909.
My Dearest Uncle Johnnie—   Your letter to Henry has just arrived & has pleased and gratified him exceedingly. The boy is doing "finely" the Doctor says in every respect. Tonight a culture is to be taken from Henry's throat & sent to Boston to ascertain if there is any germ left. His temperature is normal. Of course perfect quiet is necessary and can not tell when Henry can be up. The boys were sent away from the Hall & Henry, nurse, a care-taker and I are the sole occupants. Our meals are sent in. Henry's is the only case so far. I was answering Aunt Eva's kind letter when the telegram was handed me which brought me here… —You know dear Uncle Johnnie how anxious I am for my dear boy. Always affect. yours *Katherine*. (Virginia Historical Society)

◈ A letter from Colorado:

Dec. 16th, 1909, House.
Dear Mother and Henry—   Rah! Rah! Rah! Henry ain't got (know) [*sic*] germs. I'm off my mind to hear of it. I am very sorry you can not see our 2 plays at San Louis School, for they are going to be very good. It is going to be very lonely here at Christmas time without you or someone. If there were somebody here except Mary. I do not know what we would do without her. Mary made my costumes for the plays. One is a red and white wassel costume. Trunks, doublet, hose, and red pointed slippers. Mary says I ought to have my picture taken in it, for it is very becoming to me. My other is a tin soldier costume… Much love to Henny Penny, and keep lots for yourself your *loving son Thayer*. P.S. Mary sends her love to you and Henry.

Andover, December 19th, 1909, Phillips Hall.
My dearest Eleanor—   Yesterday I did not write you for I had one of my headaches. Not as bad as sometimes, but bad enough. Today I am all well again. We are waiting for dinner to be sent in & Henry is so hungry he can scarcely wait. He scribbled a note to you yesterday, which he says he will send to Brook Hill. He has been propped up in bed for a half hour. We fumigated Thursday & then the "fellows" returned to the Hall. Tomorrow they go for their vacation. Henry must be in bed until the 28th & he certainly gains in strength. As yet we can make no plans about leaving here. It is such a comfort this nurse can stay as long as we wish her. Henry has a beard & mustache, 4 weeks in bed today, & his hair very long. Your report was forwarded to me from home, and I was delighted with it. The Sibley girl writes home about "an adorable Eleanor Hobson," so Katherine says. —Now we have had dinner— Henry ate his with relish. It was so pathetic to see Henry, when Clement Gile came in just now to get some of his clothes & told where every day of his vacation was to be spent… & Henry said so cheerfully, "Well I hope you will have a fine time old boy." …My next letter will be sent to Brook Hill… —Kisses, *your Mother*.

Phillips Hall, Andover, Mass. December 21st, 1909.
My Dear Uncle Johnnie—   You will, I know, be glad to hear Henry is out of quarantine… I feel now greatly relieved and I shall spend Christmas with a very thankful heart… The opinion is now that all patients of this

disease must be kept quiet for some time… Eleanor has gone to Richmond to spend Xmas with the Stewarts— the trip was a short one for her to make, & there are some young girls in Richmond whom she knows. Thayer reports himself well… As always, your devoted *Katherine*. (Virginia Historical Society)

December 23, 1909, New York.
Dearest K—   Thank you for your sweet note of 21st with the good news of Henry's recovery. That is much to be thankful for. Hug the dear old boy for me & congratulate him.

It is Xmas almost. There is not much it in for me any more. All its illusions are gone & those with whom I celebrated. But there is much to be grateful for. Far, far, more than I deserve.

I have been at home for the past ten days— trying to rest & get sleep, to overcome this miserable old heart. How I would enjoy taking it out & kicking it over the fence if I could only get a new one. Don't go back to Colorado without coming here dear Katherine. I sent Sister Annie a little note & Xmas gift. Hope she will not behave foolishly about it. Goodbye. Yours affect —*John S. Wise*.

1910

Sunday, January 30th, 1910.
Dearest Mother—   You will I know be glad to hear that I have had to get glasses to study with. For the last week my eyes hurt me terribly and Miss Polly sent me to the oculist who said I had strained my eyes studying, and gave me some glasses. He said I would have to wear them only temporarily. I received your letter yesterday, also one from Henry… The exams begin tomorrow… I know I shall be an entire wreck when it is over… To think that Thayer should be fond of dancing school after the fuss he made about it last year… Had a lovely letter from the Stewarts yesterday. They say they still miss me. Best love from your very affectionate daughter, *E. W. H.*

༄ A letter from Colorado:

This amusing letter to Eleanor Hobson is actually in the handwriting of her younger brother Thayer who was in Colorado Springs. Throughout her life, her siblings occasionally called her "Piggy," the nickname that her father had given her.

House, Feb. 1st.
Oh you Peeg!   The reason I have not written lately is that it wastes ink and in these days one must be careful and not throw the lamp at Mother because it wastes the oil, and not put mush in Mother's ear because it wastes the mush, and not put overalls in Mrs. Murphies stew because it wastes the dye in the overalls. But then I do not mean to preach because you sometimes forget and do such careless things. Enclosed find Totem Pole you asked for. Also I enclose a piece of ribbon to tie your hair with. Well I thought the *Merry Widow* was first class, red plush cushioned like the railroad cars in Germany (in the olden days). I enclose also one shoe. It is morning and the sun is shining. A pretty state of affairs. If I don't see your rear attic soon I shall forget what it looks like. Mary yells that there is a robin in the yard. Well the age of miracles is not over when the moon blows, the wind chimes, and I write to you. With much love I am yours forever.   —*Mother.*

∾ A nephew to his uncle:

Phillips Hall, Andover, Mass. February 25, 1910.
Dear Uncle Johnnie—   …A year or two ago I sent a copy of *The End of an Era* to a Judge Wilson, who lives in Steamboat Springs, Colo. I hear from him at times, and he never fails to speak of you as one of our best writers, and of the book as the best he has ever read. So as I was so very successful once, I told one of the Professors here about it the other day. He is still reading it with the greatest of pleasure, and speaks of it every day. So now to live up to what I preach, I intend to read it myself very soon. I did read it once, or parts of it, several years ago. …Ever your Affec. nephew, *Henry Wise Hobson.*

Henry Wise Hobson was attending Phillips Academy in Andover, Massachusetts, and wrote this letter to his uncle, John S. Wise, whom he knew very well. Wise's book, *The End of An Era*, had been published in 1899.

St. Timothy's, March 10th, 1910.
My dear Mother—   It seems hardly possible that the second term has flown by, and that I am sending you my last report before Easter. I don't know how quickly the time has passed with you in dear old Colorado, but I can tell you that here it has been on the continuous run. I am sorry not to send you a better report, but I shall try to improve it next month… I am thoroughly enjoying the first part of an Eastern Spring.   —With dearest love believe me to be as always, Very affectionately yours, *Eleanor Whiteside Hobson.*

Colorado Springs, May 2nd, 1910.
My Dearest Uncle Johnnie—   …When I was at Andover I fell on the stairs, & I hurt a nerve in my arm— to make a long story short, I have been more or less miserable ever since, and am only lately beginning to feel at all like myself. I know you will be glad to know Henry is working on full schedule and trying to make up what he lost during his illness… Think of Katherine being twenty-one April 11th. She is working every morning in the studio… Eleanor is in love with her School… She returns there next year. Thayer is my companion now. He is an affectionate manly boy. I have just written Mamma & sent her a birthday check. She writes me she has not been well. Now dearest Uncle Johnnie, how are you? …We have twenty-six tiny chickens. Thayer has eighteen hens & supplies us with eggs— he keeps his book & buys the feed. You should have seen me hatching out six eggs on the hot-water bag…
—Your Devoted Niece, *Katherine.* (Virginia Historical Society)

St. Timothy's, May 12th, 1910.
My dear Mother—   This will be the last inspection letter I shall write you this year, and it hardly seems possible that nine months have passed almost since I was last in Colorado. School closes on the ninth or tenth, and I am becoming very much excited at the prospect of my first Commencement here… The next time you receive a report I hope to be with you, and until then, believe me to be as always,   Very affectionately yours, *Eleanor Whiteside Hobson.*

∾ Five months later:

St. Timothy's, Postmarked: October 29th, 1910.
Dearest Mother [letter addressed to Dresden, Germany]—   …It seems so funny to think that this is the last October I shall ever spend in school… I

received a letter from Mary today saying Thayer was very lonely but that he did not complain. Poor little fellow. I feel sorry for him all alone but I guess he can stand it and next year he will be having a beautiful time at school… Have not heard from Henry lately but I suppose he is very busy studying & making friends. Good night dearest Mother, loads of love, *Eleanor.*

A letter from a niece to Katherine Hobson:

Trenton, S. C., Nov. 4th, 1910.
Dear Aunt Katherine— Jennings wrote me about the agreement Grandma made with Uncle Henry concerning furniture, books & etc. The few pieces which I have of course belong to you, & you can get them whenever you want them. I do not know what Grandma has told you about my having them. I wish to explain how I come to have them— Alice & I were staying with Mother when Grandma moved from Ashland. She sent this furniture that I have to Mother's & told us we could consider it ours. We thought she meant we could have it, & when I married, Mother shipped it to me at my expense. Grandma wrote me to return it to her, for she did not give it to us, & she needed it for her parlor. It was a short while before my baby's birth. I wrote her that I was not able to see to having it packed, but would return it when I was able to. Still she certainly gave it to us, & I did not understand why she wanted us to have nothing of hers. She replied, to let the matter drop, that she would write me about it later. She has not written me about the furniture since. I also wrote her that she would have to pay packing & freight expenses on furniture when I returned it as it cost me $25.00 to get it here besides having it repaired & fixed after getting it. I did not think it would be much left of it if it took another trip on the railroad. The furniture was badly abused before when she sent it from Ashland.

I think Grandma has not acted honorably towards my brothers, sister & me, also towards you. When I was going to school at Cousin Sophie Slaughter's, she wrote me a long letter telling me to sign a paper for her, agreeing to stand for some debt of hers at her death. That I would get a small sum of money left to me by Uncle Henry at her death. Cousin Sophie told me not to sign it, & that if I did, it would not be worth anything for I was not of age. I signed it though, for I was tired of being told by Grandma that I was nothing but a pauper, & owed everything to her generosity & kindness. I think the paper called for $200. She asked the same of George. Perhaps he knows more about it as he was older. I asked Grandma the summer before I married how much Uncle Henry left to give to us at his death. She said— "Nothing— there was nothing about it in his will, & she found out there had been a mistake about his leaving us anything."

I suppose she has spent the $5,000— & we get nothing. I think Uncle Henry was a noble generous hearted man, & if he had not bought the furniture, books, & pictures from Grandma for his children, she would have sold them or pawned them like she did my father's gold watch, which belonged to Cannon, and told him he could get it when he payed [*sic*] her $20.00.

Grandma will do anything for money. I found out before I married that we owed more to Uncle Henry & you than to Grandma's generosity. I think Grandma means well, & tried to do her part by us, & I appreciate what she has done for me. Still she has not acted right towards us. She is very forgetful, especially now. Does not remember one day what she may have done the day before. From fourteen years old up, till I married, I never spent a year altogether with Grandma, & know nothing of her business affairs. I supported myself from the day I left school till I married. During that time she gave me voluntarily at different times about $50.00. Up until three years ago the Church sent her money for us... She has done less for me than any of my father's children, & knows less about me. I owe my training to Cousin Sophie Slaughter & I love Cousin Sophie more than I do my own Mother. I spent many pleasant summers with Cousin Sophie, & always felt welcome there, but never felt welcome at Grandma's. Perhaps I have taken up too much of your time & bored you considerably with my lengthy epistle. My baby boy has been playing around me, & it is hard to write well with a baby pulling at you every minute. He is over a year old, & promises to be a bright child. He favors his father's family. It took me a long time to get my health back after Colgan's birth, but I am better now. Colgan has been a very healthy baby ever since his birth. I will send you his photo when I have it taken. I have often wished to know more of you & my cousins, but we seem to drift further apart instead of nearer. I was such a small child when I last saw you that I can not remember how you looked then, but I know from the several photos Grandma had of you.

Grandma wrote me how very much she enjoyed the short visit Katherine paid her. I hear from Grandma about every three or four months, sometimes oftener. I trust this will find you & all of my cousins well. With much love for all of you—   —Your loving niece, *Mary Hobson Bryan.*

St. Timothy's. [postcard addressed to Dresden, Germany, postmarked November 15th, 1910.]
Dearest Mother—   I paid the large sum of 25 cents today to have my basketball skirt shortened. It did seem so little. I have the dickens of a cold still but I hope it will soon leave me. Miss Sally jumped on me again today about my writing, but said my inspection letter was otherwise good. —Goodnight dearest Mother. Much devoted love to you all from your devoted daughter, *Eleanor.*

November 25th, 1910. [postcard addressed to Dresden, Germany]
Dearest Mother—   Just a line tonight. I am so happy. The Brownies beat the Spiders 13-5. I felt so badly as I was the only girl on the team who did not telegraph home the results but I thought it would be useless to cable to you. I almost sent Henry a message. A year ago the darling boy had diptheria at this time.   —Dearest Love, *Eleanor.*

Brownies and *Spiders*   Two basketball teams at the St. Timothy's School.

St. Timothy's. [letter addressed to Dresden. Germany, postmarked December 6th, 1910]
Dearest Mother—   It has been snowing hard all day and there are about 8 inches of snow on the ground. It looks delightfully wintry, and we hope that there will be a lot of sledding this winter. I received a lovely long letter from Aunt Florence [Mrs. Thomas Nelson Page] today, asking me to Washington for Christmas with Henry. It seems as if you intended staying abroad. I know it will do you great good, but I feel terribly sorry for poor little Thayer. I don't know whether I think it is very good for him to be alone so long in Colo-

From the letters it is obvious that Henry and Eleanor Hobson were going to Washington for Christmas to stay with Thomas Nelson Page and his wife. Page was the Godfather to both of them. Rosewell Page would write in his brother's biography: "And it was this godson who, as a clergyman, helped at the last service in Washington when his godfather was buried."

Katie Katherine Savage Townsend, granddaughter of James Jermain, who lived in Buffalo, New York.

Aren't you glad my birthday is in the summer Eleanor is joking about the date of her birthday, which was really January 7th.

rado with only Mary. Still you know best of course. We had gym for the first time today. I am writing this during roll call so that I can be sure to get it off. Good-bye now dearest Mother, best devoted love, Ever affectionately, *Eleanor W. Hobson.*

St. Timothy's. [addressed to Dresden, Germany, postmarked December 12th, 1910]
Dearest Mother—   I thought that I should get time today to write you a long Xmas letter but I am sorry to say I did not… We are greatly delighted tonight because Miss Sally has decided to let us have self-government till Xmas. The girls last year were not good enough to get it so you can imagine we are very happy & proud… I got a letter from Aunt Florence today telling me she would expect me the 24th. As usual when in doubt, I went to Miss Sally & asked what she thought H— & I better do till the 24th. She immediately said, "The girls go home the 22nd. Get him to come here & stay with you. You can shop or do anything you like." Wasn't that sweet of her, so you can imagine H— & I encamped here for 2 days… I enclose a letter from Grandma Hobson. It is unusually interesting. I think the old lady will kill herself soon. I have written Katie we will go there the 1st & then I can come down on the 9th of January with the Rochester girls. Aren't you glad my birthday is in the summer so you can be with me. Only a little over a week more before Xmas. It hardly seems possible. I'd hope that Thayer can spend the day with the Parkers. He will be so lonely. It is frightfully cold here. Yesterday morning the ink froze as well as my wash-cloth & when I poured out the water out of the pitcher it was filled with ice… I hope Aunt Florence will let us be free in Washington & not try to send us around to parties to meet strange people. The theatre appeals to me greatly, but as Miss Sally & Miss Polly say, I am not cut out for a society belle. I think I shall be a missionary before long. Good bye now. Merry Xmas & Happy New Year to you all. Best devoted love. *Eleanor.*

Catonsville, Maryland. St. Timothy's School. [undated]
Dearest Mother—   Your postal came yesterday but I have not yet seen anything of the trunk keys… I got a letter from Grandma Hobson yesterday saying she had not heard from you for years… —As ever devotedly, *Eleanor.*

1911

Dearest Mother—   The greatest excitement of this week was going to hear *Aida*… Henry talked a lot during the vacation of Thayer's going to Andover. Please don't send him there. It would be so splendid for him to go to a school where he would have the personal supervision of a fine man and not be one of nearly 600 students. There is a lovely girl here this year whose brother is at Westminster & I have heard a lot about it… We had a splendid sermon on temperance today and I enjoyed it tremendously. Not a rampant sermon but simply statistics compiled by physicians. Miss Polly and I had a splendid talk on religion the other day. We talk very often now. I was distressed to hear you had been ill in bed. I hope it was not serious. Dearest love to you both and many kisses. As ever devotedly, *Eleanor W. Hobson.* [undated, probably early 1911]

January 6, 1911, Buffalo. [letter addressed to Dresden, Germany]
Dearest Mother—   Just a few lines before I dress for dinner… Tomorrow is my eighteenth birthday. It is so lucky that I have changed it as it would seem so funny to have your "Coming of Age" birthday without a soul knowing it where you were staying. I know, that if I told, they would think they had to celebrate so I politely refused to answer all questions. My, but we shall have a big celebration in July. I have not really had a big celebration for years. Last year we went & bought our presents together but I did not have a real birthday cake and celebration. The year before you were away and the year before that I cannot remember, so now prepare to have a big celebration. Cake, presents & lots of fuss… Yesterday was the coldest day I have ever known. We went for quite a long walk & I thoroughly enjoyed it. Katie & I are going riding tomorrow if it is not too cold… Dinner is almost ready and I am all undressed so good night now. Dearest love to all, male & female. As ever, devotedly, your affectionate daughter.   —*Eleanor W. Hobson.*

March 15, 1911, Colorado Springs, House.
Dear Pig: I suppose you have heard about K's engagement with Herbert Kraus, What do you think of it? If Herbert is what Mother pictures him, he surely is all right. I am writing with a typewriter, that we have hired for a month. I intend to get Ma to get one like it second-hand for me to do her writing for her. It only costs 50$. You need not trouble to mention it to her though. I can write fairly fast but will be an expert by the time she gets back. I am copying out all Mary's recipes for her. It is an Underwood & a very good one. I have got another poem for the Brownies. As follows:

>Brownies up in Heaven,
>Spiders down in—
>Bells on our fingers,
>Hot irons on their toes.

Appropriate hum? The only thing I can not see is the poem part, the rest is easy. But then the 1 & 2 line rhyme? the 3 & 4 also? Well, Good-by old lady & good luck. With a heartful of love & many kisses I am your own uncle Thayer. —*Thayer Hobson or Beefy.*

Herbert Kraus.

March 19, 1911, Catonsville, Maryland, St. Timothy's School.
Dearest Mother—   Welcome home dearest to thy native country… I hope you had a splendid trip and have entirely recovered from your awful experience with Salzburg… I had a long letter from Grandma Hobson today. She has been very feeble ever since she cut that artery and cannot use her head very much. Alice Hobson has a baby girl about a month old. Did you know about it?… —As ever devotedly, *Eleanor.*

New Haven, April 2nd, 1911. [addressed to the Hotel Shoreham in Washington D.C.]
Dearest Mother—   …Do, please, not try to leave Washington until the doctor says you are quite well again, for what are a few days spent quietly now, compared with the loss of an ear. So please be very careful, as I know that traveling can not be at all good for it. I do hope that the pain is less now, and

Thomas Nelson Page

that you are able to get more sleep, it distresses me to think of your suffering so. I hope the doctor you have will be very careful with you. I have written Mr. Parker that you are not able to come West for several days yet… What plans do you think would be good for Eleanor's and my vacations. If Katie still wants us, as I think she does, and if Eleanor would like to go there, it would suit me very well. I always have a good time there, and am very fond of all the Townsends… Love to all where you are with a heartful of love, ever devotedly, *Henry*.

April 30, 1911, New Haven.
Dearest Pig—   [Henry Hobson writing to his sister]   …Last Monday Uncle Tom [Thomas Nelson Page] was here giving an address at the Southern Club banquet, and it was splendid. I shall long remember his speech, and all the fellows appreciated it very much. I took him around the next morning and was most glad to be able to be with him. He introduced me to William Lyon Phelps, one of the greatest English authorities in the country, and yesterday a note came from him asking me to dinner today, and of course I went and had a very good time indeed.   —Dearest love, ever devotedly, *Henry*.

June 23, 1911, Brook Hill, Henrico Co. Virginia.
Dearest Mother—   My conscience has been pricking me terribly because I have not written to you, but really it was too hot to do anything but lie down and die. But cheer up we are now at Brook Hill being restored… Henry read aloud to me most of the way down. Grandmother met us at the station and informed me I was to stay with Cousin Virginia Wise, the boys were to stay with her. I was sincerely thankful as Cousin V— has a lovely big cool house with a *bathroom.* (You know what that means in hot weather.) We went and deposited our luggage at the various lodgings and then I went to Grandmother's. I told her of K's engagement, and she did not seem in the least excited. I then went back with Grandma and the boys to Cousin V's for supper… Thayer broke out with hives the second morning we were in Williamsburg but he is all right again now. Grandma is very much feebler than she was when I last saw her. The blow she had did not seem to weaken her memory. The boy she trained in debate just won the medal and of course she is very proud. She is heart and soul wrapt up in the College… *There were some unpaid bills in the cubby hole of the desk in the library. Do you want me to send them to you?* Maybe in the rush of getting off you forgot them. Goodnight now dearest Mother. Take good care of yourself and be good. Loads of love. Ever devotedly, —*Eleanor*.

Colorado Springs, September 12th, 1911.
My dear Uncle Johnnie—   It is just seven o'clock, a perfect morning. Pikes Peak was rose colored as the sun rose— and the light is lovely on our mountain range… Thayer enters a school in Simsbury, Connecticut, next week— he is fourteen— My Baby is getting old! Henry will be near, at New Haven— he is the finest of boys— so manly, such poise— weighs 180. I often wonder if his Father can see him. Thirteen years last month since you & I watched that precious life go from us. I can not see that one of the four are at all like their Father in looks— others see it, not I… Did you know that Eleanor passed her Bryn Mawr examinations with honors, but she is not going to College. I feel

I need her— and I am not too fond of College girls. Mary has just come in and says to give you her "best regards," she is crying most of the time, about Thayer's going away. Fifteen years of devoted service counts in this changing world. Here I have scribbled on with one of my Father's quills— and will only add my tender love to you dearest Uncle Johnnie from   —Your ever devoted niece, *Katherine*. (Virginia Historical Society)

Sept 18, 1911, Cape Charles, VA.
Dear Katherine—   …Of course I will be in Washington at the wedding, the Lord & the weather permitting. But it will be because it is you and Katherine & Henry's child. I am not able, physically or financially, to run about as of old; but this is an event— & is not to be ignored. I see Henry in every movement of young Henry. He is a fine boy & I love him for his own sake & his father's. Katherine also has physical resemblance to her father. Eleanor not so much & Thayer I do not know at all. My wife says he is a superb boy…
—*John S. Wise*.

October 13, 1911, Friday, New Haven.
Dearest Kittie Hobson—   Just a line before going down to crew. The chair is splendid and I thank you again for it. Eleanor's letters brought me joy because they told me of your improvement. Do continue to gain… The weather here is fine, and everything is going finely. I would like a Bible like the one which E— was going to get. I have nothing but a New Testament here. Also I need some bath towels, not those six foot ones, but fairly good sized. Have to leave now. Love to all.   —Ever devotedly, *Henry*.

Oct. 17, 1911, Westminster School, Simsbury, Connecticut.
Dear Piggy—   I received Mother's letter yesterday and was extremely glad to hear from her. How is she now? I am enclosing my report, which is good, except for German. The size of my window is, the curtains must be five feet long, *not longer* and my window is 3 1/2 feet broad. I do not remember Henry's curtains but I wish mine to be buff with a colored border…   Much love to ma and family, *Thayer*.

1912

May 26, 1912, 761 West Ferry Street, Buffalo, N.Y.
Mother mine!   …I have written Grandmother Hobson that I should arrive in Williamsburg the third and stay there until the sixth. I will then go to Richmond and stay there until the eleventh… Fred and Katie [Townsend] both send their dearest and best love. Be very good— as you know a lot depends upon how you get on this summer. Give my love to Mary and keep loads for yourself. As ever your devoted, *Eleanor*.

June 2, 1912.
My Own Darling Eleanor—   …I feel awfully when I think of Grandma Hobson and think how comfortable she would be in nice rooms on her income, & think of how she chooses to live and I do not see how she need have dirt & disorder…   —*Mother*.

Katherine Thayer Hobson was married to Herbert Kraus in Washington, D. C. in 1911. She had gone first to Germany in 1902 and was there for several years then with her mother, but she remained in Germany, studying art, when her mother returned to Colorado. The "wedding photograph" was taken several years after the marriage.

June 3, 1912, Williamsburg, Va.

Dearest Mother—   I left Buffalo Sunday night and arrived in Washington at 10:30. I had intended to telephone somebody, but I became sick on the car and was rather uncomfortable so I just sat & wilted until 12:01 when my train left for Richmond. I got to sleep and soon felt all right. I waited an hour in Richmond & arrived here at almost five. Grandmother met me at the station and took me to Virginia Wise's. Poor Virginia is cluttered up with Hobsons all the time. After super we came down here to see Grandmother and this morning Grandmother came to breakfast & I came back with her here. She is failing very rapidly & her memory has gone very much since I last saw her. She seems to enjoy seeing me very much… Grandmother is crazy Virginia thinks. Poor Virginia is being constantly criticized for everything she does. It is very warm here but not unbearable by any means…   —As ever devotedly, *Eleanor.*

June 5, 1912, Williamsburg, Va.

Dearest Mother—   I suppose Thayer starts for Colorado today. What a delight it will be to you to have him with you, and it will be a great relief to me to think of you not being alone. This morning I went to Grandmother's about ten. Mr. Neale took me around the College & I spent the rest of the morning listening and sleeping. Last evening Mrs. Booth, Miss Booth, and young Doctor Booth turned up. Doctor Booth escorted me to Grandmother's where just for the fun of it I told her I was a suffragette. Really you should hear her argue on the subject. It would do your heart good. She was quite disgusted with me but later I think she realized I was only joking. She gave me some photographs of Father taken when he was young. Katherine has all we had so I will divide these with the boys… Do tell Mary to answer Grandmother's letter. I have heard seventeen times about her not having written a word. Grandmother looks very badly today, and her heart is giving her a lot of trouble. It is a wonder to everybody how she keeps on living with her troubles… Give my best to Mary & Thayer & keep loads for yourself. —Devotedly, *Eleanor.*

June 7, 1912, Brook Hill, Henrico Co., Virginia.

Dearest Mother—   Yesterday when I arrived here from Williamsburg I found two letters from you, and although you did not say a word of how you are, they sounded quite cheerful so I trust you are better… Cannon Hobson has gotten a very good position owing to the business training you gave him. He is given an eight-room house and a very good salary together with all the fuel he uses… Poor Grandmother gave me up as a bad lot I am afraid. I couldn't refrain from teasing her about being a suffragette and she didn't like it a bit. I don't know what she spends her income on as I don't think she ever has what you would call a square meal. She is all the time looking out for slights and tells tales of how everybody in Williamsburg neglects her…   With a great deal of love. As ever devoted. *Eleanor.*

505 North Cascade Ave., Colorado Springs, June 24, 1912.

Dearest Eleanor—   Your letter from New London has just arrived, giving your address, and now I can write you, or rather Thayer, whom you see is an expert typewriter, will write for me. I have no idea how long you will stay in Maine, but hope this will reach you sometime… When do you go to Cooperstown? and how long do you plan to stay there. There is no reason in your hurrying out here, there is no young set for you to enjoy, and I like to have you visit your eastern friends. You can imagine how delighted Thayer and I were to hear that Henry was elected, I have tired everybody out talking about it. Mr. Parker thinks Henry is a "big" man at Yale. Of course Henry wrote about it in his usual modest manner, simply stating the fact… We have a splendid cook now, but she is going this week, she thinks the work will be too hard when all the children get home. I have heard nothing about Gladys McConnel and George Fowler. Jack Suter has been here a month at the Sturgis'. Betty Kissel has applied for a divorce, on the grounds of non-support—she wishes to take her maiden name… Thayer has shot six owls around the house. He sold them for twenty-five cents a piece… I sent my story to *Everybodys* and am going to divide the proceeds with Thayer. He is going on an allowance next month, $20 a month. With dearest love and many kisses, and love from Mary and Thayer, your devoted Mother, *Kittie*.

Henry is a "big" man at Yale
During his undergraduate years at Yale, Henry Hobson was a member of the Yale crew, General Secretary of the Yale University Christian Association, and a member of Skull & Bones.

June 28th, 1912, North Haven, Maine
Dearest Mother—   Your splendid long type written letter came today, and after the long lapse in hearing from you, it certainly was very welcome. Thayer can be a typewriter if nothing else. I leave for Cooperstown Sunday night and shall probably be with you in Colorado in about two weeks… You should see your daughter. She looks better than she has done for nearly a year. Getting nine hours sleep regularly for a week & spending the day in the open has done wonders… I have no idea when K— expects to arrive in Colorado. I really don't know where she is now in fact… Henry certainly is a "big" man… Dearest love to you and Thayer,   —Devotedly, *Eleanor*.

June 28, 1912, 505 N. Cascade Ave., Colorado Springs.
Dearest Eleanor,   Your letter from Lookout [Maine] came this morning. It must be a beautiful place. I shall look on the Atlas and find out just where it is. I had a letter from Henry… He spoke about going to Cooperstown, so I suppose he will be with you soon. I am glad that you each will have an opportunity to see what a lovely spot it is. If you go in bathing in the lake be very sure that it is a full hour after eating. Fresh water is very different from salt… It is thirty years ago, this month that I spent as a bride at Brookwood. I am glad Katie has the place [Brookwood], she always loved it so, and what a beautiful setting for her children. Give Katie and Fred love from Thayer and me. And dearest love and kisses for you and Henry.   —Your own devoted, Mother, *Kittie*.

Addressed to Eleanor Hobson c/o F. P. Townsend, Brookwood, Cooperstown, N.Y.

July 1st, 1912, Mayflower Club, Park Street, Boston.
Dearest Mother—   Here your devoted daughter is enshrined at a woman's club surrounded with cocktails and cigarettes. I find *Pall Mall* are the best in the long run… This club is a very select quiet little affair, my opening sentence to the contrary, on Park Street… I leave at 8:30 tomorrow morning for Cooperstown. Someday I hope to arrive but my notions as to how to get there are rather vague. Please give my love to Mary and Thayer. Keep oceans full for yourself and grow stronger everyday like a lady.
—Devotedly, *Eleanor*.

Hedge Lawn, home of the Jermain family on the Troy Road, Albany, New York.

Eleanor's drawing of carrying her coat and leading the boy and wagon to Hedge Lawn.

July 2, 1912, Troy Road, Albany, N.Y.
Dearest Mother— You can never tell what is going to happen. Today when I left Boston I had every expectation of being in Cooperstown tonight. I telephoned out here and found that they expected me here for tonight so here I am at Hedge Lawn with Herbert, Katherine, and Fred Townsend. Herbert came Sunday night almost dead. It was over a 100° in the convention hall & sitting up in such surroundings all night did not agree with him a bit… Fred Townsend came this afternoon and goes to Cooperstown at 7:50 A.M. tomorrow. K— & I played tennis this afternoon. I wish you could have seen me arriving this P.M. The crazy conductor carried me 4 stations beyond the Jermain's. I got out ripping mad with two very heavy suitcases and my heavy winter coat. I was just debating upon the best course when I spied a small boy with an express wagon. I inquired whether he would like to earn 10 cents. He was delighted so I piled on my bags and proceeded on my way in triumph. The suitcases fell off occasionally but after a very dusty walk we reached the Jermain's. Katherine saw me coming and nearly died laughing at the combination of me and the small boy. Here is the picture. Herbert can't see the funny part of it but K— & I have been roaring ever since. Aunt Marie sends her love… Her eyes are hurting her a little… Dearest love from us all. Devotedly, *Eleanor*.

July 4th, 1912, Brookwood at Otsego Lake, Cooperstown.
Dearest Mother— I arrived in this beautiful spot last evening after a very hot & disagreeable trip in that fiendish Delaware & Hudson road. To my great delight I found Henry who arrived yesterday morning. A letter from you also awaited me… Henry & I spent a beautiful evening sitting in one of the boats catching up with what the other one had been doing. He looks very well and is too sweet for words. When I left Hedge Lawn Herbert seemed better. They start next Monday evening for Colorado via the Yellowstone Park. I think it will probably take them about twelve days to get there… Cooperstown is certainly beautiful. I enjoyed going on the lake this morning. You poor thing. I can imagine you here at 22, a widow & how lonely you must have been. We

are both sleeping out in tents which is great fun. It seemed lovely to sleep outside again & not have to be afraid of murderers. Henry joins me in best love. I am taking 2 baths a day to make up for Colorado.   —Dearest love, *Eleanor.*

July 6th, 1912, Brookwood at Otsego Lake, Cooperstown.
Dearest Mother—   I certainly have been disgraceful not to have written you more often lately but is very hard to do so at Brookwood where we all sleep in camp… we have quite a little tent colony. There is a very nice dressing room with plumbing which makes it very comfortable. Katie has built a beautiful porch at the front of the house and we have all our meals out there… Last night we went to a large dinner at the Otesaga Hotel… Henry met Mrs. Stephen Clark last night. I told him to make the best of his opportunity and get some money for the crew… Katie sends you her dearest love. She is so devoted to you and talks about you a great deal.   —Devoted *love from your own baby daughter.*

July 8th, 1912, Brookwood at Otsego Lake, Cooperstown.
Dearest Mother—   Saturday night we went on the most beautiful picnic almost up at three-mile point. We lay around until after nine o'clock singing and talking… Henry and I are going to the Bowers' to play tennis this morning… Henry and I send our best love to you all. Be sure to rest a lot so that you will be all right when we get to Colorado. Dearest love, *Eleanor.*

July 10th, 1912, Brookwood at Otsego Lake, Cooperstown.
Dearest Mother—   Yesterday Henry and I played tennis at the Bowers'…I never enjoyed tennis more. We went swimming and then staid to luncheon. Henry took a girl canoeing after luncheon. About 4:30, just when they were coming in, two other boys in a launch, who had been at luncheon, went up and took the paddles. The consequence was the Henry & the girl sat out in the middle of the lake for 1 1/2 hours. Finally they paddled to the opposite shore & got sticks with which to paddle across to the Club. This morning we went to the village… I expect to wash my hair this afternoon. It is rather foolish to wash it just before I take a trip but it is fearfully in need of it. Dearest love to you all.   —Devotedly, *Eleanor.*

Henry Wise Hobson and his sister, Eleanor Whiteside Hobson, probably taken about 1912 in Washington, D. C.

☙ Family matters:

October 17, 1912, Cape Charles, VA.
Dear Katherine—   …How are you? I have been distressed to hear that you were sick & often intended to write, but I am in bad shape myself. I only weigh 153 lbs & am very weak…   —*John S. Wise.*

Hedge Lawn, November 11, 1912.
Dearest Uncle Johnnie   …Did your Sister Annie go to the Sea Shore this summer? I sent her one hundred dollars to use for a summer outing & accept as our birthday gift. I have had a few lines from her once since. My heart aches for her, if she has any miseries they are of her own making… Much love to Aunt Eva…   —Always your devoted niece, *Katherine.* (Virginia Historical Society)

Nov. 16, 1912, Bryn Mawr Hospital, Bryn Mawr, PA.
My Dear Katherine—   You wrote me a letter which did my innermost soul good. I love to know and feel that you realize how dear you are to me. If you had only come to see me down to the Cape— how happy we could be together.

I have been fishing on the wharf sometimes when a big fish would strike me and take away all my hooks, sinkers and break my line. Well, I thought I had got one last week when the whoppingest pain I have had yet took charge of me, and I thought I was gone sure enough, but my boys rushed at me like a football team and figuratively speaking, brought me here on their shoulders, with your Aunt Eva and old Mammie trailing behind… Concerning sister Annie, I am very sure she didn't go away. Poor old girl. I saw her enough and don't want to see her again. It was too painful both physically and mentally. Virginia Wise gave me a very funny account of her plans for going to this, that, and the other place which never culminated. She really does get less for her money than anybody I ever saw. Her mind is gone completely. She babbles on the same subjects she talked about 10 years ago and nothing else. She looked dreadfully… Well, how I have babbled on. Good-bye and God bless you all.   —Yours affectionately, *John S. Wise.*

November 12, 1912, Tuesday, Geography Class.
Dearest Piggy—   Just now the Prof. is talking about the English Plain and I'm pretty good on that so will take a few moments to write you a short note… I was distressed to hear of the further trouble at home. As soon as things seem to be going well, something slips and everything goes down again… You have not written me any of your plans for that time (Christmas). I'm sure Mother will enjoy Buffalo and Geneseo, and it ought to do her a lot of good. I do hope that her eyes are getting better & that nothing will come up to hurt them anymore… Devotedly, *Henry.*

Catonsville, Maryland, December 1st, 1912.
Dearest Mother—   Happy, happy birthday. I wrote Mary to get you whatever K— & Herbert thought best and I hope their choice was good… I am distressed that your ear is still giving you so much trouble. Of course your health is first and should you really feel unable to come East of course we will come West gladly. I do hope that this won't be the case however as we could have such a good time here in the East together… Dearest little invalid! I got your telegram this morning after church. You don't know how distressed your child is that you should have so much trouble that the doctor thinks it unwise for you to come East. Of course it is a disappointment but it is not one that can't be made up another time, and I feel confident that as soon as you really feel "fit" as the phrase goes, you will bring me East and we can do all the things we planned to do this winter & won't stay cooped up in Colorado. When you are really well, I will just spit in Mr. Parker's fan (theoretically) and tell him we are going to go East whether he approves or not. Now, about that cruise. I think [it] is rather too much for a lady who is not able to come East the end of December to start off around the world the beginning of February. Don't think of me. If you don't feel able to go I will settle down quite happily to work hard at something and wait until the time shall come when we will be

start off around the world At this time Eleanor Hobson and her mother were planning to go on an around-the-world trip in 1913.

independent of your physical condition. I don't know what I shall do until the time to start West. Probably I shall go to Richmond then possibly to Brookwood unless it would help you to have me in Colorado right away. In that case just telegraph me and I will start west at once. If Thayer gets out several days before Henry, don't you think he should start West at once so as not to miss any of his precious time with you? My dearest love and let me know whether you want me or not.   —Dearest love devotedly, *Eleanor.*

Williamsburg, Va. (undated, December 1912)
Dearest Mother—   Your telegram came last evening and I came here the first thing this morning. I am absolutely up against a wall as to what do to. Grandma H— refuses to have a nurse of any kind. I saw her this afternoon for a few moments. She was up in a chair looking like a shadow. I did not let her know that I had heard she was sick. I very soon suggested a nurse and she absolutely refused to consider having one in the house. Virginia says that she bars and bolts herself up every night in her cupboard so that anything could happen to her. The only place for her is an institution of some kind. She does not need a trained nurse. Furthermore no trained nurse would stay there. Just at this moment I am at a loss what to do. The Doctor is coming to see me tonight or in the morning and I am going to discuss ways & means with him. Probably I will go to see Dr. Oppenheimer in Richmond and ask him if he will not come down to see her. It certainly seems as if we need divine inspiration to solve it. The Doctor is rather like a tabby cat… He has no authority whatsoever over her and simply tries to sooth her. He told Virginia that he would not be surprised any day to find her dead but that she might live several years. Will write to you tomorrow when I have decided what to do… Have just returned from a basketball game between William & Mary and Richmond College. I divided my applause equally. Dearest love to you all from your composed little plotter. *E. W. Hobson.*

Dr. Oppenheimer   Most likely Dr. William T. Oppenhimer who was married to a daughter of Ellen Wise Mayo, 1844–1909.

December 8, 1912, Williamsburg, Va.
Dearest Mother—   Affairs have not been very much simplified as yet. Grandmother flares right up at the mention of her going to any hospital. The only nurse she will hear of having is one which she could wind around her little finger. No trained nurse would stay in the house. I would say that in this case it would be better just to get the nurse who is available were it not for the fact that she is running into debt so heavily. As long as she has the money why should she not be where she could get the benefit of it. The great trouble is that she refuses to be managed in any way. Tomorrow morning I am going to see Mr. Phillips, the head of the bank to see if he can throw any light on the subject of her expenditures. I am going to Richmond on Tuesday. Tomorrow I will get Grandmother's house cleaned up. If only God would solve the problem it would be such a relief. One of Grandmother's boarders took me to Church this evening. Tomorrow night he is to bring the Presbyterian minister to call. Oh Thrills! Anyway there is really nothing I can do here to alleviate things as everybody says. Anyway Grandma will not be alone at night & everybody says she cannot last very long… My dearest love to you and Mary. My, but I have a job to think about. Your devoted little puzzler. *Eleanor W. Hobson.*

December 10, 1912, Brook Hill, Henrico Co. Virginia.
Dearest Mother—   Yesterday evening three boobs came and stayed until nearly twelve so I got no opportunity to write. Grandmother got so upset when I mentioned money matters to her that afterwards she telephoned me not to go there in the afternoon. She had taken the portraits out of the library. So yesterday I calmly sent a wagon to Grandmother's, calmly took the pictures, and they will be shipped to you tomorrow as soon as they are crated. The reason I did this was that they were standing in a very dangerous place in her hall where a hole could have been knocked in them anytime and besides I heard that she was going to have a man in Williamsburg touch them up. I guess Grandmother will have a triple fit when she finds out. Tomorrow I am going to see Dr. Oppenheimer. It was perfectly evident that she did not want to see me. The only nurse available in Williamsburg everyone there advised me not to take. My trunks have not arrived so I am to wear a dress of Mary Peterkin's tonight to a box party which Cousin Caroline is giving for us…   My dearest love to you & Mary. The Stewarts join me. Devotedly *Eleanor*.

1913

In 1913 Eleanor Whiteside Hobson and her mother took a trip around the world by steamer. There are no letters or other writings about that trip, and it has always been said that they made the trip with nineteen large steamer trunks. Upon returning, Eleanor entered the Presbyterian Hospital School of Nursing in New York City.

Death in the family:

John S. Wise Dead. Ex. Congressman from Virginia and District Attorney's Father.
Princess Anne, Md. May 12—Former Congressman John S. Wise of Virginia died at noon today at the Summer residence of his son, United States District Attorney Henry A. Wise, near Princess Anne, Md. Mr. Wise had been an invalid for the last six years. He was in a hospital at Bryn Mawr, near Philadelphia, for six months. He left the hospital on May 6 for his home, Kiptopeake, in Northampton County, Va. He stopped at his son's home for a short visit, and shortly after his arrival was stricken with pneumonia. Hemorrhages from the lungs set in on Sunday.

Mr. Wise was the son of Henry A. Wise of Virginia, who at his son's birth, in 1846, was United States Minister to Brazil. Fighting on the Confederate side, young Wise was wounded in the battle of Newmarket in the civil war, but recovered, and when Gen. Lee was retreating to Appomattox, Capt. Wise carried to him the last dispatches from Jefferson Davis. After the war he practiced law, but leaped into political prominence in the Virginia State election of 1874 by a series of letters on the Knight-Johnson controversy, written for the Richmond Whig under the nom de plume of "An Old-Fashioned Man." He was the unanimous selection of the Republican State Committee as candidate for Congressman at Large in 1881, and was a member of Congress from 1883 until 1885. In the last few years he had made his home in New York.

—*The New York Times*, May 13, 1913.

August 26th, 1913.
Dearest Piggychild— [to Eleanor from her sister]   This letter will probably be forwarded to you in your new abode, and while I can quite imagine you scrubbing the floors (& perhaps the carpets) sterilizing surgical instruments & taking temperatures, I wonder where & how you will be eating, sleeping, and putting your clothes away. And especially how you will spend your free hours and occasional Saturday afternoons. I suppose now & then B.W. may condescend to take you out in his new car— but don't conceive a romantic passion for him— just because you have forsworn the frivolities of the world, & have nothing exciting to compare with the sensation of a spin in the Park! Another word of warning— and a serious one— you are in a bad big city, and your outings will probably be chiefly alone & unprotected. Never forget that you cannot be cautious enough, and remember if the Archangel Gabriel were to meet you on Fifth Ave, it would be wise to distrust him until he had been properly introduced by one of your deceased relations. Above all, never allow your humanitarian instincts to induce you to go anywhere with anybody you do not know... Never use a handkerchief, or put anything near your face, which you have dropped & anyone has returned to you on the street. Often some drug is dropped on, on the chance of the owner becoming faint on using it— upon which a couple of sympathetic passersby hurry her into a cab, and away. Also in case aught is ever spilt or thrown on your clothes, only go into a drug store, or some shop you know, to wipe it off, or repair damages. In a word— take good care of yourself my dear. I wish I were going to be in New York this winter to take care of you myself! ...But now I must get this off to the Post. I have been interrupted so often during the course of this letter that I do not think there is a coherent sentence in it. Take good care of yourself and do not overwork.   —Always devoted, *Katherine.*

Eleanor Whiteside Hobson in her nursing uniform.

September 2nd, 1913, Tuesday afternoon.
My Darling Little Girl— [to Eleanor from her mother]   It was awful to have you go away from me, but I will try & endure it. And hope you will be compensated for all the sacrifices you are making & that God will keep you in health & happiness, now & always. I am writing at the desk in the darkened sitting room. Thayer is taking a rest on the lounge and Banshee on the rug...
—*Kittie.*

Thursday, Fall 1913, The Old Home, South Cambridge, New York.
My Darling Little Girl—   It delights me to hear daily of your content and that you are seeing something of Henry. Grandma always had her bed made with a tuck, or plait, in upper sheet, at the foot. You will soon be an expert at bed making. Mary wrote for another letter of reference— as a housekeeper & I have sent her one. She says it seems a detriment, not a credit, to have lived sixteen years in one place & asked me to put in four years my housekeeper. I do hope the letter I sent will answer the purpose. Thayer & I are going to the Whitesides to call & I am glad to say it is warm... —God bless & keep you precious dear, Your own *Mother.*

Mary Faeser with Katherine Thayer Hobson. Mary was the Hobson's housekeeper for many years.

September 16, 1913, The Old Home, South Cambridge, New York.
My Darling Eleanor—   Your letter telling of Thayer's being with you, and going to the good play, I have just read... Every day I do something towards

closing up here & do not get over tired nor do I wish to lose any of those valued pounds I have added to my weight.   —Tenderest love & many kisses my own Darling Little Girl. Your ever loving *Mother*.

September 18th, 1913, The Old Home, South Cambridge, New York.
My dearest Eleanor—   You see from the date I was writing last Thursday, but there really was so little to say I stopped. Now it is Sunday, Thayer is out in the woods with Mr. Pierson to mark dead trees to be cut. We took a drive yesterday afternoon to pay the blacksmith & Mr. Lee for a cake of ice… I have been mending everything Thayer would bring me in the clothes-line. The two last letters from you told of your good outing with Henry & his friends— … I shall begin at once to get the *House* in order to leave & with Katie & John to do all the hard work, there will be nothing difficult & I shall take everything easy… I think of you most all the time my precious. How much you did for us all this summer… Your devoted *Mother*.

October 2nd, 1913, The Old Home, South Cambridge, New York.
My Precious Eleanor—   …Thayer's 1st term bill came, $475 and Jack Wise sent $450 from Watch Hill rentals. So I am paying school bill at once. I do love to pay my bills… I am so sorry Henry has any trouble with his eyes, but should think if he uses the medicines faithfully they would soon improve. Glad no glasses are necessary. Mr. Pierson came over to see me & wishes to lease the farms for another year, with privilege of three if both parities are satisfied…   —Your Devoted *Mother*.

Postmarked: October 29, 1913, New Haven.
Dearest Kitty [addressed c/o the Jermain's at Hedge Lawn in Albany, New York.]— Saturday I saw Eleanor for about a second, and she seemed in fine form. I had to come right back here after the race so got no opportunity to do more than say, hello! I'm going down this coming Friday on some work however, and hope to have a good visit then. Thayer keeps a very discreet silence at all times. The only word I've gotten from him this year being a notice of his arrival here a couple of weeks ago. This morning a letter from K— came. She seems very happy, and all is evidently going well. I do hope you finished up at the farm without getting very tired, and that you're taking a good rest now. Be very good.   —Every devotedly, *Henry*.

Troy Road, Albany, New York, Monday, November 10th, 1913.
My dearest Eleanor—   This morning I have your two letters of Saturday & Sunday. I am so glad you have a room to yourself… I went to the Jermain Memorial Church yesterday with Aunt Marie… Will you please tell me the address of Le Marquis— Aunt Marie asked me. You can look in a telephone book… —Your own *Mother*.

Nov. 26th, 1913, Paris.
Dearest Piggychild— [to Eleanor from her sister]   Well, well, for a young lady who is supposed to have sworn off the pomps and vanities of this wicked world, & taken seriously to nursing maimed humanity, it strikes me you are having a pretty gay & lively time my love. Every letter brings me accounts of parties & football games without number. You are rolling around in carriages,

wearing orchids in your dresses, and dining un-chaperoned with good looking married gentlemen. If you don't take care we will have to take you out of the hospital & put you in a sanitarium for a little rest & cure. "Yes— my sister broke down during her training at the Presb. Hospital. They so often do you know. The rapid pace and the social demands upon them are so great." I can see myself explaining. No wonder trained nursing is very popular among the debutantes nowadays! But I hope you are enjoying yourself all the same... With a great deal of the most devoted love from us both. Your affec. *Katherine.*

1914

January 3, 1914. A very easy day. Thayer came for me. We went to luncheon together. Mother still feeling badly with headache.
January 7. My birthday & a most happy one. What a change from last year.
January 16. Left @ 2 P.M. for New Haven. Had a fine time. Mother & Henry met me. To tea together. Then to dinner at the Hemingway's and to the theater to see William Hodge.   —*Diary of Eleanor Whiteside Hobson.*

January 7, 1914, New Haven.
Dearest Kittie—   Back at work again, and hoping to live a fairly quiet life for the rest of this term... You are deserted again I suppose, Thayer having left after a very long vacation. I don't know when I'll be able to get up to see him again, but hope to do so at the time of the play anyway... Will you please just make out on a piece of paper a sort of family tree for the direct line of your decent for the last three generations. Also when were you first married. When did you go to Colo? Date of your second marriage. Year Father went to Denver. Year we left Denver. Was I there every winter up till time we left? I think that's all.   —Ever devotedly, *Henry.*

January 11, 1914, New Haven.
Dearest Kittie— ...Just to tell you I'm very well and happy and to thank you a thousand times for sending along the answers to my questions about the past. Let me know about any change in your address.   —Dearest Love, *Henry.*

January 21, 1914, New Haven.
Dearest Kittie—   You certainly are prompt in sending checks even before they are asked for. Thoughtful as ever my dear, and I thank you many times for the money which will prove very useful before long. You certainly keep me well supplied... Next year I hope to be able to live without calling on you a great deal. I get a salary of $800, I think, beside my room, and my expenses will be fairly low compared with past years. Thank you for sending K's letter which I return herewith...   —Dearest Love. Devotedly, *Henry.*

April 23, 1914, New Haven.
Dearest Kittie—   A telegram came from the Stewarts today saying Grandmother was in "very precarious condition" and that Dr. Oppenheimer was much worried over condition and the fact that she had had no reply from you to two letters, and that she wished some directions in case anything happened. The telegram requested a reply, so I wired Norma to let me know any developments and that I would communicate with you. This may be one of

Between January and April 1914 Kittie was living at the Hotel Le Marquis in New York City. After the death of her brother in 1902, there was nobody left alive who called her by that name. Consequently the children, in particular Henry, used it in their letters.

Henry Hobson when at Yale. In December 1913 he wrote to his mother, "This will stand forever for what I looked like in college."

the semi-annual scares which the Oppenheimers get, and I would not worry about it. I'm writing the Stewarts in regard to the matter and I'm sure they will take care of anything that comes up. Take your tonic regularly and be good.   —Ever devotedly, *Henry.*

April 2, 1914. A busy day on the wards with two new nurses. Went shopping with Mother in morning & helped her pack in evening.
April 12. Easter day. Nobody here seemed to feel much Easter spirit. Off 10 to 4. Church and see Mother and Henry.
April 25. Joined Mother downtown & helped her buy a suit.
—*Diary of Eleanor Whiteside Hobson.*

April 28, 1914, New Haven.
Dearest Kittie—   You have done all you possibly can for Grandma Hobson, and I'm sure she'll be all right. Mrs. O— is just half crazy, and the Stewarts say that they do not consider her "reliable." Which I suppose means she's a big liar in polite language. Bad weather here still. If we could only get some real spring it would help out a lot. How about Stamford? You must come up here while you are there.   —Dearest love, *Henry.*

Wednesday, May 6th, 1914. [a post card]
Dearest Eleanor—   Fully intended to write you a letter but I have been busy over accounts from S. Oppenheimer… Of course they are out of money & I have sent another $50.00. I wrote Virginia Wise & asked her to go to the Bank to see if Grandma had any money to her credit & who cashed her cheques in January. These things I should know…   —Much love & Many kisses. Your own devoted *Mother.*

∽ Two events:

May 7, 1914. What a day. The doctors ordered every known treatment under the sun. Got off finally at 7:30. Right to bed.—
May 14. Quite a busy day with four admissions. Wonderful time with Dr. L— & Dr. Mackenzie.
May 27. Quite a busy day. Off 11:30 — 1:00. Almost spilt blood all over Dr. Mackenzie. "Oh do I look as badly as you do?"
June 4. Had a fine sleep. At P.M. came a telegram from Mother telling of Grandma Hobson's death. Will not try to go to funeral.   —*Diary of Eleanor Whiteside Hobson.*

Grandma Hobson's death   Annie Jennings Wise Hobson, 1837–1914, was the last surviving child of Henry Alexander Wise, 1806–1876.

In May 1890 Annie Jennings Wise Hobson wrote her son about her thoughts for a memorial in the Hollywood Cemetery: "My idea is a large rustic cross on rock where the names of all can be engraved." Today the four sides of the monument read:
I) Frederick Plumer Hobson son of John Cannon and Mary M. Hobson. Born in Petersburg Va. February 24, 1833. Died in Richmond Va. April 4, 1868. "Patient in tribulation made perfect through suffering."
II) Annie J. W. Hobson April 28, 1837 June 3, 1914 — Alice Hobson Haynes October 16, 1888 May 6, 1972.
III) Rev. John Cannon Hobson, son of Frederick Plumer and Annie J. Wise Hobson — Born in Richmond Va. April 25, 1857. Died in Richmond Va. February 15, 1890. "For by Grace are ye saved through faith; It is the gift of God."

Left, Hobson family plot, Hollywood Cemetery, Richmond, Virginia. Above, grave markers for Annie Jennings Wise Hobson, 1837–1914, and Plumer Hobson, 1833–1868.

IV) Children of F. P. and A. J. W. Hobson, Born & Died at Eastwood, Goochland Co VA. —Annie Wise, Born March 4, 1860 Died Aug 16, 1868 — F. Plumer, Born July 8, 1862 Died April 27, 1863 — F. Plumer, Born July 10, 1864 Died Nov. 23, 1865 — Marianne Douglas, Born April 24, Died Sept. 2, 1866.

It is not far from the Hobson plot to the Wise plot.

Stamford, June 8th, 1914.
My dearest Eleanor—   Your letter of three o'clock in the morning is here. Do be *very* careful not to get any of those animals in your hair. It is terrible to think of today. I fear you will not be able to sleep as it is fearfully hot here & if as hot in New York you must be suffering. I had a telephone from Henry last Saturday night. He arrived in New Haven at noon. Henry reached the Chapel in Cemetery [the Hollywood Cemetery in Richmond] as the first hymn started & stood in the rear of chapel. He rode to grave with Lizzie Lyons (Mrs. J—), Mary Lyons & John Lyons— Lizzie & Mary not on speaking terms except at funerals. At the grave Henry said he stood with the other Grandchildren, Cannon, Jennings, & Alice. Grandma's death was very sudden at last. Jennings "fearfully delicate looking." Henry went out to the Stewarts & left on night train. I have asked you if you saw any furniture you cared for be sure to tell me. Of course the house will have to be given up, and furniture disposed of. And I am not going to give it away. The sale of it will help pay some debts. I shall not let sentiment play any part. Mr. F— writes Mr. Parker he can get $10,500 — $7,000 for 521. Cash & the rest in mortgage & I shall sell— that is what I paid. The Hobson children only get $2,500 between them according to Papa's will. The Trust Co. have sent me word today they will settle the matter without testamentary letters & court expenses, as Grandma left no estate and I trust the whole matter can be closed soon. Jennie Wise writes about "discretion to dispose of the furniture by auction" & "bric a brac"... "wished you would give Grandpa Wise's chair to Henry Wise." No indeed. I have a Henry Wise too & Jennie added "Aunt Annie had said she wished him to have it." It is a wonder being mine, she did not send it to him. I think I have told you everything now... —Devotedly *Mother*.

June 14, 1914, New Haven
Dearest Kitty—   Finally I've made up my two exams which I missed—written by essays, spent two sleepless night and am now practically a graduate. I'll send you the tickets for commencement tomorrow. Sorry I've not written and hope you're not worried…   Devotedly, *Henry*.

July 1, 1914. Dr. Mackenzie is certainly nice to have around.
—Diary of Eleanor Whiteside Hobson.

Postcard of the *"Old Man of the Mountain,"* postmarked, "Profile House" July 26, 1914, addressed Mrs. H. W. Hobson, Point Lookout Club Lookout, Maine. Katherine Hobson had visited the Profile House in the White Mountains of New Hampshire with her parents in 1874.

We arrived at the Profile House safely about two hours ago. The trip today was the most beautiful thing I have ever seen… Tomorrow morning we proceed. All well… Much love *T.* [Thayer Hobson]

Lookout Maine, August 31st, 1914.
My Darling Eleanor—   The past two days I have had a touch of neuralgia. I stayed in bed yesterday as it was so damp… certainly is awful this war & I hope K— is safe & well. I am going down to dinner now & Henry waits. He sends love with mine, leaves Wednesday. Paying Virginia debts. Love & kisses, *Mother*.

certainly is awful this war & I hope K— is safe & well World War I, "the war to end all wars," began in August 1914 when Austria declared war on Serbia following the assassination of Archduke Francis Ferdinand and his wife in Sarajevo. Between 1914 and 1918 twenty-eight nations issued fifty declarations of war, an estimated 10 million people were killed, and another 20 million were wounded. The United States entered the war in April 1917; an armistice was declared in November 1918; and the Treaty of Versailles was signed on June 28, 1919. During the War: While recovering from wounds, Henry Hobson received a visit from Thomas Nelson Page, the old family friend and then the American Ambassador to Italy; Thayer Hobson, also wounded during the war, was first an ambulance driver for the French army and then joined the American army after the United States entered the war;

Continued next page

Sept. 6, 1914, Deer Island, Alexandria Bay, New York. [addressed to Lookout, Maine]
Dearest Kittie—   Eleanor sent me K's letters and one from you too. Of course I was delighted to get them all. The Germans seems to be having quite a hard time, but K— is most fortunate in being provided for. I have not seen a paper for several days so don't know how things are turning out. It seems a relief to get away from the awful news..… In New Haven Mrs. Camp took me around in her machine, and we looked at places for you. The place she spoke of originally was a nice one, but all the 2nd floor rooms had been given out, and the one room left was on the 3rd floor with no bathroom up there, and I feared not very good in cold weather. So we went to other places as Mrs. Camp thought we could do much better. We found a house run by a Miss Jencks. She has a room on the 2nd floor front which really has windows on three sides, South, East & West. Mrs. Camp says people she has known have been there and said the food is excellent. Also it seemed clean and Miss Jencks seemed very nice and looked like a good housekeeper. The price is $15 a week for room & board. Mrs. Camp seemed to think it would be the best place to try, and, having talked it over with Eleanor, I decided to reserve the room temporarily until you were sure you wanted it. I did not want to run the chance of losing it. It is in a very good location… Be good and you'll be happy.   —Ever devotedly, *Henry*.

Lookout Maine, September 8th, 1914.
My Dearest Eleanor—   There is nothing especially to tell you… Virginia Wise has shipped the furniture & sold the "rubbish" for enough to pay freight & carpenter for packing. Then she sends me an old bill for spectacles for "Sally." I suppose next it will be false teeth for Sally. Thayer had a lovely birthday… We will leave here, if all is well, Monday morning, & go to the Vendome. Thayer wishes to return to the School for some tutoring in Greek & German… I can sympathize with you in seeing those little babies die. It seems

awful for you to have to see so many lives go out… —A thousand kisses & tenderest love to you my blessed Baby girl, *Mother.*

Sept. 17, 1914, New Haven.
Back at work. Everything going well… Tomorrow I'm going to look further into the question of boarding houses for you and hope we can settle things up. I'll let you know what happens. Eleanor and I had a fine time in N. Y. —Dearest love, *Henry.*

Hotel Vendome, Boston, September 18th, 1914.
My dearest Eleanor—
This morning I had a letter from Henry & yesterday one from you & thought I am so glad you went to the theatre… This is such a quiet comfortable Hotel & excellent food. The porcelain filling has come off my front tooth and I am going to have the repair work done here. I have a very pretty room & bath on 2nd floor— looking out on Commonwealth Ave. The weather is lovely. I trust it will last for your trip to Oyster Bay… I have a long letter from Virginia Wise to answer, so I will stop. Love & many kisses… —Your own loving *Mother.*

Hotel Vendome, Boston, Wednesday evening, 1914.
Darling Child—   There is not a blessed thing to write except I have just written Virginia Wise & paid her in full & paid the Dr. Hawkins $150.00. It just makes me sick to have to pay bills that run back, as his does, to 1910. I also told Virginia to ship the chair to Henry… Your own devoted *Muzzie.*

Sept. 23, 1914, New Haven.
Dearest Kittie—   …Today I found a lovely place for you to stay, or rather Mrs. Camp found it. It's much nicer than the other place, and I hope to close the deal tomorrow. Very nice house and they say the food is splendid. Hope you're well… —Dearest love, *Henry.*

Oct. 22, 1914, New Haven.
Dearest Kittie—   Now that you've finally set a date for your arrival I feel that you are very much nearer. Of course there is nothing which could possibly make your coming "inconvenient." You will be a great help and of course understand when I can and when I can not be with you… I have told your people at 120 Cottage Street that you will arrive next Monday, and they will be all ready for you including the fat man and his daughter of 16 whom I've not seen… Yesterday Eleanor telephoned me just to talk a little. It was good to hear her voice.   —Every devotedly, *Henry.*

Oct. 27, 1914.
WESTERN UNION DAY LETTER
To: Mrs. Henry W. Hobson, Hotel Vendome, Boston.
Sorry you could not come today. Hope you will feel all right tomorrow. I have important meeting at 5 o'clock… Wire me which train you will take. —*H. W. Hobson.*

Oct. 31, 1914, New Haven. *SPECIAL DELIVERY*
Dearest Kittie—   …I'm terribly sorry you've been feeling badly, and I think I ought to take a trip to Boston to see how you really are. I can't break away from here just now

George Mackenzie, a physician in the U. S. Navy, participated in a number of experiments including one during which the submarine that he was on broke the time record for being submerged; and Katherine remained in Germany married to Herbert Kraus who, at the end of the war, was a member of the German delegation at the Peace Conference that ended with the Treaty of Versailles.

In the fall of 1914 Kittie was in Boston, staying at the Hotel Vendome and mail was sent to her there.

Muzzie   Katherine Hobson occasionally, but rarely, signed her letters this way.

however. The people at 120 Cottage Street don't think I have a mother. Day before yesterday I told Mrs. Camp you were coming at five and she sent the car down to the station to meet you— so you see what a royal welcome you missed... I do hope your head is better now and that by Monday you'll be feeling very well again. It's a shame to have you laid up at this time.... —Every devotedly, *Henry.*

Dec. 3, 1914.
THE WESTERN UNION TELEGRAPH COMPANY
TO: MRS. H. W. HOBSON 120 Cottage Street, New Haven.
Many Many Happy returns. Be good and you will be happy.   —*Henry.*

Hotel Vendome, Boston, December 10th, 1914.
My dearest Eleanor—   ...Have just paid another drug bill for A.J.W.H.— $35.00— There seems no end of them.   —Love & many kisses, Your own *Mother.*

December 31, 1914. Good bye year. You've taught me lots & have held lots of joys. Thank God for my family & all my blessings. Here's to the new year!
—*Diary of Eleanor Whiteside Hobson.*

1915

May 25, 1915. Henry telephoned Mother had burned her hand. Went up at two o'clock returning at 8. Condition nervous & upsetting.
May 31. Went to see Dr. Fisk in my time off. To supper at hotel with Mother and Henry. Quite a strain all-together.
June 24. Dr. MacDonald telephoned Mother was better— worked harder & felt better all day.
July 12. Another busy day. A short talk with G.M.M. [George Miner Mackenzie]
July 31. Hot as Tophet. At 3:30 started for Central Valley. Mother's condition generally improved. Lovely trip back at night.
August 21. Henry came at one & we had splendid trip to Central Valley. Mother much better. Poured coming back.   —*Diary of Eleanor Whiteside Hobson.*

Central Valley By this time Katherine Thayer Hobson was in a nursing home in Central Valley, New York.

Undated, 1915.
Dear Eleanor—   Can you get off Sunday evening for a short dinner and a walk by the ocean at Long Beach? I thought that if we could catch a train about 5:00 o'clock, we could get back in time to avoid a late pass. If you have plans to go to Central Valley or anywhere else, don't think of letting this interfere. I shall understand. It is barely possible, too, that I may have to go to Monroe... You had a rather dull and stupid companion Wednesday evening, I am afraid. Please forgive me... I have thought of you in that frightful operating room during this weather, and do hope you are not going to be used up by it. Possibly Long Beach will refresh you a bit. Hoping that you will be able to come— *George.* [George Mackenzie]

Eleanor Whiteside Hobson became engaged to George Miner Mackenzie on September 20, 1915, during an evening at Long Beach.

September 20, 1915. Six solid hours scrubbing. Great to be a trained nurse. Off with George for the evening. I know not where. The night of nights. Sep. 20 A happy happy day.   —*Diary of Eleanor Whiteside Hobson.*

September 21, 1915. Spent all day long thinking about tonight. A nice letter. Henry telephoned from New Haven. Glad he is not coming tonight though.
—Diary of Eleanor Whiteside Hobson.

Undated, 1915.
My darling George—   The first day of our happiness must not close without a word to you. All day long I have been trying to realize that yesterday was a reality. Scrubbing doesn't take much intellect so practically all day I have been with you in thought trying to fathom the feeling of quiet joyful happiness which seems to predominate in everything I do. I have wondered lots of times what it would feel like to be engaged, so far I can't realize that I really am… God has been good to send me this joy, and I hope he will make me worthy of your love. I don't think I ever realized the full significance of that quotation about "thoughts too deep for words." If yesterday all was a dream, it was a wonderful one. Good-night George. I love you. *Eleanor.* P.S. If you don't want this letter send it back…

THE WESTERN UNION TELEGRAPH COMPANY Central Valley, New York.
Sept. 22, 1915.
TO: Miss Eleanor Hobson   —Hearty congratulations on your two completed years. Dearest love. Well. *Mother.*

September 22, 1915. Washed my hair. Wrote K— & T— the important news… Thought of somebody lots.
September 23. Henry came & we dined together. Met George at 9 P.M. & we had a nice talk together. Henry very much pleased.   —Diary of Eleanor Whiteside Hobson.

☙ To a future Mother-in-law:

September 27, 1915.
My dear Mrs. Mackenzie—   Thank you so much for your sweet note of congratulations. I fully appreciate how hard it is for you all to have George become engaged to somebody about whom you know nothing. He is so splendid in every way that I couldn't help loving him, and my only hope now is that I am worthy of making him happy. Neither of us can quite realize that we are engaged yet, but we are very happy… Affectionately, *Eleanor. W. Hobson.*

September 28, 1915.
My Dearest-one—   It is ten fifteen and we are just off. Aside from loving you it is a great thing to be as happy as I am because you don't get tired… I haven't had time to look for my star tonight but I know it is up there shining as brightly as my love for you is burning. I don't quite understand it yet but it is there somewhere… —Your *Eleanor*

September 29, 1915. Dinner with Mr. Parker & the evening with the nicest man in the world.
September 30. Nice letter from George's father. Made out list of engagement announcements.

Drawing of a young George M. Mackenzie found in the letters.

October 1. Went to Central Valley to tell Mother. Found her better than I expected. George went over to Jersey City. Home late with a pass.
October 23. Went up to see Mother. Found her lonely & depressed. Left at six… A beautiful evening with my George.
—*Diary of Eleanor Whiteside Hobson.*

Undated, 1915.
Eleanor, my darling— Enclosed is a letter to your mother which I hope will be all right. If it does not meet with your approval send it back and I will write another and give it to you on the train. I am uncertain whether I have said enough or too much or the wrong things entirely, but anyhow I know this— that what seemed impossible yesterday has happened. I love you more today than I did yesterday. As for proving that you love me more that I love you— it simply can't be done; but let's not have our first quarrel about that; I am too happy to think that you love me at all. If Dr. Draper should return on Saturday would you care to make a quick trip to Monroe Sunday afternoon and see the whole family ensemble? …Ever your devoted *George.*

My Beloved Eleanor— There are a few very practical things which you and your brothers are entitled to know, so perhaps for a page or two I had better confine myself to giving you a few facts which probably you will want to know when you talk to Henry. You must have surmised that I am not rich. I haven't chosen a lucrative profession and I haven't the slightest expectation of ever inheriting anything. My family is poor and so am I. Whatever I get, I shall have to make. At present I receive $1,500 a year from the medical school and $1,200 from Dr. Draper. In addition to this I have what I make out of my own practice amounting this year I expect to about $1,200. I owe a little over $2,000 which I borrowed to go through the medical school and hospital. This I have been paying off at the rate of about $75 a month. So far as my financial condition and prospects are concerned I think this is all. There are other things which you probably will want to know and I shall tell you everything as soon as we have an opportunity. Please forgive this cold business letter and destroy it at once if you want to. I trust you understand my motive in writing thus. Your devoted *George.*

Mrs. Henry Wise Hobson, of Colorado Springs, announces the engagement of her daughter, Miss Eleanor Whiteside Hobson, to Dr. George M. Mackenzie, of 131 East Sixty-seventh Street, this city. No date has been set for the wedding.
—*Unidentified newspaper clipping.*

My Beloved Eleanor— When I come tomorrow night will you please bring the book of your father's letters down with you? I am anxious to read them… Tonight I looked up at your bright little star in the east and quite near it, the same old moon, sending down the same soft light that lighted the beach just four weeks ago tonight. The whole scene comes back so clearly— the silent walk, the great flood of love that I could not hold back, the awkward proposal, your lovely face turned up to the moonlight and looking almost frightened, the words that came so sweetly and slowly— "I have for a long time, George" and then the wonderful joy as the realization that you love me and that you were to be mine and I, yours, came over me. Since then dearest Eleanor, life has meant so much more to live for and strive for; and I have

the whole family ensemble George Mackenzie had four brothers and three sisters.

been so richly blessed with happiness, that I can never put in words what you have brought into my life. But this you know, that I love you with the deepest and strongest love a man is capable of, and I always shall. No matter what the future may have in store for us, you can always be sure of that. Good night, dear love, sweet sleep. Your devoted *George.*

Sept. 29th., 1915, Dresden.
Dearest Piggy—   The noon mail brought me your letter of Sept 5th— and I feel quite spoiled, having received three missives from you, and one from each of the boys during the last week. I also heard from Mother— a painful, you could hardly call it an epistle. Written chiefly in German, and only decipherable in spots. Herbert thought I ought to send it to you— so perhaps I will enclose it. I may be lacking in ingenuity, but can make nothing of the whole. The first page is dated August 29th. The middle, June 16th— part of it seems to be addressed to me, part to my Mother-in-law. There is evidently a description of Marschall's Infirmary & much allusion to "Golt" but the German is so extraordinary that I have wondered whether she were trying to write in that way on purpose, with the idea that the people in the Sanatorium would not be able to read it. Otherwise it throws a merciless light on what her condition still must be. Poor Lady!

   I sense a more intense tragedy in the fall this year than I ever did before. This earth in its red & golden glory of death seems an allegory of the thousands of vital young lives which are falling even as leaves, never more gloriously vital than in the hour of destruction. The French & English are trying their long announced offensive & the fighting in the West must be terrible. With tremendous losses of course on both sides. There is nothing to do but stave it off to the best of our ability… I think there is a possibility of at least peace in sight… I am very sorry that I am not in New York to take a tender and intelligent interest in your wardrobe— remodeling is especially in my line! I even have further designs on my eternal suit— once terracotta. It is so convenient to really wear out your old things. My principle nowadays— borrowed from the Parisians— is to have very few clothes, but have them chic. I have been bogged up with too many dresses all my life. And was forever carting trunks of passé garments around the globe— in excellent condition (they were so rarely worn!) but unaltered from season to season. But the supper hour approaches, so fare thee well my dear. With a great deal of love and kisses.   —Always affec. *Katherine.*

October 11, 1915, Dresden.
Dearest Henry—   Your letter of Sept 23rd arrived two days ago while I was at supper. I had a momentous feeling when I looked at it— and instead of putting it by my plate to anticipate over— as is my habit— I tore it open with a jumpy sensation, glanced down the first page & exclaimed— "Oh my prophetic soul— Mackenzie!" I can't say I was very much surprised. You & Thayer may remember my telling Eleanor she would end by marrying a doctor if she studied trained nursing— and I have been more or less awaiting his entrance on the scene ever since. Lately Sandy (my name for G. M. so that Eleanor won't think my letters to Thayer are intended for her fiancé & be jealous) aroused my suspicions to such an extent that I felt positively impelled to write E— an epistle on the pitfalls of matrimony but ten days ago. Never

Sandy For unknown reasons, Katherine's letters to her sister refer to George Mackenzie, Eleanor's fiancé, as "Sandy." He was never known by that name.

dreaming the die was already cast! It was a noble effort, but I can easily imagine it will not arouse much recognition in these early lyric days of her engagement. However, they say nothing is ever lost— so unless she destroys it, as she did all the lovely missives I wrote her when she was at St. Timothy's, perhaps her children will find it in a trunk in the attic and be saved from an impulse to do something really rash— such as eloping with father's chauffeur. Well, all things considered, I am very glad if Eleanor has found a good man, who is worthy of her, and is happy in his love. She has managed the affair with truly twentieth century independence, but apparently Sandy is a highly respectable member of society, and I am somewhat soothed by his making such a favorable impression on you in two hours! A few more intimate details concerning his person would be gratefully received however. And I wish to heaven I were where I could have the pleasure of meeting him! …I've received so many letters from you recently that I feel quite chummy. With a great deal of my best love. Yours affec, *Katherine*.

October 16, 1915.
My own precious George—   …Dearest man the ring is exquisite. Do you know of what it reminded me right away? My little star— and the best part of it is that it can't go under a cloud, but every time I look at it sends back its sparkling reassurance of your love. The part I like too about it is that it is all your choice and it is just as clear and pure as you are. Sometimes it almost scares me to think how fine you are. Don't worry about its being too tight, it is exactly right. I have had a lovely afternoon thinking about you constantly and looking forward to tomorrow night. I want to talk to you about several rather important things. The great trouble is that whenever I am with you I usually can't think of anything but perfect happiness. Good night with all my heart— *Your wife to be*.

October 17, 1915.
My dearest-one—   How I hated to leave you today… Four weeks ago tonight we really began to know each other. Dear old Long Beach never saw two happier people I am sure… Ever devotedly, *Eleanor*.

October 24, 1915.
Dearest George—   …It is getting on in time but going to sleep doesn't seem quite right unless I have really bid you good night… Mr. Sandman is very persistent just now and all I can think of is a pair of little sticks with which to prop my eyes open… As ever devotedly, *Eleanor*.

∽ Letters from his future in-laws:

Brookwood on Otsego Lake, Thursday [undated]
Dear George—   Eleanor's letter came a couple of hours ago and you do not know how glad I am that between you, you pulled it off. It is not a complete surprise, as I told Eleanor some time ago that you were the one man that I knew whom I would really want her to marry. But seriously, I am happier than I have been for a long time. For years I have unconsciously measured every girl I have met by a standard and an ideal of Eleanor, and if I did not know that she was marrying someone who really was worth her, I

Francis Thayer Hobson, date unknown.

would be wretched. You will love her more every day, just as we all do. I am not going to say that I hope you will be happy, because I know you will. I have always thought that when Eleanor became engaged, that I would feel sort of an empty place in my life, but on the contrary it does seem just the opposite. I can't help but feel that after the way I talked to Eleanor on the trip that you have chiefly me to thank for her accepting you!! She *is* pretty fresh at times George and you will have a hard time keeping her where she belongs. I speak, from eighteen years of hard and sad experience. Affectionately, *Thayer Hobson.*

October 18, 1915, Dresden.
Dear George Mackenzie—   You surely will not object to our beginning our acquaintance, and what I sincerely hope will prove a warm friendship and affection, on informal lines? To be frank, my knowledge of you is as yet rather fragmentary, occasional references to you in Eleanor's letters, rather frequent of late, so that not ten days past I felt constrained to write her an epistle, much in the spirit of St. Paul, on the subject of matrimony… I have no doubt that you are individually altogether delightful. The fact that you were able to win Eleanor is as great a compliment as any man could aspire to, and you succeeded in making an excellent impression on Henry in two hours! …I am sure Eleanor never would have promised to marry you had she not believed you worthy of her ideals… I think you will discover that the longer you know her, the more cause you have for congratulation. Living up to a woman like Eleanor, for she will demand that you amount to a great deal in yourself, will not be easy work. But there is no impetus on earth stronger than the ambition to achieve the ideal others hold of us… But now I must get this off with a letter to Eleanor, so please accept my heartiest good wishes & love before closing, Affectionately, *Katherine Kraus.*

November 7, 1915, Dresden.
My dearest Piggy—   Your last letter sounded happy in the extreme, and I am delighted that you should be— while hoping for the sake of all concerned that you will not actually reach the exploding point! Don't allow Mrs. Mackenzie or individuals like Dr. Fisk to persuade you to marry before graduating however. And if Sandy grows impatient, try knocking him over the head. It would be a thousand pities were you not to complete your training course to which you have devoted two & a half years— plus every thought & effort. And I trust you & Sandy are both sensible enough not to succumb to a triumph of matter over mind. Besides which— all-important and in view— make the most of the present beloved. Believe me, though you won't until well married, there is no period in a woman's life quite as exquisite as that of her engagement. No man will ever recognize this fact— the subconscious foundation of his desire is for someone to minister to his bodily & in modern days— spiritual needs. Courtship is a means towards securing the coveted mate & as such pleasant— but once he has her, he feels he can afford to settle down & be comfortable, while a woman always craves a lover… Marriage can prove a fine epic, or a good strong prose. There are times when a guide, philosopher & friend is more appreciated than a shepherd from Arcady. But Love's perfect moment is the anticipation of its fulfillment… So I better curtail my philosophical advice. Five years hence you will look back tenderly on your

Embassy of the United States of America
My Dearest Eleanor—   It gave us a great deal of pleasure to know the happiness that has come into your life… You are all very near to us and I am ready to accept Dr. Mackenzie and adopt him into the family. Give him my warmest congratulations. I think of you all often… the things which I dwell on most are the old things and your dear Father, then your dear Mother and then you children… I often think of little Katherine and hope she is well and happy— as happy as anyone can be in this dreadful time…

   Your devoted *Uncle Tom*
   [Thomas Nelson Page, United States Ambassador to Italy]

"first fine careless rapture." It never comes but once with the same man, *bien entendu*. Cynicism! Horrible!! "Spare us Good Lord!" I apologize most humbly. I am sure Sandy is an exception to every rule governing the average masculine being— and your ring must be lovely from your description…
—Always affec, *Katherine*.

November 4, 1915.
My dearest George—   …It came to me suddenly today that I had been offered the most important position in the world, namely that of being your wife. As usual the responsibility quite awed me. Oh foolish man reconsider! (Don't you dare!) Good-bye. I'd kiss you on Broadway if I could be with you tonight. Devotedly, *Eleanor*.

November 9, 1915. Thayer broke his leg yesterday.
November 12. At noon got letter from Central Valley which made things pretty gloomy. Dinner at the Howe's with George & Jim.
November 17. Thayer operated on & all went well. Henry down from New Haven. George wonderful as always.   —*Diary of Eleanor Whiteside Hobson.*

November 19, 1915.
Dearest Eleanor—   Don't be alarmed by the arrival of this letter. There is nothing in particular that I want to write you or ask you, but after a busy and rather hurried day, brightened by only two brief glimpses of you, I just wanted to sit down quietly for a few minutes before turning in and send you a heart full of fondest love. To bid you good night and write you a page or two about the love that has brought so much joy into my life always completes the day for me with a feeling of happiness. Happy is the man who finds what everyone longs for and so few ever find— a friend so good and true that all the feelings and facts of life are shared! a friend on whom one can always rely whatever befalls and for whom one strives with the greatest joy; to have our soul and our spirit to love and be loved from the depths of the heart— this is the God-given happiness that makes life worth while… Ever your *George*.

November 24th, 1915, Dresden.
My dearest Piggy—   The most interesting event of today was a letter from Henry this morning— otherwise it was uneventful. The dear boy gave me some affectionate advice about not getting in the way of a march of the allies, if I went to Belgium. I did not think anyone, except possibly certain uninformed classes of the allies, believed in such a possibility anymore, but you must console & cheer the family if I should ever arrive in Brussels. The only danger there would be aviators— but you can count on my making for the nearest cellar— not the roof-top like Herbert— on the first alarm… It is sad that dear Mother's progress is not more marked— from Henry's description of the visit you paid her together, I should not imagine there was any change to speak of in her mental condition, but I suppose every trouble of that kind relieves its grip very slowly & almost imperceptibly. In writing her I never have alluded to her being unwell or in the sanitorium, especially as I was unable to read the letters she wrote me on the subject & I am uncertain of my cue. I only hope she does not think me indifferent on the subject however. The pictures Henry sent me of the sanitorium never reached me, so I would

Thayer operated on   Thayer Hobson was hospitalized for three days at the Presbyterian Hospital in New York City where his sister, Eleanor, was a nursing student. The total hospital bill was $48.55 which included 5¢ for phone calls.

be glad if he would forward some more. And talking about pictures, do hurry up with a photograph of your doctor man. I am simply expiring with curiosity to see what he looks like… —With my very best love & kisses— also to Sandy. Affec. *Katherine.*

❧ Death in the family:

December 1, 1915. Dr. MacDonald telephoned that Mother was worse. Dr. Lambert went to Central Valley.
December 2. Left at one for Central Valley. Dear little Mother! These last few hours will mean so much all my life.
December 3. God took Mother.
December 4. To Albany see Mother & the boys.
December 5. Black. —*Diary of Eleanor Whiteside Hobson.*

Marie Jermain, November 1918.

December 4, 1915.
My darling [Eleanor Hobson to George Mackenzie]— Before the day starts I must write you a line. It is a little before seven. All the valley is grey this morning with hardly enough light to write. I didn't go to bed very early because I had to talk with the boys about some things before the outside world rushed in again to try to help. Then too I had to write to Katherine. When I did go to bed though it was to sleep and rest until now when I woke. My first thought was of my sorrow. My second thought was of you my precious love. Always to have you to love me! My but the wonder and glory of it makes me gasp. The feeling of your arms around me always give me the sensation of being transplanted to another world… Will you trouble to have notices put in the papers. I don't know just the form so change it as you think best. —*Hobson, Katherine Thayer wife of Henry Wise Hobson born Dec. 3rd 1859. Died Dec. 3rd 1915. Funeral and internment Troy, New York.* —Please excuse this paper. It was all I could find. The world has come in already. Goodbye my precious one. My love goes to you every minute. With all my heart I am Your *Eleanor.*

Katherine Hobson's illness and death were due to complications from pernicious anemia. She died on her birthday.

December 5, 1915, Hedge Lawn, Troy Road, Albany, New York.
My own dearest Man— …Today is very grey. William Johnston drove us out to the cemetery this morning and then back by the old house where Mother lived as a girl. Aunt Marie wanted us to bring Mother right here which we did. It is so lovely to have her near these last few days. All is peace and, really precious one, in spite of my grief I feel full of joy and thankfulness to God today. Last night I didn't sleep very well but I didn't mind because there was no worry and anxiety but perfect peace and confidence. Then too I dreamed of you and thanked God for you so many times… As ever your *Eleanor.*

December 5, 1915, Hedge Lawn.
My darling— Your letter awaited me and brought me just the reassurance of your love that must always make me inwardly rejoice… We reached here without difficulty at 2 o'clock and dear little Mother is now in the library so quiet and peaceful with lovely white lilies around her. The boys have gone to Albany to try to get clothes & I am on the way to Troy… The woman in Troy

Hedge Lawn.

to whom I am going for the clothes was a little girl in whom my Great Grandmother [Sophia Whiteside McKie] took a great interest and taught to sew. The coachman [William Johnston] at Miss Jermain's was my Grandfather's [Francis S. Thayer] coachman for years. He met us at the station, his eyes full of tears. On the way out he told of scolding Mother as a little girl for taking the stable tools away. It is lovely to be here among those who loved her and those before her. The funeral is Tuesday at two… Your ring is shining up at me as bright, clear, and beautiful as always. I don't think I ever had a gift like the one you gave me before… Good night. Love from my whole heart, your *Eleanor.*

༄ Obituary:

Mrs. Katherine Thayer Hobson, a former well-known resident of this city, died Friday at Central Valley, N. Y., where she had been ill for some months. Mrs. Hobson was born in Troy fifty-six years ago, her father being the late Senator Francis S. Thayer. Her mother, whose maiden name was Catherine Whiteside McKie, was a member of the Whiteside and McKie families of Washington County. Mrs. Hobson was educated at the Emma Willard Seminary and during her residence in Troy was a member of the First Presbyterian Church, of which her father was for many years a member of the Board of Elders. She was married twice. Her first husband was the late Barclay Jermain of the Albany Road. Some years after his death she married Henry Wise Hobson, a prominent lawyer of Denver, Col., and a grandson of former Governor Wise of Virginia. Mr. Hobson died a number of years ago. Since that time Mrs. Hobson had maintained a residence in Colorado Springs, Col., and also the ancestral home in Easton, Washington County, which had been in the Whiteside family during three centuries, and where she with her family spent occasional summers. She also spent much time in Germany, where some of her children were educated and where one daughter now resides. She is survived by two sons, Henry Wise Hobson and Francis Thayer Hobson, and two daughters, Miss Eleanor W. Hobson and Mrs. Katherine T. Kraus, the latter being the wife of Dr. Herbert Kraus of the University of Leipsic [Leipzig], Germany. Mrs. Jared L. Bacon of this city is a cousin of the deceased. The remains will be brought to Troy for interment in the family plot at Oakwood, and the funeral services will be held in the Earl Memorial Chapel tomorrow afternoon at 2 o'clock. The officiating clergyman will be Rev. C. M. Addison of Stamford, Conn., a cousin of Mrs. Hobson. Carriages will be waiting at the Oakwood Avenue entrance to the cemetery to convey any friends to the chapel.

—*An unidentified newspaper clipping.*

Following the death of Katherine Thayer Hobson, Eleanor and the other children were uncertain as to where their mother's body should be taken. After talking with "Aunt Marie," Marie Jermain, the sister of Barclay Jermain, Katherine's first husband, the body was taken to Hedge Lawn, the Jermain family home near Albany, New York. From there the body was taken to the Oakwood Cemetery in Troy, New York, where she was buried in the Thayer family plot with her parents and beside Henry Wise Hobson, her second husband and the father of her four children.

December 6, 1915. Black.
December 7. Mother's funeral.   —*Diary of Eleanor Whiteside Hobson.*

December 7, 1915, Dresden.
My own beloved children—   Your cable arrived early this morning— and I knew as soon as the maid said "a telegram" what had happened! I have been so terribly anxious about the family for the last weeks— first Thayer, & latterly our dearest Mother. On her birthday I dreampt I saw Jack Wise & he told me that Mother was so low that she would not live until I got home— and when the news of Thayer's operation came Sunday morning, I wrote Herbert that I was now simply in agony for fear something had happened to her too. Oh, dearest ones, my heart seems full to the breaking point— as heavy

Dresden, Nov. 3rd, 1915
My own sweet beloved Mother—   In order to be quite sure of your having this letter by your birthday I am taking the precaution of writing it a whole month in advance! I wish I could fold myself up in it, plus a magic spell to render me invisible so that the censor would not send me back as "too long" …this idea not seeming quite practical on account of my awkward dimensions. I am

Continued on next page

as yours must be in our mutual sorrow and loss. And were it not for the fact that I feel Mother may have been spared a great deal by this sudden release from every human trouble, I do not know how I should bear it— for no one in heaven or earth has ever meant quite as much to me as Mother. Especially during the last few years, when instead of accepting her supreme devotion with the matter of factness of childhood, I have realized more fully what it really meant— and what an adorable exquisite creature she was. Only you three know what she was too— what has gone out of our lives. No other soul, who has not been nursed at her breast & cradled by her love through the happiest of childhoods, can even in the deepest sympathy understand the supreme role she has played in our past or what we must always miss in the future. And I would to God I were with you today, when you are laying the dear, dear lady which has been her visible self beside Papa & her own family… It is so desperately hard for me to feel I will never see her again in this world— nobody has every guessed how homesick I have been during this interminable separation— how much I wished to go home. But at the beginning of the war I thought it my duty to stay here— and since her late illness I thought I better wait till she was a little better as she would wish me to help her leave the sanitarium, and my refusal to do so would only distress her, and temporarily affect her attitude towards me. At a distance she at least had the consolation & diversion of my letters. And now it is too late! I try to tell myself that my last memory of her is a happy one however. And we must all be brave together. With my whole heart's love— Always your ever affect, *Katherine*.

Undated
Dearest Eleanor—   I have just reached home and found here upon my arrival a telegram from one of the Brook Hill aunts inquiring about your mother. Although Henry had probably sent her word already, I wired her too. My dear brave girl, how I admired and loved you in the midst of your great grief, and was so filled with a helpless longing to make it easier for you. To see you suffering makes my heart ache for you. God gave you a nature that feels deeply and loves unselfishly and with such a noble spirit the great sorrow of such a loss strikes deeper than with most people; but He also gave you an unconquerable fortitude which bears bravely and helps others to bear the bereavement which He has willed to be a necessary accompaniment of going through life. Did you ever stop to think dearest, that the loss of parents is the price that every living thing must pay for the privilege of life? Remember the joy and blessing of having such a mother and all the beautiful memories of her life. As I looked on the quiet beautiful features, it all seemed so plain. The wonderful mother had passed on to her children the pure noble spirit of a beautiful life. I knew then that I should have loved your mother for herself and a thousand times more because of you. Good night, Eleanor my love. God be with you. How I wish I had the power, as I have the desire, to make it easier for you to bear. You know I love you with all my heart… Happy days and happy years together are in store for us, I am sure, Eleanor. The clouds are very dark and heavy now, but soon the sun will shine through again and all will be light and sun-shine and happiness; and the dreary days of sorrow only a memory… Be brave. I know you will. With a heart full of love and sympathy, Ever your devoted *George*.

at least packing in every specimen and variety of love & good wishes. May you have many happy returns of the day… I am enclosing an imaginary birthday cake— it has white frosting with pink ornaments… When I realize it is over two years since we were together, I feel like breaking up the furniture. In some ways it does not seem so long, for I think of you constantly & write to you often, but occasions of this kind, when I suddenly discover I do not know what your immediate needs & wishes are, make it seem an eternity! …You know I love you devotedly & tenderly— beyond the power of all human expression & it would take more than a universe of oceans to divide us in our affection. With all the love in the world & a thousand greetings. I kiss & hug you again & again— Always your own *Weanie*.

Graves of Henry Wise Hobson, 1858–1898, and Katherine Thayer Hobson, 1859–1915, Thayer family plot, Oakwood Cemetery, Troy, New York.

December 8, 1915. In Albany.
December 9. In Albany.
December 10. In Albany.
December 11. In Albany.   —*Diary of Eleanor Whiteside Hobson.*

 ~ To a future mother-in-law:

Hedge Lawn, December 9th, 1915.
Dear Mamma—   May I call you that now? In these last few days George has grown so much nearer me that I feel as if all that belongs to him must also belong to me. On Monday I return to the hospital but I am sending Thayer to you if I may. I feel that at his age he rather belongs to me. He speaks so often of how fond he is of you all and I know how much a few days with you all would mean. Thank you so much. Always affectionately, *Eleanor.*

Hedge Lawn, December 9th, 1915.
My dearest George—   About an hour ago I heard the man just starting for Albany… I have been writing notes all the morning. The more I write it seems to me the more I miss Mother. Consequently I turn from my great sorrow to you my greatest joy in life… Miss Jermain has caught cold and Thayer and I both feel guilty. We almost choke ourselves trying to prevent coughing. Poor little Thayer. He has had a hard winter and shows it… What a letter this is. No matter how many faults it has, of one thing be assured— I love you dearest with all my heart and soul. Your *Eleanor.*

December 10th, Hedge Lawn, Troy Road, Albany, New York
My dearest George— Just now I finished the fiftieth note of thanks and until the postman comes I have no more to write… A week today since this new sorrow came. It seems a thousand years ago and yet only a moment… —*Eleanor.*

December 10, 1915.
My dearest Eleanor—   What a day this has been— one of those double starred, red letter, never-to-be-forgotten, super-days. This morning first thing I received three letters from you all at once. Never did any man get such a happiness-laden mail as this. I turned them over one by one, looked at the dates on the postmarks and wondered what such a deluge of joy could mean. Of course I have been gay and happy all day— as much, at any rate, as is possible in your absence. Your little star is twinkling away tonight as brightly as ever and gave me a friendly greeting as I came home from the seminar. It is about the luckiest little star in the sky to have been adopted by you. It twinkles and shines so brightly, I guess, because it is so happy in belonging to you. Leaving out the twinkling and shining and it is just like me… I hope that miserable cough is better and that you are fast getting rested and back again to your usual blooming health… With affectionate devotion, *George.*

December 12, 1915. In Albany.
December 13. Returned to New York.
December 14. Back to work.
December 17. A terrible terrible day. Wept hard.
December 18. Things went better today. Out in evening with George.
   —*Diary of Eleanor Whiteside Hobson.*

December 13, 1915, Dresden.
Dearest Piggychild—   It is after six o'clock… When I am busy with my modeling I can forget what has happened sometimes— but although I try to believe that perhaps it is better for Mother as it is, at other moments I wander around feeling as if a part of myself had gone with her. And in looking back it seems as if I had left much undone which might have contributed to her greater happiness when she was alive. Perhaps the latter is a universal experience. I had a notice of Mother's death put in the paper, as she had been here for so long, & had quite a number of friends in Dresden. These people have written me with great regret of her death & everyone who had known her spoke of her wonderful charm & sweetness. I do not think I ever met a woman in whom personal magnetism was quite so highly developed. We, as her children, were too accustomed to it to fully recognize her powers— but everywhere she went in her old well days, the rest of the world was absolutely fascinated by that intangible something… I think of you constantly my dearest ones & wish I were with you. I am glad we have George to take care of & comfort you— for his affection will be your greatest support in these days…   —With a great deal of the most devoted love & kisses— Always affec. *Katherine.*

Dec. 29th, 1915, Dresden.
My own beloved Piggy—   When I came home last evening I found your letter of Dec. 3rd, telling me how dearest Mother had passed from us. I am glad, so glad that you & Henry were with her— and that she was her own sweet self again before her life ebbed gently away. I had been half afraid that as the end came so suddenly you might not have been able to get there. Such a death is very gentle & beautiful for the person concerned I know— and for Mother's sake I am thankful she was spared any suffering, & is now at rest— but it is very hard for those left behind in this world, & from the terrible loneliness in my own heart, I realize what your sorrow must be also. It seems so strange to me that with all the doctors you consulted on Mother's account, nobody should have suspected the existence of progressive pernicious anemia— for she must have suffered from it for a long period. If it only could have been discovered a little earlier! It would not have saved Mother, but I could have gotten home & seen her once again. Had I known she had any fatal trouble, fifty thousand wars could not have kept me away from America— as it was, the combination of circumstances & the feeling I could do nothing but antagonize her possibly by coming home before she was better, I waited. And now I shall go through life wishing I had acted otherwise! It hurts me so to feel that the dear tender creature had to ask about my letters, and I myself not be with her when she was dying! For I loved her better than anyone in heaven or earth.   —With my whole heart, Piggy dear, Always your *Katherine.*

1916

January 18, 1916, Dresden.
Dearest Piggy—   …I cannot tell you how thankful I am that your letters telling me of dearest Mother's death & funeral happened to slip through. I might still be sitting here waiting for news if they had missed the steamer they came by! And that would have been awful. I dream constantly of Mother, but

Katherine Kraus, photograph by Hugo Erfurth, Dresden 1929, where she was a sculptor and often had models posing in her studio.

always of her ill and nervous-distorted visions shadowed by half consciousness of reality, from which I usually wake with a sense of relief in feeling she is at rest… Occasionally my dreams are dreadful— almost nightmares. And yet in the midst of these I am so glad to see her again— for life seems so changed since she has gone out of it. With a great deal of the most devoted love & lots of kisses Piggy dear— always affec.. your *Katherine.*

January 19, 1916.
Dearest Darling-of-my-Heart—   Four months ago today! The memory of that moonlight scene beside the misty ocean when our lives became united in a confession and a pledge of love comes back to me to-day with a fuller and a sweeter meaning. All that has happened since that hour has brought home to me the realization of the things that make life worthwhile. The love of a beautiful woman— pure, unselfish and loving, and the happiness of giving ones whole heart and soul to the woman loved and admired more than anything else on earth— these are true values in life… Four months ago today! What happy and wonderful months for me. May all our months and years be as full or fuller of happiness and love. Good night, my dearest, Always your devoted, *George.*

February 3, 1916, Dresden.
My dear beloved Piggy—   It is two months since dearest Mother was taken from us, and I know you are thinking of that day & the changes it brought into our lives. Half the time I cannot realize she is really gone— for I had not heard from her regularly since last spring, and consequently there is no outward difference— and the other half is bitter with the consciousness of what is, and that I must live on without her. It is so difficult to accept the inevitable as irrevocable. There is some optimistic element in us which keeps crying— "It can't be so! It can't be so!" until time has softened the first violence of our grief & we have grown accustomed to that we were loth to believe. —Always your own *Katherine.*

February 17, 1916, Dresden.
My own beloved Piggychild—   Last evening when I came home, Herbert put on a most important air & bade me guess what he had in his pocket. Your letter telling me you were sending Sandy's picture having arrived the day previously, it did not take me very long to satisfy this demand & my sensations as I slowly opened your registered envelope were positively historical. So far your future husband had been nebulous. I had conceived him more or less according to what I had heard of his temperament— a sort of disembodied character & all at once he was to be revealed to me in as material terms as a photograph could manage! It was thrilling— a moment of intense suspense! My pleasure was much augmented to also find a likeness of yourself enclosed. It does not do you full justice my love— but is sweet, & as it is several years since I was last honored with one of your pictures, I am delighted to have it. The upper part of the face brings out your resemblance to Mother strongly— for an instant it quite took my breath away. But to return to Sandy— the sensation, you must forgive my lingering interest in yourself! We were both most favorably impressed by his general appearance. Herbert declares he just misses being beautiful— but while I incline to believe he shows up even better in color than black & white, he is certainly very good looking, and his

features indicate a great deal of strength & reserve power. Beside intelligence & a few such minor details— Naturally I took your word for it that he was a clean decent fellow— but every time I look at the picture which stands beside yours on my desk, the confirmation of your praise in his face gives me infinite satisfaction… So, all in all, you have given me a great deal of happiness by your two pictures— for which I thank you a great deal darling. Herbert, of course, is dying to buy silver frames for them promptly. Owing to your heads being different in size, I cannot frame them together, as custom demands in the case of bride & groom in Germany— but double frames are rarely graceful, so perhaps it's just as well… With a great deal of the most devoted love to you— & Sandy— from us both. And thank you again for the photographs. —Always affec, *Katherine.*

February 19, 1916.
Dearest Eleanor—   Just a brief message first this morning to tell you that five months after Long Beach finds me with a heart full of devotion and love for the finest woman in the world. My happiness has grown steadily fuller and deeper as the time has passed, and I have had time to realize, more perfectly, the priceless gift of your beautiful love… Tonight, I shall have to be here at the office until about seven o'clock so don't look for me before seven-fifteen. I am sorry, but it is necessary. With a heart full of love, Ever your *George.*

March 3, 1916, Dresden.
My own beloved Piggy child—   …Today my mind has been more than filled with you all— and the memories & sorrows we share together, as it is three months since Mother was taken from us. And looking ahead I wonder whether the future will ever seem less empty without her? The days succeed the days with torpid regularity— part of the time I manage to skim along the surface, half realizing a loss of which I have so far seen no material evidence— and in my other moments I wonder how I can go on living. In some way it does not seem decent or fitting for me to be alive when Mother is dead. The mere idea of her going used formerly to suggest a blank wall, the end of all things as far as I was concerned. I used to assure myself I could not stand it— and yet here I am, with the promise of a normal existence before me! Even my grief is not the passionate elemental force I should have anticipated— but as quiet and relentless as the grave itself. Were it not for the warm affection which I feel for the dear people who are left me in this world, I should believe I were psychologically frozen. My sorrow heights are terribly black and bare as I look over them trying to grasp what has happened— & in the bottom of my heart an instinct protests that it simply cannot be. I suppose you are right, that I was spared a great deal by not coming to America— but my greater comfort is the thought that she was spared losing whatever pleasure her ideal of me gave her. I hate to imagine those last dark months— & I know how hard it must be for you to remember Mother turned against you under the delusion of her illness, but Piggydear, you did everything for her which a loving tender daughter could, & you can be sure that Mother understands and appreciates your courage & noble self-sacrifice now as she would not on earth. At the time I acted from a sense of duty— but in reality you were more dutiful than I. With a great deal of the most devoted love & kisses. Always affec. *Katherine.*

March 3, 1916. Three months today. Looking back over my diary is sad with Dearest Mother how much she did for me. Out with "my George."
March 18. Two calls this morning. Off this P.M. Washing my hair & made west-side visits. Out with my George & Henry this evening.

—Diary of Eleanor Whiteside Hobson.

March 7, 1916.
Dearest—   My poor old brain is so sleepy that its eyes are all but closed, but my heart wants to send you a little message with a big meaning. With such a dull brain to guide the pen and supply the words it can't say half of what it feels and longs to tell you— of the great love for you that fills it, of the devotion to you, and the pride it feels in being yours forever and ever… Now and always your *George.*

P. S. If my mind and "common sense" had had its way to-night, I should have gone to bed without giving my heart a chance to send its message, but "common sense" has long since been in dreamland, mumbling as he fell asleep— "that fellow is more in love than anybody knows, even the angel he is in love with."

March 18, 1916.
Dear Doctor—   For the last six months I have been the subject of a very unusual malady. The chief symptom is that there is a daily increase of happiness. There has never been any lack of appetite or sign of mental excitement. All my decisions have been made with a cool judgment well backed by serious thought. To me has come a very beautiful dream which daily becomes more of a reality. A dream of perfect love of a man and woman, a love which lifts both upward and onward. A love so strong that it carries them sailing over each others' faults searching out only the best in each other. The curious part is that the dream never seems to finish. At each turn new joys appear. I do not care to recover from this malady. What I do want, doctor, is your help in learning how to meet this power, how to make the most of this wonderful life which has been given me. Knowing your ability in scientific research, aside from general perfection, can you also tell me "why?" Good bye dear doctor. Pray regard this letter as confidential as I would not want anyone except you to know how very very happy I am. "*The Lady.*"

Written on Katherine's 27th birthday.

April 11th, 1916.
My dearest children—   Your wireless arrived this evening as I was sitting alone reading after supper— and I cannot tell you how delighted I was to receive those few printed words of greeting still fresh from Henry's dictation & realize the gulf between us spanned by all but a day or so. Letters are so long on the way nowadays that they never bring us nearer than three weeks & in the interval between their composition & arrival almost anything might occur. So the feeling that a few hours ago you were well & thinking of me is a very pleasant & comfortable sensation. Thank you so much for your message, darlings… And on returning to my room, a vase of lovely red roses by Mother's picture. It was the first birthday I had ever had without her, & yet it did not pass without a kind of greeting, for in the early morning I dreampt that I received a whole package of letters in her handwriting, all addressed with the most loving terms of endearment, but I was so happy that I woke before I had time to open them! …So you see in spite of being quite alone, I had a

great deal of attention, and much to divert me before your wireless appeared as a grand finale. If the English have not interfered with my mail again, I shall probably hear from you all before long also. But now, little ones, my paper and time are both limited, so I must wish you good night and sweet slumbers. With a great deal of the most devoted love and kisses. Thank you again for your message a thousand times. Always your own affectionate *Katherine*.

 Nursing School:

May seventeenth.
Love and admiration from the proudest and happiest man in the world to the best nurse and the finest girl in the wide wide world. —*in the handwriting of George Mackenzie.*

Eleanor Hobson graduated first in her class from the Presbyterian Hospital School of Nursing on May 17, 1916.

June 3rd, 1916, Dresden.
Dearest Eleanor & Henry—   Yesterday I did not have much time for a letter, so you must share one this evening, which in a way seems quite appropriate, as six months ago you were watching together by dearest Mother, while her radiant sweet spirit gradually & gently slipped away and out of its earthly garment we knew & loved familiarly— I hoped that by chance I might hear from you children, but nothing came. Yet I know that your thoughts are constantly with me— and it is a comfort to feel the existence of this mental bond at a time when we are almost cut off from each other…   —Always affec. *Katherine*.

June 11th, 1916, Dresden.
Dearest Piggy—   As a sequel to my previous epistle— I suppose you will soon be busy apartment hunting, if you still adhere to your plans of being married in the summer. I think if I lived in New York I should prefer the neighborhood of Washington Square & Irving Place— some spot with a certain atmosphere of old fashioned refinement— although I have no doubt the air on Morningside Park may be better. Do be careful about the vicinity you choose. New York is such a queer mixed up place— & right in between quite respectable quarters will be stuck a very questionable district… Probably you will adopt some of Mother's furniture for your new house as I did. I often wonder what will happen to the house in Colorado Springs, for it does not look as if any of us would ever be able to live there. Your interests are apparently in New York, Henry's wherever he eventually gets a parish, Thayer has years of study before him 'ere he can think of living anywhere, & I am in Germany, for at least the present. (I have every reason to believe that if Herbert had a good opening in America later he would be strongly tempted to accept it— but it would not be in Colorado Springs.) So sad as breaking up an old home is, I presume the house must

Eleanor Whiteside Hobson, photographers proofs.

eventually go if there is a good opportunity to get rid of it. It seems almost a pity that Mother's sentiment did not permit her to sell it when Mrs. D. Smith was so determined to buy it. Cambridge will make a pleasant summer abode for various generations of your descendants. You considered it rather dull in your flighty youth— but when you have a lot of small children you will be more than glad to have such a quiet healthy place within easy reach of New York to take them to during the hot weather. The coal lands ought to be kept if possible, not merely from a sense of piety but because they will really be worth a great deal some day. By the way, in going through Mother's letters & papers, be careful what you throw away… I wish you would keep my letters to her. I should like to have these again, as they form a kind of diary of the past and what has been. I suppose it is wrong but just now I cannot help feeling that whatever novelty or success the future may bring, the "has been" will stand out as the Golden Age in my memory. That while I may rejoice in other people's happiness, my own must be eternally tinged with melancholy. With a great deal of the most devoted love & lots of kisses. Always affectionately, *Katherine.*

June 19, 1916.
Dearest Eleanor—   It is just nine months to-day since the lovely beach witnessed what for me was the beginning of the greatest happiness that has come into my life, and even though I shall see you this evening I can't help obeying the impulse to let you know what were my first thoughts when I awoke at five this morning. For an hour I looked back over the path we have traveled. In all these weeks and months nothing has shaken my confidence in you, nothing has interrupted my love and admiration for your beautiful self. Often I have failed, often fallen far short of the ideal I have held up for the one who aspired to be worthy of you, but I will never cease trying to rise nearer to what the man should be who has your love. Never once has the wish come that I had not spoken, nor the shadow of a regret. I love you now dearest, far more than ever, more knowingly and more ardently. I knew I loved you then, I know it now a thousand times better. To love and be loved by the woman that one admires more than anyone else in the world is indeed the greatest joy that life offers. With fondest love, dear heart, and countless kisses, good-bye until this evening. Yours forever, *George.*

At the beach, George M. Mackenzie and Eleanor Whiteside Hobson, photograph undated.

June 20, 1916.
My dearest—   The soldiers just marched by singing *Tipperary* and far from being inspired I felt like a little dump heap. It all means separation dearest. Every time I think of it, that terrible word is spelt in bigger letters. The cries of extras sound occasionally. Anna just telephoned me that you were to sleep at the armory. She also asked if we were married… Our separation & possible marriage seems to be the great topic of interest… If it seems best to be married now I feel sure no wedding could mean more under the brightest circumstances… Good night dearest. All my love I send to you… —*Eleanor.*

June 22, 1916. Married today.   —*Diary of Eleanor Hobson Mackenzie.*

~ In the news:

AMERICAN CAVALRY AMBUSHED BY CARRANZA TROOPS; Scores, Including Mexican General, Reported Slain; Pershing Shifts Army; Washington Expects Break.

— Allies Working for Peace — Talk of Mexico as Germany's Ally — Machine Gun in Action — General Pershing Is Redisposing His Entire Force — Ford Employees Lose Jobs if They Join the Militia — Women Move to Aid Soldiers' Families — Employers in Race to Honor the Flag — Women are Eager to Serve on Border — Red Cross Offices Besieged with Applications of Would-Be Nurses.
—Headlines in the *New York Times*, June 22, 1916.

BRIDES TO BE LEFT BEHIND
Many More Weddings Hastened by Mobilization Call.
Another wedding hastened by the mobilization took place yesterday afternoon at St. Thomas's Church when Miss Eleanor Whiteside Hobson of Colorado Springs, Col., became the bride of Dr. George Miner Mackenzie, instructor in the College of Physicians and Surgeons. The ceremony was performed by the Rev. Charles M. Addison of Stamford, Conn. Dr. Mackenzie is a member of the First Armored Battery, N.G.N.Y., which will be called out next week. He is a graduate of Columbia, and was Captain of the crew one year while there. The bride is the daughter of the late Mr. and Mrs. Henry Wise Hobson of Colorado Springs. Her brother, in the uniform of the Yale Battery of New Haven, gave her in marriage.
—*Unidentified newspaper clipping found in the diary of Eleanor Whiteside Hobson, now Eleanor Hobson Mackenzie.*

The wedding of Miss Eleanor Whiteside Hobson, daughter of Mrs. Henry Wise Hobson, of Colorado Springs, to Dr. George Miner Mackenzie, 131 East Sixty-seventh Street, planned for the fall, took place in St. Thomas's Church. Dr. Mackenzie is an instructor in the College of Physicians and Surgeons and was graduated from Columbia in 1908. He rowed on three varsity crews and was captain in his senior year. He is a member of the 1st Armored Motor Battery of the National Guard of New York.
—*New York Tribune, undated.*

June 29, 1916. George off for camp. Back to the hospital.
—*Diary of Eleanor Hobson Mackenzie.*

June 29, 1916.
Beloved Wife—   Keep whistling dearest as loud and long as need be. I am thinking of you this very minute and loving you with a heart full of ardent devotion. Be brave sweetheart. I'm coming back soon. Good-bye. Now and always your lover and husband. *George.*

June 29, 1916.
Beloved Husband—   Back on the ward! Outwardly I am calm as a cucumber. Inwardly there is something throbbing away telling me how much I love you and how very much I am going to miss you. It was hard waving good-bye to you but it is not for very long my husband before you are back again and I can feel your arms around me, and though I know you love me— how I always feel surer of it when I am really with you… I must settle down so good-bye now. More love than could be shipped I send to you. *Ever devotedly your wife.*

July 4, 1916.
My beloved Wife—   Twice I have run out today when they started calling the mail and twice have been disappointed. I suppose the mail is playing

camp As a result of very unfriendly relations between the United States and Mexico, and Mexican guerilla raids into Texas and New Mexico, American troops were mobilized and General John J. Pershing led 6,000 American troops into Mexico in an unsuccessful two-year attempt to capture the guerillas. At this time, George Mackenzie, married for just a week, was sent to a military camp in Peekskill, New York.

the same tricks with your letters that it played with mine. I hope you have received my lost letters before this… Sweetheart, you have been superbly brave and helpful. I love and admire you for it. But we both know that it will not be for long; that soon we shall be together again; to go on where we left off. The last mail has come and no letter. I won't believe for a second that you forgot me or failed to send even a brief message… A day without a word from my dear wife gives me a miserably lonely feeling… Tomorrow I shall get your letter, I'm sure. I love you with all my heart and all my soul, dear wife… Sweet sleep! Always your lover and husband *George.*

July 4, 1916.
Most truly beloved Husband—   …It is a glorious evening dearest one. I wish I could be very near you just now, and with your arms around me watch the close of this splendid day. A sunset is such a stirring thing as it combines the glories of the past & present with the promise of tomorrow. The past & present are beautiful for us but best of all is that future together in which we, together with our love, ought to be able to attain very nearly the summit of happiness to which man and woman can aspire. Two years ago tonight your arms were around me for the first time. I think it was the first time. In a rush the feeling came over me— "Eleanor you could love this man." I knew then I could always rejoice in being with you, that I could always feels strengthened by your great strong arms, but best of all that with all my heart I could always proudly think and dream of you as my highest ideal. I did dream dearest, and strange enough God sent love too to you so that now my highest ideal is part of my life and I can exultingly write to you "My husband I love you" …It has just occurred to me what a great long stupid letter this is. Sorry dearest. Every day away from you is one day less. …*With all my best I am Your most devoted Wife.*

July 12, 1916.
Dearest Eleanor—   For just one hour and a half this page has been out on the table waiting for me to send a good night message to my dear wife… Today has been stifling here and I have been a bit anxious about you. I know quite well what oppressive weather and the wear and tear of hospital routine does to people… It is quite interesting here to see the stamp that the various colleges have put on the men, for the most part, from the same station of life. There are a great many men who have been prominent in the colleges, a half dozen Y's, as many or more H's & P's, a few from Columbia, a few Cornell men and of course a scattering from several other colleges. Most of the men are between one and ten years out of college… I don't know why I write you this— simply letting the pen go as it pleases… Your letters, arriving by the last mail tonight, relieved a little ache in the region of my heart, an ache which sprang from a fear that I might get no word from you today. Twice I elbowed my way to the front rank of the crowd around the sergeant calling out the letters and twice I came away disappointed and empty handed. It made me that much happier, I believe, when finally it did come and the ache faded away. Each day behind us, dear, is one day less of the separation, dear heart, and one day nearer the time when we shall again be together. It is hard, very hard to be away from you so long. I don't seem to get used to it in the least. It makes me realize how deeply I love you and how dependent my inward happiness

is upon seeing you, my best friend and my beloved wife. Goodnight, my love. Sweet sleep. Your devoted *George.*

July 12, 1916.
My dearest One—   …Wasn't it strange that last night we both should have written to each other about the pleasure derived from writing? …Three weeks tomorrow I have been your wife. Oh dearest I am happy so very happy… Good night dearest one… God bless you and bring you back to me safe and as soon as your duty is done. With all my heart your *Eleanor.*

There is more to the story, but that is for another time. Very briefly, George and Eleanor Mackenzie had four children, and the "editor/author" of this book is the third son of their daughter. For many years they lived in Cooperstown, New York, where he was the Chief Physician at the Mary Imogene Bassett Hospital. Both of Eleanor's brothers had distinguished careers. Henry Wise Hobson, who once asked for a Bible for Christmas, became the Episcopal Bishop of Southern Ohio and lived in Cincinnati. Thayer Hobson, described as an "expert typewriter" in some of the letters, pursued a career in publishing and became President and Chairman of William Morrow & Company. Katherine, their older sister, was a sculptress who lived in Europe and later in New York City. Upon her death, her sculpture collection was given to the Emma Willard School, formerly the Troy Female Academy, where her mother had studied. Today there are many cousins on all sides of this family living in all parts of the country and around the world.

It is now the twenty-first century, and this nation and our lives are so changed from how everyone in this book once lived. One of the most dramatic changes in our lives is in the way that we communicate. The typewriter had not been invented when the first letters in this book were written. Few people today write a personal letter and fewer still write journals, meaning that such records will not be available for future generations to read, study, and enjoy. Today it is the telephone, WELCOME. YOU HAVE MAIL, text-messaging, and cell phones. How different from Catherine McKie Thayer writing to her daughter:

"I hear the postman's whistle and here comes a letter from you…"

FINIS

Appendix A

Selected Dates in Family History

About 1621, Adam Thoroughgood, born 1603 or 1604, leaves Lynnhaven, England, for Virginia.

1624 Adam Thoroughgood marries Sara Offley, b. 1609.

About 1630, Thomas Thayer from Braintree, Essex County, England, emigrates to Braintree, Massachusetts, with his wife, Margery Wheeler.

1635 John Wise, born 1617, sails from Gravesend, England, July 4th, and settles on the Eastern Shore of Virginia near Chesconessex Creek.

1636 John Wise marries Hannah Scarburgh who had emigrated to America with her father, Capt. Edmund Scarburgh from Norfolk, England.

1643 Edmund Bowman emigrates to Eastern Shore of Virginia.

1705 John McKie born in Bargaly Glen, Minnigaff Parish, Newton-Stewart, Galloway, Scotland.

1716 Phineas Whiteside born in County Tyrone, North Ireland.

1735–1736 Phineas Whiteside emigrates to Pequea Valley, Lancaster County, Pennsylvania.

1752 Phineas Whiteside marries Ann Cooper.

1755 Birth of Peter Whiteside in Pennsylvania, baptized March 30, 1756. Birth of John Cropper on the Eastern Shore of Virginia, December 23rd.

1760 James McKie born in Minnigaff Parish, Scotland, fifth of six children.

1765 Phineas Whiteside acquires land in Cambridge, New York.

1766 Phineas Whiteside moves from Pennsylvania to Cambridge, New York.

1767 John McKie and his wife Mary Ann Wilson come to America with four of their children.

1774 John McKie purchases land, in what is now called McKie Hollow, and moves to White Creek, New York, east of Cambridge.

Chesconessex Creek, Accomac, Virginia, near where John Wise settled in 1635.

1776–1781 American Revolution. From Virginia, John Cropper, 1755–1821, serves as a Colonel under George Washington and between 1777 and 1778 writes his wife from Philadelphia and Valley Forge. In New York, Phineas Whiteside, 1716–1793, contributes financially to the American cause and four sons are in the militia. James McKie, 1760–1843, serves with the militia from Salem and Cambridge, New York.

1782 Death of John McKie, farm passes to his son, James. John McKie buried in the Turnpike Cemetery in Cambridge, later moved to the Woodland Cemetery, Cambridge, New York, in 1865.

1785 James McKie marries Elizabeth Wilson.

1791 Birth of George McKie, fourth of eleven children of James McKie and Elizabeth Wilson McKie.

1793 Death of Phineas Whiteside, buried in Whiteside Cemetery, Cambridge, New York. Birth of Catherine Whiteside, oldest daughter of Peter Whiteside and Ann Robertson Whiteside.

1796 Birth of Sophia Whiteside, April 6th, second daughter of Peter Whiteside and Ann Robertson Whiteside.

1800 Whiteside Church in Cambridge, New York, constructed using a bequest from Ann Cooper Whiteside, widow of Phineas Whiteside. Beside the church is the Whiteside Cemetery, where the earliest graves were for infant children.

1805 Slavery in Cambridge, New York, referred to in family letters.

1806 Henry Alexander Wise born in Accomac Courthouse, Virginia, December 3rd.

1813 Death of Sara Corbin Cropper Wise, mother of Henry Alexander Wise. As his father had died in 1812, Wise and his siblings were now orphans and were raised by their maternal Grandfather, General John Cropper, and some aunts.

View from near the Whiteside Church, Cambridge, New York, overlooking The Old Home with hills of Vermont in the background. This was the farmland that Phineas Whiteside purchased in 1765.

Appendix A Selected Dates in Family History

1821 Death of John Cropper, January 15th, buried at Bowman's Folly in Accomac, Virginia.

1822 Francis S. Thayer born in Dummerston, Vermont, September 11th.

1824 Death of Catherine Whiteside, first wife of George McKie, buried in the Whiteside Cemetery.

1825 Henry A. Wise graduates from Washington College.

1827 Birth of Catherine Sophia McKie, daughter of George McKie and his second wife, Sophia Whiteside McKie, June 16th, in Cambridge, New York. In Virginia, Henry A. Wise emancipates three slaves, Elizabeth Grey and her two children, Mary Jane and William Henry.

1828 Henry A. Wise marries Ann Elizabeth Jennings, October 8th.

1833–1844 Henry A. Wise a member of Congress from Virginia. William Henry Grey, a young mulatto boy, works for Henry A. Wise in Washington.

1833 Frederick Plumer Hobson born February 24th, Petersburg, Virginia.

1835 Death of Peter Whiteside in Cambridge, New York, buried in the Whiteside Cemetery.

1836 Catherine Sophia McKie attends school in Schaghticoke, New York.

1837 Ann Jennings "Annie" Wise born, April 28th. Her mother, Ann Elizabeth Jennings Wise died on May 4th. She was originally buried in Accomac, Virginia, but her body was moved to the Hollywood Cemetery, Richmond, Virginia, in 1928.

1840 Henry A. Wise marries Sara Sergeant, November, his second marriage.

1844–1847 Henry A. Wise, Minister to Brazil.

1843 November, Catherine McKie attends Troy Conference Academy in Poultney, Vermont.

1844 Catherine McKie leaves school in Poultney, July 17th. Francis S. Thayer begins his correspondence with Catherine McKie, August 12th.

1846 George McKie goes to China, May 18th.
John S. Wise born in Rio de Janeiro, Brazil, December 27th.

1847 George McKie returns from China, March 10th.

1848 Francis Thayer writes to George McKie for permission to correspond with Catherine McKie, February 24th. Permission granted March 6th.

1849 Death of Elizabeth Wilson McKie, born 1765, December 27th in White Creek, New York. Buried in the Turnpike Cemetery and moved to the Woodland Cemetery in 1865.

1850 Francis S. Thayer marries Catherine McKie on April 30th.
Death of Sarah Sergeant Wise, buried in Philadelphia.

1851 Death of Henry McKie, April 22nd, buried in the Whiteside Cemetery.

1852 Edwin McKie robbed of $48,700 while in Cleveland, Ohio.

1853 Peter McKie leaves for Australia, February 7th.
Edwin McKie leaves for Australia, September 28th.
Henry A. Wise marries Mary Lyons, November 1st, his third marriage.

1854 George Wilson McKie moves to New York City to begin a career in the grocery business, January.
Catherine McKie Thayer has stillborn child, May 2nd. Child is buried the yard of the family house in Troy, New York.
Edwin McKie returns from Australia.
Fire in Troy destroys much of city and the home of Francis & Catherine Thayer, August 25th. Both of them write: "Our sweet home a mass of smoking ruins."
August 26th, they move to a new house and Catherine writes of the old house: "But one thing makes me love this spot. There lies our Baby. A precious mound is that to me."

1855 James McKie, 1805–1869, brother of George McKie born 1791, begins a diary on February 24th, his 50th birthday, that he maintains for fifteen years.
May 24th, Henry A. Wise elected Governor of Virginia.
Death of James "Jimie" McKie, November 1, 1855, buried in the Whiteside Cemetery.

1856–1860 Henry A. Wise Governor of Virginia.

1856 Marriage of Frederick Plumer Hobson and Annie Jennings Wise, July 9th in Richmond, Virginia.
October, body of infant child of Francis & Catherine Thayer moved to the Oakwood Cemetery, Troy, New York.
Search continues for Peter McKie, who has not been seen since 1853.

1857 Francis McKie Thayer, "Uncle Frank," born in Troy, New York, June 13th.

1858 Death of Adin Thayer, father of Francis S. Thayer, February 7th, buried in Maple Grove Cemetery (Old), Hoosick Falls, New York.
Henry Wise Hobson born at Eastwood, July 9th, baptized December 11th.
Francis & Catherine Thayer have three lame horses in their stable, September.
Edwin McKie sails to England with Cambridge Chief, November.
Fire destroys barns and sheds at Cambridge, New York, farm, November 13th.

1859 John Brown raids Harpers Ferry, October 17th. Brown was hung on December 2nd for committing murder, treason, and conspiracy against Virginia.

Katherine Sophia Thayer, later Jermain & Hobson, born in Troy, New York, December 3rd.

1860 Anne Hobson born at Eastwood, March 4th.
George Wilson McKie dies in Nashville, Tennessee, May 27th, buried in the Whiteside Cemetery.
Francis and Catherine Thayer begin construction of their home at 4 Park Street in Troy, New York.

1861–1865 American Civil War.

1861 George McKie dies in Cambridge, New York, January 15th, buried in the Whiteside Cemetery.

1862 Death of Obadiah Jennings Wise at Roanoke Island, North Carolina, February 9th, buried in the Hollywood Cemetery, Richmond, Virginia.
Death of Niel McKie, April 27th, buried in the Whiteside Cemetery.

1863–1865 Annie Jennings Wise Hobson maintains a diary at Eastwood.

1864 Dahlgren Raid at Eastwood, March.

1865 Surrender at Appomattox, April 8th. Two of the Generals present were Henry A. Wise of Virginia and his brother-in-law, George Meade, a General in the Union Army.
James McKie writes in his diary of moving the graves of "our friends," McKie family members, from the Turnpike Cemetery to the Woodland Cemetery, Cambridge, New York, October 26th.

1866–1868 Annie Jennings Wise Hobson writes a diary at Eastwood.

1867–1868 Frederick Plumer Hobson writes a daily journal of the farm at Eastwood.

1867 November, Francis S. Thayer elected State Senator from Troy, New York.

1868 Death of Frederick Plumer Hobson, April 4th, at Eastwood, buried in the Hollywood Cemetery.
Annie Hobson dies of poisoning, August 16th, at Eastwood, buried in the Hollywood Cemetery.
Francis Thayer attends the Republican National Convention in Chicago as a delegate from New York. William Henry Grey (also Gray) attends the convention from Arkansas.

1869 Death of James McKie, May 5th, buried in the Woodland Cemetery.

1871 First mention of Francis S. Thayer's asthma, May.

1872 *Seven Decades of The Union* by Henry A. Wise published by J. B. Lippincott & Co.
William Henry Grey becomes the first person of African descent to address a national political convention when he addresses the Republican Convention in Philadelphia, June 5th.

1874 Francis S. Thayer appointed Canal Auditor.
Thayer family trip to the White Mountains of New Hampshire.

1875 Francis M. Thayer takes entrance exams at Amherst College, June 30th.

1876 Henry Wise Hobson graduates from College of William & Mary, Williamsburg, Virginia.
Death of Henry Alexander Wise in Richmond, Virginia, September 12th, buried in the Hollywood Cemetery.

1877 During the summer Francis & Catherine Thayer travel to the White Mountains and Maine in search of relief from Francis' severe asthma. Francis S. Thayer, his wife, and his daughter leave Troy, New York, for Colorado, hoping to find relief for his asthma, December 9th, 2:55 P.M.

1878–1879 Francis Thayer writes columns for the *Troy Daily Times* from Colorado.

1878 Death of Sophia Whiteside McKie in Troy, New York, January 21st, buried in the Whiteside Cemetery.
Henry Wise Hobson graduates from the law school at the University of Virginia.

1879 Francis M. Thayer graduates from Amherst College, June.

1880 Francis S. Thayer dies in Colorado Springs from complications from asthma, November 26th, buried in the Oakwood Cemetery.

1881–1884 Henry Wise Hobson is a practicing attorney in Buena Vista, Colorado, and writes to his friends in Virginia about life in Colorado.

1882 Katherine Thayer marries Barclay Jermain, June 7th, in West Troy, New York.
Barclay Jermain dies at Brookwood in Cooperstown, New York, July 7th, buried in the Albany (New York) Rural Cemetery.

1885 Henry Wise Hobson appointed United States Attorney for Colorado.

1887 Henry Wise Hobson appointed Special United States Attorney for all States and Territories West of the Mississippi. He is lead counsel in United States of America vs. Church of Jesus Christ of Latter-day Saints in Salt Lake City. Supreme Court of the Territory of Utah decides in favor of the United States and Henry Hobson writes: "I am perhaps prouder of winning that case than any I ever won before."
Henry Wise Hobson marries Katherine Thayer Jermain on December 17th in Fitchburg, Massachusetts.

1889 Katherine Thayer Hobson born in Denver on April 11th.
Henry Wise Hobson travels to Europe with friends from Virginia while his wife and daughter remain in Colorado Springs.

1890 Death of John Cannon Hobson, brother of Henry Wise Hobson, February 15th, buried in the Hollywood Cemetery.
Annie Jennings Wise Hobson publishes her pamphlet and poetry about the dedication of the Lee Monument in Richmond.

Appendix A   Selected Dates in Family History   941

1891 Henry Wise Hobson born in Denver on May 16th, described by his father as a "howler."

1892 Henry Wise Hobson and Katherine Thayer Hobson build new home at 933 Pennsylvania Avenue in Denver.

1893 Eleanor Whiteside Hobson born in Denver on January 7th.
Henry & Katherine Hobson visit the Chicago World's Fair with Eleanor in the fall.

1895 Summer on the Cambridge farm. Grandma Hobson, Annie Jennings Wise Hobson, visits. Henry and Katherine Hobson travel to Europe.

1896 Henry & Katherine Hobson visit Virginia, Richmond and Eastwood, with their daughter Katherine, November.

1897 Henry Hobson, son of John Cannon Hobson, sails aboard the *Kenilworth* as a cabin boy.
Death of James Jermain, July 12th in Albany, New York, buried in the Albany Rural Cemetery.
Francis Thayer Hobson born in Denver on September 4th.
Cambridge farm renovated, running water installed.

1898 Spanish American War.
July, fire aboard the *Kenilworth* kills Henry Hobson, 1880–1898, buried at sea.
Death of Henry Wise Hobson, 1858–1898, August 13th, in New York City, buried in the Oakwood Cemetery, Troy, New York.
Henry Wise Hobson has knee surgery in Troy, New York, August 21st.

1899 *The End of An Era* by John S. Wise published by Houghton, Mifflin & Company.
The Life of Henry A. Wise of Virginia by Barton Haxall Wise published by The MacMillan Company with an introduction by John S. Wise.

1900 Katherine Thayer Hobson publishes, *Papa's Letters*, a collection of letters from Henry Wise Hobson to his children, for family and friends.
Katherine Hobson spends the summer in Watch Hill, Rhode Island, with her children.
Henry Wise Hobson's grave moved and Celtic Cross monument erected in the Oakwood Cemetery.
Katherine Thayer Hobson has surgery for breast cancer in Troy, New York.

1901 Death of Catherine McKie Thayer from pneumonia in Denver, January 4th, buried in the Oakwood Cemetery.
Death of Mary Lyons Wise, third wife of Henry Alexander Wise, July 17th, buried in the Hollywood Cemetery.

1902 Death of Francis McKie Thayer, May 24th, in Excelsior Springs, Missouri, buried in the Oakwood Cemetery.
September, Katherine Thayer Hobson sails to Europe with her four children and goes to Dresden. The family returns to America in 1905.

1908 Katherine Thayer Hobson writes to John S. Wise for assistance in preparing a "little talk" on John Brown: "Was he a fanatic, a hero, or both?"

1909 Eleanor Whiteside Hobson leaves Colorado Springs to attend St. Timothy's School in Maryland. Henry Hobson has diphtheria while a student at Phillips Academy in Andover, Massachusetts, after which he attends Yale University.

1911 Katherine Thayer Hobson marries Herbert Kraus.
Francis Thayer Hobson attends Westminster School in Simsbury, Connecticut.

1913 Katherine Thayer Hobson and her daughter Eleanor Whiteside Hobson travel around the world. After returning from the trip, Eleanor enters Presbyterian Hospital School of Nursing in New York City.
Death of John S. Wise, May 12th, buried in the Hollywood Cemetery.

1914 Death of Annie Jennings Wise Hobson, June 3rd, buried in the Hollywood Cemetery.

1915 Death of Katherine Thayer Hobson from complications of pernicious anemia, December 3rd, buried in the Oakwood Cemetery.

1916 Eleanor Whiteside Hobson marries George M. Mackenzie, June 22nd.

1985 *A Good Southerner: The Life of Henry A. Wise of Virginia* by Craig Simpson published by The University of North Carolina Press.

2006 The American Civil War Center opens in Richmond, Virginia, and over seventy descendants of Henry A. Wise attend the ceremonies including descendants of Annie Jennings Wise Hobson, Margaretta Ellen "Néné" Wise Mayo, John Sergeant Wise, and William Henry Grey.

Descendants of Henry A. Wise visit his grave in the Hollywood Cemetery, Richmond, Virginia, October 2006.

Appendix B

Handwriting Samples

It would not have been possible to do this entire book with facsimile reproductions of the letters. However, readers may be interested in reproductions of a limited number of letters from some of the principals in this story. All or portions of the letters reproduced here are included elsewhere in the book; they are reproduced here in chronological order, and only the first page of the letter is reproduced in this appendix. Some of the letters have been reduced in size to fit on the page.

Francis S. Thayer to George and Sophia McKie, February 24, 1848.....944

Francis S. Thayer to Catherine McKie, January 21, 1849......................945

Henry Alexander Wise to Mary Lyons, August 12, 1853.......................946

Annie Jennings Wise Hobson to Henry A. Wise, February 16, 1862....947

Francis S. Thayer to his daughter, Katherine Thayer, June 30, 1877.....948

Barclay Jermain to Catherine McKie Thayer, February 6, 1882............949

Henry Wise Hobson to Katherine Thayer Jermain, April 15, 1887 950

Henry Wise Hobson to Katherine Thayer Jermain, October 4, 1887...951

Katherine Thayer Jermain to Henry Wise Hobson, October 13, 1887.........952

Annie Jennings Wise Hobson to Henry Wise Hobson, January 11, 1893....953

Henry Wise Hobson to Eleanor Whiteside Hobson, May 25, 1895......954

Henry Wise Hobson to Katherine Thayer Hobson, March 9, 1896......955

Troy Febry 24th 1848

Mr. & Mrs. George McKie

Respected Friends,

    Custom and duty demand that I should make to you a disclosure which concerns alike the happiness of your Daughter and myself. A reciprocal attachment exists between Catharine and myself. I therefore as in duty bound solicit your favor to my suit and assent to a union when situation and circumstances shall render it proper. I make the request at this time in order that a correspondence & intercourse desirable to both may receive the sanction of parental authority & advice.

  You know my character & disposition and should you deem me worthy of the hand of your Daughter it will ever be my highest aim to merit the alliance.

    With the highest respect & esteem

  I am, as ever your Obedient Servant

    Francis S. Thayer

Francis S. Thayer to George and Sophia McKie, February 24, 1848, a one-page letter.

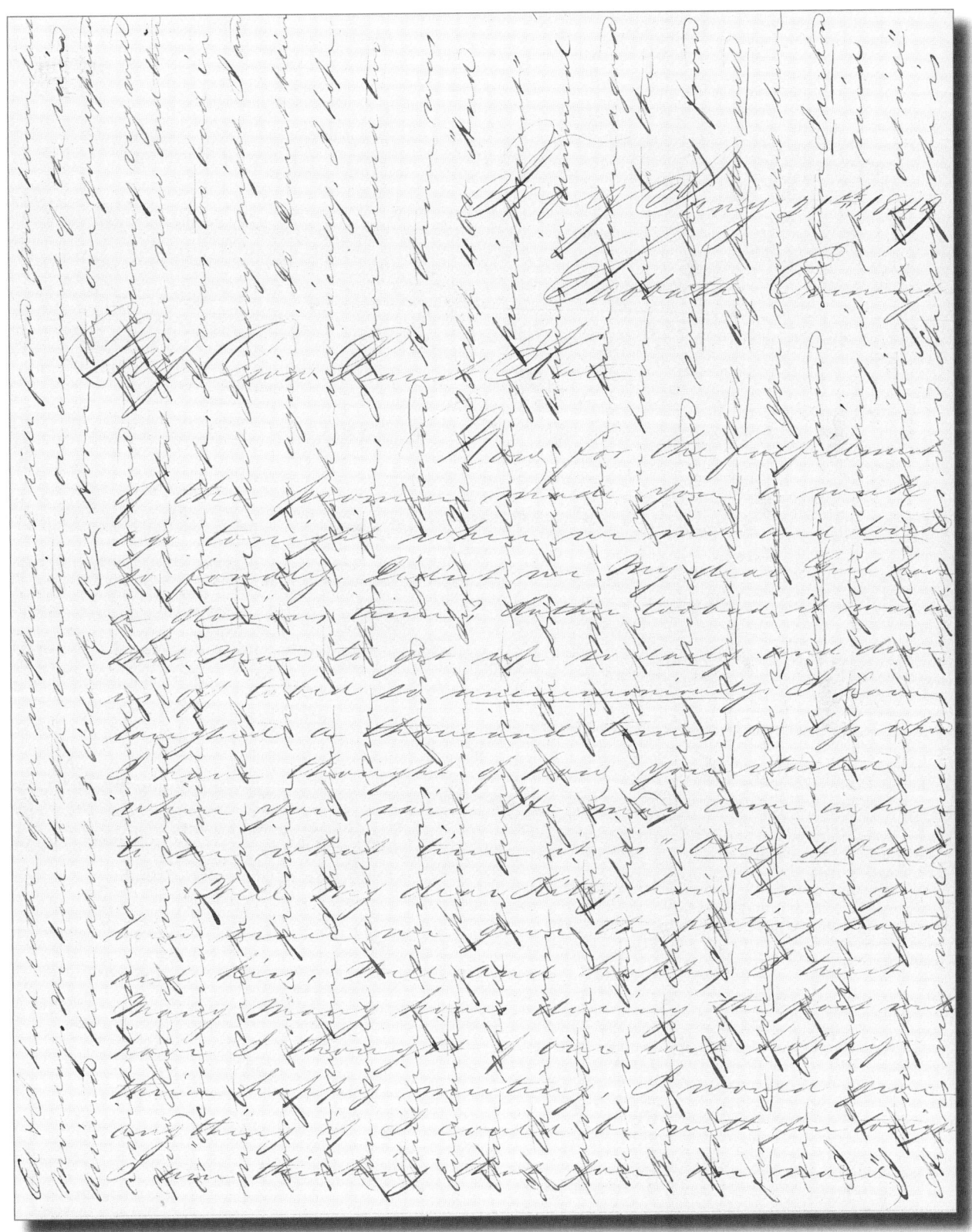

Francis S. Thayer to Catherine McKie, January 21, 1849, an example of cross-writing, a four page letter.

Only, near Onancock, V^a
Augt 13th 1853

My dearest Mary Lyons —

My heart bounds to you — it wells up to gush forth to you in its fullness & freshness. And is it so — that I am yet blest "in woman's love"? Again, again, again! I thank thee, I bless thee, I praise thee, I love thee! And this is not impious adoration, but is, truly, a part of the Divinity which stirs within us — an earnest devotion, satisfying as nature's law, which Heaven approves and sends to Earth to light it up and lift us to the grace & gladness & glory above. I may indulge it, then, and let it go free to thee. And it should bathe you as the cool, glittering waters of a pure fountain — it should illumine you as light — warm you as a lambent flame, without burning—

Henry Alexander Wise to Mary Lyons, August 12, 1853, an eleven-page letter. They were married in November 1853.

> Richmond. 16th Feb. 1862.
>
> Sunday Evening.
>
> My own dear Father,
>
> We laid our noble Hero in his last earthly resting place, at Hollywood, to day. Plumer, Dr Garnett, John & I were the only members of our own family who could follow him to the grave. On Friday, about one o'clock we heard that our worst fears were realised, & that the evening cars would bring his body with that of Capt Coles to the City. This awful intelligence came to blast hopes which had been elated to almost certainty, by previous telegrams of a far different import. The whole city was plunged in gloom — I never heard of more universal sorrow; he seems to have outlived all prejudices & all enmities; those who had been enemies in life mourn him in death; even that miserable wretch, Charles Irving grieved & said "Oh, that he could have lived!" I have been looking for him for three months to ask his forgiveness for all the wrong I have done him.'" Young & Old, rich & poor vie with one another in praising him. —— I am told that Richmond never before saw such a procession as received his remains & escorted him to the Capitol, where he was placed in the room prepared for the Senate of the C.S. Yesterday morning Plumer & I. with, Aunt Margaret, Cousin Sallie, Mary & Judge Lyons, Frank & James Wise went to look for the last time on our loved Ones face. He appeared to be placidly sleeping, after a day of weary

Annie Jennings Wise Hobson to her father, Henry A. Wise, February 16, 1862, describing the funeral for Obadiah Wise who had been killed at Roanoke Island, a six-page letter.

Crawford House
White Mts.
June 30th 1877

My dear Daughter

While your Mother is cleaning her nails and we are waiting for our breakfast at the table, I will commence this letter as it is quite late 10-15 and the mail closes in 40 minutes — Well this is a delightful spot. One of the wildest and most charming in all the mountain range. I am improving slowly but surely I hope and trust. Breakfast is now being placed before us And so good morning to you all.

Francis S. Thayer to his daughter, Katherine Thayer, June 30, 1877, written from the Crawford House in the White Mountains of New Hampshire, a three-page letter.

Hedge Lawn
Feb 6th 1882.

My dear Mrs Thayer—

Your letter of the 1st inst. reached me yesterday morning. I am glad that you can say — in speaking of Kittie's still being in the East — that you "think I will help your dear child to turn her face home". For I should feel very badly should you think I would for an hour delay her departure. Indeed I feel very sorry that I have taken away from you & Ada so much of the brightness and comfort that Kittie's presence gives you. And I know well the comfort & blessing that has

Barclay Jermain to Catherine McKie Thayer, February 6, 1882, a five page letter.

Henry W. Hobson,
  United States Attorney.

Denver, Colo. Apr 15 1887

My dear Mrs. Jermain —

You will pardon office paper, will you not, when I say that I have none other at hand —

I cannot go down I fear tomorrow morning, so will not impose on you to the extent of asking you to go by the 8 ock train, though really I never thought you had any such intention. I may go by the mid-day train but about that I will tell you this evening — Where, do you ask! Why at the Windsor, provided

Henry Wise Hobson to Katherine Thayer Jermain, April 15, 1887, a three-page letter.

Washington Octo. 4ᵃ 1887

My dearest Sweetheart—

I knew I could not receive any letter from you this morning and yet I had a hope that by some unaccountable means I would get one — I wrote you such a hurried kind of a scrawl upon yesterday that I felt almost ashamed to send it and yet dearest you knew when you received it that it was a little outpouring of my love for you — What would I not give to see you and kiss your sweet lips — Did any two lovers ever enjoy each other with more purity and sanctity that we do? I believe not, for when I am with you the world seems full of goodness and purity and you my love seem to be the center of it all — Ah Kittie! make me pure and good too, will you not?

Henry Wise Hobson to Katherine Thayer Jermain, October 4, 1887, a six-page letter.

HILL FARM, WHITE CREEK. N.Y.

October 13th '87 -

My own Darling Henry -

Yesterday morning Aunt Ada and I left New York at nine fifty. And from Albany. Where we waited a half hour, I sent you a dispatch. And to day have yours. I am relieved to hear of your safe arrival. We stopped at Uncle Allen's visited them, a few minutes

Katherine Thayer Jermain to Henry Wise Hobson, October 13, 1887, a six-page letter.

Ashland- Jan 11th 1893

My dear Son,

I had so hoped for a letter to day telling me all about the new girl and the well-doing lovely Mother.

Yet I ought to make allowance for the severe weather that has interrupted the mails, and your busy life —

We have the severest weather we have known here for many years, & most thankful was I when it moderated to day enabling me to get out with Alice & Jennings — I walked up to Mrs Binn's having heard her old Father was very sick & Sallie in bed with another severe cold — I found both better — On my return I called to see Mrs Ellar the wife of Judge Ellar the

Annie Jennings Wise Hobson to Henry Wise Hobson, January 11, 1893, a sixteen-page letter.

BOSTON & CHICAGO SPECIAL
WAGNER VESTIBULE TRAIN
Via Boston & Albany, N.Y. Central
and Lake Shore May 25th

My darling little
Piggy-Blue—
　　Papa can hardly write straight the car is shaking so and you will think what a funny old man Papa is to write just like a hen scratching in the sand— Who do you think I rode down town with the day before I left Dinner? Why with Margaret Dake in her Papa's

Henry Wise Hobson to Eleanor Whiteside Hobson, "Piggy Blue," May 25, 1895, a four-page letter, one of Papa's Letters.

Appendix B Handwriting Samples

Santa Fe Route Eating House & Dining Car System

FRED HARVEY, MANAGER.

ATCHISON, TOPEKA & SANTA FE,
COLORADO MIDLAND,
GULF, COLORADO & SANTA FE,
ATLANTIC & PACIFIC,
AND SOUTHERN CALIFORNIA
RAILROADS.

GENERAL OFFICE, UNION DEPOT, KANSAS CITY, MO.
CHICAGO OFFICE, COR. 17TH AND WENTWORTH AVE.

La Junta DEPOT HOTEL, Mch 9 1896

Darling Kate —

Here I am at La Junta until tomorrow morning and in consequence of a nice job on the part of Eddie at my office — Thursday I took from the bundle of papers on my desk the Bill of Complaint which I had gotten prepared and sworn to in N.Y. and the *one* *indispensable* *paper* at the hearing in New Mex. and without which I cannot move a peg — I told Eddie to copy it explaining to him that it must be ready by Saturday as I had to take the original with me — Yesterday morning I asked him if he had copied that Bill and he said he had — I presumed of course that he had filed the original in the only proper place in the office where it should have been filed the bundle of papers on my desk.

Henry Wise Hobson to Katherine Thayer Hobson, March 9, 1896, a thirteen-page letter.

Appendix C

Selected Portraits and Photographs

The letters and other writings published here have enabled us to establish a relationship with these people from the past that is enhanced when we study the portraits and photographs that have been included throughout the book. Studying these images can be even more interesting when a collection of pictures of the same person is printed together, but it is not always possible to find multiple images of the same person from many years ago. However, there are multiple images of Henry A. Wise, Henry Wise Hobson, and Katherine Thayer Hobson, and these are published on the following pages.

When looked at all on one page, one sees a smile on a child's face, youthful faces maturing, the self-confidence, energy, and ambition of a young man, a more serious expression, perhaps severe, on an adult's face, the same person as a small child and then as a mother with her children, the maturity of an older man, and other expressions. One can only wonder what they were thinking when these formal photographs were taken or the portraits were painted and what their reactions would be today to having these images scanned into a modern computer and published here with their letters and diaries.

Appendix C Selected Portraits and Photographs 957

Henry Alexander Wise, 1806–1876

Henry Wise Hobson, 1858–1898

Appendix C   Selected Portraits and Photographs   959

Katherine Sophia Thayer Hobson, 1859–1915

Appendix D

Bibliography

Adkins, William M., *Obadiah Jennings Wise '50: A Sketch of His Life*, Indiana University Alumni Quarterly, 1937–1938.

Brown, Rita Mae, *High Hearts*, Bantam Books, New York, 1986.

Brown, William H., *Portrait Gallery — Distinguished American Citizens with Biographical Sketches and Fac-Similes of Original Letters*, Hartford, Connecticut, 1845, Reissued 1931.

Clay, R., Foster, C., Raymond, R., Shiland, T., and Thornton, D., *Old Cambridge, 1788–1988*. Towns of Cambridge, Jackson and White Creek, New York, 1988.

Collins, Darrell L, *46th Virginia Infantry*, The Virginia Regimental Histories Series, H. E. Howard, Inc., Lynchburg, Virginia, 1992.

Cooke, John Easten, *Wearing of the Gray*, E. B. Treat & Co., New York, 1867.

Gill, Islay V. H., *The McKie Family of The Cambridge Valley*. Notes and pamphlet prepared in 1960 by Islay Gill of Greenwich, New York.

Hambleton, James P., *A Biographical Sketch of Henry A. Wise*, J. W. Randolph, Richmond, Virginia, 1856.

Hobson, Henry Wise, *Papa's Letters*, New York, 1900. Privately printed.

Jennings, Obadiah, excerpts from *Debate on Campbellism; Held at Nashville, Tennessee*, printed in Pittsburgh, Pennsylvania, by D. and M. MacLean, 1832.

Johnson, Crisfield, *History of Washington County, New York*, Everts & Ensigh, Philadelphia, 1878.

Lancaster, Jr., Robert, *Virginia Homes and Churches*, J. B. Lippincott Co., Philadelphia, 1915.

MacCarthy, James Philip, "Fitz-Mac," *Political Portraits*, The Gazette Printing Co. of Colorado Springs, 1888.

Mayo, Ellen Wise, "A War-Time Aurora Borealis," *Cosmopolitan*, June 1896.

McGuire, Judith Brokenbrough, "Diary of A Southern Refugee during the War, January–July 1862," edited by James I. Robertson Jr., from *Virginia at War 1862*, Davis, William C. and Robertson, James I., Editors, University Press of Kentucky, 2007. McGuire's book was first published in 1867 in New York by E. J. Hale & Son.

Moore, Mrs. M. B. (Maranda Branson), *The Geographical Reader for the Dixie Children*, Branson, Farrar & Co., Publishers, Raleigh, North Carolina, 1863.

Page, Rosewell, *Thomas Nelson Page: A Memoir of a Virginia Gentleman*, Charles Scribner's Sons, New York, 1923.

Prime, William C., *Boat Life in Egypt and Nubia*, Harper & Brothers, New York, 1857.

Putnam, Sallie Brock, *Richmond During the War: Four Years of Personal Observation*, G. W. Carlton & Co., New York, 1867.

Simpson, Craig M., *A Good Southerner: The Life of Henry A. Wise of Virginia*, The University of North Carolina Press, Chapel Hill and London, 1985.

Webster, Noah, Jun. Esquire. *An AMERICAN SELECTION of Leffons in Reading and Speaking. Calculated to Improve the MINDS and Refine the TASTE of YOUTH and also to Instruct them in the GEOGRAPHY, HISTORY, and POLITICS OF THE UNITED STATES. To Which Are Prefixed, RULES in ELOCUTION and DIRECTIONS for Expressing the Principal Passions of the Mind. Being the THIRD PART of a GRAMMATICAL INSTITUTE of the ENGLISH LANGUAGE, To Which is Added, An APPENDIX, Containing Several New Dialogues.* Printed at Boston, 1800.

Whiteside, Ada, *A History of Phineas Whiteside and His Family*, 1961.

Wilstach, Paul, *Tidewater Virginia*, The Bobbs-Merrill Co., Indianapolis, Indiana, 1929.

Wise, Barton Haxall, *Memoir of General John Cropper* first published in 1892 by the Virginia Historical Society and reprinted in 1974 by the Eastern Shore of Virginia Historical Society.

Wise, Barton Haxall, *The Life of Henry A. Wise of Virginia*, The Macmillan Company, New York, 1899.

Wise, Henry A., *Seven Decades of the Union*, J. P. Lippincott & Co, New York, 1871.

Wise, John Sergeant, *Diomed: The Life, Travels, and Observations of a Dog*, The Macmillan Company, New York, 1897.

Wise, John Sergeant, *The End of An Era*, Houghton, Mifflin & Co., New York, 1899.

Wood, George B., *Treatise on the Practice of Medicine*, J. B. Lippincott and Co., Philadelphia, 1858.

And the following newspapers where cited:

The Chicago Tribune
The Denver News
The Denver Republican
The Denver Times
Lake City Times
The New York Times
New York Tribune
New York Herald
The Richmond Daily Examiner
The Richmond Dispatch
The Richmond Times
The Sacramento Bee
The Salt Lake Daily Tribune
The Salt Lake Herald
The Troy Daily Times
The Washington Post
Washington County (New York) Post

Acknowledgements

THIS project would not have been possible without the assistance and suggestions from many people and institutions. First and foremost, I am indebted to the authors of the letters and to everyone who had a part in preserving them these many years.

I am grateful to the following institutions that provided assistance during my travels and research: The Virginia Historical Society, the Valentine Richmond History Center, the Library of Virginia, the Eastern Shore Public Library, the Goochland County (Virginia) Historical Society, the Historical Society of Idaho Springs, Colorado, the Rensselaer County (New York) Historical Society, the Hoosick Township Historical Society and the Louis Miller Museum in Hoosick Falls, New York, the Library and Archives at Seton Health in Troy, New York, the Eastern Shore of Virginia Historical Society, the Denver Public Library and the National Archives in Denver, Colorado, the Utah State Archives and the Church History Library for the Church of Jesus Christ of Latter-day Saints in Salt Lake City, Utah, and the Long Island Museum of American Art, History and Carriages at Stonybrook, New York.

I have used or received assistance from a number of libraries at different universities and colleges including: The Archives and Special Collections at the Amherst College Library; the Mortimer Rare Book Room in the Neilson Library at Smith College; the University Archives at Indiana University; the Special Collections Library at Duke University; the University of Virginia Law Library; the Archives Department at the College of William & Mary; the Special Collections Library at Cornell University; the Virginia Baptist Historical Society at the University of Richmond; the Dartmouth College Library; and the Griswold Library at Green Mountain College. My work would have been much more difficult without the existence of these facilities and the assistance of their professional staffs. I am grateful to all of them for their assistance and for preserving the collections that they have.

In the course of my travels and research I met a large number of people who willingly gave me their time and shared with me their knowledge, and to all of them I am very grateful. Sometimes, as when I met Dan Dudek and Gail Anderson and later Lonn and Kate Berney in Cambridge, New York, I just drove down their drive and introduced myself as a descendant of the pioneering farmer who had built their house. At a restaurant in Onancock, Virginia, I introduced myself to Robin Rinaca and Nick Covatta and they invited members of the family to visit Bowman's Folly the next day. At other times, such as when I met Grant Houston, editor of *Silver World* in Lake City, Colorado, we had exchanged e-mails before I made the long drive to Lake City. I have had assistance from a number of cousins including Hobson Goddin, George Hobson, Henry Alexander Wise, Tayloe Wise, Starita Smith, Margery Thomas, Kitty Sturtevant, Thayer Esquirol, Sarah Stowers, Helen Fries, and Dan Thomas. Other assistance has come from Don Allan, Maria Parker, Grace Campbell, Page Clark, Ellen Baber, Thomas Johnson, Charles Filkins, George & Natasha

Heinrichs, Sebastian Völcker, and John Verrill. I am indebted to Craig Simpson whose 1985 biography of Henry A. Wise, *A Good Southerner*, prompted me to wonder more about my ancestor and his family.

∾

And lastly, my mother deserves a great deal of credit for this project. For many years she preserved and read through these letters and kept saying to me, "You should take a look at 'the family letters' out in the barn." One day I did. An initial thought was that I would prepare a "pamphlet" for members of the family. It should be very apparent that the finished project gives new definition to what a pamphlet might be. As the project progressed, my mother assisted with the proof reading, answered questions about the ancestors, and made her share of suggestions.

Index

A

Addison, Ada, 460; 1887 hosts wedding of H.W. Hobson and K.T. Hobson, 560; visits Cambridge, N.Y. farm, 733; H.W. Hobson visits in Stamford, Ct., 771; *illus. 448, 520, 552*

Addison, Rev. Charles M., 1887 marriage of H.W. Hobson and K.T. Jermain, 560; 1898 funeral of H.W. Hobson, 821; 1915 funeral of K.T. Hobson, 922; 1916 marriage of E.W. Hobson and G.M. Mackenzie, 931

Appomattox Courthouse, 315

B

Beadle, Libby, 252

Birge, John, 415, 428, 444, 455

Bowman family genealogy, 8

Brown, John, raid at Harper's Ferry, 73–77; execution, 225–227; K.T. Hobson speech, 886; *illus. 77*

Brown, Rita Mae, describing funeral of O.J. Wise, 279

Bryan, Mary Hobson (1884–1947), letter to K.T. Hobson, 894–895

Burton, Sylvia, hair dye, 257

C

Cameron, William E., about H.A. Wise campaign for Governor, 68–69

Cholera, epidemics, 126–127, 134, 152, 176–180, 353–354; cause of, 464

Church of Jesus Christ of Latter Day Saints. *See* Mormon Church Case.

Civil War Monuments, 281, 326, 340–341

Coke, Henry C., H.W. Hobson speech at University of Virginia, 823; trustee in H.W. Hobson will, 832

Cooke, John Easten, describing funeral of O.J. Wise, 276–279

Corbin, George, correspondence with John Cropper, 21–31

Cropper family genealogy, 8

Cropper, John (1755–1821), letters to and from Valley Forge, 20–31; 1779 diary, 31; *illus. 34*

Cropper, Sarah Corbin (1777–1813), marriage, 32; letter to J. Cropper, 32–33; death, 41

Cuthbert, L. M., death of H.W. Hobson, 825

D

Dhalgren, Ulric., raid on Goochland County and Eastwood, 297–308

Doub, D.M., death of G.W. McKie, 235, 247–248

E

Eaton, E.R., 415, 431–432

Errington, Sophie. *See* Hobson, Katherine Thayer (1859–1915).

F

Fallon, M. E., death of H. W. Hobson, 831–832

Fires, 1837 Virginia, 46–47, 373; 1848 Albany, 122; 1849 St. Louis, 95; 1849 Troy, 130; 1850 Troy, 142; 1851 San Francisco, 153; 1854 New York, 171; 1854 Troy, 178–179, 182–183; 1858 Troy, 215; 1858 Cambridge 217; 1860 Lawrence, Massachusetts, 232; 1860 Troy, 232; 1860 Hoosick Falls, 249; 1861 Charlestown, S. Carolina, 257; 1863 Charlestown, S. Carolina, 287; 1862 Troy, 322; 1864 Dahlgren raid, 299; 1871 Chicago, 379, 386–387; 1871, Peshtigo, Wisconsin, 379, 387; 1876 at Amherst, 406; 1876 Brooklyn, 407

Fisk, Samuel, engagement of H.W. Hobson 536–537; death of H.W. Hobson, 814, 815, 840

965

G

Garland, A.H., appoints H.W. Hobson US Attorney in Colorado, 488; Mormon Church Case, 577–580

Garnett, Mary Wise (1829–1898), 54; death of child, 55

Gettysburg, battle of, 326

Golden Fleece mine, 687, 702, 704, 711, 714, 723, 733, 817–820, 846

Grey William Henry (also Gray), speech at 1872 Republican Convention, 389–391; *illus. 389*

H

Hambleton, James, about H.A. Wise campaign for Governor, 68

Handwriting samples, 935–947

Harper's Ferry. *See* Brown, John.

Hobson family genealogy, 2

Hobson, Alice Pettit (1860–1933), described by A.J.W. Hobson, 485, 486, 594, 595, 598, 607, 617–620, 621, 642, 644–645, 668–669; letter to H.W. Hobson, 641; marriage to Dr. McSparrin, 680

Hobson, Annie Jennings Wise (1837–1914), her birth and the death of her mother, 46–47; letters to her father, 61–62, 64–66, 71, 365; marriage to F.P. Hobson, 70; describing funeral of O.J. Wise, 269–272; Civil War correspondence, 282–287; Civil War diary, 288–291, 295–302, 308–315, 317–318; letters to M.L. Wise, 55, 71–72, 282–283, 285–286 345–349, 351–352, 365–366; 1866–1868 diary, 349–369; in Williamsburg, 369–370; 1881–1886 letters to H.W. Hobson in Colorado, 472–473, 477–479, 480–487, 490–493; 1887 letters, 508, 510–511, 525, 530–531, 541–542, 545, 554–555, 557–558; 1888–1889 letters, 585–586, 590, 594–595, 598–599, 602, 603–604, 607–608, 617–622; Robert E. Lee Memorial, 625–635; 1890–1897 letters, 641–642, 644–645, 648, 666–667, 668–669, 682, 690–694, 701–702, 711–714, 722–723, 727–728, 730–731, 734–739, 741, 747; 1898 letters, 800–801, 804–806, 830–831, 841, 842; 1899 letter, 847–848; in old age, 882, 883, 885, 898, 903, 905–906, 909–910; death and funeral 910–911; paying her old bills, 912, 913; *illus. 368, 370; handwriting samples, 947, 953*

Hobson, Annie Wise (1860–1868), birth 78; death 367–368; *illus. 366*

Hobson, Eleanor Whiteside (1893–1985), birth, 668; 1899 letters to T.N. Page, 849; 1900 letters to grandmother, 850; at St. Timothy's School, 888–890, 892, 895–897; 1911–1912 letters, 896–906; about A.J.W. Hobson, 898, 900, 905–906; 1913–1915 diary and letters, 907–925; death of her mother, 921–924; 1916 letters, 928, 930–933; completes nursing school, 929; marriage to G.M. Mackenzie, 930; *illus. 671, 676, 678, 700, 706, 751, 760, 850, 880, 882, 883, 884, 888, 903, 907, 929, 930*

Hobson, F. Thayer (1897–1967), birth 734; letters from, 891, 892, 897, 899, 912; service in World War I, 912–913; letter to G.M. Mackenzie, 918; 1915 knee surgery, 920; *illus. 750, 760, 850, 884, 918*

Hobson, Frederick Plumer (1833–1868), marriage to A.J. Wise, 70; describing funeral of O.J. Wise, 273; 1867 diary, 357–362; 1868 diary, 364–365; death, 365; *illus. 70, 364*

Hobson, George R. (b. 1883), letter to K.T. Hobson, 849

Hobson, Henry W. (1858–1898), birth, 71; 1876 at William & Mary, 370; moves to Colorado, 466–468; letters to friends in Virginia, 466, 470–472; appointment as U.S. Attorney in Colorado, 488–490, 493–498; term as U.S. Attorney, 498–501; 1887 letters to K. Jermain (Hobson), 503–559; appointed Special U.S. Attorney, 562–563; 1887 Mormon Church case, 561–582; 1888–1889 letters to K.T. Hobson, 585–622; 1889 trip to Europe, 608–622; resignation as U.S. Attorney, 615; 1890–1897 letters to K.T. Hobson, 639–746; 1898 letters to K.T. Hobson, 753–807; letters to J.S. Wise, 670–671, 710; letter to A.J.W. Hobson,

797; August 1898 letters and telegrams, 810–812; death, 813; funeral and obituaries, 813–816, 820–827; will, 832; hospital bill, 840; gravestone, 851–852; *illus. 282, 292, 370, 489, 505, 569, 616, 650, 726, 753, 757, 813, 833, 958; handwriting samples, 950, 951, 954, 955*

Hobson, Henry W. (1891–1983), birth, 648; knee surgery, 837–839; at Phillips Academy (Andover), 890–893, letters to his mother, 897–899, 908–910, 912–914; service in World War I, 912–913; *illus. 648, 650, 651, 673, 685, 687, 700, 706, 760, 850, 884, 903, 909*

Hobson, Henry W. (1880–1898), sails aboard *Kenilworth*, 768; death, 803–806

Hobson, Jennings (1887–1955), letter from J.S. Wise Jr., 886–887

Hobson, John Cannon (1857–1890), letters to H.W. Hobson, 469, 474, 479, 592–593; letter to A.J.W. Hobson, 602–603; death 641; *illus. 370, 593*

Hobson, John Cannon (1880–1960), on ranch in Texas, 735–739, 741; *illus. 739*

Hobson, Katherine (Catherine) Thayer (1859–1915), birth, 224–225, 227; essays written at Troy Female Seminary, 403–405; 1882–1883 letters about B. Jermain, 446–462; marriage to B. Jermain, 451; 1882 diary, 455; 1887 letters to H.W. Hobson, 505–554; marriage to H.W. Hobson, 560; 1888–1889 letters to H.W. Hobson, 584–623; 1890–1897 letters to H.W. Hobson, 639–748; 1890–1897 letters to C.M. Thayer, 711, 714, 719–721, 722–723, 724–725, 733, 747–748; 1898 letters to H.W. Hobson, 749–807; 1898 letters to C.M. Thayer 750; 1899–1901 letters to C.M. Thayer, 844, 846, 851–852; letters to J.S. Wise, 798, 807, 841, 842, 844, 846, 873–874, 876–877, 882–883, 891, 893, 898–899; Watch Hill, R.I., 850–851; short story, *My hospital Chum* by pen name of Sophia Errington, 855–869; in Dresden, 880–884; letter to A.J.W. Hobson, 881; death, obituary, and funeral, 921–922; *illus. 327, 331, 334, 383, 440, 446, 448, 451, 456, 464, 504, 506, 520, 552, 597, 606, 648, 650, 651, 655, 678, 774, 850, 881, 883, 884, 959; handwriting sample, 952*

Hobson, Katherine Thayer (1889–1982), birth, 604; poems, 432, 833, 845; marriage to H. Kraus, 899; letters to E.W. Hobson, 907, 908–909, 917–923, 925–930; 1915 letter to her mother, 922–923; *illus. 606, 616, 650, 655, 676, 700, 706, 751, 760, 850, 880, 884, 899, 907, 925*

Hobson, Mary, (1884–1947). *See* Bryan, Mary Hobson (1884–1947).

Horsbrugh, Fred, 741

J

Jenks, G. A., 578–579

Jennings family genealogy, 7

Jennings, Obadiah (1778–1832), 35–37; *illus. 36*

Jermain, Barclay (1853–1882), letter from, 449; marriage to K.S. Thayer, 451–452; illness, 446–454; death, 455; *illus. 446, 448, 456; handwriting sample, 949*

Jermain, James B. (1809–1897), 135, 191; 1882–1883 after death of B. Jermain, 456, 464; before marriage of K. Jermain to H.W. Hobson, 539–540; death of, 728–729

Jermain, Katherine Thayer (1859–1915). *See* Hobson, Katherine Thayer, (1859–1915).

K

Know-nothing movement, 68–69, 187, 316, 374

Kraus, Herbert, marriage to K.T. Hobson, 899; service in World War I, 912–913; *illus. 897*

Kraus, Katherine Hobson (1889–1982). *See* Hobson, Katherine Thayer, (1889–1982).

L

Lee, Robert E., farewell to his army, 314; memorial in Richmond, 625–635; *illus. 631, 635*

Lincoln, Abraham, 1860 election, 249; 1861 inauguration, 253; Gettysburg Address, 326; 1864 re-election, 329; 1865 inauguration, 330; death, 316–317, 330

Littleton family genealogy, 7–8

M

MacCartee, Julie, letters about death of Barclay Jermain, 454, 456–458

MacCarthy, James Philip, profile of H.W. Hobson, 511–516

Mackenzie, Eleanor Hobson (1893–1985). *See* Hobson, Eleanor Whiteside (1893–1985).

Mackenzie, George M. (1885–1952), meets E.W. Hobson, 910; service in World War I, 912–913; letters to E.W. Hobson, 914–917, 920, 923–924, 926–933; *illus. 915, 930*

Mallon, P., search for Peter Whiteside McKie, 196, 200

Mayo, Ellen Wise (1844–1909), describing the Dahlgren Raid at Eastwood, 302–308; *illus. 302*

McGuire, Judith Brokenbrough, describing funeral of O.J. Wise, 276

McKie family genealogy, 12–13

McKie, Almy (1802–1868), death 339

McKie, Catherine Sophia (1827–1901). *See* Thayer, Catherine McKie (1827–1901).

McKie, Edwin (1818–1895), 1853 letters from England and Australia, 165–167, 169, 223; 1860 letters from Ohio and Illinois, 233; 1860 letters from Liverpool, 248, 256; letter, 255; diary describing the end of the Civil War, 317; 1880 letters to Edwin McKie, 439–441; *illus. 223, 649*

McKie, George (1791–1861), letter to S.W. McKie, 83; letter to F.S. Thayer, 118; letter to C.M. Thayer, 160; death 250–253; *illus. 83*

McKie, George Wilson (1825–1860), trip to China, 102–105; trip to California, 148–151; letters to his father, 167–168, 171, 177; death in Nashville, Tennessee, 234–248; *illus. 246*

McKie, Henry (1829–1851), death 155–156; *illus. 156*

McKie, James (1805–1869), begins three volume diary, 186; 1855–1859 diary excerpts, 187–230; 1860–1861 diary excerpts, 233–257; diary describing the end of the Civil War, 317; 1862–1869 diary excerpts, 320–341; death, 341; *illus. 335*

McKie, James (1831–1855), death, 192–195; *illus. 195*

McKie, Niel Whiteside (1815–1862), described by S.W. McKie, 234; death, 321–322; *illus. 322*

McKie, Peter Whiteside (1833–1853), letters from 161–162; disappearance and search for, 174, 196, 200; *illus. 200*

McKie, Sophia Whiteside (1796-1878), letters, 90, 219–222, 234; death 431; *illus. 84, 219, 431*

McKie, William (1795–1863); death and will, 325; *illus. 325*

McQuade, Dr. H.D., death of F.M. Thayer, 878–879

Mead, General George G., 315; *illus. 315*

Miller, Ella, 1895 summer in Cambridge, 692–693, 694–696, 700–701

Minor, Raleigh C., invitation to H.W. Hobson to speak at University of Virginia, 823

Moore, Maranda Branson, excerpts from *The Geographical Reader for the Dixie Children*, 291–295

Mormon Church Case, 561–581

P

Page, Rosewell, obituary of H.W. Hobson, 821–822

Page, Thomas Nelson, letters to H.W. Hobson, 476, 488; death of first wife, 601–602; 1892 at Manhattan Beach, 658–662, 664; second marriage to F. Field, 664; letters from E.W. Hobson, 849; letters to K.T. Hobson, 869, 874, 877, 882; lectures at Yale, 898; letter to E.W. Hobson, 919; *illus. 898*

Papa's Letters, 604, 613–614, 615–616, 646, 653–654, 657, 663, 665–666, 673–676, 681, 684–688, 690–691, 693–694, 696–698, 711, 715, 717, 718, 756, 759–761, 770–771, 785; included in *My Hospital Chum*, 863, 869

Pattison, A. E., 829–830

Peters, George S., Mormon Church Case, 576–580

Prime, William, excerpt from *Boat Life on the Nile*, 72–73

Putnam, Sallie Brock, describing funeral of O.J. Wise, 274–276

S

Savage, Katherine, 1887 letters to K.T. Jermain, 538, 543; 1892 at Manhattan Beach, 658–660

Scarburgh family genealogy, 7–8

Shackelford, J. G., letter regarding education of J.C. Hobson's children, 780

Slavery in Cambridge, New York, 82–83

Stewart, Ann, death of H.W. Hobson, 827

Stewart, Lucy, death of H.W. Hobson, 827–828

Stewart, Marion, 1884 letters to H.W. Hobson, 479, 483

Stewart, Norma, 1884 letters to H.W. Hobson, 483–484

T

Thayer family genealogy, 11

Thayer, Adin (1785–1858), illness, 198; death of, 212; *illus. 212*

Thayer, Catherine McKie (1827–1901), 1836 letter to parents, 84; 1844 Poultney letters, 85–91; Poultney essays, 91–94; diary excerpts, 96, 100, 109, 113, 128, 141, 182–183, 391–392; 1846 Washington County Agricultural Society, 107; 1844–1850 letters to F. S. Thayer 97–151; 1850 marriage to F.S. Thayer, 148; 1851–1854 letters to parents, 155–183; stillborn child, 172; 1854 house-fire, 178; 1855–1859 letters and diary excerpts, 186–229; 1857 birth of son, 208; 1859 birth of daughter, 224–225; 1860–1861 letters, 243, 250, 253; 1877 letters from the White Mountains, 412–427; 1877 departure for Colorado, 427–428; 1880 to E. McKie, 439–440; letters about B. Jermain, 446–448, 450–451, 459–461; 1882 diary, 463; 1887 letters 521–522, 526, 545–548, 550–553, 555, 558; 1888–1889 letters, 584, 597, 599–600, 605; 1890–1897 letters to K.T. Hobson, 645–646, 649, 653, 655, 665, 671, 686, 691, 695, 699, 702, 716, 718–719, 721; 1898 diary excerpts, 792, 799, 810, 813, 821; 1900–1901 letters to K.T. Hobson, 836–837, 846, 853; death and obituary, 870–873; *illus. 148, 158, 334, 385, 597, 760, 871*

Thayer, Catherine Sophia (1859–1915). *See* Hobson, Katherine Thayer (1859–1915).

Thayer, Francis McKie (1857–1902), birth 208; father writes to *New York Times*, 380; applies to Amherst College, 395; letters written from Amherst College, 410, 415, 434; college term paper, 435; marriage to Harriet Jones, 785; death and obituary, 878–879; *illus. 329, 334, 395, 879*

Thayer, Francis Samuel (1822–1880), 1844–1850 letters to C. McKie and diary excerpts, 97–152; 1848 letter to G. McKie, 116–118; 1850 marriage to C. McKie, 148; 1851–1854 diary excerpts and letters, 156–182; first child, 172; 1854 house-fire, 178–179; 1855–1859 letters and diary excerpts, 186–229; 1857 birth of son, 208; 1859 birth of daughter, 224–225; 1860–1861 diary excerpts and letters, 232–257; diary describing the end of the Civil War, 316; 1862–1869 diary excerpts and letters, 320–343; 1867 elected State Senator, 336; attends 1868 Republican National Convention, 338; 1870 letter to *New York Times*, 380; 1870–1877 diary excerpts and letters, 380–428; Canal Auditor, 394; letters to son at Amherst College, 395–410; asthma, 383, 416; 1877 departure for Colorado, 427–428; 1878–1880 letters from Colorado, 430–436; letters to *Troy Times*, 436–439; death and obituary, 441–444; *illus. 148, 332, 336, 428, 442;* handwriting samples, 944, 945, 948

Thayer, Harriet Jones, marriage to F.M. Thayer, 785

Thayer, Mary Ball, death of, 328; *illus. 328*

Thoroughgood family genealogy, 9

Tracy, John Martin, 682–683

U

University of Virginia, H.W. Hobson's planned speech, 822–824

W

Washington Park, Troy, construction of house, 237; building fence, 328

Webster, Noah Jr., excerpts from *An American Selection of Lessons*, 80–82

Wheelock family genealogy, 17

Whiteside family genealogy, 14–16

White Mountains (New Hampshire), Thayer family vacations in, 394–395, 410–427

Wise family genealogy, 4

Wise, Ann Elizabeth Jennings (1808–1837), letters to H.A. Wise in Congress, 43–46; death 46–47; *illus. 43*

Wise, Annie Jennings (1837–1914). *See* Hobson, Annie Jennings Wise (1837–1914).

Wise, Barton Haxall, (1865–1899), describing H.A. Wise campaign for Governor, 69–70; describing Roanoke Island, 269; describing Appomattox, 315–316

Wise, Henry Alexander (1806–1876), youth, 41–43; first marriage, 42; death of first wife, 46–47; second marriage, 48; third marriage, 53–56; campaign for Governor, 68–70; and John Brown, 73–77, 886; Civil War letters, 268, 284, 287; Confederate roster, 318; death and obituaries, 371–378; *illus. 41, 43, 44, 49, 50, 70, 76, 77, 287, 318, 377, 957;* handwriting sample, 946

Wise, Henry A., Jr. (1834–1869), illness and death, 367

Wise, John 5th (1765–1812), letters to John Cropper, 31, 33; marriage, 32; death, 40–41

Wise, John Sergeant (1846–1913), excerpts from *End of an Era*, 73–77, 261–267, 269, 279, 317; letters to H.W. Hobson, 475, 487, 593–594, 715–716, 741–742, 748; letters to K.T. Hobson, 798-799, 828, 839–841, 842–844, 846, 848–849, 854–855, 875, 885–886, 892, 899, 903, 904; death and obituary, 906; *illus. 476*

Wise, John S. Jr. (b.1876), 802–803, 829; to Jennings Hobson, 886

Wise, Margaretta Ellen (Néné) (1844–1909). *See* Mayo, Ellen Wise (1844–1909).

Wise, Mary Elizabeth (1829–1898). *See* Garnett, Mary Wise (1829–1898).

Wise, Mary Elizabeth Lyons (1814–1901), marriage to H.A. Wise, 56; letters from, 62–64, 66; Civil War letters, 268, 286; letter to K.T. Jermain, 545; letter to H.W. Hobson, 623; death and obituary, 875–876

Wise, Obadiah Jennings (1831–1862), letters from, 47–48, 51–53, 56–61, 67; death at Roanoke Island, 269–281; *illus. 56, 273*

Wise, Richard A. (1843–1900), death, 854–855; *illus. 855*